I0884396

PREHISTORY AND HUMAN ECOLOGY OF THE VALLEY OF OAXACA

Kent V. Flannery and Richard E. Blanton
General Editors

Volume 1 *The Use of Land and Water Resources in the Past and Present Valley of Oaxaca, Mexico,* by Anne V. T. Kirkby. Memoirs of the Museum of Anthropology, University of Michigan, No. 5. 1973.

Volume 2 *Sociopolitical Aspects of Canal Irrigation in the Valley of Oaxaca,* by Susan H. Lees. Memoirs of the Museum of Anthropology, University of Michigan, No. 6. 1973.

Volume 3 *Formative Mesoamerican Exchange Networks with Special Reference to the Valley of Oaxaca,* by Jane W. Pires-Ferreira. Memoirs of the Museum of Anthropology, University of Michigan, No. 7. 1975.

Volume 4 *Fábrica San José and Middle Formative Society in the Valley of Oaxaca,* by Robert D. Drennan. Memoirs of the Museum of Anthropology, University of Michigan, No. 8. 1975.

Volume 5 Part 1. *The Vegetational History of the Oaxaca Valley,* by C. Earle Smith, Jr.
Part 2. *Zapotec Plant Knowledge: Classification, Uses and Communication about Plants in Mitla, Oaxaca, Mexico,* by Ellen Messer.
Memoirs of the Museum of Anthropology, University of Michigan, No. 10. 1978.

Volume 6 *Excavations at Santo Domingo Tomaltepec: Evolution of a Formative Community in the Valley of Oaxaca, Mexico,* by Michael E. Whalen. Memoirs of the Museum of Anthropology, University of Michigan, No. 12. 1981.

Volume 7 *Monte Albán's Hinterland, Part 1: The Prehispanic Settlement Patterns of the Central and Southern Parts of the Valley of Oaxaca, Mexico,* by Richard E. Blanton, Stephen Kowalewski, Gary Feinman, and Jill Appel. Memoirs of the Museum of Anthropology, University of Michigan, No. 15. 1982.

Frontispiece. The great Precolumbian mound of Zaachila (center) towers above the town and subvalley of the same name.

MEMOIRS OF THE MUSEUM OF ANTHROPOLOGY
UNIVERSITY OF MICHIGAN
NUMBER 15

PREHISTORY AND HUMAN ECOLOGY
OF THE VALLEY OF OAXACA

Kent V. Flannery and Richard E. Blanton
General Editors

Volume 7

MONTE ALBAN'S HINTERLAND, PART I: THE PREHISPANIC SETTLEMENT PATTERNS OF THE CENTRAL AND SOUTHERN PARTS OF THE VALLEY OF OAXACA, MEXICO

by
Richard E. Blanton
Stephen Kowalewski
Gary Feinman
Jill Appel

With contributions by Laura Finsten and Eva Fisch

ANN ARBOR
1982

Printed in the
United States of America

ISBN 0-932206-91-3

TABLE OF CONTENTS

TABLES

LIST OF FIGURES

PREFACE

In the first chapter we discuss the archaeological work in the Valley of Oaxaca and elsewhere from which we launched this project. Some of the archaeologists who did this work have aided us in other respects, through stimulating conversations, suggestions, and aid in other ways. In this regard we especially thank our Oaxaca colleagues Kent Flannery, Joyce Marcus, Ignacio Bernal, Ronald Spores, John Paddock, and Cecil Welte, as well as the staff of the Centro Regional in Oaxaca of the Instituto Nacional de Antropología e Historia, especially Manuel Esparza and Marcus Winter. Funding for this project has come primarily from the National Science Foundation (GS-28547, GS-38030, and BNS-19640). Additional funding was provided by the City University of New York Research Foundation (Grants 00230 and 10065), and an anonymous donor whose gift to the University of Arizona aided Steve Kowalewski's survey of the central part of the Oaxaca Valley. Aid from the City University of New York, Purdue University, Arizona State University, and the University of Georgia is gratefully acknowledged.

In addition to the four authors and two contributors to this volume, field crews included Pedro Castellanos, Margaret Curran, Roberto Hernández, Alexis Lee, Charlotte Lee, Fausto Olivera M., Sala Ponnech, Michael Rowley, and Jacqueline Saindon. We thank Diana Traub for her help in the lab. The following persons helped us with the coding, drafting, and typing: Linda Adams, Cameron Arcaro, Patrice Ballinger, Jean Baker, Judy Berman, Beverly Connor, Carol Edmundson, Doris Fultz, Susan Gallucci, Karen Gray, Nancy Hill, Cathy Olney, Greg Paulk, Cindy Scholte, Bonnie Spahn, and Ann Worley. We thank the following people for their suggestions, ideas, and comments on the manuscript, although we alone are at fault for errors or misinterpretations: Elizabeth Brumfiel, Bruce Byland, Geoffrey Clark, Paul Fish, Suzanne K. Fish, Robert Fry, Jeffrey Hantman, Lee Horne, Roberta Jewett, Gregory Johnson, Carol Kramer, Kent Lightfoot, Arthur Murphy, Linda Nicholas, Fred Plog, Michael Spence, Barbara Stark, Steadman Upham, Phil Weigand, and David Wilcox.

Finally, we would like to express our gratitude to the people of the Valley of Oaxaca. In the vast majority of cases these understanding people allowed us, or even encouraged us, to do our archaeological work, even though this work involved marching through agricultural fields and poking our noses into their house lots.

Chapter 1

INTRODUCTION AND COMMENTS ON METHODS

INTRODUCTION

This volume reports on the progress of the Valley of Oaxaca Settlement Pattern Project. It is the second in a series of three such reports. The first volume (Blanton 1978) presents the results of the surface survey of Monte Albán, the ancient Zapotec capital. The present volume reports on our archaeological surveys of the central and southern portions of the Valley of Oaxaca (Figs. 1-1, 1-2). The third will be devoted to the surveys of the valley's remaining areas, the Etla and Tlacolula arms (Fig. 1-2).

The Valley of Oaxaca Settlement Pattern Project is a direct outgrowth of the settlement pattern projects carried out by researchers in the Valley of Mexico (cf. Armillas 1971; Blanton 1972; Millon 1973; Parsons 1971; Sanders 1965; Sanders, Parsons and Santley 1979; Wolf, ed. 1976). The reader is referred to the relevant section of the Monte Albán volume (Blanton 1978:Chapter 1) for a detailed discussion of the nature of the methods employed by these researchers, and their goals, and how our methods and goals have grown from these studies. In shifting our arena of research from the Valley of Mexico to the Valley of Oaxaca, we were influenced by several factors. One of the most important of these is Kent Flannery's Oaxaca Human Ecology Project (Flannery et al. 1970; Flannery, ed. 1976). The work done in connection with Flannery's project is an ideal base for the development of our own research interests. Both the human ecology project and our settlement pattern project have similar goals, which are broadly speaking, to better understand the nature of human adaptation and cultural evolution in the prehispanic Valley of Oaxaca, and thereby to contribute to a more complete understanding of the nature of adaptation and evolution in general. The two projects differ in method and chronological emphasis, but, given the similarity of goals, are highly complementary. Flannery and his associates have chosen to expose living floors of hunters and gatherers, early cultivators, and early village dwellers as a primary means of data collection, while our method consists of intensive, systematic surface surveys of archaeological remains over a broad region. Given the difficulties of locating preceramic sites on the surface of the valley, we are focusing on the periods after the formation of permanent villages and the widespread use of pottery, beginning roughly 3500 years ago.

The Valley of Oaxaca, one of Mesoamerica's major "nuclear areas," has been an important focus of archaeological inquiry for nearly a hundred years because of its abundant evidence for socio-cultural evolution during the prehispanic period. Prominent features of change in the Valley of Oaxaca sequence are: 1) the transition from foraging to farming; 2) the beginnings of village life; 3) the formation of centralized "chiefdoms"; and 4) the formation and eventual collapse of a regional polity centered at Monte Albán, one of Mesoamerica's earliest cities. The Valley of Oaxaca is thus an ideal location for research on the major anthropological problems of the rise and dynamic features of chiefdoms, states, urbanism, and early civilizations (cf. Adams 1966; Fried 1965; Service 1975; Wheatley 1971; Wolf, ed. 1976). It is also an especially practical place for research on these topics due to several special features. First, since it is a semi-arid, heavily cultivated region, small prehispanic villages or even isolated residences are visible on the surface. Surface surveys of archaeological sites are thus highly productive, while at the same time simple and inexpensive relative to other archaeological methods. Second, the Valley of Oaxaca is readily accessible, and work there by anthropologists has been encouraged by the federal government of Mexico through the offices of its Instituto Nacional de Antropología e Historia (INAH). Third, there is a long tradition of interest in the spectacular ruins and tombs, which in some cases led to the collection of useful information even as early as the latter 19th century (e.g., Holmes 1897). A list of the major studies that provide a basis for contemporary work in the valley is included in the next section of this chapter.

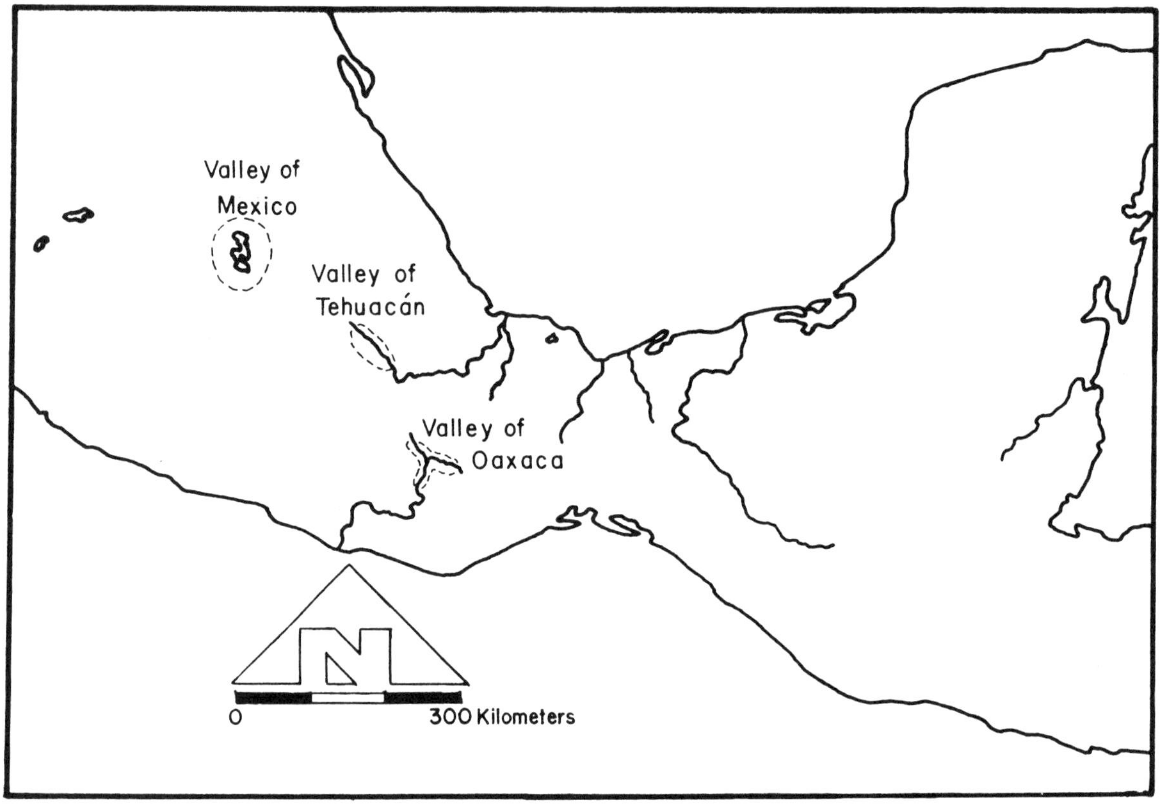

Figure 1-1. Mesoamerica, showing the location of the Valley of Oaxaca.

Thus, for the Valley of Oaxaca, we are developing a detailed, phase-by-phase picture of changing settlement patterns, covering not only the largest and most obvious centers, but the small farmsteads as well, for the 3000 year period during which the regional society underwent several major evolutionary changes. Similar information simply does not exist for other areas of the world that experienced the rise of civilization, and that includes Africa, Egypt, Europe, the Indus Valley, China, and the Central Andes. The only other major locus of the early evolution of civilizations for which comparable studies have been done is Mesopotamia. There, however, severe alluviation often precludes the kind of detailed data collection that is routine in the highland Mexican valleys (cf. Adams 1965; Adams and Nissen 1972).

PRIOR WORK IN THE VALLEY OF OAXACA

Major studies upon which our work is based include, first of all, Alfonso Caso's Monte Albán project, which involved a substantial amount of stratigraphic excavation and architectural reconstruction. The major publications reporting on this work are Caso and Bernal (1952) on the urns, Caso, Bernal, and Acosta (1967–hereafter referred to as CBA), on the ceramic sequence, and Caso (1969), describing the contents of several of the Monte Albán tombs, especially the elaborate Tomb 7. Our other major source of archaeological and relevant environmental information is that produced by participants in Flannery's Oaxaca Human Ecology Project, including Flannery et al. (1970), Flannery et al. (1967), Flannery and Schoenwetter (1970), Flannery (1968a), Drennan (1976), and Pires-Ferreira (1975) on various aspects of the Preceramic and Formative remains. As part of Flannery's project, Anne V.T. Kirkby (1973) did a study of the use of land and water resources and calculated the Oaxaca Valley's carrying capacity from the beginning of the Formative to the present day. In later chapters we will compare our population estimates with her predictions based on potential agricultural productivity. Joyce Marcus (1976a, 1976b, 1980) has continued the work on the epigraphic and iconographic materials started by Caso (1965). Summaries of the

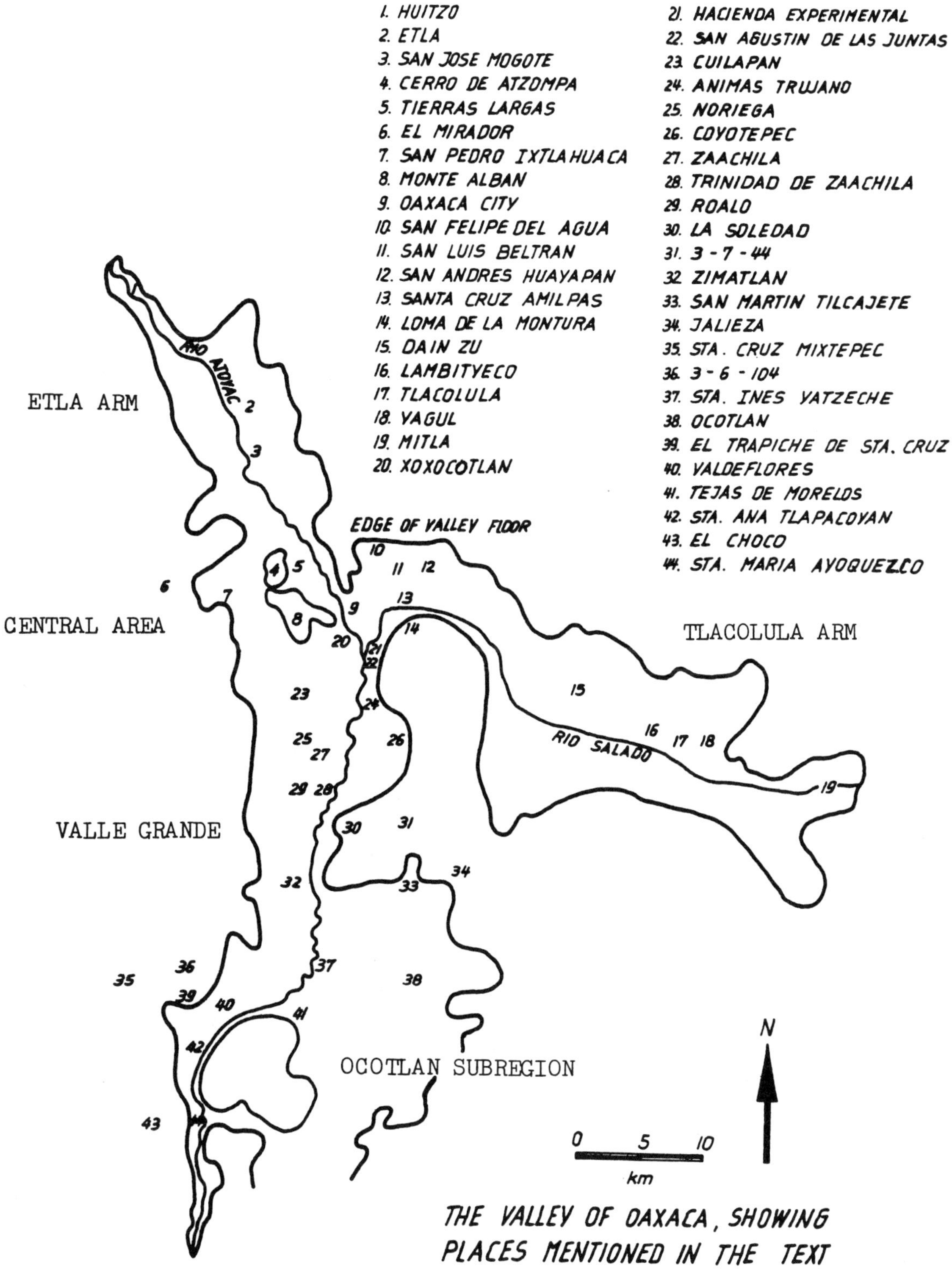

Figure 1-2. The Valley of Oaxaca, showing places and regions mentioned in the text.

archaeological sequence in the Valley of Oaxaca have been published by Bernal (1965), Paddock (ed. 1966), Flannery and Marcus (eds., in press), Flannery, Marcus and Kowalewski (1981), Blanton and Kowalewski (1981) and Blanton et al. (1979).

The Valley of Oaxaca Settlement Pattern Project began in 1971 at Monte Albán, and was continued there for three field seasons (Blanton 1978). Simultaneously, Dudley Varner (1974) initiated the survey of the Etla region (Fig. 1-2). During 1974, Steve Kowalewski (1976) completed the surface survey of the valley's Central region (Fig. 1-2). Finally, most of the southern region or "Valle Grande" was surveyed during 1977.

NATURAL ENVIRONMENT

The Valley of Oaxaca lies about one day's drive by car from Mexico City, in the rugged mountains of the Southern Highlands (16°40' - 17°20'N, 96°15' - 96°55'W). A good, brief description of the valley is given in Flannery, Kirkby, Kirkby, and Williams in one of the initial articles on the Oaxaca Human Ecology Project (1967). The best summary of the regional geomorphology is that by Lorenzo (1960), and Pires-Ferreira (1975) has mapped the outcrops of mineral resources of interest to the valley's ancient inhabitants. Modern climatic conditions have been studied authoritatively by Aceves (1976). After 3500 years of agriculture and forest cutting, the vegetation of the landscape has been almost unrecognizably altered, but Smith (1978) presents a plausible reconstruction of plant communities and their distributions before the advent of massive clearing. Additional ethnobotanical information may be found in Kappel (1977) and Messer (1978).

In the Southern Highlands of Mexico, the principal limiting factor on agriculture is flat land. In this region only a few pockets of comparatively level land—the upper drainage basins of semi-permanent rivers—exist in the otherwise continuous jumble of intersecting mountain chains. By far the largest of these patches is the Valley of Oaxaca, with a valley floor of over 1700 square kilometers. Kirkby (1973) divides the valley into four major environmental zones: mountain, piedmont, high alluvium, and low alluvium.

The *mountain* zone consists of very steep, narrow ridges generally above 2000 meters in elevation. In any other direction than along the ridge tops, transportation in the mountain zone requires strenuous exertion to cover even short distances. This zone receives more rainfall than the alluvium or piedmont, but it is cultivated less due to the steep slopes and the fact that frost is a more serious threat to crops. Mountain slopes are generally covered with dense stands of oak and/or pine. Today this zone is used more often for charcoal production and wood and plant collection than for farming.

The *piedmont* is a transition zone between the mountains and the valley floor. According to Kirkby, "the average slope of the piedmont from mountain to alluvium is 1 to 2 degrees with later dissection producing side slopes with gradients of up to 20 to 30 degrees" (1973:11). As in the mountains, piedmont soils tend to be thin and stony. Most are derived from pre-Jurassic metamorphic rocks, except for Monte Albán and portions of the eastern section of the survey areas, which are later, Cretaceous sedimentary formations. Fan gravel soils, sometimes of considerable depth, are found in a few places in the piedmont. Ancient and recent arroyo cutting makes the piedmont terrain somewhat difficult to walk over if one is headed across the drainages. We have arbitrarily divided the piedmont into *high*, *middle*, and *low* zones, since decreasing gradients, less stony and deeper soils, and greater potential for irrigation make the lower reaches of the piedmont zone more suitable for agriculture. In most places in the study area the natual plant communities of the piedmont–thorn and cactus forest at higher elevations, mesquite grasslands farther down–have been cleared and exist only as remnants in a few places (such as on archaeological mounds). The piedmont varies in width from less than 1 kilometer in many places along the eastern side of the study area, to 6 kilometers on the western side of the Valle Grande.

Most of the valley floor consists of the *high alluvium*. This zone is a nearly flat surface ranging in width from only one-half of a kilometer around Ayoquezco, to 4 or 5 kilometers in the Valle Grande and the western part of the Tlacolula arm. Today the high alluvium supports most of the valley's farming, and it was undoubtedly important in the past, though its character has probably not always been the same. To cite Kirkby's study again,

> . . . the age of the high alluvium is important to this study because although its surface now consists almost entirely of abandoned floodplains of the main rivers, evidence has been found which dates the present surface to the archaeological period. The 3 to 6 meters of alluvium which separate the present high alluvium surface from the present river level have all been deposited since about 800 B.C.-200 B.C. By the time of the Spanish Conquest in the sixteenth century, the rivers had finished aggrading

throughout most of the valley, and rapid downcutting was initiated which appears to be continuing today. [Kirkby 1973:13]

The *low alluvium* is very restricted in area and consists of the contemporary floodplain of the now-downcutting Río Atoyac. Poor soils and frequent flooding place limits on the use of the zone for agriculture today. The low alluvium as it is distributed today is of little importance for the precolumbian period, since it was not formed until after A.D. 1500.

The Valley of Oaxaca has a semi-arid climate, with rainfall ranging generally from 400 to 800 millimeters per year. The valley floor is roughly 1500-1600 meters above sea level, so that frost is not a major limiting factor on maize agriculture, as it is in the Valley of Mexico. In fact, the Valle Grande is essentially frost-free, permitting year-round cropping in that area, while nowhere on the valley floor is frost a threat for one yearly crop in the May-September growing season. The mean annual temperature is 20°C, with a daily range of 15°C (Flannery et al. 1967).

As Kirkby (1973) has shown, *within* the valley, moisture availability is the crucial variable for maize growing. Temperature, slope, and soil make relatively little difference. Crops depend on the seasonal rainfall pattern (most rain falls between June and September), on soil moisture in places on the alluvium where the water table is within two meters of the surface, and on irrigation. In a good year, the rains will support a single crop, but any attempt to assure an adequate harvest in most years, or to raise the two or three crops that are possible in some areas, implies some means of applying water in addition to rainfall. The major sources of irrigation water for prehispanic populations were shallow wells (pot irrigation) (Flannery et al. 1967; Kirkby 1973; Orlandini 1967), tributary streams (Kirkby 1973; Downing 1974; Lees 1973), various forms of floodwater irrigation (Kirkby 1973:36-40), as well as the major drainages, the Río Salado in the Tlacolula arm and the Atoyac in the Etla and southern arms.

THE VALLEY'S CERAMIC SEQUENCE

Our data pertain to the period from the earliest villages, dating roughly 1500 B.C., up to the arrival of the Spaniards some 3000 years later. This span has been divided into 11 ceramic periods (Table 1-1), based primarily on the excavated stratigraphic sequences exposed by Caso and his associates, and by Flannery and his associates. Sites we locate on our surveys are dated according to the presence of types known from this periodization. The chronology indicated in Table 1-1 has been developed by Drennan (in press). The reader should be aware that due to the present paucity of C^{14} assays for the Valley of Oaxaca, this chronology may be somewhat modified in the future. The general outline, however, is not likely to change substantially.

The Monte Albán ceramic periods were worked out by Caso, Bernal, and Acosta (1967). We have largely adhered to their suggestions, with only three important modifications (Blanton 1978; Kowalewski, Spencer, and Redmond 1978; and the reader is referred to Chapter 10 and Appendix VII in this volume). In CBA, Period I was subdivided into three phases. Given the difficulties of identifying the middle phase from surface-collected sherds, we have simplified Period I into Early I and Late I. Secondly, we interpret Period V pottery to be the marker for the Late Postclassic period in the valley, rather than as ceramic evidence for a Mixtec invasion (Blanton 1978; Blanton and Kowalewski 1981). The third modification is that we do not use Caso, Bernal, and Acosta's transitional phases (*Transición* II-IIIa, *Transición* IIIa-IIIb).

The ceramic sequence prior to the foundation of Monte Albán is known from the work of Flannery and his project members (Flannery et al. 1970; Flannery 1968a; Drennan 1976; Winter 1972). Chapter 3 in this volume, by Eva Fisch, contains a disussion of some of the problems we encountered using this ceramic typology. Appendix II in the Monte Albán volume (Blanton 1978) is a brief description of each of the categories we were able to identify in our surface collections from Monte Albán, based largely on CBA. Our only modifications involved attaching a number to each category, replacing the letter-and-number designations used in CBA, to facilitate coding, and, in a few cases CBA categories were subdivided where we thought this was justified, to facilitate such things as distributional analyses of design elements and related kinds of analysis. Appendix VII of this volume expands the ceramic category descriptions in the Monte Albán volume to include similar descriptions for the categories pertaining to periods prior to the Monte Albán sequence. Again, we have based these descriptions on published information. These descriptions are not intended to be a complete description of the pre-Monte Albán ceramic sequence; Flannery and his associates are responsible for that. Our descriptions are intended only to inform the reader of the nature of the diagnostic categories we used to date sites we located on survey. Appendix VII also contains descriptions of several Early I decorated types. For the most part, these types group several of the ce-

Table 1-1. Valley of Oaxaca Chronology

VALLEY OF OAXACA SEQUENCE		
1520		
1300		
	Monte Albán V	Late Postclassic
1100		
900		
	Monte Albán IV	Early Postclassic
700		
	Monte Albán III b	Late Classic
500		
	Monte Albán III a	Early Classic
300		
100		
A.D.		
	Monte Albán II	Terminal Formative
B.C.		
100		
	Monte Albán Late I	Late Formative
300		
500	Monte Albán Early I	
	Rosario	Middle Formative
700		
	Guadalupe	
900		
	San José	
1100		
		Early Formative
1300	Tierras Largas	
1500	Espiridión	
1700		

ramic categories that were listed in the Monte Albán report. The Monte Albán categories were lumped because very few sherds of these types were found outside Monte Albán and because the sherds of these types that were found during valley survey were normally so small and eroded that the detailed categorization developed for Monte Albán could not be used.

FIELD METHODS

Our goals in the field are to locate, describe, and date all prehispanic settlements, special function sites, workshops, and major features visible on the surface. We feel this includes virtually all sites in the valley that have been occupied long enough to leave artifactual and architectural traces, since soils are generally thin and the natural vegetation does not significantly limit visibility. There is some evidence that the number of sites lost due to alluviation, erosion, or modern occupation is minimal. Recently alluviated areas, for example, are the same areas that are exposed to seasonal or periodic flooding, probably limiting ancient settlement. A few sites are located in what is now swamp or floodplain, but these, by necessity, were generally built on platforms or natural rises, and can therefore be easily located and mapped. We are confident that few sites have been irretrievably covered; in inspecting modern and colonial wells, road cuts, foundation cuts, ditches, and so forth, as we regularly do, we have only rarely discovered sites that are not also visible on the surface. Even where alluviation has occurred, sites are not necessarily lost from view since, over the years, plowing, digging of wells, and so forth, tend to circulate sherds toward the surface.

To compensate for the problem of contemporary occupation of prehispanic sites, we surveyed all modern towns street by street, inspecting as many yards as possible. It is unlikely that our town surveys failed to locate any sites with mounded architecture, although it is possible that information on some small occupations and the actual extent of large occupations has in some cases been lost.

Places of some importance where we do feel that prehispanic remains have been significantly obscured include Oaxaca City, discussed below, the village of Tejas de Morelos (Fig. 1-2), where part of the IIIb site has been covered, and Zaachila (Fig. 1-2). Our problems at the latter site were more serious than is usual because we feel the major occupation there (Period IIIb) was dispersed to begin with, and the sherds of that period are not highly distinctive or decorated. In one case in the Central Area construction workers excavating a 5 meter deep pit at a new cement factory uncovered deeply buried cultural materials. The pit profile showed about 4 meters of gravel bands and fine alluvial soils. Below that there was a 25-30 centimeter layer of black clay. It was reported that burials without pots, but with stone tools, were found in this layer (Marc Winter, personal communication, 1974; description supplied by the workers on the site). It may be that one of the reasons we do not find many preceramic sites in the Valley of Oaxaca is that they were located on valley floor surfaces, near the main rivers, and have been buried by alluvium.

Survey conditions in Oaxaca are highly comparable to those in the Valley of Mexico (Armillas 1971; Blanton 1972; Parsons 1971; Millon 1973; Sanders 1965; Sanders, Parsons, and Santley 1979), except that in Oaxaca there has been much less of the massive erosion of the piedmont zone, and there is much less of the urban sprawl that is the major deterrent to archaeological survey around Mexico City.

The Central Area survey in 1974 included an archaeological reconnaissance of Oaxaca City which was carried out systematically. Many sites were found in the outer sections of the city, where streets are unpaved and there are open lots and exposed profiles. But in the built-up and paved core of the city, we were unsuccessful in finding sites despite the fact that building activities sometimes encounter deposits with prehispanic artifacts. We therefore did miss some sites in Oaxaca City, although none, we think, with monumental architecture. The area of Oaxaca City where sites are obscured constitutes only about 1% of the area we have surveyed so far.

We use aerial photographs at a scale of 1:5000 as field guides. These were enlarged from a set flown by the Compañía Mexicana de Aerofoto, S.A. At the 1:5000 scale, site and component boundaries can be drawn directly on the photo while in the field, and the locations of ancient buildings and other large features noted. These photos, mounted on plywood boards, are carried by the leader of each survey crew. Each crew consists of three to five people, all moving across the landscape generally parallel to one another, but zigzagging to check suspicious features, and spaced usually 25 to 50 meters apart. Since the sherd scatter associated with even the smallest sites is normally at least 25 to 35 or so meters in diameter, few if any sites are missed. Too, an experienced surveyor need not always walk directly over a site to locate it–clues can be seen from a distance such as slight mounding, soil discoloration, abundant stone debris, and light-colored sherds.

Once a site has been located, the crew is assembled for description and surface collection. This is not always done in the case of very small sites, especially the numerous small Monte Albán V sites. In these cases, the site is simply recorded on the airphoto without further description in the field. Normally, however, once a site has been located, it is described by the crew. The crew leader's first task is to walk over the site, carefully noting the limits of sherd distributions for each of the periods present. This can be a tedious job, often requiring walking and rewalking the site several times. Other crew members are at work taking notes on the site, collecting the range of information which will later be used to complete a site survey form (an example of which is included as Appendix V). If present, ancient buildings are measured by pacing the horizontal measurements and using an eye level to measure elevation, and then they are drawn on the airphoto and in the notebooks. On most sites, one or more surface collections are taken, especially if the site has more than one period. On small sites, only one collection is taken, often from the entire area of the site. On larger sites, several smaller collection areas will be chosen, usually about one hundred meters in diameter for each collection area, and these areas are noted on the airphoto. Collections are made of 50 to 100 diagnostic sherds per collection area.

Each site thus noted in the field is assigned a field number indicating its location in terms of modern administrative units. Each field number contains three abbreviated designations for administrative unit, starting with *distrito*, followed by *municipio*, then *agencia*, followed by the number. Z1M-SCM-SCM-1, for example, indicates the site is located in the ex-*distrito* of Zimatlán, *municipio* of Santa Cruz Mixtepec, and in or near the latter town and is the first site of the series located there. Appendix VI indicates the correspondences between the period site numbers and these field numbers, and translations of the abbreviations used.

Figure 1-3 shows the limits of the surveyed areas reported in this volume. This is an area of roughly 801 square kilometers, including the valley's central region and the bulk of its southern arm. A small portion

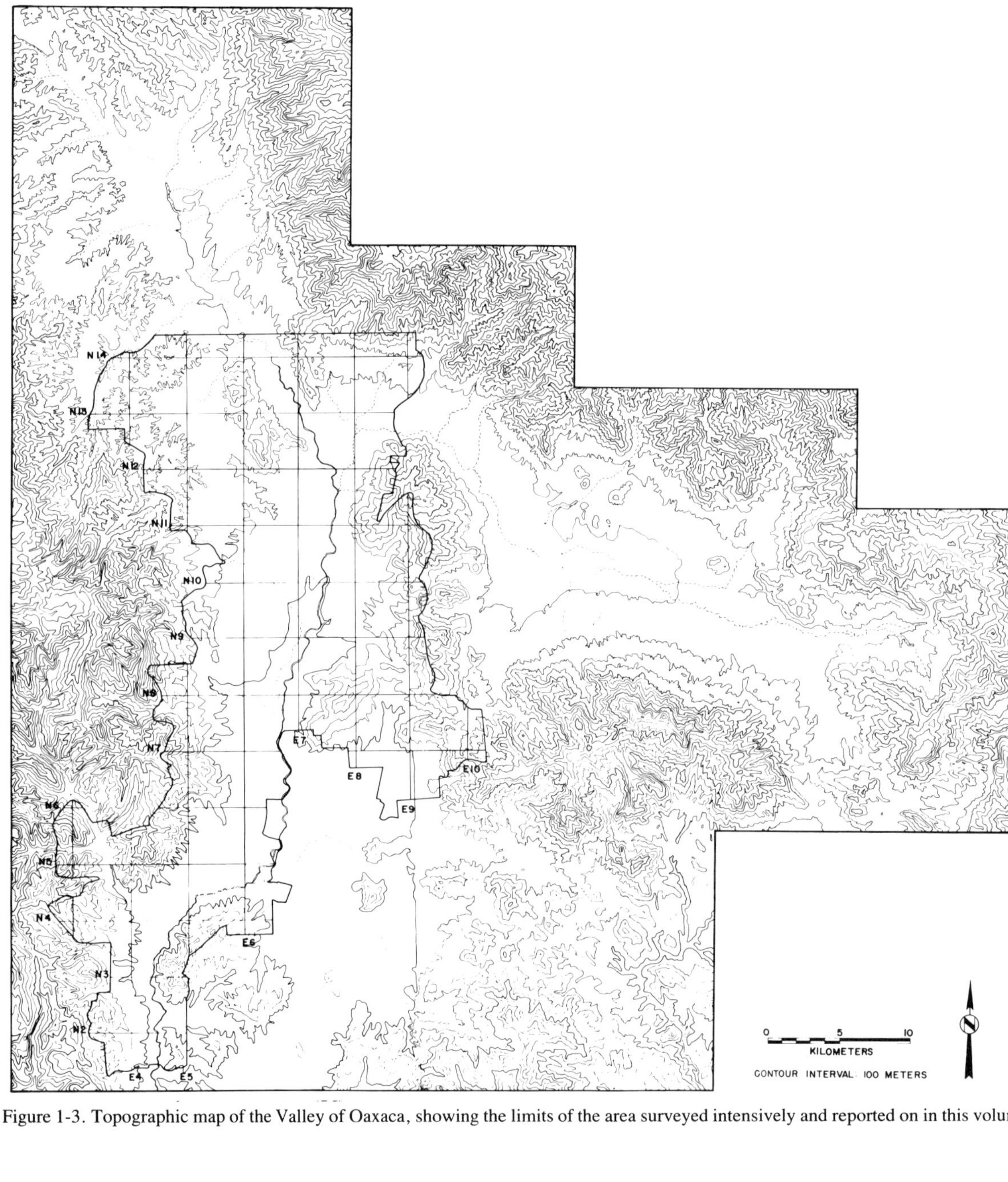

Figure 1-3. Topographic map of the Valley of Oaxaca, showing the limits of the area surveyed intensively and reported on in this volume.

of the southern arm, the Ocotlán sub-region (Fig. 1-2), could not be surveyed during our last field season and so will have to be done in our final survey season. Except where the survey boundaries are adjacent to unsurveyed areas (as along the Ocotlán sub-region, or to the north of the Central Area), the boundard corresponds to the edge of the sierra zone, or the first high ridge above the bottom line of the sierra. The sierra makes a convenient boundary for the survey since, due to poor agricultural production, few people live there now and apparently did not do so in prehispanic times either. The exception to this is several large sites built on hilltops, in some cases extending into this normally sparsely-used zone. To the south, we ended our survey near the modern town of Ayoquezco, where the valley becomes very narrow near its terminus (Fig. 1-2).

Three special features of our field methods require additional comments: determination of sherd densities, location of workshops, and mapping of terraced sites. Consistent recording of sherd densities can be somewhat of a problem since different people may differently perceive what is on the surface. The categories we use, however, are so broad that in general there is a considerable degree of consistency in recording. A trace of pottery indicates just a few sherds present, which can mean a site is present but alluviated, or that settlement was very sparse or of short duration. Most sites are listed as Very Light in density, indicating a scatter with sherds spaced every few meters. Most sites we classify as hamlets, villages, or isolated residences have Very Light sherd densities. A Light designation would indicate a nearly continuous scatter of sherds, while Moderate and Heavy indicate the rare cases where there are so many sherds that it may be possible to collect 100 or more fragments in a square meter. The correspondence of these density estimations and our population estimations for sites is discussed in the next section of this chapter.

In addition to sherd densities, we note densities of lithic and other artifacts. Unusual concentrations of such materials are taken to indicate the presence of some kind of specialized productive activity not normally found in households. We refer to such localities as production loci. (Lithic production loci are described in Appel, 1982). Ceramic production loci, as discussed in Appendix IX, are sometimes identified on other grounds, including the presence of kiln wasters, a by-product of ceramic production (and see Feinman 1980).

A number of archaeological sites in the Valley of Oaxaca, located on hill tops, necessitated the construction of terraces to provide flat spaces for residential and other construction. These sites provide a kind of information not present on valley bottom sites, since the terraces are often in good enough condition to permit measuring their dimensions. We thus have collected a large body of information of a type not usually available to the archaeologist–the sizes of what might be termed houselots. We have found the variability in these data to be useful in detecting features of social change in prehispanic Oaxaca (Blanton 1978). Similar analyses are included in subsequent chapters, based on the terrace information which is summarized in Appendix X. In mapping these sites, each terrace is located on the airphoto (sometimes a difficult task when small terraces are tightly packed along steep slopes) and assigned a number. The crew then paces the dimensions of the terrace, while noting periodization and other information, such as lithic density. Periodically, individual terraces are surface-collected. Sites were mapped in this way when we could be reasonably certain that most terraces on a site have persisted. In some cases a few terraces are present on a site, while others have eroded away. Terrace data were not collected in these latter cases, since the remaining terraces might be a biased sample of the variability in the total population.

We have chosen these field methods because they inexpensively provide information on a large number of sites over a broad area. We are sometimes asked why more intensive, systematic methods are not employed on each site, especially intensive surface collections and/or test pitting. These methods would, after all, provide a statistically meaningful sample of sherds and other artifacts, usable for a wider range of statistical hypothesis testing than is justified with our opportunistic or "grab-bag" ceramic samples or density observations of lithic artifacts. Our answer to these questions is to point out the much greater time and energy costs of doing the systematic collections, not only in the field, but including the costs of processing the millions of artifacts that would be involved. Feinman (1977) evaluated the costs of various methods and found the costs of systematic surface collections to be roughly an order magnitude greater than our simpler method (and excavation costs were another order of magnitude above these!). Our basic data are: 1) the size of sites and density of occupation by period, from which population estimates can be made; 2) the locations of sites relative to environmental and land-use zones, and other sites; and 3) the architectural complexity of sites. Our methods are highly efficient in the collection of these data. The burdensome additional costs of systematic collecting or test-pitting could not be justified in the light of our limited goals. We feel that these more intensive means of collecting data are more suited to the resolution of specific problems, involving the study of selected sites, once the total sample of sites is known. Our kind of settlement pattern study can be viewed as having a dual purpose, at once providing data on a scale not possible with other methods and serving as a necessary, preliminary foundation for an intelligent selection of cases for more detailed endeavors.

Another suggestion that is sometimes made is that we employ some method of regional sampling such as quadrat or transect sampling, rather than covering the whole region. These techniques would allow the estimation of relative numbers of sites by size categories or by environmental zones, but we are interested in far more than that. Our methods involve, for example, the measurement of distances between central places and the construction of size-rank diagrams of central places, both requiring data on all such places in a region rather than just a sample (cf. Flannery 1976a:131-36). Because our method provides information on the locations and sizes of all archaeological sites within a region, it has the additional advantage that it facilitates INAH's goal of site preservation and salvage archaeology.

LABORATORY PROCEDURES

Laboratory activities were carried out in two stages, the first while in Oaxaca, the second once we had returned to Purdue University. In Oaxaca, three major tasks were completed. First, tracings were made of the field assessments recorded on the airphotos. Secondly, we tabulated all ceramic collections according to the categorization developed by Kowalewski, Spencer, and Redmond (1978) and supplemented in Appendix VII in this volume. On each tabulation sheet, assessments of the periodization were made, and all non-diagnostics were briefly described. The sherds were then re-bagged and shipped to the storehouse of the Oaxaca Centro of the INAH. Last, the field notes, ceramic tabulations, and tracings were consulted in completing the site forms. A sample form is included here as Appendix V. Based on information from the ceramic tabulation forms and the tracings, boundaries were drawn around each site on the tracing, showing the site's maximum extent by period.

At Purdue, the work proceeded in roughly the following order:

1) Final site numbers were assigned by period. Each site designation has three parts. The first indicates survey area (0 = Monte Albán; 1 = Etla; 2 = Central; 3 = Valle Grande). The second refers to period (1 = Tierras Largas; 2 = San José; 3 = Guadalupe; 4 = Rosario; 5 = Early I; 6 = Late I; 7 = II; 8 = IIIa; 9 = IIIb; 10 = IV; 11 = V; 12 = undated sites). The third part is the site's number within that period and survey area. Our sites are thus technically "components," that is, an occupation of a particular phase at a single location. Since in a few cases numbers were assigned and later dropped and not reused, the number series for some phases is incomplete. Appendix VI shows the correspondence of these final numbers with the original field numbers. In some cases, sites with two or more field numbers have been grouped into one final site number. This was done in all cases for sites spaced less than 100 meters apart. Some additional grouping of sites was done after final site numbers were assigned for purposes of analysis. The procedures employed and the rationale for these additional groupings are explained below in Chapter 4.

2) Mound volumes were calculated, and site areas were measured from the tracings using a compensating polar planimeter. Given site area and information on sherd densities, population estimates were then made. This was done, in the general outlines, according to methods developed by Sanders (1965:50), and Parsons (1971:23), based on population densities of modern highland Mexican communities. Most commonly, sherd densities of Very Light were noted in the field, especially in the smaller sites. This translates to a density of 10-25 persons per hectare, what Sanders (1965) calls a "Compact Low-Density Village." A trace indicates what Sanders refers to as a "Scattered Village," indicating a density of 5-10 per hectare, unless other evidence is present favoring a higher density estimate (for example, the presence of abundant architectural remains). More highly nucleated communities often have ceramic densities of Light or more. These were assigned a population density of 25-50 per hectare, equivalent to Sanders' "High-Density Compact Village." Isolated residences were assigned 5-10 people, based on estimations of average household size made from 16th century Central Highlands sources consulted by Carrasco (1964) and Sanders (1970). We should note that, in general, since the majority of our sites have artifact densities in the Very Light range, most of the variation in estimated popula-

tions of settlements depends on site (component) area.

Terraced sites provide an opportunity to make even more accurate population estimations since each terrace can be considered to be a kind of "houselot" supporting one or more residences. Thus, it is possible to actually estimate the number of houses present on a site rather than just estimating its density of occupation. For all sites with more than just a few terraces, the following special method was used for population estimation. The total population is the sum of the numbers of people living in 1) non-terraced areas, 2) large houses, 3) ordinary-sized houses, each calculated as follows:

a) For occupied but non-terraced areas of a terraced site, the area was multiplied by the appropriate density figure, following the usual procedures.

b) Large residences are assumed to have had more people (10-20) than ordinary houses (5-10). A large house is defined as having a visibly raised platform with a top or enclosed area of 400 square meters or more. This includes houses that have three or four wings arranged around a rectangular or square central courtyard or patio (the kind illustrated in Figure A.X-21 in Blanton, 1978, for example). Notice that this method is somewhat different from that used on the Monte Albán survey (Blanton 1978:30), but the overall results are highly similar.

c) The number of ordinary houses was computed from the terrace-by-terrace field observations, and from the terrace dimensions. Each house is assumed to have had 5-10 people. In many cases, the person who described the terrace could identify slight rises or artifact and building stone concentrations that were probably individual houses. Sometimes these had sections of stone foundation walls still visible. If the field notes contained an estimation of the number of houses based on these kinds of information, that was followed. Otherwise, we assumed that a houselot covered about 312 square meters, a figure derived from measuring a sample of well-preserved houses and terrace areas at Monte Albán (Blanton 1978:30). This value seems reasonable since it is close to the size of what Marcus Winter calls "household clusters" at Monte Albán, a circle with a radius of about 10 meters (Winter 1974:982).

The number of houses was estimated for each terrace separately. Fractional values were not counted. We feel that this method results in a reasonable population estimate. Of course we expect that there was considerable variation in a family's size and the space it needed to carry out daily activities, both over time and within the same period, depending especially on the manner of participation in the region's economy, land use, land values, etc., but the average was probably consistently close to this figure.

Unless noted in the field, we have assumed an arbitrary ceiling of six as the maximum number of houses per terrace. Large terraces in general do not have the appearance of having been densely occupied. Artifacts and evidence of construction are often more scattered, indicating lower house densities. These large terraces may have been in general functionally distinct from smaller terraces in ways that are still unclear.

3) As the third step in our laboratory procedures at Purdue, topographic base maps were prepared, traced from a set made by the Mexican Government at a scale of 1:100,000, with 50 meter contour intervals. These were enlarged to a working scale of 1:20,000. Sites were then traced from the tracings, reduced to the same working scale, and then placed on the topographic maps. Crew leaders who had mapped sites in the field were responsible for their placement on the working maps. These placements were accomplished through a combination of measurement from known points and placement relative to features such as streams, roads, and modern communities. A few minor placement errors are probably present. Some difficulties were encountered since the topographic base maps we use contain some distortions, as did the airphotos we used to originally place sites. Thus, a measurement made between known points on the topographic map and on the tracings from the airphoto will in some cases show some variance. When compared with the monumental costs of having new and more accurate photogrammetric maps made, however, such minor errors seem inconsequential and do not constitute any major impediment to our analyses.

A grid was then imposed on our working map, with squares measuring 4 kilometers east-west by 4 kilometers north-south. The grid was positioned so that all of Monte Albán *per se* fell into one grid square, to facilitate coding and analysis. Each grid is numbered according to its north and east distance from an imaginary 0-0 square in the southwest corner of the map. Grid squares are referred to, for example, as square N6E7 (Fig. 1-3). Using this gridded map, the following information was collected for each site: grid square, elevation (to the closest 50 meter contour near the site's center), and distance to the Main Plaza at Monte Albán.

Our last task in map production was to trace final versions in ink from the working map, then pass these tracings through two stages of photographic reduction, finally arriving at the 1:300,000 maps for each period which are published in the appropriate chapters below.

4) The data were coded in three separate sections. Feinman coded all ceramic counts by collection tracts (Feinman 1980). Kowalewski and Blanton coded the site data from the site forms (Appendix 1). Appel coded lithic distribution data by field description unit (Appel 1982). Thus, all the data we collected are available in this volume, in Feinman (1980), Appel (1982), and Kowalewski (1976). For those researchers who might find it more convenient to have the data available on tape, these can be ordered from Blanton.

5) The final stage in preparing the data for analysis and publication consisted of drawing maps of most of the sites with mounded architecture, to show the dimensions and locations of architectural features (Appendix XI) and the preparation of maps of terraced sites, showing the terrace distributions, sizes, and terrace numbers, as well as other features noted on these sites, such as mounded architecture, roads, defensive walls, etc. (Appendix X).

Once the data were in these formats, we were able to begin the analysis. Many different possibilities exist for analysis and interpretation of these data. Since we have been interested primarily in a few select problems, we have by no means exhausted the analytical possibilities in preparing this report. The next chapter establishes a theoretical basis for our particular analyses, which are then carried out in the period chapters (Chapters 3-8) and in those which deal with special topics (Chapters 9 and 10).

Chapter 2

THEORETICAL BACKGROUND

INTRODUCTION

Our goal is to contribute to a better understanding of the nature of cultural evolution in the prehispanic Valley of Oaxaca. Cultural evolution can involve many things, but basically we will be concerned with three of its major features: changes in complexity, integration and scale. Complexity refers to the degree of differentiation, or in other words, the extent to which a society's members are formally divided into positions, ranks or subunits (cf. Blau 1970:203-04). Differentiation can be horizontal and/or vertical. Horizontal differentiation refers to the degree of specialization or segregation (Flannery 1972a:409) unrelated to differences in rank. The development of production specialties might be an example of an increase in horizontal differentiation. Vertical differentiation refers to specialization of parts between which there are rank differences. A more vertically differentiated society is one in which there are hierarchically segmented units arranged on different levels.

Integration refers to the degree to which there are linkages between the differentiated positions, ranks, or subunits. Scale refers to size differences, and usually, but not always, refers to differences in numbers of people, density, numbers of units integrated into a single system, or spatial size of units.

We of course do not wish to deny that cultural evolution may involve changes in such areas as technology or ideology. We feel, however, that the basic changes in human societies involve changes in complexity, integration, and scale, and that changes in other features, such as technology, can best be understood by reference to these more elementary features. We are putting social organization–in the broad sense–back into sociocultural evolution because in fact that is precisely what is changing. All other "factors," like technology and ideology, must be connected to social organization in any coherent theory of sociocultural evolution. To make these connections, these three aspects of social organization must be well defined. They must be defined abstractly and generally, so that social formations in one time and place can be compared to those elsewhere. We thus do not rely heavily on social or institutional *types*, such as chiefdom or state; nor do we study how the "economic subsystem" is affected by the "demographic subsystem." Instead, we choose to examine social organization in terms of complexity, integration, and scale, observing how each may affect the others, and how they are related to variables in the organization's environment.

TRADITIONAL APPROACHES TO THE EXPLANATION OF CULTURE CHANGE

Traditionally, the majority of the literature in anthropology on cultural evolution has dealt with the problem of the origin of states. Among scholars interested in this problem, a common approach is to evaluate the role or roles of one or more of the so-called "prime movers" (Service 1975; Flannery 1972a). These include external conflict and circumscription (Carneiro 1970), internal conflict (cf. Diakanov 1969; Fried 1965), trade and redistribution (cf. Rathje 1971; Service 1975), population growth and population pressure (cf. Smith and Young 1972; Sanders 1972; Spooner, ed. 1972), or irrigation (Millon, Hall, and Díaz 1962; Wittfogel 1957). One's analysis and writing is then devoted to promoting your pet mover, criticizing the inability of the other prime movers to cause anything, or to trying to show how all of these factors combine in concert to produce change (cf. Adams 1966). All of these approaches fail, in our opinion, because they cannot deal effectively with the problem of how some feature of human behavior (such as, for example, trade) can be a cause of cultural change in some contexts, but not in other contexts. If population growth leading to population pressure can be assumed to be a constant (as it is, for example, in most of the papers in the Spooner [ed., 1972] volume), then why did early civilizations evolve only a few times on earth, and not more generally?

An additional problem with the prime mover arguments in general is that the causal connection between the action of the prime mover and the evolution of political institutions is not well laid out. Carneiro (1970), for example, argues that the state forms as one group is able to militarily subordinate others in the context of population pressure and competition over resources. This argument is not totally convincing since it seems equally likely that warfare caused by population pressure might result in population declines, lessening stresses on resources, and permitting a return to the *status quo ante*.

The work of Wright (1969), Wright and Johnson (1975), and Flannery (1972a) contributed to the resolution of the problem of the causal linkages between the prime movers and state formation by specifying the kinds of changes that occur in political institutions in response to various kinds of stresses. Wright (1969), and Wright and Johnson (1975), for example, emphasize the role played by information overload in the growth in size and complexity of such institutions. Flannery's (1972a) argument is particularly useful since it directs attention away from the prime movers and to the more general concept of "socio-environmental stresses" as sources of change. This is an important point since no single prime mover is likely to have been important in all cases of state formation.

A recent cross-cultural review concludes that single factors such as conquest, trade, population pressure, and the class struggle do not adequately account for the diverse origins of early states–even though the same authors believed that the early states actually had much in common once they were developed (Claessen and Skalník, eds. 1978). Flannery also makes the important point, following some suggestions by Rappaport (1969), that responses to socio-environmental stresses may result in internal "pathologies," themselves creating new stresses which in turn require further responses, or which may result in breakdown.

While useful, we find the suggestions made by Wright, Johnson, and Flannery limiting for two reasons. First, they are concerned primarily with the evolution of governmental institutions, only one aspect of cultural evolution in the broad sense. Second, they are concerned with governmental *responses* to changed circumstances that produce stresses. Since they cannot predict the sources of stresses, they cannot predict change (cf. Athens 1978).

In order to begin to develop a more generalized, more explanatory approach to cultural evolution, we do two things in the following section: 1) We devise an analytical procedure that enables us to deal with change in aspects of human societies other than, but including, change in governmental institutions. 2) We discuss what we believe are some of the most important sources of socio-environmental stresses that result in change. In the final section of this chapter, we use two examples–the beginnings of chiefdom organization in the Valley of Oaxaca, and the development of the earliest state there–to illustrate how our evolutionary scheme can be applied in particular cases.

AN ANALYTICAL PROCEDURE

Our goal is to broaden our perspective to a consideration of change in whole societies, instead of focusing primarily on political evolution. Only in this way will we be able to include in our analyses explanations for things such as market system evolution, population transitions, and so on. Whole societies, though, are not themselves viable units of analysis within which we can identify the processes of change. (By processes of change we refer to the ways people cope with fluctuation–unpredictability–by altering their behavior.) Whole societies don't cope with fluctuations–people do–and, depending on the setting in which people are coping with fluctuation, the kinds of problems they are coping with will vary, and the kinds of strategies they are likely to develop to resolve problems will vary. One way to differentiate the settings within which people are coping with fluctuation is to use an analytical procedure in which one focuses attention on the processes of change at different regional scales. For example, the largest regional scale would pertain to the organization of the macroregion-involving interactions between societies. In state societies, the kinds of fluctuations pertaining to this level would involve such things as flows of long-distance trade goods, migrating people, and military activities. The actors who are developing strategies to cope with fluctuation at this regional scale are the society's highest-order elite–and their strategies would involve such things as offense-defense and diplomacy.

At the other extreme, households are a society's smallest scale unit of organization, and the actors in household decision-making are coping with an entirely different set of problems, employing a distinct set of strategies. Responses to pressures on households, for example, might involve altered behavior in the areas of fertility, production, and migration. And processes of change will have different aspects at the intermediate regional scales–villages and regions, for example.

Responses to changed circumstances are thus best

understood if viewed in terms of their regional contexts, or what we will call "organizational spheres." We will be concerned not only with the processes of change peculiar to each sphere, but the interactions–involving exchanging of energy and information–between organizational spheres. A change in one sphere may result in changes in others, and these changes may in turn feed back to further alter the first. The environment of each sphere–in other words, the source of fluctuating inputs–consists of features of the natural environment, other organizational spheres, as well as other societies. In spite of the processual autonomy of the spheres, all are interconnected, so that a change in one may cascade into changes in the others.

FLUCTUATION AND CHANGE

Cultural evolution is the result of developing strategies to cope with a fluctuating, uncertain environment (White 1959). The adjustments made in coping with fluctuation and unpredictability are of two kinds. The first, which is subsumable under the rubric of adaptation or "maximization of homeostatic abilities" (to borrow a phrase from Slobodkin, 1968), consists of gradual problem-solving, eventually leading to better performance *vis à vis* a particular environment (Holland 1975). Performance, of course, can be measured in a variety of ways and need not imply maximization. The second context for evolutionary change occurs when strategies are developed to cope with extreme, unique situations.

Any living system is capable of responding to fluctuations, whether in variables internal or external to the system, but as Prigogine (1976:121) has noted: "With fluctuations below the critical threshold, the system returns to its initial state. Beyond the threshold, it evolves to a new structure." Translated into human behavioral terms, this means that mechanisms, structures, etc., are present in all societies permitting adjustment to fluctuations (in production, fertility, or whatever). If fluctuations occur beyond critical thresholds, however, new coping strategies must be developed.

In either case, whether change is due to problem-solving in order to increase performance, or whether it occurs in the context of extreme stress, we must consider more than just the new coping strategies themselves as instances of change. Probably more important in understanding cultural evolution than the strategies themselves are the consequences of the strategies for bringing about further change. A state, for example, might institute new policies in the light of a changing interregional military environment. These directives may result in changes in other organizational spheres, which in turn may feed back to affect the state in unpredictable ways. As we will demonstrate below, seemingly minor changes in one organizational sphere can ramify through the society, resulting in significant overall change. This can happen because the actors who are developing new strategies never have perfect information concerning the consequences of their actions in terms of the natural environment or for the society as a whole (cf. Kurtz 1974; Jorde 1978; Athens 1978; Holling and Goldberg 1971; Schalk 1978). Probably this chronic lack of knowledge is due to the fact that interrelationships between the organizational spheres and between them and the natural environment and other societies are complex and involve circular, mutual feedbacks. As Rappaport (1978:67-68) has pointed out, human problem-solving tends to be linear in nature, but, as he puts it, ". . . the world is not constructed in linear fashion . . . the circularity [in causality] . . . blurs the distinction between cause and effect, or rather suggests to us that simple linear notions of causality, which lead us to think in terms of actors, objects upon which they act and the transformation of such objects, are inadequate, for purposeful behavior seldom affects only a single object . . . but usually many other objects as well, often in complex and ramifying ways. Among those being affected in unforeseen and possibly unpleasant ways may be the actor himself."

Thus, strategies employed to improve performance or to cope with unusual circumstances may have implications far greater than what was foreseen. In fact, the resulting changes may be so pervasive that it becomes unlikely that the society will ever return to anything like its original condition, even if the problem which was the source of change to begin with disappears. As Nef (1977) reminds us, coal technology, which became the energy basis for the industrial revolution, was not an invention whose potential could be forecast. Instead, people grudgingly switched to coal due to a stressful situation–an energy shortage. As Nef puts it:

> The first energy crisis, which has much to do with the crisis we now face, was a crisis of deforestation. The adoption of coal changed the economic history of Britain. . . . The substitution of coal for wood between 1550 and 1700 led to new methods of manufacturing, to the expansion of existing industries and to the exploitation of untapped natural resources. [Nef 1977: 140]

Coal proved to be such an ideal and productive energy source that, once adopted, it was not later abandoned when England reforested. Computers were developed under the stimulus of a world war to solve computational log jams. Obviously, they were not then abandoned once the war ended, since they proved to have so many varied applications, contributing to change in procedures in government, business, science, and technology.

In some cases, the adoption of a new strategy may not only create changes that ramify through a society, but it may result, unpredictably, in increased insecurity. In this case, the new strategy, while perhaps solving some problems, may actually increase the amplitude of fluctuation in some variable or variables, requiring even more coping efforts, and conceivably, more drastic changes. Perhaps the foremost example of this process in cultural evolution in general was the switch to grain agriculture. As Odum (1969) reminds us, when viewed from an ecological perspective, agriculture is a means by which humans manage successional sequences. The early stages of such sequences and the associated species are highly desirable for human use from the point of view of energy capture (and for other reasons), but, viewed systemically, the early stages are more prone to instabilities. As Gall and Saxe comment:

> Agriculture produces a condition of high energy yields, which supply a population with an additional mechanism for subsistence. As a consequence of obtaining high yields through simplified ecosystems, however, the sociocultural system becomes more vulnerable to fluctuations brought about by independent variations in rainfall, temperature, disease, and other nonsociocultural subsystems of the environment. [Gall and Saxe 1977:258-59, see also Athens, 1978]

Another feature of coping strategies is the fact that they have costs. A major change, for example the addition of a new hierarchical level in an administrative institution, may involve considerable costs in energy, time, and personnel. In preindustrial states and chiefdoms the creation of or addition to energy flows to "fund" such activities can take many forms, including militarism. Equally as common, and loaded with possibilities for secular evolution, is agricultural intensification. Such projects modify ecosystems, producing feedbacks and increased instabilities (cf. Athens 1978; Lees 1974; Farvar and Milton, eds. 1972). Since such development projects have the function of increasing state (or chiefly) revenues, they rarely if ever benefit producers. Producers may respond to the increased demands by the acceptance or development of labor-saving devices to minimize increases in work-load (and rebellion is a potential response in extreme cases), but perhaps more common are changes in the nature of "home economics," prominently involving the expansion of the size of the family as a strategy for coping with high demands (cf. Cowgill 1975; Sahlins 1972; Coontz 1968; White 1973; Blanton 1975).

As related by Jones and Woolf (1969:2), in preindustrial states

> Tax burdens were so onerous and collection was (all considered) so efficient that local consumption was kept at a low, often a subsistence level, and might be further depressed in times of stress. Any significant rise in the surplus of food produced above the subsistence level could be skimmed off by the State. . . . On the other hand, labour for food production on the family holding and to meet obligations to the State was a real asset. Probably it was this situation which encouraged population growth to meet whatever level of food supplies could be produced and retained by the bulk of the people. Even momentous agricultural advances which might have raised *per capita* real incomes–such as the medieval introduction of early ripening rice or the sixteenth century introduction of crops like the potato to China–were substantially, though not wholly, neutralized by the responsive growth of population. This response of 'static expansion'–whereby the agricultural base came to support more people without an increase in income per head–was the common historical experience of the pre-industrial world.

Population growth in a society will result potentially in new stresses as population pressure mounts. As land shortages (and other kinds of shortages) become more troublesome in the growing system, the workload of the adjudicative authority must increase in order to maintain order, necessitating, in turn, once certain built-in limits have been exceeded, additional revenue and personnel. The system thus becomes locked into a positive-feedback pattern, amplifying at each turn the magnitude and rapidity of change. The added costs of correcting for environmental degradation that can result due to intensification may be an added dimension to the new stresses and strains on the administrative subsystems (cf. Athens 1978; Lees 1974). If these subsystems cannot respond appropriately to the new conditions, breakdown is the result.

Another major feature of cultural evolution is what we refer to as institutionalization of the coping structure. A common response to extreme fluctuations is the formation of an organized group (a structure) charged with the responsibility of resolving the problem. This may result in evolutionary change if, after conditions return to normal, the new group persists rather than becoming disbanded. Secular change also results if the conditions favoring the formation of the group are becoming more frequent, warranting the maintenance of the structure.

The persistence of such a grouping, its institutionalization, even after the conditions producing it have passed, is a repetitive feature of cultural evolution. Why this is so may be a very complex problem, but perhaps a common feature of the workings of such groups is what Simon (1944:21, 1976:208, passim) calls *identification*. Here, members of the group develop loyalties to the group which may be difficult to dislodge: "It is a prevalent characteristic of human behavior that members of an organized group tend to identify with that group" (Simon 1944:21). According to Simon (ibid.:22), the psychological bases of identification include (among other factors): 1) The fact that personal success may depend on the success of the institution, and 2) that " . . . the human mind is limited in the number of diverse considerations which can occupy the area of attention at one time, and there is a consequent tendency to overemphasize the importance of those elements which happen to be within that area. To the fireman, fires are the most serious human problem; to the health officials, disease, and so forth" (ibid.:22). Thus, members of a group resist dismantling of the group no matter what. New functions may be invented, personnel kept, budget sources maintained or new sources developed. We predict that as such structures are first becoming institutionalized there will be heightened effort by the group devoted to the creation of symbols of legitimation, in order to assure continued revenue and access to power. Once fully institutionalized, such symbol production is redundant and thus falls off in quantity and costs.

A well-known example of institutionalization of a coping structure is the evolution of kingship and its associated palace institution some 5000 years ago in Mesopotamia. As summarized by Adams (1966:139), the protoliterate texts and myths indicate the presence of assemblies of elders which characteristically

> . . . met in response to a situation of crisis and temporarily delegated extraordinary powers as a war leader to one of its number. . . . By contrast, the situation portrayed in the Early Dynastic epics is one in which the presumed descendants of earlier war leaders had succeeded in varying degrees in assuming a position of permanently elevated status and authority. [Adams 1966:139-40]

Another example of this phenomenon can be seen in the political organization of the smaller Polynesian atolls. Tikopia, one of these islands, has been studied since 1929 by Raymond Firth (1936, 1939, 1959, 1961). Under the stress of land and food shortages brought on by hurricanes and drought, the Tikopia chiefdom is rigidly organized. Chiefs exercise their maximum life-and-death adjudicative powers and demand adherence to requests for labor services. Once the stress is removed, by one means or another, chiefs retain their theoretically vast constitutional powers, but in actual practice their rule is minimal and the society operates in a more egalitarian, consensual manner, while retaining the ritual precedence and symbolic importance of the chiefly hierarchy.

The creation of a coping structure can have unexpected consequences. As Simon points out, identification may result in pathological conditions:

> Organizational loyalties lead also, however, to certain difficulties which should not be underestimated. The principal undesirable effect of identification is that it prevents the institutionalized individual from making correct decisions in cases where the restricted area of values with which he identifies must be weighed against other values outside that area. This is a principal cause of the interbureau competition and wrangling which characterizes any large administrative organization. The organization members, identifying with the bureau instead of with the over-all organization, believe the bureau's welfare more important in general when the two conflict. [Simon 1944:22]

This pattern is undoubtedly related to what Rappaport has suggested may happen as an institution changes from being "system-serving" to "self-serving" (Flannery 1972a:413) and is clearly one example of the kinds of unanticipated negative consequences that may develop in a changing system.

Having established the outlines of our approach to explanation in cultural evolution, we will now turn to the Valley of Oaxaca, to illustrate how such an approach can be applied. To do this, we will briefly discuss as examples two prominent evolutionary problems in the valley, the beginnings of chiefdom organization, and the growth of the valley's earliest state, which began around 500 B.C. with the foundation of a regional capital at Monte Albán. What we say here cannot constitute a theory of cultural evolution for Formative Oaxaca. Instead, the following exercise is designed to point out what we think are the kinds of considerations that will be important in developing such a theory.

AN APPROACH FOR UNDERSTANDING THE EVOLUTION OF CHIEFDOMS IN THE VALLEY OF OAXACA

In attempting to describe and offer explanations for a society's change through time, problems in communication are immediately apparent. A society is described in terms of its natural environment, organizational spheres, and other societies with which it interacts, and how all of these interact. For example, in dealing with a period of change we may start with a description of processes in one organizational sphere. But it would be misleading to interpret this to imply that what happens there "causes" change in other spheres. Instead, the parts interact simultaneously, in mutual feedback fashion. Describing such instantaneous mutual feedback is a problem because our means of expression is more linear. Our first task is to attempt to reconstruct certain features of change in "home economics" and household time budgets from preceramic times until after the foundation of the regional capital at Monte Albán. We do this to establish a background for explaining change in other organizational spheres, but we do not intend to imply that changes in familial-level strategies should be considered to be a "prime mover" in cultural evolution.

Flannery (1968b) outlines the nature of seasonal scheduling of foragers in regions like the Valley of Oaxaca prior to the Formative. Different strategies are employed according to seasonal variation in the availability of foods, but, since food is not stored, at least not for long periods, the food quest is a year-round activity. It is possible there was abundant leisure time, as is suggested by analogy from other foragers (cf. Lee 1968), but this would have been on a day-to-day or week-to-week basis, with no long breaks in hunting/collecting.

As these populations began to depend more on those procurement systems that involved maize and other plant domesticates, schedules changed, and larger groups were a more permanent feature. As these cultigens became more productive, ". . . increased permanence of the macroband may have been *required* by the amplified planting and harvesting pattern" (Flannery 1968b:81). By analogy with other simple agriculturalists, the change from foraging to the new planting and harvesting pattern would have involved greater sedentism, given the difficulties of moving the ton or so of harvested grain a family needs for a year, and a changed yearly schedule, involving a period of more constant, intensive work during the height of the agricultural season, followed by a period of relative free time. The total amount of work versus non-work time may not have changed that much–if anything, farming implies more work inputs than foraging–but the timing of work/non-work would have been different (cf. Udy 1959:26). One of the consequences of such a shift, as discussed by Flannery (1972b:132), is a change from the *ad hoc* ritual characteristic of foragers, carried out any time in the year when abundant food supports, temporarily, larger groups for non-production activities, to the seasonally-scheduled ritual more characteristic of settled agriculturalists, which occurs regularly during the agricultural off-season, after harvesting activities are completed. We suggest there would have been an increase in two other activities during this season, long-distance raiding and long-distance trading and related interactions. Agriculturalists cannot readily move in response to production declines, so must participate in regional and interregional systems to survive extreme fluctuations. The new schedules permit such activities, given the availability of an open period after the harvest. The archaeological remains pertaining to the Early Formative support this interpretation, at least in part, as there is abundant evidence for interregional exchange in the context of what is referred to as an "interaction sphere" (Flannery 1968a; Flannery and Schoenwetter 1970). Flannery and Schoenwetter argue that long-distance exchange is a means for "banking" surpluses. Trade goods obtained in surplus years could be exchanged for food in lean years. Judging from the ethnographic literature, however, we suggest that long-distance raiding expeditions would have been viewed in certain cases as the functional equivalent of trading to account for deficits (cf. Ford 1972), as well as being a means for correcting for demographic fluctuations through abduction (Harner 1970).

We suggest, then, that warfare, including interregional raiding, would have been a more salient feature of the Mesoamerican cultural landscape after the adoption of farming than it had been earlier. It is thus probably a good example of how the adoption of a new strategy may increase the magnitude of fluctuations in one or more other variables, necessitating, in turn, the development of further coping strategies. This is by no means an argument that population pressure and "circumscription" led to increased warfare. In fact, as we will demonstrate in subsequent chapters, there is very little likelihood that the human population was anywhere near the potential capacity of the environment–there was, instead, a significant degree of underuse of agricultural resources during the early part of the Formative period. Raiding, as an alternative to trading, would have increased markedly in intensity during years when there were general production declines over broad areas, when few or no groups at all had a surplus they could supply to trade partners. Too, marginal groups not able to participate in such trade spheres (for example groups unable to produce a significant surplus even in normal years, or who lacked local products desired by other populations) might more often have had to choose raiding over trading.

Both raiding and trading, we feel, created conditions favoring secular evolutionary change in the Southern Highlands macroregion. Given the uneven distribution of agricultural resources in the Southern Highlands, the population of the Valley of Oaxaca would have had a special role to play in interregional interaction. The valley not only has the broadest expanse of cultivable alluvium in the macroregion as a whole, but it also has, in general, more sources of water suitable for simple kinds of irrigation, including a substantial area of high water table alluvium permitting "pot irrigation." It was probably the case, given the generally more suitable circumstances in the valley for farming, that extreme deficits would have been less often encountered relative to those encountered in marginal valleys. This would have had two general consequences favoring secular change: 1) A net accumulation by Valley of Oaxaca trade partners of "wealth" in the form of items exchanged for food, as well as a net accumulation of prestige, since valley trade partners would more often have been suppliers of surpluses rather than consumers of surpluses. 2) Valley populations would have been exposed to more frequent and intensive raiding pressure than groups in other areas, for similar reasons, necessitating the development in the valley of more elaborate strategies than would be necessary elsewhere to cope with extreme fluctuations in raiding pressure. An additional aspect of this to consider is that valley populations, given the greater predictability of production there, would have experienced fewer episodes of extreme depopulation due to starvation or emigration, making the valley, again, an ideal target for marginal groups interested in bolstering declining population through abduction. Exactly what kinds of strategies to cope with extremes in raiding pressure would have been developed during the early part of the Formative is unknown, but possibilities include alliance formation between villages, the "promotion" of war leaders to chief, and so on.

Our argument is that inequalities in the distribution of resources in the Southern Highlands macroregion could foster evolutionary change. Valley of Oaxaca villages would tend to accumulate "wealth" and prestige *vis à vis* marginal groups, and would, at the same time, have been more likely than marginal groups to develop elaborate coping structures to deal with military problems. To amplify this argument, we will discuss in more detail what we feel would have been some of the salient features of population dynamics at the time of early village formation, and we will consider some of its consequences for change. Again, given the shortage of data, this is meant only as a set of suggestions, not a final argument.

One of the consequences of sedentism at the extremely low population densities found in the Early Formative period (cf. Flannery, ed. 1976; Chapter 3, below) is the high probability that local populations are below a size limit making them self-contained demographic entities. In his simulation studies, Wobst (1974) found that a human population must contain 400 or more people to assure long-term persistence. Even the population of the Valley of Oaxaca during the Early Formative was probably only barely within this size range (see Chapter 3, below). Throughout the remainder of the Southern Highlands, local population aggregates would have been, no doubt, even smaller. As a consequence these peripheral populations would have been more exposed than the valley population to dangerous demographic fluctuations since, in general, the probability of fluctuations is inversely proportional to population size (cf. MacCluer et al. 1971; Skolnick and Cannings 1972; Ammerman 1975; Wobst 1974). This implies that it would have been essential for local populations to participate in macroregional networks that could be a source of wives (or husbands). To a certain extent, abduction could be the mechanism for augmenting population size, as mentioned above, but it is equally reasonable to expect personnel exchanges also through the medium of interregional marriage alliances (Friedman and Rowlands 1978). Substantial fluctuations are likely to have characterized all Early Formative populations, given the very low population densities, but, again, when viewed macroregionally, the amplitude and seriousness of fluctuations would not have been evenly distributed, favoring the larger, probably somewhat denser population of the Valley of Oaxaca. Given this, the net flow of people through the network would often have taken the form of a donor-recipient system, with Valley of Oaxaca populations more often the donors, while more marginal mountain groups would have been more often the recipients.

The following scheme is an attempt to show how this hypothesized donor-recipient pattern has embodied in it implications for evolutionary change. It is based on some suggestions by Friedman and Rowlands (1978) and Meggitt (1971, 1972) on the dynamics of tribal societies. We will make the following assumptions: 1) In a network of circulating connubia, people givers have higher status than people receivers. 2) People donors accumulate wealth as well as status since wealth moves in the direction opposite to the flow of people (e.g., in bride-price payments). 3) As the status and wealth of donors increases, more bride-price is expected to be paid to them, since the price paid reflects the status and wealth of the donors. As expressed by Friedman and Rowlands (1978:207), this " . . . relation is one where a given quantity of real wealth is exchanged for a kinship connection . . . to the source of wealth." 4) Wealth accumulated by donors can be used to further enhance prestige through feasting and prestations, increasing the size of the group with reciprocal obligations to the donors. 5) The participants consider that wealth and prosperity are controlled directly by supernatural spirits. As a result, since donor populations become more "wealthy," they are considered to have closer links to the supernatural. It is at this point that the transition to chiefdom organization can occur since donor groups are those groups that come to be mediators with the supernatural, and who can extract tribute and corvée in exchange for their mediating activities.

This set of ideas explaining the rise of chiefdom organization in Oaxaca is deficient in a number of respects. For example, we don't know at what scale an Early Formative marriage network would have operated. Would it have included only the population of the valley and perhaps a few adjacent areas? Or would the system have incorporated groups over much of the Southern Highlands? What would have been the relevant donor groups in the Valley of Oaxaca? The entire population of the valley, or more local groupings within the valley, such as specific lineages? Similarly, when discussing status differentiation and promotion to higher supernatural rank, is the relevant unit the entire population of the valley, or again, smaller groups within the valley as a whole? The archaeological evidence indicates the early predominance of one Valley of Oaxaca community, San José Mogote (Flannery, ed. 1976). Perhaps the ideal agricultural conditions around this community (Kirkby 1973) served to dampen population fluctuations there so that they more often could have continued in the role of donors, even to other Valley of Oaxaca groups.

The advantage in considering interregional differences in population sizes and inequalities in the distribution of agricultural resources is that it may be possible to explain why chiefdoms evolve in some macroregions and not others. For example, in an area containing tribal groups that interact in a circulating connubium, but where no single group can more often be donor rather than recipient, change in the direction of rank and wealth differences will not occur. Friedman and Rowlands (1978) also make the point that an emerging ranked system has increasing energy demands to support the activities of the emergent chiefly lineages. They note that in areas that are highly susceptible to environmental damage due to agricultural intensification, the emerging ranked system will collapse as energy flows decline, returning it to a more egalitarian state. The full playing-out of the evolutionary sequence can probably only occur in places like the Valley of Oaxaca, where agricultural intensification can be carried to considerable lengths without noticeable environmental consequences. The valley's relatively abundant water sources also make it possible for producers to respond to increased production demands through various kinds of irrigation projects.

An additional advantage of this kind of argumentation is that it offers explanations for change in situations in which there is no population pressure on agricultural resources. This conforms with our findings, discussed below (in Chapter 3), that populations were well below their potentials during the period in which there was a transition to ranking. Our argument pays most attention to how people cope with unpredictability, and how regional and interregional inequalities in the distribution of population and agricultural resources provide the potential for change in the context of regional and interregional interaction.

We now turn to a later period, following the formation of a regional capital in the Valley of Oaxaca at Monte Albán around 500 B.C. A fuller discussion of the set of changes during this time–Period I–is reserved for Chapter 4. The purpose of the following section is, again, to illustrate how our approach to cultural evolution can be applied in a particular case. We also hope to illustrate some of the features we feel were of importance in early state formation generally.

CONSEQUENCES OF THE FORMATION OF MONTE ALBAN

Blanton (1976a, 1978) argued that the establishment of a new regional capital at Monte Albán was a manifestation of the formation of a new political institution in the Valley of Oaxaca. This institution, he argued, was formed through the voluntary joining of several previously autonomous groups. The new capital, the center of activities of this league, was placed in a neutral position atop a high hill, central to the region as a whole, in order to avoid a setting which would unduly augment the influence of any one of the co-joining members. The carved stone monuments dating to the site's early periods indicate that the new institution was, at least initially, a military league.

The advantages of a single military organization for the Valley of Oaxaca as a whole seem obvious. Intraregional disputes would have been minimized, allowing the application of more energy, time, and personnel to minimizing external threats. An unprecedented number of soldiers could be put into the field under an unprecedented degree of centralized control. The costs, however, also are apparent: the necessity to support the new institution and the new capital. Monte Albán's marginal location suggests it could not have been locally self-supported (i.e., by its resident population) in terms of food, materials, or personnel (these topics are pursued in more detail below in Chapters 4 and 9). There are basically two means by which the new capital could have been supported during Period I: locally, in the valley, through stepped-up agricultural production and local population growth, and/or through empire formation, which would bring in resources from outside the valley. The nature of the conquest monuments at Monte Albán, however, leads to the inference that the organization of the macroregion during Period I was such that empire formation could not have been a productive or even viable strategy.

The *Danzantes* carvings of Period I were placed in what appears to have been a kind of military showcase on Monte Albán's Main Plaza (Marcus 1976a, 1980). The carvings are numerous–over three hundred are known, and more are undoubtedly incorporated into the fill of later buildings. These monuments depict individuals–perhaps captured "big-men" or chiefs who had been brought back to the capital to be humiliated and slain (Marcus 1976a, 1980). By Period II, the situation is different. The conquest glyphs by that time were fewer in number and depict the conquests of particular centers (Caso 1928; Marcus 1976a, 1980). We feel this difference in the content and frequency of conquest glyphs is relevant to a discussion of empire formation at Monte Albán. This situation reminds us of Herbert Simon's (1969) parable about the two watchmakers, Hora and Tempus. Hora built his watches in modules, then later assembled the modules into completed watches. Tempus assembled watches one element at a time. Tempus eventually goes out of business while Hora prospers. This is so because, although both are exposed to constant interruptions, Hora need not start each time from scratch as does Tempus, thus demonstrating the advantages of "modularization." Simon interprets this to imply that " . . . complex systems will evolve from simple systems much more rapidly if there are stable intermediate forms than if there are not. The resulting complex forms in the former case will be hierarchic" (ibid.:98-99). Applied to empire formation, Simon comments:

> We have not exhausted the categories of complex systems to which the watchmaker argument can reasonably be applied. Philip assembled his Macedonian empire and gave it to his son, to be later combined with the Persian subassembly and others into Alexander's greater system. On Alexander's death, his empire did not crumble to dust but fragmented into some of the major subsystems that had composed it.
>
> The watchmaker argument implies that if one would be Alexander, one should be born into a world where large stable political systems already exist. Where this condition was not fulfilled, as on the Scythian and Indian frontiers, Alexander found empire building a slippery business. So too, T.E. Lawrence's organizing of the Arab revolt against the Turks was limited by the character of his largest stable building blocks, the separate suspicious desert tribes. [Simon 1969:98]

Service (1955) reaches a similar conclusion in his article describing the nature of Indian-European relations in Latin America. In these areas of the New World where the Spaniards encountered native populations organized in large bureaucratic states, conquest was facilitated. "The manipulation of this kind of controlling mechanism was not unfamiliar to the conquerors, and they quickly placed themselves at the top of the hierarchy and governed the mass of the population through native intermediaries in the lower echelons of the bureaucracy . . . ." (Service 1955:420). Where such state bureaucracies were lacking, conquest was far more difficult and less productive materially. These groups had considerable freedom of movement. "In fact, they were able to raid and harass the Europeans as well as escape them, so much greater was their self-sufficiency and consequent mobility of their small social units. . . . Control of the Indians in [these areas] thus meant capture and enslavement of individual Indians" (ibid.:420).

We suggest that the Danzantes monuments indicate that the populations of the Southern Highlands macroregion, during Period I, were organized as numerous small, autonomous units, militarily a threat, but making empire formation by Monte Albán unlikely. By Period II, however, the processes of centralization and formation of larger regional polities were proceeding, creating the kinds of "modular units" which make empire formation a possibility. The Period II glyphs depict conquered central places, not the capture of numerous individuals.

If Monte Albán could not be substantially supported by empire until Period II, we conclude its support must have been borne during Period I largely by the local population of the region. We suggest this was accomplished through stepped-up agricultural production in the valley, and that this intensification had several important consequences, resulting in further evolutionary change. To discuss the nature of change during Period I, it will be most convenient to start again at the level of changing "home economics." We argued that during the earlier part of the Formative a single wet season crop with perhaps minimal irrigation in dry years was sufficient for subsistence and whatever minor surpluses would have been needed, leaving a dry season with little or no productive work requirements, as is typical for most tribal agriculturalists and harvest collectors. Since the formation of a regional polity in the Valley of Oaxaca necessitated stepped-up agricultural production, we suggest the response in the household organizational sphere would have included: 1) increased family size to increase the working capacity of households, and 2) a second crop and harvesting every year, necessitating, in turn, more use of irrigation. Expanding the area under cultivation during a single agricultural season is an alternative, but probably not a viable response to increased demands, since a household can only care for so much planted hectarage, and because that would have necessitated a large increase in the amount of land used per family. The latter would have been problematic in light of the very substantial population growth during Period I (Fig. 2-1) which would have meant *reduced*, not increased hectarage available to households. We believe our survey data (discussed below) strongly support a move by cultivators during Period I to canal irrigation in the piedmont zone. Flannery (et al. 1967) and his associates have noticed a similar trend toward more canal irrigation during this time. This trend, we feel, would have had major implications in terms of the evolution of the regional system.

First, an increased frequency of canal irrigation implies another re-ordering of familial time budgets, away from the Early Formative pattern, and with more time devoted to agricultural work. As Waddell has concluded from his study of Highland New Guinea agricultural systems:

> There is nevertheless, one major distinction between extensive and intensive [agriculture] systems which most authorities recognize. . . . They have contrasting rhythms of work, with the extensive systems characterized by major fluctuations in levels of agricultural activities through time, and the intensive by sustained inputs throughout the agricultural cycle. For simple social systems, like those of the Central Highlands, the former routine has the merit of providing the majority of the population with abundant opportunity for participating in the various social and ceremonial activities which serve as mechanisms for exchanging goods and services and acquiring political power. The latter tends to tie the majority of the population more closely to the land, hence providing the appropriate preconditions for the creation of a rural peasantry, where only a controlling minority is endowed with sufficient leisure time to become active in the social and political life of the society. [Waddell 1972:218]

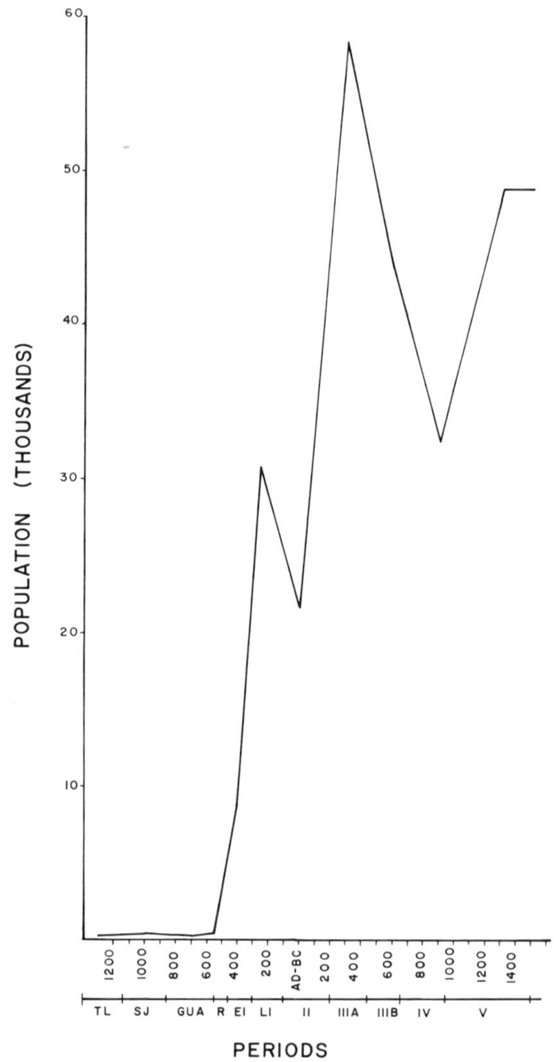

Figure 2-1. Total population estimates for the survey area (including Monte Albán), Tierras Largas through Period V.

We suggest that given the necessity of spending more time in agricultural production, producers would be willing to abandon certain kinds of time-consuming householding activities that previously could be accomplished during free periods in the agricultural cycle, and that this resulted in decreased household self-sufficiency. Work required to replace certain kinds of implements would have, in prior times, consumed a significant portion of a family's working time. Pottery, for example, is a class of implement that is constantly needed, since pots break and crack, and replacement requires considerable time and work. Clay must be obtained and prepared, vessels formed, surfaces finished, firewood obtained, then firing done. As household work budgets increasingly were devoted to agricultural production, obtaining such replacement items from outside could have been a work-minimizing strategy, if the additional agricultural surplus needed to "pay" for such items involved less additional work time than the production of the items themselves. This could have been the case if some groups in the region increasingly specialized in craft production and thus were able to take advantage of the economies of scale production. A few specialists could produce a large number of items, supplying a large number of households, in exchange for a small amount of additional agricultural surplus from each. Conditions in the valley would have been ideal for the development of such production specialties after the formation of Monte Albán for several reasons, and it is at this time, during Period I, that we can first detect surface evidence for community specialization in utilitarian items (see Chapters 4 and 10, below), a finding supported by Marcus Winter's work (1974).

How a decrease in householding (the relative self-sufficiency in production of utilitarian items) could occur, concomitant with an increase in specialized production of utilitarian items, can be understood by reference to "demand threshold." The demand threshold of an item is met if a geographic area contains sufficient customers for that good such that specialists can earn a living supplying that good. Whether an area will support specialists producing a good depends largely on population density and the degree to which households are dependent on the specialists. Both of these factors, we argue, were on the increase following the formation of Monte Albán, favoring a shift to more specialized production. One other factor is relevant. After the creation of the regional polity, there would undoubtedly have been less intraregional warfare, increasing dramatically the potential for intraregional interaction.

In Chapter 4, the data we have pertaining to specialized production in utilitarian items are analyzed in terms of the predictions of central-place theory. These results support the idea that, for the first time, a market system was present in the Valley of Oaxaca during Period I. By market system we mean a set of places in a region from which households of producers can obtain items including utilitarian goods that they could, but do not, produce at home. We want to make the distinction between market systems and what we call border-market exchanges. Border-market exchanges can occur in many kinds of societies, including tribes and chiefdoms (cf. Benet 1957; Allan 1978; Earle 1977, 1978; Helms 1979:160-62). Border-market exchange, like market system exchange, involves higgling-haggling and so is largely divorced from considerations of balanced reciprocity. The difference between the two modes of exchange, as we are defining them here, is that border-market exchange is a form of border mechanism exchange, taking place across cultural and/or linguistic and environmental boundaries, and typically involving exchanges in goods that are not locally available, including exotic items and production specialties based on environmental differences. Market system exchange, on the other hand, is intraregional exchange, largely, and involves for the most part utilitarian items that are not exotics. Market system exchange, we would argue (but not border-market exchange), develops as demands on households of producers increase, altering work schedules, thus decreasing the desirability or feasibility of household self-sufficiency in utilitarian items. Also, as we mentioned above, as a regional polity emerges, it limits intraregional warfare, thus increasing potential interaction. These, in combination with rapid population growth, mean that demand thresholds for at least some goods are exceeded, making specialized production a viable alternative for some households. A market system has started to evolve.

The stage is now set for outlining some of the probable positive-feedback processes at work during Period I that fundamentally altered the nature of the regional system. We believe that the creation of the regional polity resulted in a series of unpredictable changes. Monte Albán's original functions may have been largely offense-defense, but its effects on the valley's population produced the following changes:

1) Given an integrated regional system and the beginnings of market production and exchange, the Central area of the valley, including Monte Albán, would have been ideally located for the production of certain goods, since producers there could optimally service the valley's population as a whole. This Central area, including the city itself, would have become more commercialized. As far as we can tell from our surface surveys so far, a number of goods seem to have been produced only at Monte Albán, not only during Period

I, but during later periods as well. Included are obsidian goods, items made of jade and other rare stones, such as onyx bowls, and marine-shell items. A panregional institution like that at Monte Albán, no matter what its original functions, would, because of central-place considerations, become commercialized, adding to the functions of the community and hence to the number of people residing there. The institution created the conditions that eventually resulted in the augmentation of its regional dominance.

2) The commercial dominance of the regional capital in a bounded region like the Valley of Oaxaca is further exacerbated since competing centers away from the valley's center are closer to the region's edge and hence have fewer potential customers for each good. The ranges of goods (the areas within which a group of people are present who are willing to walk the distance necessary to obtain the good) at these other centers are small because they are ''truncated'' by rugged topography and/or military insecurity beyond the valley's edge. Demand thresholds for many goods are thus not met in these centers, and so their production cannot be supported. This limits the commercial growth of these centers, while augmenting the importance of the region's capital, where these goods are available. Regional boundedness is one factor producing a ''primate'' pattern such as that which developed soon after Monte Albán's founding, where a region's capital is unexpectedly large according to the predictions of central-place theory (or, conversely, the region's secondary centers are unpredictably small relative to the largest center) (Berry 1967; Blanton 1976b; Skinner 1977b:284-85). Center size relationships will be discussed more fully in Chapter 4.

3) Changing conditions in the valley would have required additional administrative functions, beyond those pertaining to matters of offense-defense. Several considerations would have been involved. The rapid population growth (probably to or beyond the carrying capacity in the valley's congested Central area by the end of Period I) would have increased the likelihood of land disputes, as desirable localities became rarer. Too, the rapid growth of population in the capital, which was, we think, largely fueled by immigration, could have presented the Monte Albán administrators with problems in behavior control, as is often the case in rapidly-growing cities, including Aztec Tenochtitlán (Bray 1978:380; Calnek 1978:315-16).

Two other areas of more importance may have taxed the administrative abilities of the newly-founded institution. As we mentioned earlier, there was a major move to canal irrigation during this period, especially in the vicinity of Monte Albán. We know from ethnographic studies of such simple canal irrigation systems in the contemporary valley that local groups are capable of constructing, maintaining, and operating such systems under normal circumstances, without any higher authority. But, as Downing (1974) demonstrates, such systems ultimately cannot operate without the presence of a higher adjudicative authority. Under normal circumstances, local authorities are fully capable of coordination and adjudication. In extreme circumstances, however, for example when an exceptionally large number of people are in need of water simultaneously, the ''frequency and ardor'' of conflicts over water increase, eventually overtaxing the local authority (the *síndico*). Under these circumstances, the *síndico* may switch to a system referred to as ''appropriation'' where '' . . . a three-level hierarchy of mediators buffers disputes before they reach the *síndico*. If those conflicts unresolved by the lower level in the hierarchy reach the *síndico*, they are considered much more serious . . . [they] . . . are those that could not be resolved by peers in the field or by [local] officials. The *síndico* now has public support to exercise his most coercive power–shifting the dispute to district court under the guise of a 'civil disorder.' Thus, the ultimate power for water regulation lies outside the local level'' (Downing 1974:118).

One last area demanding expanded regional administration would have pertained to the increased degree of specialization in production that was developing following the formation of Monte Albán. This need not imply total state control of the production and movement of goods. In fact that degree of control–redistribution (Polanyi 1944: Chapter 4)–is probably easily detectable archaeologically, since the administration characteristically maintains large storage facilities. Examples include the Minoan-Mycenean palaces (Renfrew 1972:291-97), Harappa and Mohenjo-Daro (Wheeler 1968), and Peruvian Chan-Chan (Mosely and Mackey 1974) and Cuzco (Katz 1978). No such features are present at Monte Albán, or in other Valley of Oaxaca sites, implying that exchange occurred largely or completely in the context of markets. Still, we suggest that some regulation would have been necessary, for example in adjudication between market participants, and that the regional polity would have been at least in part responsible, since it alone would have had pan-regional authority. Too, given the dramatic increase in the population in the region residing in cities, especially in Monte Albán, other new pressures related to production would have been created. It would probably be impossible to underestimate the importance of the state's role, in preindustrial societies, in assuring predictable, reasonably priced food supplies to urban dwellers, given the possibilities for extreme fluctuations due to factors such as variable rainfall, farmers' rebellions, and hoarding by merchants (Tilly 1975).

In short, the creation of a regional polity in the Valley of Oaxaca around 500 B.C. created a series of unprecedented new problems at the regional level, related to population pressure, irrigation agriculture, and an increase in specialized production and the proportion of the population residing in urban centers. These new problems would have added to the work-load on the new institution, increasing its scope of responsibilities, as well as its costs, and, as a result, increasing the degree of regional dominance by the institution. Our argument parallels that made by the Hunts (Hunt and Hunt 1974) regarding the role of irrigation in politics in contemporary San Juan, in the Cañada of Oaxaca. In the following quote, they refer to the role of irrigation in political centralization, but we feel the same argument could be as forcefully applied in connection with all of the areas outlined above. They conclude:

> The hypothesis which emerges from our case study is that one condition under which centralization of authority is adaptive in reducing conflict is under conditions of water scarcity (i.e., when there is pressure on land and water sources) and that this adaptive response might be particularly effective in a system of food production which is totally dependent on canal irrigation agriculture . . . .
>
> We suggest that without unified decision making, high levels of social disruption and conflict will tend to paralyze the socioeconomic system. Over long periods of time, the threat of anarchic conflict will generate further pressure to centralize the system, if it is to survive. . . .
>
> Centralization of the political system facilitates higher levels of productivity by reducing social conflict at the local levels. It also may allow the formation of an institutional frame and specialized roles which could be potential springboards to other realms of local power or control, if the social structure allows for a stratified control of resources. However, in all probability, there is a feedback loop involved here, because sustained power in other realms of the society will probably increase the likelihood of particular persons either assuming themselves, or being regularly recruited to fill, the decision-making roles connected with irrigation. At this time, we see nothing in the data which permits us to decide to make irrigation either the independent or the dependent variable when considered with other kinds of politically controlled systems within the same society. But neither can we suggest from the empirical evidence that the irrigation system is epiphenomenal to the political process or to the degrees of centralization of authority which may be most adaptive to maintain social conflict at low levels. On the contrary, irrigation appears to be for the system considered here, one of the major foci of the political field. [Hunt and Hunt 1974:118–19]

CONCLUSION

In both of these example cases, we feel that the adoption of new strategies (in the first, the switch to agriculture and sedentism, in the second, the establishment of a new capital) set in motion sets of changes that eventually transformed society. In reality, the causality involved in the two cases was probably more complex than we portrayed it and probably involved factors we have not mentioned. But, even so, we think these sketchy outlines reflect to some degree the complexity and circularity of the interactions between societies, organizational spheres, and between the human populations and their natural environments. While we have included in our sketches all of the major prime-movers–population growth, warfare, irrigation, and trade–we feel that the treatment of them here is more logically satisfying than the more linear explanations that are usually offered.

Chapter 3

THE EARLY AND MIDDLE FORMATIVE PERIODS

by Eva Fisch

INTRODUCTION

This chapter deals with the four periods making up the Early and Middle Formative (Tierras Largas, 1400-1150 B.C.; San José, 1150-850 B.C.; Guadalupe, 850-700 B.C.; and Rosario, 700-500 B.C.) in the Central and Valle Grande survey areas. What is presented here does not represent a full analysis of the settlement pattern, ceramic, or environmental data we collected in these two survey areas. The scope of this presentation has been restricted since we believe strongly that any meaningful study of these periods in the valley will have to wait until the completion of the remainder of the survey. It is already clear that the bulk of the valley occupations dating to these periods are not to be found in the Central or Valle Grande areas, but in the Etla and Tlacolula arms. Those sites with the most potential for contributing to an understanding of the development of settlement hierarchies (especially San José Mogote in the Etla arm) are located in areas that are being surveyed as of the time of this writing. Also, the opportunities that are normally inherent in the combination of survey and excavated data are close to nil in the areas we have surveyed so far, since almost all the excavated sites from these periods are located in the Etla and Tlacolula arms (Drennan 1976; Flannery et. al 1970; Flannery, ed. 1976; Flannery and Marcus 1976; Whalen 1974, 1981). The only major excavation of a site in this time range and from the survey area is at Tierras Largas (2-1-2, 2-2-4, 2-3-6, 2-4-5; Figs. 3-1 to 3-4, square N13E6) (Winter 1972).

The paucity of excavations of early sites, especially toward the southern extent of our survey area, presented us with an immediate problem on survey. The ceramic sequences established in the better-known areas are not necessarily directly applicable where we were working. This did not mean that earlier sites were more likely to be overlooked, but it did mean that at times we could not distinguish between periods. This was especially a problem in distinguishing San José from Guadalupe occupations. Where large excavation samples have been analyzed, Guadalupe phase was distinguished from San José phase by the following criteria: 1) The appearance of gray and fine gray wares as well as Guadalupe Burnished Brown; 2) the increase in frequency of Atoyac Yellow-white outleaned-wall bowls and plastic decoration of certain ollas; 3) the near disappearance of red-on-white, specular red, "several gray wares", rocker stamping, some raspada designs, and Olmec motifs (Drennan 1976:56).

Our surface collections from the Central and especially the Valle Grande survey areas included only a few Tierras Largas, San José, or Guadalupe gray wares or red-on-white wares, and no Olmec motifs. We could not, of course, determine the change in frequency of any bowl shapes. Because of this, in some cases we were able only to say that a site contained either a San José and/or a Guadalupe phase occupation. When this happened, given the marked degree of settlement continuity that has been noted at sites dating to these early periods, we assumed that both periods were present. More research is clearly warranted.

In contrast, Tierras Largas occupations were easier to identify by the presence of the Valley of Oaxaca red and red-on-buff types, which are, incidentally, quite similar to types described for the Ajalpan phase in Tehuacán (MacNeish, Peterson, and Flannery 1970:31-35, 39, 46), and Early Cruz in the Mixteca (Spores 1972). Rosario phase pottery was readily identified by specific rim forms and incised motifs (see Appendix VII).

We draw the following conclusions from our experience with identifying pre-Monte Albán settlements from their ceramics. The Tierras Largas, San José, and Guadalupe phase sites are usually recognized rather easily in the field as being "something early," even though the number of sherds on a site is usually only a small handful. Within these three phases, Tierras Largas occupations are normally distinctive and separable from succeeding occupations. In the Central and Valle Grande areas, "San José and/or Guadalupe" can be recognized, but finer identification is often problematic. Rosario phase occupations, wherever we have seen them, typically have more sherds and are fairly easy to identify in the field and in the laboratory.

SETTLEMENT PATTERNS

During the first three of the phases here discussed, insofar as we can tell from surface evidence, sites in the survey area were small and architecturally simple (i.e., lacking secure evidence of public architecture.) Most of the sites were isolated residences, or hamlets

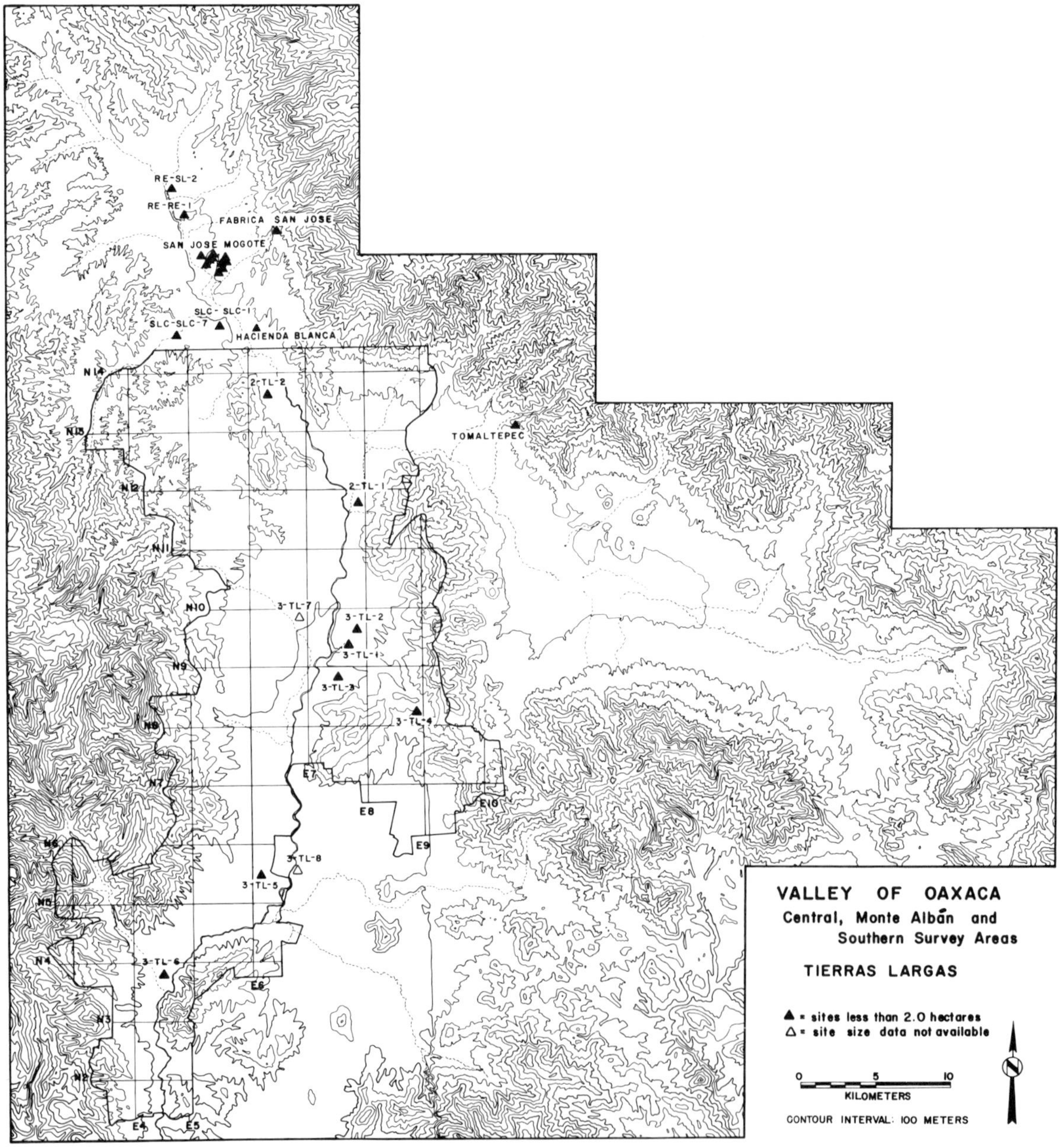

Figure 3-1. Settlements of the Tierras Largas phase. Sites shown outside the survey area in Figures 3-1 through 3-4 are those located during various prior surveys (Flannery et al. 1970; Varner 1974). Since our final systematic survey has not been completed in these areas, more sites may be found.

occupied by only a few households; few sites exceed a size indicating 50 persons (the population estimates are summarized in Tables 3-1 to 3-4). Two of the sites in this area are exceptions; Zaachila (N9E6) and Sta. Inés Yatzeche (which is located just beyond the bounds of the survey area but was partially mapped and given site numbers 3-1-8, 3-2-9, 3-4-11) were perhaps larger than average and perhaps also architecturally more elaborate. Both sites became important central places later in the sequence, as we discuss in the following chapters. The early periods at Zaachila, however, have been effectively buried under the massive constructions of the later prehistoric periods, as well as the deposits of the Colonial and recent periods. We were not allowed to map Sta. Inés in detail during the 1977 field season, but we did during the 1980 field season.

Only two sites in the survey area definitely show any tendency toward larger-than-average size: Tierras Lar-

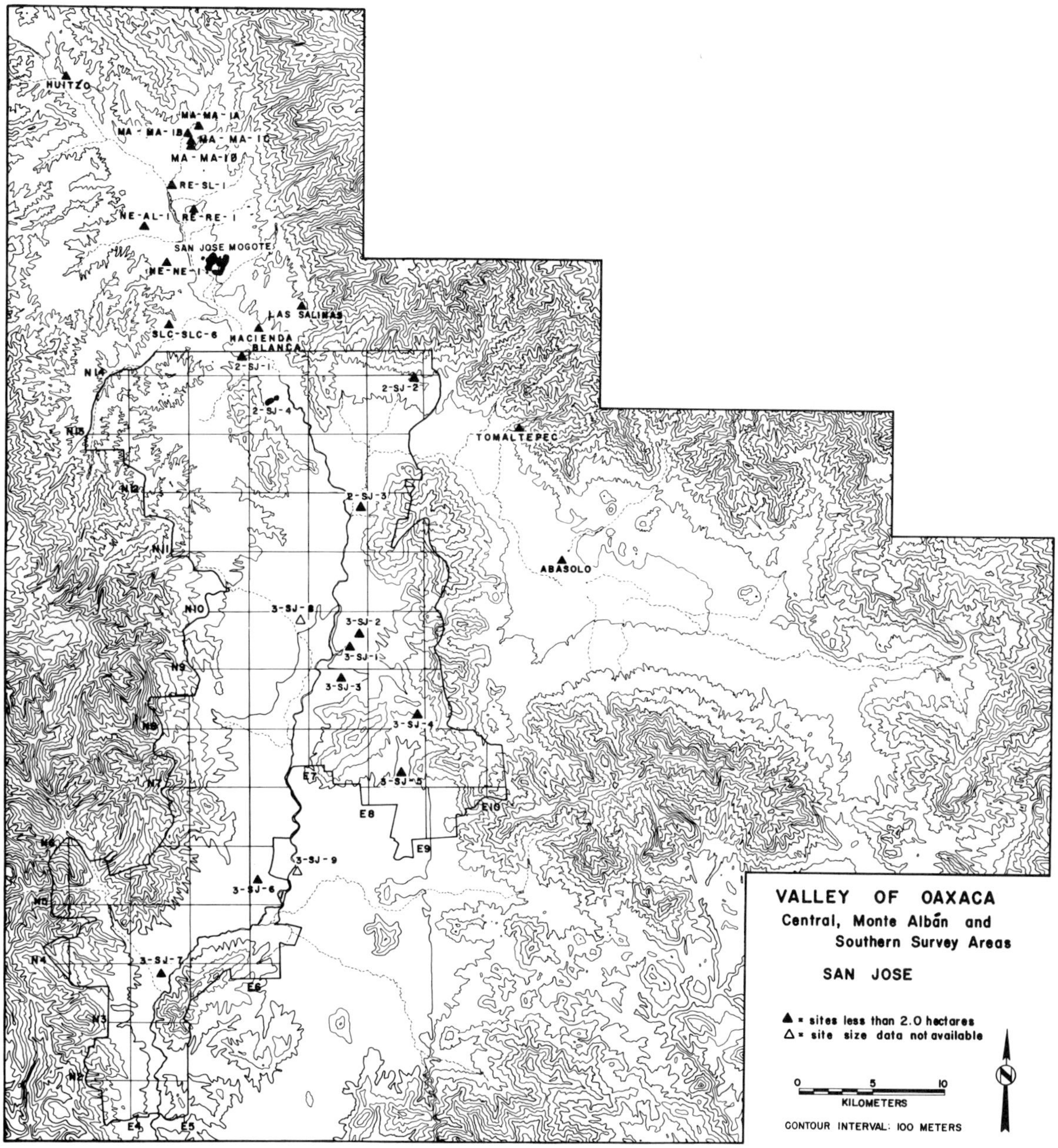

Figure 3-2. Settlements of the San José phase.

gas (N13E6; 2-1-2, 2-2-4, 2-3-6, 2-4-5) and Sta. Ana Tlapacoyan (N3E4; 3-1-6, 3-2-7, 3-3-8, 3-4-15) (Tables 3-1-4). Both are small, though, when compared with San José Mogote in the Etla arm, where population estimates are 147 for the Tierras Largas phase, 700 for the San José phase and 950 in the Rosario phase (Flannery, Marcus, and Kowalewski 1981; Marcus 1976c). Tierras Largas (2-4-5) and one site in the Valle Grande (3-4-2,18) may have had some public architecture in the Rosario phase.

The distribution of settlements from Tierras Largas phase through Rosario phase is shown in Figures 3-1 to 3-4. These figures impress one with the dominance of the Etla arm during the four pre-Monte Albán periods. Not only is the largest site known in the valley located in this arm, but there is a greater density of sites in the Etla arm compared with the Central and Valle Grande zones. Evidently these latter two zones were peripheral *vis à vis* the north until Early I. The marginality, as discussed previously, is also indicated in the ceramics.

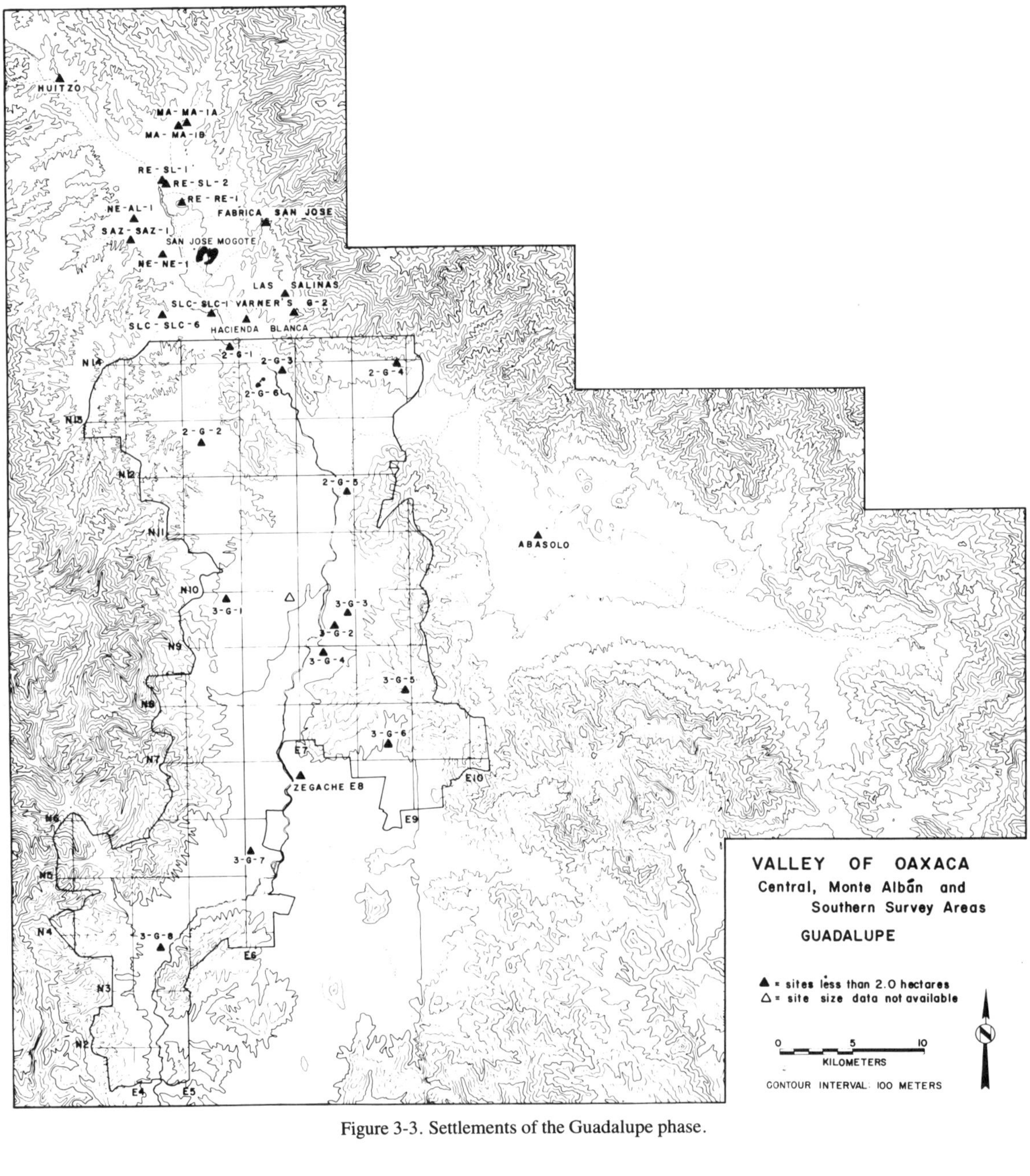

Figure 3-3. Settlements of the Guadalupe phase.

Many of the decorated types described for the northern sites (e.g. Olmec motifs) are rare south of the Central area. Why there would have been such a marked degree of intra-valley variation in these respects is a problem we hope to tackle once we have completed our survey.

One thing seems clear even now, however: the observed differences are not likely to have been due to intraregional differences in potential for agricultural production. Kirkby (1973:29, passim) discovered that the valley's richest agricultural lands are located in both the Etla arm *and* the Valle Grande. For example, she predicted that during the Tierras Largas phase, the valley's richest agricultural areas would have been near San José Mogote and near Sta. Ana Tlapacoyan (N3E4). Further, she noted that if one assumes that population will be distributed solely with respect to potential maize productivity, the total Tierras Largas population of each of these two arms would have been roughly equal, 5000 people each. The Valle Grande,

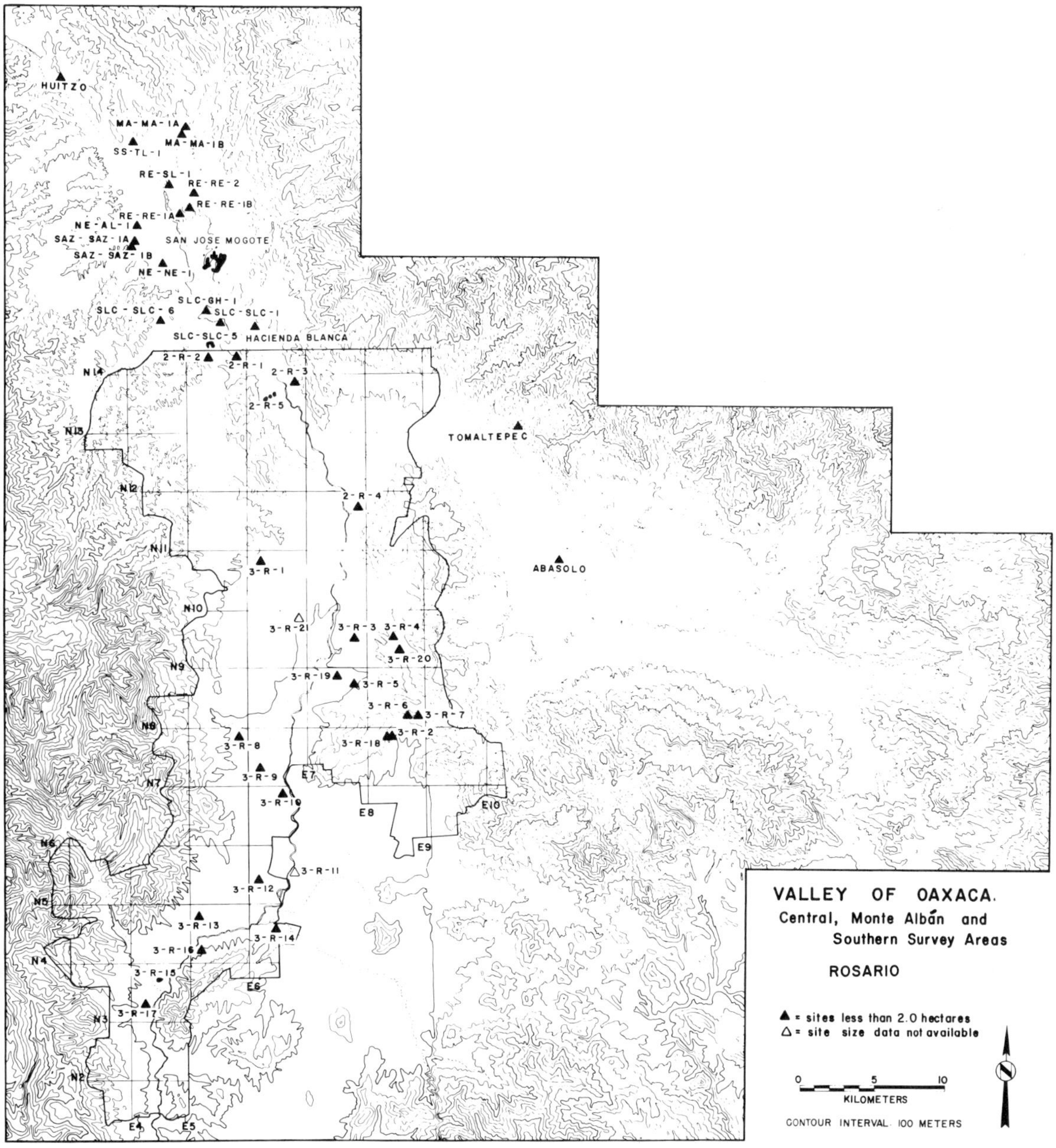

Figure 3-4. Settlements of the Rosario phase.

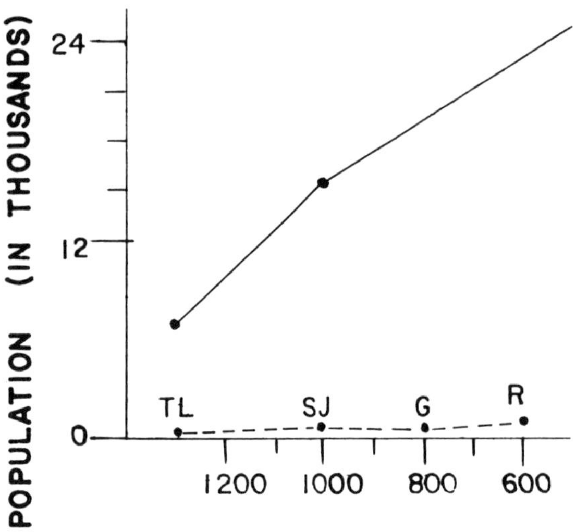

Figure 3-5. Actual estimated population of the survey area (points along the dashed line) compared with estimates extrapolated from Kirkby (1973) (solid line), Tierras Largas through Rosario phases (from Curran 1978: Fig. 1).

especially (though we expect to find that both areas were substantially under these estimated values), had many fewer people (Fig. 3-5). This unequal distribution of population continued until the foundation of Monte Albán during Early I. Environmental factors pertinent to agriculture cannot explain the observed intra-valley variation in the density of occupation during the Early and Middle Formative.

CATCHMENT CALCULATIONS

Even though on a valley-wide basis population densities cannot be predicted from potential agricultural productivity, we wondered whether such predictions might hold true within valley sub-areas. We wondered whether people tended to pay most attention, in locating their settlements, to local environmental factors, or whether other, perhaps non-environmental considerations, were more important. Did the better-situated places (in terms of agricultural potential) tend to increase in size more than poorly located places? Or again, did non-environmental factors play the most important roles in determining variation in community sizes? If potential agricultural productivity is a factor relevant to the explanation of variability in site location and size, then the larger sites should tend to be better situated *vis à vis* the best agricultural land. To begin to explore these relationships, we measured the potential productivity (in maize) of a catchment zone of 2 kilometers radius around each site for the phases from Tierras Largas through Rosario. A similar strategy was employed for sites dating to Early I and is reported in Chapter 9.

Catchment analysis relies on the assumption that people will seek to minimize the amount of energy expended in movement by farming land that is relatively close to where they live. Studies cited by Chisholm (1968:66, passim) indicate a great deal of cross-cultural regularity in this regard. He found that, generally, farmers lacking mechanized transport begin to experience declines in production when fields are more than 1 kilometer from the residence, and that beyond 3 to 4 kilometers there is a significant drop in return. We chose to measure the potential maize productivity in the catchments based on the assumption that even during the Early and Middle Formative this cultigen was the basic element of Oaxacan diets. The 2 kilometer figure was chosen because, based on Chisholm's results, this was the area around each community most likely to have been used for farming. (Compare this method with that of Vita-Finzi and Higgs [1970], who used catchment circles of 5 kilometers around each agricultural hamlet, but weighted the intensity of use of each 1 kilometer zone. In their study, land between 0 and 1 kilometers was assumed to be fully utilized. Land between 1 and 2 kilometers was weighted at 50%, land at 2-3 kilometers at 33%, and so forth [ibid.:29; cf. Flannery, ed. 1976]).

In drawing the catchment circles around each site, the outer edge of the site was used as a zero point in order that residential area was not included as part of the site's agricultural land. Thus the larger sites have somewhat larger catchments, providing a minor degree of built-in correlation between site size and potential productivity. Since most of our Early and Middle Formative sites are very small, however, we doubt this presents a serious source of error in our calculations. By far the bulk of the variation in potential maize productivity is due to variability in land types and the availability of water. In cases of catchment overlap between two sites, half of the overlap area was assigned to each site.

In arriving at the yield ranges for the various land categories found within the catchments, and in estimating the potential population supportable by each catchment, we followed Kirkby (1973), with the modifications of her method that are discussed in detail in Chapter 9 of this volume. The results of the catchment calculations are found in Tables 3-1 through 3-4. Surprisingly, in all cases (except the very few instances in

Table 3-1. Catchment Analysis: Combined Survey Area. Potential Maize Productivity and Predicted Population: Tierras Largas Phase

Site	High Water Table (Ha)	Yield Ranges[1] Low (tons)	Yield Ranges[1] High (tons)	High Alluv. (Ha)	Yield Ranges[1] Low (tons)	Yield Ranges[1] High (tons)	Pied. (Ha.)	Yield Ranges[1] Low (tons)	Yield Ranges[1] High (tons)	Potential Population[2]	Archaeolog. Population	Mean Potent. Pop.	Mean Arch Pop.
2-1-1	--	--	--	562.93	52.69-105.38	52.69-158.07	463.32	0- 92.66	46.3 -138.99	181-1856	10-25	1018	17
2-1-2	--	--	--	714.68	71.4 -142.93	71.4 -214.4	540.07	0-108	54.0 -108	246-2015	15-37	1130	26
3-1-1	--	--	--	699.7	69.97-139.94	69.97-209.91	38.9	0- 7.78	3.89- 11.67	241-1384	11-27	812	19
3-1-2	125.4	25.08-37.51	25.08-37.51	254.1	25.41- 50.82	25.41- 76.23	390.7	0- 78.14	39 -117.2	174-1443	5-10	808	7
3-1-3	48.5	9.7 -14.55	9.7 -14.55	503.3	50.33-100.66	50.33-150.99	314.3	0- 62.8	31.4 -94.29	207-1623	10-25	915	17
3-1-4	--	--	--	--	--	--	673	0-134.6	67.3 -201.9	0 -1261	5-10	630	7
3-1-5	53.43	10.68-16.02	10.68-16.02	1091.09	109.1- 218.21	109.1 -327.32	--	--	--	413-2145	5-10	1279	7
3-1-6	30.31	6.06- 9.09	6.06-9.09	597.55	59.75-119.51	59.75-179.26	450.25	0- 90.05	45 -135.07	226-2021	13-33	1123	23
3-1-7	11.5	2.3 - 3.45	2.3 -3.45	1248.68	124.8 -249.7	124.8 -374.6	--	--	--	438-2362	--	1400	?
3-1-8	--	--	--	1161.0	116.1-232.2	116.1- 348.3	--	--	--	400-2176	--	1288	?

[1] Extrapolated from Kirkby (1973: Fig. 48a,b); Kowalewski, this volume. [2] Assumes consumption of .16-.29 metric tons/person/year at high and low yields.

Table 3-2. Catchment Analysis: Combined Survey Area. Potential Maize Productivity and Predicted Population: San José Phase

Site	High Water Table (Ha)	Yield Ranges[1] Low (tons)	Yield Ranges[1] High (tons)	High Alluv. (Ha)	Yield Ranges[1] Low (tons)	Yield Ranges[1] High (tons)	Pied. (Ha.)	Yield Ranges[1] Low (tons)	Yield Ranges[1] High (tons)	Potential Population[2]	Archaeolog. Population	Mean Potent. Pop.	Mean Arch. Pop.
2-2-1	--	--	--	828.63	82.8 -248.58	82.8 -331.45	387.17	0- 95.45	38.71- 95.45	285-2668	10- 25	1476	17
2-2-2	--	--	--	34.19	3.41- 10.25	3.41- 13.67	1070.54	0-321.16	107.05-321.16	11-2092	5- 10	1051	7
2-2-3	--	--	--	526.93	52.69-158.07	52.69-210.77	463.32	0-138.99	46.33-138.99	181-2186	10- 25	1183	17
2-2-4	--	--	--	833.43	83.34-250	83.34-333.37	739.16	0-221.74	73.91-221.74	287-3469	63-157	1878	110
3-2-1	--	--	--	699.7	69.97-209.91	69.97-279.88	38.9	0- 11.67	3.89- 11.67	241-1822	11- 27	1031	19
3-2-2	125.4	37.62-50.16	37.62-50.16	254.1	25.41- 76.23	25.41-101.64	390.7	0-117.21	39.07-117.21	217-1681	5- 10	949	7
3-2-3	48.5	14.55-19.4	14.55-19.4	503.6	50.36-151.08	50.36-201.44	314.3	0- 94.29	31.43- 94.29	223-1969	5- 10	1096	7
3-2-4	--	--	--	--	--	--	673	0-201.9	67.3 -201.9	0 -1261	5- 10	630	7
3-2-5	--	--	--	259.03	25.9 - 77.7	25.9 -103.61	856.53	0-256.95	85.6-256.95	89-2253	10- 25	1171	17
3-2-6	53.43	16.02-21.37	16.02-21.37	1082.34	108.23-324.7	108.23-432.93	--	--	--	428-2839	5- 10	1633	7
3-2-7	30.31	9.09-12.12	9.09-12.12	645.23	64.52-193.56	64.52-258.09	504.05	0-151.21	50.40-151.21	253-2633	20- 50	1443	35
3-2-8	11.5	3.45- 4.6	3.45- 4.6	1236.68	123.6 -371	123.6 -494.6	--	--	--	438-3120	--	1779	--
3-2-9	--		--	1161	116.1 -348.3	116.1 -464.4	--	--	--	400-2902	--	1651	--

[1] Extrapolated from Kirkby (1973: Fig. 48a,b); Kowalewski, this volume. [2] Assumes consumption of .16-.29 metric tons/person/year at high and low yields.

Table 3-3. Catchment Analysis: Combined Survey Area. Potential Maize Productivity and Predicted Population: Guadalupe Phase

Site	High Water Table (Ha)	Yield Ranges[1] (tons) Low	High	High Alluv. (Ha)	Yield Ranges[1] (tons) Low	High	Pied. (Ha.)	Yield Ranges[1] (tons) Low	High	Potential Population[2]	Archaeolog. Population	Mean Potent. Pop.	Mean Arch. Pop.
2-3-1	--	--	--	761.21	76.12-228.36	76.12-304.48	191.83	0- 57.04	19.18- 57.54	267-2262	10-25	1264	17
2-3-2	--	--	--	247.38	24.73- 74.21	24.73- 98.95	573. 9	0-172.17	57.39-172.17	85 -1694	10-25	889	17
2-3-3	--	--	--	407.38	40.73-122.21	40.73-162.95	691.63	0-207.48	69.16-207.48	140-2315	10-25	1227	17
2-3-4	--	--	--	--	--	--	1021. 7	0-306.51	102.17-306.51	0 -1915	5 -10	957	7
2-3-5	--	--	--	526.93	52.69-158.07	52.69-210.77	463.12	0-138.93	46.31-138.93	181-2185	10-25	1183	17
2-3-6	--	--	--	780. 6	78.06-234.18	78.06-312.24	657. 5	0-197.25	65.75-197.25	269-3184	30-75	1726	52
3-3-1	--	--	--	--	--	--	1236.58	0-370.97	123.65-370.97	0 -2318	5 -10	1159	7
3-3-2	--	--	--	700. 0	70 -210	70 -280	38. 9	0- 11.67	3.89- 11.67	241-1822	10-25	1031	17
3-3-3	125. 4	37.62-50.16	37.62-50.16	254. 1	25.41- 76.23	25.41-101.64	390. 7	0-117.21	39.07-117.21	217-1681	5 -10	949	7
3-3-4	48. 5	14.55-19. 4	14.55-19. 4	503. 6	50.36-151.08	50.36-201.44	314. 3	0- 94.29	31.43- 94.29	223-1969	5 -10	1096	7
3-3-5	--	--	--	--	--	--	673	0-201. 9	67. 3-201. 9	0 -1261	5 -10	630	7
3-3-6	--	--	--	259.03	25. 9- 77.7	25. 9-103.61	856.53	0-256.95	85. 6-256.95	89 -2253	10-25	1171	17
3-3-7	53. 1	15.93-21.24	15.93-21.24	1091.09	109. 1-327.57	109. 1-436.43	--	--	--	431-2860	5 -10	1645	7
3-3-8	30.31	9.09-12.12	9.09-12.12	676.9	67.69-203.07	67.69-270.76	504.05	0-151.21	50. 4-151.21	264-1768	20-50	1016	35
3-3-9	11. 5	3.45- 4. 6	3.45- 4. 6	1236.68	123. 6-371	123. 6-494. 6	--	--	--	438-3120	--	1779	--

[1] Extrapolated from Kirkby (1973: Fig. 48a,b): Kowalewski, this volume. [2] Assumes consumption of .16-.29 metric tons/person/year at high and low yields.

Table 3-4. Catchment Analysis: Combined Survey Area. Potential Maize Productivity and Predicted Population: Rosario Phase

Site	High Water Table (Ha)	Yield Ranges[1] (tons) Low	High	High Alluv. (Ha)	Yield Ranges[1] (tons) Low	High	Pied. (Ha.)	Yield Ranges[1] (tons) Low	High	Potential Population[2]	Archaeolog. Population	Mean Potent. Pop.	Mean Arch. Pop.
2-4-1	--	--	--	761.21	76.12-304.48	76.12-380.6	191.83	0- 76.73	19.18- 76.73	262-2858	10-25	1560	17
2-4-2	--	--	--	247.38	24.73- 98.95	24.73-123.69	573.8	0-229.52	57.38-229.52	85-2207	11-27	1146	19
2-4-3		--	--	407.38	40.73-162.95	40.73-203.69	691.63	0-276.65	69.16-276.65	140-3627	10-25	1883	17
2-4-4	--	--	--	526.93	52.69-210.77	52.69-263.46	462.72	0-185.08	46.27-185.08	181-2803	10-25	1492	17
2-4-5	--	--	--	780.68	78.06-312.27	78.06-390.34	657.5	0-263	65.75-263	269-4083	30-75	2176	52
3-4-1		--	--	975.2	97.52-390.08	97.52-487.6	265.5	0-106.2	26.55-106.2	336-3711	5-10	2023	7
3-4-2	--	--	--	--	--	--	751.72	0-300.6	75.15-300.6	0-1878	5-10	939	7
3-4-3	63.35	25.34-31.67	25.34-31.67	690.63	69.06-276.25	69.06-345.31	150.34	0- 60.13	15.03-60.13	325-2731	5-10	1528	7
3-4-4	--	--	--	63.63	6.36-25.45	6.36- 31.81	479.65	0-191.86	47.96-191.86	21-1397	13-33	709	23
3-4-5	--	--	--	--	--	--	1044.15	0-417.66	104.41-417.66	0-2610	25-60	1305	42
3-4-6	--	--	--	--	--	--	341.45	0-136.58	34.14-136.58	0-853	5-10	426	7
3-4-7	--	--	--	--	--	--	253.9	0-101.56	25.39-101.56	0-634	5-10	317	7
3-4-8	--	--	--	456	45.6 -182.4	45.6 -228	49.38	0- 19.75	4.93- 19.75	157-1548	5-10	852	7
3-4-9	104.75	41.9 -52.37	41.9 -52.37	708	70.8 -283.2	70.8 -354	97.97	0- 39.18	9.79- 39.18	388-2784	5-10	1586	7
3-4-10	6.75	2.7 - 3.37	2.7 - 3.37	1073.79	107.37-429.51	107.37-536.88	159.45	0- 63.78	15.94- 63.78	379-4379	5-10	2379	7
3-4-11	--	--	--	1161	116.1 -464.4	116.1 -580.5	--	--	--	400-3628	--	2014	--
3-4-12	53.13	21.25-26.56	21.25-26.56	1082.3	108.23-432.92	108.23-541.15	--	--	--	446-3548	5-10	1997	7
3-4-13	67.81	27.12-33.9	27.12-33.9	364.85	36.48-145.94	36.48-182.42	537.68	0-215.07	53.76-215.07	219-2696	5-10	1457	7
3-4-14	--	--	--	549.98	54.99-219.99	54.99-274.99	442.07	0-176.82	44.20-176.82	189-2823	5-10	1506	7
3-4-15	30.31	12.12-15.15	12.12-15.15	627	62.7 -250.8	62.7 -313.5	294.3	0-117.72	29.43-117.72	258-2789	40-100	1523	70
3-4-16	38.38	15.35-19.19	15.35-19.19	219.57	21.95- 87.82	21.95-109.78	298.77	0-119.5	29.87-119.5	128-1552	10-25	840	17
3-4-17	--	--	--	70.75	7.07- 28.3	7.07- 35.37	682.79	0-273.11	68.27-273.11	24-1928	10-25	976	17
3-4-18	--	--	--	--	--	--	751.52	0-300.6	75.15-300.6	0-1878	15-37	939	23
3-4-19	--	--	--	568.87	56.88-227.54	56.88-284.43	196.71	0- 78.68	19.67- 78.68	196-2269	5-10	1232	7
3-4-20	--	--	--	--	--	--	390.46	0-156.18	39.04-156.18	0-976	10-20	488	15
3-4-21	11.5	4.6 - 5.75	4.6 - 5.75	1236.68	123.6 -371	123.6 -494.6	--	--	--	438-3120	--	1779	--

[1] Extrapolated from Kirkby (1973: Fig. 48a, b); Kowalewski, this volume. [2] Assumes consumption of .16-.29 metric tons/person/year at high and low yields.

which the catchment of a site is primarily piedmont) the potential population range is substantially higher than the estimated population range based on the survey results, and in every case the mean potential population is substantially higher than the mean population estimate. Clearly, all the Early and Middle Formative sites in the survey area could have been considerably larger in population and still have been comfortably supported even within these modest 2 kilometer catchments.

Are the larger sites better situated? The answer is not readily apparent by visual inspection of the tables. Some of the smallest sites have highly productive catchments, while the larger sites are not always situated in the most productive places. Some relationship, however, was recognized. For the first three of the four phases, there is a reasonably strong positive correlation between potential productivity and estimated population. For Tierras Largas, Spearman's r_S for the two variables is .423 (but not significant even at the .05 level). For San José, r_S is higher, equalling .527, a value that is significant at the .05 level. By Guadalupe, the value has again dropped somewhat, r_S equalling .424 (but not statistically significant at the .05 level). These values (and the following Rosario value) could possibly have been slightly higher if we had been able to include population estimates for Zaachila and Sta. Inés Yatzeche, assuming that they had been moderately large in size. Both have catchments that are among the highest in potential productivity (Tables 3-1 to 3-4) in the study area. We conclude that for Tierras Largas through Guadalupe, although agricultural resources were substantially underused overall, it was still the case that the larger sites tended to have better catchment potentials than the smaller sites.

For Rosario, however, that correlation began to weaken considerably. Spearman's r_S for Rosario amounts to only .132 (not significant even at the .1 level). Evidently, just prior to Monte Albán's foundation, conditions started to change such that factors other than agricultural potentials determined most of the variability in community sizes. We would suggest that political and economic systems were changing during that time and that these kinds of nonagricultural factors began to override the importance of environmental considerations in determining aspects of settlement pattern. As Kowalewski shows in Chapter 9, such man-man factors continued to overwhelm man-land relationships throughout the remainder of the sequence after Rosario. Once we have completed the survey, we hope to be able to understand precisely what changes were involved during the Rosario phase that produced the drastic declines in our correlation coefficients, as these changes no doubt were related to the eventual foundation of the new regional capital at Monte Albán.

SETTING THE STAGE FOR THE ESTABLISHMENT OF MONTE ALBAN

Monte Albán was founded on a hilltop in the center of the valley (N12E6) at the beginning of Early I, around 500 B.C. From that point on, San José Mogote was no longer the valley's largest community, and the Etla arm was no longer the valley's most densely populated area. We think these changes manifest a reorganization of the valley's population such that the region became a much more coherent entity in political and economic terms. A location central to the valley as a whole became necessary for the community that was the focus of the region-wide system. San José Mogote was not optimally located to serve in that capacity and so was bypassed in importance and size. Prior to Early I, we doubt that any community in the valley served as a center for most central-place transactions for the valley as a whole. In fact, prior to Early I, the valley's Central area was largely unused except for Tierras Largas (N13E6), a small site in square N11E7, and a couple of other small sites that have shorter occupations (Figs. 3-1 to 3-4). This relative paucity of sites may be due to the fact that the Central area, on the whole, is relatively marginal in terms of potential agricultural productivity, at least by comparison with the Etla arm and the Valle Grande (Kirkby 1973: passim; Chapter 9, this volume). But another factor may be worth considering in this regard. If, during the Early and Middle Formative, the arms of the valley had each contained one or more highly autonomous societies, which were not always on amicable terms, then the Central area may have been a risky place to live, where villages would have been subject to raiding with more than average frequency, discouraging settlement. It was not until the establishment of a region-wide polity in Early I that the Central area was heavily populated.

CONCLUSIONS

A more complete analysis of Early and Middle Formative settlement patterns will be postponed until we finish the valley survey. Yet even with the limited data we have now, several broad conclusions can be reached:

1) The focus of cultural evolution in the region was outside the completed survey area, located especially to the north in the Etla arm of the valley. The Central and Valle Grande areas remained marginal until Early I. Sites were small and few in number, and this was true even though the Valle Grande, at least, was as desirable for agriculture, or more so, than the Etla arm.

2) Population density in the survey area was nowhere near the potential as calculated by Kirkby (1973; Curran 1978; see Fig. 3-5). Clearly, factors other than shortages of food served to regulate population parameters. The increase in the numbers of people during these periods in the survey area was slight (Figs. 2-1, 3-5). Substantial growth occurred only later and seems to have been stimulated by the economic and political changes that began during Early I.

3) Our catchment analysis indicates that prior to Rosario phase, environmental factors may be relatively useful for explaining at least some aspects of settlement patterns. After Guadalupe, however, this ceases to be true. Other factors, probably especially features of regional political and economic organization, were no doubt more important than environmental ones.

4) The near-absence of any significant settlement in the valley's Central area prior to Early I suggests the presence of a fragmented regional system. This fragmentation ceased with the formation of Monte Albán. The changes related to that event in the survey area are discussed in the next chapter.

Chapter 4

PERIOD I

INTRODUCTION

Probably nobody would argue with the fact that the Rosario-Period I transition was one of the most important episodes in the evolution of human society in the Valley of Oaxaca. Even before we proceed to a closer examination of what was involved, major sets of changes are obvious, especially manifested in the formation of a new regional capital at Monte Albán, and rapid population growth unlike anything that ever occurred previously (Fig. 2-1). Two alternative models for the Rosario to Period I shift have dominated our thinking. The first argues that prior to Period I the valley had been organized into a unitary political system headed by San José Mogote. During Early I this valley-wide system expanded, and the capital was moved from San José to the top of Monte Albán.

The second, more viable model, which we elaborated in Chapter 2, argues that prior to Period I the valley had been occupied by several politically autonomous groupings; San José Mogote was just another of these, albeit the largest. At the Rosario-Period I juncture, stresses reached a level that made it worthwhile for these separate local units to join together in the establishment of a new political institution, with its headquarters at Monte Albán. Judging from the carved stone monuments at the new capital, this new organization was, at least initially, a military league (Blanton 1976a, 1978). The location for the new capital was chosen because the central part of the valley is ideal for intra-valley exchanges and because this was an area that had not been owned previously by any of the existing polities. In fact, this area had been only sparsely occupied prior to Period I. This would have helped assure the neutrality of the new capital, since locationally it would not have been highly associated with any one of the co-joining groups. The placement of the new center on the top of a high mountain, away from valuable agricultural land, further assured its neutrality.

According to this model, the formation of the new political organization in Period I need not imply that the valley became highly centralized politically. The formation of the new capital resulted in many changes in the valley, as we have shown, but the existing political units could have retained decision-making autonomy regarding local affairs. This is consistent with the findings of Joyce Marcus (1976a). In her analyses of preclassic carved stone monuments from a number of valley centers, she concluded that the range of styles present indicates a situation in which local units were not highly integrated into a valley-wide system focused on Monte Albán. Our findings, discussed below, are in agreement with this. These discoveries are of some theoretical interest. If we are correct in our interpretations, then we may conclude that a pan-regional institution evolved in the Valley of Oaxaca in the absence of the conquest of weaker polities by stronger ones. Indeed, the sequence of events in the valley may illustrate the importance of voluntarism in the pristine evolution of large-scale political institutions. Our interpretation of the origin of Monte Albán, it should be noted, has been hotly disputed by the cultural ecologists, whose theoretical position argues that force overrides cooperation in political evolution (Sanders and Santley 1978; Santley 1980; cf. Blanton 1980; Kowalewski 1980). We find it interesting and rather stimulating that data on political evolution from the valley–one of Mesoamerica's most important nuclear centers–seem to contradict the expectations of the theory that now dominates our literature (cf. Sanders, Parsons, and Logan 1976).

As interesting as the conquest-versus-cooperation debate is, we are still left with the question of why. We mentioned before that stresses may have reached the point at the end of the Rosario phase where local groups found it worthwhile to support a pan-regional polity. In Chapter 2 we made some comments about the possible role of the Valley of Oaxaca in interregional interaction during the Formative. While the factors we mentioned in that section may have been important in regional and interregional evolution, we are still at a loss to explain why Monte Albán was established when it was and not sooner or later, nor do we

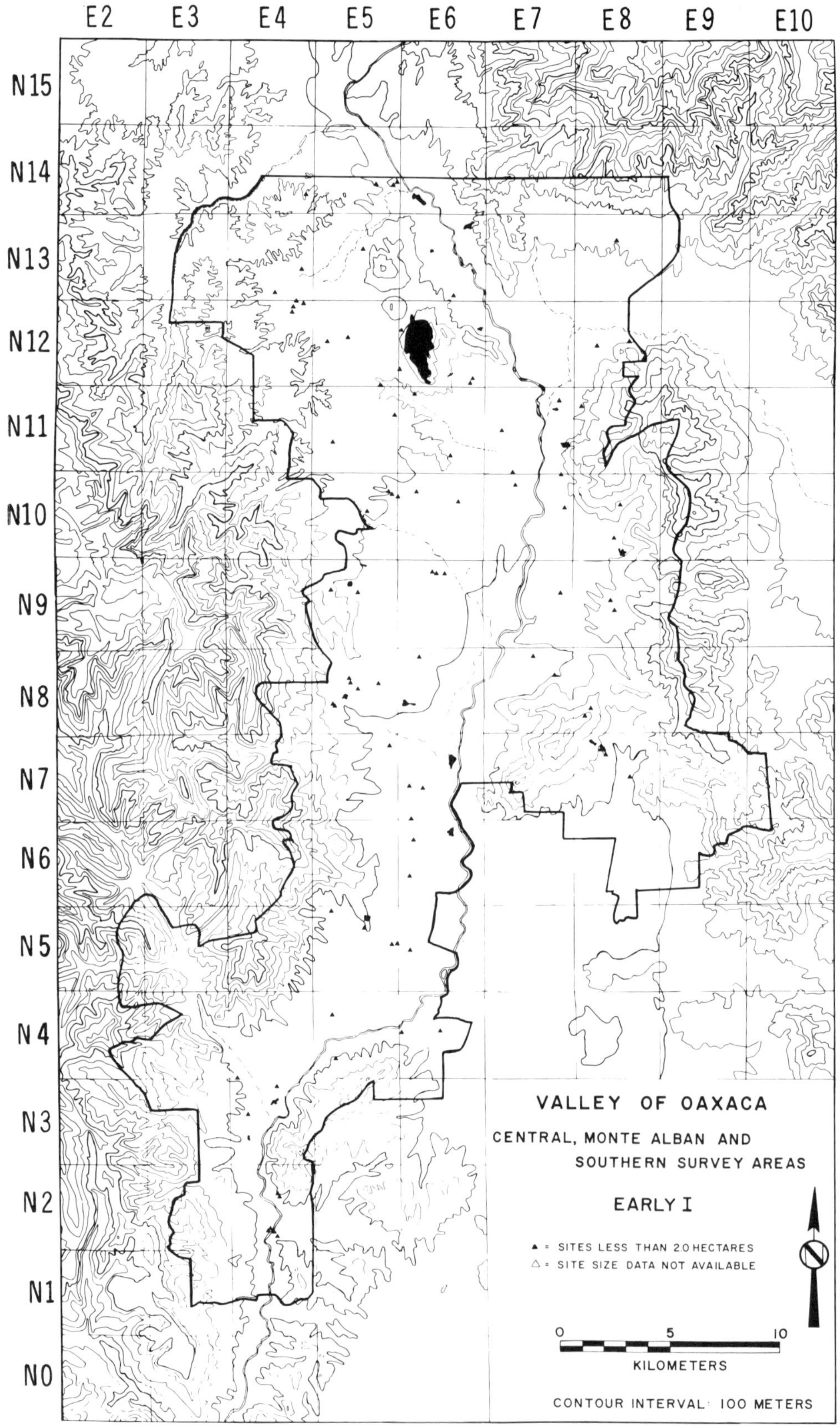

Figure 4-1. Settlements of Early I.

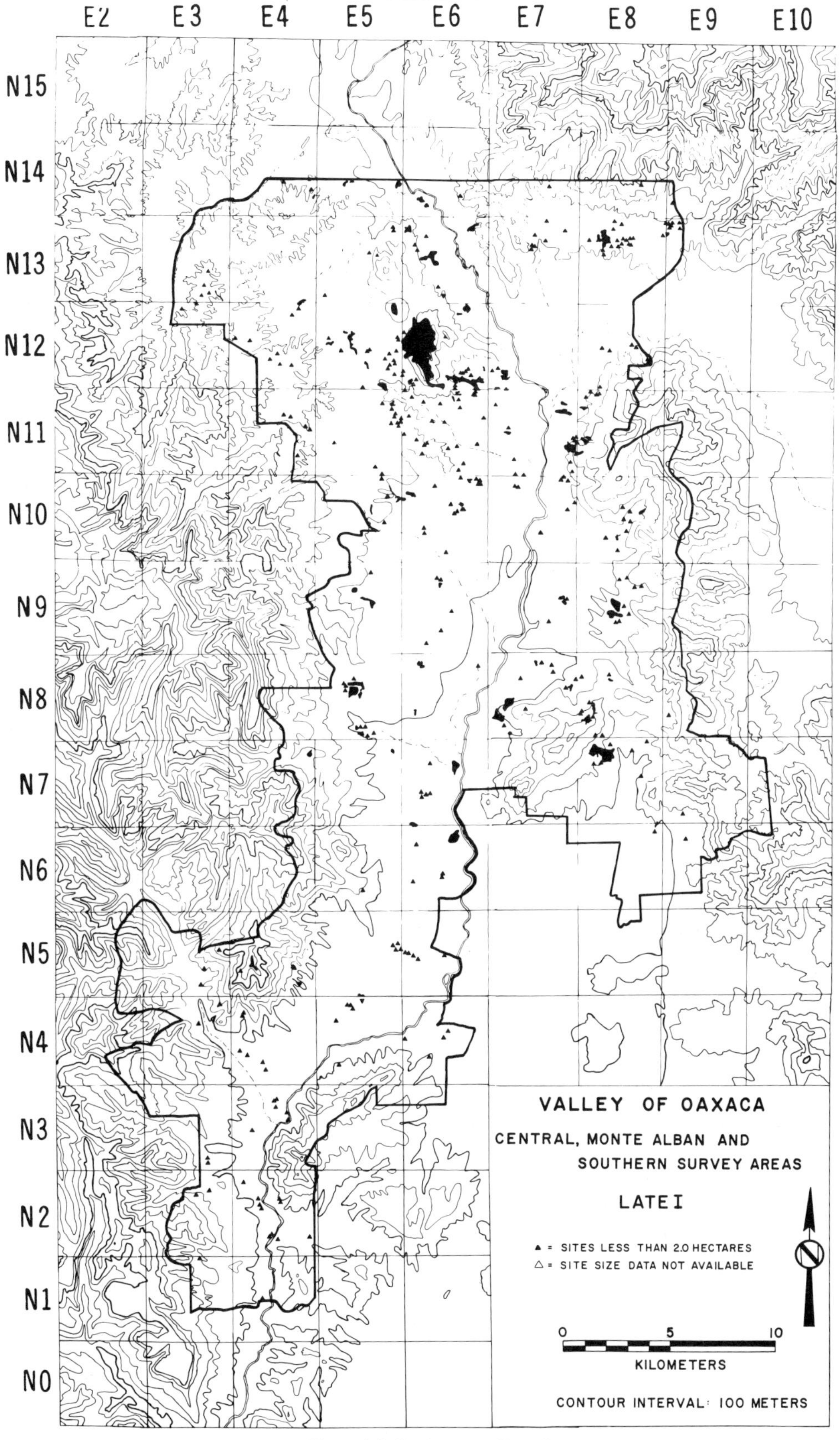

Figure 4-2. Settlements of Late I.

know precisely which factors led to its creation. The fact that the carved stone monuments at Monte Albán are militaristic in theme suggests the new institution was involved (at least initially) in problems of offense-defense (perhaps better phrased as "regional boundary maintenance," since we don't know exactly what was involved). We are still unable to explain why problems of this sort would have reached a level by the end of the Rosario phase that suddenly made it worthwhile to establish the new capital. Clearly, before such problems can be resolved we need more information from the valley and from other parts of the Southern Highlands for this critical time period.

PERIOD I SETTLEMENT PATTERNS

Figures 4-1 and 4-2 show the distributions of Early and Late I sites. (Appendix II shows the locations of the sites, with their numbers.) Not every locality in these figures has a separate site number. Discrete sherd distributions less than 100 meters apart were grouped to form a single site. Each of these combined sites was given a single number, and the data for each of these numbered sites are found in Appendix I. In some cases, additional grouping of sites was done prior to the final calculations of population sizes. Appendix IV is a list of sites combined in this manner and their final populations. In grouping sites with separate numbers, we paid most attention to the larger sites and central places, since we are particularly interested in the functions and interactions of such settlements. In some cases, similar groupings of smaller sites could be done fruitfully.

Our rationale in grouping sites with separate numbers is to arrive at a population total for the combined site that is, as much as possible, a value describing an actual sociological entity–a community. We assume that families reside in nucleated communities (as opposed to isolated residences) in order to facilitate communication and other kinds of exchanges with other families. It is possible, of course, that communities formed primarily for the purpose of defense. We are doubtful, however, that this was ever the key factor causing communal residence in the Valley of Oaxaca. There may have been some exceptions to this, including the few fortified hill-top communities found in some prehispanic periods. In general, though, communities in the valley were not sited with defense in mind, nor, apparently, were they protected by walls or palisades in the manner of, for example, Iroquois or Mississippian communities. Given this assumption, we grouped spatially discrete residences or numbered sites if the topography is such that there could have been unobstructed communication between the parts, even if the distance between the parts is somewhat greater than 100 meters. Thus sites close to 100 meters apart, but on opposite sides of a *barranca* were not combined, while similarly spaced sites stretching along the top of the same piedmont ridge would be combined. The procedure borders on the arbitrary, since we had no definite maximum distance rule. Grouping was done when, in our opinion, it resulted in more accurate estimates of community boundaries than could be achieved through some arbitrary grouping or subdividing rule. For Late I, our largest task was that of grouping a series of sherd scatters–ranging from moderate-sized sites to individual residences–that are located directly adjacent to Monte Albán, but which are not included in the Monte Albán map (Blanton 1978). These sites are on relatively flat terrain, off of Monte Albán proper (especially grid square N12E6), but so close to the main site that we feel an argument can be made that they were part of the capital's population.

GROWTH PATTERNS

Three major changes are apparent during this time period: 1) overall population growth; 2) the occupation of more marginal environmental settings, especially pronounced during Late I; and 3) an increase in the complexity of the community hierarchy. This last feature is reflected in increasing differentiation in site sizes and in architectural complexity. The nature of change in the settlement hierarchy will be discussed in a subsequent section of this chapter.

The population totals for the survey area are shown in Figure 2-1. Clearly a fundamental change in demographic processes in the region began during Early I–coinciding with the founding of Monte Albán. The rapid growth rates during Period I are especially striking in contrast with the prior six or so centuries of negligible growth. The magnitude of these differences is illustrated in Figure 4-3, which shows the estimated growth rates (r) for the survey area as a whole, for sites within 20 kilometers of Monte Albán, for sites greater than 20 kilometers from Monte Albán, and for Monte Albán itself. The instantaneous growth rate (r) was calculated from the estimated population totals using the equation $N_1 = N_0 \log_e{}^{rt}$, where

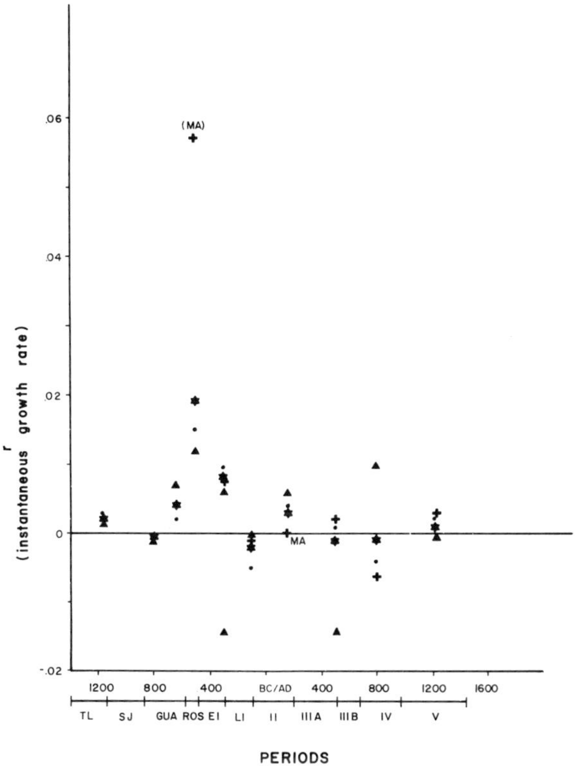

Figure 4-3. Instantaneous growth rates (r) that would account for the observed differences in population totals between periods. ✝ = Monte Albán. ● = Within 18 kilometers of Monte Albán. ★ = Total. ▲ = Greater than 18 kilometers from Monte Albán.

N_0 = population total for a period,
N_1 = population total for the subsequent period,
t = time in years, and
$\log_e$ = log to the base e.

The resultant values of r are values that could account for the observed differences in population totals between periods, although obviously the actual value of r in any given year could have been quite different. Although r cannot tell us what caused demographic transitions (or what proportion of the differences are attributable to changes in fertility, mortality, or migration), it does allow certain simple inferences. First, it is apparent that the major demographic changes occurred during Early I. A very high value of r is necessary to account for the growth from Rosario to the total estimated for Early I. Although the population of the surveyed areas also increased substantially from Early I to Late I, the overall rate of growth had slowed. That is, the additional numbers added in Late I can be accounted for with a lower growth rate than the Rosario-Early I rate since the base population involved (that of Early I) was substantially larger than the base population for the Rosario-Early I growth period.

By far the fastest growth occurred at Monte Albán itself during Early I, from a population of 0 to over 5000. The rate necessary to account for this growth, roughly 6% per year, would imply a doubling of the population every 12 years or so (assuming it was originally colonized by only a few people). In reality, according to our past arguments (Blanton 1976a, 1978), Monte Albán was probably established as a new capital, with a substantial population from the very beginning. Thus the 6% per year rate as a value of r is probably not particularly enlightening. It is interesting to note, however, that no matter what the actual growth history was, the population of the center must have increased at a rate much higher than the rates associated with the early stages of the industrial revolution and higher than the very high growth rates of the contemporary industrializing nations such as Mexico (which are in the 2 to 3% range or slightly higher). Cowgill's (1975) discussion of growth rates in human populations is useful for comparative purposes. According to him:

> Surges implying rates of natural increase of from 3 to about 7 per 1000 per year over regions up to some tens of thousands of square kilometers, sustained over two or three centuries (a doubling of population in about 240 to 100 years), have not been uncommon during the past few thousand years, but they are interspersed with periods of very slow growth or decline. Overall regional trends spanning a millennium or more show net population gains that are rarely more than what would have resulted from a steady rate of increase of 1 or 2 per 1000 per year (population doubling in 350 to 700 years), and are perhaps never over 3 per 1000 per year (doubling in about 240 years). Rates of increase as high as 10 per 1000 per year (doubling in 70 years) or even higher are suggested for the early growth surges of ancient cities such as Teotihuacan and Uruk (Adams and Nissen 1972), but these are concomitant with declining nearby rural populations and there is good reason to think that immigration contributed much to the rapid growth of these cities. It seems that rates of natural increase greater than about 6 or 7 per 1000 per year–have occurred only very briefly and locally, or during the rapid colonization of uninhabited or very weakly defended new territory. It is worth adding that even during much of the Industrial Revolution in Europe, until late in the nineteenth century, national annual growth rates were often not over 5 to 10 per 1000, and even in England and Wales before 1850 the highest rate for the decade was less than 17 per 1000 per year (Wrigley 1969:54). [Cowgill 1975:511]

A growth rate of 6% (60 per 1000) for Early I Monte Albán is very likely beyond the limits of human fertility, and while fertility may have been high at Monte Albán, still it is likely that much of the observed growth was due to immigration.

Another salient feature of the Period I growth pattern is that it was not a region-wide phenomenon. As is illustrated in Figure 4-4, the population of the survey

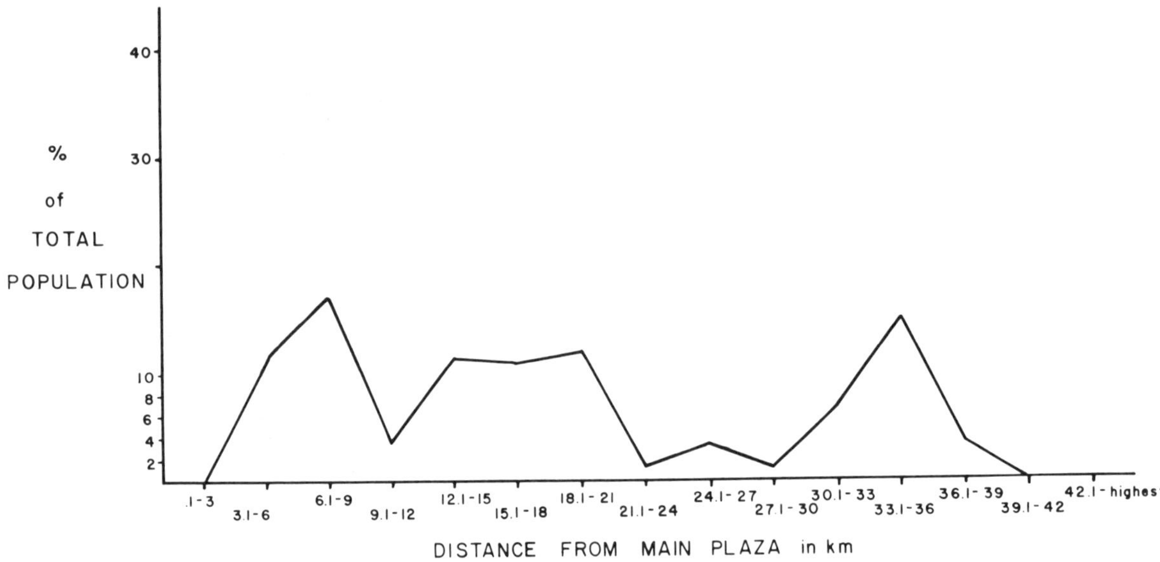

Figure 4-4. Population by distance from Monte Albán, Rosario phase.

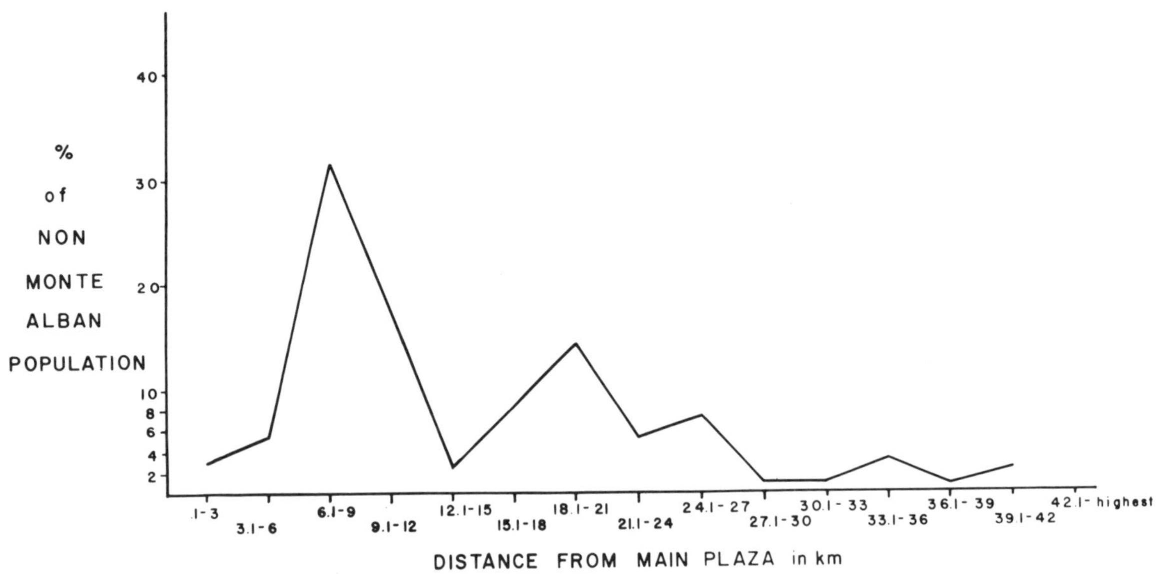

Figure 4-5. Population by distance from Monte Albán, Early I. The population estimates for Sta. Inés Yatzeche and Zaachila are included.

area was relatively evenly distributed in Rosario. By Early I (Figs. 4-5, 4-7), the population distribution was becoming skewed toward the valley's Central zone (even excluding Monte Albán). Most of the growth during this time (2134 out of total increase of 3248, or 66%), not counting Monte Albán, occurred within roughly 18 to 20 kilometers of the capital. Beyond roughly 30 kilometers from Monte Albán, growth was negligible. The relative concentration of population within a radius of about 18 kilometers of Monte Albán was even more pronounced during Late I (Fig. 4-6). Of the total estimated population increase of 10,042 from Early I to Late I outside Monte Albán, 7888, or 79%, occurred within this 18 kilometer limit (Fig. 4-8).

The growing population of Period I was increasingly exploiting more marginal environmental zones (Fig. 4-9). An increasingly smaller proportion of the total resided near the most desirable agricultural land, the high alluvium, while an increasingly larger proportion of the population occupied piedmont settings. (Kowalewski discusses these changes as they are relevant to changing agricultural strategies in Chapter 9.)

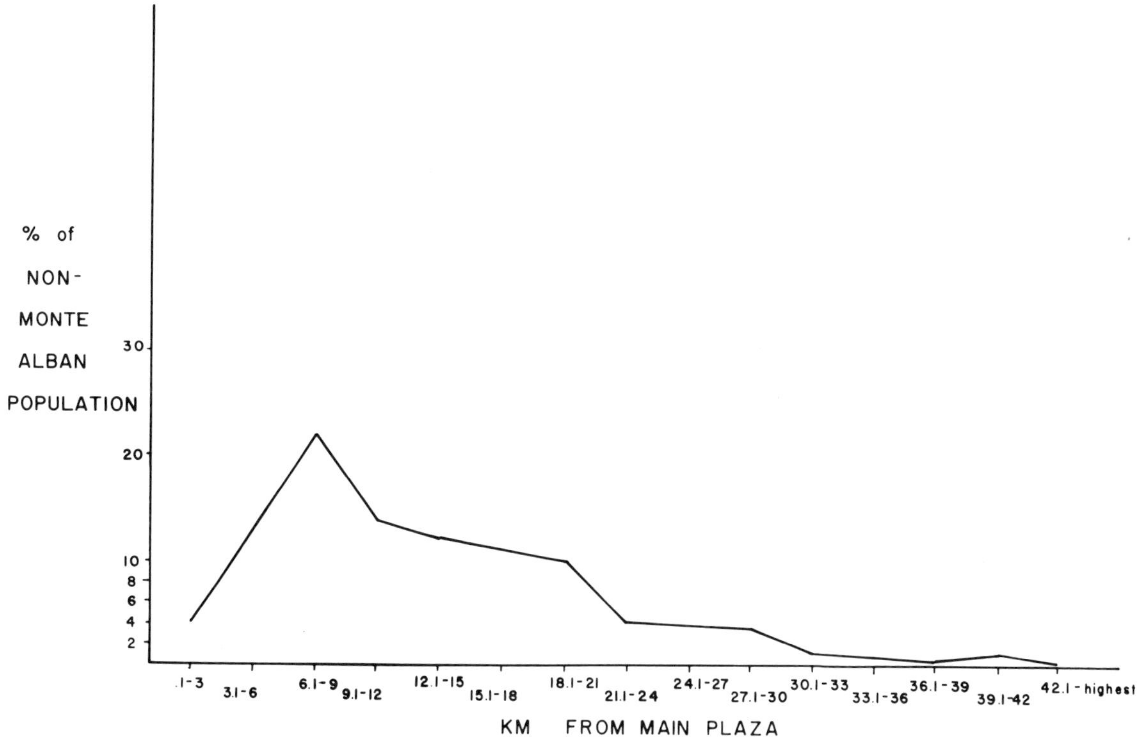

Figure 4-6. Population by distance from Monte Albán, Late I. The estimated values for Sta. Inés Yatzeche and Zaachila are included.

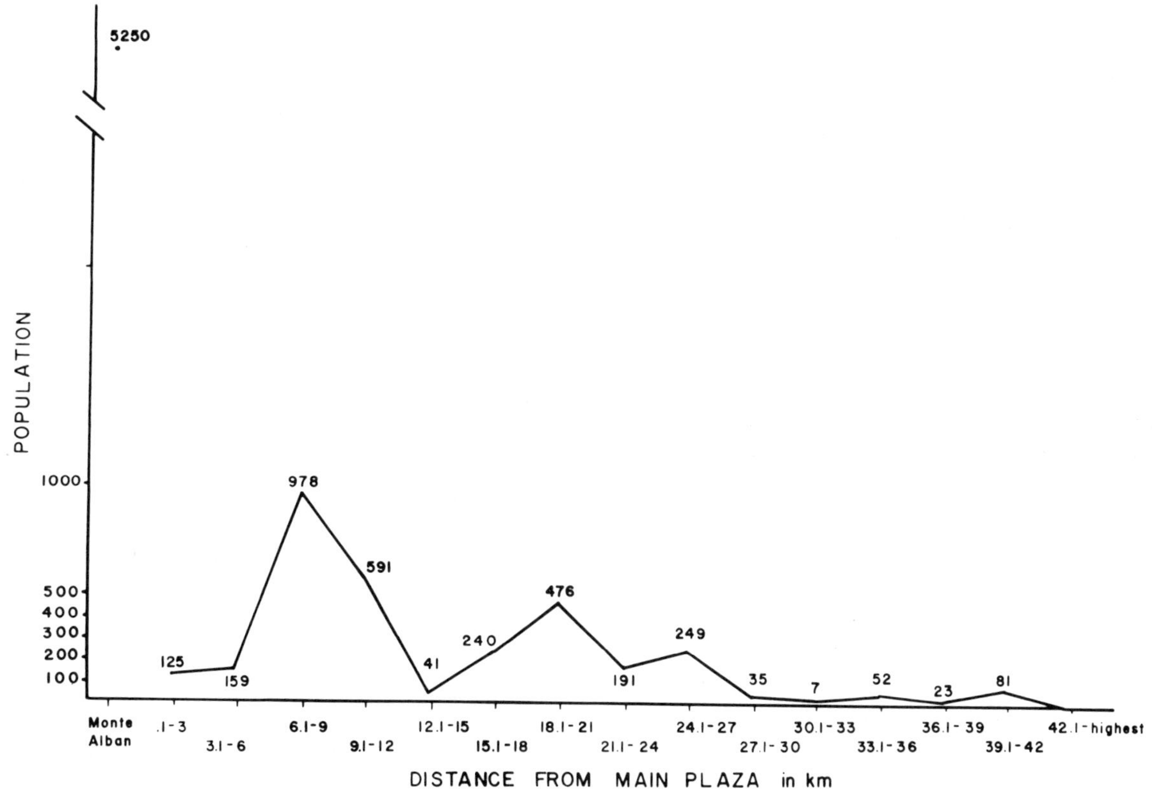

Figure 4-7. Population growth by distance from Monte Albán, Rosario to Early I.

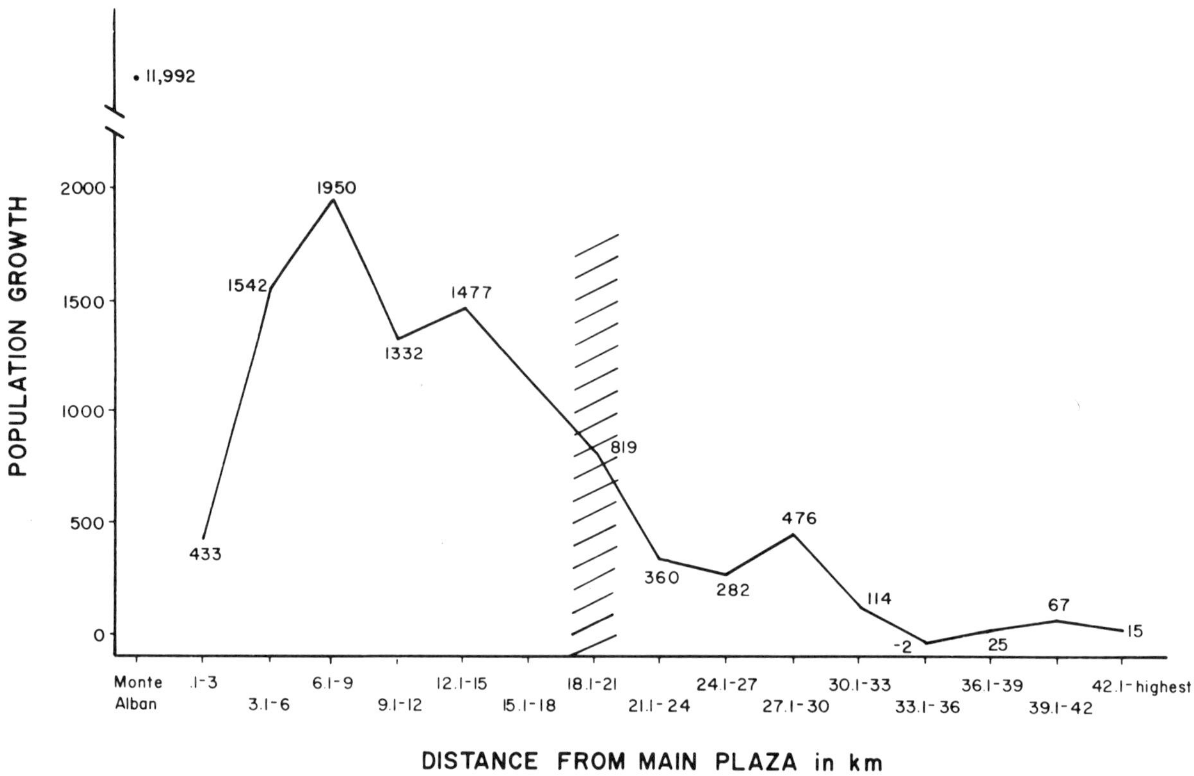

Figure 4-8. Population changes by distance from Monte Albán, Early I to Late I, including the estimates for Zaachila and Sta. Inés Yatzeche. The dashed line indicates the approximate southern limit of piedmont occupation.

As was true for population growth, the move to marginal zones was not a region-wide phenomenon. Most of the change from Early I to Late I in this regard is accounted for by the rapidly growing population of the valley's Central area. By Late I, 39% of the population of the Valle Grande survey area lived on high alluvium, while the comparable value for the Central survey area was only 7% (not counting Monte Albán). In this same Central zone 28% of the population resided in the Middle Piedmont, while only 3% of the Valle Grande population occupied this zone. The implications of these population distribution patterns will be discussed in detail in Chapter 9, but two general points can be made here. First, these developments demonstrate a lack of correspondence between environmental desirability and population distributions. The best agricultural land in the survey area is south of Zaachila (in other words, south of the N9 squares). It is this area, however, that shows the least growth during Period I. The Central area is less desirable for farming because it has less alluvium, relatively little water for irrigation, and rainfall is less predictable. Proximity to the new capital was more important as a determinant of settlement location than the availability of prime agricultural land.

A second set of inferences that can be drawn from the data on population distribution has to do with the nature of regional organization. Piedmont farming, more prominent in the Central zone, is in general riskier than alluvial farming. This is true for several reasons, to be discussed more fully in Chapter 9. In part the relative riskiness of the piedmont is due to the fact that fields are more exposed to erosion once the natural vegetation is cleared and the fact that the thin, sandy piedmont soils retain less moisture than do the deeper, loamy alluvial soils. Several strategies can be adopted in response to unpredictable piedmont production: 1) reduced consumption, 2) emigration, 3) construction of irrigation and soil-preservation facilities, and 4) stepped-up intraregional exchange, so that deficit areas can be supplied from surplus areas. The first two responses would have been undesirable, both from the point of view of the farmers themselves and that of an administrative institution hoping to milk some production surpluses from the piedmont. The latter two responses may therefore have been more important during Period I. The first direct archaeological evidence for piedmont irrigation systems in the survey area pertains to Period I (one at 2-5-20, and one southeast of Monte Albán [Mason et al. 1977]). Also, two new

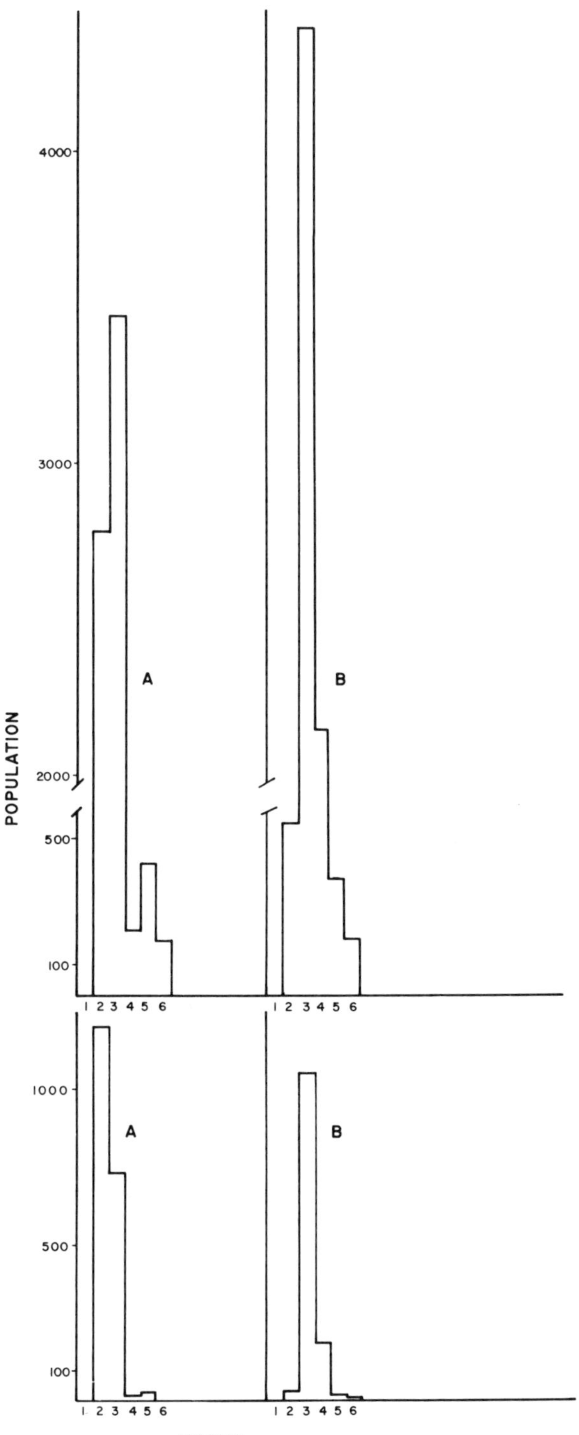

Figure 4-9. Distribution of population by environmental zone, Early and Late I. The lower bars are Early I (A = Valle Grande, B = Central Survey Area). The upper bars are Late I (A = Valle Grande, B = Central Survey Area). The numbers correspond to zones as follows: 1 = Low Alluvium, 2 = High Alluvium, 3 = Low Piedmont, 4 = Middle Piedmont, 5 = High Piedmont, 6 = Mountain.

Period I sites in the Valle Grande (3-5-16,17 and 3-5-18, etc.), both within 18 kilometers of Monte Albán, are situated in the piedmont directly adjacent to permanent tributaries suitable for canal irrigation.

We know less about intraregional movement of food, but indirect evidence of several sorts (discussed in Chapters 9 and 10) does suggest the presence of a more integrated regional system, especially by Late I. Exactly how the regional system was integrated, however, is not easily determined. In part, we feel that increased regional interaction may have occurred in the context of an evolving market system. Perhaps even more important than this is the likelihood that during Period I, and especially Late I, there was an increase in the amount of administrative orchestration of regional production and distribution. As Kowalewski (1976:812) argued, piedmont cultivation implies more regional organization problems than does alluvium cultivation. As we discussed in Chapter 2, this has to do in part with the high level administrative requirements of canal irrigation, but another part of it may have to do with the problems of moving food from surplus to deficit areas. We feel these problems were handled primarily through an increase in the complexity of the region's administrative network, including an enhanced role played by Monte Albán in regional government and exchange.

REGIONAL ORGANIZATION

In the more complex human societies, certain transactions–those in the realm of administrative and/or marketing institutions–do not take place randomly in space, but in a structured spatial organization referred to as a central place hierarchy. Central places, the loci of the transactions, are situated over the landscape in order to minimize the energy and time costs of information and materials movement (cf. Blanton 1976b; Christaller 1933; Johnson 1977). Central places are special communities in that the transactions carried out in them pertain not only to the population of the community itself, but to an area containing additional population that the central place services (its sustaining or complementary area or population). The simplest central-place system would be a region containing a few villages and a single center, the chief's village. (Note that in this very general model, "central-place theory" applies not only to modern, industrialized societies, but probably to all sedentary societies.) In a larger system multiple central places will exist since distance costs prohibit the interaction of all communities with only one center. Not only will multiple centers exist, but they will also exhibit a hierarchical ordering. This is due to the fact that the central-place transactions themselves have a hierarchical ordering.

Some central-place transactions are local ("low-order" transactions), while others pertain to larger regional units ("high-order" transactions). Low order transactions would, ideally, take place in a large number of local central places, each situated optimally to service its small, local sustaining population. Since higher-order transactions pertain to larger regional units, there will be fewer higher-order central places. Higher-order places will also generally have larger populations than the low-order places. High-order central places have more central place functions in total than do low-order places since the former include low-order functions (servicing the local population) as well as the other functions (servicing a larger region). Low-order central places are restricted to the low-order central place functions alone. This is translated into variable size for central places since the "functional size" of central places (i.e., the number of central-place functions present there) correlates positively with population size (cf. Haggett 1966; Berry 1967; Webber 1972; Johnson 1977), although it would be unwise to depend totally on population size as an index of functional size (Crissman 1976).

To what extent is the observed hierarchy of site sizes in the survey area during Period I a hierarchy of central places? Several major implications of the presence of such a hierarchy are the following:

1) There is a decreasing number of sites with evidence for central-place functions as you ascend the hierarchy.

2) There should be regular spacing of central places with the same-order functions, since each services a sustaining area.

3) A corollary of these two implications is that the mean distance between central places of higher order is larger than the mean distances between lower-order places.

Many extrinsic factors can distort a central-place system so that these expectations are not met (e.g., the presence of topographic complexities, uneven distribution of population), but they can serve as a convenient and simplified starting-point for the discussion here.

In order to compare our settlement data with these expectations, our first task is to identify places we think may have had central-place functions and distinguish low-order from high-order places. Christaller (1933), who developed many of the implications about the size and spacing of central places, showed that a region's system of central places may respond to the needs of both administrative and marketing activities. Marketing systems, however, are notoriously difficult to study archaeologically because the locations of commercial transactions may not always be identifiable archaeologically. Nor is it the case, apparently, that specific artifact classes are associated with commercial transactions in areas like prehispanic Mexico. Later in this chapter we show that some indirect measures strongly suggest the existence of a marketing central-place hierarchy in Period I. Fortunately, we are in a better position to elucidate the nature of the hierarchy of administrative places because of the presence of archaeological evidence for administrative functions. Our major evidence for administrative activities is the presence of pyramid-mounds and related features that undoubtably functioned as civic buildings and elite residences. Blanton (1978) discusses these features at Monte Albán. Some of these buildings may have functioned as religious buildings rather than in the context of administration. Given the close isomorphism of ecclesiastical and administrative activities in chiefdoms and the primitive states, however, we doubt this presents a serious problem for our interpretations. Another potential problem is the possibility that some mounded architecture functioned as residences of an elite who had access to resources and labor for construction projects, but who had no direct role in regional decision-making, i.e., families with high prestige or economic status that for some reason did not owe their position to their place in the regional decision-making hierarchy. Here, we would argue that in societies of the type in question here there is little distinction between the class of elites and the society's administrators. We concur with Elman Service's conclusion that:

> All the archaic civilizations, and the ethnographically known primitive states . . . did have strata: basically there were two, the *governors* and the *governed* . . . The difference was in political and religious power. . . [1978:32; cf. Claessen and Skalník 1978]

We might further assume that sites with larger-scale buildings would be higher-ranking central places, combining low-order functions with the higher-order administrative functions carried out by the highest-ranking elite. These elite would presumably have had most access to the power and resources required to carry out the construction of larger-scale buildings. Low-order places might be expected to have correspondingly smaller-scale construction. To a large extent these assumptions no doubt hold true, but perhaps an even better method for identifying a center's relative status would be to take into consideration population size as well as size of buildings. A higher-order administrative central place usually has more total functions, as discussed previously, and this should be reflected in the size of the resident population involved in administration or supporting administrators as servants or retainers. In doing our rankings of central places, then, we considered both population size and total mound volume. This eliminates from consideration large communities lacking architectural evidence for administrative activities and properly, we think, accounts for sites with sizeable mounds but low population (the latter is rarely a significant problem, however). Although a site lacking mounds could still have been a central place if it had been a commercial center lacking any administrative functions, the present discussion is limited to administrative functions.

Since many sites have multiple components, it is not always easy to determine the size of buildings in any one period. We often can tell whether there was *some* mounded construction from an earlier period, but we can't directly measure how big it was. To resolve this problem, we again turned to population as an indicator variable. In such situations, we assume that the volume of mounded construction for a period at a given site is the same proportion of the site's total mound volume as the population size of that period is a proportion of the site's maximum population size. When structures can be dated directly, their volume is simply added to the volume estimate made according to the proportional method. For example, if a site reached its maximum size during Period IIIa, then we assume that 100% of the site's mounds were in use at that time. If the population of the site during Late I was half the IIIa size, and the mounds are within the limits of the Late I site, *and we had archaeological reason to believe that there may have been Late I mounded construction*, then we infer that the Late I mound volume was equal to 50% of the total mound volume. A value derived in this way is referred to as a mound volume index in Table 4.1, the central-place summary for Early I. This method is potentially misleading, but it is the best means we could devise for estimating mound volumes short of excavating the hundreds of mounds that have multiple periods of occupation, a task so vast that it will probably never be accomplished. Our problems in the identification of administrative places, given the presence of multicomponent sites, are not so serious as they might seem. Often the dating of mounds can be done by the inspection of fill in looter's pits. At Monte Albán, the favored orientation of buildings changed after the beginning of the Classic period, making it possible to tentatively identify buildings that were built before that time (Blanton 1978). Even for Periods I and II, some administrative sites have only a single component and, for Periods IIIa through V, many sites with mounds have only one component.

For a period like Early I it is not easy to discover the nature of the hierarchy because there are so many multicomponent sites. Too, for this and the other periods, we realize that the final interpretations of hierarchies will have to await the completion of the valley survey. Within the survey area in question here, however, we think we can make a reasonable argument for three and perhaps four levels of administrative central places for period Early I. The region's highest category consists of one site–Monte Albán. A second level consists of sites 2-5-33 and 3-5-52,54, both of relatively large population size, and both containing what appears to be a substantial amount of mounded architecture that we think can be attributed at least in part to this (Fig. 4-10, Table 4-1). A third tier is made up of a group of smaller sites with more modest architecture. In some cases sites in this level have relatively high mound volume indexes (e.g. 3-5-9 and 3-5-34,35), but their population sizes were modest, and we were less sure,

Table 4-1. Central-place Summary, Early I

SITE	POPULATION	MOUND VOLUME m^3	RANK
2-33	179	9320*	2
3-9	17	12,199*	3
3-21, 57	29	1432*	3
3-25	31	2725*	3
3-27	255	4180*	market?
3-30	143	3763*	3
3-34, 35	49	13,933	3
3-36	(202)	?	2
3-37, 38	43	7907*	3
3-43	89	1564*	3
3-52, 54	225	6873*	2
3-59	114	8458*	3
3-64	(202)	?	2
		* Index	

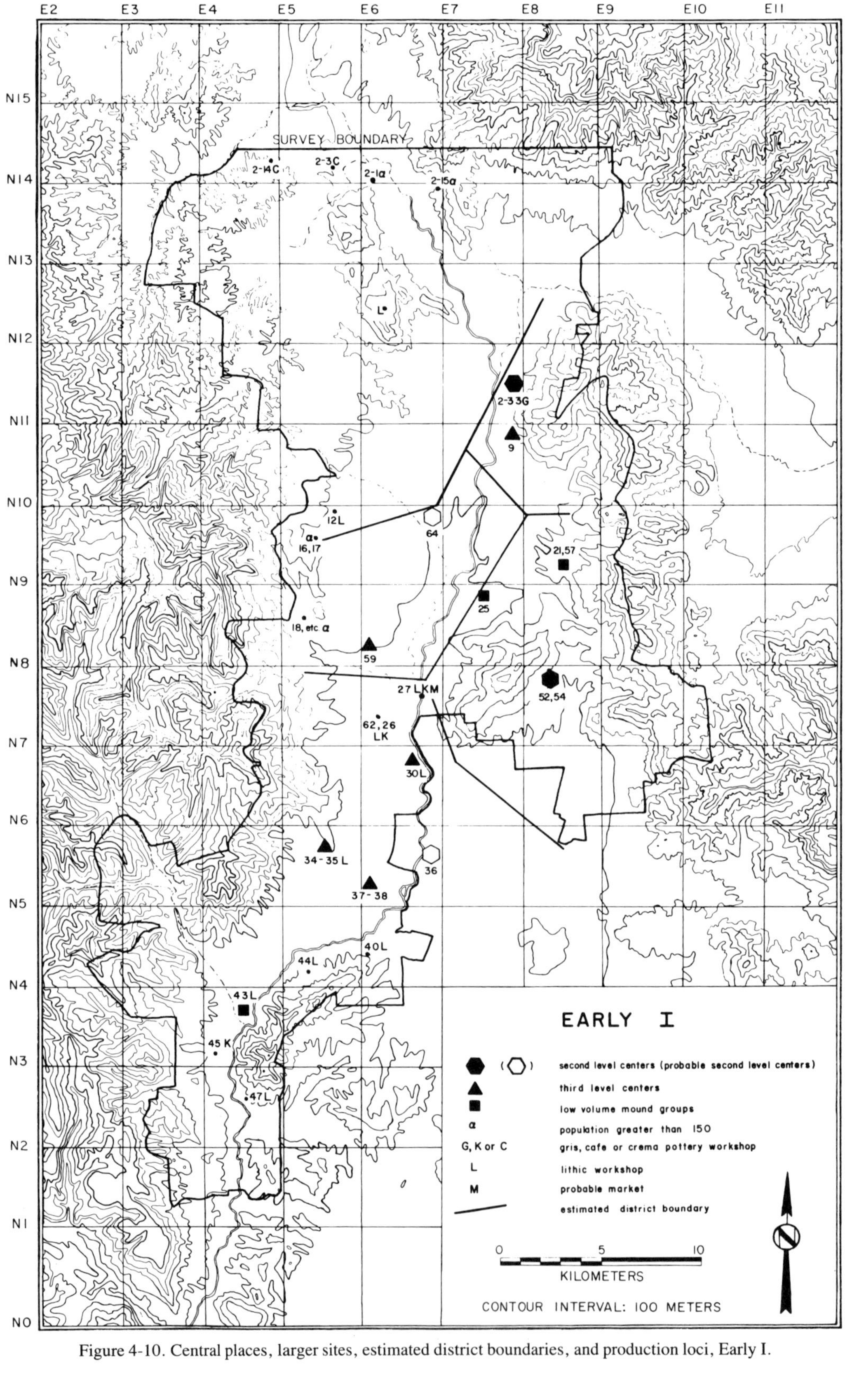

Figure 4-10. Central places, larger sites, estimated district boundaries, and production loci, Early I.

based on surface evidence, of the dating of the mounded construction. Our fourth group, referred to in Figure 4-10 as "low volume mound groups" have so little evidence for mounded construction that we are not at all sure they should be interpreted as central places. Figure 4-10 also includes two other centers that are indicated as having rank-2 status, Zaachila (3-5-64) and Sta. Inés Yatzeche (3-5-36). These two sites have been included at this rank because, although neither was ever as large as Monte Albán at its height, both were apparently very important central places for long periods of time, with mounded architecture at a scale far in excess of our class-3 sites. Our problem is that for these sites we lack information on prehispanic population size by period. Such data could not be collected at Zaachila due to the heavy Colonial and Modern overburden (IIIb is the only period measurable, since the site at that time was larger than the contemporary town). Early I pottery is abundant around the main Zaachila mounds (which are described in Appendix XI), however, so we assume it was an important central place at that time. The population size of Sta. Inés will be determined once we have completed the regional survey. For now, we will assume that the population sizes of these two centers are equivalent to the mean size of the other two secondary centers.

The location of the highest ranking center at the confluence of the valley's three arms, ideally situated to provide administrative services for the entire valley makes sense in central place terms. The distribution of class-2 centers also conforms very nicely to the expectations of central-place theory, since they form a very regular lattice extending south from Monte Albán. The mean distance between rank-2 centers (including Monte Albán, since it presumably had rank-2 functions along with its higher-order functions) is 8.93 kilometers, with a standard deviation of only 1.429. This supports the idea that each of these settlements was a central place, administering a distinct complementary area.

Several alternative interpretations of the locations and spacing of centers are less satisfactory. Certainly the locations of these centers could not be predicted in strictly environmental terms. Monte Albán and 3-5-52,54 are very poorly located in terms of local agricultural potential (see below, Chapter 9). The dictates of center spacing resulting from distance-minimization seem to have overridden other locational factors. It is also possible that regularity in spacing was due to military competition between the centers. We feel this is unlikely for several reasons: 1) Only Monte Albán and, to a lesser extent, 3-5-52,54, are in elevated positions that could be interpreted as defensive. 2) None of these sites has evidence for defensive features in Early I. 3) No shatter zones, that is, open areas that were unused due to military competition, can be identified in the surveyed area between these centers.

Thus we argue that the placement of Monte Albán and the rank-2 centers in Early I is the outcome of development of an administrative central-place hierarchy in which these centers were optimally situated from the point of view of regional administration. This need not imply that the locations were dictated entirely from Monte Albán; in part the Early I system at this level was simply an outgrowth of pre-existing patterns. Both Zaachila and Sta. Inés Yatzeche have long occupational histories and no doubt were important places prior to the formation of the new capital, and 3-5-52,54 was an important Rosario phase place.

In contrast with the distributions of the rank-2 centers, the distribution of the third-ranking centers (and the "very low volume mound groups") does not conform to the simplified predictions of central-place theory outlined above. Although there are more third rank places than second rank places (6 versus 4, not counting the smallest sites), and the distances between them are less than the distances between higher-order centers (4 kilometers versus 8.9— which includes distances to the higher ranking centers, since these would have had rank-3 functions), they are not evenly distributed over the landscape. Most such centers are in the vicinity of Sta. Inés Yatzeche, while none are found in the near vicinity of Monte Albán. While the distribution of the rank-1 and rank-2 centers in the survey region seems to support our contention that there was an administrative central-place hierarchy, the distribution of the smaller centers indicates a divergence from the central-place predictions. In later sections we will consider the implications of this divergence.

ASPECTS OF THE ADMINISTRATIVE CENTRAL-PLACE HIERARCHY, PART I: PRIMACY

An outstanding feature of the Early I settlement hierarchy is the extremely large size of one center, Monte Albán, relative to other centers (this pattern is present in other periods also and is discussed further below). The size relationships of communities in a region can be illustrated by plotting them according to rank and population size on log-log paper (a rank-size graph) (cf. Berry 1967; Haggett 1966; Blanton 1976c;

Johnson 1977). Although rank-size graphs are difficult to interpret in terms of what precisely they indicate about the structure and function of regional systems (Johnson 1977), a few rather secure inferences can be made. Rank-size relations range from ''primate'' or ''concave'' in form–where there is a large drop from the rank-1 center to lower-ranking centers, to ''convex,'' where two or more of a region's higher-order centers are nearly equivalent in size. In the first case, the relatively large size of the largest center often means that that center has a relatively large proportion of the region's total central-place functions. This implies more regional dominance than is present in less primate systems. At the other extreme, the convex case, a primate center is lacking. Instead, the highest-ranking centers in a region are more equivalent in size. This should indicate a more dispersed, less focused distribution of the region's central-place functions. These nearly-equivalent centers can be considered to be ''competing'' insofar as they have similar functions, and not one of them has a monopoly of regional control. The competition involved need not be manifested as warfare, and indeed in some cases the convex distribution simply indicates little interaction between centers.

Intermediate between the concave and convex rank-size forms is the ''log-normal'' distribution, where a center's population is equivalent to

$$P_n = P_1(n)^{-1}$$

where n = the rank of the center in question

P_1 = the population of the region's rank-1 center

A large literature exists offering explanations for why some regions correspond closely to this equation (cf. Berry 1961; Zipf 1949; Simon 1955; Johnson 1977). For our purposes here we will simply interpret this distribution as a situation intermediate between one in which there are multiple, nearly equivalent centers and one in which there is strong dominance by a single primate center.

Figure 4-11 is the rank-size graph for the survey region in Early I. The reader should keep in mind the important fact that these are all preliminary graphs. They show the rank-size relationships of sites in the survey area, which is not a complete, self-contained region. The final rank-size graphs and the final interpretations of center-size relationships cannot be completed until the completion of the valley survey. The Early I graph illustrates the strong primacy of Monte Albán. Line A in the figure shows the location of the log-normal line, calculated from Monte Albán. Below the level of

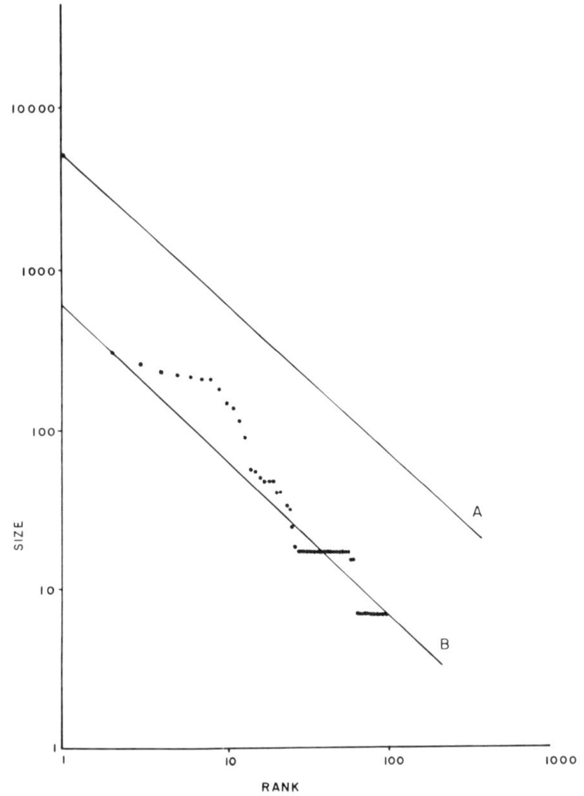

Figure 4-11. Rank-size graph, Early I. Line A is log-normal as calculated from the size of the rank-1 center. Line B is log-normal as calculated from the size of the rank-2 center.

Monte Albán, the next few centers illustrate a convex pattern (line B is the location of the log-normal line calculated from the rank-2 center). The Early I line is thus what is sometimes referred to as ''concave-convex'' in shape (Johnson, in press). This may be interpreted to mean overall primacy centered on Monte Albán, but with the presence of a series of functionally nearly equivalent centers below rank-1. A factor complicating this interpretation is that of the eight places ranking just below Monte Albán in size, three have little or no evidence for mounded buildings that would indicate administrative functions, and another, 3-5-27, has very unusual architecture probably not indicative of elite activities. Obviously factors other than administrative activities alone must be considered in evaluating size-rank relationships. These will be discussed more fully in the course of this chapter.

In Chapter 2 we briefly discussed the basis for primacy in the valley. The general argument was that the valley's size–most of it is within a day's walk from the center–and bounded topography limit the growth of secondary centers since their sustaining areas are so sharply delimited by mountainous terrain. This would have been especially important as a factor limiting the growth of secondary centers if the valley's boundaries had been highly impermeable, that is, if the flows of materials and information were primarily intraregional, rather than interregional. Secondary centers in such a situation would have serviced only the Valley of Oaxaca population, not populations exterior to the valley, sharply limiting the potential sizes of sustaining populations.

Several more points can be made about the tendency toward primacy in Early I:

1) Only Monte Albán had a sustaining area equivalent to the entire valley. All secondary centers have sustaining areas that were at most equivalent to one arm, or a portion of one arm. The only other location in the valley suitable for a center serving a more extensive area is in the vicinity of N7E9 and E10–where easy transport is possible between the east side of the Valle Grande and the western portion of the Tlacolula arm. No Period I center was located in this position. Exchanges between these two zones, then, may have been largely through Monte Albán, amplifying its regional importance. Monte Albán's central location would have been ideal for coordinating intraregional exchanges. In general, stepped-up intraregional movement of goods would have increased Monte Albán's importance.

2) We have already argued that the military themes in Monte Albán's Period I carved stone monuments (and their absence elsewhere) indicate it served as the region's center in offense-defense activities. Activities such as diplomacy and long-distance exchange probably added functions to the capital not present elsewhere. Evidence that long-distance exchange was controlled by Monte Albán might be difficult to come by, although it is perhaps relevant that all the obsidian production loci found to date are in the capital (and obsidian is obtainable only through interregional exchange).

Our provisional conclusions are that the rank-size graph for Early I implies a regional organization highly focused on one center, but with the presence of a series of much smaller secondary centers of nearly equivalent functional size, each administering a local zone. The presence of local styles in iconographic and epigraphic materials suggests the retention of some local autonomy in some of the centers in this secondary level (Marcus 1976a). Several communities were as populous as the secondary centers, but they had no administrative functions.

ASPECTS OF THE ADMINISTRATIVE CENTRAL-PLACE HIERARCHY, PART 2: REGIONAL INTERACTION

Another method for approaching the analysis of regional organization is to consider patterns of community interaction. Although such interactions are very difficult to reconstruct archaeologically, they are subject to two types of constraints that can be measured with data of the sort we have collected. First, distance is relevant because interaction is subject to movement costs. This means that we may justifiably infer that interaction decreases with increasing distance. Second, the intensity of interaction is related to the numbers of people who are potentially involved in interaction. The potential interaction between two villages is less than the potential interaction between two cities, all other things being equal, and assuming they are at similar distances.

Geographers have combined these constraints into a deductive formula called the gravity model, used to predict the intensity of interaction between communities (cf. Haggett 1966:35-40; Johnson 1977; Olsson 1965). This model is derived directly from Newtonian physics and suggests that the amount of interaction between two communities is proportional to the product of their population sizes and inversely proportional to the square of the distance between them. That is,

$$I_{1,2} = \frac{P_1 P_2}{d^2}$$

where $I_{1,2}$ is the interaction between communities 1 and 2,

d is the distance between the two communities,

P_1 is the population of community 1

P_2 is the population of community 2.

While we utilize this equation as a means of characterizing certain features of the regional system, we are doing this with the model's limitations in mind. The gravity model cannot be considered either a cultural "law" applicable in all situations, or a direct measure of interaction. It is simply a deductive model which has been shown to have considerable empirical validity in a variety of situations (cf. Carrothers 1956; Zipf 1949;

Johnson 1977). The equation as we are using it here contains certain simplifications. The major factors that could result in misleading potential interaction values are the following:

1) The actual interacting population may not be equal to the total population (Olsson 1965). Elite, for example, may be more likely to interact across substantial distances than non-elite (Johnson 1977).

2) Travel time may be a more useful means of calculating interaction potential than distance, given the possibilities of topographic obstacles (Johnson 1977). Given the relatively flat valley floor, however, we assume relative uniformity in travel time as a function of distance in the Valley of Oaxaca. It should be remembered, though, that the Río Atoyac could have impeded movement between some places during part of each year.

3) Geographers have found that other distance exponents may in some cases make better empirical sense than the d^2 used here. The major determiner of exponent best-fit seems to be technology, especially transportation technology. $PP/(d)^{-1}$, for example, makes more empirical sense for interaction rates in the contemporary United States, given the reduced costs of mechanized movement, electromagnetic communication, and the like. In less industrialized situations, however, the larger exponent for d is supported (cf. Haggett 1966:35-40). Since we are using our interaction measures as a means of calculating interaction potentials at particular points in time and for comparison of interaction potentials between periods within the same region, during which transport technology remained relatively unchanged, the value used as exponent is actually relatively unimportant anyway, so we will use d^2.

For Early I, two sets of interaction potential (hereafter shortened to *IP*) measurements were made. The first set of measurements involved administrative centers only. The second set of measurements included all sites in the top 10% of Early I range in population size. The latter measures, we thought, might provide some clues as to the nature of the larger sites that lack any architectural evidence for administrative functions. Our primary goal in examining *IP* between administrative centers was to assess the importance of horizontal interaction between same-level centers relative to their vertical interaction with higher-level centers, especially Monte Albán. Interaction measures were calculated in each case for first and second nearest-neighbors, as well as for Monte Albán (even if Monte Albán was not a first or second nearest-neighbor). For administrative centers, interaction was measured for each tertiary center (which includes our category "very low volume mound groups") and its first and second tertiary center neighbors; between each tertiary center and its nearest two secondary neighbors; and for each secondary and tertiary center and Monte Albán.

In all of the *IP* calculations, the populations of Zaachila and Sta. Inés Yatzeche are assumed to be equivalent to the mean size of the other two secondary centers (202 people). A nearest-neighbor of two of our large population sites (2-5-1, 2-5-15) is located just outside of the survey area, at San Lorenzo Cacaotepec. We have mapped this site (estimated population of 252), but since it is in the as-yet incomplete Etla survey zone, it is not included in this report. It is not used as an additional site in these calculations since its nearest neighbors, in turn, are not securely known.

The conclusions we can make from the measures of *IP* are tentative, but nonetheless intriguing:

1) *IP* between tertiary centers ($\overline{nn}_1 = 194.5$, $\overline{nn}_2 = 98.3$) is less than *IP* between tertiary centers and their nearest-neighbor secondary centers ($\overline{nn}_1 = 625.7$, $\overline{nn}_2 = 184$). This implies relatively little horizontal interaction between the low-order administrative centers in comparison with the intensity of vertical interaction.

2) In turn, these measures argue for much more interaction between secondary centers and Monte Albán (mean = 7555.9) than existed between the secondary centers themselves ($\overline{nn}_1 = 527.3$, $\overline{nn}_2 = 309.8$). These patterns are probably typical of highly primate administrative systems, where a large proportion of the region's total interactions are focused on a single center. These systems therefore tend to have a strongly vertical rather than horizontal directionality.

3) The total amount of *IP*, as we measured it, involving the large population sites (which total 13, including Monte Albán), is considerably greater than the total for sites we have identified as administrative sites. The total of *IP* "units" for administrative sites (not counting nearest-neighbor pairs) is 39,939, while that for the large sites totals 135,998 (both populations contained 13 sites). Obviously some non-administrative sites are accounting for a significant amount of the region's *IP*. In both cases, Monte Albán accounts for over 75% of the total *IP*.

If we consider *IP* among this group of larger sites other than Monte Albán in terms of the percentage each accounts for of the region's total for the larger sites, some additional interesting features of interaction become apparent (Table 4-2). In this group, four sites

Table 4-2. Percent of Total Interaction Potential of Large Sites, Not Including Interactions with Monte Albán

Site	%	Site	%
2-1	9.8	51	1.3
2-15	7.5	52,54	1.2
2-33	1.1	59	4.1
27	6.5	64	1.4
30	3.6	18, etc.	2.9
36	1.9	16,17	1.1

stand out as contributing more than the average to the interaction measures. Of these, 3-5-27 is the site that was originally considered to be a third-rank administrative center, but which has architecture unlike the other administrative places. This site is also unusual in having the largest number of mentions (4) as a nearest-neighbor among the larger sites. This is more than the nearest-neighbor mentions of the secondary administrative places (3-5-64 = 3, 2-5-33 = 1, 3-5-52,54 = 0, and 3-5-36 = 1). The relative centrality and accessibility of this site, in combination with the nature of the architectural and other archaeological remains (discussed below), lead us to suggest it was a marketing/production center, not an administrative place. The relative accessibility of this site contrasts strikingly with the nearby administrative site 3-5-52,54, which accounts for only a very small proportion of *IP* and has no mentions as a nearest neighbor. In the next section of this chapter, we will try to explain why an administrative place would have been so poorly located.

Another site categorized as an administrative central place of third rank, 3-5-59, accounts for an above average potential interaction. Interestingly, this site is in the upper range of tertiary-level sites in terms of population (Table 4-1). Although it would probably not be reasonable to argue that this site alone could comprise an administrative level intermediate between secondary and tertiary centers, the site certainly was an important tertiary center, as is indicated by its relatively elaborate elite residential architecture (Appendix XI).

Two other Early I sites account for a relatively large proportion of the total *IP* among the larger sites, 2-5-1, and 2-5-15. Neither has architectural remains suggestive of administrative functions. These two sites, plus one other (3-5-18, etc.), accounting for a higher than average share of the *IP* total, are all located within 18 kilometers of Monte Albán, in the area where there was the most rapid population growth during Early I. The closeness of these sites to Monte Albán and the absence of similar sites farther away from the capital (in fact none of the large population sites lacking administrative functions are in the southern part of the survey region) suggest that the area around Monte Albán was not only distinct in terms of population growth and land use, as discussed previously, but also in the nature of intercommunity interaction and administration. This possibility can be explored by examining each of the Early I "administrative districts."

ASPECTS OF THE ADMINISTRATIVE CENTRAL-PLACE HIERARCHY, PART 3: EARLY I ADMINISTRATIVE DISTRICTS

In the absence of written materials dealing with jurisdictional matters, we can only approximate the boundaries of the areas administered by the four secondary centers. Our method assumes that the size of the area administered is proportional to the population of the center administering that area (we are in some trouble applying this method since we have only approximations of the sizes of two of the centers involved). Presumably, centers administering more people would have had more people involved in administration, hence larger population sizes. Our method thus supplies only a rough approximation of administrative districts since it demarcates areas irrespective of population densities or population sizes within the areas. A better method would demarcate districts in which center sizes and district populations vary proportionately, but, to our knowledge, no such method has been developed. An additional problem with our method is that Monte Albán's population may have been larger than that of other district capitals due to its wider range of functions pertaining to the region as a whole, rather than to the number of people administered within its own district. We have thus probably overestimated the size of its district.

Keeping these limitations in mind, we can demarcate the administrative districts using the method of weighted Thiessen polygons (Blanton, 1978, used a similar method in identifying site subdivisions at Monte Albán. See also Hammond 1972; Haggett 1966: 247-48; Hodder and Hassall 1971). The vertices of the polygons are located at lines drawn between each two centers. The location of the boundary between two centers is determined by the relative sizes of the centers in question, so that the line is proportionately closer to the smaller center–the exact place a function of the population sizes of the centers. Figure 4-10 shows the polygons for Early I. The boundaries of the districts adjacent to the Tlacolula and Etla regions cannot be finalized until the completion of the valley survey.

Divided up in this way, the survey area has five districts, distributed in such a way that three distinct administrative "zones" are present from north to south. The northernmost zone is the administrative district of Monte Albán. This is the most populous of the five districts, including 38 sites in addition to the capital, and a population of 1159, not counting Monte Albán. None of these sites can be securely identified as an Early I administrative place. Even the relatively large sites 2-5-1 and 2-5-15 lack any evidence for mounded buildings. On the basis of this evidence, it seems likely that even low-order administration was done directly from the capital itself in this district, severely restricting the degree of community autonomy. This high degree of administrative control by the capital was probably only feasible in the newly developed central area. Elsewhere in the valley, older communities dating back to the Rosario phase or earlier were more autonomous in their local affairs.

The second administrative zone, including the districts around 2-5-33, 3-5-64, and 3-5-52,54, is unlike the Monte Albán zone in having evidence for local administration at the tertiary level (3-5-9, 3-5-59, 3-5-25, 3-5-21,57). Still, even in this zone, some relatively large communities apparently lacked any administrative functions (3-5-16,17, 3-5-18, etc.). A total population, not residing in administrative places, of 658 is estimated for this zone (2-5-33 = 306, 3-5-52,54 = 49; 3-5-64 = 303). The site numbered 3-5-52,54 is unusual in having so few people (49) in its district apart from the population of the center itself. Like the Monte Albán district, this district is highly centralized. The only candidates for tertiary centers are the "very low volume mound groups" at 3-5-21,57, and at 3-5-25. The district capital is also enigmatic in being located in an environmentally marginal position on a ridge, at some distance from both farmland and people to administer. We mentioned earlier that of the larger sites, 3-5-52,54 had no nearest-neighbor mentions and accounts for only a very small proportion of the total *IP* (Table 4-2).

The location of 3-5-52,54 may be explicable in terms of the changes that occurred during Early I. Specifically, the location of this secondary center may make sense given that the regional system was becoming so much more vertically-oriented toward the new capital. Steponaitis (1978) has demonstrated that under centralized circumstances an administrative place is optimally located close to the "demographic center of gravity" (*DCG*) of its sustaining area (a point where distance costs to the total sustaining population are minimized). But if ". . . the low order center pays tribute to a higher-order center . . . then the ideal location of a minor center is no longer at the *DCG*, but is closer to the capital . . . The greater the degree of political centralization, the further is the optimal location deflected away from the *DCG* and toward the capital" (Steponaitis 1978:433). Given the increasing importance of a new regional capital in Early I, it may be possible that a center administering the Ocotlán area south of 3-5-52,54 was moved to the location on the ridge, where interposed between the Ocotlán area and Monte Albán, it was optimally situated for administration. This can be tested when we do the survey of the Ocotlán sub-region.

The third administrative zone, comprising the district around Sta. Inés Yatzeche (3-5-36), is clearly unlike the other two zones. Within this zone there are three definite tertiary centers (3-5-34,35, 3-5-30, and 3-5-37,38) and another possible center at that level (3-5-43). This probably indicates a more decentralized mode of localized administration around Sta. Inés, in contrast with the more northerly zones. Other features of this district indicate that its organization was unique:

1) Other than the population in the administrative place, 307 people resided in this district, in 21 communities with a mean size of 14.6. Ninety percent of these communities are isolated residences or hamlets (i.e., less than 30 in population size). In the Monte Albán district, in contrast, the 40 communities apart from the center itself averaged 29 in population size, and only 80% of these were hamlets or smaller. The average size of non-administrative communities in the middle administrative zone is an intermediate 21.2 people. The larger size of communities north of the southern zone may reflect one aspect of the more centralized administration toward the valley's center. One possibility is that in these more centrally administered zones, populations were nucleated to facilitate administration and taxation.

2) The population of the southern zone remained, throughout Period I, largely oriented to the alluvium. For Early I, 92% of the sites in this area are situated on the alluvium, and no sites are located in the high piedmont or mountain zones. The Monte Albán and middle zones are both more piedmont-oriented. In the Monte

Albán district only 8% of sites are on the alluvium; for Ocotlán the figure is 11%, for Zaachila, 50%. Ocotlán and Monte Albán have, respectively, 22% and 5% of their sites in the high piedmont and mountain zones. In part this distribution of alluvium sites is a function of the less abundant alluvium in the valley's central area, but we believe it may also be due to a policy by the highest administrative institution for development of the piedmont. The southern zone, based on the evidence we have presented here, was obviously not affected as much by the administration of the center and so remained unaffected in terms of population dynamics and land-use. Judging from our results so far, it seems that when discussing changing patterns of administration, one must maintain a regional perspective. New administrative patterns are not established necessarily as a monolithic structure in a region; the magnitude of difference seems to be largely a function of distance from the region's center. We have noted that the Monte Albán district seems to have been administered from the capital itself. Secondary administration is evident only in the second administrative zone, which begins some 8 to 10 kilometers from the center. This pattern may be related to travel time. Given that the administrator would have to descend and later ascend a high mountain, and in some cases travel over piedmont terrain, the maximum distance he might be able to go, accomplish work, then return in one day may have been limited to an area with a radius of about 8 to 10 kilometers. Beyond that range, secondary administration would have required a permanently staffed secondary administrative center. A second factor to consider is the maximum distance village dwellers are willing to travel to a service center. In societies where such travel is on foot or by cart, centers tend to be placed roughly 10 kilometers apart (Hodder and Orton 1976:57-60). Greg Johnson's comparable distance value for capital-based local administration at Susa is about 20 kilometers, more than double the estimate we have derived (Johnson, in press). The differences may have to do with the greater extent of flat terrain around Susa, plus the possibility for use of animal-powered transport in the Near East.

MARKETING IN EARLY I

Up to this point, our discussion has focused on administrative functions. We now turn to a consideration of the commercial organization of the region. Marketing institutions were a prominent feature of prehispanic Mesoamerican societies, in contrast with other early civilizations such as those in the Central Andes, where economies tended to be more directly administered by governments (cf. Murra 1956; Isbell 1978; Cieza de León 1945; Rowe 1967; Sanders 1956; Sahagún 1952:IV; Torquemada 1969:II; Díaz del Castillo 1956:218-19). We suggested in Chapter 2 that a marketing system may have first evolved in the Valley of Oaxaca in Period I. Proving this will be very difficult, since marketing activities are difficult to identify archaeologically. Most of our argument will dwell on various kinds of indirect, but highly suggestive, information. We cannot at this time be highly specific about what such an early market system would have looked like in terms of details of functioning or scale. It is not likely to have been the equivalent of the market system that the Spaniards observed in operation in Aztec Tenochtitlán and the surrounding Valley of Mexico (cf. M. Smith 1979). Such markets were no doubt the product of hundreds of years of evolutionary change.

One interesting bit of evidence suggesting market system evolution during Period I is the substantially greater specialization by community in ceramic production. A few potential ceramic production loci in the Central Survey Area may date to Rosario, but none are definitely that early (Winter, 1974, concurs with this finding). Craft specialization in utilitarian items like pottery need not indicate the presence of markets, of course, since such specialization may also occur in redistributive systems (cf. Peebles and Kus 1977; Earle 1978) or even in simpler exchange networks based on reciprocity (cf. Chagnon 1968). With respect to redistributive systems, as we argued previously, the absence of evidence for state storage facilities, a prominent byproduct of the redistributive economies, suggests the presence of a different mode of exchange. This is not to suggest that no storage or redistribution whatsoever was done by governmental agencies in Oaxaca, but that if present this must have been on a relatively small scale given the absence of major archaeologically identifiable features. Our most important evidence favoring the presence of marketing institutions beginning in Early I is the development and distribution of ceramic production loci.

In order to develop our argument for the presence of markets in Period I, several assumptions will be made (these are based on several sources, cf. Christaller 1933; Haggett 1966; Berry 1967):

1) People are only willing to travel so far to obtain goods because of transport costs. Longer trips will be

made to obtain costly items, but since such items are consumed less frequently, few such trips will be made. Less costly, more frequently consumed items will be obtained locally.

2) Families want "costly" goods, either because they manifest prestige and/or are more useful because they are of better quality. But, given finite resources, they consume these more costly goods at a lower rate than less costly items. Overall, then, the demand for costly items is lower and their demand thresholds are higher. Fewer producers of costly items can be supported in a region, compared with the numbers of producers of less costly items. Distribution points for the more costly items should be centrally located with respect to a large sustaining area, in order to service the maximum number of consumers.

3) Less costly but more frequently consumed items have relatively low demand thresholds. More producers of less costly goods can be supported in a region, and the distribution points should be more scattered to minimize transport costs for consumers.

4) Producers of bulky, fragile items like pottery will tend to produce near distribution points to minimize transport costs, assuming that raw materials are widely available. For pottery-makers in Oaxaca, this is generally the case.

5) The costliness of an item is proportional to the work effort required in its production. In Chapter 10, Feinman develops a method for calculating the relative costliness of the Valley of Oaxaca ceramic types, which he calls the "production step index." In essence, he reconstructs the number of steps required in the production of pots of different types. We assume that the types with more production steps were costlier than those with fewer steps. Briefly, for the Early I ceramic assemblage, the paste categories rank from high to low in costliness in the following order: *gris*, *crema*, and *café*. In general the gray wares are better burnished than the other categories; they exhibit more shapes, and often they have intricate decoration in fine-line incising (e.g., the G-15's and G-16's).

We might expect the *gris* categories in Period I to be produced and distributed near the valley's Central Area, serving the entire region, while the least costly *cafés* would be produced in several localities in each of the valley arms, where producers can be supported by smaller, local populations because of the greater demand for these lower-order types. These predictions work out very nicely for the Early I ceramic production loci we have located to date (Appendix IX is a list and description of all these sites). The only *gris* production site we have been able to identify is near the center of the valley at 2-5-33 (Fig. 4-10). *Crema* production is also restricted to this central zone, in two localities (2-5-3 and 2-5-14), just north of Monte Albán. Three *café* production sites have been identified, at 3-5-27, 3-5-26, and at 3-5-45 (Fig. 4-10). Feinman's preliminary work with the Etla arm ceramic collections indicates the presence there of a number of *crema* and probably *café* production sites, but none of *gris*. The ratio of *gris*, *crema*, and *café* production sites found so far (not counting the Etla sites) is thus 1:2:3, and only *cafés* are produced deep in the valley's southern arm. The clay sources themselves are rather widely distributed throughout the Valley of Oaxaca, so the natural occurrence of clay soils does not explain the distribution of the production loci. The numbers of sites for each paste category, their locations, and the fact that they are specialized, hierarchically ordered centers producing wares of varying costliness in considerable volume all are consistent with market system patterns of production and distribution.

Several additional lines of evidence are suggestive of market activities in the survey area:

1) Blanton (1978) found several open areas, in Monte Albán, whose locations adjacent to major roads and clusters of public buildings led him to suggest the possibility that they functioned as markets, but, of course, dating is problematical.

2) The site numbered 3-5-27 has an architectural feature that could be interpreted as a marketplace (Appendix I, part 2). The feature is a large artificial terrace, built on a small batholith located near the Atoyac. The terrace is buttressed by large boulders and measures roughly 55 meters north-south by 38 meters east-west. Present at the site is evidence for craft production involving quartz. *Café* kiln wasters were also noted. A quarry was discovered cut into the batholith, in the form of a tunnel following a vein of biotitic (metallic) quartz. This feature cannot, of course, be securely dated. Previously we mentioned the fact that the site's location is ideal for a site functioning as a market. Of the large population sites, it has the largest number of nearest-neighbor mentions, and it accounts for a relatively large proportion of the region's total *IP*. Interestingly, the site is located near the boundaries of three administrative districts–where it would have been optimally situated to service all three districts (Fig. 4-10).

Very provisionally, two points can be made concerning the functioning of the proposed Early I market system:

1) Production loci and administrative activities tend to be spatially separated, probably implying a market system largely "disembedded" from the government. In this inference we make the assumption that administrators desirous of controlling production activities would locate those activities within administrative places. Only one ceramic production locus (2-5-33) is within an administrative center. Given this, we should probably amend our statement to include the possibility that at least some high-order goods (like *gris* ceramics) were more administered, while lower-order goods were more administration-free. Note also that this production site is near the valley's center, only 8 kilometers from Monte Albán. The low-order lithics–the local quartz and cherts, are also spatially separated from administrative places, at least in the Valle Grande (Fig. 4-10). The absence of these production sites around Monte Albán is suggestive that even low-order lithics were produced in the capital for the population of the central region. Obsidian, though, a high-order good because it is not locally available, must have been worked only in the capital, given the absence of surface evidence for production loci anywhere else. (The problem of administration-market relations is discussed more fully by Feinman in Chapter 10.)

2) A market system like the one we believe evolved in Early I, characterized by predominantly vertical flows to a primate center, is referred to as dendritic (cf. Smith 1974). Such systems create inequalities in access to markets, since consumers at a greater distance from the system's center "pay" more for goods because they have greater time and energy costs in movement. Although low-order goods may be readily available everywhere in the region, high-order goods are available only near the system's center: thus consumers at a distance have less access to higher-order goods. Distant consumers are therefore "poorer" since, relatively speaking, they lack access to the region's full range of goods.

The inequalities in the Early I regional system can be seen in the nature of artifact distributions. Obsidian is a good example of a desirable but rare product in the prehispanic Valley of Oaxaca; we might expect it to show a center-centric distribution if a dendritic system operated. Of the Early I sites within the Monte Albán administrative district, 46% had obsidian present on the surface (some of this, of course, may pertain to other periods in the case of multicomponent sites). By contrast, only 23% of the sites in the southern administrative zone (around 3-5-36) had obsidian noted on the surface. Presumably, blades are the most useful form of obsidian tool (more so, probably, than the flakes or "chunks" we often find–cores are rarely found anywhere in the valley). Blade distributions demonstrate the regional inequalities even more clearly. Forty-one percent of the sites in the Monte Albán district have obsidian blades; the figure for sites in the southern zone is 9%.

Ceramic distribution data also support the hypothesis that the Early I market manifested regional inequalities. Following our arguments above, we would expect consumers living in sites closer to the regional center to have access to the full range of ceramic types, while consumers living in more distant sites, with fewer marketing choices, would have access to a more limited range of types. Also, there may be non-market reasons to expect a greater variety of ceramic types to be found toward the center of the region, especially in the capital itself. Since the area near the center has a greater number of towns with diverse functions, there are correspondingly greater numbers of roles and, proportionately, a larger number of people with higher wealth, power, and prestige. The greater density of people in different statuses toward the center of the system means greater variety in the means for acquiring price-differentiated goods and perhaps greater desire or demand for differentiated goods with which to express status nuances. Figure 4-12 shows the distribution of sites in the survey area according to distance from Monte Albán and numbers of Early I types found. Unpredictably, the sites situated just a few kilometers from Monte Albán have relatively few types, but, in general, sites within 20 to 25 kilometers of the capital have more types than more distant sites. Administrative places tend to have more types than non-administrative places, but even in this case distance is a factor. Several non-administrative sites close to Monte Albán (e.g., 2-5-15, 3-5-3, 3-5-8) have roughly as many types as the secondary administrative center at 3-5-52,54.

The foregoing, so far as we know, is the first archaeological study of the pristine emergence of a market system. Existing studies of market evolution have been based on recent data and are really studies of secondary market formation–that is, the growth of market systems in an undeveloped area, but where impinging groups already have such systems (cf. Vance 1970; Skinner 1965; Appleby 1976; Schwimmer 1976). Therefore, our data may have considerable intrinsic theoretical value for evaluating theories of market origins and evolution, since we can discuss features of the system with a minimal amount of concern for

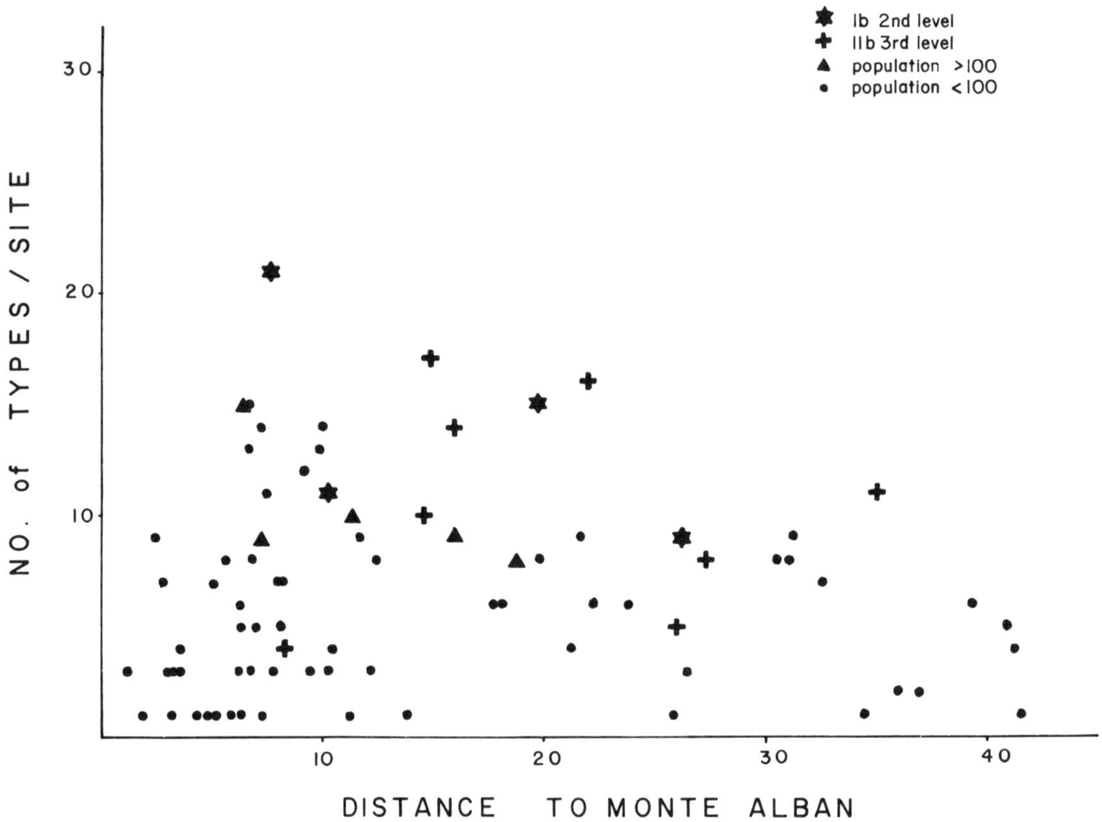

Figure 4-12. Types per site by site category and distance from Monte Albán, Early I. The data are found in Appendix VIII.

complicated recent historical factors. Two basic schools of thought dominate theories of market system origins. The one school argues that market systems evolve from "the bottom up," while the other argues that they evolve from the "top down" (cf. Berry 1967; Polanyi et al. 1957; Smith 1974, 1976). According to the "bottom up" theories, market systems will develop as the result of several factors operating among agricultural village dwellers, especially the assumed propensity for people to truck, barter, and exchange goods (as Adam Smith phrased it), but also including such things as the development of surplus-producing technologies (Berry 1967:108), population growth (Skinner 1965; Hodder and Ukwu 1969), and topographic and climatic diversity (Sanders 1956). In this interpretation, the impetus is, in other words, internal. Market evolution will occur, if conditions are appropriate, without external stimulation.

The opposing school, begun by Polanyi, argues that market exchange is not likely to develop on its own and is, instead, the product of external influences. Most commonly this is considered to be some form of long-distance exchange (cf. Pirenne 1936; Vance 1970), but it may also include urban food needs (Appleby 1976), or the demands of an elite in stratified societies. As Smith (1974:193) put it: "The marketing system would be instituted by an elite class that requires regular and efficient food provisioning. Elite groups or rulers do not necessarily give up control of the economy by instituting marketplaces, for by controlling the places, conditions, and means of exchange, they can allow the peasant to become a petty capitalist, competing with other peasants, without fear of economic competition themselves. In fact, marketing can be seen as a cheaper and more efficient means of compelling tribute, the peasant capitalist probably producing more for the state than his tribute-paying forbearers. Certainly all the evidence to date indicates that most marketing systems are controlled by some kind of political authority. So the state would seem to predate and be a condition for marketing systems if not market exchange."

We doubt that our data totally support or refute the contentions of either school of market system origins. In part our data are not of the sort that would allow such judgments to be made, especially concerning certain features of the "bottom-up" arguments. It is doubtful, for example, that we will ever know whether humans have a "natural propensity" to develop market systems. What about surpluses, environmental complexity, and population growth? We have no evidence indicating some Period I technological innovation that made it possible for people to produce more surpluses. They probably were producing more surpluses by that time, but no doubt this was because they had to do so. We doubt that the existence of surpluses alone explains the origins of market systems. We are unable to comment on the potential importance of environmental complexity in market system origins, since the classes of materials (especially pottery) we are able to identify as being produced and exchanged in market contexts are utilitarian items that presumably could have been produced virtually anywhere. Period I was a time of rapid population growth, but we doubt that this alone was responsible for market system origins, although it may have been an important variable, one that we have considered in the scheme presented above. We doubt that population growth in the absence of the kinds of changes in household economics that we argued for would engender market system growth, however.

If we may conclude that market systems are not likely to have evolved exclusively in "bottom up" fashion, does that imply that they were instituted due to external factors? Long distance exchange is the most frequently cited external force in this regard, but we are doubtful of its role in the Valley of Oaxaca. We have no evidence for changes in the pattern of long distance exchanges during Period I that could account for the formation of a market system, although we must admit we know relatively little about long distance exchange at that time. The problem of urban food needs for the expanding population of Monte Albán seems as though it would be a promising arena to explore in understanding the causes of market system formation. In a well-documented case, however, Appleby (1976) found that while urban food needs in the Puno, Peru, did cause marketplace formation, they did not result in the development of an integrated market system. This example brings into question the nature of the causal links between urban food needs and market system formation. We doubt, too, that the Period I market system was instituted in the manner suggested by Carol Smith. Our evidence from Early I indicates that this earliest market system was relatively free of administrative control.

Our contribution to the problem of market system origins, we feel, is in demonstrating the likelihood that the causality involved is circular, not linear, and that "top-down" and "bottom-up" factors may have operated simultaneously. An important factor not considered by those who have talked about market system origins is the nature of household time budgets–"home economics." We argued previously that as a large proportion of the farmers in the valley turned from a one-crop to a two-crop regime in response to the increased costs of supporting a new regional polity and capital, they would have been less able to produce certain utilitarian items at home, making it more likely that they would obtain these items from specialist producers, and a market system originated as a result. In turn, we suggested, the evolution of this new form of regional integration (along with the move to more canal irrigation) would have augmented the work-load of administrators, resulting in further growth of those institutions and even greater administrative costs. This is not an argument that the market system was instituted by the state, but, on the other hand, it is entirely possible that the pressures on families of producers created by the evolution of the new form of government resulted in conditions in which market-system origins were highly probable. Too, the demands of the state cannot be seen strictly in terms of the food requirements of the new capital. The energy costs of a new regional political institution in the valley would have included more than simply the feeding of the urban population. Military expeditions, for example, could have been costly, if, as we suggested, they could not have resulted in empire formation as early as Period I. We cannot even be sure that the population of Monte Albán was fed through the market system. It is at least as plausible that food flowed to the capital as tribute. We feel that the market system that evolved was one that serviced the rural population (as a source of utilitarian items, at least in part), as well as, perhaps, the urban population.

As we see it, the origin of a market system in the Valley of Oaxaca illustrates how a change in one sphere of organization (regional political integration) results in changes in other spheres (increasing potential interaction between households, changing agricultural strategies, changing household time budgets), which in turn result in the evolution of a new form of regional integration (a market system), which in turn has implications for change in regional political organization (e.g., due to increasing administrative costs involved in market management).

Testing the hypotheses presented here will require more detailed information concerning production,

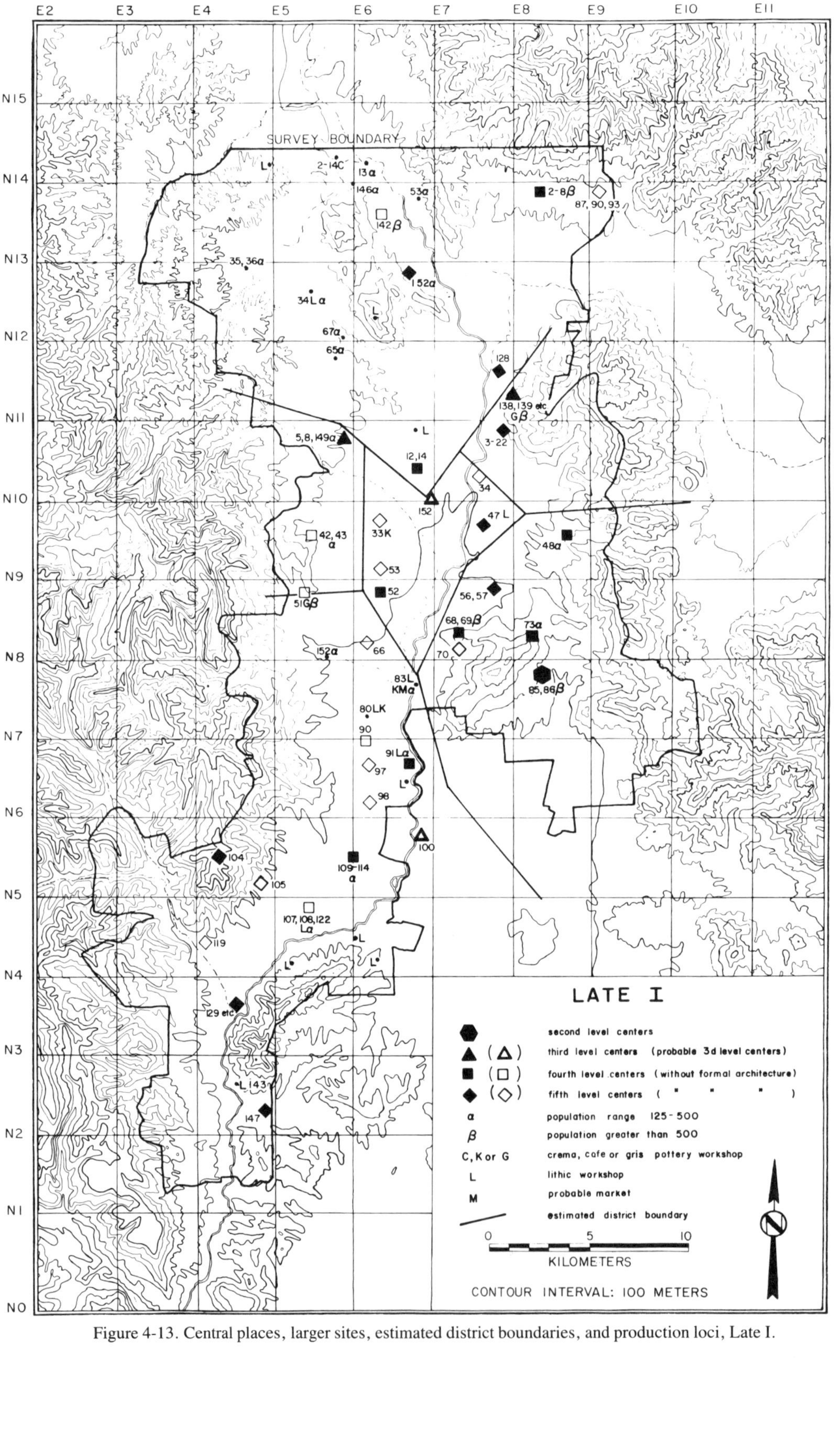

Figure 4-13. Central places, larger sites, estimated district boundaries, and production loci, Late I.

household activities, and so forth, information which can only come from more intensive projects involving systematic surface collections, excavations, and artifact analyses.

ADMINISTRATIVE ORGANIZATION IN LATE I

The administrative central-place hierarchy in Late I was larger and more complex than its Early I predecessor. Figure 4-13 shows the distribution of central places and the estimated district boundaries for Late I. The following are the major features of continuity and change from Early I to Late I in regional administration:

1) Late I shows a striking increase in the total population of sites with evidence for administrative functions. While the total population in the survey area increased from Early to Late I by a factor of 3.46 (8960 to 30,994), the total population of administrative places increased by a factor of 3.84 (6573 to 25,245). This increase occurred primarily in administrative central places other than Monte Albán. The total growth in this latter category was by a factor of 6.05 (1323 to 8003). Monte Albán's growth by a factor of 3.28 (5250 to 17,242) was not only much less than this, but was also less than the region's overall growth.

Assuming that population size is proportional to functional size, these changes in population may indicate a reduction in the degree of centralized control exerted at Monte Albán after Early I, with an increase in the amount of lower-level administration. Overall, these data seem to indicate an increase in the amount of administration per capita (since the rate of growth in administrative places was much faster than in non-administrative places); this, in turn, probably implies an increase in administrative costs. In part these increased costs may have stimulated the continuing development of the piedmont, which we have already discussed. Another possibility, which is explored in a later section of this chapter, is that government revenues were augmented through expanded control and taxation of production and distribution.

2) Monte Albán, with a population of over 17,000 and with abundant evidence for massive construction activities (CBA; Blanton 1978), still ranked as the region's number one administrative central place. Below that level there was not only substantial population growth in administrative centers generally, but also an increase in the degree of hierarchy formation. Some new centers were added. The secondary center in the northern part of the Ocotlán sub-region, 3-6-85,86 (formerly 3-5-52,54), grew in size and increased in architectural complexity more than the center across the river from Monte Albán at 2-6-136-9 (formerly 2-5-133). This places 3-6-85,86 in a position in the hierarchy intermediate between Monte Albán and 2-6-136-9. Below the level of 3-6-85,86, there are two sites consisting of 2-6-136-9 and a new center at Cuilapan (3-6-5,8,149) (N10E5). Another site similar to this group in mound volume, 3-6-12-14 (N10E6), is not indicated in Figure 4–13 as functioning as an administrative center at this level; due to its small population (only an estimated 91 people), it was pushed down one level. For Early I, we decided to include Zaachila and Sta. Inés at the rank-2 level, given the monumentality of architecture in both places. For Late I we have the problem of deciding whether these two sites should be grouped with 3-6-85,86, or with the sites in the level just below that. Both sites were occupied in Late I, and both were probably important places. Based on the limited evidence at our disposal, we decided to include them with the third group (2-6-136-9, and 3-6-5,8,149). We did this because we do know that the periods of most substantial growth at the two centers were later-IIIa for Sta. Inés (3-6-100), and IIIb for Zaachila (3-6-152), perhaps indicating the growth from Early I to Late I was not as substantial in these two places as at 3-6-85,86. Also, population growth in the surveyed area around Sta. Inés Yatzeche was very slow from Early I to Late I, which suggests that growth at the center was relatively slow too. Provisionally, therefore, we estimated the populations for these two centers by averaging the populations of 2-6-136-9 and Cuilapan, giving a value of 474.

Below the level of what we are calling district centers (that is, levels 2 and 3) there is considerable variability among the sites with evidence for public construction (Table 4-3). None have the combination of large population size and substantial public architecture (that we could be reasonably sure in attributing to this period) that is seen in the district centers. Somewhat arbitrarily, we decided to divide the remaining sites into two groups, a fourth level and a fifth level. Fourth level centers are those ranging in population from the fifties to about one-hundred people (in some cases members of this group are larger in population size than sites in level three but lack evidence for public construction on a large scale), while fifth-level centers are those among the smallest in mound volume and/or population size.

Our data, although difficult to interpret given that so

Table 4-3. Central-Place Summary, Late I

SITE	POPULATION	MOUND VOLUME m^3	RANK
2-8	607	2722*	4
3-5, 8, 149	289	26,948*	3
3-12-14	91	68,803*	4
2-87, 90, 93	115	2341	5
2-128	99	2865	5
2-136-139	658	10,512	3
2-142	555	4384*	4
2-152	173	923	5
3-22	25	12,861	5
3-33	64	2305*	5
3-34	17	19,137*	5
3-42, 43	260	3444*	4
3-47	95	3541*	5
3-48	263	11,962*	4
3-51	605	6458*	4
3-52	95	33,162*	4
3-53	23	4412*	5
3-56, 57	51	4352*	5
3-66	41	3039*	5
3-68, 69	616	3826*	4
3-70	41	3431*	5
3-73	301	4316*	4
3-83	255	4180	market?
3-85, 86	879	26,847*	2
3-90	111	11,182*	4
3-91	343	9023*	4
3-97	17	6323*	5
3-98	17	8108*	5
3-100	?	?	3
3-104	143	186*	5
3-105	77	1026*	5
3-107, 108	137	16,325*	4
3-109-114	138	25,415*	4
3-119	17	8955*	5
3-129, etc.	59	1027*	5
3-147	33	1184*	5
3-152	?	?	3
		* Index	

many Late I sites have later periods of occupation, thus indicate the possibility that a four- or five-level administrative hierarchy in Late I replaced the three levels of Early I. Whether the administrative institutions were actually conceived in this way is not yet known, and other interpretations are possible, including one that would include Monte Albán's site subdivisions as another tier. A fuller picture should emerge with the completion of the valley survey and additional analysis. But for the present we think that an apparent shift from a three-level to a five-level system as recognized through the same interpretive lens does indicate a move in the direction of change of administrative structure and function. This may imply a restructuring of some features of regional organization. The second-level center at 3-6-85,86, for example, may have assumed certain administrative functions for an area wider than its own particular district (the wider area perhaps including much of the Valle Grande), reducing some of the administrative work-load on Monte Albán. The growth rates of the two centers support this interpretation. Monte Albán increased in population from Late I by a factor of 3.28, while 3-6-85,86 increased by a factor of 3.9.

A restructuring of the regional administrative system is also indicated by the formation of the new center at Cuilapan (3-6-5,8,149). This new center would have been ideally located for the administration (and taxation) of the growing piedmont population just south of the site (in squares N8-10, E5). We suggest that rapid population growth in the piedmont, combined with the greater organizational requirements of piedmont cultivation, made it necessary to subdivide Zaachila's former district by establishing a new Late I center at Cuilapan.

LATE I INTERACTION POTENTIAL MEASURES

The first set of measures involved the large population sites (those with over 125 inhabitants–roughly the upper 10%), their first and second nearest-neighbors, and Monte Albán. Several conclusions can be drawn from these values:

1) The total amount of interaction between large population sites is much higher in Late I than in Early I.

For Early I, there was an average of 11,333 *IP* ''units'' per large site, while for Late I the average value is 159,282. In part population growth accounts for this, but the value is enhanced by the fact that most of this growth occurred in the valley's congested Central area, reducing the distances between larger sites (for Early I, the mean distance to first nearest-neighbor for these sites equals 4.25 kilometers; the Late I value is 2.89 kilometers).

2) As is apparent from the Late I rank-size graph (Fig. 4-14), the regional system as we know it remained strongly primate. Some decentralization seems to have occurred, however, as we argued in the previous section. The *IP* measures of the large population sites support this interpretation. Although the share of the total *IP* between these sites (counting the nearest-neighbor pairs only once) accounted for by Monte Albán increased from the Early I value of 78% to the Late I value of 89.6%, most of this increase occurred within Monte Albán's own district. *IP* within this district, in fact, accounts for 68% of the regional total for the larger sites. For Early I, the comparable value was only 41% of the total *IP*. So while interaction within Monte Albán's district increased in Late I, there was proportionately less *IP* between Monte Albán and sites in other districts. This supports our argument that 3-6-85,86 may have assumed some of the administrative functions for the Valle Grande sub-region that had previously been centered in the capital. For Early I, that same site (3-5-52,54) accounted for only 1.2% of the *IP* for the larger sites. The Late I value is 2.9%.

A second set of *IP* measures was calculated for administrative places only. These calculations are identical to those made for the Early I sites, where for each site *IP* is calculated for the first two nearest-neighbors at that level, then with the first two nearest-neighbors at the next level up. For the sake of brevity, only those fourth-and fifth-level sites are included that have evidence for the kind of residential architecture with an enclosed patio. These are the kinds of structures which Blanton (1978) argued were elite residences at Monte Albán; they are indicated on Figure 4-13 as having ''formal'' architecture. Site 2-6-8 is excluded from these calculations, because its proximity to the edge of the survey region means that its nearest-neighbors could be located in the unsurveyed Tlacolula arm.

As was the case for Early I, the values indicate that most of the administrative interaction was vertical. Tertiary centers and 3-6-85,86 have more *IP* with Monte Albán than among themselves, and the same is true for the smaller centers *vis à vis* the middle-level centers. The secondary center at 3-6-85,86 has, in spite of its distance, more *IP* with Monte Albán than do the third-level centers. Sta. Inés Yatzeche (3-6-100) continued to be by far the lowest in *IP* with Monte Albán, although its *IP* with Monte Albán is larger than its *IP* with 3-6-85,86 (11,998 versus 3851).

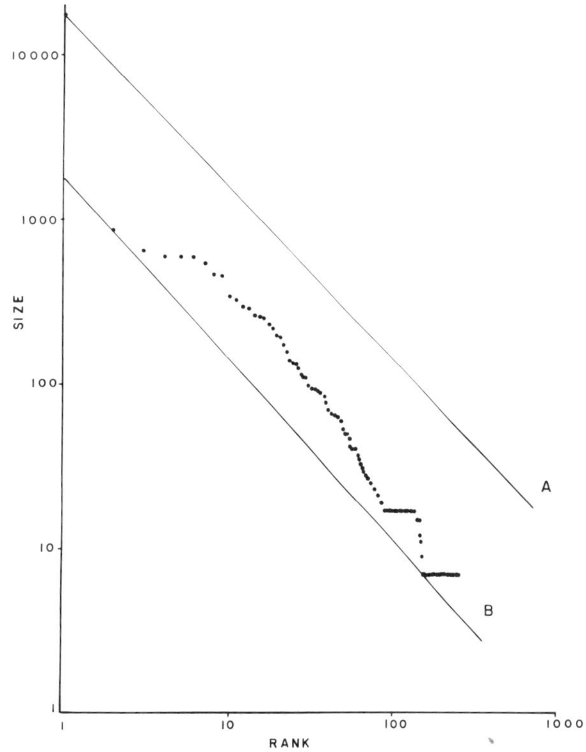

Figure 4-14. Rank-size graph, Late I. Line A is log-normal as calculated from the size of the rank-1 center. Line B is log-normal as calculated from the rank-2 center.

We can compare the relative amount of *IP* accounted for by administrative sites by calculating the percentage their total represents of the *IP* of the large population sites. For Early I, administrative *IP* is 29.4% of the *IP* of the larger sites. For Late I, the figure is somewhat reduced, amounting to 23.4%. This seems contrary to our argument that there was more administration per capita in Late I than there had been in Early I. Again, though, these values are misleading from that point of view because of the great concentration of large population sites lacking administrative functions adjacent to Monte Albán. If we divide the total administrative *IP* by the *IP* of the larger sites not including those in Monte Albán's zone, then administrative *IP* is 89.8% of the *IP* of the larger sites. This

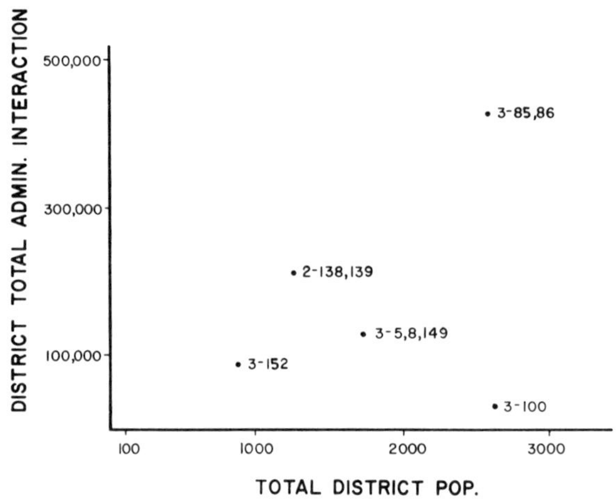

Figure 4-15. District total administrative interaction by total district population, Late I.

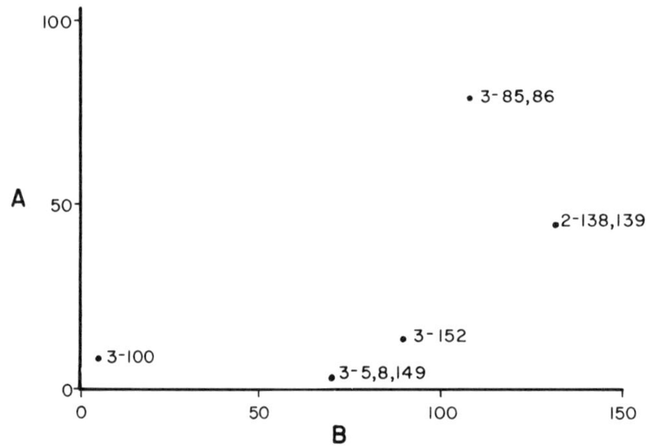

Figure 4-16. Scatter diagram, index of internal administration (A) by the index of external administration (B).

$$\text{Internal administration} = \frac{\text{District Internal Administrative } IP}{\text{District Rural Population}}$$

$$\text{External administration} = \frac{IP \text{ of District Secondary Center with Monte Albán}}{\text{Total District Population}}$$

value is high because, outside the Monte Albán district, most of the large population sites have administrative functions, while those within Monte Albán's district less often have such functions.

A second measure of administrative *IP* includes only those interactions that were likely to have been in operation given the administrative scheme we have proposed for Late I. Here, a quaternary center will interact with a secondary center in its own district if there are no tertiary centers in the district. Each center interacts only with centers in its own district, except for the highest ranking centers, which interact with Monte Albán. The bulk of the total *IP* for fifth-level centers has to do with one site, 2-6-152, located in the Monte Albán district. For the quaternary centers, the bulk of the *IP* is made up by three sites in the 3-6-85,86 district, 3-6-48, 3-6-68,69, and 3-6-73. This is 84.5% of the total *IP* for that administrative level, quite a difference as compared with Early I, when there were no administrative centers other than the main center in that district.

The results of this second set of administrative *IP* measures have been used in the preparation of Figures 4-15 and 4-16. The first of these two figures shows the relationship between total administrative *IP* by district and total population by district. Excluding Sta. Inés Yatzeche (3-6-100), there is a strong positive correlation between these two variables. As in Early I, the southern administrative district was unique (it will be discussed more fully below). Figure 4-16 shows the relationship between two administrative indices, the index of internal administration (district internal administration, i.e., the total administrative *IP* divided by the district population not residing in administrative centers) and an index of district *IP* with Monte Albán (*IP* of district center with Monte Albán divided by the total district population). This plot shows a positive correlation between the level of internal administration and the amount of *IP* with Monte Albán.

Based on these two figures, we suggest some additional changes in the nature of regional administration during the course of Period I. In both Late I and Early I it is possible to distinguish three administrative zones: Monte Albán and its highly centralized district, a middle zone, and a southern zone. By Late I, however, the middle zone may be divisible into eastern and western "sub-zones." The western "sub-zone," consisting of the Cuilapan (3-6-5,8,149) and Zaachila (3-6-152) districts, had very close ties with Monte Albán and poorly developed local administration. The eastern zone, including 2-6-138,139 and 3-6-85,86, also had close ties with Monte Albán, but much more in the way of local administration, perhaps implying more decentralization.

As in Early I, the southern zone was least affected by change. It exhibited the slowest rate of population growth from Early to Late I, and it continued into Late I as a largely alluvium-oriented district. (Fifty-nine percent of the sites in the southern district were located in the alluvium, while only 5% of the sites in the Monte Albán district were alluvial.) Given the relative lack of influence from Monte Albán, it seems possible that in Late I the southern district continued to be near the limits of the area administered by Monte Albán. Although there was no direct evidence for this proposition for Early I, some evidence exists for Late I. Site 3-6-104 (N5E4) is located on the very top of one of the highest mountains bordering the southern part of the Valle Grande. Given its location, this site clearly would not have had access to sufficient agricultural land to support its population. On the other hand, the view from this mountain-top includes not only a vast expanse of the southern part of the valley, but also the Mixtepec Valley to the south and west (in the vicinity of N4,5, E3,4). This setting is an ideal place for a military garrison for the purpose of border defense. It is suggestive that, at least to the south, the limits of the regional political unit were isomorphic with the limits of the Valley of Oaxaca.

CHANGES IN MARKET ORGANIZATION IN PERIOD I

The locations of Late I production loci are shown in Figure 4-13. The ceramic production loci are reasonably well-dated (see Appendix IX), but the lithic sites cannot be as accurately dated, due to the presence of some multiple components. In some respects the regional production/distribution system probably remained unchanged from Early to Late I. On the whole, for example, obsidian continued to be more available to the population of the Monte Albán district than to the populations in other districts. Sparse obsidian was noted on 30% of the sites around Monte Albán, while only 19% of the sites in the Sta. Inés Yatzeche district had comparable amounts of obsidian. But even these data, while somewhat difficult to interpret, because of the presence of multicomponent sites, seem to indicate change. The comparable percentages of sites for these two districts for Early I were 46% and 23%, respectively. Tentatively, we interpret this to mean that the degree of differential access to obsidian by distance from Monte Albán was less during Late I than it had been in Early I. The major features of change in the region's system of marketing from Early to Late I, as we can infer them from our surface data, are the following:

1) The population increase from Early to Late I was not matched by an increase in the number of production loci. For lithic production sites, we estimate one locus for every 224 people in Early I (counting the 40 concentrations of lithics found within the bounds of the Early I site at Monte Albán). For Late I, we estimate one lithic production locus for every 544 people. In large part this difference may be due to the fact that we are counting as Early I loci places that may actually date, as production sites, only to Late I. Our data on ceramic production sites, however, which are much more securely dated, support the veracity of these statistics. For Early I, we estimate the presence of one ceramic production site for every 1493 people; for Late I the value is one for every 5166 people. The response to increased demand due to population growth must have been to step up production rather than to proliferate production places.

The number and locations of the ceramic production places suggest other changes in regional marketing during Period I. Although the *café* production sites still numbered three by Late I, their locations are somewhat different (Fig. 4-13). The southern-most place dropped out, while a new place was established at 3-6-33 (N6E6). By Late I, a *gris* production site is located in the Valle Grande, at 3-6-51 (N8E5). This makes the ratio of *gris*, *crema*, and *café* sites 2:0:3. The addition of the *gris* site away from the central part of the valley is probably related to the substantial population growth north of the southern district and the lower cost of Late I *gris* ceramics relative to their Early I counterparts (see Chapter 10). Both factors would have lowered the demand thresholds for *gris* pottery sufficiently to support additional production loci. Interestingly, *gris* production continues in a secondary administrative center (2-6-138,139) and is started in a new locality (3-6-51) which although lacking any formal elite residential architecture, has mounded buildings perhaps indicative of administrative functions. Included among these buildings is a ball court. Judging from the paucity of sherds this ball court was contructed in Late I (along with several other buildings at the site), but never used, or used for only a short period before the Period II population declines. The *café* production sites are still largely non-administered, judging from the absence of mounded buildings, except for the new *café* site at 3-6-33. These data seem to denote an increase of administrative control of ceramic production in Late I, since more sites are associated with mounded buildings–three out of five, compared with one out of six in Early I.

2) In some respects, Late I was a more "affluent" period than Early I, if affluence can be measured in terms of numbers of ceramic types found per site. Our values for number of types per site are somewhat difficult to interpret, given that the sherds were not collected so as to assure statistically comparable samples from each site. The samples are comparable, however, in the sense that our technique in surface collection was essentially the same site to site. Still, unusual values from individual sites could be misleading and will not be discussed here. Too, the collections from Zaachila and Sta. Inés Yatzeche were not made according to our usual procedures and so have artificially small numbers of types in our tabulations (for Sta. Inés we based our periodization on one collection provided by Kent Flannery). In discussing numbers of types per site, we will be restricted to discussing general regional and diachronic trends–patterns in the frequency of types that show considerable repetitiveness, and which are probably not due, therefore, to sampling errors. Following our previous argument, more types indicate more marketing choices and less standardization, i.e., more opportunities to obtain vessel types suited to particular tasks, to obtain costly as well as less costly types, and so on. The average number of types per site increased from Early I to Late I even though the total number of types was about the same (EI = 85, LI = 88), but the increases vary significantly along two distinct axes. Although there was some increase in the average number of types per non-administrative site from Early to Late I (5.6 to 6.9), the real increases were in the administrative places. For Early I the mean value of number of types per site with administrative functions is 11.7. For Late I the value is 17.9. If we drop the Late I fifth-level administrative places from the calculations, the difference is even more pronounced, giving a mean of 21.5, almost twice the average for comparable Early I administrative sites and three times the average for Late I non-administrative sites. We interpret this to mean that more movement of pottery products in Late I was through administrative channels–increasing the "affluence" of administrators, but decreasing the availability of goods to non-administrators. This is not to argue for a totally administered economy in Late I, but simply to point out the likelihood that a larger proportion of the region's ceramic production (and perhaps production in other craft categories as well) may have been administratively distributed rather than moving entirely through a non-administered market organization.

The idea of a more administered economy is supported by the increased association of ceramic production and mounded buildings, as discussed previously. Further support comes from a consideration of the site that was tentatively identified as a market in Early I (3-5-27, N7E6). The site continues into Late I (3-6-83), but its position in the regional hierarchy seems to have changed considerably. Although population growth in the survey region generally was by a factor of roughly 3, from Early to Late I, the evidence indicates that this site did not increase in size from Early to Late I. One interpretation of this lack of growth in what appears to have been a market is that goods were increasingly flowing through non-market channels.

It is of some interest to compare the histories of the proposed marketplace and an administrative central place situated the same distance from Monte Albán–the site in the north part of the Ocotlán sub-region (3-6-85,86, 3-5-52,54). In Early I the administrative center accounted for only a very small proportion of the region's total *IP* of large sites (1.2%), while the proposed marketplace accounted for more of the region's *IP* of larger sites than any other site in the Valle Grande (6.5%). By Late I the tables had turned. Of the large

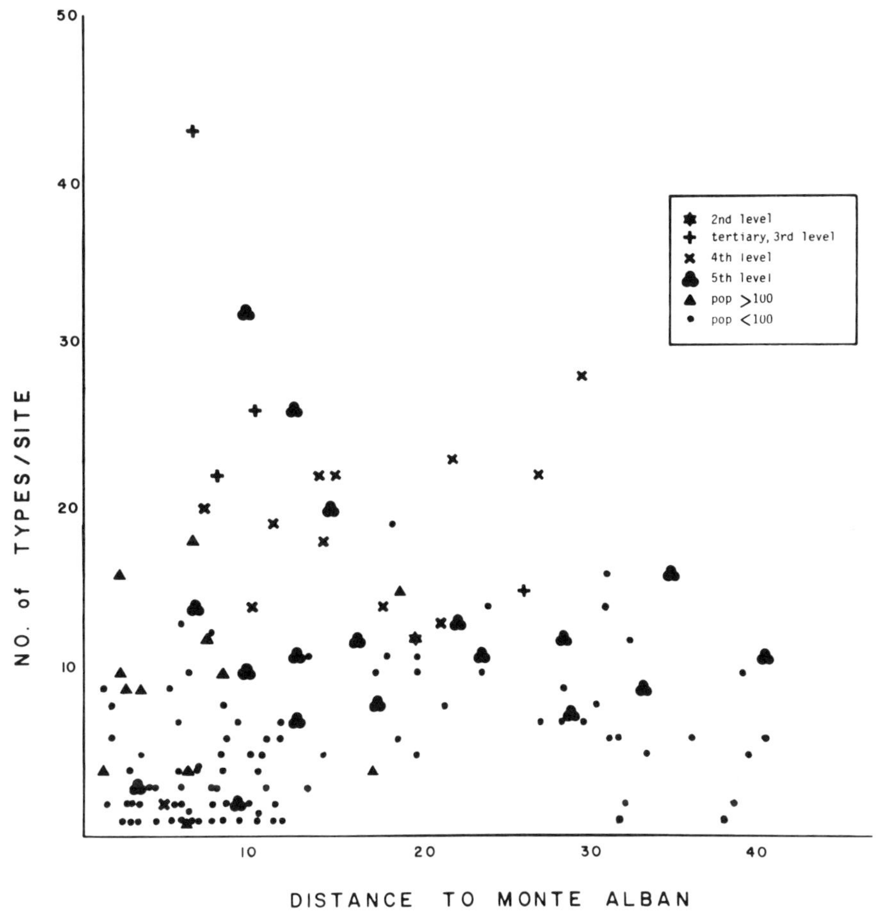

Figure 4-17. Types per site by site category and distance from Monte Albán, Late I. The data are found in Appendix VIII.

population sites, 3-6-85,86 accounted for the largest proportion of *IP* of any site in the survey region other than Monte Albán (2.9%), while 3-6-83 accounted for only .6%. Arguably, it may have been the case that the relatively rapid growth of sites with administrative functions during Late I could have been due in part to these communities having more commercial functions than they had earlier in the period.

3)We are suggesting an overall increase in the degree of overlap between administration and marketing by Late I. This may have been the result of the growth of administration relative to population and the consequent increase in administrative costs per capita. Production and distribution of craft items may increasingly have become a source of revenue for administrators. The degree of administrative control of markets, however, does not appear to have been the same everywhere in the region. As is to be expected based on our prior discoveries, change occurred at different rates in different places. The most influential variable is distance from Monte Albán, although by Late I an additional important variable is the presence or absence of administrative activities on a site. Figure 4-17 shows the number of types per site for Late I by distance from Monte Albán and according to whether sites are administrative or not. Again, as in Early I, there are overall differences between administrative and non-administrative sites, but the differences are more pronounced by Late I. In Early I (Fig. 4-12), small non-administrative sites within 5 kilometers of Monte Albán have relatively few types and beyond a 5 kilometer radius, as distance increases there is a general trend downward in numbers of types per site for both administrative and non-administrative sites. Late I was different; the number of types per site steeply increases with distance from Monte Albán, out to about 15 kilometers. Beyond 15 kilometers, however, the number begins to decline again, reaching a low in the isolated southern district. We interpret these data to indicate that communities close to Monte Albán were administered from the capital, and they were administratively supplied with a very limited choice of ceramic products. A middle range of sites was further from Monte Albán and less directly tied to it administratively, but still near enough to the centers of production and distribution to assure access to a relatively wide range of products. A third zone, far to the south, was probably least administered from the capital, but people there lacked access to a wide range of goods because they were situated at the peripheries of the system and were therefore poorly connected to it.

In Figure 4-17, most of the values of 5 or fewer Late I types per site are found within 10 kilometers of Monte Albán–an area roughly isomorphic with Monte Albán's own administrative zone. These data can be interpreted to mean that the increases in administrative control over ceramic production and distribution were greatest near the capital, and much less severe in the middle and southern zones. This argument makes sense if it is reasonable to suppose that a concomitant of increased administrative control of ceramic production/distribution was increased standardization. This argument is developed in more detail in Chapter 10, but its essential point is that administrators desirous of stepped-up revenues "flood" the market with highly standardized (and therefore inexpensive to produce) goods. If this had been happening in the valley's Central zone in Late I, it could help explain the loss of the *crema* poduction sites, since these are relatively costly ceramics which may have been "pushed out" by the now less costly and more standardized *gris* pottery. According to Feinman's calculations, the Late I *gris* types were less costly than the Early I *gris* types.

PERIOD I: CONCLUSIONS

We will make our final conclusions in Chapter 12 and in Chapters 9, 10, and 11, where it will be possible to make cross-period generalizations and comparisons. Here we restrict ourselves to a few specific topics: 1) We amplify several points that were brought up in Chapter 2 concerning the impact of the formation of Monte Albán and consider the nature of some of the long-term changes in Period I; 2) We consider in more detail some aspects of the origins of Monte Albán; and 3) We address ourselves briefly to the problem of the origin of the state in the Valley of Oaxaca.

In Chapter 2, we developed a theoretical model causally linking, in positive-feedback relationships, the major features of culture change in the Valley of Oaxaca after the formation of Monte Albán. This model included population growth, piedmont development, increased political centralization, the growth of Monte Albán, changing familial strategies and time budgets, and the origin of markets. Now that we have reviewed the Period I data, these suggestions can be further refined. First, the suggested causal interrelationships between these variables did not fully develop everywhere in the region. Instead, the most pronounced changes were restricted to the area proximate to Monte Albán, and, to a lesser extent, to the middle administrative zone. The southern zone remained relatively immune to change. This points up the importance of the new institution of Monte Albán as an "instrument," so to speak, of culture change; beyond what we think was its realm of fairly direct influence, relatively little occurred evolutionarily.

Our data seem to indicate that a product of the proposed set of interrelationships between variables after the foundation of Monte Albán was a faster rate of increase in the amount of administration than in the rate of general population growth and a more vertically hierarchical administration. We have argued that this would imply increased administrative costs per capita, and it may be related to expanded administrative control of markets. This, in turn, may have had certain negative consequences, especially in the increasing dichotomy in "affluence" between those places with administrative functions and those without. Communities close to Monte Albán seem to have been particularly affected by these changes, having overall the lowest numbers of types per site in the region. Proximity to the capital, by the end of Late I, may have become less and less desirable, especially given the crowded conditions in the valley's Central zone (most of the squares with excess population compared with potential agricultural resources are in this zone–see Chapter 9). Monte Albán in Late I has, of course, all the 88 ceramic types in our categorization, while most of the sites within 10 kilometers of the capital have fewer than 5 types–suggesting that the increasing differential between administrative and non-administrative places was most pronounced in the Central zone.

Given these facts, we feel justified in arguing that the regional system was becoming less viable during the course of Period I, the result of strained agricultural resources in the Central zone, burgeoning administrative costs, and an expanding dichotomy between the haves and have-nots. The system developing in this fashion may have reached the limits of viability toward the end of Late I. By Period II a kind of "devolution" had occurred, the nature of which is discussed at length in the next chapter.

THE ORIGINS OF MONTE ALBAN

As we mentioned in the introduction to this chapter, Blanton (1976a, 1978) suggested that Monte Albán had been located in a neutral place, ideal in terms of political factors, but with little regard to local agricultural potential. Kowalewski's analysis of potential agricultural production by grid square in Chapter 9 supports this hypothesis. The site was located in one of the region's more marginal localities, not only in terms of the potential productivity of its own grid square, but in terms of the potential productivity of adjacent squares. Now that we have collected more settlement pattern data, Blanton's comments on the founding of Monte Albán can be amplified.

The importance of Monte Albán's central valley location is apparent–travel costs to all three valley arms are minimized there, an important feature for the location of what was undoubtedly even in Early I a pan-valley institution. The location of the site in the Central zone is a clear indication that political factors outweighed potential agricultural production in importance, since the valley's best agricultural land is located in the Etla arm and to the south of Zaachila (Kirkby 1973; and see Chapter 9 in this volume). Another factor may have been important in the decision to place the new capital in the Central zone. The near absence of sites in much of this zone during the Rosario phase (Fig. 3-4) suggests the zone may have been a "no-man's land" or "shatter-zone" between competing political entities. No other explanation seems reasonable for why the Central zone was so sparsely used. Although this zone is not the region's most productive, it clearly could have supported more people than it evidently did. The fact that the Central zone was relatively unused prior to the establishment of Monte Albán could have been an additional important factor in the placement of the capital and its subsequent growth, for two reasons:

1) While the "ownership" of agricultural land and other resources would have been firmly established within the context of the valley's existing territorial corporate and/or political entities, the contested, largely unoccupied Central zone would have had much less firmly established, less firmly legitimated, prior proprietorship. Thus the new institution would have been able to claim tenancy of the Central zone without seriously upsetting existing claims. Assuming the absence of prior claims, we may infer that the proceeds from the development of this zone could have gone directly to the new institution. Such a directly-controlled, undisputed resource base ("free-floating resources" in the phraseology of Eisenstadt [1963]), is probably essential for the growth and continued functioning of a political institution like Monte Albán. A parallel can be drawn with the growth of the political institution of Tenochtitlán. There, the Culhua Mexica were able to develop a highly productive, independent resource base by reclaiming a saline swamp (Lake Mexico) that had been so marginal it had not been claimed by any existing political entity.

2) Given that the Central zone was largely unoccupied prior to Early I, and given the very high population growth rates in and directly around Monte Albán during Period I, we may infer that much of the original population of the capital and its district were immigrants. Initially, at least, the capital would have been attractive to immigrants–offering the chance to gain prestige and wealth in military expeditions, location close to the region's commercial core, and so on. An important feature of an immigrant population is that, divorced from the corporate descent groups and territorial political units they left, the newcomers could become more directly attached politically (as well as economically) to the new institution. The newcomers would have few or no other affiliational responsibilities. In effect, they can readily become "citizens" of a political institution, and as such are under the direct control of the capital's political hierarchy.

Given a "free-floating" resource base and a populace with direct allegiances to Monte Albán, the new capital would thus have been better able to perpetuate itself in spite of the apparent lack of totally unified political control of the region by the capital during Period I.

THE ORIGIN OF THE STATE IN THE VALLEY OF OAXACA

One final point deserves attention before we begin the discussion of Period II. Does the evolution of a regional system centered on Monte Albán signify the formation of the state in the Valley of Oaxaca? Although our interest is in the evolution of a regional system and not exclusively in the evolution of the state *per se*, our data are certainly relevant to this problem. In trying to establish the point in time of state origins, we are of course hampered by definitional problems–since most such definitions involve features of administrative behavior, such as the monopoly of power (cf. Service 1975), which are not detectable archaeologically. Wright and Johnson (1976; cf. Johnson 1973) suggest that states are possibly detectable archaeologically if they are viewed as internally differentiated control mechanisms containing minimally three levels of administrative hierarchy above the general population. These hierarchical levels are detectable archaeologically as levels of settlement hierarchy in sites with administrative functions. By Early I, we identified minimally three administrative levels–tertiary sites (plus the "very low volume mound groups"), the secondary centers, and Monte Albán. Early I, we may thus conclude, meets the requirements of this definition of the state. (By Late I, five levels of administrative sites are identified.) Keep in mind, however, that this need not imply the presence in the valley of a monolithic or even highly articulated regional governmental institution in Period I. Three levels of administrative hierarchy above the general population were apparently present, but at least some local territorial political units may have retained considerable autonomy *vis à vis* the capital. At any rate we feel justified in referring to the regional political organization as the state, however centralized or decentralized it may have been.

In Chapter 2, we evaluated the so-called "prime-mover" arguments that are so often associated with state-formation studies. While we argued that these excessively linear explanations are relatively unproductive, we feel it will be worthwhile here to briefly evaluate these arguments with our Period I data. The major prime-movers are irrigation management, population pressure, trade, and warfare (cf. Flannery 1972a). As we see it, the role of each in the origin of the state in the Valley of Oaxaca is as follows:

1) *Irrigation management*. Our evidence indicates the beginnings of the construction of piedmont irrigation systems in Period I (cf. Flannery et al. 1967), associated with the increasing emphasis on piedmont development. These irrigation systems, we feel, signal the beginnings of a general move by agricultural producers in the valley from a predominantly one-crop to a predominantly two-crop regime, the latter requiring a period of dependence on irrigation. As we have already argued, following the ethnographic work of the Hunts (1974) and Ted Downing (1974), even these smallish systems required some form of high-level authority for long-term functioning. This need not imply, however, that irrigation management caused the formation of the state. We see the development of the piedmont and the switch to more irrigation as long-term processes that proceeded during Period I, associated with the growth of Monte Albán. On the one hand, farmers had to produce additional surpluses to support the new regional institution, but, on the other hand, the move to irrigation would have resulted in more cases in which government officials had to intervene to resolve disputes, amplifying their importance, and enhancing the costs of administration, and requiring even more production of surpluses. The causal linkages between irrigation management and state formation would have been, in other words, more circular than linear.

2) *Population pressure*. As Eva Fisch demonstrated in Chapter 3, populations in the valley were operating at well below the agricultural potential during the periods leading up to Early I. As Steve Kowalewski shows, in Chapter 9, this situation continued for the valley as a whole during Period I, in spite of substantial population growth. We are secure in concluding that population pressure did not cause state formation in the Valley of Oaxaca. The formation of the new political institution in Period I seems, in fact, to have been a spur to population growth, probably because family size increased in response to increased demand for labor, as we discussed in Chapter 2, and perhaps also because there was immigration into the valley.

3) *Trade*. Admittedly, our evidence is somewhat shaky in this area, especially concerning long-distance exchange, but we have no evidence favoring the idea that changes in patterns of exchange or shortages of key resources (cf. Rathje 1971) caused the formation of the state. We have argued that the evolution of the new regional polity created conditions favoring market system evolution and that this, in turn, may have created additional administrative problems, perhaps requiring growth in the governing institutions. Again, though, the causality involved was probably highly circular, meaning that trade did not cause state formation.

4) *Warfare*. The question of the relationship between military problems and the formation of Monte Albán is a complex one for which we have no answer at this time. The military orientation of the Monte Albán Danzantes suggests the institution was initially involved with offense-defense activities (perhaps the more vague phrase "boundary maintenance" would

be more apt, since we're not really sure exactly what was involved). We are at a loss to explain why stresses related to boundary maintenance would have reached a critical point toward the end of the Rosario phase, necessitating the costly creation of a pan-regional political institution. Clearly, if there was one, the military threat was coming from groups in the Southern Highlands. They would have been able to raid valley communities quickly, then escape into the surrounding mountains. Their activities may have been viewed as pesky, devastating, and difficult to control. None of this implies a threat to the valley by some empire building polity in a distant region. No society in the Valley of Mexico, the "Olmec" area, or the Maya area had, in 500 B.C., the capacity to expand militarily over such a broad area. Even mighty Teotihuacán, so far as we know, was unable to incorporate the Valley of Oaxaca into its massive Classic period empire. Obviously the question of warfare in the formation of Monte Albán is an important one deserving close attention in future research in the Southern Highlands macroregion.

Chapter 5

PERIOD II

INTRODUCTION

Before discussing the trends in Period II settlement patterns, it will be necessary to broaden our perspective temporarily, to consider the nature of change through time in the role of the population of the Valley of Oaxaca in a larger geographical context. This digression to a consideration of evolving patterns in interregional interaction, we feel, is relevant for explaining certain features of change in patterns of settlement, population density, and ceramic assemblages we have observed in our survey area.

To put Period II into perspective, we will consider the broad outlines of change in modes of interregional interaction from the Early Formative to the Classic period. Broadly speaking, during this long period three stages can be identified by considering most of Mesoamerica as a regional unit:

1) The first, dating to the Early and Middle Formative, is characterized by a considerable amount of interregional exchange, manifested in part by the presence of similar ceramic categories over widely separated areas (cf. MacNeish, Peterson, and Flannery 1970: Chapter 12). Given the relative simplicity of societies in Mesoamerica at that time, the most reasonable explanations for the interactions involve the use of ethnographic analogs from pre-state societies, such as the Kula ring (Malinowski 1922), or the Vitiaz Straits (cf. Harding 1967; Flannery 1968a; Flannery and Schoenwetter 1970; Pires-Ferreira 1975). Archaeological analogs would include Hopewell (Caldwell and Hall, eds. 1964) and Chavín (Willey 1962).

The uniformity of ceramic styles over wide areas is apparently the result of relatively high levels of participation in interregional exchange by the general population in the context of border mechanisms such as trade partnerships and/or border markets.

2) After about 500 or 600 B.C., this level of interregional similarity begins to dissolve, as more locally distinct ceramic styles appeared. For example, the Late Formative Ticomán ceramic complex in the Valley of Mexico is vaguely similar in some respects to the Period I pottery of the Valley of Oaxaca, in that both contain vessels with composite silhouettes and hollow supports, but there is no overlap of specific ceramic types between the two areas. This branching in ceramic styles surely implies less interregional interaction of the kind that would influence ceramic styles after the Middle Formative. This may be related, perhaps, to the increased levels of complexity in local systems evident by that time (cf. Pires-Ferreira 1975).

In spite of the pan-Mesoamerican decline in ceramic resemblances after the Middle Formative, some local interregional stylistic traditions persisted, at least for a few centuries more. Pottery very much like our Early I *gris* vessels with incised decoration, for example, can be found all the way from the Grijalva depression and the Isthmus of Tehuantepec to the Tehuacán Valley (Lowe and Mason 1965; MacNeish, Peterson, and Flannery 1970: Chapter 12). If we look at two regions which have well known ceramic sequences and whose pottery assemblages were similar at about 500 B.C., the valleys of Oaxaca and Tehuacán, we can further trace the process of regional divergence in the latter part of the Formative. The *gris* ceramics of the Late Santa María phase in the Tehuacán Valley (ca. 500 B.C. to 150 B.C.) are described by MacNeish, Peterson, and Flannery (1970:143-44) as being most like Monte Albán I. Actually, as they are described and illustrated in that volume, these categories are most similar to our Early I fine-line incised types and other incised types, especially the G-15's and G-16's in the CBA nomenclature. It does not seem to be possible to distinguish the equivalent of our Early and Late I during the Late Santa María phase, mostly due to the absence, as far as we can tell from the description of the variability in the Late Santa María types, of that "workhorse" of Late I, the plain G-12 bowl with a combed bottom. This difference in ceramic assemblages may be explicable given the much greater degree of societal complexity that developed in the Valley of Oaxaca, as compared with Tehuacán. By Late I, we argued, some of this increased complexity may have been "funded" through the replacement of the costly Early I types with the more standardized, utilitarian G-12's in the context of an administration using ceramic production as a source of revenue. The absence of a comparable powerful political entity, engaged in modifying production/distribution systems, would help explain the persistence of more costly types in the Tehuacán Valley.

After the Late Santa María phase, the ceramics of the valleys of Oaxaca and Tehuacán became markedly distinct (MacNeish, Peterson, and Flannery 1970: Chapter 12). Period II pottery is found in other places outside the Valley of Oaxaca proper, but these deposits are surely indicative of the emergence of new modes of interregional interaction. One site with Period II pottery, in the Oaxacan Cañada, has been excavated by Charles Spencer and Elsa Redmond (1979), who identify it as a military outpost of Monte Albán. It has long been noted that the Monte Albán II ceramic complex has certain resemblances to southeastern Mesoamerica, resemblances that do not appear earlier than Period II or in the Classic (CBA:256ff). It may be significant that these similarities occur in the "costlier" types of pottery (streaky red-on-orange painting, hollow globular supports, rim and basal flanges, stucco-and-painted wares) rather than the bulk of the assemblages, which continue to be mass produced. These general similarities, however, do not mean that Oaxaca and the Maya area were politically linked in the same "empire"–there is no evidence of this.

3) The new methods of organizing macroregions for which we first see evidence in Period II are fully developed over wide areas of Mesoamerica by the Classic period. Widespread ceramic similarities again appear, especially in terms of the ubiquity of Teotihuacán-style materials and several specific pottery types such as Thin Orange. Of course, not all of the people in Mesoamerica used Teotihuacán-style ceramics during the Classic period, but the influence is nonetheless widespread. Although the Mesoamerica-wide ceramic similarities in the Classic period parallel those of the Early and Middle Formative periods, we would surely be unwise to revert to our Vitiaz Strait and related analogs for elucidation. Surely by this time we are talking about some mixture of empire formation and commercial production for export as sources of long-distance similarities, although a fuller explanation might involve some other factors such as stylistic imitation.

Two conclusions that will provide a backdrop for our continued discussion of the settlement patterns of the Valley of Oaxaca can be drawn from this digression into interregional exchanges. First, the presence of Early I-like *gris* ceramics over a broad area surely does not imply the presence of a Monte Albán empire of that period extending from Chiapas to Tehuacán. Instead, we feel this phenomenon is best viewed as the last gasp of an Early-Middle Formative variety of long-distance interaction, dying out because the "tribal" exchange modes were being replaced. We are probably safe, however, in concluding that the presence of Period II and later pottery pertaining to the Monte Albán sequence outside the Valley of Oaxaca is explicable in terms of conquest and/or the establishment of commercial exchange networks. Extra-regional conquest by Monte Albán is supported by two lines of evidence, including the military outpost in the Cañada mentioned previously. The other class of evidence consists of the Structure J conquest glyphs at Monte Albán (Caso 1947; Marcus 1976a, 1980). As we noted in Chapter 2, the Period I Danzantes seem to commemorate the capture of individuals, while the Period II glyphs commemorate the conquest of named central places. Marcus (ibid.) feels that one of the 40-odd conquered places indicated on Structure J is Miahuatlán, a place located in the Atoyac drainage, south of the valley. Interestingly, this probable extension southward of Monte Albán's polity corresponds with the abandonment of 3-6-104, the Late I site near the valley's southern terminus, which we interpreted as a military garrison. Such a site would no longer have been necessary if territory south of the valley became politically incorporated. In a survey of the larger archaeological sites around Miahuatlán, Brockington (1973) found pottery like that of Period II of the Valley of Oaxaca on several sites.

The beginnings of empire formation at Monte Albán in Period II, we feel, had important consequences for the Valley of Oaxaca population. After reviewing the nature of the changes in the valley after Late I, we will offer an explanation for how they are systematically interrelated to the newly-developed mode of interregional interaction.

PERIOD II: POPULATION TRENDS AND SETTLEMENT DISTRIBUTIONS

Figure 5-1 is the settlement pattern map for Period II. The most striking change apparent in this map is the near-abandonment of the valley's central zone. Figures 5-2 and 5-3 indicate the magnitude of this change. By Period II, population was more evenly distributed, although there is still a substantial drop-off in numbers of sites towards the valley's southern end.

Figure 2-1, the population totals by period, shows the magnitude of the overall change in numbers of

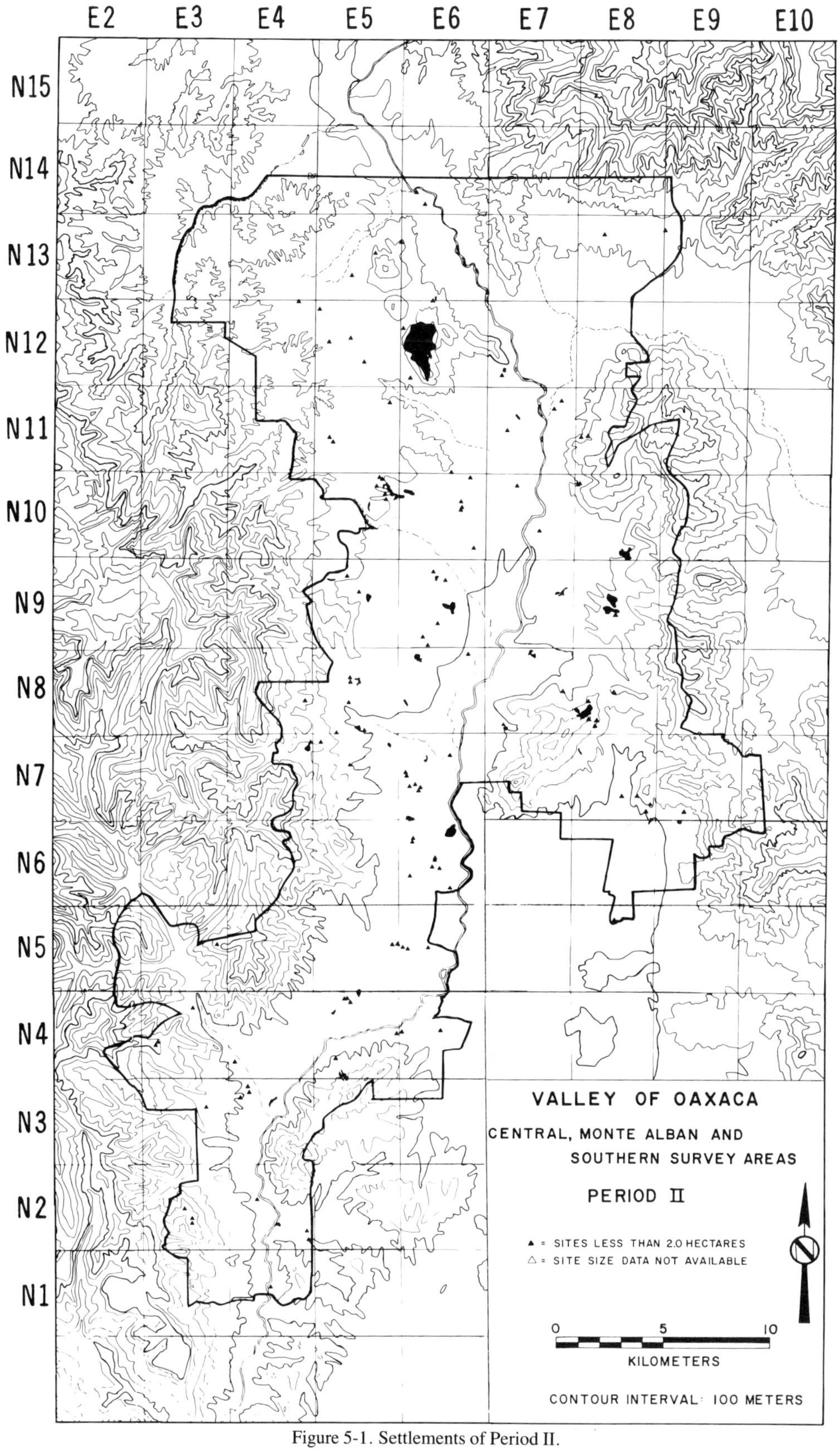

Figure 5-1. Settlements of Period II.

Figure 5-2. Population by distance from Monte Albán, Period II. Included are the estimated population values for Sta. Inés Yatzeche and Zaachila.

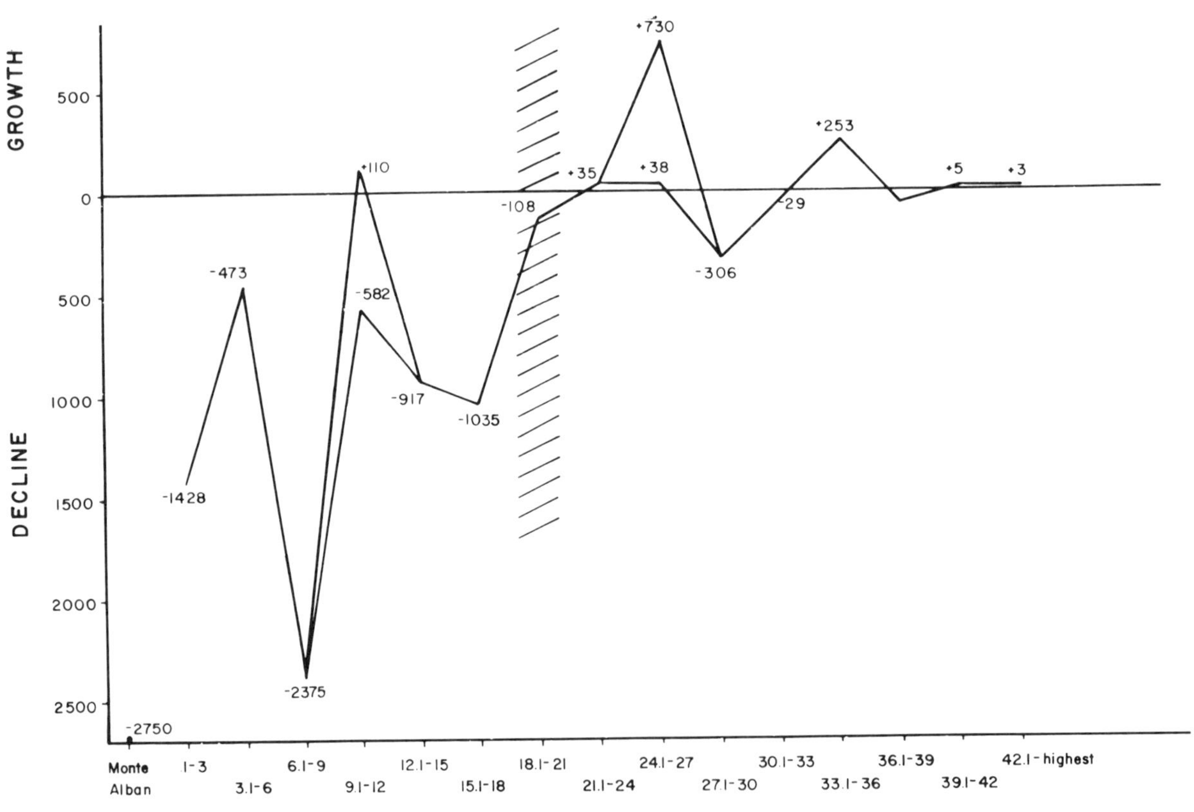

Figure 5-3. Population changes by distance from Monte Albán, Late I to II. The multiple values at 9-12 kilometers are due to the addition of the estimate for Zaachila. The multiple values for 24-27 kilometers are due to the addition of the estimate for Sta. Inés Yatzeche. The dashed line indicates the approximate southern limit of piedmont occupation during Period Late I.

people–a total loss in the survey area of 30% from Late I. Figure 4-3 contains the values of *r* that would account for the observed differences in population totals between Late I and II. The total population decline from Late I to II in the survey area was 9314. Of this, 2750 is accounted for by the decline in the population of Monte Albán, representing a loss of 16% of its Late I population. Most of the population decline in the survey area occurred within 18 kilometers of Monte Albán, amounting to 6226, or 95% of the total decline of the non-Monte Albán population (all of these figures assume populations of 692 for Zaachila and Sta. Inés Yatzeche. The derivation of this value will be discussed below). The southern zone, beyond 18 kilometers from the Main Plaza, actually increased slightly according to our calculations, by 1.3% over the Late I estimate (again, assuming a population of 692 for Sta. Inés Yatzeche).

Most of the decline in the non-Monte Albán population happened in the area within 18 kilometers of the Main Plaza. This zone had been the scene of extensive piedmont development in Late I. Thus, a much smaller proportion of the total Period II population resided in the piedmont, and a correspondingly higher proportion of sites were in the alluvial zone (Fig. 5-4). This change, we believe, has implications in regional organization and administrative costs to which we will return below.

PERIOD II: ADMINISTRATIVE CENTRAL PLACES

Monte Albán, with a population of over 14,000 and continued massive construction and monument erection (cf. CBA; Acosta 1965; Caso 1947), remained the rank-one center in Period II. Below that level we have identified the administrative central place hierarchy according to the procedures laid out in the Period I chapter. Two centers stand out as intermediate between Monte Albán and all other centers, Cuilapan (3-7-1-5,7) and 3-7-44,46(N8E8). The latter site is located north of the Ocotlán sub-region, very near the site of the Late I center at 3-6-85,86. Again, it is our impression that Zaachila (3-7-106) and Sta. Inés Yatzeche (3-7-73) are best placed in the hierarchy of administrative places at this second level, just below Monte Albán. We could not be sure, however, that our usual method for population estimation for these two centers (the mean of two other similarly-ranked centers) would work for Period II, since, in Late I the Ocotlán site was considerably larger than the other higher-order centers, perhaps indicating wider administrative responsibilities. On the other hand, to use the population of Cuilapan as an estimate could have been misleading, perhaps, since that would have meant an estimate for these two sites less than the estimate for Late I, while all other centers at this level actually increased in size into Period II. An alternative method is to assume that these two sites increased in population from Late I to II at the same rate of growth as the rate of growth at Cuilapan (46% increase from Late I to II), producing an estimate of 692 (which is very close to the mean size for Cuilapan and Ocotlán, 701).

Again, as in Late I, there is considerable variability among the centers that were left after we identified our first and second ranks. Following our procedure for Late I, we divided this group, again somewhat arbitrarily, into third and fourth levels. Third level centers generally have populations in the hundreds of people, but less secure evidence for public architecture of the scale of the rank-2 centers. The fourth level consists of sites usually less than 100 people, or with only small amounts of mounded architecture. Figure 5-5 shows the locations of the administrative places so identified, with the weighted Thiessen polygons around the higher-order centers to approximate administrative districts. The major features of continuity and change from the Late I to the Period II hierarchy of central places are the following:

1) Monte Albán declined in population, but at a rate less than the overall declines. The capital's immediate administrative district obviously underwent a major reorganization as is indicated by the near-abandonment of the piedmont zone here. We interpret this to mean a cessation of the policy of local agricultural development that had been a prominent feature of Late I. The implications of this will be explored below.

2) Second-level administrative locations are very similar to Late I, given the continued occupation of Cuilapan, Zaachila, Sta. Inés Yatzeche, and the presence of 3-77-44,46 very close to 3-6-85,86, north of Ocotlán. A major change at this level is indicated by the abandonment of the secondary center at 3-6-138,139 (N11E7,8); its functions may have been assumed by the new fourth level center at 2-7-15,16 (N11E7). The abandonment of a secondary center and its replacement by such a small place could be simply a reflection of the general population declines and deemphasis on piedmont development near Monte Albán, but this interpretation begs the question of why Cuilapan, also close to Monte Albán, would have persisted. For some reason, in spite of general population declines close to Monte Albán, Cuilapan not only

continued, but increased in population by 46% and became a center of both *gris* and *crema* ceramic production (Appendix IX).

3) Below the second administrative level the major changes from Late I to Period II involve the abandonment of several centers in the Monte Albán district and in the districts around old 3-6-138,139 and 3-6-85,86. To the south of Cuilapan and Zaachila, and west of the Atoyac, considerable continuity from Late I is apparent. Third-level centers such as Roaló (3-7-31, N8E6), 3-7-60 (N6E6), San Pablo Huixtepec (3-7-80-82) (N5E5,6), Sta. Ana Tlapacoyan (3-7-93, N3E4), and 3-7-101 (N2E4) persisted from Late I. The major change in this latter area is the abandonment of the suggested military garrison at 3-6-104 (N5E4) and the establishment of a new third-level center at 3-7-95 (N4E5).

When viewed from the perspective of population changes, the administrative places can be an important source for understanding the changes in the Valley of Oaxaca after Late I. The decline in the population of all administrative places (from 8225 to 5606) other than Monte Albán amounted to a 32% loss, less than the total population decline (48%) in the survey area apart from Monte Albán. Proportionately, the decline in the population of Monte Albán and the other administrative places was less than the total population decline in the survey area–meaning that relative to Late I more people were living in centers with administrative functions in Period II. Perhaps this indicates that such places had an increasing number of functions. This interpretation is supported by our data on production and distribution discussed below.

The patterning of population transitions in administrative places illustrates other features of organizational change from Late I. Sixty-one percent of the population decline in administrative centers occurred in the piedmont zone. At the same time, the population of administrative sites in the alluvium actually increased, from 2922 for Late I to 3536, a gain of 21% (this does not include the population of Monte Albán). This is no doubt indicative of a substantial move away from administered agricultural development of the piedmont. Based on what we have previously argued about piedmont development, we believe this change would have resulted in substantially lowered administrative costs in the region, given the regulatory problems and relative unpredictability of piedmont agriculture (compared with the relative simplicity of most alluvium strategies). This change also implies, of course, a substantial loss in agricultural productivity, especially around Monte Albán.

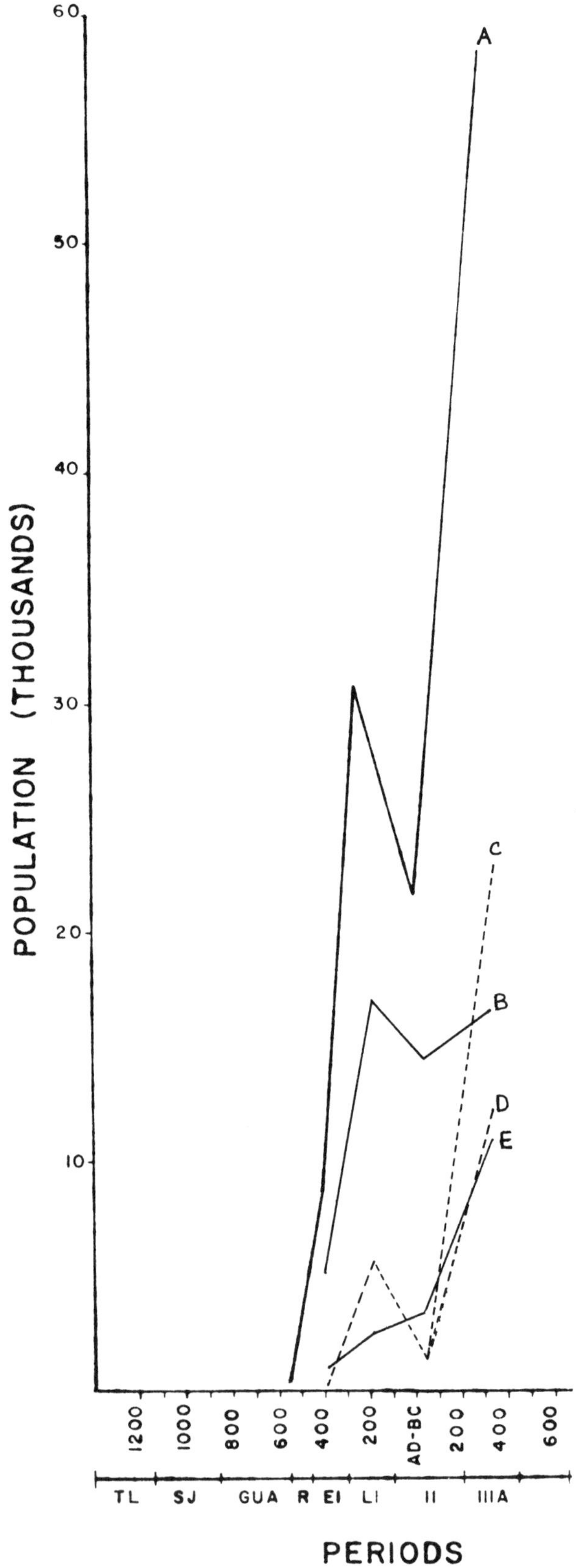

Figure 5-4. Population totals of sites with administrative functions, Early I through IIIa. A = Total population of the survey area. B = Monte Albán. C = Piedmont administrative total. D = Piedmont administrative total, not including IIIa Jalieza. E = Alluvium administrative total.

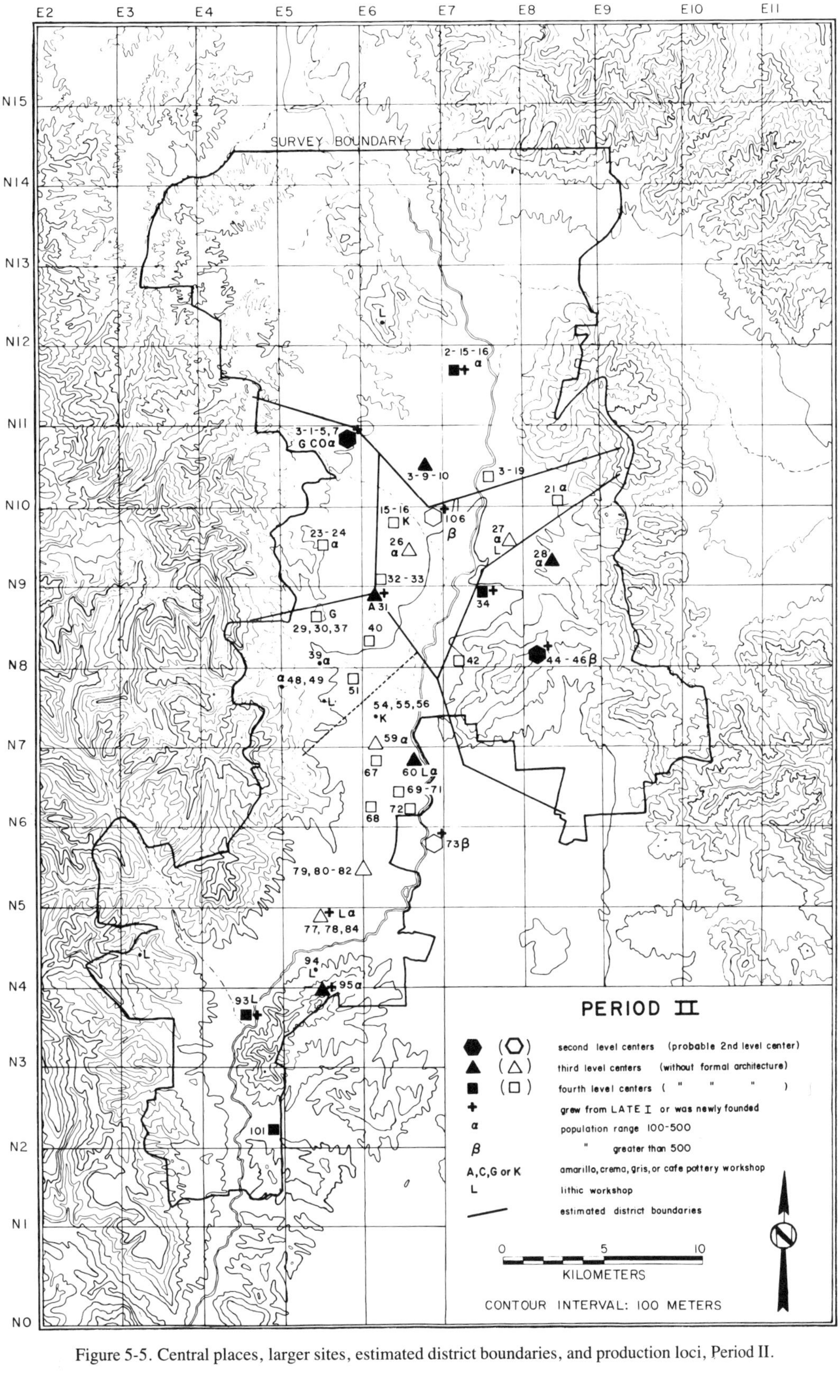

Figure 5-5. Central places, larger sites, estimated district boundaries, and production loci, Period II.

Another feature of administrative change is a continuation of a pattern that was initiated in Period I: decentralization. That is, by Period II secondary centers in the survey area appear to have had more autonomy *vis à vis* Monte Albán. While Monte Albán's population was 16% less in Period II than it had been in Late I, secondary center populations actually increased–and this is especially striking in light of the overall population declines. Cuilapan increased in population by 46%, and Ocotlán by 11%. Third-level centers declined an average of 28% (which is less than the overall non-Monte Albán declines), while the total population of the lowest-ranking centers stayed roughly the same as the total for Late I.

Overall, we infer, administrative places other than Monte Albán, especially the second-rank centers, had more functions in Period II than they had in Late I. At the same time, we believe that Monte Albán's level of regional dominance within the valley proper declined somewhat. This is apparent in the Period II rank-size graph (Fig. 5-6). Although the system continued in a markedly primate mode, the gap between the first-and second-rank center was smaller by Period II. In Early I, for example, the population of the second-rank center was only 4.3% of Monte Albán; by Late I this had increased to 5.1%, and by Period II the value is 6.8%.

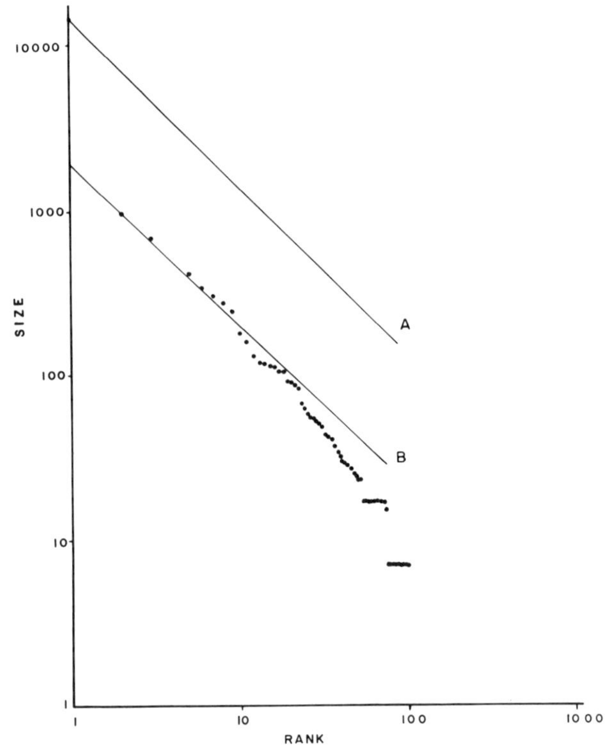

Figure 5-6. Rank-size graph, Period II. Line A is log-normal as calculated from the size of the rank-1 center. Line B is log-normal as calculated from the size of the rank-2 center.

Table 5-1. Central-Place Summary, Period II

SITE	POPULATION	MOUND VOLUME m^3	RANK
2-15,16	105	4652*	4
3-1-5, 7	423	39,356*	2
3-9, 10	48	36,235*	3
3-15-17	63	4430*	4
3-19	17	19,137*	4
3-21	308	1274*	4
3-23, 24	132	1748*	4
3-26	277	3405*	3
3-27	104	3880*	3
3-28	249	11,325*	3
3-29, 30, 37	83	885*	4
3-31	121	42,238*	3
3-32, 33	40	7664*	4
3-34	90	1690*	4
3-40	53	3928*	4
3-42	41	3431*	4
3-44-46	979	13,953*	2
3-51	41	1790*	4
3-59	111	11,182*	3
3-60	343	9023*	3
3-67	15	5584*	4
3-68	17	8108*	4
3-69-71,etc.	29	7770*	4
3-72	17	3087*	4
3-73	(692)	?	2
3-77, 78	161	19,181*	3
3-80-82	87	16,023*	3
3-93	93	1631*	4
3-95	182	6899*	3
3-101	34	1184*	4
3-106	(692)	?	2
		* Index	

PERIOD II INTERACTION MEASURES

Three measures of interaction potential (*IP*) were made for Period II, first including those sites in the top 10% of population size (referred to as the "larger sites") and then two measures involving administrative sites alone. The *IP* of the group of larger sites illustrates some of the changes from Late I to II that we have already mentioned. By Period II, Monte Albán accounted for only 77% of the *IP*, down from the 89.6% for Late I. This is largely due to the decline in numbers and sizes of sites in Monte Albán's district and reflects the declining orientation of the capital to local agricultural development. This reduction in *IP* in Monte Albán's district also accounts for a large proportion of the decline from Late I in the total number of *IP* "units" for the larger sites, from 4,189,742 for Late I to 649,003 for Period II.

For the first measure of administrative *IP*, as discussed previously, *IP* is measured from each center to its first two nearest-neighbors of the same level, then to its first two nearest-neighbors of the next higher administrative level. As was true for Period I, most administrative *IP* is vertical–that is, more *IP* exists between centers of a given level and higher-order centers than exists between centers of a given level. The decentralization in administration from Late I to II is also indicated in these figures. Given the decline in the number of communities lacking local administrators, the amount of administrative *IP* is larger proportionate to the amount of *IP* between the larger sites–amounting to 58% in Period II, but only 23% for Late I. More of the larger sites, in other words, have evidence for administrative functions by Period II.

The second method of measuring administrative *IP*, as before, involves measures of each center's *IP* with a nearest-neighbor in its own administrative district, at the next highest administrative level (or two levels higher if no other center is present). These figures again illustrate the increased autonomy of administrative centers from Late I to Period II. The total administrative *IP* "units" using this measure for Late I amounted to 1,308,303, while by Period II they add up to only 462,253. At each administrative level, the values of *IP* are lower than they were for Late I. Mean *IP*, for example, between secondary Period II centers and Monte Albán is 75,336, while for Late I the *IP* value for 3-6-85,86 (the lone secondary center) and Monte Albán is 276,564; the mean value for all Late I secondary and tertiary centers with Monte Albán is 133,190 (97,347 less 3-6-85,86).

Thus the *IP* measures support the idea that by Period II Monte Albán's role was somewhat diminished, especially its role in piedmont agricultural development in its own district. These measures also support the idea that secondary centers were more autonomous in Period II, in contrast with the prior period.

PRODUCTION/DISTRIBUTION IN PERIOD II

The phrase production/distribution is used here instead of market organization since the changes evident by Period II make us less certain of the exact mode of product movement. Markets probably existed, but the degree of administrative intervention was such that the system may have involved more of what could be termed redistribution. The architectural evidence still does not indicate an administered economy to the extent indicated, for example, by the prehispanic Central Andean systems, but we still hold out the possibility that market places *per se* were on the decline as a means of exchange in Period II. The evolution of production/ distribution activities from Late I to Period II, as we know it from our surface evidence, can be approached by viewing three major processes:

1) Our evidence indicates less region-wide exchange, i.e., the presence of fewer and/or less important linkages between local systems in the valley. This change is probably related to the evidently reduced role of Monte Albán in valley affairs and to the reduced rates of interaction at lower levels. The evidence, which is discussed more fully in Chapter 10, is the appearance of more Period II ceramic types that have relatively discrete distributions. The CBA category A-9, for example, produced at Roaló (3-7-31), is largely a Valle Grande type found only infrequently in the other arms of the valley. Kowalewski's land-use analysis in Chapter 9 also supports this suggestion of reduced region-wide linkages.

2) The degree of spatial isomorphism between administrative central places and production loci continued to increase from Late I into II (Fig. 5-5). By Period II, only one ceramic production site–at 3-7-54-56 (N7E6)–has no evidence for mounded architecture indicative of administrative functions. Cuilapan (3-7-1-5,7) has evidence for production of both *gris* and *crema* pottery. *Gris* production continued at 3-7-29, 30,37 (Late I 3-6-51). Café production continued at 3-7-15,16 (3-6-33), associated with mounds. Amarillo production was centered at the third-level center at Roaló (3-7-31). Only one ceramic (*café*) production

site lacks significant evidence for administrative functions (3-7-54,56 [N7E6], old 3-6-80).

This increased association of production activities and administrative activities is also indicated by the location of lithic production sites in Period II (Fig. 5-5). Only two of these sites are spatially unrelated to evidence for administrative activities, one at 3-7-11 (N10E6), and one at 3-7-94 (N4E5), and the latter site is only a few hundred meters down-slope from a tertiary administrative place (3-7-95). All other lithic production sites occupied in this period are in administrative places, and, so far as we can tell, obsidian was worked only at Monte Albán. For Late I, 10 of 13 sites with surface evidence for production involving lithics have no evidence for administrative activities.

Again, these data are difficult to interpret and need not imply a totally administered economy–nor is it the case that all administrative places have evidence for production activities. At the largest secondary center, 3-7-44-46, for example, we noted no evidence for production. On the other hand, these data can be interpreted to imply more (or at least a continued level of) movement of goods through administrative channels in Period II. This interpretation is supported by looking at our suggested marketplace (3-6-83, N7E6), which by Period II was reduced to an isolated residence or hamlet, lacking any evidence for craft production. The Period II sherds on the site are not even adjacent to the large platform that we earlier identified as a market place. If it was the case that administrative places had more economic functions by Period II, this could help explain why, as was discussed above, relatively more people lived in communities with administrative functions in Period II than in Late I.

3) Judging from the numbers of types per site, Period II was a time of greater affluence than Late I had been, and this is supported by Feinman's production step index, which is higher for Period II than for Late I (see Chapter 10). For all non-administrative Period II sites, the average number of types per site is 8.8. For Late I the comparable value is 6.9. Another way to illustrate this difference is to point out that of the non-administrative sites, 10 out of 72 for Period II have more than 15 types, but only 9 out of 109 for Late I have more than that number of types. These figures are especially striking since there are only a total of 53 Period II types, while for Late I we count a total of 88 types.

Administrative places in Period II show a different pattern. The average number of types for all administrative centers in Period II is 15.8, down from the average value of 17.9 for Late I. Or, excluding the lowest-order centers for both periods, only 7 of the 19 Late I centers have fewer than 15 types, while 6 of 13 Period II centers have fewer than 15 types. Clearly, some of the Late I differences between administrative and non-administrative places in terms of access to a wide variety of types were undone by Period II. This leads to the seemingly counter-intuitive conclusion that although exchange and production may have been more administered in Period II, there was nonetheless more general access to goods by the entire population than had been the case in Late I. Actually, we feel these data are not as contradictory as they seem at first, since, as we will argue below, the key variable seems to have been how production is affected by administrative institutions, not how much overlap there is between administration and production/distribution.

Figure 5-7 shows the number of types per site by distance from Monte Albán. Again, it is apparent that the administrative places, on the whole, have more types per site than non-administrative places, but the dichotomy is not as sharp as it had been in Late I. Too, the cluster of sites with very few types that is visible on the Late I graph (Fig. 4-17) close to Monte Albán is not present in Period II. Instead, there is a more or less continuous group of points representing small non-administrative places with relatively few types extending from around Monte Albán to the southern end of the survey region. Most of the sites with extremely large values are sites we have identified as production places.

The ceramic distribution data seem to indicate that access to locally manufactured items was improving in general from Late I into II. This may not have been the case for items obtained through long distance exchange. For the Period II sites within Monte Albán's district, 38% have obsidian on the surface (30% in Late I), while obsidian was noted on only 17% of the sites in the southern administrative district (19% in Late I). Although these data are difficult to interpret, they may indicate that goods obtained through long distance exchange, probably involving Monte Albán's intervention, were less available to distant consumers than to those closer to the capital. This could be another reflection of weaker ties between Monte Albán and local valley systems–implying fewer channels (or more restricted channels) through which non-local items could have moved.

Explaining the Period II developments in patterns of production/distribution probably will require consideration of several variables. Feinman discusses problems specific to ceramics below. In general, however, we feel that the most important factors governing changes in this arena from Late I to II are the following:

1) We believe it likely that administrative costs in Period II were lower than in Late I. This reduction in costs would have been due largely to two factors. First, there was a much reduced commitment to the piedmont zone–and considerably reduced amount of administration in the piedmont. This would have substantially lowered overall administrative work-load in the region, especially since, presumably, piedmont development implies the necessity for maintaining a valley exchange network capable of supplying large numbers of piedmont cultivators in deficit years. Alluvium cultivation is less risky and can be successfully carried out using very simple irrigation strategies. Piedmont development, especially the way it had been done around Monte Albán, would have required adjudication in the context of tributary stream water rights, as well as in the context of land disputes, since the area was heavily overpopulated by Late I. A second and perhaps even more important feature of reducing administrative costs to local producers was the fact that Monte Albán may have been supported to a much larger extent from its newly-conquered external sources. The response at Monte Albán was to cease the policy of local agricultural development and to reduce the levels of production of highly standardized, less costly ceramics. The result was a higher average number of types per site, and a higher overall ceramic production-step index by Period II.

2) A second factor to consider in comparing Periods

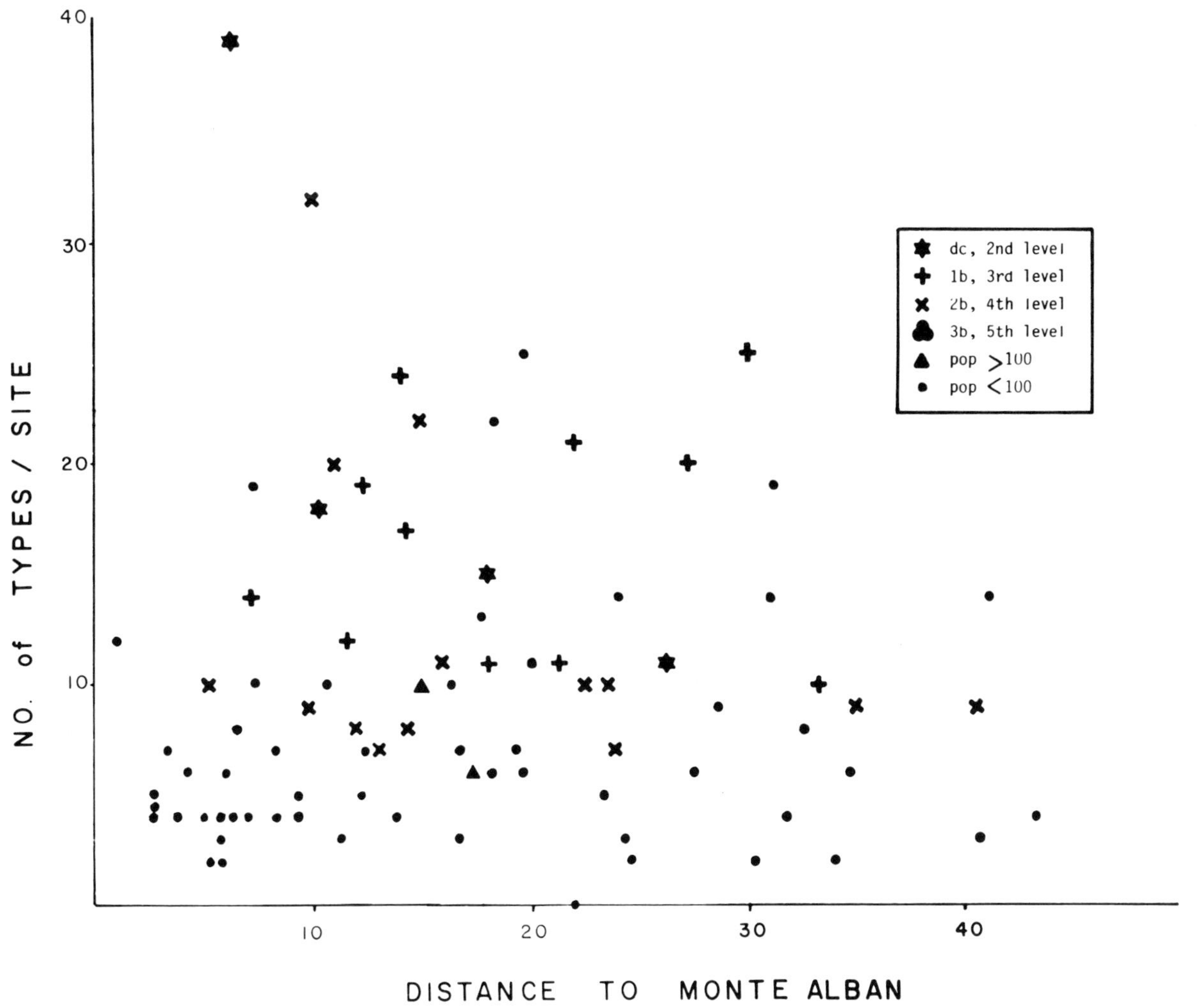

Figure 5-7. Types per site by site category and distance from Monte Albán, Period II. The data are found in Appendix VIII.

I and II has to do with the increasing permeability of the valley's boundaries. As the area militarily and politically secured by Monte Albán increased, there could have been an increase in the amount of movement of people, information, and materials across the valley's boundaries (as well as an increase in the inflow of energy from outside). This implies a larger area of potential economic integration, which, in turn, would have meant that the sustaining areas of secondary centers could have increased, amplifying the possibilities for commercial activities in these centers, and contributing to the greater population growth we observed for secondary centers.

PERIOD II: CONCLUSIONS

The evidence that Monte Albán first extended its hegemony beyond the boundaries of the Valley of Oaxaca during Period II seems firmly based on both archaeological and epigraphic grounds. The major implications of this new development for the local system were, briefly:

1) Population decline, due to the reduced production demands on the valley population, as Monte Albán's support-base shifted to a wider area.

2) Much reduced emphasis on administered development of the piedmont zone, due, again, to the reduced necessity for local sources of energy to support the population of Monte Albán and the activities of the institution based there.

3) Reduced levels of interaction between Monte Albán and local valley systems, again probably reflecting the decreased importance of local systems as sources of energy and/or personnel for the regional institution.

4) An increase in the number of ceramic categories per site, on the average, due to a reduction in the importance of standardization in ceramic production. In addition, lower administrative costs would have lowered the cost per transaction in the exchange of goods. Since markets were less of a source of administrative income, costlier types were more widely available.

5) An increase in the permeability of the valley's boundary, increasing the sustaining areas of local centers.

6) Increased local autonomy is indicated by the growth of local administrative centers *vis à vis* the population of Monte Albán. This is explicable if Monte Albán was becoming more oriented toward interregional activities, allowing local systems to operate with less direct control. This is related to the decreased amount of exchange between local systems in the valley.

Given the evidence at hand, we are better equipped to discuss the consequence of interregional military expansion than to discuss its causes. In Chapter 2 we pointed out the likelihood that interregional military expansion would not have been a productive strategy until regional systems outside the valley reached some minimal level of complexity and territorial inclusiveness. Was it the case that conquest had been a constant goal of the Monte Albán administrators from the beginning, but that it was not until Period II that military expansion finally proved worthwhile considering costs and benefits? An alternative possibility is that beginning in Late I the local system was becoming so congested and costly to administer that new sources of revenue had to be developed in order to assure the preservation of the state. External groups were eyed as sources of revenue. Evidence favoring one or the other of these possibilities will be important since it may supply us with one clue as to why conquest-oriented warfare becomes state policy.

Chapter 6

PERIOD IIIa

INTRODUCTION

Period IIIa represents the beginning of what Caso, Bernal, and Acosta called the "Zapotec" ceramic tradition (CBA: 311). They mean by this that beginning at that time the ceramics of the Valley of Oaxaca branched away from the other Mesoamerican patterns. For example, although Teotihuacán-style pottery is present in many other Mesoamerican regions, only a few such sherds are found in the IIIa assemblages. While some IIIa pottery has been found outside the valley, for example in the vicinity of Miahuatlán (Brockington 1973), for the most part during this period and the remainder of the Classic Period the valley was a ceramic isolate. The valley's ceramic divergence probably reflects a decline, after Period II, in interregional interaction of the sort influencing ceramic styles. Survey and excavations by Spencer and Redmond (1979) in the Cañada have elucidated one aspect of this change. By Period IIIa, the military garrison guarding access to the Cañada was abandoned, and there is no further evidence of Monte Albán's presence in the area. Obviously the Monte Albán empire had retracted sometime during Period II. At the same time there is increasing evidence of Teotihuacán influence in the nearby Tehuacán Valley, manifested both in the presence of actual Teotihuacán pottery types and in the production of local Tehuacán types displaying the Teotihuacán "Horizon Style" (Drennan and Nowack 1977; MacNeish, Peterson, and Flannery 1970: 175-76). These same Tehuacán assemblages, by contrast, show little affiliation with the Monte Albán IIIa types, although a few IIIa-looking sherds have been noted (ibid.).

It is likely that as Teotihuacán expanded its sphere of influence and control, the area controlled from Monte Albán was pushed back to include a smaller, but as yet undefined territory. Monte Albán's role in the larger sphere of Mesoamerican interregional interaction would have been reduced further if Teotihuacán had increasingly redirected long-distance exchange channels to itself and away from the Zapotec capital. Acting in concert, these two factors could have contributed significantly to the parochialism evident in the "Zapotec ceramic tradition."

Previously, Blanton (1978) suggested that one consequence of the expansion of Teotihuacán hegemony and influence was that Monte Albán's functions as a center coordinating offense-defense activities for the Valley of Oaxaca became more important. As a consequence, he reasoned, it was more heavily "funded" after Period II, as reflected in the growth of the population residing in the center (from an estimated 14,492 in II to 16,507 in IIIa) and in the ample monumental construction in the Main Plaza area (Acosta 1965). Our new data on sites other than Monte Albán provide us with an opportunity to expand our analysis of the nature of the transition from Period II to IIIa.

PERIOD IIIa: POPULATION GROWTH AND AGRICULTURAL DEVELOPMENT

The population of the survey area increased rapidly after Period II (Figs. 2-1, 6-1), reaching levels in IIIa higher than any prior or subsequent prehispanic period (an estimated total of 58,677). The Valle Grande, in fact, had nearly as many residents in IIIa as it has today (38,000 versus roughly 40,000 in the survey area). Figure 4-3 indicates the estimated growth rates for the transition from II to IIIa. Of the territorial units shown in this figure, Monte Albán shows the slowest rate of growth ($r = .0003$). Totally unlike the other periods we have discussed so far, the fastest rate of population growth occurred in the area more than 18 kilometers from the Main Plaza, an area that had remained relatively stationary in terms of numbers for centuries. The total increase beyond this 18 kilometer line amounted to 29,715, or 70% of the total non-Monte Albán increase. Some population growth occurred closer to the capital, but very little of it within the Central area (Fig. 6-2). As in Period II, this latter area was largely unused except for the capital itself–the only major change here being the growth of the large site at Xoxocotlán (2-7-17, N11E7).

Forty-three percent of the increase in the population

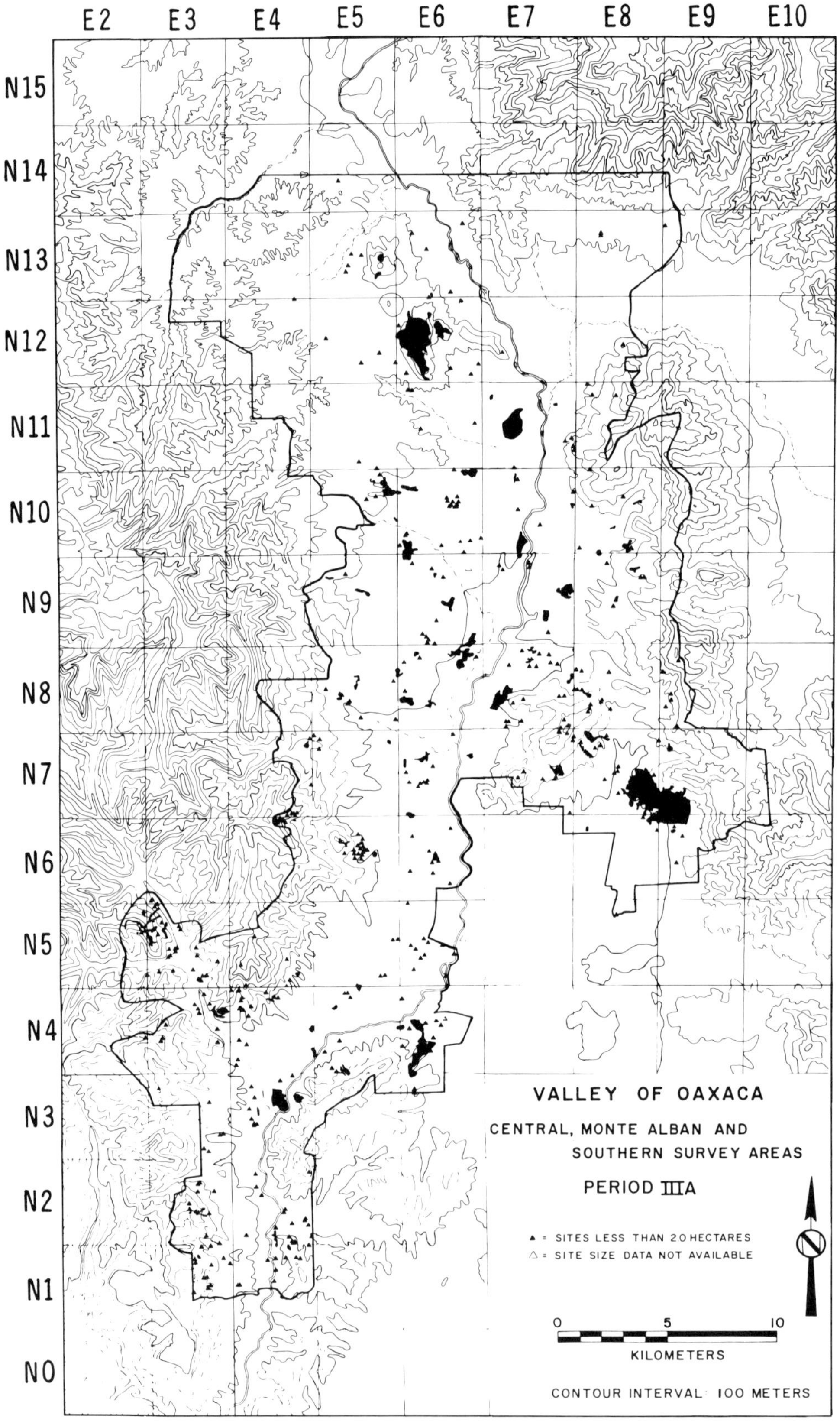

Figure 6-1. Settlements of IIIa.

residing 18 kilometers or more from the Main Plaza can be attributed to the growth of the new center near Sto. Tomás Jalieza (3-8-136,150-152, N7E8). (This site will be referred to from now on simply as Jalieza.) Amazingly, this site increased in population from close to 0 to a number (estimated at 12,385) more than one-half the size of Monte Albán in IIIa. Note that this is a growth rate even higher than that of Monte Albán in its first period of occupation (which was from 0 to over 5000). As we argued previously in connection with Monte Albán in Early I, growth rates of that magnitude are far in excess of human reproductive potential, implying a great deal of immigration. Like Monte Albán, Jalieza was built on a hilltop, at least in part, necessitating terrace construction. Figure 6-3 is a map of these terraces, and Appendix X contains a summary of the terrace descriptions made in the field.

Most of the population increases in the southern sector other than that at Jalieza occurred in a series of piedmont sites, including several medium-sized new centers. Included here are the sites at Rancho Tejas (3-8-233-9,241, N4E6), Sta. Cruz Mixtepec (3-8-177-179, N5E2), and "El Choco" near Ayoquezco (3-8-272-274, N2E3).

The "filling out" of the piedmont in the southern sector in IIIa resulted in a more even distribution of population in the region by distance from Monte Albán (Figs. 6-1 and 6-4) than existed in prior Monte Albán periods, and a population "peak" at 21-24 kilometers from the Main Plaza, produced by Jalieza. The southern end of the valley would have looked attractive because of its relatively adequate rainfall and because its piedmont was then essentially virgin farmland–very few people had ever lived there.

Period IIIa was a return to the Late I pattern in several respects. One of these is the increase in the occupation of the piedmont zone–at a rate of growth much higher than the growth in the alluvium, resulting in an overall distribution of population by environmental zone considerably unlike the more alluvium-oriented Period II (Fig. 5-4). We interpret this to imply a return to a policy (like that of Late I) of agricultural development of the piedmont. Judging from the rapid growth in the population of piedmont sites with evidence for administrative functions, this development was probably not something that was simply the product of decisions at the familial level. It is much more likely to have been the result of state decision-making, leading

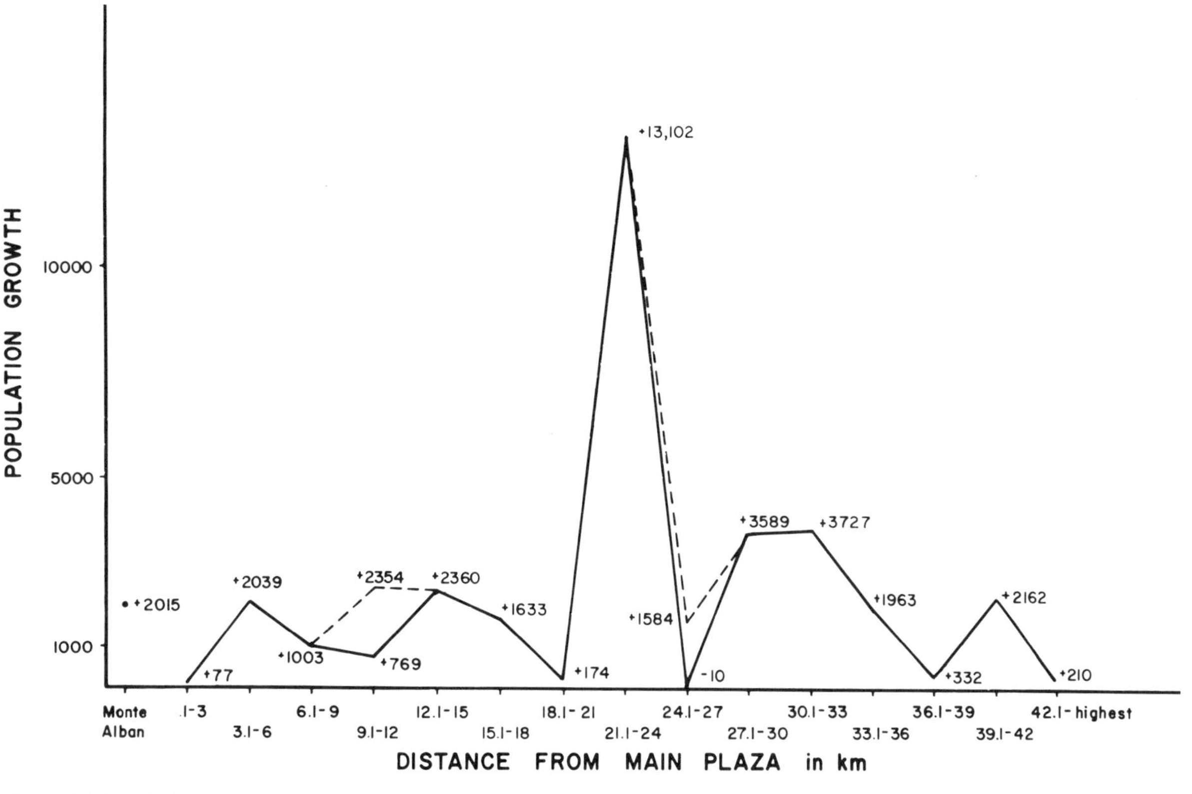

Figure 6-2. Population changes by distance from Monte Albán, Period II to IIIa. The dashed lines indicate the addition of the estimates for Zaachila (at the 9-12 kilometer point) and Sta. Inés Yatzeche (24-27 kilometers).

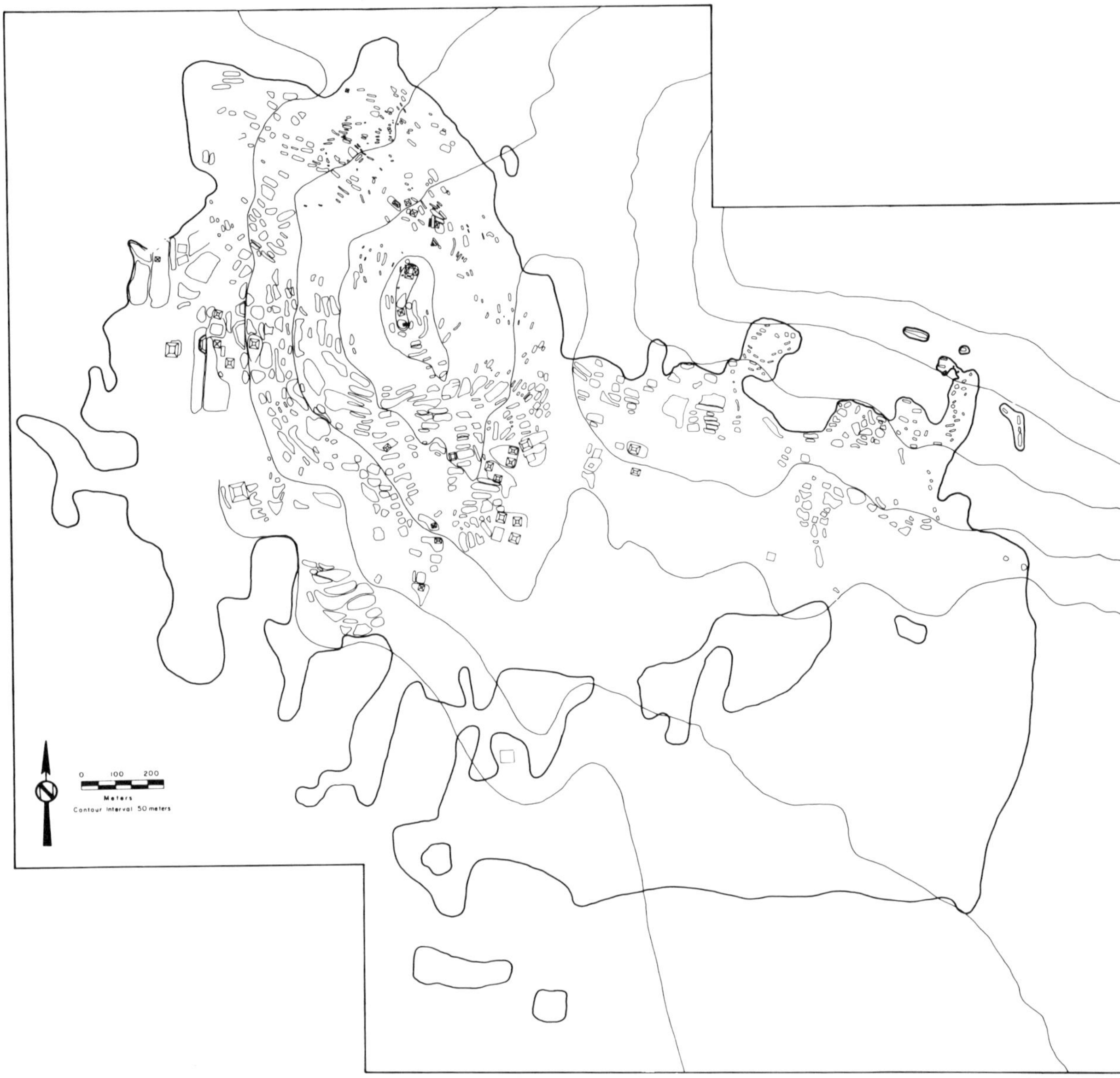

Figure 6-3. Terraces and estimated site boundaries, IIIa Jalieza.

to administered development. Unlike the Late I round of piedmont development, however, the IIIa development was no longer in the area adjacent to the capital. By IIIa the area most intensely utilized was the valley's southern sector.

In the prior Monte Albán periods, we argued that the valley's southern sector had been poorly integrated into the system centered at the capital. The substantial development of the piedmont in this same area in IIIa is indicative of the growth of the territory directly integrated into the Monte Albán system. How this was accomplished administratively will be considered in the next section. Evidence favoring this interpretation comes from Joyce Marcus' analyses of the IIIa stone monuments in the Valley of Oaxaca. Prior to IIIa, she points out, regional styles in the carving of these monuments persisted, indicating some level of continued autonomy, but, ". . . all regional styles were abandoned by Monte Albán III-A times and those sites that continued to carve monuments did so in the Monte Albán style'' (Marcus 1976a:136).

PERIOD IIIa: ADMINISTRATIVE CENTRAL PLACES

In interpreting the nature of the administrative hierarchy for Periods Early I through II, we took into consideration both mounded architecture and population size. Our major obstacle was the fact that although we had some information concerning the distribution and scale of public architecture, most sites had many subsequent periods of occupation. For those periods including and subsequent to IIIa, however, we have much better information on the periodization of mounded buildings. Many sites, for example, had their major occupation during IIIa, so that we were often quite sure that the morphology of the buildings that we can see today was the morphology during IIIa. Too, for the periods after IIIa there were drastic shifts in settlement patterns, leaving many buildings with only one or two periods of occupation. This conceivably could make it possible to interpret administrative hierarchies on the basis of architecture alone, but at the same time we wanted to consider the population size of centers as well. We decided that a simple index of administrative importance could be derived by multiplying population size times mound volume. This technique would surely separate out those sites with substantial populations and architecture from those sites ranking lower in either or both of these variables.

Figure 6-5 is the Period IIIa histogram of values of population times mound volume estimates. In preparing this figure, some combining of nearby sites was done, following the method outlined in prior chapters. Appendix IV lists the combined sites and their population totals. Five categories of administrative places have been identified from the histogram. Monte Albán, not included in the histogram, clearly maintains its position in IIIa as the rank-1 center in the region, with a population of roughly 16,500 and substantial new IIIa construction, probably including the addition of the South Platform (Acosta 1965). Jalieza stands alone in a second rank below Monte Albán, with

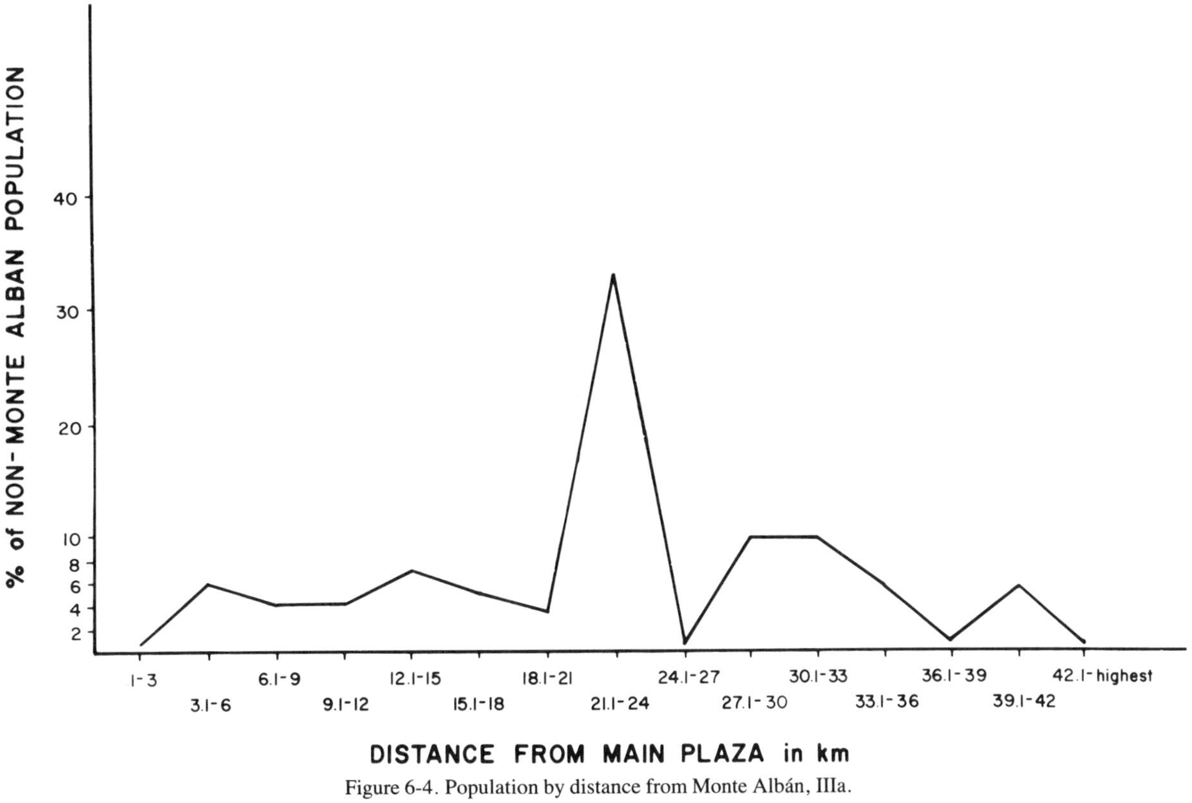

Figure 6-4. Population by distance from Monte Albán, IIIa.

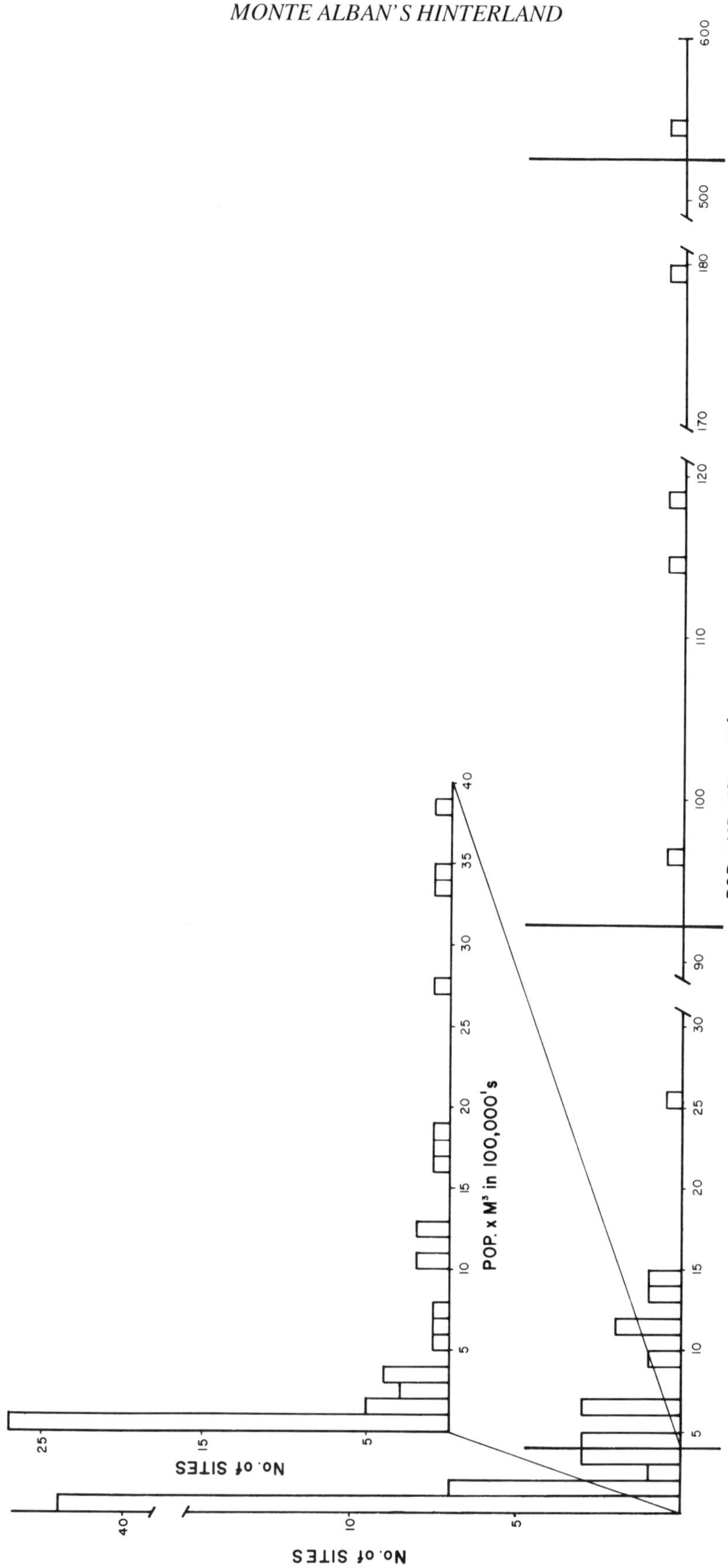

Figure 6-5. Histogram of mound volume times population, IIIa.

a population of more than half that of Monte Albán and a mound volume times population value of over 5.43×10^8 (Monte Albán's estimated value is roughly 1.03×10^{10}).

Four sites make up the third rank in our hierarchy of sites: Cuilapan (3-8-2-6,8), Xoxocotlán (2-8-17), the new site at 3-8-65 (N8E6), and the new site at Rancho Tejas (3-8-233-239,241). Of these, only 3-8-65 lacks what we have previously referred to as "formal" elite residential architecture (the site consists of a number of low platforms), perhaps implying that its functions were somewhat different than the other rank-3 centers.

Given what little we know about mound volumes and population sizes at Sta. Inés Yatzeche (3-8-175) and Zaachila (3-8-37), we had some difficulty deciding where these sites should fit into the ranking of central places. We do know that Zaachila could not have been as populous as Jalieza in IIIa (Zaachila reached its maximum population in the subsequent period IIIb), so we reasoned it should be placed with the rank-3 centers. Sta. Inés Yatzeche was also placed in this rank. Ignacio Bernal (field notes) visited this site and suggested that it reached its maximum size during Period IIIa. If we assume that all of the mounds we were able to observe at the site were in use in that period, then our total mound volume estimate for Sta. Inés of roughly 80,000 cubic meters fits very nicely within the range of mound volume estimates for the other rank-3 centers (Cuilapan = 120,302 m^3, 3-8-65 = 93,321 m^3, Rancho Tejas = 59,280 m^3, and Xoxocotlán = 89,224 m^3). The population estimates for Zaachila and Sta. Inés we then calculated as the mean size of the known rank-3 centers (excluding 3-8-65, due to its somewhat more equivocal position in the hierarchy), or 1585 people.

Surprisingly, from the point of view of mound volume total, Jalieza actually falls below the range of the rank-3 centers, with a total estimate of only 42,363 cubic meters. We cannot explain this discrepancy, but we do believe that our relative ranking of sites is still justified given the very large size of Jalieza, substantially above the estimates for the rank-3 centers.

Figure 6-6 shows the locations of the administrative centers and the weighted Thiessen Polygons drawn around Monte Albán and sites we felt were the administrative district capitals (and see Table 6-1). No separate district is indicated for 3-8-65, given its unusual architecture, although it is reasonable to suppose that it could have been the center of an alluvium district comparable to Zaachila's.

The major features of change and continuity in the administrative central place hierarchy from Period II to Period IIIa are the following:

1) To a large extent, sites with administrative functions in the alluvium persisted into IIIa, although in almost all cases there was an increase in both population and architectural complexity in IIIa. Sites with occupational continuity included Xoxocotlán, Cuilapan, 3-8-10, etc. (N10E6), Zaachila, Roaló (3-8-62, N8E6), Sta. Inés Yatzeche, and several sites in its vicinity, especially in grid square N6E6 (except for 3-8-146, which by IIIa apparently no longer had administrative functions), and Sta. Ana Tlapacoyan (3-8-251, N3E4). Major changes in the alluvium after Period II include the addition of 3-8-65, the dramatic growth in size and complexity of Xoxocotlán, and the overall population growth from an estimated 2626 for Period II to an estimated 9333 for IIIa.

2) The most noticeable discontinuity from II to IIIa was the filling up of the piedmont zone in the Valle Grande, including the rapid growth of a number of sites with administrative functions. The total increase in the piedmont and sierra population in the area south of and including the N10 row of grid squares was an estimated 26,099, increasing from 2820 to 28,919. In several cases sites with administrative functions increased in population from close to nothing to populations in the thousands, or, in the case of Jalieza, over 10,000. We infer that this implies a great deal of immigration into the piedmont because of the new demand for agricultural labor.

3) A second set of changes from II to IIIa is in the spatial organization of administration. By IIIa, Monte Albán's district appears to have been smaller than previously; new districts were centered on Xoxocotlán and Rancho Tejas, and Jalieza's district expanded in size at the same time that the Zaachila and Sta. Inés Yatzeche districts diminished in area. It is likely that the Rancho Tejas district could be subdivided, producing subdistricts around Sta. Ana Tlapacoyan, Sta. Cruz Mixtepec (3-8-179, N5E2), and "El Choco" (3-8-272-274, N2E3).

Another feature of organizational change as we see it is the increased hierarchical complexity at the rank-2 and rank-3 levels. For Period II, the data seem to indicate approximately similar functional sizes for Ocotlán (3-7-44-46), Cuilapan, Zaachila, and Sta. Inés Yatzeche. By IIIa, Jalieza stands out as representing a distinct hierarchical level interposed between Monte Albán and the other district capitals. Jalieza was a very large community of about 12,000 people in 4 square kilometers, with roughly 700 residential terraces (Appendix X; Fig. 6-3). It is possible that this reflects the addition of administrative functions for an area lar-

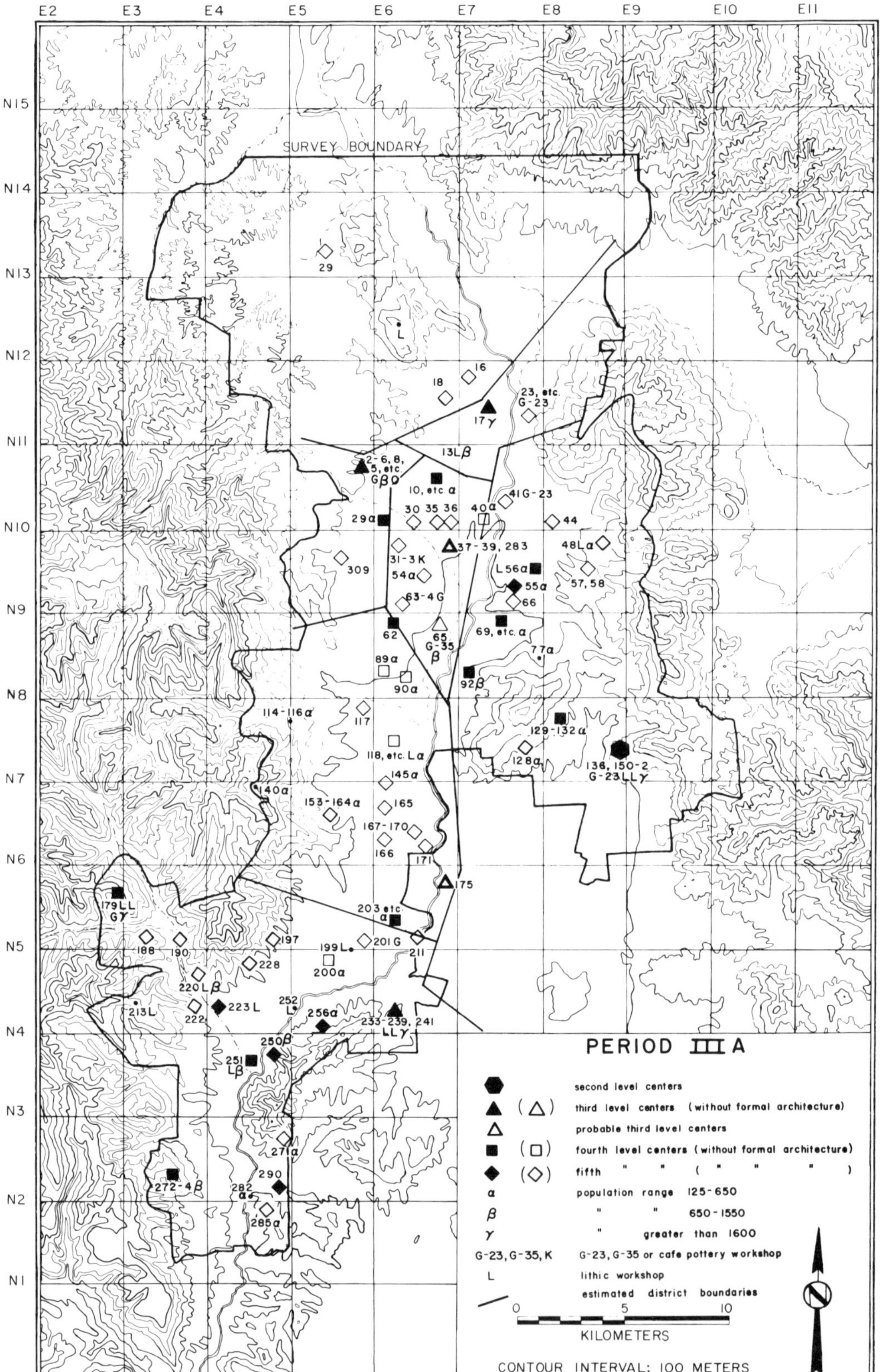

Figure 6-6. Central places, larger sites, estimated district boundaries, and production loci, IIIa.

Table 6-1. Central-Place Summary, Period IIIa

SITE	POPULATION	MOUND VOLUME m^3	RANK
2-16	53	9870	5
2-17	2014	89,224	3
2-18	17	832	5
2-23, etc.	47	416	5
2-29	49	662	5
3-5, etc.	803	120,302	3
3-10, etc.	135	102,070*	4
3-29	254	46,003*	4
3-30	31	6917*	5
3-31-33	64	4430*	5
3-35	7	1545	5
3-36	17	2564	5
3-37	?	?	3
3-40	455	7351*	4
3-41	17	19,137*	5
3-44	17	15,283*	5
3-48	211	224	5
3-54	315	3874*	5
3-55	215	7936	5
3-56	565	21,077	4
3-57-58	42	1910*	5
3-62	72	37,731*	4
3-63-64	81	15,755*	5
3-65	1265	93,231*	3
3-66	28	1464	5
3-69, etc.	309	20,336	4
3-89	286	21,197*	4
3-90	137	24,948*	4
3-92	814	5054	4
3-117	41	1790	5
3-118, etc.	197	19,580	4
3-128	169	985	5
3-129-32	556	16,982*	4
3-136	12,835	42,363	2
3-145	135	13,604	5
3-153-164	296	2499	5
3-165	28	10,418	5
3-166	15	8108*	5
3-167-70	83	19,828	5
3-171	17	3087*	5
3-175	(1585)	80,000*	3
3-179, etc.	3219	7845*	4
3-188	17	754	5
3-190	73	2235	5
3-197	53	706*	5
3-200, etc.	193	22,993*	4
3-201	42	7192*	5
3-203, etc.	158	28,546*	4
3-211	7	1456*	5
3-220	1177	1000	5
3-222	120	276	5
3-223	17	8955*	5
3-228, etc.	119	513	5
3-236, etc.	1937	59,280	3
3-250	825	1286	5
3-251	901	15,801	4
3-256	182	6899*	5
3-271	225	165	5
3-272	1305	5059*	4
3-285	503	719	5
3-290	33	1184*	5
3-309	116	2676*	5
		* Index	

ger than Jalieza's own district–perhaps including much of the Valle Grande. Its location near a pass into the western portion of the Tlacolula arm suggests it could have serviced the population of that area also.

4) Changes can also be pointed out from II to IIIa in terms of Monte Albán's role in the region and in terms of the overall amount of administration. Sites with evidence for administrative functions (other than Monte Albán) increased in total population from II to IIIa by a factor of 6.6. This was a rate of growth higher than the overall growth of the non-Monte Albán population, which was by a factor of 5.8 (and Monte Albán increased in population by a factor of only 1.1). We interpret this to indicate more administration, overall, in IIIa than was the case in II. Most of these increases had little to do with Monte Albán directly. This may sound contradictory in light of what we said before–that the territorial extent of Monte Albán's control within the Valley of Oaxaca increased in IIIa. This extension seems to have been accomplished without increasing dramatically the number of administrative functions at the capital. Instead, compared with prior periods, a more integrated administrative system was developed by expanding the roles of secondary centers, and through the establishment of some new centers. There was, in other words, more overall administration, but it was more decentralized. IIIa was the first period in which the total population of administrative places in the survey area exceeded the population of Monte Albán (roughly 22,800 versus 16,507). The IIIa rank-

size graph (Fig. 6-7) also supports this interpretation. The graph shows that the region no longer had the strongly primate organization we noted for Periods Early I through II. Instead, IIIa is nearly log-normal. However, there is still some indication of top-heavy high-level administration given the drop in size from the rank-2 to the rank-3 centers, so that most sites below the first two in rank fall below the log-normal line drawn from Monte Albán.

Given the impressive development of the southern part of the valley, coupled with rapid population growth to levels never before reached, we believe that IIIa represents a scale of organization never before reached in this region. If so, then the decentralization apparent during the period can probably be explained at least in part in scale terms. By this we mean that organizational changes involving decentralization may have been required to cope with problems of growing system size. Perhaps the major problem in the growth of administrative institutions is that, disproportionately, communication costs increase. According to the sociologist Kasarda (1974:26) ". . . organizational size has substantial implications for the composition of the administrative tasks whose primary functions are communication and management . . . however, . . . communicative functions increase with organizational size at a much faster rate than managerial functions. The net result is a disproportionate amount of human resources being drawn into communicative functions in larger organizations" (see also Boulding 1956). Based on some findings of administrative science, we would expect that if communications costs were becoming oppressively high, the Monte Albán administrators might have employed two related strategies: 1) more management through indirect controls, and 2) more vertical differentiation in the control hierarchy (Blau 1968, 1970). Indirect controls imply that higher-order administrators are less concerned with day-to-day problem solving. This can be accomplished, as Blau points out, through " . . . devising impersonal control mechanisms that constrain operations to follow automatically the policies and programs specified by top executives. The substitution of indirect mechanisms of control for direct control requires that an orientation to abstract universalistic standards replace reliance on personal judgements" (Blau 1968:465). We may have some evidence of the application of uniform, bureaucratically conceived standards as opposed to more flexible adaptation to local conditions. This lies in the area of "housing and community development", and the evidence consists of obvious uniformities in residential terrace dimensions and layouts in newly established settlements in IIIa. Further work on this is planned. The institution of more impersonal controls implies an increase in the degree of vertical differentiation, with the highest-order elite concerned more with the formulation of broad policy, while day-to-day operations are delegated to lower officials. Because controls are exercised indirectly, however, does not necessarily imply that decentralization of power has occurred. Indirect control can be what the sociologist Fesler refers to as "pseudo-decentralization", in which the *work-load* is decentralized, but not administrative power. In fact, he says that "To move work load out of the capital may be efficient and convenient for the public and may even promote a feeling that government is close to the people. But it may not involve any decentralization of power, that is, it may not provide the opportunity to exercise substantial local discretion in decision making" (Fesler 1968:373).

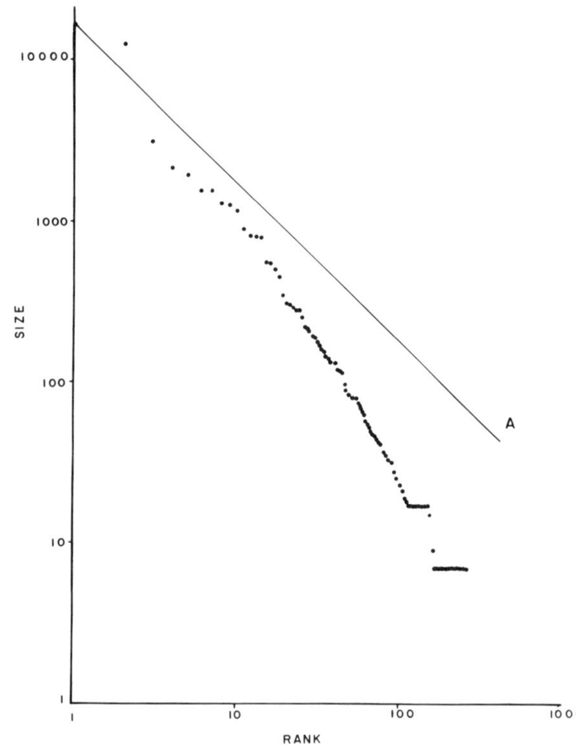

Figure 6-7. Rank-size graph, Period IIIa. Line A is log-normal calculated from the size of the rank-1 center (Monte Albán).

The purpose of this foray into administrative science has been to demonstrate that it is possible to talk, simultaneously, of a growing system which is becoming more integrated and more decentralized. The carved-stone monuments of IIIa indicate a level of control in the valley by Monte Albán greater than any prior period (Marcus 1976a), while our data indicate more decentralization. The two processes are compatible, and are, in fact, what one might expect in the context of scale changes in a growing system.

We interpret the data on Period IIIa administrative activities to indicate a return to a round of administered piedmont development in IIIa analogous in some features to that of Period Late I. In IIIa, however, the administration in the piedmont occurred largely at a lower level in the region's administrative hierarchy–centered at a series of places ranking from 2 to 4 in our scheme, and including sites in the southern zone like Jalieza, Rancho Tejas, Sta. Cruz Mixtepec, and El Choco. During Late I, most piedmont administration, we argued, emanated directly from the capital and secondarily from a series of second and third-order sites. But there was an increase in the degree of administrative division of labor by IIIa, such that the elite of Monte Albán were no longer so directly involved in local production problems. Instead, they were probably more involved in higher order decision-making tasks including offense-defense, diplomacy (cf. Marcus 1980), and long-distance exchange. In addition to the problems of system size, the more serious threat of Teotihuacán expansionism must have made such high-order functions a great deal more momentous and time consuming than had been the case in prior periods, necessitating a reordering of priorities that resulted in a more decentralized system. The total amount of local administration increased coming into IIIa, however, since the loss of at least some portion of empire meant that new sources of energy had to be developed locally in order to maintain some acceptable level of revenues to support Monte Albán.

PERIOD IIIa: INTERACTION ESTIMATES

The same three measures of interaction potential (*IP*) were made for the IIIa sites as were made for the earlier periods–one involving sites in the upper 10% of population sizes, and two measures involving the sites with administrative functions. Several features of the *IP* measures for the larger sites highlight the changes that occurred in the regional system from Period II to IIIa. First, the total amount of *IP* among the larger sites is considerably higher in IIIa–amounting to a total of 6,309,508. This is an average of 166,040 per site. The Period II values are 649,003, total, or 38,177 per site. Monte Albán's share of the total in IIIa is lower–amounting to 48%–than for Period II, when it contributed 77% of the total *IP* measured in this way. In IIIa, several sites in particular have high values of *IP*, and these tended to be in the southern sector. In Period II, the highest *IP* values other than Monte Albán were for sites in the "second" administrative zone, including Zaachila and two smaller nearby sites, 3-7-26 and 3-7-28. By IIIa, the larger *IP* values other than Monte Albán are accounted for by Jalieza (8.6%), 3-8-251 (Sta. Ana Tlapacoyan), and 3-8-250 (N3E4), both with about 19% of the total *IP*. These values reflect the intense development of the piedmont zone south of Sta. Inés Yatzeche.

The first administrative *IP* measures involve each site's first two nearest-neighbors at the same administrative level and each site's first two nearest-neighbors at the next higher level. These values help to clarify some additional characteristics of the period. First, of course, the sum for this set of measures is higher than the value for Period II–5,364,828 (an average of 243,856), versus 378,693 (an average of 29, 130). For IIIa, the total administrative *IP* value amounts to 85% of the total value for the larger sites, compared with only 58% for Period II. This means that fewer of the large sites in IIIa lack evidence for administration. Period IIIa can be especially contrasted in this regard with Late I, when a number of large sites, particularly those in Monte Albán's administrative district, lacked any evidence for mounded buildings. In Late I, this administrative *IP* measure amounted to only 23% of the total *IP* for the larger Late I sites.

For Period II, we argued that the local subsystems focused on the district capitals were relatively autonomous. For IIIa, this first administrative measure of *IP* hints at the presence of a regional system more integrated than that of Period II. In II, the total *IP* among the secondary centers amounted to only 15% of their *IP* totals, including the values of their interactions with Monte Albán. By IIIa, this value (considering Jalieza plus the other district capitals) had increased to 40%. This means that more of the region's total *IP* was among district capitals–perhaps indicative of the breakdown of some of the local autonomy of the district capitals seen in Period II.

The second set of administrative *IP* measures was made between each site and its nearest-neighbor of next-highest level, but only for a site within its own administrative district. These values also support the idea that there was an increase in regional integration from II to IIIa. For II, this second administrative *IP* measure-total 462,553 - is larger than the total of the first administrative *IP* measure, 378,693. More *IP* is indicated within administrative districts, in other words, than is indicated when the measures ignore district boundaries. By IIIa the situation was reversed. The first set of measures, which ignores district boundaries, totaled 5,364,828, while the second measure, involving *IP* only within the districts, totals 4,292,584. In a more unified regional system, district boundaries may have had fewer functions, and more of the region's total administrative interactions were between centers in different districts rather than among centers in discrete districts.

PRODUCTION/DISTRIBUTION IN PERIOD IIIa

Our evidence pertaining to production and distribution in IIIa suggests some important departures from the Period II pattern, departures that are reminiscent of some of the features of change we noted in the transition from Early I to Late I. Just as IIIa was a return to a round of intensive piedmont occupation of the sort that we noted in Late I, IIIa also was characterized by increased standardization in ceramic production (see Chapter 10). The highly standardized G-12 bowl was the ceramic "workhorse" of Late I. The IIIa analogs were, first and foremost, the plain G-35 bowl and the carved G-23 bowl. There is other evidence for an increase in standardization in ceramic production: 1) a substantial reduction in the average production-step index from II to IIIa (see Chapter 10); and 2) a decline in the numbers of types exhibiting discrete spatial distributions. In Period II, some types, such as the A-9, are mainly restricted to localized areas, implying relatively spatially discrete systems of production and distribution, poorly articulated with other local systems. IIIa lacks evidence for such discrete distributions, supporting the previous suggestion that by IIIa the valley system was generally more integrated, in terms of exchange as well as administration. The more uniform distribution of IIIa pottery types could be the result of a more unified administrative system producing a particular set of ceramic forms for wide distribution. A more detailed discussion of the IIIa types and their distributions is included in Chapter 10.

Both production standardization in ceramics and increased integration of the regional system are aspects of how the system "gears up", so to speak, for increased levels of local productivity designated for government revenues. In both Late I and IIIa an important strategy was to tap the agricultural potential of the piedmont by attracting immigrants into an administered structure. This kind of development has two implications for regional exchange. First, as we pointed out previously, piedmont cultivation can produce a surplus, but is relatively unpredictable. Thus it cannot exist in the absence of a region-wide network capable of effectively moving food to deficit areas in bad years. In both Late I and IIIa this seems to have been accomplished through an increase in the degree of vertical differentiation in administration, along with an increase in the amount of administration, especially in the piedmont. In both periods, sites that were more important than the other district centers, and interposed between Monte Albán and the other centers, were identified in the area north of Ocotlán. In the transition from Early to Late I, we noted the possibility that there was an increase in the degree to which goods moved through administrative channels, given the growth in the dichotomy between administrative and non-administrative sites in numbers of types per site (along with the decline in relative importance of our marketplace). In Period II this difference in numbers of types per site was less pronounced, suggesting that even non-administrative places could be more fully incorporated into the region's system of production and distribution. By IIIa the dichotomy in numbers of types per site between administrative and non-administrative sites is again pronounced. Table 6-2 illustrates the changes in this regard from Early I through IIIa (the data are found in Appendix VIII).

We made the argument in the Late I section that many of the people participating in the expanding piedmont development were immigrants. As such, we suggested, they could be more readily incorporated into an administrative structure, which then supplied them with the highly standardized, state-produced goods, including pottery. Thus sites within Monte Albán's district, the most intense zone of piedmont development, tended to have five or fewer pottery types, while most other sites had many more. By IIIa, two clusters of sites display very few types (again, less than five)–those, within roughly 10 kilometers of Monte Albán and those in the heavily piedmont-oriented and heavily administered district south of Rancho Tejas (beyond about 30 kilometers from the Main Plaza). We argue that these areas were most directly incorporated into an administrative structure that supplied standardized pottery.

The survey area's middle zone, from roughly Sta. Inés Yatzeche north to Zaachila, was different. This

Table 6-2. Mean Number of Types per Site. The Numbers in Parentheses are the Percentage Each Number Represents of the Total Number of Types for the Period

	Early I (88 types)	Late I (85 types)	II (53 types)	IIIa (33 types)
all centers	11.75(14)	16(18)	15.6(29.4)	11.75(36)
all non-admin.	5.6(6.6)	5.8(6.6)	7.2(13.6)	4.8(14)
non-admin. > 100	10.2(12)	9.3(10.6)	8(15)	11.75(36)
non-admin. < 100	5.26(6)	5.3(6)	6.8(12.7)	4.3(13)
district capitals	14(16)	***23.6(27)	20.75(39)	**18.7(57)
one rank below district capitals	*10.6(12.5)	18(21)	16.6(31)	16.3(49.5)
two ranks below district capitals	--	12.4(14)	12.3(23)	8.4(25.5)

* includes "very low-volume mound groups"

** includes Jalieza

*** includes Ocotlán

area remained largely alluvium-oriented in IIIa and overall has more types per site (Fig. 6-8). Although the evidence points to the fact that this area was more tightly woven into the Monte Albán system in IIIa than it had been in the past (especially the Sta. Inés district) still, these data suggest that this alluvial zone may have been less directly controlled than the piedmont areas, and thus less directly tied to a system churning out highly standardized pottery. Interestingly, the large alluvial site within what had been Monte Albán's administrative district, at Xoxocotlán, has only 13 types, far below the mean for the other district centers, and even lower than the mean value of centers one level below the district capitals (Table 6-2). The site's location, close to Monte Albán, suggests it was more directly tied to the Monte Albán state, probably making it the analog of the Early and Late I district capitals at 2-5-33 and 2-6-138,9.

Further evidence that the survey zone's middle area was not so heavily tied into the regional administrative system is the fact that, overall, the difference in the numbers of types per site by administrative and non-administrative function is less pronounced than elsewhere. Non-administrative sites in this central zone average 62% of the number of types found in the sites with administrative functions. The comparable value for the survey area as a whole (not counting Monte Albán) is 41%. In addition, both sets of values, that is, for numbers of types per site for administrative and non-administrative sites, are higher in this middle zone than the values for the survey area as a whole. Administrative sites in the alluvium have a mean number of 12.5, while non-administrative sites average 8 types per site (the comparable values for the survey area as a whole are 11.7 and 4.8, respectively).

IIIa: CONCLUSIONS

Previously, Blanton (1978) argued that the growth of Monte Albán and its valley-wide influence was the product of changes in the Mesoamerican regional system–specifically the expansion of Teotihuacán's empire. The Classic period was thus a time of Mesoamerica-wide increases in the scale of regional organizations, comparable perhaps to expansion in the size of what Frederic Lane calls the "natural monopoly of force" in Europe. As he put it: "In much of medieval Europe, governing more territory than one province brought disadvantage of scale. In contrast, by the seventeenth century it had become almost impossible for a government to maintain against outsiders its monopoly of even a single province unless its military establishment was strong enough to conquer a national kingdom. The size of the natural monopolies has changed, and there have been periods of competition

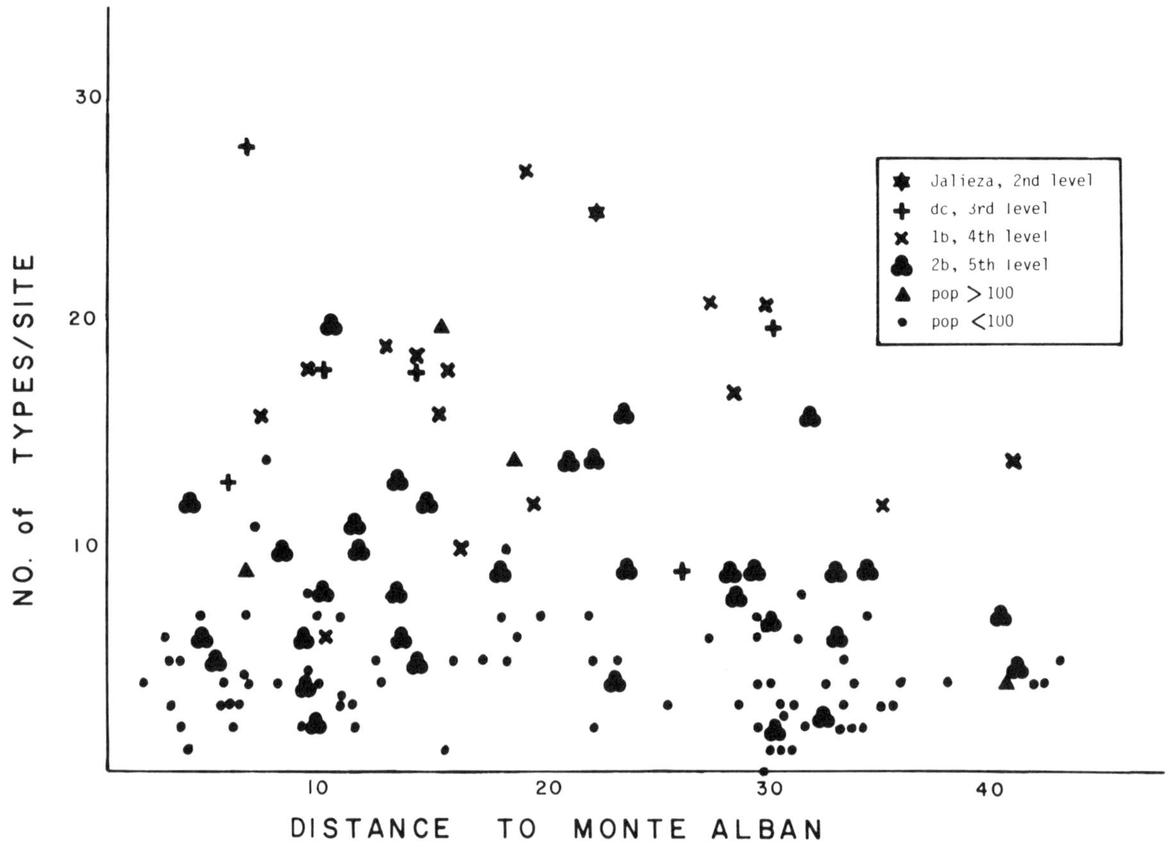

Figure 6-8. Types per site by site category and distance from Monte Albán, IIIa. The data are found in Appendix VIII.

and higher costs of protection while new natural monopolies in accord with new techniques were being established'' (Lane 1966:415-16). We don't necessarily feel that the changes in scale of regional organizations in the Mesoamerican Classic were due to a shift in the ''natural monopoly'' caused by technological advances, but, whatever the causes, the consequence for Monte Albán was a change in the competitive environment. The associated ''increased costs of protection'', we think, required new internal structures that would motivate greater production and reproduction–thus the changes we see in the settlement patterns. These changes were:

1) Population growth. As in Late I, this was especially pronounced in the piedmont zone.

2) An increased degree of vertical differentiation in administration. This was manifested by the growth of the Jalieza district capital far beyond the size ranges of the other district capitals, suggesting it assumed functions beyond those pertaining to its district alone. Perhaps it was involved in certain kinds of regional affairs that had been centered at Monte Albán. This, again, is reminiscent of Late I, when the center at 3-6-85,86 seemed to have had a similar regional role. The G-23 carved bowl, the valley's chief decorated type, is most frequently found in the Valle Grande, and its center of distribution may have actually been at Jalieza. Monte Albán has very few G-23's per capita. This marks the first time that a universally-distributed, top-of-the-line pot type was not found most frequently at Monte Albán, suggesting again a distinctive role for Jalieza.

3) Compared with Period II, we feel there may have been more administration per capita. Sites with administrative functions increased in population size more rapidly than the general population growth, except for Monte Albán. By far the most pronounced growth rates in administrative sites were found in the piedmont zone in the south where a major round of administered development took place.

4) There was an increase from Period II in standardization in ceramic production, implying more governmental intervention in production and distribution. As in Late I, areas we suspect were most closely

involved in state administration show the most evidence for standardization, manifested as few types per site.

5) As in Late I, we feel that the increased levels in state control of production and distribution systems resulted in a greater gulf between administrative and non-administrative sites in numbers of types per site. The differences were less pronounced in II. This dichotomy in IIIa, however, is not so pronounced in the alluvial zone as compared with the piedmont.

6) We found evidence for an increased level of regional coherence by IIIa. This is suggested by the *IP* measures and is attested to by the absence of any discretely-distributed ceramic types of the sort that we did note for Period II.

Based on these interpretations, we feel we can identify two modes of operation of the regional system after the founding of Monte Albán. We would contrast the growth periods (Late I and IIIa) with the more stationary Period II. Early I is a growth period when viewed from the perspective of Monte Albán, but in other regards it is like Period II. In Early I there was little piedmont development, a relatively simple hierarchy of central places, little evidence for standardization in ceramic production, and the presence of discretely-distributed ceramic types suggestive of less regional coherence than existed in Late I and IIIa. We cannot argue, however, that the regional system started out in the more stationary mode, developed into a growth phase, then simply cycled back through this sequence again in Periods II and IIIa. Although alternate modes of organization are identifiable, the system was also undergoing directional change during this 900 year period. Compared with Late I, the IIIa growth period occurred in the context of a system of considerably increased scale and total population size. The IIIa system also manifested, we feel, considerably more hierarchical specialization of administrative labor than did the Late I system. By IIIa Monte Albán's elite seem to have delegated administration of piedmont agriculture. While the capital undoubtedly benefited from piedmont development, the actual administration of it had been delegated to lower levels in the administrative hierarchy, and it took place at some distance from the capital. Finally, although pottery was standardized in both Late I and IIIa, the very low production-step index for IIIa compared to Late I (see Chapter 10) suggests an even greater degree of standardization in IIIa.

Given the limitations of our data base, we cannot hope, at this time, to fully explain the changes through time in the Valley of Oaxaca regional system. Our data do permit, however, the construction of what might be called an explanatory sketch that takes into consideration what we think may have been some of the more salient dynamic properties of the valley and the human system resident there after the foundation of Monte Albán. In the final paragraph of the section of production and distribution, we noted that the alluvium from roughly Sta. Inés to Zaachila is in some ways distinguishable from the remainder of the survey area having, overall, more types per site and a less pronounced dichotomy between administrative and non-administrative sites in numbers of types per site. This area in IIIa was also distinct in remaining largely alluvium-oriented. Most of the increases in piedmont population occurred around Jalieza and in the Rancho Tejas district. In this regard, IIIa is somewhat reminiscent of Late I, when the alluvium south of Zaachila similarly exhibited stability while most of the population growth occurred around Monte Albán.

These observations have led us to suggest that to varying degrees, but generally speaking, the alluvial zone was organized differently than the zones more directly controlled from Monte Albán. Previously we argued that this alluvium-piedmont dichotomy arose because in developing "free floating" resources, the new institution at Monte Albán had to focus primarily on the relatively marginal and probably largely unclaimed piedmont. The longer-established local systems located in the alluvium south of Zaachila were no doubt tied into the regional system, but were not so directly controlled as were the piedmont communities. This would explain why the most pronounced evidence for ceramic standardization was found in the Monte Albán-controlled areas, since, again, this had been a strategy for producing "free-floating" revenues.

Comparing the piedmont and alluvial systems provides some insight into the workings of the regional system as a whole. Clearly these two modes of organization represent very different kinds of organization with different dynamic properties. First, the piedmont systems were considerably more transitory, exhibiting periods of rapid growth followed by decline. This is illustrated in Figure 5-4, which shows the change through time in the population of administrative places by environmental zone. While the population of the administrative places in the alluvium continued to grow more or less constantly from Early I to IIIa, the piedmont population fluctuated. These changes in the population of administrative places in the piedmont are weakly but definitely mirrored in the population changes at Monte Albán, strengthening our argument that a direct tie existed between Monte Albán and the piedmont developments. The piedmont sites with administrative functions were also more transitory than the alluvial places in terms of location. Of all the alluvial places with administrative functions from Early I through IIIa, 84% have occupational continuity with at least one other of these four periods. The value for the piedmont centers is only 47%. This suggests that piedmont development could not become as stable a form of adaptation as could the alluvial adaptation.

Thus, explaining the dynamic features of the Valley of Oaxaca regional system from Early I to IIIa involves a consideration of at least the following factors:

1) In periods in which the Monte Albán elite are desirous of developing new sources of revenue locally, one of the major strategies is to develop the piedmont. This strategy, however, results in an increase in the frequency and severity in fluctuations in production in the region, given the unpredictability of the piedmont zone. In other words, the growth of the new regional institution can, under certain conditions, become a factor promoting disequilibrium. This we think in turn required corrective actions, including increasing the degree of regional coherence to facilitate the movement of food from surplus to deficit areas more effectively than is possible in a region with more autonomous local systems. This increase in integration was achieved through increasing the amount of government and by more vertical differentiation in regional government. A consequence of this, in turn, is even higher revenue demands to support the exchange system, necessitating even more means for capturing energy. "Meddling" in ceramic production was undoubtedly one of the strategies employed to support the more costly regional system. Another factor to consider here involves the consequences of increased levels of regional coherence. The elimination of "buffers" between local systems might actually have had the result of increasing the severity of production fluctuations. In a more buffered situation, extreme fluctuations in one part of a system do not pose a serious threat to the system as a whole since the parts are poorly articulated. If buffers are eliminated, however, the system may become "hypercoherent" (cf. Flannery 1972a; Rappaport 1978), meaning that extreme fluctuations in one local system can ramify through the larger entity, creating problems of a wider regional scope, which in turn would necessitate even more costly remedial measures.

2) The regional political institution may also have had another feature promoting disequilibrium. The bulk of the fluctuation in population size in the region from Early I through IIIa is accounted for by Monte Albán and the piedmont population. Our data seem to indicate that this involved at least in part the alternate coming and going of migrants. Although we cannot be sure where these migrants are coming from (or going to), it is possible that in part they were attracted from (or perhaps even abducted or bought) from outside the valley. One of the early readers of this manuscript, Suzanne K. Fish, noted that this would make sense given that populations from more marginal areas in the Southern Highlands would have been more accustomed to piedmont-like agriculture and could thus be more readily incorporated into an expanding piedmont-oriented system. At any rate, a system dependent largely on immigrants would have been "open-ended" in the sense that it can increase in numbers as fast as immigrants can be brought into the system. The alluvium systems, in contrast to those of the piedmont, tended to exhibit relatively stationary population size or slow, steady growth. This could be explained if the alluvial systems were organized as corporate communities or corporate descent groups in which membership and therefore access to land is by birth. Such systems are more likely to be "closed" in the sense that growth is largely a product of the reproductive potential of the population alone. Only the piedmont systems, then, are likely to exhibit extremely high growth rates and thus have the potential to grow quickly to levels above production potentials. Thus the regional administrative system, desirous of increasing local productivity by importing or attracting labor from outside, may further promote regional disequilibrium as some over-populated areas become even more exposed to the risk of disastrous agricultural years. A second factor to consider in connection with this is that rapid population growth in the piedmont can have serious environmental consequences. The piedmont zone in general is a fragile environment. The steeper slopes and thinner soil mean that over-use can lead to production declines due to soil erosion (Smith 1978).

Our view of the regional system after the foundation of Monte Albán through Period IIIa is one in which has evolved a political institution capable of rapid development of energy sources locally through the importation of labor and piedmont development. But in so doing that institution substantially increases the likelihood of whole-system failure and collapse. It may have been that in the early stages of a growth cycle production was high relative to administrative costs. As population grew, however, and the severity of fluctuations necessitated expansion in governmental activities, costs increased to the point that the administrative superstructure could no longer be supported, and collapse resulted. Our data indicate that the IIIa system did just that–it collapsed. In the next chapter we describe the considerably reduced system that was the result.

Chapter 7

PERIOD IIIb

INTRODUCTION

We interpreted Period IIIa as a time of intense local development of energy sources by Monte Albán in response to a diminishment in empire revenues and an increased threat from Teotihuacán. The settlement patterns of IIIb seem to stand as testimony to the failure of the development strategy. Figure 7-1 is the map of the IIIb sites in the survey area. Even a cursory glance of this map convinces one that major changes occurred in the survey area after the climax in population density during IIIa. By the time the pottery types that we identify as IIIb were in use, there were many fewer sites occupied, and there was a reorientation of the regional system as we know it to the valley's Central zone. For reasons we can only guess at, the massive development of the southern region proved not to be a viable strategy for the long run. We return to a further consideration of this issue below.

The reader should keep in mind the difficulties we had in producing the IIIb settlement pattern map, given the knotty problem of distinguishing the ceramics of IIIb and IV. We feel that, on the whole, we are on firm ground in our periodization, but, as we mention in Chapter 1, some problems remain. Sites we identified as IIIb have ceramic assemblages similar to that we noted at Cerro Atzompa during the course of our Monte Albán survey, since we think this was a nearly pure Late Classic occupation. Pottery we identified as Period IV differs from the Atzompa assemblage in several respects, although the differences are not always that easy to detect, especially when the surveyor is looking at muddy, eroded sherds in the field. Although the IV assemblages are somewhat variable within the region, they are generally distinguishable from the IIIb assemblages in that they 1) show more affinity to the pottery from Lambityeco (Paddock, Mogor, and Lind 1968), 2) contain in some cases known Period IV markers such as imitation Fine Orange, and, 3) finally, are in some cases obviously transitional to Period V in containing G-3M sherds but not in the Monte Albán V forms. Our biggest problem remaining in this regard is the possibility that small areas of IIIb occupation could be "swamped" in the larger IV sites, such as Jalieza. We are convinced, though, that no major IIIb occupations have been overlooked, even within these larger Period IV sites.

Figures 2-1 and 7-2 portray quantitatively the nature of the population shifts that occurred in the transition from IIIa to IIIb. Figure 7-3, which shows the proportion of non-Monte Albán population by distance from the Main Plaza, is reminiscent of comparable Late I (Fig. 4-6) in that by IIIb there was an extreme concentration of population in the central sector, especially within 15 kilometers of Monte Albán. The small "bump" in this graph at 30.1 to 33 kilometers is due to the presence of a large Late Classic site at Rancho Tejas, the last remnant of the impressive IIIa developments in the south.

The total population decline in the survey area from the IIIa maximum to the IIIb maximum was 16,090 people. This value, however, masks the actual magnitude of population shifts. As is illustrated in Figure 7-2, the declines in the area south of a line 12 kilometers south of Monte Albán were substantial, amounting to a total estimated loss of 32,815 persons (of which nearly 14,000 is accounted for by the abandonment of Jalieza) (see also Fig. 4-3). Population increase in the IIIa to IIIb transition was largely confined to Zaachila (3-9-31,37-42,71,72), the area north and west of Monte Albán, and Monte Albán itself (with a total estimated population of 24,189, an increase of nearly 8000 people over IIIa) (the preliminary survey of the Etla area indicates IIIb growth there also). Our population estimate for Monte Albán in IIIb is somewhat higher than the value given by Blanton (1978) because in the survey of the Central zone done by Kowalewski, a number of small sites were found that are located so close to the Monte Albán terraces that we thought they should be included in the site's final population total (Appendix IV).

Both I and IIIb were periods of growth in the capital and in its immediate hinterland. These two periods are also comparable insofar as most of the non-Monte Albán population in this central area resided in settings higher than the alluvium. Zaachila and Cuilapan (3-9-

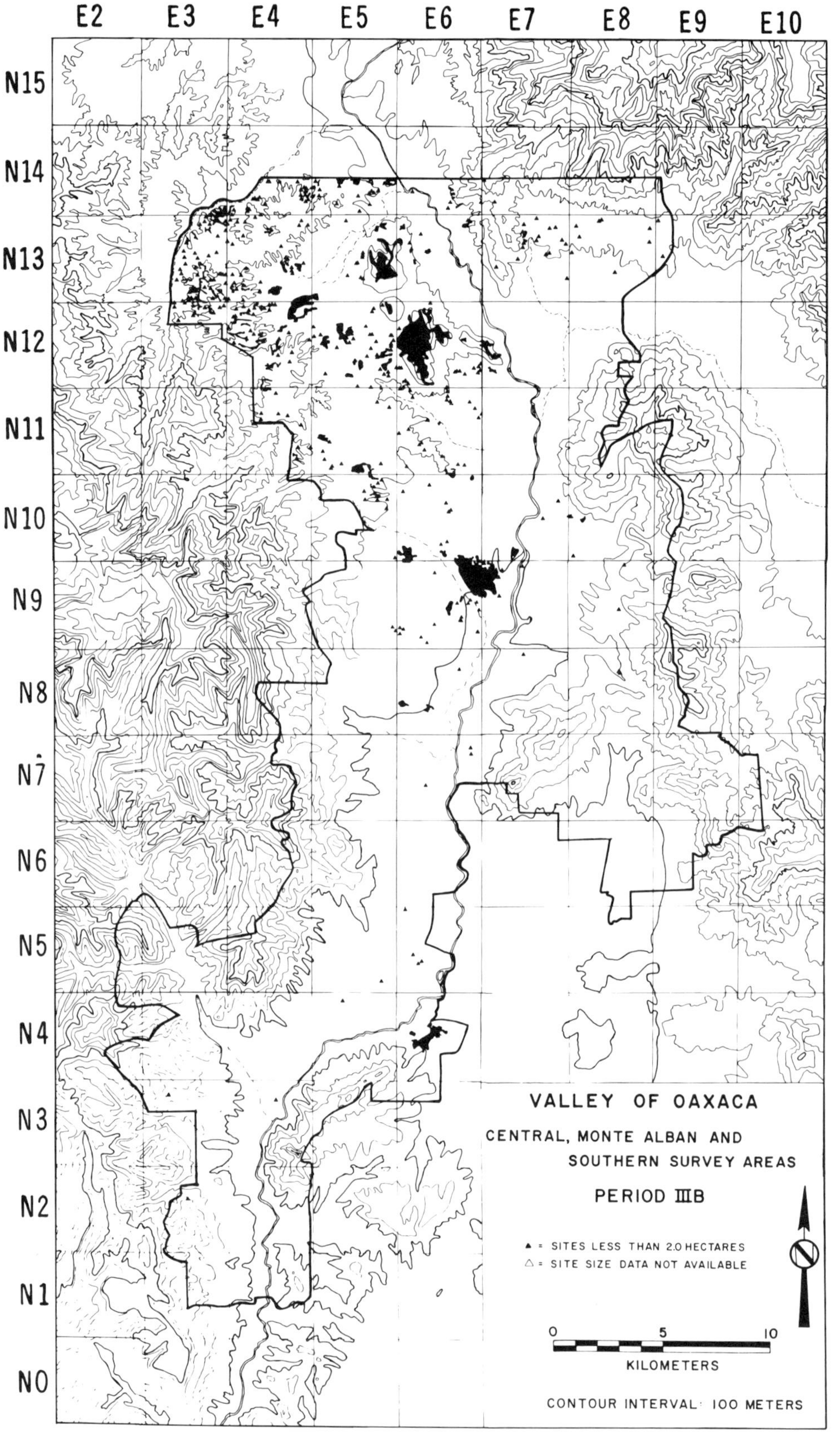

Figure 7-1. Settlements of IIIb.

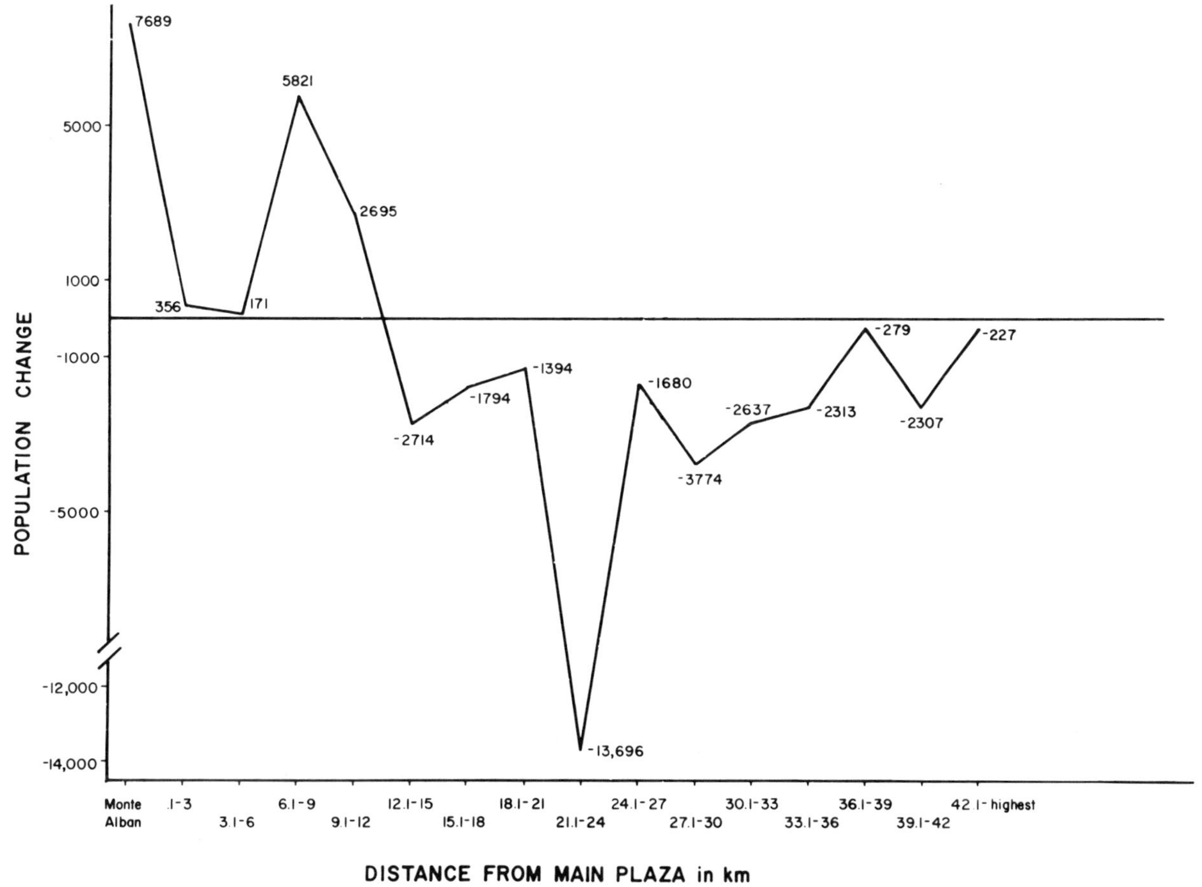

Figure 7-2. Population change by distance from Monte Albán, IIIa to IIIb.

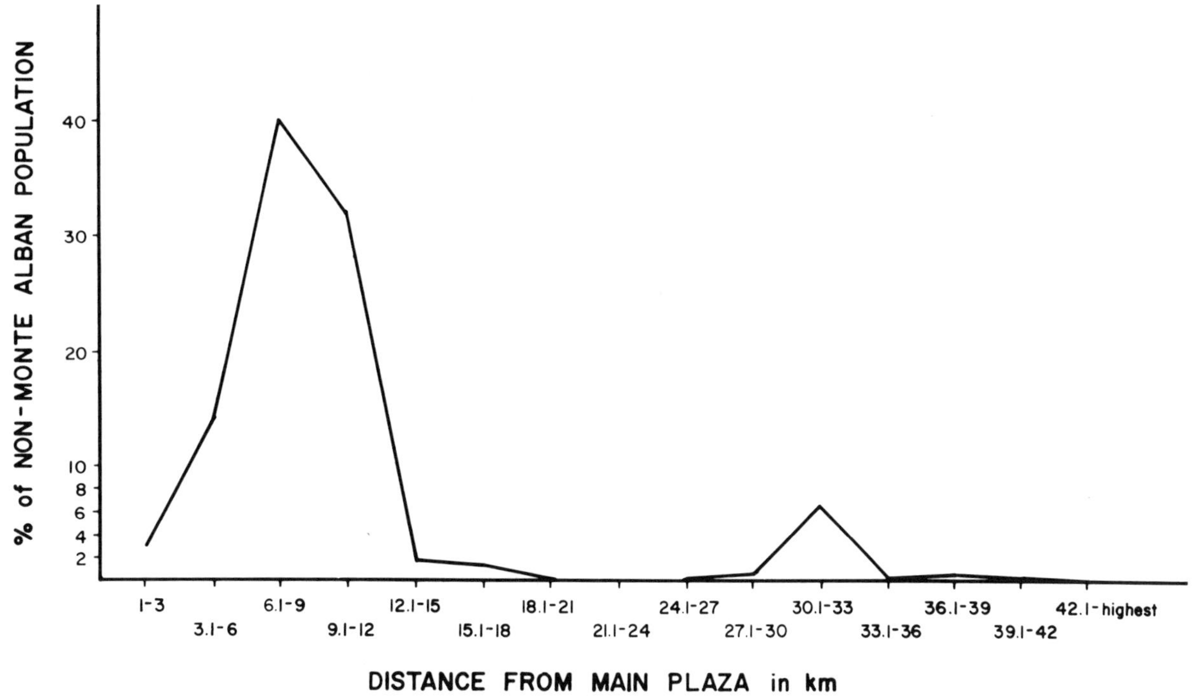

Figure 7-3. Population by distance from Monte Albán, IIIb.

8-18) are the only large sites not situated in the piedmont or higher. In his report on the Central Valley Survey, Kowalewski documents the nature of the IIIb occupation and offers an interpretation. According to him, in Period IIIb, as in Late I:

> . . . all environmental zones from the mountains to the high alluvium were occupied. But a greater percentage of the population resided at higher elevations in the Late Classic: 21% vs. 2% in the mountains and 12% vs. 2% in the high piedmont. One large village (2-9-1), with six platform mounds and a ball court, was located at an elevation of over 2000 m near the western border of the survey area. In fact, the mountain and high piedmont ridges west of San Pedro Ixtlahuaca were unexpectedly productive of habitation sites. Perhaps as many as 2000 people were living in the area. Except for the main ridge at 2-9-1, none of these sites were densely occupied. Habitational debris was found to be very sparse, but persistently scattered along the ridge tops in places where soil deposits are deepest and the hilltops relatively wide and gently sloping, so that the sites tended to be strung out in a linear, branching fashion (as at 2-9-37,53,114, and others).
>
> It is interesting to speculate about what circumstances would make this mountainous zone favorable for habitation in IIIb, when the only previous occupations were a few tiny sites in Late Monte Albán I. The area is distinctly unfavorable for agriculture today, and it was in the past (Kirkby 1973:Fig. 52). The hilltops might have been easily defended locations, but the highly dispersed nature of the settlements and the lack of any archaeological evidence for fortification suggest that defense was not a consideration.
>
> I propose as an alternative hypothesis that people living in the mountains and high piedmont in the western part of the survey area were involved heavily in procuring and moving mountain products to meet the demands of a growing population at Monte Albán. Without the support of a valley floor economic base, such a heavy occupation of this area . . could not have existed. Copal, wild flowers, game, fruits, and nuts were probably trekked out of the western mountains in appreciable quantities, but perhaps the most important product was wood: pine, oak, and mesquite for charcoal, roof beams, and the huge amounts of firewood necessary for lime plaster manufacture, cooking, and heating.
>
> Several objections might be raised to this hypothesis. The demand for mountain products existed long before Monte Albán IIIb (see Flannery, 1976b: 105-111), so why was it not until that time that the area was heavily occupied? This may be answered in several ways. First, in prior times mountain resources may have been obtained on an individual household or individual community basis, while mesquite firewood was available on the slopes of Monte Albán itself and quite possibly in as-yet uncleared sections of the lower and middle piedmont closer to the Valley floor. The low hills within 3 km to the west and south of Monte Albán, for instance, are now barren and eroded, but may have supported stands of mesquite before IIIb. Second, it can be argued that the earlier woodcutting close to Monte Albán meant that the energy costs of obtaining wood would have been much higher during IIIb, when population and building activity at Monte Albán increased sharply. Therefore the demand sufficient to support large numbers of mountain product specialists may not have existed before that time.
>
> It might also be asked why Monte Albán sought mountain resources from the west, while the same products grew in the mountains at comparable or even closer distances to the northeast and east. I think the answer to this might be that the latter mountainous areas lie on the opposite bank of the Rio Atoyac, which during a good part of the year is a hindrance to travel. No such barrier existed on the west. [Kowalewski 1976:480-83]

ADMINISTRATIVE PLACES IN PERIOD IIIb

So far we have emphasized the similarities between IIIb and Late I. Now we will turn to some of the differences. In IIIb Monte Albán clearly continued as the region's highest-ranking center. It reaches its all-time population high and its maximum in terms of architectural complexity and scale (CBA, passim; Blanton 1978), but the spatial arrangement of other sites with mounds is unlike that of any prior period, including Late I. Not only was the piedmont in the southern district largely abandoned, but so also was the alluvium in the south. Sta. Ana Tlapacoyan (3-9-70), for example, a site with a history of occupation stretching well back into the Formative, was much reduced in size compared with its IIIa maximum. The most striking set of abandonments in the alluvium occurred around and including the site of Sta. Inés Yatzeche. The decline of this site, which had been a district capital probably since pre-Rosario times, indicates the Late Classic was a period of fundamental changes in the operation of the regional system. This change includes a reversal of the trend of steady population growth in the alluvium south of Zaachila (Fig. 7-3).

Two other important IIIa alluvial sites, 3-8-65 (N8E6) and Xoxocotlán (2-8-17, N11E7) were no longer occupied by Period IIIb. Zaachila, an alluvial site with a long occupational history, by contrast, not only survived into IIIb, but actually increased substantially in population. IIIb, in fact, is the only period in which we have been able to attempt an estimate of the population size of Zaachila. Earlier periods here are so obscured by the colonial and modern debris that we have had to derive a population estimate from the sizes of other district capitals. Period IIIb is the only period in which the ancient sherds spill out beyond the limits of the modern town, making measurement a possibility. We still have the problem, of course, that we cannot determine the population density of the major part of the site (where it is covered by modern houses). Where we *can* see IIIb debris, the density appears very light and the habitation loci are scattered. Whether the center of the site was similarly scattered or more densely occupied cannot be determined, so we assume the overall density is comparable to that area we have been able to see firsthand. Thus, we may have underestimated the population of the site: we give a figure of over 2000 people–the modern town, which is densely occupied, has a population of 7000 (1970 Census).

At Zaachila we also could not make an effective estimate of the total mound volume. This is in part due

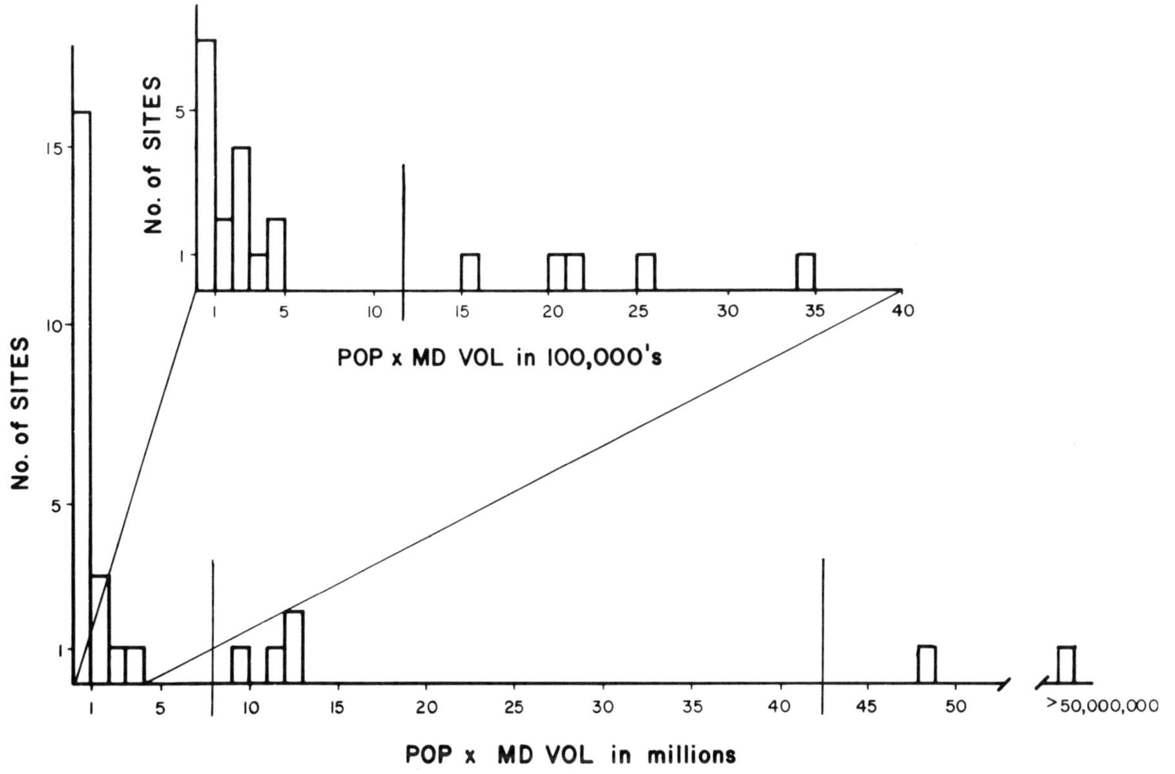

Figure 7-4. Histogram of mound volume times population, IIIb.

to the modern occupation, but estimating the mound volume is further complicated by the fact that the mounds are situated on a batholith in such a way that it is very difficult to determine what proportion of the mounding is natural, and what is cultural. Since IIIb is the largest period on the site, we assume that all the construction was in use at that time (so far as we can tell the Period V occupation of the site was minimal, perhaps consisting only of a few palace-like structures). Following the rough map of Zaachila included in Gallegos (1962,1963), reproduced in Appendix XI, we estimate the mound volume total at over 50,000 cubic meters.

Figure 7-4 is the histogram of values of mound volumes times population estimates for sites other than Monte Albán. Although the capital is not included in this figure, we can put it into perspective. The values for the two district capitals, Zaachila and Ixtlahuaca (2-9-63, N12E4), are in the vicinity of 10^7 or 10^8, while a rough estimate for Monte Albán puts it at about 2.4×10^{10}. Figure 7-5 shows the locations of the administrative places we have identified based on the histogram (and see Table 7-1). Below the two district capitals already mentioned is a group of rank-3 sites including 2-9-1, etc. (N12E4), Cuilapan (3-9-8-18, N10E5), Noriega (3-9-26, N10E6), and Rancho Tejas (3-9-62,63, N4E6). Within this latter class, two of the sites (Cuilapan and Rancho Tejas) lack formal architecture in IIIb, so they are indicated in the figure with distinct symbols. For this period, as in the other periods, we are unable to evaluate the importance or significance of the architectural differences.

Finally, two groups of lower-ranking administrative places have been identified from the histogram (Fig. 7-4). One of these, at 3-9-65 (N3E4), may be an analog of the hypothesized Late I garrison at 3-6-105 (N5E4) (Appendix I, Part 2). Like 3-6-105, this site is situated on the very top of the highest mountain in that area, affording distant views in all directions. A small mound is present, as well as terraces and two defensive walls. Unfortunately, the ceramic assemblage is so shoddy we are unclear as to whether both IIIb and IV are present, or only Period IV. If we are correct in attributing the site to both periods, then we may have evidence that the southern terminus of the Valley of Oaxaca was the approximate boundary of the political unit centered at Monte Albán. Such a garrison could have functioned in protecting the system's southern

Table 7-1. Central-Place Summary, Period IIIb

SITE	POPULATION	MOUND VOLUME m^3	RANK
2-1, etc.	1677	5522	3
2-29, 30	221	1478	5
2-32	17	700	5
2-39	339	1320	5
2-63	1655	29,115	2
2-92-100	869	187	5
2-114	103	149	5
3-9, etc.	839	15,179*	3
3-21, 22	53	38,353*	4
3-25	59	232*	5
3-26	270	47,512*	3
3-27-29	120	20,918	4
3-31	2135	?	2
3-32	289	7351*	4
3-34	17	15,283*	5
3-48	17	15,827*	5
3-49	30	6401*	5
3-51	97	16,172*	4
3-52	137	24,948*	4
3-57	17	3421*	5
3-59, 60	35	6220*	5
3-61	7	1456*	5
3-62, 63	1215	9436	3
3-65	53	4914*	5
3-68, 47	31	14,363*	5
3-70	7	7612*	5

*Index

boundary. The peculiar placement of the site at Rancho Tejas, away from the other large sites, also can be interpreted in these terms. That is, it could have been an outpost near the region's edge, placed for the purposes of boundary defense. We will no doubt be able to evaluate such ideas with more certainty than now once we have completed the survey of the Ocotlán subregion.

One class of sites with mounds was found only in IIIb. These are isolated mounds with little resident population (Fig. 7-5). All are located in the congested Central zone. Kowalewski (1976) suggested these may have been boundary markers demarcating the territorial limits of local social, political, or economic units. If this interpretation can be supported, they may constitute evidence that in this heavily-occupied zone disputes over land were so serious they resulted in the establishment of means of boundary identification more formal than anything we have noted earlier in the sequence.

The layout of the estimated administrative boundaries is also indicated in Figure 7-5. We have identified a southern district centered on Rancho Tejas, a central district centered on Zaachila, but also containing Cuilapan and Noriega, a mountain district west of Monte Albán centered on Ixtlahuaca, and a Monte Albán district. For Late I, we suggested the numerous piedmont sites within the Monte Albán district were administered directly from the capital, since there was virtually no architectural evidence for administration apart from Monte Albán. The center, in other words, had a direct role in agricultural production in its immediate hinterland. By IIIa, this was no longer the case: such administration was by that time emanating from secondary centers. The latter situation also largely characterizes IIIb. Although the IIIb pattern was one involving a renewed round of agricultural development near Monte Albán, it appears to have been administered primarily from secondary and tertiary centers such as Ixtlahuaca, 2-9-1, etc., and Cuilapan. Following the IIIa pattern, Monte Albán in IIIb was probably oriented in part to regional boundary maintenance and diplomacy. The capital must have had functions in addition to these, however. Otherwise, how can we explain why it grew so much from IIIa to IIIb?

As we know it so far, the Late Classic regional system was of a smaller spatial scale than the Early Classic system had been. The Late Classic system was also simpler than it had been in IIIa. Fewer districts were present, and the hierarchy of central places was simpler. In spite of this smaller scale and more simplicity, however, we feel the evidence should be interpreted to mean the IIIb regional system was more highly centralized than its immediate predecessor. One bit of evidence favoring this interpretation is the return, in IIIb, to the extreme primacy in size-rank relationships, after a period nearer to log-normality in Period IIIa (Fig. 7-6). Monte Albán, in other words, was unexpectedly large in IIIb. Although the final word on this awaits the completion of the regional survey, as of now we will suggest that in IIIb a larger proportion of the region's total central place functions were concentrated in the one center than had been the case in IIIa.

The disposition of secondary centers is also indicative of a highly centralized IIIb system. Recall the suggestion made by Steponaitis (1978) that in highly

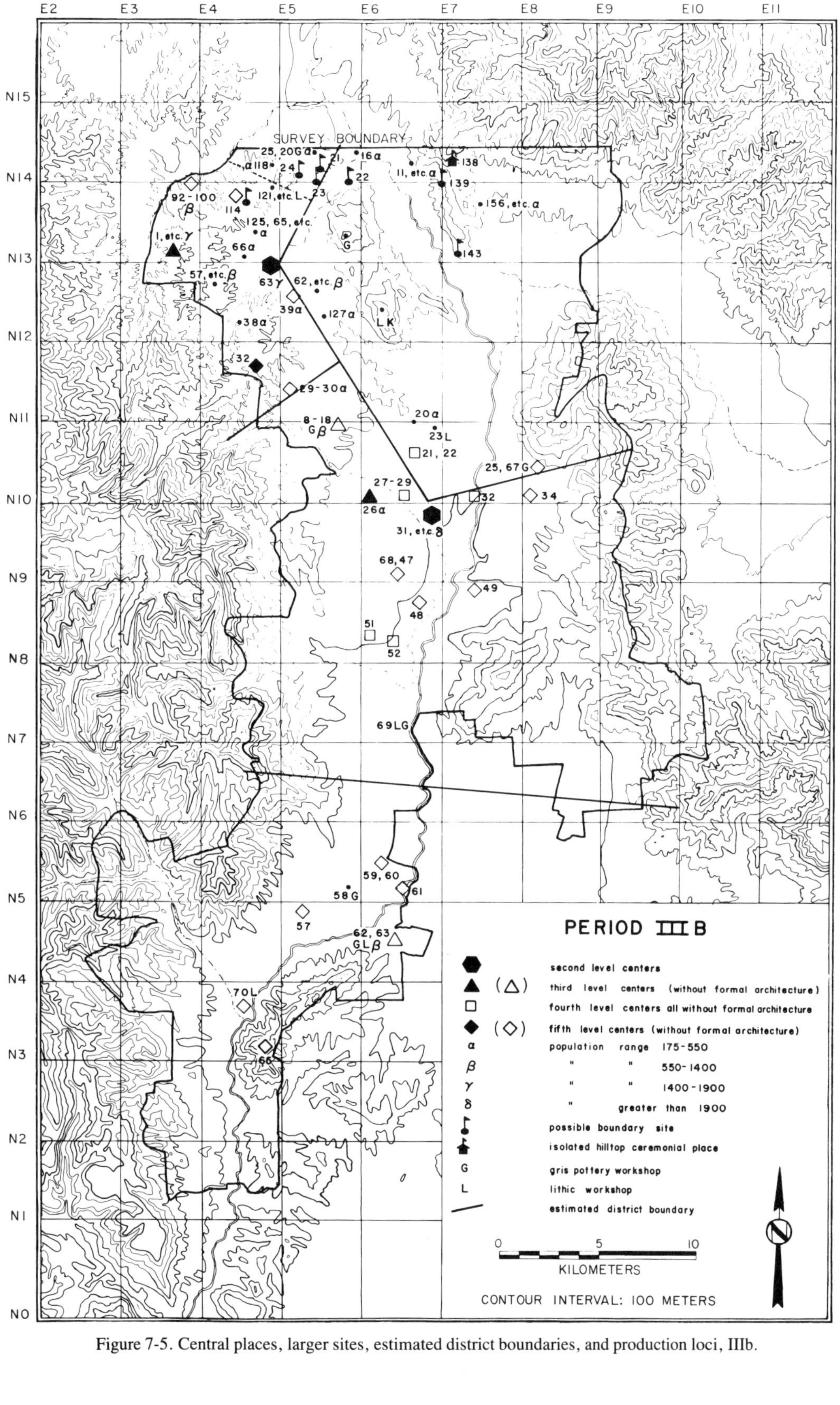

Figure 7-5. Central places, larger sites, estimated district boundaries, and production loci, IIIb.

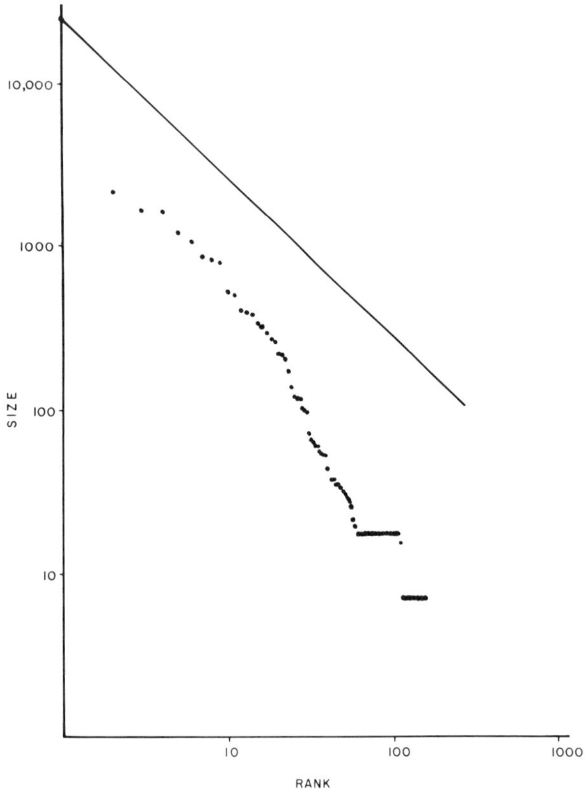

Figure 7-6. Rank-size graph, IIIb. The line is log-normal as calculated from the size of the rank-1 center.

centralized regional systems the linkages between the largest center and secondary centers are more important (and therefore more costly) than the linkages between secondary centers and the communities they administer. The optimum location for secondary centers in such a situation is close to the capital and away from the demographic center of gravity of their own districts. They are, in a sense, "pulled" toward the capital, interposed between their administrative districts and the main center. Except for the site at Rancho Tejas (which we have provisionally identified as a military outpost), this kind of "pulling-in" of secondary centers seems to have been characteristic of IIIb. In such a centralized system, Zaachila (and to a lesser extent Cuilapan and Noriega) would have been ideal places to administer the entire Valle Grande; Ixtlahuaca would have been ideally located for the administration of the area to the west of Monte Albán; and the Cerro de Atzompa (N13E5) would have been an ideal place for the administration of the area north of Monte Albán. If the latter interpretation makes sense, then Atzompa should be considered a district capital rather than as part of Monte Albán. Roughly speaking, it would fit into the district capital size range, with a population times mound volume of roughly 2.5×10^8 (with a total population of 3692).

PERIOD IIIb: INTERACTION POTENTIAL MEASURES

The interaction potential (*IP*) measures provide another window for viewing the IIIb regional system. Again, three measures were made–the first involving sites in the upper 10% of population size, and the usual administrative measures. Surprisingly, the total *IP* for the larger sites, amounting to 10,228,121 *IP* "units", is larger than the total for the comparable IIIa measure (which amounts to 6,309,508). This means that although IIIb was a smaller regional system, by comparison with the preceding period, it was nonetheless a system with a high *IP*, mostly "packed" into a small area in high density fashion. Monte Albán's share of this total *IP* (77%) for Period IIIb is higher than it had been in IIIa (48%), adding some confirmation to our suggestion that the IIIb system was more focused on the center than it had been in IIIa.

The measures of *IP* for the administrative sites also reflect the relatively high degree of centrality of the Late Classic regional system. First, the amount of *IP* between tertiary centers is negligible compared with the *IP* they have with their district capitals, and the same is true with respect to the *IP* between district capitals compared with their *IP* with Monte Albán. This is indicative of a system much more vertically organized than the IIIa system–that is, more flows of energy and material probably existed between centers and their next-highest-order neighbors than between centers of equivalent rank. For IIIa, the total *IP* for first nearest neighbors for the district capitals amounted to 11% of the *IP* of these same places with Monte Albán. In IIIb, the comparable value is only .9%.

Another facet of the relative centrality of the IIIb system is illustrated by the *IP* measures. In IIIa, most of the larger sites have evidence for administrative functions *in situ*, in the form of mounded buildings. Thus, for this period the first measure of administrative *IP* is equal to 85% of the *IP* among the larger sites. By IIIb, a number of large sites exist without any architectural evidence for administrative functions. In this case, then, the *IP* among administrative places using the first administrative measure amount to only 19% of the *IP* among the larger sites. In IIIb, we would argue, these larger sites would have been administered either directly from Monte Albán or from secondary centers like Ixtlahuaca and 2-9-1, etc. IIIb administration, in other words, had more tendency than before to be concentrated in a few places. In IIIa, in contrast, we feel there had been more in the way of local administration.

PRODUCTION/DISTRIBUTION IN PERIOD IIIb

Feinman's analysis of the IIIb pottery (Chapter 10) points to an increase in the degree of standardization in ceramic production from IIIa to IIIb. This, we think, may indicate even more administrative "tampering" with systems of production and distribution in the Late Classic as compared with the Early Classic. The average of the production step indices for the IIIb categories is the lowest we have seen in the sequence so far (Table 10-5). IIIb is also the period with the lowest number of types per site that we have seen to this point (Tables 6-2 and 7-2).

Table 7-2. Mean Number of Types per Site. Numbers in Parentheses are the Percentage Each Value Represents of the Period's Total Number of Types

	IIIa (33 types)	IIIb (22 types)
all centers	11.75 (36)	6.4 (29)
all non-admin. places	4.8 (14)	3.5 (16)
non-admin.> 100	11.75 (36)	4 (19)
non-admin < 100	4.3 (13)	3.2 (14)
district capitals	18.7 (57)	8.5 (39)
one rank below district capitals	16.3 (49.5)	10.5 (48)
two ranks below district capitals	8.4 (26)	7 (32)

Again in IIIb, as in Late I and IIIa, our evidence indicates that sites closest to Monte Albán were most directly keyed into a system of production and distribution that was supplying them with very few types, as well as highly standardized types (Fig. 7-7). This graph, which shows the number of types per site class and distance from Monte Albán, clearly indicates that a number of communities near the capital had very simple ceramic assemblages. Most sites in the area with three or fewer types are within 12 kilometers of Monte Albán. Many of the households in this zone apparently had access to little more than the minimum number of ceramic types that a household would need for its basic cooking, storage, and food-serving. Typically, such a minimal assemblage, common in the Central area, would consist of plain G-35 bowls, G-1 or G-3 *ollas* (storage vessels very much like the G-35 bowls), perhaps a *sahumador* and/or a G-35 with supports, and little else. This is quite a contrast with the variability in form and in decoration of assemblages from Early I or II sites. Not only are the IIIb assemblages limited in the number of types, but also the G-35's in Period IIIb are so poorly made they probably broke, cracked, and leaked more often than would the better-made pottery of other periods, not to mention that these ubiquitous Late Classic vessels have almost no surface treatment and look terrible.

The locations of the ceramic producing sites support the idea that the state is somehow involved in production. Most of the ceramic production took place at Monte Albán proper, Atzompa, Cuilapan, and possibly Rancho Tejas (Appendix IX). The latter two sites lack formal administrative architecture, but the presence of mounded buildings probably indicates high-level functions of some kind. Three sites have evidence for ceramic production without any mounded buildings, but two of these are only isolated residences or very small hamlets (3-9-69, N7E6, and 3-9-58, N5E5). Only one intermediate size site has evidence for ceramic production in the absence of any mounded architecture (2-9-20,25, N14E5).

In our Late I and IIIa chapters, we argued that the pronounced differences in numbers of types in administrative sites contrasted with non-administrative sites indicated more flow of pottery through administrative channels. Populations of sites with administrative functions, we reasoned, had access to a wider range of goods because administrators were well connected to the source of supply. Given our argument here that the IIIb system was highly centralized and that there was much administrative involvement in production and distribution, we would predict a similarly marked disparity in numbers of types between those sites with and those sites without evidence for administrative functions. Such a disparity exists, but it is not as marked in IIIb as it had been in Late I or IIIa (Tables 6-2 and 7-2). In fact, the IIIb values are more in line with the less-administered periods Early I and II (Fig. 7-8). This seems at first glance to challenge our interpretations based on other data, but in reality we believe it does not. This is because in IIIb, the values of types per site for *both* administrative and non-administrative sites were very low (except for Monte Albán, which has all of the 22 types). This means that even the populations

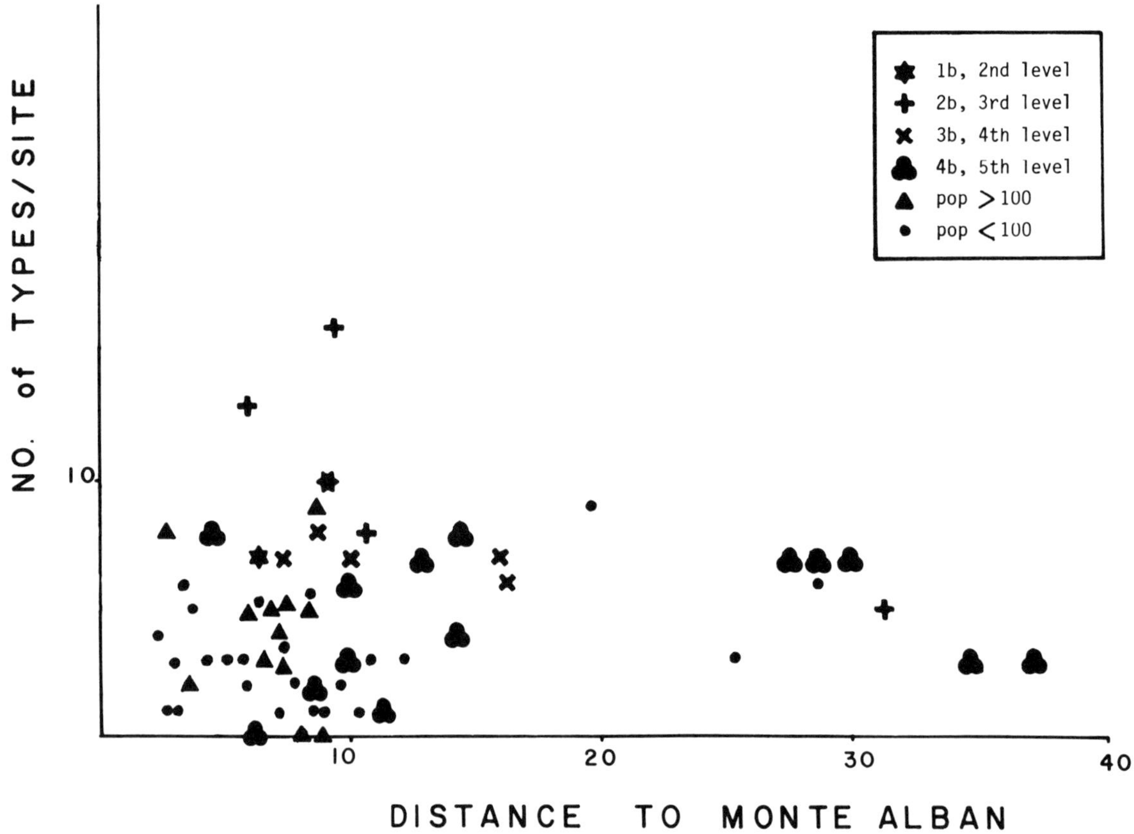

Figure 7-7. Types per site by site category and distance from Monte Albán, IIIb. The data are found in Appendix VIII.

of the district capitals had access to only a small range of types. The values of types per site could simply not be much lower for the non-administrative sites since, as they stand, they represent close to the minimum number of categories needed for basic domestic activities. Even the populations of administrative centers (other than Monte Albán), however, were getting little more than this minimal variability in ceramics. The IIIb system may have been so centralized that only the population of the capital itself could obtain more than close to the minimum number, but the total number of types even at the capital was only 22.

PERIOD IIIb: CONCLUSIONS

The major changes associated with the reduction in scale of the Valley of Oaxaca system from IIIa to IIIb included:

1) Population decline, due primarily to the collapse of the piedmont system in the Valle Grande, and the abandonment of other large areas including the alluvium around Sta. Inés Yatzeche and the area east and southeast of Monte Albán.

2) The initiation of a round of administered development of the piedmont and mountains west of Monte Albán.

3) A "pulling inward" of district capitals to positions closer to Monte Albán. This, in combination with the reassertion of a primate mode in size-rank relations is indicative of a more centralized regional system.

4) A decline in the quality of ceramics and in the numbers of types per site, indicative, we feel, of more standardization in ceramic production than we have observed in any prior period, and indicative of more administrative control of ceramic production and distribution than we have seen in the sequence so far.

In the last chapter, we argued that the IIIa developments were unstable because of rapid population growth in environmentally limited piedmont settings, coupled with the necessarily increased administrative costs of achieving a high degree of regional coherence. The latter process, we argued, may have resulted in the growth of a system so tightly integrated it became

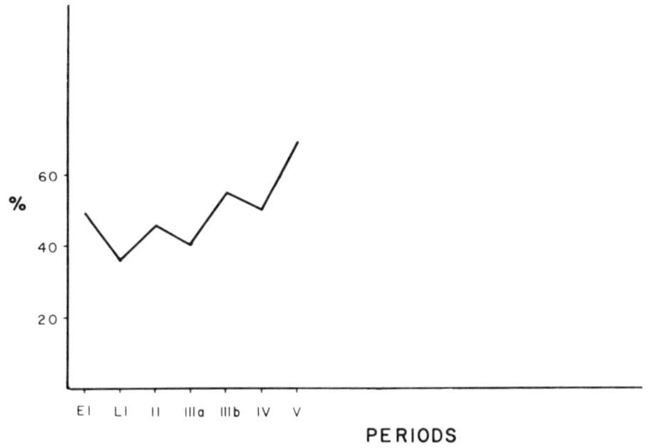

Figure 7-8. Types per site (average) of non-administrative sites as a percentage of the average number of types per site of sites with administrative functions.

"hypercoherent." The abandonment of the alluvial zone in and around Sta. Inés Yatzeche and Sta. Ana Tlapacoyan may stand as evidence for the importance of hypercoherence in explaining the nature of the transition from IIIa to IIIb. This alluvial zone had been occupied continuously and relatively densely from the very earliest ceramic phases, and, we concluded earlier, may have remained relatively autonomous and unchanged through time *vis à vis* the remainder of the regional system. The collapse of this long-lived local system after the IIIa maximum in population size may reflect the fact that in IIIa this local system became so firmly tied to the larger regional system that when the larger system collapsed, the alluvial communities by necessity collapsed also. Exactly why this would have happened is not clear given the paucity of data. The contrast with the transition from Late I to II is striking. That was also a period of major reorganization in the valley, but the Sta. Inés area was not particularly affected. Perhaps in IIIa the Valle Grande communities on the alluvium were coaxed by the state into investing heavily in the development of the southern piedmont. Earlier they had always been able to avoid this kind of entanglement. When the piedmont strategy ultimately failed, it pulled the traditional alluvial communities down too.

The abandonment of the area east of Monte Albán also presents a series of knotty problems which can't be resolved until we complete the survey of the valley (if then). Perhaps, as Kowalewski argued, this area may have been excluded from a symbiotic network focused on Monte Albán because of the problems the river poses for transportation. On the other hand, this area seems to have been effectively tied into a Monte Albán system in prior periods (e.g., Late I). An alternative explanation for the abandonment of this eastern zone is that it was at that time a shatter-zone–a militarily contested area between Monte Albán and an autonomous, competing Tlacolula arm. If so, and we should know this once the Tlacolula survey is complete, then we are dealing with a Monte Albán system in IIIb much more reduced in areal extent and total population than we have previously thought possible. It is possible that Monte Albán's control was largely limited to the western part of the Central zone and the northern part of the Valle Grande (eventually, we will also know more about how the Etla arm fit into the Monte Albán system; Varner's preliminary survey indicates a large population).

By the subsequent Period IV, the Main Plaza at Monte Albán was no longer in use. Its buildings were beginning to collapse (CBA:passim). Thus, the political institution that had been the focus of government in the Valley of Oaxaca for roughly 1200 years dissolved. In the next chapter, we document the nature of the regional organization that replaced the one that had been for so long focused on Monte Albán and offer some suggestions for why such a venerable institution failed.

Chapter 8

THE POSTCLASSIC

INTRODUCTION

From the founding of Monte Albán to its collapse, the two most prominent features of the Valley of Oaxaca regional system were: 1) a hierarchy of central places capped by a center containing the monumental Main Plaza structures, the center of regional government during that 1200 year period; 2) a regional system that was dynamic rather than stable. Within the 1200 years of Monte Albán's preeminence, five ceramic periods are identifiable, each with its own distinct settlement pattern and population density.

Our argument has been that these two features of the "Monte Albán system" were interrelated. The governmental institution centered at the Main Plaza was capable of initiating periods of rapid population growth and piedmont development cycles–but, in each case the result was overextension leading to collapse and reorganization. The failure of the IIIb system took Monte Albán down with it, and from that point on, new modes of regional organization were present in the valley. The major points of dissimilarity between these and the earlier systems are the following. 1) No center that was precisely the functional equivalent of Early I to IIIb Monte Albán ever developed in the Postclassic. The most obvious evidence is the fact that no feature comparable to the Main Plaza in scale or format was ever built after Monte Albán's demise. In fact, in the Postclassic generally there was much less construction of mounded buildings–of all types–compared with the Monte Albán periods (Fig. 8-1). Apparently, the governmental systems of the Postclassic did not have as much access to labor for the construction of buildings as they had in prior periods; and secondly, there was no central focus of regional government of the sort that had existed in the Main Plaza complex, although other factors may have been at work. In the Postclassic, for example, labor costs might have increased, or labor may have been differently organized or perhaps more productively employed elsewhere. An additional possibility is that the kind of signalling that goes on through the medium of monumental construction was no longer necessary or at least no longer as important. 2) The Postclassic was a period of over 800 years, in which only one ceramic transition is readily discernible. The Period V ceramic assemblage lasts for nearly 600 of those years. We suggest that the conservatism in ceramic styles indicates a more stable regional system in the Postclassic. It could be argued, of course, that major shifts *which we are unable to detect in the absence of finer chronological control* occurred *within* Period V. We have argued, however, that the changes observable in the ceramic assemblages of the Monte Albán periods were consequences of changing political and economic organization. The relative absence of change in the Late Postclassic ceramics, then, we hold, is strong evidence that this period was comparatively stable.

Following our earlier argument, we suggest that these distinctive features of the Postclassic are interrelated. We hypothesize that the relative stability of the Postclassic was due to a large degree to the fact that not only was there less governmental control overall, but also that no single, centralized source of governmental control was capable of the massive reorganization of energy flows necessary to effect major changes in the

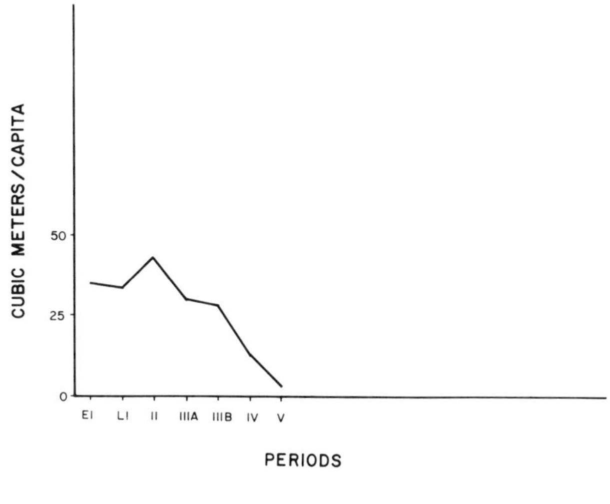

Figure 8-1. Cubic meters of mound fill (estimated) per capita, Early I through V.

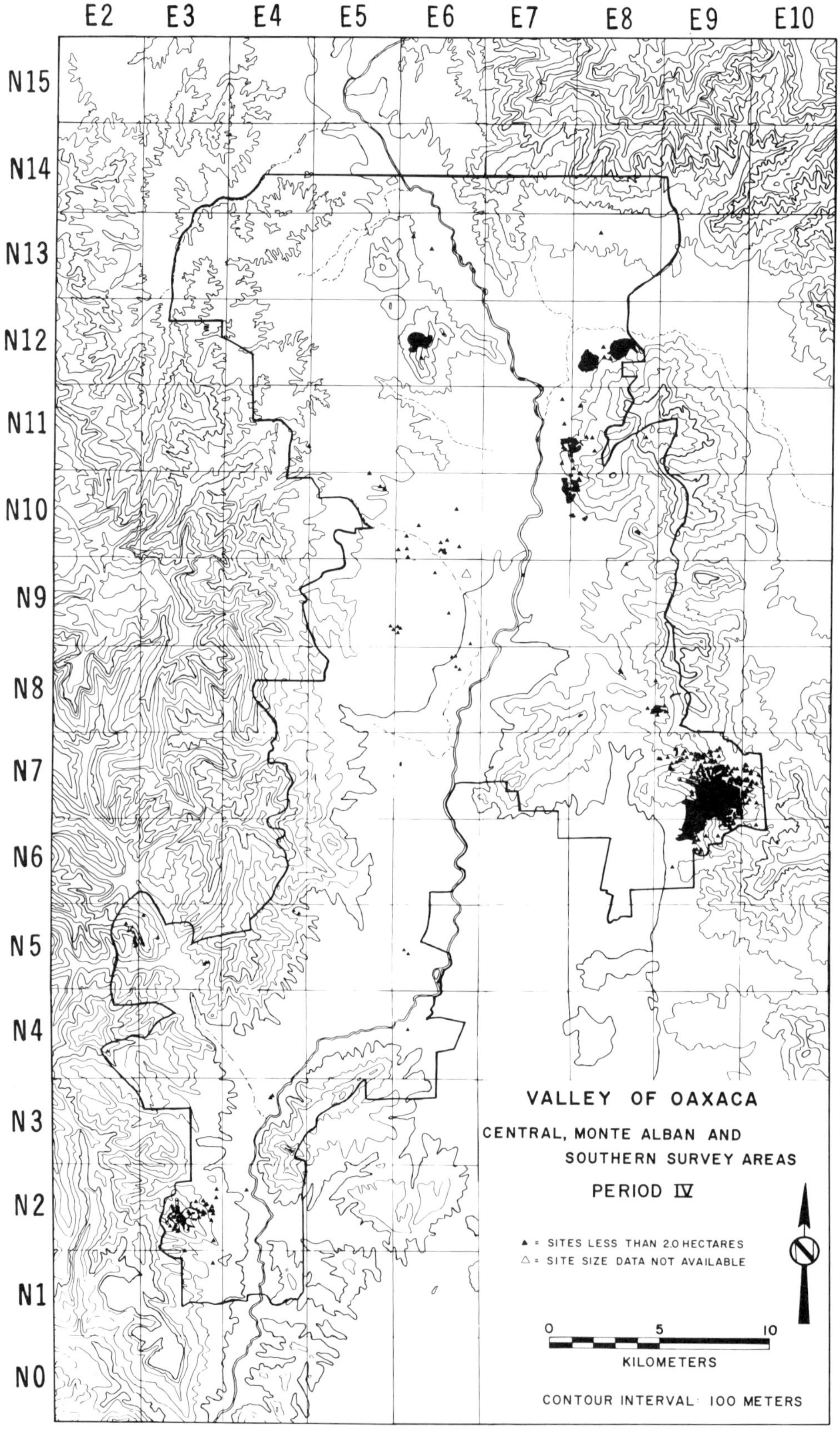

Figure 8-2. Settlements of Period IV.

region's settlement pattern, population density, administrative organization, and system of production and distribution. We argue that the nature of regional organization in Period V is a reflection, in large part, of numerous individual decisions made at lower levels in the organizational hierarchy. During the Monte Albán periods, by contrast, we feel that to a much greater degree the form of the regional system was the product of decision-making at the highest governmental levels. Thus, the Valley of Oaxaca archaeological sequence presents us with an opportunity to explore another theoretically interesting problem: comparing the properties of centralized versus decentralized regional organization.

POSTCLASSIC SETTLEMENT PATTERNS AND POPULATION TRANSITIONS

The Period IV settlement pattern in the survey area (Fig. 8-2) is dominated by a series of large sites separated by extensive tracts of unused land. We interpret this to indicate the presence of a series of autonomous, competing political units, each surrounded by contested, unused land–a "Balkanization" of the regional system. Steve Kowalewski describes the Period IV occupation of the Central Survey Zone as follows:

> During the Central Valley survey, no sites were found with pottery complexes like that of Lambityeco, a Period IV site studied by Paddock (Paddock, Mogor and Lind 1968). However, two spatially separate groups of sites in the survey area may have had Monte Albán IV occupation.
>
> 1. In the north and west some of the Late Classic sites could have persisted into the Early Postclassic without any appreciable ceramic changes, especially if supplies from the Cacaotepec (2-9-20, 25)-Atzompa manufacturing centers were never jeopardized. Here one might make a case for ceramic continuities between the "*gris-cremosa*" wares of the Classic, distributed from Cacaotepec-Atzompa, and an obviously Postclassic sandy cream complex. The latter consists of utility wares and finer "Huitzo Polished Red-on-Cream" vessels (Paddock 1966:208). Sherds of these types are found mainly on the western part of the central area, often on the same sites as earlier forms of G-3M's (a usually Postclassic gray ware), and in many places in the Etla Valley. They are not found at Monte Albán, and are very rare in the Tlacolula Valley. The red-on-cream pottery is very similar to that from Nochixtlán (Spores 1972), but when it was first made and how long it lasted in the Valley of Oaxaca is not known. Tentatively I would suggest a marked decline in population at the beginning of Monte Albán IV in the northwestern part of the Valley, with perhaps some persistence in small settlements in the western part of the central area, and the concentration of remaining groups in the Etla Valley around several fortified hilltop locations.
>
> 2. Another group of possible Monte Albán IV settlements was located in the hills just east of the confluence of the Rio Salado and the Atoyac. Fourteen of these settlements were less than 3 hectares in extent, but there were larger sites of 38.4,84.7, and 103.4 hectares. The latter is the site of Loma de la Montura (2-10-2, N12E8), initially described by Bernal. The occupation is spread over the top and sides of a high hill at the edge of the valley floor. There are 133 residential terraces, and a separate administrative precinct with considerable mounded architecture at the crest of the hill. Analysis of the traffic patterns here shows that the formal and rather tight access controls were directed toward the site's own population, rather than being part of a system of fortifications against military threats from the outside. Loma de la Montura, with its satellites, may be an example of the smaller, localized polities that arose after the balkanization of the Late Classic Monte Albán state. The impressive public buildings at San Luis Beltrán (2-10-1 N13E8) excavated by Bernal and re-surveyed in 1974 are still not adequately dated. If they pertain to Monte Albán IV, as Bernal suggested (1965:807), then the site might have been linked to this group. (It might be noted, however, that the same area covered by this proposed Monte Albán IV pattern had few IIIb sites, suggesting that the occupation began while Monte Albán was still going strong. This possibility cannot be dismissed with the data at hand.)
>
> Early Postclassic components in this area are defined by the preponderance of undecorated gray wares, including G-35's and early G-3M's distinct from the pottery of Monte Albán and Lambityeco, and perhaps different in some respects from the Postclassic material from Yagul and Cuilapan. The closest parallel may be the G-3 and G-35 to G-3M-and G-35M continuity suggested by Brockington's work at Miahuatlan (1973). All of this indicates the existence of several ceramic production centers with separate distribution spheres: one near Atzompa, an early one at Lambityeco, perhaps one at Coyotepec, and possibly a few others. [Kowalewski 1976: 514-17]

Monte Albán continued to be occupied into Period IV (CBA: passim), although it is difficult to identify the precise limits of the occupation. We do know from the excavations of Caso, Bernal, and Acosta that the Main Plaza was not in use, but we cannot be sure which if any other public or elite residential buildings may have been occupied. We have attempted to estimate the site's Period IV occupation by tracing out the limits of occurrence of a known Period IV type, the A-7 (our category 3030). These sherds were found in parts of Monte Albán site subdivisions 2, 4, 6, 7, and 12 (Blanton 1978). Assuming a population density equivalent to that of the prior periods, we estimate a population of 4062.

South of the Central area most of the population in Period IV resided in several large communities, including 3-10-7, etc. (N10E7), Sta. Cruz Mixtepec (3-10-72, etc., N5E2,3), El Choco (3-10-83, etc., N2E3), and Jalieza (3-10-46, etc., N7E9). Our ceramic collections suggest the possibility of some continued occupation of Zaachila into IV, although we were so unsure of this that while in the field we did not assign a site number for this period (N9E6). Since we have no way to determine Zaachila's Period IV population directly, we reasoned that for purposes of our analyses here we could devise a population estimate if we assume that the decline in numbers at the site from

Figure 8-3. Terraces and estimated site boundaries, Period IV Jalieza.

IIIb to IV was proportional to the decline of the rural population in Zaachila's immediate area (squares N10E5,6, N9E5,6, and N8E6). This method gives a Period IV population for the site of 432 people, a figure that must be viewed with considerable suspicion.

El Choco (3-10-83, etc.) reached its maximum extent in Period IV (Fig. A. XI-43,44). Nearly all of its 524 terraces were occupied at this time, so we assume that most of the mounded buildings at the site were in use also. The main group of these structures stretches along the dominant ridge and consists of what appears to be a series of platforms, elite residences, and a ball-court.

By far the largest Period IV site in the survey area is Jalieza (3-10-46, etc.). Fortunately, the IV area of the site is not significantly coterminous with the IIIa and V occupations, so we can view it as essentially a single-component site. Due to its extremely large size (1156 terraces, an area of 4.63 square kilometers, and a population estimated at 16,117), Jalieza becomes the rank-1 center in the survey area for Period IV (Fig. 8-3). The differences between the IIIa occupation and the IV occupation at this site are illustrative of some of the changes in the region associated with the Classic-Postclassic transition. Laura Finsten has summarized these changes as follows:

In the Early Classic (IIIA), Jalieza had a clearly defined administrative area, both topographically and architecturally. Two or three small peaks at the top of the easternmost hill have been extensively modified. The southernmost one has been flattened completely, and has a fairly small mound in one corner of the resulting plaza area. The size of the mound suggests that it probably was not residential in function. A second small peak to the north is joined to the first by a long "saddle", which again takes the form of a plaza, with at least two and possibly three different levels, as well as two small mounds at the southern end directly adjacent to the southern peak. The second peak is occupied by a fully enclosed four mound group which in all likelihood housed the highest status individual(s) at Jalieza. Access to this summit area is extremely difficult from all sides except the eastern, which slopes away relatively gradually . . . . The west and north sides are considerably steeper, but have terraces with generally very well preserved retaining walls in the areas surrounding the summit. These may have functioned in part to regulate access to the administrative area. The southern face, near the top, in many places approaches vertical and is often sheer rock. Our first expedition to the summit was via this route, and we never took it a second time! Needless to say, there were no suitable locations for occupation, and the largest near-horizontal areas were the numerous goat trails which wound through, and incidentally did have sherds on them.

The other mounds in this sector tend to occur just beyond the major break in slope (middle to low piedmont). Several mounds, probably residences of high status individuals, are so situated near the western periphery of the site. Many more are located southeast of the summit. Although there are several potential clusters of mounds there, there are no groups which consist of more than two structures situated on the edges of a patio. All of these again are probably elite residences.

By the Late Classic, the area just described is completely abandoned. There is, in fact, no discernible significant Period IIIb occupation at Jalieza. In the Early Postclassic the locus of occupation shifts to the eastern area of the site, centering around the north-south running ridgeline which forms the eastern Valle Grande boundary . . . .

In Period IV there is no visible administrative core. Instead, a series of elite residential mound groups are strung along the ridgetop at reasonably regular intervals, except for a somewhat denser clustering of mound groups toward the southern end of the ridgeline, and especially on a secondary ridge running east of this part of the main ridge.

At least one mound, and frequently several associated with a patio or plaza, occurs on almost every secondary ridge east of the main one. This, in view of the lack of any apparent administrative core, suggests that in Period IV Jalieza consisted of a series of smaller local subunits each with one or more higher status individuals who may have wielded power within, and perhaps only within, that locality. [Finsten 1978:3-6]

Not only were the Period IV structures at Jalieza more dispersed and more accessible than the IIIa structures, but they were also, on the average, smaller. Thirty-four structures mapped at the site were attributed to IIIa. These total 34,692 m^3, and average 2,040.7 m^3. Thirty-nine mounds were attributed to Period IV. These totalled only 24,257 m^3, and have a mean value of only 621.97 m^3 (Finsten 1978).

Finsten draws the following conclusions based on her analyses of the Jalieza materials:

On the average, elite residences at Jalieza entailed far greater energy expenditures in Period IIIa than in Period IV. This likely indicates a greater command over labour in the Early Classic and may indicate greater "social distance" or social differentiation at this time. The presence in Period IIIa of a small administrative core to which access was limited indicates the presence of a small group of elites with considerably higher status (and power?) than the other residents of the site. This higher centralized administrative level is absent in Period IV. No part of this component is more tightly closed and inaccessible, neither architecturally nor topographically, than any other. Instead, mounds and mound groups are scattered at fairly regular intervals along the tops of the main and secondary ridges, suggesting that Jalieza may have been broken up into a series of small, "locally" controlled subdivisions, similar to the subdivisions defined by Blanton (1978) for Monte Albán in Period IIIb, but without any higher order control administering all of them. Thus the degree of social differentiation appears to be somewhat diminished in Period IV.

Access to the main ridge line is fairly open everywhere from the east, where a tributary stream flows toward the Tlacolula Valley through the easily-travelled middle and upper piedmont slopes. It is again easily accessible on the west, from the floor of the Valle Grande, toward the northern end where the ridge is lowest and the most probable area for a pass into the Tlacolula Valley occurs. The ridge is highest and the slope steepest, rendering access most difficult, on the western face at the southern end. Thus access patterns suggest that no part of the long north-south running ridge enjoyed more limited access than any other, with the possible exception of the southernmost area. This would seem to be the logical place for an administrative centre, if one existed. But as I have already pointed out, although there is a slightly higher density of mound construction in the southern portion of the Period IV component of the site, the bulk of this occurs not on the main ridge top, but on a secondary ridge which adjoins it, and is very readily accessible from the east. [ibid.]

Thus, Jalieza, in microcosm, illustrates some of the more general features of the Classic-Postclassic transition: government on a smaller scale, and less centralized government in the Postclassic. This is evident even when comparing the rank-1 center of IV with the rank-2 center of IIIa.

Along with the breakup of the IIIb regional system, there was some population decline in the survey area, from a IIIb total of 42,587 to 32,436 (Fig. 2-1). Most of the declines occurred in and around Monte Albán, although our ability to monitor this set of changes is somewhat clouded, as Kowalewski (1976) noted, due to the conservatism in ceramic production in the Atzompa-Cacaotepec area. The Valle Grande experienced growth from IIIb to IV, mostly due to the reemergence of large populations at El Choco and Jalieza.

By Period V (Fig. 8-4), the valley's central region had again become the zone of highest population densities and was again the locus of the rank-1 center. The changes were accompanied by overall population growth (although probably at very slow rates, given the vast amount of time involved) (Fig. 2-1 and 4-3). Too, by Period V there was much "filling in" of areas that had been unused during the prior period, probably indicative of a less "Balkanized" regional system.

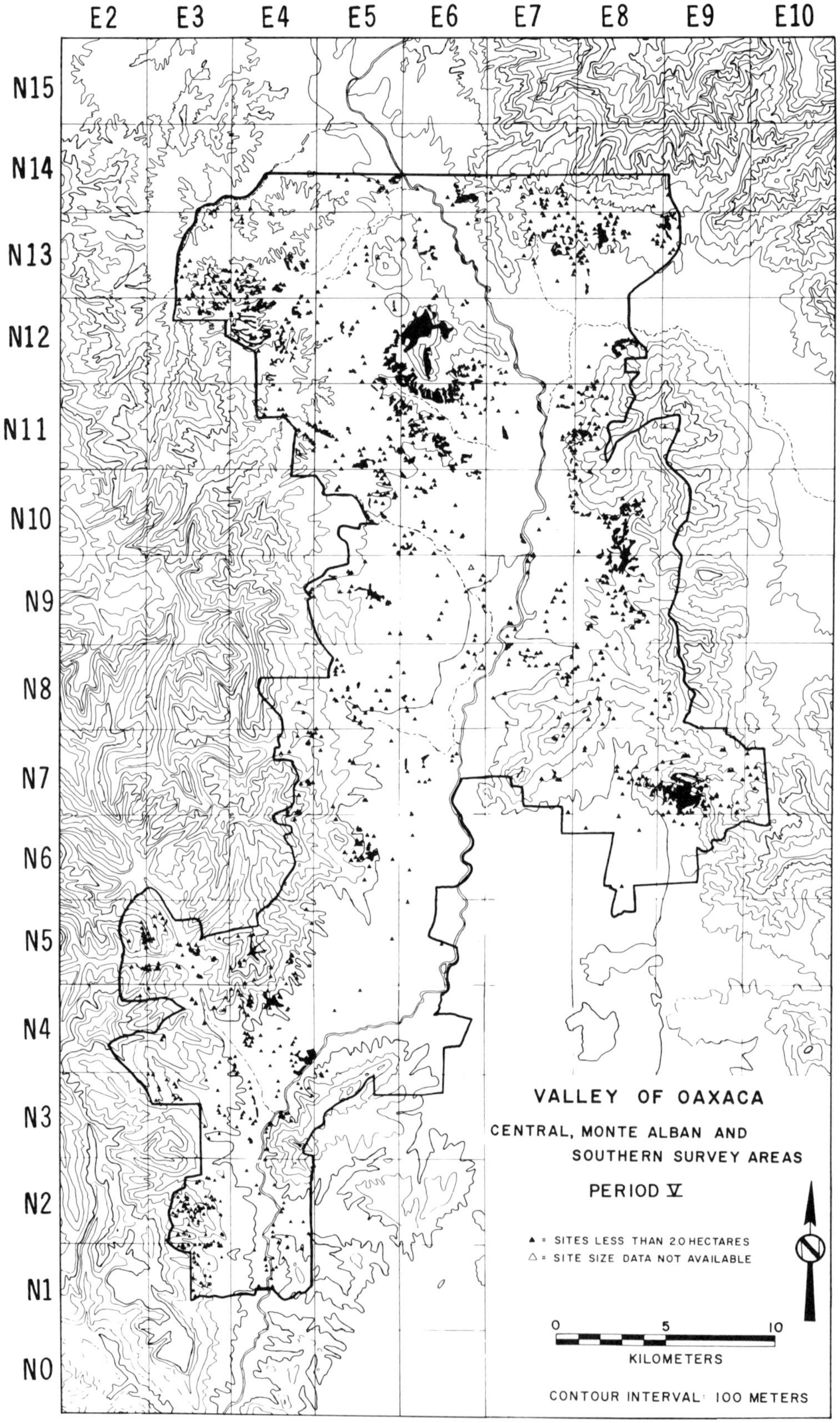

Figure 8-4. Settlements of Period V

There is an important exception to the latter process, however, in the vicinity of squares N5E5,6 and somewhat to the north of these. This break in the Period V settlement may indicate the continuation of a contested political boundary between polities to the north and those to the south and southwest. This isolated southern subregion was not only spatially separated from the remainder of the survey area, but was also distinct from the rest of the Period V areas ceramically. Several ceramic categories found in this southern zone–*cafés* with abundant mica temper (micaceous *cafés*)–are rarely if ever found in other parts of the valley. Fortunately, other V diagnostics, especially the G-3M's, are present, making possible the periodization of sites.

Jalieza (3-11-259) continued into V as a large site (Appendix X; Fig. 8-5), with a total of 690 terraces and an estimated population of 6649. By the Late Postclassic the site was stretched primarily along and just below the site's major east-west trending ridge, still in a good position from the point of view of providing access to both the Ocotlán region and the western portion of the Tlacolula arm, but, on the other hand, generally located at a very high elevation (the view of Monte Albán from the highest part of the site is *very* nice, but it takes considerable time and energy to get up to that point). This location is ideal for defense and is a rather commanding position *vis à vis* the pass to the Tlacolula arm. No mounded buildings were noted within the boundaries of the V site.

Those IV sites with mounds that we noted in the central zone to the east of Monte Albán (2-10-2,5,11, 3-10-7, etc.) were abandoned by Period V. Replacing them was a series of villages, some rather large, lacking any mounded architecture. Two new sites with mounded structures, however, were established in this general area by V–Coyotepec (3-11-58, etc., N10E8), and the smaller site at 2-11-235 (N13E9).

Zaachila was definitely occupied in V, as attested to by the Late Postclassic tombs and elite residences excavated by Gallegos (1962, 1963). Since little Period V pottery was found on or around the site, however, we feel the occupation may have consisted largely of a small group of elite without much total population. We return below to a consideration of the role of the population of Zaachila in the Late Postclassic regional system.

By Period V, Monte Albán was again the rank-1 center in the survey region, with a total population estimated at 13,573. The V occupation here, however, is not at all like the site that had been the rank-1 center for so many other periods. First, the Main Plaza continued to be unused during V, and no new feature was built that could be described as its functional or scale equivalent. In fact, Blanton (1978) doubted that much if any new construction within the boundaries of the ancient capital could be attributed to the Late Postclassic. A second major distinction between Monte Albán in the Late Postclassic and the earlier periods is that the population resident here was no longer compactly situated along the upper slopes of the mountain. Instead, the site consisted of a number of spatially distinct but closely-packed settlement loci extending like a giant "C" from site subdivision 12 to the northeast (Blanton 1978), then west and south along the lower extension of terraces of the earlier periods (but generally within the site's major set of walls), then completing the bottom of the "C" to the south with a string of sites extending along the slopes of the hill, but stretching all the way to the northern outskirts of modern Cuilapan. This large cluster of sites was combined in calculating the final population total for the site following our past practice of uniting sites that, although spatially separated, are situated such that interaction between components would have been very easy. Because the site extends all the way from Monte Albán to Cuilapan, we named the site "Cuiban," a term we will use for the site from this point on.[1]

ADMINISTRATIVE PLACES AND INTERACTION POTENTIALS IN THE POSTCLASSIC

Since we have not completed the survey of the entire Valley of Oaxaca, these comments should be considered to be highly provisional. This is true, of course, for all periods, but applies especially to the Postclassic, given the presence of important sites in areas we have not yet worked, including Lambityeco (Paddock, Mogor, and Lind 1968), Yagul (Bernal and Gamio 1974), and Milta (Caso and Rubín de la Borbolla 1936).

The histograms of mound volume times population for the two Postclassic periods are found in Figures 8-6 and 8-7. Based on breaks in these histograms, we identified the hierarchies of administrative places, then located these on Figures 8-8 and 8-9 (and see Tables 8-1 and 8-2). These figures also include the estimated

[1] "Cuiban" is a term coined to describe the series of settlements of various sizes which, during Monte Albán V, extended from Cuilapan to Monte Albán. It is not the name of a Prehispanic settlement.

Figure 8-5. Terraces and site limits, Period V Jalieza.

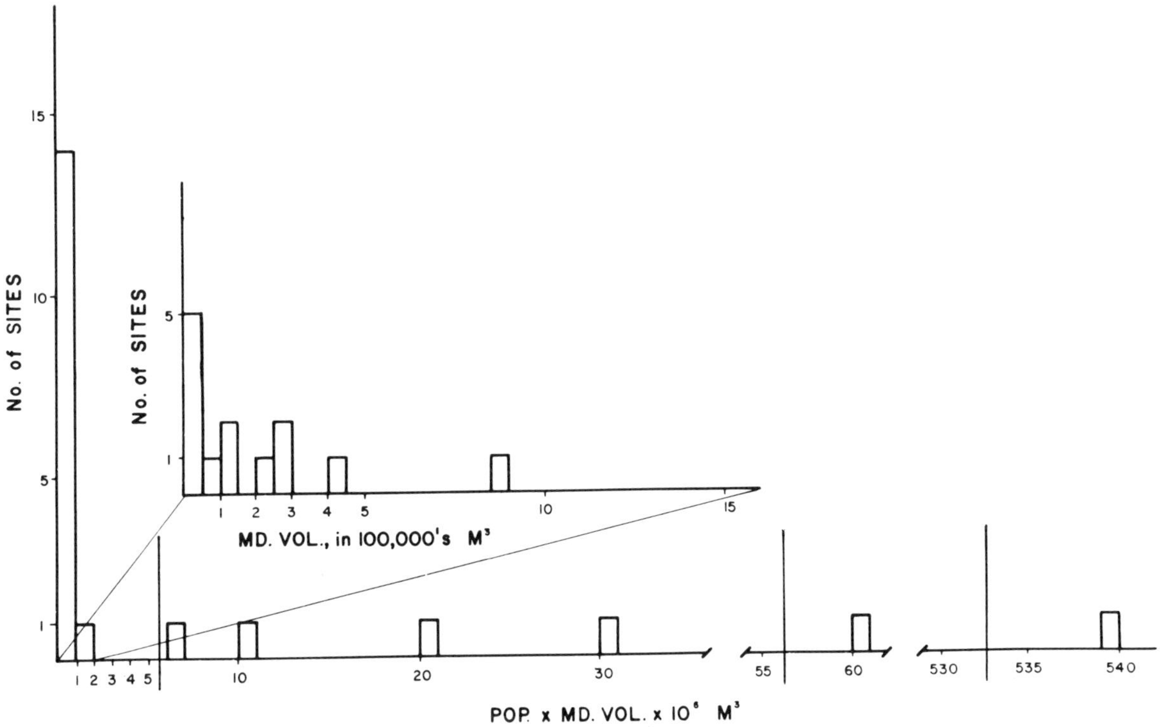

Figure 8-6. Histogram of mound volume times population, Period IV.

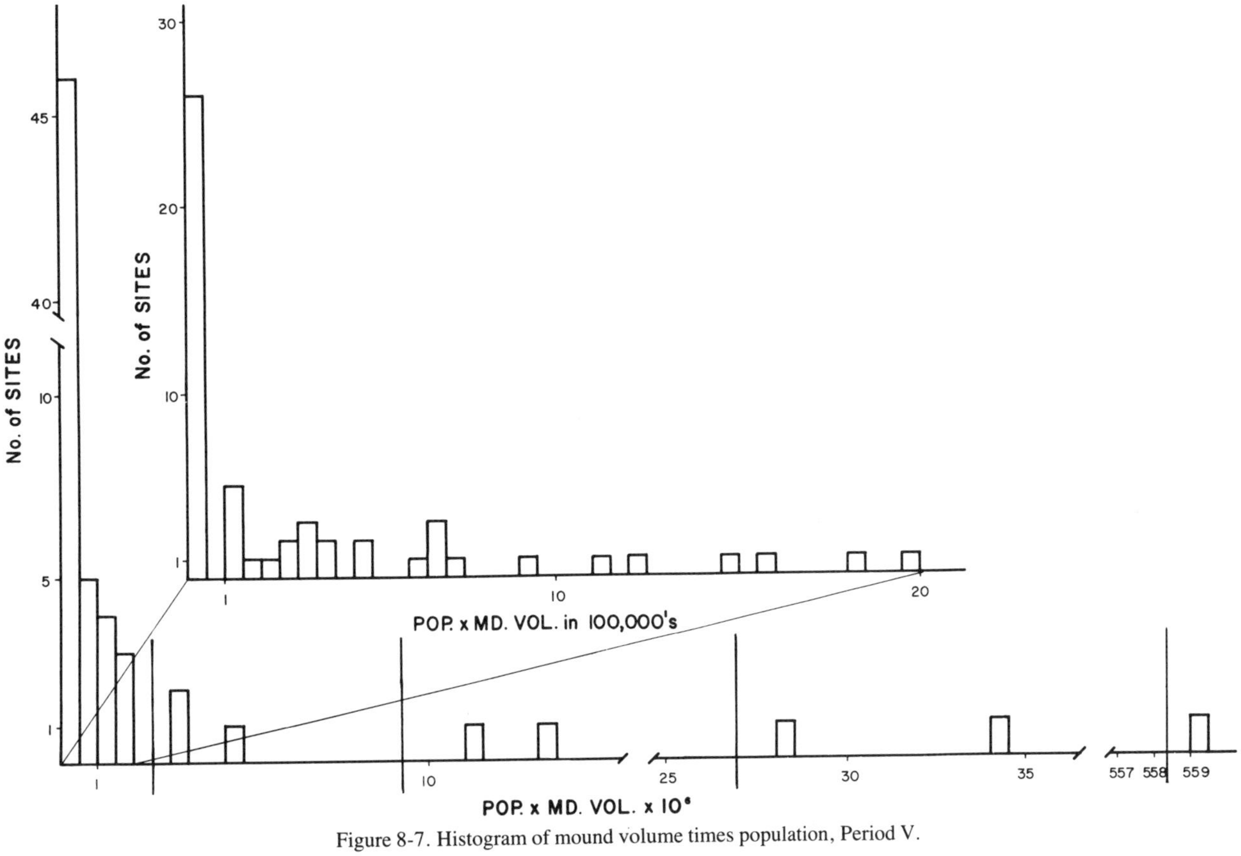

Figure 8-7. Histogram of mound volume times population, Period V.

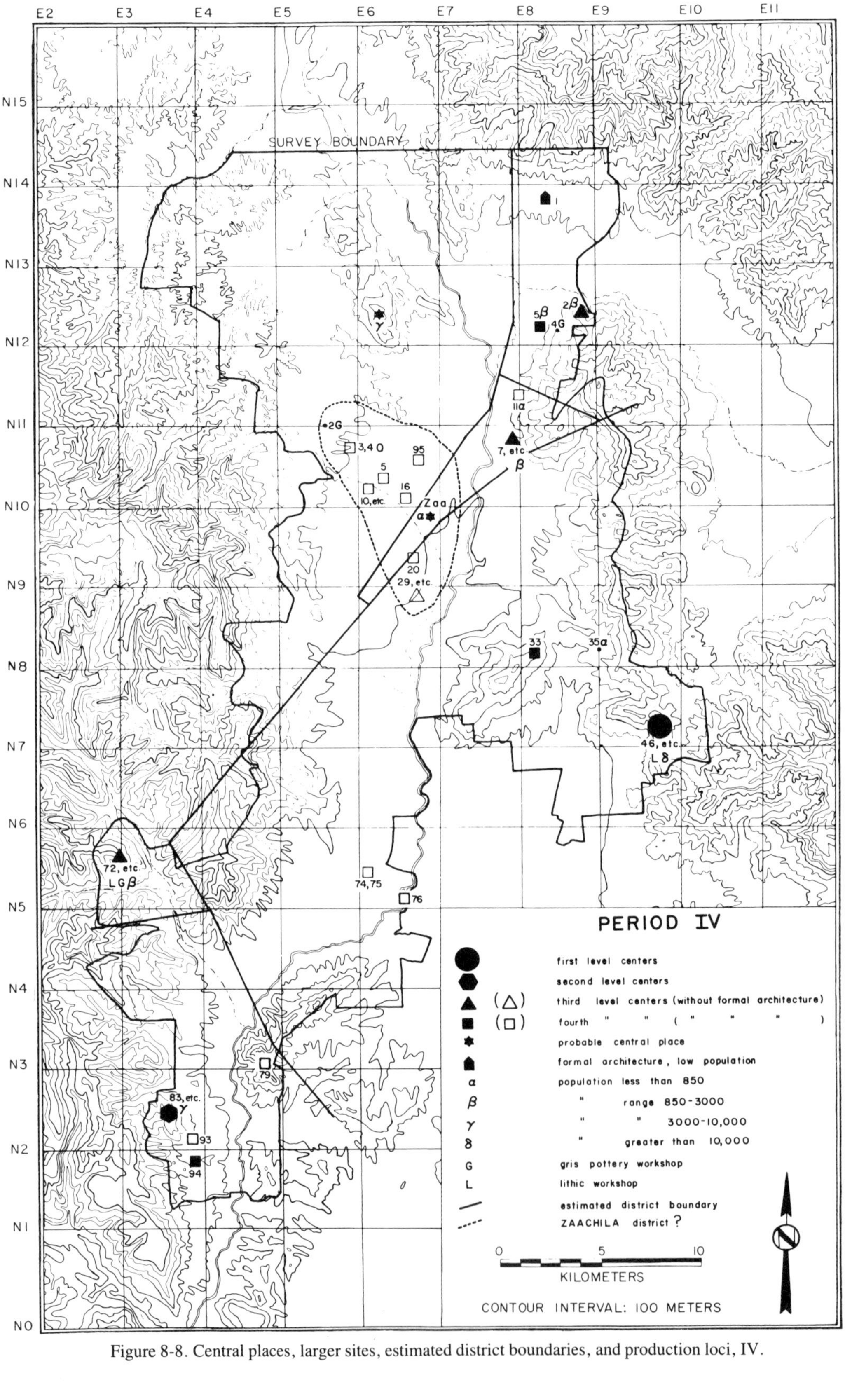

Figure 8-8. Central places, larger sites, estimated district boundaries, and production loci, IV.

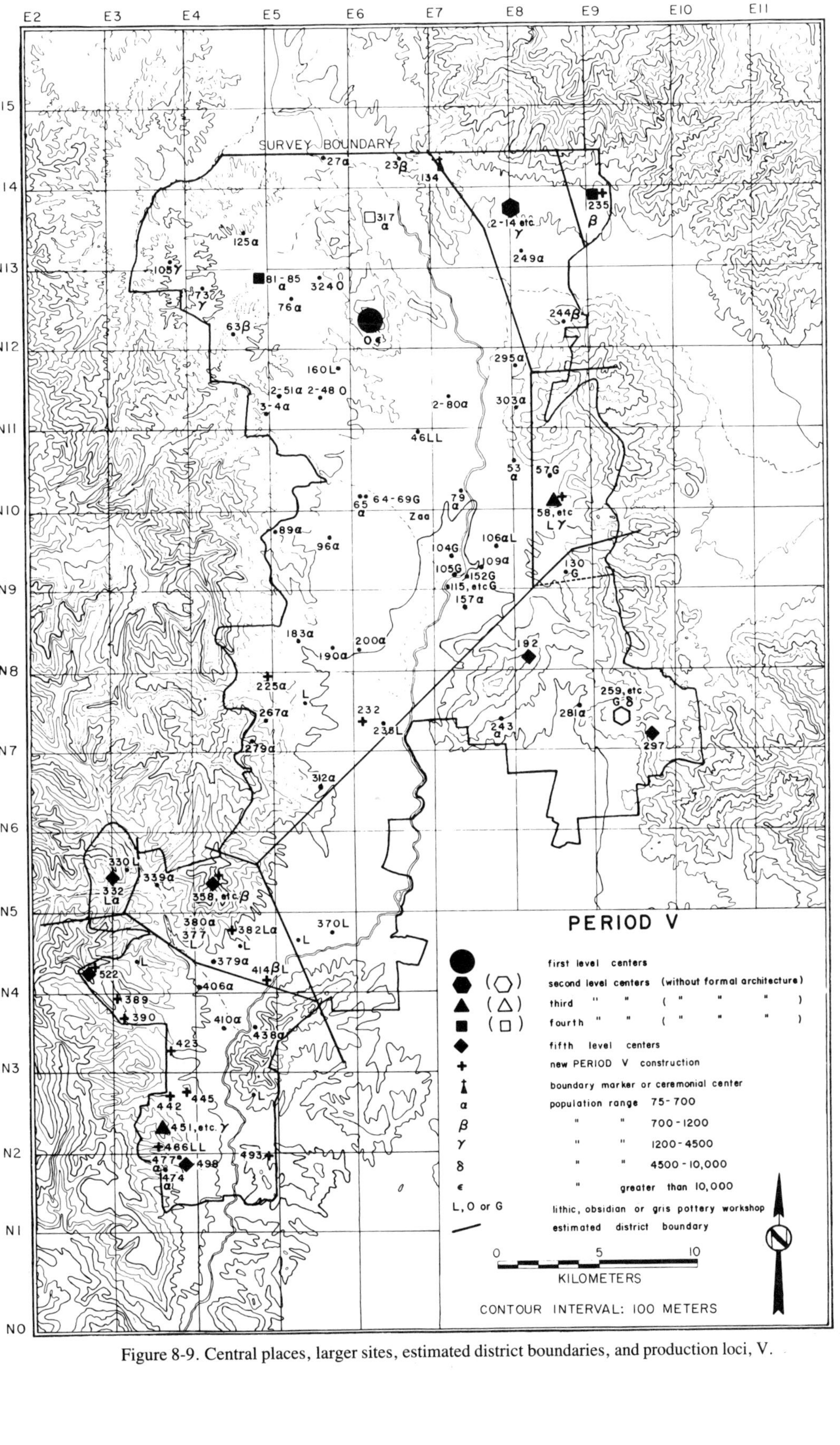

Figure 8-9. Central places, larger sites, estimated district boundaries, and production loci, V.

Table 8-1. Central-Place Summary, Period IV

SITE	POPULATION	MOUND VOLUME m^3	RANK
2-2, etc.	1929	16,010	3
2-5	1482	1000	4
2-11, etc.	718	385*	4
3-3, 4	7	11,858*	4
3-5	17	2420	4
3-7, etc.	1121	18,058	3
3-10, etc.	43	3135*	4
3-16	105	8255*	4
3-20	23	1611*	4
3-29, etc.	95	65,032*	3
3-33	41	11,575*	4
3-46, etc.	16,117	33,503	1
3-72, etc.	1501	7283*	3
3-74, 75	25	4395*	4
3-76	7	1456*	4
3-79	53	4914*	4
3-83, etc.	4047	15,158	2
3-93	17	76	4
3-94	7	406*	4
3-95	17	13,923*	4
Zaa.	?	?	2(?)
Monte Albán	4062	?	2(?)
		* Index	

Table 8-2. Central-Place Summary, Period V

SITE	POPULATION	MOUND VOLUME m^3	RANK
2-14, etc.	2506	11,267	2
2-84	329	10,281	4
2-235	774	6424	4
2-317	506	6455	4
CUIBAN	13,573	41,226	1
3-58, etc.	1939	4923	3
3-192	55	12,078?*	5
3-259	6649	0	2
3-297	7.5	5966	5
3-332, etc.	285	1352*	5
3-358	793	2325	5
3-451, etc.	1627	8016*	3
3-498	7	406*	5
3-522	7.5	99	5
		* Index	

district boundaries and locations of production sites.

Our method of identifying the administrative central-place hierarchies, which we feel has considerable utility for Periods Early I through IIIb, may have relatively little meaning for the Postclassic periods. The highly segmented, "Balkanized" Period IV, in fact, may not even contain a hierarchy of central places in the sense that this was true in the earlier periods. Such a hierarchy implies a largely integrated system of places, each place with a range of central-place functions, but each, in turn, tied into one or more higher-ranking centers with an even greater range of functions, culminating finally in the rank-1 center. We cannot be certain that in Period IV there was such a regional division of labor in administrative functions. The large abandoned areas separating sites suggest a situation in which sites were in competition with one another, rather than being parts of a common hierarchical system. Two sources of information–the interaction potential (*IP*) measures and the terrace size data–support this contention.

For Period IV, two measures of *IP* were made, both involving the sites in the upper 10% in population size. In the first case, we followed our procedure from earlier periods, counting Monte Albán as the rank-1 center. In these measures, as expected, Monte Albán's share of the *IP* total was very small, dropping from the IIIb value of 77% to 19%. We also calculated the values using the same procedure, but considering Jalieza as the rank-1 center. Its share of the total *IP* is higher than Monte Albán's,–amounting to 29%–but this figure is still substantially lower than the proportion of *IP* accounted for by the rank-1 center during the Monte Albán periods.

The *IP* totals are also proportionately much lower than for any of the Monte Albán periods. While the decline in population after IIIb amounted to roughly 24% of the IIIb total, the decline in *IP* "units" for the larger sites was from 10,228,121 in IIIb to 2,429,923 in IV, a decline of 76% of the IIIb total. All of these *IP* measures are suggestive of a situation in which there was so little interaction between centers that it would be a mistake to regard them as having been actors in an integrated regional system. Of course, these values cannot constitute proof that no regional system operated, since we have no way of knowing what, if any, might be the lower limits in *IP* below which a group of sites in a region can no longer be considered to be a regional unit.

We will know more about regional organization when we complete the survey of the remainder of the

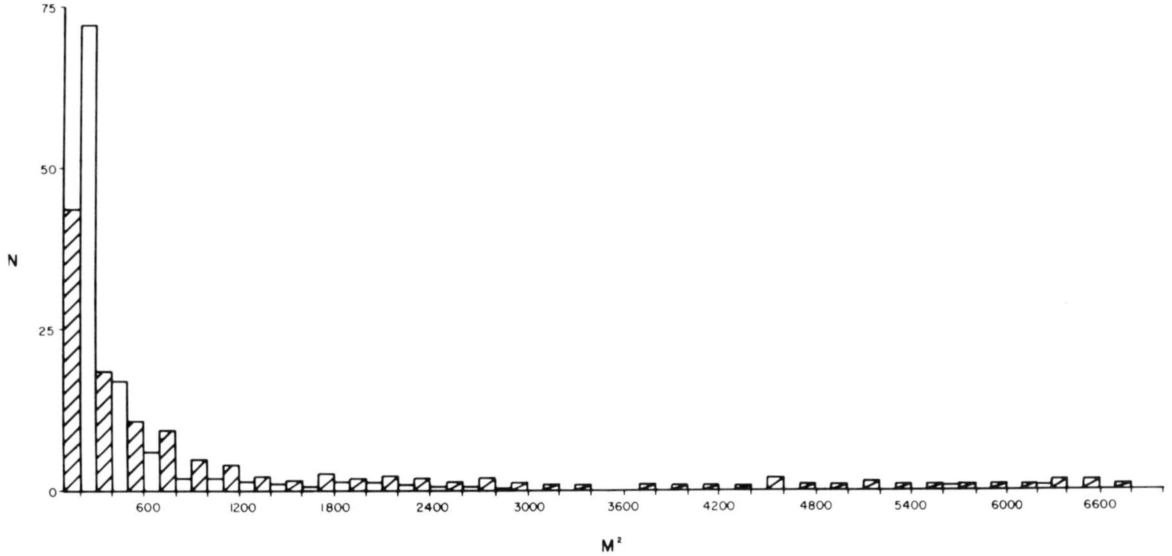

Figure 8-10. Histogram of terrace areas, Jalieza. The cross-hatched bars represent the IIIa values, and the non-hatched are the Period IV values.

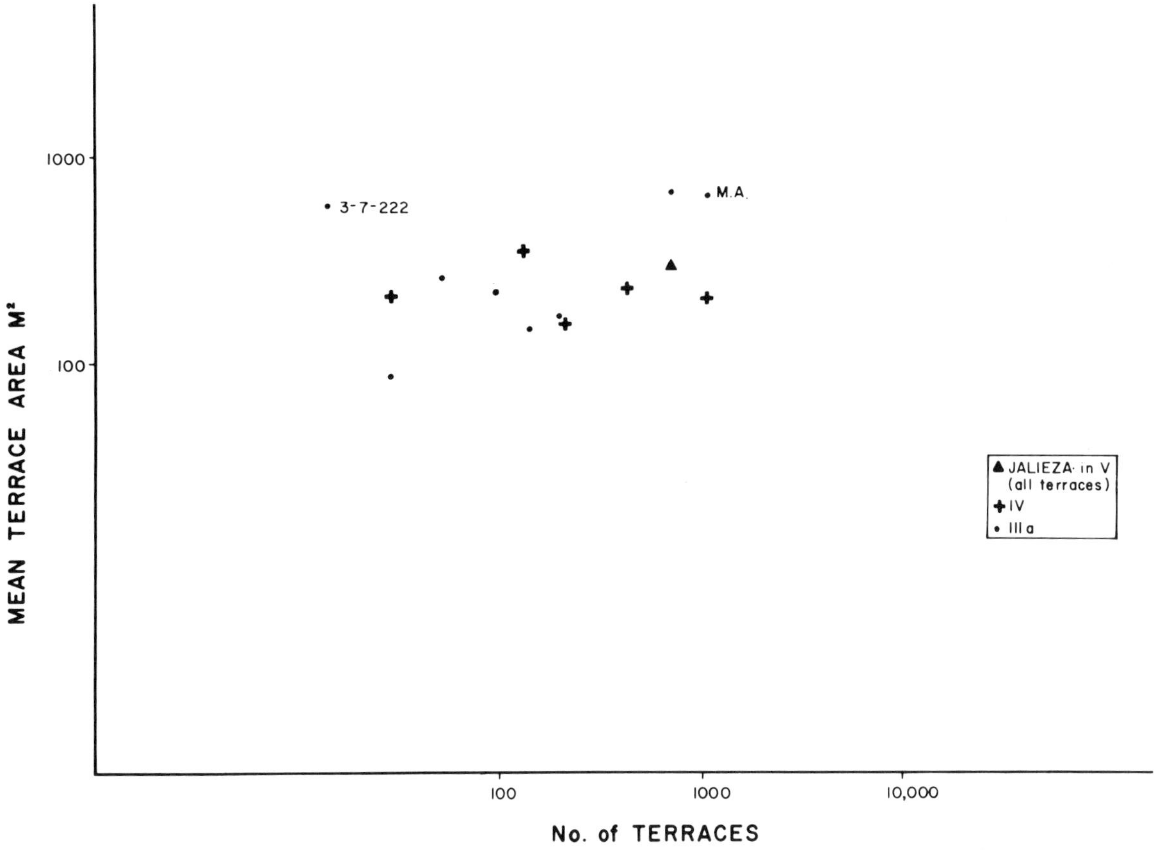

Figure 8-11. Scatter diagram, mean terrace area and number of terraces, for IIIa, IV, and Jalieza in Period V.

valley, especially the Tlacolula arm. Lambityeco, a Period IV site in the latter area, does seem to have evidence for specialized production of goods (salt, perhaps pottery) for a wider market (Peterson 1976).

The terrace size data similarly do not support the idea of a hierarchy of central places in an integrated regional system in Period IV. Sites higher in the hierarchy of central places should be larger in population size, have larger terraces on the average, and should have a wider range in terrace sizes. This should be so because higher-ranking sites have a wider range of activities present, and more members of a higher-ranking elite population who probably build larger than normal terraces because they have more servants, have larger than normal living quarters, and so on. For Period IIIa, these predictions proved to be largely correct (Table 8-3). Jalieza, the highest-ranking site in IIIa with terraces (and which was mostly a single-component site so we could be sure of the accuracy of the terrace measurements for the period), has the most variability in terrace area ($V = 2.8$) and the largest mean terrace size (709 m^2) (and see Fig. 8-10). For Period IIIa, a high correlation ($r = .63$) exists between the number of terraces and mean terrace size (the value is .93 when the small and anomalous 3-8-222 is deleted).

In IV the situation is very different. None of the sites, including Jalieza (which is considerably larger in IV than it had been in IIIa), has much variability in terrace size (Table 8-3)–the highest value, Jalieza's, is only $V = 1.6$. The correlation for Period IV between number of terraces and mean terrace area is negative ($r = -.48$) (Fig. 8-11).

We conclude that although the rank-size distribution for Period IV (Fig. 8-12) is of the primate form (although not as strongly so as for most of the Monte Albán periods), it is doubtful that this represents a situation of regional dominance by Jalieza analogous to the earlier dominance of the region by Monte Albán. The architectural and terrace size data suggest that although Jalieza was an exceptionally large site, it was probably just one of several large, autonomous Period IV centers, all with essentially the same range of functions. Keep in mind, though, that these conclusions are tentative. Final understanding of the nature of the Period IV regional system will depend on the completion of the Tlacolula arm survey, the location of the large and important site of Lambityeco.

Even with the data at hand, certain problems and anomalies are present with this interpretation of Period IV. Earlier, based on what we know about alluvium

Table 8–3. Summary of Terraced Sites, Indicating Number of Terraces and V (Standard Deviation Divided by the Mean)

	SITE	n	V
IIIa	Jalieza (3-8-259)	694	2.8
	Sta. Cruz Mixtepec (3-8-326, etc.)	197 (392*)	1.25 (1.24)
	3-8-220	141	1.18
	3-8-250	91	.69
	3-8-285	54	1.3
	3-8-271	29	.69
	3-8-222	13	.9
	* The total number of terraces with IIIa pottery.		
IV*	Jalieza (3-10-46, etc.)	1156	1.6
	El Choco (3-10-83, etc.)	432	1.13
	2-10-2	133	1.08
	3-10-7	28	1.12
	* Sta. Cruz Mixtepec not included since virtually all the terraces were built in IIIa.		
V (Jalieza)		690*	2.68*
		536**	1.39**
	* All terraces with V.		
	** Excludes those that also have IIIa.		

versus piedmont agriculture, we suggested that the massive populating of piedmont areas such as happened during Late I and IIIa could only have occurred in the context of a region organized so as to assure the efficient flow of food to deficit from surplus areas. Period IV, which our evidence indicates was probably not organized in this integrated fashion, was nonetheless a period in which piedmont settings were common (at least in the area we have surveyed so far). How did these populations cope with the inherent unpredictability of piedmont agriculture? It is interesting to note that Period IV may have been relatively short, perhaps indicating that this kind of regional pattern is unstable. The subsequent period was one in which there is again evidence for higher levels of regional integration.

Judging from the *IP* measures, by Period V many sites in the region may have again participated in an integrated regional system. While the population increases from IV to V in the survey area amounted to 16,523 (51% more people than in IV), the total *IP* "Units" of the larger V sites increased from the Period IV total of 2,429,923 (where Jalieza was considered the rank-1 center) to a total 6,202,200, an increase of 155%. This new regional organization was, again, focused on Monte Albán (now called "Cuiban"). By V, this site accounted for 60% of the total *IP* measured in this way.

This value for the proportion of the *IP* total is reminiscent of the days when Monte Albán was a regional capital, but by Period V the site was different than it had been in any of the prior periods. First, as we mentioned previously, although Cuiban was a large site, there is little evidence for new construction of mounded buildings. The major structures in use within the Period V limits of the site were structures that had been, as far as we can tell, built during the Classic period or earlier. The most important of these are the structures on Monte Albán terraces 453 and 1453 (Blanton 1978).

We conclude that although some administrative functions may have been centered in the Cuiban district, the paucity of mounded buildings suggests these functions accounted for a relatively small proportion of the site's total population size. The same can be said concerning Jalieza–only more so. Period V Jalieza is the survey region's second largest site (with a population of 6649), but it lacks anything at all reminiscent of a pyramid or platform mound. In addition, during the Late Postclassic, Zaachila was said to be the residence of the Zapotec ruler–and yet the archaeological evidence points to only a small resident population during that time. Obviously in a number of respects the Late Postclassic is unlike the Monte Albán periods, even though in some superficial ways there are similarities.

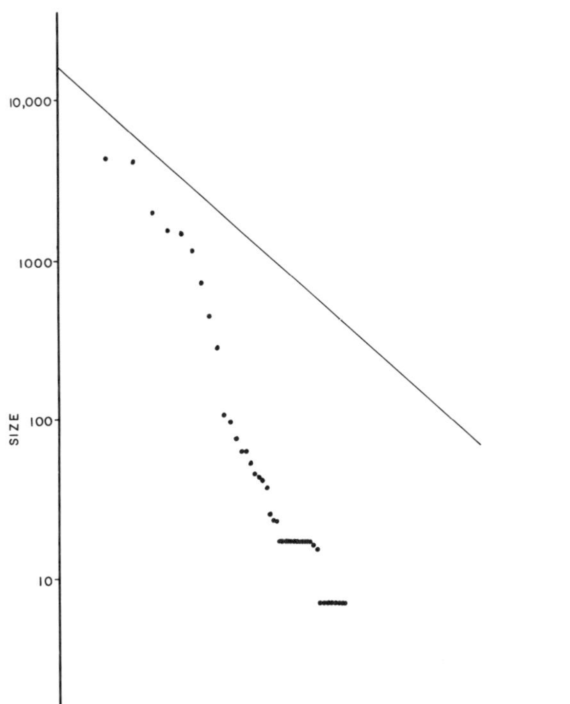

Figure 8-12. Rank-size graph, Period IV. The line is log-normal calculated from the rank-1 center.

Given the peculiarities in the nature and distribution of the Period V mounded architecture, we cannot be sure that the hierarchy of places we have identified (Fig. 8-9) is a hierarchy of the sort we identified for the region from Early I through IIIb. The differences between the Classic and Postclassic in this regard can be illustrated by noting, for each period, the relationship between mound volume and population sizes of centers. In a hierarchy of administrative central places of the sort we have identified for the Monte Albán periods, sites higher in the order of central places should have 1) more and larger structures, reflecting the larger number and importance of administrative functions, and 2) larger population sizes. While direct measures of mound volume are difficult for Periods Early I through II (because so many of the sites have multiple components), such measures can be reasonably accurate for the later periods. On virtually all of the IIIa sites, the maximum population of the site is reached at that time, making it reasonable to assume that all the structures visible were in use at that time. By Period IIIb, substantial shifts in settlement patterns occurred, so that in most cases we can directly date mounded buildings. The latter is largely, though not entirely, true also for the Postclassic sites.

In Figure 8-13, we plotted the values of population and mound volume for Periods IIIa through V. Figure 8-14 shows the least-squares regression lines for each of the periods derived from these values (for each of the regression lines, we did not include the values for the rank-1 center). As predicted, the IIIa and IIIb lines slope upward and have positive correlations between population and mound volume (for IIIa, $r = .24$, for IIIb, $r = .36$). These two periods are also similar in occupying roughly the same space in the regression line graph. The Period IV regression line is different from those of IIIa and IIIb. It is lower than the lines for

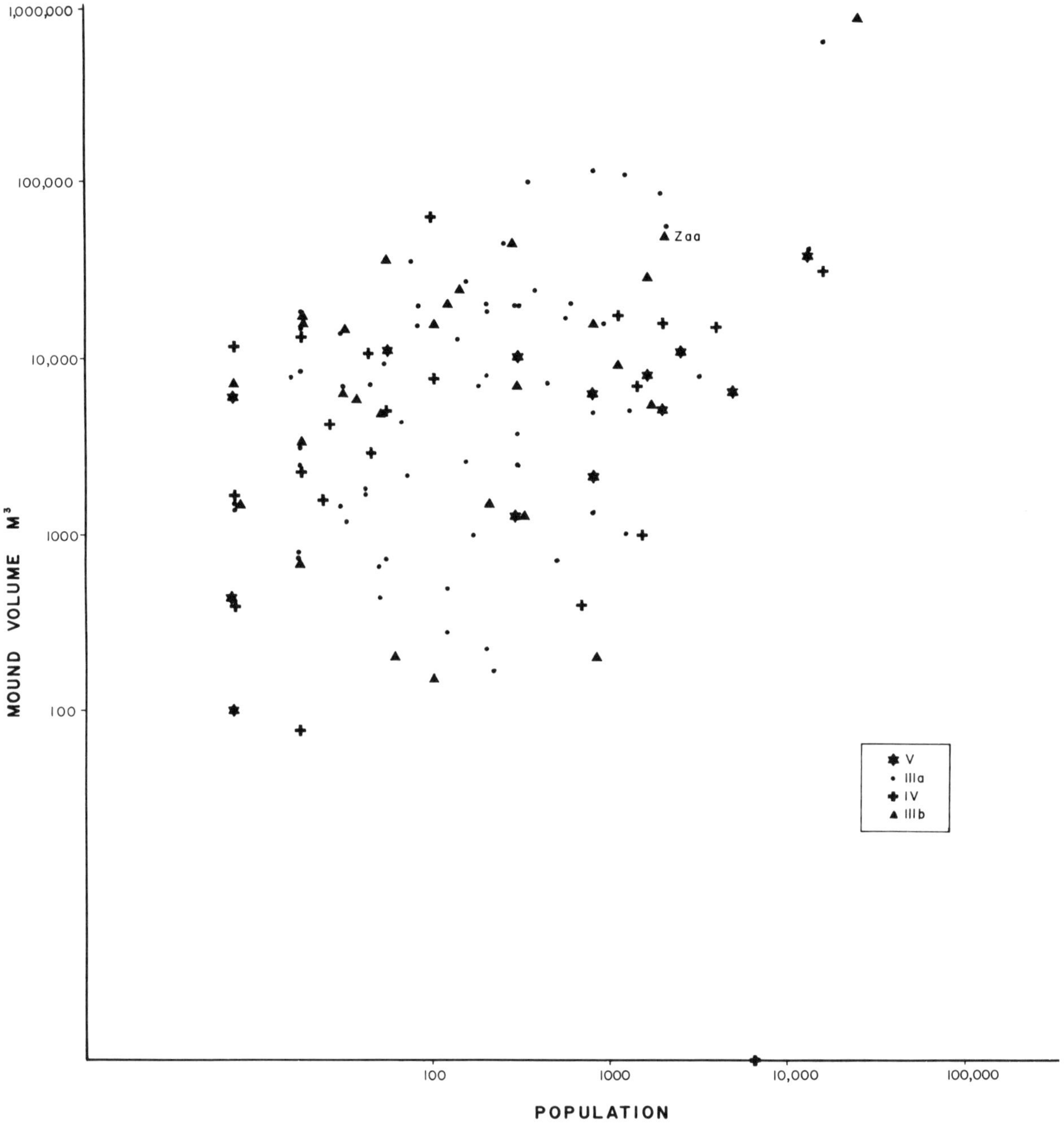

Figure 8-13. Scatter diagram, mound volume and population, for IIIa through Period V.

the prior periods, indicating less mounded architecture per capita, and there is little or no correlation between site size and volume of mounded architecture ($r=.083$). By V, the regression line is located even lower than the IV line, indicating even lower mound volume per capita. Since Jalieza has no mounded architecture in Period V, the correlation is negative ($r=-.11$).

We conclude from this analysis that during the Postclassic, administrative functions accounted for relatively little of the variation in population sizes of the central places. Given that in Period IV a hierarchically-organized regional system may not have operated, we cannot account for the differences in the population sizes of the centers. By Period V, we suggest, a regional system had evolved again, but one, we feel, tied together in ways having relatively little to do with governmental administration. Instead, we feel that the basis for regional integration during the Late Postclas-

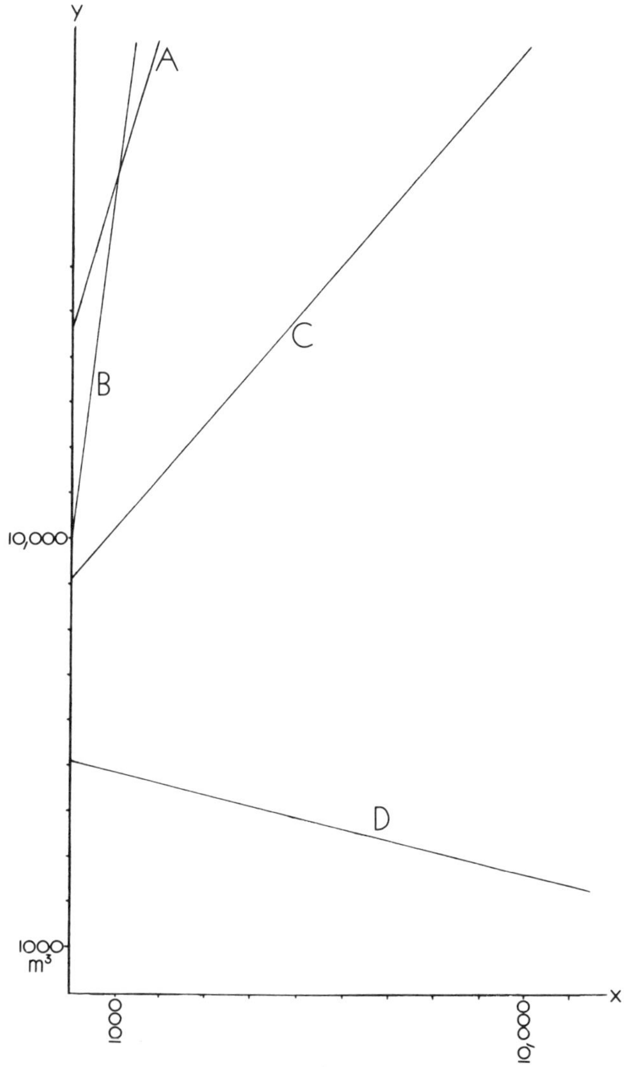

Figure 8-14. Least squares linear regression lines for mound volume (y axis), Periods IIIa through V. Line A is Period IIIb (y = 9872 + 8.48x, r = .36). Line B is Period IIIa (y = 14,523 + 3.68x, r = .24). Line C is Period IV (y = 9152 + 1.16x, r = .083). Line D is Period V (y = 5099 − .238x, r = −.11).

sic was a system of markets. The hierarchy of central places in V, in other words, was more a hierarchy of commercial places than a hierarchy of administrative ones, and it is to a consideration of such matters that we now turn.

PRODUCTION AND DISTRIBUTION IN THE POSTCLASSIC

As usual, our best evidence for the nature of production and distribution activities comes from ceramics. Our analysis is based on both the forms of pottery and the number and locations of ceramic production sites.

Following Caso, Bernal, and Acosta (1967), we had considered the Period IV ceramics to be largely a continuation of the IIIb forms, in spite of the fact that numerous changes occurred from the point of view of regional organization after IIIb. It is true that, during Period IV, as in IIIb, few ceramic types were present (only a total of 19 for IV), and that most of these were crude and mass produced, giving the period a very low mean production step index (Chapter 10, Table 10–5). Now that we have surveyed other parts of the valley, however, we are becoming aware of the complexities of the IV ceramics. By Period IV, for example, there was less regional uniformity in pottery than had been present in IIIb–with assemblages in some ways distinct from those at Monte Albán present in the western part of the central zone, at Jalieza, at El Choco, and at Lambityeco. This is no doubt the product of a situation in which there was less interaction between centers involving material exchanges. Once these Period IV ceramic assemblages are better understood, it is likely they will be found to contain more types and a higher production step index.

Steve Kowalewski, who tabulated the sherds, believes that the IV collections from the Valle Grande had what appeared to be many "one-of-a-kind" pots–probably indicating greater variability than our existing typology is capable of handling. In fact, this variation itself–even though we don't understand it very well–was sometimes used as a Period IV marker. One possible explanation for this increased ceramic variability is that with a combination of reduced governmental costs after the collapse of Monte Albán and the break-up of a regional marketing system, many households reordered their time budgets and production strategies and resumed at least some home production of pottery.

Although our data on types per site indicate that people during IV were still relatively "poor" (in the sense of having access to only a relatively small number of types, on the whole), still, there was some improvement over IIIb. In IIIb, centers averaged 6.4 types, while non-administrative places averaged 3.5; by IV, the values are 7 and 3.6 respectively. Although only to a very small extent, this reverses a trend which had begun after Period II in which the values in types per site were lower and lower through time (see Appendix VIII and Figs. 8-15 and 8-16). By V, the reversal of this trend was even more pronounced. Centers in V still averaged 7 types per site, but non-administrative places had increased to 4.8. Thus, by V the gap in numbers of types per site between administrative and non-administrative places was smaller than in any of the periods since Early I (Fig. 7-8).

The latter statistic shows that in Period V, people in non-administrative sites had relatively more access to a wider range of types, indicating, we think, less control of ceramic production and distribution through administrative channels. We refer to this process whereby there was more "affluence" in non-administrative settings as "commercialization." The relative commercialization of the Late Postclassic is indicated by several other statistics: 1) Period V is the first period since the establishment of Monte Albán in which the mean number of types per non-administrative site greater than 100 in population (7.7) is larger than the mean value for all administrative places. These larger sites may have had more commercial functions than did the administrative places overall, meaning that their populations had access to more types than did the populations of the administrative places; 2) the Period V ceramics were the best-made of any period since the foundation of Monte Albán (Table 10-5). In his chapter below, Feinman argues that this was the consequence of competition between potters producing for a market system that was largely free of administrative control; 3) during the Monte Albán periods, especially those phases characterized by a high degree of standardization in ceramic production, sites close to Monte Albán had the fewest types per site than sites in any other subregion. We argued that this was because these groups were getting their pottery from a highly-administered production structure centered in the capital. By V this was no longer true. Non-administrative sites within 10 kilometers of the Main Plaza in V had roughly an average number of types (4.6) (Table 10-1) for that category while sites within the area that we identified as the Cuiban district (Fig. 8-9) have higher than the average number of types (5.3) (Table 10-1) per non-administrative site. It was thus no longer an economic

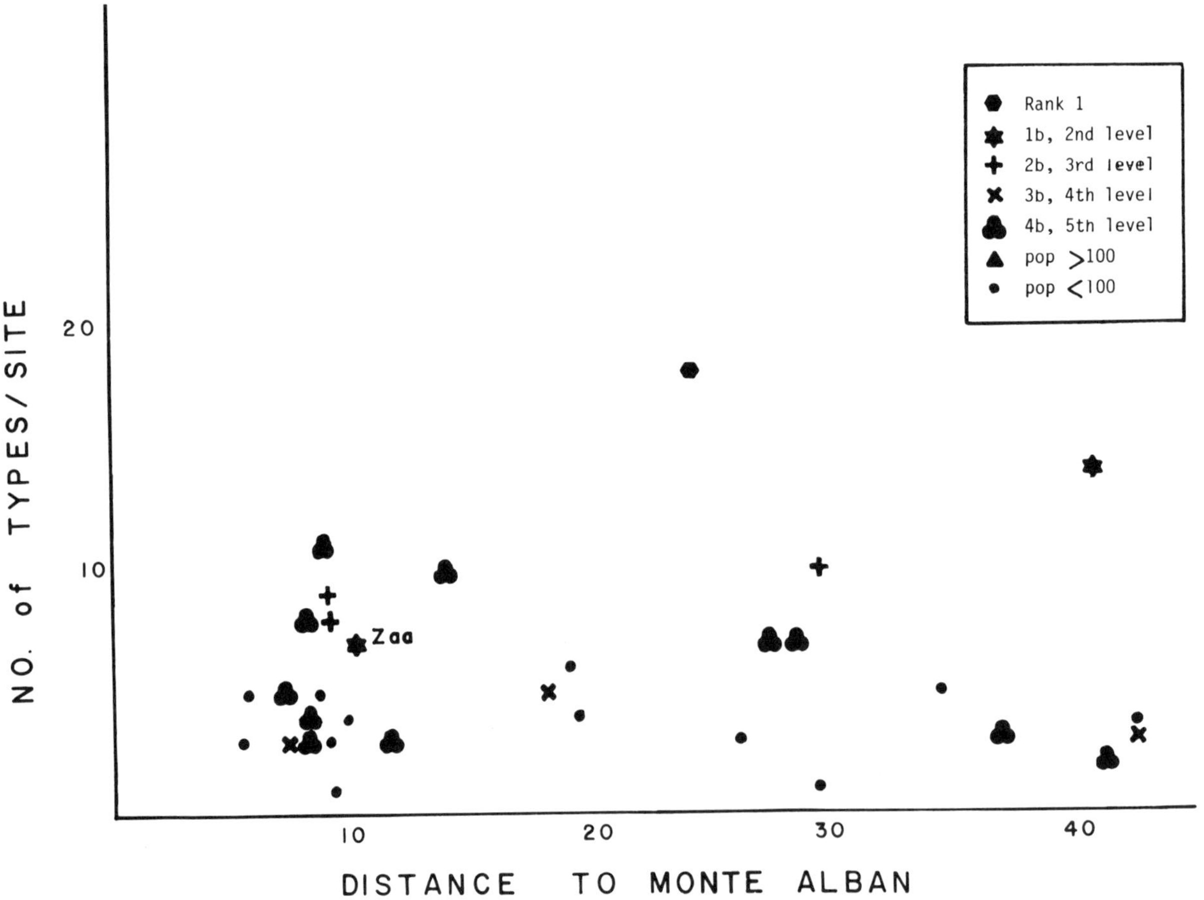

Figure 8-15. Types per site by site category and distance from Monte Albán, Period IV.

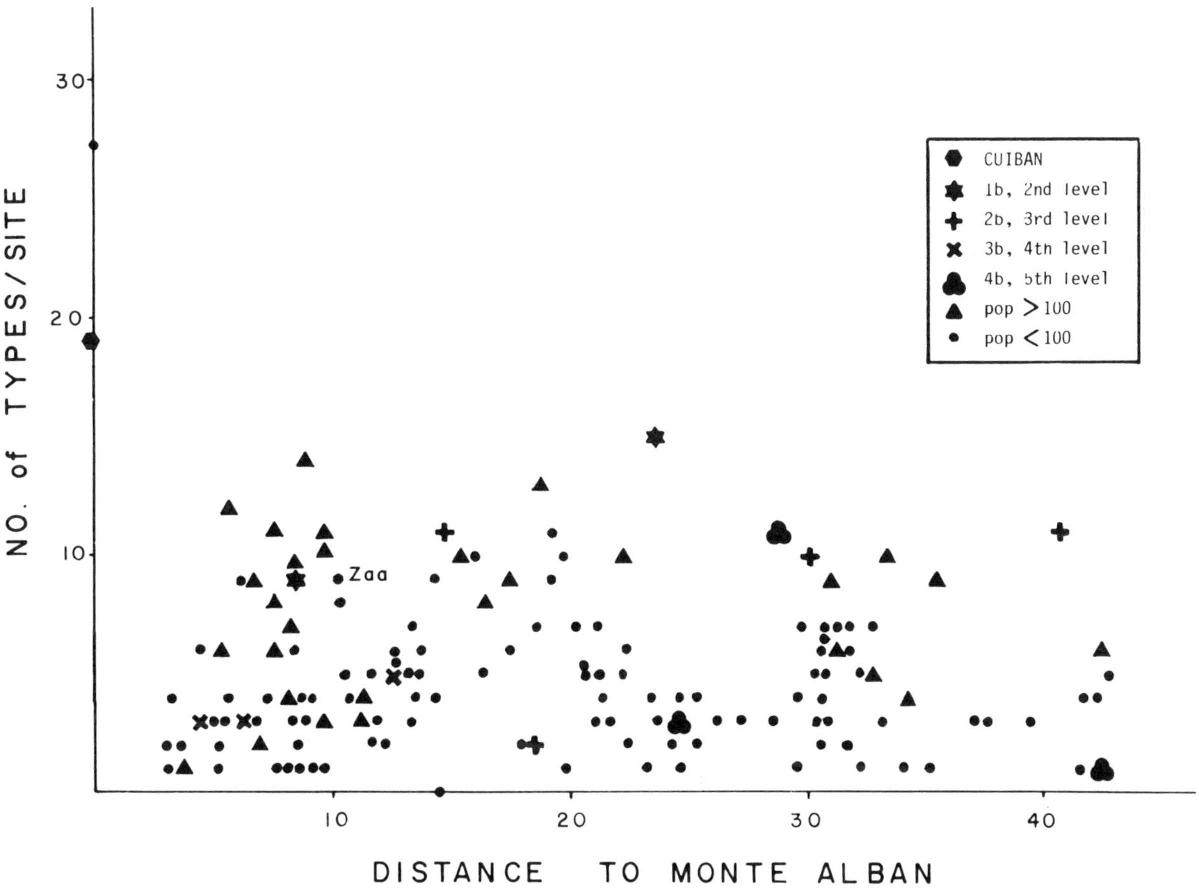

Figure 8-16. Types per site by site category and distance from Monte Albán, Period V. The data are found in Appendix VIII.

disadvantage (from the point of view of access to ceramic types) to live in the vicinity of the rank-1 center.

In Period V, ceramic production sites are largely "disembedded" from the administrative central-place hierarchy (Fig. 8-9). Interestingly, most of these production sites are located in an area midway between the Cuiban district and Jalieza, an area lacking any significant evidence for administrative architecture (the only exceptions being the rank-3 center at Coyotepec, and at Zaachila, but these are at some distance from most of the actual production places). The locations of these ceramic production sites would have been ideal for potters producing for distribution in several large centers, but their locations would not have been optimal from the point of view of administrators wishing to control or tax production. The possible exception, again, is Zaachila. The production sites, however, are not in or very near this site. Note that this general area was, during Period IV, directly along what we take to have been the boundary between the areas controlled by Monte Albán and Jalieza–right in the middle, in other words, of what might have been politically contested land. This kind of setting, midway between two large centers, but in a location probably not directly under the control of either, would have been an ideal place for the growth of administration-free commercial enterprises. No single polity could claim jurisdiction over residents of this zone, we suggest, reducing the likelihood of extensive taxation or control of production.

In this same vein, it is perhaps of some importance to point out that Zaachila–the residence of the Late Postclassic Zapotec ruler of the Valley of Oaxaca (see the addendum to this chapter)–is also located in this "neutral" tract. We suggest that this is so because the Zapotec kingship in V was a neutral institution, serving to lace together a series of largely independent polities, but maintaining some distance–probably political as well as spatial–from each one so as to avoid becoming primarily associated with one component of the regional system at the expense of the others. Zaachila, in other words, in Period V, perfectly fits the definition of a disembedded capital as defined by Blanton (1976b).

THE POSTCLASSIC: CONCLUSIONS

The Classic-Postclassic transition in the Valley of Oaxaca (as we know it, of course, from our survey area) and the reorganization of the regional system in the Late Postclassic may have considerable theoretical importance for students of human societies. Our data indicate that this set of changes is a fundamental one in the nature of regional organization, and it provides us with an opportunity to compare two nearly diametrically opposed organizational modes. We suggest that the "glue" cementing the region together from Early I through IIIb consisted primarily of government, focused on a dominating regional institution located in Monte Albán's Main Plaza. After this particular form of regional glue dissolved, the region was temporarily segmented, but out of this a regional system evolved in which integration was primarily commercial, not governmental (although, of course, governmental institutions still existed). Below, a hypothesis is posed explaining why commercial institutions overrode governmental ones. The following is a tentative listing of the systemic features of the Late Postclassic that we believe are most important in distinguishing it from the Early I through IIIb time span. This is also a listing of what our data indicate may be the differences, in general, between regions organized on the basis of centralized government versus those in which nongovernmental commercial institutions are important:

1) As we already noted, the Late Postclassic was a long period of relative stability. It did not evidence the kinds of major upheavals and reorganizations more typical of Early I through IIIb. This, we argued, was due to the fact that in the Late Postclassic the form of the regional system was the product of numerous decisions made at lower levels of organization. No single institution was present that was capable of the massive shifts of energy flows that become manifested in rapid change in settlement patterns, rapid population transitions, and reorganization of systems of production and distribution. During the prior periods the concentration of power at Monte Albán was such that shifts of this sort could be carried out, and at several points in time they were.

2) Period V was a time of very slow population growth by comparison with some of the prior periods (Fig. 4-3) (note also the very slow growth rates associated with the periods prior to the formation of Monte Albán). During the Late Postclassic, overall population densities remained far below the productive potentials of the region (see Chapter 9). In part, this more stationary demographic pattern may have been due to the fact that given a much lower level of support necessary for governmental institutions, large family size was less often a necessary economic strategy in the Postclassic. Small families, in other words, may have been as economically viable as large ones since labor demands on families would have been reduced (cf. Blanton 1975). Another aspect of this, though, has to do with immigration. We argued that in prior periods this was an important component of rapid population growth. We know that during the Late Postclassic immigration (of Mixtec peasants) was encouraged by valley elite, through marriage alliances with Mixtec elite, but, again, given the very low growth rates of the Late Postclassic, this practice was apparently having little effect. Lacking in the Late Postclassic was the kind of structure (which we assume had been present at Monte Albán) capable of encouraging or forcing the massive importation of people that produced the very high growth rates we have observed at certain junctures in the valley's history.

3) Lastly, and especially in contrast with the Classic period as a whole, our evidence indicates that during the Late Postclassic, more people had access to a wider range of goods, and the quality of those goods was higher than had been the case in any prior period. Governmental institutions, we would argue, during the Late Postclassic, were not able to direct, control, or reorganize systems of production and distribution for purposes of generating revenue.

One last point deserves some attention. Recall that one of the Monte Albán periods (II) was a time of relatively less centralized control, in which Monte Albán's influence in the valley seems to have been considerably diminished in contrast with Periods Late I or IIIa. Note that this period was, to a degree, like Period V. Growth rates were low or negative. This was by far the longest ceramic period we have from the foundation of Monte Albán to its collapse (lasting nearly 400 years, as far as we can tell), indicating relative stability. And, last, the ceramics of Period II were the closest of all periods since the foundation of Monte Albán to Period V in the mean value of the production-step index, indicating the manufacture of high-quality ceramics during that time.

The question before us now is what, if any, were the interrelationships between the observed declines in centralized governmental control, on the one hand, and commercialization, on the other. Declines in centralized control are probably not unusual in early civilizations, although we cannot be certain that this is a general characteristic of all such societies. An example is given by Rathje (1975:437-38, Figs. 40,41) for the Old and Middle Kingdoms of Egypt. There too the resources expended in monumental state constructions (especially pyramids) diminished over time. As traced by Rathje, the trend includes:

> 1) resources changed from multiton Tura limestone blocks to small rubble and mud brick, which were easier to procure; (2) quantity of resources and labor and organizational requirements decreased from the mammoth Giza pyramids to the diminutive later ones; and (3) skill needs were reduced by making the pyramid a solid mass instead of including a mortuary chamber and intricate passageways. [Rathje 1975:437-38]

Rathje discusses similar trends in the Lowland Maya area. There

> Resource concentration/commodity ratios, measured by quantity of resources invested for housing, changed between the Classic and Late Postclassic. In the Classic, in both the southern and northern lowlands, the building of temple and palace structures entailed skill in executing block masonry and functional corbeling. Masonry blocks were well cut and fitted and sometimes beautifully carved; in addition, structures were covered with a coat of plaster and often sculpted stucco. Human labor and materials were concentrated not only in care and detail of construction, but also simply in size of construction. The two largest Maya buildings are temples built during the Classic Period at Izamal and Dzilam (Andrews, 1965: 299). The Izamal pyramid is 700,000 cubic meters of rubble (Segovia, personal communication, June, 1973), almost ten times the size of the largest Late Postclassic pyramid. As a result of the quantity of invested materials and human labor and skill, many large Classic construction units, such as palace A-V at Uaxactun (cf. A.L. Smith, 1950) and the North, Central, and South acropoli at Tikal (cf. Coe, 1967, and Culbert, 1974) were foci of tremendous resource concentration.
>
> One example of Late Postclassic (''Decadent'' Period) architecture, comparable to Tikal in many functional respects, is Mayapan, a walled city of perhaps ten thousand residents, measuring about four square kilometers. The main temple in the ceremonial precinct at Mayapan was small, about eighty thousand cubic meters. No other structure was the focus of large-scale resource concentration of the type found in Classic structures and construction units . . . . Not only did size of structures decrease, but so did demands for expertise in organization and construction. The quantities of stone and human labor and skill needed for corbeled roofs were replaced by the simpler requirements of thatch and beam-and-mortar roofing. The need for careful cutting and sculpting of stone was replaced by reuse of previously cut stone (with a decrease in precision of fit) and heavy application of plaster. The result of this cost-control implementation is the critique that Mayapan's ''monuments were thrown together with a minimum of skill'' (Andrews, 1968). [Rathje 1975:421-422]

Rathje also notes that these changes in the Classic-Postclassic transition in the Maya area are associated with an increased commercialization:

> Thus while Classic populations were to a large extent integrated through the costly maintenance of an elite minority, Postclassic populations were most probably integrated through a rising standard of living locked into large-scale population participation in a commerce which emphasized economic efficiency and mass consumption. From this viewpoint, transformations within material culture production-distribution systems may hold one important key to describing and understanding the nature of the differences between the Classic and Postclassic Maya cultural systems. [ibid.:436]

These conclusions parallel our own discoveries in the Valley of Oaxaca that the decline in the degree of centralized control was associated with an increase in commercialization.

We are struck with the similarities between the Classic-Postclassic transition, insofar as we are able to reconstruct the changes and events following the collapse of the Romanized polities in Western Europe after about the 8th century A.D.

We are aware that there has been an active debate over the nature of the growth of the European economic system during the Middle Ages (cf. Pirenne 1936, 1957; Lopez 1976), a debate we are not qualified to join. We think, however, that certain basic trends can be seen in the period after the 8th century A.D. that may be relevant to an understanding of culture change in the Postclassic of Oaxaca and perhaps other parts of Mesoamerica. According to Pirenne the Roman administrative foundations of these European polities, under the Carolingians, ''. . .crumbled away to nothing. . .the first to go was the very conception of royal power'' (Pirenne 1957:266). These states, he argues, were politically weaker than the prior Romanized states largely due to ''. . .the disorder of the financial administration. . . . No more surveys of land, no more registers of taxes, no more financial functionaries; hence no more archives, no more offices, no more accounts'' (ibid.:266, 268). The impost, the financial mainstay of the Romanized governments, was abandoned during the 8th century. After this time, new markets could be founded, normally, without royal authorization. Coins were minted in a variety of places, no longer under royal control–''coins were struck in most cities. . . . In 920 some of the churches obtained the right to mint coins with their own superscription. This was a complete usurpation, the natural consequence of the King's abandonment of his proper rights'' (ibid:247). Interestingly, coincident with the decline of state control over the economy, the number of retail markets increased markedly (cf. p. 253), even though long-distance trade had declined due to the insecurities of travel on the Muslim-controlled Mediterranean. Although Pirenne does not discuss this increase in frequency of local markets in any detail, it seems reasonable to infer from this an increase in commercialization. Pirenne would disagree with this since he was more concerned with declining long-distance exchange. He regularly denied the importance of local market systems, a fact which is amply demonstrated in the following passage:

> The large number of [9th-century] markets might seem at first sight to contradict the commercial paralysis of the age, for from the beginning of the ninth century they increased rapidly and new ones were continually being founded. But the number is itself proof of their insignificance . . .there were only innumerable small weekly markets, where the peasants of the district offered for sale a few eggs, chickens, pounds of wool, or ells of coarse cloth woven at home. The nature of the business transacted appeared quite clearly from the fact that the people sold *per deneratas*, that is to say, in quantities not exceeding a few pence in value. In short the utility of these small assemblies was limited to satisfying that instinct of sociability which is inherent in all men. They constituted the sole distraction offered by a society settled in work on the land. Charlemagne's order to the serfs on his estates not to ''run about to markets'' shows they were attracted much more by the desire to enjoy themselves than by considerations of trade. [Pirenne 1936:10-11]

We disagree with Pirenne's explanation for the existence of these markets, and we take their growth in numbers to indicate an increase in the importance of marketing systems beginning at that time and an increase in the level of participation in marketing by the general population, points which are supported by Lopez (1976).

Our question has been: what are the interrelationships between decreased governmental control and the apparent increases in commercialization noted in these cases? Skinner (1977a) offers an explanation for the decline in governmental control in relation to commercialization in China that occurred from roughly A.D. 200 to Late Imperial times. In A.D. 180, the empire was divided into 1180 county-level administrative units, giving an average of 50,000 people per unit. As the population of China grew, however, the number of units did not increase correspondingly; in fact the number of such units tended to remain essentially stationary (ibid.:23-24). This implies less administrative control per capita. A concomitant development was a ''medieval revolution'' that began as early as the 8th century. The major features of this revolution were, as summarized by Skinner:

> . . .(1) a relaxation of the requirement that each county could maintain only one market, which had to be located in the capital city; (2) the breakdown and eventual collapse of the official marketing organization; (3) the disappearance of the enclosed marketplace, along with the walled-ward system, and their replacement by ''a much freer street plan in which trade and commerce could be conducted anywhere within the city or its outlying suburbs'' (Twitchett, 1966:231); (4) the rapid expansion of particular walled cities and the growth of commercial suburbs outside their gates; and (5) the emergence of ''great numbers of small and intermediate-sized towns'' (ibid.:203) with important economic functions. These changes. . .were accompanied by the increased monetization of taxation and trade; by a growth in the numbers, wealth, and power of merchants; and by a softening of social and official attitudes disparaging trade and the merchant class. [Skinner 1977a:23-24]

Skinner argues that this increased commercialization, in addition to population growth, forced the Chinese state to reduce its span of control. As he sees it, given

> . . . the growing scale of commerce and the decline in the number of *yamens* per unit of population, the system of administered trade became increasingly arduous and expensive to enforce. Through a process of trial and error–the secular trend was punctuated by the periodic reimposition of controls–there occurred a general withdrawal by government from the minute regulation of commercial affairs. [ibid.:24-25]

We doubt that Skinner's hypothesis suffices as a general explanation for the observed interrelationships between changes in span of control and commercialization for all of the cases we reviewed here. Population growth on a massive scale as occurred in China during the period in question was not present during the Classic-Postclassic transition in Mesoamerica. In the Maya area, Postclassic population densities may have been lower, on the whole, than those of the Classic period. In the Valley of Oaxaca, our estimates indicate the Late Postclassic population was the same as, or somewhat less than, the IIIa level. It is harder to assess the increased difficulty of administration, given a growing scale of commerce in the valley, but this factor, too, seems unlikely as an explanation for why there was a decline in governmental control. We suggest an alternative hypothesis, and one which may be applicable in the other cases mentioned here, including the Chinese case, based on our general view of human societies as fluctuating structures.

To reiterate, our argument has been that extreme fluctuations require costly adaptive responses to assure continuity–and that these responses may in turn so restructure a society that a return to prior conditions is not possible. Prior to the statement of the hypothesis, three assumptions will be made: first, that systems of production, specialization, and exchange require mechanisms for regulation to assure the steady flow of commodities, more or less dependable incomes for producers and prices for consumers, means for protection against banditry, and means for adjudication of disputes among market participants. Secondly, we assume that once some level of specialization and market dependence develops in a region, the participants, both as producers and consumers, will try to maintain at least that minimal level. Decreases in exchange mean losses of income for producers who may have no other sources of income and increases in the time costs of householding for consumers of craft goods. Thirdly, we assume that the natural institutional matrix for the administration of markets as they are first formed is the state (or chiefly institution). This seems confirmed by the overwhelming number of ethnographic examples where this is true. Markets, at least initially, we argue, are normally dependent on some degree of state control. The ability of the state to carry out these functions, however, is a fluctuating variable–the state's ability to properly administer markets varies depending on many circumstances, including such things as fluctuations in state revenues, pressing border problems, internal disorders, bureaucratic inefficiencies, and so on. We argue that, given some minimal level of required administration for markets, disruptions in state power could disrupt trade, at least during some critical periods. The collapse of a major political institution like that centered on Monte Albán, or those of the western Romanized polities in Europe, would create especially serious problems for continued market operation. Under these circumstances, we argue, market participants respond through the formation of various kinds of non-governmental mechanisms for regulation and control. That is, in the light of fluctuations, coping strategies adopted by market participants make markets more self-regulatory, controlled by what Skinner refers to as "informal governance" (1977b:336-44, 721, footnote 48) or "informal parapolitical structures" (ibid.:338). This produces a secular trend toward decreased governmental control over the long run, and increased market autonomy, since, once established, such mechanisms would be difficult to dislodge by the state, even after a return to normal levels of state administrative abilities. State control cannot be easily reasserted, even during periods of reascendency of state power, and this increasingly limits state activities to such areas as offense-defense and long-distance exchange. The level of state control even in these areas may be affected, however, since market-produced revenues may be significantly reduced. Decline in state control of markets has another consequence. Given the reduced ability of the state apparatus to control and tax markets, increased commercialization is the result. In part this may have to do with the built-in spatial contradictions between marketing and administrative regional organization (Blanton 1976b), but probably more importantly, state regulation of markets is in general more costly to market participants than the self-regulatory mechanisms, especially if the state uses market revenues to fund other activities such as militarism. A good example is the decline of the Roman impost in Europe in A.D. 791. The abandonment of such a tax in effect lowers the cost per transaction, and therefore raises the purchasing power of consumers. This in turn has several consequences: 1) some goods that previously could not be produced by specialists now can be because the increased purchasing power of consumers pushes such goods above their demand thresholds; 2) the ranges of all goods increase. The relatively lower costs of goods means that consumers who originally were beyond the range of a good now find it worthwhile to absorb the costs of travel to obtain that good. Thus, consumers who reside in what had been marginal localities, poorly serviced by markets, can now more fully participate in the region's economic system; and 3) reduced costs per transaction not only mean that more goods can be offered to a wider range of consumers, but that more people will have access to more "costly" goods, because the prices of these goods become relatively less.

We argue that as markets are increasingly governed by "informal parapolitical structures" there would have followed an increase in commercialization, including more goods offered in markets, more participants in marketing, and a greater distribution of "costly" items. This would be accompanied by a secular decrease in state controls, and, probably, in state revenues. A partial listing of the kinds of structures regulating production and exchange (through adjudication, policing, price regulation, canal maintenance, market cleanup, etc.) in Late Imperial China includes lineages (Skinner, ed. 1977:721; Baker 1977:500, passim), clans (cf. Baker 1977:501, passim; De Glopper 1977:638, passim), surname groups (Baker 1977:501, passim; De Glopper 1977:638, passim), *Landsmannschaften* (common origin associations) (cf. Skinner, ed. 1977:539, passim), guilds (cf. Golas 1977), religious foundations and neighborhood cult associations (Skinner, ed. 1977:721; van der Sprenkel 1977:614-15; Schipper 1977), irrigation societies (Skinner, ed. 1977:721), and "Gentry Directors" of water-control projects (Elvin 1977).

Addendum to Chapter 8: The Postclassic

A SUMMARY OF THE ETHNOHISTORIC INFORMATION RELEVANT TO THE INTERPRETATION OF LATE POSTCLASSIC SETTLEMENT PATTERN DATA, THE CENTRAL AND VALLE GRANDE SURVEY ZONES

By Jill Appel

INTRODUCTION

While a number of ethnohistoric records bear on the Valley of Oaxaca in Period V, the main body of this chapter has considered only archaeological data from the survey area. This has been done in order to preserve continuity with the discussions of previous periods, for which no other records exist. These comments are intended to supplement the discussion of archaeological data on Period V political organization with details drawn mainly from published primary sources and secondary works which document information from unpublished sources. The first section considers local administration, as a basis for more detailed interpretation of settlement patterns, as well as for understanding the dynamics of the regional system. The second section describes regional integration and regional administration, with emphasis on evidence for political change within the long time span represented by Period V archaeological remains. Because of the emphasis placed in the main part of the chapter on the relationship between political and economic activities, details on commercial activities will be treated separately in the final section of these comments. It will be necessary to consider a number of communities outside the survey area, both because of their ties with the survey area and because there are gaps in the records for any one part of the valley which can be filled in with information from other areas. For reference, Figure 8A-1 shows the communities that are mentioned.

DOCUMENTARY SOURCES

The major documents available for the Valley of Oaxaca are the *Relaciones Geográficas* (Paso y Troncoso 1905, Vol. IV, here abbreviated as PNE IV; Caso 1928a; Barlow 1945) and Fray Francisco de Burgoa's (1934 edition) *Geográfica Descripción* (here abbreviated as GD). The *relaciones* are a survey of political and economic conditions in New Spain, conducted between 1579 and about 1585 at the instigation of Philip II. Reports are based on a comprehensive questionnaire which included requests for information on prehispanic customs and political organization. (Table 8A-1 lists the extant complete *relaciones* from the Valley of Oaxaca. With the exception of the colonial capital of Antequera, it can be seen that the Tlacolula arm has the best coverage, while there are disappointingly few *relaciones* from the Valle Grande and Etla arms.) A less detailed series of reports, the *Suma de Visitas* (PNE I), was compiled in the mid-16th century. Burgoa's work was intended as a history of the Dominican order in the Oaxaca region, although it is sprinkled with numerous comments on prehispanic and colonial Indian life in the valley. Its late date (ca. 1670) somewhat weakens its value as a record of pre-Colonial customs. In addition, Burgoa's interweaving of Biblical history with Oaxacan history at times makes his grip on reality seem questionable. Against these drawbacks can be weighed the facts that Burgoa had lived in Oaxaca since his birth in 1600, and that he drew on native oral traditions that at least in some cases were based on native manuscripts not available at present (cf. GD II:345). Some additional information can be gleaned from Aztec political histories which mention the Valley of Oaxaca in a pre-Conquest setting and from published 15th century administrative documents. An especially valuable secondary source, because it contains a wealth of well-documented information from archival sources, is Taylor's (1972) study of land tenure in colonial Oaxaca.

LOCAL ADMINISTRATION

The following discussion is a generalized, static description of local administrative units. Most deviations

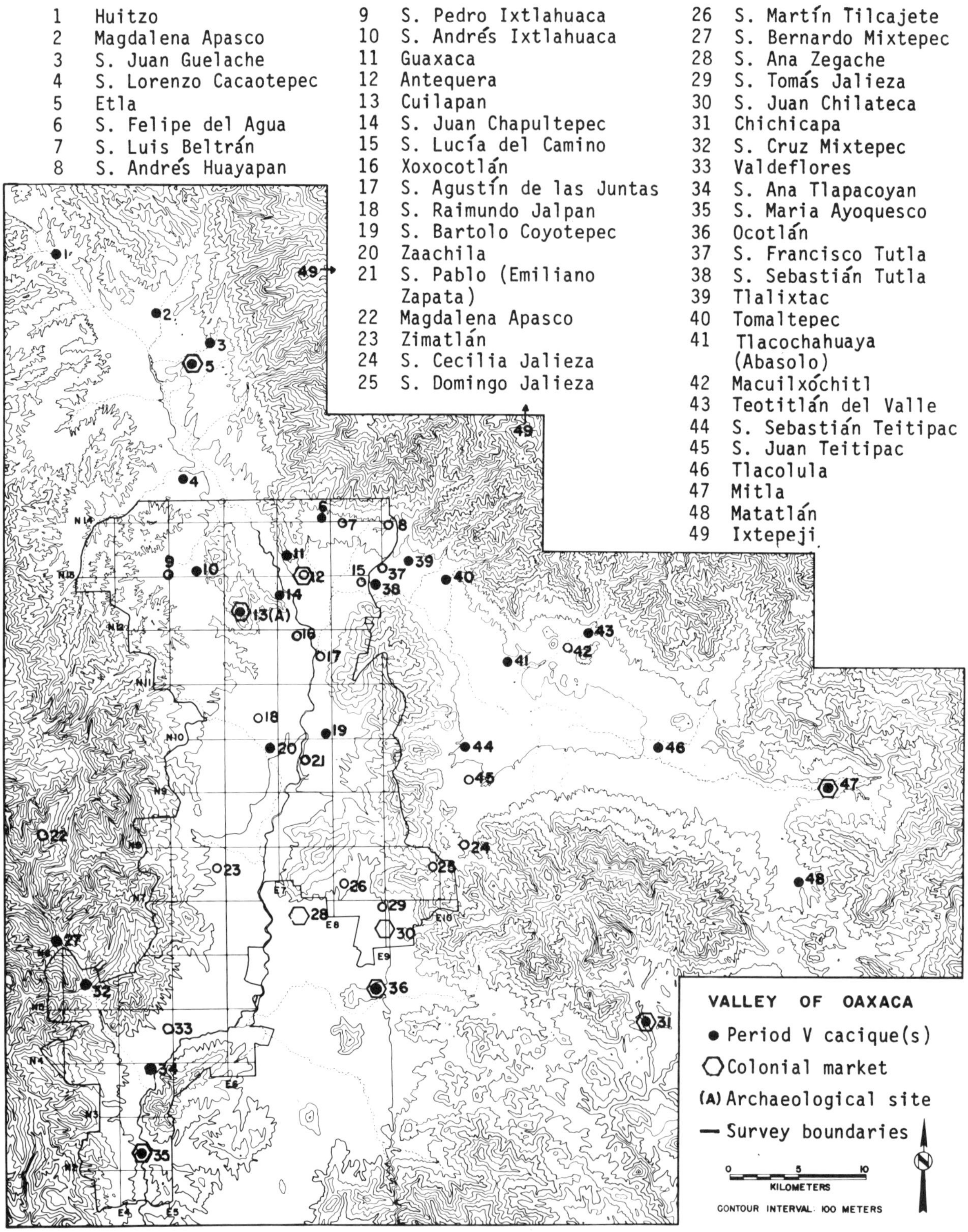

Figure 8A-1. The Valley of Oaxaca: reference map for comments on Period V ethnohistory.

from this pattern are best understood in a diachronic framework and will be treated in the next section.

Local administration was directed by *caciques*, or native lords, who were members of the highest-ranking lineage (Whitecotton 1977:154). The cacique resided in a head town, which together with outlying subject villages, hamlets, and/or farmsteads formed the unit of local administration. A glance at the Period V settlement pattern map (Fig. 8-4) shows that in most cases in the survey area, these units were not highly nucleated. However, "the same term is applied to both a subdivision of a town and a *sujeto* or *estancia* in ancient Zapotec" (Whitecotton 1977:150), indicating that all were cognized as belonging to the same political and social community. Following Spores (1967) and Kowalewski (1976), these units will be referred to as petty kingdoms.

Often a single cacique is reported for a kingdom, as for Huitzo (PNE IV:199) and Santa Cruz Mixtepec (Caso 1928a:181). In other cases, there appear to have been multiple caciques, a pattern which has also been noted for some Late Postclassic political units in the central Mexico region (cf. van Zantwijk 1973; Brumfiel 1982). Tomaltepec, for example, had four caciques in early colonial times (Taylor 1972:41). Burgoa refers to "*caccicíques* and *principales* [lower-ranking nobility]" for various communities such as Chichicapa, Teitipac, and Ocotlán (GD II:51,76,141). Three caciques are reported for the pre-Conquest period from Ixtepeji (PNE IV:12), and Cuilapan as well had more than one cacique (Taylor 1972:46).

There are some ethnohistoric clues to the processes that account for variability in numbers of caciques, as well as to the administrative division of labor in places with multiple caciques. The Ixtepeji caciques were reportedly descended from three lords who emigrated from a Chinantla town in the 6th or 7th century A.D. They founded three settlements which remained separate until roughly 100 years before the writing of the *relación* (in 1579), when the caciques united in a single town (PNE IV:14-15). Since the approximate date is close to the period of Aztec intrusions into the Valley of Oaxaca region during the reigns of Moctezuma I (1440-1468) and Ahuitzotl (1486-1502), it is possible that the spatial alliance of the Ixtepeji caciques had to do with defense. In Miahuatlán (directly south of the valley), a cacique's two sons ruled jointly after his death; the elder son "divided the people that he had and gave half to his younger brother." However, at some point the younger son and his followers conquered a Chontal town and set up residence there (*Colección. . .* IX:225).

All of these cases imply that multiple caciques were each independently responsible for part of the population subject to a head town. In the cases cited, they arose through either fission or fusion, apparently as a result of practical considerations such as facilitating communication and defense, inheritance conflicts, and successful attempts by lower lords at building an independent base of support. Multiple caciques might also result from the marriage of a female cacica to a male cacique (ibid.:38). Not only is there no single cause of multiple caciques, but evidently in the long run a kingdom could fluctuate between rule by a single cacique and multiple caciques. Overall, the impression is one of considerable fluidity within the general structure of kingdoms.

The local administrative responsibilities of the Oaxaca caciques which are explicitly mentioned in the sources are tribute levies (Caso 1928a:181; PNE IV:111), mediation of disputes (PNE IV:199), judgement of adulterers (PNE IV:198), and coordination of military activities (PNE IV:12,179). Probably supervision would also have been required for managing the caciques' lands (see Taylor 1972:41-43). In one case, *mayordomos* are mentioned as aides in managing the caciques' household (Caso 1928a:181). These are separate from the administrative aides (*tequitlatos*) who were appointed as the local administrators of each barrio and estancia and were entitled to receive labor services in their own right (ibid.; PNE IV:129, 199). *Tequitlatos* were members of the nobility rather than commoners (Spores 1965:967; Whitecotton 1977:144).

From the beginning of Spanish occupation of the valley, colonial administrators recognized the traditional rights of the Oaxaca caciques, and throughout the colonial period the caciques retained their hereditary titles (Taylor 1972:36,64). Taking the presence of a cacique as the criterion for the existence of a local administrative unit or kingdom, ethnohistoric sources indicate that there were at least 27 such units in the valley in 1579-80. Table 8A-1 lists these units; it was compiled by identifying names of communities founded in the pre-Conquest period which can be documented as the residences of caciques in colonial times. With one exception, survey area sites in or adjacent to the communities on this list were also independently identified as administrative centers according to the methods described in Chapter 4. The exception is Santa Ana Tlapacoyan, visible archaeologically as a cluster of dispersed occupation lying north-

Table 8A-1. Residences of Caciques in the Valley of Oaxaca in the Pre-Colonial or Colonial Periods

AREA OF VALLEY	COMMUNITY NAME	REFERENCE*	CORRESPONDING ARCHAEOLOGICAL SITE (IF IN SURVEY AREA)
Central	San Juan Chapultepec	Taylor, p.40	None
	Cuilapan	Barlow; Taylor, p.40	
	Guaxaca	Taylor, p.42	None
	S. Andrés Ixtlahuaca	Taylor, p.45	2-11-81, etc.
	San Felipe del Agua	Taylor, p.48	2-11-14, etc.
Etla	Huitzo	PNE IV; Taylor, p.41	
	Etla	Taylor, p.42	
	San Lorenzo Cacaotepec	Taylor, p.45	
	San Juan Guelache	Taylor, p.63	
	Magdalena Apasco	Taylor, p.16	
Valle Grande	San Bartolo Coyotepec	Taylor, p.52	3-11-56, etc.
	Zaachila	PNE IV	3-11-76
	Ocotlán	Taylor, p.55	
	Santa Cruz Mixtepec (formerly Iztepec)	Caso	3-11-332, etc.
	Santa Ana Tlapacoyan	Taylor, p.74	3-11-385, etc.
	San Bernardo Mixtepec (formerly Tepecimatlan)	PNE I	
	Ayoquezco	Taylor, p.230; Gerhard, p.48**	3-11-451, etc.
	Chichicapa	PNE IV	
Tlacolula	Tlalixtac	PNE IV; Taylor, p.40	
	Tomaltepec	Taylor, p.64	
	San Sebastián Teitipac	PNE IV; Taylor, p.45	
	San Sebastián Tutla	Taylor, p.38	
	Teotitlán del Valle	PNE IV; Taylor, p.64	
	Tlacolula	PNE IV; Taylor, p.64	
	Mitla	PNE IV; Taylor, p.40	
	Tlacochahuaya	Taylor, p.64	
	Matatlán	Taylor, p.52	

* References to PNE IV, Caso (1928), or Barlow (1945) document the presence of caciques in period V. References to Taylor (1972) document their presence in the colonial period.

** I have been unable to find a specific reference to an Ayoquezco cacique. However, it was known as a head town in early colonial times, according to the document cited by Taylor; Gerhard's study of the political geography of colonial Mexico also refers to Ayoquezco as a separate kingdom prior to the Conquest (Gerhard 1972).

east of the modern town, with an estimated population of 851 (488-1215). Further Period V occupation may underlie the modern community. The prehispanic population of Tlapacoyan was said to be over 2000 (Caso 1928a:183). In addition, two communities on the list (San Juan Chapultepec and Guaxaca) which fall within the present city of Oaxaca were not visible on survey. Guaxaca was adjacent to the colonial capital of Antequera (*Colección* . . . VI:511). The Aztec occupation of Guaxaca is reported to have comprised about 900 families (Durán 1951:243). Its status before the Aztec conquest is unclear, although it was evidently occupied before that time (ibid.:234; PNE IV:16).

Several other sites that were identified archaeologically as Period V administrative centers do not appear on the list compiled from ethnohistoric sources. A major example is Jalieza (3-11-245, etc.), the second largest V site in the survey region. Jalieza does not appear on Aztec tribute lists dating from the second half of the 16th century, even though they include a number of other major valley centers (see Barlow 1949). In 1532, a Spanish administrator who listed Cuilapan, Zaachila, Zimatlán, Tlapacoyan, and Chichicapa as important towns in the southern part of the valley failed to mention Jalieza (Paso y Troncoso 1940, III:142). Since Chichicapa is located in the mountains southeast of the valley, Jalieza's relatively remote location cannot account for its exclusion. The colonial towns closest to the archaeological site were Santa Cecilia Jalieza, Santo Tomás Jalieza, and Santo Domingo Jalieza. According to the *relaciones*, Santo Tomás was a small dependency of Chichicapa (PNE IV:115), while Santa Cecilia was subject to Zaachila (ibid.:192-93); Santo Domingo is not mentioned. Although at present there is no known way to distinguish visually between Early and Late V pottery, these lines of evidence suggest that Jalieza was no longer a major center by the time of the Spanish Conquest.

The status of three other relatively large sites which were archaeologically identified as administrative centers but which do not appear on the list of towns with caciques, San Andrés Huayapan (2-11-235, etc.), Valdeflores (3-11-358,etc.) and 2-11-317, etc., (Fig. 8-9) is even more ambiguous. Possibly their exclusion is the accidental result of missing records, and they were either independent centers or part of kingdoms with multiple caciques. Alternatively, any one could have been the residence of an influential *tequitlato* rather than a cacique. The fact that none were colonial head towns somewhat diminishes the likelihood that they had been independent centers at Conquest, although both San Felipe del Agua and San Andrés Ixtlahuaca had caciques in spite of their dependent colonial administrative status. The site we called Valdeflores is on a mountain directly east across the river from modern Santa Cruz Mixtepec (ancient Iztepec), and appears to fall within the area that Welte (1975) postulated as the kingdom of Iztepec according to measurements given in the *Suma de Visitas*. Thus it could also be a residence of a Santa Cruz cacique, an Early V administrative center which preceded the later center of Santa Cruz, or an earlier, distinct kingdom which was later subsumed by Santa Cruz or abandoned. 2-11-317, etc. may also have been more important in Early V. But its nearness to the 16th century *congregación* town of San Jacinto Amilpas (Taylor 1972:26), as well as the fact that it adjoins a community with the revealing name of Pueblo Nuevo, implies that it was probably occupied in Late V. Huayapan, on the other hand, may date exclusively to Late V, since it was said to be founded by Cuilapan in the last years before the Conquest (GD I:395).

In addition to these four sites, there is a group of very small sites which were originally classified as fifth level Period V administrative centers but which lack ethnohistoric documentation. None of these should be considered head towns. The largest (3-11-192, with an estimated population of 55) sits on a ridge adjoining the hill known as María Sánchez, west of San Martín Tilcajete. Both Burgoa (GD II:348) and the Zaachila *relación* (PNE IV:195) state that the Zaachila ruler used this hill as a fortress. Thus the occupation at 3-11-192 (and at 3-11-239, on the hilltop itself) is probably related to this purpose. The remaining four fifth level "centers" are all small, isolated four-mound groups or enclosed courtyards. One (2-11-134), which we initially identified as a fifth-level center but then dropped, was defined as serving ritual functions because it appeared to lack evidence for a residential population and because unusually large numbers of *sahumadores* were found. Its isolated, mountaintop location is consistent with ethnohistoric descriptions of Period V shrines (PNE IV:198; GD II:119), although it may have served simultaneously as a boundary marker. Two other sites (3-11-522 and 3-11-498) had pottery which was too sparse and eroded to provide clues to their function, but their settings and architecture imply that they were similar to 2-11-134. The final site in this group, 3-11-297, appears to be a Period V occupation of a formal mound group built at Jalieza in Period IV; whether special or administrative functions were performed by the Period V residents is unclear.

REGIONAL INTEGRATION AND REGIONAL ADMINISTRATION

In the previous section, a generalized picture of the Valley of Oaxaca kingdoms was presented–as if all were copies of a single pattern. With allowances for differences in subsistence bases and size, this is probably a valid way to view the kingdoms at the local administrative level. Within the regional system, however, each kingdom was the focus of a unique, dynamic set of interactions which overlapped but never replicated those of other kingdoms. These ties will be discussed as background to understanding 1) the formal integrating mechanisms that existed beyond the local level, and 2) the dynamics of political change within Period V.

Marriages between ruling families of various kingdoms were a major basis for regional integration (Spores 1974; Whitecotton 1977:44), establishing access to resources from outside the boundaries of a particular kingdom. For example, they helped to establish and solidify military alliances (Spores 1974) and trading relationships (ibid.; PNE IV:16). They may further have served to establish channels for boosting followers and agricultural manpower through immigration. The influx of Mixtecs into the Valley of Oaxaca following the marriage of a sister of the wife of the Zaachila lord to a lord from the Mixteca Alta (PNE IV:190) was probably advantageous from this point of view (Blanton, in press). From another perspective, of course, marriages could provide access to land–as implied by the fact that these Mixtecs came to the flat, fertile Valley of Oaxaca from what is described as a "very rough and rugged" part of the Mixteca Alta (Barlow 1945:23).

Unfortunately, there is at present no detailed genealogical information on Zapotec elite marriages comparable to the contents of the Aztec chronicles or the Late Postclassic Mixtecan codices. If Zapotec elite marriage customs were comparable to those of Mixtecan elites, then only one of a cacique's multiple wives would have been the senior wife designated as the mother of the heir to his estate (Herrera 1947, III:320). An additional type of kinship relation is suggested by Herrera's (ibid.) report that the Mixtecan nobility considered it an honor to send their daughters to serve in the cacique's household; they bore him children and were subsequently married to other nobility and merchants. It is not clear whether these liaisons reinforced vassalage ties with nobility from inside or outside the cacique's kingdom, or both.

Despite the lack of good genealogical data, the limited number of marriages mentioned in the ethnohistoric sources helps to indicate the extent and complexity of marriage alliances. The Ixtepeji caciques exchanged daughters with Cuilapan, Zaachila, Guaxaca, and two sierra towns, Teocuicuilco and Chicomesuchitl (PNE IV:16). Shortly after the Conquest, the son of the Zaachila ruler married a woman from Tlacochahuaya (GD II:117). Zaachila and the Mixteca Alta were linked through marriage, as indicated by a 13th century marriage between a lord of Zaachila and a Mixtecan woman. Evidently the relationship between Zaachila and the Mixteca Alta persisted for a long time and ultimately involved a marriage link with Cuilapan as well, as the sister of the wife of the Zaachila ruler and the Mixtecan noble whom she married shortly before the Conquest resided in Cuilapan (PNE IV:190). Given the association between kinship and military alliances, perhaps another set of marriages can be inferred from the alliance between Huitzo, Etla, Guaxaca, and Cuilapan (ibid.: 199). Clearly, considering the political and economic benefits of elite marriages, it would have been advantageous to establish many linkages. A more specific idea of the extent of elite marriage networks is given by the Huitzo *relación*, which states that the cacique had 15 to 20 wives (ibid.:197).

The Valley of Oaxaca kingdoms also tended to be interdependent in commercial and religious activities. For example, aside from the trading relationships which were mentioned above in conjunction with marital alliances, major marketplaces were apparently not located in every kingdom. (These data will be discussed in detail in the final section of this paper.) With regard to religious interdependence, it is evident that shrines in some communities served regional rather than local functions. Mitla was a major pilgrimage center, the site of an elaborate religious complex, the residence of the highest Zapotec priest, and the reputed burial place of Zaachila rulers (PNE IV:149, 151-52; GD II:121-25). Two other important shrines were noted by Burgoa. One at Teotitlán del Valle attracted people from all parts of Oaxaca (GD II:119), while lower-ranking valley nobility were buried at one at Teitipac (ibid.:65,70). In addition, the abandoned Monte Albán Main Plaza adjacent to Cuilapan may have retained special regional ritual significance; one local Zapotec term for the site is *Danibaan* or 'sacred mountain' (Cruz 1946:157-64).

The system which has been described up to this point is one in which the valley kingdoms were politically autonomous at the local level, but bound by complex sets of crosscutting ties at the regional level. Ethnohistoric sources also suggest that there was a formal level of regional control, represented by Zaachila.

Zaachila is repeatedly mentioned as the capital of the ruler of most of the Valley Zapotecs. Reported to have been vassals of the Zaachila king are the nobility of Tlacolula (PNE IV:145), Macuilxóchitl (PNE IV:101), Teitipac (PNE IV:111), Chichicapa (PNE IV:116), Tlalixtac (PNE IV:179), Mitla (PNE IV:149), Teotitlán del Valle (PNE IV:105), Magdalena Mixtepec (GD II:348), and perhaps Etla (GD II:2). The period of Zaachila's pre-eminency dates from at least A.D. 1375 (CBA:381-82) to at least 1485 or 1495, when an Aztec codex refers to Zaachila as the head town of the Valley of Oaxaca (Schmieder 1930:16; PNE IV:194, footnote 1).

It was argued in the main part of the chapter that Zaachila was actually a disembedded capital–in this case, a neutral capital maintained in a situation where there is a balance of power among competing polities. Archaeological indicators were the absence of mounded construction dating to Period V at Zaachila, the lack of evidence for any extensive Period V occupation of the site, and the fact that there was very little occupation of the area around Zaachila. Ethnohistoric accounts tend to corroborate our field evidence. Burgoa, who lived at Zaachila in the 1600s, had examined the massive mounds that can still be seen today in the center of Zaachila. Local tradition at that time maintained that the mounds were ancient religious or commemorative structures, and he did not regard them as evidence of "the houses, and palace of the cacique." He commented, "I have been unable to discover any signs of large buildings, or continued occupation such as one finds in other places that persist since ancient times" (GD I:414).

It should be noted, too, that while we originally interpreted Zaachila's pre-Conquest population as minimal, there is some ethnohistoric data that contradicts this interpretation. In the mid-1500s, Zaachila had 1097 households (PNE I:287); it is not clear whether this figure includes outlying dependencies. The 1581 *relación* reported that in pre-Conquest times there were many people there, including many nobles (PNE IV:191). Many of these, of course, could have been visitors to the court or part-time residents of the town. Burgoa's observations, quoted above, do imply that the town had grown considerably since the pre-Conquest period. And Zaachila's population evidently swelled in the last years before the Conquest, as a Mixtec barrio was reported to date from the time that Mixtecs expanded into Zaachila's territory (GD I:396). Considering all of this evidence, perhaps a better interpretation of Zaachila's population during the time that it was indisputably the Zapotec capital is that it fell within the size range of head towns which were smaller than Jalieza.

Neither the evidence that Zaachila's population was larger than we originally believed nor the evidence that it had a local administrative district contradicts our interpretation of the town as a disembedded capital. Of seven places reported in the *relaciones* to have been former subjects of Zaachila (Chichicapa, Tlacolula, Macuilxóchitl, Teitipac, Tlalixtac, Teotitlán del Valle, and Mitla), six mentioned payment of tribute and services. Three towns reported tribute payments varying from a contribution of game and honey (Teitipac; PNE IV:111) to the more costly payments of cotton mantles, feathers, and military service (Teitipac; PNE IV:179) and gold dust, cotton, fowls, chile, and slaves (Teotitlán del Valle; PNE IV:106). Of the remaining three towns, one (Mitla; PNE IV:149) only occasionally planted a cornfield and gave fowls and honey, while two, Tlacolula (PNE IV:145) and Macuilxóchitl (PNE IV:101), paid no tribute other than assistance in warfare.

It has been suggested (Whitecotton 1977,128) that Zaachila may have at some point attempted to take more direct control. The *relación* of Macuilxóchitl states that the town was once ruled by a governor appointed by Zaachila (ibid.; PNE IV:102) and Burgoa (GD II:70) commented that Zaachila had also placed lords in Teitipac. In addition, Zaachila apparently tried to increase the resources at its disposal by leading an alliance of Mixtecs and Zapotecs in the conquest of Tehuantepec (GD I:393), a populous coastal market center about 150 kilometers southeast of the valley. Once conquered, Tehuantepec was ruled directly through the Zaachila dynasty; at the time of the Spanish Conquest, its cacique was the son of the Zaachila ruler (GD II:346; Whitecotton 1977:130-31). The benefits of the conquest are readily apparent from comparing the preceding list of tribute goods paid to Zaachila by Valley of Oaxaca towns with the following list of items paid by Tehuantepec: gold dust, gold jewelry, *chalcihuites* (semi-precious stones), green feathers, tiger skins, cotton clothing, fowls, corn, chile, beans, honey, deer, fish, and fruit (Caso 1928b:169). At Tehuantepec, the Zapotec ruler was powerful enough to resist an Aztec attempt to take over the center (ibid.; Durán 1951:438). However, within the valley, Cuilapan was formally replacing Zaachila's position.

For a time, towns such as Teotitlán del Valle which had previously paid tribute to Zaachila continued to pay the ruler at Tehuantepec (PNE IV:116-117). But by the time of the Conquest, places such as Teotitlán, Mitla, and Teitipac which formerly paid tribute to Zaachila or Tehuantepec gradually came under the influence of the Mixtecs of the region we have called "Cuiban".[1] When the Spaniards arrived, several sources state that the Zaachila ruler was fighting Cuilapan from his hill-top stronghold near San Martín Tilcajete (GD II:348; PNE IV:116). The only Zaachila allies who are mentioned are the nobility of Magdalena Mixtepec (GD II:348). With Mixtec aid, Cuilapan had already established the towns of San Raimundo Jalpan and San Pablo (Emiliano Zapata) on Zaachila's territory and had gone on to found Xoxocotlán, Huayapan, San Francisco Tutla, San Sebastián Tutla, and Santa Lucía del Camino (GD I:395).

A second source of valley conflict was probably the Aztecs. The Aztec version of their first expedition into the valley implies that they had difficulty fighting so far away from their base; a reason which they gave for planning to destroy the town of Guaxaca was that it would be too much trouble to return if future rebellions occurred (Durán 1951:234). It is almost inconceivable that the valley's large population would have been unable to resist, had they been united against the Aztecs. In fact, in the section of the *relaciones* where all informants were asked to state who they fought with prior to the Conquest, only 3 out of 11 valley towns named the Mexica (Table 8A-2). One of the three towns is Mitla, which is consistent with Aztec statements that Mitla provoked the first expedition by murdering several Aztec merchants (Durán 1951:229). Interestingly, Mitla is one of the few valley towns which is also named as an adversary by other valley towns. Zaachila is another town reporting warfare with the Aztecs, but this probably refers to a later conflict within the valley around 1495 (Torquemada 1944, I:186; PNE IV:194,footnote 1) or to the clash between Tehuantepec and the Aztecs which took place after 1502 (Durán 1951; Caso 1928b:169). With regard to the Aztec garrison, the Zaachila *relación* specifically states that it was placed in the valley "by way of friendship and without war" (PNE IV:194).

As argued previously (see also Spores 1974), the complex interactions of Late Postclassic kingdoms formed a regional system which was very unstable when viewed from the perspective of any individual kingdom, but very stable at a macroscopic level. To permanently transform such a system, by developing more strongly centralized control, would have been extremely costly. Cuilapan's well-documented record of exploiting the Spaniards to further consolidate its power within the valley after the Conquest (Taylor 1972) could be the extension of a strategy begun by the Mixtecs of the "Cuiban" region. In essence, this involved drawing on resources from outside the valley without the risks or costs of territorial expansion beyond the valley. Zaachila, in conquering and occupying Tehuantepec, had clearly also attempted to gain control of new resources. The occupation of Tehuantepec was a success insofar as it led to control of a major marketplace, provided a wealth of tribute goods, and bolstered the Zaachila dynasty's influence in the Mesoamerican system (as indicated by the marriage of a daughter of Moctezuma II to the Tehuantepec ruler [Durán 1951:438]. At the same time, however, Zaachila's loss of its position within the valley might be partly attributed to the strain of trying to maintain an empire over a large area through flimsy administrative mechanisms.

[1] "Cuiban" is a term coined to describe the series of settlements of various sizes which, during Monte Albán V, extended from Cuilapan to Monte Albán. It is not the name of a Prehispanic settlement.

Table 8A-2. Summary of Reports on Pre-conquest Warfare, from the *Relaciones Geográficas*

COMMUNITY	ADVERSARIES	REMARKS	REFERENCE
Zaachila	Tututepec, Tlaxiaco, Mexicans		PNE IV, 193-194
Huitzo	Teocuicuilco, Coatlan, Miahuatlán, Chichicapa, Nexapa		ibid., 199
Tlalixtac	Not mentioned	Warfare was frequent.	ibid., 179
Macuilxóchitl	Mitla	Also fought with other places where they were sent by the ruler of Zaachila.	ibid., 102
Teotitlán del Valle	Mexicans		ibid., 106
Teitipac	Indians of the sierra	Fought only as ordered by the ruler of Zaachila.	ibid., 111
Chichicapa	Surrounding groups	Continual warfare.	ibid., 117
Tlacolula	The Mixes, Mitla	Warfare was frequent.	ibid., 145
Santa Cruz Mixtepec	-------	They did not recall having wars.	Caso, 1928, 181
Mitla	Tututepec, Mexicans		PNE IV, 149
Cuilapan	Zaachila		Barlow, 1945, 25

COMMERCIAL ACTIVITIES

There is a paucity of published information on commercial life in the Valley of Oaxaco in Period V. The lack is certainly partly attributable to the overriding emphasis on political matters in Spanish sources. However, the Aztec state's concern with long-distance trade is reflected in a number of explicit references in their chronicles to major market centers which serviced the pan-Mesoamerican system with luxury goods. In the vicinity of Oaxaca, three such markets were Coixtlahuaca, Miahuatlán, and Tehuantepec. Coixtlahuaca, in the Mixteca Alta, dealt in gold, feathers, cacao, fine *jícaras*, clothing, cochineal, and dyed rabbit yarn (Durán 1951:188). Miahuatlán, directly south of the valley, specialized in slaves (PNE IV:125). In the 16th century, following the Conquest, Tehuantepec functioned as an important port and center for the distribution of cotton, salt, and cacao (Caso 1928b:174; García Pimentel 1904:62). The Aztecs' professed interest in trading in Tehuantepec (Durán 1951:395; PNE IV:194), as well as Oviedo's (1851-55, IV:161)remark that after the Spanish Conquest of Tehuantepec, "the Indians. . .carried on their markets and commerce as before" indicate that Tehuantepec had played a similar role before the Conquest.

The absence of any mention of a major long-distance market in Oaxaca, in spite of the fact that neighboring centers are explicitly referred to in the documents, strongly suggests that the valley was not a focus for production and distribution of goods to traders servicing the pan-Mesoamerican system. Instead, both the Aztecs and the Spanish commented on the valley's agricultural productivity and fertility (Durán 1951:243; Motolinía 1950:31; Cortés 1971:269). This evidence implies that the valley tended to specialize in the production of food as its major exchange item. Preliminary examination of information on Aztec tribute reinforces this suggestion. According to the *Codex Mendocino* (Molíns Fábrega 1956:25), a total of 19 provinces in the Aztec empire were required to contribute grains. All of these provinces except Coyolapan (of which the Valley of Oaxaca is the major part) cluster around the Valley of Mexico, in a zone covering northern Puebla, northcentral Guerrero, Morelos, and Hidalgo. Coyolapan stands alone as the only province in the rest of the empire, the area encompassing southern Guerrero, southern Puebla, Veracruz, and northeastern Oaxaca state, which contributed grains (ibid., facing 48). It is noteworthy, too, that the total value of Coyolapan's tribute is among the lowest in the empire– and, if the value per tributary town is used as an index, it is also the lowest (Table 8A-3). This is attributable to the fact that low-value staple foods form the bulk of the Coyolapan tribute, while other provinces contributed greater amounts of exotic goods and craft items. It

Table 8A-3. Value of Aztec Tribute Assessments by Province

PROVINCE	# OF TOWNS[1]	TOTAL VALUE OF GOODS[2]	TOTAL VALUE: RANK	VALUE OF GOODS PER TOWN	VALUE OF GOODS PER TOWN: RANK
Tuxtepec	15	88,528	1	5,902	5
Tuxpan	7	71,728	2	10,247	3
Cihuatlan	16	71,600	3	4,475	9
Tepecuacuilco	23	65,178	4	2,834	13
Taxco	11	55,048	5	5,004	7
Cotastla	6	48,598	6	8,100	4
Jilotepec	12	39,154	7	3,262	10
Cicoaque	8	28,328	8	2,916	12
Atlan	2	26,400	9	13,200	2
Huastepec	26	25,804	10	992	24
Ojitipa	1	25,600	11	25,600	1
Huatusco	5	25,200	12	5,040	6
Acolman	25	24,592	13	984	25
Cuernavaca	17	23,372	14	1,375	18
Tlatlauquitepec	15	22,528	15	1,502	17
Tlalcocauhtitlan	5	22,528	15	4,626	8
Coixtlahuaca	19	22,418	16	1,180	22
Petlacalco	10	22,160	17	2,216	14
Axacuba	10	13,528	18	1,353	19
Atotonilco de Pedraza	4	12,968	19	3,242	11
Cahuacan	14	11,744	20	839	29
Tlatelolco	6	11,720	21	1,953	16
Hueypoxtla	10	11,272	22	1,127	23
Atotonilco el Grande	5	11,056	23	2,211	15
Tlapa	12	10,918	24	910	28
Toluca	13	10,408	25	801	30
Ocuilan	7	8,944	26	1,278	20
Cuatitlan	7	8,592	27	1,227	21
COYOLAPAN	33	6,400	28	194	34
Tlapacoya	7	5,528	29	790	31
Chalco	4	3,728	30	932	26
Tlachquiauco	4	3,704	31	926	27
Yoaltepec	13	3,644	32	282	33
Quiauhteopan	3	2,029	33	676	32

[1]Barlow (1949). Compiled by Saindon (1977, 70).
[2]Values as measured in quachtli, a standard mantle of approximately 5½ feet Calculations per Borah and Cook (1963). Compiled by Saindon (ibid.).

could be argued that the Coyolapan tribute was set at an unusually low value for political reasons. Still, the fact that the valley is spatially isolated as a province contributing agricultural staples seems to be good evidence that these actually were its major products.

The destiny of at least some of the tribute food was Coixtlahuaca (PNE IV:198), which may parallel the movement of part of the valley's non-tributary goods in exchange for craft items. Miahuatlán also reported importing salt from the valley in pre-Colonial times (ibid.:129), although it has been noted that the Valley's salt deposits may not have been large enough to meet local demand in Period V (Taylor 1972:16–17). Markets which were reported in the *relaciones* to have provided salt and/or cotton to valley traders in the 1580s may indicate other sources of goods in Period V. Judging from the number of towns which cited each market, Tehuantepec (PNE IV:103, 107, 113, 119, 147, 181, 204; Caso 1928a:182, 184) was the most important, followed by neighboring Xalapa (PNE IV: 103, 107, 147, 181; Caso 1928a:182,184). Nexapa (PNE IV:103, 181), Tututepec (ibid.:204; Caso 1928a:182), Teposcolula (PNE IV:204, Xoquilla (Caso 1928a:182), and Tequicistlan (PNE IV:103) were also mentioned. That Valley of Oaxaca residents were active in trade in precolonial times is implied by a 1531 letter in which an Antequera administrator complained about the effects of a Spanish ordinance forbidding transport of goods by natives:

> . . . the natives of New Spain always had and still have the custom of transporting goods and by that they make their living . . . I appeal to your Majesty to grant permission to the people of said town [Antequera] so that by paying said natives for their work according to their tradition they may transport moderate amounts of goods. [Paso y Troncoso 1940, II:100]

One of the few direct references to prehispanic local exchange in the valley, which appears to take the presence of local markets for granted, is the comment in the Teotitlán del Valle *relación* that some peasants sold game in order to pay their tribute (PNE IV:160). Also, Burgoa explicitly states that a market at San Juan Chilateca, serving to provision Indians from the mountains, dated from before the Conquest (GD II:63). It has been argued (Cook and Diskin, 1976, with reference to Taylor, 1971) that the only Spanish interference in the pre-existing valley market system was the establishment of the Antequera market for the purpose of provisioning the urban population, while

> . . . the prehispanic Indian marketplaces in Ocotlan, Ayoquezco, Etla and other Valley towns were essentially undisturbed by Spanish meddling. The paternalistic colonial policy of segregating Indians from Spaniards and castes led the viceregal government to support the autonomy and independence of the Indian marketing system in the Valley. [Cook and Diskin 1976:11]

This statement indicates why there are few colonial references to prehispanic markets, but we do not know how many colonial marketplaces recorded in ethnohistoric sources were already in operation in Period V. Aside from the new Antequera market, documented colonial markets are Etla (GD II:8), Chilateca (GD II:55,63) Santa Ana Zegache (GD II:61), Cuilapan (GD I:410), Chichicapa (PNE IV:118), Mitla (Taylor 1972:103), Ocotlán, and Ayoquezco (Taylor 1972:99).

Considering this list of markets in the context of ethnohistoric data on local and regional administration, some additions can be made to the commentary on the relationship between administrative and commercial hierarchies in the main part of the chapter. Six of the eight markets are located in ethnohistorically documented administrative centers. Yet it is significant that most of the ethnohistorically-documented administrative centers appear to lack markets–or, more certainly, to lack markets large enough to be considered noteworthy in colonial sources. In the overall context of the regional system, then, this implies a lack of isomorphism between commercial and administrative functions–in the sense that the lattice of commercial central places is not equal to the lattice of administrative central places.

The two markets which are located in non-administrative places are Santa Ana Zegache and San

Juan Chilateca. Zegache, as noted above, was in the territory contested by Cuilapan at the time of the Conquest and is therefore assumed to have been a local dependency of Zaachila before that time. Chilateca was administratively related to Zegache in the 17th century (GD II:63), and it is thought to have been a 16th century subject of Cuilapan (Welte 1975:10). Considering these relationships, and its nearness to Santa Ana Zegache, Chilateca can probably also be safely assumed to have been formerly located in Zaachila's local administrative district. At the top of the formal Period V hierarchy, then, is the clearest case for a separation between commercial and administrative functions. This absence of high-order commercial functions is characteristic of disembedded capitals (Blanton 1976b), reinforcing previous arguments that Zaachila functioned as a disembedded capital in the context of the competing polities of Period V.

However, there are signs that such segregation did not last throughout the period. First, Zaachila conquered and occupied a major market center, Tehuantepec, on which most Valley of Oaxaca kingdoms depended. It can be suggested that this was a strategy adopted in a situation where Zaachila's position as a local and regional administrative center was threatened by the growing competition of the "Cuiban" region, and where it lacked the real power to establish strong control over such centers. Zaachila apparently exploited the power that it did have (coordination of military activities) in order to establish firm political and economic control over a major market center outside the valley.

Chapter 9

POPULATION AND AGRICULTURAL POTENTIAL: EARLY I THROUGH V

by Stephen Kowalewski

INTRODUCTION

In Chapter 3 we showed that for the first thousand years of settled farming life in the Valley of Oaxaca the numbers of people that might have been living at any one time were far fewer than the resources of the land could support. This should not be surprising. To produce the food to feed more people requires more labor from the existing population. There has to be a reason why people should work harder, or more efficiently, to do that. Given the picture of a small scale, ranked society that is sketched in Flannery's *The Early Mesoamerican Village* (1976) and in Chapter 3, it is not clear where that kind of demand for greater production would have come from.

A vastly increased economic demand and increased population apparently did not come about until Monte Albán Early I, with the founding of the new and much larger capital at Monte Albán. Within a hundred years or so of 500 B.C. entirely new demands were placed on the valley's economy. The most salient difficulty was the provisioning of roughly 5000 people at Monte Albán. How was that accomplished? In the "rural" area, that is, the rest of the valley, what might account for the universal increase in population and the emergence of larger towns as well as villages and hamlets? (These trends in the countryside probably began on a small scale in the Rosario phase, but in Monte Albán Early I the growth pattern becomes clear and is of a greater magnitude.)

These basic questions–how as much as half the total valley population was sustained on its mountaintop, and why the rural population was distributed the way it was–are the themes of this chapter. The emphasis is on the possible relationships between agricultural productivity and the distribution of population. To what extent did the natural distribution of agricultural land and water resources influence the evolution of the valley's settlement system? In the present chapter we take up this question for each phase from Monte Albán Early I through V. The problem is conceived here as a search for regularities in the relationships between population abundance and distribution, on the one hand, and agricultural productivity on the other, within each archaeological phase and between phases.

VARIABLES AND ASSUMPTIONS

There is little direct evidence of the cultural patterns of ancient agricultural production. Since the Valley of Oaxaca has been intensively inhabited and farmed for 3000 years, remains of ancient fields are rare. In a few cases we have found what we believe to be ancient agricultural terraces. For example, just southeast of El Choco (3-8-272-274, N2E3), there are terraces similar in construction to the prehispanic residential terraces that are part of the ancient community a short distance upslope. These terraces, however, are larger than the usual residential terraces, and they have no artifactual evidence of habitation. Lacking that, of course, they are hard to date. Similarly, in square N8E7 an area of more than 1.2 square kilometers in the middle piedmont has been modified for agricultural terraces. Again, they are difficult to date. In the field we thought they might have been built in the Colonial period, because of the proximity of the hacienda La Soledad. Possible agricultural terraces were spotted in several other piedmont areas. On the valley floor the traces of old fields have long been erased by subsequent farming and, in a few places, alluviation.

We are not likely to know about important features of ancient farming systems such as land tenure or crop diversity. Therefore it is necessary to use indirect methods to approximate some of the constraints facing the ancient inhabitants. The principal kind of association between population and agricultural resources is spatial. Spatial association may mean proximity, as in the catchment analysis discussed in Chapter 3. Eventually we will carry out different kinds of catchment analyses for every site in the valley. Another kind of spatial association involves the quantification of resources and ancient population within delimited spatial areas of specified sizes. As in the catchment analyses where one measures the distance between resource patch and population cluster, this kind of spatial association also relies on the assumption that people tend to live near their fields. Thus in this chapter we will investigate relations between population density and agricultural resource density insofar as these may be understood indirectly by their relative spatial associations. We consider aspects of technology, land and water, climate and weather, labor, and consumption. Each of these factors is discussed in the following pages.

Technology

For the purpose of this study we assume that even the earliest farmers in the valley had the cultural knowledge and tools and techniques necessary to carry out successful agriculture. That is, we assume that the history of farming in the valley was neither held back nor propelled forward by the lateness or miraculous appearance of new inventions. Presumably the most important technology would have been that of irrigation and drainage. The principles of that technology are simple and basic, and there is in fact archaeological evidence of wells, conceivably for pot irrigation, at least as early as the latter part of the Guadalupe phase (Flannery et al. 1970: 90-93), and irrigation canals dating to Monte Albán Early I (2-5-20, N12E8; 2-5-25, 26, 28, N12E6). The amount or scale of the application of drainage and irrigation technology would seem to be best explained not by the genius of invention, or diffusion, but by the particular requirements of the political and economic system. The causal arrow, we think, does not run the other way.

Knowledge about the breeding of corn, however, does seem to have played a significant role. Perhaps the long trend toward increased maize cob length, and hence greater yield, might be considered technological. Using archaeological specimens of corn cobs from dry caves in Tehuacán and Oaxaca, Anne Kirkby (1973:126) described an increase in cob length through the archaeological period. Since yield is directly related to the length of the cob, Kirkby concluded that maize yields per unit area of land were probably increasing at what we may assume to be a constant rate over the span of time of interest here. For each time period from Early I through V, we have estimated the average yields per hectare for the different kinds of land as a percentage of the present yield for these land types.

The increase in maize production through time is important for many of the conclusions in this study. Kirkby's curve showing increasing cob length in seven archaeological collections tends to be substantiated by information from another source, the Zapotec funerary urns. These were made during Monte Albán III-IV, and a number of them have ceramic replications of actual maize ears. Mary Dunn was able to obtain measurements on ten specimens (1975:313). The lengths range from 5.9 to 19 centimeters, with an average of 10.5 centimeters. The mean cob length suggested by Kirkby for the mid-point of this time period is between 9.5 and 10.0 centimeters, a figure that agrees rather well with the urn measurements. (The archaeological cobs range in size from less than 1 centimeter in preceramic times to more than 14 centimeters in the latest context.) While this does not irrevocably settle the issue, on the basis of the present knowledge we seem justified in accepting Kirkby's curve.

Land and Water

In the analysis that follows, we rely heavily on Anne Kirkby's *The Use of Land and Water in the Past and Present Valley of Oaxaca, Mexico* (1973). After reviewing her procedures carefully, with the perspective of almost ten years of further research in the area since her work was undertaken, and including our remeasurement of farm land, we find ourselves in essential agreement with Kirkby's assessment of the valley's resources for growing maize. Kirkby's study also contains an important chapter on past population and agricultural potential. At the time she wrote, there was only a very preliminary notion of the ancient settlement pattern. Now that we have systematic archaeological evidence, we are able to cast our data in a new model. This and the need to quantify ancient agricultural potentials for specific small areas and for time periods other than those used by Kirkby are the reasons for our rebuilding of Kirkby's model. In the course of this analysis we have made a number of modifications in the assumptions–simplifying here, complicating there–which we give in detail below. It should be clear then that our aim and our results are not a test or refutation of Kirkby's study.

We assume that maize was the single most important food of the ancient inhabitants of the Valley of Oaxaca.

Other plants were certainly integral parts of the diet as well. Beans, squash, chiles, tomatoes, amaranth, tree legumes, fruits, and miscellaneous herbs and "weeds" probably could not have been omitted from the diet without deleterious effects. But it is difficult to reconstruct crop mixes and agricultural specializations, so we use maize yields as a proxy for the general agricultural productivity.

Classification of Land Types

In Chapter 1 the Valley of Oaxaca environment was described in general terms, and broad environmental zones were defined (high alluvium, low piedmont, etc.). As Kirkby shows, these zones are not appropriate for understanding variability in maize growing potential. (Similarly, Flannery [1968b] notes that procurement systems may focus on particular resources that often cross-cut broadly defined environmental zones.) Kirkby demonstrates that water, more than any single factor or set of factors, determines how much maize a hectare of land can at present be made to produce. Soil, temperature, and slope differences in themselves are not nearly so significant. (Yields increase with slope angle in dry farming areas in Tlacolula and Etla, [1973:63, Fig. 23], but this is largely a function of the greater rainfall at higher elevations). Rainfall, the availability of moisture from the water table, and irrigation are thus the crucial factors determining the size of the maize yields modern peasants are able to obtain. Water is an almost constant preoccupation of modern farmers, as anyone who has had sustained conversation with a rural Oaxaqueño knows. There is no reason to suggest that this priority would have been different in the past.

The land type classification and the evaluation of average maize yields for each land type are derived from Kirkby (1973:19,48,66-69). The land types are defined on the basis of moisture availability. Kirkby recognizes six types; we have consolidated these into three based on the close similarity of average yields.

Type I Land consists of "water table" and "canal irrigable" land. Water table land has a high enough (0.5-2.0 meters) water table to allow crops to get moisture by capillary action. By canal irrigable, we refer to land that could be irrigated by water from the main river or its tributaries given prehispanic technology. On a long tributary stream, the amount of land irrigated depends on the volume of water. If nearly all the water is diverted at the head, downstream land cannot be irrigated. In practice this does restrict agricultural potentials, but because we have no way of knowing how water use was organized in the past, we include all potentially irrigable land. It is difficult to tell how much this inflates the overall estimates of potentials under past conditions, but given present water use (see Lees 1973) its effect should be quite minor. Including the possibility of more than one harvest per year, Type I land presently has an average yield of 2.0-2.8 tons per hectare per year.

Type II Land combines "marginal water table" land and "good floodwater farming" land. The former consists of land with a water table varying around 2-3 meters, and good floodwater land means that water in addition to rainfall comes in the form of storm floods that can be controlled and directed onto fields. For good floodwater land, this happens at least once every year. While recognizing that the hydrological conditions that allow for water table farming here, canal irrigation there, and floodwater farming in yet another place are subject to change over time, we do not see evidence of any radical alteration in their relative proportions during the archaeological time since 1500 B.C. If anything, conditions should have been better earlier in the history of farming, because of the lack of soil erosion and the richer vegetation (see Smith 1978). Average yields for Type II land are highly variable–0.4-2.8 metric tons per hectare per year, depending on rainfall.

Type III Land is defined as "poor floodwater land," where floodwater is available, but not every year; and dry farming land, where the only moisture comes from rainfall. In years with poor rainfall, yields are essentially zero, while in good years average yields may be as much as 1.2 tons per hectare.

All three land categories thus show variability in expected yields. This variation was probably significant for the ways in which food energy was moved through the valley system. The structures of ancient exchange systems seem to reflect this uncertainty in production, and this is discussed further in the sections on climate and weather, across-phase results, and the phase-by-phase results.

The Distribution of Land Types

All arable land in the study area (the Monte Albán, Central, and Valle Grande sections) was classified according to the above typology, using the 1:20,000 air photo mosaics taken in a rainy season in the middle 1960s, Kirkby's published maps, present agricultural practices, environmental and land use information we recorded on the 1:5000 air photos, our field notes, and our memory of local environment and land use. The classification used here is not an assessment of present-day land use, but of maximum potential agricultural production given prehispanic conditions. Therefore we had to omit the effects of well diggers, pumps, oxen, and alfalfa.

Since it is likely that the Atoyac was aggrading rather than downcutting during the time under consideration (Kirkby 1973:13) this too had to be taken into account. It is a factor of some importance. At present it is difficult to canal irrigate from the main river, because the river flows in a deep channel running through flat land, and because floods during the rainy season are capable of considerable destruction. However, before A.D. 1500 when the river began its present downcutting, conditions may have been somewhat similar to the area around Tlacolula, where the Río Salado loses its channel. That area is marshy. For farmers in our present study area, not irrigation but drainage is the problem, especially since greater volumes of stream water as well as rainfall are involved in the Valle Grande than are ever seen in Tlacolula. Such marshlands may have been major resources for collectable plant and animal food and other materials, but agriculture was very possibly a competing use provided that there was a labor force sufficient to dig drainage works large enough to control floodwater. Drainage canals are numerous and essential for the high productivity today around Valdefores, Santa Gertrudis, and Tejas de Morelos (N4E5, 6; N5E5); more efficient drainage would be desirable in other places farther upstream. Salinization would have been a long-term problem, as can be seen today in the valley in low lying areas such as near Loma Larga, San Bartolo Coyotepec (N9E6), and Zaachila (N10E7). Another difficulty with managing the marshlands for agriculture would be that one would have to control the flow of water in the tributary streams as well as having to react to the changing volume of the main stream.

Though there would have been difficulties farming the marshlands in some periods, the return might have justified the investment. The soils have the highest organic content of any in the valley, and water could have been applied almost whenever necessary, given the high water table.

We have tentatively mapped the distribution of possible marshlands along the Atoyac in the study area. With some qualifications, places that would have been marshland in the past are now recognizable because of the present-day soil type, a distinctive dark gray clay, relatively high in organic content and usually without sand. In places, such as around San Raymundo Jalpan and Zaachila, the gray clay overlies the typical sandy brown soil of the high alluvium, and near the main river gray clay may be covered by silt or sand. Although we are not able to demonstrate this conclusively, it seems likely that the gray clay soil deposits were formed under marshy or *ciénaga* conditions sometime prior to A.D. 1500.

At present the gray clay soils are used in two quite distinctive agricultural regimes. Along the east side of the Atoyac from San Bartolo Coyotepec (N10E7) south to Sta. Catarina Quiané (N7E6), and on the west side from San Raymundo Jalpan (N10E6) south through N7E6 there are bands of gray clay from 100 meters to 1 kilometer wide, paralleling the river. Today these areas may be irrigated with pumps and deep wells, dry farmed, or left fallow. The main crops are corn and alfalfa, but in general these areas are less productive than other parts of the alluvium, for several reasons, including inadequate drainage, lack of water, difficulty in working the soil, and even land disputes. In general many of these difficulties (except for the land disputes) were brought on by the Atoyac's downcutting, which left these areas high, dry most of the time, and subject to floods at other times. In the past we think that the gray clay paralleling the river would have been as productive as the gray clay zones in which the second kind of agriculture is practiced. These are located away from the main river, along tributaries on the west side of the Atoyac, from Zaachila south through Valdeflores (N4E5). This is some of the most productive land in the valley today. Fallowing is virtually unnecessary, at least with alfalfa in the rotation, and as many as three crops a year are possible. A wide variety of crops besides maize can be grown. In these areas, water is regularly supplied by canals that tap the tributary streams, by pumps, and by the naturally high water table. The tributary stream itself, plus the slightly higher gradient typical at 1 kilometer from the river, are adequate to handle the necessary drainage.

Topographic features seemed to have constrained the distribution of marshlands (and the gray clay by which they are recognized). In the Central area gradients are too steep and the flow of the main river too fast for the formation of marshes. As the valley broadens out in the Valle Grande area, however, the river slows down. The larger watershed from the high mountains to the west (compared to the smaller watershed and lower mountains on the east) mean more runoff, more erosion, and more alluviation in the west.

In a way this has pushed the channel of the Atoyac toward the east between Monte Albán and Santa Ana Zegache (roughly N6E7). Much the same thing probably accounts for the position of the Río Salado channel in the western Tlacolula Valley.

All of the tributary streams on the western side of the Valle Grande flow directly to the east only as long as they are in the piedmont. Once in the high alluvium, they slow considerably and turn to the south, in some cases because of anomalies such as the batholiths near the river at Zimatlán (N8E6), often for as much as 3 kilometers. (By the time they reach the Atoyac they usually have no water.) It is along these relatively slow moving streams where one finds what is today the most productive gray clay. Precisely how much of the Valle Grande would have been marshy at any one time in the past is difficult to determine. We have counted all of the possible marshlands as Type I or occasionally Type II land, depending on local conditions.

Pot irrigation (see Lorenzo 1960; Flannery, Kirkby, Kirkby, and Williams 1967; Kirkby 1973), involving hand-carrying water drawn from shallow wells to individual plants, is a technique that can be used to achieve very high yields from small fields, if one is willing to invest considerable labor every day of the growing season. Because of the ability of pot irrigation to absorb labor, it is practiced today on less than 1% of the valley land. We treat pot irrigation simply as another practice possible on high water table land, and not as a separate land category.

Measuring Land Areas

The areal extent of different land types was traced separately for each grid square at a scale of 1:20,000. The area taken up by the Atoyac and the larger tributary streams was subtracted from the total, but that occupied by modern towns and roads was of course included. No allowance was made for ancient villages, roads, or field borders, but these areas would be very small. In the high piedmont and mountain zones, however, slopes are often too steep and rocky, and soils too thin for cultivation. To account for this, a distinction was made in Type III land between land that is nearly 100% cultivable, and land that is very rocky and steeply sloped–considered here, somewhat arbitrarily, as 10% arable.

The land areas of each type are shown in the grid square maps (Appendix III). The measured areas for each grid square we show in Table 9-1. The area of each type was estimated by counting quarter-centimeter blocks (at 1:20,000, each block is 1 hectare). A check for counting mistakes showed an error of usually less than 2%. Errors over that figure were unacceptable and were recounted. Given the room for misinterpretation of water availability and its past variation, the measurement error is relatively insignificant. The general characteristics of the distribution of land types of different potential for growing maize are discussed in the following paragraphs.

Canal irrigated land is found in small patches in several places along the major tributaries west of Monte Albán. In N13E6, N12E7, and N11E7 the main techniques in use along the Atoyac are floodwater farming, then dry farming, with canal irrigation other than that which relies on deep wells and pumps of lesser importance. In this area, the valley is narrow, and the frequent and often destructive floods would limit the practice of canal irrigation. Therefore the Atoyac alluvial land nearest to Monte Albán is considered best suited for floodwater farming and marginal water table farming rather than canal irrigation.

The most important expanses of Type I land lie to the south of Zaachila (roughly N10) on the west side of the Atoyac. Water table farming is possible along the line formed by the eastern edge of the fine sandy brown soil and the gray clay, also coinciding with the locations of all of the larger modern towns in this area. All of the pot irrigation in the Valle Grande also falls along this line. Canal irrigation can be practiced in the same area, as well as farther upstream along the tributaries, where these break out of the steep slopes in the middle piedmont. Some of the land along the Atoyac in the southern part of the study area above Tlapacoyan (N4E4) is also designated Type I rather than good floodwater or marginal water table, because of the nearby piedmont streams and, in the past, the possibility of tapping the main river. In N5E6, we found evidence of ancient water control on the main channel of the Atoyac, but it is unclear how this might have fitted into a grander scheme of water use. At present most of the immediate vicinity is dry farmed or well-and-pump irrigated. The total extent of Type I land in the study area is 5341 hectares, 10.4% of the total arable land.

Good floodwater land, and in places (along the Atoyac) marginal water table land, is nearly as productive as Type I land. It occurs along portions of the tributary streams and the Atoyac is not suitable, in general, for canal irrigation though canals may in fact be used to divert flood-water. Type II land makes up 9.6% of the total arable, or 4931 hectares.

Dry farming or poor floodwater farming, the least

Table 9-1. Land (in Hectares) of Each Type of Agricultural Potential

Grid Square	Surveyed	Type I	Type II	Type III	Mean Annual Rainfall (low is less than 700 mm)	Grid Square	Surveyed	Type I	Type II	Type III	Mean Annual Rainfall (low is less than 700 mm)
N1E3	680		13	68	High	N8E8	1600			287	High
N1E4	874		21	573	"	N8E9	495			49	"
N2E3	1007		10	101	"	N9E4	37			4	"
N2E4	1530	56	63	1343	"	N9E5	1485	113		872	"
N3E2	26			1	"	N9E6	1600	312		1288	"
N3E3	967		14	462	"	N9E7	1600	641	245	700	Low
N3E4	1559	163	77	936	"	N9E8	1600			871	High
N3E5	468			47	"	N9E9	307			31	"
N3E6	191			191	"	N10E5	1016	59		808	"
N4E2	312			31	"	N10E6	1600	141	32	1405	"
N4E3	1434	105		368	"	N10E7	1600	45	579	881	Low
N4E4	1600	399		932	"	N10E8	1600			589	High
N4E5	1600	557	60	902	"	N10E9	421			42	"
N4E6	959	257	196	506	"	N11E4	667			67	"
N5E2	497		10	49	"	N11E5	1600	236	39	329	"
N5E3	1238	115	1	112	"	N11E6	1600	94	263	1201	Low
N5E4	1400			140	"	N11E7	1600		623	760	"
N5E5	1600	54		1546	"	N11E8	1223			293	"
N5E6	818	121	70	611	"	N11E9	136			14	High
N5E8	65			65	"	N12E3	293	8		29	"
N6E2	16			16	"	N12E4	1376			402	"
N6E3	33			33	"	N12E5	1600	86	127	1026	"
N6E4	521			52	"	N12E6	1600		69	713	Low
N6E5	1600			892	"	N12E7	1600		629	829	"
N6E6	1178	208		953	"	N12E8	1067		297	400	"
N6E7	39			39	"	N13E3	891	43		85	High
N6E8	982		127	855	"	N13E4	1600		65	630	"
N6E9	830			538	"	N13E5	1600	156	128	617	"
N6E10	50			5	"	N13E6	1600		446	714	Low
N7E4	487		7	172	"	N13E7	1600		19	1079	"
N7E5	1600		16	1538	"	N13E8	1482		25	1457	"
N7E6	1366	395	44	893	"	N13E9	170		18	152	"
N7E7	1278			823	"	N14E3	68	6		44	High
N7E8	1600			1503	"	N14E4	559		18	218	"
N7E9	1556			760	"	N14E5	687		90	291	"
N7E10	1307			142	"	N14E6	672		204	279	Low
N8E4	500			50	"	N14E7	680			93	"
N8E5	1485	32	47	1113	"	N14E8	680			119	"
N8E6	1600	805	194	585	"	N14E9	63			22	"
N8E7	1600	134	45	1277		TOTALS	80,128	5341	4931	40,913	

productive kinds of farming, are the only agricultural strategies possible in most of the area. Type III land makes up 79.9% of the arable, or 40,913 hectares. Dry farming is practiced in all environmental zones from the high alluvium into the mountains. It is the riskiest, yields varying from zero to 1.2 tons per hectare. No more than one crop a year is possible, and the harvest depends on the critical timing of the highly seasonal rainfall pattern. The remaining 28,943 hectares of the surveyed area are uncultivable, given prehispanic technology.

Climate and Weather

Though the past climatic conditions of the Valley of Oaxaca are far from perfectly understood, the existing paleoenvironmental evidence for Oaxaca and the Tehuacán Valley, 150 kilometers to the northwest, indicate relative stability at least from 1500 B.C. into the historic period (Schoenwetter 1974; Byers 1967). As of yet, no long term secular trends in temperature or rainfall that might have been responsible for major societal readjustments have been detected. More important for corn agriculture and the organization of the human system than secular trends are the ceaseless year-by-year and local variations in rainfall. Partial series of mean annual rainfall data are available from 19 stations in the valley (Table 9-2). Table 9-2 shows that there is at present considerable variation in rainfall within one arm of the valley, and even within one arm, from one valley floor station to another. This variation is caused by the multiple and overlapping rain shadow effects of the valley's complex topography, and by the fact that it is influenced by both Pacific and Gulf weather systems. Storms may come from almost any direction. As the ethnographer Theodore Downing notes,

> Precipitation's random spatial distribution adds. . . uncertainty to farming. Most rains occur as cloud bursts or severe local thunderstorms which drench a small area–often no larger than a few square kilometers–while adjacent lands remain dry. Rainfall's varying annual magnitude and uneven spatial distribution combine to make dry farming a risky enterprise. [Downing 1974:113]

In the summer of 1972 there were days when the crew surveying Atzompa was drenched by rain, while less than 3 kilometers away the Monte Albán crews worked in the sunshine, and the reverse happened, too.

In general the floor of the Tlacolula Valley is usually–but not always–the driest area in the Valley of Oaxaca. This is reflected in corn production today. Kirkby found that the yield for dry farming in the Tlacolula Valley was between 0-0.4 tons per hectare. Almost half of the dry farmed area of the Zaachila arm yielded between 0.4-1.2 tons (1973:65, 68, 70). The isohyet that best isolates the precarious dry farming portions of the valley is that of 700 millimeters (from Kirkby 1973:19, *Carta de Climas* 1970; Aceves 1976:Fig. 41). Grid squares that generally have less than 700 millimeters of rain per year have estimated present corn yields of 0-1.2 tons per hectare for Type III land (dry and poor floodwater farming), while those receiving more than 700 millimeters on the average have yields of 0.4-2.0 tons per hectare. The estimated yields for high and low rainfall conditions for each of the three land types are shown in Table 9-3, which also gives the yield estimates adjusted for corn cob length for every phase back to Early I.

Thus far we have stressed local spatial variation in rainfall. Temporal variation from year to year is significant as well. The only available year-by-year figures of total annual rainfall are those for Oaxaca City from 1941 to 1962 (eight years missing, World Weather Records, 1941-1972, in Kappel 1977:308), Tlacolula from 1926 to 1968 (five [?] years missing, Kirkby 1973:158) and a complete series from the western edge of the *municipio* of Tlalixtac de Cabrera (N13E9) from 1968 through 1977 (Cecil Welte, personal communication, 1978). The standard deviations for each of these are, respectively, 91.9 (mean 597.4), 160.7 (mean 529.7), and 137 (mean 788.6), all in millimeters. What this means is that even in one place the adequacy of rainfall for maize farming is highly unpredictable.

Rainfall thus varies widely over space in the same year, and from year to year in the same place. Is there a dependent relation between the amount of rain received in one place in a year and the amount received at another place in the valley? An intuitive answer based only on our own experience is that some variance might be due to a valley wide pattern, but that local, essentially random variation would be the most important component of the variance at any single station. In the figures cited above there are only ten years that have data from more than one rainfall station in the same year–a sample far too small to be reliable, but, for its value as the only extant information, it is noteworthy that there are an equal number of cases of negative and positive correlation.

In the absence of better data it may be interesting to examine some of the possible consequences for organizing social systems in the valley if we assume that 1) rainfall at one spot is independent of that at other places in the valley in the same year; 2) rainfall in one year is independent of that in previous years. In other words,

Table 9-2. Mean Annual Rainfall for 19 Stations in the Valley of Oaxaca

Station	Rainfall, in mm	Station	Rainfall, in mm
1 Cuilapan	700	11 Mitla	521
2 Tlalixtac	700	12 Matatlan	593
3 El Tule	700	13 Teotitlan	540
4 Coyotepec	700	14 Zaachila	719
5 Etla	678	15 Zimatlan	721
6 Huitzo	721	16 Huixtepec	721
7 Telixtlahuaca	765	17 Tlacolula	530
8 Ocotlan	747	18 Oaxaca	597
9 Taxiche	644	19 NW of Tlalixtac	789
10 Tlacochahuaya	500		

* Sources: 1-16 -- Aceves 1976:Appendix 41; 17 -- Kirkby 1973:158; 18 -- Kappel 1977:308; 19 -- Cecil Welte, personal communication, 1978.

given the limits of best and worst years established by the modern rainfall measurements, rainfall might be said to be unpredictable in both space and time. Since the mean rainfall figures hover around 500 to 750 millimeters per year, just the range of marginal adequacy for corn, farming has probably always been fairly risky, and that risk would have had to have been adjusted for in any social organization after the threshold of dependency on sedentary life and maize agriculture. The assumption of random rainfall distribution outlined above has certain implications for organizing the valley system that can now be explored.

The risk of failure, and the products of an exceptionally good harvest, might be spread out by integrating a number of farmers into one system. The question is, how large should this system be? If it is assumed that all farmers employ basically the same strategy, but do so in different places, then the appropriate measure of "size" for a system in this sense is areal size. Rephrasing the question, how much of the valley would be necessary for the smallest viable social system given these climate and weather limitations on agricultural yields? This question is best addressed by considering the probabilities of harvest failure on Type III land, since what we want to know is whether farmers in local parts of the valley are able to produce a surplus, or whether they will produce nothing for potential exchange. Irrigated land is less affected by rainfall than dry farming land–its yield is constantly high. The real *increment* in maize production derives from the 80% of the arable land that is most affected by rainfall. Since we know that at least from Early I on, the society supported numerous non-agricultural specialists, as well as, perhaps, other agricultural special-

Table 9-3. Yield Ranges for Land Types through Time, in Metric Tons per Hectare per Year

Archaeological Phase	Type I Rainfall		Type II Rainfall		Type III Rainfall	
	Low	High	Low	High	Low	High
EI	0.5-0.6	0.5-0.6	0.1-0.6	0.3-0.6	0-0.3	0.1-0.5
LI	0.6-0.8	0.6-0.8	0.1-0.8	0.4-0.8	0-0.4	0.1-0.6
II	0.7-1.0	0.7-1.0	0.1-1.0	0.4-1.0	0-0.4	0.1-0.7
IIIA	0.8-1.1	0.8-1.1	0.2-1.1	0.5-1.1	0-0.5	0.2-0.8
IIIB	1.0-1.4	1.0-1.4	0.2-1.4	0.6-1.4	0-0.6	0.2-1.0
IV	1.1-1.5	1.1-1.5	0.2-1.5	0.7-1.5	0-0.7	0.2-1.1
V	1.4-1.9	1.4-1.9	0.3-1.9	0.8-1.9	0-0.8	0.3-1.4
Present	2.0-2.8	2.0-2.8	0.4-2.8	1.2-2.8	0-1.2	0.4-2.0

Note: Present yields per annum are derived from Kirkby 1973 (see especially Fig. 27, p. 68) and related discussion; variation back through time is extrapolated from her Fig. 48 (p. 126).

ties, potential for exchange and not simply bare subsistence is key. Therefore we choose an annual rainfall figure of 600 millimeters per year as the critical level below which Type III land will produce an inadequate harvest.

It is assumed that the chances of having a "bad year"–less than 600 millimeters of rain–are equal to the frequency of such years where we have year to year records. For Tlacolula, that frequency of less-than-600 millimeter years is 70%; for Oaxaca, 64%; and for Tlalixtac de Cabrera, 10%. Presumably, the higher the average annual rainfall, the less the chance of having a bad year. This relationship might be expressed as an S-shaped probability curve, so that the probability of having a bad year might be estimated, very roughly, from the annual average. We did this for each of the rainfall stations in Table 9-2 and arrived at an average low-rainfall probability for sub-areas of the valley by using the mean of all probabilities within each sub-area. This procedure allows for cultural practices that would tend to even out differences in a year's harvest *within* the sub-area (see the discussion under "Changing the Scale of Analyses", below). The differences between sub-areas are shown in Table 9-4.

Table 9-4. Probability of an Excessively Dry Year, by Sub-Area

Valley Sub-area	Estimated Probability
Etla	.30
Central	.49
Tlacolula	.61
Zimatlán	.30
Ocotlán	.40

The lowest chance of a bad year, 30%, occurs in Etla and Zimatlán; the highest, 61%, is in Tlacolula; the Central area (with few stations reporting) is highly variable, with a 49% chance of a bad year. These figures are at best approximations, since the available rainfall data even for the recent past are scanty. We are also forced to ignore the problem of specifying the distance necessary between stations for them to be said to vary independently. However the approach does seem to match our assessment of the long-run results of dry farming attempts in the valley and, hence, should give the clear idea that no single sub-area, even Etla, could be a viable, independent economic unit. (Raiding between sub-areas is of course a possibility.) Given the overall reliance on rainfall farming, the valley would have had to have been organized as sets of two or more sub-areas perhaps from the earliest times. Table 9-5 shows the probabilities of having a bad year over a whole system if the system consists of two or more sub-areas, assuming that rainfall between sub-areas behaves independently.

Notice in Table 9-5 that no combination of only two contiguous sub-areas reduces the chances of overall failure to less than 12%. The most favorable combination of three contiguous sub-areas would be Etla, Central, and Zimatlán, at 4%. Only with combinations of four sub-areas can the probability of failure be reduced to less than 5% if Etla is excluded.

Table 9-5. Probability of an Overall Excessively Dry Year, for Combinations of Sub-Areas

Sub-areas	Estimated Probability	Sub-areas	Estimated Probability
C,T	.30	Z,T,O	.07
O,T	.25	C,Z,O	.06
Z,T	.18	C,O,E	.06
E,T	.18	E,T,Z	.05
E,C	.15	E,C,Z	.04
C,Z	.15	E,C,T,O	.04
Z,O	.12	C,T,Z,O	.04
C,T,O	.12	E,Z,O	.04
E,C,T	.09	E,C,T,Z	.03
C,T,Z	.09	E,C,Z,O	.02
E,Z	.09	E,T,Z,O	.02
E,T,O	.07	E,C,T,Z,O	.01

Key: C = Central
T = Tlacolula
O = Ocotlán
Z = Zimatlán-Zaachila
E = Etla

Good years, here defined as those with more than 700 millimeters of rainfall, are less frequent and mirror the distribution of bad years at the stations for which there are records over the years—Tlacolula 11%, Oaxaca 21%, and Tlalixtac 60%. Thus, the higher the average rainfall, the greater the chances of having a "good year".

This consideration of bad and good years cannot tell us how the ancient Oaxacans handled deficits or surpluses, what they viewed as an acceptable risk, or what they did when failure was widespread. But it does suggest that rainfall variability could have been a powerful reason to maintain economic integration over a wide area of the valley, presumably as wide as possible without entailing unacceptably high costs of communication and administration.

Labor

An exhaustive coverage of variation in output per

unit input of human labor is beyond the scope of this study. It would be interesting to know, for example, what the marginal returns on increments of labor on different kinds of land would be if the rural labor force could have been cajoled into greater efforts. Short of a series of experiments that no one has yet conducted, this aspect of agricultural production will remain unknown. In the present study we rely on Anne Kirkby's estimate that a man can cultivate 2 hectares using the traditional Middle American hoe, the *coa* (1973:73). Estimates of the size of the labor force must also depend on ethnographic analogy. Here we rely on Wayne Kappel's study of the present and historical demography of four communities in the eastern Tlacolula Valley (1977). Using archival evidence, Kappel constructed age and sex distributions for these populations. A random sample of years drawn from his tables for Mitla, Loma Larga, and Xaaga showed that the percentage of the population over the age of 15 and under age 60 varied around 55% for Mitla, the largest community, with 45% for Loma Larga and 48% for Xaaga, two smaller villages (Kappel 1977:425-55). In itself this variation is interesting; however for our purposes we will assume a work force of 50% of the archaeological population estimate. This of course is a maxium size interpretation, since we are not allowing for other kinds of rural specializations, nor for differences between male and female workers.

The amount that one person can cultivate, and the estimated size of the labor force, will be used below to estimate how much maize populations could have produced given the estimated fertility of the land.

Consumption

The number of people that a resource might support will vary inversely with its rate of consumption. It would be wrong to assume that the ancient population of the Valley of Oaxaca was limited only by maize, and likewise it would be misleading to say that consumption rates are inflexible. In the first regard we consider that potential maize yields only hypothetically form ceilings for actual populations. Actual population variables are in practice controlled by many factors and interactions.

A perusal of ethnographic accounts of average maize consumption shows that this may be highly variable. In his article on *chinampa* agriculture in the Valley of Mexico, Parsons estimates a subsistence level of 160 kilos of maize per person per year, and with enough for exchange for other necessary foods, 200 kilos (1976:243-44). Nash (1958:39) published a weekly diet for Guatemalan families whose maize consumption works out to 211 kilos per year per person. Redfield and Villa Rojas give an equivalent of 218 to 273 kilos per person (1962:56). Among the Tzotzil Maya of highland Chiapas, a maize harvest of 5 *fanegas*, the equivalent of 240 kilos per person per year, is required for one household for food alone (Collier 1975:34-37). Chamula in lowland Chiapas are said to require about 214 kilos per person per year (Wasserstrom 1977:459). Two-hundred kilos is the figure used by Coe for maize consumption (1969:14). Elsewhere, native farmers in Zambia require 236 kilos (Allan 1965:39). Among the Pima, where it is said that only 60% of food is cultivated, the figure is 238 kilos (Castetter and Bell 1942).

Within the Valley of Oaxaca three ethnographic studies supply details on maize consumption. Four families studied by Granskog (1974:142-66) had actual annual maize consumptions of 260, 216, 172, and 180 kilos per person per year. Kappel reports that annual consumption in Loma Larga is 200 kilos, in Xaaga 261 kilos, and in Corral del Cerro, 289 kilos, based on housewives' estimates for persons over five years old (1977:128). Teresa Graedon (personal communication, 1978) found that a family of six (two adults, four children) will eat an *almud* of corn a day, and sometimes, a kilo of beans. This would be equal to 243 kilos per person per year. In Oaxaca today actual amounts of corn eaten will vary with economic status, as these ethnographic studies show. Generally, poor families eat relatively more maize because they do not have access to other kinds of food. The figure used by Kirkby (1973:90, 127), 480 kilos, is far higher than all the other estimates and undoubtedly includes animal fodder–not a factor in pre-Hispanic times–as well as subsistence and exchange for other foods (see the pages of Granskog cited above). On the basis of these data we may conclude that consumption needs may vary from a low of 160 kilos to a corn-fed high of 290 kilos per person per year. This range is preserved in the analysis to emphasize the elasticity in this aspect of carrying capacity.

Calculating Potential Population

In the analysis that follows we try to answer the question, "how many people could a specific area of land support, ignoring external exchange and other limiting factors on population?" This hypothetical limit is referred to here as *potential population*. To

Table 9-6. Potential Yields in Metric Tons (Monte Albán Early I)

Grid Square	Type I	Type II	Type III	Total	High Pot. Pop.[1]	Low Pot. Pop.[2]	Ave. Pot. Pop.[3]	Arch. Pop. Est.	No. of Sites
N1E3		3.9 - 7.8	6.8 - 34	10.7 - 41.8	67 - 261	37 - 144	127		
N1E4		6.3 - 12.6	57.3 - 286.5	63.6 - 299.1	397 - 1869	219 - 1031	879		
N2E3		3.0 - 6.0	10.1 - 50.5	13.1 - 56.5	89 - 353	45 - 195	169	7	1
N2E4	28.0 - 33.6	18.9 - 37.8	134.3 - 671.5	181.2 - 742.9	1133 - 4643	625 - 2562	2241	73	3
N3E2			0.1 - 0.5	0.1 - 0.5	1 - 3	0 - 2	1		
N3E3		4.2 - 8.4	46.2 - 231.0	50.4 - 239.4	315 1496	174 - 826	703		
N3E4	81.5 - 97.8	23.1 - 46.2	93.6 - 468.0	198.2 - 612.0	1239 - 3825	683 - 2110	1964	155	4
N3E5			4.7 23.5	4.7 - 23.5	29 - 147	16 - 81	68		
N3E6			19.1 - 95.5	19.1 - 95.5	119 - 597	66 - 329	278		
N4E2			3.1 - 15.5	3.1 - 15.5	19 - 97	11 - 53	45		
N4E3	52.5 - 63.0		36.8 - 184.0	89.3 - 247.0	558 - 1544	308 - 852	815		
N4E4	199.5 - 239.4		93.2 - 466.0	292.7 - 705.4	1829 - 4409	1009 - 2432	2420	7	1
N4E5	278.5 - 334.2	18.0 - 36.0	90.2 - 451.0	386.7 - 821.2	2417 - 5133	1333 - 2832	2929	25	2
N4E6	128.5 - 154.2	58.8 - 117.6	50.6 - 253.0	237.9 - 407.2	1487 - 2545	820 - 1404	1564	15	2
N5E2		3.0 - 6.0	4.9 - 24.5	7.9 - 30.5	49 - 191	27 - 105	93		
N5E3	57.5 - 69.0	0.3 - 0.6	11.2 - 56.0	69.0 - 125.6	431 - 785	238 - 433	472		
N5E4			14.0 - 70.0	14.0 - 70.0	87 - 437	48 - 241	204		
N5E5	27.0 - 32.4		154.6 - 773.0	181.6 - 805.4	1135 - 5034	626 - 2777	2393	89	4
N5E6	60.5 - 72.6	21.0 - 42.0	61.1 - 305.5	142.6 - 420.1	891 - 2626	492 - 1449	1364	17	2
N5E8			6.5 - 32.5	6.5 - 32.5	41 - 203	22 - 112	95		
N6E2			1.6 - 8.0	1.6 - 8.0	10 - 50	6 - 28	23		
N6E3			3.3 - 16.5	3.3 - 16.5	21 - 103	11 - 57	48		
N6E4			5.2 - 26.0	5.2 - 26.0	33 - 163	18 - 90	76		
N6E5			89.2 - 446.0	89.2 - 446.0	557 - 2787	308 - 1538	1298		
N6E6	104.0 - 124.8		95.3 - 476.5	199.3 - 601.3	1246 - 3758	687 - 2073	1941	179	3
N6E7			3.9 - 19.5	3.9 - 19.5	24 - 122	13 - 67	57		
N6E8		38.1 - 76.2	85.5 - 427.5	123.6 - 503.7	773 - 3148	426 - 1737	1521		
N6E9			53.8 - 269.0	53.8 - 269.0	336 - 1681	186 - 928	783		
N6E10			0.5 - 2.5	0.5 - 2.5	3 - 16	2 - 9	7		
N7E4		2.1 - 4.2	17.2 - 86.0	19.3 - 90.2	121 - 564	67 - 311	265		
N7E5		4.8 - 9.6	153.8 - 769.0	158.6 - 778.6	991 - 4866	547 - 2685	2272	7	1
N7E6	197.5 - 237.0	13.2 - 26.4	89.3 - 446.5	300.0 - 709.9	1875 - 4437	1034 - 2448	2449	285	4
N7E7			82.3 - 411.5	82.3 - 411.5	514 - 2572	284 - 1419	1197		
N7E8			150.3 - 751.5	150.3 - 751.5	939 - 4697	518 - 2591	2186	233	3
N7E9			76.0 - 380.0	76.0 - 380.0	475 - 2375	262 - 1310	1106		
N7E10			14.2 - 71.0	14.2 - 71.0	89 - 444	49 - 245	207		
N8E4			5.0 - 25.0	5.0 - 25.0	31 - 156	17 - 86	73		
N8E5	16.0 - 19.2	14.1 - 28.2	111.3 - 556.5	141.4 - 603.9	884 - 3774	488 - 2082	1807	143	6
N8E6	402.5 - 483.0	58.2 - 116.4	58.5 - 292.5	519.2 - 891.9	3245 - 5574	1790 - 3076	3421	121	2
N8E7	67.0 - 80.4	13.5 - 27.0	127.7 - 638.5	208.2 - 745.9	1301 - 4662	718 - 2572	2313	49	2
N8E8			28.7 - 143.5	28.7 - 143.5	179 - 897	99 - 495	418	35	2
N8E9			4.9 - 24.5	4.9 - 24.5	31 - 153	17 - 84	71		
N9E4			0.4 - 2.0	0.4 - 2.0	3 - 13	1 - 7	6		
N9E5	56.5 - 67.8		87.2 - 436.0	143.7 - 503.8	898 - 3149	496 - 1737	1570	165	4
N9E6	156.0 - 187.2		128.8 - 644.0	284.8 - 831.2	1780 - 5195	982 - 2866	2706	23	3
N9E7	320.5 - 384.6	24.5 - 147.0	0.0 - 210.0	345.0 - 742.0	2156 - 4635	1190 - 2577	2635	17	1
N9E8			87.1 - 435.5	87.1 - 435.5	544 - 2722	300 - 1502	1267	19	2
N9E9			3.1 - 15.5	3.1 - 15.5	19 - 97	11 - 53	45		
N10E5	29.5 - 35.4		80.8 - 404.0	110.3 - 439.4	689 - 2746	380 - 1515	1333	23	3
N10E6	70.5 - 84.6	9.6 - 19.2	140.5 - 702.5	220.6 - 806.3	1379 - 5039	761 - 2780	2490	59	3
N10E7	22.5 - 27.0	57.9 - 347.4	0.0 - 264.3	80.4 - 638.7	503 - 3992	277 - 2202	1744	53	3
N10E8			58.9 - 294.5	58.9 - 294.5	368 - 1841	203 - 1016	857	168	3
N10E9			4.2 - 21.0	4.2 - 21.0	26 - 131	14 - 72	61		
N11E4			6.7 - 33.5	6.7 - 33.5	42 - 209	23 - 116	97		
N11E5	118.0 - 141.6	11.7 - 23.4	32.9 - 164.5	162.6 - 329.5	1016 - 2059	561 - 1136	1193	15	2
N11E6	47.0 - 56.4	26.3 - 157.8	0.0 - 360.3	73.3 - 574.5	458 - 3591	253 - 1981	1571	25	2
N11E7		62.3 - 373.8	0.0 - 228.0	62.3 - 601.8	389 - 3761	215 - 2075	1610	285	5
N11E8			0.0 - 87.9	0.0 - 87.9	0 - 549	0 - 303	213	17	1
N11E9			1.4 - 7.0	1.4 - 7.0	9 - 44	5 - 24	20		
N12E3	4.0 - 4.8		2.9 - 14.5	6.9 - 19.3	43 - 121	24 - 67	64		
N12E4			40.2 - 201.0	40.2 - 201.0	251 - 1256	139 - 693	585	40	4
N12E5	43.0 - 51.6	38.1 - 76.2	102.6 - 513.0	183.7 - 641.0	1148 - 4005	633 - 2210	1999	43	3
N12E6		6.9 - 41.4	0.0 - 213.9	6.9 - 255.3	43 - 1596	24 - 880	636	5399	6
N12E7		62.9 - 377.4	0.0 - 248.7	62.9 - 626.1	393 - 3913	217 - 2159	1671	7	1
N12E8		29.7 - 178.2	0.0 - 120.0	29.7 - 298.2	186 - 1864	102 - 1028	795	43	3
N13E3	21.5 - 25.8		8.5 - 42.5	30.0 - 68.3	188 - 427	103 - 236	238		
N13E4		19.5 - 39.0	63.0 - 315.0	82.5 - 354.0	516 - 2213	284 - 1221	1058	25	2
N13E5	78.0 - 93.6	38.4 - 76.8	61.7 - 308.5	178.1 - 478.9	1113 - 2993	614 - 1651	1593	17	1
N13E6		44.6 - 267.6	0.0 - 214.2	44.6 - 481.8	279 - 3011	154 - 1661	1276	265	3
N13E7		1.9 - 11.4	0.0 - 323.7	1.9 - 335.1	12 - 2094	7 - 1156	817		
N13E8		2.5 - 15.0	0.0 - 437.1	2.5 - 452.1	16 - 2826	9 - 1559	1102	7	1
N13E9		1.8 - 10.8	0.0 - 45.6	1.8 - 56.4	11 - 353	6 - 194	141		
N14E3	3.0 - 3.6		4.4 - 22.0	7.4 - 25.6	46 - 160	26 - 88	80		
N14E4		5.4 - 10.8	21.8 - 109.0	27.2 - 119.8	170 - 749	94 - 413	356	17	1
N14E5		27.0 - 54.0	29.1 - 145.5	56.1 - 199.5	351 - 1247	193 - 688	620	61	2
N14E6		20.4 - 122.4	0.0 - 83.7	20.4 - 206.1	127 - 1288	70 - 711	549	309	2
N14E7			0.0 - 27.9	0.0 - 27.9	0 - 174	0 - 96	68		
N14E8			0.0 - 35.7	0.0 - 35.7	0 - 223	0 - 123	87		
N14E9			0.0 - 6.6	0.0 - 6.6	0 - 41	0 - 23	16		

Notes: [1] Potential population at .16 tons per person per year.
[2] Potential population at .29 tons per person per year.
[3] Mean potential population.

simplify calculations, an *average potential population,* or just *potential population,* is convenient. It is the mean of the potential population figures for the upper and lower estimates of yield per hectare. Again, to simplify the handling of the data, the *archaeological* population estimates are the means of the upper and lower archaeological estimates.

Maize yields were calculated for each grid square separately. The yields per hectare, expressed as the upper and lower ends of a range, are shown in Table 9-3. Yields vary through time and also depend on whether the grid square normally receives high or low rainfall (shown in Table 9-1). The lower and upper estimates of yield for each land type were multiplied by the number of hectares of each land type in the grid unit. The lower estimates for all three land types were added together; then so were the upper estimates. The resulting figure is the range of potential maize yields, in metric tons. Potential populations were calculated by dividing the maize yields by .16 and .29 tons, respectively. An example of the results–those of Early I –are shown in Table 9-6.

A second question that we try to answer is "how much food could be produced from a given area of land by the archaeological estimated population?" This question is not the same as the previous one, since it takes into account the fact that what is produced depends on the amount of labor that can be applied, as well as the fertility and amount of land.

The calculation of the amount of maize the existing labor force could have produced proceeds first by determining the total amount of land that could have been farmed with that labor force. The hectares that could be worked is a number equivalent to the archaeological population, since the labor force is half the population but each worker can farm 2 hectares (these figures are discussed in the section on labor, above). This amount is then spread between the three different land types according to the proportion that each land type makes up of the total cultivable land. These three new figures are multiplied by the appropriate (for phase and rainfall) yield per hectare and then summed. The result is yield in hectares, but this figure is not allowed to be larger than the total yield that the land itself is capable of producing, even if the available work force is very large. Examples of these calculations are discussed in the sections on Early I, IIIa, and IIIb.

No single quantitative measure can faithfully express every interesting aspect of the complex relations between land, labor, capital, and the relations of production. Therefore we use one measure to illustrate a particular feature, another to bring out another aspect. But this of course means that each statistic has limitations and inherent distortions. Therefore the methodological manipulations and assumptions made to produce these measures should be well understood beforehand. As with any index values, these are interpretations of data, not observational facts.

The kind of areally-based (grid square) analysis used here has the advantages of scale manipulability, facility, and freedom from assumptions about matching particular tracts of land to particular communities. Nevertheless it has the drawback of not even pretending to represent actual cultural practices regarding access to land, as is true with settlement-based catchment analysis. Also, a different placement of the arbitrary grid over the landscape does result in different statistical results, though not enough on the regional scale to fundamentally alter our conclusions. Thus, for us the comparison of results between periods of time with the same grid is more important than the absolute values of indices in any one period. This especially applies to the correlation coefficients discussed below. Clearly the size of the grid units matters. We exploit this variation by examining patterning as it appears at the 4 × 4 kilometer grid square scale, through several larger areal units up to the scale of whole study area. Finally, not all grid squares were fully surveyed because they were on the boundary of the survey area. To drop incomplete squares would bias, usually, against dry farming on steep slopes; so instead, where unequal sizes of cases would distort the meaning of the results, we shift from the absolute values to densities per unit area surveyed.

THE RESULTS: ACROSS PHASES

Potential Population

Potential population increases linearly from about 75,000 in Early I to 218,000 in Monte Albán V. The increase is due to the improvement in the maize plant that resulted in higher yields. Table 9-7 gives the calculated values of potential population for the study area, and these are plotted in Figure 9-1 along with the total archaeologically estimated population with and without the population of N12E6, Monte Albán. Because Monte Albán pertains to the unsurveyed part of the valley as well as the study area, we might add one-half of the city's population to that of the study area when comparing potential with actual population. In Early I, actual population (counting half of Monte

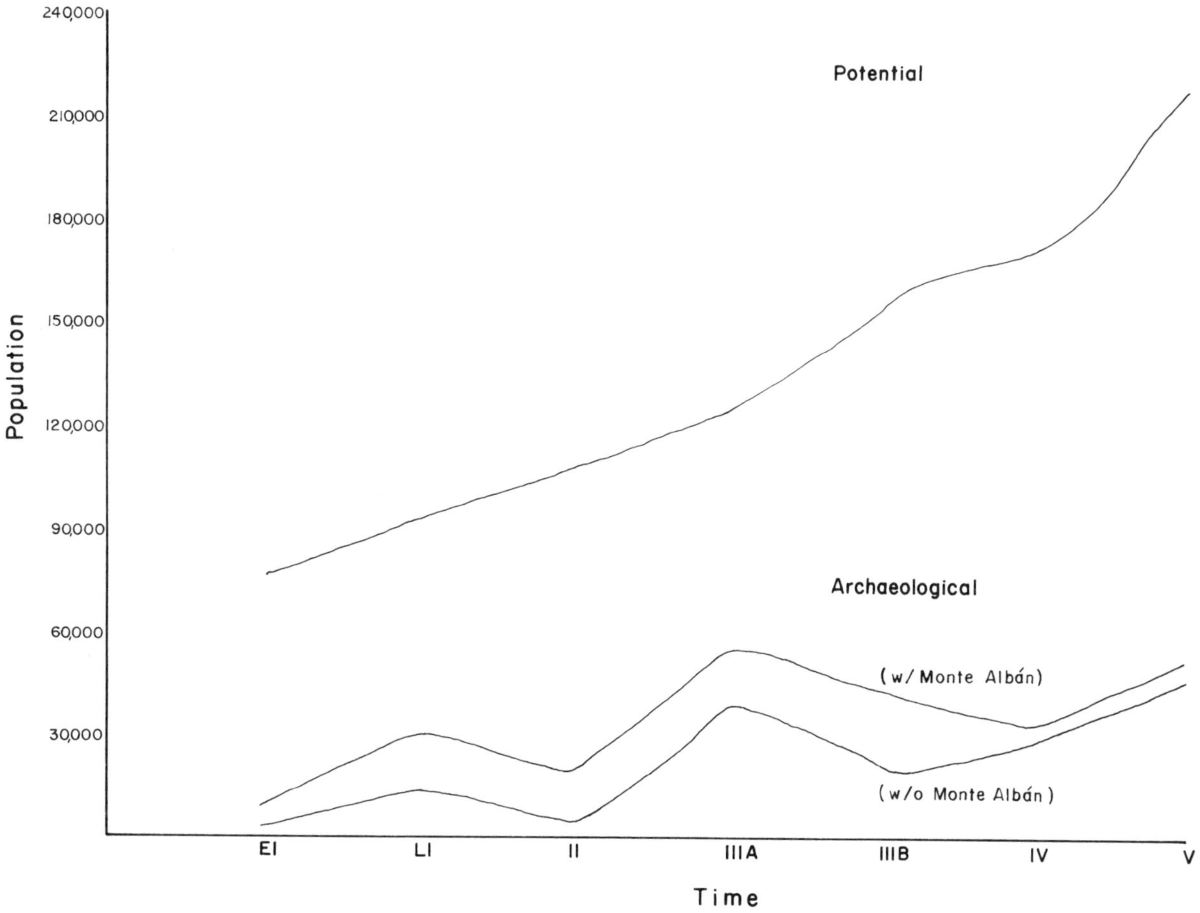

Figure 9-1. Potential and actual population, Early I through V.

Albán) is 8% of potential; it is 24% in Late I, 12% in II, 37% in IIIa, 20% in IIIb, 17% in IV, and 22% in V. The overall rate of increase in population potential is 86 persons per year (using the span between the midpoints of Early I and Monte Albán V), and the overall increase for the actual population is 25.7 persons per year. Thus the actual population increase, in general, is not as steep as the assumed increase in potential population due to the improvement in the maize plant. Perhaps the clearest case of even growth in population (that is, *in situ* increase instead of major shifts in the settlement pattern itself) occurs from Monte Albán Early I to Late I. Archaeologically it appears that the population growth should be spread over the 400 year length of Early and Late I, and this would be an increment of roughly 40 persons per year, very close to the 42 person per year increase if the potential population increase is also spread over 400 years. That population increases faster than the increase in potential yields is known, however, from Monte Albán II to IIIa, and perhaps we might conclude that that particular growth in numbers outpacing growth in food potential could have happened only in the context of the kind of reorganization of the political and economic system that did occur between those two phases.

Overall, potential population density increases through time with the increase in maize productivity. In the analytical model used here, the relative potential density of grid squares does not change through time, though the absolute values do. A map of the relative densities is shown in Figure 9-2. Generally the highest potential densities are in squares with water available in addition to rainfall. The lowest third of the cases are squares of steep slope, and the middle third are by and large dry farmed.

According to the productivity assumptions discussed in previous sections of this chapter, through time there is an increasing divergence in potential population density. In Early I, half the grid squares could have supported less than 60 persons per square kilo-

Table 9-7. Potential Population and Archaeological Population Estimates

Phase	Average Potential Population	Archaeological Population Without Monte Albán	Archaeological Population With Monte Albán
EI	75,532	3,146	8,545
LI	92,379	13,407	30,037
II	106,221	5,771	20,264
IIIA	128,693	38,784	55,399
IIIB	156,623	19,811	42,584
IV	170,684	28,361	28,361
V	218,351	45,930	50,617

meter, and none could have supported more than 240. By Monte Albán V the frequency of squares with different potential densities is more evenly distributed, with a range from below 30 to over 630 people per square kilometer.

Is this divergence in potential densities matched by a corresponding divergence in actual population densities? To an extent, yes. Generally the histograms of actual densities have a reverse-J shape, with many low density cases and less frequent, unevenly occurring examples of higher densities up in the squares containing the largest settlements. Thus the forms of the potential and actual density histograms are somewhat similar, but the way people were actually distributed was patchier than the resource distribution. A way of expressing this is to use the coefficient of variation, a statistic designed to compare relative dispersal around the mean when means of two or more samples are different. The coefficient of variation is the standard deviation divided by the mean. In Figure 9-3 the lower line represents the coefficients of variation of potential population for all grid squares occupied (excluding the squares of the extreme cases of Monte Albán [N12E6] and in IIIa and IV, Jalieza [N7E9]). The upper line shows the coefficients of variation for the actual populations. Actual populations are more deviant than the agricultural resources, consistently; and in general the difference between the coefficients is greater in the later periods than in earlier periods. Roughly speaking, all of these observations about envionmental variability versus settlement variability show that there are greater differences–more variation–in settlement than there are in the population's principle resources. It would thus seem difficult on this count to account for

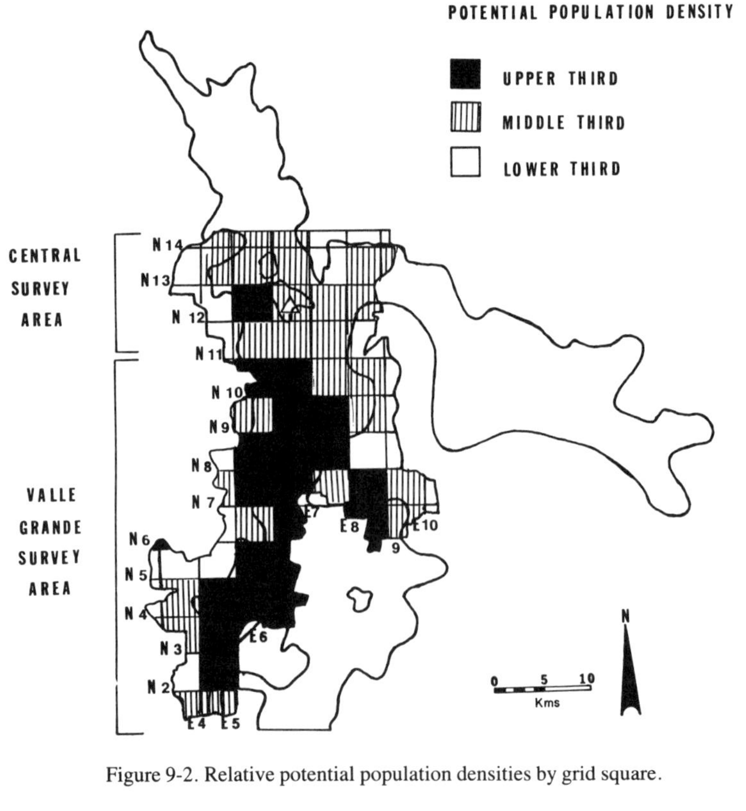

Figure 9-2. Relative potential population densities by grid square.

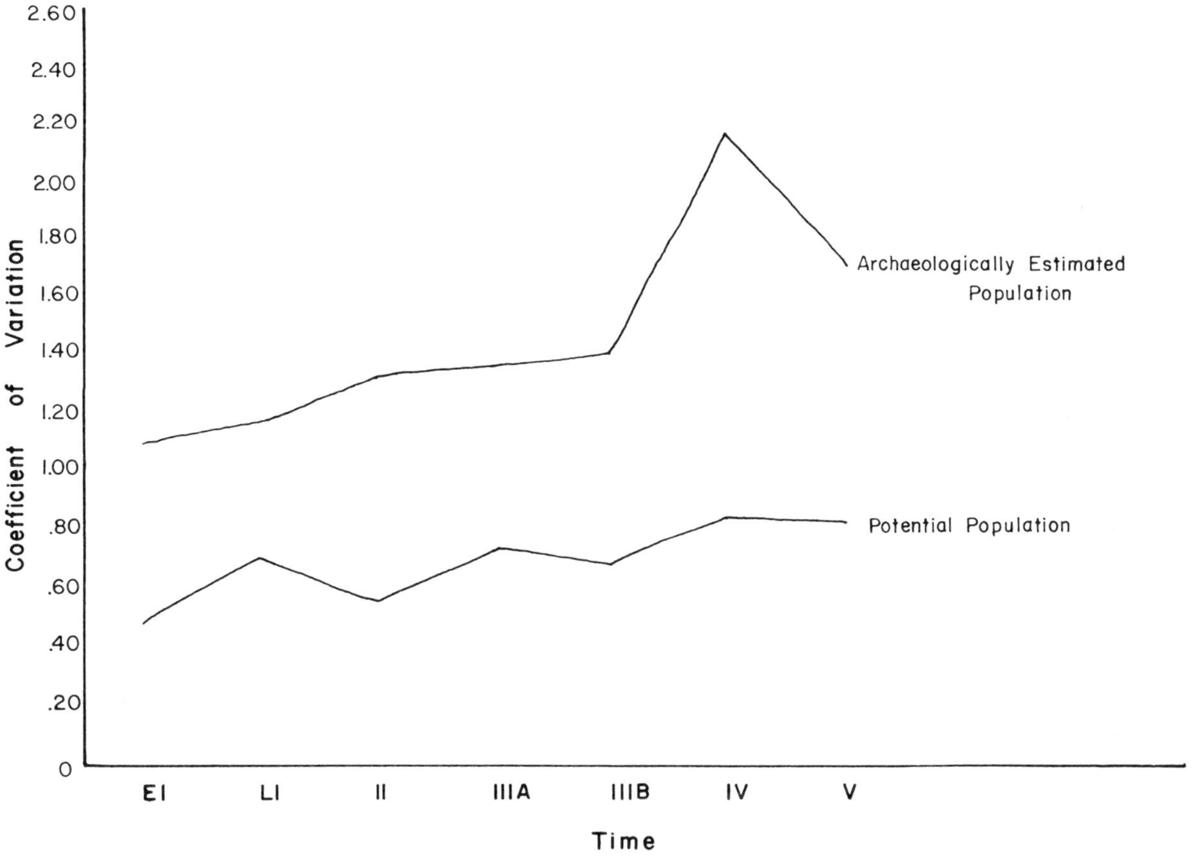

Figure 9-3. Coefficients of variation for potential and actual population of the grid squares, Early I through V.

variability in settlement by invoking variability in resources, but there are other ways of investigating this relationship, and we continue with them below.

Especially from Monte Albán Early I to Monte Albán II, the grid squares actually occupied (those with sites, of any size, from that phase) do tend to be those squares with relatively high potential population density. In these phases the distinction between occupied and unoccupied squares in terms of their potential densities is strong and statistically significant. This is especially true in Early Monte Albán I. By IIIa. however, the potential densities of unoccupied squares are similar to those of all grid squares. In Monte Albán V almost all squares have some occupation, so instead of examining occupied vs. unoccupied squares, we use low density (25 people or less per square kilometer) vs. high density, and again there seems to be obvious preference for squares with high quality land (i.e., land with water) as in the earlier phases.

Correlation and Regression

If people chose to live in squares with high population density potential, meaning high quality land, do their numbers correspond in some way to the amount of potential production of food? Is there an association between potential productivity, as an independent variable, and the archaeological population estimates as the dependent variable? We examined this possible relationship by means of correlation and regression, where each grid square, or partial grid square if the unit was on the survey boundary, represents a separate case. Average population potential and actual population were scatter-plotted for each phase. None of these plots for any phase suggest the slightest linear or curvilinear association, even when just low population or high population squares are examined separately. Squares of low potential have high and low actual populations, and squares with high potential have high and low actual population. Best fit linear regression lines were drawn for all phases, but each has a flat slope (some slightly positive, others slightly negative) indicating little sensitivity between the two variables, and there is a great dispersal of points on either side of the line. An example of these scattergrams is shown in Figure 9-4.

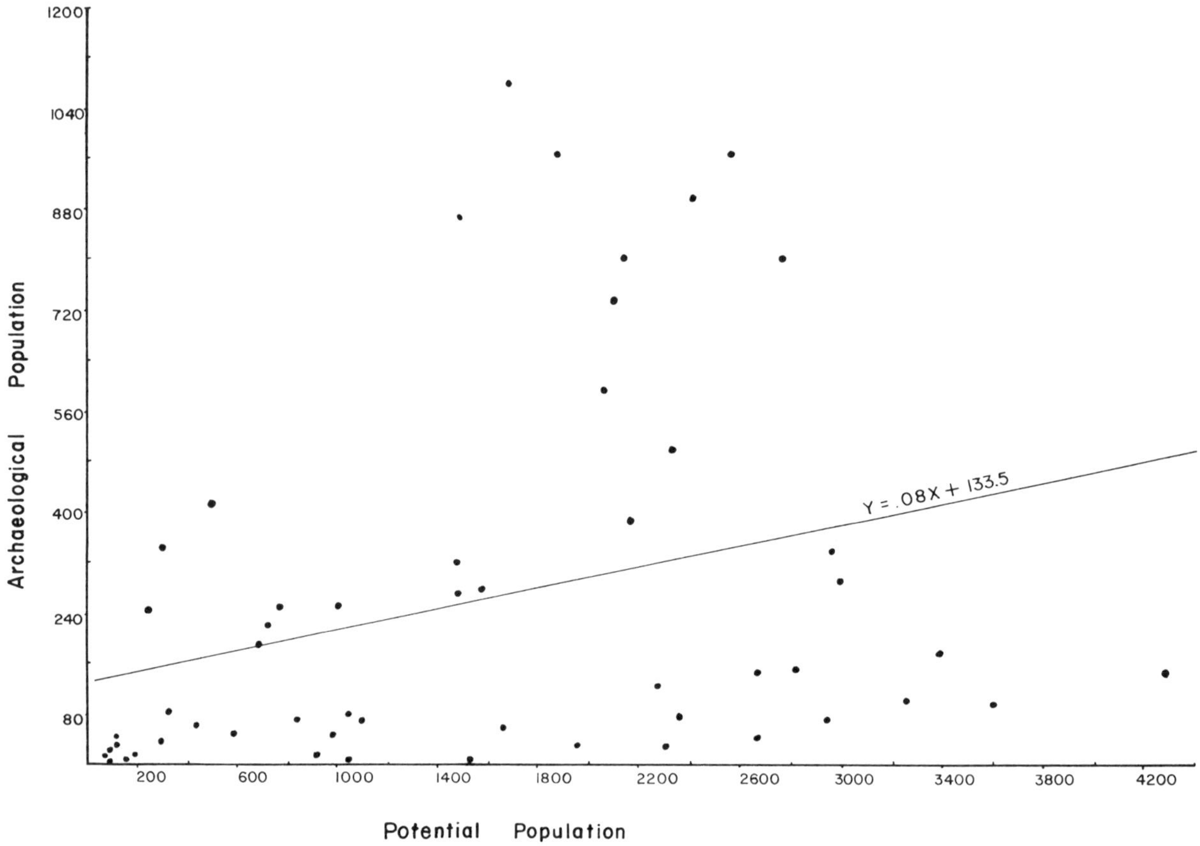

Figure 9-4. Scatter diagram of potential and actual population by grid square, Period Late I.

To measure the relative strength of association between potential and actual population, linear correlation coefficients were calculated. These are given in Table 9-8. Because of the statistical difficulties involved in using this kind of analysis, we should be stringent in requiring a high level of significance, and we set this therefore at .01. None of these *r* values are statistically significant at that level. The IIIa value may be significant at the .05 level, but the presumed relationship would account for less than 9% of the variance, and the scatterplot strongly suggests no real relationship (Fig. 9–5).

The relative changes in correlation coefficients from one phase to the next are of somewhat doubtful meaning. One might expect that from Early I to Late I there would be an increasingly finer tuning of population to resources with the growth of population in the same settlement framework, and this seems to be the case since *r* increases somewhat between the two phases. The settlement pattern reorganization at the end of Late I might be suspected of lowering *r*, and this also happens. In IIIa, with the tremendous development of the

Table 9-8. Correlation Coefficients at Three Analytical Scales

Phase	n = 78	n = 14	n = 6
EI	.08	.46	.53
LI	.29	.59	.63
II	.11	.65	.63
IIIA	.25	.39	-.12
IIIB	-.02	.02	.19
IV	-.21	--	--
V	-.01	.47	.28

Valle Grande, the value is up again. All of these changes, though slight and not statistically significant, are in the direction that one would predict given an assumption that denser populations must be dispersed with keener regard to critical resources than less dense populations. But why the final three phases show a negative association between population and resources can't be accounted for by this assumption. Why in Monte Albán V the *r* value is lower than other periods of expansion (Late I, IIIa) is also a question difficult to answer with this assumption. Intra-valley exchange and political concerns are probably more powerful factors in determining settlement pattern variability.

It should be noted, however, that there are difficulties in the interpretation of linear correlation and regression statistics when these are applied to help interpret data arranged by quadrat. As noted above, changing the quadrat size may make a difference (we increase the scale below). Incomplete squares on the boundary conceivably might make the individual observations unequal in character. This was checked by examining frequency distributions of x and y variables for squares that were less than 25% complete, and with the exception of less than a half-dozen squares, low y values were at least as likely to be due to low x values as to sampling error. Since the survey boundary was almost always drawn to include sites rather than skip them, the border squares if anything are allowed to have higher than expected populations.

A third problem with regression and correlation is the fact that shifting the grid in space (while retaining the same quadrat size) does change the value of r. Our experiments with artificial data (not reproduced here) demonstrate that differences in the value of the correlation coefficient can be produced by moving the grid. It may thus be that shifting the grid within Early I, for example, will give different square-to-square results for that phase though it does not greatly affect the overall pattern, and there is no reason to believe that using that new grid placement in the succeeding phases would change the strength of the association between the two variables in any consistent direction.

Finally, in each instance we checked for and deleted extreme values of actual population (there are considered to be no extreme values of potential population). Thus, Monte Albán's grid square was always dropped, as was Jalieza's in some periods. Zero values of actual population were likewise not included. Keeping them inflates the value of r, but since we already knew that people did not prefer to live on the worst land, the question was whether differences in potential were associated with differences in the number of people present in the squares that they did occupy.

While these analytical limitations should be recognized, it remains appropriate to conclude that there is

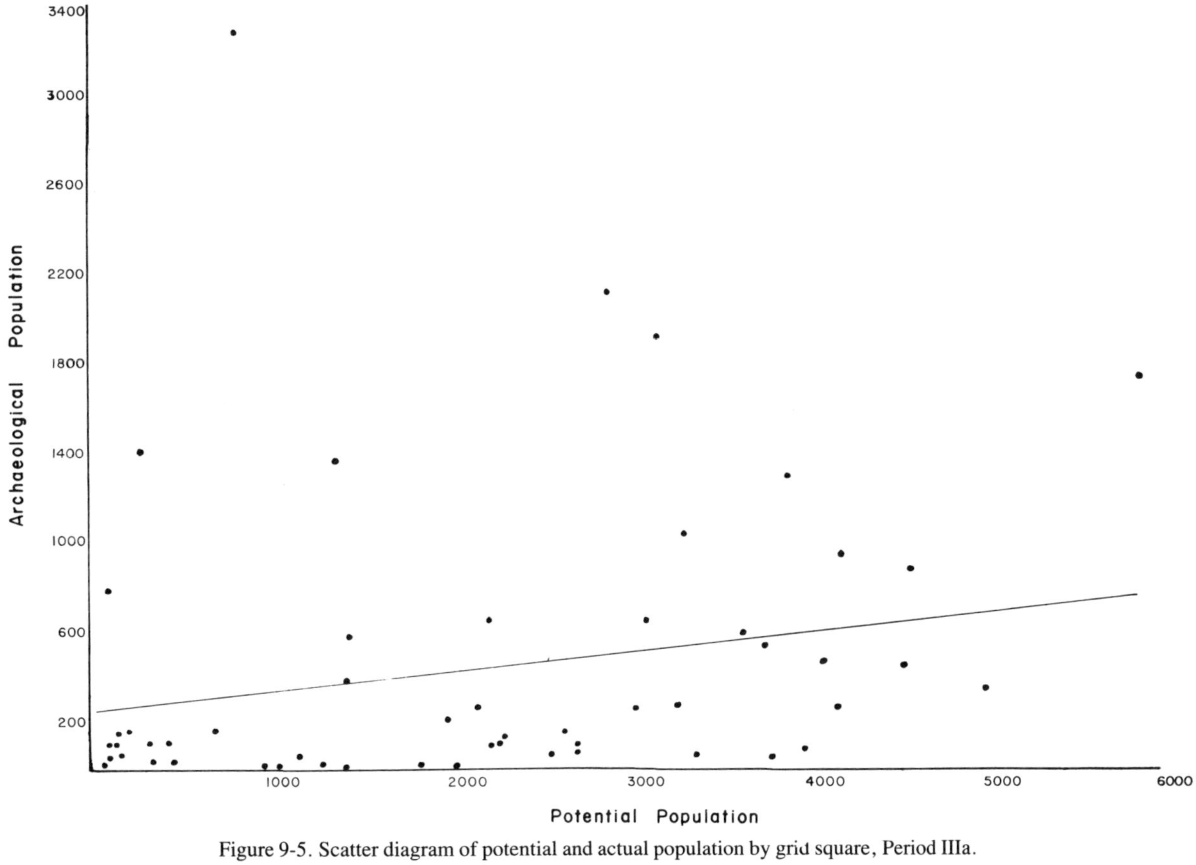

Figure 9-5. Scatter diagram of potential and actual population by grid square, Period IIIa.

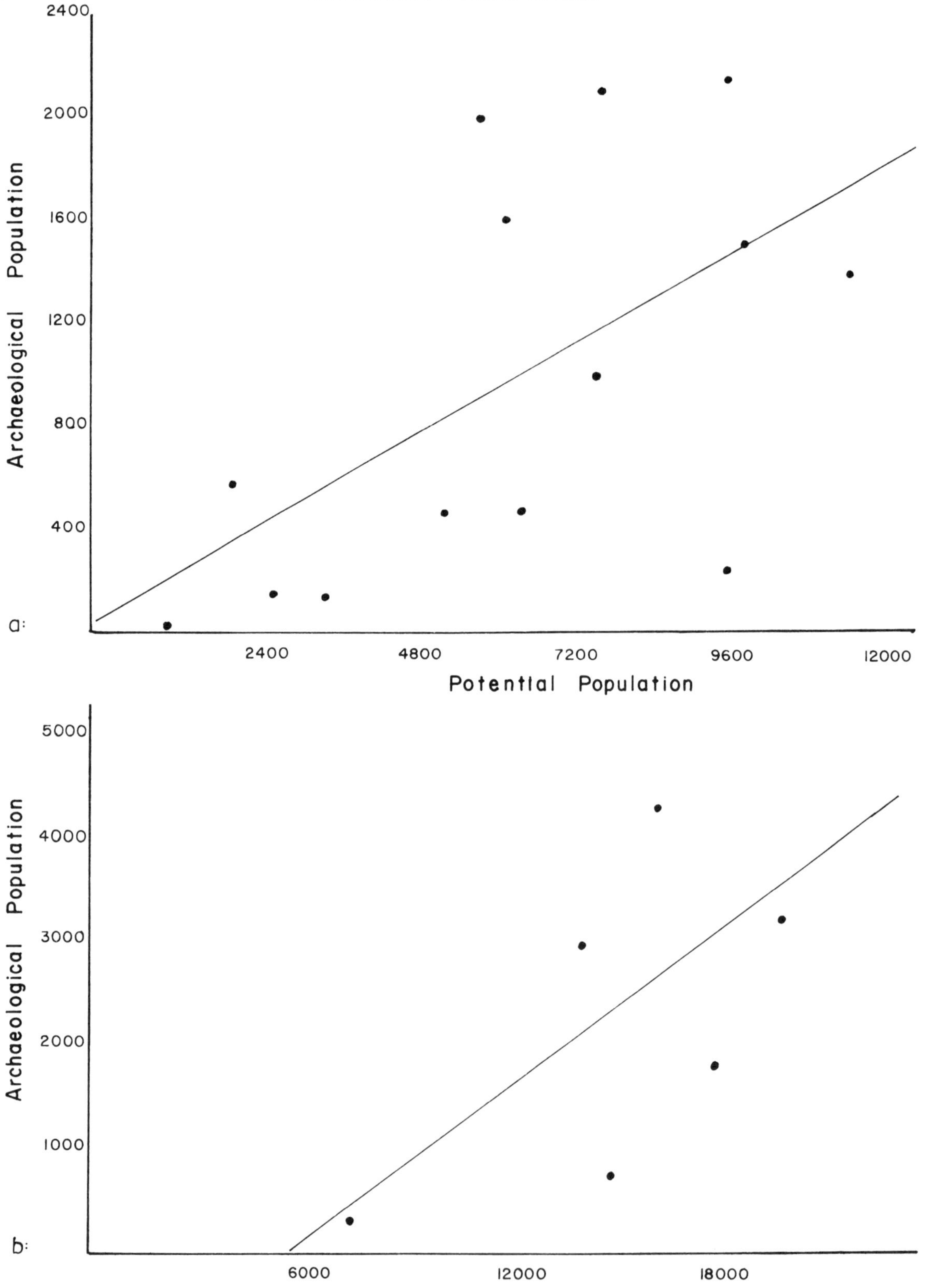

Figure 9-6. Scatter diagrams of archaeological and potential population estimates, Period Late I. a is the N = 14 scale, while b is the N = 6 scale.

no evidence indicating a regular, predictable association between the amount of potential maize yield in specified areal units and the number of people estimated by archaeological means to have lived in the same units. This conclusion can only apply of course to the 4 × 4 kilometer scale used so far. It may be that if larger areal units are chosen, a closer association will be found, since perhaps farmers held land in different envionmental zones and since local exchange of labor and produce quite likely crossed quadrat lines. These larger scales are examined next.

Changing the Scale of Analysis

In order to increase the chances of detecting adjustments between population and resources made possible by movement between environmental zones, we use larger spatial units that are cross sections of the valley–mountain to piedmont to valley floor to uplands again. The most convenient way of doing this is to treat all the grid squares along an east-west strip (all of the N7s, for example) as a single unit, recognizing however, that these units will then be of somewhat different sizes. There are 14 such strips, and when we discuss this scale of analysis, we refer to it as "n = 14", n being the number of data points or cases. A larger grouping is also utilized, because local exchange systems probably entail movement longitudinally as well as across the valley, for more than 4 kilometers. We thus use blocks that are two grid squares (8 kilometers) wide. There are six of these, N1,2,3; N4,5; N6,7; N8,9; N10,11; and N12,13,14 and this scale is labeled n = 6. The differences in area sizes and the irregular shape of the study area require that caution be exercised in the interpretation of the data.

Population potential and archaeological population estimates were computed for both scales, n = 14 and n = 6, scattergrammed, (examples are shown in Figure 9-6) and characterized with linear regression and correlation statistics. The more particular results of this procedure are discussed below in the sections on each separate phase. Now we address the general, long-term aspects of the possible association of population and resources with the larger spatial blocks.

Figure 9-7 and Table 9-8 give the linear correlation coefficients for potential population, the variable treated as independent, and actual population, the dependent variable. As in the previous analysis, grid squares containing the one (or two, in IIIa) leading settlements are deleted because their actual populations are out of range. As before this biases the results toward finding a

Figure 9-7. Linear correlation coefficients for potential population and actual population, Early I through V, at three scales.

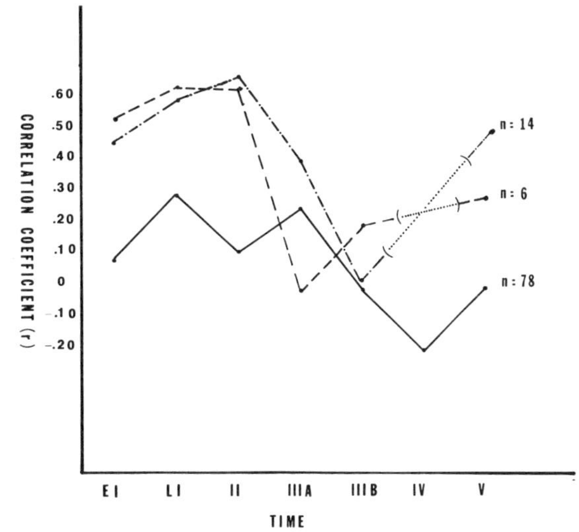

regular relationship between the two quantities. Monte Albán IV is not included in this analysis, since it is likely to make little sense until the Tlacolula Valley is surveyed.

As can be seen in Figure 9-7, all correlation coefficients at the scale n = 6 and n = 14 are larger than those at the same phase for the single grid square scale (where n = 78), with the exception of the n = 6 value for Monte Albán IIIa. The fact that almost all are higher may indicate that processes such as flows between environmental zones or local exchange of labor or produce might be operating to even out the discontinuities seen at the smaller scale.

It should be remembered though that only one *r* value, that of Monte Albán II where n = 14, is significant at the .01 level, and only one other coefficient is significant at the .05 level (that for Monte Albán Late I at n = 14). Only in these two cases might we accept a nonrandom association between population and resource distribution in the direction expected, and here only about 36-40% of the variance in population could be accounted for by the value of resource availability.

It is possible nonetheless to draw certain tentative conclusions from the *relative* strengths of the association between population and resources at different scales in each phase. We suggest that the reason our variables are usually more strongly associated at the larger scales is that a variety of exchange mechanisms were organized at the local levels in such a way that population and food resource balances are not detectable at the finest scale. Though we cannot be sure, such mechanisms might involve the practice of having fields in widely dispersed locations to take advantage of soil, irrigation, and rainfall possibilities. Irrigation or drainage systems might be best seen at larger than the 4 × 4 kilometer scale. Cooperative labor efforts in agricultural production, local redistribution, periodic or traveling markets, or complimentary crop specializations are all possibilities. At the n = 6 scale mechanisms more likely to be regulated by local administration might be operating, while the unregulated flows are more typical of the n = 14 scale.

Assuming for the time being that this assessment of the scale differences is close to the truth, we may add further interpretations. Through Monte Albán II the *r* value for n = 6 is about equal to that for n = 14, but in IIIa it is much lower, and the coefficient for the grid square scale is rather high. This could mean that large parts (though not necessarily every part) of the system have little in the way of regulated flows on the local exchange level, while maintaining unregulated movement, that is, exchanges not administratively controlled, on the smaller scale. In IIIb, with the concentration of population around Monte Albán, the grid square level adjustment to resources is absent and so is any adjustment at n = 14, the 4 kilometer wide cross section, but there is a small degree of regulated local exchange at the n = 6 level. Clearly here all of the smaller scale debits and credits in the population/resource balance are being transacted at the full system level, probably through Monte Albán. Finally, in Monte Albán V, unregulated movements at the n = 14 scale are most important, followed by regulated exchange, while at the smallest scale that we use there is no association. Administration-free movement of goods, energy, people, and information is precisely the kind of mechanism that we think–on the basis of other evidence discussed in Chapter 8–was important in Monte Albán V.

Special attention should be given to the relative strengths of the population/resource association at different scales in Early I, II, and V. These are the phases whose ceramic complexes contain the largest proportions of costly decorated types. As proposed in Chapter 10, the predominance of costly pottery in these phases, contrasted with plain wares in the other phases, may be a feature of light administrative control at the higher levels of the production/distribution system. The analysis in the present chapter (on data of an entirely different sort) supports this idea. Whenever the smallest-scale population/resource association is low *and* the local exchange systems are strong (resulting in more correspondence between population and resources at the larger scales), pottery production does exhibit design florescence (see Fig. 9-7 for the *r* values at the three scales for Monte Albán Early I, II, and V). Conversely, in IIIa and IIIb there is evidence of attenuation in n = 6 and n = 14 flows, made up for by exchange mediated and controlled at the whole system level. In IIIa the smallest scale, unregulated flows may be more prevalent than regulated exchange, while the latter is relatively more important (though still dominated by central control) in IIIb. This might have something to do with the ceramic production index differences between IIIa and IIIb discussed in Chapter 10.

Superficially, Late I appears to be anomolous to this interpretation. Local exchange, regulated and unregulated, is healthy by our assumption, but potters are producing the fairly plain pots thought to be typical of periods of central administrative meddling. But Late I is the only phase in which the population/resource associations are relatively high at each scale (grid square, n = 14, n = 6), and given the steady growth in size of population within the same basic settlement pattern from Early I to Late I, this most probably indicates an increasingly finer tuning of population to resources wherein every level below Monte Albán is uniformly determined by its tributary relation to the capital.

Population/Resources and Distance from Monte Albán

The general lack of correspondence between population and resource values means that the existing spatial distribution of agricultural resources was used in a variety of ways by the valley's population instead of in a single, determined way. Resource distributions may not directly determine population densities in any detectable way, but there are population/resource relations that have patterns we think are generated by the nature of exchange networks, in a general sense, or the degree of access to exchange networks. In this chapter we can't specify very much about the institutional form of these networks, or whether what was being exchanged was mainly material goods, information (e.g., administrative decisions), or labor services. These questions are explored using other evidence in other chapters. However, there are long-term population/resource patterns that vary regularly and seem to be influenced by distance (and hence the factor of transport costs) to the main focus of region-wide exchange.

To begin simply with the archaeological population

estimates, expressed as densities, it may be readily shown that in particular periods dense concentrations of populations occur near Monte Albán, in the center of the Valley of Oaxaca, the hub of exchange activity and the place with the best physical access to markets and services. Monte Albán V is instructive in this regard. In this phase there is little evidence of a powerful, centralized, valley-wide state, but population is concentrated toward the center of the system. To correct for differences in width of the study area, we converted the population figures to densities. In Monte Albán V it makes sense to divide the frequency distribution of densities into two parts, low (25 people per square kilometer or less) and high (more than 25 people per square kilometer). Ninety-five percent of the low density cases are more than 9 kilometers from Monte Albán, whereas 43% of the high density squares (n = 37) are less than 9 kilometers from Monte Albán. Similar observations can be made in other periods.

We may also examine, in addition to density itself, the relation between actual and potential population as this varies with distance from Monte Albán. The effects of many variables–noise–usually makes it hard to see this operating on the grid square (n = 78) scale, but it is seen in almost every phase at the n = 14 and n = 6 scales. The curve is similar to that of the distribution of population with distance from Monte Albán, even though here we are comparing actual to potential population. Probably the higher than usual densities compared to potential densities nearer to the high order central places meant differences in the intensity of land use, the organization of labor, and crop specialization, but we have no evidence bearing on that.

Finally, the regression analysis using the larger areal blocks also provides evidence of a change in the association of actual and potential population with distance from Monte Albán. For heuristic purposes in describing scatterplots of actual vs. potential population, we refer to data points as being above the best fit linear regression line (that is, having higher actual population than predicted from the potential value), or below it (lower actual population than predicted from the potential value). Generally, areas near Monte Albán fall above the line, with a slight tendency toward the upper end of the potential population range; areas away from Monte Albán had lower than expected populations, and slightly lower potential. To a certain extent this relationship also holds for the largest secondary centers in some phases. Thus the intensity of land utilization probably varies with proximity to exchange networks, as in the geographer von Thünen's ideal landscape (Hall 1966).

In the previous sections we have discussed regularities in population and resources across phases. Here we present particular aspects of consumption and labor, as they are seen in each phase.

THE RESULTS: PHASE-BY-PHASE

Early I

The preference for site location near land of high production potential has already been noted. This is especially true in Monte Albán Early I. Occupied squares do tend to have high productive potentials; unoccupied squares do not. The mean potential density values of occupied and unoccupied squares are significantly different. Furthermore, we may say that there is a preference for high quality land. Occupied squares more often than expected have Type I (high water table and canal irrigable) land, and unoccupied squares usually have no Type I land. The same holds for Type II land and either Type I or II land–occupied squares more often than expected have high quality land, unoccupied squares usually only dry farming or poor floodwater farming possibilities. This may be shown by chi square tests. For Type I land, $X^2 = 15.6$; Type II, $X^2 = 17.5$; and with the presence of either Type I or II, $X^2 = 26.0$ (see Table 9-9). All values are significant at the .01 level.

Table 9-9. X^2 Values for Land Types and Presence/Absence of Occupation

Phase	Type I	Type II	Types I or II
EI	15.6*	17.5*	26.0*
LI	12.8*	5.7	23.9*
II	23.7*	10.7*	16.0*
IIIA	5.7	4.7	4.4
IIIB	9.1	12.0*	17.0*
IV	1.1	1.3	0.1
V	0.03	2.7	3.3

*significant at the .01 level

However, while knowing where the good land is would allow us to guess where Early I sites are, it does not tell us how many sites there are nor how large they are. Correlation coefficients for the amounts of each land type versus the archaeological population estimates are .03 for Type I, .20 for Type II, and .09 for Type I or Type II. None are significant at the .05 level. As with all the correlations, Monte Albán is not included because it is an extreme value, and zero cases of values for actual population are excluded because we want to know about the nature of the association where sites are present. We may conclude that the Early I population needed to be near *some* low risk, high yield agricultural land, but perhaps patches of this kind of land were so large, and populations so small, that the size and number of settlements were hardly affected by the size of the patch of high quality land the settlements were near.

As discussed earlier in this chapter in the section on consumption, the number of people that could be provided for from maize harvests may vary considerably. Consumption, ethnographically, varies between 160 and 290 kilos per person per year. Each grid square also has a range of potential maize yields, the width of the range depending on rainfall variation. In bad years, or with very high populations, the alternative of lowering consumption would be inadequate, and maize would necessarily have to be obtained from elsewhere. We can list the grid squares for which these choices were probably necessary. Referring to Table 9-6, for example, if the archaeological population estimate exceeds the lower limit of the range of the estimate that uses a high consumption figure, then that population either may reduce consumption or obtain corn from elsewhere in years of low rainfall. In Early I this was probably true for the squares N11E7,8; N12E6; N13E6; and N14E6. These areas lie in the zone of low and highly erratic rainfall in the central part of the valley, but they were also relatively heavily populated in Early I. In addition, N11E8, N12E6, and N14E6 had populations that exceed the lower limit of the low consumption population potential, so in those areas lowering consumption would not have been feasible, and in bad years dependence on exchange is suggested.

If one were to choose the grid square with the highest potential density it would be N8E6; N4E5, N9E6, and N9E7 also have high population potentials. Interestingly, the square chosen in Early I as the location for the new capital of the regional system, N12E6, has a potential population only in the middle third of the range. If we include the ring of eight 4 kilometer grid squares around a given square as possible farm land for the center square, then any of the six squares in the middle of the northern Valley Grande would have been more suitable places for the capital. Even some places far to the south (such as N4E4,5) would have had the local resources to support higher population densities than N12E6. As far as agriculture is concerned the problems with the Central area in general are that much of the land has to be dry farmed, rainfall is erratic, there is less potential for irrigation than in other areas, and the alluvium is susceptible to destructive flooding and deposition by the Atoyac. It is unlikely that the location for Monte Albán was chosen to take advantage of local agricultural resources. Central location *vis à vis* the entire Valley of Oaxaca area was probably the key factor, in order to minimize the cost of administration and exchange between different arms of the valley. In this respect it is interesting to note that N12E6 in fact has the *lowest* population potential of any of the full squares in the central part of the valley. It was probably rather undesirable for Formative period farmers. But a large population was settled there, rather suddenly, in Early I, and in the area around the capital new settlements arose and old ones grew in much the same way as elsewhere in the valley. There is thus no settlement pattern evidence suggesting that the way the land around Monte Albán was used was different from land and labor used in the rest of the valley. We see no evidence of an urban population organized for farm labor in the vicinity of Monte Albán.

This raises the question of whether Monte Albán could have been provisioned from its hinterland without the city population being involved in farm work. The method of estimating production was discussed in the section on calculations above. The total amount of maize that the rural work force can produce in Early I is equal to the number of workers times the amount of land one worker can cultivate times the productivity per hectare. The rural population is defined as the whole population of the study area (less that of Monte Albán), 3147. The labor force is one-half of the population, or 1573. The amount of land one worker can cultivate by traditional methods is assumed to be 2 hectares. The Early I preference for Type I and II land has already been demonstrated. Productivity of these two types of land is not as greatly affected by rainfall variation as it is for Type III land, so we do not take rainfall variation into account any more than that already expressed in the range of average production for the two land types. The productivity ranges for Type I land in Early I are 0.5-0.6 tons per hectare, and for Type II, 0.3-0.6 tons per hectare. The range 0.3-0.6 tons per hectare will be used here.

The estimates for total amount of maize producible by the rural population is 1573 people × 2 hectare ×

0.3 tons per hectare = 944 tons, and 1573 × 2 × 0.6 = 1888 tons. The food requirements for the rural population, at .16 to .29 tons per year per person, are 504-913 tons. The differences between the amount producible and the amount needed for the food–the surplus–are:

high production, low consumption	1384 tons
low production, low consumption	440 tons
high production, high consumption	975 tons
low production, high consumption	31 tons
average	707 tons

Monte Albán's requirements for food range between 864 and 1566 tons per year, depending on consumption rates. The average figure is 1215 tons. The surplus producible by the rural population of the study area is an average of 707 tons, 58% of the amount required to provision Monte Albán. This is about the percentage of the valley area included in the study area, and if, as we suspect, the rest of the valley (Etla, Tlacolula, and Ocotlán) was contributing in proportion to its area at approximately the same rate as in the study area, then with all the valley integrated in the same system in Early I, Monte Albán could have been provisioned by the rural population. And according to this analysis, that could have been done without the urban population being involved in farm work.

In summary, for Early I population potential densities range up to 240 people per square kilometer, but about one-third of the grid squares have potential densities of less than 30 per square kilometer. Almost all of these very low density squares are unoccupied, while most of the squares over 60 people per square kilometer in potential are occupied, and all of the highest potential (over 150 per square kilometer) are occupied. There is thus a clear preference for the most reliable and most productive type of farming, and this can be further developed by chi square analysis to show that sites are quite likely to be located in areas with irrigation, water table, or good floodwater possibilities.

Correlation and regression analysis at the 4 × 4 kilometer scale, however, shows no relationship between population potential, determined by land and water resources, and archaeological population estimates. At the scale (n = 14) where we can cross-section the valley, there is a weak but nonsignificant improvement in the correlation, and there is a slight further increase (still not statistically significant) in the association at the scale designed to detect local exchange (n = 6). At n = 6 the cases are clearly segregated into those near Monte Albán and those far away, with areas near the city tending to have higher than expected populations compared to resources. Areas outside the area of direct Monte Albán administrative reach have lower than expected populations.

Relative to later periods there would seem to be low intrinsic demand for exchange between local rural areas in the study area, since only 4 of the 78 grid squares have populations that were chronic food importers in bad years. In later periods there are more of these cases. Clearly the main burden on the rural population, however, was the provisioning of Monte Albán. A preliminary estimate based only on the non-Monte Albán population of the area studied so far indicates a very close correspondence between the food needs of Monte Albán and the estimated amount of surplus the rural population can produce. We find no evidence that Monte Albán was founded where it is to take advantage of local agricultural resources; in fact, the agricultural catchment of Monte Albán is poorer than similar sized catchments for many other parts of the valley. The land use analysis reviewed in this chapter suggests, however, that Monte Albán's function and location were determined by other factors: (1) Whatever its function, the city would have to be located so as to be able to efficiently supply itself. Central location *vis-à-vis* the inhabited parts of the rest of the valley would be optimal. (2) Monte Albán perhaps had a role in maintaining the kind of valley-wide integration that we think was necessary because of the local variation in rainfall and harvests. Wide integration would be important to assure survival of local communities in dry years and to assure that sufficient surplus is generated for the city in better years. In Early I we suspect that the mitigation of local disaster is not as great a factor as the assurance of continuous supply for the city, because in this phase there is less dependence on dry farming and relatively more emphasis on Type I and Type II farming. Monte Albán had important functions in its regional system in Early I, aside from these two, and these are discussed in Chapter 4.

Late I

As in the early half of Monte Albán I, in Late I there is an unmistakable preference for land that supports higher population densities. In this phase the highest potential density for any square is 270 people per square kilometer, while about one-fourth of the squares have potential densities of less than 30 people per square kilometer. Of these last, almost half have some Late I occupation, indicating a shift toward less desirable land between Early and Late I. However, the preponderance of occupied squares have potential densities over 60 people per square kilometer, so that in general we may still say that there is a general preference for higher quality land. There is a statistically significant difference in the mean potential population densities for occupied (113.7 persons per square kilometer) vs. unoccupied (72.6 persons per square kilometer) squares.

The chi square value for nonrandom distribution of occupied/unoccupied squares and squares with and without Type I land is almost as high as in Early I (12.8 vs. 15.6), showing again a preference for canal irrigable and high water table land. Less clear, and not significant at the .01 level, is the association between occupation and Type II land, but for either Type I or Type II land, the value is almost as high as in Early I (23.9 vs. 26.0). The slight drop in the chi square values probably reflects the fact that more people live in dry-farming-only areas in Late I than in Early I.

On the other hand, beyond a simple relationship between presence of sites and presence of Type I and II land in the same grid square, there is no demonstrable relationship between the *amount* of Type I and Type II land and the *number* of people estimated to have lived in the square ($r = .04$, $n = 42$). A somewhat stronger association exists between the amount of Type III land and the *increment* in population in each grid square between Early I and Late I. This was suspected given the apparent increase in central administrative concern for increasing production, possibly by emphasizing dry farming (see Chapter 4) ($r = .34$, $n = 55$, y est $= .59x + 73.6$, significant at the .05 level–but only 11% of the variance is accounted for). There is no such relationship between the added population in Late I and Type I or II land ($r = .02$).

For all grid squares (except Monte Albán) the association between average population potential and archaeological population is slight ($r = .29$) but significant at the .05 level. There are actual populations ranging from 80 persons or less to over 1000 per square (the top end of the scale) for the middle third of the potential population range, so the association is hardly convincing. At the larger groupings $n = 14$ and $n = 6$, though, there is a stronger relationship, probably reflecting local exchange. This pattern emerges at the $n = 14$ scale, though it is still rather diffuse. Areas with higher-than-predicted populations for given potentials tend to be near Monte Albán. Some of these areas are also the ones that are intensively developed for the first time in Late I. Areas at a greater distance from Monte Albán have lower than predicted populations. This relationship becomes clearer at the scale $n = 6$ (where the study area is divided into six large units instead of 14 or 78 smaller ones). "Near" and "far" zones separate out fairly distinctly. The linear correlation coefficient is .63, not significant at .05 (y est $= .24x$-1303.5). Examination of the scattergrams suggests that perhaps a *J*-shaped curve might give a better fit than a straight line, but the most reasonable interpretation of that curve would be the operation of another variable besides the population potential of resources. Distance from Monte Albán, important because of the differences in travel costs, would seem to be important. As in Early I, actual population reaches a higher percentage of potential population the closer one is to Monte Albán, and the relationship is rather regular. At the $n = 14$ scale, for every 4 kilometers of distance from Monte Albán, there is a roughly 5% drop in the proportion of the potential population that the actual population attains (starting at a high of 36% for N11).

In Late I the number of squares that would have had either to reduce consumption or obtain maize from elsewhere in bad years increases from 4 to 26 (one-third of the total number of grid squares). Most of these are in the Central area of the valley. In fact, of the 25 grid squares north of N11, 16 (64%) would have to rely on exchange or decrease consumption. Fifteen grid squares in all could not rely only on reducing consumption, but would have to be involved in exchange. Given the proximity to Monte Albán and the lack of evidence for rural administrative centers in the Central area, this exchange must have been mediated by Monte Albán itself.

Monte Albán II

In this phase the highest potential population density permitted by maize yields is 330 people per square kilometer. Approximately 60% of the grid squares fall in the range of 60 to 240 people per square kilometer, and three-fourths of the squares with Monte Albán II sites fall within this range. Very few Period II sites are found in the least desirable areas, less than in the previous phase. This could mean that there is less reason for attempting much dry farming in marginal areas. The difference between the mean potential values of occupied vs. unoccupied squares is statistically significant, and we conclude that there is some preference for squares of higher population potential.

There are very few squares left unoccupied that have Type I land, and the same, to a lesser extent, can be said for Type II land. In other words, there is also a preference for living near irrigable, water table, or good floodwater land. The chi square values for non-chance association between presence/absence of occupation and presence/absence of Type I land is 23.7. For Type II land it is 10.7, and for Type I and II it is 16.0. All of these are statistically significant at least at the .01 level, and the association between occupation and Type I land is the highest of any phase. This might suggest a relatively greater role for canal irrigation in Monte Albán II, but that conclusion is far from clear and there is little we can say in the absence of a detailed, settlement-centered catchment analysis.

None of this association between high quality land and occupation in Monte Albán II can be carried further to predict the size of population from the amount of Type I or II land. The correlation coefficients for Type I, Type II, and Type I and II land against archaeological population are .26 or less, and none are significant at the .05 level. Similarly, there is no evidence of linear correlation between overall potential and archaeologically estimated population at the n = 78 scale ($r = .11$).

When the grid squares are grouped into larger areal units, the association between potential and actual population is stronger and is significant at the .01 level for the scale n = 14 ($r = .65$ for n = 14, $r = .63$ for n = 6). We think that the stronger association reflects greater exchange at the local level and perhaps somewhat less dependence on Monte Albán-centered exchange in Period II. In Monte Albán I, especially Late I, locally organized exchange may have been greatly overshadowed or even interfered with by the exchange focused on the primate center. By Monte Albán II there seems to be less concern on the part of Monte Albán for activity on every level of the settlement hierarchy, and there does appear to be more evidence of population/resource balances being controlled at the local level.

Supporting evidence for this interpretation comes from examination of the scattergrams of actual against potential population at the larger areal scales. At n = 14 the areal units divide into two groups, those near the best-fit linear regression line or having lower populations than predicted by the best-fit linear equation, and those having higher than predicted populations (these are at the higher end of the range of potential populations). The first group includes cases at the greatest distance from Monte Albán, as in Late I, indicating that development requires proximity to exchange networks. But this first group also includes the areas closest to Monte Albán. The second group of data points are those of N8, N9, and N10, at moderate distance from Monte Albán. As in Period I, distance from Monte Albán is implicated in the determination of both population density and population-to-resource ratios. But in Monte Albán II, population was very far below resource potential in the Central area, above average (for the phase) between 10 and 18 kilometers, and again low compared to resource potential farther away. Close in, Monte Albán may have on the one hand suppressed locally organized exchange, possibly to prevent competition while the state was preoccupied elsewhere; at the same time Monte Albán did nothing to control and administer low-level exchange in the Central area, as it had done earlier. Without local centers, the exchange we think necessary for maintenance during dry years, at the minimum, would be so inefficient that it might have been virtually impossible to live in that area. This problem is discussed in greater detail in Chapter 5.

Grid squares having to import food or cut consumption in Monte Albán II are N5E8, N7E4, N8E8, N10E8, N11E8, and N13E8— far fewer than in Late I. Of these only N8E8 is of any significance. This was the location of a secondary center large enough that it is not surprising that it could not produce enough to feed itself from its high piedmont surroundings.

Monte Albán IIIa

The population/resource relations for Monte Albán IIIa are of considerable interest since this phase is a time of great population expansion in the Valle Grande. The same topics reviewed in the earlier phase summaries are discussed here, with the analytical details, but a summary of conclusions for the phase follows at the end of the Monte Albán IIIa section.

The frequency distribution of population potentials for grid squares in IIIa is trimodal, with 23% of the squares having potentials of less than 30 people per square kilometer, 20% falling between 120 and 180 people per square kilometer, and 14% between 240 and 270 per square kilometer. The highest value is 390 per square kilometer. In itself this is simply a state of the initial maize yield assumptions. But it is of note that those (57) squares *occupied* are distributed conformably to the distribution of the potential densities, except that somewhat fewer of the lowest density squares are occupied. Thus the squares with IIIa sites are more representative of the total range of potential than in any previous phase. By this measure there is less preference for the most fertile land than before, though a slight tendency to avoid some poorer land is seen.

Preference for different types of agricultural land is likewise not as strong in IIIa. Occupied squares actually, more often than not, do not have Type I land, and occupied squares are split about evenly between those that have Type II land and those that don't. Unoccupied squares, in contrast, are overwhelmingly without Type I land, and the same holds for Type II. Overall the chi square values are 3.7 for Type I land, 4.7 for Type II, and 4.4 for Types I and II taken together. These values are much lower than in the previous phases and are only significant at the .05 level. There is a strong tendency to occupy squares with irrigable, water table, and good floodwater land, but many squares without high quality land are also occupied.

Because the number of unoccupied squares is low (22), the archaeologically estimated population densities of occupied squares were histogrammed and split into two groups, those with high density (greater than 50 persons per square kilometer) and those with low (50 persons per square kilometer or lower). The latter were combined with the unoccupied squares, and the 2× 2 tables reexamined. The chi square values are small and show no significant distribution, but the number of high density squares is small (n = 17). The point of interest is that the squares with the high actual population densities tend to be fairly evenly divided between those that have Type I land (and to a lesser extent, Type II land) and those that don't, meaning that high densities occur often in the absence of the more fertile land.

With all cases except Monte Albán and Jalieza, whose populations are out of range and would distort any association, there is no statistically demonstrable association between population and resource potential at the grid square scale. In fact, three of the six highest archaeological population cases have potential populations in the lowest third of the population potential range–an incongruous circumstance if one had expected population to be distributed evenly with regard to food resources.

In the northern half of the study area, however, dense concentrations of people did tend to live in areas with higher-than-median potential productivity (again excluding Monte Albán and Jalieza). This remains true even though a large portion of the Central survey area was essentially abandoned. In the southern end of the study area, dense concentrations of people lived in even marginal zones (a fact we try to interpret momentarily). Clearly this southern end of the study area is different, and an improvement in the association between population and resource potential might be sought by eliminating squares N1E3 through N6E7. With that modification, the linear correlation coefficient *r* is .59 (n = 32, *y* est = .215 *x*-139.7), significant at the .01 level. This would still account for less than 35% of the variance, but it is a strong relationship compared to most of the poor fits we have. At that it is probably spurious, which becomes clear when we examine the n = 14 scale.

The best fit linear regression line for actual versus potential population at the n = 14 scale neatly splits the 14 cases in half, where the halves obviously represent the operation of several processes other than regular and close adjustment of population and resources. Areas of long prior occupation with little new development and comparatively little administration all have lower than "expected" populations; newly developed areas, with intensive administration, have higher than "expected" populations. The fairly high correlation between population and resources, then, is a coincidental compromise, an average that obscures the real but contradictory processes. One might note that at the n = 6 scale there is no association between population and resource values (*r* = -.12), linear regression operating on the data with the definitiveness of a surgeon's scalpel in a bowl of oatmeal.

Some of the same aspects of differences in land use in IIIa can be brought out in another and somewhat simpler way. For each grid square we divided the actual population by the potential population, in order to see the performance of population against local capacity. All but ten of the grid squares (excluding Monte Albán) have actual populations that are at or less than 50% of potential. Every grid square, with one exception, from the northern limit of the study area to 23.5 kilometers distance from Monte Albán is below 40% of population potential. The one exception is N11E7, where there is a large, new administrative center at Xoxocotlán. Beyond 23.5 kilometers, the majority of the grid squares also have populations less than 40% of potential. A second class of squares has populations closer to a 1:1 ratio between actual and potential population (60%-110%). This group consists of two piedmont squares on the boundary of the survey area, not considered significant, and five quadrats that have large, new administrative centers (N11E7, N7E9, N5E2, N4E6, and N4E3). These areas may have fewer farmers and more nonagricultural specialists, but presumably they are supplied partly by their commanding position in exchange or tribute. Three more squares have much higher densities, with actual populations four to seven times potential. These are also all new administrative centers, 30 kilometers or more from Monte Albán, but in each case we surveyed only a short distance beyond the boundaries of the major site, so the grid square's potential is underrepresented. With the exception of Monte Albán, then, most squares have populations below 40% of average potential, and those that have ratios closer to 1:1 are new, large, administrative centers no closer than 23.5 kilometers from Monte Albán. Note however that these ratios are based on average potential. Year to year and place to place variation in rainfall could mean that at any one time the ratios will be more variable than they appear to be here, thus emphasizing the importance of movement of produce, labor, people, or information between local areas.

Table 9-10 lists the grid squares that in bad years would have to import food or cut consumption, and those for which cutting consumption is not possible and importing is the only alternative, and those for which the archaeological population estimates exceed even the maximum population potential estimates. Most of these areas lie far to the south, in the part of the survey area newly developed in Monte Albán IIIa, the area administered by second-or third-level centers other than Monte Albán. The grid squares receiving less than 700 millimeters average annual rainfall in the Central area are in better shape, by and large, in IIIa because of the low populations.

The southern part of the Valle Grande merits more scrutiny because IIIa is the only phase in which it has very large populations. The total lower estimate of potential population under the assumption of relatively high maize consumption for grid squares N1E3 through N6E7 (roughly the southern third of the study area) is 14,100 people. The archaeologically estimated population for the same area is very close–13,591–easily within the limits of error. More specifically, for the area of new development south of the old administrative center at Sta. Inés Yatzeche (N5E6), the respective figures are 10,021 for potential and 12,576 for actual population. Thus the southern part of the Valle Grande *as a whole* must import or cut consumption in dry years–purely local exchange probably is not sufficient, or is just barely so.

If it is true that the whole southern area is relatively precarious, why are there so many people living here? We think the answer lies in what can happen in good years. In the best years in Monte Albán IIIa, this area could produce a surplus above that required for local consumption even at high consumption rates, sufficient to feed as many as three and one-half times its own population. This one area alone could provide enough to feed Monte Albán, and it could do so fairly easily in most years. For the whole regional system, then, the investment in the necessary administration and in insurance against bad years would be more than recouped by the immense potential for producing surplus.

We arrive at this conclusion in the following manner. The land itself (for grid squares N1E3 through N5E4) is capable of producing 2906-7737 tons of maize per year, according to the assumption discussed earlier in this chapter. Calculating what the labor force of Monte Albán IIIa in that area would be capable of producing involves the assumption that people in IIIa in that area farmed the different land types in the proportion in which these are present. They may not have done so, but in the absence of better data, it is the simplest assumption. Each land type has its estimated yield. An average of the yield estimates weighted to reflect the proportional amounts of the three land types in the area in IIIa is .36-.87 tons per hectare. The production by the existing labor force is calculated as 6288 workers × 2 hectares farmed by each worker × .36-.87 tons per hectare = 4527-10,941 tons. This figure is noticably higher than the 2906-7737 tons that the land can theoretically yield, so this case is land, not labor, limited.

In the best years the land could yield 7737 tons, of which local consumption is 12,576 × .16-.29 = 2012-3647 tons, leaving 4091-5725 tons as surplus, enough

Table 9-10. Grid Squares Reducing Consumption or Importing Maize in IIIa

Squares where the archaeological population estimate exceeds the lower limit of potential population, with consumption at .29 tons/person:

N1E3	N4E6	N6E4	N10E7
N1E4	N5E2	N7E4	N11E7
N2E3	N5E3	N7E9	N11E8
N3E5	N5E4	N8E4	N12E6
N4E3	N6E3	N8E9	N13E8

Squares where the archaeological population estimate exceeds the lower limit of potential population, with consumption at .16 tons/person:

N1E3	N5E3	N11E7
N2E3	N6E4	N11E8
N3E5	N7E9	N12E6
N4E3	N8E4	
N5E2	N8E9	

Squares where the archaeological population estimate exceeds the lower limit of potential population, with consumption exceeding all estimates of potential population:

N2E3
N3E5
N5E3
N7E9
N12E6

to feed 14,105-34,783 people. In an average year 5326 tons could be produced, leaving a surplus of 1679-3314 tons, enough for 7462-14,728 people. There is no hard evidence about how often good and bad years occurred over this sector in IIIa, and unfortunately the nearest modern rainfall station is San Pablo Huixtepec, 6 kilometers from the northern edge of the area. There, we guess that dangerously dry years for dry farming occur perhaps one out of every three years, but about two in five years would have "good" harvests. This station of course is on the valley floor, but we suspect from the site locations that in IIIa much of the farming was on the piedmont slopes, which receive more rainfall, in general, than valley floor locations. More than 75% of the cultivable land in this southern area is dry or poor floodwater farmed. It appears that the IIIa strategy was to develop the area by massive emphasis on dry farming or small scale floodwater farming for the purpose of providing a substantial surplus (more often than not). In some ways this strategy is similar to that employed in the Central area and the Cuilapan administrative district in Late I, but in this instance there is heavy administration on the local level, as opposed to the apparent lack of administration in the Central area in Late I. The difference is probably due to the latter area's proximity to the main center, permitting direct administration by the capital. The southern tail of the valley in IIIa is beyond a day's round trip journey, necessitating heavier investment in local level administration. The southern tail, then, could potentially produce more than the Central area, mainly because of its higher rainfall, but to do so would require a regional system of sufficient scale to fund the necessary local organization of exchange and administration, and associated transport costs. That was possible in IIIa, but not in the smaller scale Late I system.

In summary, there is less evidence for site locations being determined by proximity to high quality land in IIIa than in earlier phases. Potentially irrigable and high water table land is occupied, but so are large areas where only dry farming is possible. High population densities are found about as often in resource-poor areas as in high population potential areas. The best fit or regular covariation between potential population and archaeological population estimates occurs at the scale of the 4 kilometer cross sections of the valley (n = 14), but even this is a weak correlation. What seems to account for the degree to which resource potential is reached by population is position in the region's central-place hierarchy. Quadrats with low order places, and possibly commercial centers, tend to have populations that are less than 40% of potential capacity, while quadrats with important secondary and tertiary administrative centers have populations that are from 60% to somewhat over potential capacity. Populations relatively high compared to resources are manifest especially in areas a little more than 20 kilometers from Monte Albán, this distance being roughly a day's journey for the round trip. If communities are to be viable and well-integrated into the rest of the regional system at more than 20-25 kilometers from Monte Albán, a qualitatively greater administrative investment must be made, as discussed in Chapter 6, and this is exactly what is seen in the southern third of the study area in IIIa: a large population and considerable administration. The population was so large that in dry years it would have had to cut consumption of maize back to the lowest amounts possible, or import corn from other areas. But we suggest on the basis of the interpretation in this chapter that the reason that this population–so large and well integrated with the rest of the regional system–is occupying an area previously under-utilized is because of the rather good chances of producing a large maize surplus with dry or poor floodwater farming.

Monte Albán IIIb

Average potential populations for grid squares are more evenly distributed in IIIb than in earlier phases (though the distribution is not as flat as it is in Monte Albán V). The highest potential is 480 people per square kilometer, and the lowest is less than 30 people per square kilometer. Occupied and unoccupied squares have similar potential density characteristics, except at the extremes, where the areas of the least potential are usually unoccupied, and the four squares of the highest potential are all occupied. In general, however, there is no clear trend toward favoring areas of different potential population.

Chi square analysis of presence or absence of sites and Types I and II land shows significant nonrandom distributions. (The values are 9.1 for Type I, 12.0 for Type II, and 17.0 for Types I and II together. The latter two are significant at the .01 level, the former at .05.) People in IIIb tend not to live in areas without Type I land, while favoring areas with Type II land. It is not entirely clear, however, that land type is the main or only determinant of settlement location. Much of the Type I land is in the Valle Grande, while the Central area has more Type II (good floodwater and marginal water table land) than Type I land. Since the Central area has more of the population, there is a split in favor of Type II land, but settlement location in this case might be more influenced by proximity to Monte Albán, presence of Type II land having little to do with it. On the other hand, the high chi square value for Types I and II taken together do seem to indicate a preference for living in areas that have either Type I or Type II land. Potential yields for these two categories are much higher than those of Type III, and Type II yields are not that much lower than Type I. So it does appear that in IIIb there is a site location preference for areas with higher yield land, whether this is in the Valle Grande where populations are low or in the central areas where populations are high.

At no scale analyzed from the grid square up is there any suggestion of covariance between an area's population potential and its actual population. In general, areas near Monte Albán have the highest population, but only moderate agricultural potentials. Similarly the highest percentages of potential capacities are also reached near Monte Albán.

Neither the n = 14 nor the n = 6 scale shows any significant evening out of population/local resource balances from their highly variable states at n = 78. Perhaps the transactions that would serve to even out spatio-temporal fluctuations in resources were handled mainly through Monte Albán itself.

Table 9-11 gives the grid squares in which the archaeologically estimated population exceeds a) the lower limit of potential population with high rates of consumption, b) the lower limit of potential population with the lowest rate of maize consumption, and c) the maximum population potential. All of these squares are in the Central area. Grid squares N12E3,4, and N13E3 have larger populations than could be supported by locally grown maize even under the best circumstances. After the completion of the Central area survey in 1974, one of us suggested (Kowalewski 1976:482-83) that precisely the area of these grid squares may have been the scene of specialized production and distribution involving mountain products, especially wood for fuel. This remains a reasonable interpretation given the available evidence. Given the land and labor limitations examined for each grid square, the sum of estimated maize production is 3319-11,256 tons. At average consumption rates (225 kilos per person), the rural population of 19,812 persons would require 4458 tons to feed itself. This is close to the lower estimate of production, meaning that under poor conditions there will be no surplus for Monte Albán coming from the bounds of the study area. Under the best conditions a surplus of 6798 tons could be achieved, enough to feed 30,215 people, more than the population of Monte Albán. Given the local variations in rainfall from year to year, Monte Albán's hinterland for foodstuffs included more than the present study area. Probably the large population known to be present throughout the Etla Valley was essential for maintaining Monte Albán.

Table 9-11. Grid Squares Reducing Consumption or Importing Maize in IIIb

Squares where the archaeological population estimate exceeds the lower limit of potential population, with consumption at .29 tons/person:

N11E4	N12E6	N13E8	N14E7
N11E6	N13E3	N13E9	
N12E3	N13E4	N14E4	
N12E4	N13E6	N14E5	
N12E5	N13E7	N14E6	

Squares where the archaeological population estimate exceeds the lower limit of potential population, with consumption at .16 tons/person:

N11E4	N13E3	N14E4
N12E3	N13E4	N14E5
N12E4	N13E6	
N12E5	N13E7	
N12E6	N13E8	

Squares where the archaeological population estimate exceeds the lower limit of potential population, with consumption exceeding all estimates of potential population:

N12E3
N12E4
N12E6
N13E3

Monte Albán IV

Until the rest of the Valley of Oaxaca is surveyed, we must restrict our interpretations of Monte Albán IV settlement and land use to the most general level. Grid squares with Period IV sites are outnumbered by unoccupied squares, 29 to 50. The unoccupied squares would actually seem to be about as representative of the range of variation of potential population densities as the occupied squares. More than one-third of the occupied squares would support fewer than 120 people per square kilometer. There is no significant association whatever between occupation and different types of land, suggesting that sites were not primarily located for reasons of agricultural land preference. (The chi square values for occupied vs. unoccupied grid squares and Type I, Type II, or Type I and II land are, respectively, 1.1, 1.3, and 0.)

With or without Jalieza, by far the largest settlement in Monte Albán IV, there is no significant correlation between population potentials and actual populations for the occupied grid squares. If anything, the slope of the best-fit linear regression line is slightly negative.

In ten grid squares–almost one-third of those occupied–actual population exceeds the lowest estimate of potential population, meaning that population would have to reduce consumption or obtain maize from elsewhere in dry years. In eight squares, even with reduced consumption, maize would have to be obtained from other areas. All of these squares but one on the survey boundary contain the large, nucleated communities that are the outstanding features of the Monte Albán IV settlement pattern. In three squares–N2E3, N5E2, and N7E9–actual population is greater than the potential population even with reduced consumption in the best years. Whether the harvest differences that must have existed between Period IV communities were ameliorated by having large catchment areas in the unoccupied land around each community, or by trade between communities, cannot be determined with the presently available evidence. We anticipate that the Tlacolula Valley survey may provide the essential pieces to the puzzle.

Monte Albán V

Compared to all other phases, the greatest proportion of all grid squares is occupied in Monte Albán V–71 out of 79. Those that do not have any sites are very small cases on the survey boundary, so that their lack of sites may mean very little. Potential population densities are distributed more widely and more evenly than in any other phase, one-third falling below 150 persons per square kilometer, one-third between 150 and 330, and one-third between 330 and 660 persons, potentially, per square kilometer.

In order to determine whether site locations might be influenced by agricultural potential, actual population densities for the occupied squares were divided into two classes, high (greater than 25 persons per square kilometer, n = 38) and low (less than 25 persons per square kilometer, including the zero cases, n = 41). The distribution of high and low actual densities was then compared to that of potential densities. The frequency of high density occupations closely parallels the distribution of potential population densities, except for the high extreme, where the eight highest potential density cases have low actual density. Other than that there is no clear pattern of potential density preference for light or heavy occupation.

As in all previous periods, chi square tables were constructed and values computed to examine possible nonchance association between occupied (here, high density) and unoccupied (and low density) squares on the one hand and higher quality land types on the other. The general trend through time is from strongly significant nonrandom association in the early periods to no significant association beginning in Monte Albán IIIa.

Period V continues the general trend–there is no significant association again. (The chi square values are .03 for Type I land, 2.75 for Type II, and 3.34 for Types I and II.) Neither is there an association between high and low density occupation and squares with more than or less than one-half of the surveyed area classified as Type III land ($X^2 = 3.1$). We consider this lack of statistically significant associations to mean that site location–and whether an area was settled lightly or heavily–had little to do, at least directly, with proximity to particular kinds of agricultural land.

As in all other phases, there is in Monte Albán V no significant correlation between actual and potential population where each data point or case is a grid square (or partial square if it lies in the survey boundary) ($r = .0145$, n = 69, y est = .007x + 711.4). At the scale of larger units of area, 4 kilometer wide cross sections of the study area, there is a stronger–but still not significant–correlation between potential and actual population ($r = .47$, n = 14, y est = .138x + 739.7). This may be an accidental average between two separate relationships. In the ten cases relatively far from the center of the valley (and its commercial functions) an argument might be made for a fairly strong relationship between potential and actual populations. But the best fit line would have a more gradual slope, so that comparatively large increases in population potential are associated with small increases in actual population–an artifact, perhaps, of the smaller areas of the farthest cases, but also presumably influenced by the coincidental fact that the more fertile land south of N10 is that which is closest to Monte Albán.

A separate and different kind of relationship may obtain for the four remaining cases. Here there might also be a strong association, but with a steep slope on which smaller movements of potential population are accompanied by large increases in actual population. Three of these cases are in the central part of the valley, the other is a square containing the second largest central place in the study area. The sample size is small, and again the matter is somewhat equivocal because of the irregularly shaped study area. But this may be reflecting the varying actual-to-potential population ratios made possible by differences in the organization of local exchange, higher densities per potential capacity in the well-serviced areas near the center of the valley, and low densities in poorly serviced sections.

At the n = 6 scale whatever relationship existed at the n = 14 scale deteriorates. One might, cautiously, interpret this to mean that the boundaries of the 8 kilometer wide cross sections of the valley are drawn too widely to detect local exchange networks, whereas these are better circumscribed at the n = 14 scale. This possibility requires further refinement and testing with other kinds of data.

In Monte Albán V, 35% of all the grid squares in the study area have archaeologically estimated populations higher than the lowest potential estimate, indicating some degree of difficulty at least during dry years (see Table 9-12); most of these are in the Central survey area. We expect that the Central survey area should show the most evidence for specialization and exchange that would serve, among other things, to even out spatio-temporal variation in resource distributions.

For IIIb we suspected that the people of squares N12E3,4 and N13E3,4 were involved in moving mountain products to Monte Albán. The same might hold for Monte Albán V, as there is again a substantial population in this high piedmont and mountain zone.

Table 9-12. Grid Squares Reducing Consumption or Importing Maize in Period V

Squares where the archaeological population estimate exceeds the lower limit of potential population, with consumption at .29 tons/person:

N1E3	N7E9	N11E6	N12E8	N13E9
N2E3	N9E4	N11E7	N13E3	N14E6
N3E5	N9E8	N11E8	N13E4	N14E7
N5E2	N10E8	N12E3	N13E6	N14E8
N5E4	N11E4	N12E4	N13E7	
N7E4	N11E5	N12E6	N13E8	

Squares where the archaeological population estimate exceeds the lower limit of potential population, with consumption at .16 tons/person:

N1E3	N9E4	N12E6	N14E6
N2E3	N11E4	N12E8	N14E7
N3E5	N11E6	N13E4	N14E8
N5E2	N11E8	N13E7	
N5E4	N12E3	N13E8	
N7E9	N12E4	N13E9	

Squares where the archaeological population estimate exceeds the lower limit of potential population, with consumption exceeding all estimates of potential population:

N2E3
N7E9
N12E3
N12E6
N14E7

GENERAL CONCLUSIONS

In this chapter we have outlined features of the Valley of Oaxaca natural environment that were important for one of the major preoccupations of Oaxaqueños–maize farming. We examined in a systematic, quantified way what the land could have yielded and what its ancient inhabitants could have produced from the land. What is the logical status of our results? The results are based on observed facts, which we acknowledge are limited in certain ways; ethnographic analogies; assumptions, some with more substantiation, some with less; estimates and indices; and conclusions, which we regard as tentative. We have tried to present the analytical procedures in as detailed a manner as space permits, believing that one can't understand a model without knowing precisely how it is constructed. The conclusions reached here will not show exactly how people behaved in the past in the Valley of Oaxaca, but they will allow us to understand some of the important factors and constraints under which this regional system, as a dynamic functioning whole, has evolved.

Throughout this chapter our search has been for the nature of the relationship between the ancient population and their principle food resources. Has the natural environment determined how people have been distributed on the landscape? Has it determined organizational features of society? Has change in the environment determined the course of change in the regional system? The answer, of course, is a qualified but emphatic no. Environments and their subsistence resources are broad fields upon which many different–but not an unlimited number–of games may be played. On the same field the participants have the capacity–and are often forced–to change the rules and to change games. This is not to say that sociocultural systems are independent of their natural environmental fields, in fact there is important interaction, as this chapter clearly shows, and these interactions are the essence of modern anthropological ecology. But interaction does not mean unilateral determination. It is awkward and anachronistic to have to reiterate these statements in this day and age–they have been said before by Marx, Spencer, Steward, and many others. But there are still some anthropologists who believe that there is no satisfactory explanation without an environmental prime mover, and it is to them that the preceding remarks are directed.

We have suggested that from the time of the first known sedentary villages in the Valley of Oaxaca, considerations of exchange probably played an important role in the regional settlement system. By the time of the founding of Monte Albán the necessity of maintaining system-wide coherence, by means of an urban center that absorbed not quite half the population of the society, implied a means of insuring the flow of goods, people, or information from one part of the social system to another. Environmental uncertainty was a major reason for these networks of exchange and, hence, for maintaining particular levels of sociocultural integration. Overall the system integration is detected on the regional scale, but we suggest that subunits related hierarchically to the whole are seen at smaller scales. Roughly those might be tentatively connoted by the terms "local community" and "district." Since even at the smaller scales of analyses the association between agricultural resources and population is usually weak, these subunits were probably dependent on considerable exchange. What kinds of exchange–a very general term, purposely chosen–is a question that we cannot answer with this population/resource analysis, but other information discussed in Chapter 10 does bear on the question.

Chapter 10

PATTERNS IN CERAMIC PRODUCTION AND DISTRIBUTION, PERIODS EARLY I THROUGH V

by Gary Feinman

INTRODUCTION: ASSUMPTIONS, THEORETICAL FRAMEWORK AND PROBLEM ORIENTATION

This chapter will examine the organization of the ceramic production and distribution system in the prehispanic Valley of Oaxaca, Mexico. The research strategy for this investigation is based upon three premises. The initial premise follows directly from the work of Anna O. Shepard (1977:16). She argued that broad regional reconnaissance and not single site excavation was necessary if the organization of ceramic production was to be understood. The second tenet is that the organization of ceramic production and distribution in a region is likely to change through time. Therefore, one should not expect this organization at any one point in time (i.e., the present) to approximate the organization in other phases (Charlton 1976:146). The third premise stems from the regional analytic approach in anthropology (Blanton 1976b; G. Johnson 1977; Skinner 1964, 1965; Skinner, ed. 1977; C. Smith 1976; C. Smith, ed. 1976). It suggests that although the ceramic production industry in Oaxaca can be examined as if it had an independent linear trajectory of its own, it is more useful to view changes in ceramic production and distribution in the broader context of shifts in the organization of exchange, agricultural production, political administration, and population.

The theoretical basis for this research has been derived from studies of regional system organization (Blanton 1976b; Christaller 1933; E.A.J. Johnson 1970; G. Johnson 1977, in press; Skinner 1964, 1965; C. Smith, ed. 1976; Steponaitis 1978). These studies outline a continuum in the cross-culturally observed pattern of articulation between economic and administrative institutions. At one end of the continuum are regional systems in which there is a considerable degree of overlap between administrative and economic channels of interaction. The administrative hierarchies in these systems often extend a certain degree of control over economic institutions. Competition is therefore limited and consumers as well as small-scale, rural producers have few economic choices (Blanton 1976b; E.A.J. Johnson 1970; Kelley 1976; Skinner 1964; C. Smith 1976:30-31). At the other end of the continuum are regional systems marked by the segregation of administrative and economic networks. In these systems economic transactions and/or market exchanges are relatively autonomous of administrative institutions. Political boundaries therefore tend not to limit or constrain economic choices and consequently competition is more developed in the regional system (Blanton 1976b:258-61; Skinner 1976:359).

Based on this theoretical continuum of regional organization, a set of expectations can be generated about the organization of ceramic production-distribution systems. It is expected that as the extent of administrative control over economic transactions increases, the extent of such control over production, including ceramic production, should also increase. Ceramic manufacturing was one of the principal craft industries in prehispanic Mesoamerica (Durán 1951:278; Millon 1976:232). Therefore, the monopolistic control over the production and distribution of these craft products would have provided a potentially rich source of revenue and coercive power for administrative officials (Davies 1973:137; Soustelle 1961:68-69).

It is predicted that a high degree of administrative control over ceramic manufacturing influenced the ceramic production industry in several ways:

1) The spatial concentration of ceramic production would have been encouraged in order to take advantage of the economies of scale. A centralized, politically controlled ceramic production industry could have employed the large scale production techniques that small decentralized producers could not have used efficiently.

2) The large scale production loci would have been

concentrated in political centers so that the costs of administering these production loci could have been minimized.

3) The adoption of specialized, large scale production techniques would have resulted in a more standardized ceramic production process (Balfet 1965; David and Hennig 1972:25; Irwin 1978:300). This relationship has been noted by Irwin who based on his study of prehistoric pottery production in coastal Papua has argued that:

> the work of specialists reflects a firm unity leading to standardization of production methods, shapes, sizes, and decoration . . . . (*t*)he Mailu Islanders held a pottery-making monopoly in the region and the industry at that time was technologically and stylistically homogeneous. [Irwin 1978:300]

4) In an area like the Valley of Oaxaca in which pottery clay is readily available throughout the region (S. Plog 1976), an increase in the spatial concentration of potters would have led to a reduction in the number of different clay types or sources that were being utilized.

5) In an administratively controlled economic system, the reduced amount of competition between craft producers (including potters) (Blanton 1976b; E.A.J. Johnson 1970; Skinner 1964; C. Smith 1976:30-31) along with the increased scale of the production process would have resulted in the reduction in the amount of energy expended in the production of each craft item (i.e., pot) (van der Leeuw 1976:403). This expectation is based upon several ethnographic studies of contemporary ceramic producers (Fontana et al. 1962:53; Foster 1965:52-56) which have implied that potters will decrease the amount of energy that they will expend in the preparation of a single ceramic vessel when the competition between these potters is diminished. Alternatively, increased competition between potters has been shown to result most frequently in the production of a wide variety of ceramic vessels which often require a large expenditure of energy to produce (Birmingham 1975:381-82; Foster 1965:52-56). This relationship is perhaps best expressed by Foster who has argued that:

> The negative fashion in which the market may act to maintain traditional forms is through the absence of a competitive situation. That is, where a market is essentially non-competitive, there is no particular stimulus pushing potters to come up with a new or better product. [Foster 1965:55]

In summary, it is then expected that when pottery is produced in the context of reduced competition and increased concentration, the ceramic complex would be expected to exhibit greater standardization and a comparatively small amount of energy input per vessel.

This analysis is designed specifically to examine the relationship between changes in the nature of regional administrative organization and shifts in the ceramic production-distribution system. In order to assess this relationship both settlement and ceramic distributions from the last seven temporal phases of the prehispanic sequence in the Valley of Oaxaca are studied. The analysis has been designed to focus on ceramic production as opposed to other craft production industries for three reasons. 1) Ceramics are comparatively well preserved and can easily be collected in the large quantities necessary for analysis during survey. 2) Ceramics can be dated, and therefore certain changes in their production process can be noted and compared through time; lithic artifacts, which are also readily available on site surfaces, are more difficult to date securely. 3) Clay beds are present throughout the Valley of Oaxaca (S. Plog 1976:263). Clay can be procured from the riverbeds as well as from parts of the piedmont zone (Shepard 1967). Thus for any given time, the size and location of ceramic production loci are most likely functions of the nature of the economic and political organization of the valley, not the differential distribution of clay resources.

In this study, four sets of related problems are addressed. Initially, certain aspects of the settlement pattern analysis (see Chapters 4-9) are briefly summarized and some additional insights into the changing patterns of settlement in the valley are made using ceramic data. Secondly, additional ceramic analyses are utilized to construct a preliminary interpretation of the shifting organizational structure of ceramic production in the prehispanic Valley of Oaxaca. The third aspect of this investigation compares through time the changing administrative organization of the valley to the recognized shifts in the ceramic production-distribution system. This comparison permits an evaluation of the hypothesized relationships between these two systemic components. Finally, the research focus is broadened and the diachronic interrelationship between administrative organization and ceramic production is interpreted in relation to changes in other components of the prehispanic Oaxacan system. Long-term shifts in long-distance exchange connections, population distributions, and agricultural production strategies are examined in order to improve our understanding of the trajectory of economic and political change in prehispanic Oaxaca.

ANALYTICAL FRAMEWORK: VARIABLES, MEASURES, AND INDICES

To evaluate the long-term interrelationships between ceramic production and administrative organization in the Valley of Oaxaca, a series of analytical indices and measurements were devised. Two of these measures were utilized in conjunction with settlement pattern analyses to examine the changes in the relative degree of overlap between administrative and economic institutions. First, it was expected that in those phases in which there was relatively more administrative control over production, a larger percentage of the ceramic production loci (see Appendix IX) would be located in settlements with mounded architectural construction (see Chapter 4). The second measure compared the mean number of ceramic types found at administrative sites with the mean number of ceramic types found at non-administrative sites (Table 10-1). It was presumed that the number of contemporary types found in the collections from a given site was reflective of the relative access that site had to a variety of ceramic products during that phase. The larger the number of types found at a site, the greater the access to ceramic products. Given the somewhat opportunistic nature of our ceramic collections, we hardly expect a perfect ordering of the number of types per site versus site function or importance. Individual cases might not mean very much in themselves. But if we are right in our basic political-economic hypotheses, the expected patterns should hold for each phase, and especially, the cross-phase patterns should conform to our expectations.

The differentials between administrative and non-administrative sites were expected to be greatest during those phases when economic networks were isomorphic with administrative networks. Alternatively, it was predicted that the differences in the mean number of types found at the two classes of sites would be reduced in those phases when the production and distribution of ceramics was relatively segregated from administrative activities (Skinner 1977a:23-26; Twichett 1966).

The organization of ceramic production-distribution was examined diachronically through an analysis of five indices: 1) the number and size of the ceramic production locations; 2) the differential distributions of specific ceramic categories and wares; 3) a preliminary analysis of the specific production techniques used for constructing certain ceramic vessels (van der Leeuw 1976); 4) a contingency table analysis designed to examine the relative homogeneity-heterogeneity of each complex's distribution across the survey region; and 5) a mean production-step index for each ceramic complex.

It was expected that ceramics would be produced in

Table 10-1. Mean Numbers of Types/Site

		Mean Number of Types				
Phase	Total Number of Types	All Centers Excluding Monte Albán	All Non-Administrative Settlements	Non-Administrative Sites ≥ 100 People	Non-Administrative Sites < 100 People	Ratio Mean Non-Administrative / Mean Administrative
Early I	85	11.8	5.6	10.2	5.3	47.4%
Late I	88	16.0	5.8	9.3	5.3	36.3%
II	53	15.1	7.1	8.0	7.1	47.0%
IIIA	33	11.9	4.6	11.8	4.3	38.6%
IIIB	22	6.4	3.5	4.1	3.2	54.7%
IV	19	7.0[a]	3.6	--	3.6	51.4%
V	20	7.9[b]	4.9	8.1	4.0	62.0%

a includes Jalieza

b includes Cuilapan-Monte Albán

fewer locations during those periods when production was administratively controlled. It was also hypothesized that when production occurred at fewer sites, the pottery would show more evidence of mass production. During those phases when ceramic production was highly centralized, greater homogeneity in the ceramic complex was also expected. That is, fewer clay sources and pigments should have been utilized. In addition, for those phases, we expected to find very little variation in the specific ceramic categories present in different parts of the survey region.

The analysis of ceramic distributions and the contingency table analysis included the data from the ceramic collections made during the preliminary survey of the Etla area. The analyses of the ceramic production locations and of the number of types per site were restricted to the data from the Central and Valle Grande survey areas. These analyses were limited because the settlement pattern analysis of the Etla area has not been completed. The ceramic distributional analyses, because they did not consider either settlement size or rank, could utilize the data from the Etla area.

The ceramic distributions were analyzed as sherd densities per hectare of surface collected area. These calculations were made for each 4 square kilometer grid unit within the Central, Valle Grande, and Etla survey areas. Ten (less than 1%) of the ceramic collections that were made were not included in these analyses. These collections had sherd densities so low (less than two sherds per collected hectare) that they severely skewed the calculations.

The *contingency table analysis* was designed to examine the relative homogeneity-heterogeneity of the distribution of each ceramic complex across the survey region. This measure was devised to supplement the distributional analyses of specific ceramic categories and wares. It was expected that certain phases would be characterized by spatially discrete ceramic distributions. This indeed proved to be the case. Yet, focusing on only the distributions of a few ceramic categories per phase does not necessarily present a complete picture of changes in ceramic variation. Thus, this contingency table analysis was devised in order to examine and compare the spatial distribution of each entire complex across the survey area (see Feinman 1980: Tables 10-16).

The rows in the contingency tables were composed of each bowl or jar category (Kowalewski, Spencer, and Redmond 1978; see Appendix VII in this volume) that was represented by a minimum of 15 samples in the collections dated to a particular phase. The four columns in the tables represented the four horizontal segments into which the survey area was divided for this analysis. Each cell in the table, therefore, represented the total number of sherds of a given ceramic category that were found in the collections dated to a particular phase within one of the four east-west sections of the survey area.

A phi coefficient (ϕ^2) was used to measure the relative homogeneity of each complex's distribution. The phi coefficient was used instead of chi square, because unlike the latter, phi has been rendered independent of sample size (Thomas 1976:419). This consideration was important because of the large and variable sizes of the samples examined in the contingency analyses. High coefficients suggested heterogeneity and the likelihood that discrete ceramic style zones existed within the valley. Low values suggested that the ceramic categories were distributed uniformly across the region.

Two steps were taken in order to minimize the number of expected values that were smaller than five in the contingency tables (Thomas 1976:298). First, in each table a sample of 15 sherds was chosen as an arbitrary cut-off point for the inclusion of a specific ceramic category in the analysis. Second, the survey region was collapsed into four east-west cross sections. These four sections were chosen because each represents an area that had its own distinct trajectory of settlement pattern change. The settlement pattern shifts within each of the blocks was relatively homogeneous. The northernmost block (grid units N 14-18) represents most of the Etla Arm of the valley. The second section (N 12-14) includes the area adjacent to and immediately north of Monte Albán. The third block is composed of both the southern half of the Central Valley survey area and the northern half of the Valley Grande survey area, while the southernmost block (N 01-05) is made up of the southern half of the Valle Grande area.

The *production step measure* was designed as a rough index of the amount of work imparted per pot. This measure was calculated for each ceramic category identified in the classification of pottery from the surface collections. The measure is based on a series of ethnographic studies that described the step-by-step manufacturing process used by potters who work without the wheel (Chapman 1970; Fontana et al. 1962; Foster 1965; van de Velde and van de Velde 1939). The actual ceramic shaping process was not counted as a production step because all vessels undergo this construction step. Unfortunately, the surface sherd collections did not provide us with enough information to determine systematically the specific shaping process utilized in the production of each ceramic vessel. Intelligent postulations regarding the production processes of certain Oaxacan vessels are possible (van der Leeuw, personal communication), but these analyses are not complete enough to allow us to integrate these findings into the production step measure calculations. An eventual expansion of the production step measure is intended and hopefully it will better address the recognized variability in vessel formation (van der Leeuw 1976).

Painting, slipping, burnishing, smoothing, and incising were all counted as production steps (see Table 10-2). The placement of clay appliqués (supports, everted rims, handles, etc.) onto the basic ceramic vessel body also was included as a production step because these features are usually added on after a vessel is formed, shaped, and dried an initial time (van de Velde and van de Velde 1939:32). In addition, a production step was added for those ceramic vessels made with fine paste clays. The production of vessels that contain only small amounts of non-plastic substances require a longer time for both firing and drying (Payne 1970:3-4; Shepard 1977:13; Stolmaker 1976:194).

Table 10-2. Production-Step Measure

Attribute	Point
Appliqués	
Handle	1
Flange	1
Shelf	1
Hollow support	1
Everted rim	1
Nubbin support	1
Paste	
Fine	1
Surface Finish	
Wiped, Scraped, Smoothed, Lightly Burnished	1-2 (by side)
Burnished (in addition to points awarded for above)	1-2 (by side)
Decoration	
Incision, Carving, Combing or Pattern Burnished	1-2 (by side)
Complex incision - usually requiring more than one tool (in addition to points awarded for above)	1-2 (by side)
Painting or Slipping (1 color)	1-2 (by side)
Painting: Design (in addition to points awarded for above)	1-2 (by side)
Additional Color (per vessel)	1
Differentially Fired Bands	1

Each ceramic category received a production step measure (Table 10-3), and then two cumulative production step indices were calculated for each temporal component. One index calculated a mean production step measure for all but a few of the ceramic vessel categories that were present in each phase. This index was devised by simply adding the production step measures for each category dated to a particular phase and then dividing this sum by the number of categories. Only those few categories that were devised for miscellaneous and unidentifiable sherds were not included in this mean production step index. A second index calculated the mean production step measure for all the categories of ceramic bowls that were present in each phase. This second index minimizes the role of functional variability. The extent of the temporal variation in the production process was best expressed with the latter measure, perhaps because bowls as a rule were the most highly decorated form in the prehispanic Oaxacan ceramic sequence. It must be pointed out, however, that all Oaxacan vessels, including bowls, were much more highly decorated in certain phases than in others.

It was expected that the mean production step measures would co-vary inversely with the degree of administrative control over ceramic production-distribution. To recapitulate, it was expected that when administrative control over production was extensive, the ceramics would have been mass-produced and relatively little energy would have been expended in the production of each vessel. Alternatively, it was predicted that the mean production step indices would be high for those phases when production was relatively independent from administrative institutions. During these times, a considerable degree of competition was expected between a comparatively large number of decentralized ceramic producers (Foster 1965:52-55) and thus more work input per vessel was predicted.

ANALYSIS, INTERPRETATIONS, AND RESULTS

The results of these analyses are presented sequentially. Interpretive emphasis has been placed on a comparison of the observable patterns of change in the set of analytical measures that were described above. The changing relationships between these measures were not all expected to conform to the specified predictions. The organization of a regional system is too complex to expect that it should change in an easily predictable or strictly repeatable fashion (Wallerstein 1974:3-11). Obviously, each phase was characterized by very important differences in the spatial organization of land utilization, population, craft production, administration, and exchange. Yet, certain general reg-

Table 10-3. Production-Step Measure for Each Ceramic Category

Ceramic Category	Present in Phase(s)	Production Step Measure
0001	II	8.5
0002	II	9.5
0003	II	9.0
0004	II	10.0
0005	II	9.5
0006	Not calculated: ceramic description is not detailed sufficiently	
0008	EI, LI	2.5
0016	EI, LI	5.5
0018	EI, LI	7.0
0021	II	9.0
0022	EI, LI	4.0
0023	II	7.0
0031	EI, LI	3.0
0032	EI, LI	4.0
0038	EI, LI	4.0
0056	EI, LI	3.5
0057	LI, II, IIIA	8.0
0121	EI, LI	2.5
0122	EI, LI	2.5
0123	EI, LI	2.5
0374	EI, LI, II	1.5
0375	EI, LI, II	1.5
0376	EI, LI, II	2.0
0377	Not calculated: ceramic description is not detailed sufficiently	
0378	Not calculated: ceramic description is not detailed sufficiently	
0379	EI, LI, II	2.5
0380	EI, LI, II	6.0
0381	EI, LI	4.0
0382	EI, LI	2.5
0383	EI, LI	4.0
0384	EI, LI	2.5
0385	EI, LI	2.5
0386	Not calculated: ceramic description is not detailed sufficiently	
0387	EI	6.5
0388	Not calculated: ceramic description is not detailed sufficiently	
0389	EI, LI	5.5
0390	EI, LI	4.5
0391	EI, LI	4.0
0393	EI, LI	5.0
0394	EI, LI	4.0
0395	Not calculated: ceramic description is not sufficiently detailed	
0396	EI, LI	5.0
0397	EI, LI	3.75
0398	EI, LI	4.5
0399	EI, LI	4.0
0400	EI	6.0
0401	EI, LI	6.0
0402	EI, LI	7.0
0403	EI, LI, II	5.0
0404	LI, II, IIIA	4.5
0405	II, IIIA	8.0
0406	II	8.0
0407	II	7.0
0423	V	3.5
0424	V	5.0
0561	EI, LI	2.5
0610	Not calculated: ceramic description is not detailed sufficiently	
1102	V	7.0
1103	V	7.5
1104	V	5.0
1105	V	5.0
1106	V	5.0
1107	V	6.0
1108	V	5.0
1109	V	4.5
1111	EI, LI, II	4.0
1120	IIIA, IIIB, IV	2.5
1122	IIIB	2.5
1123	IIIA, IIIB, IV	2.5
1125	IIIB	2.5
1126	IIIA, IIIB, IV	2.25
1137	IIIB, IV	2.5
1138	IIIA, IIIB, IV	2.25
1140	IIIA, IIIB, IV	4.0
1141	EI, LI, II, IIIA, IIIB, IV	1.5
1143	EI, LI, II, IIIA, IIIB, IV	2.5
1144	Not calculated - unknown periodization	
1194	II, IIIA	4.0
1207	LI, II, IIIA	4.0
1227	LI, II	5.0
1241	LI, II, IIIA	5.0
1258	LI, II, IIIA	5.0
1259	IIIB	3.0
1262	EI, LI	4.0
1263	IIIA, IIIB, IV	3.25
1264	IIIA	5.0
1265	IIIA	5.5
1268	LI, II, IIIA, IIIB, IV	2.0

Ceramic Category	Present in Phase(s)	Production Step Measure
1274	IIIA, IIIB, IV	3.25
1275	Not calculated - unknown periodization	
1277	IIIA, IIIB, IV	1.0
1297	LI	4.0
1312	IIIA	4.0
1319	EI, LI	6.0
1320	Not calculated: ceramic description is not detailed sufficiently	
1330	Not calculated: ceramic description is not detailed sufficiently	
1332	EI	6.0
1338	EI	5.0
1341	EI, LI	4.0
1343	EI	7.0
1345	EI, LI	5.5
1348	EI	6.0
1349	EI	6.5
1358	EI	6.0
1359	EI, LI	4.5
1360	EI, LI	6.0
1366	LI	4.5
1370	EI	5.0
1372	EI, LI	5.5
1373	EI	6.0
1400	V	5.0
1419	II	5.0
1420	II	6.0
1421	IIIA	7.0
1422	IIIB, IV	1.0
1507	II, IIIA	5.0
1508	IIIA, IIIB, IV	2.0
1509	EI, LI	4.5
1510	LI	5.0
1511	EI	4.5
1512	Not calculated: ceramic description is not detailed sufficiently	
1513	EI	5.0
1514	EI, LI	6.0
1515	EI, LI	6.0
1516	EI	4.5
1517	EI	4.83
1518	EI	5.83
1519	EI, LI	5.0
2009	LI, II, IIIA	2.5
2010	EI, LI	5.0
2011	LI, II	1.5
2013	LI, II, IIIA	1.5
2014	IV, V	2.5
2015	Not calculated: Periodization unknown	

Ceramic Category	Present in Phase(s)	Production Step Measure
2040	LI, II	1.5
2042	LI	6.5
2052	EI, LI, II	3.0
2061	II	5.0
2064	LI	6.0
2065	Not calculated: ceramic description is not detailed sufficiently	
2072	EI, LI	2.5
2073	EI, LI, II	3.0
2076	EI, LI	3.0
2077	EI, LI	4.0
2078	LI, II	3.0
2079	EI, LI	3.0
2080	Not calculated: ceramic description is not detailed sufficiently	
2083	IIIB, IV	1.0
2085	EI, LI, II	3.5
2086	IIIA, IIIB, IV	1.5
2220	Not calculated: ceramic description is not detailed sufficiently	
2221	V	2.5
2222	V	1.5
2223	V	6.0
2224	V	3.0
2411	EI	4.0
2412	EI	5.0
2413	EI, LI, II	5.0
2414	LI, II	4.5
2415	EI, LI	5.5
2416	II	5.0
2417	II	4.0
2418	IIIB, IV	3.5
3030	IIIB, IV	5.5
3033	EI, LI, II	6.5
3035	IIIA, IIIB	7.0
3066	LI, II	5.5
3408	II	6.0
3409	II	8.0
3410	IIIA	7.0
3411	Not calculated: exotically produced	
5000	Not calculated: exotically produced	
5007	V	10.5
5425	V	8.0

ularities have been observed in the relationships between these variables and it is these regularities that are focused upon here.

Rosario Phase

Rosario phase political organization and ceramic production were both structured differently than they were in the succeeding phases. Therefore, it is important to have some notion of the organization of the Oaxacan population in the Rosario phase so that the magnitude of the changes that occurred during Period I can be understood. Monte Albán was not yet occupied in the Rosario phase. San José Mogote was the largest settlement in the region and most of the valley's known Rosario phase public architectural construction was concentrated there. Below San José Mogote, there was a single tier of settlements containing non-domestic architectural construction. It seems likely that the population of the valley was organized at the pre-state, chiefdom level.

Although very little information exists, it appears that ceramic production was more decentralized in the Early and Middle Formative Periods than it was in the later Monte Albán phases. Excavations (Flannery and Winter 1976) have provided evidence of the specialized production of certain tools and ornaments but not of pottery during the pre-Monte Albán periods. The survey analysis has not identified any ceramic production locus for the Tierras Largas, San José or Guadalupe phases. Consequently, ceramic production during these phases is assumed to have occurred at small and dispersed locations.

Two Rosario phase sites in the Central Valley survey area and one in the Valle Grande may have been loci of ceramic production, however the evidence is not exactly overwhelming. One of the sites (2-4-1) was occupied in several phases, including the Rosario phase. It does seem to have been a locus of ceramic production, but the dating of the production activities at the site is uncertain. It may be that the production activities at the site also date to Early I (2-5-3).

The second possible Rosario production site (2-4-2) was a single component occupation, however we are unable to date it securely to either the Rosario phase or to Monte Albán Early I. Whatever the dating, *cremas* were produced at this site, which was small and contained no evidence of mounded construction. The Valle Grande production locus (3-4-44) manufactured *café*-ware ceramics, but the sherds collected suggest that it was probably an Early I and not a Rosario phase manufacturing location.

Four preliminary observations can be drawn regarding ceramic production in the Rosario phase.

1) Only three possible ceramic production locations have been identified, and the scale of ceramic production at these sites does not appear to have been as massive as it was at certain later production locations.

2) If village specialization of ceramic manufacturing did occur in the Rosario phase, it occurred at several small settlements, all of which lack evidence of mounded architectural construction.

3) Although the evidence is meager, it seems probable that an initial transition to more specialized strategies of production did take place during the Rosario phase.

4) Two of the three pottery making places are located in the interstitial zone between the valley's semi-autonomous Rosario phase polities indicating independence from political domination.

The nature of ceramic assemblages of the Early and Middle Formative periods suggests that pottery was produced in a more decentralized, less standardized manner at this time (S. Plog 1976:262). Great variability has been noted in plastic decoration (Drennan 1976; S. Plog 1976; Pyne 1976). The Monte Albán period ceramics were, in general, far more standardized. Consequently it appears that whereas the pottery of the Monte Albán phases may have been made in large part by specialized ceramic producers, the pre-Rosario phase pottery may have been made locally at most villages. The great variation and the lack of standardization in the pre-Monte Albán pottery may have been a consequence of the large number of dispersed, decentralized ceramic producers. The fact that these producers probably made their pottery only intermittently throughout the year also enhanced the likelihood that the ceramics from each production event would have been quite variable (Balfet 1965). This too would have lessened the degree of standardization in the Early and Middle Formative Period complexes. Interestingly, as compared to *prior* phase complexes, the variation in the Rosario phase ceramics did seem to reflect greater standardization. Drennan (1976:67-69) has noted that the Oaxacan ceramic assemblage underwent a relatively rapid transformation between the end of the Guadalupe phase and the outset of Period I. These observations permit me to speculate that the transition from individual household ceramic production to a more specialized pottery producing industry may have been initiated in the Rosario phase. However, it also seems clear that by Early I the evidence for this change is much more convincing.

Monte Albán Early I

The regional political and economic organization of the Oaxaca Valley changed markedly during Early I. Monte Albán was founded, and the administrative organization of the valley increased in hierarchical complexity. In spite of this development, we have argued that the valley's administrative and economic hierarchies still appear to have been relatively more segregated from each other in Early I than they were in most of the later phases.

In Early I important changes also occurred in both the intraregional exchange system and the organization of ceramic production. Three principal points will be made in the following discussion:

1) Specialized village ceramic production increased in importance during Early I.

2) The Early I system of ceramic production appears to have been less centralized and freer of administrative control than in all the other Monte Albán phases (perhaps excluding Monte Albán V). Since the regional economic and political institutions appear to have been relatively segregated in Early I, the relationship between ceramic production and regional organization seems to conform to the principle research expectations outlined in the introduction to this chapter.

3) If a segment of the Early I ceramic complex was produced under administrative control, it was the highly decorated gray ware.

In Early I, the organization of ceramic production in the Valley of Oaxaca clearly continued to shift in the direction that it had begun to change in the Rosario phase. Six loci of ceramic production were identified in the Central and Valle Grande survey areas. An additional location was found in the Etla area (Table 10-4). The majority of these seven sites were clearly locations where ceramics were produced in quantity during Early I. Several other factors also suggest that ceramic production was more specialized at this time. The very variable plastic decoration commonly found on the utilitarian pottery from the pre-Monte Albán phases was found only on a small proportion of the Early I ceramic utility ware (Drennan 1976). In addition, each ceramic production location appeared to produce pottery of only one ware. Three sites in the Valley Grande made *café* vessels. Two settlements in the Central area and one site in Etla produced *crema* pottery. And the one identified gray ware producing site was in the Central area. The fact that each of these sites only produced ceramics of one ware also suggests that ceramic production was a specialized craft in Period I (cf. Winter 1974:13). Although each production location made pottery of only one ware, the great majority of Early I occupations had surface pottery of at least two and often all three wares. Thus, it appears that the "consumers" of ceramics had access to the pottery from more than one production location. No evidence of Period I ceramic production was found at Monte Albán (Blanton 1978; Winter 1974). This is in marked contrast to the Late Classic period for which the evidence of ceramic production was easily discernible. It seems that Monte Albán must have imported at least some of its pottery in Early I. This again suggests that by Early I at least a portion of the ceramic complex was produced by village specialists for consumers in other communities.

The ceramic measures support the interpretations based on settlement analysis, which suggested that political and economic institutions were segregated in Early I. The differential in the mean number of types per site between administrative and non-administrative sites was less in Early I than it was in Late I, II or IIIa (Table 10-1). This suggests that the access to ceramic goods was not solely a function of the level of a particular settlement in the administrative hierarchy. In addition, non-administrative settlements with estimated populations larger than 100 had access to almost as many types as were found at administrative centers (Table 10-1).

As predicted given the structure of the regional organization in Early I, ceramic production appears to have been relatively free of administrative control. Of the seven production locations, only two were in settlements that had mounded architecture (Table 10-4). The *gris* production location was situated in the closest (7.8 kilometers) second rank center (2-5-33) to Monte Albán. The *crema* production location in the Etla Arm (ET-SLC-SLC-5) also had several small mounds that were occupied in Early I.

The production step (Table 10-5) and contingency table analyses (Table 10-6) also suggest that relative to the other Monte Albán phases (excluding V), the production of Early I ceramics was free of administrative control. The mean production step measures indicate that a relatively large amount of energy was put into the production of a rather costly ceramic complex. Only the pottery from Monte Albán II and V had higher mean production step measures. The contingency table analysis shows that the Early I complex was distributed relatively heterogeneously across the valley. More specifically, *crema* ware ceramic vessels were most abundant in the Etla Arm (Feinman 1980:67-72,177). *Café* pottery was found somewhat more frequently in

Table 10-4. Ceramic Production Locations

Phase	Number of Identified Production Locations in Surveyed Region	Additional Locations Identified in Etla Area	Additional Locations Identified in the Tlacolula Arm	Total Number of Identified Ceramic Production Locations	Number Located in Administrative Places
Early I	6	1	0	7	2
Late I	5	1	0	6	4
II	5	0	0	5	4
IIIA	9	0	0	9	9
IIIB	6	0	0	6	3
IV	3	0	1	4	3
V	7	0	1	8	2

the southern part of the valley (Feinman 1980:79-80). On the other hand, the highly decorated Early I gray ware bowls (Caso, Bernal, and Acosta 1965:30–35) were comparatively under-represented in the Valle Grande (Feinman 1980:75).

A lack of valley-wide economic integration in Early I is also indicated by the fact that no single category of pottery had a very wide distribution (Table 10-7). Of the 50 grid squares that had evidence of Early I occupation, the most dispersed category of bowl (T2052) was only found in 27 squares. In comparison, the Late I G-12 bowl (T1207) was collected from 57 of the 63 squares that were occupied in that phase (Table 10-7). These findings independently support our land use study (Chapter 9), which suggested that in Early I local exchanges in sub-areas of the valley were probably more important than were broad, valley-wide movements of goods.

A final point concerning Early I ceramic production relates to the initial imposition of administrative control. If the production of any of the Early I complex was administered, it was the gray ware. While none of the *café* production loci were in settlements with mounded architecture, and only one of the three *crema* production places was in a settlement that had Early I architecture, the only known locus of *gris* production was in a major administrative center. It seems that the administrators were interested initially in controlling access to the most costly segment of the ceramic complex. Gray ware was the most elaborately decorated segment of the Rosario phase complex. The mean production measure for Early I *gris* bowls (5.2) was higher than the mean production step measure for *crema* (4.6) or *café* (3.9) bowls. Interestingly, administrative control over *gris* production appears to have been maintained in Late I, by which time the *gris* bowls were less elaborately decorated and more widely distributed.

Monte Albán Late I

The political administration of the valley appears to have expanded its control over production and exchange during Late I. The rate of population growth of administrative centers was much more rapid than the growth of non-administrative sites. Increased isomorphism between administrative and economic channels was observed. Compared to Early I, greater standardization of the Late I ceramic complex was found, and ceramics were more homogeneously distributed across the valley.

Several measures suggest that relative access to ceramic goods was principally a consequence of administrative function in Late I. Four of the six Late I ceramic production places were in administrative settlements. This contrasts markedly with the location of production loci in Early I, when only two of seven were in administrative settlements. The differential in the mean number of types found at administrative versus non-administrative places was larger in Late I than it was in Early I. Almost three times as many ceramic types were found at administrative places as compared to non-administrative places in Late I. This represents the largest differential for any of the seven Monte Albán phases (Table 10-1). In addition, whereas the mean number (10.2) of pottery types found at the non-administrative places with populations above one hundred was almost as large as the mean number (11.8) found at administrative places in Early I, this was not so for Late I. Late I administrative places had greater access to ceramic products than did the large occupations that did not serve administrative functions (16.0 mean types/administrative site versus 9.3 mean types/non-administrative site).

As predicted, the increased isomorphism between economic and administrative networks in Late I was associated with greater standardization in the production and distribution of the pottery. The existence of more standardized production is suggested by several factors. The mean production step measure was lower for the Late I complex than for the Early I complex (Table 10-5). Yet the relatively small differential between the Early I and Late I mean measures does not reflect adequately the extent of the differences between the two complexes. In calculating the mean production step indices, the production step measure for each ceramic category was weighted equally. In Late I, however, a few *gris* bowl categories were especially abundant. The abundant types were basically the *gris* bowl categories not made in Early I. The mean production step measure for these eight bowl categories was 4.31 as compared to 4.60 for all Late I *gris* bowls and 4.54 for all Late I bowl types. The most abundant Late I ceramic category (T1207) had a production step measure of 4.00. The abundance of the standardized, relatively plain *gris* bowl (T1207) in the Late I complex also marks a major difference between Late I and all earlier Oaxacan ceramic complexes. More specialized, mass production in Late I is also suggested by the fact that there were more than three times as many people per identified ceramic production locus in Late I than there were in Early I.

The distribution of Late I ceramics also was apparently more uniform and spatially homogeneous than in Early I (Feinman 1980:177, 181). The contigency table analysis indicated that pottery was more evenly distributed in Late I than in Early I (Table 10-6). In addition, whereas the most widely distributed Early I bowl category (T2052) was found in just over half of the grid units occupied in that phase, the G-12 (T1207) (Table 10-7) was found in 57 of the 63 grid squares occupied in Late I. The most widely distributed Late I *olla* (T2013A) was found in 54 of the 63 occupied grid squares; thus it also was more widely distributed than any Early I *olla* category (Table 10-7).

In Late I, *cremas* were still somewhat more abundant in Etla and *cafés* were found more frequently in the Valle Grande. But the ceramic categories that were most prevalent were for the most part distributed more evenly across the valley in Late I than was the case in Early I (Feinman 1980:85,86,240-43).

Table 10-5. Mean Production-Step Measure by phase

Phase	All Types	All Bowls	Rank
Early I	4.39	4.80	3
Late I	4.10	4.54	4
II	5.09	5.56	2
IIIA	3.85	4.11	5
IIIB	2.68	2.90	6
IV	2.45	2.58	7
V	5.14	5.88	1

Table 10-6. Contingency Table Analysis Results

Phase	Phi Coefficient Value	Rank
Early I	.419	2
Late I	.308	3
II	.200	6
IIIA	.111	7
IIIB	.222	5
IV	.295	4
V	.533	1

phi coefficient value ranges from a minimum of zero to a maximum of three.

The preceding analyses suggest that we may accept the predicted relationship between a high degree of isomorphism between political and economic channels of interaction and a more highly standardized ceramic production industry for Period I. But why was the control of production and exchange a more viable or essential strategy for administrators to adopt in Late I as compared to Early I? How were rural producers affected by these changes in administrative decision-making strategies? What were the effects of the large Late I urban population at Monte Albán on the production and distribution of both agricultural and craft goods?

Chapter 9, on human-land relationships, shows that although the total population was below the potential agricultural productivity in both phases, in Late I a much larger proportion of the population would have found it necessary to either reduce consumption or import maize in bad years. More specifically, with the

Table 10-7. Distribution of Well-Dispersed Vessel Categories

Phase	Number of occupied grid squares in which collections were made*	Most well-distributed bowl category	Number of squares containing bowl category	Percentage of total	Most well distributed olla category	Number of squares containing olla category	Percentage of total
EI	50	T2052	27	54%	T0121	32	64%
LI	63	T1207	57	90%	T2013A	44	70%
II	56	T1207	51	91%	T2013A	39	70%
IIIA	57	T1126	57	100%	T1120	45	79%
IIIB	42	T1126	40	95%	T1120	38	90%
IV	26	T1126	26	100%	T1120	26	100%
V	71	T1104	66	93%	T1109	56	79%

*In the Valle Grande, Central and Etla Survey Areas

marked population increase in and around Monte Albán during the later half of Period I, the central portion of the valley most likely would have had to import agricultural produce periodically.

In Late I there also was an increase in the percentage of the population that resided in the piedmont zone (Table 10-8), especially in the Central area. In the piedmont, agriculture would have been both risky and largely dependent on irrigation techniques. Periodically, the valley-wide movement of grain would have been necessary to buffer local shortages. It appears that the intensification of agricultural production in the piedmont was one mechanism for coping with these local imbalances. Yet the encouragement of piedmont farming would have only worked if a dependable valley-wide exchange system operated to buffer the populations in those areas that lost their crops. Consequently, it is not surprising that production and exchange appear to have been administratively controlled or influenced in Late I, as well as in IIIa and IIIb (Table 10-8). All three of these phases were characterized by low mean production step indices and by highly standardized ceramic complexes (Table 10-5). It thus appears that ceramics as well as other craft goods may have been centrally produced during these phases and then exchanged for agricultural produce from the piedmont through tribute or administered exchange networks.

Elizabeth Brumfiel (1976) has argued convincingly that the Aztec elite during the Late Aztec period fostered the production of craft goods in urban centers in order to encourage intensive, specialized agricultural production in rural areas. Brumfiel (1976) further suggested that the manipulation of the cost and availability of craft items was used as a means for stimulating rural producers to intensify their production of agricultural surplus. That at least some of this centralized craft production was directly influenced by the policies of the Aztec elite was suggested by Davies who wrote that:

> . . . quite apart from the ruler's own property, the goods which the merchants themselves traded must also have been partly manufactured from raw materials obtained as tribute. Thus by monopolistic commerce the ruler multiplied his tribute, sometimes even imposing unfair terms of trade on conquered provinces and selling them goods which they did not value. [Davies 1973:137]

This kind of control over production and exchange would have required increased administrative activities and facilities. Thus it is not surprising that Late I, IIIa, and IIIb were all characterized by the construction of a large amount of administrative architecture (Table 10-8). In two other regional studies, Skinner (1977a:20-31) and Johnson (in press) also have found

Table 10-8. Rank Order of Certain Key Variables by Phase

Phase	% of Total Population in Piedmont and mountain zones[a]	Volume Occupied Mounded Architecture[a]	Volume Occupied Mounded Construction at Monte Alban
EI	7	5	6
LI	4	3	3
II	5	4	4
IIIA	3	1	2
IIIB	2	2	1
IV	1	6	7
V	6	7	5

[a]Includes Valle Grande, Central and Monte Albán Survey Areas

that increases in the spatial density of administrative places were related to expanded bureaucratic control over economic affairs.

The increasingly powerful urban elite at Monte Albán must have derived an additional advantage by controlling the production and/or distribution of craft goods and promoting intensification and specialization of rural agricultural production. The increasing extent of economic specialization in agricultural as well as craft production must have intensified the dependence of both urban and rural segments of the population on the mediating, administrative institution that fostered exchange. Wright (1977) has pointed out that the administrators in early states often attempted to encourage this kind of organic integration in order to strengthen their central position (see also Uzoiqwe 1972:427, 450-52). In Oaxaca during Period I the increased specialization and thus dependence of local populations must have served to solidify the economic and political unification of a region that seems to have been divided into more than one political unit prior to the foundation of Monte Albán.

Monte Albán II

Several similarities are evident between the Monte Albán Late I-II transition in the Valley of Oaxaca and the model of Imperial Chinese expansion that has been put forth by Skinner (1977a). These similarities may help to provide insight into the changes in ceramic production and distribution that occurred in Oaxaca at this time. Skinner has noted that when the size of the Imperial Chinese system was increased the extent of centralized administrative control over taxation, marketing, and trade in most parts of the system was actually decreased. As we have shown (Chapter 5) for the Valley of Oaxaca, the intensity of administrative control over the local system was not maintained as the size of the system expanded. Skinner (1977a:25) also found, similar to Period II in Oaxaca, that both the autonomy and the functional diversification of the local elite residing at secondary centers often increased during periods of expansion.

It appears that Monte Albán II was characterized by: 1) the decentralization of administrative control, 2) the reduced importance of intraregional exchange ties with the shift away from intensive strategies of piedmont farming, and perhaps 3) a reduction in the intensity of administrative control over production and exchange. This latter point is not clearcut and the somewhat contradictory data must be addressed.

The hypothesis that the degree of overlap between administrative and economic networks in the valley was reduced in Monte Albán II compared to Late I is supported by the analysis of the mean number of types found at administrative versus non-administrative sites (Table 10-1). While the mean number of types found at administrative sites was roughly constant in Late I (16.0) and II (15.1), non-administrative sites had access to a larger number of types in the latter phase (7.1 versus 5.8). The magnitude of this differential is even more significant when it is pointed out that there are 88 identified types for Late I and only 53 for II. Thus, in Late I, non-administrative localities had access to an average of 6.6% of the total number of types, while in II, this site class had access to 13.4% of the total complex. Non-administrative localities were thus able to procure a larger percentage of the available ceramic products in the latter phase.

The identification of four of the five Period II ceramic production loci at administrative sites does not support the proposed hypothesis that administrative control of production was reduced in this phase (Table 10-4). Yet, in part this may be due to the nature of our survey region. Considerable ceramic variability has been noted at Period II sites in both the Etla and Tlacolula arms of the valley. Some of the ceramic vessel types found in these areas (John Paddock, personal communication) were not even noted in our surveys of the Central and Southern areas. Thus, it is possible that when the production loci from these rather rare categories of ceramic vessels are identified they may be located in sites without administrative architecture.

The degree of overlap between administrative and

economic networks was apparently less in Early I than in either Late I or II. Yet it does appear that at least the distribution (if not the production) of craft products was more segregated from the administrative sphere in Period II than in Late I. Given the general research focus of this study it was expected that the Period II ceramic complex would be less standardized, more highly decorated, and more heterogeneously distributed than the Late I complex. These predictions were only supported partially by the ceramic analytic measures. The mean production step measure for Monte Albán II was 5.09 as compared to 4.10 for Late I (Table 10-5). Only the Monte Albán V complex had a higher mean production step measure than Period II. The mean production step measure confirms numerically that Monte Albán II complex had some very highly decorated vessels. Several of these highly decorated types were distributed rather discretely in different sections of the valley. For example, the Caso, Bernal, and Acosta (1967; Fig. 48, 49) category A-9 (T3408), which was manufactured at Roaló (3-6-31), was found exclusively in the Central and Valle Grande survey areas (Fig. 10-1). Only a few (4) A-9's were found in the collections from Etla. In addition, John Paddock (personal communication) found examples of a ceramic category that he termed "black and white" in the excavated collections from several Period II occupations at sites in the Tlacolula Valley. This vessel type was not found in any of the survey collections made in the Etla, Central, or Valle Grande survey areas. Finally, highly decorated *crema* bowls were both proportionately more abundant and more variable at the Period II sites in the five northernmost grid squares. These *crema* vessels, however, were present in smaller quantities throughout the Central and especially the Valle Grande survey areas (Feinman 1980:186). The heterogeneous distribution of some of the highly decorated Period II vessel categories suggests that the distribution of at least the "fancy" pottery was less centrally controlled than was the distribution of the Late I complex. It also supports the suggestion that there was less exchange and interaction between the valley's local subsystems (see Chapters 5 and 9). This was expected with the reduced reliance on the risky strategies of piedmont farming during Period II.

The results of the contingency table analysis (Table 10-6) indicated that the more abundant Period II ceramic types were distributed relatively homogeneously across the survey area (Feinman 1980:186). Thus, at least certain utilitarian *gris* and *crema* ceramic types may have been administratively distributed in Period II. Interestingly, the identified production loci for these types were all situated in administrative centers. Consequently, it is suggested tentatively that many of the utilitarian ceramics were still produced and distributed in a manner similar to the way they were in Late I. However, as suggested above, the highly decorated Period II serving bowls were produced and distributed through different, less centralized economic networks (Caso and Bernal 1965:876).

Monte Albán IIIa

As noted above, in IIIa, there was a return to the Late I pattern of administered development of the piedmont (see Chapters 6, 9). The major difference, however, was that in IIIa, this administration occurred largely at the lower levels of the political hierarchy, whereas in Late I most piedmont administration emanated directly from the capital and secondarily from smaller centers (see Chapter 6). Given the expanded reliance upon intensive piedmont farming strategies in IIIa, an increased administrative involvement in the production and exchange system was expected. The ceramic measures support this interpretation. There was the second largest percentage differential in the mean number of types per site between administrative and non-administrative sites in this phase (Table 10-1, column 6). There was an average of only 4.6 types found at the non-administrative sites dating to this phase as compared to the average of 11.9 types which were found at administrative centers. Thus, the access to ceramic products was markedly reduced for those inhabitants of non-administrative settlements in IIIa.

The relationship between piedmont farming and relatively intense periods of administrative control over production and exchange is further supported for Late I and IIIa by the analysis of the number of types per site. As stated above, in Late I the most intensive piedmont farming was undertaken in the central part of the valley. In IIIa, the most intensive area of piedmont population buildup was in the southern half of the Valle Grande. In Late I the most standardized ceramic complexes, with the least variability, were located in Monte Albán's central district. These sites tended to have five or fewer pottery types while the other Late I sites averaged many more. In IIIa, two areas of sites were found to have very few (less than five) types per site: those sites within 8 kilometers of Monte Albán, and those more than 30 kilometers from the Main Plaza. Interestingly, those few IIIa sites that were located in the alluvial zone were found in the area between

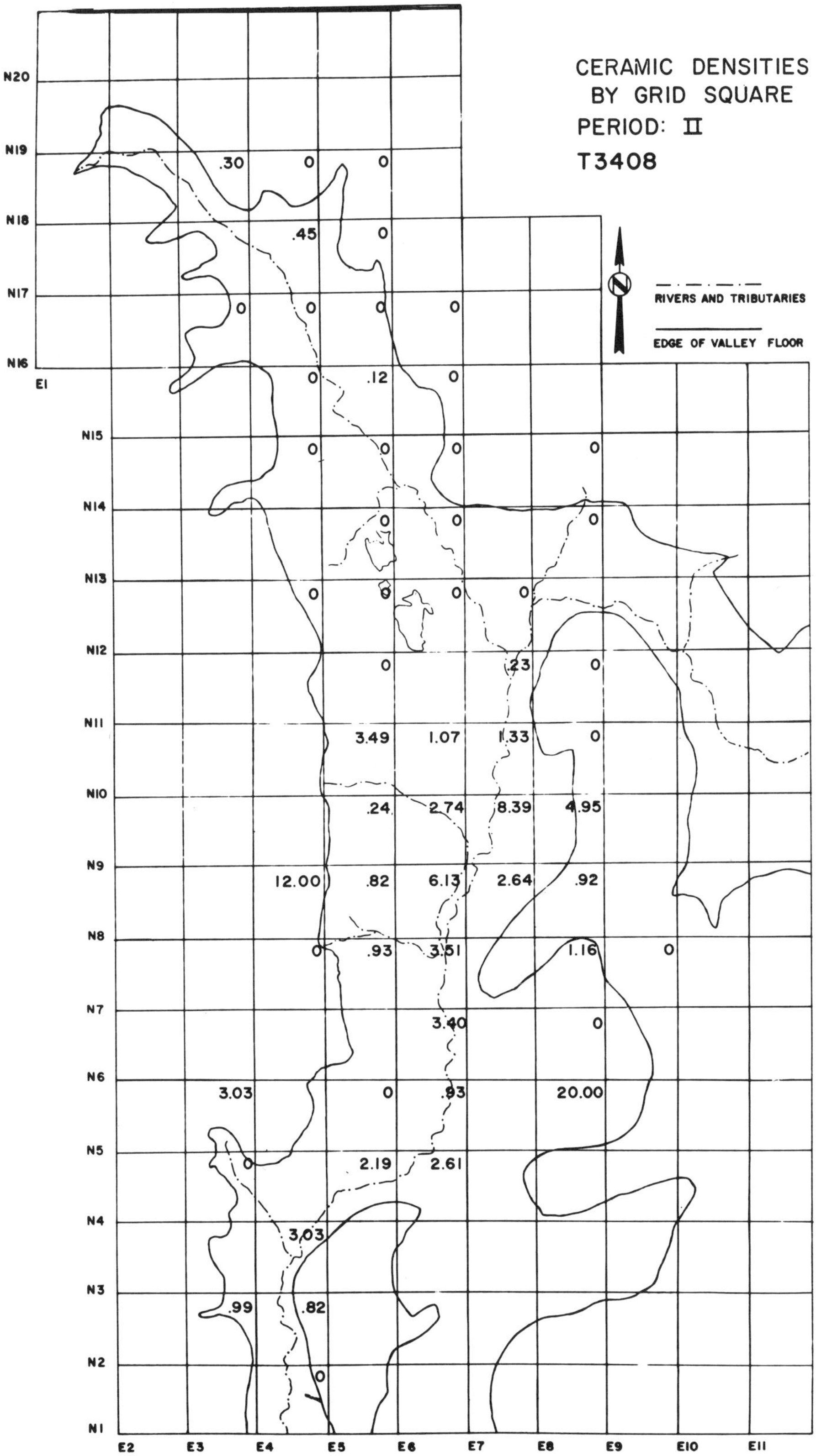

Figure 10-1. Ceramic densities by grid square, Period II, category T3408.

Zaachila and Santa Inés Yatzeche. In this area, an average of more IIIa types were found per site and there was less differential in the number of types per site between administrative and non-administrative localities. Non-administrative sites in this zone averaged 62% of the number of types found in sites with administrative functions. The comparable figure for the Central and Valle Grande areas was 41%. Thus, the primarily alluvial area in IIIa was less connected than most of the rest of the survey region into the heavily administered production and exchange system. This interpretation was supported independently by certain aspects of the settlement analysis (see Chapter 6).

A high degree of administrative control over production and exchange in IIIa is also suggested by the location of the ceramic production places. All nine were situated in settlements that had administrative functions (Table 10-4). These nine included both Jalieza and Santa Cruz Mixtepec, two of the largest Early Classic administrative settlements. No hard evidence for Early Classic ceramic production at Monte Albán has as yet been found. However, the very large number of Classic Period kiln wasters found on the surface of an area of Late Classic ceramic production at Atzompa does at least raise the possibility that ceramic production may have been initiated at the site in the Early Classic. Additional surface, and perhaps subsurface, research will be necessary to examine this hypothesis.

Based upon the analyses of settlement and ceramic information, the Early Classic in the valley is thought to have been characterized by intensive administrative involvement in production and exchange. Consequently, administrative control over ceramic production was predicted for this phase. The IIIa ceramics therefore are expected to have been more highly standardized, more homogeneously distributed, and less highly decorated than the Period II pottery.

These predictions are strongly supported by this study. Unlike all earlier phases, Oaxacan ceramics dated to the Early Classic period were made almost entirely in one ware (*gris*). This remained basically characteristic of the ceramics throughout IIIb and IV. Only 3 *crema*, 6 *café*, and 3 *amarillo* ceramic categories were identified in the IIIa assemblage as compared to 21 *gris* types. Most of the non-*gris* ceramic types were relatively rare, and at least 75-85% of typical IIIa collections are *gris*. The increased standardization of Early Classic pottery is also indicated by the great frequency of plain G-35 (T1126) bowls (Table 10-7). The G-12 (T1207) *gris* incised bowl was plentiful in Late I and II ceramic collections, but comparatively the G-35 was even more abundant in the Classic. In all but one of the 57 grid squares where IIIa collections were made, G-35's were collected.

In addition to its greater abundance, the G-35 bowl was less costly and even more likely to have been mass manufactured than the G-12 bowl. The production step measure for the standard G-12 was 4 while the standard G-35 had a production step measure of 2.25. Also, whereas the G-35's were often found with bolstered rims, the G-12's were not. This is significant because according to Sander van der Leeuw (personal communication), bolstered rims on G-35's were probably the consequence of very rapid, somewhat careless, production. This technique entailed the folding over and smoothing down of surplus clay on the exterior of a bowl rather than the removal of the surplus clay and the creation of the more finished rim.

The greater standardization of the IIIa complex is also indicated by the fact that for the first time, the most abundant bowl (T1126) and jar (T1120) categories were both made in the same ware. In fact, these two ceramic vessels were similar in almost every attribute save those related to form. It thus seems very likely that the same ceramic production loci must have produced both kinds of vessels in the Classic. Consequently, with the relative decline in the abundance of both *café* and *crema* jars in the Early Classic (a trend intensified in the Late Classic) it seems safe to suggest that ceramic production was restricted to a relatively small number of places that utilized large scale production techniques.

The IIIa ceramic complex was the most homogeneously distributed according to the contingency table analysis (Table 10-6). Spatially discrete distributions of highly decorated types were not found in IIIa (Feinman 1980:190) as they were in Monte Albán II (i.e., T3408). The hypothesis that the valley-wide exchange network was better integrated in IIIa than it was in II is well supported.

Finally, the results of the mean production step measure support the contention that on the average a greater number of steps was employed in the production of Monte Albán II as compared to IIIa ceramic vessels. The mean production step measure was 5.09 for the former phase as compared to 3.85 for the latter (Tables 10-3, 10-5). This differential does not completely describe the degree of contrast between the pottery of these two phases, because the highly decorated Period II vessels were relatively abundant in the collections dated to that phase while the "costly" IIIa types

(T0057, T3410) were a comparatively small segment of the Early Classic complex (Feinman 1980:190).

Monte Albán IIIb

In IIIb, more than 75% of the occupied monumental construction in the survey area was built at Monte Albán. Thus, it seems clear than most political functions were concentrated at the valley capital. For the only time in the prehispanic sequence it is clear that pottery production was important at Monte Albán. Two known loci of IIIb ceramic manufacturing were found at this site: one excavated (Winter and Payne 1976) and the other mapped by us at Atzompa. In the Atzompa site subdivision, 34 Classic period kiln wasters were collected (Blanton 1978). This represented just less than one-third the number of wasters collected during the entire survey of the Central, Valle Grande and Monte Albán areas. It seems safe to suggest that ceramic production at Atzompa must have been rather massive in scale. The characteristic Atzompa diorite-tempered G-35 *ollas* (T1120) (Feinman 1980:119) and bowls (T1126) (Feinman 1980:120) were noted in large quantities at Monte Albán, throughout much of the Central survey area, and in the southern half of the Etla Arm. If this entire area was serviced in large part by the Atzompa potters then the scale of production must have indeed been huge.

This concentration of economic activities at the capital seems to have been largely a Late Classic period phenomenon. As we have suggested, far fewer economic functions were centered at Monte Albán during its initial phases of occupation. Thus it is suggested that the capital was established principally as an administrative center (Blanton 1976a), but that its role in the region had shifted by the Late Classic. By IIIb, Monte Albán was the primary economic center in the valley as well. In the ancient Near East similar transitions often occurred. New rulers often built their administrative palaces in isolated localities separated from existing urban centers (Olmstead 1923:99, 270; Oppenheim 1964: 117-18, 124). Yet through time, these administrative capitals often became economic centers of considerable importance (Oppenheim 1964:104, 117-18).

It seems clear that first order administrative and economic functions were *both* centered at Monte Albán during Monte Albán IIIb. There also appears to have been a considerable degree of isomorphism between economic and administrative networks throughout the rest of the IIIb settlement system. The location of ceramic producing localities offers some support for this interpretation. Although three sites without mounded architecture had evidence of ceramic manufacturing, two of these were isolated residences or very small hamlets (3-9-69; 3-9-58). The bulk of ceramic production apparently occurred at some of the larger administrative centers (Monte Albán proper, Atzompa, Cuilapan [3-9-8-18], and possibly Rancho Tejas [3-9-62,63]).

Since the regional system in the Late Classic period was highly centralized, with considerable administrative involvement in economic activities, it was predicted that a similarly marked disparity in the quantity of types found at administrative versus non-administrative sites would be found. A disparity existed, but it was not as pronounced in IIIb as it had been in either Late I or IIIa (Table 10-1). In fact, the differential was less marked than that found for the less-administered phases Early I or II. But the IIIb values of types per site for *both* administrative and non-administrative sites were very low. Compared to Monte Albán, which had all 22 types, the populations of all other sites had access to relatively little ceramic variety. The most important distinction in the access to ceramic products was between Monte Albán and all other settlements. These settlements averaged only 4.7 types/site. This differential corresponded to the marked distinction between the capital and all other settlements in both population and architectural construction. In this regard, it is important to point out that the mean values of the numbers of types per site could not have been much lower for the non-administrative sites. A mean of three to four types (actually 3.5) represents close to the minimum assortment of ceramic vessels necessary for basic familial activitics. Even the populations of administrative centers had access to little more than this minimal variability in ceramics. Thus the IIIb system may have been so centralized that only the capital population could have obtained a fairly wide assortment of ceramic vessels.

Again in IIIb, as in Late I and IIIa, the area of most intensive piedmont development was more closely tied into an administered system of production and exchange. The sites in the central portion of the valley, adjacent to Monte Albán, had access to small numbers of types per site. Most of those sites with three or fewer types were within 12 kilometers of Monte Albán. The inhabitants of this zone often had access only to the minimum number of ceramic vessels that a household would need for basic cooking, storage, and food-serving tasks. Typically these collections would include only plain G-35 bowls (T1126), plain G-35 jars

(T1120) and either a *sahumador* (T1123) or a *comal* (T1125) and/or a G-35 bowl with hollow (T1263) or solid nubbin (T1274) supports.

As expected almost the entire IIIb ceramic complex was both highly standardized and mass produced (Bernal 1965:806). Almost the entire complex was manufactured in *gris* paste. Only five relatively rare categories were *cafés* (T2083, T2086, T2418) or *amarillos* (T3030, T3035). No *crema* ceramics date to IIIb. The tremendous uniformity in ceramic jars is especially revealing since jars, unlike flat-bottomed or cylindrical bowls, cannot be stacked and thus are much more difficult and expensive to transport (Lightfoot, n.d.; Whittlesey 1974). The fact that IIIb has only three jar categories, all *gris* (T1120, T1141, T1508) suggests that administrative involvement in production and exchange was intensive. The local production of jars in the piedmont *café* and *crema* clays must have been discouraged either through administrative sanction, the exaction of high demands for agricultural tribute on communities, forcing the individuals within these communities to concentrate entirely upon farming (Brumfiel 1976), and/or the large-scale production of very inexpensive *ollas,* which in spite of the distribution costs were still cheaper than locally produced jars.

The mean production step measure (2.68) for IIIb shows that little energy was imparted in the production of Late Classic period pottery (Tables 10-3, 10-5). As with the IIIa assemblage, the vessel categories that were found most frequently in the collections (T1126-2.25; T1120-2.50) had lower production step indices than the mean value calculated for the phase. Evidence for the importance of large scale production processes in IIIb ceramic manufacture is indicated by the great frequency of bowls with "incipient bases" (T1138, T2083) and bolstered rims (T1122) (Feinman 1980:194). Both of these attributes, which suggest the employment of mass manufacturing techniques, were more prevalent in IIIb than in any prior phase. Interestingly, these two attributes often co-occured on the G-35 bowls that were found at Monte Albán (Caso, Bernal, and Acosta 1967:390).

The IIIb complex was also distributed rather homogeneously throughout the region. Of the 42 grid squares occupied in IIIb, G-35 bowls (T1126) and *ollas* (T1120) were found, respectively, in all but 2 and 4 of the grid squares (Table 10-7). As in IIIa, no clear ceramic style zones were apparent, although the few *cafés* (e.g., T2086, T2418) found seemed to be most abundant at Monte Albán proper (Blanton 1978:88) and in the area just south of the capital (Feinman 1980:283). There was so little surface decoration on IIIb pots that nothing similar to the partially discrete clustering of highly decorated Monte Albán II vessels was discernible.

The contingency table analysis showed that the IIIa types were distributed very homogeneously across the valley, and it was expected that IIIb pottery would have been distributed just as homogeneously. Instead, IIIb pottery was distributed only about as evenly as that of Monte Albán II (Table 10-6). As discussed above, this was in part due to the fact that some of the II types that were distributed discretely could not be included in the contingency table analysis because they were too rare. Yet, it was also due to the unequal distribution of some of the varieties of Late Classic period G-35's in the survey region.

It should be pointed out that most of the Classic period types were G-35's that were distinguished almost entirely by formal attributes. This is quite different from the Monte Albán I and II complexes, in which categorical distinctions could be drawn also according to paste and surface treatment. In the IIIb complex, types were based for the most part either on differences in vessel shape or by the presence or absence of particular attributes on G-35 bowls (i.e., incipient bases, nubbin supports, hollow supports, bolstered rims). Interestingly, the five G-35 bowl and jar categories, distinguished according to the form T1120 (*olla*), T1126 (conical *cajete*), T1141 (*tecomate*), T1143 (*apaxtli*) and T1259 (vertical walled bowl with flanged rim), were distributed even more homogeneously than was the IIIa complex ($\phi^2 = .016$) (Table 10-9). Yet several varieties of G-35 bowls (T1122, T1138, T1263, T1268 and T1274) were distributed unevenly (Table 10-10). The distribution of these varieties was very revealing. It was argued previously that bolstered rims and incipient bases were evidence of mass production. These varieties were expected to be most prevalent in the areas where exchange was most heavily administered (in and around Monte Albán). This was indeed the case (Caso and Bernal 1965:890). More than twice as many (1009) bolstered rim G-35 bowls (T1122) were collected at Monte Albán than were found in the entire Etla, Central, and Valle Grande survey regions. None were found in IIIb collections south of grid line N10. The distribution of the G-35 bowls with incipient bases (T1138) was very similar. Only 12 were found outside Monte Albán, while 148 were collected at the capital. None were found in IIIb collections south of grid line N11.

The distribution of the G-35 bowls with basal supports (T1263, T1274) (Feinman 1980:116-17) was somewhat different. Interestingly, these bowls were both more costly to produce and more difficult to stack and transport than bowls without supports. Both bowl types were again most abundant at Monte Albán where, if they were made at the capital itself, distribution would not have been a major problem. Both of these vessel types were very rare in Etla and Central survey areas, a region perhaps serviced by administratively produced ceramics. G-35's with supports were most abundant (excluding Monte Albán) in the less heavily administered area south of grid line N9. Although IIIb settlements were sparse in this portion of the Valle Grande, 30 of 45 hollow-supported G-35's (T1263) and 89 of 103 nubbin-supported G-35's (T1274) were recovered in the IIIb collections made south of this line.

Table 10-9. IIIb *Gris* Ware Distributions: Vessel Shape Variants

Observed:

Grid Squares	Ceramic Categories 1120	1126	1141	1143	1259	Total
N 15 - 18	382	1638	18	16	25	2079
N 12 - 14	142	716	9	15	4	886
N 6 - 11	256	639	10	9	2	916
N 1 - 5	40	133	1	3	0	177
Total	820	3126	38	43	31	4058

Expected:

Grid Squares	Ceramic Categories 1120	1126	1141	1143	1259
N 15 - 18	420	1602	19	22	16
N 12 - 14	179	683	8	9	7
N 6 - 11	185	706	9	10	7
N 1 - 5	36	136	2	2	1

Table 10-10. IIIb *Gris* Ware Distributions: Technical Variants

Observed:

Grid Squares	Ceramic Categories 1122	1263	1268	1274	Total
N 15 - 18	248	1	9	1	259
N 12 - 14	142	0	11	2	155
N 6 - 11	11	19	80	64	174
N 1 - 5	0	25	0	36	61
Total	401	45	100	103	649

Expected:

Grid Squares	Ceramic Categories 1122	1263	1268	1274
N 15 - 18	160	18	40	41
N 12 - 14	96	11	24	25
N 6 - 11	108	12	27	28
N 1 - 5	38	4	9	10

Monte Albán IV

Almost the entire Monte Albán IV population resided in the piedmont zone. Although the population in the survey area as a whole was not particularly dense, each settlement cluster was rather nucleated. Almost 97% of the IV population was clustered in nine settlements, seven of which were the head towns of settlement clusters. The organization of each settlement cluster may have approximated the structure of the Late Classic settlement system in miniature.

Consequently, food procurement may have been a problem for Period IV head towns, as it was for Monte Albán in IIIb. The problem may have been particularly serious in dry years if the amount of intraregional exchange did indeed diminish in IV. Thus, it is proposed that ceramic production may still have been both administratively controlled and centrally produced in the Early Postclassic. But pottery was not expected to have been distributed as homogeneously as in IIIb. With the "balkanization" of the valley into a series of relatively autonomous polities, exchange was expected to be more localized and the degree of spatial variability in the Period IV complex was predicted to increase.

These expectations were supported by the ceramic analytic measures. Three of the four Period IV ceramic production places were in large settlements with mounded architecture (2-10-2-4; 2-10-67-72; Lambityeco [Paddock, Mogor, and Lind 1968; Payne 1970]). In addition, the distinctiveness of the complex at Jalieza suggests that ceramics may have been manufactured at that center as well. The low mean production step measure for Monte Albán IV (Table 10-5) also suggests that most ceramics may have been centrally produced through large-scale production processes. The fact that the mean production step measure was even slightly lower than the IIIb measure is somewhat surprising; however, this may be in part due to our less than total understanding of variability in the Period IV complex. The projected survey of the Tlacolula arm should familiarize us with a greater variety of Period IV types. When these types are figured into the mean production step calculations the Period IV index most probably will increase (see Paddock, Mogor, and Lind [1968] for an indication of the extent of the IV variability noted in excavations in the Tlacolula arm).

Interestingly, the one IV production locus not situated in an administrative center was within the Zaachila settlement cluster. This cluster was distinct from the other IV clusters in several respects. The population of Zaachila was considerably smaller than the population of any other head town. In addition, the population within this cluster resided primarily in the alluvial zone, which was largely uninhabited throughout most of the rest of the survey area. Given these differences it is not surprising that the non-administrative settlements in the Zaachila cluster had access to a wider variety of ceramic types than did the non-administrative settlements in the other clusters. It is also not surprising that the differential between the mean number of types found at administrative versus non-administrative settlements ws less marked in the Zaachila cluster than in any other cluster (Table 10-11).

Table 10-11. Mean Number of Types per Site: Monte Albán IV

Administrative Cluster	Mean Number of Types Administrative Center	Mean Number of Types Non-administrative Site
Jalieza	9.25	4.33
Santa Cruz Mixtepec	10.00	1.00
El Choco	5.75	3.50
Monte Albán	19.00	3.00
Animas	6.00	3.00
2-10-2-4	5.00	N.C.[a]
Zaachila	6.67	5.33

N.C.[a] none of the non-administrative sites in this district were collected.

In the Classic the highly standardized IIIa and IIIb complexes were homogeneously distributed across the survey region. The highly standardized Period IV pottery, however, was not. The contingency table analysis showed that the IV pottery (Feinman 1980:196) was more heterogeneously distributed than that of IIIa or IIIb (Table 10-6). The G-35 *olla* (T1120) (Feinman 1980:127) and bowl (T1126) (Feinman 1980:128) were the principal types, and they were found in each settlement cluster, but the remainder of the IV complex associated with each cluster of settlements was distinct. The Monte Albán IV occupations in the eastern portion of the Central area had ceramics that in several ways differed from the IIIb-IV assemblages at Monte Albán. The IV assemblages at Lambityeco (Paddock 1968; Paddock, Mogor, and Lind 1968), Jalieza, El Choco, and Etla were also all somewhat different from each other. Tan and grayish-brown colored wares made with alluvial clays were most prevalent in the Jalieza settlement cluster. In the Etla area, which was sparsely populated in IV, *café* ceramics (T2086) were proportionally more abundant (Feinman 1980:196). The large plain *gris* storage jars (T1508), however, were most abundant in those IV settlement clusters located in the southern half of the Valle Grande (El Choco, Santa Cruz Mixtepec, Jalieza). These jars were rarely found in the central and northern portions of the valley. Thus, ceramic diversification and the redevelopment of strong local ceramic traditions were both initiated with the fall of Monte Albán and the "balkanization" of Period IV.

Monte Albán V

In the Late Postclassic the valley's largest center (Cuiban)[1] did not serve valley-wide administrative functions comparable to those served by Monte Albán between Early I and IIIb. Although the V population of the survey area was quite large, periodic food shortages could have been remedied solely through the operation of local exchange networks. Similar to Early I and II, there was less intensive occupation of the piedmont zone and the importance of local, rather than regional, exchange networks increased.

Thus, the settlements in the Valley of Oaxaca apparently were not integrated by administratively controlled exchange networks in Monte Albán V as they were in IIIa and IIIb. The spatial segregation of administrative and economic activities in the Late Postclassic was indicated by several facts. Ethnohistoric materials generally have agreed that an important political center in the valley at the time of conquest was Zaachila (Whitecotton 1977:128-29). Yet Cuiban was the most populous settlement, as well as the survey area's most important locus of obsidian production. It also was the site with the greatest assortment of different Monte Albán V ceramic vessels. The distributional analysis of obsidian (Appel 1982) also suggests that valley administrative and economic networks were largely distinct in Monte Albán V.

The distribution of the Monte Albán V ceramic production loci also supports this interpretation. Six of the eight known ceramic production places were located in non-administrative centers (Table 10-4). Not since Early I had the majority of identified loci been in non-administrative sites. Interestingly, all of the known V production sites were making *gris* pottery. Traditionally, the production of this ware was often administratively controlled while *crema* and especially *café* pottery usually was made in smaller non-administrative

[1]"Cuiban" is a term coined to describe the series of settlements of various sizes which, during Monte Albán V, extended from Cuilapan to Monte Albán. It is not the name of a Prehispanic settlement.

settlements. Thus it seems probable that the percentage of Monte Albán V ceramic production loci within administrative sites was possibly even over-represented in our sample.

The locations of the ceramic production places are also revealing. The Tlacolula locus was in a piedmont cave removed from any administrative place (Flannery et al. 1970). Many of the Valle Grande ceramic manufacturing places were located midway between Cuiban and Jalieza in small sites lacking administrative construction. The locations of these sites were both near alluvial clay beds and within servicing distance of several large centers of population. From the point of view of the potters, the location would have been optimal. Yet these locations were not especially advantageous for any administrators who wanted to tax or control ceramic manufacturing.

The results of the mean-number-of-types-per-site analysis for this phase were also consistent with the previously discussed findings. The percentage differential between the mean number of types found at administrative versus non-administrative settlements was less marked than in any prior phase. When the results from V are compared with the findings from IIIb and IV (the only phases with a comparable number of ceramic categories) an interesting relationship emerges. The access to ceramic products at non-administrative sites increased throughout this three-phase sequence with the most significant increase occurring between IV and V (Table 10-1).

It seems evident that access to at least certain goods was not primarily a function of administrative importance in Period V. For the first time since the establishment of Monte Albán, the mean number of types (8.1) found at non-administrative places with populations greater than 100 was larger than the mean number (7.9) recovered at administrative locations (Table 10-1). It seems likely that the production and distribution of goods occurred primarily through commercial (market) exchanges that were not controlled administratively. The differences between this system of exchange and the network of exchange that operated during the Classic period can be shown by examining the changes in the access to ceramic products in the Central part of the valley. During the Classic, rural settlements close to Monte Albán had access to few ceramic types. These sites only had access to the highly standardized vessels that were produced and distributed administratively. In V, however, the non-administrative settlements located within Cuiban's administrative district averaged 5.3 types per site, or more than the mean found in all non-administrative sites (4.9). The non-administrative settlements within 10 kilometers of Monte Albán averaged 4.6 types per site, a figure just below the regional mean for non-administrative settlements. Thus greater articulation with the valley's largest center may have served to increase, and certainly no longer acted to decrease, the flow of goods into non-administrative settlements. At the same time, those non-administrative sites furthest from Cuiban (in the El Choco administrative district) had access to only a mean of 3.85 types per site.

Economic transactions in V were for the most part both localized and segregated from administrative control. The degree of interaction between Valley of Oaxaca settlements was apparently substantial. This interaction was primarily commercial. Relative to earlier phases, increased competition between ceramic producers was therefore expected. If this were indeed the case, an expanded energy input per vessel would be predicted. Additionally, the ceramics of V were expected to have been relatively variable and heterogeneously distributed. In short, the Monte Albán V ceramic complex should have been the diametric opposite of the IIIb complex.

These expectations were borne out in this analysis. The Monte Albán V ceramics had the highest mean production index (5.4) of any phase in the valley sequence (Tables 10-3, 10-5). The most "costly" ceramic category, polychromes (T5007), with the highest production step index, dated to the Late Postclassic. In addition, the most abundant plain *gris* vessels (T1104) were much better fired and far more carefully finished than were the most common Classic period vessels (G-35's). This bowl type had a production step index of 5.00, while the index for its counterparts, the G-12 and G-35, were 4.00 and 2.25 respectively.

The Monte Albán V complex was less standardized and more variable than the IIIb or IV complexes. No one ceramic vessel was as predominant as the G-35 bowl in IIIb and IV. The number of different ceramic wares also increased. *Cremas,* which were not produced in IIIb and IV, were again manufactured in V. The greatest change, however, was the marked increase in the number of different jar types. No longer were jars manufactured primarily in a single paste. Late Postclassic period jars were made in *gris* (T1109), *café* (T2221, T2222) and *crema* (T0423).

As the area of our survey has been expanded, the recognized variability in Period V ceramics has been increased significantly. In part this has been due to the considerable spatial variability that existed in this com-

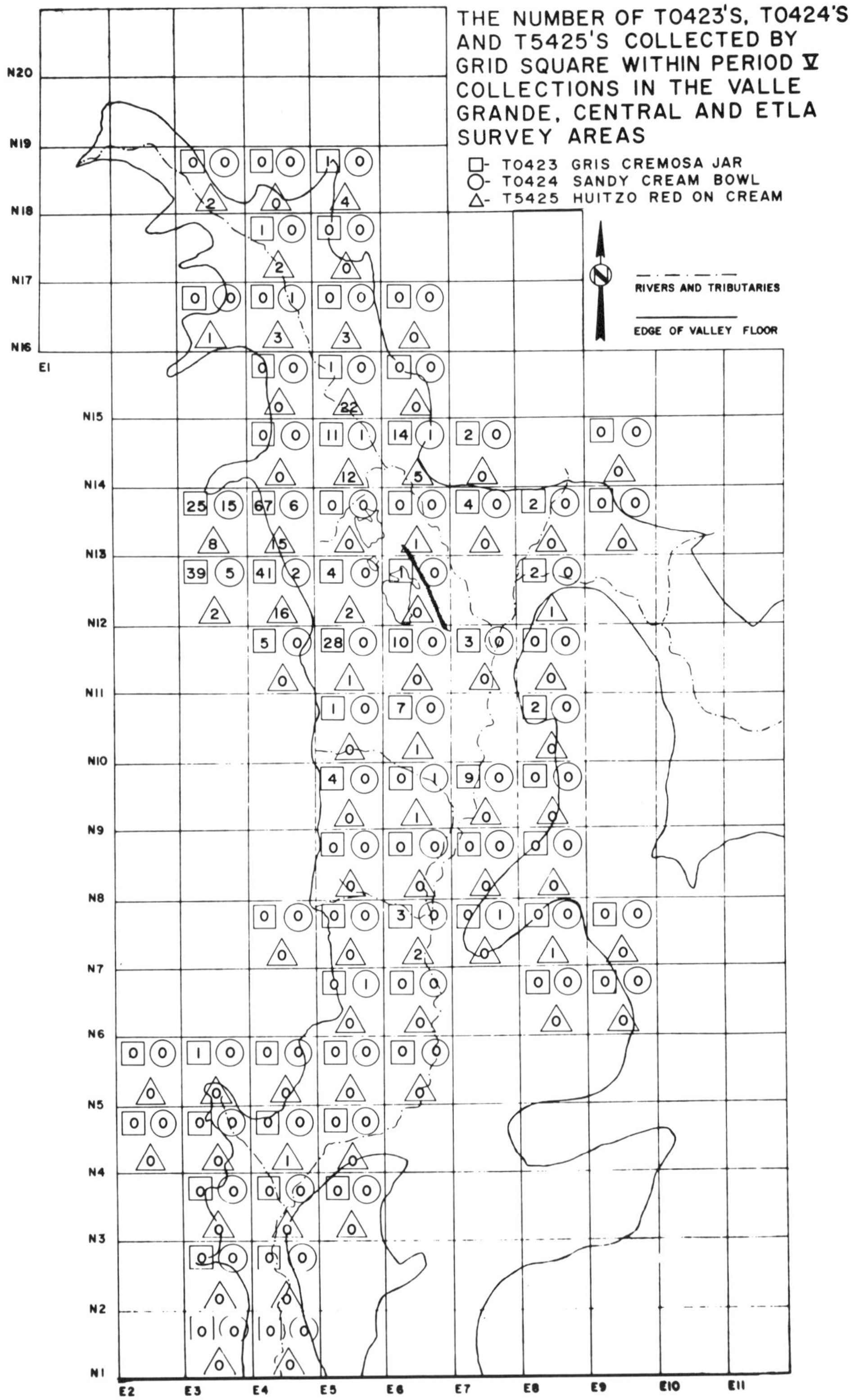

Figure 10-2. The number of T0423's, T0424's, and T5425's collected by grid square within Period V collections in the Valle Grande, Central, and Etla survey areas.

plex. As with the Monte Albán IV ceramics, it seems possible that the known variability (and consequently the number of identified ceramic categories) in the V assemblage will be expanded when the Tlacolula arm has been investigated.

The contingency table analysis reveals that the Monte Albán V pottery complex was distributed more heterogeneously (Feinman 1980:198) than the complex of any other phase (Table 10-6). The plain G-3M (T1104) (Feinman 1980:307) bowls were found throughout the region, in 66 of 71 of the grid squares occupied in V (Table 10-7). But the distribution of *ollas* was less uniform. The predominant *olla* type (T1109) (Feinman 1980:308) was only found in 56 of the 71 grid units (Table 10-7). The fact that bowls were distributed more evenly was expected given the comparative ease of transporting these vessels as compared to jars.

The non-*gris* wares were found to be most abundant in different sub-areas of the valley (Figs. 10-2, 10-3, 10-4). All three *crema* ceramic types (T0423, T0424, T5425) were most commonly found in the western portion of the Central area (Feinman 1980:146–48). The four *café* types (T2221, T2222, T2223, T2224) (Feinman 1980:141-44) were most densely distributed in the southern half of the Valle Grande area. Most of the *gris* vessels were found throughout the survey region, although they were most abundant in the Central area (Feinman 1980:313-15). Polychromes (T5007) were also found to be most common in the Central and Etla portions of the valley (Feinman 1980:316).

SUMMARY

Several conclusions can be drawn from the research reported on in this chapter. The general hypothesis that the relative degree of overlap between economic and political networks was generally associated with the structure of valley-wide ceramic production and distribution through time was supported. Relatively high degrees of overlap (i.e., Late I, IIIa, IIIb, IV) were associated with centralized, administratively controlled production and/or distribution while relatively low degrees of overlap (i.e., Early I, II and V) were associated with more localized, autonomous ceramic production/distribution networks. These latter networks were associated with competition between producers and a high amount of energy investment per pot while the former were associated with the predominance of large scale production techniques.

In addition, it was noted that large scale ceramic production industries operated during those phases (Late I, IIIa, IIIb) when periodic, localized food shortages and the supplying of Monte Albán must have been serious problems for valley administrators. At these times, large scale ceramic production was apparently part of a valley-wide strategy that included intensive farming in the piedmont zone and the operation of region-wide systems of exchange. Alternatively, more decentralized ceramic manufacturing strategies were shown to have existed during those phases (Early I, II, V) when valley agriculture was oriented more toward the less risky alluvial zone and when temporary population-resource imbalances could have been resolved through the operation of localized exchange networks alone.

Thus it may be concluded that in the prehispanic Valley of Oaxaca, the organization of ceramic production did change, as predicted, in response to specific systemic variables (i.e., political organization). Consequently, the organization of ceramic production can perhaps best be understood in this broader systemic context. Simple models of linear or progressive change in technological processes, or waves of outside influence, do not satisfactorily explicate the complex cycles of change in the ceramic production industry.

Although the predicted relationship between the organization of the ceramic production-distribution system and the degree of the isomorphism between economic and political networks in the valley was well supported when examined within each of the seven Monte Albán phases, the predictions were met even more closely when the relationship was examined as a series of processual transitions between phases (Table 10-12). Consequently, it is suggested that in studying change one must not only examine the strength of the

Table 10-12. Transitional Changes in the Degree of Isomorphism Between Economic and Political Networks and the Organization of Ceramic Production-Distribution

Phase - Phase Transitions	Degree of Isomorphism between Economic and Political Networks	Organization of Ceramic Production-Distribution
Early I - Late I	increased	increased scale
Late I - II	decreased	decreased scale
II - IIIA	increased	increased scale
IIIA - IIIB	relatively constant; perhaps slight increase in scale	relatively constant; perhaps slight increase in scale
IIIB - IV	decreased	relatively constant; perhaps slight decrease in scale
IV - V	decreased	decreased scale

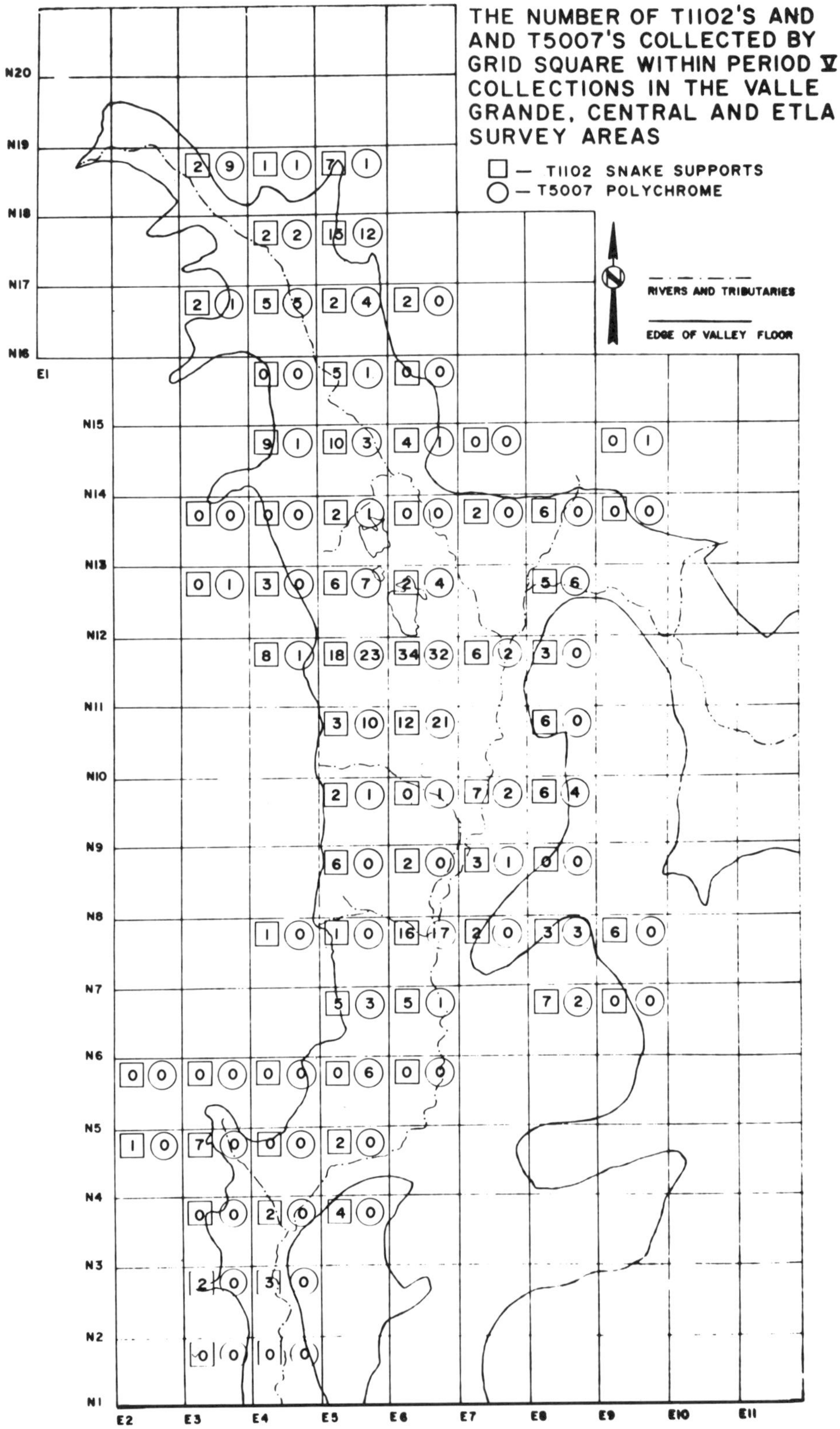

Figure 10-3. The number of T1102's and T5007's collected by grid square within Period V collections in the Valle Grande, Central, and Etla survey areas.

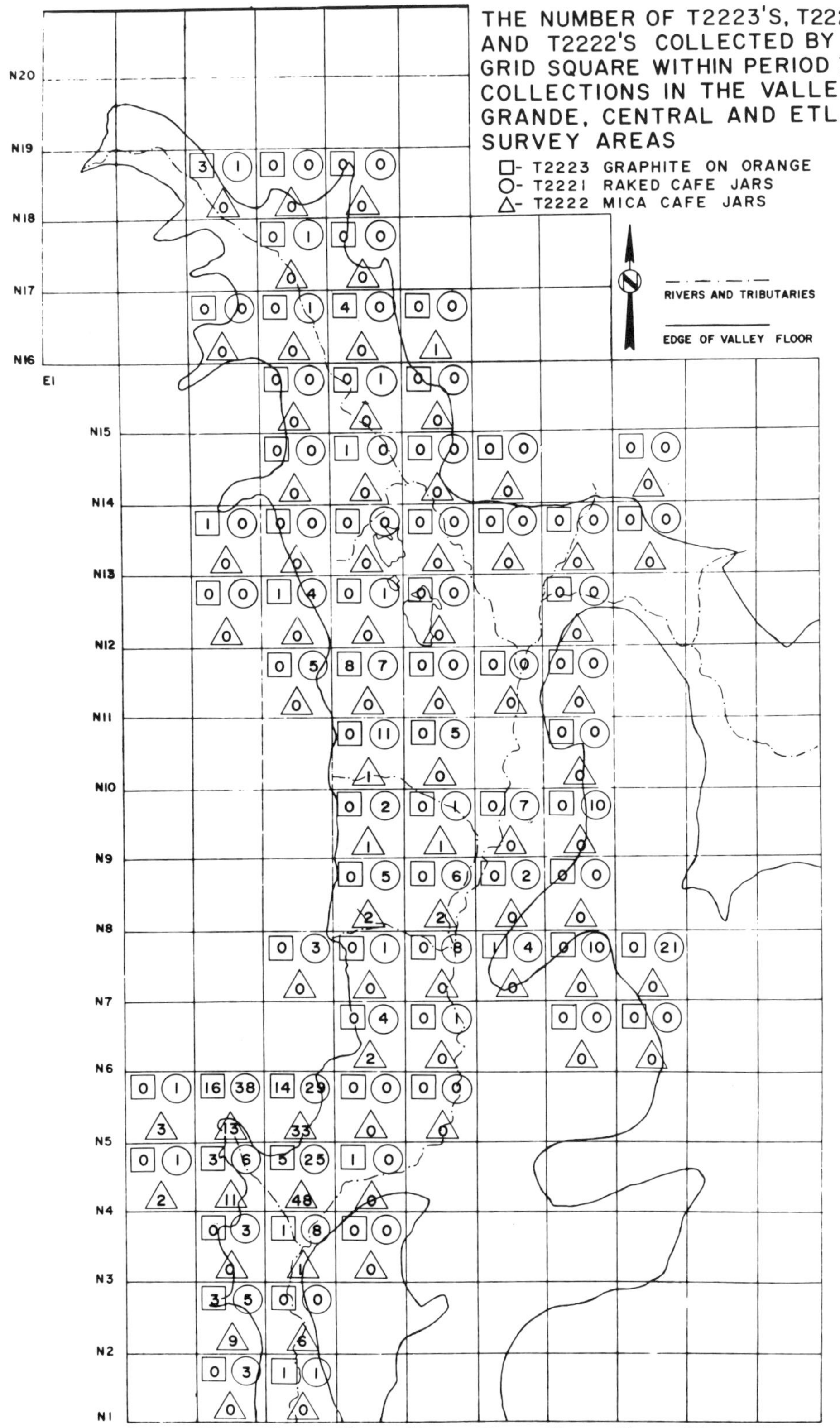

Figure 10-4. The number of T2223's, T2221's, and T2222's collected by grid square within Period V collections in the Valle Grande, Central, and Etla survey areas.

correlations or associations between specified variables within certain temporal units, but one should also examine the patterning in the transformations themselves, a point that has also been made by F. Plog (1979:223) and Renfrew (1979:38-39).

Finally, it is recognized that this research represents only a preliminary attempt to address some very complex relationships. The primary intent has been to ask a set of new questions about societal change which can then be initially operationalized through the analysis of data from regionally-oriented research projects. Future research will hopefully far surpass this study in both the sophistication of the questions asked and the rigor of the analytical methods employed.

Chapter 11

SYNTHESIS

In synthesizing our conclusions, we will look at change in the Valley of Oaxaca from three perspectives. First, we will examine processes of change from the "bottom up," looking at the household organizational sphere and considering the causes and consequences of change there. Then we will look at "middle-level" changes, and finally, we will look at the system from the "top down," examining change in macroregional organization, and the causes and consequences of this set of changes. We are using this approach to synthesis solely as an organizational device and do not mean to imply that household, middle-level, or macroregional spheres are somehow the "prime movers" in cultural evolution.

THE VIEW FROM THE BOTTOM

Direct archaeological evidence from the Valley of Oaxaca for change in household structure and function is highly limited (cf. Drennan 1976; Paddock, Mogor, and Lind 1968; Whalen 1981; Winter 1974, 1976), especially for the periods after Monte Albán I. Our data, however, lend themselves to inferences concerning changing household time budgets, production strategies, and fertility and migration strategies. The major changes of interest to us were those associated with the growth of Monte Albán. Period I is the first period in which there is evidence for substantial interregional migration, both to the new capital itself and into the piedmont within a radius of about 18 kilometers of the capital. This was accompanied by a shift to more canal irrigation, signifying a move to a two-crop agricultural cycle, away from the one-crop cycle of prior times. The heightened production demands on households that were the reason for the change in production strategies may also have resulted in changed fertility strategies to increase the working capacity of households, bringing population growth, especially in those areas most directly affected by Monte Albán. Unfortunately our data do not permit an assessment of the relative contributions of immigration and fertility shifts in explaining the rapid population growth that occurred subsequent to the foundation of the new capital.

Changes in household strategies during Period I were the result of changes in other spheres, but in turn these changes fed back, causing changes especially at the regional level. We argued that altered household time budgets, coupled with population growth and increased potential interaction, resulted in the evolution of a regional marketing system. This would have represented a novel mode of regional integration, with consequences for growth in regional government, as the new institution would have required some degree of regional-level control in order to function.

Similarly, the importance of high-level controls would have been heightened in connection with the need for adjudicative authority in canal irrigation. Inter- and intraregional squabbles over land no doubt increased in frequency in the ever more crowded central portion of the valley, necessitating increased governmental intervention. The growth of a city–a kind of community never before seen in Mesoamerica–would have forced the elite at Monte Albán to confront a wholly new set of problems, ranging from behavior control to assuring a steady supply of food to the urban population.

After Period I we made additional inferences about changes in household strategies. In other periods, too, fertility and migration decisions were affected by the degree of centralized control and integration in the region. In IIIa and to a lesser extent in IIIb (in the area adjacent to Monte Albán), families again moved to the piedmont, in spite of the inherent risks there. Growth in the scale and vertical complexity of government permitted this piedmont in-migration by assuring families of a tie to a tightly integrated regional network which could be a source of food in bad years (and which also became a source of implements such as pottery). Growth in government, in turn, implied increased demands on each household, creating a climate favoring large family sizes and thus population growth.

The Postclassic marked the end of the recurring association between population growth/piedmont immigration/growth in government that we observed after the formation of Monte Albán (with only Period II representing a long-running reversal of these trends). After the collapse of region-wide government, we observed a reduction in population density, probably due to reduced family size and/or emigration. By Period V, a new order of things was beginning to emerge, involving a resurgence of regional integration, albeit on a basis different from that of the prior periods. Evidently, government was less demanding, and we think this is reflected in several things, including extremely low population growth rates and population density far below what the region was capable of supporting. Judging from our data, life was also becoming more satisfying materially. Pottery was better, and obsidian was more generally available. This, we argued, was symptomatic of the growth in importance of a marketing system as the key means of regional integration.

From Period I through IIIb, highly centralized regional government had been a major feature of the environment of households, causing alterations in family size, location, and production strategies. By Period V, this was no longer the case. By that time, although governmental action was no doubt important, we feel the market system had become more of a focus of activity. We infer this in spite of the fact that we know relatively little about the structure or function of this market system. It is likely that this would have been a system relatively free of governmental controls, regulated by "parapolitical" institutions analogous to European or Chinese guilds, or autonomous commercial cities. Demonstrating how this market system worked presents a set of problems requiring the application of more fine-grained archaeological methods and problem-oriented research with ethnohistoric and colonial archival sources.

THE VIEW FROM THE MIDDLE

Our second view of the major trends in the evolution of the Valley of Oaxaca regional system is from the perspective of the middle-level sociocultural formations that we have identified. Between the household level and the regional state or commercial system were, at different times, local communities, local exchange spheres, administrative districts, and, at a few of the largest urban centers, "site subdivisions." Each of these had their own reasons for existence, interests, and emergent properties distinct from those at the household level or the larger regional or macroregional scales. In our settlement pattern analysis, in fact, many important relationships were detected only at this middle scale, reflecting distinct economic, political, and ecological processes. Too, the formation, persistence, and dissolution of these middle level units can be related directly to coping strategies initiated at the household, regional, or macroregional scales.

Some kind of "district" level formation probably existed in the Valley of Oaxaca from as early as the Early Formative. These units, each encompassing part of an arm of the valley, became smaller in territory, larger in population, and better-defined as chiefdom and early state institutions were established. Originally politically autonomous in local affairs, some districts later became simply administrative appendages of the Monte Albán state. The degree to which district level autonomy could be maintained depended on the pressure for state control of piedmont agriculture and the relative openness of the system's boundary at the regional scale. The more the pressure for agricultural surplus, the more state control over administrative matters at the district level. The districts in the valley's alluvium showed considerable autonomy and persistence of tradition, while the piedmont districts were subject to the whims of the state and the complaints of households trying to survive in a too-variable and ultimately inadequate economy. Correspondingly, the more open the regional system boundary, the more autonomous the district level organizations. However, concurrently, another process affected middle-level units. Since 1) the valley shows a secular trend toward greater economic specialization, and 2) control of agriculture passed from central administrators to increasingly lower level administrators from 500 B.C. to A.D. 1500, districts found themselves increasingly opposed to state controls. It was the withdrawal of support by elite with district-level interests that led to the collapse of the Monte Albán state and the formation of smaller, equally stratified political units, which were organized at the older "administrative district" scale. For much of the Postclassic, then, political administration was apparently most efficiently carried out at this scale. On the other hand, local exchange spheres, which had tended to vary in their vitality depending on the degree of state level political interference, grew into an integrated, valley-wide commercial system in the Postclassic.

THE MACROREGIONAL PERSPECTIVE

Beginning as early as the Early Formative, the extent to which households in the general population were the units involved in interregional exchange was declining. The increasing divergence in ceramic styles interregionally during the Formative period reflects this change. Increasingly, only an elite group were involved in this type of interaction, and increasingly, this is indicated by the fact that the only ceramic types that can be identified stylistically with distant areas are the more costly types.

The reduction in the amount of household-to-household exchange was probably due to the following interrelated factors:

1) Shifts in time schedules of agricultural producers in the direction of more time committed to agricultural production reduced the time available for long-distance raiding and trading expeditions. The governing elite became representatives of non-elite households in this organizational sphere.

2) A governing elite increasingly restricted the general population's freedom of movement in order to limit emigration and hence to assure a steady, dependable labor supply (cf. Earle 1978). Immigration, of course, may be encouraged or forced.

3) A governing elite increasingly monopolized long-distance exchange as a source of revenues.

4) Growing population sizes reduced the necessity for local population aggregates to participate in interregional marriage alliances since larger populations are less prone to wild fluctuations (Wobst 1974).

Warfare is an arena for interregional interaction for which we have little data until late in the Formative. We are intrigued, but frustrated due to the shortage of data, by the possibility that Monte Albán's foundation was at least in part due to the stresses of regional boundary maintenance. The Monte Albán Danzantes and other monuments offer clues as to the nature of warfare after the formation of the new capital. The abundance and relative uniformity of the Danzantes implies to us that during Period I Monte Albán was dealing militarily with a plethora of "big men"–important people, perhaps, but people whose capture does not seem to have brought with it territorial aggrandizement. Military efforts may have focused primarily on reducing the frequency and severity of raids on valley villages by neighboring groups. The not-inconsiderable amount of energy expended in constructing the Danzantes signified more than just the success of these ventures–these monuments would also have served to build the legitimation of a fledgling organization that was in the process of becoming institutionalized. During later periods many fewer such monuments were put up, and those that were, evidently were not destined for public display, located as they were in an increasingly closed-off Main Plaza. Symbols of power became less important as control was assured through other channels.

In Period II, the conquest monuments suggest the military domination of named central places whose conquest may have brought under the capital's control sizable dependent populations. We suggested that there was a connection between these conquests and settlement pattern changes in the valley. Some of Monte Albán's support may have been shifted to this macroregional scale, away from the local population. The consequences in the valley were population decline, cessation of piedmont development, and a less vertically differentiated administrative central-place hierarchy.

We related the Period II changes to what Herbert Simon called "modularization." As larger regional units–"modules"–developed throughout the Southern Highlands, it was progressively easier for Monte Albán to assemble the parts, through the conquest of key places, into a relatively easy-to-manage hierarchical system that could be a source of substantial tribute. Unfortunately, from the point of view of the Oaxacan capital, this modularization process was evidently proceeding in other areas of Mesoamerica as well. By Monte Albán IIIa, in fact, Teotihuacán was beginning to assemble an empire on a scale far greater than even that of Monte Albán. This created an unprecedented set of problems for the Valley of Oaxaca capital, and the response was the development of a set of strategies to increase the valley's production and reproduction on a scale theretofore unheard of, involving a massive round of population growth and piedmont development, as well as a new level of governmental meddling in market transactions. The shoddy pottery of the Classic was one result.

From the time of the earliest villages through the Classic, changing patterns of macroregional interaction played a critical role in societal form and change in the Valley of Oaxaca. Can the same be said of the Postclassic? According to the modularization argument, in empire formation large, centralized components are assembled, creating a hierarchical structure that produces tribute but requires relatively little administration from the highest levels (existing hierarchical structures in each module solve local problems). Empire formation would have taken on a different complexion during the Postclassic if it had generally been the case that the power of centralized governments declined, and as commercial institutions became the major foci of regional-level and perhaps interregional-level organization. This would have represented a kind of "demodularization" since commercial networks lack the kind of centralized control typical of governments; instead of decision-making by a few elite, a commercial system operates through the individual decisions of participants at all levels of participation. This may help explain why the Aztec "empire" was never an empire in the sense that Teotihuacán's had been. Relatively little artifactual or architectural evidence can be seen of the Aztec presence outside the Valley of Mexico, while Teotihuacán's presence is indicated in both of these ways in a number of places. Even in the Valley of Mexico, the Tenochcan expansion left secondary centers and the market system with a considerable degree of autonomy (cf. M. Smith 1979; Blanton 1976c), and in Oaxaca it seems clear that neither Zaachila nor "Cuiban" exercised the kind of control that Monte Albán had exerted earlier.

THE DYNAMIC

Each of the growth periods (I, IIIa, IIIb) was followed by reorganization, giving the valley system a kind of cyclic dynamic up to the collapse of Monte Albán's hegemony. As we see it, the dynamic was due in large part to the following factors:

1) A growth period is instigated from Monte Albán to assure stepped-up levels of production and reproduction, and, possibly, immigration. In the early stages of the growth period productivity is high, both because the lands being brought into cultivation are essentially virgin farmland, and because administrative costs are low.

2) As growth continues, the best farmland is gradually used up, as are the most desirable sources of water for irrigation, resulting in disputes. Administrative costs increase due to the increased need for adjudicative authority.

3) As the number of people committed to the piedmont increases, the state assumes a larger and larger responsibility for supplying food to deficit areas.

4) As the piedmont is a relatively delicate environment, its soils begin to show signs of wear and tear, and production begins to decline.

When the combination of production declines and increased administrative costs reach a critical point, reorganization is carried out. This is seemingly an argument that overpopulation and environmental degradation eventually bring an end to periods of political growth, but the limits to growth involve other factors, especially the kinds of scale problems in growing administrative organizations that we discussed earlier. This has to do with the fact that communication costs increase at a disproportionate rate, lessening the efficiency of the organization, so that full expansion of piedmont agriculture may have been limited more by administrative costs than by environmental degradation. If it can be said that Period V was a growth cycle, it was surely different than those of Periods I, IIIa, and IIIb, in that 1) there was a high degree of retention of district-level political autonomy, 2) population growth rates were very slow, and 3) there was an increase, not the usual decrease, in commercialization.

CONCLUSION

If one were to ask, "What *did* bring about the evolution of culture in Oaxaca?", our true answer, which we would give confidently and without the least embarrassment, is that every facet of this development is very complicated. The question is linear. It asks for a single, simple solution. As the reader of this book is by now aware, there are no simple solutions. The key processes involve a series of mutually interacting causes, so "the answer" must by the very nature of our human language involve us in quite a busy discussion. The world appears more interesting with this "systems" approach, but not idly so. This way is more realistic, since civilizations are complicated. We believe we have contributed some new insights about processes of change and specific events in cultural evolution that have been previously ignored.

Appendix I

SITE DATA

Information that could be conveniently coded in numerical form is included in Part 1 of this Appendix. The coding scheme is described and discussed beginning in the next paragraph. Features noted on sites that are not amenable to coding are included as Part 2, "Comments". In many cases this involves quoting passages directly from the field notebooks, or summarizing such passages. To obtain data on our ceramic collections, see Feinman (1980). For data on lithic information by collection tract (rather than by site, as it is presented here) see Appel (1982).

EXPLANATION OF TERMS USED IN CODING SITES

The coding scheme used here is based on that employed for the Monte Albán data (Blanton 1978), but it is modified in several respects to meet the requirements of survey in the valley. Here we discuss in detail the definitions of some of the terms used in the new code book which are not immediately obvious.

To achieve the maximum possible uniformity, all Valle Grande sites, and Monte Albán, were coded by one person, Blanton, and all Central area sites were coded by Kowalewski. Between us we did have some minor differences in the interpretation of a few terms, all of which are discussed here. Finally, it is important to remember that all of these coded descriptions apply only to the archaeological sites themselves, and not necessarily to the area surrounding the sites. For example, for the column "alluviation", the value "significant" applies only to alluviation on the site itself, and not to alluviation 200 meters or 1 kilometer away.

Card 1, cols. 17, 18, 19, 20: Elevations were read from the Departamento Geográfico Militar 1:100,000 topographic maps, rounded to the nearest 50 meters. When a large site crossed several contours, the middle figure was used.

Card 1, col. 21: The *low alluvial zone* is the present floodplain of the main river, formed after the archaeological period. The *high alluvium* is the principal zone of the valley floor. It is a nearly flat surface that, according to Anne Kirkby

> consists almost entirely of abandoned floodplains of the main rivers. . . . The 3 to 6 meters of alluvium which separate the present high alluvium surface from the present river level have all been deposited since about 800 B.C.–200 B.C. By the time of the Spanish Conquest in the sixteenth century, the rivers had finished aggrading throughout most of the valley. . . . [Kirkby 1973:13]

The *piedmont* is a transitional zone between the mountains and the valley floor. According to Kirkby, "the average slope of the piedmont from mountain to alluvium is 1 to 2 degrees with later dissection producing side slopes with gradients up to 20 to 30 degrees" (1973:11). We have divided the piedmont into thirds (*high, middle, and low*), since decreasing gradients, less stony and deeper soils, and greater potential for irrigation make the lower reaches of the piedmont much more suitable for agriculture. The *mountain* zone consists of very steep, narrow ridges separated by deep barrancas. This zone usually begins above 1800 meters. More information on environmental variability, beyond these simple categories, is available in Chapter 1 of the present volume. If a large site lies in several different environmental zones, it is coded as being in the predominant or the average zone.

Card 1, col. 23: Hilltop or ridgetop means a clearly elevated location in the high piedmont or mountain zones, a location generally without higher ground in the immediate vicinity. This may be more liberally interpreted in a few instances in the Valle Grande.

Card 1, col. 26: Soil types are defined as in Kirkby (1973:Fig. 5), except for the use of the term "loam", which we use for a mixture of varying proportions of sand, silt, and clay. Kowalewski, for the Central area sites, distinguished between "mostly sand" and "sandy loam", such that to be classified as the latter, a soil had to have an obvious clay, silt, or humic component. In cases of thin, weathered, and eroded bedrock soils, thus, the classification used was "mostly sand". Blanton, for the Valle Grande, used "mostly sand" only when the note-takers emphasized that the soils were even sandier than usual, so category 2 was used more often. We believe that for most purposes classes

1 and 2 are essentially equivalent, and that the important distinctions are between these two taken together and all the others.
Card 1, col. 28: Mountain and piedmont soils in the northwestern part of the Central area, from San Lorenzo Cacaotepec southwestward to a line drawn from San José Atzompa west to the Río Jalapillas, are dazzlingly white in color, and are referred to here as *tierra blanca*. Cretaceous sedimentary formations usually have brownish soils, while the earlier Jurassic bedrock soils are reddish (or orange). The dark gray/black color class was used for *ciénaga* clay deposits.
Card 1, col. 29: Erosion here usually refers to the cutting of small washes or arroyos, as this is more common and more important than the movement of material in sheets across wide surfaces. The descriptions apply to current erosion. If we were able to see evidence of past erosional conditions or change in erosional patterns, this is discussed in the comments section, Appendix I, Part 2.
Card 1, col. 30: Significant means that either alluviation contributed recognizably to the formation of the depth of the archaeological deposit, or that the archaeological deposit was probably obscured by subsequent alluviation. These instances are rare, and are discussed in each case in Appendix I, Part 2.
Card 1, col. 31: These are distinguishable soil zones with different drainage characteristics in the high alluvium, and their possible importance is detailed in Chapter 1.
Card 1, cols. 32, 33: From the edge of the site. Rounded to the nearest 100 meters.
Card 1, cols. 35, 36: 98 and 99 are essentially equivalent. Water table depth was assessed by peering into hand-dug wells, which are by no means uniformly distributed over the valley floor.
Card 1, col. 38: "Requires drainage" means either that the site is soggy, or that people now or in the past have taken measures to prevent that.
Card 1, col. 44: Since the sites were visited only once during the year, this information is not a complete land use record.
Card 1, 46: Same as Parsons (1971:22-23).
Card 1, col. 48: Sparse means one or two pieces per hectare of site area. Abundant means more than five pieces per square meter.
Card 1, 62: Chert projectile points were coded as chert blades, but are always noted in Appendix 1, Part 2.
Card 1, cols. 64, 66: Cores include, in a few instances, chunks that were not always definitely cores in the strict sense.
Card 2, col. 36: These are the other lithic workshops as they were observed as such by field crews. Some of these were deleted from the list of workshops by Jill Appel (1982) if she felt, during the course of her reevaluation of the field notes, that insufficient evidence was present.
Card 2, col. 54: Central area isolated residences, which always have population estimates of 5-10, are coded with population density category 3, "other". The same phenomena in the Valle Grande were coded using density category 1, 10-25. This is not an actual difference in population estimates or density, since the Valle Grande isolated residences always have population estimates of 5-10.

CODING SCHEME FOR SITES VALLEY OF OAXACA SETTLEMENT PATTERN PROJECT

Column(s)	Variables	Values
1	Area Prefix	Monte Albán-0 Etla-1 Central Valley-2 Valle Grande-3 Tlacolula-4 Ocotlán-5
2,3	Phase	TL-01 SJ-02 Gua-03 Ros-04 EI-05 LI-06 II-07 IIIa-08 IIIb-09 IV-10 V-11 undated-12
4,5,6,7	Site Number	
8	Card Number	(1)
9,10,11,12	Grid square	(*north* value followed by *east* value)
13,14,15	Distance to Center of Main Plaza in km	(00.0)
16	Major Recorder	Blanton-1 Kowalewski-2 Feinman-3 Appel-4
17,18,19,20	Elevation above sea level in meters	(000.)
21	Environmental Zone	Low Alluvium-1 High Alluvium-2 Lower Piedmont-3 Middle Piedmont-4 High Piedmont-5 Mountain-6 M.D.-9
22	Slope	Flat-1 Shallow-2 Moderate-3 Steep-4 M.D.-9
23	Hilltop or Ridgetop?	No-0 Yes-1 M.D.-9
24	Soil Character	Alluvium-1 Bedrock-2 M.D.-9
25	Gravel?	Absent-0 Present-1 M.D.-9
26	Soil Texture	Mostly Sand-1 Sandy Loam-2 Loam-3 Clayey Loam-4 Dark Clay-5 Sandy Clay-6 M.D.-9
27	Soil Depth	Shallow (0-20 cm)-0 Medium (20 cm-1 m)-1 Deep (over 1 m)-2 M.D.-9
28	Soil Color	White-0 Light Brown-1 Reddish-2 Dark Brown-3 Dark Gray/Black-4 M.D.-9
29	Soil Erosion	None-9 Light-1 Moderate-2 Heavy-3 M.D.-9
30	Alluviation	Insignificant-0 Significant-1 M.D. 9
31	Is the Site on the Boundary of the Brown Loam and the Bajío/Ciénaga?	No-0 Yes-1 M.D.-9
32,33	Distance to Nearest Water	(Km. 0.0) M.D.-9.9
34	Type of Water Source	Main River-0 Tributary Stream-1 Arroyo-2 Spring-3 Well-4 M.D.-9
35,36	Depth of Water Table	(closest meter) Deep but Depth in Meters Not Known-98 M.D.-99
37	Type of Irrigation	None-0 Well-1 Well With Pump-2 Valley Floor Canal-3 Piedmont Canal (now or in the recent past)-4 Flood-Water-5 Portable Pump From Stream-6 Terracing Only-7 M.D.-9
38	Drainage	Well Drained-0 Requires Drainage-1 M.D.-9
39	Recency of Plowing	Never-0 This Year-1 Sometime in the Past-2 M.D.-9
40	Pot-Hunting	None-0 Some-1 Heavy-2 M.D.-9
41	Scientific Excavation	None-0 Present-1 M.D.-9
42	Vegetation (predominant type)	Cleared-0 Chamizo/Willow (riverine)-1 Mesquite-2 Cactus-3 Grass-4 Oak-5 Pine-6 M.D.-9
43	Modern Land Use	Collecting/Hunting-0 Town-1 Farming-2 Industrial-3 Grazing-4 Garbage-5 M.D.-9
44	Crops (predominant type)	None-0 Milpa-1 Alfalfa-2 Castor Beans-3 Tobacco-4 Truck Gardening-5 Sugar Cane-6 Carrizal-7 Maguey-8 M.D.-9
45	Special Resources	None-0 Quarryable Stone-1 Clay for Pottery-2 Salt-3 Chert-4 Mica-5 Magnetite-Hematite-6 Other Ores-7 Other-8 M.D.-9
46	Sherd Density	None-0 Trace-1 Very Light-2 Light-3 Moderate-4 Heavy-5 M.D.-9
47	Can Observed Lithics be Attributed to This Phase Only?	No-0 Yes-1 M.D.-9

48	Obsidian Density	None-0 Sparse-1 Moderate-2 Abundant-3 M.D.-9
49	Obsidian Color	None-0 Gray-1 Green-2 Black-3 Gray and Green-4 Green and Black-5 Gray and Black-6 Gray, Green, and Black-7 Other-8 M.D.-9
50	Obsidian Points	None-0 Present-1 M.D.-9
51	Obsidian Blades	None-0 Present-1 M.D.-9
52	Obsidian Flakes	None-0 Present-1 M.D.-9
53	Obsidian Cores	None-0 Present-1 M.D.-9
54,55	Number of Whole or Fragmentary Manos	More than 96-97 Present But Not Counted-98 M.D.-99
56,57	Number of Whole or Fragmentary Metates	More than 96-97 Present But Not Counted-98 M.D.-99
58	Mortars	(number of present but not counted-8 M.D.-9) More than 6-7
59	Pestles	(number of present but not counted-8 M.D.-9) More than 6-7
60	Celts	(number of present but not counted-8 M.D.-9) More than 6-7
61	Other Ground Stone	Absent-0 Present-1 M.D.-9
62	Chert Blades	Absent-0 Present-1 M.D.-9
63	Chert Flakes	Absent-0 Present-1 M.D.-9
64	Chert Cores	Absent-0 Present-1 M.D.-9
65	Quartz Flakes	Absent-0 Present-1 M.D.-9
66	Quartz Cores	Absent-0 Present-1 M.D.-9
67	Adobes	Absent-0 Present-1 M.D.-9
68	Building Stone	Absent-0 Present-1 M.D.-9
69	Plaster Floors	Absent-0 Present-1 M.D.-9
70	Stone Floors	Absent-0 Present-1 M.D.-9
71	Burned Daub	Absent-0 Present-1 M.D.-9
72	Other Evidence for Burning	Absent-0 Present-1 M.D.-9
73	Carved Stone	Absent-0 Present-1 M.D.-9
74	Burials Visible	Absent-0 Present-1 M.D.-9
75	Number of Tombs Visible	(M.D.-9) More than 7-8
76,77,78,79,80	Site Area	(hectares 0000.0)
1	Area Prefix	
2,3	Phase	
4,5,6,7	Site Number	
8	Card Number	(2)
9,10	Number of Units Making Up the Site	
11,12,13	Number of Structures 1m or Less in Elevation (indicates only those attributable to this phase)	M.D.-999
14,15,16	Number of Structures 1m or More in Elevation (indicates only those attributable to this phase)	M.D.-999
17,18,19, 20,21,22	Total Volume of Mounds definitely in Use During This Phase (mounds present but date of construction and use not known-999998)	M.D.-999999
23,24,25,26	Number of Terraces	M.D.-9999
27	Defensive Walls	Absent-0 Present-1 Present and Definitely Attributable to This Phase-2 M.D.-9
28	Ancient Dams	Absent-0 Present-1 Present and Definitely Attributable to This Phase-2 M.D.-9
29	Ancient Agricultural Terraces	Absent-0 Present-1 Present and Definitely Attributable to This Phase-2 M.D.-9
30	Ancient Quarries	Absent-0 Present-1 Present and Definitely Attributable to This Phase-2 M.D.-9
31	Shell Workshop(s)	Absent-0 Present-1 Present and Definitely Attributable to This Phase-2 M.D.-9
32	Obsidian Workshop(s)	Absent-0 Present-1 Present and Definitely Attributable to This Phase-2 M.D.-9

33	Mano Workshop(s)	Absent-0 Present-1 Present and Definitely Attributable to This Phase-2 M.D.-9		
34	Metate Workshop(s)	Absent-0 Present-1 Present and Definitely Attributable to This Phase-2 M.D.-9		
35	Ceramic Workshop(s)	Absent-0 Present-1 Present and Definitely Attributable to This Phase-2 M.D.-9		
36	Other Lithic Workshop(s)	Absent-0 Present-1 Present and Definitely Attributable to This Phase-2 M.D.-9		
37	Salt Workshop(s)	Absent-0 Present-1 Present and Definitely Attributable to This Phase-2 M.D.-9		
38	Other Workshop(s)	Absent-0 Present-1 Present and Definitely Attributable to This Phase-2 M.D.-9		
39	Burnishing Stone(s)	Absent-0 Present-1 Present and Definitely Attributable to This Phase-2 M.D.-9		
40	Kiln(s)	Absent-0 Present-1 Present and Definitely Attributable to This Phase-2 M.D.-9		
41	Shell	Absent-0 Present-1 Present and Definitely Attributable to This Phase-2 M.D.-9		
42	Greenstone or Jade	Absent-0 Present-1 Present and Definitely Attributable to This Phase-2 M.D.-9		
43	Misc. Artifacts	Absent-0 Present-1 Present and Definitely Attributable to This Phase-2 M.D.-9		
44,45,46,47,48	Lower Population Estimate			
49,50,51,52,53	Upper Population Estimate			
54	Density of Population	5 to 10-0 10 to 25-1 25 to 50-2 Other-3 M.D.-9		
55	Continuity of Occupation	No prior or Subsequent Phase-0 One Immediate Subsequent Phase-1 One Immediate Prior Phase-2 Two Immediately Adjacent Phases-3 M.D.-9		
56	TL	Absent-0	Present-1	M.D.-9
57	SJ	Absent-0	Present-1	M.D.-9
58	Gua	Absent-0	Present-1	M.D.-9
59	Ros	Absent-0	Present-1	M.D.-9
60	EI	Absent-0	Present-1	M.D.-9
61	LI	Absent-0	Present-1	M.D.-9
62	II	Absent-0	Present-1	M.D.-9
63	IIIa	Absent-0	Present-1	M.D.-9
64	IIIb	Absent-0	Present-1	M.D.-9
65	IV	Absent-0	Present-1	M.D.-9
66	V	Absent-0	Present-1	M.D.-9
67	Published Information	Absent-0	Present-1	M.D.-9
68	Comments? None-0	Yes-1		

Appendix I: Part I, Coded Data

```
20100031111070662160032020211000010993010002102000000000000000000000000000000004
2010001201000000000000000000000000000000000000010000251111111111100101
201000211306050216003202021300009099001110210201101000000000000000000000000000015
2010002201000000000000000000000000000000000000015000371111111110111111
301000110907131215003102021100001299001000210200000000400000000111011000000000011
3010001201000000999998000000000000000000000000011000272111100101 00100
30100021090712621550310102210010040100110022020000000000000000000000100000000000002
3010002201000000999998000000000000000000000000050001011111111111 00000
30100031080714921500320202120000329900110021020000000000000000000000100000000000004
30100032010000009999980000000000000000000000000100002511111111111 00000
301000410808194216004202021120000299001000210200000000000000000000000000000001000001
30100042010000000000000000000000000000000000000500010111111100000000
301000510506274114502101032100100404201000220201100100100000001000001000000000003
301000520100000099999800000000000000000000000005000101111111110101001
3010006103043501145021010221100050990021002302000000000000000000010101100000100013
30100062010000009999980000000000000000000000013000331111111111100000
30100071090610221500210103230010040100011010020120100000000000000011110010299999
301000720100000099999800000000000000000000009999999999911111111110111
3010008105062611145022120211201004021009001019099999999999999999999999999999999999
301000829999999999999998999999999999999999999999999999999999999991110111110000 1
202000111405082216003202011200010099001000212200000000010000000101000000000000003
202000120100000000000000000000000000000000000000100002511011110001 0101
2020002113081062165042020111000012990010002102000000000000000000000100000000000001
20200022010000000000000000000000000000000000000050001030010011000000 1
2020003111070662160032020111000010990010002102000000000000000000000000000000000004
202000320100000000000000000000000000000000000000010000251311111111100101
202000411306050216003202021300009099001110210201101000001000000000000000000000063
20200042010000000000000000000000000000000000000063001571311111110111111
302000110907132215003102021100001299001000210200000000400000000111011000000000011
3020001201000000999998000000000000000000000000011000272311100101 00100
30200021080712621550310102210010040100110022020000000000000000000000100000000000002
302000220100000099999800000000000000000000000005000101311111111100000
302000310807149215003202021200003299001100210200000000000000000000000100000000000001
302000320100000099999800000000000000000000000005000101311111111100000
3020004108081942160042020211200002990010002102000000000000000000000000000001000001
30200042010000000000000000000000000000000000000050001013111110000000001
302000510708222215003212021120000299009000290200000000000000000000100000000000000005
302000520100000000000000000000000000000000000000100002511011000110000 0
302000610506274114502101032100120304201000220201100100100000001000001000000000003
302000620100000099999800000000000000000000000005000101311111110101001
3020007103043501145021010221100050990021002302000000000000000000010101100000100020
302000720100000099999800000000000000000000000200005013111111111100000
30200081090610221500210103230010040100011010020120100000000000000011110010299999
3020008201000000999998000000000000000000000099999999999311111111110111
30200091050626111450221202112010040210090010190999999999999999999999999999999999999
3020009299999999999999989999999999999999999999999999999999999999921101111100001
203000111405082216003202011200010099001000212300000000010000000101000000000000006
203000120100000000000000000000000000000000000000100002513011110001 0101
203000211204062216503202021200003199001100210201201100100000000000000000000000010
203000220100000000000000000000000000000000000000100002510001011111 0101
2030003113060622160032020212000050980010002101000000000000000000000000000000000003
20300032010000000000000000000000000000000000000000100002511001111 0010001
203000411308109216504202011210001298001000210200000000000000000100000000000000002
203000420100000000000000000000000000000000000000500010300010010000101
2030005111070662160032020211000010990010002102000000000000000000000000000000000010
203000520100000000000000000000000000000000000000010000251311111111100101
2030006113060502160032020211000090990011102102000000000000000000000000000000000030
203000620100000000000000000000000000000000000000300007513111111011111 1
3030001109051001160032020221000022980020002302100000000010000000110000000100000001
303000120100000000000000000000000000001000000000000050001010001000 0000000
3030002109071322150031020211000012990010002102000000000400000000111011000000000008
3030002201000000999998000000000000000000000000010000251211101010 0100
30300031090712621550310102210010040100110022020000000000000000000000100000000000002
303000320100000099999800000000000000000000000005000101311111111100000
30300041080714721500320202120000329900110021020000000000000000000000100000000000001
303000420100000099999800000000000000000000000005000101311111111100000
3030005108081942160042020211200002990010002102000000000000000000000000000001000001
303000520100000000000000000000000000000000000000500010131111100000 0000
303000610708222215003212021120000299009000290200000000000000000000100000000000000005
303000620100000000000000000000000000000000000000100002512011000110000 0
302000710506274114502101032100120304201000220201100100100000001000001000000000003
303000720100000099999800000000000000000000000005000101311111110101001
3030008103053501145021010221100050990021002302000000000000000000010101100000100020
303000820100000099999800000000000000000000000200005013111111111100000
30300091090610221500210103230010040100011010020120100000000000000011110010299999
3030009201000000999998000000000000000000000099999999999311111111110111
204000111405082216003202011200010099001000212300000000010000000101000000000000006
204000120100000000000000000000000100000000000000100002513011110001 0101
2040002114050852170042020110200002980010002124111001000000000010000000100000000011
2040002201000000000000000000000002000200000000011000271000010000000011
2040003113060622160032020112000050980010002102000000000000000000110000000000000003
204000320100000000000000000000000000000000000000100002513001111001 0001
2040004111070662160032020211000010990010002102000000000000000000000000000000000010
204000420100000000000000000000000000000000000000010000251311111111100101
2040005113060502160032020111000090990011102102012010000010000000000000000000000030
204000520100000100207100000000000000000000000000300007513111111011111 0
30400011100606221550210102210000019930100021020000000000000000000100000000000000003
304000120100000000000000000000000000000000000000500010110001100100000
304000210708202215503202022120002299001000210200000000000000000000000000000000000001
304000220100000099999800000000000000000000000000500010110001110000000
304000310907124215503101022100100401001100220200000000100000000000001100000000000002
304000320100000099999800000000000000000000000005000101311111111100000
3040004109081434165032120211200022990000044002000000000000000001000000000000000000013
304000420100000099999800000000000000000000000013000330100011110000000
3040005108071592150032020201200002990010002102000000000000000000000000000000000000011
30400052030000000000000000000000000000000000000025000601110011000000000
304000610808192216003202021110000239001000210210000000000000000000000000000000000002
304000620100000000000000000000000000000000000000500010100001000000000
304000710808194216004202021120000239001000210200000000000000000000000000000001000001
3040007201000000000000000000000000000000000000000500010121111000000000
3040008107051791150021010221000004052010002102011999900010000000010110000000000002
304000820100000099999800000000000000000000000005000101100011111 00100
3040009107062001150021010524001004011010002202000000000000000010000100000000000003
304000920100000099999800000000000000010000000000050001011000111110000 1
3040010106062201145023120211200020390001021020000000000000000011100100000000001
3040010201000000999998000000000000001000000000005000101100011111 00001
30400111050626111450221202112010040210090010190999999999999999999999999999999999999
304001129999999999999899999999999999999999999999999999999999999991110111110000 1
304001210506274114502101032100120304201000220201100100100000001000001000000000003
304001220100000099999800000000000000000000000005000101311111110101001
304001310405305314502101022100100499201100230100000000100000000000001100000000001
304001320100000099999800000000000000000000001000050001011000111110010 0
3040014104063102150032120222100120990010002102000000000000000000000001000000000000003
304001420100000099999800000000000000000000000500010110001111110000
3040015103043501145021010221100030990021002302011999900000000000010111100000100040
304001520100000099999800000000000000010000000000040001001311111111110001
30400161040532511550321202211000129900200029020000000004000001111000000010000000009
3040016201000000000000000000000000001000000000010000251100011110000 01
3040017103043682145021011222100040393010002102000000000000000000000000001000000010
3040017201000000000000000000000000001000000000000100002511000110000000 1
```

```
30400181070819721600320202212000129900110021020000000000000000000000000000000015
3040018201000000999998000000000000000000000000150003711000111010000
30400191080714721500320202120000329900110021020000000000000000000000100000000001
3040019201000000999998000000000000000000000000500010131111111100000
30400201090815031650321202112000229900010440020140100000000000100011100000000003
3040020202000000999998000000000000000000000001000020010001111100100
30400211090610221500210103230010040100011010020120100000000000300111100102999999
3040021201000000999998000000000000000000000099999999999311111111110111
00500011120600118003312021120000299001110211201711119797676111111911191108032400
0050001201000000999998045011011111010110111035000700031000011111111
20500011140607321600320201012000109900100021030120110020000000100101000000100017
2050001201000000000000000000000000000000000000172004301100000111000000
20500021140508121600320201111000509800110021230140110010000001100001000000000031
2050002202000000000000000000000000000000000000031000771100001100100101
20500031140508221600320201120001009900100021230000000001000000010100000000000002
2050003201000000000000000000000000100000000000050001032011110001010101
20500041110605021600420201023000049900100021020140110010000000100000000000000009
2050004201000000000000000000000000000000000001000025100000100000101
20500051110505621650320201112000119900100021020140110020100200000000000000000001
2050005201000000000000000000000000000000000000500010300000100000101
20500061120504320650420202110000319800100021020140100000100000100000000000000005
2050006201000000000000000000000000000000100000100002511000011111010100
20500071120503421650310201010000319800100021020110100020000101100000000000000001
2050007201000000000000000000000000000000000000500010310000111010101
20500081120405821650320201121000129800100021021000000000000000000000000000000002
2050008201000000000000000000000000000000000000500010300000100000001
20500091120406221650320201121000319900110022020000000000000000100000000000000002
2050009201000000000000000000000000000000000000500010310000110010001
20500101120406221650320201120000219900110021020120110010000000000000000000000010
2050010201000000000000000000000000000000000001000025110010111110100
20500111120406221650320201020000219800010440020000000000000000000000000000000002
2050011201000000000000000000000000000000000000500010300000100010001
20500121130406721650320201102000219900100021020110010010000101000000000000000007
2050012201000000000000000000000000000000000001000025100000100010101
20500131130407321650320201111000049900100021020000000000000000000000000000000001
2050013201000000000000000000000000000000000000500010300000100010101
20500141140409221700530201102000029900100021241000000000000000000000000000000008
2050014201000000000000000000000200000000000001000025100000100000001
20500151130606521600320202131000309900100011020120100040000201100001000000000120
2050015201000000000000000000000000000000000012000300130011110110100
20500161140607921700620201112000529800100021020000000000000001100000000000000002
2050016201000000000000000000000000000000000000500010300000100000101
20500171110503021650420101023000029800100021020120110010000000000000000000000001
2050017201000000000000000000000000000000000000500010300000100000101
20500181120502321600320201022000319800100021030140110010000000100000000000000006
2050018201000000000000000000000000000000000001000025110000110000100
20500191130810421600420201111000029800100021020000000000000000000001000000000001
2050019201000000000000000000000000000000000000500010310100110000001
20500201120810321700430201111000029800100021020000000000000000000001000000000002
2050020201000000000000000000100000000000000001000025110000110000001
20500211120809521600320202130000200301100021020000000000000000000001000000000001
2050021201000000000000000000000000000000000000500010300000100001101
20500221120808121600310101310000709900010240020000000000000000000001000000000004
2050022201000000000000000000000000000000000100010000251100001100000001
20500231120601121650320201023000519800200440020140110000000000100001000000000004
2050023201000000000000000000000000000000000001000025110000110010101
20500241110601821600320201021000419800100021020120100000000000000000000000000001
2050024201000000000000000000000000000000000000500010300000100000101
20500251120601721600420201121000229800100021020000000000000000000000000000000023
20500252010000000000000000200000000000000000002300057110000110100111
```

```
20500261120602721600420201121000229800100021020000000000000000000000000000000007
2050026201000000000000000020000000000000000000010000251100001101000011
20500271120703521600320201120000229800100021020000000000000000000100000000000002
2050027201000000000000000000000000000000000000500010310000110000101
20500281120602721600320201021000129800100021020111010000000000000000000000000002
2050028201000000000000000000000000000000000001000025110000110000000
20500291110705121600210112210100119931100022020000000000000000000000000000000003
2050029201000000000000000000000000000000000001000025110000110100100
20500301110706721600320202110000109900110021020000000000000000000001000000000027
2050030201000000000000000000000000000000000027000671311111111100100
20500311110706721600210112210000309900100021020120100010000000000000000000000009
2050031201000000000000000000000000000000000001000025110000110000100
20500321110807721600320201231000229800100021020000000000000000000001000000000007
2050032201001000000104000000000000000000000001000025110000110001101
20500331110707821600320202111000609800120221030120100010000000100101100000000102
2050033201002006009320000000000000000000100000001020025511000011010101101
20500341130505621600320201121000119900100021020110100000000000100001000000000004
2050034201000000000000000000000000000000000100002510000010000010100
20500351120603121600420202131000409800100028020000000000000000000000000000000032
2050035201000000000000000000000000000000000320008010000010000100
20500361130603221600320202121001009900100021020000000000000000000000000000000003
2050036201000000000000000000000000000000000000500010300000100100001
20500371130604921600320202120000909900211040010000000000000000000001000000000030
2050037201000000100316200000000000000000000000450005033111111001111
30500011100506831600210102210000119930110021020000000001000000001010010000000003
3050001201000000999998000000000000000000000050001011000011110000
30500021100506541600210102210000019930100021020000000000000001010101000000000002
3050002201000000000000000000000000000000000000500010110000111100100
30500031100606631600320202111000019900100021020140101010000010100000000000000008
3050003201000000000000000000000001000000000001000025110000111100001
30500041100507511600320202021000219800100021020120100010000000000000000000000002
3050004201000000000000000000000000000000000000500010110000111100100
30500051100606221550210102210000019930100021020000000000000001000000000000000003
3050005201000000000000000000000000000000000000500010120001100100000
30500061100607021550210102230110410210100022010000000000000000000001000000000019
3050006201000000999998000000000000000000000000000190004811000011110000001
30500071110706221550210101210000519901000440020000000000000000000011100000000014
3050007201000000000000000000000000000000000014000351100001101000000
30500081100707320550210106230000010101210440020000000000000000000011000000000006
3050008201000000999998000000000000000000000001000025110000111100000
30500091100708441550310202111000029900000450010000000000000000000011000000000006
3050009201000000999998000000000000000000000001000025110000110000001
30500101100709521550210102210000429900100022020000000000000000000000000000000003
3050010201000000000000000000000000000000000001000025110000110100000
30500111100811241700430202023000029800000440020000000000000000000000000000000006
3050011201000000000000000000000000000000000001000025110000110000000
30500121090511711600320202111000119900200021030110010000000100110000001000000027
3050012201000000000000000000000001000000000002700068110000110000101
30500131090609811500210102210010040210100025020129999000000000000000000000000004
3050013202000000000000000000000000000000000001000020410000111111000
30500141100812131600210102210000029900100021020000000000000000000000000000000008
3050014201000000000000000000000000000000000001000025110000110100100
30500151090510411600321202012000219900100021021110100020000100000000101000000001
3050015201000000000000000000000000000000000000500010100000100000000
30500161090511311600220102210000119900110021020000000000000000000000000000000045
3050016201000000999998000000000000000000000000450011311000011000000
30500171090511311600220102210000019930110021020140110000000000000000000000000018
3050017201000000999998000000000000000000000000180004511000011110100
30500181080516011550320202112000029900000440020000000000000000000000000000000023
3050018201000000000000000000000000000000000000230005810100010000100
```

30500191090712-21550310102210010040100110022020000000001000000010100100000000000007
3050019201000000999998000000000000000000000000000100025131111111100000
305002010805156115503302020220003199001000210101101000000000000000000000000003
3050020201000000000000000000000000000000000000005000101100001101001000
305002110908148416503212021120002299000104400201201000000000000100011100000000003
3050021201000000999998000000000000000000000000005000100300011110000000
305002210805151116003312020220002199001100210200000000000000000000001000000000006
3050022201000000999998000000000000000000000000010000251100001110000000
305002310805153115503202021220000199401000210210000000000000000000000000000000005
3050023201000000000000000000000000000000000000010000251000001000000000
305002410806138115002101032100100402101100210200000000000000000000001000000000002
3050024201000000999998000000000000000000000000005000101100001111000000
305002510807148215003202021200003299001100210200000000000100000000001000000000018
3050025201000000999998000000000000000000000000018000451311111111000000
305002610706199115002101052400100401101000220201201000000000000100001000000000005
3050026201000000999998000000000000100000000000100002003000111110010100
305002710706189115002312020130001099001000217200000000010100000011010000000000146
30500272010000009999989999000100001100000001001460036511000011110010100
305002810708216115002201021100000299001000210201201100101000000000000001000000001
3050028201000000000000000000000000000000000000050001010000010000010000
305002910706213115002102032300100401101000220200000000000000000000000000000000001
3050029201000000999998000000000000000000000000005000101100001111001000
305003010606220114602312021120002099000102102000000000030100000111001000000000082
3050030201000000999998000000000000000100001000008200205130001111100001
305003110606222115002101032300100403101000220200000000000000000100011000000000006
3050031201000000999998000000000000000000000000010000251100001111001000 *
305003210606239115002101032300100499201000220201999990200000001011010000000000006
3050032201000000999998000000000000000000000000010000251100001111001000
305003310505259114503202020220001199201000210110000000000000000000001000000000001
3050033201000001000253000000000000000000000000005000101000001000000001
305003410505265314502101022330000199201000230211601000000000000000001000000000001
3050034201000000000000000000000000000000000000005000101000001000000001
305003510505260115002101022110000199001100230110000000000000000001010100100000000065
3050035201000005013933000000000000000200000000000330006600000010000000001
305003610506261114502212021120100402100900101909999999999999999999999999999999999
305003629999999999998999999999999999999999999999999999311011111000001
305003710506274114502101032100100404201000220201100100100000100000100000000000003
3050037201000000999998000000000000000000000000010000251311111101010001
305003810505272114502101032100100404201000220200000000100000000011001001000000009
3050038202000000999998000000000000000000000000150003511000011110010000
305003910405305314502101022100100499201100290200000000100000000000000110000000000001
3050039201000000999998000000000000000000000100005000101300011111001000
305004010406311115502201022100002099001000290200000000000000000011100000000000000003
3050040201000000999998000000000000100000000000500010110000111100001
305004110406310215003212022210012099001000210200000000000000000000001000000000003
3050041201000000999998000000000000000000000000005000101300011111100000
305004210304342114502101022100007099002000290210000000000000000000000000000000002
3050042201000000000000000000000000000000000000050001010000010000000000
305004310304350114502101022110003099002100230201199990000000000101111000001000051
3050043201000000999998000000000000000100000000005100128131111111110101
305004410405325115503212022110001299002000290200000000400000111100000010000000009
3050044201000000000000000000000000001000000000001000025130001111000001
305004510304368214502101122210004099301000210200000000000000000000000001000000023
3050045201000000000000000000000001000000000000230005812000110000000001
305004610304359215002101022100006099001000210100000000000000000000001000000000007
3050046201000000999998000000000000000000000000010000251000001001000000
305004710204392115502201021220002099001000210200000000000000001100000000000000019
3050047202000000000000000000000000000000000000023000581100001100000000
305004810204409214502201042300101099001000210200000000000000000000000000000000004
3050048202000000000000000000000000000000000000100002011000011000000001
305004910204411214502201062210102001001000210210000000000000000000000000000000006
3050049201000000000000000000000000000000000000010000251000001000000000
305005010906100115002101022100100402101000250210000000000000000000000000000000001
3050050201000000000000000000000000000000000000005000101000001000000000
305005111008120216003212020130000299000104400201101000000000000000001000000000076
3050051201000000999998000000000000000000000000007600190100000101100100
305005210708202216003202022120000299001100210200000000100000000001000000000077
3050052201000000999998000000000000000000000000080001981300011101000000
305005310203415214503201022100100099001000210200000000000000000000000000000000003
3050053201000000000000000000000000000000000000005000101100001101001010
305005410708194216503202022120000299001000210200000000000000000000001000000000049
3050054201000000999998000000000000000000000000049001231100001101000000
305005510807159215003202020120000299010000210200000000000000000000000000000000005
3050055201000000000000000000000000000000000000010000251200011000000000
305005610805154115503312020220001199001100210200000000000000000000111000000100011
3050056201000000999998000000000000000000000000011000281100001110000000
305005710908143316503212021120002299000004400200000000000000000100000000000000015
3050057201000000999998000000000000000000000000080001603000111110000000
305005810805165115503202021110000299001000210201101000000000000000000001000000019
3050058202000000000000000000000000000000000000023000581000001000001000
305005910806160115002101022100000499201000210201101000501000010000100000000000065
3050059201000000999998000000000000000000000000065001631100001111010000
305006010808183218005312021120000299001100210301201000000000100000001100000000016
3050060201000000999998000000000000000000010000016000401100001110011000
305006110808180217505312021120000299001000210300000000000000000000000000000000001
3050061201000000999998000000000000000010000000500010110000111100000
305006210706198115002101052400000401101000220200000000000000000000001000000000002
3050062201000000999998000000000000000000000000005000100000000101100001
305006310705179115002101022100000405201000210201199990001000000101100000000000002
3050063201000000999998000000000000000000000000005000101300011111001000
305006410906102215002101032300100401000110100201201000000000000000011110010299999
3050064201000000999998000000000000000000009999999999311111111101110
305006510404344215003102022110101299001000210200000000000000000000000000000000003
3050065201000000000000000000000000000000000000005000101000001000001000
006000111206000118003312021120000299001110211301711119797676111111911191118044200
0060001204000000999998116911011111010111111120020400330001111111111
206000111303107218506212010230009298002104410200000000000000010000010000000000002
2060001201000000000000000000000000000000000000050001030000010010001
206000211203105218506212010230009298000105400200000000000000000000001000000000001
2060002201000000000000000000000000000000000000050001030000010010001
206000311303103218006312010230009298002004402000000000000000000001000000000000003
2060003201000000000000000000000000000000000000010000251000001001010000
206000411303106218006312010230009298002005400200000000000000000000001000000000002
2060004201000000000000000000000000000000000000050001030000010010101
206000511303107218006312010230011298000004400200000000000000000000001000000000002
2060005201000000000000000000000000000000000000050001030000010010101
206000610303098218006212010230008298002005400200000000000000000000000000000000029
2060006201000000000000000000000000000000000000029000721000001001010000
206000711203114217505302041210000298401000210210000000000000000000000000000000001
2060007201000000000000000000000000000000000000050001030000010000001
206000811308100216003202122210001298401110210201401100800000011110110000000000347
2060008203005005002722000500000000000000000000034700086711000011110111
206000911308094216003201162220001298001000210200000000000000000000000000000000004
2060009201000000000000000000000000000000000000050001030000010000101
206001011308107216506520206121000129800100021020000000000000000000000000000000002
2060010201000000000000000000000000000000000000050001030000010000101
206001111308105216504202061210001298002004400200000000000000000000000000000000002
2060011201000000000000000000000000000000000000050001030000010000101
206001211406078216005302010230001298000004400201211010300001001000000000000000011
2060012201000000000000000000000000000000000000110002710000010010100

```
20600131140607321600320201112000109900100021030140110000000000011000100000000000115
2060013202000000000000000000000000000000000000000115002871300001110000000
206001411405082216003202011110001099001100212301401100300000110000100000000000091
20600142010000000000000000000000000000000000009100227120000110010101
20600151140508321650420202101000229800100021020000000000000000000000000000000000037
20600152010000000000000000000000000000000000037000921000001011000
20600161140508921600320102210000239401000210200000000000000000000000000000000000016
20600162010000000000000000000000000000000000001600040100000010010000
20600171110604421600420201122000129800100021020000000000000000000000000000000000002
20600172010000000000000000000000000000000000005000103000000010000101
20600181110604321600420201121000129800100021020000000000000000000000000000000000001
20600182010000000000000000000000000000000000005000103000000010000101
20600191110503321650620201023000329800000440020120100000000000000000000000000000001
20600192010000000000000000000000000000000000005000103000000010000101
20600201110505921650410201023000219870100021020110110000000000000010000000000000004
20600202010000000000000000000000000000000000001000025110000011010100
20600211110406221700520202112000119870100021020140000000000000000000000000000000001
20600212010000000000000000000000000000000000005000103000000010000101
20600221110406321700520202113000019800100021020190101000000000000000000000000000001
20600222010000000000000000000000000000000000005000103000000010010101
20600231110406721700621201023000229800100421020000000010000000000000000000000000001
20600232010000000000000000000000000000000000005000103000000010010001
20600241110407021750621201023000229800100441020000000010000000000000000000000000001
20600242010000000000000000000000000000000000005000103000000010010101
20600251120406621750621201023000529800100441020000000000000000000000000000000000001
20600252010000000000000000000000000000000000005000103000000010010101
20600261120504321650420202211000319900110021020140100000100000100001000000000000051
20600262010000000000000000000000000000000100000510012713000011111010100
20600271120504421650320202210000299001000210200000000100000000000000000000000000010
20600272010000000000000000000000000000000000001000025100000010010000
20600281120406721750631201023000629800000440020110110000000100100000000000000000001
20600282010000000000000000000000000000000000005000103000000010010101
20600291120407121950631201023000629800000440020000000000000000000000000000000000001
20600292010000000000000000000000000000000000005000103000000010000001
20600301120406121750621201122000429800000441020110110000000000000000000000000000001
20600302010000000000000000000000000000000000005000103000000010000101
20600311120408021750621201122000229800100021020000000000000000000000000000000000001
20600312010000000000000000000000000000000000005000103000000010010101
20600321120408521800621201023000629800000541020000000000000001100000000000000000001
20600322010000000000000000000000000000000000005000103000000010010101
20600331120503821650430201023000219800000440020000000000000000000000000000000000001
20600332010000000000000000000000000000000000005000103000000010010001
20600341120503521650420201023000219800100441020110100020000101100011100100000000189
20600342020000000000000000000000000000010000000001890047213000011101010101
20600351120406221650320202120000219900100021020120110010000000000000100000000000071
20600352010000000000000000000000000000000000007100177130010111110101
20600361120406221650320201122000119900100021020000000000000010000000100000000000008
20600362010000000000000000000000000000000000001000025120000110010001
20600371120406321650320111221100019900100021020110110000000000000000000000000000001
20600372010000000000000000000000000000000000005000103000000010010101
20600381130505421650320201111000129900100021020000000000000000000000000000000000003
20600382010000000000000000000000000000000000005000103000000010010001
20600391140410421700410201013000229800100021020000000000000000010000100000000000005
20600392010000000000000000000000000000000000001000025100000010010001
20600401140409121700521201012000129800100021030000000000000000001000110001000000024
20600402010000000000000000000000000000001000000000240006010000010010001
20600411140409421700420202220000299001000210200000000000000000000000000000000000004
20600412010000000000000000000000000000000000005000103000000010010001
20600421120501521600320206123000419900100021020110100000000000000000000000000000008
20600422010000000000000000000000000000000000001000025100000010010100
20600431120501421650420202032000319900210411020100100000000000100000000000000000006
20600432010000000000000000000000000000000000001000025100000010000100
20600441120501521650420202132000129800100021020000000000000000000000000000000000006
20600442010000000000000000000000000000000000001000025100000010010100
20600451120502621650320202122000119900100021020110100030000000100001000000000000037
20600452010000000000000000000000000000000000037000921200000011110101
20600461120501321650420201023000129900200040020140110000000100100011000100000000015
20600462020000000000000000000000000000000100000150003710000010010100
20600471120501621600320201022000129900100021020140100000000100000000000000000000003
20600472010000000000000000000000000000000000005000103000000010010101
20600481120501521600320201121000319900100021020120100020000100000000000000000000002
20600482010000000000000000000000000000000000001000025100000010000100
20600491120501721600320202112000319970100021020000000000000000000000000000000000002
20600492010000000000000000000000000000000000001000025100000010010100
20600501120502521650320202112000229900100021021000000000000000000000000000000000013
20600502020000000000000000000000000000000000001300032100000010000000
20600511120501321650420201022000519970200040020120100000000000000000100000000000001
20600512010000000000000000000000000000000000005000103000000010010101
20600521120501721600320201121000319900100021020140101000000000010000000000000000005
20600522010000000000000000000000000000000100000500010300000010110101
20600531130606521600320202121000309900100011020120100040000201100000000000000000133
20600532010000000000000000000000000000000000013300332120011110110100
20600541110503521650420201023000329800100002102011010000000000000000000000000000002
20600542010000000000000000000000000000000000005000103000000010010101
20600551110604021600520201123000529800100021020120010000000000100000000000000000004
20600552020000000000000000000000000000000100000251000000010010100
20600561110603821600420201023000529800100021020000000000000000000000000000000000004
20600562010000000000000000000000000000000000005000103000000010000101
20600571110603121600320202120100019900100021020000000000000000000000000000000000008
20600572010000000000000000000000000000000000001000025100000010010101
20600581110602921600330202112000319870100021020110100000000000000000000000000000011
20600582010000000000000000000000000000000001100027100000010010101
20600591110503221650521201023000429800100021020000000010000000000000000000000000003
20600592020000000000000000000000000000000000001000025100000010000100
20600601110503021650420201023000299002000300200000000000000000000000000000000000001
20600602010000000000000000000000000000000000005000103000000010000101
20600611110602721600420201123000229900100021020000000000000000000000000000000000002
20600612010000000000000000000000000000000000005000103000000010000101
20600621110502921650420201023000529800200040020000000000000000000000000000000000003
20600622010000000000000000000000000000000000005000103000000010000101
20600631110503021650420201023000429800100021020000000000000000000000000000000000003
20600632010000000000000000000000000000000000005000103000000010000101
20600641110502821600420201023000329900100021020120110010000000000000000000000000014
20600642010000000000000000000000000000000000014000351000000010000100
20600651110502621600320201023000129900100021020140110000000010000000000000000000072
20600652020000000000000000000000000000000000072001801200000011000100
20600661110502821600320201022000129900100021020140100000100000000000000000000000000
20600662010000000000000000000000000000000000005000103000000010010101
20600671120502221600320201111000119900100021020140110040000001000000000000000000126
20600672010000000000000000000000000000000126003151200000110010100
20600681120503121600320201022000219900100021020141100000000000000000000000000000017
20600682010000000000000000000000000000000000017000421000000010010100
20600691130708421650420201022000029900000440020110100010000000000000000000000000002
20600692010000000000000000000000000000000000005000103000000010010101
20600701130708721650420202110000229800100022020000000010000000100000000000000000002
20600702010000000000000000000000000000000000005000103000000010010101
20600711130707621650420201013000119800100021020140110030000100000000000000000000006
20600712010000000000000000000000000000000000001000025100000010010100
20600721130707121650520201023000219800000410020000000000000000000000000000000000001
20600722010000000000000000000000000000000000005000103000000010010101
```

```
20600731130707221600420201023000119800000410020190100010000000000000000000000002
20600732010000000000000000000000000000000000000500010300000010010101
20600741130707021650520201023000119800000440020000000000000000000000000000000008
20600742010000000000000000000000000000000000010000251000000100010100
20600751130809321600420201022000129800100021020000000000000000000000000000000005
20600752010000000000000000000000000000000000010000251000000010010100
20600761130707721600420201021000119800100021020000000000000000000000000000000002
20600762010000000000000000000000000000000000500010300000010010101
20600771140709821750520201022000298000004400201900100100000000000000000000000001
20600772010000000000000000000000000000000000500010300000010000101
20600781130810221600410201021000029800200440020110010020000000100000000000000003
20600782010000000000000000000000000000000000010000251000000010000100
20600791130810921650420112222000029800100021030000000000000000100000000000000003
20600792010000000000000000000000000000000000010000251000100010000101
20600801130810421600420201111000129870100021020000000000000000000000010000000001
20600802010000000000000000000000000000000000500010320100110000001
20600811130810621650420201022000129800200430021000000000000000100001000000000001
20600812010000000000000000000000000000000000500010300000010000001
20600821130810721650420201121000229800210440020000000000000000000000100000000001
20600822010000010001160000000000000000000000000500010300000010000101
20600831130810921650420201023000229800200441021000000000000000000000000000000003
20600832010000000000000000000000000000000000500010300000010000001
20600841130811121650410201021000329800210441020000000000000000000000100000000006
20600842010000010010970000000000000000000000010000251000000010000100
20600851130810821600420201022000129800200441620000000000000000100001000000000006
20600852020000000000000000000000000000000000010000251000000010000101
20600861140813421750521201023000129800200440020120100000000010010010000000000005
20600862010000000000000000000000000000000000010000251000000010000101
20600871130812321700420202111000029800110021020000000000000000000000100000000020
20600872050000020015030000000000000000000000020000501000000100010100
20600881130913321700420201021000129800100021021000000000000000000000000000000002
20600882010000000000000000000000000000000000500010300000010000001
20600891130913121700420201022000029800100021020000000000000000000000000000000002
20600892010000000000000000000000000000000000500010300000010000101
20600901130812621650420112211000029940110021020000000000000000000000100000000042
20600902010000020008380000000000000000000000004200105110000011100100
20600911130810321600420101221000029800200440020000000000000000000000000000000001
20600912010000000000000000000000000000000000500010300000010000101
20600921140812822000631201023000129800000440021000000000000000000000000000000004
20600922010000000000000000000000000000000000010000251000000010000000
20600931130812321650420202122000229900100021020000000000000000000000000000000001
20600932010000000000000000000000000000000000500010300000010000101
20600941120810221700420202111000819800100021020000000000000000000000100000000014
20600942020000000000000000010000000000000000014000351200000110000001
20600951120809821600320202130000213900000440020000000000000000000000100000000002
20600952010000000000000000000000000000000000010000251000000010001100
20600961120809521600320202130000219901100021020000000000000000000000100000000001
20600962010000000000000000000000000000000000500010300000010001101
20600971120808521600310111110000719800010240020000000000000000000000110000000001
20600972010000000000000000000000000000000000500010300000010001101
20600981120808121600310111110000719900110241020000000000000000000000110000000004
20600982010000000000000000000000000000000000100010000251200001100001
20600991110605321600320201122000429800100021020000000000000000000000000000000007
20600992010000000000000000000000000000000000010000251000000010010100
20601001120501121650320201023000619800100021020141110000000001000100001000000023
20601002020000000000000000000000000000000000023000571200001100010101
20601011120601221600320201023000619800200020020114011000000000000000100000000078
20601012020000000000000000000000000000000000078001951100000111110100
20601021110501621600320201023000219800100040020000000000000000000000000000000006
20601022010000000000000000000000000000000000010000251000000010010100
20601031110601821600320201123000319800100021020000000000000000000000000000000015
20601032010000000000000000000000000000000000150003710000010000100
20601041110602321600320201123000219800100021020000000000000000000000000000000004
20601042010000000000000000000000000000000000010000251000000010000100
20601051110602221600320201023000219800100021020000000000000000000000000000000001
20601052010000000000000000000000000000000000500010300000010000101
20601061110602921600220201122000519800100021020000000000000000000000000000000002
20601062010000000000000000000000000000000000500010300000010000101
20601071110602421600320201122000519800100021020000000000000000000000000000000025
20601072010000000000000000000000000000000000250006210000010010100
20601081110602321600420201023000129800100021020000000000000000000000000000000040
20601082010000000000000000000000000000000000400010010000010000100
20601091120602221600420201122000129800110021020111010000000000010000110000000457
20601092050000000000000000010000000000000000457011421200001101000111
20601101120602021600420201122000029800100021020000000000000000000000100000000013
20601102030000000000000000000000000000000000013000321000000010010100
20601111120602421600420201120000029800100021020000000000000000000000000000000007
20601112010000000000000000000000000000000000010000251000000010010100
20601121120602921600420201121000029800100021020000000000000000000000100000000023
20601122010000010001310000000000000000000000023000571000000010110100
20601131120602221600420201123000229800200100210000000000000000000000100000000001
20601132010000019999990000000000000000000000500010300000010000001
20601141120703421600430201023000429800000040020000000000000000000000100000000005
20601142000000000000000000000000000000000000500010300000010010001
20601151120703821600320202121000309870110021020000000000000000000000100000000220
20601152010000010007880000000000000000000000022000550110000011010100
20601161110603021600320202220000229800110021020000000000000000000000100000000011
20601162030010000003080000000000000000000000011000271000000010000100
20601171120603621600310202120000129800110021020000000000000000001001110010000041
20601172010010030057920000000000000000000000000410010212000011000100
20601181110704021600320202220000209800200010020000000000000000000000000000000003
20601182010000000000000000000000000000000000010000251000000010000100
20601191110703921600320202120000129800000440020000000000000000000000000000000015
20601192010000000000000000000000000000000000150003710000010100100
20601201110604021600320202220000129800100021020000000000000000000000000000000004
20601202010000000000000000000000000000000000010000251000000010010000
20601211120601021650430201023000819800000440020000000000000000000000000000000002
20601212010000000000000000000000000000000000500010300000010000101
20601221110705121600210112210100129801111021020000000000000000000000100000000054
20601222020000000000000000000000000000000000054001351300001111100100
20601231110706221600210112210100229831100021021000000000000000000000000000000004
20601232010000000000000000000000000000000000010000251000000010000000
20601241110707121600210106210101009831200421021000000000000000000000000000000003
20601242010000000000000000000000000000000000010000251000000010000000
20601251110605421600320201220000029800100021020000000000000000000000000000000002
20601252010000000000000000000000000000000000010000251000000010000100
20601261110604421600310202220000019800100021021000000000000000000000000000000002
20601262010000000000000000000000000000000000010000251000000010000000
20601271110604721600210102210000319830100022020000000000000000000000000000000004
20601272010000000000000000000000000000000000010000251000000010000100
20601281110706821600320201110000129800110021020000000200000000000000100000000114
20601282010010050028650000000000000000000000114002851311111111100101
20601291110706821600310212210000309800110021020120100010000000000000100000000053
20601292010000010002330000000000000000000000053001321300001110001101
20601301120808221600430201012000229800200440020000000000000000000000000000000003
20601302010000000000000000000000000000000000500010300000010000101
20601311110807721600320201112000129800100021020000000000000000000000000000000008
20601312010000000000000000000000000000000000010000251000000010100100
20601321110808021600420201013000129800200441020000000000000000000000000000000003
20601322010000000000000000000000000000000000500010300000010000101
```

20601331110808221600420201012000129800200441020000000000000000000000000000000003
20601332010000000000000000000000000000000000000500010300000010000101
20601341110807621600320202111000229800100021021000000000000000000000000000000002
20601342010000000000000000000000000000000000000050001030000010000001
20601351110807721600320202111000229800110021020000000000000000000001000000000048
20601352010010000001040000000000000000000000004800120120000110001100
20601361110707821600320112212000029800100021020000000000000000000000000000000017
20601362030000000000000000000000000000000000000170004210000010000100
20601371110708021650320202111100129800100021420000000000000010000000000000000003
20601372010000000000000000000000000000000000000500010300000010001001
20601381110808321650320202112000298701104410301101000100000000100001000000000128
20601382020000020009800000000000000000000000012800320110000011001100
20601391110708021650220202111000609800010241030120100010000000100111100000000227
20601392010000090095300000000000000000100000022700567120000110101100
20601401110708321650320201112000229800000240020000000000000000000000000000000002
20601402010000000000000000000000000000000000000500010300000010000001
20601411110708621650320201112000129800000240021000000000000000000000000000000002
20601412010000000000000000000000000000000000000500010300000010000001
20601421130604821600320202121000029800111021020110100000100000000011000000000317
20601422010020020043840000000000000000000000031700792121111110111110
20601431130605021600320201121000239800100021021000000000000000000000000000000003
20601432010000000000000000000000000000000000000500010300000010000001
20601441130605721600310201121000309800100021020000000000000000000000000000000007
20601442010000000000000000000000000000000000010000251000000010010100
20601451130605321600420202101000129800000440020000000000000000000001000000000009
20601452010010000000390000000000000000000000001000025100000010010100
20601461130606121650531202033000129800200440020000000000000001000000000000000112
20601462010000000200000000000000000000000000011200280100000010010001
20601471130505521650320201122000119800100021020000000000000000000001000000000002
20601472010000000000000000000000000000000000000500010300000010010001
20601481130506221650421202033000229800200440021000000000000000000001000000000009
20601482020000000000000000000000000000000000010000251000000010000001
20601491130603421600320202111000129800200028021000000000000000000000000000000003
20601492010000000000000000000000000000000000000500010300000010000001
20601501130603121650421202112000129800100021021000000000000000000000000000000029
20601502010000000000000000000000000000000000000290007210000010000000
20601511120602721600420201023000129800200410021000000000000000000000000000000027
20601512010000000000000000000000000000000000002700067100000010000000
20601521120603221600320202122000298002004400201401000000000000000001000000000099
20601522010010020009230000000000000000000000009900247100000010100100
20601531110602621600320201121000719800100021020000000000000000000000000000000020
20601532010000000000000000000000000000000000002000050100000010000100
20601541120603121600320202121000129800100021020000000000000000000000000000000002
20601542010000000000000000000000000000000000000500010300000010000101
30600011110407541700531202121000129800100021020000000000000000000000000000000010
30600012020000000000000000000000000000000000001000025100000010010100
30600021110505531650320202111000019900100021020000000000000000000000000000000008
30600022010000000000000000000000000000000000001000025100000010010100
30600031110505831600210102210000199301000210201201000000000000000000000000000001
30600032010000000000000000000000000000000000000500010100000010100100
30600041100506041600210102210000119930100021020000000000000000000000000000000003
30600042010000000000000000000000000000000000000500010110000011000100
30600051100506531600210102210000199301110210301100109801010101001100000000000108
30600052010000003999960000000000010000010000010800270130000111100101
30600061100507411600320202021000219800100021020120100100000000000000000000000033
30600062010000000000000000000000000000000000000003300083120000111100100
30600071100507931600310202122000298601000290201100100100000001000000000000000008
30600072010000000000000000000000000000000000001000025100000010000100
30600081100606311550210102210000199301000210200000000000000000001100000000000053
30600082010000009999980000000000000000000000005300133110000011110101
30600091100608321550210102110000919900100021020000000000000000001000000000000001
30600092010000000000000000000000000000000000000500010100000010001100
30600101100605821550210102220000719930100021020000000000000000000000000000000006
30600102010000000000000000000000000000000000001000025100000010010100
30600111100605821550320202121000149930100021020000000001010000000001000000000001
30600112010000000000000000000000000000000000000500010100000010010000
30600121100606921550210101210000510500100021020000000000000000000000000000000003
30600122010000000000000000000000000000000000000500010100000010110000
30600131100607321006210102230110010210100022010199999030100100000010000000000007
30600132020000009999980000000000000000000000001500030100000010110101
30600141100607021550210102230110410210100022010000000000000000001000000000000035
30600142010000009999980000000000000000000000000350088130000111100001
30600151050329741650330202023000019900100021021000000000000000000000000000000001
30600152010000000000000000000000000000000000000500010100000010000000
30600161100606221550310202021010029900100021020000000000000009999000000000000004
30600162020000000000000000000000100100000000010000201000000010100101
30600171100606121550310202021010129900100021020000000000000009999000000000000001
30600172010000000000000000000000100100000000000500010100000010110001
30600181100605921550310202021010129900100021020000000000000009999000000000000003
30600182010000000000000000000000100100000000000500010100000010110101
30600191100605921550310202021010029900100021020000000802000099999010000000000030
30600192010000000000000000000000100100000000003000075110000011100101
30600201110706221550210101210000519901000440020000000000000000001110000000000014
30600202010000000000000000000000000000000000001400035120000110100000
30600211100707221540210106230000010101210440020000000000000000001100000000000018
30600212020000009999800000000000000000000000002300058130000111100000
30600221100708441550310202111000299000004500100000000000000000001100000000000007
30600222020000009999080000000000000000000000001500035120000110000001
30600231100708521550321202022000299000004400200000000000000000000000000000000003
30600232010000000000000000000000000000000000000500010100000010001000
30600241100708521550321202022000299000004400200000000000000000000000000000000005
30600242010000000000000000000000010000000000010000251000000010001001
30600251100709521550210102210000429900100022020000000000000000000000000000000006
30600252010000000000000000000000000000000000001000025120000110100000
30600261100811721650320202012000029900000440020000000000000000000000000000000016
30600262010000000000000000000000000000000000008001600000000010000100
30600271100812421600421202023000029900000440020000000000000000001000000000000037
30600272010000009999980000000000000000000000037000931000000010100100
30600281100811621650320202012000029900000440010000000000000000000000000000000001
30600282010000000000000000000000000000000000000500010100000010000100
30600291100812121600310202210000299001000210200000000000000000000000000000000005
30600292010000000000000000000000000000000000000500010000000010000100
30600301100811241700430202023000029800000440020000000000000000000000000000000006
30600302010000000000000000000000000000000000001000025120000110000000
30600311100608011550210103210000319920100022021000000000000000000000000000000006
30600312010000000000000000000000000000000000010000251000000010000000
30600321100609111550210103210010040310100021020110001010000000010000000000000011
30600322010000009999980000000000000000000000011000281000000010111100
30600331090609811500210102210010040210100025020149919030000010111001000000000032
30600332030000009999980000000000000000000000003800090130000011111100
30600341100709831550210102210005099301000210200000000000000000001000000000000008
30600342010000009999980000000000000000000000010000251100000011100000
30600351100812121600210102210000299001000210200000000000000000000000000000000039
30600352010000000000000000000000000000000000003900098120000110100100
30600361100812021600210102210000299001000210200000000000000000000000000000000019
30600362010000000000000000000000000000000000001900048100000010000100
30600371090813731600321202013000029900000440020000000000000000000000000000000004
30600372010000000000000000000000000000000000000500010000000010000100
30600381090813431600321202013000023900000440020000000000000000000000000000000004
30600382010000000000000000000000000000000000000500010000000010000100

```
30600391100811841550210102210000029900100021021000000000000000000000000000000009
3060039201000000000000000000000000000000003010000251000000100000000
30600401090814141650320202012000029900000440011000000000000000000000000000000013
3060040201000000000000000000000000000000000700014000000010000000
30600411090814441700320202012000029900000440020000000000000000000000000000000007
3060041201000000000000000000000000000000000500010000000001010000
30600421090511311600220102210000119900110021020000000000000000000000000000000045
3060042201000000099999800000000000000000000004500113120001100000
30600431090511311600220102210000019930110021020140110000000000000000000000000103
306004320100000099999800000000000000000001001030025813000011100100
30600441090612211500220106240010040110100021020000000000000000001001000000000003
306004420100000000000000000000000000000000005000101100000011110100
30600451090611521500210103210010040110100021021000000000000000000000000000000002
306004520100000000000000000000000000000000005000101000000010000000
30600461090713221500310202110000129900100021020120100050000000011101100000000015
306004620100000009999980000000000000000000000150003810111010100100
30600471090712621550310102210010040100110022020110110110000000011100110000100074
306004720100000099999800000000000000000000000780011313111111100100
30600481090814341650321202112000022990001044002017011001000000010011100000000341
306004820300000099999800000000000000000000001750035003000111100100
30600491090814141650320202012000129900000240021000000000000000000000000000000003
306004920100000000000000000000000000000000000500010000000010000000
30600501090815041650321202013000029900000440020110010000000000100010000000000008
306005020100000000000000000000000000000000001000025100000010010100
30600511080515011600331202122000019940110021020110100010000000000011100000100337
306005120700000300407300000000000001000000000034800863130000111100101
30600521080614011500210103210010040210110021020110010000100101110111000000000054
306005220100000099999800000000000000000000000540013513000011110000
30600531090612911500210102210000229900100023020000000002000000010100100000000013
306005320100000099999800000000000000000000001300033110000011110000
30600541080614221500210102210110040210100021020000000000000000010000000000000003
306005420100000099999800000000000000000000005000101000000010100100
30600551080715321500210105240010310330100022021000000000000000000000000000000012
306005520100000000000000000000000000000000001200030100000010000000
30600561090714821500320202120000329900110021020000000000010000000000100000000025
306005620100000099999800000000000000000000002500063131111111100000
30600571090714921500320202120000329900100021020000000000010000010100100000000002
306005720100000099999800000000000000000000005000101000000101010010
30600581080715021500320202122000229900100021020000000000000000000000000000000002
306005820100000000000000000000000000000000005000101000000010100000
30600591080715421500430202122000429900100021020000000000000000000000000000000004
306005920100000000000000000000000000000000010000251000000010100100
30600601080716421550320202012000029900100021020110010000000000000001000000000036
306006020200000099999800000000000000000000040000981000000010100100
30600611080716221550320202012000029900100021020000000000000000000000000000000008
306006120100000000000000000000000000000000010000251000000010000100
30600621080816121550320202111000029900100021020000000000000000000000000000000002
306006220100000000000000000000000000000000005000101000000010100100
30600631080816721650521202013000029900000440021000000000000000000001000000000035
306006320200100200303000000000000000000000035000881000000010100000
30600641080517211500210102220000019900100021021110100020000000000000000000000105
306006420500000000000000000000000000000000095002283100000011100100
30600651080517311500210102220000119900100021021000000000000000000000000000000020
306006520100000000000000000000000000000000020000501000000010000000
30600661080616111500210102210000049920100021020000000101000000100010000000000023
306006620100000099999800000000000000000000002300058120000110100000
30600671080717511500320202111000029900100021020000000000000000000000000000000003
306006720100000000000000000000000000000000005000101000000011000000
30600681080716821500331202012010609900100021020000000000000000000000000000000174
30600682010000000000099900000000000000000000017400435100000010100100

30600691080716321500331202012010609900100021020000000000000000000000000000000178
30600692010000099999899990000000000000000000017800445100000010100100
30600701080717521500320202111000029900100021020000000000000000000100000000000023
306007020100000099999800000000000000000000002300058110000011100100
30600711080716721650430202122000429900100021020000000000000000000000000000000001
306007120100000000000000000000000000000000005000101000000010100000
30600721080818121800531202112000029900100021020000000000000000000000000000000007
306007220200000000000000000000000000000000015000351100000011000100
30600731080817821750531202112000029900110021030120100000000100000001100000000168
306007320400000099999800000000000000000010000172004291300001111101100
30600741080818921700430202012000129900100021021000000000000000000000000000000002
306007420100000000000000000000000000000000005000101000000010000000
30600751080819021650320202112000129900100021021000000000000000000000000000000004
306007520100000000000000000000000000000000010000251000000010000000
30600761080919921650421202131000119900100021020000000000000000000000000000000011
306007620100000000000000000000000000000000011000281000000010100100
30600771070418811700321202122000319900110021020000000020000100000000100000100048
306007720100000099999800000000000000000000004800120110000011100100
30600781070518011500210102210000040520100021020119999000100000001011000000000023
306007820100000099999800000000000000000000002300058130001111100100
30600791070618411500210104240000040210100022020000000000000000101101100000000012
306007920100000099999800000000000000000000006000120100000011100101
30600801070619811500210105240000040110100022020000000000000000000010000000000003
306008020100000099999800000000000000000000005000100000000010000101
30600811070619911500210105240010040110100022020000000001000000011001000000000004
306008120100000099999800000000000000000000005000100000000010100001
30600821070619911500210105240010040110100022020120100000000000100001000000000005
306008220100000099999800000000000010000000000100002023000111100101
30600831070618911500231202013000109900100021720000000010100001101000000000000146
306008320100000099999899990001000011000000100146003651200001111100101
30600841070820221600320202121000029900100021020000000000000000000000000000000003
306008420100000000000000000000000000000000005000101000000010100000
30600851070820021600320202212000029900110021020000000001000000000001000000000497
306008520200000099999800000000000000000000004990124512000111010000
30600861070819621550320202212000129900100021020000000000000000000000000000000002
306008620100000000000000000000000000000000005000101000000010100000
30600871070820421500220106210000029900100021021000000000000000000000000000000002
306008720100000000000000000000000000000000005000101000000010000000
30600881070821511500220102111000029900100021020000000001000100000101000000000009
306008820100000000000000000000000000000000010000251000000010000100
30600891070820421650430202912000429900100021021000000000000000000000000000000003
306008920100000000000000000000000000000000005000101000000010000000
30600901060621311500210203230010040110100022020110010000000000001001000000000063
306009020100000099999800000000000000000000006300158130000111100101
30600911060622011450231202112000209900010210200000000030100000111101000000000196
306009120100000099999800000000000100001000019600490130001111100001
30600921070824021500320202012000029900100023020000000000000000000001000000000021
306009220100000099999800000000000000000000002100053110000011100000
30600931070824221500320202012000029900100023020000000000000000000001000000000007
306009320100000000000000000000000000000000010000251000000010100000
30600941060924121600310202112000029909000021020000000000100000000000000000000001
306009420100000000000000000000000000000000005000101000000010100100
30600951060925421500320202112000029909000290200000000000000000000000000000000001
306009520100000000000000000000000000000000005000101000000010001000
30600961060524511600320202022000029900100021021000000000000000000000000000000001
306009620100000000000000000000000000000000005000101000000010000000
30600971060622311500210103230010040310100022020000000000000000010001100000000006
306009720100000099999800000000000000000000010000251300001111100100
30600981060623911500210103230010049920100022020199999020000000101101000000000006
306009820100000099999800000000000000000000010000251300001111100100
```

```
3060099106062381145021010221000100990010002202000000001000000010000100000000000004
306009920100000099999800000000000001000000000100002011000011100001
3060100105062611145022120211201004021003001019099999999999999999999999999999999
306010029999999999999999999999999999999999999999930001111100001
3060101105033054155032120221200021994012002402014011001000000000000011000000000004
306010120100000099999800000000600000000000000010000251000000010100000
306010210503287419506412021220002299002004400200000000000000010000001000000000016
3060102201000000999998000000000000000000000000160004011000011000100
3060103105042983205064120201200992990000440021000000000000000000000010000000000002
30601032010000010002080003000000000000000000000500010100000010000000
30601041050428912100641202112000229900010440020000000000000000000000011100003000082
3060104201000000999998999900000000000000000000082002051000000010000101
306010510504293115003212021120000299001000210200000000010000000000011000000000044
306010520100000099999800000000000000000000000004400110100000010100001
306010610504285115504212020230000299401000210200000000000000000000000000000000004
30601062020000000000000000000000000000000000010000201000000010000100
30601071050529511450210103230010040110100021020000000003000000011110100000000000044
30601072010000009999980000000000000100000000000044001101100000011100101
306010810405300114502101022100100401101000210200000000000000000011110100000000000025
30601082010000000999998000000000000000000001000300007511000001111 0001
3060109105062771145021010321001004042010002202011001002000000100000110000000000008
306010920200000099999800000000000000000000000000001000025222111110111001
30601101050627111450210104240000040420100022021000000000000000010000100000000000006
3060110201000000000000000000000000000000000001500030100000010000000
306011110506271114502101032100100404201000220201100100100000010101000000000000005
306011120100000000000000000000000000000000010000251100000011000001
306011210505272114502101032100100404201000220201100100400000001111010010000000024
306011220100000099999800000000000000000000000000026000651300000111100100
306011310505269114502101022100002499001000210210000000010000000100000001000000004
306011320100000000000000000000000000000000001000025100000010000000
306011410505269114502101022100001499001000210210000000000000000000000001000000000008
306011420100000000000000000000000000000000001000025100000010000000
30601151050627311450231202012000209900200021010140110000000000101001000000000000001
30601152010000009999980000000000000000000000005000101000000010100101
3060116104033224160032120221100002994010002402000000000000000000000000000000000001
306011620100000000000000000000000000000000005000101000000010100000
3060117104033113170054120202300032990000024002100000000000000000000000000000000000001
306011720100000000000000000000000000000000000500010100000010000000
306011810403318415503402020130003199001000210200000000101000000001001000000000000021
30601182010000000000000010000000001100000000002100053100000010100101
306011910404334415002101022100002199301200240200000000010000000101001000000000008
30601192010000009999980000000000000000000000001000025100000010100000
306012010404335315002101021110003199301000240200000000100000000001100000000000002
306012020100000000000000000000000000000000000500010100000010100100
30601211040431631500430202112000023940100024020000000000000000000000001000000000000003
3060121202000000999998000000000000000000000000010000201000000010100100
306012210405305314502101022100100499201100290100000000010000000000000011000000000001
30601222010000009999980000000000000000000000010000500010130001111100100
306012310406311115502201022100002039001000290200000000000000000000111000000000000003
306012320100000099999800000000000001000000000000500010130000111100001
306012410406319215503212022210014099001000210200000000000000000009999010000000000002
306012420100000099999800000000000000100000000005000101000000101100001
306012510406310215003212022210012099001000210200000000000000000000000001000000000003
3060125201000000999998000000000000000000000000000500010130001111110000
306012610406310215003212022210012099001000210200000000000000000000000000000000000002
306012620100000000000000000000000000000000000500010100000010110000
30601271040433111500231202012000129900110021020120100000000000101001000000000000010
306012720100000099999800000000000000000000000010000251000000010000101
306012810404335115002201042100000510330100021021000000000000000000000000000000000008
30601282010000000000000000000000000000000000001000025100000010000000
```

```
306012910304346114502101022100006099301000210200000000000000000000000000000000000006
3060129202000000000000000000000000000000000001000020100000010100000
3060130103043501145021010221100030990021002302011999900000000010101100000000100011
3060130201000000999998000000000000000000000000000000110000281311111111100000
306013110304354114002101022110000099002100210200000000000000000000000000000000000002
30601312010000000000000000000000000000000000005000101000000010100000
306013210405325115503212022110001299002100290200000000040000111110001001000000018
30601322010000009999980000000000000100000000001800045130001111000001
3060133103033822155042120212100011990010002101000000000000000000000000000000000000006
30601332010000000000000000000000000000000000001000025100000010100000
3060134103033802155042020201200002990010002102100000000000000000000000000000000000001
306013420100000000000000000000000000000000005000101000000010000000
306013510304362214502201022100005099001000210201100100100000000000001000000000000011
306013520100000000000000000000000000000000011000281000000010100100
306013610304350114502101022110000099002100230200000000000000000000000000000000000010
306013620100000000000000000000000000000000100010000251000000010100000
30601371020339821650530202012000029900100021020000000000000000000000000000000000000002
306013720100000000800000000000000000000000000005000101000000010000100
3060138102033962155042020202200012990010002102000000000000000000000000000000000000002
30601382010000000000000000000000000000000000500010100000010000100
306013910204387214503202021220000299001000210210000000000000000000000000000000000011
306013920100000000000000000000000000000000001100028100000010000000
306014010204393214502101062100000299001000240200000000000000000000000000000000000012
3060140201000000000000000000000000000000000012000301000000010100100
306014110204396214502101062100001099301000210200000000000000000000000000000000000003
30601412010000000000000000000000000000000000005000101000000010100000
306014210204396214502101062100001099301000210200000000000000000000000000000000000003
306014220100000000000000000000000000000000005000101100000011100100
306014310204392115502201021220002099001000210200000000000000000000110000000000000019
30601432020000000000000000000000000000000002300058120000110000000
3060144101034272170053120201200012990010002102000000000000000000000000000000000000002
30601442010000000000000200000000000000000000500010100000010100100
306014510204409214502201042300101099001000210200000000000000000000000000000000000004
3060145202000000000000000000000000000000000001000020120000110000001
306014610204415214503201022100100099001000210200000000000000000000000000000000000001
30601462020000000000000000000000000000000005000101200001101000101
3060147102054072145032020211201041990012002102000000000000000000001100000100019
306014720100000099999800000000000000000000000190004811000001110000
306014810104439214502101042300002099001000210200000000000000000000000000000000000001
30601482010000000000000000000000000000000000500010100000010000100
30601491100506841600210102211000129930110021020110010980000000001001100000000000001
3060149201000000999998000000000000000000000000500010110000011100000
306015011008122216003212020120000299000004400201401000000000000000000000000000000013
30601502010000000000000000000000000000000000001300033100000010000100
306015110905117116003202021110001199002000210301100100000000100110000000100000001
306015120100000000000000000000000000000000000500010120000110000100
306015210906102215002101032300100401000110100201201000000000000000011110010299999
306015220100000099999800000000000000000000000999999999931111111110111
00700011120600011800331202112000029900111021130171111979767611111191119111804160
0070001203000000999998103011011111010111111096501930033000011111111
20700011130801021600320202121000229800100021030140110020000000011110100000000000001
207000120100000000000000000000000000000000000500010330000011201100
20700021140607021600320201112000109800100021020000000000000000010000000000000000002
207000220100000000000000000000000000000000000500010320000111000001
20700031140607621600320102210000109900100021020000000000000000000000000000000000003
207000320100000000000000000000000000000000001000025100000001010100
207000411105057216504202011230002198701100210200000000000000000000000010000010000001
2070004201000000000000000000000000000000000500010320000011010101
20700051110505721650420202122000119870110021020000000000000000000000000000000000008
2070005201000000000000000000000000000000000001000025100000001010100
```

```
20700061120504321650420202211000313800110021020140100010100000100001000000000013
2070006201000000000000000000000000000000010000130003213000011111010
20700071120503421650310201110000219800100021030110100200001011000000000000000001
2070007201000000000000000000000000000000000000100002512000011110101
20700081120405221650420201110000129800100021020110100000100100000010000100000002
2070008201000000000000000000000000000000000000500010300000001010101
20700091120406221650320201120000219800110021020120110010000000001000000000000005
2070009201000000000000000000000000000000000000100002513001111110101
20700101120502721600420201122000319800100021020000000001000001000000000000000002
2070010201000000000000000000000000000000000000500010320000011010001
20700111110502621600320201022000419800100021020140110000000000100000000000000002
2070011201000000000000000000000000000000000000500010320000011000101
20700121130812521650410112210000129800110021020000000000000000000000000000000006
2070012201000000000000000000000000000000000000100002513000011100100
20700131120601121650420201023000819800200040030000000000000000000000000000000002
2070013201000000000000000000000000000000000000100002513000011100100
20700141120703721600320202121000229800100021020000000000000000000000000000000001
2070014201000000000000000000000000000000000000500010320000011000001
20700151110705221600210112210100519800111021020000000000000000000001000000000036
2070015201000000000000000000000000000000000000360009011000001100101
20700161110705221600210112210100329801111021020000000000000000000000000000000024
2070016201000000000000000000000000000000000000240006013000011100001
20700171110706521600320201110000109900110021020000000000000000000000000000000008
2070017201000000000000000000000000000000000000100002513111111100100
20700181110706721600320112210000409800100021030120100010000000000001000000000003
2070018201000000000000000000000000000000000000500010320000111000001
20700191110808221650320202110000129800110021020110100000000000100001000000000009
2070019201000002000980000000000000000000000000100002512000011000100
20700201110808421600320201023000129800100021030000000000000000100000000000000008
2070020201000000000000000000000000000000000000100002512000011001100
20700211130505021600320201122000219800110021020000000000000000000000011100000000001
2070021201000001000381000000000000000000000000500010310000001110000
20700221130602721600420201123000129800200440020000000000000000001000000000000033
2070022202000000000000000000000000000000000000330008211000001100100
20700231120703821600330201122000309800200441020000000000000000000000000000000038
2070023201000000000000000000000000000000000000380009512000011010000
30700011100505941600210102210000119930100021020120100000100000000000000000000002
3070001202000000999998000000000000000000000000100002013000011110100
30700021100506831600210102210000319900100021020110010000000100101000100000000001
3070002201000000999998000000000000000000000000500010110000001110000
30700031100506531600210102210000019930111021030140110980101010101001100000100168
3070003201000000999998000000000000000100001000016800420130000111101101
30700041100506341600210102211000129930110021020110010980000000001001100000000001
3070004201000000999998000000000000000000000000500010130000011100000
30700051100506831600210102210000129930100021020000000000000000000000000000000001
3070005201000000000000000000000000000000000000500010110000001100000
30700061100507411600320202021000219800100021020120100100000000000000000000000031
3070006201000000000000000000000000000000000000310007813000011100100
30700071100606311550210102210000019930100021020000000000000000000000110000000053
3070007201000000999998000000000000000000000000530013313000011110100
30700081110605721550320202121000149930100021020110010000000000000000000000000017
3070008201000000000000000000000000000000000000170004310000001010100
30700091100607121550210102210010110230110022020000000000000000000000110000000010
3070009202000000999998000000000000000000000000150003513000011101000
30700101100607021550210102230110410210100022010000000000000000000000100000000013
3070010201000000999998000000000000000000000000130003313000011100001
30700111100606021550310202021010029900100021020000000000501000000000000000000002
3070011201000000000000000000000100100000000000500010110000011100101
30700121100707321550210106230000010101210440020000000000000000000000110000000006
3070012201000000999998000000000000000000000000100002513000011100000
```

```
30700131100809421650321202022000029900000440020000000000000000000000000000000003
3070013201000000999993000000000000000000000000100002010000001001000
30700141090510631600320202020000229900200023020110110000000000100000000000000002
3070014201000000000000000000000000000000000000500010110000001100100
30700151090610111500210102210010040210100025020149919030000010111001000000000028
3070015201000000999998000000000000000000000000280007013000011100100
30700161090609811500210102210010040210100025020129999000000000000000000000000002
3070016201000000000000000000000000000000000000500010130000111100000
30700171090610411500210102210010040210100025020110100000000001100000000000000001
3070017201000000999998000000000000000000000000500010110000001100000
30700181100609420500200102210000410210100021020000000000000000000000110000000003
3070018201000001001545000000000000000000000000500010110000001100000
30700191100709831550210102210000509930100021020000000000000000000000100000000008
3070019201000000999998000000000000000000000000100002513000011100000
30700201060924321600430202012000029900900029020000000000000000000000000000000002
3070020201000000000000000000000000000000000000500010110000001100100
30700211100812021600321202013000029900010440020110100000000000000000100000000176
3070021201000000999998000000000000000000000000176004401100001011100100
30700221090511111600320202022000119900100021020140100000000000000000000000000032
3070022201000000000000000000000000000000000000320008011000001100100
30700231090511411550220102210000019930110021020140110000000000000000000000000018
3070023201000000999998000000000000000000000000180004513000011100100
30700241090511411550220102210000019930110021020140100000000000000000000000000057
3070024201000000999998000000000000000000000000570014313000011100100
30700251090612211500220106240010040110100021020000000000000000100100000000000003
3070025201000000000000000000000000000000000000500010130000011110100
30700261090611621500210103210010040110100021020000000000000000100010000000000158
3070026201000000999998000000000000000000000000158003951100000111100
30700271090712521550310102210010040100110022020110010050000000111001000001000059
3070027201000000999998000000000000000000000000590014813111111100100
30700281090814331650321202112000229900010440020170110010000001000111000000000325
3070028203000000999998000000000000000000000000166003320300011100100
30700291080515111600331202022000319900000440020000000000000000000000000000000026
3070029201000000999998000000000000000000000000260006513000011100000
30700301080514811600331202022000219900110021020000000000000000000001000000000006
3070030201000000999998000000000000000000000000100002512000011100000
30700311080614011500210103210010040210110021020110010000100010111011100000000069
3070031201000000999998000000000000000000000000690017313000011100001
30700321090613211500210102210000049910100023020000000000000000000000000000000004
3070032201000000000000000000000000000000000000100002511000001100000
30700331090612911500210102210000229900100023020000000002000000101001000000000013
3070033201000000999998000000000000000000000000130003313000011110000
30700341090714421500320202120000029900110021020110100000000001010001000000000051
3070034201000000999998000000000000000000000000510012813111111100100
30700351080416711750441202023000229900100021021000000000000000000000000000000001
3070035201000000000000000000000000000000000000500010100000001000000
30700361080516311550320202122000119900100021020110100010000000000000000000000005
3070036201000000000000000000000000000000000000100002510000001000100
30700371080515411550331202022000119900110021020000000000000000000001110000100011
3070037201000000999998000000000000000000000000110002812000011100000
30700381080517811550210102220000019900100021021000000000000010000001000000000014
3070038201001000000203000000000000000000000000140003510000001000000
30700391080517411500210102220000019900100021021000000010000000000000000000000068
3070039201000000000000000000000000000000000000680017012000011000100
30700401080616011500210102210000499201000210201999902000000000000100000000000030
3070040201000000999998000000000000000000000000300007511000010110100
30700411080717511500320202111000029900100021020000000000000000000000000000000003
3070041201000000000000000000000000000000000000500010100000011000000
30700421080717521500320202111000029900100021020000000000000000000001000000000023
3070042201000000999998000000000000000000000000230005813000011100100
```

```
30700431080716821600430202011000329900000440021000000000000000000000100000000000015
30700432010010020006890000000000000000000000000015000381000000001000000
30700441080818521800531202112000029900110021030120100000000100000000110000000000543
30700442020000009999980000000000000000000010000552013781300000111101100
30700451080818921700430202012000029900100021021000000000000000000000000000000000002
30700452010000000000000000000000000000000000000050001010000000001000000
30700461080818721750421202012000129900000440021000000000000000000000000000000000002
30700462010000000000000000000000000000000000000050001010000000001000000
30700471080817721700420202111000429900100021021000000000000000000000000000000000001
30700472010000000000000000000000000000000000000050001010000000001000000
30700481070418811799321202122000119900110021020000000002000010000000110000010000050
30700482020000009999800000000000000000000000000053001301300000011100100
30700491070518411650220102210000019940100021020000000000000000000000000000000000013
30700492010000009999980000000000000000000000000130003311000000001100100
30700501170520011550320202121000129900100021020000000002000000001010010000000000015
30700502010000001000619000000000000000000000000015000381000000001000100
30700511070518011500210102210000040520100021020119999000100000000101100000000000023
30700512010000009999980000000000000000000000000230005813000111110100
30700521070619311500210103210010040210100021020000000000000000000000100000000000009
30700522020000000000000000000000000000000000000100002001000000001100100
30700531070618411500210104240000040210100022020000000001010000110110110000000000029
30700532010000009999980000000000000000000000000150003003000011100101
30700541070619811500210105240000040110100022020000000000000000000000100000000000002
30700542010000009999980000000000000000000000000050001001000101100001
30700551070619711500210105240000040110100022021000000000000000000000000000000000002
30700552010000001000478000000000000000000000000050001000000000001000001
30700561070619811500210105240010040110100022020000000000000000010000100000000000005
30700562010000009999980000000000000010000000000010000200300011110001
30700571070618211500231202013000119900100021020000000000000000000000000000000000004
30700572010000000000000000000000000000000000000010000251200011000001
30700581070819621650320202121000029900100021020000000000000000000000000000000000021
30700582010000000000000000000000000000000000000021000531100000001100000
30700591060621311500210203230010040110100022020110010000000000001001000000000000063
30700592010000009999980000000000000000000000000063001581300001111001001
30700601060622011450231202112000209900010210200000000030100000011110100000000000196
30700602010000009999980000000000000100001000019600490130000111100001
30700611070822821500330202112000029900100021020000000001000000000000000000000000001
30700612010000000000000001000000000000000000000050001011000000001100000
30700621070822221500321202112000029900900029020000000000000000000000100000000000005
30700622010000000000000000000000000000000000000010000251101100001100000
30700631070823421500320202012000129900900029020000000000000000000000100000000000001
30700632010000009999980000000000000000000000000050001011000000001100000
30700641070823521550320202012000023900900021020000000000000000000000000000000000001
30700642010000000000000000000000000000000000000050001011000000001100000
30700651070824021500320202012000029900100023020000000000000000000000100000000000021
30700652010000009999980000000000000000000000000210005313000000111100000
30700661060924621550330202112000229900900028020000000000000000000000000000000000024
30700662010000000000000000000000000000000000000240006011000000001100100
30700671060622211500210103230010040310100022020000000000001000000000110000000000005
30700672010000009999980000000000000000000000000010000201300001111100100
30700681060623911500210103230010049920100022020199999020000000010110100000000000006
30700682010000009999980000000000000000000000000010000251300001111100100
30700691060623111450210102210001009900110022020000000001000000000000100000000000004
30700692010000009999980000000000000000000000000010000201100000001100000
30700701060623611450210102210001009900100022020000000000000000000000100000000000002
30700702010000009999980000000000000000000000000050001011000000001100000
30700711060623711450210102210001009900100022020000000000000000100001000000000000001
30700712010000009999980000000000000000000000000050001013000000011100000
30700721060624311450210106210000309900100022010000000000000000000000100000000000006
30700722010000009999980000000000000000000000000010000251100000001100000
```

```
30700731050626111450221202112010040210090010190999999999999999999999999999999999999
30700732999999999999999899999999999999999999999999999999993000111110001
30700741050827521450210104210000040430100025020000000000000000000000100000000000016
30700742010000000000000000000000000000000000000016000401100000001100001
30700751050330142000641202122000029900100021020000000000000000000000000000000000003
30700752010000000000000400000000000000000000000050001011000000001101100
30700761050328741950641202122000229900200440020000000000000100000001000000000000016
30700762010000009999980000000000000000000000000016000401200000011000100
30700771040529511450210103230010040110100021020000000002000000001111010000000000035
30700772010000009999980000000000000100000000003500088130000011100101
30700781040530011450210102210010040110100021020000000000000000001111010000000000025
30700782010000009999980000000000000000000000001000300007513000001111000
30700791050627411450210102210000040420100022020000000000000000000000100000000000007
30700792010000009999980000000000000000000000000010000251100000001100000
30700801050627211450210103210010040420100022020110010010000001010100000000000000005
30700802010000000000000000000000000000000000000010000251200000011000001
30700811050627111450210105240000040420100022021000000000000000000000100000000000005
30700812010000001000370000000000000000000000000050001010000000001000000
30700821050526911450210103210010040420100022020110010040000000011110100100000000024
30700822010000009999980000000000000000000000000026000651300001111100100
30700831040334021950641202013000529900000540020000000000000000001000000000000000007
30700832020000009999980003000000000000000000000015000351100000001100101
30700841040530531450210102210010049920110029010000000001000000001010011000000000026
30700842010000009999980000000000000000000000001000260006513000111110100
30700851040631111550220102210000209900100029020000000000000000001110000000000000003
30700852010000009999980000000000001000000000000050001013000001111100001
30700861040531111550220102210000209900100029020000000001000000001111000000000000010
30700862010000009999980000000000000000000000000010000251100000001100000
30700871040631021500321202221001209900100021020000000000000000000000100000000000003
30700872010000009999980000000000000000000000000050001013000111111110000
30700881030335921550410202210000229900100029020000000000000000000000100000000000001
30700882010000009999980000000000000000000000000050001011000000001100000
30700891040433621500320202212000019900100021020000000000000000000000000000000000001
30700892010000000000000000000000000000000000000050001010000000001000100
30700901030434621500210102110000219900100021020000000000000000000000100000000000007
30700902010000000000000000000000000000000000000010000251000000001000100
30700911030434721500320202111000219900100021030000000000000000000000000000000000013
30700912010000000000000000000000000000000000000130003311000000001100100
30700921030435121500320202112000329900100021021000000000000000000000000000000000007
30700922010000000000000000000000000000000000000010000251000000001000000
30700931030435011450210102211000309900210023020119999000000000001011110000001000053
30700932010000009999980000000000000100000000000053001331311111111110001
30700941040532511550321202211000129900210029020000000000040000001111000100100000016
30700942010000009990980000000000000100000000000018000451200011111000001
30700951040533311650541202022000239900220023020000000000000000001111011000000000104
30700952010000009999980000000000000000000000000104002601100000001100000
30700961020439621450210106210000109930100021020000000000000000000000000000000000004
30700962010000000000000000000000000000000000000010000251300000011100100
30700971020341021850541202012000029900100021020120100000000000000000100000000000002
30700972010000009999980001000000000000000000001000050001010000001001101
30700981020341321850541202012000029900110021520110010010000000001000000000000000013
30700982010000009999980013000000000000000000000017000401100000001101101
30700991020340921850541202012000029900100021020000000000000000001000000000000000001
30700992010000000000000001000000000000000000000050001011000000001101101
30701001020440721450110102210000109920100021021000000000000000000000100000000000029
30701002010000000000000000000000000000000000000029000731000000001000001
30701011020440721450320202112010419900120021020000000000000000000000110000010000011
30701012010000009999980000000000000000000000000019000481300000011100000
30701021020441021500321202120010222340100021020000000000000000000000100000000000002
30701022010000000000000000000000000000000000000050001010000000001000100
```

```
30701031010443+21450320202920000009990010002102000000000000000000000000000000000009
30701032010000000000000000000000000000000000001000025110000001100100
3070104108061392150021010221011004021010002102000000000000000000010010000000000003
3070104201000000999998000000000000000000000000000050001011000001100100
3070105104033184160032120202100002390010002402000000000000000000000000000000000002
3070105201000000000000000000000000000000000000005000101100000001100100
3070106109061022150021010323001004010001101002012010000000000000000111100102999999
3070106201000000999998000000000000000000000000999999999931111111110111
00800011120600011800321202112000029900111021120171111979776111111191119111804750
0080001207000000999998119611011111010111111110002200023000011111111
2080001113080982160032020212100012980010002102011010000000000100100000000000000005
20800012010000000000000000000000000000000001000025120000011101100
2080002114050892160042020210100032980010002102000000000000000000000000000000000002
2080002201000000000000000000000000000000000100002511000001010110000
2080003112050432165042020211000031980011002102014010000010000100000000000000000013
20800032010000000000000000000000000000001000001300032130000111110100
2080004112040622165032020212000011980011002102000000000000000000000001000000000010
208000420100000000000000000000000000000000001000025110000110110001
2080005112050182160032020112200031980011002102014010100000000001000000000000000005
2080005201000001000361000000000000000000100000100002511000001010110100
2080006113060642160032020102200012980020041002012010004000000000000000000000000004
2080006201000000000000000000000000000000000100002511001110110101
2080007112050272160032010122010011990010002102000000000000000000000000000000000005
2080007201000000000000000000000000000000001000025110000010110100
2080008111060362160032020102200022980020044002112011000000000000000000000000000002
2080008201000000000000000000000000000000000500010300000000100001
2080009113081252165042011121000002980010002102000000000000000000000001000000000002
2080009201000000000000000000000000000000000500010320000011100101
2080010112080922170054020213000023980010002102000000000000000000000000000000000001
2080010201000000000000000000000000000000000500010300000000101001
2080011112050112165043020102300012980020044002014011001000000000000000000000000001
2080011201000000000000000000000000000000000500010300000000100101
2080012111060182160032020112210041980010002102000000000000000000000000000000000002
2080012201000000000000000000000000000000000500010300000000100101
2080013111060182160032020112100041980010002102000000000000000000000000000000000003
2080013201000000000000000000000000000000001000025100000000100100
2080014112060172160042020212100012980010002102000000000000000000000000000000000007
2080014201000000000000000000000000000000001000025100000110100100
2080015112060272160042020112200022980010002102000000000000000000000000000000000003
2080015201000000000000000000000000000000001000025100000110100000
2080016111060382160032020102100001980020044002012010000000000000000110000000000030
2080016201000003009870000000000000000000000300007510000000100100
2080017111070552160021011221010011980111102202012010000000000001000111000100001151
208001720100001508922400000000000000000000115102877120000111100111
2080018111060432160021010221010011990020001002100000000000000000000011000000000004
2080018201000010008320000000000000000000001000025100000000100000
2080019111070662160032020211100010980011002102000000000000000000000011000000000025
2080019201000000000000000000000000000000002500062121111111100101
2080020111080772160032020111200012980010002103000000000000000000000000000000000002
2080020201000000000000000000000000000000000500010300000010100101
2080021111080802160042020101200012980010044002000000000000000000000001000000000001
2080021201000000000000001000000000000000000500010300000000100101
2080022111080912180052120203300012980000044002100000000000100000000001000000000011
2080022201001000000024000000000000000000001100027100000000100000
2080023111070802170032020213200090980011002102000000000000000000000101000000000027
208002320100000100041600000000000000000100000002700067100000110100100
2080024111070782160032020111100070980010002102000000000000000000000000000000000010
20800242010000000000000000000000000000000100002510000011010101000
2080025111070822170042020103100012980020024102000000000000000000000000000000000003
2080025201000000000000000000000000000000000500010300000010101001
2080026111070842170042020103100012980000024004000000000010000010000000000000000001
2080026201000000000000100000000000000000000500010300000000101001
2080027113060492160032020121100012980010002102000000000000000000000000000000000020
2080027201000000000000000000000000000000200005011111110111111
2080028113060562160032020112200002980010002102000000000000000000000000000000000001
2080028201000000000000000000000000000000000500010300000000101001
2080029113050502160032020121011001980011002102011001000000000000000000000000000028
2080029201001000000662000000000000000000002800070130000001110100
2080030113050522160032020112200011980010002102100000000000000001000000000000000010
2080030201000000000000000000000000000000001000025100000000100000
2080031113050562160031020102100011980010002102100000000000000000000001000000000003
2080031201000000000000000000000000000000000500010300000000100001
2080032113050522160032020102300012980020044002012010001000000000000000000000000002
2080032201000000000000000000000000000000000500010300000000100101
2080033113060272160042020102200012980020044002000000000000000000001000010000000033
2080033202000000000000000000000000000000000033000821200000001100101
2080034113060322160032020112100100980010002102000000000000000000000000000000000003
2080034201000000000000000000000000000000000500010300000100100000
2080035112060322160032020112200080980011001102014010000000000000000001000000000037
2080035201000000000000000000000000000000003700092100000010100100
2080036112060292160042020112100022980010002102000000000000000000000001000000000001
2080036201000000000000000000000000000000000500010300000010100101
2080037112060112165042020102300081980020044002014011000000000000000001000000000002
2080037201000000000000000000000000000000000500010320000011100101
3080001111050583165032020211100001990010002102000000000000000000000000000000000011
3080001201000000000000000000000000000000000600011010000000110100
3080002111050583165021010221000001993010002102012010000000000000000000000000000001
3080002201000000000000000000000000000000000500010100000010100100
3080003110050594160021010221000011993010002102012010000010000000000000000000000001
3080003201000000999998000000000000000000000500010120000001100000
3080004110050653160021010221000031990010002102011001000000010010100010000000000027
3080004201000000999998000000000000000000002700068130000001110000
3080005110050624160021010221000001993011102102014011098020101010100110000000100320
3080005201000000999998000000000000100001000003200080013000011111101
3080006110050704160031020202100032054010002102100000000000000000000000000000000002
3080006201000000000000000000000000000000000500010100000000100000
3080007110050731160032020202100021980010002102012010001000000000000000000000000005
3080007201000000000000000000000000000000001000025110000111100101
3080008110060631155021010221000001993010002101019999900010000100001100000000000099
30800082010000030147950000000000000000000000990024813000111110101
3080009111060582055032020212100014993010002102000000010100000000001000000000000009
3080009201000000000000000000000000000000001000025110000000110000
3080010110060702155021010121000051050010002102000000000000000000000000000000000018
3080010202000001019290000000000000000000002200053110000010110001
3080011110060712155021010223011001021010002201019999903010010000000111000000000021
3080011207000003016971000000000000000000004500105130000011111101
3080012110060702155021010223011041021010002201000000000000000000001000000000000013
3080012201000000999998000000000000000000001300033120000111100001
3080013110060612155031020202101002990010002102011999908030010999990100000000000201
30800132010000000000000000000100100000000020100503130000011110101
3080014111070622155021010121000051990100044002000000000000000000000011100000000002
3080014201000000000000000000000000000000000500010100000110100000
3080015110070722055021010623000001010121044002000000000000000000000001100000000046
30800152020000009999980000000000000000000000460011512000011100000
3080016110070852055021010221000021042000044002112010000000000000000000000000000003
3080016201000000000000000000000000000000000500010100000000100000
3080017110080953180041020201300022980000044002000000000000000000000000000000000006
3080017201000000000000000000000000000000001000025100000000100100
3080018110070932160032120202200012990000044002000000000000000000000000000000000005
3080018201000000000000000000000000000000001000025100000000101000
```

```
30800191100709521550210102210000429900100022020000000000000000000000000000000010
30800192010000000000000000000000000000000000000100002510000011010000
30800201100709821550321202022000029900004400200000000000000000000000000000000023
30800202010000000000000000000000000000000000000012000240000000100100
30800211100810721600321202022000029900004400210000000000000000000001000000000007
30800212010000010004390000000000000000000000001000025100000000100000
30800221080717021650430202111000299001000210210000000000000000000000000000000001
30800222010000000000000000000000000000000000000500010100000000100000
30800231100812121600421202023000029900004400200000000000000000000001000000000046
30800232010000009999980000000000000000000000004600115000000010100100
30800241100711321700430202023000029900004400200000000000000000000000000000000014
30800242010000000000000000000000000000000000001400035100000000100100
30800251100507811550220102110000119800210011021000000000000000000000000000000023
30800252010000000000000000000000000000000000000230005810000000100000
30800261090510631600320202020000229900200023020110110000000000100000000000000002
30800262010000000000000000000000000000000000000500010120000001100100
30800271100608411550210102211000129930100020021000000000000000000000000000000005
30800272020000000000000000000000000000000000000100002010000000101100
30800281090609611550210102210000129901000210211101000000000010000000000000000002
30800282010000000000000000000000000000000000000500010000000000100000
30800291100609211550210102210010029900120021302012011012010000011101110000000300
30800292020000010013890000000000000000000000001540030801000000111101
30800301100609111550210103210010040310100021020110001010000000010001000000000018
30800302010000010015200000000000000000000000001800045110000010111100
30800311090610111500210102210010040210100025020149919030000010111001000000000028
30800312010000009999980000000000000000000000002800070130000011100100
30800321090609811500210102210010040210100025020129999000000000000000000000000002
30800322010000000000000000000000000000000000000500010120000111100000
30800331090610411500210102210010040210100025020110100000000001100000000000000001
30800332010000009999980000000000000000000000000500010120000001100000
30800341100609121550210102210000040210100021020000000000000000000110000000000008
30800342010000000000000000000000000000000000001000025100000000101000
30800351100609421500200102210000410210100021020000000000000000000110000000000003
30800352010000010015450000000000000000000000000500010120000001100000
30800361100609221550210102210000810210100021021000000000000000000010000000000005
30800362010000020025640000000000000000000000001000025100000000100000
30800371090709121500210103230010040110100021020000000000000000000000000000000006
30800372010000000000000000000000000000000000001000025110000000110000
30800381090710721500210103230010040110100021020000000000000000000000000000000006
30800382010000000000000000000000000000000000001000025110000000110000
30800391090710511500210103230010040110100021020000000000000000000000000000000002
30800392010000000000000000000000000000000000000500010110000000110000
30800401100710021500210106230000099301000210200000000000200001000010000000000283
30800402010000009999980000000000000000000000002830070811000000110100
30800411100709831550210102210000509930100021020000000000000000000010000000000008
30800412010000009999980000000000001000000000001000025120000011100000
30800421080710841500210106240000009920100022020000000000000000000010000000000002
30800422010000000000000000000000000000000000000500010110000000110100
30800431090711031500210102210000109920100021011000000000000000000000000000000001
30800432010000000000000000000000000000000000000500010100000000100000
30800441100811631550210102210000129900000010010000000000000000000010000000000013
30800442010000009999980000000000000000000000001000025110000000110101
30800451100812021600210102210000029900100021020000000000000000000000000000000021
30800452010000000000000000000000000000000000210005300000000110100100
30800461100812921650321202013000029900010440020110100000000000000000010000000000090
30800462020000009999980000000000000000000000009600240120000101100100
30800471090813031600210102210000029900100021020000000000000000000000000000000006
30800472010000000000000000000000000000000000000500010000000000100100
30800481090813931750421202013000029900000440120000000010000000000001000000000058
30800482010000009999980000100100100000000000002900058000000000100100
30800491100812641600210102240010029900100021020000000000000000000000000000000038
30800492010000000000000000000000000000000000003800095100000000100100
30800501090814441700320202012000029900004400200000000000000000000000000000000003
30800502010000000000000000000000000000000000000500010000000010100000
30800511090814741650330202013000129900004400110000000000000000000000000000000001
30800512010000000000000000000000000000000000000500010100000000100000
30800521090511111600320202022000119900100021020140100000000000000000000000000032
30800522010000000000000000000000000000000000003200080120000001100100
30800531090612211500220106240010040110100021020000000000000000010010000000000003
30800532010000000000000000000000000000000000000500010130000011110100
30800541090611621500210103210010040110100021020000000000000000100010000000000180
30800542010000009999980000000000000000000000001800045013000001111100
30800551090713321500310202110000129900100021020120100050000000011101100000000123
30800552010000009999980000000000000000000000012300308101110010100100
30800561090712821550310102210010040100110022020110010050000000111001000000000323
30800562020000009999980000000000000000000000003230080812111111100100
30800571090814431650321202112000229900004400201501100100000010000110000000000041
30800572010000009999980000000000000000000000002100042020000011100100
30800581090815031640321202112000229900004400201101000000000000000011000000000013
30800582010000009999980000000000000000000000000700014020001011100100
30800591080515211600331202022000319900004400201101000000000000000000000000000069
30800592020000009999980000000000000000000000006900173020000111100100
30800601080614311500210103230010040111100022021000000000000000000000000000000003
30800602010000010014130000000000000000000000000500010100000000100000
30800611080414931550220102210010020110100021020000000000000101000000000000000067
30800612010000000000000000000000000000000000006700168100000000100100
30800621080614111500210103210010040210110021020110010000100010111011100000000041
30800622020000009999980000000000000000000000004100103120000111100000
30800631090613011500210102210000129910100021020000000003000000010100100000000021
30800632040000009999980000000000000000000000003800078130000011110100
30800641090613311500210103210010510500000010011000000000000000000011000000000013
30800642010000020046420000000000000000000000001300033100000000100000
30800651080614121500210102210110040210100021020140110100100101100110000000000720
30800652030000150933210000000000000000000000100724018081300011111100
30800661090714121500320202121000429940100021020000000000101000000000000000000016
30800662010000010014640000000000000000000000001600040100000000100100
30800671080714121500210102210010229930100022021000000000000000000000000000000003
30800672010000000000000000000000000000000000000500010100000000100000
30800681080715421500210105240000400320100022020000000000000000000000000000000002
30800682010000000000000000000000000000000000000500010100000000100100
30800691080715021500320102111010629900100021021000000000000001000010000000000056
30800692010000000000000000000000000000000000005600140100000000100100
30800701080715521500430202121000129900100021020000000000000000000000000000000005
30800702010000000000000000000000000000000000001000025100000000100100
30800711090714521500320202120000029900110021020110100000100001010001100000000053
30800712010000009999980000000000000000000000005300133131111111110100
30800721090714921500320202120000329900100021020000000000010000010100100000000003
30800722010000009999980000000000000000000000000500010100000010100100
30800731080715221500320202122000229900100021020000000000000000000000000000000019
30800732010000000000000000000000000000000000001900048100000010100000
30800741080715421500421202121000719900100021020000000000000000000000000000000004
30800742010000000000000000000000000000000000001000025100000000100100
30800751080715421500430202122000429900100021020000000000000000000000000000000004
30800752010000000000000000000000000000000000001000025100000010100100
30800761080715821500420202121000029900100021020000000000000000000000000000000005
30800762010000000000000000000000000000000000001000025100000000100100
30800771080716521550320202012000029900100021020110010000000000000001000000000074
30800772010000009999980000000000000000000000007400185100000010100100
30800781080816121550320202111000029900100021020000000000000000000000000000000003
30800782010000000000000000000000000000000000000500010100000010100100
```

```
3080079108081642155032020212200002990010002102100000000000000000000000000000000000003
30800792010000000000000000000000000000000000000005000101000000000100000
3080080108081702165052120201300002990000044002000000000000000000000000000000000000001
30800802010000000000000000000000000000000000000500010100000001010000 0
3080081108091852180064120201200022990000060002100000000000000000000000000000000000002
30800812010000000000000000000000000000000000000500010100000000010000 0
3080082108091853205064120201200999990000050001100000000000000000000101000000000001
30800822010010000000250000000000000000000000000500010100000000010000 0
3080083108051601155032010221100002990010002101100000000000000000000000000000000002
30800832010000000000000000000000000000000000000500010100000000100001
3080084108051591155020010221000002990010002102000000000000000000000000000000000043
30800842020000000000000000000000000000000000004700115100000000100100
3080085108051641155032020212200011990010002102100000000000000000000000000000000004
30800852030000000000000000000000000000000000001500030100000000100000
3080086108051721150032020211100002990010002102100000000000000000000000000000000015
30800862020000000000000000000000000000000000001900045100000001010000 0
3080087108061543150021010221000004992010002302100000000000000000000000000000000001
30800872010000000000000000000000000000000000000500010100000000010000 0
3080088108051703150021010211200041990010002301100000000000000000000000000000000003
30800882010000000000000000000000000000000000000500010100000000010000 0
3080089108061601150021010221000004992010002102011011007030000100001000000000000159
30800892010000000999998000000000000000000000015900398130000111110100
3080090108061621150021010321001004991012002202000000000000000000000110000000000078
30800902010000000999998000000000000000000000078001951100000000110101
3080091107061771150021010221001011993010002202100000000000000000000000000000000001
30800912010000000000000000000000000000000000000500010100000000010000 0
3080092108071652150033120201201060990010002102000000000000000000000000000000000465
30800922010000000999998999900000000000000000465011631000000010100100
3080093108071671160049120201200022039000002900210000000000000000000000000000000006
30800932010000000000000000000000000000000000010000251000000000100000
3080094108071752150032020211100002990010002102000000000000000000000001000000000025
30800942030000000000000000000000000000000000032000781200000011100101
3080095108071762150032020291100002990010002102100000000000000000000000000000000001
30800952010000000000000000000000000000000000000500010100000000010000 0
3080096108071672165043020212200042990010002102000000000000000000000000000000000001
30800962010000000000000000000000000000000000000500010100000001010000 0
3080097108071702165043020211100042990010002102100000000000000000000000000000000001
30800972010000000000000000000000000000000000000500010100000000010000 0
3080098108081702160032020212100052990000002102100000000000000000000000000000000001
30800982010000000000000000000000000000000000000500010100000000010000 0
3080099108081722165032020211100022990010002102100000000000000000000000000000000001
30800992010000000000000000000000000000000000000500010100000000010000 0
3080100108071862180054120201300022990000044002100000000000000000000000000000000002
30801002020000000000000000000000000000000000010000201000000000100000
3080101108071842185054120201300012990000044002100000000000000000000000000000000001
30801012010000000000000000000000000000000000000500010100000000010000 0
3080102108071812180054120201300002990000044002100000000000000000000000000000000013
30801022010000000000000000000000000000000000013000331000000000100000
3080103108081752170053120211200002990010002102000000000000000000000000000000000046
30801032010000000000000000000000000000000000046001151200000111000000
3080104108081802170053120211200002990010002103000000000000000000000000000000000009
30801042010000000999993000000000000000000100001000025120000111100100
3080105108081832185053120211200002990010002103000000000000000000000000000000000004
30801052010000000000000000000000000000000000010000201200000111000000
3080106108081862160043020201200012990010002102000000000000000000000000000000000003
30801062010000000000000000000000000000000000000500010100000000100100
3080107108081812170043020202300012990000044002100000000000000000000000000000000001
30801072010000000000000000000000000000000000000500010100000000010000 0
3080108108081812165043020201200022990000044002000000000000000000000000000000000003
30801082010000000000000000000000000000000000000500010100000000100100
3080109108081732165043020201200002990010002102100000000000000000000000000000000001
30801092010000000000000000000000000000000000000500010100000000010000 0
3080110108091992165042120213100011990010002102000000000000000000000000000000000016
30801102010000000000000000000000000000000000001600040100000010101100
3080111108092102175061120201200062990000044002100000000000000000000000000000000001
30801112010000000000000000000000000000000000000500010100000000010000 0
3080112108091982170053120201100031990000054002000000000000000000000000000000000001
30801122010000000000000000000000000000000000000500010100000000100100
3080113108091352175053020201200002990000054002000000000000000000000000000000000002
30801132010000000000000000000000000000000000000500010100000000100100
3080114107041881170032020212200001990011002102000000000200010000000110000001000065
30801142030000000999998000000000000000000000068001681200000111100100
3080115107051841165022010221000001994010002102000000000000000000000000000000000013
30801152010000000999998000000000000000000001300033120000001100100
3080116107051891170033020202300012990020002102100000000000000000000000000000000002
30801162010000000000000000000000000000000000000500010100000000010000 0
3080117107051801150021010221000004052010002102011999900010000001011000000000000023
30801172010000000999998000000000000000000002300058120001111100100
3080118107061921150021010321000004021011002101512010000000000000000000000000000044
30801182010000000999998000000000000000000002200044100000000101101
3080119107061941150021010321001004021010002102000000000000000000000001000000000010
30801192020000000000000000000000000000000000010000200000000001100100
3080120107061871150021010424000004021010002202014011101010001101101100000000000123
30801202010000000999998000000000000000000000620012402000011100101
3080121107061841150021010424000004021010002202100000000000000000100010000000000002
30801212010090000999999000000000000000000000050001000000000100001
3080122107061981150021010524000004011010002202000000000000000000000001000000000002
30801222010000000999998000000000000000000000050001002000010110000 1
3080123107061981150021010524001004011011002202011010001000000101101100000000000025
30801232010000000999998000000000000010000000000270005403000111110101
3080124107061872150032020222001004021010002202112010000000000000000000000000000047
30801242010000000000000000000000000000000000047001181000000000100000
3080125107072022185053120201200022990000044002000000000000000000000000000000000013
30801252010000000000000000000000000000000000013000331000000000100101
3080126107072052160033020201300002990000044002100000000000000000000000000000000001
30801262010000000000000000000000000000000000000500010100000000010000 0
3080127107071882190042020201200002990000044002100000000000000000000000000000000003
30801272010000000000000000000000000000000000000500010100000000010000 0
3080128107072052160031020222100002990012002102000000000100000000001100000000000075
30801282100000000999998000000000000000000000010200235100000000100101
3080129107081992165032020212100002990010002102000000000000000000000000000000000071
30801292090000000000000000000000000000000000078001851200000111001100
3080130107081962160032020221200002990010002102100000000000000000000000000000000003
30801302010000000000000000000000000000000000000500010100000000010000 0
3080131107081972160032020221200012990010002102000000000000000000000000000000000013
30801312010000000999998000000000000000000001300033100001110100000
3080132107081942165032020221200002990010002102000000000000000000000001000000000225
30801322020000000999998000000000000000000002250056310000011010000 0
3080133107082142150032020221000012990010002102100000000000000000000000000000000001
30801332010000000000000000000000000000000000000500010100000000010000 0
3080134107082142150033020211200002990010002102000000000000000000000000000000000001
30801342010000000000000000000000000000000000000500010100000000100100
3080135107082122150033020211200002990010002102000000000000000000000000000000000002
30801352010000000000000000000000000000000000000500010100000000100100
3080136107092232160043120202300001990011002112014010011080021111100110001000408 1
30801362050005037027633057601010010110000000103185173903201100111100111
3080137107082102160042020211100002990010002102100000000000000000000000000000000001
30801372010000000000000000000000000000000000000500010100000000010000 0
3080138107092162160043120201200031990010002102100000000000000000000000000000000048
30801382010000000000000000000000000000000000048001201000000000100000
```

```
30801391070420611750320202112000029940100021020120010000000000000000000000000014
30801392010000000000000000000000000000000000001400035100000000100100
30801401060422312000540202022000429950100021021000000000000000000000000000000021
30801402080000000000000000000000000000000000004500095100000000100000
30801411060422211950540202022000429950100021021000000000000000000000000000000011
30801412010000000000000000000000000000000000011000281000000000100100
30801421060422311850540202022000229950100021020000000000000000000000000000000001
30801422010000000000000000000000000000000000050001010000000000100100
30801431060421911950540202022000329950100021020000000000000000000000000000000008
30801432040000000000000000000000000000000000250005510000000000100100
30801441060522411500320202012000119940100021021000000000000000000000000000000003
30801442010000000000000000000000000000000000050001010000000000100000
30801451060621411500210203230010040110100022020110010000000000001001000000000076
30801452010000009999800000000000000000000000077001931200000111100101
30801461060622011450231202112000209900010210200000000000000000011100100000000001
308014620100000099998000000000000010000000000000500010120001111100001
30801471060823321500310102112010521000100021020000000010000000000000000000000026
30801472010000000000000000000000000000000000026000651000000000100100
30801481070722321500310202120000129900100021020120100010000000000000000000000006
30801482010000000000000000000000000000000000100002510000000000100100
30801491070821421550430202111000429900100021021000000000000000000000000000000003
30801492010000000000000000000000000000000000050001010000000000100000
30801501070822321500210106210000129900100021021000000000000000000000000000000003
30801502010000000000000000000000000000000000050001010000000000100000
30801511060823721500210106210010329900900290210000000000000000000000000000000013
30801512010000000000000000000000000000000001300033100000000100000
30801521060924721500210106210000023900100021021000000000000000000000000000000004
30801522010000000000000000000000000000000000100002510000000000100000
30801531060522811800491202013000329900000440021000000000000000000000100000000043
30801532010000020002499000900000000000000000004300108100000000100001
30801541060522311650330202122000419900000440020000000000000000000000000000000001
30801542010000000000000000000000000000000000050001010000000000100100
30801551060523611550330202122000019900000440020000000000000000000000000000000003
30801552010000000000000000000000000000000000050001010000000000100100
30801561060523411550330202122000319900000440020000000000000000000000000000000003
30801562010000000000000000000000000000000000050001010000000000100100
30801571060523511550330202122000019900000440020000000000000000000000000000000003
30801572010000000000000000000000000000000000050001010000000000100100
30801581060522611500320202112000029900100021021000000000000000000000000000000002
30801582010000000000000000000000000000000000050001010000000000100000
30801591060522811600320202112000023900100021020000000000000000000000000000000028
30801592040000000000000000000000000000000000370008510000000000100100
30801601060523511650320202112000029900100021020000000000000000000000000000000002
30801602020000000000000000000000000000000000100002010000000000100100
30801611060523511650320202112000029900100021021000000000000000000000000000000002
30801612010000000000000000000000000000000000050001010000000000100000
30801621060523411500320202112000129900100021021000000000000000000000000000000010
30801622020000000000000000000000000000000000150003510000000000100000
30801631060523111600320202112000029900100021021000000000000000000000000000000001
30801632010000000000000000000000000000000000050001010000000000100000
30801641060523211500320202112000029900110022020120100000000000000110000000000034
30801642010000009999800000000000000000000000034000851000000000100101
30801651060622311500210103230010040310100022020140100000200000010001100000000016
30801652010000009999800000000000000000000000160004012000111100100
30801661060623911500210103230010049920100022020199999020000000101101000000000006
30801662010000009999800000000000000000000000100002052000111100100
30801671060624111450210102210001009900100022021000000001000600000101000000000003
30801672010000010062140000000000000000000000050001010000000000100000
30801681060623611450210102210001009900100022020000000000000000000000000000000002
30801682010000009999800000000000000000000000050001012000000001100000
30801691060623411450210102210001003900110022020000000020000000010000100000000017
30801692010000009999800000000000010000000000040000801200000011100001
30801701060623111450210102210001009900100022021120100010000000000001000000000002
30801702010000010031170000000000000000000000050001010000000000100000
30801711060624311450210106210000303900100022010000000000000000000010000000000006
30801712010000009999800000000000000000000000100002512000000001100000
30801721060823321500210106210000049920100025021000000000000000000000000000000001
30801722010000000000000000000000000000000000050001010000000000100001
30801731060925621550410202211000299401000210210000000000000000000000000000000003
30801732010000000000000000000000000000000000050001010000000000100001
30801741050625411450210102110000499201000220201100100000000000000000000000000003
30801742010000000000000000000000000000000000050001011000000000110100
30801751050626111450221202112010040210090010190999999999999999999999999999999999
30801752999999999999999999999999999999999999999999999920001111100001
30801761050827521450210104210000404301000250200000000000000000000100000000000019
30801762010000000000000000000000000000000000024000601200000001100001
30801771060328221600431202112000219900100021021000000000000000000000000000000007
30801772010000000000000000500000000000000000150003510000000000100000
30801781050229021800541202112000519900100021021000000000001000000000100000000024
30801782010000030003920019000000000000000000115002303000000000100000
30801791050328641900641202122000029900110021020110110020200111101101100000300494
30801792050010020001700366000001000100000010201004033320000001101101
30801801050328911550320202122000119940100021011110010000000000000000000000000010
30801802010000000000000000000000000000000000200005010000000000100000
30801811050329941600420202122000129900100021021000000000000000000000000000000007
30801812010000000000000000000000000000000000100002510000000000100000
30801821050329811550330202122000419940100021020000000000000000000000000000000016
30801822030000000000000000000000000000000000210004810000000000100100
30801831050330241600320202111000219900100021021000000000000000000000000000000008
30801832020000000000000000000000000000000000200005010000000000100000
30801841050329731650431202012000429900000280200000000000000000000000000000000004
30801842010000000000000099990000000000000000100002510000000000100100
30801851050329841550430202012000119930100021010120100000000000000000000000000001
30801852010000000000000000000000000000000000050001010000000000100100
30801861050331511750431202012000229900100021021000000000000000000000000000000002
30801862010000000000000000000000000000000000050001010000000000100001
30801871050331211600340202012000319900000440020110100000000000000000000000000001
30801872010000000000000000000000000000000000050001010000000000100100
30801881050330811700421202022000229900010028020130100000000000000010000000000007
30801882010000009999800000000000000000000000100002510000000000100100
30801891050330411600220112210000119900100026010110100000100000000000000000000012
30801892010000000000000000000000000000000000120003010000000000100100
30801901050330641550321202212000219940120024020140110010100000000110000000000019
30801902010000009999800000000000000000000000450010010000000010100100
30801911050329711600430202013000229900000440020000000000000000000000000000000002
30801912010000000000000000000000000000000000050001010000000000101100
30801921050430211800521202122000429900200021020000000000000000000100000000000003
30801922010000000000009999000000000000000000050001010000000000100100
30801931050429842050641202112000229900100021020000000000000000000100000000000006
30801932010000000000000300000000000000000000200004510000000000100100
30801941050428932100641202111000329900000540020110100000000000001001000000000003
30801942010000009999800030000000000000000000050001010000000000100100
30801951050430011550420202013000029900100021020000000000000000000000000000000001
30801952010000000000000000000000000000000000050001010000000000100100
30801961050429611500421202013000029900100021021000000000000000000000000000000001
30801962010000000000000000000000000000000000050001010000000000100000
30801971050429311500321202112000029900100021020000000001000000000110000000000030
30801972010000009999800000000000000000000000300007510000000010100000
30801981050428811650321202012000029900100021011110010000000000000000000000000003
30801982010000000000000000000000000000000000050001010000000000100000
```

```
3080199104052951145021010323001004011010002102000000000200000000111101000000000044
30801992010000009999980000000000000001000000000440011002000011100101
308020010405300114502101022100100401101000210200000000000000001111010000000000025
30802002010000009999980000000000000000000000100030000751300000011110000
308020110505288314502201022100007299201000210200000000000000000100010000000000021
3080201201000001001995000000000000100000000000240006011000000110000
308020210506274114502101022100000404201000220210000000000000000000000100000000008
30802022010000010056840000000000000000000000001000025100000000100000
308020310506281114502101022100000404201000220200000000000000000000001000000000016
30802032020000010019430000000000000000000000000200005011000000110000
308020410506275114502101022100000404201000220200000000000000000000001000000000007
308020420100000099999800000000000000000000000001000025120000001100000
308020510506273114512101022100000404201000220210000000000000000000001000000000005
30802052010000000000000000000000000000000000100002510000000100000
308020610506277114502101032100120404201000220200000000010000000000001100000000005
30802062010000009999980000000000000000000000010000251100000010111000
308020710506274114502101032100120404201000220201100100100000010000010000000000003
30802072010000009999980000000000000000000000000000500010101111110101001
308020810505269114502101032100120404201000220201100100400000001111010010000000024
308020820100000099999800000000000000000000000000002600065120000111100100
308020910506273114502312020120002099002000210201401100000000001010010000000000001
3080209201000000999998000000000000000000000000005000101000000010100101
308021010506278114501101012100000001101000210210000000000000000000000000000000001
30802102010000000000000000000000000000000000000500010100000000100001
308021110506189114501101012100000099001000260200000000103000000000100000000000001
30802112010000009999980000000000000000000000000050001011000000111001
308021210402341220506412029120002299000205400210000000000000000000001000000000002
30802122010000010006960000000000000000000000000050001010000000100001
308021310403340219506412020130005299000005400200000000000000000000000000000000007
30802132020000009999980003000000000000000000000015000351200000011100101
308021410403332217505402020120004299000000210110000000000000000000000000000000010
30802142010000000000000000000000000000000000001000025100000000100000
308021510403318416003212020210000299001000240100000000000000000000000000000000003
30802152010000000000000000000000000000000000000500010120000001100100
308021610403320316003302020110003199002000290210000000000000000000000000000000001
30802162010000000000000000000000000000000000000500010100000000100000
308021710403322416003212022110000299401000240100000000000000000000000000000000001
30802172010000000000000000000000000000000000000500010100000010100001
308021810403312315004302020220003199002000290210000000000000000000000000000000001
30802182010000000000000000000000000000000000000500010100000000100000
308021910403315415503302020120002299002000210210000000000000000000000000000000002
30802192010000000000000000000000000000000000001000020100000000100000
308022010403320415504412020130005199001200218200000000101000000011011000000000110
3080220202000002001000014100010000110000001007850157030000010100101
308022110403326315503312021100000199001000210210000000010000000000000000000000001
30802212010000000000000000000000000000000000000500010100000000100000
308022210403332417004312021120004199001100210111101000200100000000100000000000010
30802222010010020002760013000000000000000000000800016030000000100001
308022310404334415002101022100002199301200240200000000010000000101001000000000008
30802232010000009999980000000000000000000000001000025100000010100000
308022410404335315002101021110003199301000240200000000010000000001100000000000002
30802242010000000000000000000000000000000000000500010100000010100100
308022510404316415503212022100002299001000290200000000000000000000000000000000007
30802252010000000000000000000000000000000000001000025100000000100100
308022610404316315004302021120000299401000240200000000000000000000001000000000013
30802262020000009999980000000000000000000000002000045100000000100100
308022710404308316004302021120000299401000240200000000000000000000001000000000024
30802272020000009999980000000000000000000000003000075100000010100100
308022810404306116003312021120000299401100210200000000100000000000001100000000043
30802282030000009999980000000000001000000000000560014010000000100101
```

```
308022910404306116003312021120000299401000210200000000000000000000000000000000012
30802292010000000000000000000000000000000000001200030100000000100100
308023010404316114502101022100101199301000220210000000000000000001010100000000055
30802302010000000000000000000000000000000000005500138100000000100000
308023110405320115002201021100003099001000290211100100101000001010000000000000002
30802312010010000000108000000000000000000000000500010100000000100001
308023210405305314502101022100100499201100290100000000010000000101001100000000036
3080232201001000000636000000000000000000000010003600090120001111100100
308023310406311115502201022100002099001000290200000000010000000011110100000000066
308023320100000100374000000000000000010000000000660016512000111100001
308023410406309115502201022100003099001000290210000000000000000000000000000000006
30802342010000000000000000000000000000000000001000025100000000100000
308023510406320316002201022200011099001000290210000000000000000000000000000000004
30802352010000000000000000000000000000000000001000025100000000100000
308023610406315215503212022210002099001200210200000000020100001110001100000000993
3080236203006030048011000000000000000200000000099902495110000010111001
308023710406318215503212022210012099001000210210000000001000000000100000000000008
30802372010000010006200000000000000000000000001000025100000000100001
308023810406307215003212022210009099001000210200000000000000000000000000001000003
30802382010000000000000000000000000000000000000500010110000000110001
308023910406310215003212022210012099001000210200000000000000000000001000000000003
30802392010000009999980000000000000000000000000500010130001111110000
308024010406299115002101022100000499201000220210000000000000000000000000000000003
30802402010000000000000000000000000000000000000500010100000000100000
308024110406308215003212022210012099001000210200000000000000000000000000000000002
30802412010000000000000000000000000000000000000500010110000010110000
308024210303363218006412020120003299000006400200000000000000000000001000000000001
30802422010000009999980000000000000000000000000500010100000000100100
308024310303359215504102022100002299001000290200000000000000000000001000000000001
30802432010000009999980000000000000000000000000500010120000001100000
308024410404337215003202021120000199001000210210000000000000000000000000000000005
30802442010000000000000000000000000000000000001000025100000000100000
308024510404341215003202022120002199001000210200000000000000000000000000000000007
30802452010000000000000000000000000000000000001000025100000000100100
308024610304347215003202021110002199001000210300000000000000000000000000000000007
30802462010000000000000000000000000000000000001000025120000001100100
308024710304352215002101022210002099301000210201201000000000000000001000000000018
30802472010000000000000000000000000000000000001800045100000000100100
308024810304339114502101022100002099001000210110000000000000000000000000000000002
30802482010000000000000000000000000000000000000500010100000000100000
308024910304342114502101022100007099002000290210000000000000000000000000000000003
30802492010000000000000000000000000000000000000500010100000000100000
308025010305349115503312020220003099001100210110000000000000000000001000000100137
30802502010000040012860092000000000000000000005500110030000000100000
308025110304353114502101022110000099002100230201191990000000001011110000000100515
30802512010010000002360000000000000100000010051501288131111111111101
308025210404329114502101022100100099301000217201201000000000101100000000000000045
30802522010000009999980000000000000100000000000510012810000000100100
308025310405326114503212021120002099002000230210000000000000000000000000000000001
30802532010000000000000000000000000000000000000500010100000000100000
308025410405333116004202020120001299002000290210000000000000000000001000000000002
30802542010000000000000000000000000000000000000500010100000000100001
308025510405335116504412020120000299001000210210000000000000000000000000000000010
30802552010000000000000000000000000000000000001000025100000000100000
308025610405333116505412020220002399002200230200000000000000000111101100000000104
308025620100000099999800000000000000000000000010400260120000001100000
308025710303382215504312020120000299000004400210000000000000000000000000000000004
30802572010000000000000000000000000000000000001000025100000000100000
308025810303382215504212021210001199301000210200000000000000000000000000000000006
30802582010000000000000000000000000000000000001000025100000010100000
```

```
30802591030337321500320202021000319900100021020000000000000000000000000000000002
30802592010000000000000000000000000000000000000500010100000000100100
30802601030337121500320202121000019900120021021000000000000000000000000100000000001
30802602010000019999990000000000000000000000000500010100000000100000
30802611030436521450210102212010109930100021020000000010000000000000000000000000003
30802612030000000000000000000000000000000000001500030100000000100100
30802621030436221450220102210000509900100021020110010010000000000000010000000000011
30802622010000000000000000000000000000000000001100028100000010100100
30802631030435921500210102210000609900100021020000000000000000000000010000000000003
30802632010000009999980000000000000000000000000500010100000100100000
30802641030435521450210102220010209930100021020110010000000000000000000000000000033
30802642010000000000000000000000000000000000003300083100000000100100
30802651020340321700431202011000029900100021021000000000000000000000000000000000012
30802652010000000000000000000000000000000000001200030100000000100000
30802661020339821650530202012000029900100021020000000000000000000000000000000000010
30802662010000009999989999000000000000000000001500035100000000100100
30802671020340021600410202022000129900100021021000000000000000000000010000000000001
30802672010010000000190000000000000000000000000500010100000000100001
30802681020438731450310202919000219900100021021000000000000000000000000000000000001
30802682010000000000000000000000000000000000000500010100000000100000
30802691020439321450210106210000029900100024010000000000000000000000000000000000003
30802692010000000000000000000000000000000000000500010100000010100100
30802701020439621450210106210000109930100021020000000000000000000000000000000000016
30802702010000000000000000000000000000000000001600040120000011100100
30802711020438221750531202022000329900004400210000000000000000000000010000000000014
30802712010000020001650029000000000000000000001500030030000000100000
30802721020341321800541202012000029900110021520140110050000000110001100000000091
30802722010000009999980157000000000000001000087001740320000500110 1101
30802731020340921850541202012000029900100021020000000000000000010000000000000001
30802732010000000000000100000000000000000000000500010120000001101101
30802741020341121700541202023000729900004400200000000000000000000000000000000000001
30802742010000000000000000000000000000000000000500010100000000101000
30802751010342721700531202012000129900100021020000000000000000000000000000000000002
30802752010000000000000020000000000000000000000500010100000010100100
30802761010343121700421202110000129900100021020000000000000000000000010000000000021
30802762010000000000000000000000000000000000002100053100000000100100
30802771020342221650530202112000129900100021020000000000000000000000010000000000003
30802772010000000000000000000000000000000000000500010100000000100100
30802781010342521550421202112000029940100024020000000000000000000000000000000000009
30802782010000000000000000000000000000000000001000025100000000100100
30802791020342421550431202022000129900100021020000000000000000000000010000000000022
30802792020000000000000000000000000000000000002500060100000000100100
30802801020541621500320202120000529900100021021000000000000000000000000000000000001
30802802010000000000000000000000000000000000000500010100000000100000
30802811020440221450320202120000029900100021020000000000000000000000010000000000013
30802812020000000000000000000000000000000000001600038100000000100100
30802821020441021450320102210010009900100021020000000000000000000000000000000000092
30802822010000000000000000000000000000000000009200230100000110100100
30802831090610221500210103230010040100011010201201000000000000000000111100102 99999
30802832010000009999980000000000000000000000999999999931111111110111
30802841020440621450320202120004139900100021021000000000000000000000000000000000004
30802842010000000000000000000000000000000000001000025100000000100000
30802851010441621550431202121000529900110021021000000000003000010001101000000031
30802852010000020007190054000000000000000000033500670300000000100100
30802861020441321500430202112000029900100021021000000000000000000000000000000000007
30802862030000000000000000000000000000000000001500030100000000100000
30802871020441321500320202122000129900100021020000000000000000000000000000000000002
30802872010000000000000000000000000000000000000500010100000000100100
30802881020440521450420202122000129900100021021000000000000000000000000000000000001
30802882010000000000000000000000000000000000000500010100000000100000
30802891020440521450320202110000229900100021021000000000000000000000000000000000001
30802892010000000000000000000000000000000000000500010100000000100000
30802901020440721450320202112010419900120021020000000000000000000000011000001000 19
30802902010000009999980000000000000000000000001900048120000011100000
30802911020441121500321202120010220340100021021000000000000000000000010000000000002
30802912010000000000000000000000000000000000000500010100000000100000
30802921010441521500210106230000129900100021021000000000000000000000000000000000003
30802922010000000000000000000000000000000000000500010100000000100000
30802931010343221800531202022000129900004400200000000000000000000000000000000000006
30802932010000000000000000000000000000000000001000025100000000100100
30802941010340821650531202122000029900100021020000000000000000000000000000000000001
30802942010000000000000000000000000000000000000500010100000000100100
30802951010343321650421202122000229900004400200000000000000000000000000000000000002
30802952010000000000000000000000000000000000000500010000000000100100
30802961010342721500410202120000129900100021020000010000000010000110000000000 3
30802962010000009999980000000000000000000000000500010100000000101101
30802971010342921500421202121000229900004400210000000000000000000000000000000000002
30802972010000000000000000000000000000000000000500010100000000100000
30802981010340021600541202112000129900100021020000000000000000000000000000000000016
30802982020000000000000000000000000000000000002000048100000000100100
30802991010340421650521202111000029900100021020000000000000000000000000000000000004
30802992020000000000000000000000000000000000001500035100000000100100
30803001080514911550210102210010029910100021021000000000000000000000000000000000005
30803002010000000000000000000000000000000000001000025100000000100000
30803011010440121500421202121000129900100021021000000000000000000000000000000000003
30803012020000000000000000000000000000000000001000020100000000100000
30803021010443421450320202920000039900100021020000000000000000000000000000000000009
30803022010000000000000000000000000000000000001000025120000001100100
30803031010443021450210104230000009900100021020000000000000000000000000000000000003
30803032010000000000000000000000000000000000000500010100000000100100
30803041010442621450210104230000209900100021020000000000000000000000000000000000002
30803042010000000000000000000000000000000000000500010100000000100100
30803051010442421450210104231000009900100021020000000000000000000000000000000000001
30803052010000000000000000000000000000000000000500010100000000100100
30803061010442421500320202122000509900100021020000000000000000000000000000000000004
30803062010000000000000000000000000000000000001000025100000000100100
30803071010442121550531202022000029900004400110000000000000000000000010000000000006
30803072010000000000000000000000000000000000001000025100000000100001
30803081010442021550531202013000029900100021121000000000000000000000000000000000001
30803082010000000000000000000000000000000000000500010100000000100001
30803091090511311550220102210000019930110021020140110000000000000000000000000000072
30803092010000009999980000000000000000000010007200160120000111100100
30803101080718521900521202012000029900004400200000000000000000000000000000000000001
30803102010000009999980000000000000000000000000500010100000000100100
30803111070618211500231202013000309900100021020000000000000000000000000000000000011
30803112010000000000000000000000000000000000000600011000000110100101
30803121070720021950531202012000229900004400201101000100000000000000010000000000003
30803122010000009999980000000000000000000010000500010000000000100101
30803131070819221750320202121000029900100021021000000000000000000000000000000000004
30803132020000000000000000000000000000000000001000020100000000100000
30803141030634131500420202012000029990100021021000000000000000000000000000000000004
30803142010000000000000000000000000000000000001000025100000000100000
30803151030634031500420202012000129990100021021000000000000000000000000000000000004
30803152010000000000000000000000000000000000001000025100000000100000
30803161040430641800441202023000329900300029020000000000000000000000010000000000003
30803162010000000000000000002000000000000000000500010100000000100100
30803171040430731650431202012000029900003990200000000000000000000000000000000000003
30803172020000000000000000000000000000000000001000020100000000100100
30803181040431231650430202112000029940100021020000000000000000000000000000000000001
30803182010000000000000000000000000000000000000500010100000000100100
```

```
30803191010340721750 6-120202300042990000044002100000000000000000000000000000000001
308031920100000000000000000000000000000000000000500010100000000100000
00900011120600011800331202112000029900111021130171221979777712222291119111806500
0090001207007053912080200611021111220122222150003000033000011111111111
20900011130310721850621201123000719800110501020160110160410211100001110000000357
2090001216000007005522003500100000000001000000554012273000000010010101
20900021120310421800631201023000129800200500020000000000000000000001000000000024
2090002201000000000000000000000000000000000000240006010000000000010100
20900031120310721850631201023000529800100541020000000000010000000001000000000008
2090003202000000000000000000000000000000001000100002530000000000010101
20900041120311321850631201022000419800200540021000000000000000000000000000000001
2090004201000000000000000000000000000000000000050001030000000000010001
20900051120311621750621201023000219800200540020000000000000000000000000000000016
2090005202000000000000000000000000000000000000016000401000000000010100
20900061120311221800631201023000519800200540020000000000000000000000000000000030
2090006205000000000000000000000000000000000000030000751000000000010100
20900071130311821800621201023000219800200540020000000000000000000000000000000051
2090007202000000000000000000000000000000000000051001271000000000010100
20900081130311721750521201023000419800200540021000000000000000000000000000000008
2090008201000000000000000000000000000000000000100002530000000000010000
20900091130311821750521201023000319800200540020000000000000000000000000000000006
2090009201000000000000000000000000000000000000100002530000000000010100
20900101130810521650320201221000129800100021020000000000000000000000000000000009
2090010202000000000000000000000000000000000000100002530000000000010100
20900111140607821600520201122001009800004400201211010300010030000000000000000080
2090011203000000000000000000000000000000000000800020010000000010010101
20900121140607321600320112210000409800100021031000000000000000000001000000000001
2090012201000000000000000000000000000000000000050001020000000000010001
20900131140607021600320114210000409830100022020000000000000000000000000000000007
2090013201000000000000000000000000000000000000100002530000000000010100
20900141140607321600320211122000809800100021020000000000000000000000000000000031
2090014201000000000000000000000000000000000000031000771000000000010101
20900151140607621600320112210000109800100022020000000000000000000000000000000004
2090015201000000000000000000000000000000000000100002530000000001010100
20900161140508121600320202111000109800110021230140110030110001100001000000000230
2090016201000000000000010000000000000000000000023000575100000110010101
20900171140508421600320201121000619800100021220000000010000000101000000000000037
2090017202000000000000000000000000000000000000037000921011111100010101
20900181140507921600420202012000319800100441021140100000000000010001000000000024
2090018203000000000000010000000000000000000000024000601000000000010101
20900191140507921600420201022000319800100441020000000000000000000000000000000007
2090019201000000000000000000000000000000000000100002530000000000010100
20900201140508621600320202122000510400100021041000000000000001000111001000000105
2090020202000000000000000000000000000000000000105002621000000000010001
20900211140509921600521201123000229800200441021000000000000000000001000000000001
2090021201000002000074000000000000000000000000100002530000000000010001
20900221140507421600320201022000519800100441021000000000000100001000000000000018
2090022201000002000456000000000000000000000000180004510000000000010001
20900231140507221600531201013000329800200440021000000000000000000001000000000001
2090023201001000000610000000000000000000000000050001030000000000010001
20900241140508021700621201003000229800210441021000000000000000000001000000000001
2090024201000002000266000000000000000000000000100002530000000000010001
20900251140508921650420202101000129800100021231140110000000000100001000000000115
2090025202000000000000000000000010000000000001150028712000000010110101
20900261110605221600420201023000329800100021020140100000000000010000000000000004
2090026201000000000000000000000000000000000000050001030000000000010101
20900271110604821600520201023000729800100029020000000000000000000000000000000007
2090027201000000000000000000000000000000000000100002530000000000010101
20900281110604421600530201023000129840100021020000000000000000000000000000000001
2090028201000000000000000000000000000000000000050001030000000000010101
```

```
20900291110505721650420201023000319800100021020110110000000000000000000000000004
2090029201000000000000000000000000000000000000100002530000000011010101
20900301110505921650420201121000019800110011020000000000000000000001000000000116
2090030201000002001478000000000000000000000000116002901000000001010101
20900311110406321700520201123000119800100021020190101000000000000001000000000001
2090031201000000000000000000000000000000000000050001030000000010010101
20900321110406721700621201123000229800110021020000000010000000000001000000000008
2090032201000040007000000000000000000000000000100002530000000010010001
20900331110407121750631201023000229800100441020000000010000000000000000000000005
2090033201000000000000000000000000000000000000100002530000000010010100
20900341110407921800621201023000129800100541020000000000000000000000000000000011
2090034201000000000000000000000000000000000000011000271000000000010100
20900351110407821800621201023000229800100441020000000000000000000000000000000005
2090035201000000000000000000000000000000000000050001030000000000010101
20900361110406921650621201123000229800100441020000000000000000000000000000000005
2090036201000000000000000000000000000000000000050001030000000000010101
20900371120407421800621201023000729800100441020000000000000000000000000000000066
2090037201000000000000000000000000000000000000066001651000000000010100
20900381120406821750621201023000629800100441020000000000000000011000100000000115
2090038201000000000000000000000000000000000000115002871000000010010101
20900391120504421650320202111000119800110021020140100010100000100011100000000194
2090039201000020013200000000000000000000000100019400485120000111110100
20900401120404921650430202112000129800100021031000000000000000010000000000000001
2090040201000000000000000000000000000000000000100002530000000000010000
20900411120504721650420201112000129800100021021000000000000000000000000000000001
2090041201000000000000000000000000000000000000050001030000000000010001
20900421120405121650420202211000029800100021020000000000000000000000000000000004
2090042201000000000000000000000000000000000000100002530000000000010101
20900431120405121700430201112000029800100021021000000000000000000000000000000001
2090043201000000000000000000000000000000000000050001030000000000010001
20900441120406021750621201123000429800100021020000000000000000000000000000000011
2090044201000000000000000000000000000000000000011000271000000000010100
20900451120405921750621201122000329800100441020000000000000000000000000000000006
2090045201000000000000000000000000000000000000100002530000000000010100
20900461120406621700621201123000229800100441020140110000000010010000000000000100
2090046202000000000000000000000000000000000000100002501000000010010101
20900471120406621700620201122000229800100441020000000000000000000000000000000001
2090047201000000000000000000000000000000000000050001030000000000010101
20900481120406121700420201023000029800100021020000000000000000000000000000000004
2090048201000000000000000000000000000000000000100002530000000000010101
20900491120406921650421201112000229800100441020000000000000000000000000000000067
2090049201000000000000000000000000000000000000067001671000000000010100
20900501120407621700620201122000129800100021020000000010100000000000000000000137
2090050202000000000000000000000000000000000000137003421000000000010100
20900511120408721800621201122000229800100441020000000000000000000000000000000004
2090051201000000000000000000000000000000000000100002530000000000010100
20900521120407421700520201122000129800100021030000000000000000000000000000000038
2090052201000000000000000000000000000000000000038000951000000000010100
20900531120408421800621201023000229800200541020000000000000000110000000000000099
2090053201000000000000000000000000000000000000099002471000000010010101
20900541120407921750620201023000229800200441020000000000000000000000000000000013
2090054202000000000000000000000000000000000000013000321000000000010100
20900551120408221750621201023000229800200441020000000000000000000000000000000028
2090055201000000000000000000000000000000000000028000701000000000010100
20900561120309021800621201023000229800000540020000000000000000000000000000000004
2090056201000000000000000000000000000000000000100002530000000000010100
20900571120408721800621201023000229800100441020000000000000000000000000000000063
2090057203000000000000000000000000000000000000063001571000000000010101
20900581120408321750621202112000229800100421020140100010001100000000000000000096
2090058204000000000000000000000000000000000000096002401000000000010100
```

```
20900591120407821700520201023000119800100421020000000000000000000000000000000096
209005920500000000000000000000000000000000009600240100000000010100
20900601120407321700320202111000119800100021020000000000000000000000000000000024
209006020300000000000000000000000000000000002400060100000000010100
20900611120408821700520201122100119850100021021000000000000000000000000000000001
209006120100000000000000000000000000000000000500010300000000010001
20900621120503621650320202113000119800100021020110100020000101100011000000000444
209006220400000000000000000000000000000000000044401110100000111010101
20900631120406121650320202112100119800110021020140110020100200000111001000000946
20900632010000090291150000000000000000000000094602365120011111110101
20900641130406921650320201102000119800100021020110010010000010100000000000000103
209006420200000000000000000000000000000000000010300257100000100010101
20900651130407221650320201102000219800100021020000000000000000000000000000000013
209006520300000000000000000000000000000000001300032100000000010100
20900661130407321650320202111000119900100021020120100000000000000000000000000218
209006620100000000000000000000000000000000000021800545100000100010001
20900671130408021700420201023000329800100421020000000000000000000000000000000017
209006720100000000000000000000000000000000000170004210000000010100
20900681130408121650420201023000319800000440020000000000000000000000000000000009
209006820100000000000000000000000000000000001000025300000000010100
20900691130408821700621201023000229800100541020000000000000000000000000000000011
209006920100000000000000000000000000000000001100027100000000010100
20900701130409121700621201023000329800100421020000000000000000000000000000000006
209007020100000000000000000000000000000000001000025300000000010100
20900711130409321700621201023000629800100541020000000000000000000000000000000007
209007120100000000000000000000000000000000001000025300000000010100
20900721130409521700620201123100129800000540020000000000000000000000000000000004
209007220100000000000000000000000000000000001000025300000000010100
20900731130310021750621201020000329800000440020000000000000000000001000000000013
209007320400000000000000000000000000000000001300032100000000010101
20900741130310221800621201023001329800000540020000000000000000000000000000000005
209007420100000000000000000000000000000000000500010300000000010101
20900751130309621700621201023000629800000540020000000000000000000000000000000007
209007520100000000000000000000000000000000001000025300000000010100
20900761120310021800620201020000229800000540020000000000000000000000000000000003
209007620100000000000000000000000000000000001000025300000000010100
20900771130309821800620201023000129800100541020000000000000000000000000000000034
209007720100000000000000000000000000000000003400085100000010010100
20900781130309721800620201023000229800100541020000000000000000000000000000000015
209007820100000000000000000000000000000000001500037100000000010100
20900791120309521750620201123000129800100421020000000000000000000000000000000037
209007920400000000000000000000000000000000003700092100000000010101
20900801120408621700520101222100119800100021020000000000000000000000000000000001
209008020100000000000000000000000000000000000500010300000000010101
20900811120309521750620201020000419800100421021000000000000000000000000000000003
209008120100000000000000000000000000000000000500010300000000010001
20900821130409121750621201122001219800100421020000000000000000000001000000000034
209008220200000000000000000000000000000000003400085100000000010100
20900831130409321750621201023000629800100421020000000000000000000000000000000005
209008320100000000000000000000000000000000000500010300000000010101
20900841130408621700620201122000429800100021020110100010100001000000000000000041
209008420100000000000000000000000000000000004100102100000000010101
20900851130311221800621201023000429800000540021000000000000000000000000000000002
209008520100000000000000000000000000000000001000025300000000010000
20900861130311421700621201023000329800100441021000000000000000000000000000000004
209008620100000000000000000000000000000000001000025300000000010000
20900871130311621700621201023000419800100541020000000000000000000000000000000009
209008720100000000000000000000000000000000001000025300000000010100
20900881130311821700520201023000319800100441021000000000000000000000000000000003
2090088201000000000000000000000000000000000000005000103000000000100010
```

```
20900891130311921700520201023000219800100441021000000000000000000000000000000003
209008920100000000000000000000000000000000000500010300000000010001
20900901130312021700420201102000219800100021021000000000000000000000000000000005
209009020200000000000000000000000000000000001000025300000000010000
20900911130311821700420201102000119800100021021000000000000000000000000000000031
209009120100000000000000000000000000000000003100077100000000010001
20900921130311821700420201002000219800100021021000000000000000000000000000000006
209009220100000000000000000000000000000000001000025300000000010001
20900931130311721700520201102000329800100021021000000000000000000000000000000006
209009320100000000000000000000000000000000001000025300000000010000
20900941130311821700420201003000129800100021020000000000000000000000000000000005
209009420100000000000000000000000000000000001000025300000000010100
20900951130311321750421201102000119800100021020000000000000000000001000000000396
20900952060000010001870000000000000000000000039600990100000000010101
20900961130410421700420202112000129800100021020000000000000000000000000000000005
209009620100000000000000000000000000000000000500010300000000010101
20900971130310721750530201003000329800100021021000000000000000000000000000000002
209009720100000000000000000000000000000000000500010300000000010001
20900981130311421750521201002000329800100021020120100030000001100000000000000048
209009820100000000000000000000000000000000010004800120100000000010101
20900991130311421700520201103100129800100021021000000000000000000001000000000001
209009920100000000000000000000000000000000000500010300000000010001
20901001130310921750630201003000829800100021021000000000000000000000000000000003
209010020100000000000000000000000000000000001000025300000000010000
20901011130310321750621201103000829800100041021000000000000000000000000000000003
209010120100000000000000000000000000000000001000025300000000010000
20901021130410121750621201103000829800100041021000000000000000000000000000000002
209010220100000000000000000000000000000000000500010300000000010001
20901031130310621750621201003000529800100541021000000000000000000000000000000002
209010320100000000000000000000000000000000000500010300000000010001
20901041130310821800621201003000629800100541021000000000000000000000000000000004
209010420100000000000000000000000000000000000500010300000000010001
20901051130408221700521201122000129800100541020120100000000000000000000000000018
209010520100000000000000000000000000000000001800047100000000010100
20901061130409921700420101111100129800100021021000000000000000000000000000000003
209010620100000000000000000000000000000000000500010300000000010001
20901071130410221700320101111100129800100021021000000000000000000000000000000004
209010720100000000000000000000000000000000000500010300000000010001
20901081130409921750521201003000129800100541021000000000000000000000000000000008
209010820100000000000000000000000000000000001000025300000000010000
20901091130409821700430201103000129800100021021000000000000000000000000000000014
209010920100000000000000000000000000000000001400035100000000010000
20901101140410021700420201101000229800100021021000000000000000000000000000000003
209011020100000000000000000000000000000000000500010300000000010001
20901111140410421700420201102000229800100021020000000000000000000000000000000025
209011120300000000000000000000000000000000002500062100000000010100
20901121140410521700420201102000219800100021021000000000000000000000000000000021
209011220400000000000000000000000000000000002100052100000000010000
20901131140410621700320201101000119800100021021000000000000000000000000000000008
209011320200000000000000000000000000000000001000025300000000010001
20901141130408921800621201102000429800110021021000000000000011000001000000000059
209011420100001000149000100000000000000000005900147100000000010001
20901151140410321700410202013000229800110441020000000000000000010001000000000005
209011520100000000000000000000000000000000000500010300000010010001
20901161140409821700430201003000129800200441021000000000000000000000000000000002
209011620100000000000000000000000000000000000500010000000000010001
20901171140409221700520201103000129800100021020000000000000000000000000000000040
209011720700000000000000000000000000000000004000100100000110010000
20901181140409021750520201102000129800100021020000000000000000001000000000000103
209011820500000000000000000000000000000000000010300257100000010010001
```

```
20901191140409221700520201003000129800200441021000000000000000000000000000000141
20901192040000000000000000000000000000000000014100352100000000010000
20901201120501421650430201123100129800100021020140101000000000100000000000000166
20901202080000000000000000000000000000001000016600415120000010110101
20901211130408221750520201002000129800200440121120010000000000001000000000000003
20901212010000000000000000000200000000000000000500010300000000010001
20901221130408221700621201013000629800200440021000000000000000000000000000000004
20901222010000000000000000000000000000000000000500010300000000010001
20901231130407921700621201013000529800200440021000000000000000000000000000000006
20901232010000000000000000000000000000000000001000025300000000010000
20901241130408121700621201013000629800100021020000000000000000000000000000000002
20901242010000000000000000000000000000000000000500010300000000010101
20901251130407521700320202111000129800100021020000000000000000000000000000000119
20901252040000000000000000000000000000000000011900297100000000010100
20901261120501521650430202112000229800100021020000000000000000000000000000000014
20901262020000000000000000000000000000000000001400035100000010010100
20901271120502721600320202122000119800100021020110100030100001000110011000000185
20901272020000000000000000000000000000000000018500462120000011110101
20901281120501621600320202121000219800100021020000000000000000000000000000000003
20901282010000000000000000000000000000000000000500010300000000010101
20901291120501621600320202121000319800100021020000000000000000000000000000000004
20901292010000000000000000000000000000000000000500010300000000010101
20901301120501821600210101211100119850100021020000000000000000000000000000000006
20901302010000000000000000000000000000000000001000025300000000010101
20901311120501821600320202122100119800100021020140110000000011010000000000000118
20901312020000000000000000000000000000000100011800295100000010010101
20901321120502321600320201122000119800100021021000000000000000000000000000000004
20901322010000000000000000000000000000000000000500010300000000010001
20901331120502221650220101211100119850100021021000000000000000000000000000000006
20901332010000000000000000000000000000000000001000025300000000010001
20901341120502021650320201022000119800100021021000000000000000001000000000000011
20901342010000000000000000000000000000000000011000271000000000010001
20901351120502421650420201023000129800100441021000000000000000000000000000000016
20901352010000000000000000000000000000000000001600040100000000010000
20901361120503121650420201023000129800200441021000000000000000000000000000000008
20901362010000000000000000000000000000000000001000025300000000010000
20901371120502721650520201023000429800100441021000000000000000000000000000000002
20901372010000000000000000000000000000000000000500010300000000010001
20901381140608621950621201023000229800010540020141100000000010100001000000000002
20901382010000100006600000000000000000000000000000000030000000010101
20901391140607721700520201023000129800003400210000000000000000001000000000000002
20901392010000100006470001000000000000000000000500010300000000010001
20901401140707921700621201013000829800200440021000000000000000000000000000000005
20901402010000000000000000000000000000000000001000025300000000010001
20901411130606521600320202121000129800200011020000000000000001100000000000000097
20901412020000000000000000000000000000000000009700242120011110110101
20901421130707821650420201122000129800100021020000000000000000000000000000000009
20901422010000000000000000000000000000000000001000025300000000010101
20901431130705421750621201023000329800010540020000000000000000000100000000000021
20901432010000000000000000000000000000000000021000521000000000010101
20901441110503721650420201023000229800100021020110100000000000000000000000000002
20901442010000000000000000000000000000000000000500010300000010010101
20901451110604021600520202122000529800110021020000000000000000000001000000000006
20901452020000000000000000000000000000000000001000025300000010010101
20901461110603321600320201122000119900200011020000000000000000000000000000000025
20901462010000000000000000000000000000000000002500062100000010010101
20901471120708321650420201023000129800000044002011010000000000000000000000000002
20901472010000000000000000000000000000000000000500010300000010010101
20901481110603421600420201023000129800100021020190100010000000110000000000000010
20901482010000000000000000000000000000000000001000025300000000010101
20901491110603021600320201123000519800100021020110100000000000000000000000000011
20901492010000000000000000000000000000000000011000271000000010010101
20901501110502821600420201023000419800200440020000000000000000000000000000000002
20901502010000000000000000000000000000000000000500010300000000010101
20901511110502821600320201023000129800100021020140100000100000000000000000000001
20901512010000000000000000000000000000000000000500010300000010010101
20901521110502321600320202122000119800100021020000000000000000000000000000000034
20901522010000000000000000000000000000000000003400085100000010010101
20901531120504121600420201022000229800100021020170100000500000000010000000000008
20901532010000000000000000000000000000000000001000025300000000010100
20901541120503121600320201022000319800100021020000000000000000000000000000000020
20901542010000000000000000000000000000000000002000050100000010010100
20901551120503321600320202122000219800100021020110110010000001000010000000000054
20901552010000000000000000000000000000000000005400135100000000010101
20901561130707421650520201023000129800210010020140110000400100000000000000000097
20901562040000000000000000000000000000000000009700242100000010010001
20901571130707721600420201022000119800100021020000000000000000000000000000000020
20901572020000000000000000000000000000000000002000050100000010010101
20901581130707021650520201023000119800200440020000000000000000000001000000020
20901582010000000000000000000000000000000000002000050100000010010101
20901591130706421600420201023000419800200440020000000000100100000000000000000004
20901592010000000000000000000000000000000000001000025300000000010101
20901601130708421650420201020000229800200440020000000000000000000000000000000002
20901602010000000000000000000000000000000000000500010300000000010101
20901611130708721650420202111000229900100022020000000100000001000000000000000003
20901612010000000000000000000000000000000000001000025300000010010100
20901621130709521650420202112000229800100021020000000000001001000000000000000020
20901622010000000000000000000000000000000000002000050100000000010100
20901631130809321600420201022000329800100021020000000000000000000000000000000005
20901632010000000000000000000000000000000000000500010300000010010101
20901641130708521600410201022000229800200010020000000000000000000000000000000005
20901642010000000000000000000000000000000000001000025300000000010100
20901651130709321600420201122000129800200010020000000000000000000000000000000003
20901652010000000000000000000000000000000000000500010300000000010101
20901661130707721600420201022000329800200010020000000000000000000000000000000003
20901662010000000000000000000000000000000000000500010300000000010101
20901671130707621600410201022000129800200010020000000000000000000000000000000019
20901672010000000000000000000000000000000000001900047100000000010100
20901681130808821600410201022000129800200010020000000000000000000000000000000003
20901682010000000000000000000000000000000000000500010300000000010101
20901691130812821700410112112100029800100021020000000000000000000000000000000002
20901692010000000000000000000000000000000000001000025300000010010101
20901701130812221650420201022000429800100021020000000000000000000000000000000001
20901702010000000000000000000000000000000000000500010300000000010101
20901711130811921650320201122000129800100021021000000000000000000000000000000003
20901712010000000000000000000000000000000000000500010300000000010001
20901721130912321600320201022000129800100021020000000000000000000000000000000003
20901722010000000000000000000000000000000000001000025300000000010100
20901731130809921600210101211009999800100021021000000000000000000000000000000003
20901732010000000000000000000000000000000000000500010100000000010001
20901741110605421600320202122000529800100021020000000000000000000000000000000012
20901742010000000000000000000000000000000000012000301000000010010101
20901751110605621600320202122000329800100021021000000000000000000000000000000004
20901752010000000000000000000000000000000000001000025300000000010001
20901761120504421650320202121000129800100021020000000000000000000000000000000009
20901762010000000000000000000000000000000000001000025300000000010101
20901771120501021650420201023000819800200041020140110000000001000000000000000011
20901772030000000000000000000000000000000000011000271000000110010101
20901781120601421600420201023000619800200040020000000000000000000000000000000065
20901782010000000000000000000000000000000000006500162100000010010101
```

```
20901791110601621600320201023000619800100021020000000000000000000000000000000004
20901792010000000000000000000000000000000000001000025300000000010100
20901801110601921600320201123100319800100021020000000000000000000000000000000004
20901802010000000000000000000000000000000000001000025300000000010100
20901811110601921600420201023000519800200040020000000000000000000000000000000002
20901812010000000000000000000000000000000000001000025300000000010101
20901821110602421600320201123000519800100021020000000000000000000000000000000032
20901822020000000000000000000000000000000000003200080100300010010100
20901831110602621600320202122000029800100021020000000000000000000000000000000001
20901832010000000000000000000000000000000000000500010300000000010101
20901841110602821600320202222000029800100021020000000000000000000000000000000011
20901842010000000000000000000000000000000000001100027100000000010100
20901851110602221600530201023000129800000240020000000000000000000000000000000001
20901852010000000000001000000000000000000000000500010300000000010101
20901861120602021600520201023000129800000240020000000000000000000000000000000002
20901862010000000000000000000000000000000000000500010300000000010101
20901871120602721600420201022000329800100021020000000000000000000000000000000012
20901872010000000000000000000000000000000000001200030100000000010100
20901881120602921600420201022000329800100021020000000000000000000000000000000024
20901882020000000000000000000000000000000000002400060100000010010000
20901891120703521600320201022000509800100021020000000000000000000011000100000060
20901892010000000000000000000200100000000000000600015010000011010101
20901901120602121600420201122000129800100021020000000000000000000000000000000016
20901902030000000000000000000000000000000000001600040100000010010100
20901911120602421600420201122000029800100021020000000000000000000000000000000011
20901912010000000000000000000000000000000000001100027100000010010000
20901921120603021600320201121000029800100021020000000000000000000000000000000006
20901922010000000000000000000000000000000000001000025300000000010100
20901931120603021600320201121000129800100021020000000000000000000000000000000002
20901932010000000000000000000000000000000000001000025300000010010100
20901941110603321600320201221000129800100021021000000000000000000000000000000002
20901942010000000000000000000000000000000000000500010300000000010001
20901951110603621600320201221000229800100021021000000000000000000000000000000003
20901952010000000000000000000000000000000000001000025300000000010000
20901961110604121600320202221000129800100021020000000000000000000000000000000004
20901962010000000000000000000000000000000000001000025300000010010001
20901971110604121600320202221000129800100021020000000000000000000000000000000005
20901972010000000000000000000000000000000000001000025300000000010100
20901981130604421600420201111000229800100021021000000000000000000000000000000038
20901982010000000000000000000000000000000000003800095100000000010000
20901991130604821600320202111000129800101021020000000000000000000010000000000068
20901992010000000000000000000000000000000000006800170131111110111111
20902001130604821600420201112000129800100021021120010000000000000000000000000036
20902002020000000000000000000000000000000000003600090100000000010000
20902011130605621600320201121000909800100021020000000000000000000000000000000007
20902012010000000000000000000000000000000000001000025300000010010101
20902021130605221600420202112000129800100021020000000000000000000000000000000016
20902022010010000000390000000000000000000000001600040100000010010101
20902031130606021650521202013000229800210440020000000000000000100001000000000066
20902032010000000000000000000100000000000000006600165100000010010001
20902041120503021650420201023000229800200440021000000000000000000000000000000001
20902042010000000000000000000000000000000000000500010300000000010001
20902051120503021650420201023000529800200440021000000000000000000000000000000005
20902052010000000000000000000000000000000000001000025300000000010001
20902061120502921700430201023000429800000440021000000000000000000000000000000001
20902062010000000000000000000000000000000000000500010300000000010001
20902071130504421700520201023001019800200240021000000000000000000100001000000004
20902072020000000000000000000000000000000000001000025300000000010001
20902081130505021600320201122000219800100021020000000000000000000000000000000001
20902082010000000000000000000000000000000000000500010320000001110001
20902091130505221600320201123000219800200240021000000020000010000010000000000006
20902092020000000000000000000000000000001000001000025300000000010001
20902101130505421600320201023000219800100041020000000000000000000001000000000008
20902102030000000000000000000000000000000000001000025300000010010101
20902111130506221650420202013000219800200440021000000000000000000010000000000055
20902112010000000000000060000000000000000000005500137100000000010001
20902121130506321650421201013000129800200440021000000000000000000000000000000095
20902122010000000000000000000000000000000000009500237100000000010001
20902131130507121650420201103000129800100021021000000000000000000000000000000006
20902132010000000000000000000000000000000000001000025300000000010001
20902141120602521650420201023000029800000240021000000000000000000000000000000002
20902142010000000000000000000000000000000000000500010300000000010001
20902151120503821650420201023000219800200440020000000000000000000000000000000001
20902152010000000000000000000000000000000000000500010300000010010001
20902161130707821600320201022000129800200010020000000000000000000000000000000001
20902162010000000000000000000000000000000000000500010300000000010101
30900011110406641700320202112000211000100321020000000000000000000000000000000004
30900012010000000000000000000000000000000000001000025110000000011100
30900021110506441650210103230000219830100021020000000000000000000000000000000010
30900022010000000000000000000000000000000000001000025100000000010100
30900031110407141700421202112000129800100021021000000000000000000000000000000001
30900032010000000000000000000000000000000000000500010100000000010000
30900041110407541700531202121000129800100021020000000000000000000000000000000025
30900042020000000000000000000000000000000000003100078100000010010100
30900051110506531650320202012000329800200221021000000000000000000000000000000002
30900052010000000000000000000000000000000000000500010100000000010000
30900061110506651650430202122000029800100021020000000000000000000000000000000004
30900062020000000000000000000000000000000000001000020100000000010100
30900071110506241650210102210000119830100022021000000000000000000000000000000012
30900072010000000000000000000000000000000000001200030100000000010000
30900081110505231600210102230000210730100021020000000000000000000000000000000004
30900082010000000000000000000000000000000000001000025100000000010100
30900091110505931650320202111000019900100021020140101010000001010100100000000307
30900092010000009999980000000000000000000000030700768120000010110100
30900101100505931600320202111000019900100021020000000000000000000000000000000001
30900102010000000000000000000000000000000000000500010100000000010100
30900111100506141600210102210000219930100021020000000000000000000000000000000002
30900112010000000000000000000000000000000000000500010100000000010100
30900121100506931600210102210000319900100021020110010000000010010100010000000027
30900122010000009999980000000000000000000000002700068120000001110000
30900131100506841600210102210000219930100021020120010000100001010000000000000013
30900132010000000000000000000000000000000000001300033120000000110000
30900141100507241600210102210000419930100021021000000000000000000000000000000001
30900142010000000000000000000000000000000000000500010100000000010000
30900151100506841600310202021000320540100029020110010000000000100000000000000069
30900152020000000000000000000000000000000000007500183100000000010100
30900161100506711650330202012000029840100021021000000000000000000000000000000004
30900162010000000000000000000000000000000000001000025100000000010000
30900171100507011650320202122000419800100021020000000000000000000000000000000006
30900172010000000000000000000000000000000000001000025100000000010100
30900181100606111550210102210000019930100021020000000000000000000110000000000015
30900182010000009999800000000000000000000000001500038100000011110100
30900191100605821550210102220000719930100021020000000000000000000000000000000006
30900192010000000000000000000000000000000000001000025100000010010100
30900201110606021550320202121000149930100021020149919050100000000010000000000116
30900202010000000000000000000000000000000000001160029012000011110100
30900211100607021550210101210000510500100021020000000000000000000000000000000017
30900212010000010192900000000000000000000000001700043110000010110001
30900221100607320550210102230110010210100022010199999030100100000001000000000006
30900222020000009999980000000000000000000000001500030120000010110101
```

```
30900231100606121540310202021010029900100021020119999000000000000000000000000040
30900232010000000000000000000000100100000000004000100120000010110101
30900241100709221550210102210000129900100021021000000000000000000000000000000003
30900242010000000000000000000000000000000000001000025100000000010000
30900251100810621550321202022000029900000440020000000000000000010000010000000038
30900252010000009999980000000000000000000000001900038010000000011100
30900261100609411550210102210010029900120021020120110110000000111011100000000359
30900262010000009999980000000000000000000000001800036003000000111101
30900271100608911550210103210000319900100021020000000000000000000001000000000001
30900272010000000000000000000000000000000000005000101100000000011000
30900281100608711550210103210000219900110021020000000001010000000000100000000002
30900282010000000000000000000000000000000000005000101100000000011000
30900291100609011550210103210010040310100021020119991020000000010000000000000060
30900292010000009999980000000000000000000000006000150130000010111100
30900301090609811500210102210010040210100025020000000000000000000000000000000002
30900302010000000000000000000000000000000000005000101100001100011000
30900311090709121500210103230010040100011010020120100000000000200011110010202326
30900312030000020063320000000000000000000001011410234102111111110111
30900321100710021500210106230000009930100021020000000020000000100010000000000165
30900322000000009999980000000000000000000000001650041312000000110000
30900331090710841500210106240000009920100022020000000000000000000001000000000006
30900332010000000000000000000000000000000000001000025120000000110100
30900341100811531550210102210000129900000010010000000000000000000001000000000013
30900342010000009999980000000000000000000000001000025120000000110101
30900351090813631700321202013000029900000440020000000000000000000000000000000003
30900352010000000000000000000000000000000000005000101100000000011100
30900361090612211500220106240010040110100021020000000000000000000010010000000009
30900362010000000000000000000000000000000000001000025120000011110100
30900371090611621500210103210010040110100021020000000000000000000001000000000125
30900372010000009999980000000000000000000000001250031313000001111000
30900381090611121500210102210000220310100021021000000000000000000000000000000005
30900382010000000000000000000000000000000000001000025100000000010000
30900391090611221500210113210000205001000210200000000000000000000000000000000027
30900392010000000000000000000000000000000000002700068100000000010100
30900401090611521500210102210000029900100021021000000000000000000000000000000011
30900402020000000000000000000000000000000000002000050100000000010000
30900411090611521500210102210000719900100021021000000000000000000000000000000004
30900412010000000000000000000000000000000000001000025100000000010000
30900421090711421500210105040000709901100022021000000000000000000000000000000007
30900422010000000000000000000000000000000000001000025100000000010000
30900431090814841650321202013000029900000440020110010000000000100001000000000015
30900432010000000000000000000000000000000000001500038100000010010100
30900441090512511550321202121000029900100021020000000000000000101001000000000006
30900442010000000000000000000000000000000000001000025110000000011001
30900451090612511550321202121000029900100021020000000000000000101001000000000032
30900452010000000000000000000000000000000000003600090110000000011001
30900461090612711550321202121000029900100021020000000000000000101001000000000003
30900462010000000000000000000000000000000000005000101100000000011001
30900471090613111500210102210000129910100021020000000000000000000000000000000002
30900472010000009999980000000000000000000000005000101000000000110100
30900481080614521500210102210110040210100021020000000000100000000001000000000006
30900482010000009999980000000000000000000000001000025120000000110000
30900491090714621500320202120000129900110021020000000000000000000110000000000017
30900492010000009999980000000000000000000000001700043120000000110100
30900501080817421600421202121000029900100021020000000000000000000000000000000002
30900502020000000000000000000000000000000000001000020110000000011000
30900511080616011500210102210000049920100021020110110050200000101001000000000055
30900512010000009999980000000000000000000000005500138120000101110100
30900521080616211500210103210010049910120022020000000000000000000001100000000078
30900522010000009999980000000000000000000000007800195120000000110101
```

```
30900531100709331550210102210000309900100021021000000000000000000000000000000001
30900532010000000000000000000000000000000000005000101000000000010000
30900541070618521500320202210010040210100022021000000000000000000000000000000002
30900542010000000000000000000000000000000000005000101000000000010000
30900551070618121500320202210010140210100022021000000000000000000000000000000002
30900552010000000000000000000000000000000000005000101000000000010000
30900561050625411450210102110000499201000220201100100000000000000000000000000003
30900562010000000000000000000000000000000000005000101200000000110100
30900571040530011450210102210010040110100021020000000000000000000110010000000010
30900572010000009999980000000000000000001000100002512000000011110000
30900581050528831450220102210000729920100021020000000000000000000001000000000007
30900582010000009999980000000000001000000000001000025120000000110000
30900591050628111450210102210000040420100022020000000000000000000001000000000016
30900592010000009999980000000000000000000000001000025120000000110000
30900601050627711450210103210012040420100022020000000000100000000011000000000005
30900602010000009999980000000000000000000000001000025130000010111000
30900611050628911450110101210000009900100026020000000000103000000001000000000001
30900612010000009999980000000000000000000000005000101300000000111001
30900621040631222500321202221000409900100021020000000000000000000000000000000044
30900622020000009999980000000000000000000000004400110130000000111000
30900631040630721500321202221000809900100021020000000000000000000001000001000645
30900632020000009999980000000000001000000000006500162512000111110001
30900641030336021650430202011000029900000340021000000000000000000001000000000002
30900642010000000000000000000000000000000000001000023100000000010001
30900651030437111900541202111009999900000440010000000000000000000000101000000030
30900652010000009999989991000000000000001000003000075110000000011101
30900661020340221700530202023000029900100021021000000000000000000000000000000002
30900662010000000000000000000000000000000000005000101000000000010000
30900671100810121550321202022000029900000440020000000000000000000000000000000040
30900672010000000000000000000000000000000000002000043010000000011100
30900681090612911500210102210000229900100023020000000000200000101001000000000013
30900682010000009999980000000000000000000000001300033120000011110000
30900691070619811500210105240010040110110022020000000000000000101001100000000003
30900692010000009999980000000000001000000000005000100200000000110101
30900701030434811450210102211000309900210023020000000000000000001111000000000001
30900702010000009999980000000000001000000000005000101200011011110001
30900711090611921500210102210010040330100022020000000000000000010000001000000002
30900712010000019999980000000000000000000000005000101000000000010100
30900721090612221500210102210010020330100022021000000000000000000001000000000014
30900722030000020074780000000000000000000000002000045100000000010000
30900731090612821500210103230000909930100021021000000000000000000000000000000001
30900732010000000000000000000000000000000000005000101000000000010000
01000011120600011800331202112000029900111021190179999999999999999999999999999999
01000012999999999999999999999999999999999999999999999999300011111111
21000011130810021600320212111000129800111021020000000000000000000011000000000020
21000012010000050076060000000000000000000000000000000310000011101111
21000021120809321700421202112000100200110241030170110060610390110011100000001034
21000022010000140160100133000000000000200003120502555310000110101101
21000031120808821600430202013000129800000440021000000000000000000000000000000008
21000032010000000000000000000000000000000000001000025300000000001000
21000041120808521600320202033000129800200240021000000000000000000000000000000018
21000042010000000000000000000000000000000000001800045100000000001000
21000051120807721650421202013000209800010240121110100000000001000011000000000847
21000052010020010010000000100000000000000000008470211711000000001101
21000061120808421600310101111000809800210240021000000000000000000011000000000001
21000062010000000000000000000000000000000000005001031000000010001101
21000071110706921600320201211000609900100021021000000000000000000000000000000002
21000072010000000000000000000000000000000000005000103000000000001001
21000081110807621600320202211000229800100021020000000000000000000000000000000001
21000082010000000000000000000000000000000000005000103100001100001101
```

```
210000911107074216003202022110001298001000210210000000000000000000000000000000001
2100009201000000000000000000000000000000000000050001030000000001001
210001011108086217003202010130001298001000210200000000000000000000000000000000013
2100010201000000000000000000000000000000000001300032110000011001100
21000111110708221700421201113000609800010241020110100010100001010010000000000384
2100011202000002000385000000000000000000003840096011000011010101101
210001211107079216003202021130000298001000210200000000000000000000000000000000012
2100012202000000000000000000000000000000000001200030110000110101100
210001311107083216003202010130001298000002400210000000000000000000000000000000002
2100013201000000000000000000000000000000000000050001030000000001001
210001411107088216504202010130001298000002400200000000000000000000000000000000006
2100014201000000000000000000000000000000000001000025310000000001100
210001511007090216004302010120001298000002400200000000000000000000000000000000026
2100015201000000000000000000000000000000000002600065110000000001100
210001611107086217004202010120003298000002400210000000000000000000000000000000004
2100016201000000000000000000000000000000000001000025300000000001000
210001711108092217506202010130002298000005400200000000000000000000000000000000001
2100017201000000000000000000000000000000000000050001031000000001101
210001811108088217505202010130001298000004400200000000000000000000000000000000003
2100018201000000000000000000000000000000000000050001031000000001101
210001911306055216003202011231000298001000210200000000000000000000000000000000004
2100019201000000000000000000000000000000000001000025300000000101001
210002011306050216003202021110001298001010210200000000000000000000000000000000010
2100020201000000000000000000000000000000000001000025331111110111111
310000111104066417003202021120002110001003210200000000000000000000000000000000004
3100001201000000000000000000000000000000000001000025130000000011100
310000211005058416002101022100002199301000210200000000000000000000000000000000006
3100002201000000000000000000000000000000000001000025130000000011100
31000031100506341600210102210000219930100021020210011000000010000000000000000002
3100003201000000000000000000000000000000000000500010110000001101100
31000041100506331600210102210000219930101021020000000000000000000011000001000003
3100004201000000999998000000000000000000000005000101000000001101000
31000051100608321550210102110000319900100021020000000000000000001000000000006
3100005201000001002420000000000000000000000001000025110000010001100
31000061110809231700431202012000029800000240011120100000000000000000000000000001
3100006201001000000182000000000000000000000000050001010000000001000
31000071100709321660321202022000029900020440020140110000000000101001010000000529
3100007204001004013684002800000000000000000006260148331000011101101
310000811008101215503212020220000299000004400200000000000000000000000000000000040
3100008201000000000000000000000000000000000002000040030000000011100
31000091100810621550321202022000029900000440020000000000000000010000100000000038
3100009201000000999998000000000000000000000001900038030000000011100
310001011006084115502101022110012993010002002100000000000000000000000000000000005
3100010201000000000000000000000000000000000001000025110000000101100
31000111100609111550210102210010129900110021020000000000000000000000100000000003
3100011201000000999998000000000000000000000000050001003000000111101
31000121100608911550210102210010129900100021020000000000200000000000000000000014
3100012201000000999998000000000000000000000000700014030000000111101
31000131100609411550210102210010029900100021020120100020000000000000110000000002
3100013201000000999998000000000000000000000000050001003000000111101
31000141100608911550210103210000319900100021020000000000000000000000100000000001
3100014201000000000000000000000000000000000000050001012000000011000
31000151100608711550210103210000219900110021020000000010100000000000100000000002
3100015201000000000000000000000000000000000000050001012000000011000
31000161100609011550210103210010040310100021020119991020000000010000000000000060
3100016201000000999998000000000000000000000006000150130000010111100
310001710906098115002101022100100402101000250200000000000000000000000000000000002
3100017201000000000000000000000000000000000000050001012000010011001
310001810908121317003212020130000299000004400200000000000000000000000000000000003
3100018201000000000000000000000000000000000000050001012000000011100
```

```
3100019110081293185042120211200012990000024002100000000000000000000000000000000043
3100019201000000000000000000000000000000000004300108100000000001000
31000201090611821500210103210010040110100021020000000000000000000010000000013
3100020201000000999998000000000000000000000001300033120000001111000
31000241090711221500210106240010000131100021020000000010000010000000100000000004
3100024201000000000000000000000000000000000001000025110000000001100
31000251090612511550321202121000029900100021020000000000000000101001000000000006
3100025201000000000000000000000000000000000001000025120000000011001
31000261090612511550321202121000029900100021020000000000000000101001000000000032
3100026201000000000000000000000000000000000003600090120000000011001
31000271090612511550321202121000029900100021020000000000000000101001000000000003
3100027201000000000000000000000000000000000001000025120000000011001
31000281080614521500210102210110040210100021020000000020000000000000100000000017
3100028202000000999998000000000000000000000002200055110000000101100
31000291080613921500210102210110040210100021020120100000000000000000110000000023
3100029202000000999998000000000000000000000002800070110000000101100
31000301090613521500210102210110040210100021020000000010000000000000000000000002
3100030201000000999998000000000000000000000005000101100000000101100
310003110808174216004212021210000299001000210200000000000000000000000000000000002
3100031202000000000000000000000000000000000001000020120000000011000
310003210808185217006412020120001299000006000210000000000000000000000000000000001
3100032201000000000000000000000000000000000000050001010000000001000
31000331080818321750531202112000029900110021030120100000000010000000110000000023
3100033201000000999998000000000000000000010000023000581100011001100
310003410808192216504202021110000299001000210210000000000000000000000000000000004
3100034201000000000000000000000000000000000001000025100000000001000
3100035108091992165042120213100001990010002102000000000000000000000000000000000139
3100035206000000000000000000000000000000000015300375110000010101100
3100036108091962185 05-1202031000429900000540021000000000000000000000000000000036
3100036201000000000000000000000000000000000003600090100000000001000
31000371070619211500210103210000040210100021010120100000000000000000000000000021
3100037201000000000000000000000000000000000001100021010000000101100
3100038107092172155042120211200001990010002102100000000000000000000000000000000017
3100038202000000000000000000000000000000000001900045100000000001000
310003910709219216004202020130002199001000210210000000000000000000000000000000003
3100039201000000000000000000000000000000000000050001010000000001000
31000401070921821650420202011000219900100021021000000000000000000001000000000034
3100040202000001000191000000000000000000000003800093100000000001000
3100041107092202165042120202200001990010002102100000000000000000000000000000000012
3100041202000000000000000000000000000000000001500035100000000001000
310004210709225217504312020230001299000004400210000000000000000000000000000000004
3100042201000000000000000000000000000000000001000025100000000001000
31000431070922421600431202022000119900100021021000000000000000000000100000000084
3100043208000000000000001500000000000000000001340029731000000001100
310004410709224219006412020120000299000004400200000000000000000000000000000000001
3100044201000000000000000000010000000000000000050001011000000001100
310004510709228218005302021120000299001000210210000000000000000000000000000000003
3100045202000000000000000000000000000000000001000020100000000001000
31000461070924321600541202023000019900110021020170110101300001010011100110005344
3100046262003049024398111201000000010000000103799211453100001001101
310004710709229218505302021120006299001000210210000000000000000000000000000000001
3100047201000000000000000000000000000000000000050001010000000001000
310004810709229218005312021120006299001000210210000000000000000000000000000000002
3100048202000000000000000000000000000000000001000020100000000001000
310004910709229218005212021110004199001000210210000000000000000000000000000000001
3100049201000000000000000000000000000000000000050001010000000001000
310005010709223217504202021130003199000004400210000000000000000000000000000000002
3100050201000000000000000000000000000000000000050001010000000001000
310005110709231218004302021120001199001000210210000000000000000000000000000000006
3100051201000000000000000000000000000000000001000025100000000001000
```

```
31000521070923821750430202112000119900100021021000000000000000000000000000000000004
31000522020000000000000000000000000000000000010002010000000000001000
31000531071024321750420202122000019900100021021000000000000000000000000000000000005
31000532030000000000000000000000000000000000001500030100000000001000
31000541071024521750420202112000019900000001102000000000000000000000000000000000008
31000542050000000000000000000000000000000000002500050110000000001100
31000551071024621800421202122000219900000440120000000000000000000000000000000000007
31000552020000000000000000000000000000000000001500035110000000001100
31000561071025021800531202022000619900000440021000000000000000000000000000000000001
31000562010000000000000000000000000000000000000500010100000000001000
31000571060925821800531202012000719900000240021000000000000000000000000000000000003
31000572010000000000000000000000000000000000000500010300000000001001
31000581060926121950641202023000919900000540021000000000000000000001000000000002
31000582010000000000000000000000000000000000000500010100000000001000
31000591061026821950641202023000329900000500021000000000000000000000000000000000001
31000592010000000000000000000000000000000000000500010100000000001000
31000601071025921850521202013000429900000440021000000000000000000000000000000000007
31000602010000000000000000000000000000000000001000025100000000001000
31000611060926521550421202123000029901000215210000000000000000000000000000000000001
31000612010000000000000000000000000000000000000500010100000000001000
31000621100609121550210102210000040210100021020000000000000000000011000000000008
31000622010000000000000000000000000000000000001000025100000000101000
31000631060925921650430202012000329900000440021000000000000000000000000000000000001
31000632010000000000000000000000000000000000000500010100000000001000
3100064106092612155042020202200002990090002102100000000000000000000000000000000018
31000642040000000000000000000000000000000000003500080100000000001000
31000651050426211500320202111000019940100021021000000000000000000000000000000000004
31000652010000000000000000000000000000000000001000025100000000001001
31000661050426311500320202111000019940100021020150100000000000000000000000000004
31000662010000000000000000000000000000000000001000025110000000001101
31000671050329721800431202112000419900100021020110100000000000000000000000000007
31000672010000000000000002000000000000000000001000025100000000101000
31000681050229542000641202122000029900110021020110010010000001000000000000100119
31000682010000009999980090000010001000000000004850097031000000101101
31000691050329541750541202122000719900100021020110100000000001100000000000000060
31000692010000009999980047000000010000000000002850057030000000101001
31000701050229941950641202122000029900110021020110100000000000001000000000100002
31000702010000000000000002000000000000000000001000025100000000101000
31000711050230141950641202122000029900110021020110100000000000100001000000000030
31000712010000009999980028000000000000000010014000280310000001101101
3100072105023021170044020202300002990010002102000000000000000000000000000000000038
31000722080000000000000002000000000000000000006100140110000000001101
31000731050329611600430202013000229900000440010000000000000000000000000000000000006
31000732040000000000000000000000000000000000002500050110000000101101
31000741050627711450210103210010040420100022020000000000010030000001100000000005
31000742010000009999980000000000000000000000001000025120000010111000
31000751050627411450210103210010040420100022020110010010000001000001000000000003
31000752010000009999980000000000000000000000000500010101111110101001
31000761050628911450110101210000000990010002602000000001030000000100000000000001
31000762010000009999980000000000000000000000000500010120000000111001
31000771040630921550321202221000409900100021020000000000000000000000000000000000002
31000772010000000000000000000000000000000000000500010120000000011000
31000781110811132150641202012009999900200020011000000000000000000000000000000000001
31000782010000000000000000000000000000000000000500010100000000001000
31000791030437111900541202111009999900000440010000000000000000000010100000000030
31000792010000009999989999100000000000001000003000751300000000011101
31000801020340021550420202919000129900100021021000000000000000000000000000000000001
31000802010000000000000000000000000000000000000500010100000000001000
31000811020339620550320202919000019900100021021000000000000000000000000000000000001
31000812010000000000000000000000000000000000000500010100000000001000
```

```
31000821020439321450210106210000299001000240110000000000000000000000000000000000003
31000822010000000000000000000000000000000000000500010100000000001000
31000831020341021800541202012000029900110021520140110050000001110000000000000534
31000832170010040023680431001000000000001000259505225310000001101101
31000841020340821650431202022000029900100021021190010000000000000010000000000007
31000842030000000010000000000000000000000000002000045110000000001100
31000851020340821650431202022000029900100021021000000000000000000010000000000004
31000852030000000010000000000000000000000000001500030100000000001000
31000861020340321600421202011000029900100021021000000000000000000000000000000000007
31000862010000000000000000000000000000000000001000025100000000001001
31000871020340321600431202122000129900100021021000000000000000000010000000000005
31000872020000000000000000000000000000000000001000020100000000001001
31000881020340421600421202110000129900100021020000000000000000000000000000000000004
31000882010000000000000000000000000000000000010100025110000000001101
31000891020340621550441202022000329900100021021000000000000000000000000000000000004
31000892010000000000000000000000000000000000001000025100000000001001
31000901020340921600541202023000129900100021020000000000000000000000000000000000001
31000902010000000000000000000000000000000000000500010110000000001101
31000911020341121700541202023000729900000440020000000000000000000000000000000000001
31000912010000000000000000000000000000000000000500010100000000101000
31000921010342721700521202121000229900100021020110100000000000010000000000000004
31000922010000000000000000000000000000000000001000025110000000001101
31000931020341921650521202111000129900010440020110100000000000001000000000000008
31000932010000009999980003000000000000000000001000025110000000001101
31000941010342721500410202120000129900100021020000000001000000100001100000000003
31000942010000009999980000000000000000000000000500010110000000101101
31000951100607121550210102210010010230100022020000000000000000000011000000000008
31000952010000009999980000000000000000000000001000025100000001101000
31000961030434811450210102211000209900210023020000000000000000000000000000000000003
31000962010000000000000000000000000000000000001000020100000000101000
01100011120601911800331202112000029900111021130171111979727711111191119111801760
01100012070000009999980367110102110100111110277405549320000011111111
2110001112031162180062120102300021980000044002000000000000000000000000000000000012
21100012020000000000000000000000000000000000001200030100000000010101
21100021120310621850631201023000429800100541020000000000000000000010000000000015
21100022030000000000000090000000000000000000045000903000000000010101
21100031120310321850621201023000729800000540030000000000000000000000000000000000001
21100032010000000000000000000000000000000000000500010300000000010101
21100041120310121800630201023000729800000500020000000000000000000010000000000008
21100042020000000000000000000000000000000000001000025300000000010101
21100051120310521850621201023000629800000441021000000003010100000010000000000025
21100052010000000000000020000000000000000000002500062100000000010101
21100061120310521850631201023000629800000440020000000000000000000000000000000000005
21100062010000000000000000000000000000000000001000025300000000010100
2110007112031122180063020102300062980000044002000000000000000000000000000000000026
21100072040000000000000000000000000000000000002600065100000000010100
21100081130310721850631201023000729800000500020000000000000000000000000000000000004
21100082010000000000000000000000000000000000001000025300000000010100
21100091130310721850621201123000929800100421020160100090100101110001000000000104
21100092050000000000000070000000000000000000010400260100000010010101
21100101130311221800621201023000719800000440020000000000000000000000000000000000004
21100102010000000000000000000000000000000000000500010300000000010101
21100111130311821750531201023000219800000440020000000000000000000000000000000000005
21100112010000000000000000000000000000000000000500010300000000010101
21100121130311821750521201023000219800000440020000000000000000000000000000000000006
21100122010000000000000000000000000000000000001000025300000000010100
21100131130310621806212011230008198001100210201100100101100000000010000000100001
21100132010000000000000000000000000000000000000500010300000000010101
21100141130809921600320102222000129800101021020140110080000011110100000000000439
21100142010000000000000000000000000000000000043901097120000011101111
```

```
21100151130809721600320201221000129800100021021000000000000000000000000000000002
21100152010000000000000000000000000000000000001000025300000000000101
21100161130810321600320202121000129800100021021000000000000000000000000000000002
21100162010000000000000000000000000000000000000500010300000000000101
21100171130810421650320201121000129800100021020000000000000000000000000000000007
21100172010000000000000000000000000000000000010000253000000010000100
21100181130810421650520201121000129800100441020000000000000000000000000000000009
21100182010000000000000000000000000000000000010000253000000000010100
21100191130810421650520201122000129800100021021000000000000000000000000000000005
21100192010000000000000000000000000000000000000500010300000000000101
21100201130810921650530201122000129800200441020000000000000000000000000000000005
21100202020000000000000000000000000000000000010000253000000010000100
21100211140810421700520201122000129800200441021000000000000000000000000000000004
21100212010000000000000000000000000000000000000500010300000000000101
21100221140810621700630201023000229800000440021000000000000000000000000000000003
21100222010000000000000000000000000000000000000500010300000000000101
21100231140607621650420211123000029800200040020121101010000100100001000000000439
21100232040000000000000670000000000000000000043901097100000010010101
21100241140607421600320111211000409900100021021000000000000000000000000000000002
21100242010000000000000000000000000000000000000500010300000000000101
21100251140607021600320111210000409930100021020000000000000000000000000000000007
21100252010000000000000000000000000000000000010000253000000000010101
21100261140607621600220102210100119900100021020000000000000000000000000000000004
21100262010000000000000000000000000000000000010000253000000001010101
21100271140508221600320201122000209800110021220140110050110001100001100000000144
21100272010000000000000002000000000000000000014400360100000110010101
21100281140508221600320201121001009800100021220000000001000001101000000000000001
21100282010000000000000000000000000000000000000500010301111100010101
21100291140508221600320201112000219800200441031000000000000000000000000000000001
21100292010000000000000000000000000000002000000500010300000000000101
21100301140508421600420201022000419800200441030120100000000001000000000000000005
21100302030000000000000000000000000000000000010000253000000000010100
21100311140507721600320201221000219900100021031000000010000000000000000000000001
21100312010000000000000000000000000000000000000500010300000000000101
21100321140508821600430201002000229800200440030000000000000000000000000000000005
21100322010000000000000000000000000000000000010000253000000000010100
21100331140509121600420201002000229800100041031000000000000000000001000000000015
21100332010000000000000000000000000000000000000150003710000000000101
21100341110605121600420201121000129900100021020000000000000000000000000000000133
21100342020000000000000000000000000000000000013300332100000000010101
21100351110605021600320101211100229900100021021120100010000000101001000000000013
21100352010000000000000000000000000000000000000130003210000000000101
21100361110604821600320201122000129900100021021000000000000000000000000000000020
21100362010000000000000000000000000000000000000200050100000000000100
21100371110604921600521201023000629800200440021000000000000000000000000000000002
21100372010000000000000000000000000000000000000500010300000000000101
21100381110604921600520201123000529800100021031140110010100000000000000000000001
21100382010000000000000000000000000000000000000500010300000000000101
21100391110604821600520201023000629800200040021000000000000000000000000000000002
21100392010000000000000000000000000000000000000500010300000000000101
21100401110604421600520201123000129800200040030140100010000000000000000000000003
21100402020000000000000000000000000000000000010000253000000010000100
21100411110604421600420201023000319800200041020140110010000000100000000000000410
21100412020000000000000000000000000000000000041001025100000110010101
21100421110604321600530201023000129800200040020000000000000000000000000000000001
21100422010000000000000000000000000000000000000500010300000000010101
21100431110504621600320201123000119840100021021140100000000000000000000000000026
21100432060000000000000000000000000000000000000260006510000000000101
21100441110504721600420201022000129800100021021000000000000000000000000000000027
21100442010000000000000000000000000000000000000270006710000000000100
21100451110504621600420201023000229800100041021190900000000000000000000000000005
21100452010000000000000000000000000000000000000500010300000000000101
21100461110504321600520201023000329800100041021000000000000000000000000000000005
21100462020000000000000000000000000000000000010000253000000000000100
21100471110503421650630201023000329800200440020120100010000000000000000000000003
21100472020000000000000000000000000000000000010000253000000010000101
21100481110505021650320201122000229800100021021240111000000000000000000000000044
21100482010000000000000000000002000000000000044001101000000000000101
21100491110505721650320201112000119800100021030140110020100000000000000000000012
21100492010000000000000000000000000000000000001200030100000100000101
21100501110505721650420201123000219800110021020110110000000000000000000000000004
21100502010000000000000000000000000000000000010000253000000011010101
21100511110505921650420201022000119800100421020140101000000000000001000000000165
21100512090000000000000000000000000000000000016500412100000011010101
21100521110505721650630201023000129800000440021000000000000000000000000000000001
21100522010000000000000000000000000000000000000500010300000000000101
21100531110407021750621201123000229800200441020000000010000000000000000000000001
21100532010000000000000000000000000000000000000500010300000010010101
21100541110407221750621201023000329800000440021000000000000000000000000000000001
21100542010000000000000000000000000000000000000500010300000000000101
21100551110407021700521201123000119800100441021120100000000000000000000000000006
21100552030000000000000000000000000000000000010000253000000000000100
21100561110407921800621201023000129800100441020000000000000000000000000000000011
21100562010000000000000000000000000000000000011000271000000000010101
21100571110407821800621201023000129800100441020000000000000000000000000000000005
21100572010000000000000000000000000000000000000500010300000000010101
21100581110406821750621201023000329800100441020000000000000000000000000000000005
21100582010000000000000000000000000000000000000500010300000000010101
21100591110407121800621201023000629800100441021000000000000000000000000000000013
21100592010000000000000000000000000000000000000130003210000000010100
21100601120407221800621201023000129800100441020000000000000000000000000000000046
21100602010000000000000000000000000000000000000460011510000000010100
21100611120406821750621201023000329800100441020000000000000000000000000000000105
21100612010000000000000000000000000000000000010500262100000010010100
21100621120504421650420201112000219800100021030140100000100000100000000000000028
21100622020000000000000000000000000000001000002800070100000111110100
21100631120406521700621201023000229800100441020140110010300100100011000100000179
21100632050000000000000000000000000000000010017900447100000010010101
21100641120406021700640201023000229800000440021000000000000000000000000000000001
21100642010000000000000000000000000000000000000500010300000000000101
21100651120406821700320201122000119900100021021000000000000000110001000000000019
21100652010000000000000000000000000000000000000190004710000000000101
21100661120405921700621201123000329800100441020000000000000000000000000000000006
21100662010000000000000000000000000000000000010000253000000000010100
21100671120406121700420201023000029840100021030000000000000000000000000000000004
21100672010000000000000000000000000000000000010000253000000000010101
21100681120406621700320201122000219800100021020000000000000000000000000000000009
21100682010000000000000000000000000000000000010000253000000000010100
21100691120406421650320201013000119800100441020000000000000000000000000000000043
21100692020000000000000000000000000000000000000430010710000000010100
21100701120405121650420201222000029900100021020000000000000000000000000000000004
21100702010000000000000000000000000000000000010000253000000000010101
21100711120407721750520201023000229800100441020190100010100001100001100101000409
21100712060000000000000000000000000000000000040901022100000010010101
21100721120407721700521201023000129800200541021000000000000000000000000000000010
21100722010000000000000000000000000000000000010000253000000000000101
21100731120408321750520201023000229800100511020140110050001000000001000100000539
21100732060000000000000004000000000000000000005390134710000000010101
21100741120309121800621201023000229800200541021000000000000000000000000000000004
21100742020000000000000000000000000000000000010000253000000000000100
```

```
21100751120309021800621201023000229800000540020000000000000000000000000000000006
21100752010000000000000000000000000000000000001000025300000000010100
21100761120503921650320201112000119800100021020110100200001011000000000000000079
21100762010000000000000000000000000000000000000790019710000111010101
21100771120503421650420201023000419800200440020000000000000000000000000000000021
21100772010000000000000000000000000000000000002100052100000010010100
21100781120503421650420201023000229800200440020000000000000000000000000000000006
21100782020000000000000000000000000000000000001000025300000010010100
21100791130505521600320201112000219900100021021000000000000000000000000000000002
21100792010000000000000000000000000000000000000500010300000000000101
21100801130405621600320201112000319900100021020000000000000000000000000000000004
21100802010000000000000000000000000000000000000500010300000000010101
21100811120405621650320201122000129800100021020000000000000000000000000000000004
21100812010000000000000000000000000000000000000500010300000000010101
21100821120406221650320201112000119900100021020120110000000000000000000000000031
21100822010000000000000000000000000000000000003100077100000111110101
21100831120406221650320201122000119900100021020000000000000000000000000000000003
21100832010000000000000000000000000000000000000500010300000000010101
21100841120406221650320201123000119900100021020110110010000000000000000000000144
21100842010000000000000000000000000000000000014400360100000010010101
21100851120405621650420201023000229800200440020000000000000000000000000000000005
21100852010000000000000000000000000000000000000500010300000000010101
21100861120405521650420201112000129900100021021000000000000000000000000000000002
21100862010000000000000000000000000000000000000500010300000000000101
21100871120405221650420201112000129900100021020120100010000100000010000100000002
21100872010000000000000000000000000000000000000500010300000010010101
21100881130406921650320201102000119800100021020110010010000000100000000000000084
21100882020000000000000000000000000000000000010008400210100001000010101
21100891130407021650320201102000119900100021020000000000000000000000000000000014
21100892010000000000000000000000000000000000000140035100000000010100
21100901130407221650320202111000049900100021020120100000000000000000000000000023
21100902020000000000000000000000000000000000002300057100000000010101
21100911130407421650320202111000049900100021020000000000000000000000000000000144
21100912010000000000000000000000000000000000014400360100000100010100
21100921130408021700420201123000129800100021020000000000000000000000000000000017
21100922010000000000000000000000000000000000001700042100000000010100
21100931130408021700420201023000329800200440020000000000000000000000000000000009
21100932010000000000000000000000000000000000001000025300000000010100
21100941130408321700520201023000229800100441021000000000000000000000000000000002
21100942010000000000000000000000000000000000000500010300000000000101
21100951130408521700520201023000129800100021021000000000000000000000000000000001
21100952010000000000000000000000000000000000000500010300000000000101
21100961130408821700621201023000229800100421020000000000000000000000000000000011
21100962010000000000000000000000000000000000000110027300000000010100
21100971130409121700621201023000229800100441020000000000000000000000000000000012
21100972020000000000000000000000000000000000001200030300000000010100
21100981130409321700621201023000429800100541020000000000000000000000000000000007
21100982010000000000000000000000000000000000001000025000000001010100
21100991130409521750620201123100129800000540020000000000000000000000000000000004
21100992010000000000000000000000000000000000000500010300000000010101
21101001130309921800621201023000329800000540020000000000000000000000000000000013
21101002040000000000000000000000000000000000001300032300000000010100
21101011130310221800621201023001329800000440030000000000000000000000000000000005
21101012010000000000000000000000000000000000001000025300000000010100
21101021130309921800621201023001029800000540021000000000000000000000000000000003
21101022010000000000000000000000000000000000000500010300000000000101
21101031130309621800620201023000629800000540031110100000000000000000000000000009
21101032020000000000000000000000000000000000001000025300000000010100
21101041130309821800620201123000429800000540020000000000000000000000000000000006
21101042010000000000000000000000000000000000001000025300000000010100
```

```
21101051120309821800620201123000129800100541020140100040100010000100010000000224
21101052110000000000000000000000000000000000002240056010000010010101
21101061120408221700520112233100119800100021031000000010000000000001000000000001
21101062010000000000000000000000000000000000000500010300000000010101
21101071130409021750620201023000129800000440021000000000000000000000000000000004
21101072010000000000000000000000000000000000001000025300000000000100
21101081130408821750621201123000429800100021020110100101000001000000000000000129
21101082020000000000000000000000000000000000001290032210000000010101
21101091130409421750621201023000629800100441020000000000000000000000000000000005
21101092010000000000000000000000000000000000000500010300000000010101
21101101130408421700620201122000119800100021021140100020000000100000000000000036
21101102030000000000000000000000000000000000003600090100000000000101
21101111130408121700530201122000029800100021021140100010000000000000000000000018
21101112020000000000000000000000000000000000001800045100000000000100
21101121130311721750621201023000429800100441020000000000000000000000000000000009
21101122010000000000000000000000000000000000001000025300000000010100
21101131130311521750520201103000329800100021020000000000000000000000000000000003
21101132010000000000000000000000000000000000000500010300000000010101
21101141140311821700320201103000219800100021020000000000000000000000000000000002
21101142010000000000000000000000000000000000000500010300000000010101
21101151140311721700320201202000119800100021020120100030000000000000000000000003
21101152010000000000000000000000000000000000000500010300000000010101
21101161140411021700320201102000119800100021020000000000000000000000000000000002
21101162010000000000000000000000000000000000000500010300000000010101
21101171130310921750520201103000329800100021020000000000000000000000000000000002
21101172010000000000000000000000000000000000000500010300000000010101
21101181130410501700420202112000129800100021020000000000000000000000000000000005
21101182010000000000000000000000000000000000000500010300000000010101
21101191130410421700420202112000129800100021021000000000000000000000000000000003
21101192010000000000000000000000000000000000000500010300000000000101
21101201130409021700521201122000129800100021020120100000000000000000000000000018
21101202010000000000000000000000000000000000001800045300000000010100
21101211130409621700520201202100229900110021021000000000000000000010000010000007
21101212010000000000000000000000000000000000001000025300000000000101
21101221140410521700320201102000129900100021020000000000000000000000000000000007
21101222010000000000000000000000000000000000000500010300000000010101
21101231130311921700420201103000419800100021020000000000000000000000000000000005
21101232010000000000000000000000000000000000001000025300000000010100
21101241130408221750620201013000629800200441020000000000000000000000000000000002
21101242010000000000000000000000000000000000000500010300000000010101
21101251130407621700320201111000129900100021020000000000000000000000000000000119
21101252040000000000000000000000000000000000001190029710000000010100
21101261120501421650320201023000129800100021020140101000000001000000000000000111
21101262040000000000000000000000000000000100001110027710000010110100
21101271120501421650420202112000329800200411020120100000000001000110001000000001
21101272010000000000000000000000000000000000000500010300000010000101
21101281120501521650420201022000129900100441020000000000000000000000000000000010
21101282020000000000000000000000000000000000001000025100000010010100
21101291120502721650420201123000129800100441020000000001000001000000000000000004
21101292010000000000000000000000000000000000000500010300000000010101
21101301120502721650320201122000219800100021020110100300000000100000000000000006
21101302010000000000000000000000000000000000001000025300000010110100
21101311120501821600210101211100119900100021020000000000000000000000000000000006
21101312010000000000000000000000000000000000001000025300000000010100
21101321110601821600420201023100119900100041020171111050000011100011000100001960
21101322150000000000000000000000000000001000196004900100000111110101
21101331140608021750620202113000629800100441020000000000000011000000000000000002
21101332010000000000000000000000000000000000000500010300000100000101
21101341140608821950621201023000329800105400201411000000000010100000000000000002
21101342010000016006000000000000000000000000000000030000000000010101
```

```
21101351140708621800620201023000129800200441021000000000000000000000000000000005
21101352010000000000000000000000000000000000000000050001030000000101
21101361140709521750530201112000129800200021021000000000000000000000000000000014
21101362010000000000000000000000000000000000000140003510000000000100
21101371140708921750520201123000229800100021021000000000000000000000000000000005
21101372010000000000000000000000000000000000000100002530000000000100
21101381140709021700520201123000129800100021021000000000000000000001000000000019
21101382020000000000000000000000000000000000000190004710000000000100
21101391140708621700520201123000129800100021021000000001000001100001000000000020
21101392010000000000000000000000000000000000002000050100000000000101
21101401130606421600320102112000129900100021020000000000000000000000000000000005
21101402010000000000000000000000000000000000000100002530000110010101
21101411130606721600320201122000129900100021020000000000000000000000000000000003
21101412010000000000000000000000000000000000000500010300000110010101
21101421130707821650420201123000129800100021020000000000000000000000000000000004
21101422010000000000000000000000000000000000000500010300000000010101
21101431130705521750621201023000329800000440020000000000000000000000000000000006
21101432010000000000000000000000000000000000000100002530000000010100
21101441110503721650420201123000219800100021020110100000000000000000000000000002
21101442010000000000000000000000000000000000000500010300000010010101
21101451110504021650320201123000219800100021021000000000000000000000000000000002
21101452010000000000000000000000000000000000000500010300000000000101
21101461110603921650420201123000129800100021021140100000000100000000000000000006
21101462020000000000000000000000000000000000000100002530000000000100
21101471110603921600420201023000229800100021021000000000000000000000000000000002
21101472010000000000000000000000000000000000000500010300000000000101
21101481110604221600320201123000329800100021021000000000000000000000000000000002
21101482010000000000000000000000000000000000000500010300000000000101
21101491110603921600420201123000529800100021120120010000000000010011000100000031
21101492030000000000000000000000000000000000000310007710000010010101
21101501110603721600420201023000129800100021020140110020000001100011000100000214
21101502040000000000000000000000000000000000002140053510000010010101
21101511110603621600320201023000129800100021020000000000000000000000000000000011
21101512010000000000000000000000000000000000000110002710000000100101
21101521110603221600320201123000119900100011020000000000000000000000000000000067
21101522010000000000000000000000000000000000000670016710000010010101
21101531110603121600320201123000129800100021021000000000000000000000000000000038
21101532010000000000000000000000000000000000000380009510000000000100
21101541110603221600420201123000129800100021021000000000000000000000000000000005
21101542010000000000000000000000000000000000000500010300000000000101
21101551110603021600420201113000219800100021021120110000000000000000000000000049
21101552010000000000000000000000000000000000000490012210000000000101
21101561110503321650520201023000429800100021020000000001000000000000000000000003
21101562010000000000000000000000000000000000000500010300000010000101
21101571110603021600320201123000519800100021020110100000000000000000000000000011
21101572010000000000000000000000000000000000000110002710000010010101
21101581110502621600420201123000129800100021020140110050000000100000000000000418
21101582080000000000000000000000000000000000004180104510000011000101
21101591110502821600320201023000129800100021020040100000010000000000000000000001
21101592010000000000000000000000000000000000000500010300000010010101
21101601110503521650420201023000129800000041041140110040702000000011000100000001
21101602010000000000000000000000000000000000000500010300000000000101
21101611110502821600420201123000229800100021021000000000000000000000000000000033
21101612010000000000000000000000000000000000000330008210000000000100
21101621110502521600320201123000219800100021021000000000000000000000000000000020
21101622010000000000000000000000000000000000002000050100000000000100
21101631120502221600320201122000119800100021030110010000000000100011000100000147
21101632020000000000000000000000000000000000001470036710000010010100
21101641120503021600320201123000219800100021020141100000000000000010000100000019
21101642010000000000000000000000000000000000000190004710000010010101
21101651120503321600320201123000229800100021020110110010000000100000000000000049
21101652010000000000000000000000000000000000000490012210000000010100
21101661140709821750520201023000129800004400201900100100000000000010000000000002
21101662010000000000000000000000000000000000000500010300000010000101
21101671140709321700520202022000229800000440021000000000000000000010000000000010
21101672010000000000000000000000000000000000000100002510000000000101
21101681140709421700520201223000129800100021021000000000000000000000000000000002
21101682010000000000000000000000000000000000000500010300000000000101
21101691140710121750520201023000119800000440021000000000000000000000000000000005
21101692010000000000000000000000000000000000000500010300000000000101
21101701140709921750520201123000129800000441021000000000000000000000000000000002
21101702010000000000000000000000000000000000000500010300000000000101
21101711140709921700520201023000129800000441021000000000000000000000000000000004
21101712010000000000000000000000000000000000000100002530000000000100
21101721140709721700530201023000129800200441021000000000000000000000000000000003
21101722010000000000000000000000000000000000000500010300000000000101
21101731140709721700520201023000119800100441021000000000000000000000000000000005
21101732010000000000000000000000000000000000000100002530000000000100
21101741140709421650420201123000119900100021021000000000000000000000000000000003
21101742010000000000000000000000000000000000000500010300000000000101
21101751140709321650420201123000119900100021021000000000000000000000000000000003
21101752010000000000000000000000000000000000000500010300000000000101
21101761140709721700520201023000229800200441021000000000000000000000000000000004
21101762010000000000000000000000000000000000000100002530000000000100
21101771140709621650520201123000229800100021021000000000000000000000000000000007
21101772010000000000000000000000000000000000000100002530000000000100
21101781130709321650420101223100129800100021021000000000000000000000000000000004
21101782010000000000000000000000000000000000000100002530000000000100
21101791130709321650420201113000229800100021021000000000000000000000000000000003
21101792010000000000000000000000000000000000000500010300000000000101
21101801130709521650420201113000229800100021020000000000010010000000000000000020
21101802010000000000000000000000000000000000002000050100000000010100
21101811130709221650420201123000129800100021021000000000000000000000000000000002
21101812010000000000000000000000000000000000000500010300000000000101
21101821130708921650420201123000329800100021121000000000000000000000000000000003
21101822010000000000000000000000000000000000000500010300000000000101
21101831130708721650420201122000429800200010021000000000000000000000000000000003
21101832010000000000000000000000000000000000000100002530000000000101
21101841130708721650410201122000229800100022020000000000000000000000000000000015
21101842010000000000000000000000000000000000000150003710000010010100
21101851130708921650410201122000229800100021021000000000000000000000000000000004
21101852010000000000000000000000000000000000000100002530000000000100
21101861130708721650420201022000319800200440021000000000000000000000000000000002
21101862010000000000000000000000000000000000000500010300000000000101
21101871120808421600310111111000809800210240020000000000000000001100000000000001
21101872010000000000000000000000000000000000000500010320000010001101
21101881130708521650420201022000229800200440020000000000000000000000000000000010
21101882010000000000000000000000000000000000000100002510000000010100
21101891130708421650420201122000229800200410021000000000000000000000000000000003
21101892010000000000000000000000000000000000000500010300000000000101
21101901140708921650420201122000119800200441021000000000000000000010000000000120
21101902040000000000000000000000000000000000001200030010000000000101
21101911140708621650420201023000229800200441011000000000000000000000000000000002
21101912010000000000000000000000000000000000000500010300000000000101
21101921130708521650420201122000129800200441020110100100000000000000000000000012
21101922020000000000000000000000000000000000000120003010000010010100
21101931130707521650520201023000219800000210020140110040000100000000000000000099
21101932050000000000000000000000000000000000000990024710000010010101
21101941130707821600420201023000119800200410020000000000000000000000000000000080
21101942030000000000000000000000000000000000000800020010000010010101
```

```
21101951130707121650520201023000219800000240020000000000000000000000000000000020
21101952010000000000000000000000000000000000000200005010000010010100
21101961130706421600420201023000419800200440020000000000100100000000000000000016
21101962010000000000000000000000000000000000001600040100000000010100
21101971130706621600420201122000119800100021021000000000000000000000000000000002
21101972010000000000000000000000000000000000000005000103000000000101
21101981130706552160042020112200019900100021021000000000000000000000000000000002
21101982010000000000000000000000000000000000000005000103000000000101
21101991130708221600420201123000029800200411021000000000000000000000000000000005
21101992010000000000000000000000000000000000000010000253000000000100
21102001130708321600420201122000329800200410021000000000000000000100000000000052
21102002010010000000000000000000000000000000000052001301000000000101
21102011130708621600420201122000229800200411020000000000000000000000000000000046
21102012020000000000000000000000000000000000000046001151000000010100
21102021130708921600420201122000229800200410021000000000000000000000000000000029
21102022010000000000000000000000000000000000000029000721000000000100
21102031130709221650420202113000229800000440121000000000000000000000000000000001
21102032010000000000000000000000000000000000000005000103000000000101
21102041130709221650420201122000129800100021021000000000000000000000000000000003
21102042010000000000000000000000000000000000000005000103000000000101
21102051130809321650420201023000229800100021020000000000000000000000000000000005
21102052010000000000000000000000000000000000001000025300000010010100
21102061130809221600420201022000229800100021021000000000000000000000000000000002
21102062010000000000000000000000000000000000000005000103000000000101
21102071130708021600420201022000129800200411021000000000000000000000000000000002
21102072010000000000000000000000000000000000000005000103000000000101
21102081130707821600420201122000229800200010020000000000000000000000000000000114
21102082030000000000000000000000000000000000001140028510000000010101
21102091130708021600420201022000429800200410021000000000000000000000000000000002
21102092010000000000000000000000000000000000000005000103000000000101
21102101130708221600420201122000129800200410021000000000000000000000000000000005
21102102010000000000000000000000000000000000000010000253000000000100
21102111130708221600420201122000229800200410021000000000000000000000000000000002
21102112010000000000000000000000000000000000000005000103000000000101
21102121130708221600420201022000229800200410021000000000000000000000000000000002
21102122010000000000000000000000000000000000000005000103000000000101
21102131130808821600420201122000129800200411020000000000000000000000000000000005
21102132010000000000000000000000000000000000001000025300000000010101
21102141130708621600420201122000229800200411021000000000000000000000000000000005
21102142020000000000000000000000000000000000000010000253000000000100
21102151130708421600420201022000129800200410021000000000000000000000000000000002
21102152010000000000000000000000000000000000000005000103000000000101
21102161130808721600420201122000229800100011021000000000000000000000000000000002
21102162010000000000000000000000000000000000000005000103000000000101
21102171130708521600420201122000229800100021021000000000000000000000000000000003
21102172010000000000000000000000000000000000000005000103000000000101
21102181130708321600420201122000129800100011021000000000000000000000000000000002
21102182010000000000000000000000000000000000000005000103000000000101
21102191130808721600420201122000229800100021021000000000000000000000000000000003
21102192010000000000000000000000000000000000000010000253000000000100
21102201130708421600420201122000129800100021041000000010000000000000000000000008
21102202010000000000000000000000000000000000001000025300000000000101
21102211130708121600420201122000129800200010021000000000000000000000000000000002
21102212010000000000000000000000000000000000000005000103000000000101
21102221130707921600420201122000229800200010021000000000000000000000000000000004
21102222010000000000000000000000000000000000000010000253000000000100
21102231130810321600410201122000129800200021020110010010000100000000000000000003
21102232010000000000000000000000000000000000000050001030000010000101
21102241130810421600410111222000129800100021020000000000000000000000000000000001
21102242010000000000000000000000000000000000000050001030000010000101
```

```
21102251130810521600420111223000129800100021021000000000000000000000000000000003
21102252010000000000000000000000000000000000000005000103000000000101
21102261130810721650420111223000029800100021021000000000000000000000000000000005
21102262020000000000000000000000000000000000001000025300000000000101
21102271130811021650420111223000029800100021020000000000000000000000000000000002
21102272010000000000000000000000000000000000000050001030001110000101
21102281130810021600320201222000029800100021021000000000000000000000000000000010
21102282010000000000000000000000000000000000001000025100000000000101
21102291130810821650430201023000429800100021021110100000000000000010000000000008
21102292020000000000000000000000000000000000001000025300000000000101
21102301130810721650420201023000229800200440020000000000000000000001000000000002
21102302010000000000000000000000000000000000001000025300000010000101
21102311130810721650420201023000129800000441620000000000000010000000000000000001
21102312010000000000000000000000000000000000000050001030000010000101
21102321130811021650420201122000329800200441020000000000000000000000000000000011
21102322010000000000000000000000000000000000000110002700000011000101
21102331140812621700420111223000229800100021021000000000000000000000000000000006
21102332010000000000000000000000000000000000001000025300000000000100
21102341140813521750521201013000229800200440020120100000000100100100000000000005
21102342010000000000000000000000000000000000001000025300000010000101
21102351130812821700420202112100029900110021021000000000100000000001000000000368
21102352030000070038480000000000000000000000003680092010000011110101
21102361130812221650320201121000129800110021021000000000000000000001000000000008
21102362010000010002350000000000000000000000001000025300000000000101
21102371130812021650310101211000129900100021021000000000000000000000000000000005
21102372020000000000000000000000000000000000001000025300000000000101
21102381130811821650420201122000129800100021021000000000000000000000000000000003
21102382010000000000000000000000000000000000001000025300000000000100
21102391130812121650320201122000129800100021021140100000000000000000000000000006
21102392010000000000000000000000000000000000001000025300000000000101
21102401130912321650320201122000129800100021020000000000000000000000000000000003
21102402010000000000000000000000000000000000001000025300000000010100
21102411130912521650320201122000129800100021021000000000000000000000000000000003
21102412010000000000000000000000000000000000001000025300000000000101
21102421130913221650430201122000129800100021021000000000000000000000000000000002
21102422010000000000000000000000000000000000000005000103000000000101
21102431130812121650210101221000219800100021021000000000000000000000000000000004
21102432010000000000000000000000000000000000001000025300000000000100
21102441120809821600310202111000100201100021020170110040400300110001000000000324
21102442010000000000000520000000000000001000051001075320000111001101
21102451120809321700620202012000239800002400200000000000000000000000000000000001
21102452010000000000000000000000000000000000000050001032000000001101
21102461120807721600320202012000229800200240020000000000000000000000000000000010
21102462010000000000000000000000000000000000001000025320000000001101
21102471110605321600320201122000229800100021020000000000000000000000000000000140
21102472010000000000000000000000000000000000014000350100000010010101
21102481120504421650320201122000129900100021020000000000000000000000000000000009
21102482010000000000000000000000000000000000001000025300000000010100
21102491130808221600320101222000129900100021021120100000000000000000000000000065
21102492010000000000000000000000000000000000006500162100000000000100
21102501130808521600320201121000229800100021021000000000000000000000000000000029
21102502010000000000000000000000000000000000000029000721000000000100
21102511120602421600420201122000329800003400210000000000000000000000000000000003
21102512010000000000000000000000000000000000001000025300000000000100
21102521120602521600420201122000129800100021021000000000000000000000000000000017
21102522030000000000000000000000000000000000001700042100000000000100
21102531120602721600420201122000429800100021020000000000000000000000000000000012
21102532010000000000000000000000000000000000001200030100000010010100
21102541120602021600420201122000129800100021020000000000000000000000000000000017
21102542030000000000000000000000000000000000001700042100000010010100
```

```
21102551120602321600420201122000129800100021021000000000000000000000000000000006
21102552010000000000000000000000000000000000001000025300000000000100
21102561120603021600320201111000129800100021020000000000000000000000000000000049
21102562010000000000000000000000000000000000004900122100000010110100
21102571120703621600320201122000329800100021020000000000000000000000000000000021
21102572010000000000000000000000000000000000002100052100000010010100
21102581120703721600320201122000229800100021020000000000000000000000000000000002
21102582010000000000000000000000000000000000005000103000000010000101
21102591120703921600320201122000409800100021020000000000000000000000000000000001
21102592010000000000000000000000000000000000005000103000000010000101
21102601120602021600420201221000129800100021020000000000000000000000000000000002
21102602010000000000000000000000000000000000005000103000000010000101
21102611120602121600420201122000129800100021020000000000000000000000000000000002
21102612010000000000000000000000000000000000005000103000000010000101
21102621120602321600420201122000129800100021020000000000000000000000000000000002
21102622010000000000000000000000000000000000005000103000000010000101
21102631120602421600420201122000329800100021020000000000000000000000000000000002
21102632010000000000000000000000000000000000005000103000000010000101
21102641120603021600320201122000329800100021020000000000000000000000000000000002
21102642010000000000000000000000000000000000005000103000000010000101
21102651120703621600320201221000329800100021020000000000000000000000000000000049
21102652010000000000000000000000000000000000004900122100000110000101
21102661120602921600320201221000329800100021020000000000000000000000000000000154
21102662010000000000000000000000000000000000001540030810000010000100
21102671110602821600320201221000229800100021021000000000000000000000000000000002
21102672010000000000000000000000000000000000005000103000000000000101
21102681110602921600320201122000129800100021021000000000000000000000000000000002
21102682010000000000000000000000000000000000005000103000000000000101
21102691110603221600320201221000429800100021021000000000000000000000000000000006
21102692010000000000000000000000000000000000001000025300000000000101
21102701110603521600320201122000129800100021021000000000000000000000000000000007
21102702010000000000000000000000000000000000001000025300000000000100
21102711110603621600320201122000129800100021021000000000000000000000000000000003
21102712010000000000000000000000000000000000001000025300000000000100
21102721110604021600320201221000129800100021021000000000000000000000000000000008
21102722010000000000000000000000000000000000001000025300000000000100
21102731110604021600320201221000129800100021020000000000000000000000000000000005
21102732010000000000000000000000000000000000001000025300000000010100
21102741110704421600210111210100019931100021021000000000000000000000000000000010
21102742010000000000000000000000000000000000001000025100000000000100
21102751110603521600320201221000129900100021021000000000000000000000000000000002
21102752010000000000000000000000000000000000005000103000000000000101
21102761110603721600320201221000129800100021021000000000000000000000000000000002
21102762010000000000000000000000000000000000005000103000000000000101
21102771110603821600320201122000129900100021020130100000000000000000000000000027
21102772010000000000000000000000000000000000002700067100000010100101
21102781110704021600320201221000329900100021020000000000000000000000000000000003
21102782010000000000000000000000000000000000001000025300000010000100
21102791110705221600210111210100629900103021020000000000000000000000000000000006
21102792010000000000000000000000000000000000001000025300000010100101
21102801110705321600210111210100229930101021020140100000000000100000000000000135
21102802010000000000000000000000000000000000001350033710000110100101
21102811110605521600320201222000129900100021020000000000000000000000000000000007
21102812010000000000000000000000000000000000001000025300000010000100
21102821110604821600210111210100419930100022020000000000000000000000000000000005
21102822010000000000000000000000000000000000001000025300000010000100
21102831110604121600210111210100229900100021021000000000000000000000000000000002
21102832010000000000000000000000000000000000001000025300000000000100
21102841110707021600320201222000309800100021020000000020000000000000000000000063
21102842010000000000000000000000000000000000006300157100000111100100
```

```
21102851110706721600320111211000309900100021020000000010000000000000000000000039
21102852010000000000000000000000000000000000003900097100000111000100
21102861120808221650420201012000329800200440020000000000000000000000000000000003
21102862010000000000000000000000000000000000005000103000000010000101
21102871110808021600420201013000229800200440121140100000000000100000000000000046
21102872020000000000000000000000000000000000004600115100000010000101
21102881110807821600320201013000129800200441021110100000000000100000000000000038
21102882010000000000000000000000000000000000003800095100000010100100
21102891110707021600310111210100509900100021021000000000000000000000000000000006
21102892010000000000000000000000000000000000001000025300000000000101
21102901110707521600320201112000129800200441021000000000000000000000000000000042
21102902010000000000000000000000000000000000004200105100000000000100
21102911110808121650420201013000229800000440020000000000000000000001000000000002
21102912010000000000000000000000000000000000005000103000000000100101
21102921110808521700420201013000129800000440021000000000000000000000000000000002
21102922010000000000000000000000000000000000005000103000000000000101
21102931110808721750540201013000129800000440121000000000000000000001000000000005
21102932020000000000000000000000000000000000001000025300000000000101
21102941110707321600320201211000129900100021021000000000000000000000000000000020
21102942010000000000000000000000000000000000002000050100000000000100
21102951110807721600320201211000229800100021020000000000000000000000000000000007
21102952010000000000000000000000000000000000001000025320000110001100
21102961110808321700420201112000329800200441021000000000000000000000000000000012
21102962010000000000000000000000000000000000001200030100000000000100
21102971110809021750520201013000129800000440021000000000000000000000000000000001
21102972010000000000000000000000000000000000005000103000000000000101
21102981110708021600320111212100129900100021021000000000000000000000000000000002
21102982010000000000000000000000000000000000005000103000000000000101
21102991110808421700320111211000129800100021021000000000000000000000000000000003
21102992010000000000000000000000000000000000005000103000000000000101
21103001110808721750420201013000129800000240021000000000000000000000000000000002
21103002010000000000000000000000000000000000005000103000000000000101
21103011110808821800520201013000229800000440021000000000000000000000000000000010
21103012010000000000000000000000000000000000001000025100000000000100
21103021110808821800420201013000129800000440021000000000000000000000000000000002
21103022010000000000000000000000000000000000005000103000000000000101
21103031110808321650420201112000029800100021020130110020200001011000000000000231
21103032090000000000000000000000000000000000002310057712000011001100
21103041110707721600320202212000129900100021021000000000000000000000000000000003
21103042010000000000000000000000000000000000005000103000000000000101
21103051110708121700320202212000329800100021020000000000000000000000000000000008
21103052010000000000000000000000000000000000001000025320000010101100
21103061110707621600320202211000809900100021020000000000000000000000000000000007
21103062020000000000000000000000000000000000001000025300000110000100
21103071110708021650320202212000329900100021020140100000000000000000000000000001
21103072010000000000000000000000000000000000005000103000000110000101
21103081110708221700320202013000909800200240020000000000000000000000000000000004
21103082010000000000000000000000000000000000005000103000000000001101
21103091110708321700420202112000129800200240021000000000000000000000000000000002
21103092010000000000000000000000000000000000005000103000000000000101
21103101110708521700420202112001209800200240020000000000000000000000000000000006
21103102020000000000000000000000000000000000001000025320000000001100
21103111110708621650420202112000129800000240021000000000000000000000000000000024
21103112010000000000000000000000000000000000002400060000000000000100
21103121110708821650420201013000229800000240020000000000000000000000000000000005
21103122010000000000000000000000000000000000001000025320000000001100
21103131100709021600420201012000129800000240020000000000000000000000000000000005
21103132010000000000000000000000000000000000001000025320000000001100
21103141110809321800620201013000229800000540020000000000000000000000000000000006
21103142010000000000000000000000000000000000001000025320000000001101
```

```
21103151110809821750520201013000129800000440020000000000000000000000000000000002
21103152010000000000000000000000000000000000000500010320000000601101
21103161110809821750520201013000129800000240021000000000000000000000000000000002
21103162010000000000000000000000000000000000000500010300000000000101
21103171130604721600320201221000129800111021020110100000100000000000000000000213
21103172030000000000000000000000000000000000021300532131111110111111
21103181130604921600420201122000129800100021021000000000000000000000000000000002
21103182010000000000000000000000000000000000000500010300000000000101
21103191130605121600420201122000129800100021021000000000000000000000000000000006
21103192010000000000000000000000000000000000010000253000000000000100
21103201130605321600420201123000129800100021021140100010000000000000000000000035
21103202010000000000000000000000000000000000003500087100000010010100
21103211130605721600320201122000129800100021020000000000000000000000000000000007
21103212010000000000000000000000000000000000010000253000000010010101
21103221130606221600320201222000229800200440021140100000000000010000000000000013
21103222010000000000000000000000000000000000000130003210000000000100
21103231120503321650420201023000329800200440021000000000000001000000000000000001
21103232010000000000000000000000000000000000000500010300000000000101
21103241120503121650420201023000529800200440021120110000000000000000000000000001
21103242010000000000000000000002000000000000000500010300000000000101
21103251130503821700420201023000529800200440021120100000100000000000000000000001
21103252010000000000000000000000000000000000000500010300000000000101
21103261130505121600320201211000119900100021020000000000000000000000000000000001
21103262010000000000000000000000000000000000000500010300000000100101
21103271130505221600320201023000319800200040021000000000000000000010000100000001
21103272010000000000000000000000000000000000000500010300000000000101
21103281130505021600320201023000129800200440020120100010000000000000000000000002
21103282010000000000000000000000000000000000000500010300000000100101
21103291130505321600320201122000419800200440020000000000000000000000000000000001
21103292010000000000000000000000000000000000000500010300000000010101
21103301130505621600320201122000119800100021020110100000000000010000100000000003
21103302010000000000000000000000000000000000000500010300000100000101
21103311120603021206420202112000229800200010020000000000000000000000000100000001
21103312010000000000000000000000000000000000000500010300000100000101
21103321130603921600320201122000229800100021021000000000000000000000000000000002
21103322010000000000000000000000000000000000000500010300000000000101
21103331130602721600420201123000129800200440020000000000000001000000000000000006
21103332020000000000000000000000000000000000010000253000000001100100
21103341120603221600320201123000909800200010020140100000000000000000000000000028
21103342010000000000000000000000000000000000028000701000000010100100
21103351120503021600320201121000129800100041020000000000000000000000000000000012
21103352010000000000000000000000000000000000001200030100000010100100
21103361130707821600320201122000129800200010020000000000000000000000000000000001
21103362010000000000000000000000000000000000000500010300000000010101
21103371130707021600320201122000129800200010021000000000000000000000000000000001
21003372010000000000000000000000000000000000000500010300000000000101
21103381140810721750540201023000229800000440021000000000000000000001000000000001
21103382000000000000000000001000000000000000000500010300000000000101
21103391130310421800630201023000229800200540021000000000000000000000000000000006
21103392010000000000000000000000000000000000010000253000000010010100
31100011110406831700330202012000119840100421021120100000000000000000000000000008
31100012010000000000000000000000000000000000010000251000000000000100
31100021110406941700330202012000119840100421021000000000000000000000000000000010
31100022020000000000000000000000000000000000001500035100000000000100
31100031110406741700330102112000119840100321021000000000000000000000000000000011
31100032010000000000000000000000000000000000011000281000000000000100
31100041110406641700320202112000211000100321020000000000000000000000000000000004
31100042010000000000000000000000000000000000010000251200000000011100
31100051110506441650210103230000219830100021020000000000000000000000000000000010
31100052010000000000000000000000000000000000010000251000000000010100
```

```
31100061110407541700531202121000129800100021020000000000000000000000000000000030
31100062020000000000000000000000000000000000003600090100000010010100
31100071110406941700430202012000129800100021011000000000000000000000000000000001
31100072010000000000000000000000000000000000000500010100000000000100
31100081110506641650430202122000029800100021020000000000000000000000000000000003
31100082010000000000000000000000000000000000000500010100000000010100
31100091110506241650210102230000219830100022021000000000000000000000000000000017
31100092010000000000000000000000000000000000001700043100000000000100
31100101100506641650320202111000029800100021021000000000000000000000000000000019
31100102010000000000000000000000000000000000001900048100000000000100
31100111110505441650220102230000010530100021021000000000000000000000000000000002
31100112010000000000000000000000000000000000000500010100000000000100
31100121110505541650210102230000210530100021021000000000000000000000000000000003
31100122010000000000000000000000000000000000000500010100000000000100
31100131110505741650210102230000011030100022021000000000000000000000000000000001
31100132010000000000000000000000000000000000000500010100000000000100
31100141110504741650210102210000519830100021021000000000000000000000000000000002
31100142010000000000000000000000000000000000000500010100000000000100
31100151110505141640210102230000419830100021021000000000000000000000000000000001
31100152010000000000000000000000000000000000000500010100000000000100
31100161110505441600210102230000010530100021021000000000000000000000000000000002
31100162010000000000000000000000000000000000000500010100000000000100
31100171110505241600210102230000210730100021020000000000000000000000000000000004
31100172010000000000000000000000000000000000010000251000000000010100
31100181110506231650320202111000019900100021020140101010000010100000000000000217
31100182010000009999980000000000000000000000217005431000000010110100
31100191100507511650320202122000029840100021021000000000000000000000000000000001
31100192010000000000000000000000000000000000000500010100000000000100
31100201100507211640330202012000029800000440021000000000000000000000000000000001
31100202010000000000000000000000000000000000000500010100000000000100
31100211110505931650210102210000019930100021020140111000000010101001000000000065
31100212030000000000000000000000000000000000007300178120000011111100
31100221100506341600210102210000219930100021020000000000000000000000000000000002
31100222010000000000000000000000000000000000000500010100000000010100
31100231100506341600210102220000019930110021020110010010100000100001100000000018
31100232010000009999980000000000000000000000001800045100000011110100
31100241100506341600210102210000219930100021020210011000000000100000000000000002
31100242010000000000000000000000000000000000000500010120000001101100
31100251100506841600210102210000019930100021020000000000010101000100000000000023
31100252030000009999980000000000000000000000003000073100000111100100
31100261100506831600210102210000129930100021020000000000000000000000000000000002
31100262010000000000000000000000000000000000000500010100000000100100
31100271100506841600310202021000320540100029020110010000000000100000000000000004
31100272010000000000000000000000000000000000010000251000000000010100
31100281100506941600310202021000320540100029020110010000000000100000000000000019
31100282020000000000000000000000000000000000002100050100000000010100
31100291100507111650320202122000419800100021020000000000000000000000000000000003
31100292010000000000000000000000000000000000000500010100000000010100
31100301100507411600320202021000219800100021020120100010000000000000000000000027
31100302020000000000000000000000000000000000003200080100000111100100
31100311100507111600320202211000119800100021021000000000000000000000000000000002
31100312010000000000000000000000000000000000000500010100000000000100
31100321100507231600320202022000029800200021021110100000000000000000000000000001
31100322010000000000000000000000000000000000000500010100000000000100
31100331100507931600310202122000029860100029020110010010000000100000000000000053
31100332010000000000000000000000000000000000005300133100000010000100
31100341100605711600320202012010319800000-10021000000000000000000000000000000050
31100342010000000000000000000000000000000000000500012510000000000101
31100351100606111550210102210000019930100021020000000000000000000110000000000015
31100352010000009999980000000000000000000000001500038100000011110100
```

```
31100361100606521550210102210000019930100021020000000000100000000000000000000021
31100362040000000000000000000000000000000000300068100000000100100
31100371100505621550320202120001019840100021021000000000000000000000000000000001
31100372010000000000000000000000000000000000005000101000000000000100
31100381100606721550210102210000019930100022021110100000000000000000000000000007
31100382010000000000000000000000000000000001000025100000000000100
31100391100608321550210102110000919900100021020000000000000000000000010000000000001
31100392010000000000000000000000000000000000500010120000010001100
31100401100606321540210101210000319900100021021100100000000000000010000000000001
31100402010000000000000000000000000000000000050001010000000000100
31100411100605821550210102220000719930100021020000000000000000000000000000000006
31100412010000000000000000000000000000000010000251000000010010100
31100421100606221550210101210000319930100021021100100000000000000000000000000006
31100422010000000000000000000000000000000010000251000000000000100
311004311106057215503202021210001499301000210201499990000000000000010000000000064
31100432010000000000000000000000000000000000640016010000000001010100
31100441100607321550210102230110010210100022010000000010100000000001000000000005
31100442010000009999980000000000000000000000010000251000000010110101
31100451090610211500210102210010040210100025020149919020000100010000000000000004
31100452010000009999980000000000000000000000010000251000000011100100
31100461100606021550310202021010029900100021020000000002010000999990100000000101
31100462030000000000000000000010010000000001020025510000000010110101
31100471100809531800410202013000229800000440020000000000000000000000000000000006
31100472010000000000000000000000000000000000100002510000000000100100
31100481100809421650321202022000029900010440020140100000000000000001010000000001
31100482010000009999980000000000000000000000000500010120000000001100
31100491100709021600321202022000029900000440020000000000000000000000000000000014
31100492010000000000000000000000000000000000140003512000000000001100
31100501100708721600321202022000029900000440020000000000000000000000000000000011
31100502010000000000000000000000000000000000110002812000000000001100
31100511100809621600321202022000029900000440020000000000000000000000000000000004
31100512010000000000000000000000000000000000010000251200000000001100
31100521100709521550321202022000029900000440020000000000000000000000000000000019
31100522010000000000000000000000000000000000019000481200000000001100
31100531100710021550321202022000029900000440021000000000000000000000000000000055
31100532030000000000000000000000000000000003000060000000000000000100
31100541100810421550321202022000029900000440020000000000000000010000001000000044
31100542010000009999980000000000000000000000015000300200000000011100
31100551100709631550210102210000110310100021021000000000000000000000000000000001
31100552010000000000000000000000000000000000005000101000000000000100
31100561100810921600320202023000029900000440011999990000000000000000000000000003
31100562010000000000000000000000000000000000005000101000000000000100
31100571100811621650331202023000029900000440020120110010000000100001000000000404
31100572170010000000400000000000000000000000034700807300000010100100
31100581090814831600321202013000029900010440120140100010000001101001000000001126
31100582080000009999989999100100100000000000000583011640200001111111101
31100591100811341700430202023000029900000440020000000000000000000000000000000011
31100592010000000000000000000000000000000000001100281000000000100100
31100601090510631600320202020000229900200023020110110000000000010000000000000002
31100602010000000000000000000000000000000000005000101000000001100100
31100611090510631600320202020000229900200023021000000000000000000000000000000003
31100612010000000000000000000000000000000000005000101000000000000100
31100621090510531600320202020000229900200023021000000000000000000000000000000005
31100622020000000000000000000000000000000000010000201000000000000100
31100631090511711600320202111000119900200021030110010000000100110000001000000003
31100632010000000000000000000000000000000000005000100000000110000100
31100641100603411550210102211000129930100020021220110000000000000000000000000028
31100642010000000000000000000000000000000000028000701200000000101101
31100651100608511550210102211000129930100020021000000000000000000000000000000001
31100652010000000000000000000000000000000000005000101000000000000100
```

```
31100661100509011550210102210000229900100021021000000000000000000000000000000003
31100662010000000000000000000000000000000000005000100000000000000100
31100671100609011550210102210010029900110021020000000003000000011100010000000114
31100672020000009999980000000000000000000000005700114020000000111101
31100681100609411550210102210010029900100021020120100020000000000011000000000020
31100682010000009999980000000000000000000000001000020020000000111101
31100691100609111550210102210010129900100021020000000000000000000000000000000001
31100692010000000000000000000000000000000000005000100000000000110100
31100701100608010550210103210000319920100022021000000000000000000000000000000002
31100702010000000000000000000000000000000000005000101000000000000100
31100711100608011550210103210000319920100022021000000000000000000000000000000002
31100712010000000000000000000000000000000000005000101000000000000100
31100721100608511550210103210000519900100021021000000000000000000000000000000001
31100722010000000000000000000000000000000000005000101000000000000100
31100731100609211550210103210010040310100021020110001010000000010000000000000023
31100732010000009999980000000000000000000000023000581200000010111100
31100741090610811500210103210000040100000010020000000000000000000000000000000001
31100742010000000000000000000000000000000000005000101000000000010100
31100751100608721550210102210000040210100021021120100000000000000001000000000003
31100752020000000000000000000000000000000000010000201000000000000100
31100761090610621500210103230010040110100021020000000000000000000000000000000006
31100762010000000000000000000000000000000000010000251000000000010100
31100771090610721500210103230010040110100021020000000000000000000000110000000006
31100772010000000000000000000000000000000000010000251000000000010100
31100781090610821500210103230010040110100021020000000000000000000000000000000002
31100782010000000000000000000000000000000000005000101000000000010100
31100791100709521500210106230000009930100021020000000000000000000000000000000077
31100792010000000000000000000000000000000000077001931000000000100100
31100801100709931550210102230000709930100021021000000000000000000000000000000001
31100802010000000000000000000000000000000000005000101000000000000100
31100811100710731500210102230000209920100021021000000000000000000000000000000001
31100812010000000000000000000000000000000000005000101000000000000100
31100821090710841500210106240000009920100022020000000000000000000000100000000006
31100822010000000000000000000000000000000000010000251000000000110100
31100831100811531550210102210000129900000010010000000000000000000001000000000003
31100832010000009999980000000000000000000000005000101000000000110100
31100841100810741550310102210000029900100021021000000000000000000000000000000003
31100842010000000000000000000000000000000000005000101000000000000100
31100851100812641600210102240010029900100021020000000000000000000000000000000053
31100852010000000000000000000000000000000000053001331000000000100100
31100861090813241600320202111000029900100021021000000000000000000000000000000038
31100862040000000000000000000000000000000000036000720000000000000100
31100871090814641650310202012000029900000440021000000000000000000000000000000001
31100872010000000000000000000000000000000000005000101000000000000100
31100881090814841650330202023000129900000440021000000000000000000000000000000001
31100882010000000000000000000000000000000000005000101000000000000100
31100891090511211650220102110000019900100021020140100000000000000000000000000105
31100892020000000000000000000000000000000000069001540000000001100100
31100901090412011650330202112000019900100021021000000000000000000000000000000003
31100902010000000000000000000000000000000000005000101000000000000100
31100911090412011700430202012000119900100021021000000000000000000000000000000002
31100912010000000000000000000000000000000000005000101000000000000100
31100921090412311700320202012000019900100021021000000000000000000000000000000003
31100922010000000000000000000000000000000000005000101000000000000100
31100931090511610600330202022000019900100021021000000000000000000000000000000002
31100932010000000000000000000000000000000000005000101000000000000100
31100941090511511600330202012000219900100021021000000000000000000000000000000001
31100942010000000000000000000000000000000000005000101000000000000100
31100951090511211600210103130000019930100021021000000000000000000000000000000004
31100952010000000000000000000000000000000000010000251000000000000100
```

31100961090511311550220102210000019930110021020140110000000000000000000000000291
31100962010000009999380000000000000000000100291007281000001111100100
31100971090512011550310102121000219900100021021000000000000000000000000000000001
31100972010000000000000000000000000000000000000500010100000000000100
31100981090511641550430202212000199401000210211401100000000000000000000000000007
31100982030000000000000000000000000000000000001500030100000000000100
31100991090612211500220106240010040110100021020000000000000000001001000000000003
31100992010000000000000000000000000000000000000500010100000011110100
31101001090612211500210103210010040110100021021000000000000000000000000000000002
31101002010000000000000000000000000000000000000500010100000000000100
31101011090611421500210103210010040110100021021000000000000000000000000000000002
31101012010000000000000000000000000000000000000500010100000001100100
31101021090611921500210102210010040330100022020000000000001000000010000000000002
31101022010000019999980000000000000000000000000500010100000000010100
31101031090611221500210113210000205001000210200000000000000000000000000000000003
31101032010000000000000000000000000000000000000500010100000000010100
31101041090712621500210102210100209900100021021000000000000000000000000000000018
31101042010000000000000000000000000100000000000180004510000000000010
31101051090713221500210102230000009900100021031000000000000000000010000000000012
31101052010000000000000000000000000100000000000150003510000000000010
31101061090712821550320202121010020200100021021000000000000000000000000000000028
31101062020000000000000000000000000000000000002800070100000000000100
31101071090713321500310202110000129900100021020120100050000000011101100000000020
31101072010000009999980000000000000000000000020000501011100010100100
31101081090713921550320202921000429900100021021000000000000000000000000000000002
31101082010000000000000000000000000000000000000500010100000000000100
31101091090713721500210105240000402201000220210000000000000000000000000000000005
31101092010000000000000000000000000000000000001000025100000000000100
31101101090711421500210106240010000131100021020000000001000001000000100000000004
31101102010000000000000000000000000000000000010000251200000000001100
31101111090712521550310102210010040100100022020000000000000000000000000000000003
31101112010000000000000000000000000000000000000500010100000001100100
31101121090712421550310102210010040100100022020110010010000000000101000000000001
31101122010000099999800000000000000000000000000500010100000011100100
31101131090712521550310102210010040100100022020000000400000001010010000010000019
31101132010000099999800000000000000000000000001900048100000011100100
31101141090813041600320202012000029900200029011000000000000000000000000000000001
31101142010000000000000000000000000000000000000500010100000000000100
31101151090713721500210105240000309920100022021000000000000000000000000000000003
31101152010000000000000000000000000100000000000050001010000000000010
31101161090814541600320202111000129900100021021000000000000000000000000000000036
31101162010000000000000000000000000000000000000180036000000000000100
31101171090814241650320202012000129900004400110000000000000000000000000000000003
31101172010000000000000000000000000000000000000500010000000000000100
31101181090814031650321202112000229900004400200000000000000000000000000000000008
31101182010000000000000000000000000000000000000500010000000011000100
31101191090814331650321202112000229900004400201500100000000000100001100000000028
31101192010000099999800000000000000000000000001400028000000011100100
31101201090815031640321202112000229900004400201101000000000000000110000000000003
31101202010000099999800000000000000000000000000500010000001011100100
31101211090815141650321202112000229900004400211100100000000000000100000000000023
31101212020000020066090000000000000000000000001500030000000010000100
31101221090814141650310202012000029900004400210000000000000000000000000000000003
31101222010000000000000000000000000000000000000500010100000000000100
31101231090814041640330202013000129900004400210000000000000000000000000000000002
31101232020000000000000000000000000000000000001000020100000000000100
31101241090814841700330202013000129900004400210000000000000000000000000000000016
31101242010000000000000000000000000000000000001600040100000000000100
31101251090815141650321202013000029900004400201100100000000001000010000000000025
31101252020000000000000000000000000000000000002800068100000010010100
31101261090815441650320202013000129900004400210000000000000000000000000000000003
31101262010000000000000000000000000000000000000500010100000000000100
31101271090815531650321202023000229900010440011000000000000000100001000000000010
31101272010000010062520000000000000000000000000500010000000000000100
31101281090815141700420202012000029900004400210000000000000000101000000000000005
31101282030000000000000000000000000000000000001500030100000000000100
31101291090815741750430202013000029900004400211200100000000000000000000000000002
31101292020000000000000000000000000000000000001000020100000000000100
31101301090815931700421202023000129900004400211401000000000000000000000000000042
31101302010000000000000000000000000000001000004200105100000000000101
31101311090816041750430202013000029900004400210000000000000000000000000000000003
31101312010000000000000000000000000000000000000500010100000000000100
31101321090816241700421202023000129900004400110000000000000000000000000000000005
31101322010000000000000000000000000000000000000500010000000000000100
31101331080514711550321202111000019900100021021000000000000000000000000000000002
31101332010000000000000000000000000000000000000500010100000000000100
31101341080514911550321202111000119900100021021000000000000000000000000000000002
31101342010000000000000000000000000000000000000500010100000000000100
31101351080515511550321202111000119940100021021000000000000000000000000000000010
31101352030000000000000000000000000000000000002000045100000000000100
31101361080515211550321202111000119900100021021000000000000000000000000000000009
31101362010000000000000000000000000000000000001000025100000000000100
31101371090613011550210102110000129900100021021000000100000001010010000000000010
31101372010000000000000000000000000000000000001000025000000000000100
31101381090513111550210102110000029900100021021000000000000000000000000000000003
31101382010000000000000000000000000000000000000500010100000000000100
31101391080514311550210102210000629900100021021000000000000000000000000000000002
31101392010000000000000000000000000000000000000500010100000000000100
31101401080414911550210103210000419930100021021000000000000000000000000000000002
31101402010000000000000000000000000000000000000500010100000000000100
31101411080514931550220102210010020110100021020000000000001010100000000000000004
31101412010000000000000000000000000000000000001000025100000000100100
31101421090613111500210102210000129910100021020000000100000010100100000000000017
31101422020000099999800000000000000000000000001700034300000000110100
31101431080614621500210102210110040210100021020000000000000000010000000000000007
31101432020000099999800000000000000000000000001500035120000000101100
31101441080614221500210102210110040210100021020000000000000010000000000000000006
31101442010000099999800000000000000000000000001000025100000010100100
31101451080614121500210102210110040210100021020000000300000001001000000000000026
31101452010000099999800000000000000000000000002600065100000001100100
31101461090613221500210102210110040210100021020000000000000000000000000000000009
31101462010000000000000000000000000000000000001000025100000000100100
31101471090613521500210102210110040210100021020000000100000000000000000000000002
31101472010000099999800000000000000000000000000500010120000000101100
31101481080714321500210105230000309900000022021000000000000000000000000000000003
31101482010000000000000000000000000001000000000500010100000000000100
31101491080614621500210105240000409920100022021000000000000000000000000000000002
31101492010000000000000000000000000000000000000500010100000000000100
31101501080614821500210105240000309920100022021000000000000000000000000000000002
31101502010000000000000000000000000000000000000500010000000000000100
31101511080714821500210105240000209920100022021000000000000000000000000000000005
31101512010000000000000000000000000000000000001000025100000000000100
31101521090713521500210105240000003201000220310000000000000000000000000000000001
31101522010000000000000000000000000100000000000050001010000000000010
31101531090714121500320202121000429940100021020000000101000000000000000000000016
31101532010000000000000000000000000000000000001600040100000000100100
31101541080714221500210105240000009930100022021000000000000000000100000000000063
31101542010000000000000000000000000000000000006300158100000000000100
31101551080714821500210105240000499999999999210000000000000000000000000000000003
31101552010000000000000000000000000000000000000500010100000000000100

```
31101561080715421500210105240000400320100022020000000000000000000000000000000000002
31101562010000000000000000000000000000000000000500010100000000100100
31101571080715021500210102210010329900100021021000000000000000000001000000000099
31101572010000000000000000000000000000000000009900248100000000100100
31101581080715521500430202121000129900100021020000000000000000000000000000000005
31101582010000000000000000000000000000000000001000025100000000100100
31101591090714621500320202120000329900100021020000000000100001010010000000000012
31101592020000009999980000000000000000000000001600038100000010100100
31101601080715421500421202121000719900100021020000000000000000000000000000000004
31101602010000000000000000000000000000000000001000025100000000100100
31101611080715421500420202121000719900100021021000000000000000000000000000000003
31101612010000000000000000000000000000000000000500010100000000000100
31101621080715421500430202122000429900100021020000000000000000000000000000000003
31101622010000000000000000000000000000000000000500010100000010100100
31101631080715721500420202121000029900100021020000000000000000000000000000000003
31101632010000000000000000000000000000000000000500010100000000100100
31101641080716321550320202012000029900100021020110010000000000000001000000000103
31101642040000009999980000000000000000000000001070026510000010100100
31101651080715721500320202132000329900100021021000000000000000000000000000000002
31101652010000000000000000000000000000000000000500010100000000000100
31101661080815321500310202131000029900100021021000000000000000000000000000000001
31101662010000000000000000000000000000000000000500010100000000000100
31101671090814921600320202121000229900100021021000000000000000000000000000000013
31101672030000000000000000000000000000000000002500060100000000000100
31101681080815421500310106210000019900100021021000000000000000000000000000000002
31101682010000000000000000000000000000000000000500010100000000000100
31101691080816121550320202111000029900100021020000000000000000000000000000000006
31101692020000000000000000000000000000000000001000020100000010100100
31101701080817021600420202011000229900000440021000000000000000000000000000000001
31101702010000000000000000000000000000000000000500010100000000000100
31101711080817021650430202022000029900000440021000000000000000000000000000000002
31101712010000000000000000000000000000000000000500010100000000000100
31101721080816621600420202011000029900000440021000000000000000000000000000000002
31101722010000000000000000000000000000000000000500010100000000000100
31101731080816421650420202012000529900000440011000000000000000000001000000000001
31101732010000000000000000000000000000000000000500010100000000000100
31101741080816121600420202011000319900000440021000000000000000000000000000000001
31101742020000000000000000000000000000000000001000020100000000000100
31101751080816021600320202012000029900100021021000000000000000000000000000000016
31101752010000000000000000000000000000000000001600040100000000000100
31101761070716421550310206231000029900100021091000000000000000000000000000000001
31101762010000000000000000000000000000000000000500010100000000000100
31101771090816021700420202112000029900000240021000000000000000000000000000000002
31101772020000000000000000000000000000000000001000020100000000000100
31101781080417211700440202023000129900000440021000000000000000000000000000000002
31101782010000000000000000000000000000000000000500010100000000000100
31101791080417611750440202022000029900100021021000000000000000000000000000000001
31101792010000000000000000000000000000000000000500010100000000000100
31101801080516111550120202112000029900100021021000000000000000000000000000000003
31101802010000000000000000000000000000000000000500010100000000000100
31101811080516611550320202111000029900100021010110100000000000000000001000000019
31101812020000000000000000000000000000000000002300058100000100000100
31101821080516311550200102210000029900100021020000000000000000000000000000000010
31101822010000000000000000000000000000000000001000025100000000100100
31101831080515911550320202112000029900000440020000000000000000000000000000000005
31101832010000000000000000000000000000000000001000020100000100000100
31101841080516311550320202122000119900100021020110100010000000000000000000000005
31101842010000000000000000000000000000000000001000025100000001000100
31101851080515811550330202022000319900100021020110100000000000000000000000000032
31101852010000000000000000000000000000000000003200080100000110100100
```

```
31101861080516711500320202012000013940100021021000000000000000000000000000000001
31101862010000000000000000000000000000000000000500010100000000000100
31101871080516611500320202012000113940100021021000000000000000000000000000000001
31101872010000000000000000000000000000000000000500010100000000000100
31101881080517211500210102220000019900100021021110100010000000000000000000000029
31101882020000000000000000000000000000000000003300080100000010000100
31101891080517311500210102220000019900100021021000000010000000000000000000000003
31101892020000000000000000000000000000000000001000020100000011000100
31101901080517311500320202111000219900100021021000000000000000000000000000000002
31101902010000000000000000000000000000000000000500010100000000000100
31101911080516611500210103210000319900100021021140100000000000000000000000000035
31101912010000000000000000000000000000000000003500088100000000000100
31101921080818021750531202112000029900100021030000000000000000000000000000000001
31101922010000009999980000000000000000001000000500010100000111100100
31101931080515611500210102210000129900100021021000000000000000000000000000000003
31101932020000000000000000000000000000000000001000020100000000000100
31101941080515711550220102211000129900100021021000000000000000000000000000000001
31101942010000000000000000000000000000000000000500010100000000000100
31101951080516111500210102210000819900100021021000000000000000000000000000000002
31101952010000000000000000000000000000000000000500010100000000000100
31101961080516531500210102112000519900100023011000000000000000000000000000000003
31101962010000000000000000000000000000000000000500010100000000000100
31101971080616631500210102110000240300100021011000000000000000000000000000000002
31101972010000000000000000000000000000000000000500010100000000000100
31101981080616431500210102110000240300100021011000000000000000000000000000000002
31101982010000000000000000000000000000000000000500010100000000000100
31101991080617031500210102110000819900100023011000000000000000000000000000000003
31101992010000000000000000000000000000000000000500010100000000000100
31102001080616011500210102210000049920100021020110110050200000101001000000000047
31102002010000009999980000000000000000000000004700118100000101110100
31102011080616211500210103210010049910120022020000000000000000000011000000000021
31102012010000009999980000000000000000000000001000021000000000110101
31102021080716421500331202012010609900100021020000000000000000000000000000000001
31102022010000000000000000000000000000000000000500010100000010100100
31102031080616321500331202012000809900100021020000000000000000000000000000000001
31102032010000000000000000000000000000000000000500010100000010100100
31102041080717521500320202111000029900100021020000000000000000000001000000000023
31102042010000009999980000000000000000000000002300058100000011100100
31102051080717121640430202111000129900100021021000000000000000000000000000000001
31102052010000000000000000000000000000000000000500010100000000000100
31102061080716821600310202011000129900100021021000000000000000000000000000000002
31102062010000000000000000000000000000000000000500010100000000000100
31102071080718021750541202012000229900000440021000000000000000000000000000000001
31102072010000000000000000000000000000000000000500010100000000000100
31102081080817721700531202112000029900100021020000000000000000000000000000000003
31102082010000000000000000000000000000000000000500010100000010000100
31102091080818621750531202112000029900100021020000000000000000000000000000000002
31102092010000000000000000000000000000000000000500010100000001000100
31102101080818321750531202112000029900110021030120100000001000000011000000000023
31102102010000009999980000000000000000001000002300058120000011001100
31102111080819221650320202012000029900100021021000000000000000000000000000000001
31102112010000000000000000000000000000000000000500010100000000000100
31102121080819121550320202111000029900100021021000000000000000000000000000000002
31102122010000000000000000000000000000000000000500010100000000000100
31102131080818621600430202012000129900100021020000000000000000000000000000000003
31102132010000000000000000000000000000000000000500010100000000100100
31102141080818121650430202012000229900000440020000000000000000000000000000000003
31102142010000000000000000000000000000000000000500010100000000100100
31102151080818021700430202023000429900000440021000000000000000000000000000000001
31102152010000000000000000000000000000000000000500010100000000000100
```

```
31102161080817221650430202012000329900000440021000000000000000000000000000000001
31102162010000000000000000000000000000000000000500010100000000000100
31102171080819321650420202110000199001000210210000000000000000000000000000000001
31102172010000000000000000000000000000000000000500010100000000000100
31102181080819421650421202131000119900100021021000000000000000000000000000000002
31102182010000000000000000000000000000000000000500010100000000000100
31102191080919921650421202131000119900100021020000000000000000000000000000000001
31102192010000000000000000000000000000000000000500010100000010100100
31102201080919821700531202011000319900000540020000000000000000000000000000000001
31102202010000000000000000000000000000000000000500010100000000100100
31102211080919521750530202012000029900000540020000000000000000000000000000000002
31102212010000000000000000000000000000000000000500010100000000100100
31102221070419711800531202023000119940100021021000000000000000000000000000000001
31102222010000000000000000000000000000000000000500010100000000000100
31102231070419511750531202023000219940100021021000000000000000000000000000000001
31102232010000000000000000000000000000000000000500010100000000000100
31102241070418711700320202012000029900000440021000000000000000000000000000000001
31102242010000000000000000000000000000000000000500010100000000000100
31102251070418811700320202122000019900110021020120100020000100000001100000100082
31102252060090020015810000000000000000000000009300228100000011100101
31102261070518411650220102210000199401000210200000000000000000000000000000000013
31102262010000009999980000000000000000000000001300033100000001100100
31102271070519011650210102210000299001000210210000000000000000000000000000000001
31102272010000000000000000000000000000000000000500010100000000000100
31102281070520011550320202121000129900100021020000000020000001010010000000000001
31102282010000000000000000000000000000000000000500010100000001000100
31102291070521111550210102111000029940100021021000000000000000000000000000000002
31102292010000000000000000000000000000000000000500010100000000000100
31102301070519211500210102210000299301000210210000000000000000000000000000000007
31102302010000000000000000000000000000000000001000025100000000000100
31102311070518011500210102210000+0520100021010119999000100000000101100000000000002
31102312010000009999980000000000000000000000000500010100001111100100
31102321070619211500210103210010040210110021020120100000000000000000100000000068
31102322020000009999980000000000000000000000003400068020000001101101
31102331070619111500210104240000040210100022020140111010100001101101000000000073
31102332010000009999980000000000000000000000003900078000000011100101
31102341070619811500210105240000040110100022020000000000000000000001000000000003
31102342010000009999980000000000000000000000000500010000000010000101
311023510706198115002101052400100401101100?220201101000000000010110110000000013
31102352010000009990980000000000000100000000001000020000000110110101
31102361070618811500231202013000409900100021020000000000000000000000000000000019
31102362010000000000000000000000000000000000001900048100000110000101
31102371070618211500231202013000309900100021020000000000000000000000000000000002
31102372010000000000000000000000000000000000000500010100000110100101
31102381070618611500231202013000109900100021020000000000000000000000000000000002
31102382010000000000000000000000000000000000000500010100000110000101
31102391070720121850531202012000229900000440020110100010000000000000100000000033
31102392010000009999899990000000000000000100003300083100000000100101
31102401070720521600330202013000029900000440021000000000000000000000000000000001
31102402010000000000000000000000000000000000000500010100000000000100
31102411070718921900591202013000229900000440021000000000000000000000000000000010
31102412020000000000000000000000000000000000001500035100000000000101
31102421070718921850410202012000129900000440021000000000000000000000000000000001
31102422010000000000000000000000000000000000000500010000000000000100
31102431070720521600310202221000029900120021020000000100000000000000110000000043
31102432040000009999980000000000000000000000000510012610000000100101
31102441070813921650320202121000029900100021020000000000000000000000000000000011
31102442020000000000000000000000000000000000001500035100000000100100
31102451060924121800641202012000029900000440020000000000000000000000000000000002
31102452010000000000000300000000000000000000000500010120000000001100
```

```
31102461060622311500210103230010040310100022020140100000200000000001100000000011
31102462010000009999980000000000000000000000001100028100000111100100
31102471070821421500330202112000029900100021020000000000000000000000000000000004
31102472010000000000000000000000000000000000001000025100000000100100
31102481070821221500330202112000029900100021020000000000000000000000000000000002
31102482010000000000000000000000000000000000000500010100000000100100
31102491070821611500220102110000029900100021010120110010100000000000001000000001
31102492010000000000000000000000000000000000000500010100000100000100
31102501070821511500220102111000029900100021020000000000010000100000001000000009
31102502010000000000000000000000000000000000001000025100000010000100
31102511070922821700430202112000029900100021020000000000000000000000000000000001
31102512010000000000000001000000000000000000000500010100000000100100
31102521070922321700430202112000029900100021020000000000000000110000000000000001
31102522010000000000000001000000000010000000000500010100000000100100
31102531070922421850430202112000029900100021020000000000000000000000000000000001
31102532020000000000000003000000000000000000000500010100000000100100
31102541070822221650430202012000029900100021021000000000000000000000000000000001
31102542010000000000000000000000000000000000000500010100000000000100
31102551070922021600420202013000219900000440021000000000000000000000000000000001
31102552010000000000000000000000000000000000000500010100000000000100
31102561070921621700431202111000029900100021021000000000000000000000000000000001
31102562010000000000000000000000000000000000000500010100000000000100
31102571070922321600431202022000119900100021020000000000000000000001000000000011
31102572030000000000000000000000000000000000000250006012000000001100
31102581070922321650431202022000119900100021021000000000000000000000000000000001
31102582010000000000000000000000000000000000000500010100000000000100
31102591070923621750641202023000029900010540020170110090900101011011110000001491
31102592080000009999980640010000001000000104299088103200000000101101
31102601070924121500430202012000029900000440020000000000000000000000000000000003
31102602020000000000000000000000000000000000001000020120000000001100
31102611071024821750430202012000029900000440021000000000000000000000000000000001
31102612010000000000000000000000000000000000000500010100000000000100
31102621071025021800420202012000029900000440020000000000000000000000000000000012
31102622010000000000000000000000000000000000001200030120000000001100
31102631070923121800430202112000219900100021021000000000000000000000000000000002
31102632020000000000000000000000000000000000001000020100000000000100
31102641071024021750210102210000110400100021021000000000000000000000000000000001
31102642010000000000000000000000000000000000000500010100000000000100
31102651071024421750420202112000019900000011020000000000000000000000000000000002
31102652010000000000000000000000000000000000000500010120000000001100
31102661071024621800421202122000219900000440120000000000000000000000000000000004
31102662010000000000000000000000000000000000001000025120000000001100
31102671070420611750320202112000029940100021020120010000000000000000000000000022
31102672040000000000000000000000000000000000003400080100000000100100
31102681070420611800320202112000029940100021021000000000000000000000000000000012
31102682010000000000000000000000000000000000001200030100000000000100
31102691070421311950541202013000229900000440011000000000000000000000000000000003
31102692010000000000000000000000000000000000000500010100000000000100
31102701060422311950540202022000429950100021020000000000000000000000000000000013
31102702020000000000000000000000000000000000001700040100000000100100
31102711060522011950540202022000329950100021020000000000000000000000000000000009
31102712040000000000000000000000000000000000002500055100000000100100
31102721060422311850540202022000229950100021020000000000000000000000000000000001
31102722010000000000000000000000000000000000000500010100000000100100
31102731070521411600330202112000029900100021021000000000000000000000000000000008
31102732010000000000000000000000000000000000001000025100000000000100
31102741070520911500210102122000029930100021021000000000000000000000000000000002
31102742020000000000000000000000000000000000001000020100000000000100
31102751060521911550330202012000029900100021021000000000000000000000000000000001
31102752010000000000000000000000000000000000000500010100000000000100
```

```
31102761060522211500210102012000019900100021021000000000000000000000000000000005
31102762030000000000000000000000000000000000001500030100000000000100
31102771060621411500210203230010040110100022020110000000000000000001000000000038
31102772010000009999980000000000000000000000003800095100000111100100
31102781060823321500210102112010521000100021020000000000100000000000000000000002
31102782010000000000000000000000000000000000000500010100000000100100
31102791070722321500310202120000129900100021020120100010000000000000000000000006
31102792010000000000000000000000000000000000001000251000000000000100100
31102801060823421500210106210000229900100021021000000000000000000000000000000003
31102802010000000000000000000000000000000000000500010100000000000101
31102811070821831500320203949900229900200023011000000000000000000000000000000005
31102812020000000000000000000000000000000000001000020100000000000100
31102821070822221700330202112000029900100021020000000000000000001000000000000031
31102822040000090009000120000000000000000000003900095100000000100100
31102831070822221500330202112000029900100021020000000000100000000000000000000005
31102832010000000000000000000000000000000000001000025100000000100100
31102841070822521500320202112000129900900029020000000000000000000000000000000003
31102842010000000000000000000000000000000000000500010100000000100100
31102851060824321500210106240010429900100022021000000000000000000000000000000012
31102852010000000000000000000000000000000000001200030100000000000101
31102861070823221500430202012000029900100029020000000000000000000001000000000005
31102862010000009999980002000000000000000000001000025100000000100100
31102871070822521750541202112000029900100021020000000000000000000000000000000002
31102872020000000000000200000000000000000000001000020100000000100100
31102881070924121500320202012000029900900029020000000000000000000000000000000002
31102882010000000000000000000000000000000000000500010100000000100100
31102891070924221550320202012000029900900029020000000000000000000000000000000006
31102892010000000000000000000000000000000000001000025100000000100100
31102901060924921550320202012000029900900029020000000000000000000000000000000012
31102902010000000000000000000000000000000000001200030100000000100100
31102911060925221550320202112000029900900029020000000000000000000000000000000011
31102912010000000000000000000000000000000000001100028120000000001100
31102921070825121550320202112000029900900029020000000000000000000000000000000001
31102922010000000000000000000000000000000000000500010120000000001100
31102931070924721650430202112000029900900029020110010000000000000000000000000001
31102932010000000000000002000000000000000000000500010110000000001100
31102941070924521600420202112000029900100021020000000000000000000000000000000004
31102942020000000000000000000000000000000000001000020120000000001100
31102951070925021600430202112000029900900021020000000000000000000000000000000002
31102952010000000000000000000000000000000000000500010120000000001100
31102961070924921650430202112000029900900021020000000000000000000000000000000001
31102962010000000000000000000000000000000000000500010120000000001100
31102971070924821550541202012000029900000440020000000000000000000000000000000003
31102972010000009999980003000000000000000000000500010120000000001100
31102981070924621850531202012000129900000440020000000000100000000000000000000001
31102982010000000000000100000000000000000000000500010120000000001100
31102991070924821830641202013000129900000540020000000000000000000000000000000003
31102992010000000000000000000000000000000000000500010120000000001100
31103001030434611450320202012000129901000210210000000000000000000000000000000006
31103002010000000000000000000000000000000000001000025100000000000100
31103011070925421800641202012000129900000540020000000000000000000000000000000001
31103012010000000000000000000000000000000000000500010120000000001100
31103021070925621800530202112000029900900029020000000000000000000000000000000001
31103022010000000000000000000000000000000000000500010120000000001100
31103031070925821800540202012000129900900029020000000000000000000000000000000001
31103032010000000000000000000000000000000000000500010120000000001100
31103041071025721850430202012000229900100021021000000000000000000000000000000001
31103042010000000000000000000000000000000000000500010100000000000100
31103051060523411500330202122000419900000440020000000000000000000000000000000001
31103052010000000000000000000000000000000000000500010100000000100100
31103061060523711550330202122000019900000440021000000000000000000000000000000001
31103062010000000000000000000000000000000000000500010100000000000100
31103071060523411550330202122000319900000440020000000000000000000000000000000003
31103072010000000000000000000000000000000000000500010100000000100100
31103081060523511500330202122000019900000440020000000000000000000000000000000003
31103082010000000000000000000000000000000000000500010100000000100100
31103091060523211500330202122000019900000440021000000000000000000000000000000001
31103092010000000000000000000000000000000000000500010100000000000100
31103101060523511500330202122000019900000440020000000000000000000000000000000005
31103102020000000000000000000000000000000000001000020100000000100100
31103111060522511500220102211000029900100021021000000000000000000000000000000013
31103112010000000000000000000000000000000000001300033100000000000101
31103121060522811600320202112000029900100021020000000000000000000000000000000029
31103122050000000000000000000000000000000000004600108100000000100100
31103131060523411600320202112000029900110022020120100000000010000001100000000164
31103132040000099999800000000000000000000000017400433100000000100101
31103141040432811500210102210000629930100024021000000000000000000000000000000005
31103142010000000000000000000000000000000000001000025100000000000100
31103151060523811600441202122000429900000440021000000000000000000000000000000001
31103152010000010002010000000000000000000000000000000030000000000101
31103161060524511550320202022000029900100021021000000000000000000000000000000001
31103162010000000000000000000000000000000000000500010100000000000100
31103171060522511500320202110000129900100023021110100000000100000001000000000001
31103172010000000000000000000000000000000000000500010100000000000100
31103181060523331500320202112000529900100021021000000000000100010000000000000001
31103182010000000000000000000000000000000000000500010100000000000100
31103191060623911500210103230010049920100022020199999020000001011010000000000006
31103192010000099999800000000000000000000000001000025100001111100100
31103201050426211500320202111000019940100021020150100000000000000000000000000004
31103202010000000000000000000000000000000000001000025120000000001100
31103211050426911400321202022000129900100021021000000000000000000000000000000001
31103212010000000000000000000000000000000000000500010100000000000100
31103221050625411450210102110000043920100022020110010000000000000000000000000003
31103222010000000000000000000000000000000000000500010100000000110100
31103231060826521500210106230000401101000350210000000000000000000000000000000001
31103232010000000000000000000000000000000000000500010100000000000101
31103241050229642000641202122000029900104400200000000000000001100001100000000003
31103242010000099999800050000000001000000000000500010120000000101101
31103251050329741900641202122000029900100021020000000000000000000000000000000004
31103252010000000000000004000000000000000000001000025020000000101100
31103261050329441850441202022000819900100021020210100000100000010010000000000018
31103262010000000000001100000010000000000000019000451000000000100101
31103271050329011800431202112000419900100021021000000000000000000000000000000002
31103272010000000000000100000000000000000000000500010000000000100100
31103281050328921650431202112000219901000210210000000000000000000000000000000002
31103282010000000000000200000000000000000000000500010000000000100100
31103291050329131700441202022000219901000210200000000000000000001000000000000025
31103292020000000000000012000000000000000000002800681000000000100101
31103301050329541800541202122000719900100021020110100000000001011000000000000005
31103302010000099999800090000000000100000100001000025100000000100101
31103311050230041950641202122000029901000210200000000000000000001000000000000003
31103312010000000000000004000000000000000000000500010100000000100100
31103321050230241750641202122000029901100210201101000000000000000001000000000049
31103322110000099999800100000000000000000000100510018512000001101101
31103331040331731550351202013000719800100021020000000000000000000001000000000001
31103332010000000000000100000000000000000000000500010100000000100100
31103341050230211700430202111000119900100021021000000000000000000000000000000002
31103342010000000000000000000000000000000000000500010100000000000100
31103351050230611300541202113000219900100021021000000000000000000001000000000011
31103352010000000000000008000000000000000000110002810000000000000100
```

31103361050330111650220104230000219900100022011000000000000000000000000000000001
31103362010000000000000000000000000000000000000500010100000000000101
31103371050329-415503202021110002199001000210210000000000000000000000000000000001
31103372010000000000000000000000000000000000000500010100000000000100
31103381050329731650431202012000429900000028020000000000000000000000000000000004
31103382010000000000000999900000000000000000000100025100000000100100
31103391050329841550430202012000119900100021020120100000000000000000000000000016
31103392080000000000000000000000000000000000000500010510000000100100
31103401050240611700431202111000319900100021021000000000000000000000000000000004
31103402010000000000000000000000000000000000000100025100000000000100
31103411050330311650431202012000029900100021021000000000000000000000000000000001
31103412010000000000000000000000000000000000000500010100000000000100
31103421050331511650431202012000129900100021021000000000000000000000000000000006
31103422030000000000000000000000000000000000000150003010000000000100
31103431050330011550330202122000419940100021020000000000000000000000000000000005
31103432020000000000000000000000000000000000000100020100000000100100
31103441050331311750441202012000319940100021021120100000100000000001000000000010
31103442010000000000000000000000000000000000000100025100000000000100
31103451040232612000540202122000229900100021521120100000000000000000000000000001
31103452010000000000000000000000000000000000000500010100000000000100
311034610403321117504-020201200012990010002102100000000000000000000000000000001
31103462010000000000000000000000000000000000000500010100000000000100
31103471050331111600340202012000319900000440020110100000000000000000000000000003
31103472030000000000000000000000000000000000000150003010000000100100
31103481050331711650210102111000019900100021021000000000000000000000000000000001
31103482010000000000000000000000000000000000000500010100000000000100
31103491050330611600421202022000229900010028020170110000000000000001000000000002
31103492030000099999800000000000000000000000000100020100000000100100
31103501050330411600220112210000119900100026020110100000100000000000000000000012
31103502010000000000000000000000000000000000000120003010000000100100
3110351105033074155032020221200021 99-0120024-02014011000100000000000000000000009
31103512010000000000000000000000000000000000000300006510000000100100
31103521050329611600430202013000229900000440020000000000000000000000000000000006
31103522040000000000000000000000000000000000000250005012000000101100
311035310503287419506-1202122000229900200440020000000000000100000010000000000016
31103532010000099999800000000000000000000000000160004010000011000100
31103541050429942000611202210000129900200021021000000000000000000000000000000002
31103542010000000000000000000000000000000000000500010100000000000100
31103551050430211800521202122000429900200021020000000000000000000001000000000003
31103552010000000000000999900000000000000000000500010100000000100100
311035610504298420506-1202112000229900100021020000000000000000000001000000000013
31103562020000010004870008000000000000000000000300007010000000100100
31103571050429842100641202112000229900110021021000000000000010000001000000100005
31103572010000000000000050000000000000000000000250005010000000000100
31103581050428942100641202112000229900010-40021110100000100000000011100013001 97
31103582010020010007 5-99990000000000000000010004600920300000010000101
311035910504289321006412021110003239000005-0020110100000000000000001001000000000005
31103592020010000003900030000000000000000000000100020100000000100100
31103601050429911800430202013000129900100021021000000000000000000000000000000001
31103602010000000000000000000000000000000000000500010100000000000100
31103611050429711800430202013000329900100330021000000000000000000000000000000001
31103612010000000000000000000000000000000000000500010100000000000100
31103621050429411800431202013000229900100330021000000000000000000000000000000001
31103622010000000000000000000000000000000000000500010100000000000100
31103631050430011550420202013000029900100021020000000000000000000000000000000001
31103632010000000000000000000000000000000000000500010100000000100100
31103641050429711500310202023000029900100021021000000000000000000000000000000007
31103642010000000000000000000000000000000000000100025100000000000100
31103651050429811500321202023000129900100021021000000000000000000000000000000001
31103652010000000000000000000000000000000000000500010100000000000100
31103661050029411500320202112000029900100021021000000000000000000000000000000005
31103662010000000000000000000000000000000000000100025100000000000100
31103671050428911500320202111000029900100021021000000000000000000000000000000001
31103672010000000000000000000000000000000000000500010100000000000100
31103681050428911600421202122000299001102100010000000000000000000000000000000010
31103682040000000000000000700000000000000000000250055100000000000100
31103691050428511550421202023000029940100021020000000000000000000000000000000004
31103692020000000000000000000000000000000000000100020100000010000100
31103701040529511450210103230010040110100021010000000010000000000000000000000001
31103702010000099999800000000000000100000000000500010100000011100101
31103711050527211450210103210010040420100022020110010030000000101101000000000005
31103712010000099999800000000000000000000000000100025100000111100100
31103721050627311450231202012000209900200021010140110000000000101001000000000001
31103722010000099999600000000000000000000000000500010100000010100101
311037310403340219506-1202013000529900000540120000000000000001000000000000000007
31103732020000099999800030000000000000000000000150003510000001100101
31103741040331841600321202021000029900100024010000000000000000000000000000000002
31103742010000000000000000000000000000000000000500010100000001100100
31103751040332241550320202012000229900200029021000000000000000000000000000000002
31103752010000000000000000000000000000000000000500010100000000000100
31103761040331141650530202112000029900100021021000000000000000000000000000000001
31103762010000000000000000000000000000000000000500010100000000000100
31103771040331941550340202013000319900100021020000000010100000000100100000000013
31103772010000000000000007000000001100000000000130003310000010100101
31103781040432931500210102111000313930100024020000000010000000000011000000000070
31103782090000000000000000000000000000000000000910022110000010100100
31103791040432431500210102111000619930100024021000000010000000000011000000000005
31103792010000000000000000000000000000000000000100025100000000000100
31103801040431031550430202112000029940100021020000000000000000000001000000000071
31103802130000999900989999000000000000000000000116002661000010100100
31103811040430811700641202112000429900200029021000000000000000100001000000000004
31103812010000000000000000600000000000000000000100025100000000000100
31103821040431111600331202112000029940110021020000000100000000000011000000000317
31103822070000099999800000000000000010000000000334008311000000100101
31103831040431011600331202112000329940100021021000000000000000000000000000000005
31103832020000000000000000000000000000000000000150003510000000000100
31103841040431911500220102122000029900200023011000000000000000100000000000000022
31103842010000000000000000000000000000000000000220005510000000000100
31103851040432111500210102210000029900100021021000000000000000000000000000000014
31103852040000000000000000000000000000000000000390009310000000000100
31103861040530531450210102210010049920110029010000000010000000000001100000000001
31103862010000099999800000000000000000000001000500010100001111100100
31103871030335821850641202012000329900000540021000000000000000000000000000000002
31103872010000000000000000000000000000000000000500010100000000000100
31103881110911832150641202012009999900005400110000000000000000000000000000000001
31103882010000000000000000000000000000000000000500010100000000000100
31103891030335721800531202013000029900000540011000000000000000000001000000000005
31103892010010000000150000000000000000000000000100025100000000000101
31103901030336821850620202112000129900000640011000000000000000000001000000000006
31103902010000010000480000000000000000000000000100025100000000000100
311039110303362218006412020120003299000006-40020000000000000000000001000000000001
31103912020000099999800000000000000000000000000100020100000000100100
311039210303358217505312020120002299000000-40011000000000000000000000000000000001
31103922010000000000000000000000000000000000000500010100000000000100
31103931030335821650430202012000029900100021021000000000000000000000000000000001
31103932010000000000000000000000000000000000000500010100000000000100
31103941030335721650430202012000029900100021021000000000000000000000000000000001
31103942010000000000000000000000000000000000000500010100000000000100
31103951030336321700610202022000229900100021011000000000000000000001000000000001
31103952010000010001320000000000000000000000000500010100000000000100

```
31103961030336421700620202022000329900000640021000000000000000000000000000000001
31103962010000000000000000000000000000000000000500010100000000000100
31103971030336421700620202012000299000006400110000000000000000010000000000000000001
31103972010000000000000000000000000000000000000500010100000000000100
31103981030336321700521202012000129901000210210000000000000000000000000000000001
31103982010000000000000000000000000000000000000500010100000000000100
31103991030335521600320202112000229900100021021000000000000000000000000000000003
31103992010000000000000000000000000000000000000500010100000000000100
31104001030335131600499202199000129900990021021000000000000000000000000000000001
31104002010000000000000000000000000000000000000500010100000000000100
31104011030335421550320202121000419900100021021000000000000000000000000000000001
31104012010000000000000000000000000000000000000500010100000000000100
31104021040334421550320202112000229900100021021000000000000000000000000000000001
31104022010000000000000000000000000000000000000500010100000000000100
31104031040334121550320202112000029900100021021000000000000000000000000000000005
31104032010000000000000000000000000000000000001000025100000000000100
31104041040433721500320202112000129900100021021000000000000000000000000000000020
31104042010000000000000000000000000000000000002000050100000000000100
31104051040433621500320202212000019900100021020000000000000000000000000000000005
31104052010000000000000000000000000000000000001000025100000001000100
31104061040434121500320202212000219900100021020000000000000000000000000000000006
31104062020000000000000000000000000000000000000100002010000000100100
31104071040434321500310202210000129900100021021000000000000000000000000000000010
31104072030000000000000000000000000000000000002000045100000000000101
31104081030434621500210102110000219900100021020000000000000000000100000000000007
31104082010000000000000000000000000000000000001000025100000001000100
31104091030434721500320202111000219900100021030000000000000000000000000000000013
31104092010000000000000000000000000000000000001300033100000001100100
31104101030435321500210102221000209930100021020120100000000000000010000000000042
31104102010000000000000000000000000000000000004200105100000000100100
31104111040433111500231202012000129900110021020120100000000000101001000000000010
31104112010000000999998000000000000000000000001000025100000010000101
31104121040433111500210102210000629930100024021000000000000000000000000000000002
31104122010000000000000000000000000000000000000500010100000000000100
31104131040433611500210102210000619990100021011000000000000000000000000000000001
31104132010000000000000000000000000000000000000500010100000000000100
31104141040433211450210102210010009930100021720120100000000000110000000000000447
31104142060000000999998000000000000000000000044901122100000000100101
31104151030434211500320202012000009900100021021000000000000000000000000000000013
31104152020000000000000000000000000000000000001600038100000000000100
31104161030434311550320202012000029900100021021000000000000000000000000000000002
31104162010000000000000000000000000000000000000500010100000000000100
31104171030434211450210102210000709900200029210000000000000000000000000000000003
31104172010000000000000000000000000000000000000500010100000000000100
31104181030434611450210102211000409900210023020000000000000000000000000000000001
31104182010000000000000000000000000000000000000500010100000000100100
31104191030435611450210102211000309900210023020000000000000000000000000000000010
31104192010000000000000000000000000000000000001000025100000100100100
31104201030533511600320202112000029900100021021000000000000000000000000000000003
31104202030000000000000000000000000000000000001500030100000000000100
31104211040533311600311202111000129901000021021000000000000000000000000000000004
31104212010000000000000000000000000000000000001000025100000000000100
31104221030337221600420202110000219900100021021000000000000000000000000000000001
31104222010000000000000000000000000000000000000500010100000000000100
31104231030337721550320202122010129940110023021000000010000000000000010000000000012
31104232010000010002170000000000000000000000001200030100000000000100
31104241030337021550420202011000419900100021021000000000000000000000000000000002
31104242010000000000000000000000000000000000000500010100000000000100
31104251030337321500320202021000319900100021020000000000000000000000000000000002
31104252010000000000000000000000000000000000000500010100000000100100
31104261030436521500210106210001319900100021021000000000000000000000000000000002
31104262010000000000000000000000000000000000000500010100000000000100
31104271030336721550320202021000029900100021021000000000000000000000000000000003
31104272020000000000000000000000000000000000001000201000000000000100
31104281030336021550320202121000229900100021021000000000000000000000000000000001
31104282010000000000000000000000000000000000000500010100000000000100
31104291030436921450210106230000029900100021021000000000000000000000000000000001
31104292010000000000000000000000000000000000000500010100000000000100
31104301030537221450210112220010909930100021021000000000000000000000000000000011
31104302030000000000000000000000000000000000000200045000000000000100
31104311030536521450210102212010109930100021020000001000000000000000000000000019
31104312020000000000000000000000000000000000002300055100000000100100
31104321030436221450220102210000509900100021020110010010000000000000100000000000011
31104322010000000000000000000000000000000000001100028100000010100100
31104331030436421500210112220000909900100021021000000000000000000000000100000000001
31104332010000000000000000000000000000000000000500010100000000000100
31104341030436221500210112220000809900100021021000000000000000000000000000000007
31104342020000000000000000000000000000000000001500030100000000000100
31104351030435821450210102220010209930100021020110010000000000000000000000000040
31104352010000000000000000000000000000000000004000100100000000100100
31104361030437511550330202013000009900004400210000000000000000000000000000000003
31104362020000000000000000000000000000000000001000201000000000000100
31104371030436811500330202013000009900004400210000000000000000000000000000000018
31104372050000000000000000000000000000000000003500080100000000000100
31104381030435811500220104230000109900100021011000000000000000000000000000000038
31104382060000000000000000000000000000000000005500130100000000000100
31104391030436011500320202112000509900004400110000000000000000000000000000000013
31104392010000000000000000000000000000000000001300033100000000000100
31104401030437111900541202111000999990000440010000000000000000000000000000101000000000030
31104402010000009999989999100000000000000001000003000007512000011101
31104411020339821650530202012000029900100021020000000000000000000000000000000010
31104412020000009999989999000000000000000000001500035100000010100100
31104421020339021550430202022000029900000140021000000000000000000000000000000001
31104422010000000000000000000000000000000000000500010100000000000100
31104431020339621550420202022000129900100021020000000000000000000000000000000002
31104432010000000000000000000000000000000000000500010100000001000100
31104441020339521550420202122000029901000021021000000000000000000000000000000014
31104442010000010003380000000000000000000000000140003510000000000100
31104451020339221600511209029000429900100021011000000000000000000010000100000000001
31104452010000010000610000000000000000000000000500010100000000000100
31104461020438621450310202919000119900100021021000000000000000000000000000000001
31104462010000000000000000000000000000000000000500010100000000000100
31104471020439321450210106210000029900100024020000000000000000000000000000000013
31104472010000000000000000000000000000000000001300033100000010100100
31104481020439621450210106210000109930100021020000000000000000000000000000000010
31104482010000000000000000000000000000000000001000025100000011100100
31104491030337911550320202012000309900100021021000000000000000000000000000000002
31104492010000000000000000000000000000000000000500010100000000000100
31104501020439211550220102122000209900100021021000000000000000000110000000000000013
31104502010000000000000000000000000000000000001300032100000000000100
31104511020340621700541202012000029900110021520140110010000000010001100000000186
31104512230000009999980143001000000000000100003900160032000001101101
31104521020341321850641202013000029900000540020000000000000000000000000000000005
31104522010000000000000080000000000000000000001000025120000000001101
31104531020341221850641202013000029900000540020000000000000000000000000000000004
31104532020000000000000000000000000000000000001000201200000000001101
31104541020341421800641202013000029900000540020000000000000000000000000000000001
31104542010000000000000000000100000000000000000500010120000000001101
31104551020341521800641202013000029900000540020000000000000000000000000000000001
31104552010000000000000010000000000000000000000500010120000000001101
```

```
311045610203419216505312020120000199000000-4002000000000000000000000000000000002
31104562010000000000000000000000000000000000050001012000000000001101
31104581020341421800541202012000029900100021020000000000000000000000000000000003
311045820200000000000003000000000000000000000100002012000000000001101
31104591020341321750541202012000029900100021020000000100000000000000000000000015
3110459201000000999998001500000000000000000000012000240320000000101101
31104601020340321600421202011000029900100021021000000000000000000000000000000002
311046020100000000000000000000000000000000000000500010100000000000100
31104611020340321600431202122000129900100021021000000000000000000100000000000003
311046120200000000000000000000000000000000000000100002010000000000000100
31104621020340421600421202110000129900100021020000000000000000000000000000000004
311046220100000000000000000000000000000000000010000251200000000001100
31104631020340921600541202023000129900100021020000000000000000000000000000000001
3110463201000000000000000000000000000000000000500010120000000001100
31104641020342511850541202022009929900110021021000000000000000100000000000000001
3110464201000001001458000000000000000100000000000000003000000000000101
31104651020342411800541202022000229900120021021000000001000001010000100000100001
3110465201000000000000000000000000001000000000000500010100000000000101
31104661020342111800541202022000129900110021021000000000100000100001000000000011
311046620100000100480600000000000000000000000150003510000000000101
31104671010342711850531202022000229900100021011000000000000000000100000000000001
3110467201000000999999000400000000000000000000000000300000000000101
31104681010342711800531202022000229900100021021000000000000000000000000000000001
31104682010000000000000000000000000000000000500010100000000000100
31104691010342811800531202022000229900100021021000000000000000000000000000000002
31104692020000000000000000000000000000000000100002010000000000100
31104701010342711800531202022000129900100021021000000000000000000000000000000001
311047020100000000000000000000000000000000000500010100000000000100
31104711010342721700521202121000229900100021020110100000000000100000000000000004
31104712010000000000000000000000000000000000010000251200000000001100
31104721010343021700531202022000129900004400210000000000000000000000000000000004
311047220100000000000000000000000000000000010000251000000000000100
31104731010342721700531202012000129900100021021000000000000000000000000000000019
31104732010000000000000001600000000000000000000085001753000000010100100
31104741010343121700421202110000129900100021020000000000000000000100000000000021
311047420100000000000000000000000000000000002100053100000000010100
31104751010342721600421202012000129900100021021000000000000000000000000000000001
311047520100000000000000000000000000000000000500010100000000000100
31104761020342221650530202112000129900100021020000000000000000000100000000000003
3110476201000000000000001000000000000000000000500010100000000100100
31104771010342521550421202112000029940100024020000000000000000000000000000000009
3110477204000000000000000000000000000000000025000551000000000100100
31104781020342421550431202022000129900100021020000000000000000000100000000000022
31104782020000000000000000000000000000000000250006010000000000100100
31104791010342421550431202022000129900000440021000000000000000000000000000000003
311047920300000000000000000000000000000000001500030100000000000100
31104801020341921650521202111000129900010440020110100000000000100000000000000009
3110480202000000999998000300000000000000000000100002512000000000001101
31104811010442421500210102210000709900100021021000000000000000000000000000000001
311048120100000000000000000000000000000000000500010100000000000100
31104821020439821500411202122000029900100021021000000000000000000100000000000002
311048220100000000000000000000000000000000000500010100000000000100
31104831020440221450320202120000023900100021020000000000000000000100000000000013
31104832020000000000000000000000000000000000160003810000000000100100
31104841020441521450320102210010009900100021021000000000000000000000000000000011
31104842010000000000000000000000000000000001100028100000000000000100
31104851020441121450220106221010200100100021020000000000000000000000000000000015
3110485202000000000000000000000000000000000200005010000000000100100
31104861020441021450220106221010200100100021021000000000000000000000000000000001
311048620100000000000000000000000000000000000500010100000000000100
31104871020442021500320202122000409900100021021000000000000000000000000000000001
311048720100000000000000000000000000000000005000101000000000000100
31104881020440621450320202120000419900100021021000000000000000000000000000000003
311048820100000000000000000000000000000000005000101000000000000100
31104891010441621550431202121000529900110021021000000000000000000000000000000002
31104892020000000000000200000000000000000000010000201000000000100100
31104901020441321500320202122000129900100021020000000000000000000000000000000002
31104902010000000000000000000000000000000000050001010000000000100100
31104911020440621450320202110000229900100021021000000000000000000000000000000001
311049120100000000000000000000000000000000050001010000000000000100
31104921020441021500321202120010220340100021020000000000000000000100000000000004
31104922010000000000000000000000000000000001000025100000001000100
31104931010441821500320202131000229900100021021000000000000000000000000000000001
311049320100000000000000000000000000000000005000101000000000000100
31104941010343221800531202022000129900000440020000000000000000000000000000000006
311049420100000000000000000000000000000000010000251000000000100100
31104951010340821650531202122000029900100021020000000000000000000000000000000001
311049520100000000000000000000000000000000005000101000000000100100
31104961010343421650521202022000029900100021021000000000000000000000000000000001
311049620100000000000000000000000000000000005000101000000000000100
31104971010343321650421202122000229900000440020000000000000000000000000000000013
311049720100000000000000000000000000000000001300033100000000100100
31104981010342721500410202120000129900100021020000000001000000100000110000000003
3110498201000000999998000000000000000000000000500010120000000101101
3110499101034422165064-1202023000329900000540021000000000000000000000000000000001
311049920100000000000000000000000000000000005000101000000000000100
31105001010340021600541202112000129900100021020000000000000000000000000000000019
311050020200000000000000000000000000000000000230005510000000100100
31105011010340421600521202111000029900100021021000000000000000000000000000000002
311050120200000000000000000000000000000000010000201000000000000100
31105021010340421650521202111000229900100021021000000000000000000000000000000001
311050220100000000000000000000000000000000005000101000000000000100
31105031010340121600521202111000029900100021020000000000000000000000000000000004
31105032010000000000000000000000000000000010000251000000000100100
31105041010443921450210104230000209900100021020000000000000000000000000000000005
311050420100000000000000000000000000000000010000251000000010000100
31105051010443821450320202122000209900100021021000000000000000000000000000000001
311050520100000000000000000000000000000000005000101000000000000100
31105061010443321450320202920000009900100021020000000000000000000000000000000004
311050620100000000000000000000000000000000010000251000000001100100
31105071010443021450210104230000009900100021020000000000000000000000000000000001
31105072010000000000000000000000000000000000500010100000000100100
31105081010442921500320202122000209900100021021000000000000000000000000000000001
311050820100000000000000000000000000000000005000101000000000000100
31105091010443121450210104230000209900100021021000000000000000000000000000000001
311050920100000000000000000000000000000000005000101000000000000100
31105101010442921450210104230000209900100024021000000000000000000000000000000001
311051020100000000000000000000000000000000005000101000000000000101
31105111010442521450210104230000209900100021020000000000000000000000000000000003
31105112020000000000000000000000000000000000100002010000000000100100
31105121010442421450210104231000009900100021020000000000000000000000000000000001
31105122010000000000000000000000000000000000500010100000000100100
31105131010442421500320202122000509900100021020000000000000000000000000000000004
31105132010000000000000000000000000000000010000251000000000100100
31105141090714921500320202120000129900100021020000000000000000000100000000000001
3110514201000000999998000000000000000000000000500010100000000110100
31105151090713321550310202120000329900100021021000000000000000000000000000000001
311051520100000000000000000000000000000000005000101000000000000100
31105161080718521900521202012000029900000440020000000000000000000000000000000001
3110516201000000999998000000000000000000000000500010100000000100100
```

```
31105171020340421650541202012000029900100021020000000000000000000000000000000008
31105172010000000000000000000000000000000000100002512000000000001101
31105181010340721750641202023000429900000440021000000000000000000000000000000001
31105182010000000000000000000000000000000000000500010100000000000100
31105191010340921750641202023000229900100021021000000000000000000000000000000004
31105192010000000000000000000000000000000001000025100000000000000100
3110520104043064180044120202300032990030002902000000000000000000100000000000003
31105202010000000000000002000000000000000000000150003010000000100100
31105211040331741600330202111000129900100021021000000000000000000000000000000001
31105212010000000000000000000000000000000000000500010100000000000100
31105221040235322000641202023000329900000540011000000000000000000000000000000001
31105222010030010001580000000000000000000000000500010100000000000101
31105231040430731650431202012000029900000399620000000000000000000000000000000002
31105232010000000000000000000000000000000000000500010100000000100100
31105241050428442050641202012000062990000054001100000000000000000001000000000001
31105242010000000000000000000000000000000000000500010100000000000100
31105261100609211550210103210010040210100021011000000000000000000000000000000014
31105262010000000000000000000000000000000000000700014000000000000100
31105271060925421600420202112000029900900029020120100000000000000000000000000001
31105272010000000000000000000000000000000000000500010120000000001100
31105281090610221500210103230010040100011010020120100000000000000011110010299999
31105282010000009999980000000000000000000009999999999011111111110111
31105291080616011500210102210000499201000210200000000010100001000010000000000001
31105292010000099990980000000000000000000000000500010100000110100100
21200011140799921700421201122000329800200441000000000000000001100000000000000009
21200012010000000000000000000000000000000000000000000000000000000001
31200011090811431550321202121000129900110021009220100000000000000001100000000002
31200012010010050030720000000000000000000000000000000300000000000001
31200021090512511750441202023000229800000440001000000000000000000000000000000001
31200022010040020001620000000000000000000000000000000000000000000001
31200031050527911450220102111000029900110021001000000000000000000001000000000001
31200032010000010004960000000000000000000000000000000300000000000000
31200041030436111700541202013000229900000440000000000000000000000001000000000002
31200042010010000000509999000000000000000000000000000300000000000000
31200051030535411800441202023000129900000440000000000000000000000001000000000001
31200052010000010004910000000000000000000000000000000300000000000000
31200061020449621500310202922000229900110021010000000000000000000110000000000001
31200062010000010002130000000000000000000000000000000300000000000001
31200071020438211750541202013000329900000440000000000000000000000001000000000001
31200072010010000000150000000000000000000000000000000300000000000000
31200081090510411600321202012000219900100021000000000000000000000001000000000001
31200082010010000000008800000000000000000000000000000300000000000001
31200091050528211450320202112000029900900029011000000000000000000000000000000003
31200092010000000000000000000000000000000000000000000300000000000001
```

Appendix I: Part II
COMMENTS ON SITE DATA

SITE	COMMENTS
2-1-2	Excavated and described by Marcus C. Winter (1972). For the Early Tierras Largas phase, Winter suggests that ten households occupied an area of 0.93-1.58 ha; in Late Tierras Largas ten households existed on 0.81-2.24 ha.
2-2-1	Near the gray clay source.
2-2-3	Obliterated by the modern paved highway.
2-2-4	In Early San José there were five households on 0.15-0.95 ha; and in Late San José there were eight households on 0.42-1.59 ha (Winter 1972:Tables 12 and 13).
2-3-2	Very sparse Guadalupe phase sherds were found in a general collection from the Late Classic mound group.
2-3-6	Marc Winter's excavations at the eastern end of the site (Winter 1972:107-11) produced a median estimate of 19 households dating from 850-500 B.C., on an area of 3 to 4 ha. The surface survey did not identify this large an occupation here, but found very sparse and scattered Guadalupe phase debris farther upslope to the west, for a rough total of 3 ha.
2-4-2	*Crema* ceramics outnumber gray wares by better than 6:1. The temper or grog in the *crema* sherds appears to be the same material as the rock found in the clay mined at the site. No kiln wasters were found, but six unformed chunks of fired clay, and two smooth pebble polishing stones may indicate pottery making. It should be noted that this site is also a magnetite source (Pires-Ferreira 1956).
2-4-3	Almost totally destroyed by modern building activities.
2-4-4	Site destroyed by highway.
2-5-2	On the top of the hill is a heavily plowed and eroded architectural complex consisting of a 1 m high mound and a rectangular terrace or plaza abutting the mound on the south side. On the west and south edges of the terrace there are remains of rock rubble retaining walls. Late Monte Albán I sherds outnumber those of Early I in the vicinity of this structure, but whether the construction and use date to Early I, Late I, or both cannot be determined with the present evidence.
2-5-3	One possible kiln waster was found. This was made of a *gris* paste, and it might belong to any of the site's occupations after the Guadalupe phase.
2-5-4	The collection could perhaps be from the preceding Rosario phase.
2-5-8	The sherds could also be from the Rosario phase.
2-5-12	One "bark beater".
2-5-14	*Crema* ceramics, in a great variety of forms, are overwhelmingly more abundant than gray wares. The sherds are unusually large. These facts suggest that *crema* pottery may have been produced at this site, which is in a similar topographic situation to 2-G/R-2, another suspected Middle Formative pottery manufacturing center.

SITE	COMMENTS
2-5-16	Chert projectile point coded as chert blade.
2-5-20	Part of an ancient irrigation canal runs through the site. The downslope edge of the canal was built up and held in place by a retaining wall. In places, the upslope side was cut into the slope. The channel, constructed of stone slabs, is about 0.75 m wide. The canal was followed for 450 m.
2-5-22	Stone bead.
2-5-23	The terrace at the upper end of the site was probably residential, and measures 22 by 18 m, but it could date to one of the other occupations.
2-5-25	The occupation straddles an ancient irrigation canal, which has its beginning at a rubble dam farther up the barranca on the lower slopes of Monte Albán. The canal runs along the top to the ridge for a distance of almost 2500 m. The system probably was begun in Early Monte Albán I (Mason et al. 1977).
2-5-26	The site is located on an irrigation canal built in Monte Albán I (Mason et al. 1977).
2-5-32	On the eastern side of the site is a rubble and earthen platform, no more than 1.0 m high, and measuring 15 m N-S by 8 m E-W. On the west side of this structure is a 15 m long stone wall, with an orientation of N 6°W. The rest of the Early I occupation spreads out to the west of the mound.
2-5-33	"*Casi no se puede ver la tierra por los tepalcates*," Fausto Olivera, the survey team leader, noted.
2-5-37	Winter's excavation at the eastern end of the spur uncovered a number of Early I features. Projecting from the sampling results to the universe of his study area, Winter suggests a median of 18 Early I households, on 3.0 ha (Winter 1972:107, 113). Near the eastern end of the ridge is a 5 m high mound. At the base it measures roughly 39 m N-S by 35 m E-W. Winter believes that this structure may date from Early Monte Albán I, though it continued to be occupied later in the period (1972:121-22).
2-6-8	Lacking diagnostic sherds from exposed construction fill, the mounds at San Luís Beltrán are dated less satisfactorily by pottery found on the surface. Of the 15 mounds noted at the site, 10 are considered to belong to the Late I component. Almost all are being plowed away.
2-6-14	An architectural complex. Consists of a 1 m high mound adjoining a long, rectangular plaza or terrace. One chert projectile point coded as chert blade.
2-6-32	Two chert projectile points coded as blades.
2-6-34	Unusually large quantities of chert flakes.
2-6-35	Although the last construction phase of these mounds was in the Late Classic, they may have been built over Late I structures.
2-6-36	The Late Classic mounds were constructed on top of

SITE	COMMENTS
	pre-existing Late I structures.
2-6-39	The remains of a structure, consisting of the corner of a stone wall (orientation N 11°E), may date to this occupation or the Late Classic component.
2-6-40	Chipped stone, especially white chert, is unusually common.
2-6-45	The eastern part of the site may be covered by the modern town of Arrazola.
2-6-57	The size of the occupation is obscured by alluviation and the modern use of the area.
2-6-58	Heavy plowing by tractor has probably spread the cultural deposits out over a wider area than that occupied by the Late I community.
2-6-79	Pottery clearly belongs to Monte Albán I, but good Early I or Late I diagnostics are absent.
2-6-81	A probable house wall runs for 9 m, with an orientation of N 11°E.
2-6-85	Several chunks of magnetite were found in the vicinity.
2-6-86	A number of stone wall fragments, possibly four houses.
2-6-94	See 2-5-20.
2-6-98	One stone bead.
2-6-100	22 by 18 m residential terrace.
2-6-109	A small irrigation system, involving a 2 km long canal running down the top of the ridge from a dam on the barranca above the site, was probably begun in Early Monte Albán I and reached its greatest extent during Late I (Mason et al. 1977).
2-6-114	27 by 23 m terrace.
2-6-128	Most of this spur has been modified by ancient and more recent landscaping. Dating these constructions is problematical, but the associated ceramics suggest that the major building activities took place in Monte Albán IB-IC.
2-6-129	At the southern edge of the occupation is an easily distinguishable sparse concentration of sherds covering a slight (0.5 m) rise about 20 m in diameter, interpreted as a low house platform.
2-6-137	The local limestone contains nodules of good quality brown chert, flakes of which are found in these fields.
2-6-146	On the crest of the hill is a low, rock rubble mound near the north end of a small, rectangular terrace or platform. The nature of this construction, and its dating, are uncertain, as it is very poorly preserved.
2-6-148	Stone wall fragments form three right angles, suggesting a structure that measured 6 m N-S by 7 m E-W.
2-7-4	Most of the Monte Albán II sherds were found in the profile and backdirt of a shallow pit dug into a human burial.
2-7-7	2 chert projectile points.
2-7-9	Monte Albán II sherds were found in a general collection from Sts. 5-8 of 2-9-63.
2-7-15	Substantial alluviation and massive buildings of III make an accurate estimate of the Period II site impossible.
2-7-16	Alluviation and Early Classic construction has obliterated the nature and extent of the Period II site.
2-7-18	Light-moderate quantities of pottery are found on a heavily plowed rise that may have been a house platform.
2-8-4	Very sparse Early Classic pottery was found around St. 4, a 6 m high mound whose last construction phase was in IIIb (2-9-63). On St. 3, 65 m to the west, a few possible IIIa sherds were found. These occurrences may indicate a IIIa occupation of the area, and possible of the mounds themselves.
2-8-6	The International Highway has cut through and destroyed most of this site.
2-8-17	Pottery is generally sparse and light on the mounds, but usually nonexistent on the surface more than 10 to 30 m from any structure. Because habitational debris is almost completely absent except on the mounds, an empirical estimate of the site size cannot be made. There are grounds for believing that there was occupation in the intervening space, and that the Early Classic settlement did not simply consist of a set of isolated platforms. The evidence is supplied by Saville (1899a, 1899b), who excavated at the site in the 1890s and noted that there was ancient construction several meters below the 1897 ground surface in several places between the large platforms where farmers had plowed up the plaster floors of ancient houses. In addition, Saville mapped several low mounds that are today undetectable. Both the geographer Kirkby (1973:13) and the historian Taylor (1972:94) agree that the present surface on the valley floor has been built up by alluviation relatively recently. Apparently, then, the portions of the ancient settlement that were not constructed on high platforms are now buried under several meters of soil. The figure of 115.1 ha for the site area is only a very crude calculation arrived at by drawing a closed figure around the periphery of the set of 15 platforms. Saville's excavations showed that these earth and adobe platforms were the foundations of multi-room structures, often with patios and elaborate sub-floor tombs. It seems possible that all of these structures were residences, with the larger ones also serving administrative purposes.
2-8-19	The greatest concentration of IIIa pottery occurs on and around a low, partially destroyed platform at the north edge of the spur (St. 6 of 2-6-128).
2-8-26	A polished, white piece of marble, and two pieces of ceramic drain pipe were found.
2-8-27	Tierras Largas (See Winter 1972).
2-8-33	The main ridge was probably used in Colonial times.
2-9-1	Three chert projectile points.
2-9-3	Stone bead.
2-9-11	Just below the southern part of the site, a number of pots were found during the construction of Hotel Loma Bonita, indicating that the site may have extended farther downslope than was apparent from the survey.
2-9-14	The western edge of the site has probably been destroyed by the building of the International Highway. The rest of the land has become a suburban development, and it is rapidly being covered over with houses and streets.
2-9-16	Potters from Sta. María Atzompa obtain their fine textured, gray alluvial clay from the source west of the hill. Residential terrace 15 by 7 m.
2-9-17	Atzompa potters obtain their fine textured gray clay from

SITE	COMMENTS
	the extensive beds east of the site.
2-9-18	18 by 10 m residence terrace.
2-9-20	Sherds are generally sparse or very sparse on the upper part of the site, except for seven very distinct concentrations often marked by soil discoloration, interpreted as separate houses. The dimensions of the concentrations vary from 10 by 9 m to 41 by 41 m (mean 29.8 by 25.2 m, mean area 832.5 m^2). This distance between a concentration and its closest neighbor ranges between 15 and 55 m (mean and mode 28.4m). One concentration has heavy, two have light-moderate, and four have light sherd densities.
2-9-21	There are two small mounds or platforms oriented roughly along the east-west trending ridge line, and separated by about 8 m. The eastern mound is better described as a 1 to 2 m high outcrop, with the space between the boulders filled in with earth and rock rubble. The structure measures 7 by 6 m. The western mound, also about 1 to 2 m in height, and likewise constructed of large boulders, rubble, and earth, measures 5 by 5 m. This may be a special function site.
2-9-22	On the top of the ridge there are two 1 m high mounds constructed by adding earth and rock rubble fill to prominent bedrock outcrops. The mounds are oriented roughly to the ridge line. The eastern mound measures 15 by 15 m, and the western, 20 by 15 m.
2-9-23	There is a 15 by 11 m jumble of unshaped, 0.25 to 1 m size rocks that may be the remains of a structure. This may be a special function site.
2-9-24	A 15 by 15 m, 1 m high platform was constructed on the highest ground, with a 9 by 7 m, 1.5 m high mound 17 m to the north. The orientation of the larger mound is about N 13°E and that of the second mound is N 1°E.
2-9-25	Should be treated as the southern extension of the Etla survey's M.A. IIIb-IV-11 (Varner 1974). There is some evidence suggesting that *gris* or *gris cremosa* pottery was made at or near this site. The modern Atzompa potters' source of "coarse" clay lies at the base of the ridge, only 250 m southeast of the site. *Gris*, and what would be called *gris cremosa* pottery is abundant and gives the impression of unusual variety in forms. In addition, one hollow *sahumador* handle that may be a kiln waster, and a fragment of a mold for a Classic period funerary urn, were found in the southeastern part of the site.
2-9-29	Several shallow ditches have been dug across the fields to check soil erosion. It does not appear that they are effective.
2-9-30	On the top of the ridge are two mounds, separated by a flat, possible plaza area.
2-9-32	The highest ground is taken up with what is apparently an ancient architectural complex consisting of four badly plowed and eroded 1 m high mounds grouped around a 21 by 19 m plaza. The largest of the mounds is about 30 by 14 m.
2-9-38	In a plowed field near the eastern end of the site is a 13 by 13 m concentration of sherds, stones, burned adobe, and ash.
2-9-42	Small scale canal irrigation would be feasible in the area.
2-9-46	Sherds are not continuous, but tend to concentrate in and around thicker deposits of soil.
2-9-48	The site is next to a small concrete dam or *toma* from which water is led through short canals into the gently sloping fields at the base of the hills. Tomatoes, onions, and chili peppers are grown in the early spring, and corn in the summer.
2-9-53	Two chert projectile points coded as chert blades.
2-9-57	Grazing, firewood cutting on the upper slopes, and rainfall cultivation of corn on the ridge tops.
2-9-62	Two chert projectile points are coded as chert blades. There is also a chert blade.
2-9-63	In San Pedro Ixtlahuaca.
2-9-64	One "bark beater" coded as other ground stone.
2-9-66	Soils are darker in color in some fields because of the household garbage that modern farmers spread around.
2-9-73	The four habitation areas measure 0.3, 0.2, 0.5, and 0.3 ha.
2-9-79	The four areas measure 1.3, 1.6, 0.6, and 0.2 ha.
2-9-84	One chert projectile point coded as chert blade.
2-9-91	The Río Jalapillas flows past the tip of the ridge. At that point the river has been dammed up for irrigation and flood control.
2-9-92	Floodwater farming and canal irrigation on the valleys below.
2-9-95	A projectile point similar in form to the Tehuacán Valley preceramic Trinidad type.
2-9-98	One chert projectile point coded as chert blade.
2-9-113	The arroyos along the base of the hill have been channelized in places to facilitate floodwater irrigation.
2-9-114	There is a 13 by 12 m, 1.3 m high mound on the highest point at the site. The orientation is N 14°E. About 40 m to the north and east of this structure is a stone retaining wall, following the contour around the knob on which the mound was built, at about the point where the slope becomes steeper. Soil deposits are thicker upslope of the wall, and except for one outlier, the wall marks the edge of the habitation in this area. The construction is not freestanding, but consists of a line of stones embedded in the soil. In places this is simply one line of rocks, but frequently there are several parallel lines. The total length is 165 m.
2-9-115	The corner of a stone structure, with an orientation of N 11°E, still exists on the top of the hill. This may date either to Late I or IIIb.
2-9-156	On top of the north ridge there is a mound of dirt and rock that has the appearance of an ancient construction. However, it is badly destroyed, and no sherds were found in the fill.
2-9-157	The eastern limit of the site is formed by the Colonial aqueduct that brought water to the city from San Felipe del Agua, and the Calzada Porfirio Díaz.
2-9-158	A human burial was found on the roadway that had been bulldozed across the tip of the ridge. Evidently the body was extended, face up, and buried in a pit dug into the shaley bedrock. The tractor blade removed the overburden and the top half of the skeleton. No offering was found, and it is not clear whether the burial pertains to the Late Classic or the Postclassic occupations.

SITE	COMMENTS
2-9-159	Surrounded on all sides by modern houses, including the Colonia ISSSTE on the north, and the Colonia La Cascada on the southeast.
2-9-169	Some canal irrigation in the vicinity.
2-9-174	A small canal flows eastward at the base of the rise, 450 m southeast of the site. A main tributary of the Atoyac, canalized for flood control and irrigation, lies 1100 m to the east.
2-9-175	Even with the canalization of the streams in this area, farmers still experience severe crop losses due to flooding.
2-9-176	The site is taken up by maize and castor bean fields, and the dispersed house lots of the community of Tiracoz.
2-9-177	Most of the area is eroded badlands. There are a few maize fields where soil depth permits cultivation, and some fields that appear to have been abandoned.
2-9-178	Very sparse sherds over 6.5 ha, with a few sparse concentrations probably marking individual residences.
2-9-189	On the northwestern edge of the site are three long, narrow terraces, one above the other, which, from the paucity of artifacts, might be agricultural terraces. Roughly 125 m southeast of this on a steep, rocky slope, there is a 27 by 23 m well-preserved residential terrace. Just south of this is a 30 by 26 m concentration of sherds, stone, and burned adobe, probably indicating a house. About 10 m east of this is a long, broad terrace that may date to this period.
2-9-196	Some canal irrigation in the vicinity.
2-9-199	Tierras Largas.
2-9-201	Sherds are concentrated primarily on an area of 48 by 41 m.
2-9-202	At the western edge of the occupation is a 0.5 m high, rock rubble platform measuring 10 m N-S by 9 m E-W.
2-9-203	Several badly eroded terrace-like features might belong to the Late Classic occupation of the hill. One, T.3, consists of a 120 m long retaining wall remnant.
2-9-205	The area consists of narrow, gently sloping ridge crests and steep barrancas cut deeply into the friable metamorphic bedrock. This area just west of Monte Albán, El Gallo, and Atzompa has all the characteristics of badlands topography.
2-9-206	The site occupies an apparently natural terrace about 75 m in length and less than 15 m in width. Part of the El Gallo sector of the Late Classic Monte Albán urban complex.
2-9-207	The site consists of two distinct artifact concentrations (in three fields) separated by an open slope of about 75 m. With the upper concentration was a small patch of burned adobe. In this badlands terrain sites are small and widely dispersed, but they tend to be found at the tops of ridges in relatively flat places where there is sufficient soil depth for maize cultivation.
2-9-209	Two concentrations of sparse pottery with some building stones and two manos on areas of 72 by 56 m and 52 by 30 m. A single G-12 suggests an earlier (Late I, II, or IIIa) occupation.
2-9-210	The site consists of three artifact concentrations (38 by 32 m, 100 by 40 m, and 47 by 38 m).
2-9-211	Thin, dark brown, limestone bedrock soil, with caliche. The hillside appears to have been eroded very heavily in the past, but the erosion has ceased and the slope is stabilized under a closecropped grass cover.
2-9-212	There were hints, never confirmed, of a Monte Albán V occupation here. Likewise we were not successful in localizing any prehispanic settlements within Sta. María Atzompa.
2-9-213	On the western side of the site is a 50 cm high rise that, before the field was plowed, might have been a mound.
2-9-216	The site is on a lot at the northwest corner of Geranios and Eucaliptos in the Colonia Las Flores in the eastern part of Oaxaca City.
2-10-1	San Luís Beltrán. The site was tested by Bernal. On the strength of his conclusions (1965:804), the site's biggest construction—a ball court and a large quadrangular structure— are assigned to Monte Albán IV. However, the present survey found no evidence of IIIb or IV occupation outside the mounds, and no diagnostic sherds were discovered in any exposed mound fill.
2-10-2	Loma de la Montura. The Río Salado, permanent and enchanneled in this part of the valley, runs along the northern edge of the site. There are several functioning springs on the lower part of the northern slope and one on the west side of Loma de la Concepción, overlooking the saddle. Maize and alfalfa are intensively cultivated on the high alluvium just north of the site. Some of these fields are canal irrigated, but flooding and inadequate drainage often ruin the summer crop. Several square kilometers of fields along this part of the Río Salado were under water while we were mapping the hillside. For purposes of describing the cultural remains, the site is divided into seven zones: *1. South and west sides, lower slopes of Loma de la Cruz*: about 17% of the site area. The amount and persistence of habitational debris clearly indicate that this part of the hill was used for residences, but there are many fewer residential terraces than on the north side, perhaps because the south and west sides are better drained and face away from the main expanse of alluvial land. Nine residential terraces are found in this zone, mainly on its south side. Lengths range from 11 to 42 m (mean 23.6 m), widths from 7 to 15 m (mean 11.0 m), and surface areas from 77 to 555 m^2 (mean 266.6 m^2). *2. North side, lower slopes, Loma de la Cruz*. This zone includes about 13% of the site area. Sherds are most common on the residential terraces, but are also found in quantities from very sparse to light on the surrounding gentle and moderate slopes. The occupation is confined to the higher ground and does not extend more than a few meters out into the alluvium. There are 46 residential terraces in this zone. Lengths range from 9 to 127 m (mean 26.4 m), widths range from 3 to 20 m (mean 10.1 m), and surface areas range between 36 and 1778 m^2 (mean 293.1 m^2). Many of the larger terraces are reminiscent of certain features at Monte Albán, where there is sometimes a clear retaining wall along the leading edge of a terrace, with one or more house platforms built 2-4 m back from the terrace edge, leaving a long, narrow, clear area in between, possibly for use as a walkway. *3. North side, lower slopes, Loma de la Concepción*. About 27% of the site area. It is clear that what is today unbroken, moderate or gentle slope was being used as a habitation space. There is no indication of a Period IV

SITE	COMMENTS
	utilization of the Monte Albán I irrigation canal (2-5-20, 2-6-94) just 60 m from the eastern boundary of the site. In Zone 3, 44 residential terraces were mapped. Lengths vary from 9 to 105 m (mean 30.6 m), widths range from 3 to 26 m (mean 11.4 m), and surface areas vary from 36 to 2730 m (mean 406.4 m^2).
	4. Upper slopes, Loma de la Cruz. This zone takes in the top half of the hill, but does not include the topmost knoll, which is treated separately as Zone 7. About 26% of the site area, with 17 terraces. Terrace lengths range from 12 to 46 m (mean 21.1 m), widths vary from 6 to 36 m (mean 12.2 m), and surface areas from 90 to 1748 m^2 (mean 301.9 m^2). One group, consisting of at least three and perhaps five terraces built as a unit, is a probable high status residence. Aside from its exceptionally high (9 m) bank on the front (north) side, the principal feature is an approximately 16 by 16 m sunken court, surrounded by low mounds, indicating an elaborate residence. A second prominent group is composed of four mounds built around a 15 m square plaza. A looter's pit in the north mound revealed five superimposed plaster floors. This mound group also might have been an elaborate residence.
	5. Upper slopes, Loma de la Concepción. About 11% of the site area. Eight residential terraces were mapped, all overlooking the pass or saddle between the two hills. Terrace lengths vary from 20 to 27 m (mean 24.9 m), widths range from 14 to 26 m (mean 20.4 m), and surface areas from 280 to 676 m^2 (mean 510.7 m^2).
	6. Saddle between Loma de la Cruz and Loma de la Concepción. About 4% of the site area. In terms of directed access, or traffic flow, this was a key sector of the site. The pass appears to have been leveled and taken up with buildings and plazas. The dominant unit is a 32 by 30 m plaza and mound group. Access into or through the saddle is impeded by a roughly 1.5 m high rock wall, which runs along the north and east sides of the ditch, and then turns east and runs part way up the slope of Loma de la Concepción. On either side of this arm of the wall are two large, open plazas (57 by 20 m, 40 by 17 m). North-south traffic most probably moved through this sector in the following manner: ascend the north slope via a path from the northwest, or another path from the north that runs just east of, but well screened off from, the high status residence described for Zone 4. These two paths join about 100 m north of the saddle. Then, follow the outside of the rock wall around the northernmost structure, onto the first open plaza. This is the key point for access to the four mound group. Traffic through the saddle would be routed through a break in the rock wall at the end of this plaza, along a narrow path around the edge of the eastern mound, onto another open plaza at the southern end of the saddle, and then down the slope.
	7. Top, Loma de la Cruz. About 2% of the site area. This is a steeply sloping knoll just to the west of the saddle. Its top has been built up as a platform to support a 25 by 24 m plaza with mounds at the north and south ends. This group is isolated on all sides by a steep slope, and access to it must have been from a more reachable plaza (33 by 20 m) abutting the north side of the north mound, via a stairway on the north side of the north mound. On the steep slope east of this group, overlooking the saddle, are six apparently residential terraces. Lengths range from 9 to 23 m (mean 14.3 m), widths from 4 to 13 m (mean 7.5 m), and surface areas from 52 to 208 m^2 (mean 107.2 m^2) One hundred and thirty artificially constructed terraces, 14 mound structures, and several plazas were recorded for the site as a whole. Most of the site's population was living on the lower slopes (Zones 2 and 3), on terraces constructed for one or more houses. The upper slopes and the south and west sides of the site (Zones 4 and 1) were probably less intensively occupied. Two elaborate residences were identified on the slopes between the main concentration of population and the large mound groups at the top of the hill. There are considerable size differences between terraces. While the mean terrace dimensions of Zones 1-4 are quite similar, those from Zones 5 and 7 are anomalous. Zone 7 terraces are smaller than usual, and those of Zone 5 are exceptionally broad. The artifactual evidence gives no indication of special function, but it is suspicious that both sets of terraces are contiguous to what was probably the administrative precinct (Zone 6). An analysis of probable ways of access shows that elaborate measures were taken to restrict or control traffic entering the monumental buildings of Zone 6 from the direction of the most populous area of the site, whereas access to the same sector from outside the site was comparatively easy. This implies that access restrictions, at least in this case, have more to do with internal social stratification than with defense against outside invasion.
2-10-5	Several structures were noted on the top of the hill. Structure 1 consists of a hollow square formed by 0.5 m high rubble piles, interpreted as a residence. Structures 2 and 3 have been so badly destroyed by caliche mining that their forms are difficult to determine. What Structures 2 and 3 were used for, and their relationship to each other is unclear, but one possibility would be that the complex served as a minor palace with residential and administrative functions.
2-10-11	The highest point of the hill has a small, heavily eroded, rock rubble and earth platform. A ca. 30 by 40 m, flat, cleared area extends away from the northeast side of the structure. Another mound (St. 11) located on the western slope of the hill, may pertain to this period, though its dating is very insecure.
2-10-13	Tiny, unidentifiable potsherds occur elsewhere on this hill, so it might be possible that this occupation is three to five times larger.
2-10-17	The occupation here might be Late IV, or Early V, or both.
2-10-18	The site may pertain to both Monte Albán IV and V, or it might be a single, short occupation dating from the end of IV or the beginning of V.
2-10-19	Sherds found eroding out of a shallow arroyo cut, indicating some post-occupational deposition in this area.
2-10-20	Tierras Largas. No definite Monte Albán IV artifacts were found on the survey (though IIIb-IV G-35's were noted). However, in his excavation of Early Formative features at the site, Winter did encounter Monte Albán IV deposits similar to materials from Lambityeco (Winter, personal communication, 1974).
2-11-1	Arable land is relatively scarce, though there seems to be enough water for irrigation.
2-11-2	Mean terrace length is 24 m, width is 16 m, and surface area is somewhat less than 340 m^2.
2-11-3	Area 25 m in diameter with a light concentration of pottery, indicating a house, and very sparse pottery sur-

SITE	COMMENTS
	rounding this spot.
2-11-4	A concentration of pottery and several cut stones on an area of level ground suggests a house site.
2-11-5	Two terraces built during Monte Albán IIIb were reused in Monte Albán V.
2-11-9	Of the 14 residential terraces in this area occupied during IIIb times, only six have Monte Albán V debris. The lowest and easternmost outlier has a 20 by 10 m rectangular terrace. Two chert projectile points coded as chert blades.
2-11-12	Rainfall, floodwater, and canal irrigated farming are practiced in the alluvium below the site.
2-11-13	Plowing, and subsequent investigation by the farmer or passersby, revealed a human burial in a shallow pit, apparently accompanied by an offering of three manos, a stone grinding slab, and a large assortment of fragmentary Sandy Cream and Polished Cream bowls, one *sahumador*, one *patojo*, one unknown complex bowl form, one *comal*, and 12 large sherds from big jars. Notably absent were Monte Albán V gray wares.
2-11-14	San Luís Beltrán.
2-11-15	A fairly reliable arroyo has been diverted for irrigation purposes north of the site. One of its channels runs between 2-11-14 and 2-11-15.
2-11-23	Artifact distributions are difficult to observe in the southern part of the site because of recent construction. Seven residential terraces were found on the moderately sloping southwestern flank of the mountain. These vary from 10 to 37 m in length (mean 21.4 m), from 8 to 17 m in width (mean 10.2 m) and have areas ranging from 80 to 629 m^2 (mean 246 m^2).
2-11-25	The site is plowed and irrigated by small ditches.
2-11-26	Alfalfa and corn are grown on the alluvium, with the aid of the high water table and irrigation canals.
2-11-27	One chert projectile point coded as chert blade. Two residential terraces, 28 by 18 m, and 15 by 7 m.
2-11-33	Rainfall cultivation of corn on the gentler slopes and a small amount of floodwater farming (using check dams in the arroyo at the edge of the site).
2-11-34	Over much of the site the Monte Albán V sherds are mixed with occasional Colonial or recent pottery.
2-11-35	In the alluvium, a network of irrigation canals permits tomatoes, chili peppers, squash, and alfalfa to be grown year round.
2-11-41	It is clear from the stratigraphic evidence that a great deal of the arroyo cutting has taken place subsequent to the Monte Albán V occupation.
2-11-43	11 modern agricultural terraces.
2-11-47	Very eroded residential terrace.
2-11-48	On the southern part of the western slope is 9 by 19 m concentration of obsidian (six green blade fragments, 80 green flakes, three gray flakes, two striated gray flakes). 200 m north of this, a 20 by 25 m concentration yielded three chunks of magnetite, six green obsidian blades, three green blade cores, nine green flakes, and one blade core with the color that thinly sprayed gold paint shows on a black surface. Obsidian occurs elsewhere on the site in lesser frequencies. This surface distribution suggests that there were at least two areas where obsidian blades, mostly green in color, were produced.
2-11-49	Canal irrigated corn and alfalfa fields on the alluvium.
2-11-50	Several shallow ditches have been dug across the fields to check soil erosion. It does not appear that they are effective.
2-11-51	Northwest of El Carrizal, on the opposite side of the stream, are the ruins of a Colonial structure. This may be the Carrizal listed by Taylor (1972:124-25) as an 18th century Spanish secular estate. Locally it is known as El Trapiche, and is said that "in the past" the entire length of the narrow valley was planted in sugar cane. On top of the sixth bluff upstream from El Carrizal is a roughly square terrace, about 45 m on a side, and well-defined by rubble and earth retaining walls. This is interpreted as a residential and agricultural terrace, with a house situated on a rise near the center, and fields around the sides of the unit.
2-11-56	Hamlet, perhaps two houses.
2-11-63	Obsidian bead.
2-11-64	Area about 120 m^2. Several large bowl fragments were found 10 to 20 cm below the ground surface in a 3 m deep arroyo cut. Careful inspection of the surrounding area revealed a few small sherds. This is one of the few instances of artifacts being found on a steep slope below the crest of a high ridge. There is no indication of habitation on the ridge line above this site, and while the situation is unusual, it is likely that there was at least one house on this spot.
2-11-65	Several concentrations of ash, burned adobe, and building stones were found. The owner of the land reported plowing up a number of house foundations.
2-11-67	The site is next to a small concrete dam or *toma* from which water is led through short canals onto the gently sloping fields at the base of the hills. Tomatoes, onions, and chili peppers are grown in the early spring, and corn in the summer.
2-11-70	Small-scale canal irrigation would be feasible in this area.
2-11-71	Human bone and ash were found. Two chert projectile points counted as chert blades. One "bark beater."
2-11-72	Farther down the slope of the hill is an abandoned Colonial or recent adobe house. Two similar ruins are found to the east and west along the stream. Informants from San Pedro said that this *ranchería* was abandoned because of hostilities involving the neighboring mountain community of San Pablo Cuatro Venado.
2-11-73	The site is a good example of "rural sprawl." Evidence of ancient occupation is spread over the ridges and hills of an area measuring 2250 m by 1350 m, on four major east-west trending ridges, the side ridges of the northern and lowest of these ridges, and the broad spurs extending down from this to the high alluvium. In the mountains the occupation is confined to the narrow, gently sloping ridge tops, with no evidence of habitation on the steep side slopes or in the barrancas. The northern ridge has seven fairly wide side ridges, and all of these were occupied. Toward the east this ridge broadens out into a series of gently and moderately sloping low hills. On the northern part of the site are the remains of four residential

SITE	COMMENTS
	terraces. Measurements could be obtained from two of the terraces: 25 by 12 m and 19 by 8 m.
2-11-76	One chert projectile point coded as chert blade.
2-11-82	Sts. 5-8 of 2-9-63 are on the southern part of the site, but there is no indication of any construction on the mounds after the Late Classic.
2-11-84	Much of the site lies in the town, but San Pedro is a fairly dispersed community.
2-11-88	One "bark beater."
2-11-90	Scattered modern house compounds and fields cover the area.
2-11-105	Four residential terraces. Measurements were obtained on three (12 by 9 m, 8 by 6 m, and 9 by 7 m). One chert projectile point coded as chert blade.
2-11-106	18 by 20 m.
2-11-108	One chert projectile point coded as chert blade.
2-11-110	Pottery on the lower slopes is distributed in distinct concentrations, probably the locations of ancient house compounds. For example, the small habitation area on the opposite bank of the arroyo from the main part of the site consists of three sherd concentrations, separated by 9 to 12 m of sparse or very sparse pottery densities. (It was in this last area that a possible Plumbate sherd was found.)
2-11-121	While surface sherds are infrequent, in two places plowing and subsequent investigation by the farmer has turned up more sherds, some building stone, and several fragments of human bone. Apparently the site has been partially covered by material washing in from above.
2-11-127	Sherds, animal bone, and burned adobe fragments were found in a 1.5 m profile of a modern house terrace.
2-11-132	Of the total site area, roughly 75% has very sparse pottery, 24% has sparse, and 1% has higher densities. Concentrations of pottery, obsidian, ground stone, burned adobe, and building stone were observed on areas of 18 by 18 m, 18 by 22m, 30 by 30 m, and 35 by 40 m, probably indicating individual residences. Burned adobe seemed relatively common, particularly on the south and west sides.
2-11-133	One chert projectile point coded as chert blade.
2-11-134	On the top of the highest peak in the vicinity. Sherds are sparse and consist of an unusually large number of *sahumador* handles and what may be figurine fragments or vessel supports, as well as the common domestic wares. On the highest point on the site is a fairly well preserved, stone masonry mound and courtyard complex. One ground stone pendant. Abutting the mound on the west side is a 23 by 20 m, wholly enclosed courtyard with a small *adoratorio* located on the east side. While there are no apparent habitation areas around this structure, the variety of vessel forms present suggest that cooking and eating took place on the site, perhaps as ritual activities. Isolated hilltop ceremonial place.
2-11-139	One chert projectile point coded as chert blade.
2-11-140	Stony, orange-brown soil overlain by 0.5 to 2 m deposits of a fine, brown, alluvial material. The deposition of this upper layer apparently began before the Monte Albán V occupation of the site, and continued after that time as well.

SITE	COMMENTS
2-11-149	At the top of the hill on the southwestern end of the site is a well-preserved masonry structure. The wall stubs stand to a height of 1.5 m and are constructed with a rubble core, and cut stones cemented into place for the facing. Wall thickness is 0.9 m. There is a low banquette on all four sides on the interior. The structure is rectangular, with an orientation of N 36°W. It measures 8.4 by 7 m. The construction dates to sometime during or after the Late Classic. Burned adobe was found in one area about 150 m northeast of the structure along the ridge line. There is a possible quarry (for mano and metate stone?) on the lower slopes on the northeastern part of the site.
2-11-150	The outstanding characteristic of the area is its heavy erosion. The slopes are laced with washes and barrancas. It is apparent from the sherd distribution that at least part of the erosion has occurred after the Late Postclassic occupation. One chert projectile point coded as chert blade.
2-11-151	An earth and rubble dam has been built about 200 m east of the site to trap the water draining off the hills to the west. The maximum area covered by the reservoir is 6 ha.
2-11-152	The nature of the occupation is difficult to discern because of the modern house compounds.
2-11-155	Parts of the north slope of the hill have been plowed by tractor, exposing the soil to erosion. Attempting to combat this, the owners of the land have built several terraces. But the terraces are not altogether successful, as several washes have begun to cut through the fields.
2-11-157	Portions of the site have been plowed by tractor, and to combat erosion, the landowners have dug a series of parallel ditches running along the contours of the hill.
2-11-158	Much of the erosion has apparently taken place after the Monte Alban V use of the area. The occupation is confined to the gentler slopes that have deeper soil deposits.
2-11-160	Cut by several washes. The washes clearly postdate the ancient occupation.
2-11-164	A 60 by 60 cm area of fire cracked rock and burned adobe was found near the center of the site.
2-11-166	Clearly visible are the outlines of a structure, defined by what may be the foundation stones. It measures 15 by 4 m, and may have three interior walls. Another wall parallels the long axis of this structure, 5.7 m to the east.
2-11-167	There are stone wall fragments for at least two free-standing structures on terraces, one of which is probably a house measuring 6 by 2 m.
2-11-182	A limestone quarry 100 m east of the site is being worked today.
2-11-183	The area is used as a refuse dump for Oaxaca City.
2-11-190	A low platform was noted, on top of which are two free standing constructions measuring 6 by 4 m and 4 by 3 m. Orientation is N 14°E. The edges of the low platform are marked by short retaining wall fragments. The surface artifacts suggest a Monte Albán V date. Elsewhere on the top of the same hill there are several other less well preserved stone alignments.
2-11-193	On top of the north ridge there is a mound of dirt and rock that has the appearance of an ancient construction. However, it is badly destroyed, and no sherds were found in the fill.

SITE	COMMENTS
2-11-194	There are a few houses on the site, and more on the north and east. The Calzada Porfirio Díaz and the Colonial aqueduct from San Felipe del Agua run along the eastern edge of the site, but a portion of the Monte Albán V occupation is found on the eastern side of the street, north of the Escuela Normal.
2-11-200	The cultural deposits appear to be thin. A short section of a plaster floor is exposed in the profile of a street that cuts through a poorly preserved, 0.4 m high mound. The structure is probably a Monte Albán V house.
2-11-213	The site is cut by a dirt road.
2-11-220	The heaviest concentration of artifacts occurs on an area of 32 by 25 m.
2-11-226	The site is in an area of deep, alluvial fan deposits, perhaps of Pleistocene age.
2-11-228	Just to the south is an area of sandy alluvial soil measuring about 14 ha that is irrigated by water from a canal that taps the stream at the edge of the site.
2-11-229	16 by 4 m residential terrace.
2-11-230	A 1 m high earth and stone platform stands on the top of the ridge. The structure measures 15 m east-west, and 9 m north-south. One wall fragment has an approximate orientation of N 20°E. The use of the platform could date to the Late Monte Albán I or Monte Albán V occupations.
2-11-232	On the flat ridge top at the north end of the site is a single mound and plaza. The mound is 35 by 34 m at the base, stand 2 m high, and has a top area of at least 110m^2. The orientation is N 5°E. The plaza extends out from the base of the mound to the west. It measures 50 by 31 m, and varies from 1 to 2 m above the surrounding ground. The construction and use of these features could date to Monte Albán Late I or V.
2-11-234	Several stone wall fragments, possibly from houses, were found on the top of the knoll. Whether these belong to the Monte Albán Late I or the Monte Albán V occupation could not be determined.
2-11-235	Some of the terraces do not have the amount of habitation debris usually associated with residential terraces, and they may have served instead as public plazas.
2-11-236	On the top of the hill is a 1.5 m high earth and rock rubble platform, dated to Monte Albán V by the sherds within the fill.
2-11-237	There is some doubt whether the sherds represent ancient habitation, or whether they were deposited with the refuse that modern farmers have deposited on the fields.
2-11-238	There are intermittent arroyos flowing along the sides of the ridge, one of which has a small, modern dam at a point 210 m southwest of the site.
2-11-239	In addition to the occupation at the top of the hill, sherds were found in the profile of a dirt road that was along the gently sloping western side of the hill.
2-11-241	A dam provides a reservoir of irrigation water for farmers with fields in the alluvium to the south.
2-11-244	The occupation is thin, superficial, and spotty. People were living on the residential terraces built in Monte Albán IV (as well as elsewhere on the gentle slope), but there is no indication of any major building or terrace modification. The principal mound groups above the site do not show any signs of use during Period V.
2-11-246	One piece of Late Monte Albán V polychrome pottery turned up in a general collection from the Period IV site, but we failed to localize a Period V settlement. Nevertheless it seems likely that there was a small Monte Albán V site, probably on the southern or eastern flank of the hill.
2-11-247	Rainfall cultivation of maize and peanuts on the hill, and canal irrigated alfalfa and maize on the alluvium. Despite the canalization of all watercourses in the area, fields on the alluvium are subject to destructive seasonal floods.
2-11-265	The four low mounds on the site were probably built during Late Monte Albán I, though they may have been reused as house platforms in Period V.
2-11-277	The mound and terrace construction at the site dates to Monte Albán IIIa, but the presence of a few sherds on two of the mounds (Sts. 1 and 3) might indicate the re-use of these in Period V.
2-11-279	Very sparse sherds appear on, around, and to the east of Structure 1 of the Early Classic occupation.
2-11-280	The site area estimate is inexact, as the area has been subjected to considerable alluviation since Monte Albán V.
2-11-287	There is an 8 m long retaining wall for a small terrace, with an approximate orientation of N 10°E. An artifact scatter measuring 55 by 12 m around this feature suggests residential functions. Another wall remnant measures 3.4 m in length, with an artifact concentration (ca. 10 by 7 m).
2-11-289	Intensive cultivation of maize.
2-11-291	Residential terrace 33 by 40 m.
2-11-293	On the hillside opposite the site are several pits where limestone was mined sometime during the past.
2-11-314	The occupation might be Late IV, Early V, or both.
2-11-317	Tierras Largas.
2-11-321	Rainfall maize cultivation on the higher ground, and intensive maize and alfalfa growing, sometimes using small scale canal irrigation, on the alluvium. All of the arroyos in the vicinity have been channelized for irrigation, flood, and erosion control.
2-11-323	A 2 cm long, triangular, side-notched, indented base, chert projectile point.
2-11-324	Green obsidian was unusually frequent (seven blades, five flakes). The blades are very thin, and appear to be mis-struck. This might be taken as evidence for blade manufacture on the site, though not necessarily manufacture for commerical purposes.
2-11-327	The site consists of a few sherds and burned adobe found in the backdirt of a hole dug by someone recently for reasons unknown. Several crew members called the feature an oven, which, among other things, it might have been.
2-11-331	A bulldozer exposed a human burial and several accompanying pots. Several other features in the vicinity suggested that this area was a Monte Albán V habitation area.
2-11-334	The site is largely covered by Colonia Lázaro Cárdenas.
2-11-336	On a lot at the northwest corner of Geranios and Eucalip-

SITE	COMMENTS
	tos in the Colonia las Flores in the eastern part of Oaxaca City.
2-11-337	The site is in a vacant lot at the corner of Dalias and Costa Rica, just north of the International Highway, in the Colonia Reforma.
2-11-388	There is a small, 0.4 m high terrace, with a retaining wall measuring 6 m across the front, and 3.75 along the side. Scattered building stone on the hillside might indicate other, now destroyed structures.
3-1-5	A modern well has been dug directly through the middle of Structure 2, where most of the early sherds were found.
3-1-7	Our periodization is based on two sets of surface collections (an earlier one by Flannery and his associates and one made by Blanton and Varner in 1970), made around the large mounds. Sherds do not extend far away from the slopes of the mounded area, probably due to the deep Colonial and recent deposits. Additional collections from the mound area were not made during the 1977 field season since during the reconnaissance of the site's peripheries we were stoned by a group of students who also vandalized one of our trucks, making us nervous about returning to the site. See Gallegos (1962, 1963) for a description of his excavation of a Period V palace. His map of the mounded area is reproduced in Figure A-XI-29.
3-2-4	We are somewhat uncertain about this component. The pottery is miserable.
3-2-6	(see 3-1-5)
3-2-8	(see 3-1-7)
3-3-7	(see 3-1-5)
3-3-9	(see 3-1-7)
3-4-9	"A lot of chert."
3-4-10	Site on a batholith. Evidence for specialized activity is "lots of. . .cut granite, chert and flint nodules (Structure 2). . .a lot of flint, chert, quartz, and granite chunks (Structure 6)."
3-4-11	Sta. Inés Yatzeche. We were not given permission to survey the *municipio* on foot, so we are dependent in our periodization on a surface collection made some years ago by Flannery and his associates. This collection was evidently made near the train-stop. We made a map of the mounds while passing through town on the train, so our estimate of mound volume is only approximate. We have no way of knowing whether the site extends continuously from the southern group of mounds to the northern mound. Judging from the Flannery collection and comments made by his crew concerning the number of G-23's, we feel the site must have peaked in IIIa.
3-4-12	(see 3-1-5)
3-4-13	Mica noted.
3-4-15	Structure 1 has "much white quartz, worked and unworked around it."
3-4-16	"Lots of chert cores, flakes, and chunks, and an unusual number of manos noted. One ground-stone "pounder" noted."
3-4-17	"*Possible café* pottery-making. One burned clay lump noted, one possible kiln waster, and a large proportion of *cafés* to gray wares for this area."
3-4-21	(see 3-1-7)
3-5-2	Several "bark beaters" noted.
3-5-3	Two probable kilns noted, but they are probably associated with the 3-6-5 site (or with 3-7-3).
3-5-6	Alluviation here may have covered some occupation.
3-5-9	Date of construction of the mounds here is uncertain, although Structure 6 is probably Late I only. "The relative openness of mound groups and the sparsity of sherds suggest primarily public rather than residential functions. There is no suggestion of a residential population immediately surrounding the mounds (unless the evidence has been buried by the modern town of Animas Trujano)."
3-5-12	Chert-working evidence can tentatively be attributed to Early I since this component dominates the site.
3-5-26	(see 3-4-9)
3-5-27	Site located on a batholith. *Café* kiln wasters noted. Early I pottery well represented, as is Late I. Period II was found only in a small area along the site's north edge. No mounds were noted, but within the bounds of the Early and Late I site, near the top of the batholith (but easily accessible) a large platform was contructed measuring 55 m north-south by 38 m east-west, and bordered along its north edge by very large boulders. The openness of the platform and its accessibility suggested the possibility this had been a dance platform or ritual structure, but the adjoining evidence for specialized production activities led us to suggest this had been a marketplace. These activities are indicated both by the presence of the kiln wasters and by the relatively dense quantity of chert and quartzite. Too, a tunnel was noted, dug vertically into the batholith, evidently following a vein of biotitic quartz. Two circular bedrock features were noted that would have served in some grinding or pounding operation. One bark-beater was noted. Blanton estimates there may have been as many as 40 to 50 terraces on the site, but most are now eroded away.
3-5-30	(see 3-4-10)
3-5-33	Isolated mound. Function unknown.
3-5-34	The site is in danger of being eroded away by a river.
3-5-35	Around Structures 1,2, and 5, there are a lot of chert, flint, and quartz chunks.
3-5-36	(see 3-4-11)
3-5-37	(see 3-1-5)
3-5-39	Mica noted.
3-5-40	Around Structure 1 there is "abundant quartz and lots of utilized chert of good quality."
3-5-43	(see 3-4-15)
3-5-44	(see 3-4-16)
3-5-45	(see 3-4-17)
3-5-48	Shoddy assemblage, difficult to periodize
3-5-53	Shoddy assemblage, difficult to periodize.
3-5-62	The mounds here are probably residential only (i.e. not indicative of central-place activities), built to elevate residential space from the surrounding *bajío-ciénaga*.

SITE	COMMENTS
3-5-64	(see 3-1-7)
3-6-5	Cuilapan. The abundance of G-12's around Structure 15 may indicate a ceramic workshop. Also, two kilns were noted just to the west of Structure XX. These were damaged, but were probably originally more than 1 m in diameter and 2 m deep. The earth around them is cooked to a bright red. An unusual abundance of *cremas* in the area is also of interest. As discussed in Appendix VII, the most likely date for ceramic production here is Period II. Several "bark-beaters" were noted in this part of the site. Abundant evidence exists in several places in the Cuilapan site for the construction of low, broad terraces, probably to create flat spaces for residential architecture, as well as, perhaps, flood-control.
3-6-8	Large, broad terracing is common here, probably ancient.
3-6-13, 14	(see 3-5-6)
3-6-16-19	The abundance of chipped stone, large chipped cobbles, and manos over the site suggests stoneworking, but no date can be established.
3-6-22	(see 3-5-9)
3-6-24	A lump of burned clay *could* suggest ceramic production, but other evidence is lacking and dating uncertain.
3-6-33	One alabaster "doughnut" noted.
3-6-43	A ceramic "tool" noted, consisting of a slab of pottery with a hole in it and a groove along the top. Function unknown.
3-6-51	Clear G-12 waster noted. Three structures were noted across the river, west of the site, that have very little pottery–although what is there appears to be Late I. These buildings were evidently built but then never used, or were used only for a short time.
3-6-52	"Bark beater" noted on Structure 1.
3-6-79	Mounds here were probably residential only (i.e. not indicative of central-place functions), built to elevate residential space from the surrounding *bajío-ciénaga*.
3-6-80,81	(see 3-5-62)
3-6-82	(see 3-4-9)
3-6-83	(see 3-5-27)
3-6-90	St. 3 has a Colonial/recent kiln dug into it.
3-6-91	(see 3-4-10)
3-6-99	"Lots of flint" and some quartz nodules.
3-6-100	(see 3-4-11)
3-6-102	Basin ground into bedrock noted.
3-6-104	At the very top of the mountain, there is a flattened area roughly 38 m in diameter, on which there are four low mounds (now nearly shapeless and covered with dense vegetation) facing a common patio. This may have been an elite residence as access is restricted. A number of terraces are visible within the site boundaries (and see 3-11-358), but most have eroded away. We noted two other mounds on a large terrace just to the south of the four-mound group, and on the saddle between this mountain and the next to the west, a probable reservoir was noted.
3-6-105	Several remnants of residences noted, some attributable to Late I only.
3-6-107	"Lots of chert and flint" noted around Structures 3 and 5. Two or three possible Tierras Largas sherds were noted, but no other evidence for Early Formative.
3-6-108	One hammerstone noted. This site may start as early as Early I, but the collection was not conclusive.
3-6-109	(see 3-1-5)
3-6-111	Chert point noted.
3-6-115	Site sits on a small batholith.
3-6-118	One kiln waster noted. Terrace 141 has "lots of mica, perhaps indicating production activities."
3-6-122	Mica noted.
3-6-123	(see 3-5-40)
3-6-124	"Lots of chipped stone." This, however, and the structures probably date to 3-8-236.
3-6-127	Site sits on a small hill that sticks out from the high alluvium.
3-6-132	(see 3-4-16)
3-6-136	Mica noted.
3-6-145	(see 3-5-48)
3-6-146	(see 3-5-53)
3-6-152	(See 3-1-7)
3-7-3	(See 3-6-5)
3-7-7	(See 3-6-8)
3-7-9	(see 3-5-6)
3-7-10	(See 3-5-6)
3-7-11	(see 3-6-16-19)
3-7-15	(see 3-6-33)
3-7-24	(see 3-6-43)
3-7-31	A-9's noted eroding out of Structure 1 from a cut near the top of the mound. "Bark beater" noted on Structure 1.
3-7-53	(see 3-6-79) One chert point noted.
3-7-54	(see 3-5-62)
3-7-55	(see 3-5-62) Almost no pottery present. Two A-9's were noted. The structure may not have been used much after it was built.
3-7-56	(see 3-4-9)
3-7-59	(see 3-6-90)
3-7-60	(see 3-4-10)
3-7-73	(see 3-4-11)
3-7-74	Four possible cream-slipped jar sherds noted. The limits of the site may be somewhat different than is indicated here. We were unable to complete our survey in this area because of a theft by the local people of the airphoto.
3-7-76	(see 3-6-102)
3-7-77	(See 3-7-107)
3-7-78	One hammerstone noted.
3-7-80	Chert point noted.
3-7-83	Shoddy assemblage. Periodization somewhat uncertain.

SITE	COMMENTS
3-7-84	Mica noted.
3-7-85	(see 3-5-40)
3-7-93	(see 3-4-15)
3-7-94	(see 3-4-16)
3-7-97,98,99	El Choco. Notes are found under 3-10-83.
3-7-100	Shoddy assemblage, difficult to periodize.
3-7-106	(see 3-1-7)
3-8-5	(see 3-6-5)
3-8-7	Periodization uncertain.
3-8-8	(see 3-6-8)
3-8-10	The mound here possibly dates to IIIa.
3-8-11,12	(see 3-5-6)
3-8-13	(see 3-6-16-19)
3-8-29	Sherds are found mostly on or around the mounds. We thought this could be due to alluviation, but later changed our minds. A series of excavations were noted, all a meter or more in depth, near Structure 8 (for tree-planting), showing the presence of abundant cultural debris, including ash deposits and sherds, near the mound, but trailing off away from the mound.
3-8-31	(see 3-6-33)
3-8-44	Periodization is somewhat uncertain, although definitely falling somewhere in Period III, and probably the first half of that.
3-8-48	A small area on a ridgetop. Two possible defensive walls noted, but their date is uncertain (they could pertain to 3-11-58). Quarrying is in evidence, but, again, the date is unknown. An unfinished mano may indicate specialized mano production, but date unknown. One chert point noted.
3-8-61	One unidentifiable ground-stone fragment noted.
3-8-62	A "bark-beater" was noted on Structure 1.
3-8-65	Ceramic "drain-pipe" noted.
3-8-83	Poor assemblage. Periodization somewhat uncertain.
3-8-90	Carved stone noted outside a residence, just to the west of the site.
3-8-94	The IIIa pottery is generally not found in the vicinity of the mounded buildings.
3-8-118	A colonial hacienda, now in ruins, was built directly over the prehispanic mound, largely obscuring it.
3-8-120,121	(see 3-6-79). One chert point noted at IIIa-120.
3-8-122	(see 3-5-62)
3-8-123	(see 3-4-9) Around Structure 7 there is "a lot of quartz."
3-8-125	On or near the top of the "Teta de María Sánchez."
3-8-128	"The mound here was probably constructed in IIIa."
3-8-136	Jalieza. Several small dams noted, probably not indicative of organizational effort beyond the household level. A very large pile of roughly-worked stone blanks (mano blanks?) was noted at the west edge of the IIIa site-suggesting a date of IIIa. The pile sits along the lower slope of the hill and measures roughly 36 m wide at the top, 56 m wide at the base, and runs for 41 m down the slope. The depth cannot be estimated accurately, but Blanton estimates a volume for the deposit of roughly 4000 m^3. The stone size is relatively uniform—most are around 20 to 30 cm in length. One partially completed mano was noted in this same area. The bedrock over much of this part of the site, the same material composing the "mano blank pile", was often used as a material for carved-stone implements found in the valley. Carved stones: Several can be found around the church in Santo Domingo, perhaps dating to Period IV. One was noted in the lower piedmont in the IIIa site, and one in front of the *municipio* in Santo Tomás is probably IIIa in date. The southwest boundary of 3-10-46 and the southeast boundary of 3-8-136 are tentative, due to the paucity of sherds, especially good diagnostics. For all the periods here, roads are not prominent archaeological features. Where they can be observed, they tend to lead down from residential areas to farmland below, rather than connecting various parts of the community together. Too, they are all small, looking more like paths and ramps. The modern cart road from Sto. Tomás to Sto. Domingo cuts through mound groups and terraces and so is not an ancient road. Mound clusters are not well serviced by roads.
3-8-140-143	Located in a hidden plateau at the base of the Sierra zone. Few IIIa diagnostics present. No G-23's were noted, but there are IIIa-looking G35's, G-12's, and outleaned-wall bowls.
3-8-145	(see 3-6-90)
3-8-146	(see 3-4-10)
3-8-153	Dating a little questionable due to the poor quality of the assemblage, but one probable G-23 was noted, and the G-35's looked IIIa.
3-8-164	Possible mound noted, but we were not able to determine whether it was only a Colonial/recent agricultural terrace, or whether in the construction of the terrace an ancient mound was modified. A pot-hole reveals a possible plaster floor.
3-8-169	(see 3-6-99)
3-8-172	The site may be larger than we indicate. Complete mapping was impossible due to the theft of the airphoto by a group of *campesinos*.
3-8-173	Poor assemblage, dating somewhat uncertain.
3-8-175	(see 3-4-11)
3-8-176	(see 3-7-74)
3-8-186	Shoddy assemblage. Date uncertain.
3-8-199	(see 3-6-107)
3-8-200	(see 3-6-108)
3-8-201	Several kiln wasters noted.
3-8-207	(see 3-1-5)
3-8-209	(see 3-6-115)
3-8-210	Site sits in a location suggesting it was at the head of a canal.
3-8-211	Shoddy collection, probably mostly IIIa. Site is adjacent to what was probably a canal in ancient times. Some Colonial construction here also.

SITE	COMMENTS
3-8-212	Shoddy assemblage, probably IIIa.
3-8-213	(see 3-7-83)
3-8-217	Assemblage mostly Late I. IIIa presence not definite.
3-8-218	Shoddy assemblage, probably IIIa.
3-8-220	Quarryable quartz abundant in several places on the site.
3-8-222	Pottery sparse. Short occupation?
3-8-228	"Lots of worked chert."
3-8-230	Shoddy assemblage. Probably IIIa.
3-8-231	Shoddy assemblage. Probably IIIa.
3-8-232	Mica noted.
3-8-233	(see 3-5-40)
3-8-236	Carved stone noted in town (Tejas de Morelos). Much evidence for chert working at Structures 9, 2-4, and 24.
3-8-237	A second possible structure was noted, but it is largely destroyed by modern occupation.
3-8-238	Pits were noted in recent land-grading cuts north of Tejas de Morelos, exposing IIIa and IIIb sherds, charcoal, and one human burial.
3-8-242	Site could be larger than is indicated, but is obscured by deep grass.
3-8-251	(see 3-4-15) Shoddy IIIa assemblage. G-23's hard to find.
3-8-252	Graphite source located just across the river. One "hammerstone" noted. "Chert is abundant."
3-8-254	Shoddy assemblage, difficult to periodize.
3-8-267	Ceramic evaluation: III-IV. Scraped-exterior G-35's suggest IIIa, but the number of brown-surfaced sherds suggests IV. Inadequate collection.
3-8-272	El Choco. Notes are found under 3-10-83.
3-8-283	(see 3-1-7)
3-8-296	Shoddy assemblage, difficult to periodize. One chert knife noted.
3-8-307	Periodization: III-IV, best guess is IIIa. Two probably residential structures present, reasonably well preserved. Several probably ancient agricultural terraces noted.
3-8-308	Large quartz outcrop.
3-8-309	(see 3-6-43)
3-8-312	On or near the top of the "Teta de María Sánchez."
3-8-317	Shoddy assemblage; best guess is Period IIIa.
3-9-9	Calcite core and polishing tool.
3-9-21	(see 3-8-10)
3-9-22	(see 3-5-6)
3-9-23	(see 3-6-16-19)
3-9-26	(see 3-8-29)
3-9-31	Establishing site limits and estimating density of occupation at Zaachila is problematic. See Gallegos (1962, 1963) and Acosta (1972) for descriptions of excavations carried out here. Ceramic drain-pipe noted at Structure 1.
3-9-34	Periodization uncertain. IIIa is a possibility.
3-9-44-46	The IV component here is questionable.
3-9-52	(see 3-8-90)
3-9-57	One hammerstone noted.
3-9-58	(see 3-8-201)
3-9-61	(see 3-8-211)
3-9-63	(see 3-8-236) The IIIb occupation might continue under Tejas de Morelos, but is not easy to detect there.
3-9-64	Two non-mounded structures noted, with walls fairly well preserved.
3-9-65	Shoddy assemblage. We're not sure that both IIIb and IV are present. Mound volume indicated is the mound alone. Low platforms noted were not included in the calculation. At the very top of the mountain there is a platform roughly 50 m east-west by 25 m north-south, on which is situated a mound roughly 17 m north-south by 25 m east-west at the top. The latter contains some stone alignments and a possible sunken patio. The volume of this whole complex is estimated at somewhat less than 5000 m^3. Several other stone alignments were noted downslope from the mound, along with a number of fragmentary terraces and two defensive walls.
3-9-69	(see 3-5-62) "Lots of quartz noted near Structure 7."
3-9-70	(see 3-4-15)
3-9-71	"Possible hammerstone."
3-10-7	(see 3-6-24) Twenty-eight terraces were measurable, but many more have been damaged by erosion.
3-10-10	Most of the obsidian here is in that part of the site that is predominantly Period V in date.
3-10-11-13	(see 3-8-29)
3-10-17	Evaluated as IIIb-IV since so few diagnostics are present.
3-10-24	Hammerstone noted.
3-10-25-27	The IV component here is problematical.
3-10-46	(see 3-8-136)
3-10-55	Red stone (jasper?) outcrop 300 m to the north.
3-10-57	Sherds found scattered around some large boulders. No habitation space present, so this is possibly not a habitation site.
3-10-65, 66	Poor assemblage. Periodization uncertain.
3-10-68	Chert point noted. Chert working?
3-10-69	Poor assemblage, difficult to periodize.
3-10-71	Stone doughnut noted.
3-10-72	The precise extent of Period IV in this area is difficult to determine.
3-10-73	Difficult to periodize.
3-10-75	(see 3-1-5)
3-10-76	(see 3-8-211)
3-10-79	(see 3-9-65)
3-10-83	El Choco. The site is largely Upper Piedmont but extends into the Oak-Pine zone on the upper slopes. What appear to be ancient agricultural terraces were noted on the High

SITE	COMMENTS
	Piedmont ridges southeast of the site.
3-10-86-90	Early IV.
3-10-92	*Probable* IV, possibly early IV.
3-10-93	Ancient agricultural terraces cover most of this broad ridge. Dating is problematical.
3-10-94	(see 3-8-296)
3-10-95	(see 3-5-6)
3-11-18	(see 3-9-9)
3-11-25	Several ''bark beaters'' noted.
3-11-34	Located largely under the *Convento* in Cuilapan. An exposed structure at the south end of the *Convento* is apparently not prehispanic.
3-11-44, 45	(see 3-5-6) One alabaster ''doughnut'' noted at 45.
3-11-46	(see 3-6-16-19)
3-11-58	(see 3-9-48)
3-11-64	(see 3-10-10)
3-11-67, 68	(see 3-8-29)
3-11-96	(see 3-6-43)
3-11-105	Sits on a low mound with enough space for 2 to 3 houses. Pottery is early V or late IV.
3-11-110	Hammerstone noted.
3-11-130	Two unusable kiln wasters noted.
3-11-141	Unidentifiable ground-stone fragment noted.
3-11-148	''Some specialized activity involving thin gray ollas-perhaps their manufacture.''
3-11-201	(see 3-8-90)
3-11-225	An area north of the main part of the site has three small, shapeless mounds, probably attributable to the Period V occupation, but almost no pottery could be found on or around them.
3-11-232	(see 3-8-118)
3-11-233	(see 3-6-79) One chert point noted.
3-11-234,235	(see 3-5-62) ''Lots of quartz noted'' where the site is isomorphic with 3-8-123.
3-11-239	(see 3-8-125)
3-11-241	Unique assemblage, probably pure Early V.
3-11-243	(see 3-8-128)
3-11-259	(see 3-8-136)
3-11-266	(see 3-10-55)
3-11-270,272	(see 3-8-140-143)
3-11-280	Unusual assemblage, but seems to fit within the Period V range in variation.
3-11-285	Poor assemblage. V is present, and some earlier period *may* be present.
3-11-311	Pottery is unusually fancy.
3-11-313	(see 3-8-164)

SITE	COMMENTS
3-11-315	Small hilltop mound, probably not residential.
3-11-323	Site limits unsure due to intensive cultivation.
3-11-329	Periodization somewhat unsure.
3-11-332	(see 3-10-71)
3-11-336	Site limits unsure due to intensive cultivation.
3-11-353	(see 3-6-102)
3-11-357	One stone ball noted. One ground-stone fragment with groove noted.
3-11-358	This site may start in Period IV, but the assemblage does not permit a definite statement on this, nor can we estimate the size of the potential IV site. A possible reservoir noted. Much of the assemblage here is the typical pottery of Period V closer to the center of the valley, rather than the crummy micaceous stuff which is more common in this area. The people living here must have been able to import the better pottery from further north in the region (see also 3-6-104).
3-11-370	(see 3-6-107)
3-11-372	(see 3-6-115)
3-11-373	(see 3-7-83)
3-11-377	(see 3-6-118)
3-11-382	(see 3-8-228)
3-11-386	(see 3-4-13)
3-11-389	Shoddy assemblage, difficult to periodize.
3-11-391	(see 3-8-242)
3-11-407	The portion of the site closest to the river has two rims of possible Rosario/Early I date.
3-11-411	(see 3-6-127)
3-11-414	(see 3-8-252)
3-11-464	''Lots of worked chert flakes.''
3-11-465	''Early V or IV/V. Lots of chipped chert. One polished chert piece.''
3-11-466	Extra large metate noted, roughly 60 cm on a side and roughly 30 cm deep.
3-11-467	Hilltop mound with 4 terraces, but almost no pottery other than a few micaceous *cafés*.
3-11-480	(see 3-10-93)
3-11-498	One chert knife noted.
3-11-510	V is present, but about half the collection consists of unidentifiable ''crudware'' that is either Colonial, or goes with the V but is unusual, or represents some earlier period.
3-11-522	Pottery very sparse. Dating somewhat uncertain. Hilltop ceremonial center? Boundary marker?
3-11-528	(see 3-1-7)
3-12-1	Two small mounds and a possible ball-court, but with few or no sherds. The site does seem to have been used for some period of time, however, as indicated by the superimposed plaster floors visible in a cut.
3-12-6	Three sherds recovered. Dating is probably later than Late I but earlier than V.
3-12-8	Probably associated with 3-5-15, but no datable sherds were noted.

Appendix II

SITE MAPS

This appendix has two parts. The first part includes the maps of sites, by period, and including site numbers, for the Central survey region (Kowalewski 1976). The second part consists of the Valle Grande sites, with numbers, by grid square. Each grid square represents a 4 kilometer by 4 kilometer area. Their numbering scheme is discussed in Chapter 1 (and see Fig. 1-3). In some of the more congested grid squares, the periods were segregated, so that, for example, square 0907A includes Tierras Largas through Period II, while 0907B includes sites of IIIa through V.

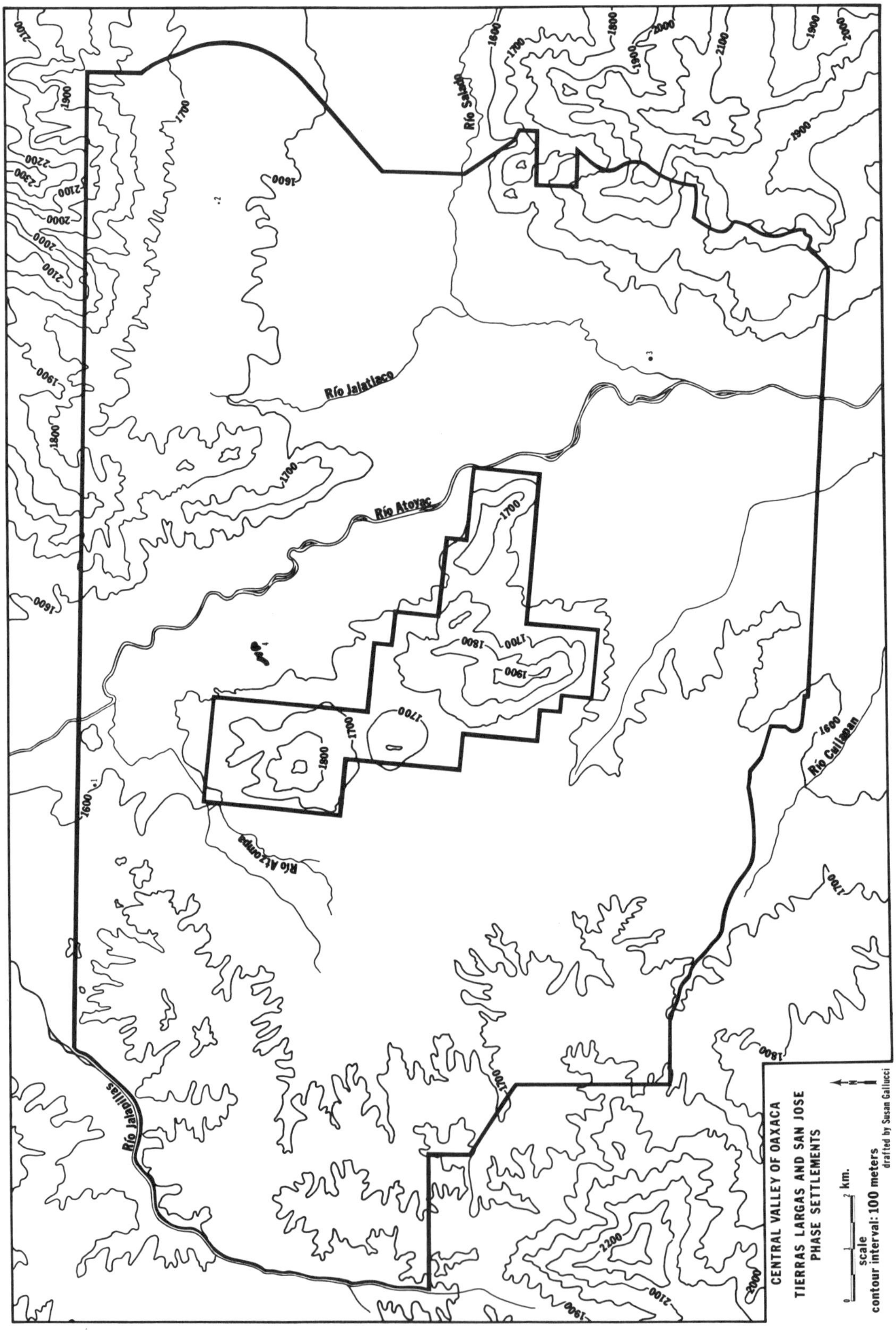
Río Salado
Río Jalatlaco
Río Atoyac
Río Atzompa
CENTRAL VALLEY OF OAXACA
TIERRAS LARGAS AND SAN JOSE
PHASE SETTLEMENTS
scale
0 2 km.
contour interval: 100 meters
drafted by Susan Gallucci

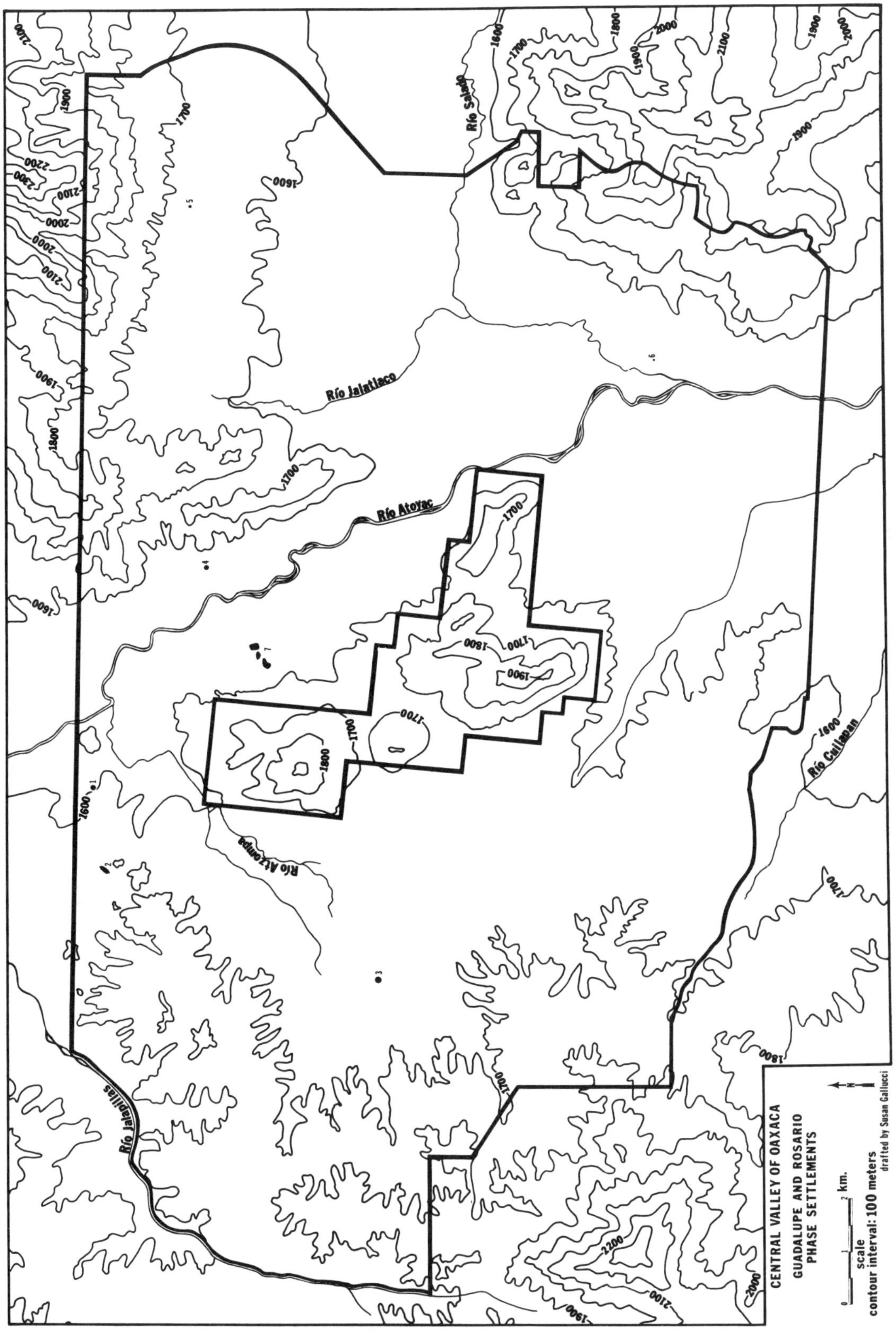
Río Salado
Río Jalatlaco
Río Atoyac
Río Atzompa
Río Cuilapan
Río Jalapilla
CENTRAL VALLEY OF OAXACA
GUADALUPE AND ROSARIO PHASE SETTLEMENTS
scale
km.
contour interval: 100 meters
drafted by Susan Gallucci

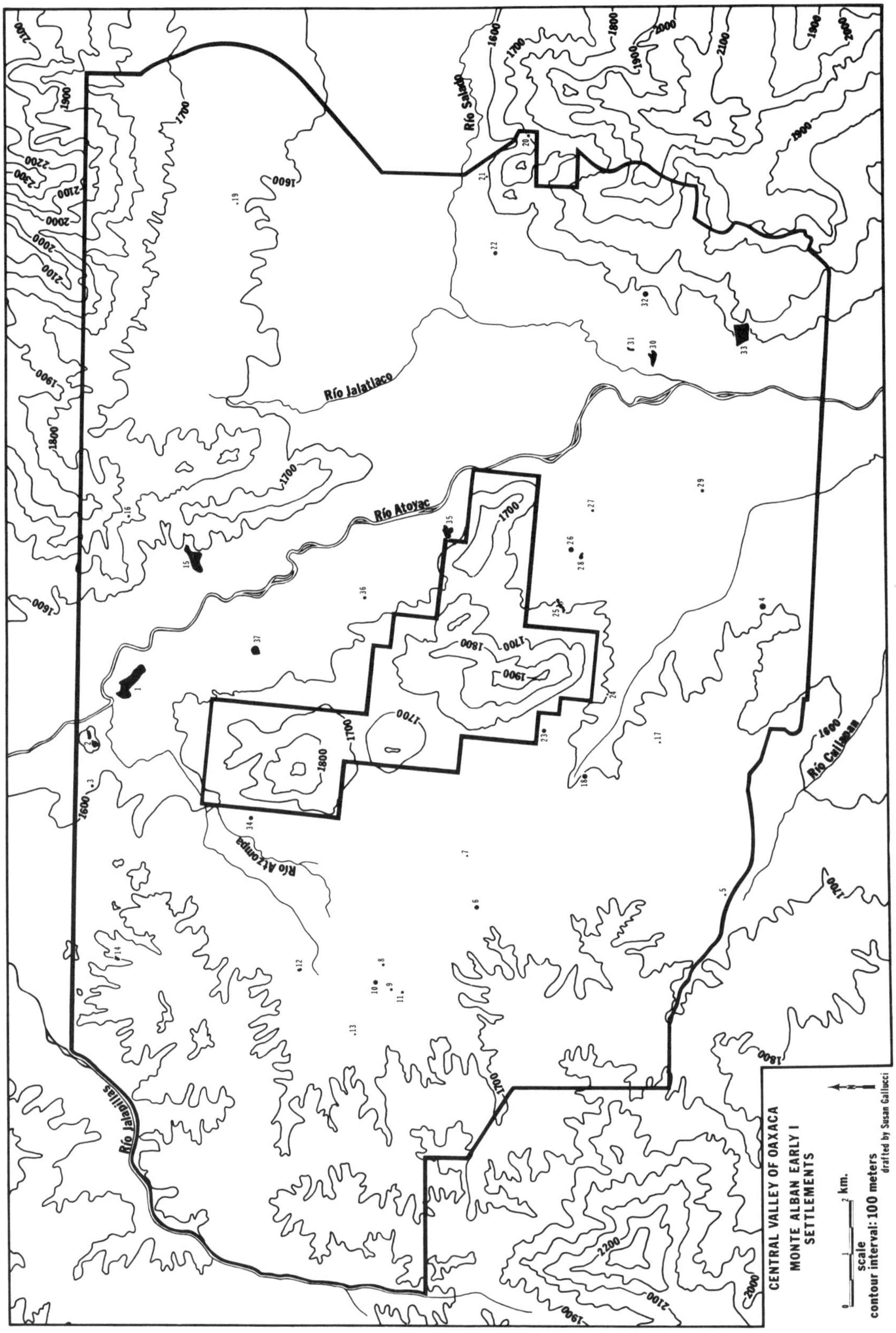
CENTRAL VALLEY OF OAXACA
MONTE ALBAN EARLY I
SETTLEMENTS
scale
2 km.
contour interval: 100 meters
drafted by Susan Gallucci
Río Salado
Río Jalatlaco
Río Atoyac
Río Atzompa
Río Jalapilla
Río Callapan

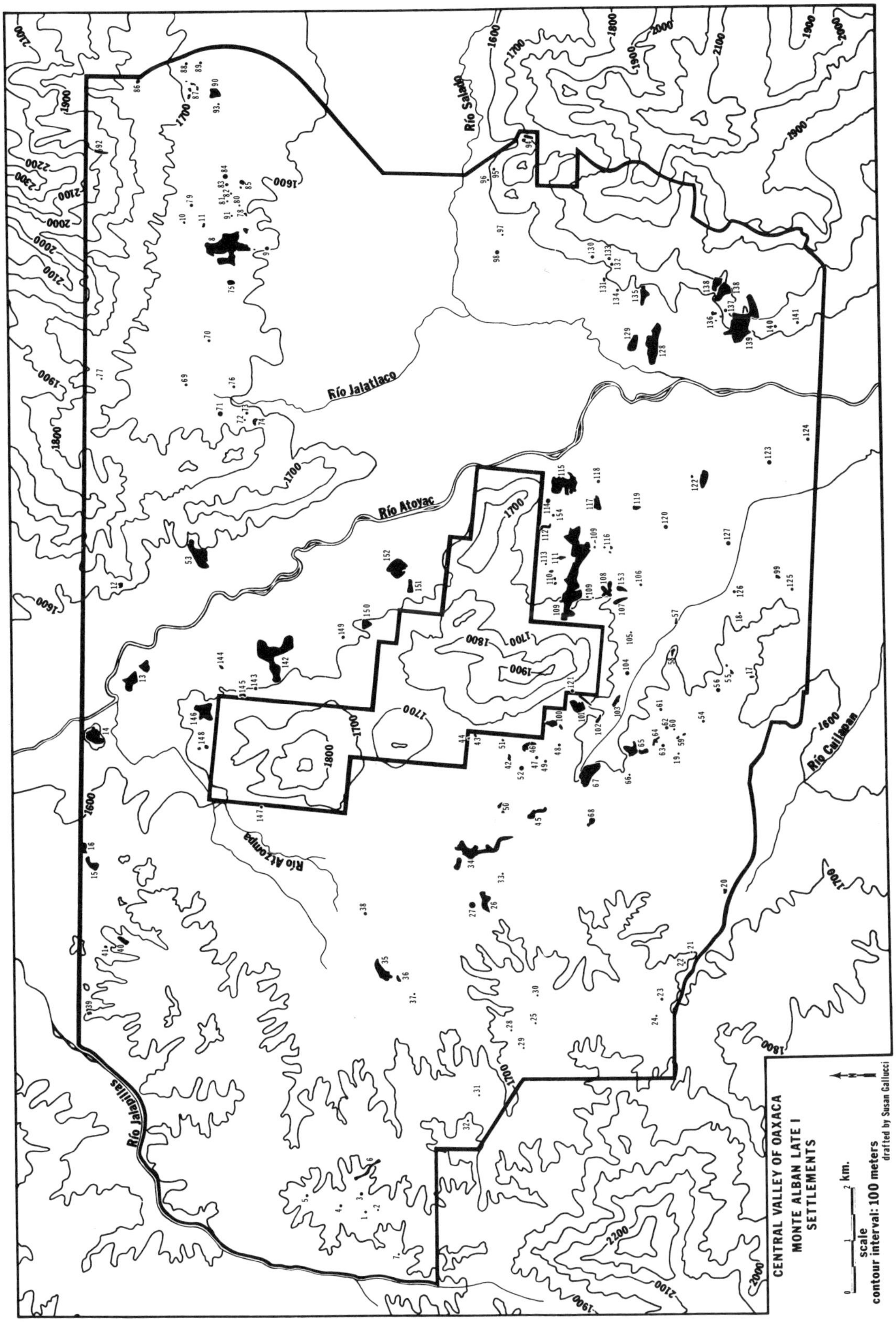
CENTRAL VALLEY OF OAXACA
MONTE ALBAN LATE I
SETTLEMENTS
scale
0 2 km.
contour interval: 100 meters
drafted by Susan Gallucci
Río Salado
Río Jalatlaco
Río Atoyac
Río Atzompa
Río Cuilapan
Río Jalapilla

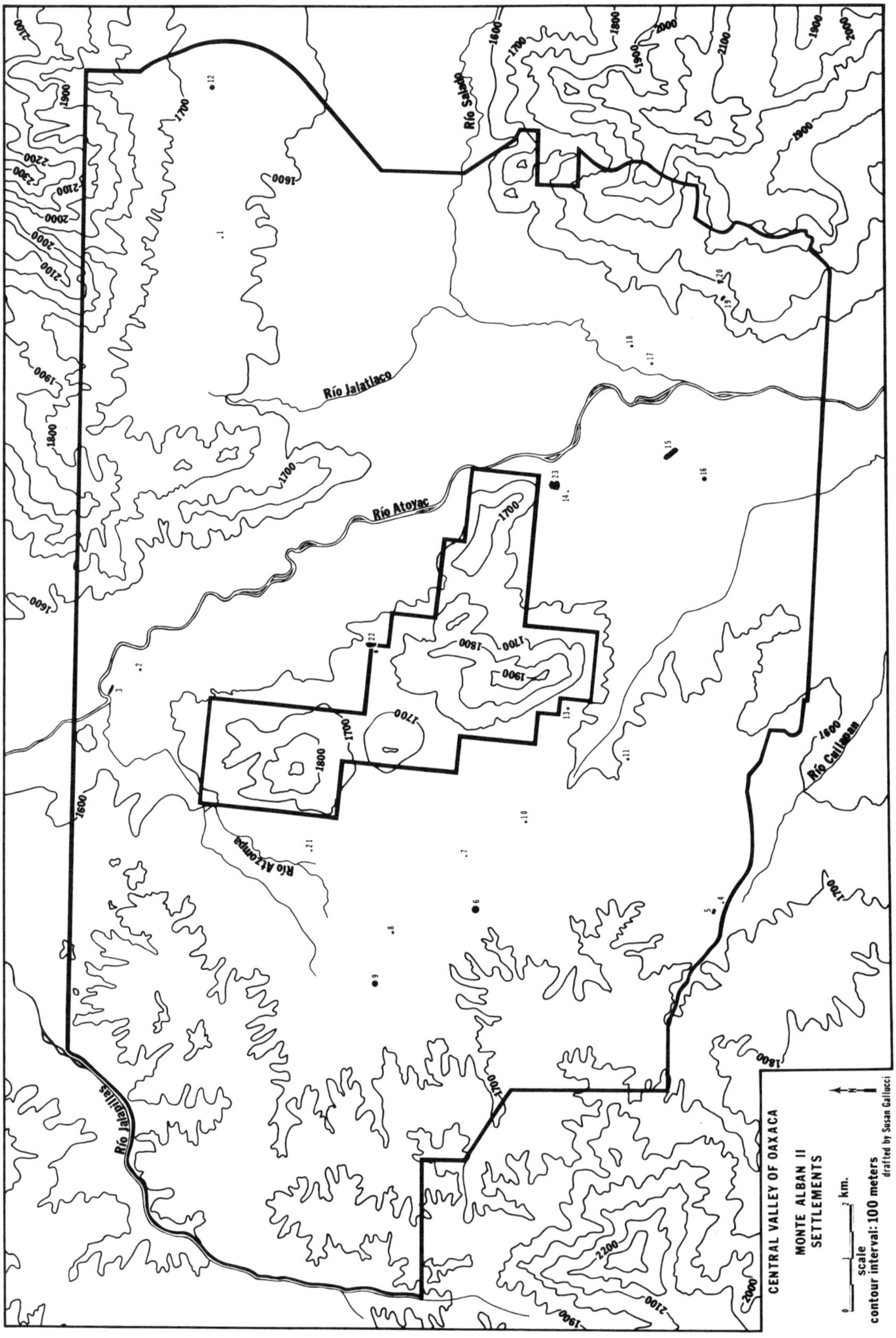
CENTRAL VALLEY OF OAXACA
MONTE ALBAN II
SETTLEMENTS
scale
0 1 2 km.
contour interval: 100 meters
drafted by Susan Gallucci
Río Salado
Río Jalatlaco
Río Atoyac
Río Atzompa
Río Jalapilla
Río Cuilapan

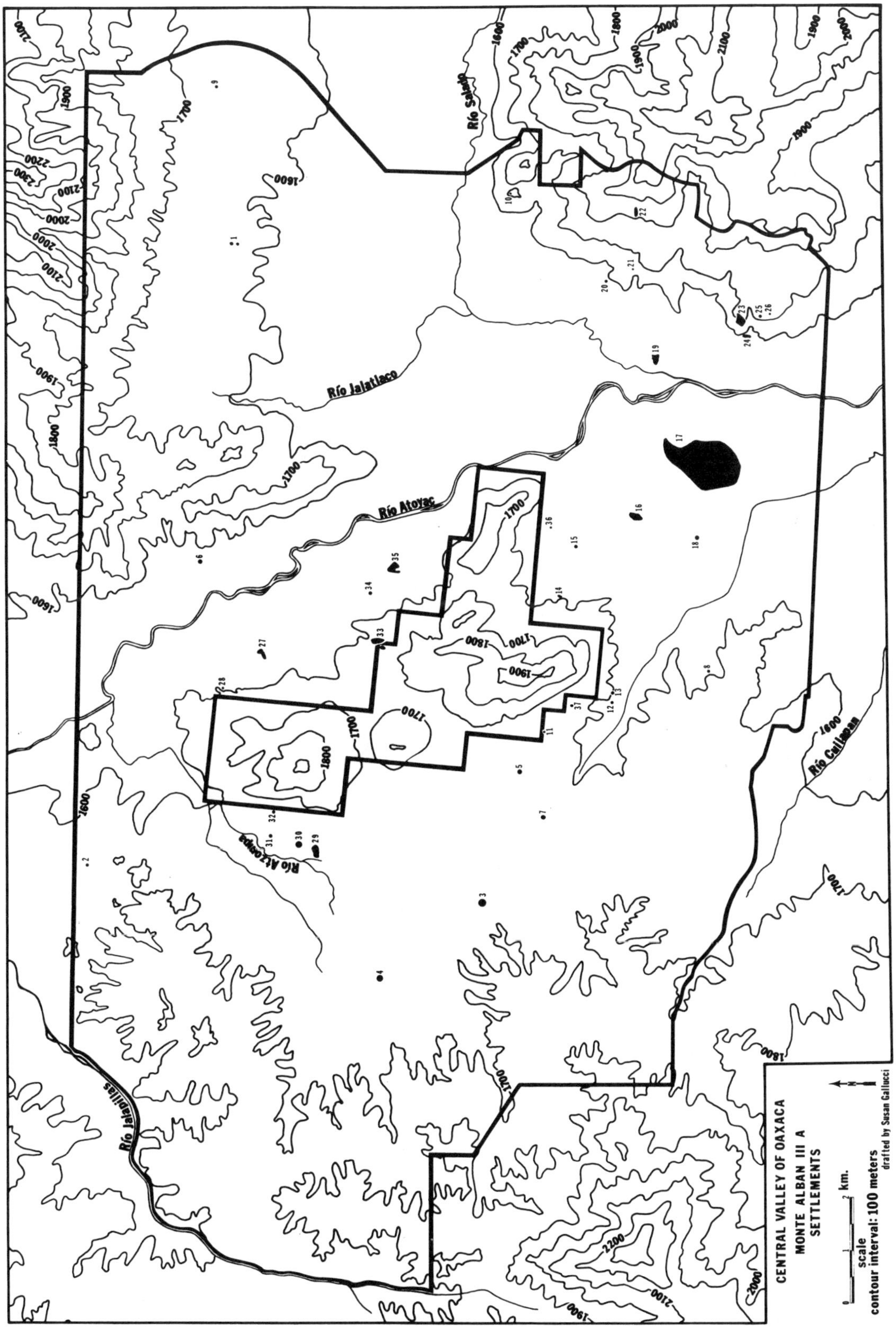
CENTRAL VALLEY OF OAXACA
MONTE ALBAN III A
SETTLEMENTS
scale
0 1 2 km.
contour interval: 100 meters
drafted by Susan Gallucci
Río Salado
Río Jalatlaco
Río Atoyac
Río Atzompa
Río Jalapilla
Río Calipam

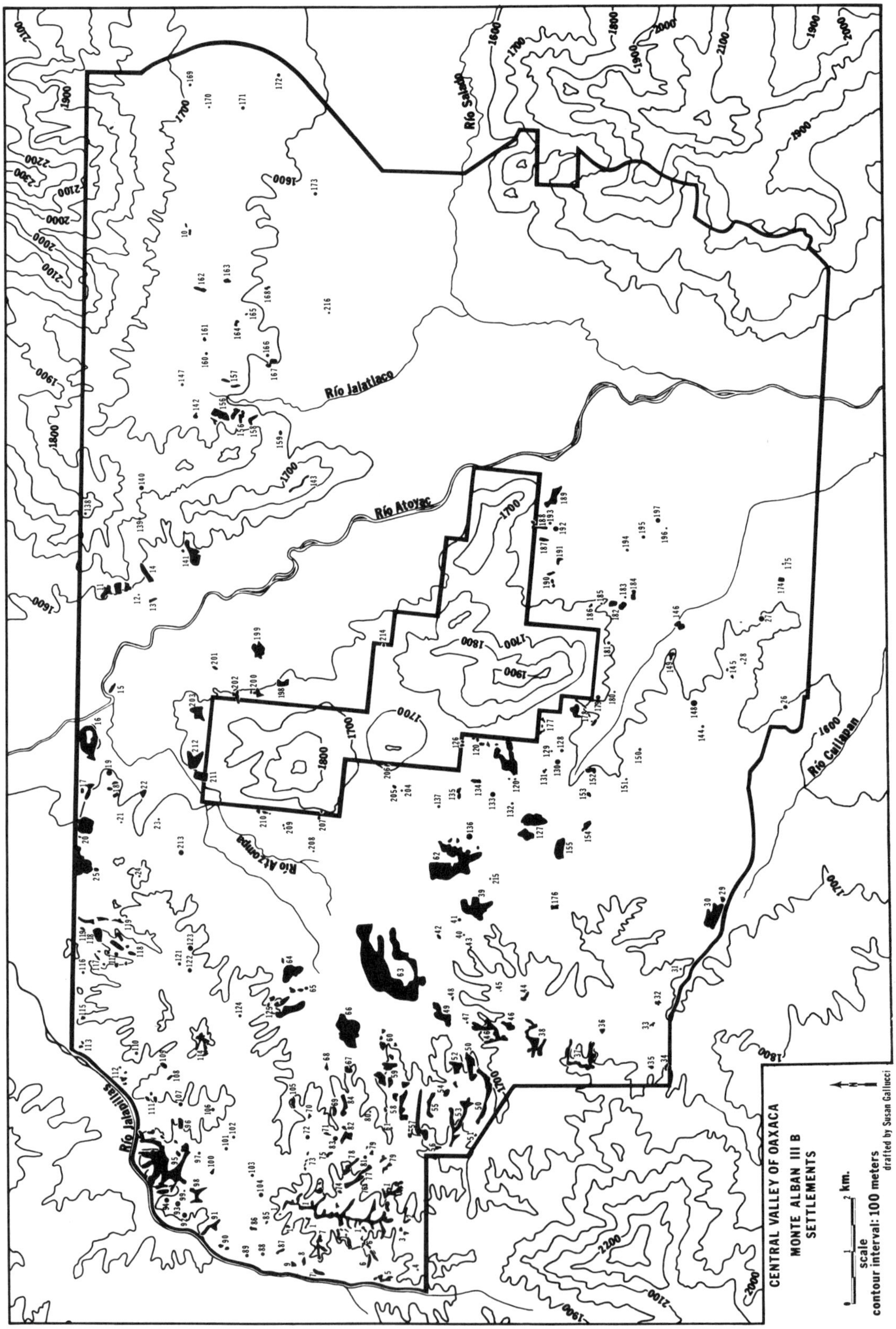
CENTRAL VALLEY OF OAXACA
MONTE ALBAN III B
SETTLEMENTS
scale
2 km.
contour interval: 100 meters
drafted by Susan Gallucci
Río Salado
Río Jalatlaco
Río Atoyac
Río Atzompa
Río Jalapilla
Río Cuilapan

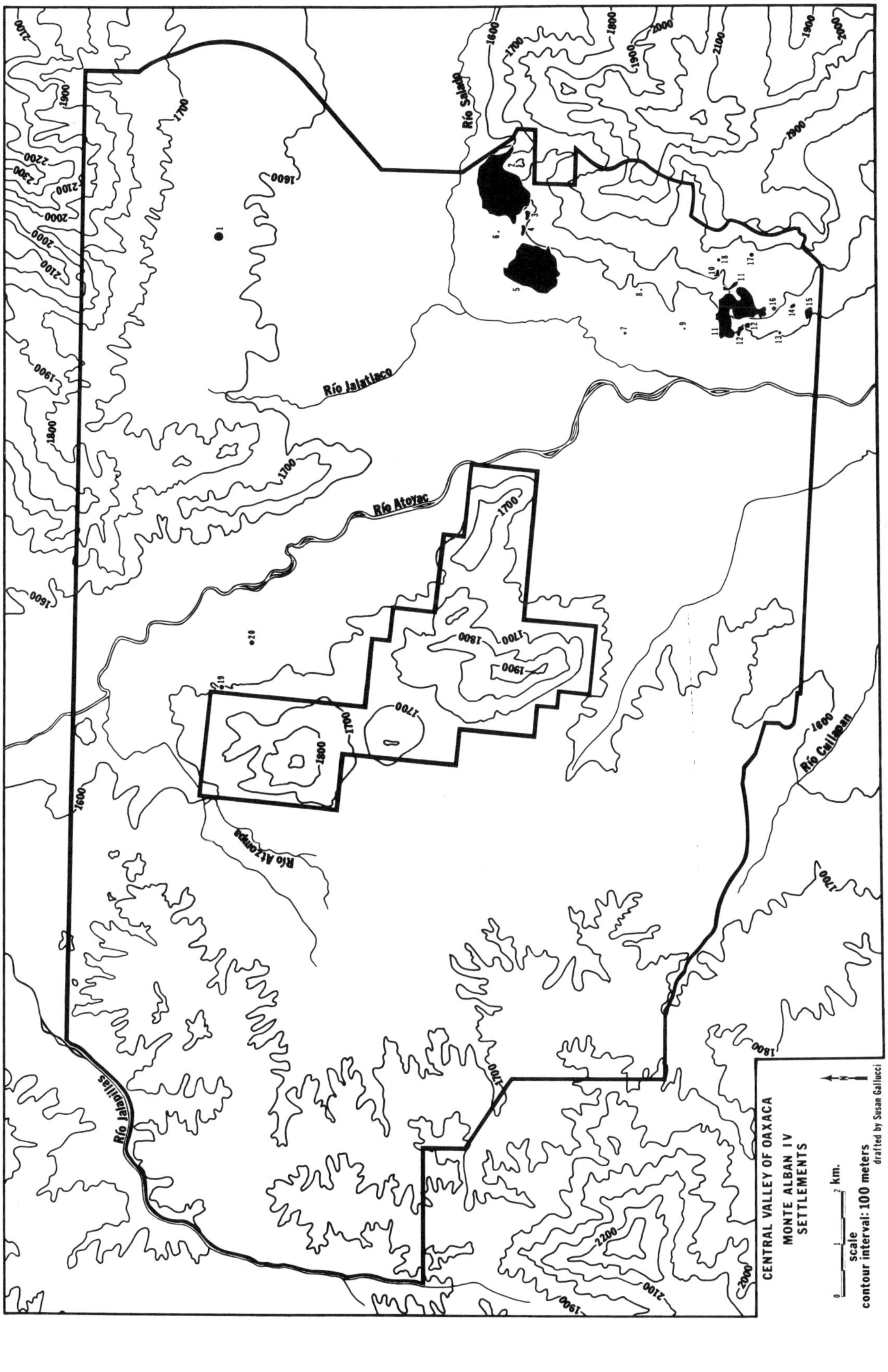
CENTRAL VALLEY OF OAXACA
MONTE ALBAN IV
SETTLEMENTS
scale
0 1 2 km.
contour interval: 100 meters
drafted by Susan Gallucci
Río Salado
Río Jalatlaco
Río Atoyac
Río Atzompa

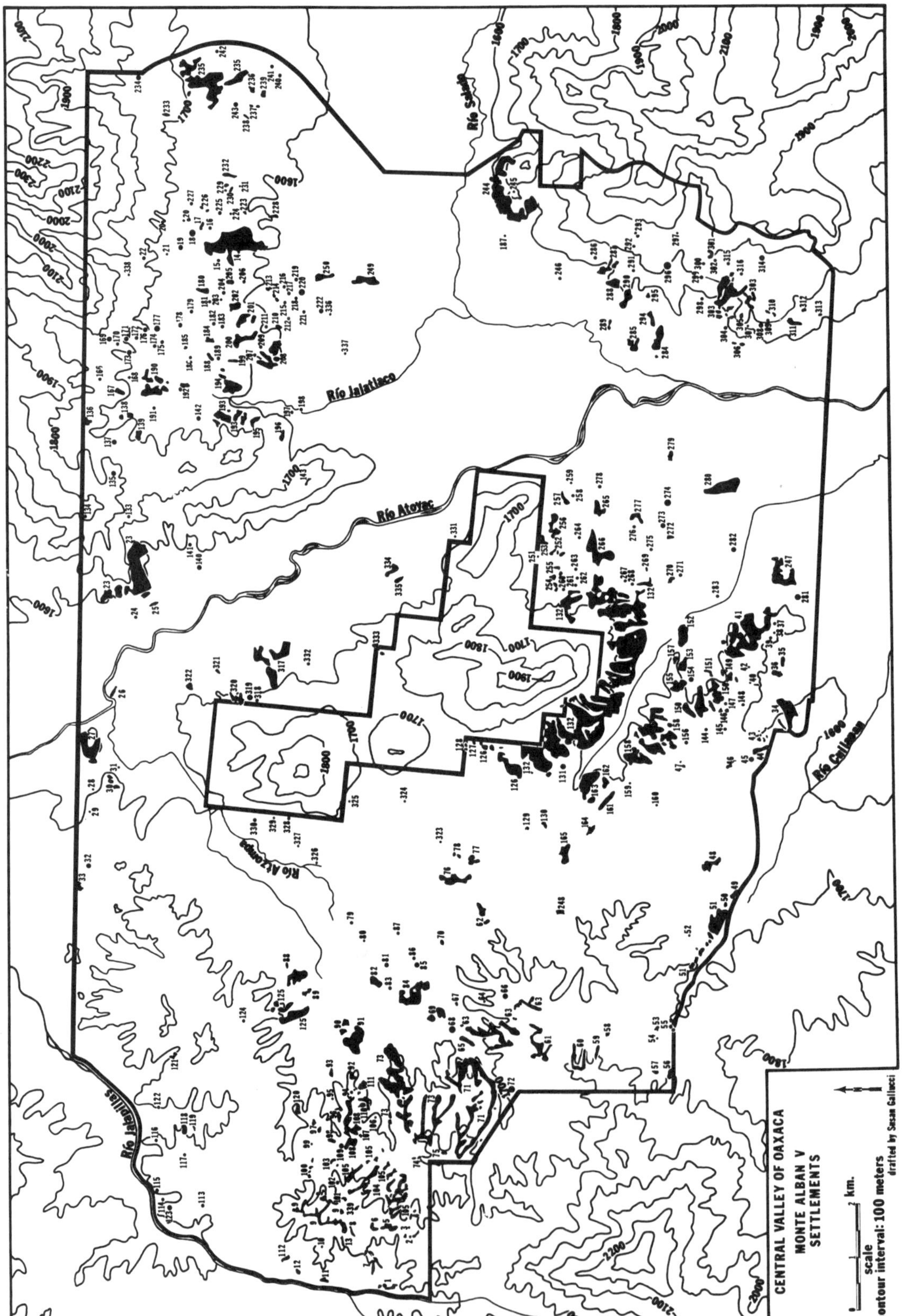
CENTRAL VALLEY OF OAXACA
MONTE ALBAN V
SETTLEMENTS
scale
2 km.
contour interval: 100 meters
drafted by Susan Gallucci
Río Atoyac
Río Jalatlaco
Río Salado

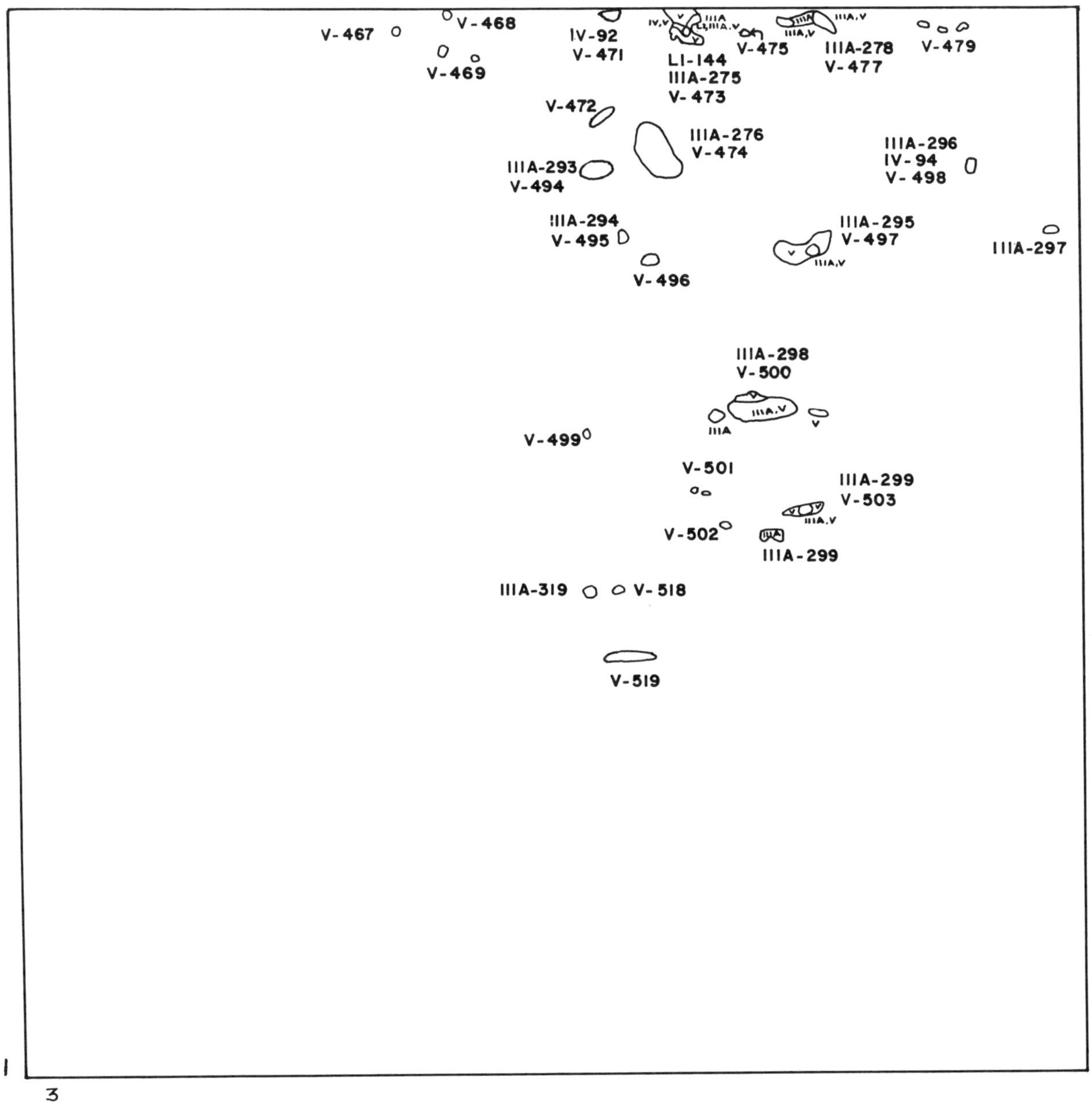
V-467
V-468
V-469
IV-92
V-471
LI-144
IIIA-275
V-473
V-475
IIIA-278
V-477
V-479
V-472
IIIA-276
V-474
IIIA-296
IV-94
V-498
IIIA-293
V-494
IIIA-294
V-495
IIIA-295
V-497
IIIA-297
V-496
IIIA-298
V-500
V-499
V-501
IIIA-299
V-503
V-502
IIIA-299
IIIA-319
V-518
V-519
1
3

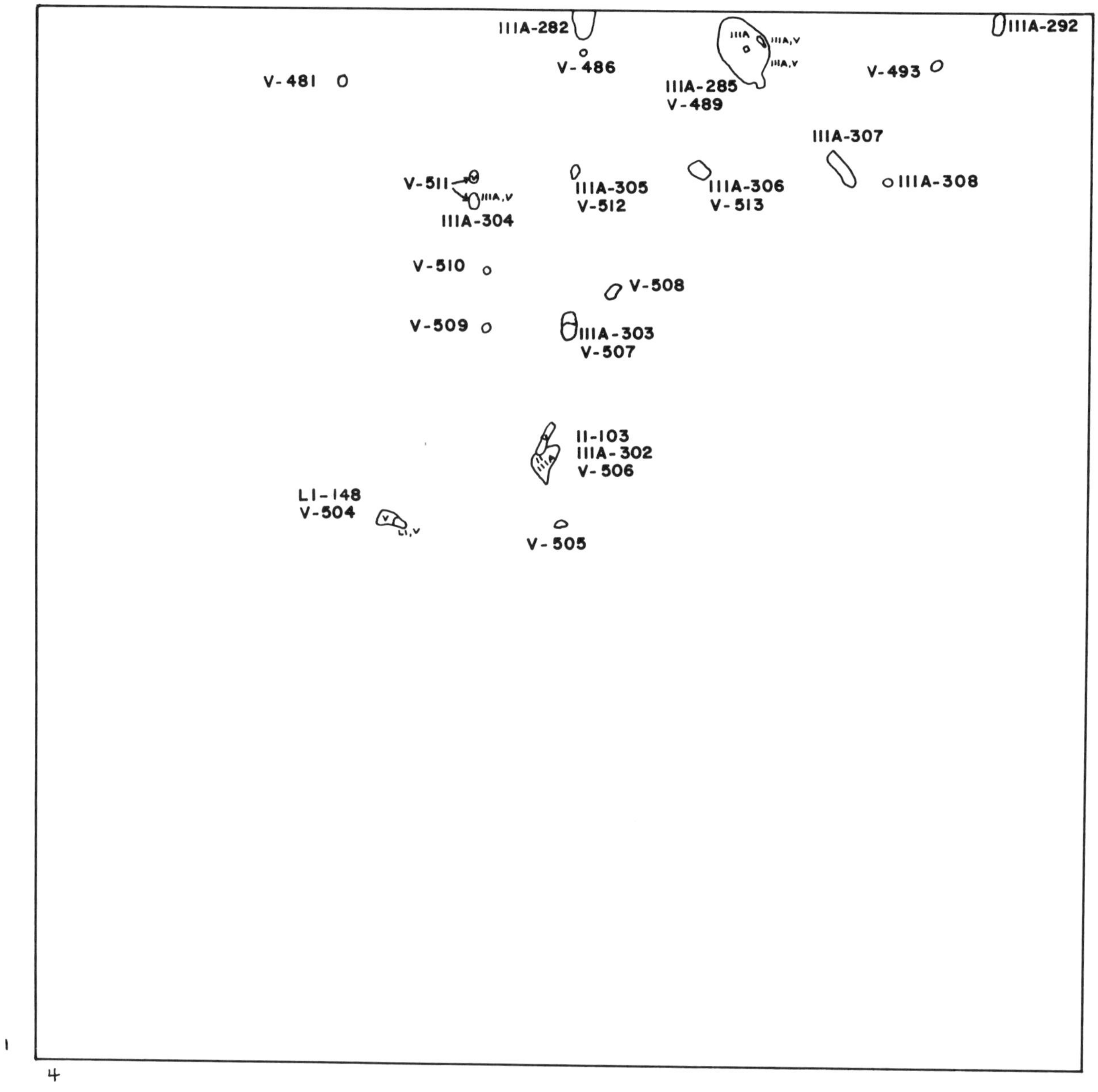
IIIA-282
V-486
IIIA
IIIA,V
IIIA,V
IIIA-285
V-489
IIIA-292
V-481
V-493
IIIA-307
V-511
IIIA,V
IIIA-304
IIIA-305
V-512
IIIA-306
V-513
IIIA-308
V-510
V-508
V-509
IIIA-303
V-507
II-103
IIIA-302
V-506
L1-148
V-504
V
L1,V
V-505
1
4

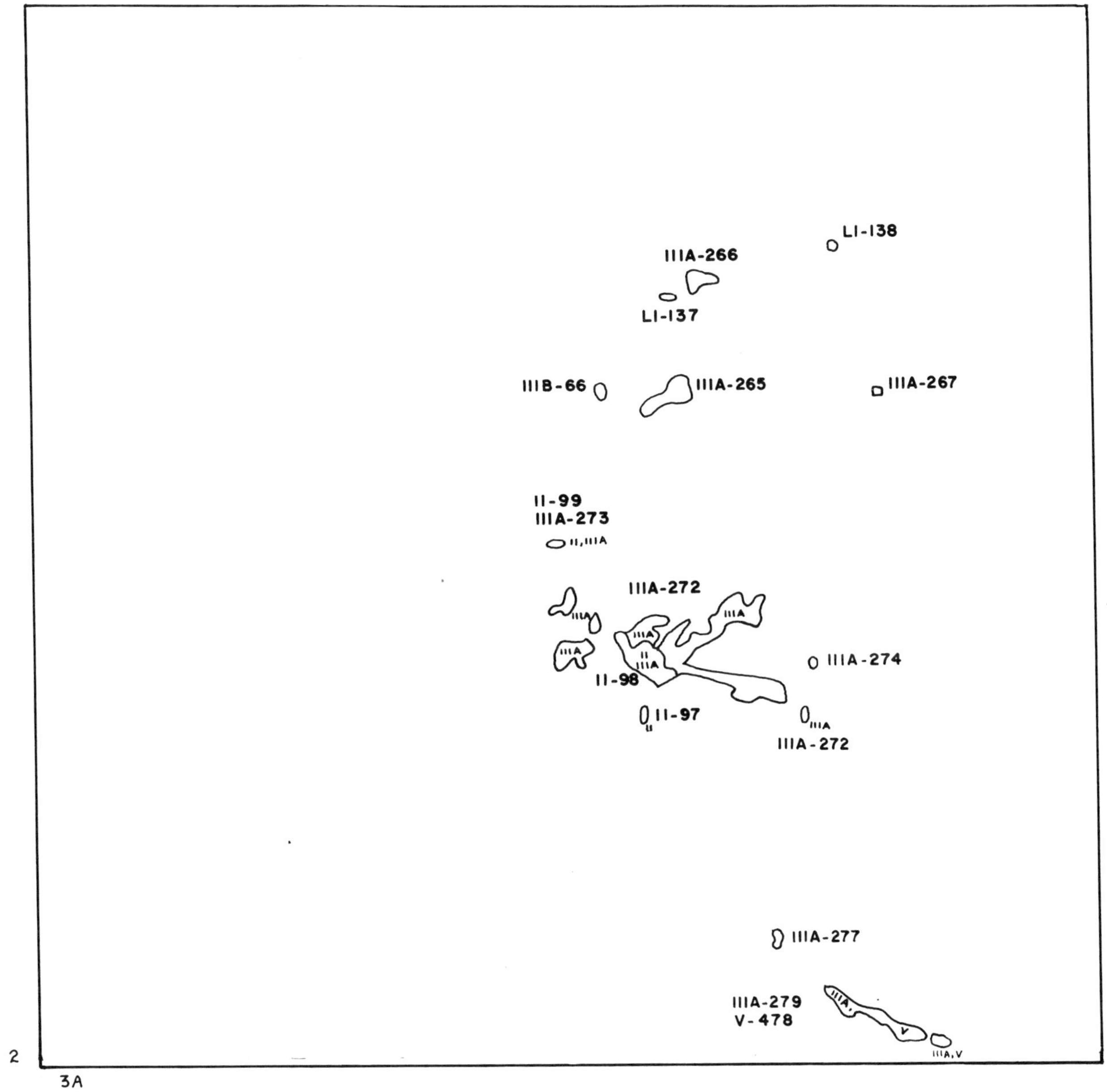
LI-138
IIIA-266
LI-137
IIIB-66
IIIA-265
IIIA-267
II-99
IIIA-273
II, IIIA
IIIA-272
IIIA
IIIA
IIIA
IIIA
II
IIIA
IIIA-274
II-98
II-97
II
IIIA
IIIA-272
IIIA-277
IIIA-279
V-478
IIIA
V
IIIA, V
2
3A

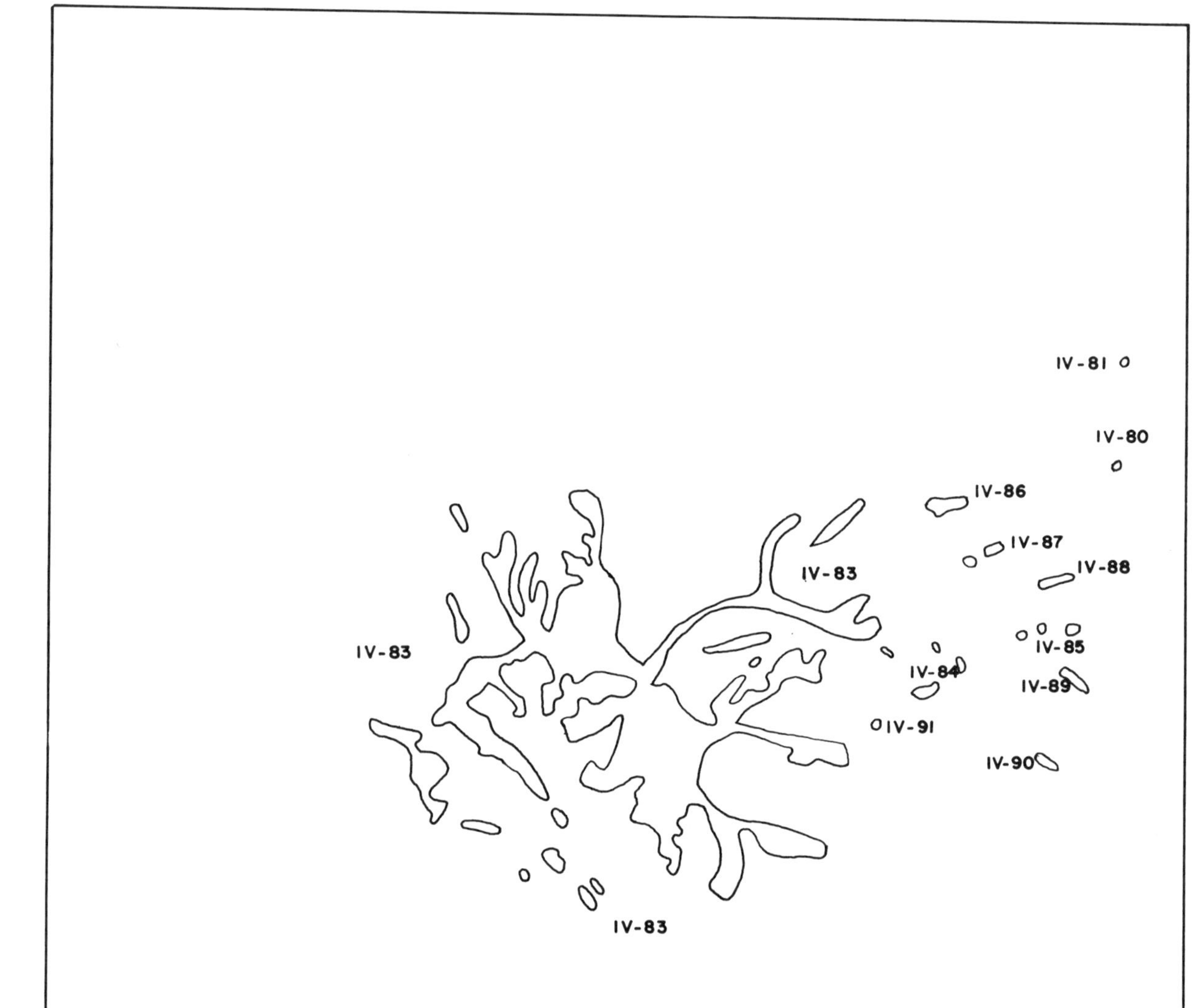
IV-81
IV-80
IV-86
IV-87
IV-88
IV-83
IV-83
IV-85
IV-84
IV-89
IV-91
IV-90
IV-83
IV-93
2
3B

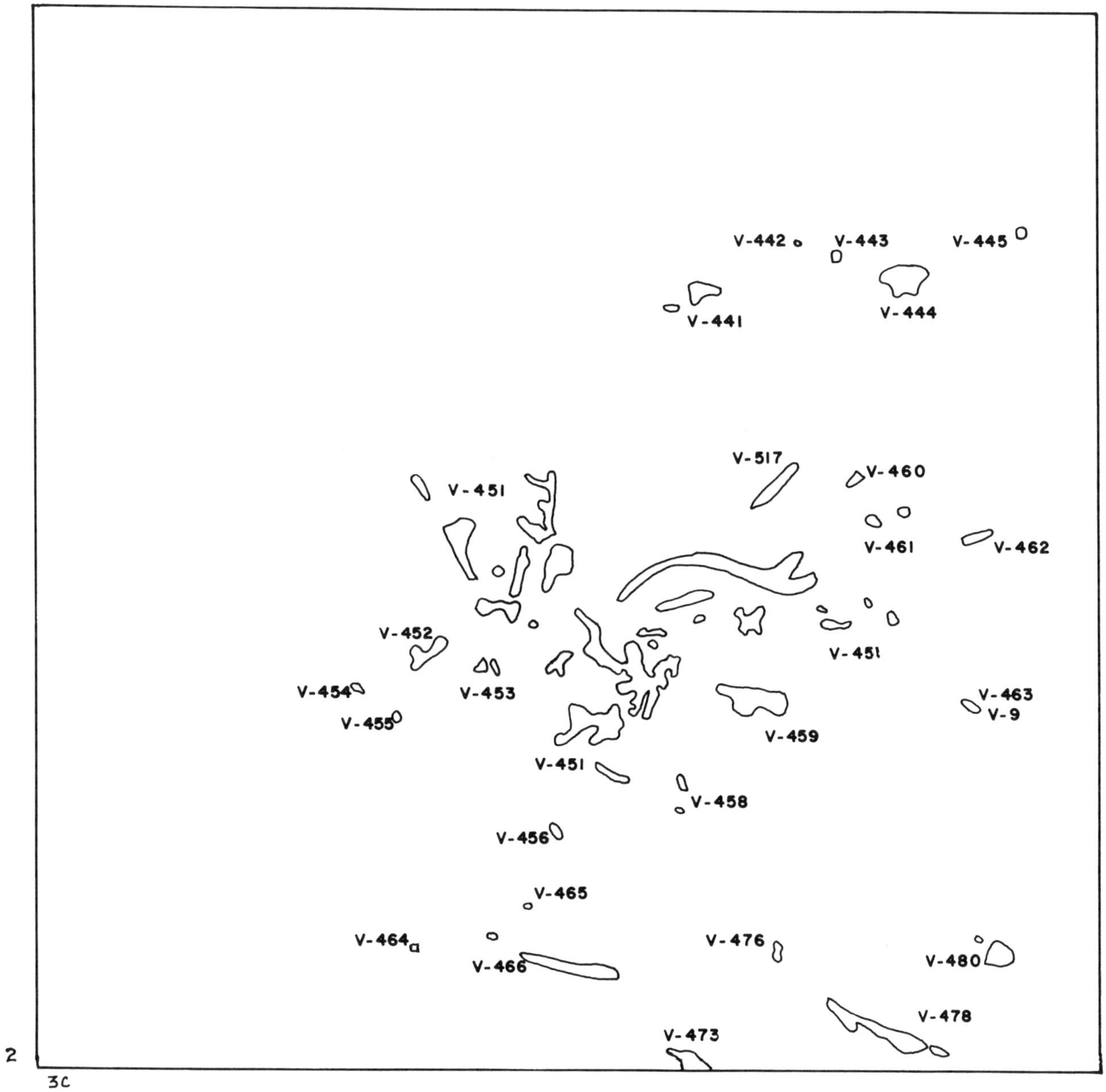
V-442
V-443
V-445
V-441
V-444
V-517
V-460
V-451
V-461
V-462
V-452
V-451
V-454
V-453
V-463
V-9
V-455
V-459
V-451
V-458
V-456
V-465
V-464a
V-476
V-480
V-466
V-478
V-473
2
3C

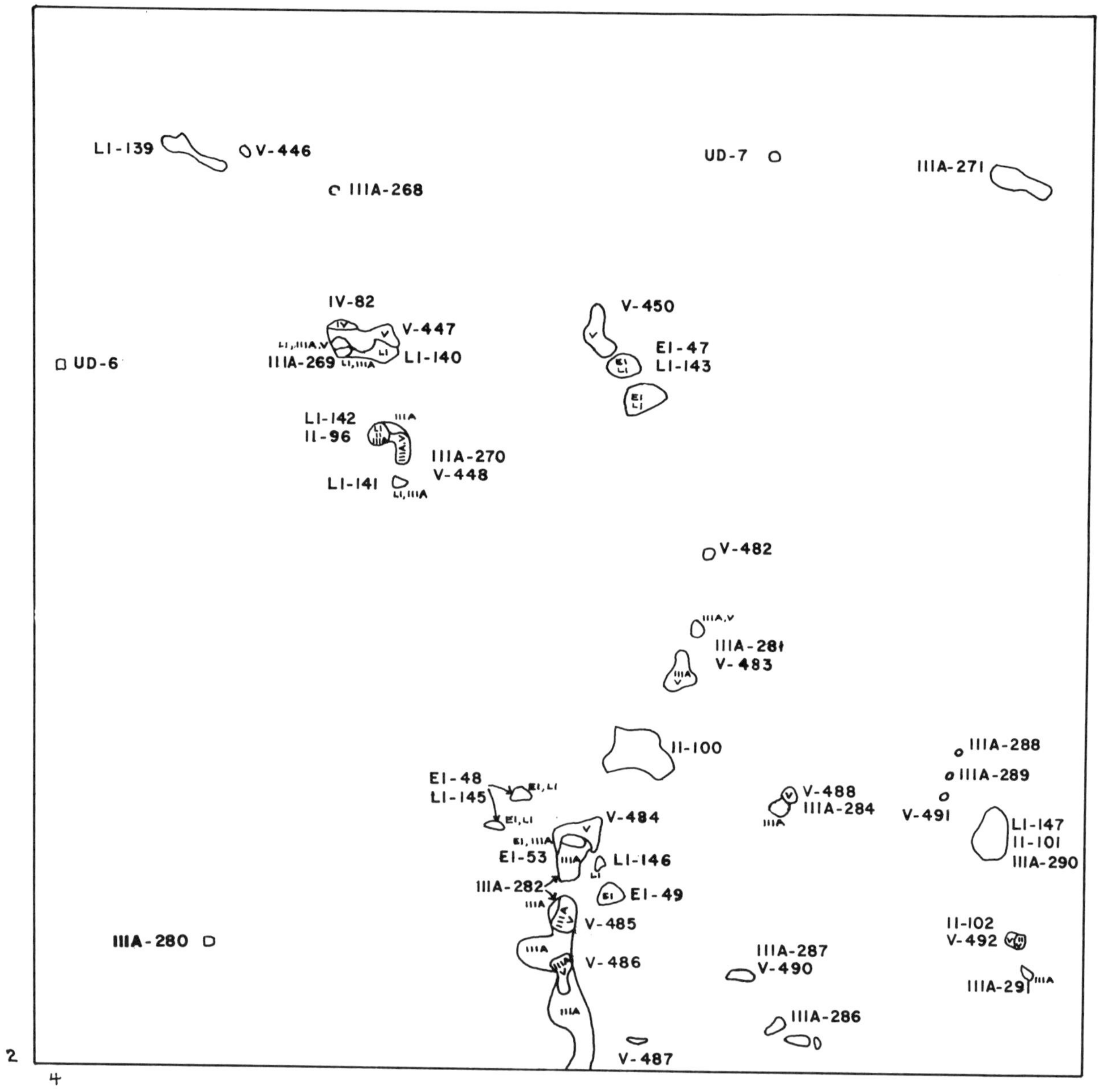
LI-139
V-446
IIIA-268
UD-7
IIIA-271
IV-82
V-447
IIIA-269
LI-140
UD-6
V-450
EI-47
LI-143
LI-142
II-96
IIIA-270
V-448
LI-141
V-482
IIIA-281
V-483
II-100
IIIA-288
IIIA-289
EI-48
LI-145
V-488
IIIA-284
V-491
V-484
LI-147
II-101
IIIA-290
EI-53
LI-146
IIIA-282
EI-49
V-485
II-102
V-492
IIIA-280
IIIA-287
V-490
V-486
IIIA-291
IIIA-286
V-487
2
4

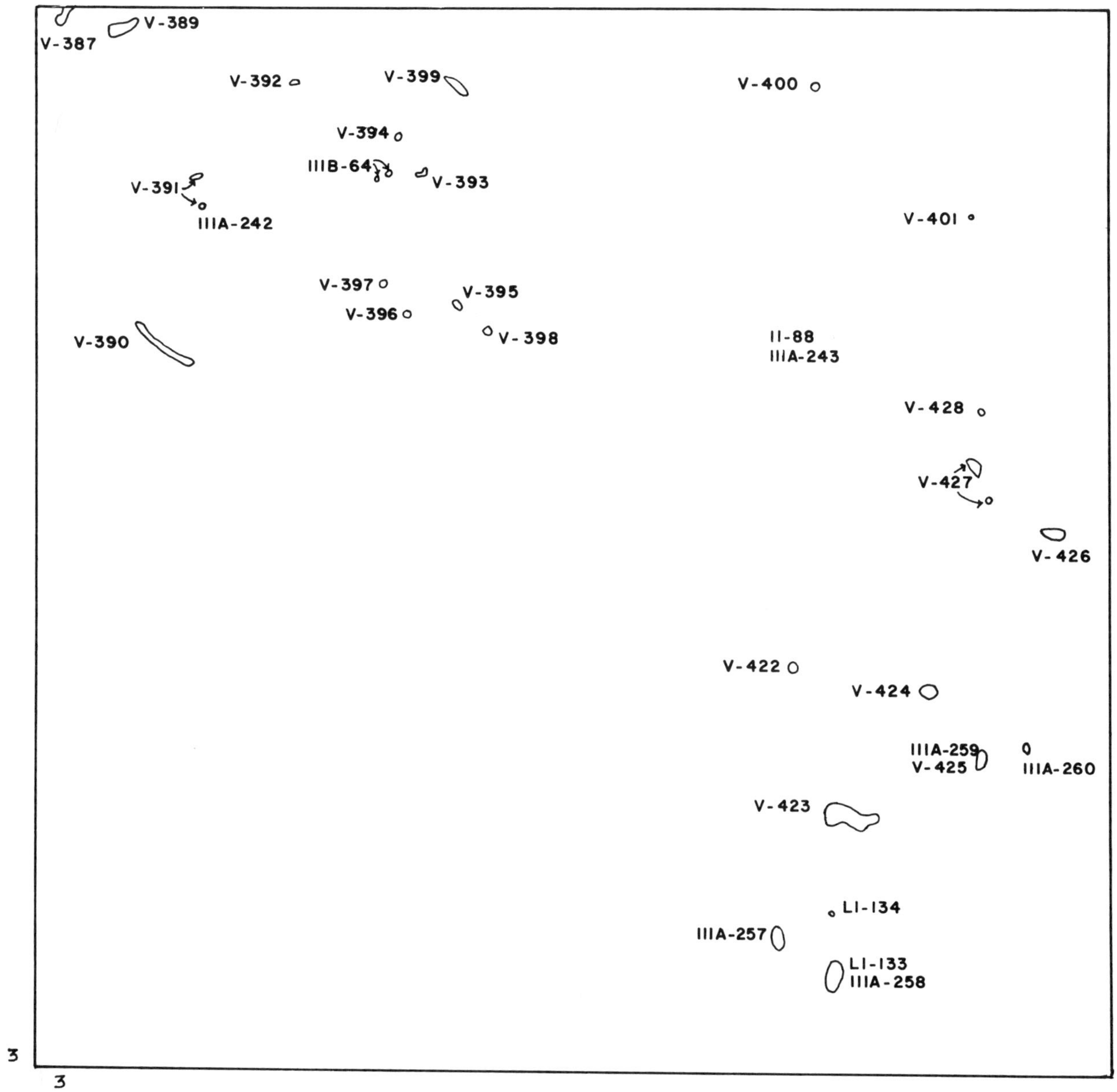
V-387
V-389
V-392
V-399
V-400
V-394
IIIB-64
V-393
V-391
IIIA-242
V-401
V-397
V-395
V-396
V-390
V-398
II-88
IIIA-243
V-428
V-427
V-426
V-422
V-424
IIIA-259
V-425
IIIA-260
V-423
LI-134
IIIA-257
LI-133
IIIA-258
3
3

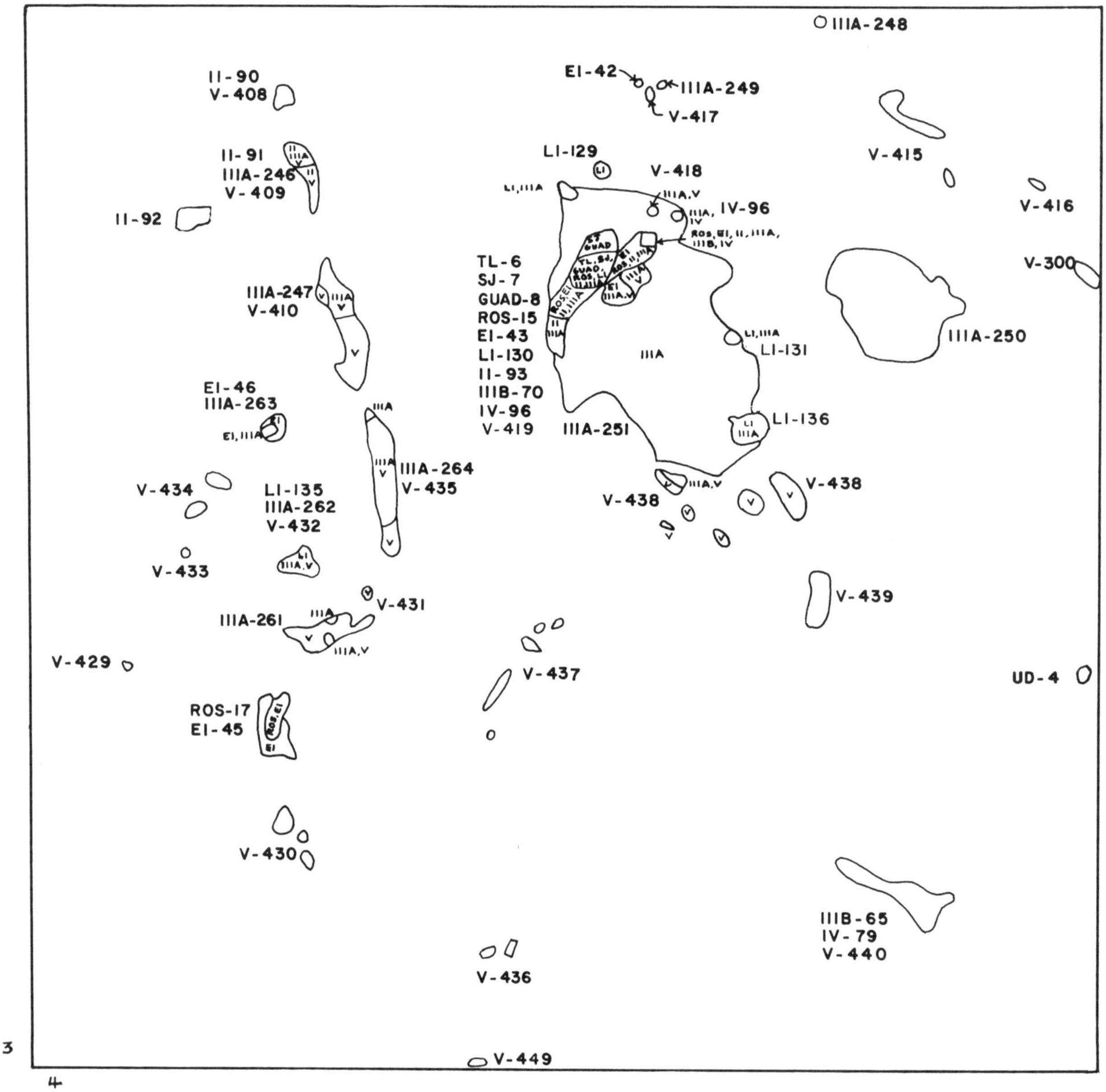

V-420
UD-5
3
5

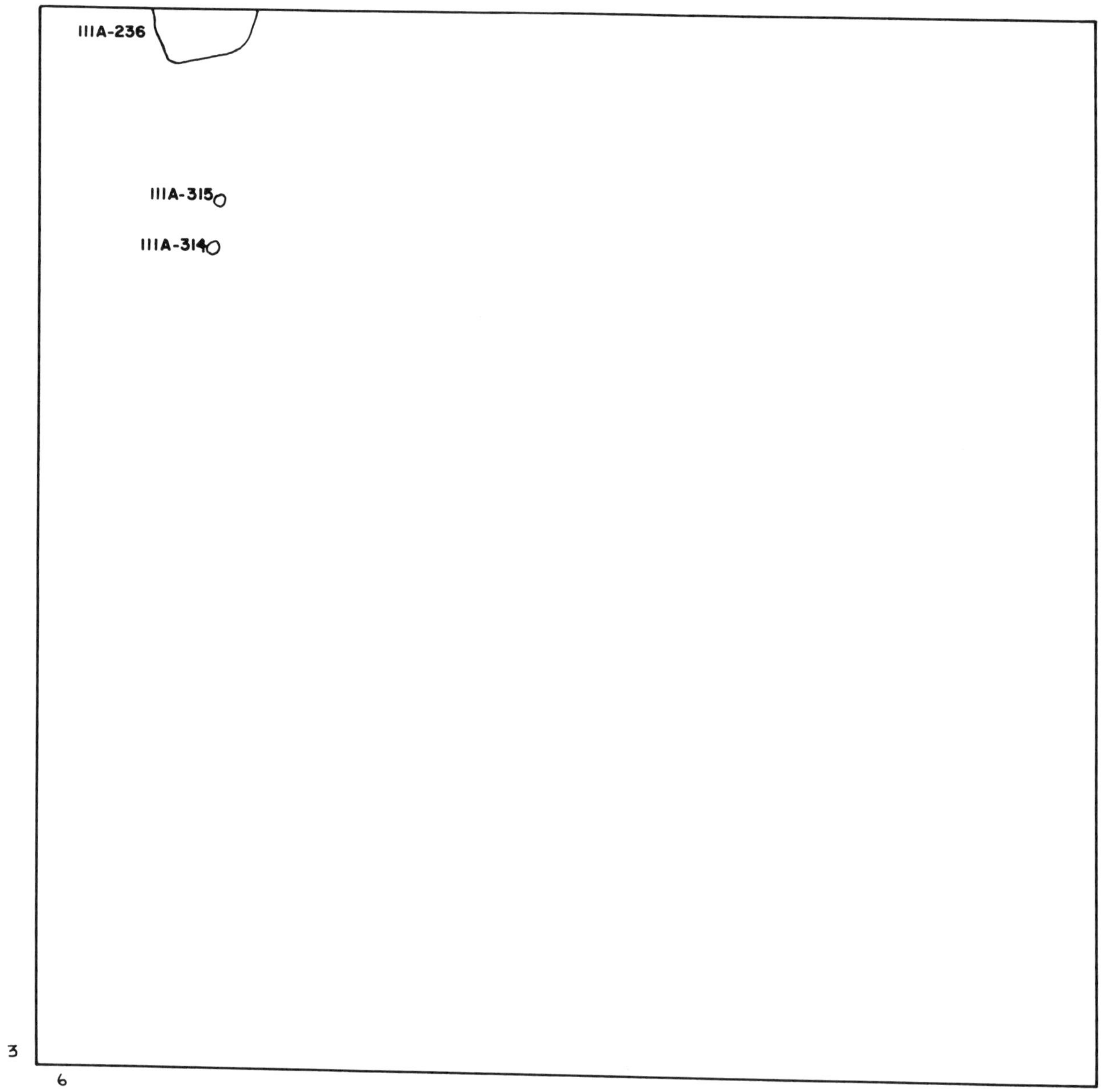
IIIA-236
IIIA-315
IIIA-314
3
6

V-345
IIIA-212
V-522
4
2

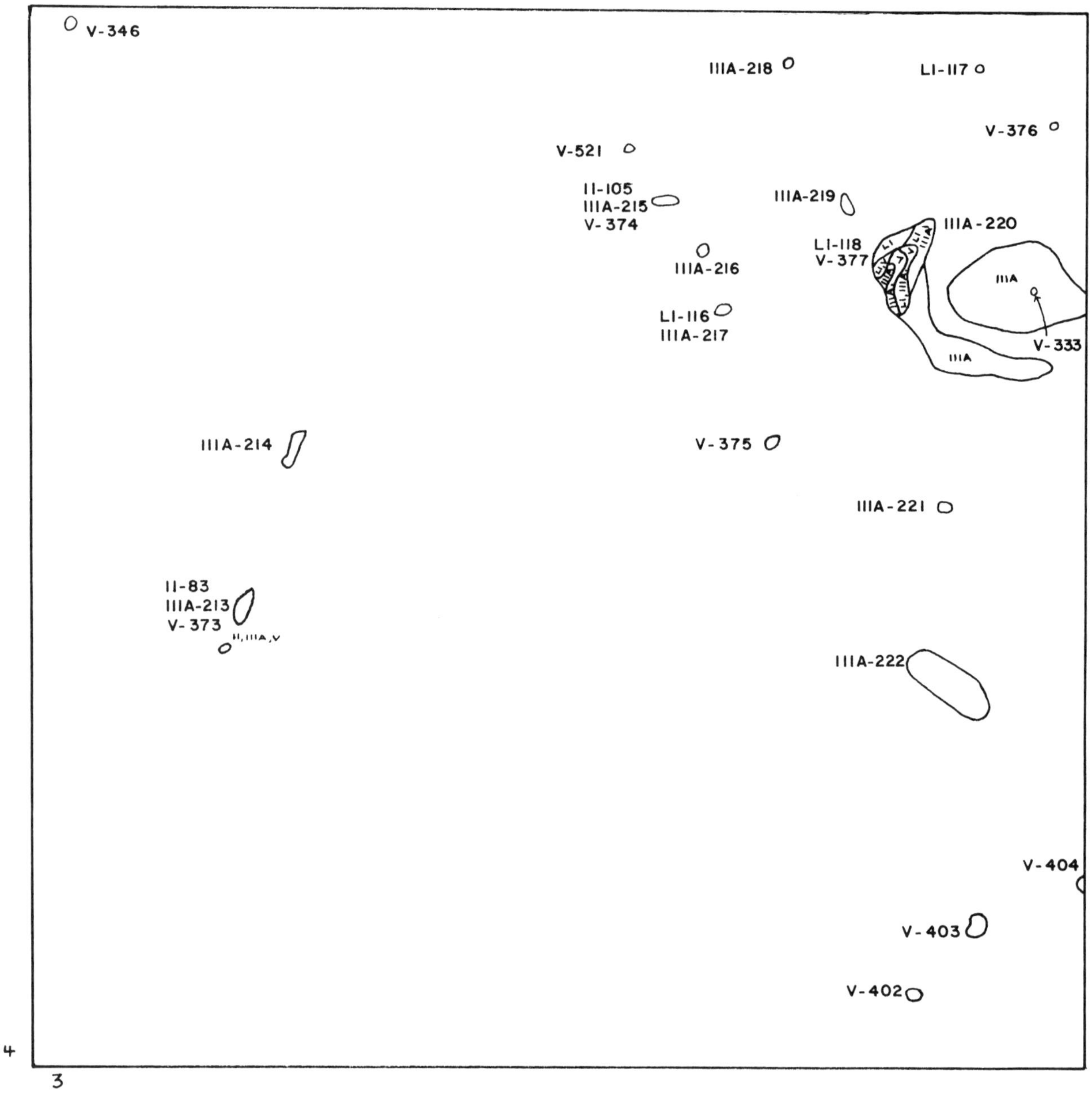
V-346
IIIA-218
LI-117
V-376
V-521
II-105
IIIA-215
V-374
IIIA-219
IIIA-220
LI-118
V-377
IIIA-216
IIIA
LI-116
IIIA-217
V-333
IIIA
IIIA-214
V-375
IIIA-221
II-83
IIIA-213
V-373
II, IIIA, V
IIIA-222
V-404
V-403
V-402
4
3

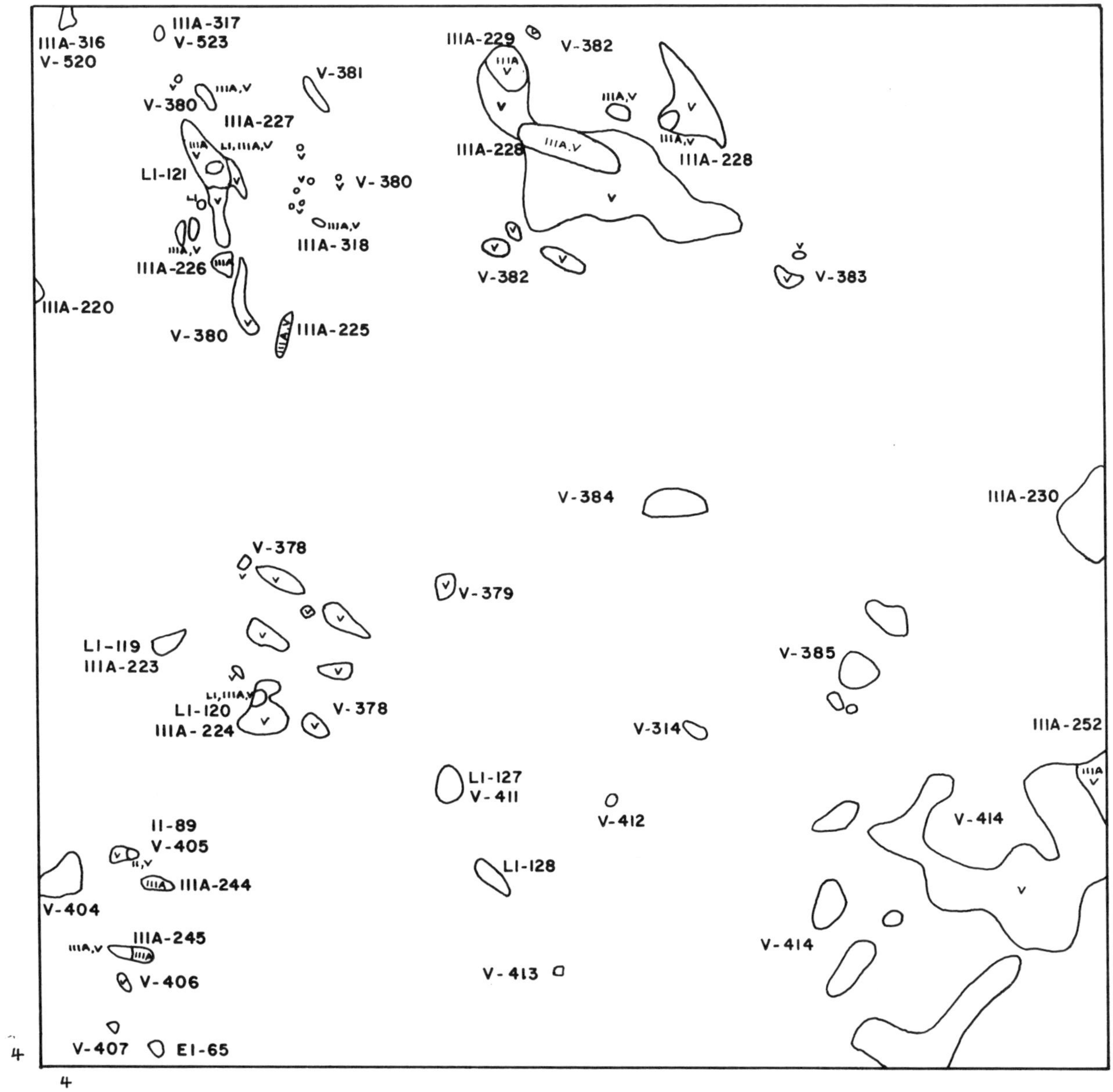
IIIA-316
V-520
IIIA-317
V-523
IIIA-229
V-382
V-381
V-380
IIIA-227
IIIA-228
IIIA-228
L1-121
V-380
IIIA-318
IIIA-226
V-382
V-383
IIIA-220
IIIA-225
V-380
V-384
IIIA-230
V-378
V-379
L1-119
IIIA-223
V-385
L1-120
IIIA-224
V-378
V-314
IIIA-252
L1-127
V-411
V-412
V-414
II-89
V-405
L1-128
IIIA-244
V-404
IIIA-245
V-414
V-413
V-406
V-407
E1-65
4
4

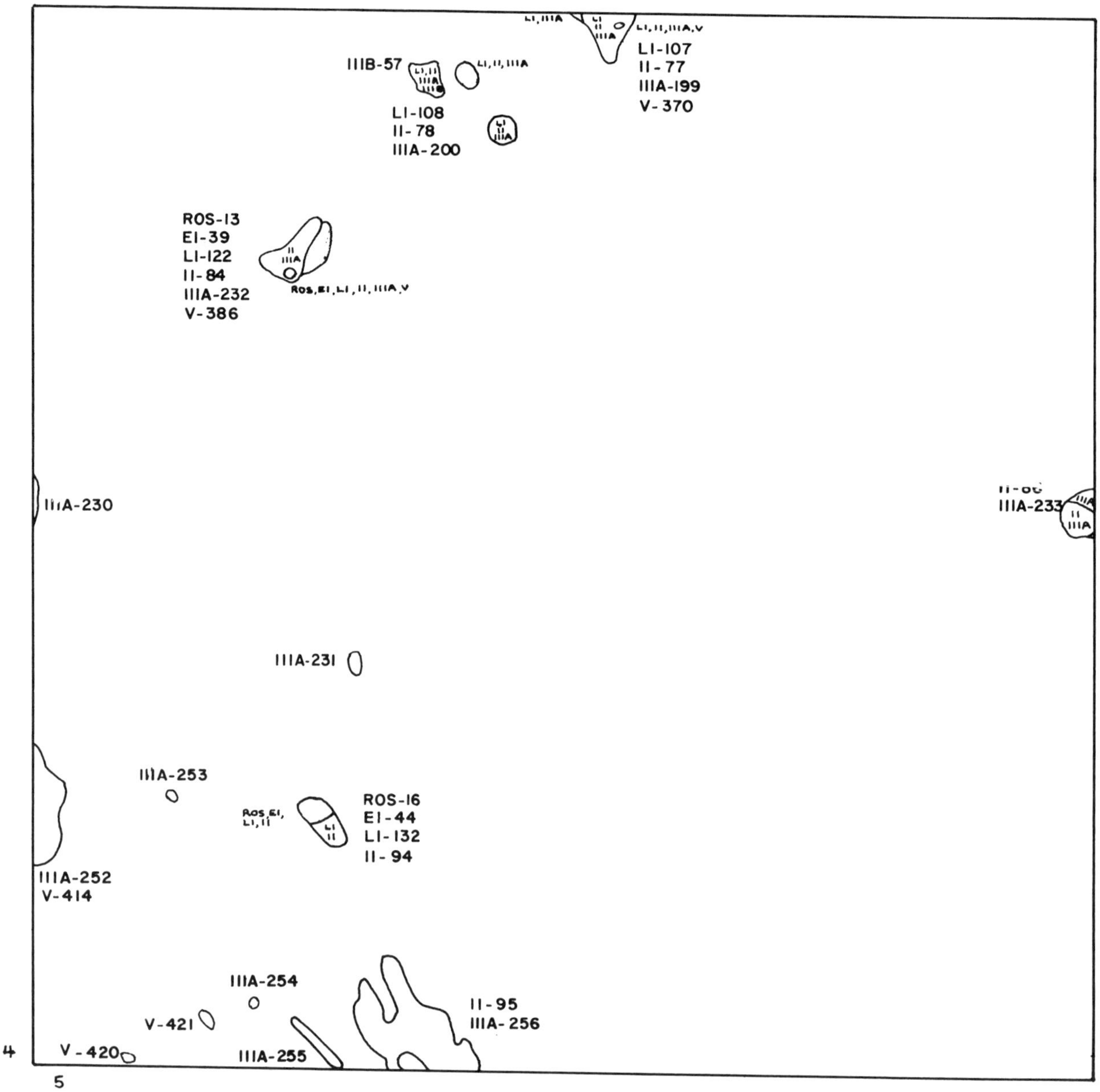
IIIB-57
LI-107
II-77
IIIA-199
V-370
LI-108
II-78
IIIA-200
ROS-13
EI-39
LI-122
II-84
IIIA-232
V-386
IIIA-230
IIIA-233
IIIA-231
IIIA-253
ROS-16
EI-44
LI-132
II-94
IIIA-252
V-414
IIIA-254
II-95
IIIA-256
V-421
V-420
IIIA-255
4
5

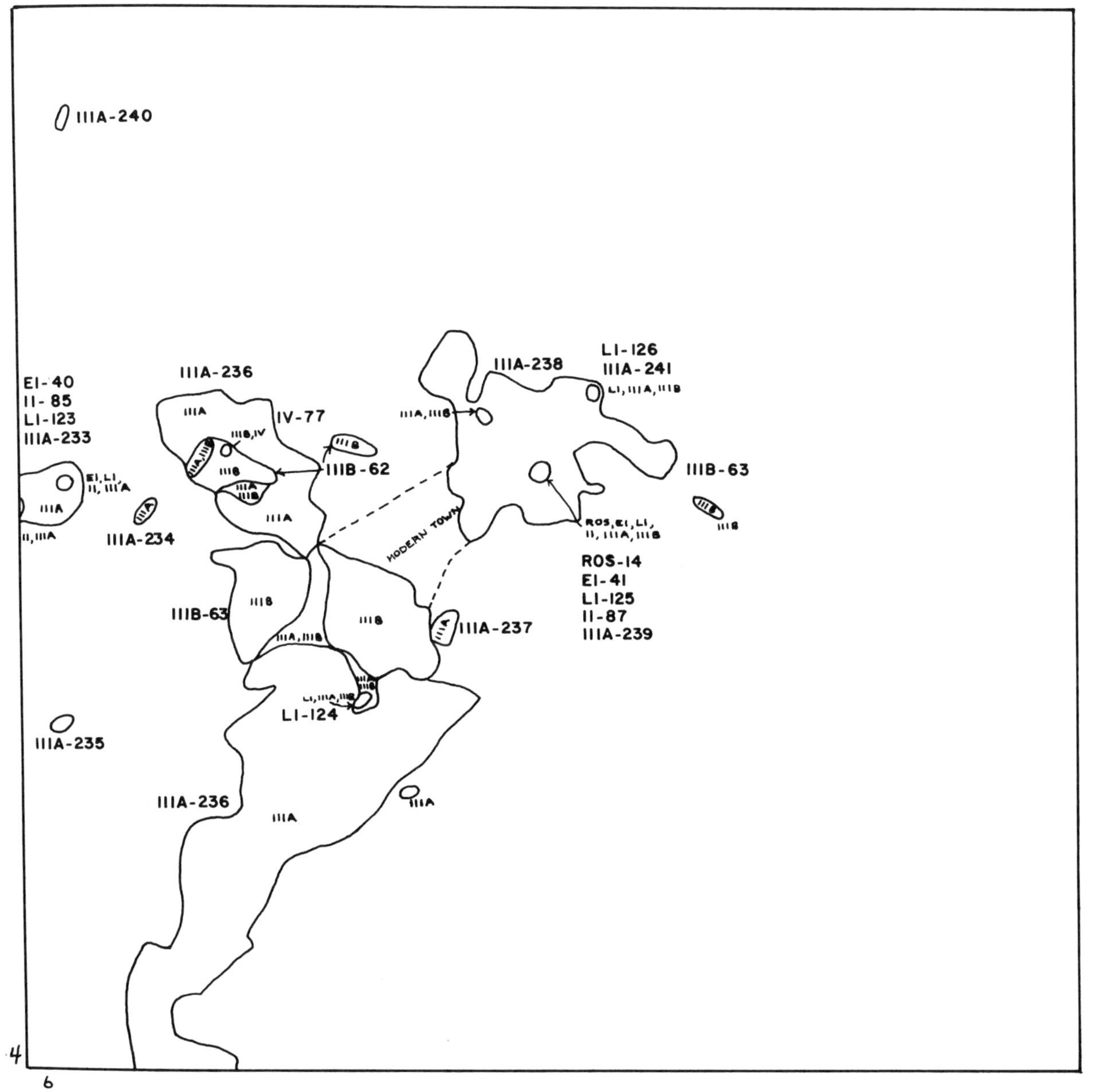
IIIA-240
EI-40
II-85
LI-123
IIIA-233
IIIA-236
IV-77
IIIA-238
LI-126
IIIA-241
IIIB-62
IIIB-63
IIIA-234
MODERN TOWN
ROS-14
EI-41
LI-125
II-87
IIIA-239
IIIB-63
IIIA-237
LI-124
IIIA-235
IIIA-236
4
6

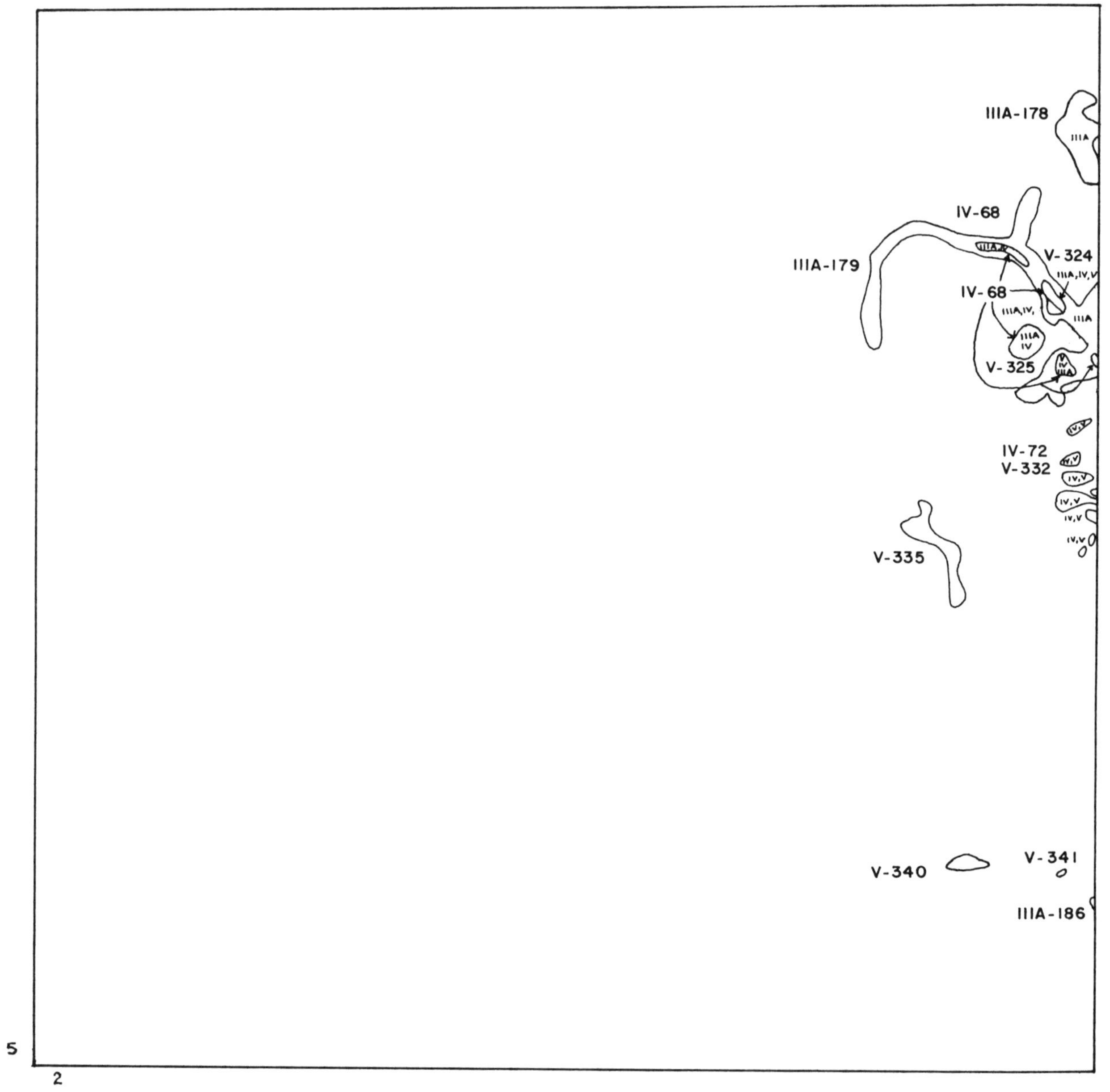
IIIA-178
IIIA
IV-68
IIIA-179
V-324
IIIA,IV,V
IV-68
IIIA,IV,
IIIA
IIIA
IV
V-325
IV-72
V-332
IV,V
IV,V
IV,V
IV,V
V-335
V-340
V-341
IIIA-186
5
2

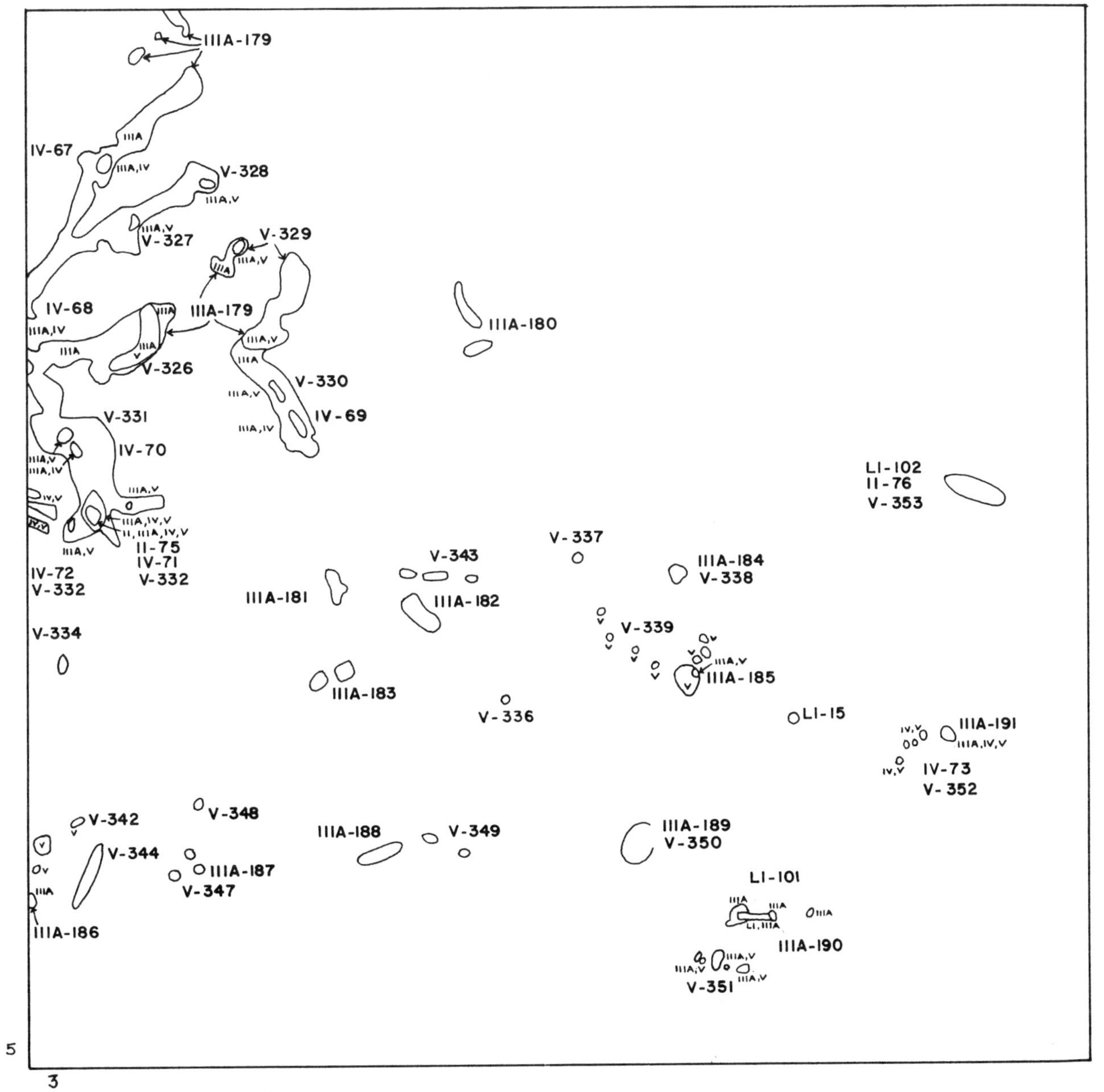
IIIA-179
IV-67
V-328
V-327
V-329
IV-68
IIIA-179
IIIA-180
V-326
V-330
IV-69
V-331
IV-70
LI-102
II-76
V-353
II-75
IV-71
V-332
IV-72
V-332
V-337
V-343
IIIA-184
V-338
IIIA-181
IIIA-182
V-334
V-339
IIIA-185
IIIA-183
V-336
LI-15
IIIA-191
IV-73
V-352
V-342
V-348
IIIA-188
V-349
IIIA-189
V-350
V-344
IIIA-187
V-347
LI-101
IIIA-186
IIIA-190
V-351
5
3

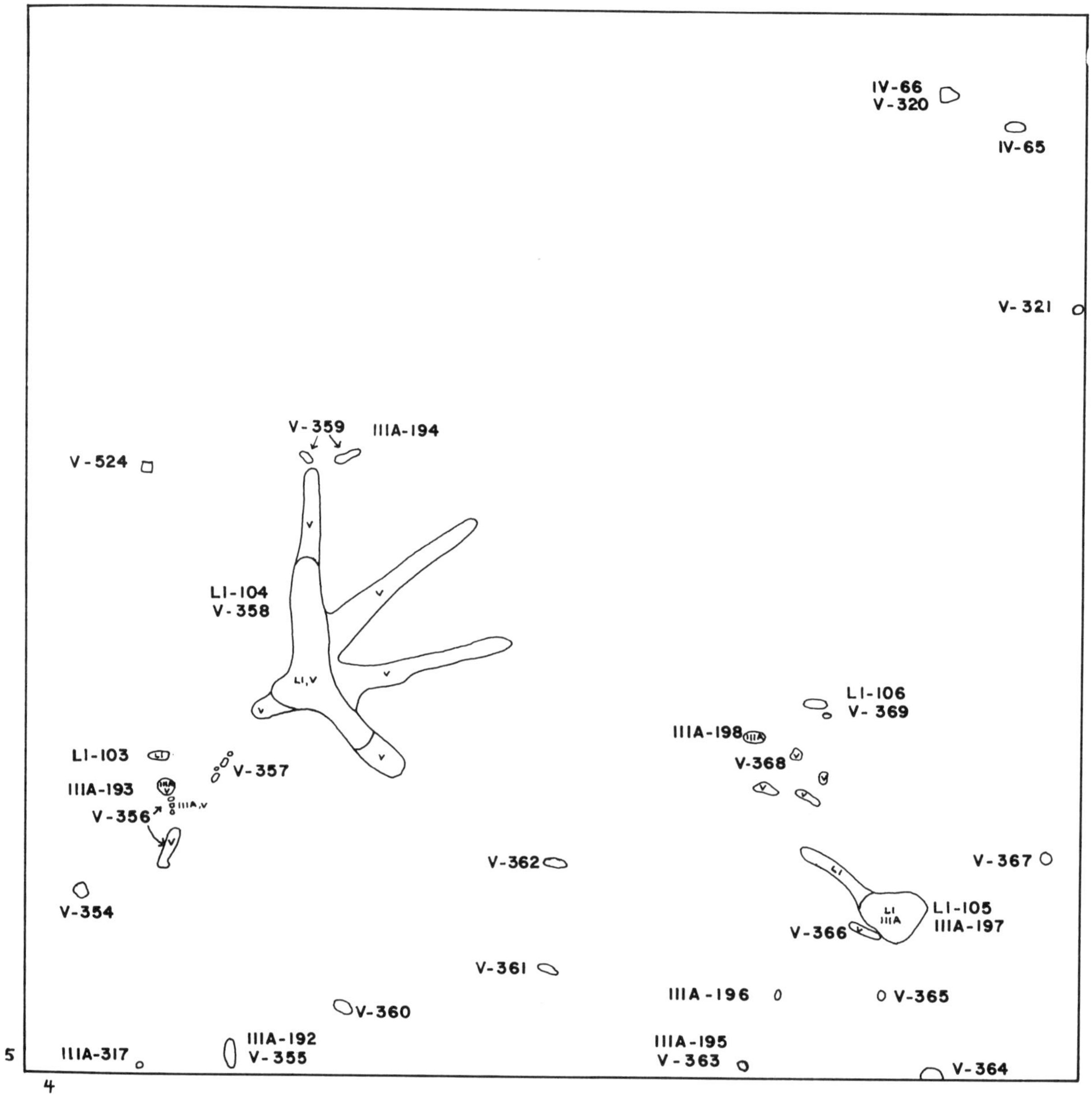
IV-66
V-320
IV-65
V-321
V-359
IIIA-194
V-524
LI-104
V-358
LI,V
LI-106
V-369
IIIA-198
V-368
LI-103
V-357
IIIA-193
IIIA,V
V-356
V-362
V-367
V-354
LI-105
IIIA-197
V-366
V-361
IIIA-196
V-365
V-360
IIIA-317
IIIA-192
V-355
IIIA-195
V-363
V-364
5
4

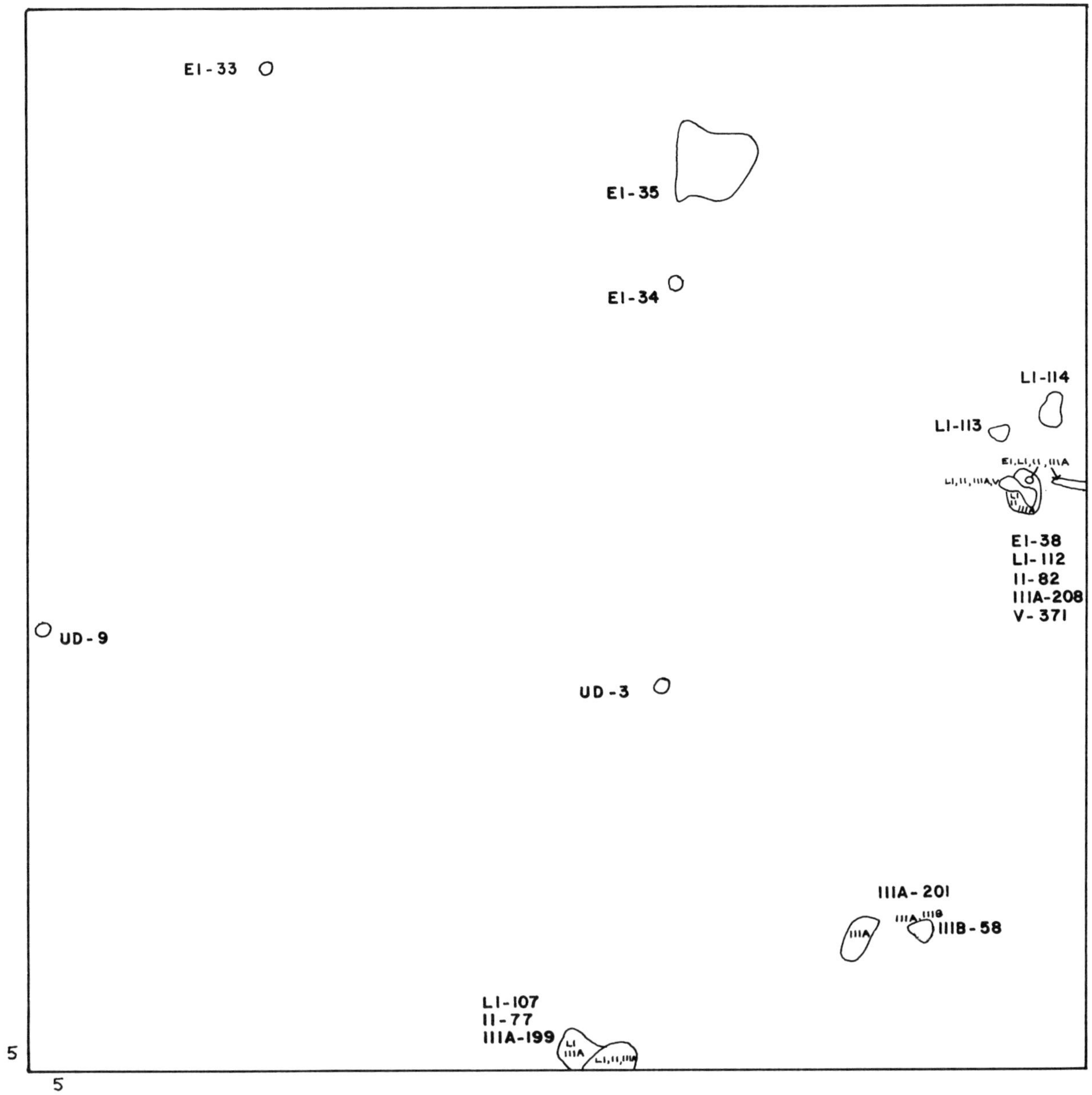
EI-33
EI-35
EI-34
LI-114
LI-113
EI-38
LI-112
II-82
IIIA-208
V-371
UD-9
UD-3
IIIA-201
IIIB-58
LI-107
II-77
IIIA-199
5
5

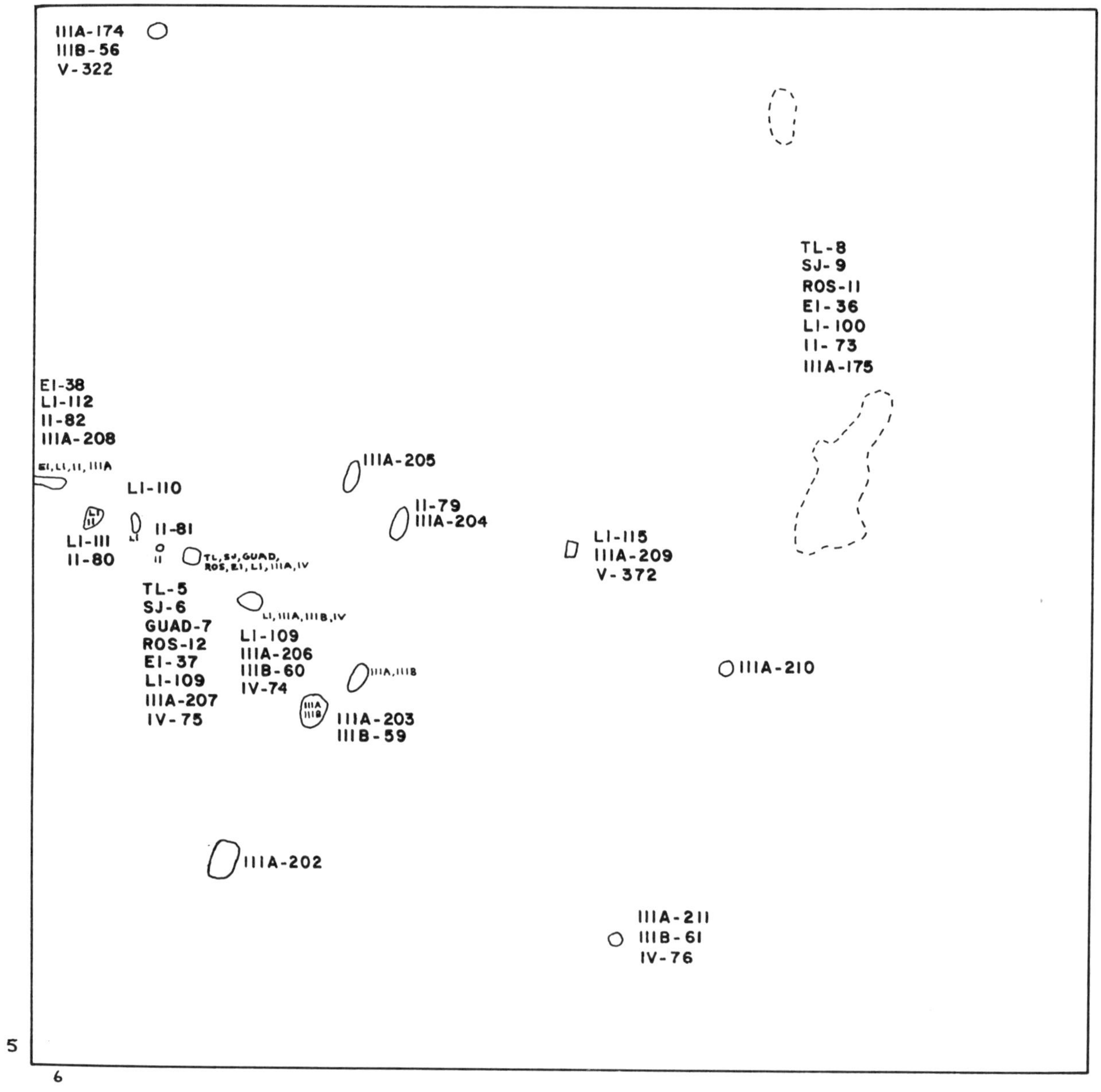
IIIA-174
IIIB-56
V-322
TL-8
SJ-9
ROS-11
EI-36
LI-100
II-73
IIIA-175
EI-38
LI-112
II-82
IIIA-208
EI, LI, II, IIIA
LI-110
IIIA-205
II-79
IIIA-204
LI
II
II-81
LI-111
II-80
II
TL, SJ, GUAD, ROS, EI, LI, IIIA, IV
LI-115
IIIA-209
V-372
TL-5
SJ-6
GUAD-7
ROS-12
EI-37
LI-109
IIIA-207
IV-75
LI, IIIA, IIIB, IV
LI-109
IIIA-206
IIIB-60
IV-74
IIIA, IIIB
IIIA-210
IIIA
IIIB
IIIA-203
IIIB-59
IIIA-202
IIIA-211
IIIB-61
IV-76
5
6

II-74
IIIA-176
II, IIIA
5
8

IIIA-177
IIIA-179
6
3

IIIA
V
IIIA-141
V-270
IIIA-142
V-272
IIIA-140
6
4

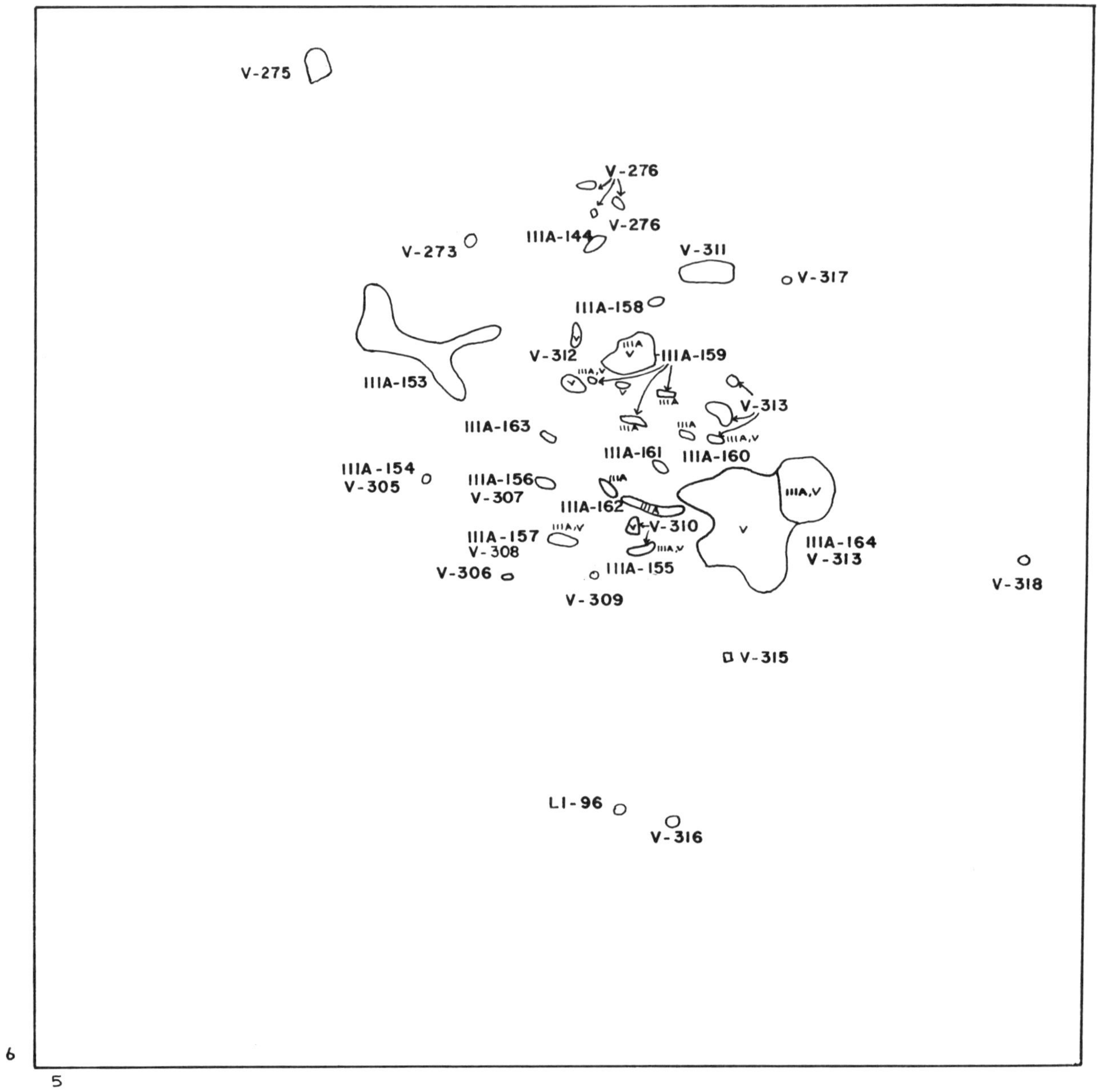
V-275
V-276
V-276
IIIA-144
V-273
V-311
V-317
IIIA-158
IIIA-153
V-312
IIIA-159
V-313
IIIA-163
IIIA-161
IIIA-160
IIIA-154
V-305
IIIA-156
V-307
IIIA-162
V-310
IIIA-157
V-308
IIIA-164
V-313
V-306
IIIA-155
V-309
V-318
V-315
LI-96
V-316
6
5

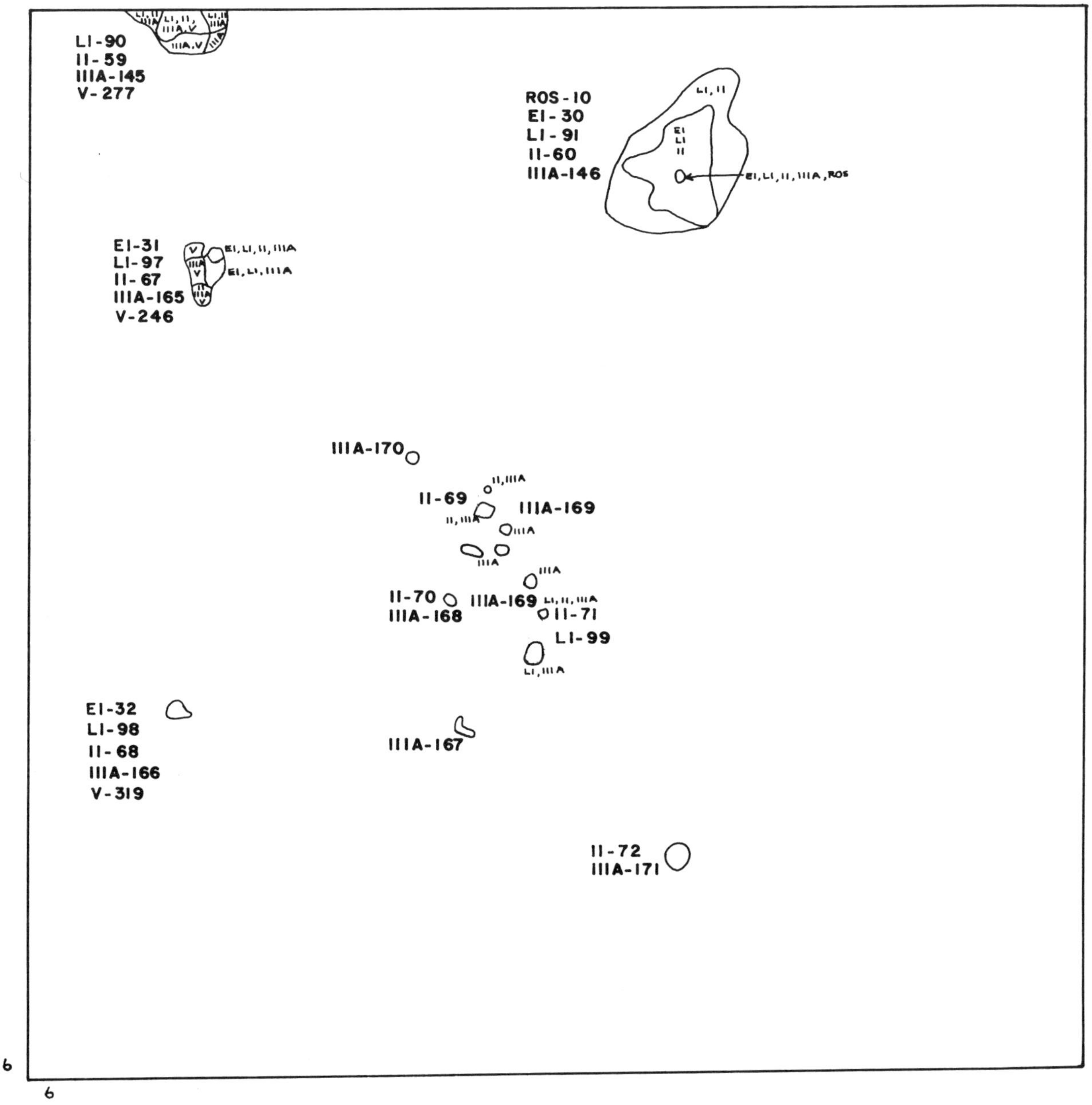
LI-90
II-59
IIIA-145
V-277
ROS-10
EI-30
LI-91
II-60
IIIA-146
EI-31
LI-97
II-67
IIIA-165
V-246
IIIA-170
II-69
IIIA-169
II-70
IIIA-168
IIIA-169
II-71
LI-99
EI-32
LI-98
II-68
IIIA-166
V-319
IIIA-167
II-72
IIIA-171
6
6

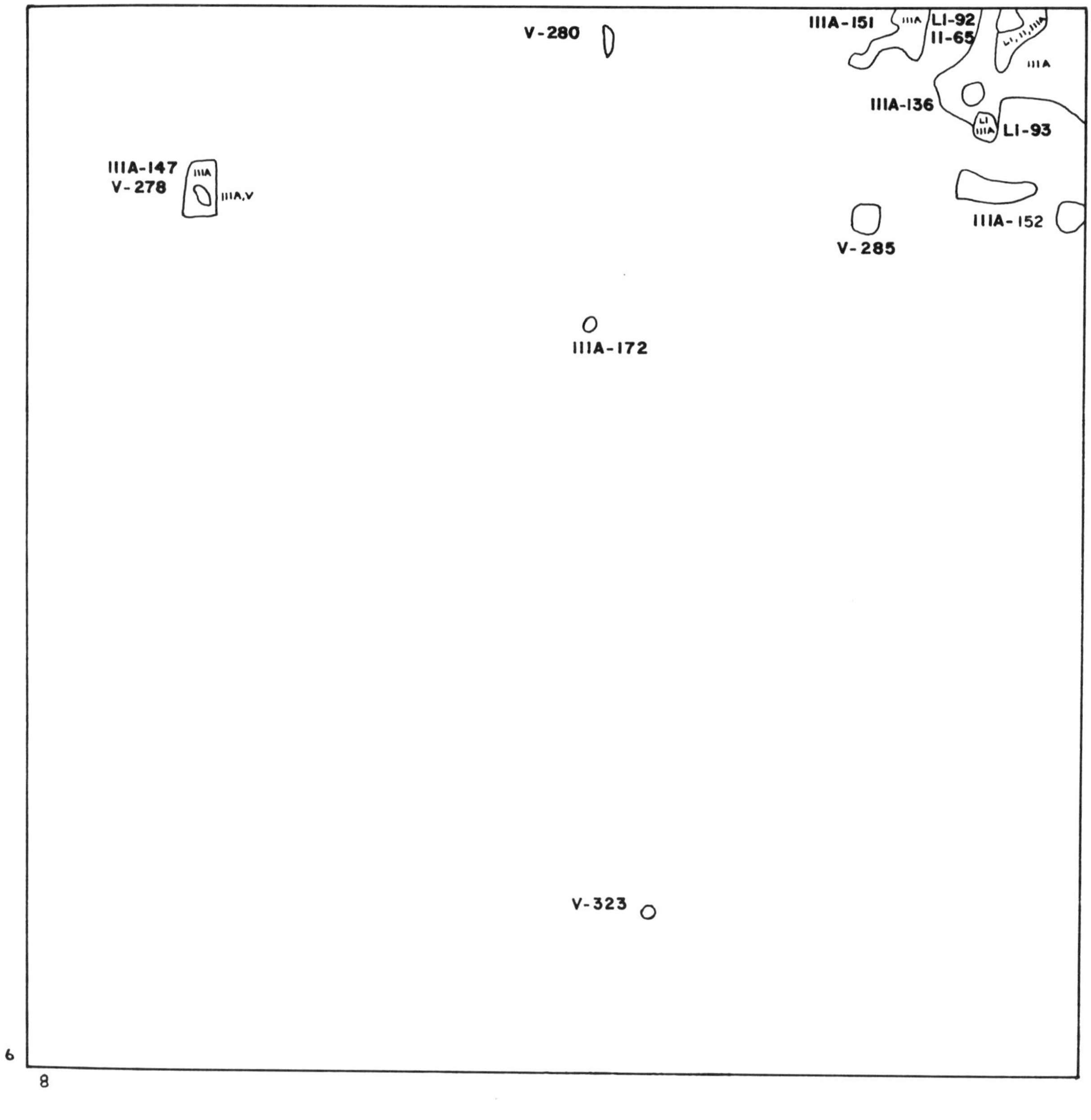
V-280
IIIA-151
IIIA
LI-92
II-65
LI, II, IIIA
IIIA
IIIA-136
LI
IIIA
LI-93
IIIA-147
V-278
IIIA
IIIA,V
IIIA-152
V-285
IIIA-172
V-323
6
8

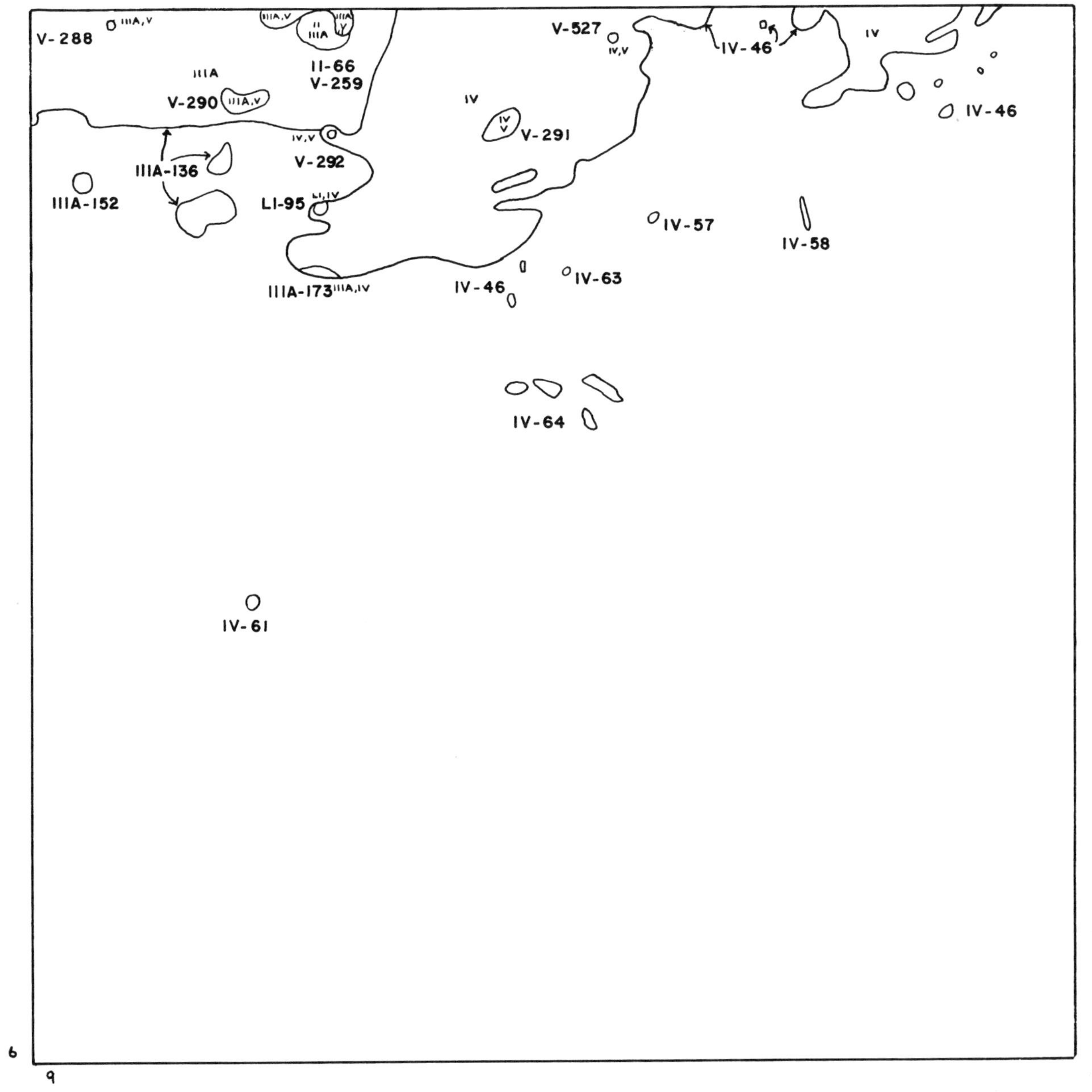
V-288
IIIA,V
IIIA,V
II
IIIA
IIIA
V
IIIA
II-66
V-259
V-290
IIIA,V
IV,V
V-292
IIIA-136
IIIA-152
LI-95
LI,IV
IIIA-173
IIIA,IV
V-527
IV,V
IV-46
IV
IV
IV
V
V-291
IV-46
IV-57
IV-58
IV-46
IV-63
IV-64
IV-61
6
9

IV-46
IV-59
6
10

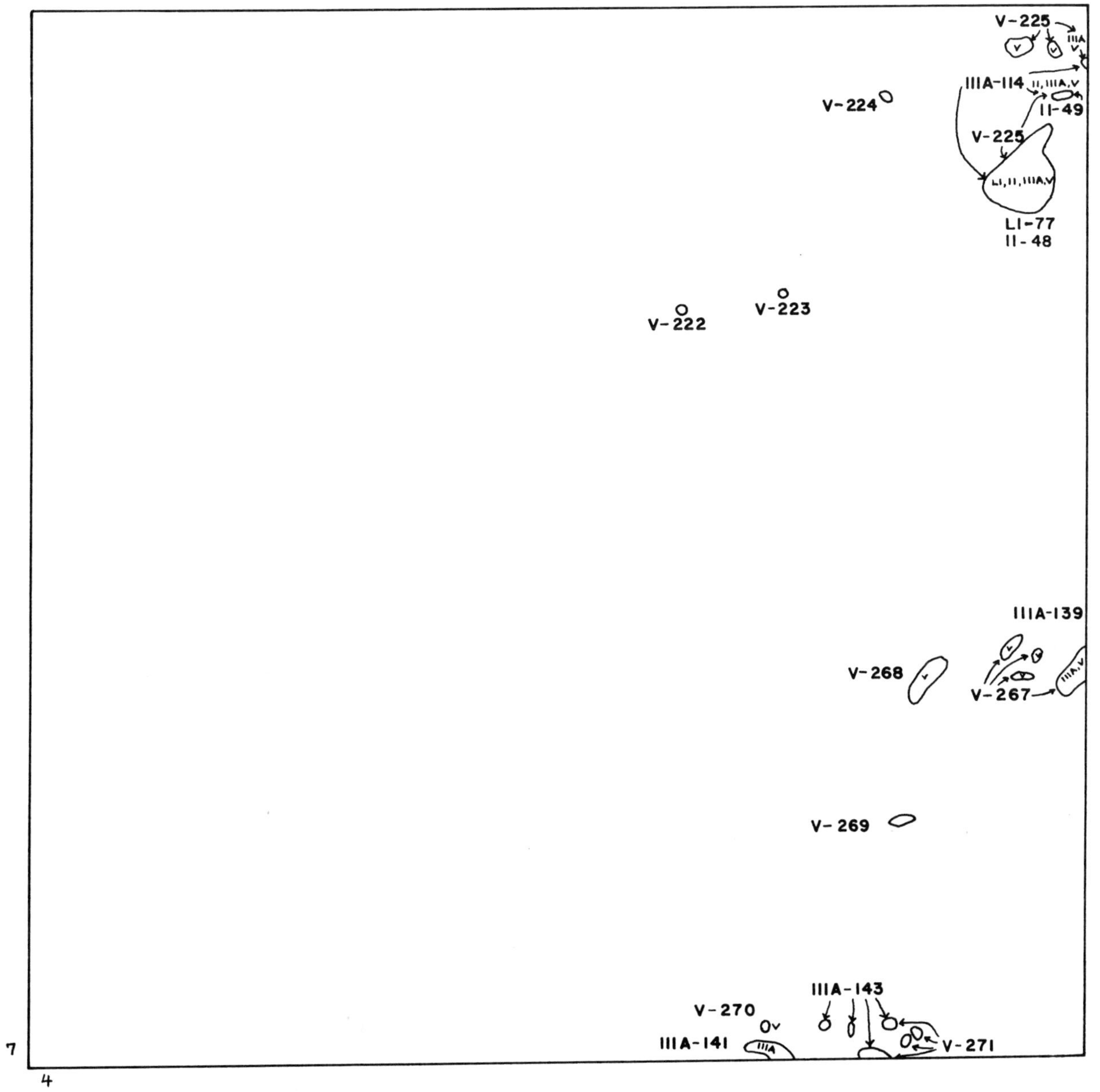
V-225
IIIA
V
IIIA-114
II,IIIA,V
II-49
V-224
V-225
LI,II,IIIA,V
LI-77
II-48
V-222
V-223
IIIA-139
V-268
V-267
IIIA,V
V-269
IIIA-143
V-270
IIIA-141
IIIA
V-271
7
4

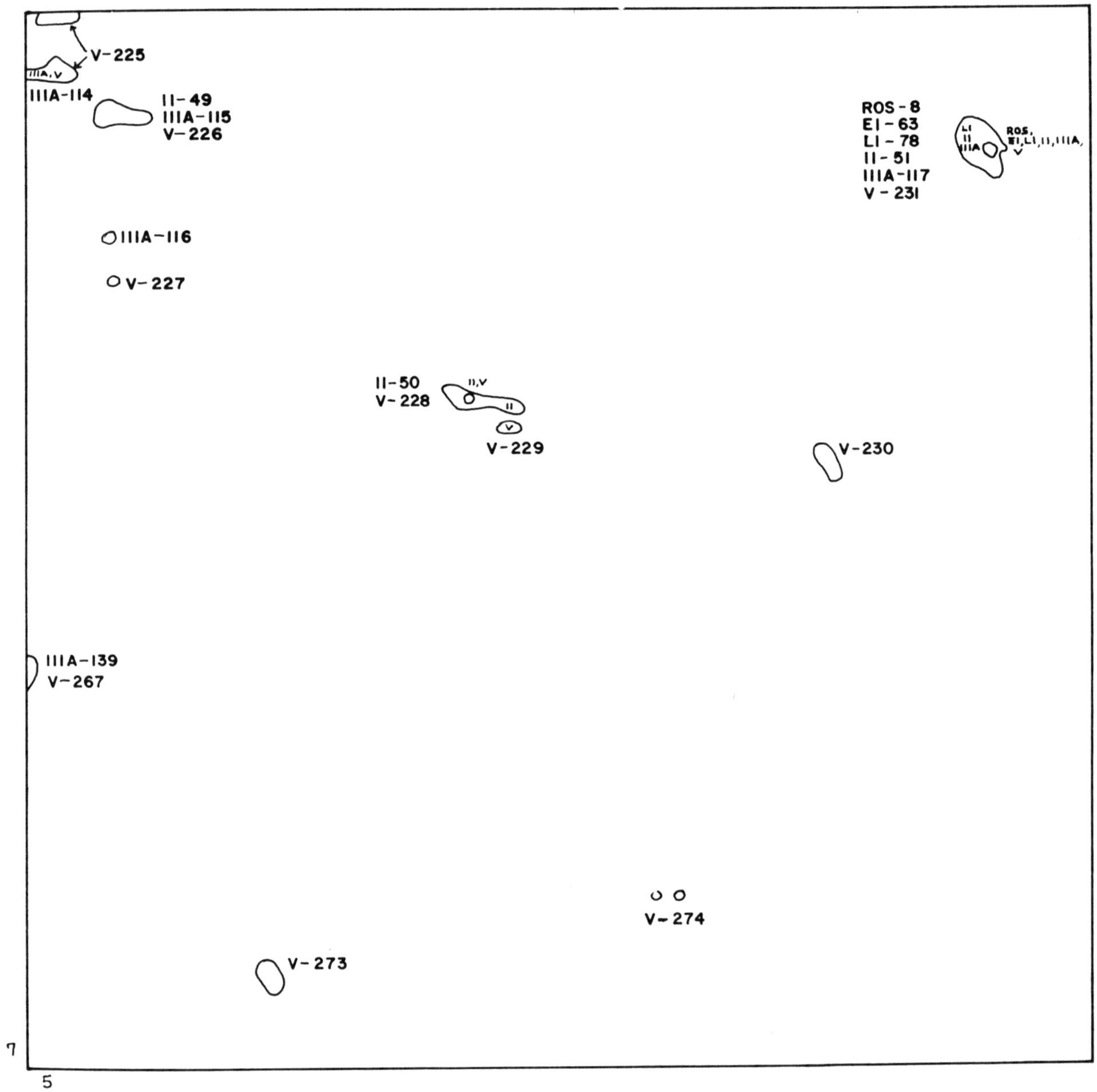
V-225
IIIA,V
IIIA-114
II-49
IIIA-115
V-226
ROS-8
EI-63
LI-78
II-51
IIIA-117
V-231
ROS,
EI,LI,II,IIIA,
V
IIIA-116
V-227
II-50
V-228
II,V
II
V
V-229
V-230
IIIA-139
V-267
V-274
V-273
7
5

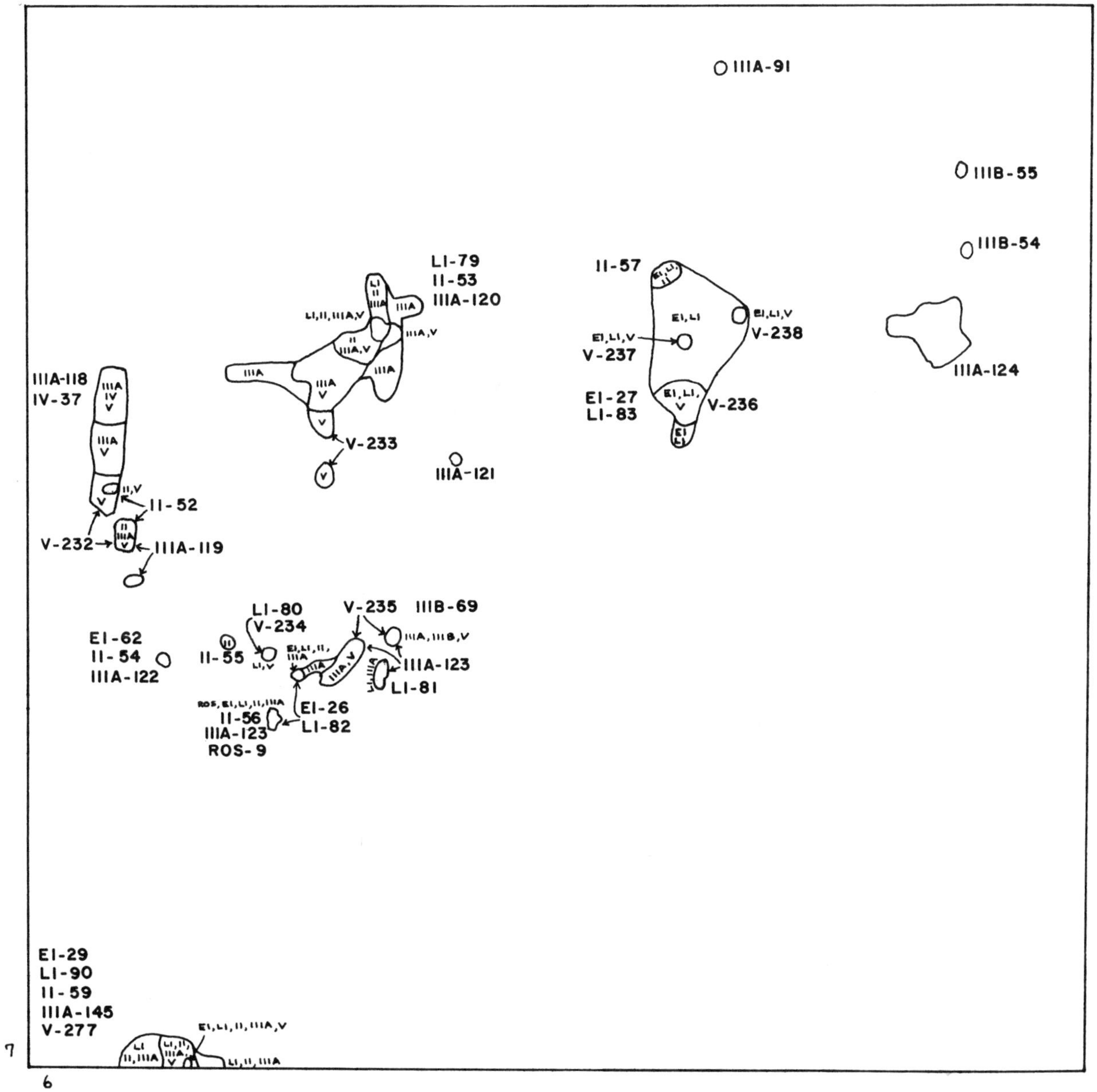
IIIA-91
IIIB-55
IIIB-54
LI-79
II-53
IIIA-120
II-57
V-238
V-237
EI-27
LI-83
V-236
IIIA-124
IIIA-118
IV-37
V-233
IIIA-121
II-52
V-232
IIIA-119
LI-80
V-234
V-235
IIIB-69
EI-62
II-54
IIIA-122
II-55
IIIA-123
LI-81
EI-26
LI-82
II-56
IIIA-123
ROS-9
EI-29
LI-90
II-59
IIIA-145
V-277
7
6

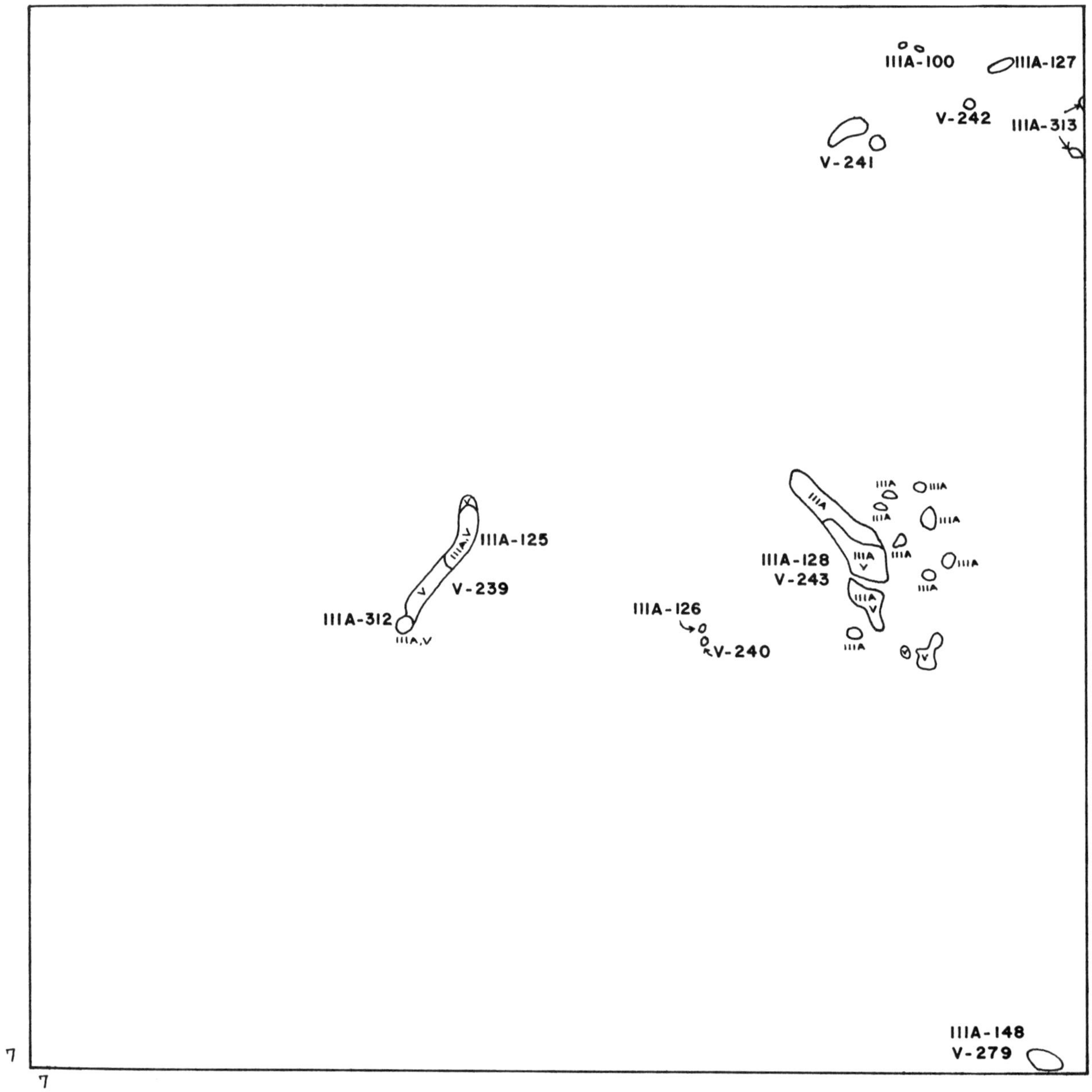
IIIA-100
IIIA-127
V-242
IIIA-313
V-241
IIIA-125
V-239
IIIA-312
IIIA,V
IIIA-128
V-243
IIIA-126
V-240
IIIA-148
V-279
7
7

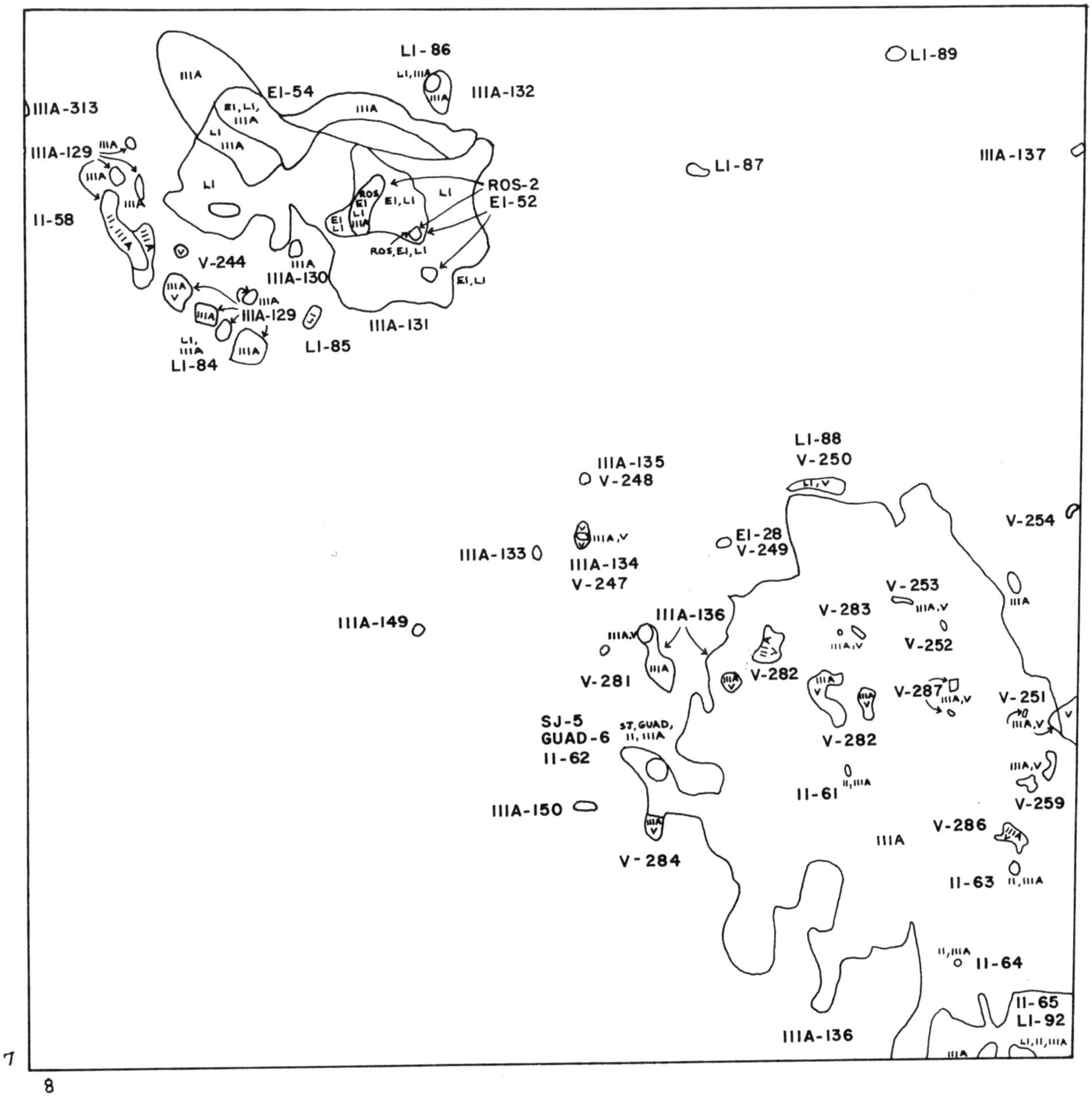
LI-86
LI-89
IIIA-132
EI-54
IIIA-313
IIIA-129
LI-87
IIIA-137
ROS-2
EI-52
II-58
V-244
IIIA-130
IIIA-129
LI-85
IIIA-131
LI-84
LI-88
V-250
IIIA-135
V-248
V-254
EI-28
V-249
IIIA-133
IIIA-134
V-247
V-253
V-283
IIIA-136
IIIA-149
V-252
V-281
V-282
V-287
V-251
V-282
SJ-5
GUAD-6
II-62
II-61
V-259
IIIA-150
V-286
IIIA
V-284
II-63
II-64
II-65
LI-92
IIIA-136
7
8

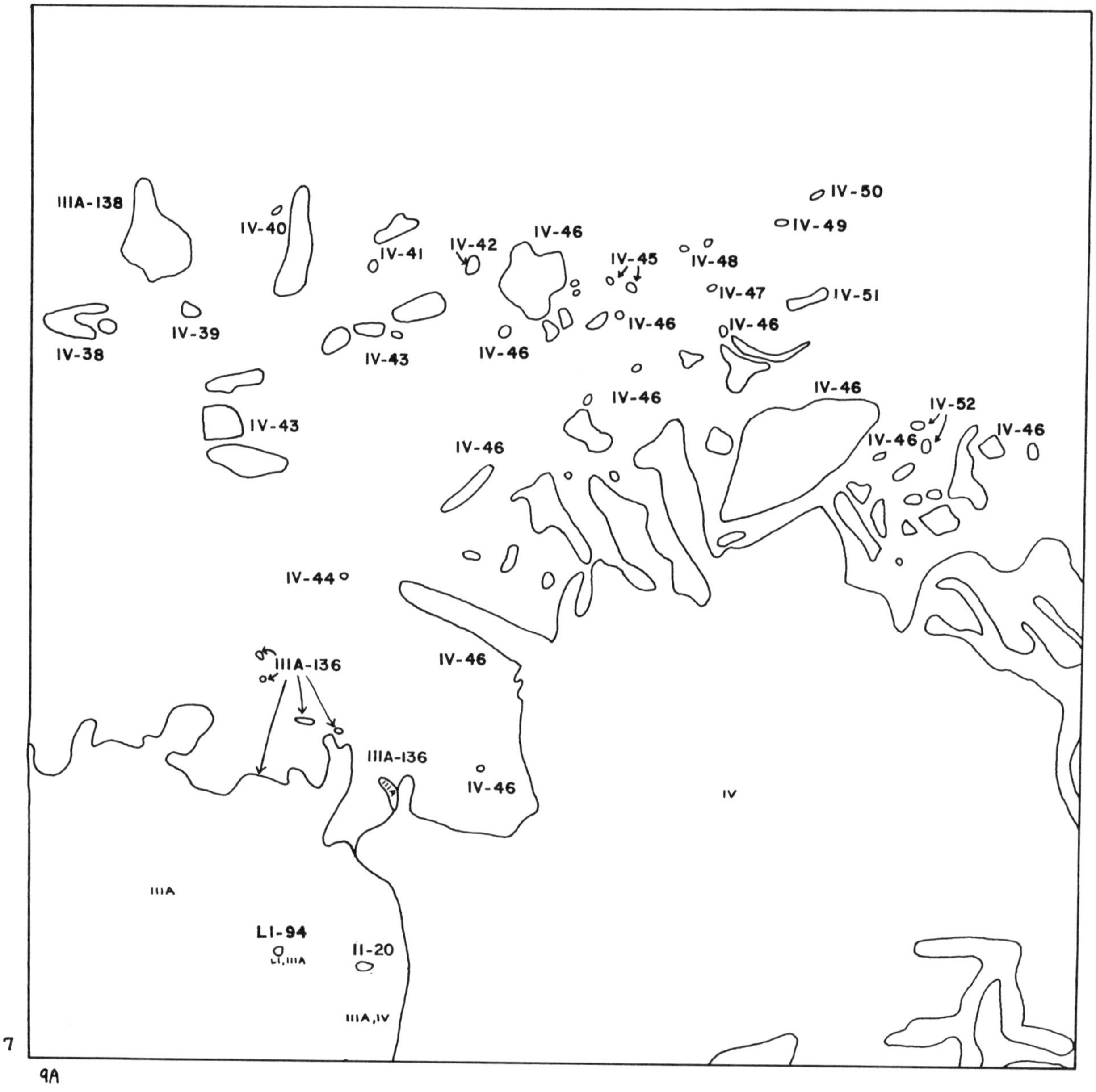
IIIA-138
IV-40
IV-41
IV-42
IV-46
IV-45
IV-48
IV-50
IV-49
IV-47
IV-51
IV-38
IV-39
IV-43
IV-46
IV-46
IV-46
IV-46
IV-43
IV-46
IV-52
IV-46
IV-46
IV-46
IV-44
IIIA-136
IV-46
IIIA-136
IV-46
IV
IIIA
LI-94
LI, IIIA
II-20
IIIA, IV
7
9A

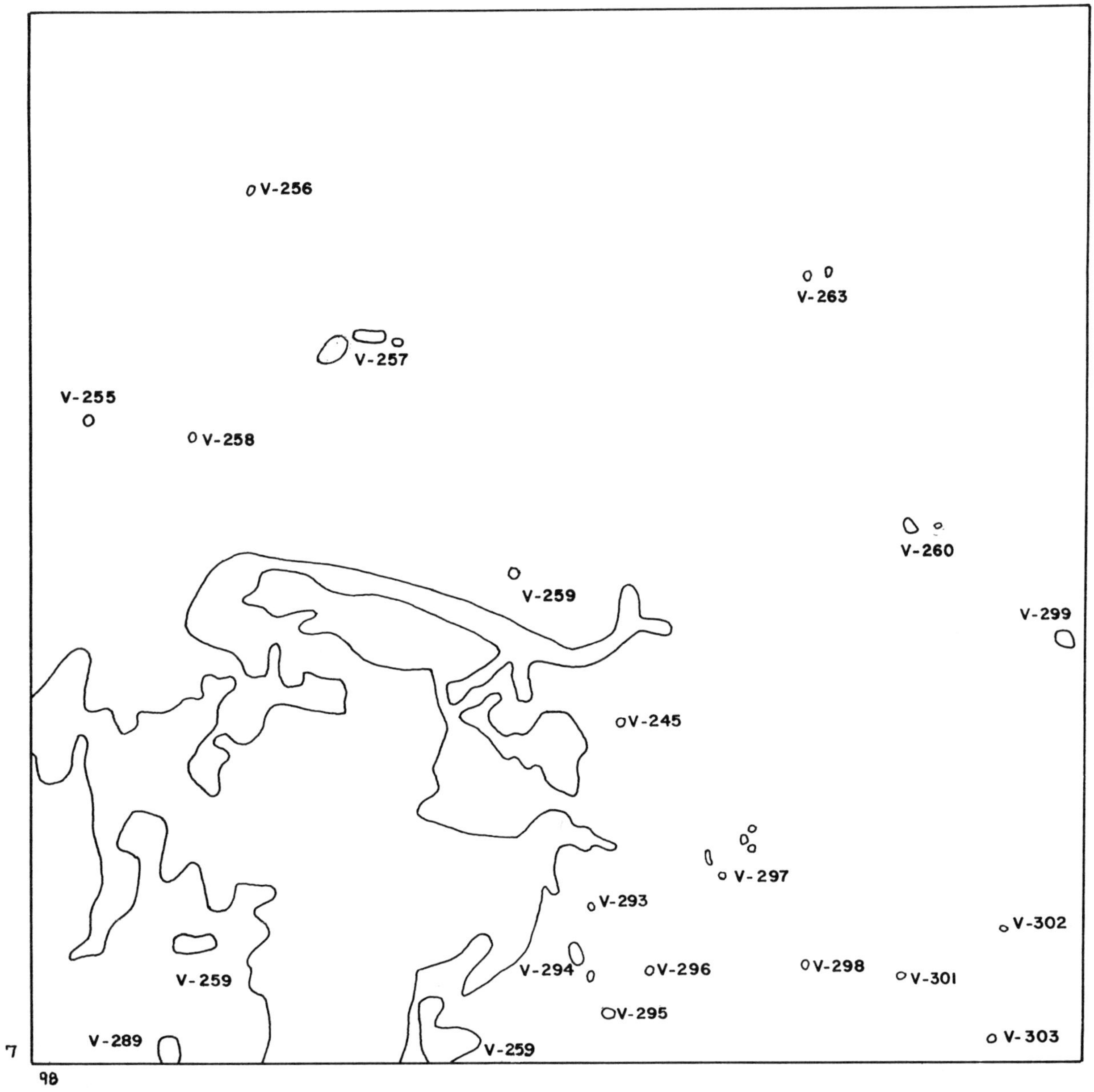
V-256
V-263
V-257
V-255
V-258
V-260
V-259
V-299
V-245
V-297
V-293
V-302
V-259
V-294
V-296
V-298
V-301
V-295
V-289
V-259
V-303
7
98

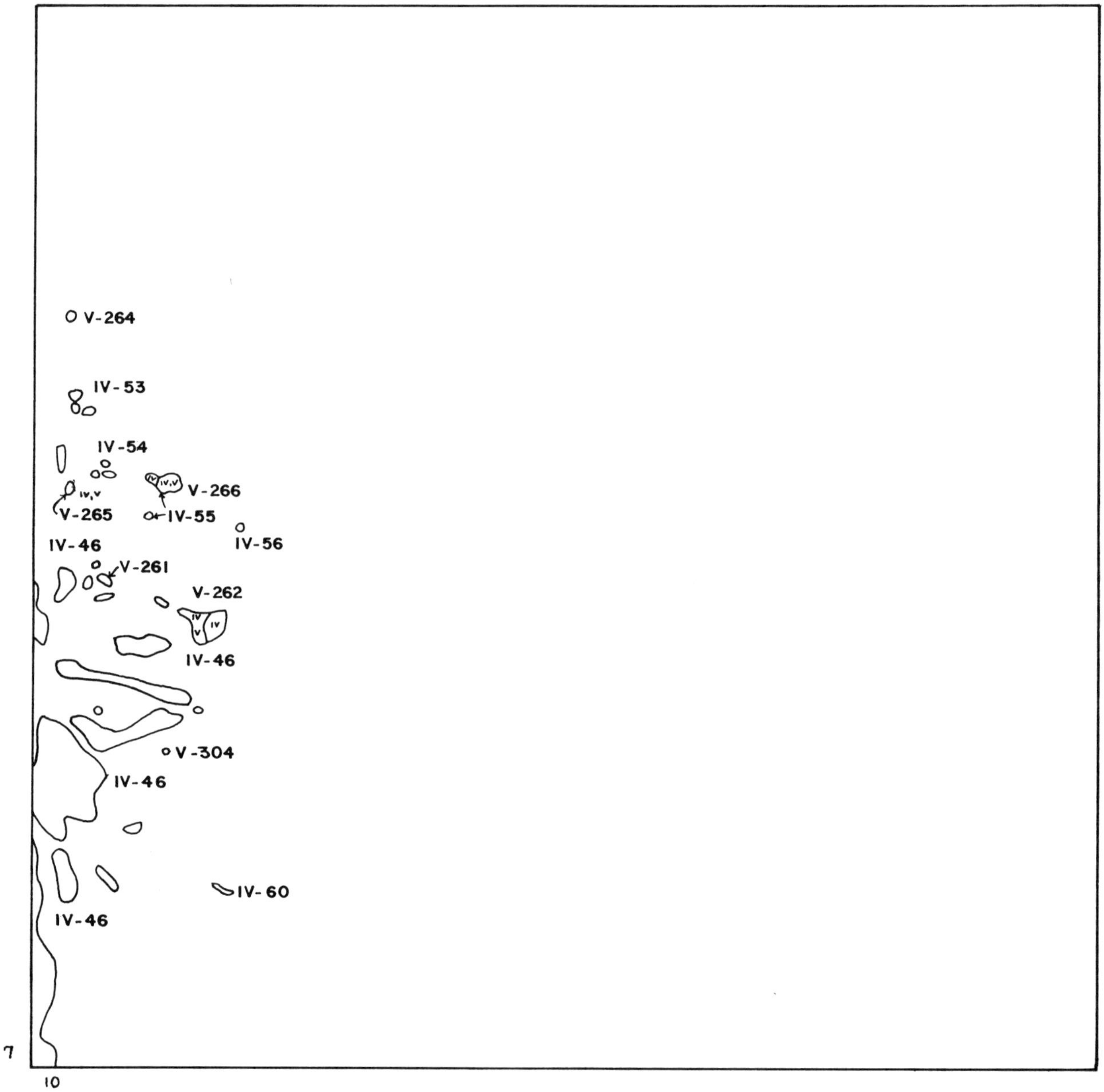

V-264
IV-53
IV-54
IV,V
V-265
IV
IV,V
V-266
IV-55
IV-56
IV-46
V-261
V-262
IV
IV
V
IV-46
V-304
IV-46
IV-60
IV-46
7
10

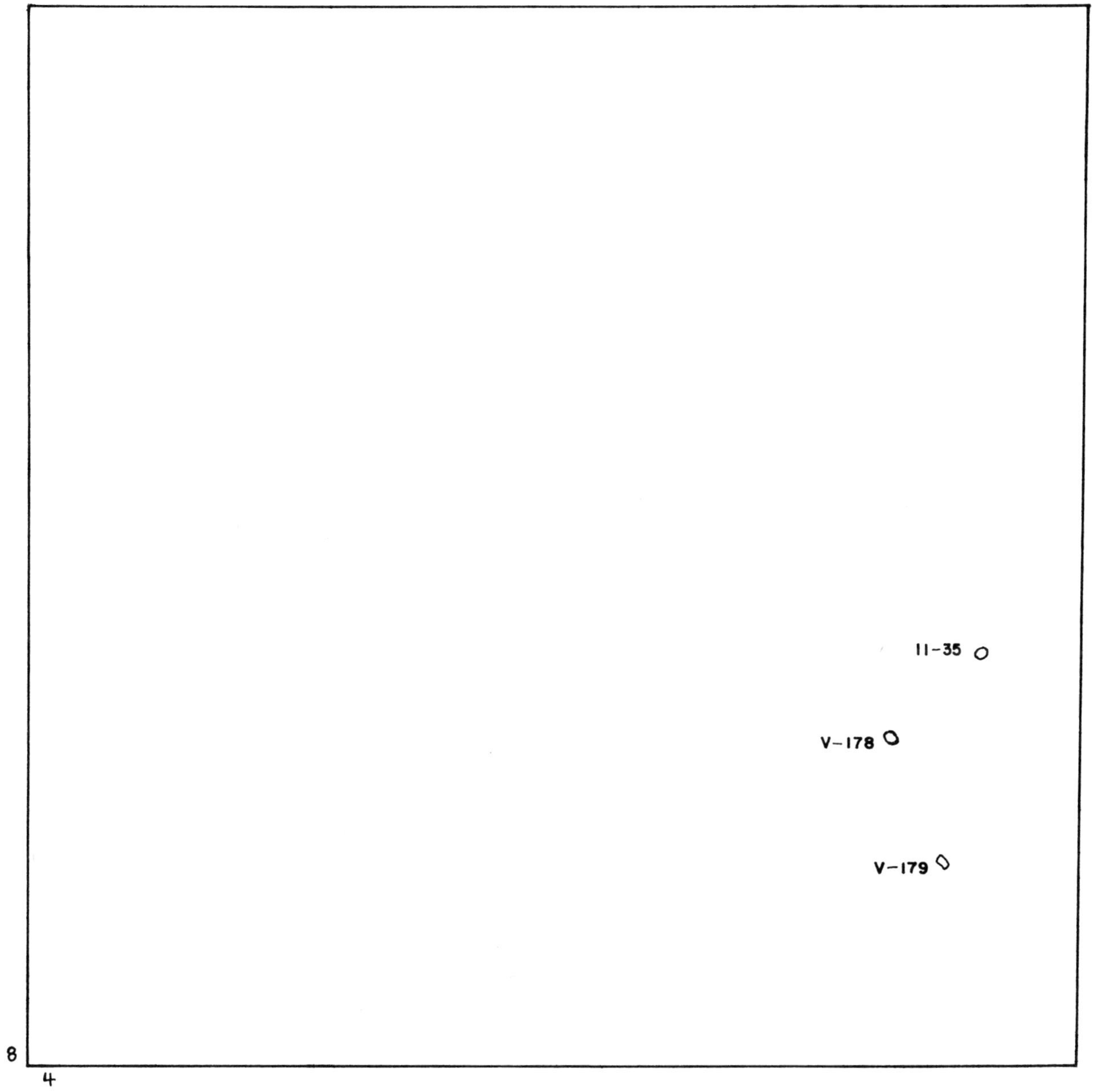
11-35
V-178
V-179
8
4

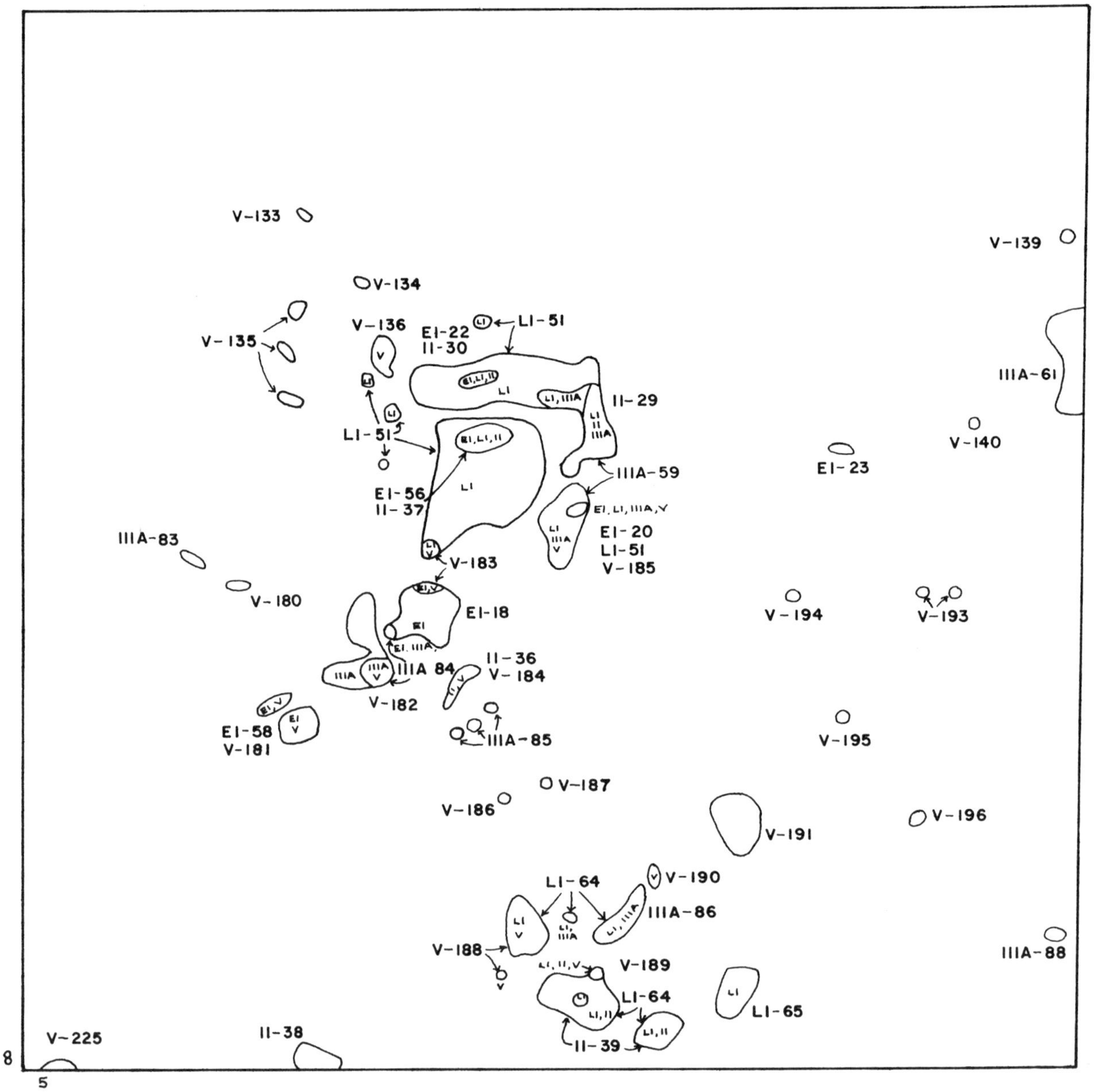
V-133
V-139
V-134
V-136
E1-22
II-30
L1-51
V-135
IIIA-61
II-29
L1-51
V-140
E1-23
IIIA-59
E1-56
II-37
E1-20
L1-51
V-185
IIIA-83
V-183
V-180
E1-18
V-194
V-193
IIIA 84
II-36
V-184
V-182
E1-58
V-181
IIIA-85
V-195
V-187
V-186
V-196
V-191
V-190
L1-64
IIIA-86
V-188
IIIA-88
V-189
L1-64
L1-65
V-225
II-38
II-39
8
5

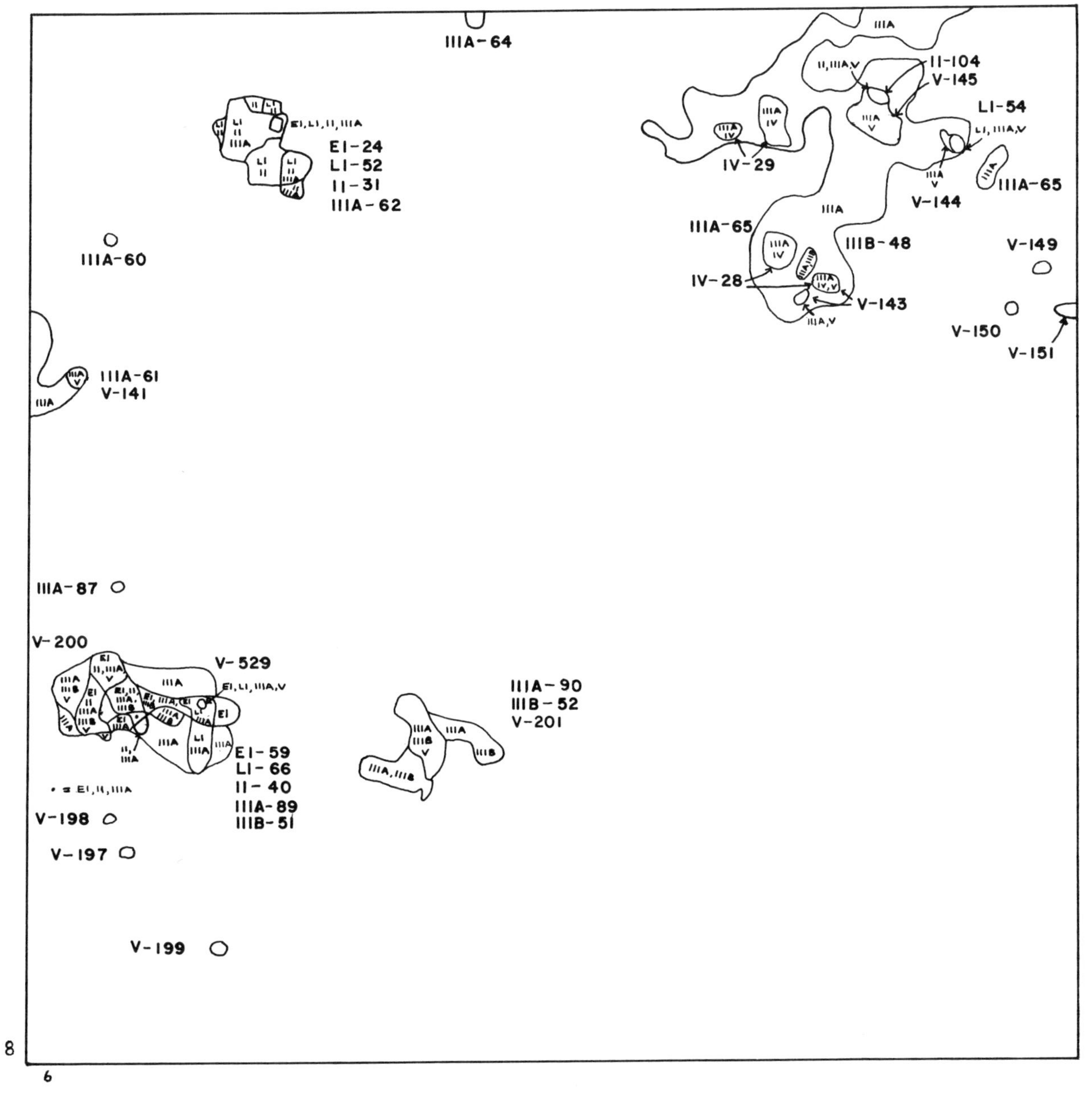
IIIA-64
EI-24
LI-52
II-31
IIIA-62
IIIA-60
IIIA-61
V-141
IV-29
II-104
V-145
LI-54
IIIA-65
V-144
IIIA-65
IIIB-48
V-149
IV-28
V-143
V-150
V-151
IIIA-87
V-200
V-529
IIIA-90
IIIB-52
V-201
EI-59
LI-66
II-40
IIIA-89
IIIB-51
• = EI, II, IIIA
V-198
V-197
V-199
8
6

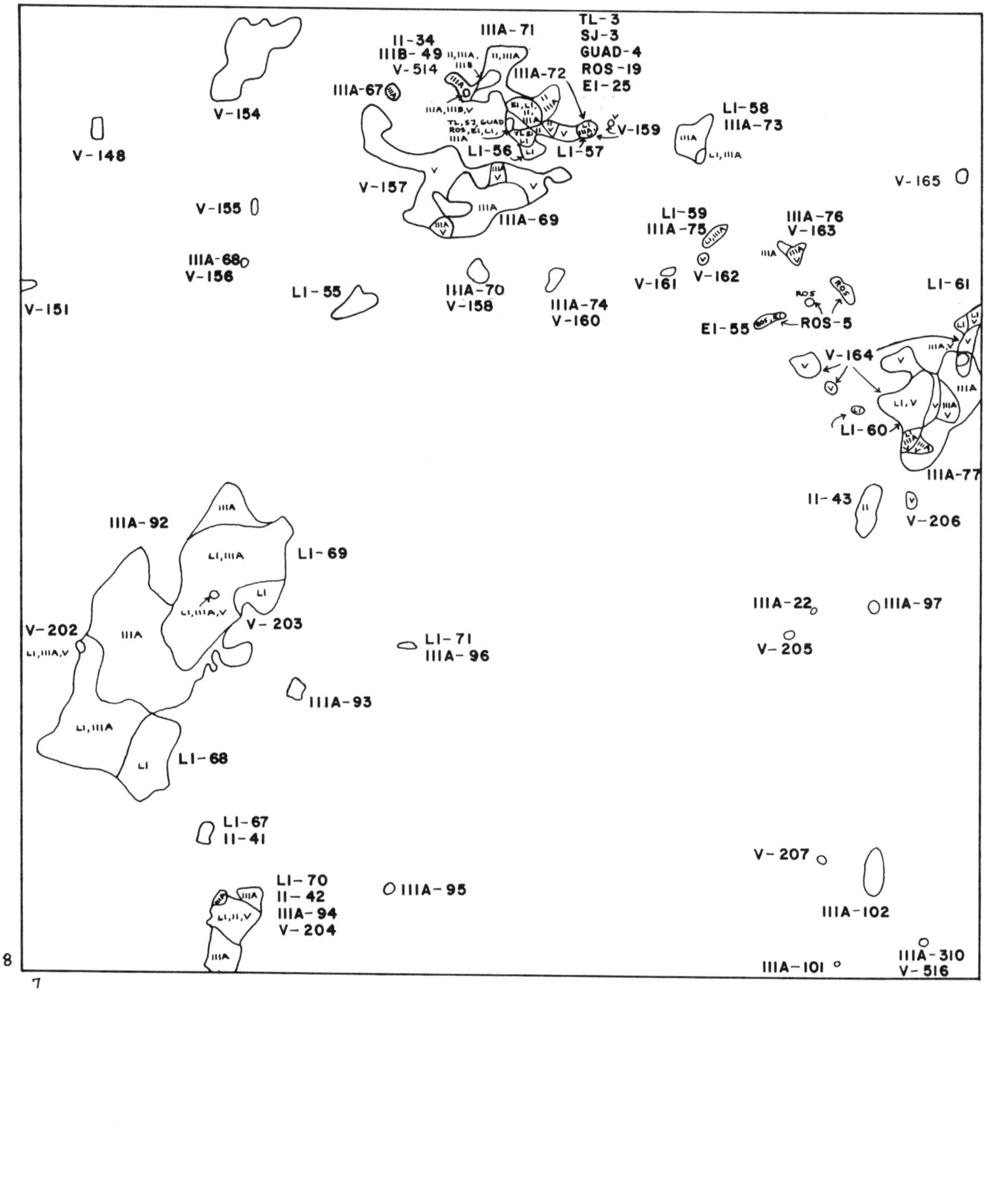
II-34
IIIB-49
V-514
IIIA-71
TL-3
SJ-3
GUAD-4
ROS-19
EI-25
IIIA-72
IIIA-67
V-154
V-148
LI-56
LI-57
V-159
LI-58
IIIA-73
V-157
IIIA-69
V-165
V-155
LI-59
IIIA-75
IIIA-76
V-163
IIIA-68
V-156
V-162
V-161
LI-55
IIIA-70
V-158
IIIA-74
V-160
LI-61
V-151
EI-55
ROS-5
V-164
LI-60
IIIA-77
II-43
V-206
IIIA-92
LI-69
V-202
V-203
IIIA-22
IIIA-97
V-205
LI-71
IIIA-96
IIIA-93
LI-68
LI-67
II-41
V-207
LI-70
II-42
IIIA-94
V-204
IIIA-95
IIIA-102
IIIA-101
IIIA-310
V-516
8
7

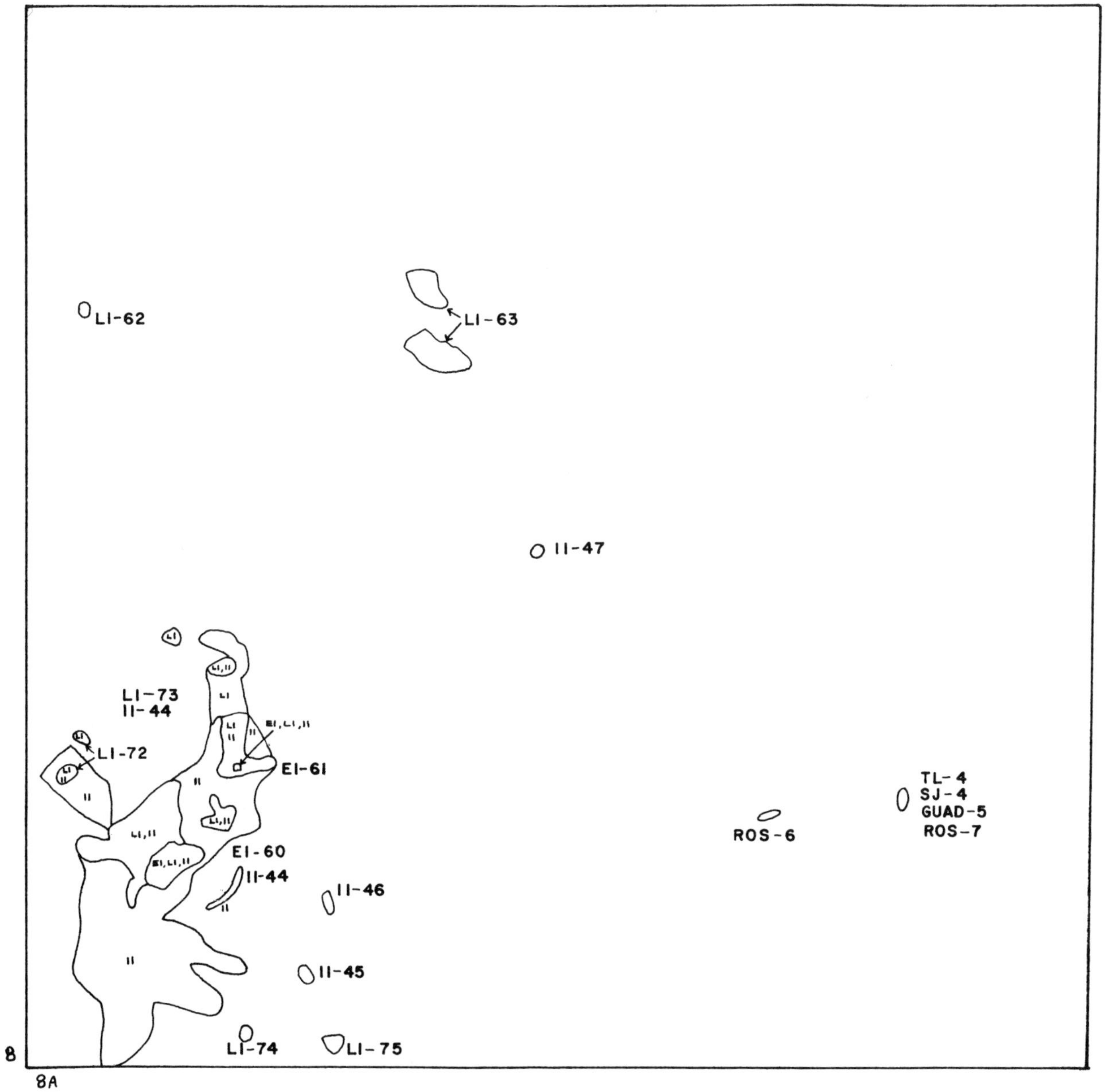

LI-62
LI-63
II-47
LI-73
II-44
LI-72
EI-61
EI-60
II-44
II-46
II-45
LI-74
LI-75
ROS-6
TL-4
SJ-4
GUAD-5
ROS-7
8
8A

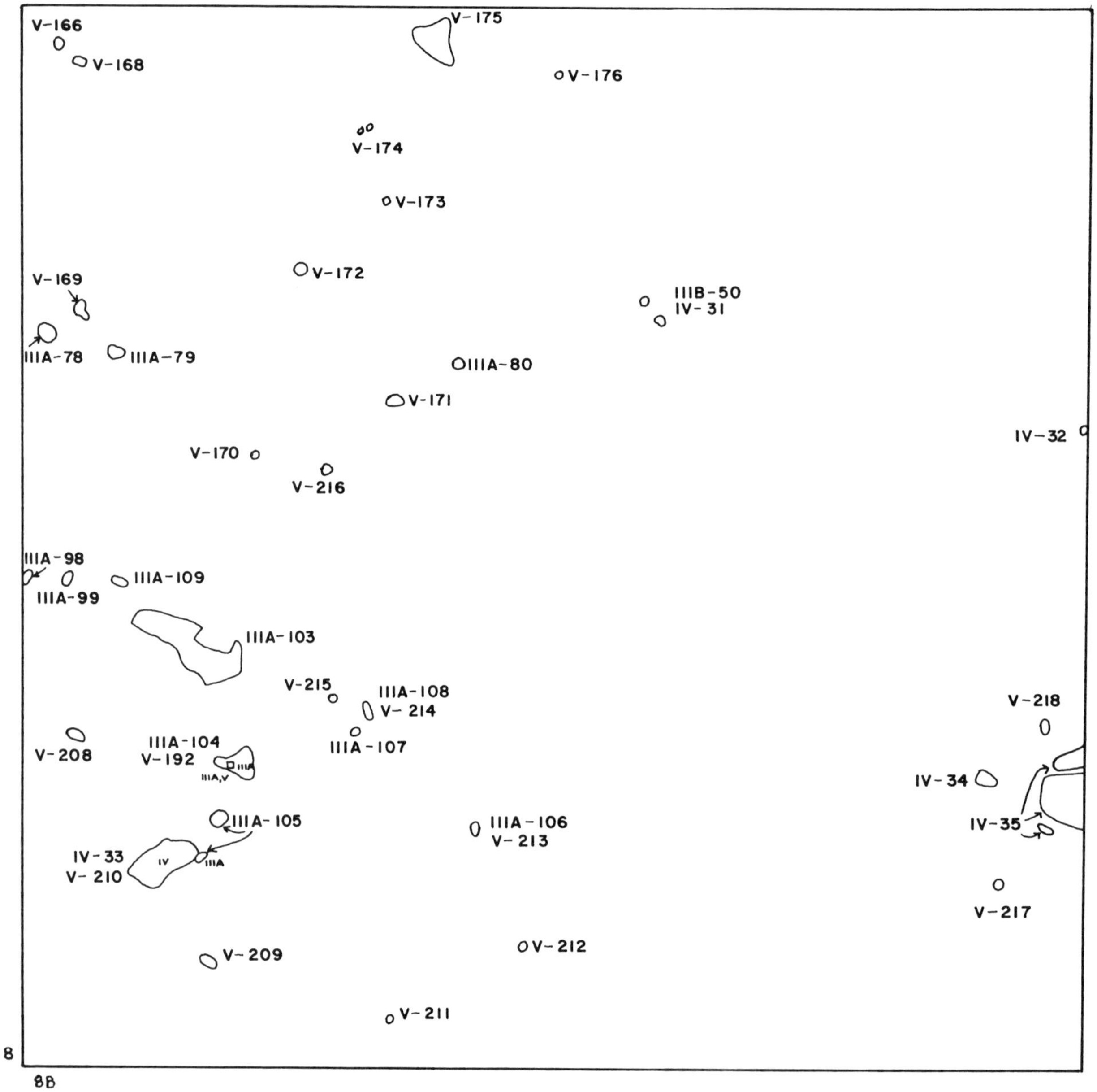
V-166
V-168
V-175
V-176
V-174
V-173
V-172
V-169
IIIB-50
IV-31
IIIA-78
IIIA-79
IIIA-80
V-171
IV-32
V-170
V-216
IIIA-98
IIIA-109
IIIA-99
IIIA-103
V-215
IIIA-108
V-214
V-218
V-208
IIIA-104
V-192
IIIA
IIIA,V
IIIA-107
IV-34
IIIA-105
IIIA-106
V-213
IV-35
IV-33
V-210
IV
IIIA
V-217
V-209
V-212
V-211
8
8B

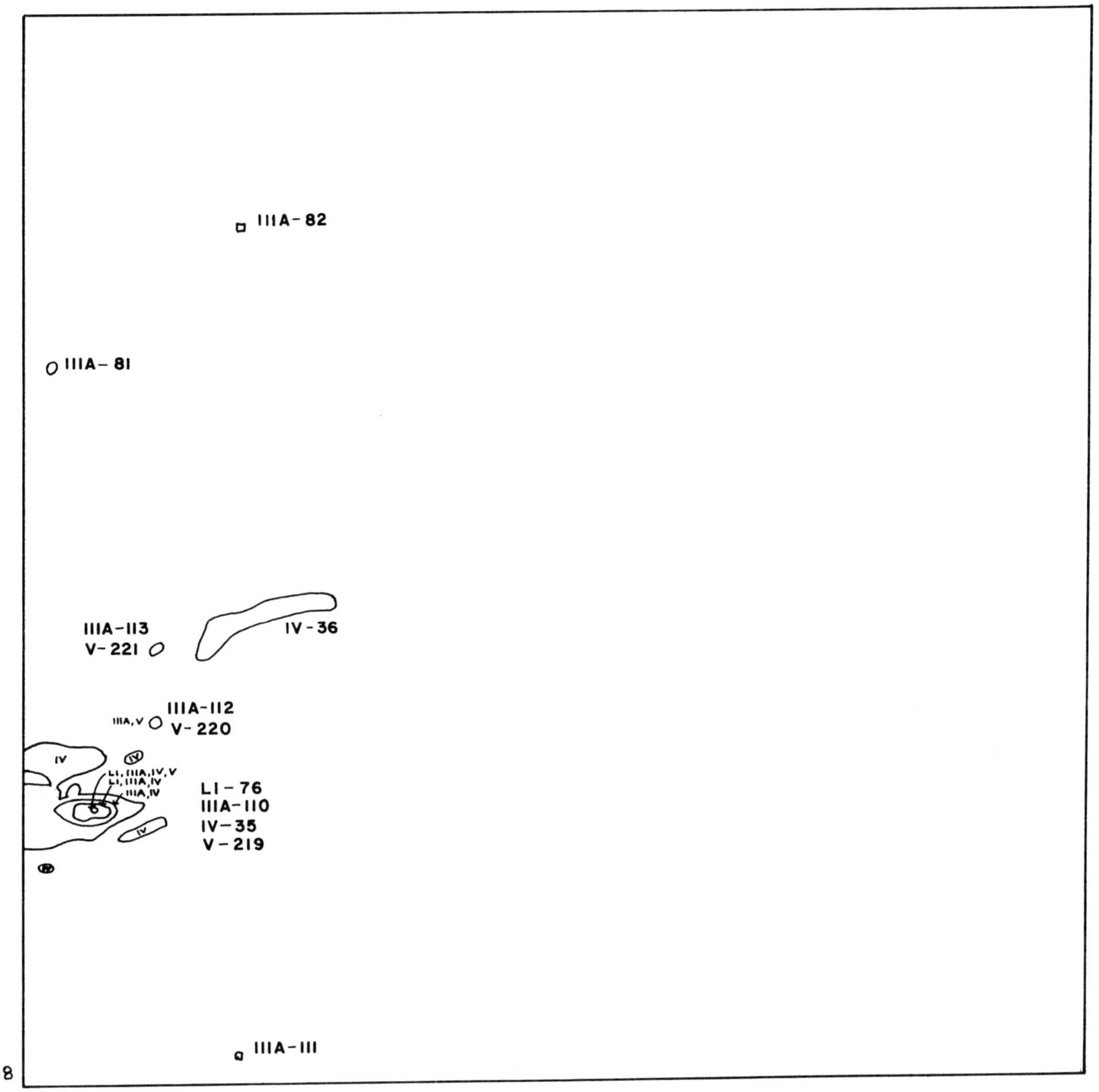
IIIA-82
IIIA-81
IIIA-113
V-221
IV-36
IIIA-112
V-220
IIIA,V
IV
L1, IIIA, IV, V
L1, IIIA, IV
IIIA, IV
L1-76
IIIA-110
IV-35
V-219
IV
IIIA-111
8
9

V-90
V-91
V-92
9
4

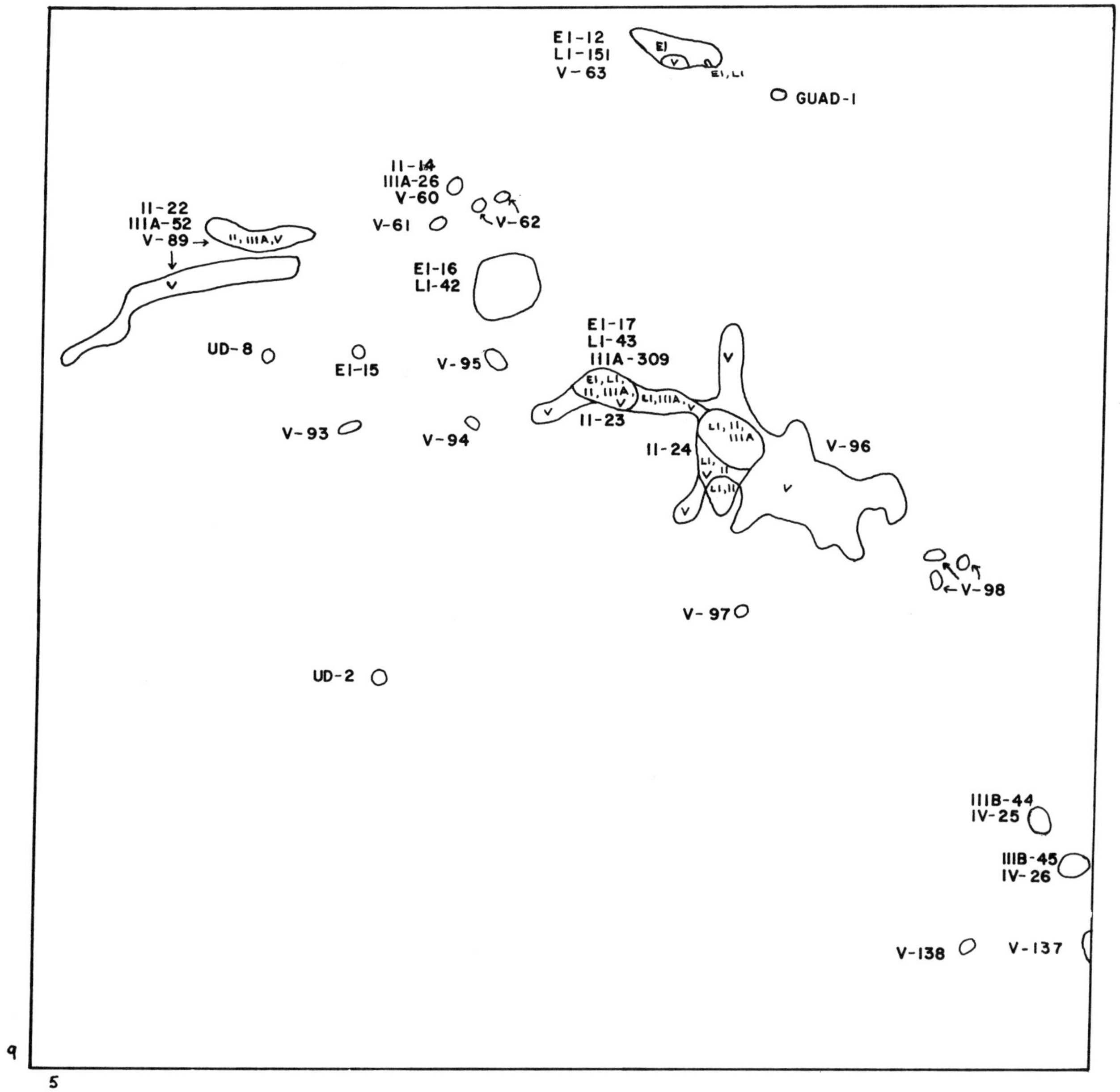
EI-12
LI-151
V-63
EI
V
EI, LI
GUAD-I
II-14
IIIA-26
V-60
V-61
V-62
II-22
IIIA-52
V-89
II, IIIA, V
V
EI-16
LI-42
EI-17
LI-43
IIIA-309
UD-8
EI-15
V-95
EI, LI, II, IIIA, V
LI, IIIA, V
V
II-23
V-93
V-94
II-24
LI, II, IIIA
LI, II
LI, II
V-96
V-98
V-97
UD-2
IIIB-44
IV-25
IIIB-45
IV-26
V-138
V-137
9
5

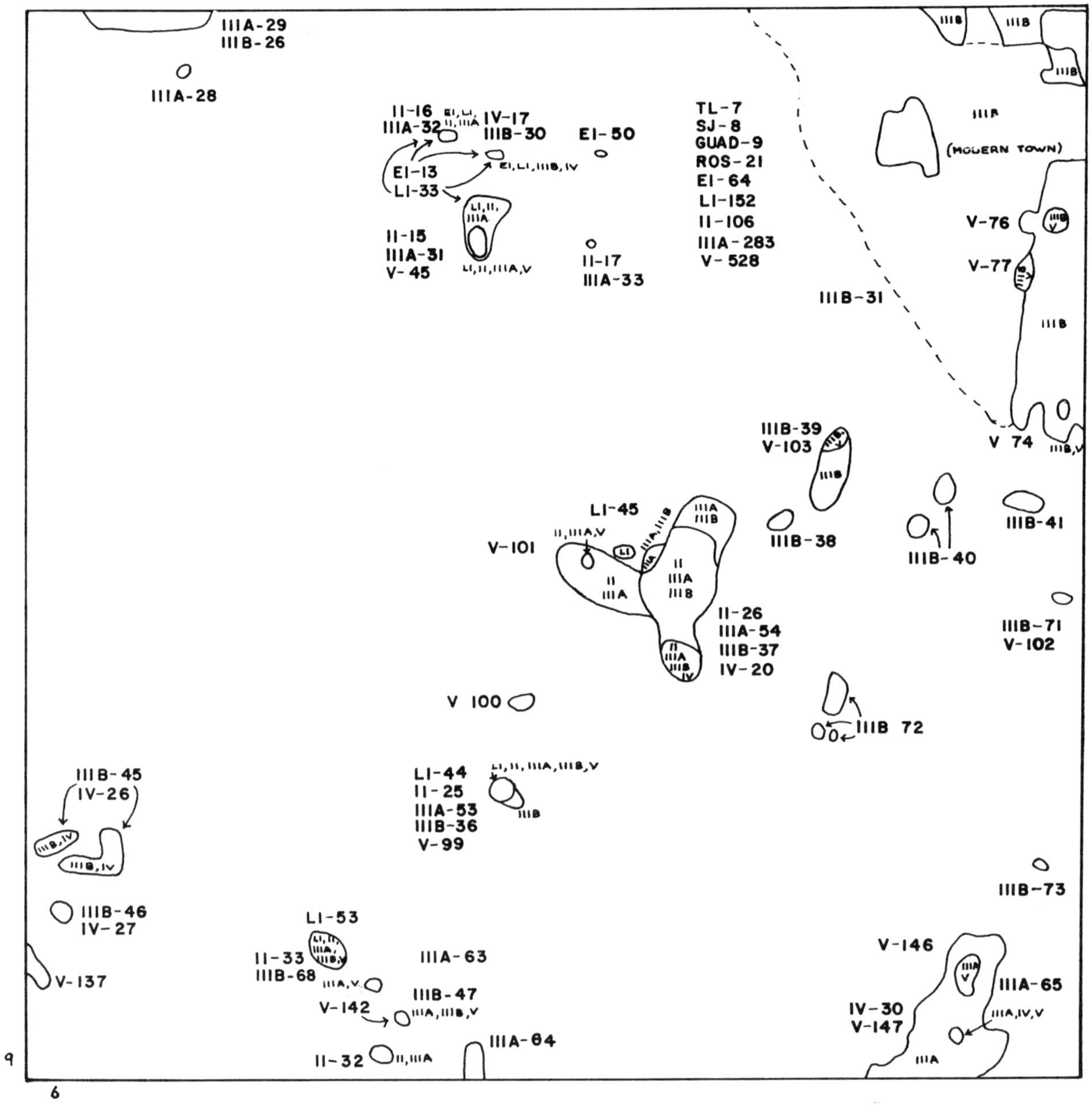
IIIA-29
IIIB-26
IIIA-28
II-16
IIIA-32
IV-17
IIIB-30
EI-50
TL-7
SJ-8
GUAD-9
ROS-21
EI-64
LI-152
II-106
IIIA-283
V-528
(MODERN TOWN)
EI-13
LI-33
II-15
IIIA-31
V-45
II-17
IIIA-33
V-76
V-77
IIIB-31
IIIB-39
V-103
V 74
LI-45
V-101
IIIB-38
IIIB-40
IIIB-41
II-26
IIIA-54
IIIB-37
IV-20
IIIB-71
V-102
V 100
IIIB 72
IIIB-45
IV-26
LI-44
II-25
IIIA-53
IIIB-36
V-99
IIIB-73
IIIB-46
IV-27
LI-53
II-33
IIIB-68
IIIA-63
V-137
IIIB-47
V-142
V-146
IIIA-65
IV-30
V-147
II-32
IIIA-64
9
6

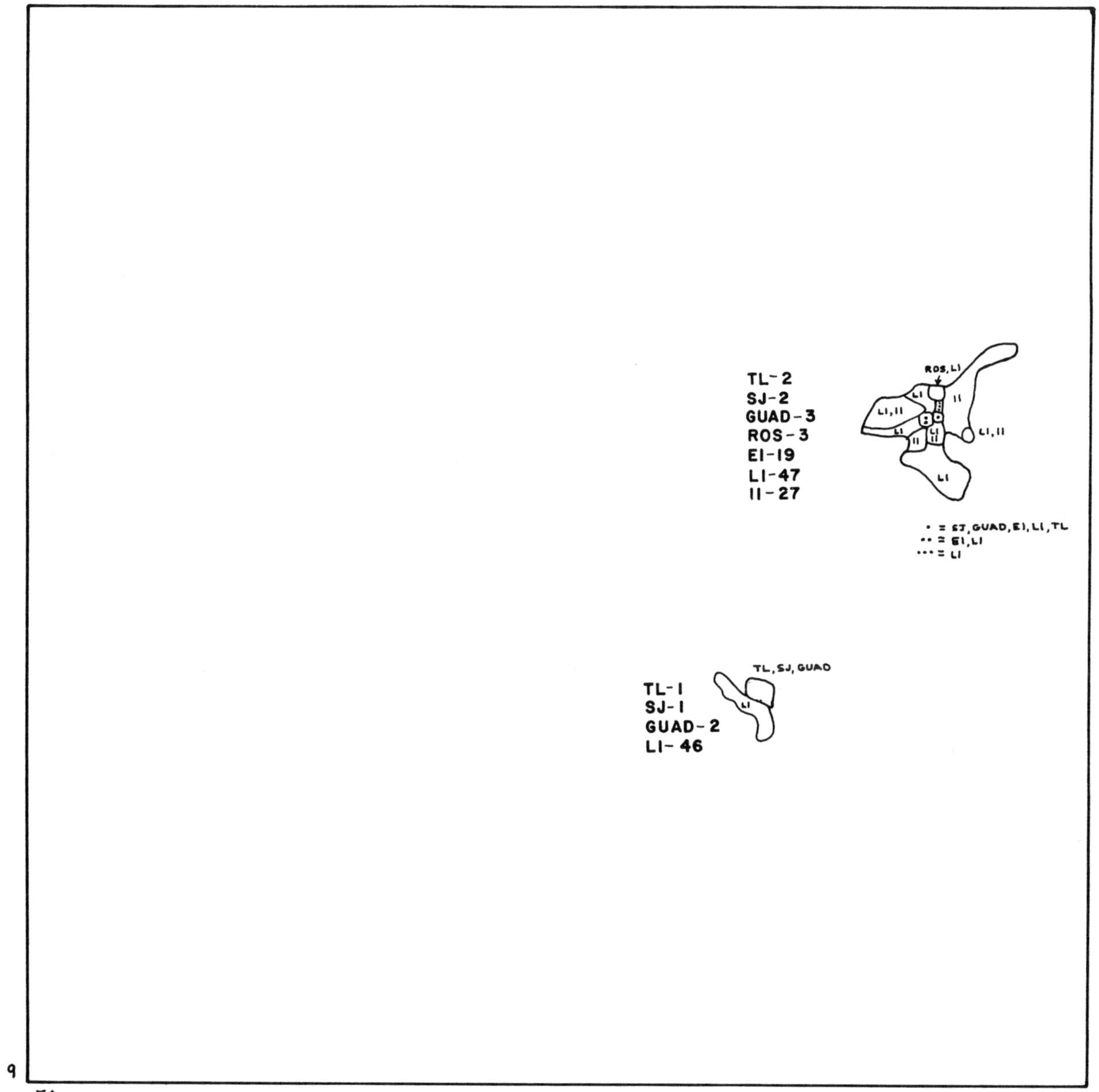
TL-2
SJ-2
GUAD-3
ROS-3
EI-19
LI-47
II-27
ROS, LI
• = SJ, GUAD, EI, LI, TL
•• = EI, LI
••• = LI
TL-1
SJ-1
GUAD-2
LI-46
TL, SJ, GUAD
9
7A

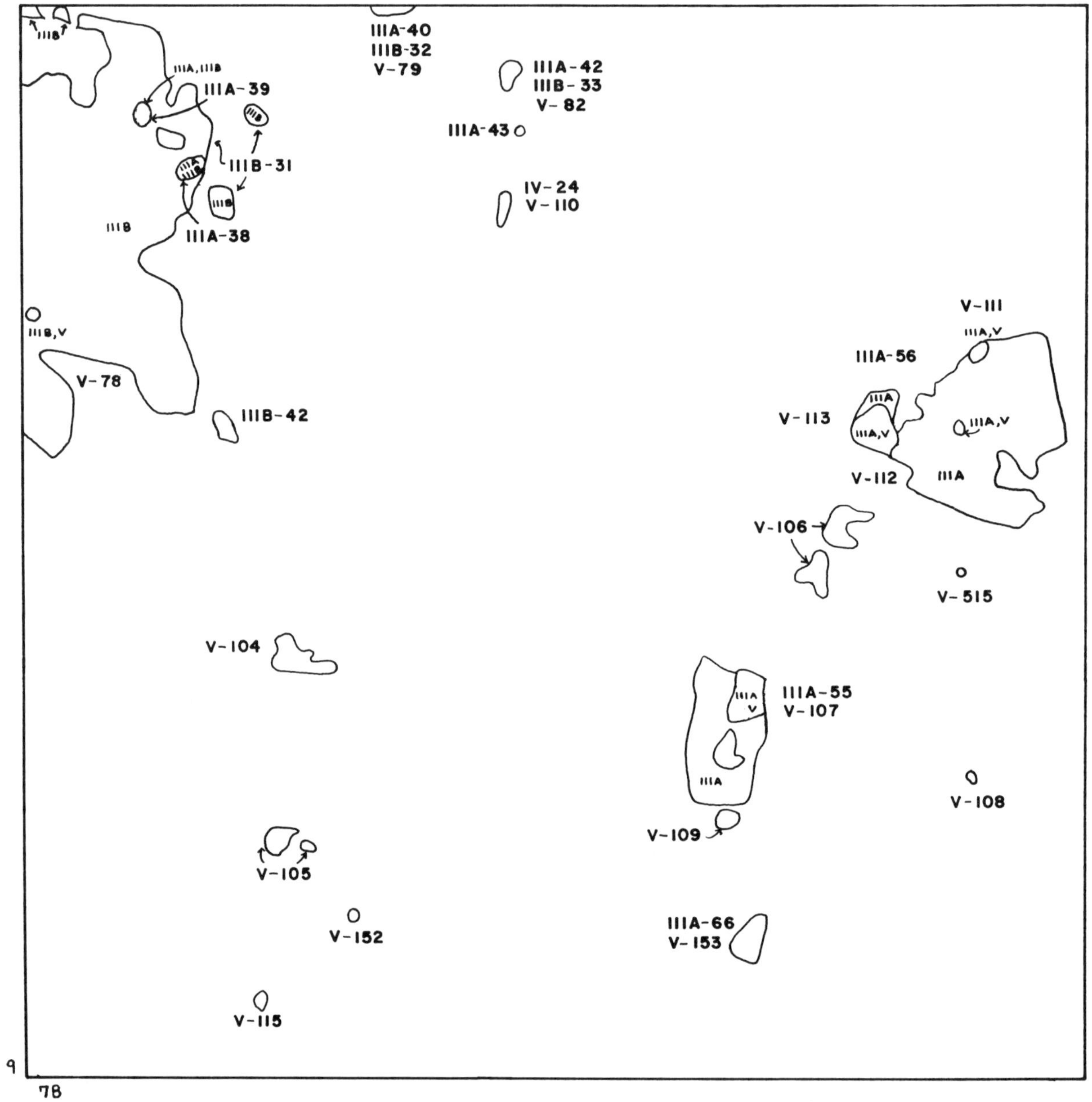
IIIB
IIIA-40
IIIB-32
V-79
IIIA, IIIB
IIIA-39
IIIA-42
IIIB-33
V-82
IIIA-43
IIIB-31
IV-24
V-110
IIIB
IIIA-38
IIIB, V
V-78
IIIB-42
V-111
IIIA, V
IIIA-56
IIIA
V-113
IIIA, V
IIIA, V
V-112
IIIA
V-106
V-515
V-104
IIIA
V
IIIA-55
V-107
IIIA
V-108
V-109
V-105
V-152
IIIA-66
V-153
V-115
9
78

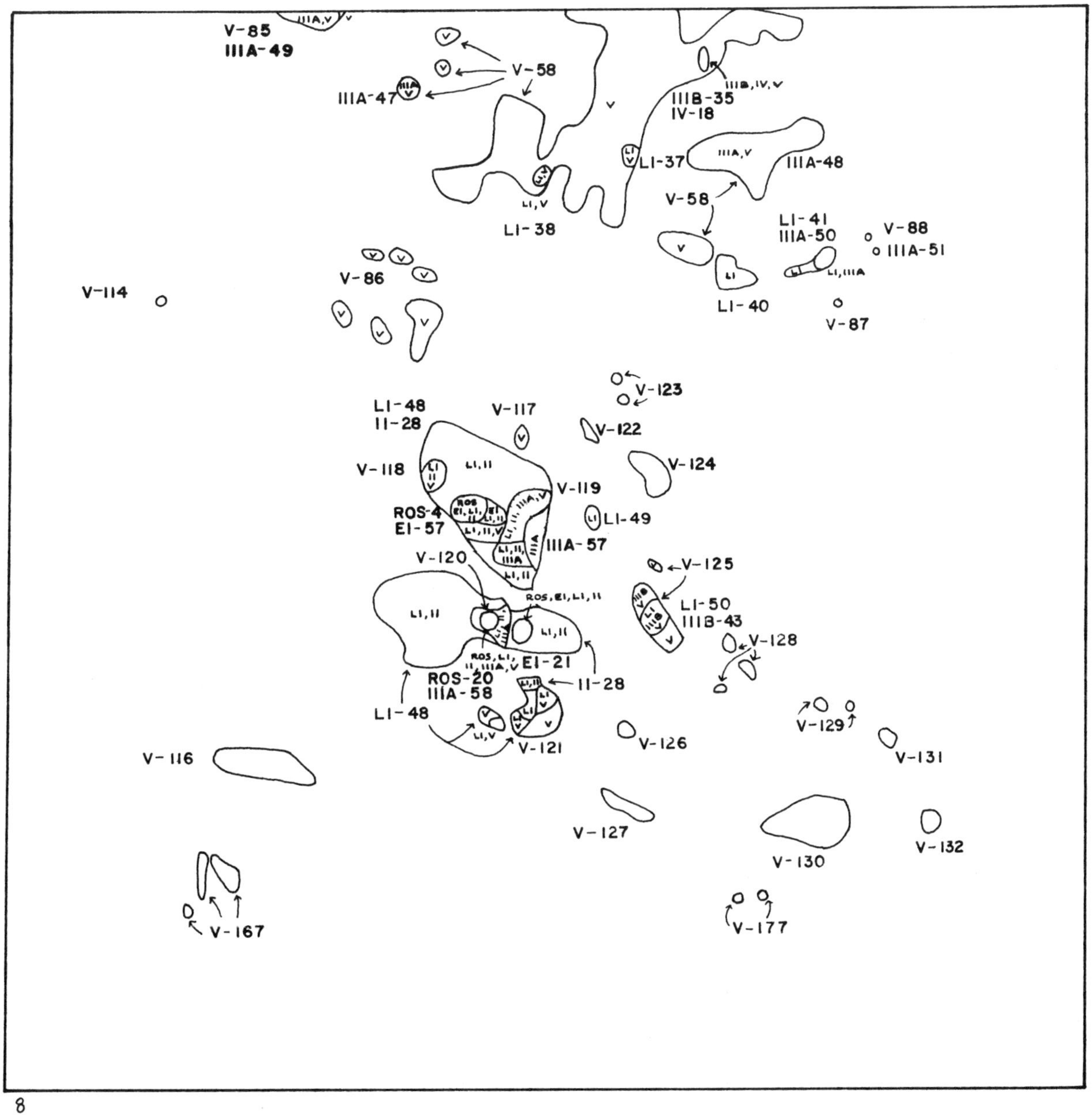
V-85
IIIA-49
V-58
IIIA-47
IIIB-35
IV-18
LI-37
IIIA-48
V-58
LI-38
LI-41
IIIA-50
V-88
IIIA-51
V-114
V-86
LI-40
V-87
V-123
LI-48
II-28
V-117
V-122
V-124
V-118
V-119
ROS-4
EI-57
LI-49
IIIA-57
V-120
V-125
LI-50
IIIB-43
V-128
EI-21
ROS-20
IIIA-58
II-28
LI-48
V-129
V-121
V-126
V-131
V-116
V-127
V-130
V-132
V-167
V-177

9
8

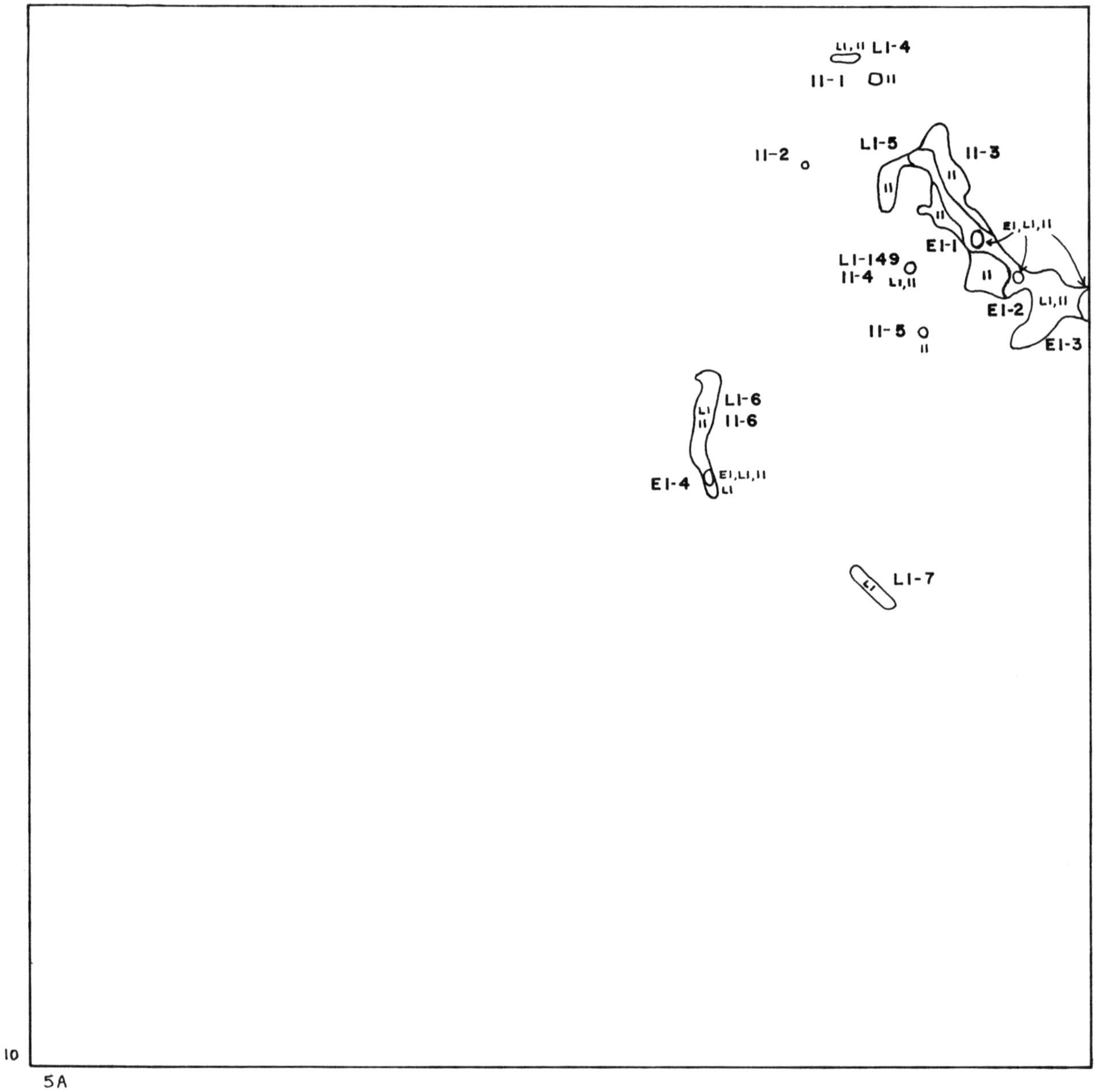
L1, II L1-4
II-1 II
II-2
L1-5
II-3
E1, L1, II
E1-1
L1-149
II-4 L1, II
E1-2 L1, II
E1-3
II-5 II
L1-6
II-6
L1 II
E1-4 E1, L1, II L1
L1-7
L1
10
5A

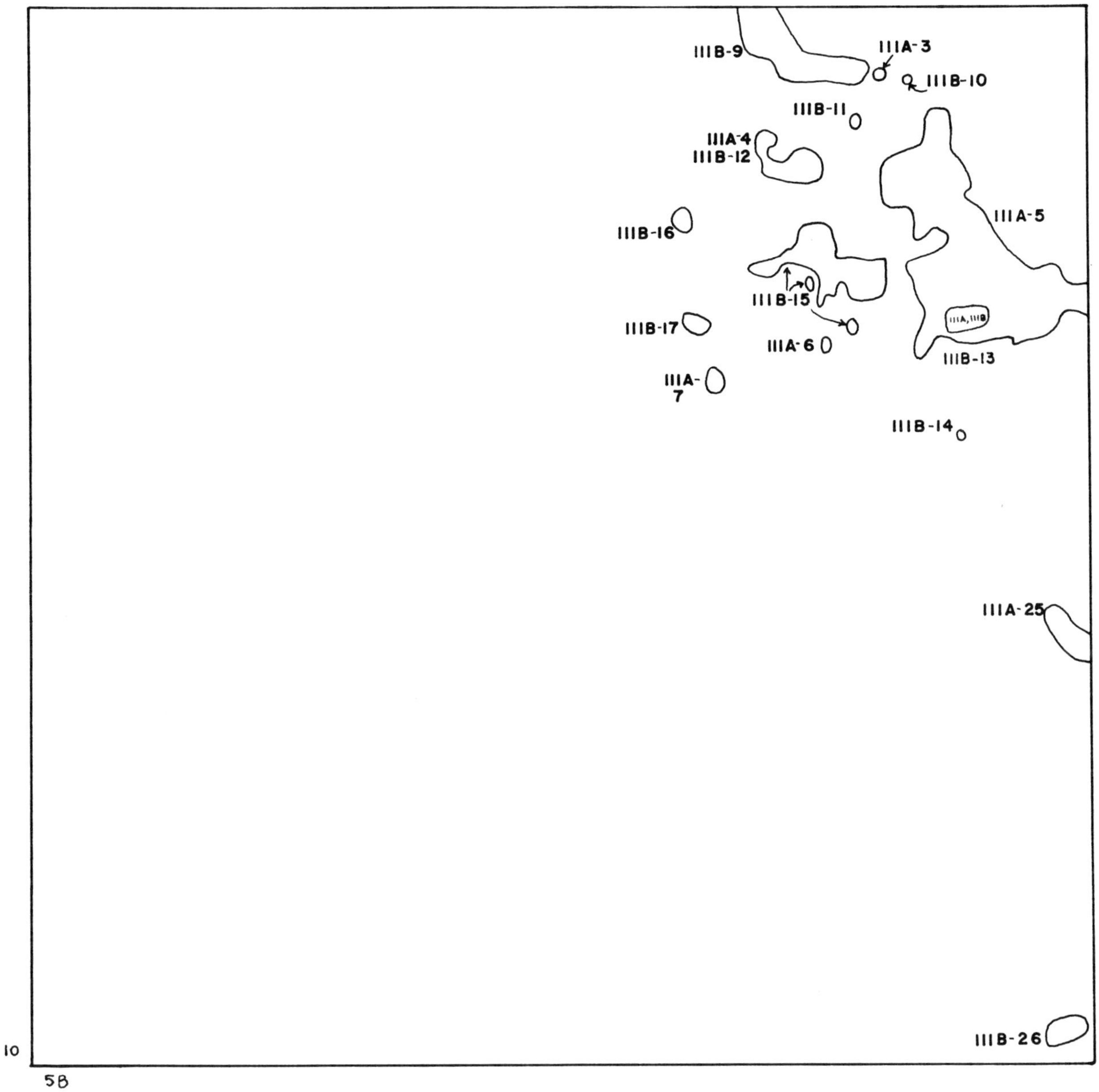
IIIB-9
IIIA-3
IIIB-10
IIIB-11
IIIA-4
IIIB-12
IIIA-5
IIIB-16
IIIB-15
IIIB-17
IIIA-6
IIIA, IIIB
IIIB-13
IIIA-7
IIIB-14
IIIA-25
IIIB-26
10
5B

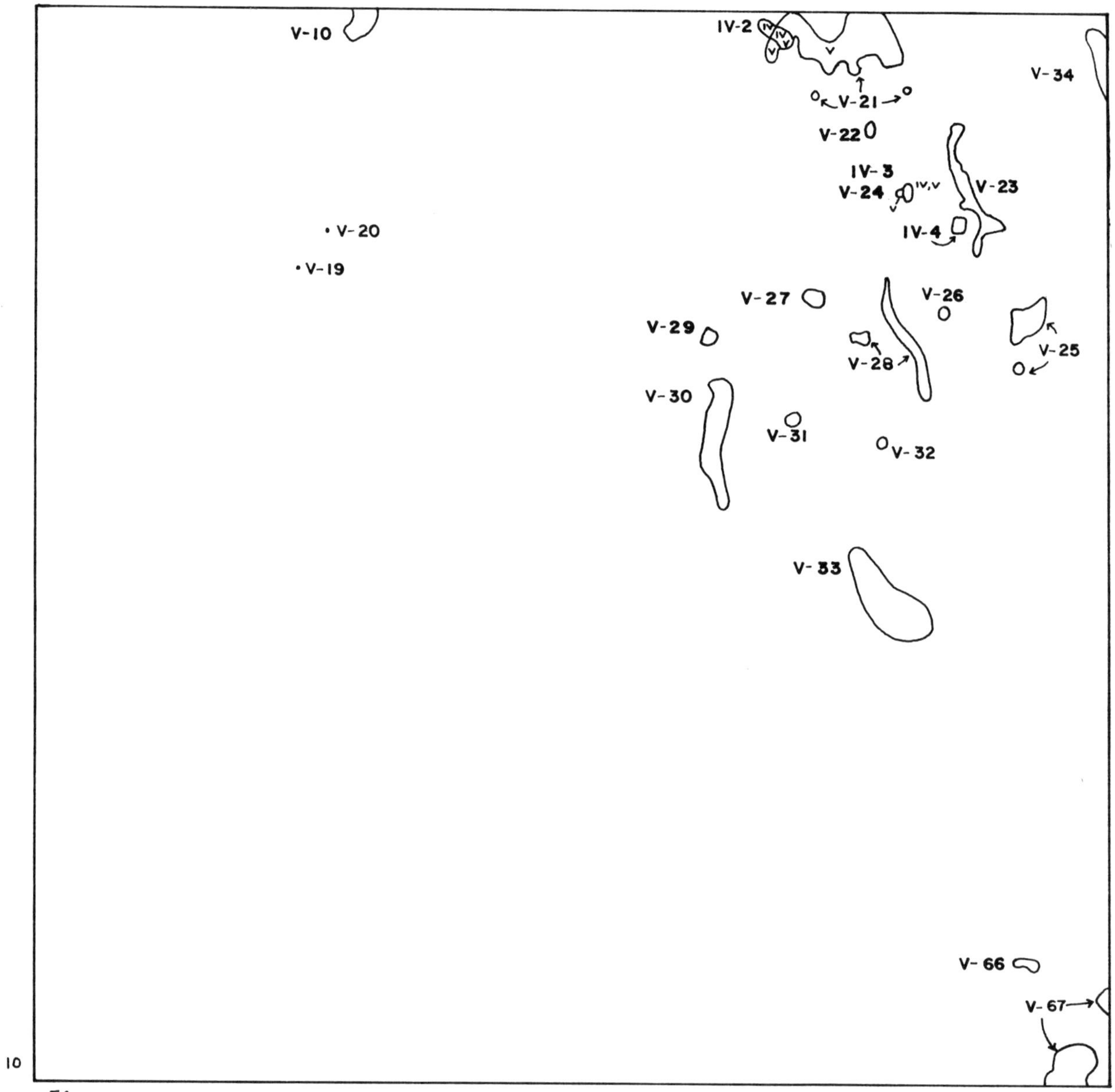

V-10
IV-2
IV
IV
V
V
V
V-21
V-34
V-22
IV-3
V-24
IV,V
V
V-23
IV-4
V-20
V-19
V-27
V-26
V-29
V-25
V-28
V-30
V-31
V-32
V-33
V-66
V-67
10
5C

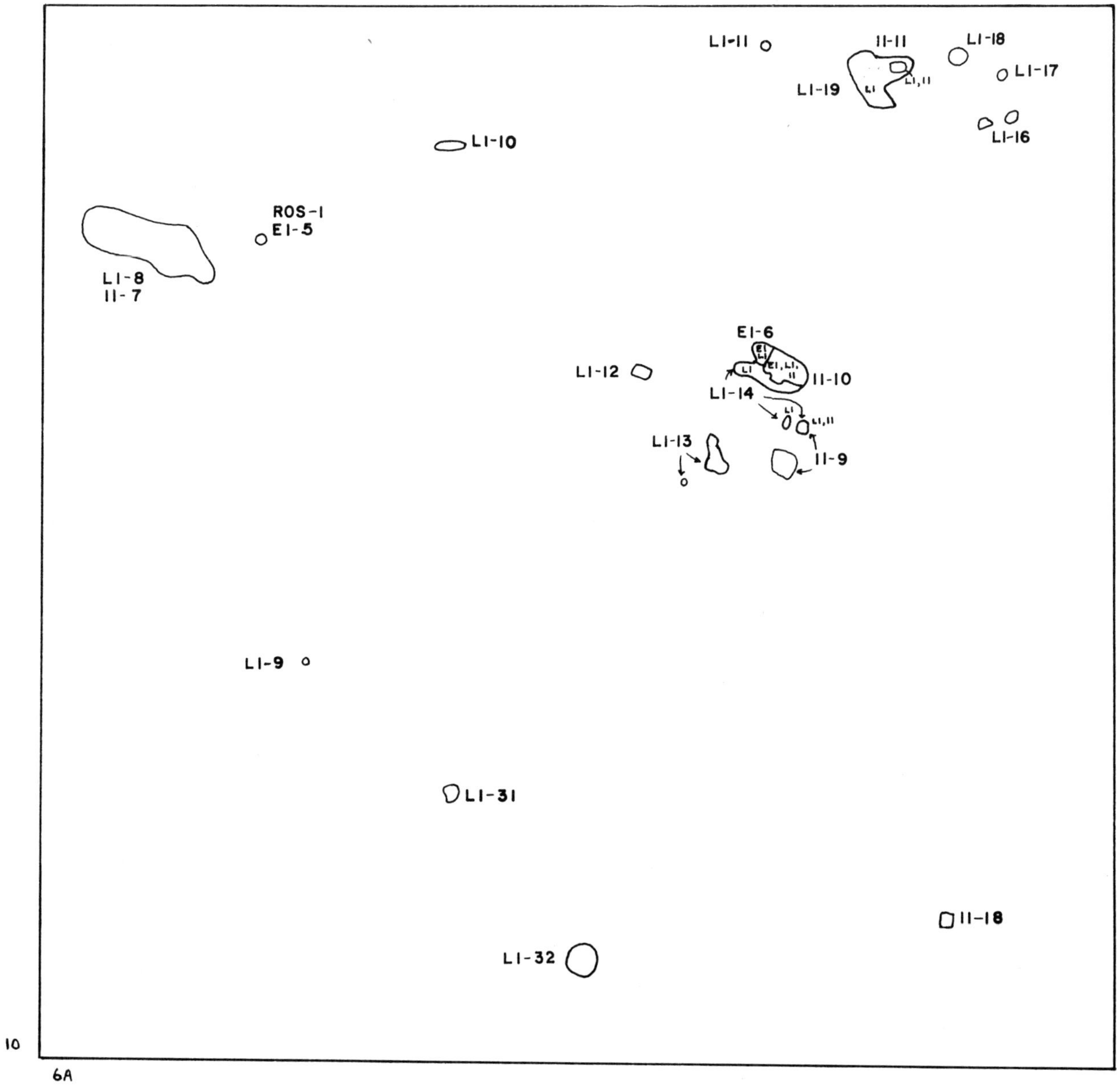
L1-11
11-11
L1-18
L1-17
L1-19
L1-16
L1-10
ROS-1
E1-5
L1-8
11-7
E1-6
L1-12
11-10
L1-14
L1-13
11-9
L1-9
L1-31
11-18
L1-32
10
6A

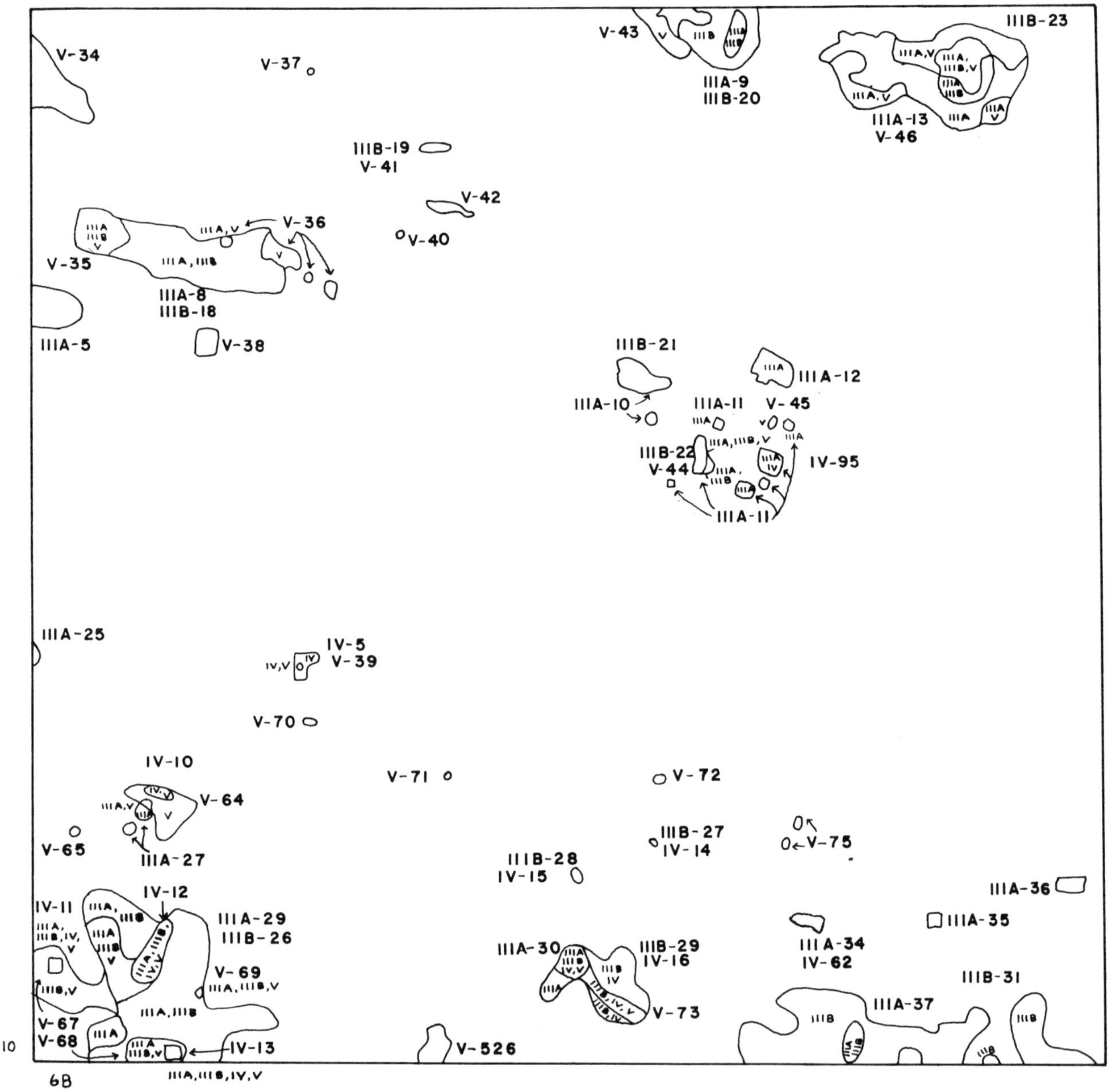
V-34
V-37
V-43
IIIA-9
IIIB-20
IIIB-23
IIIA-13
V-46
IIIB-19
V-41
V-42
V-36
V-40
V-35
IIIA-8
IIIB-18
IIIA-5
V-38
IIIB-21
IIIA-12
IIIA-10
IIIA-11
V-45
IIIB-22
V-44
IV-95
IIIA-25
IV-5
V-39
V-70
IV-10
V-64
V-71
V-72
V-65
IIIA-27
IIIB-27
IV-14
V-75
IIIB-28
IV-15
IIIA-36
IV-11
IV-12
IIIA-29
IIIB-26
IIIA-35
IIIA-30
IIIB-29
IV-16
IIIA-34
IV-62
V-69
IIIB-31
V-67
V-68
IV-13
V-73
IIIA-37
V-526
10
6B

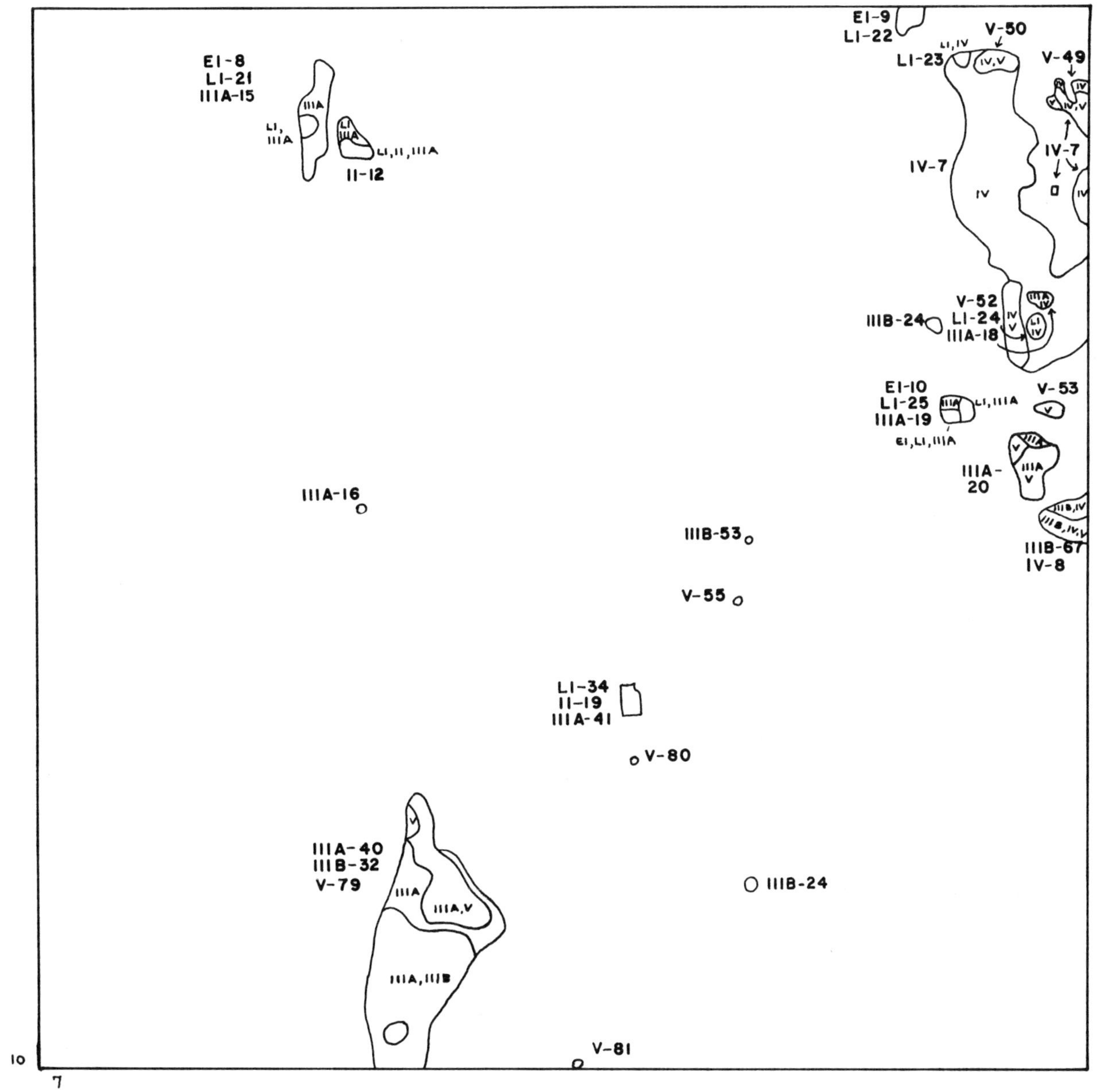
EI-8
LI-21
IIIA-15
LI, IIIA
IIIA
LI,II,IIIA
II-12
EI-9
LI-22
LI-23
LI,IV
V-50
IV,V
V-49
IV-7
IV
V-52
LI-24
IIIA-18
IIIB-24
EI-10
LI-25
IIIA-19
EI,LI,IIIA
LI,IIIA
V-53
IIIA-20
IIIB-67
IV-8
IIIA-16
IIIB-53
V-55
LI-34
II-19
IIIA-41
V-80
IIIA-40
IIIB-32
V-79
IIIA
IIIA,V
IIIA,IIIB
IIIB-24
V-81
10
7

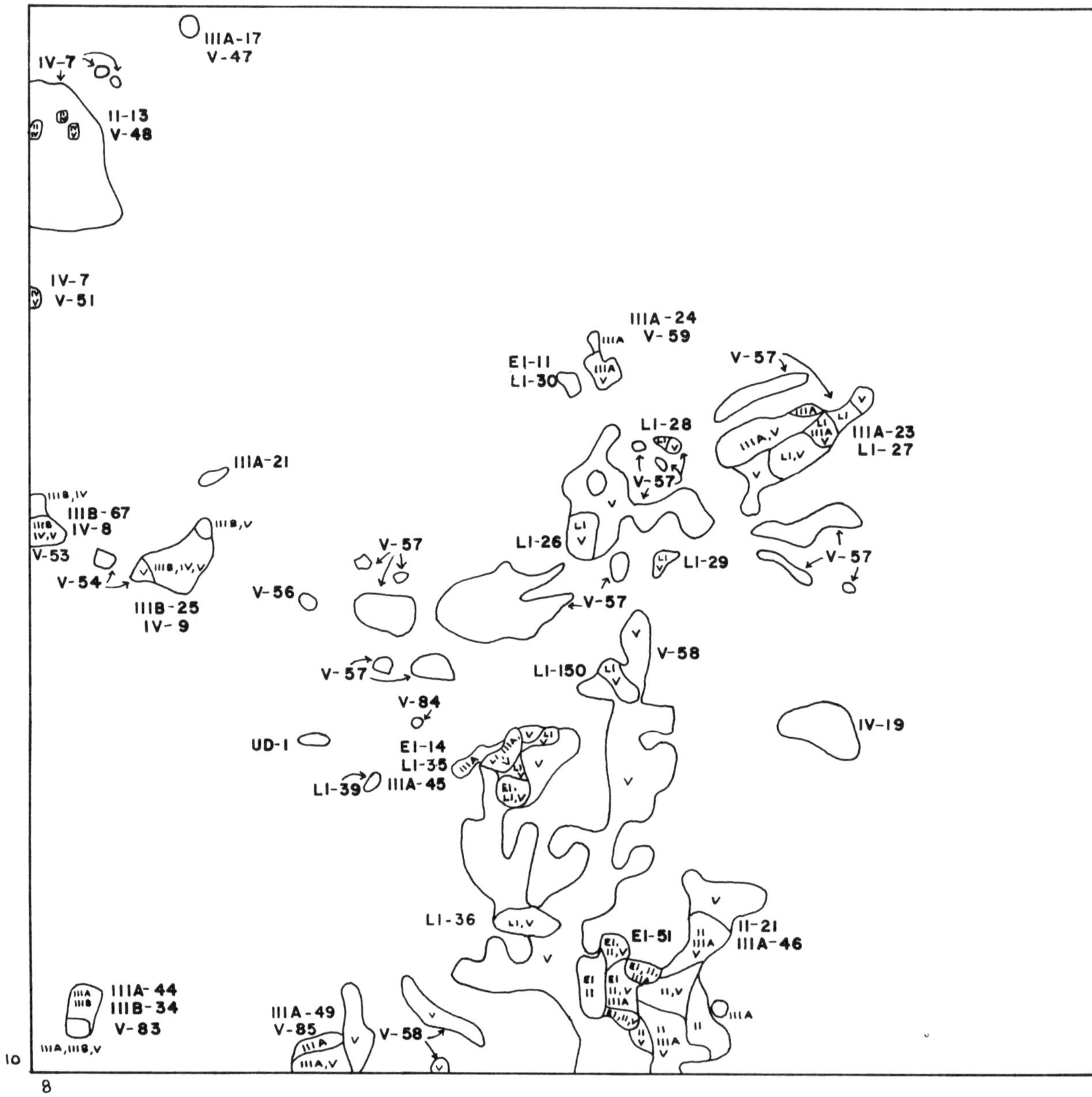
IIIA-17
V-47
IV-7
II-13
V-48
IV-7
V-51
IIIA-24
V-59
EI-11
LI-30
V-57
IIIA-23
LI-27
LI-28
V-57
IIIA-21
IIIB-67
IV-8
V-53
V-54
IIIB-25
IV-9
V-57
V-56
LI-26
LI-29
V-57
V-57
V-58
LI-150
V-57
V-84
IV-19
UD-I
EI-14
LI-35
LI-39
IIIA-45
LI-36
EI-51
II-21
IIIA-46
IIIA-44
IIIB-34
V-83
IIIA-49
V-85
V-58
10
8

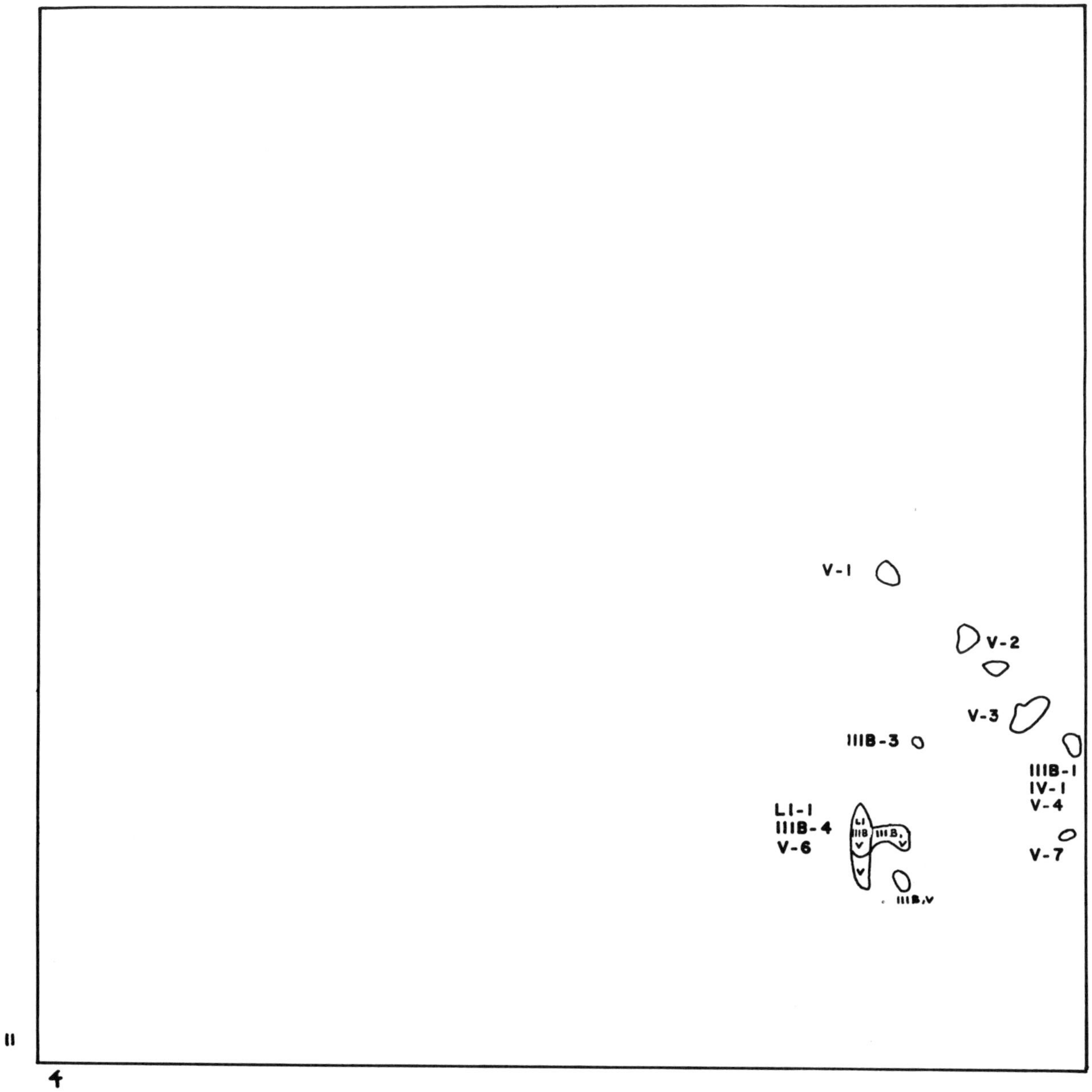
V-1
V-2
V-3
IIIB-3
IIIB-1
IV-1
V-4
LI-1
IIIB-4
V-6
V-7
IIIB,V
11
4

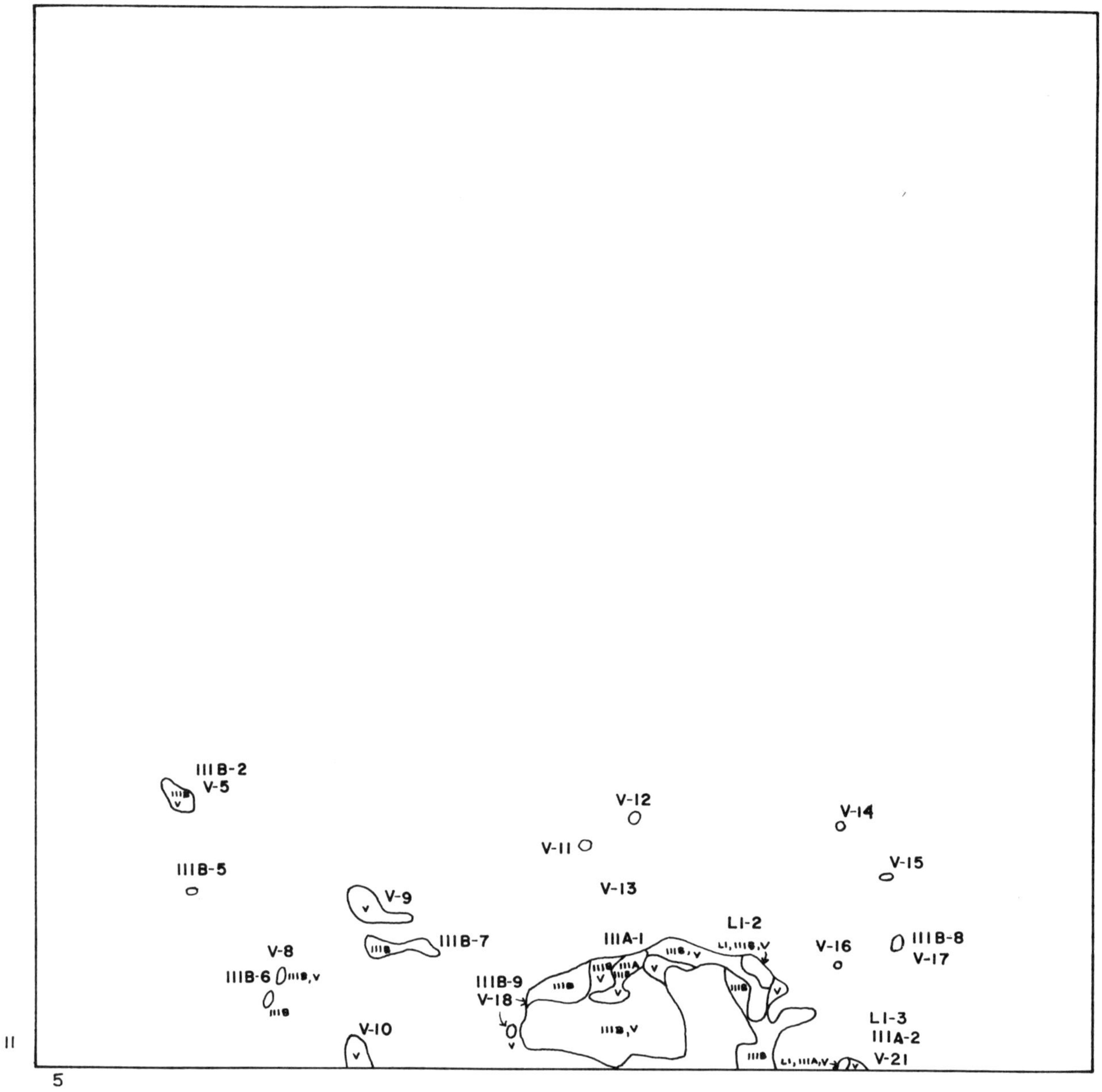
IIIB-2
V-5
V-12
V-14
V-11
IIIB-5
V-15
V-9
V-13
L1-2
V-8
IIIB-7
IIIA-1
V-16
IIIB-8
V-17
IIIB-6
IIIB-9
V-18
L1-3
IIIA-2
V-10
V-21
11
5

II-8
V-43
IIIB-20
V
IIIB
V
V
IIIB
II,V
11
6

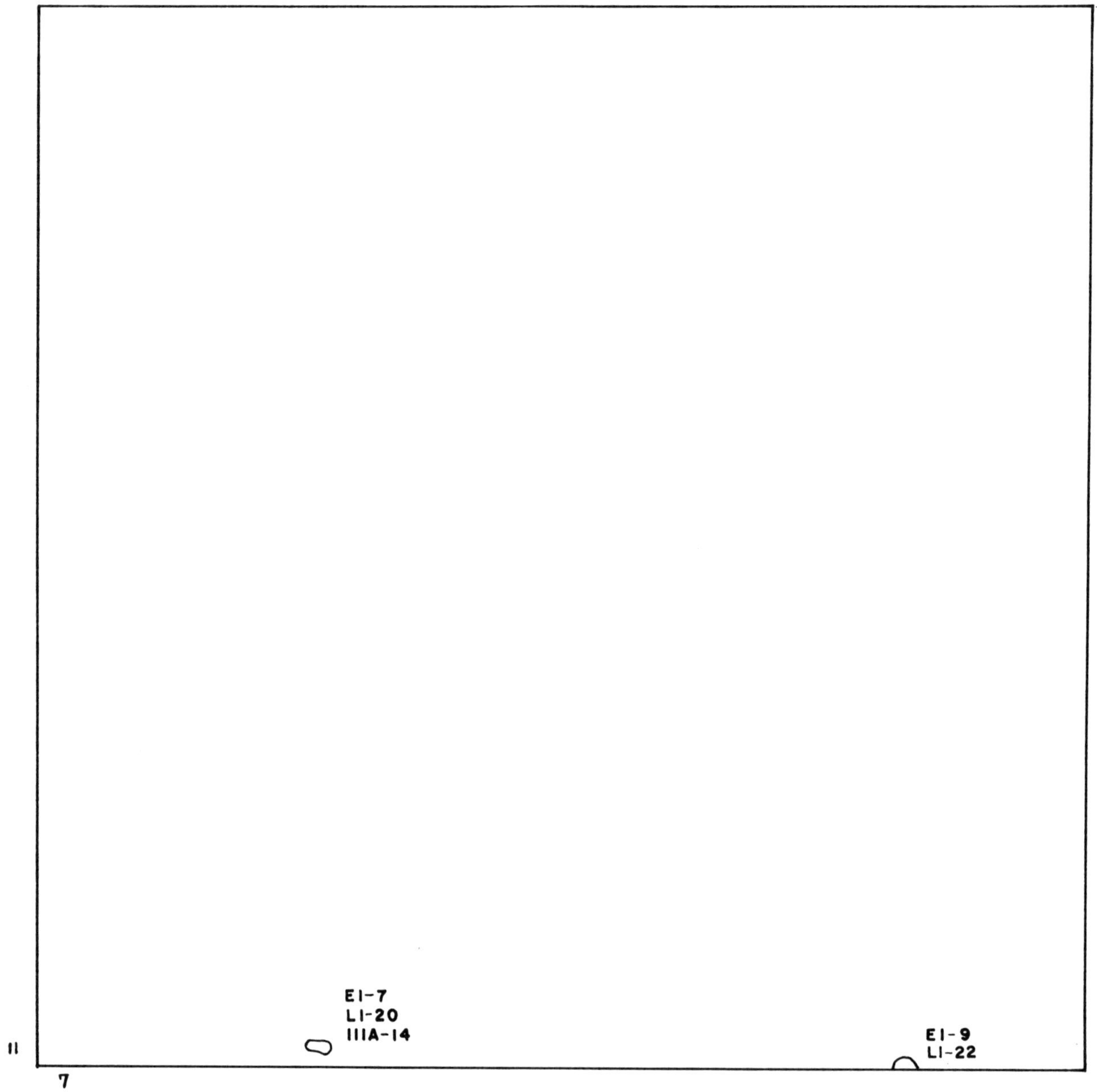
E1-7
L1-20
IIIA-14
E1-9
L1-22
11
7

IV-78
11
8

V-388
11
9

Appendix III

DISTRIBUTION BY GRID SQUARE OF THREE LAND TYPES

Appendix III presents the distribution by grid square of the three land types defined in Chapter 1. Type I is the most productive; Type III is the least productive. The accuracy of these maps is limited by the scale at which observations were made, so that finer details cannot be shown, even when these were recognized in the field. There are also some inconsistencies, which for our purposes here are of minor consequence, due to difficulties in aligning the grid on the 1:20,000 airphotos. This accounts for the apparent irregularities on the edges of some grid squares. The standards of accuracy employed, however, should be sufficient for the designed task of showing broad-scale (4 x 4 kilometer) intra-regional differences in potential maize productivity.

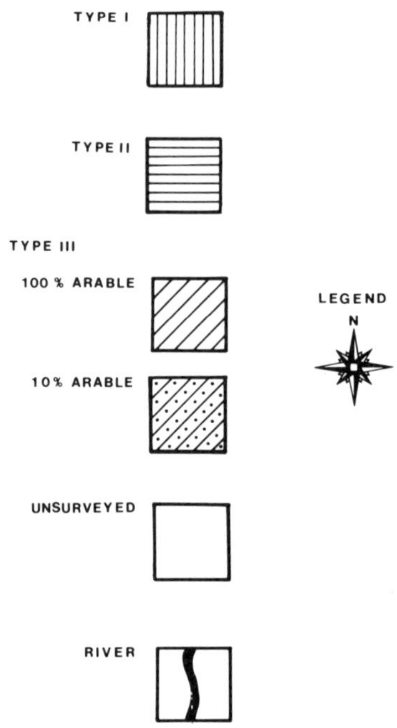
TYPE I
TYPE II
TYPE III
100 % ARABLE
10% ARABLE
UNSURVEYED
RIVER
LEGEND
N

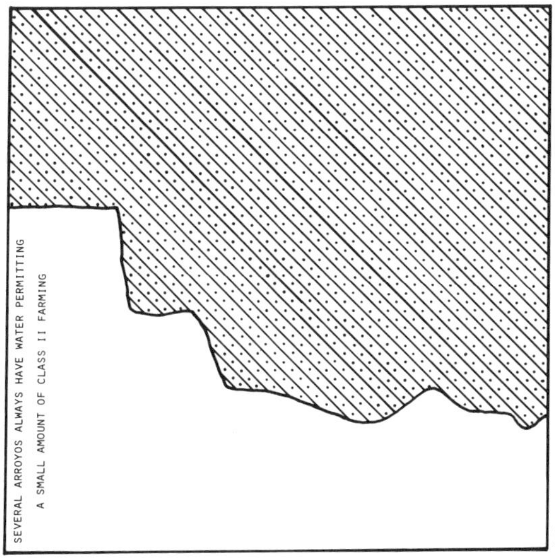

N2E3

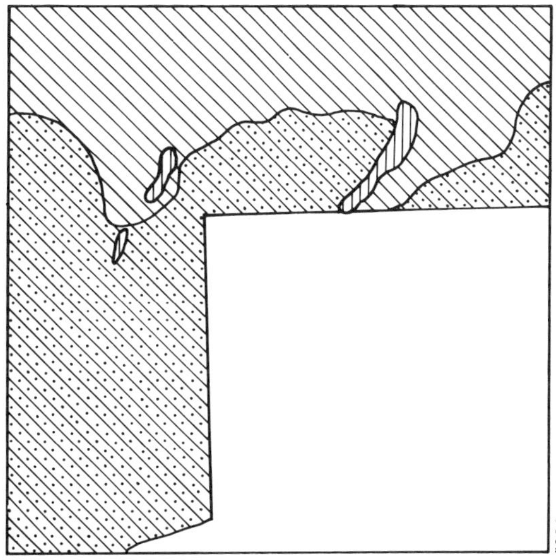
N3E3

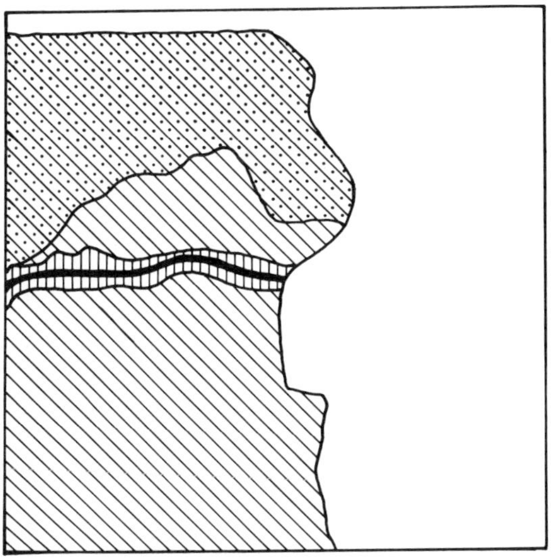
N1E4

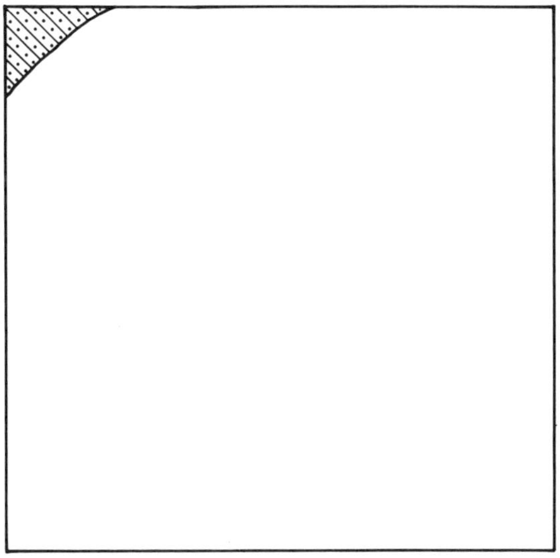
N3E2

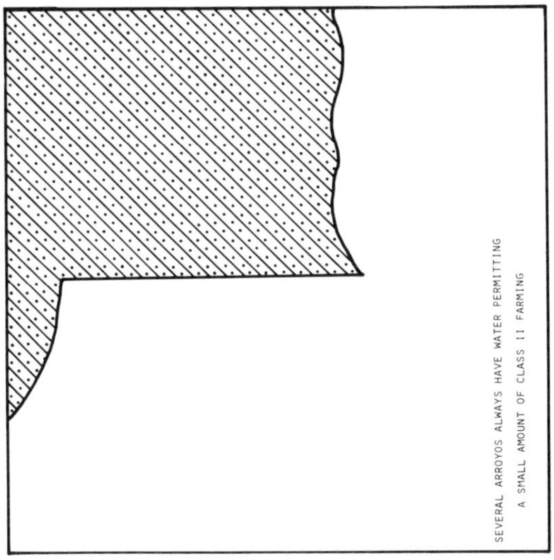

N1E3

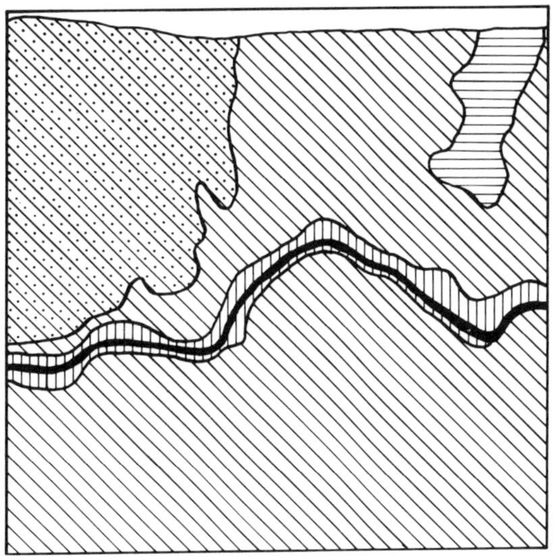
N2E4

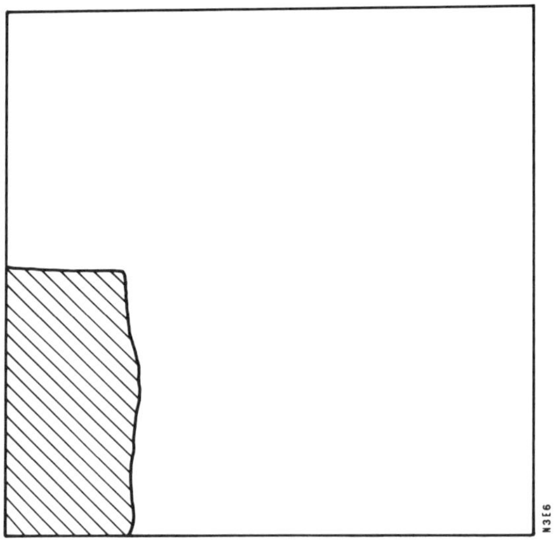
N3E6

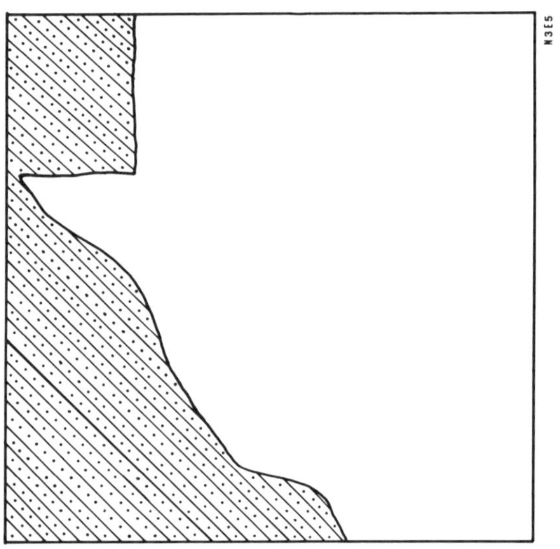
N3E5

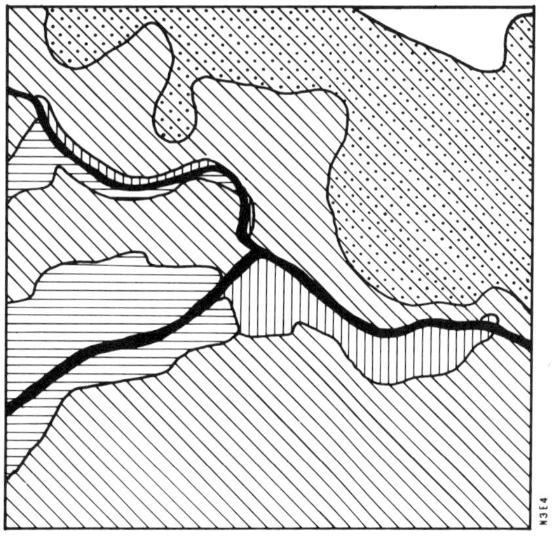
N3E4

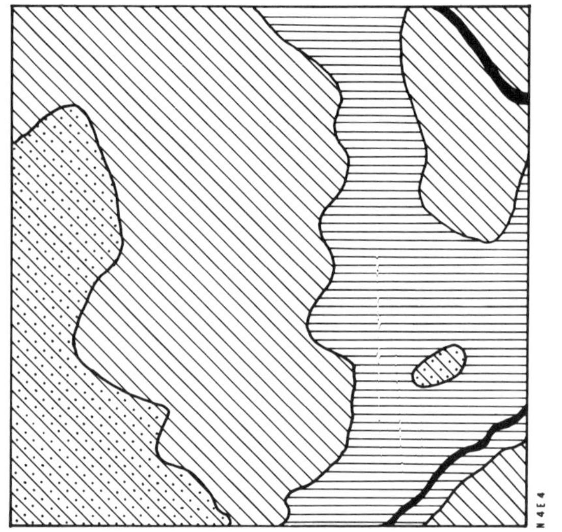
N4E4

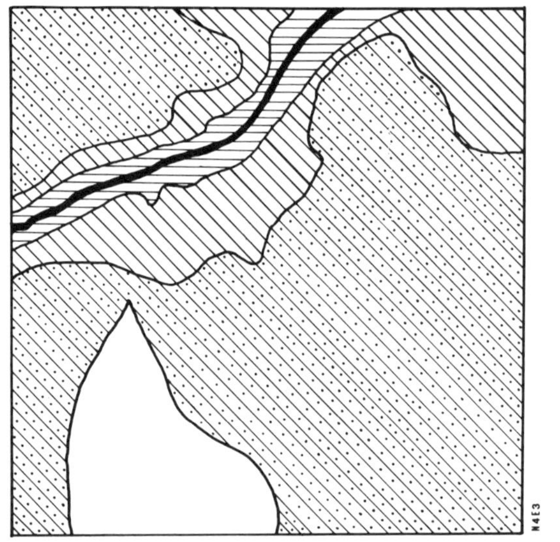
N4E3

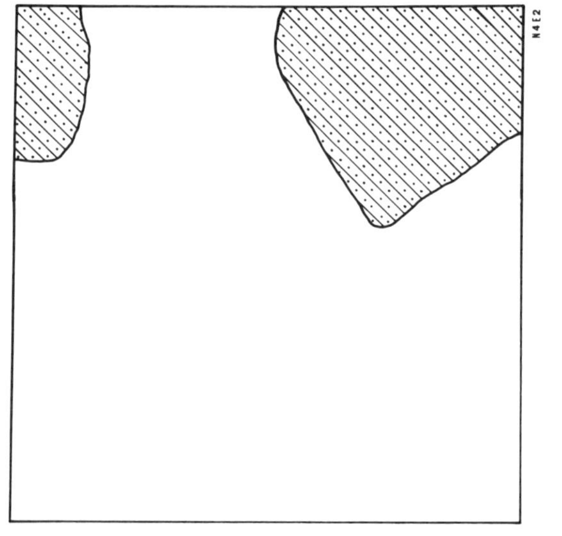
N4E2

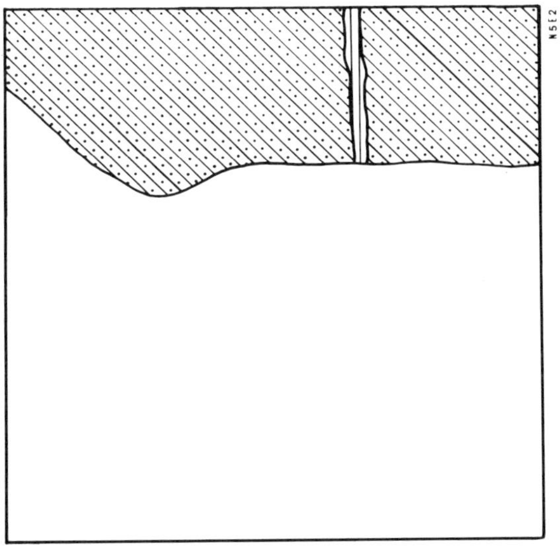
N5E2

N5E5

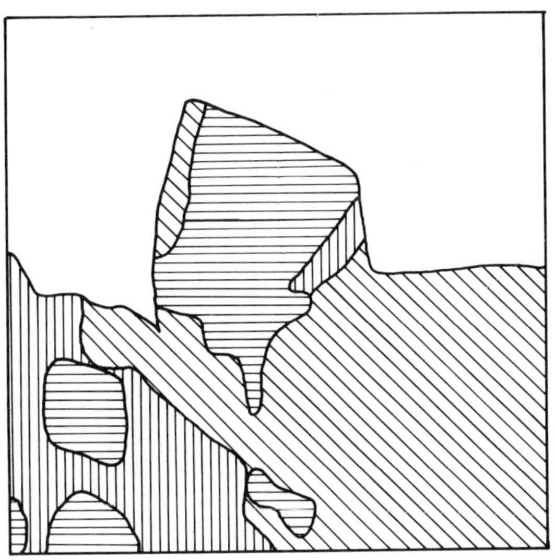
N4E6

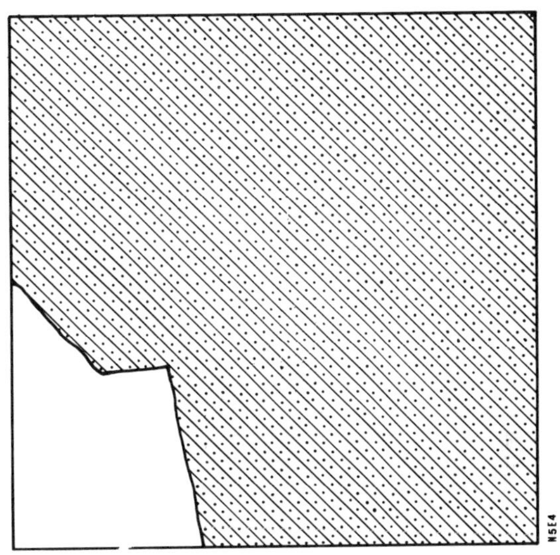
N5E4

N4E5

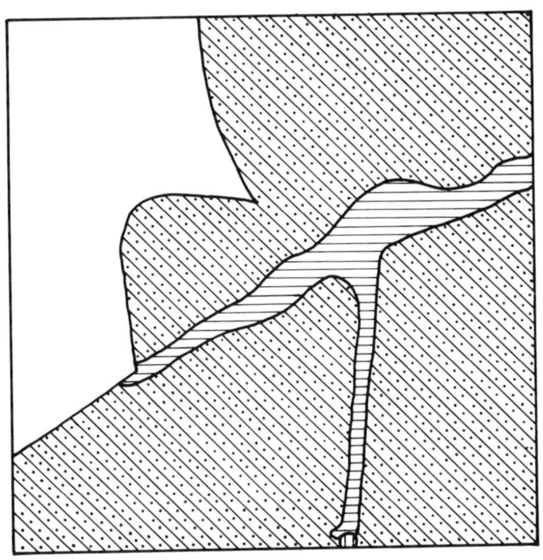
N5E3

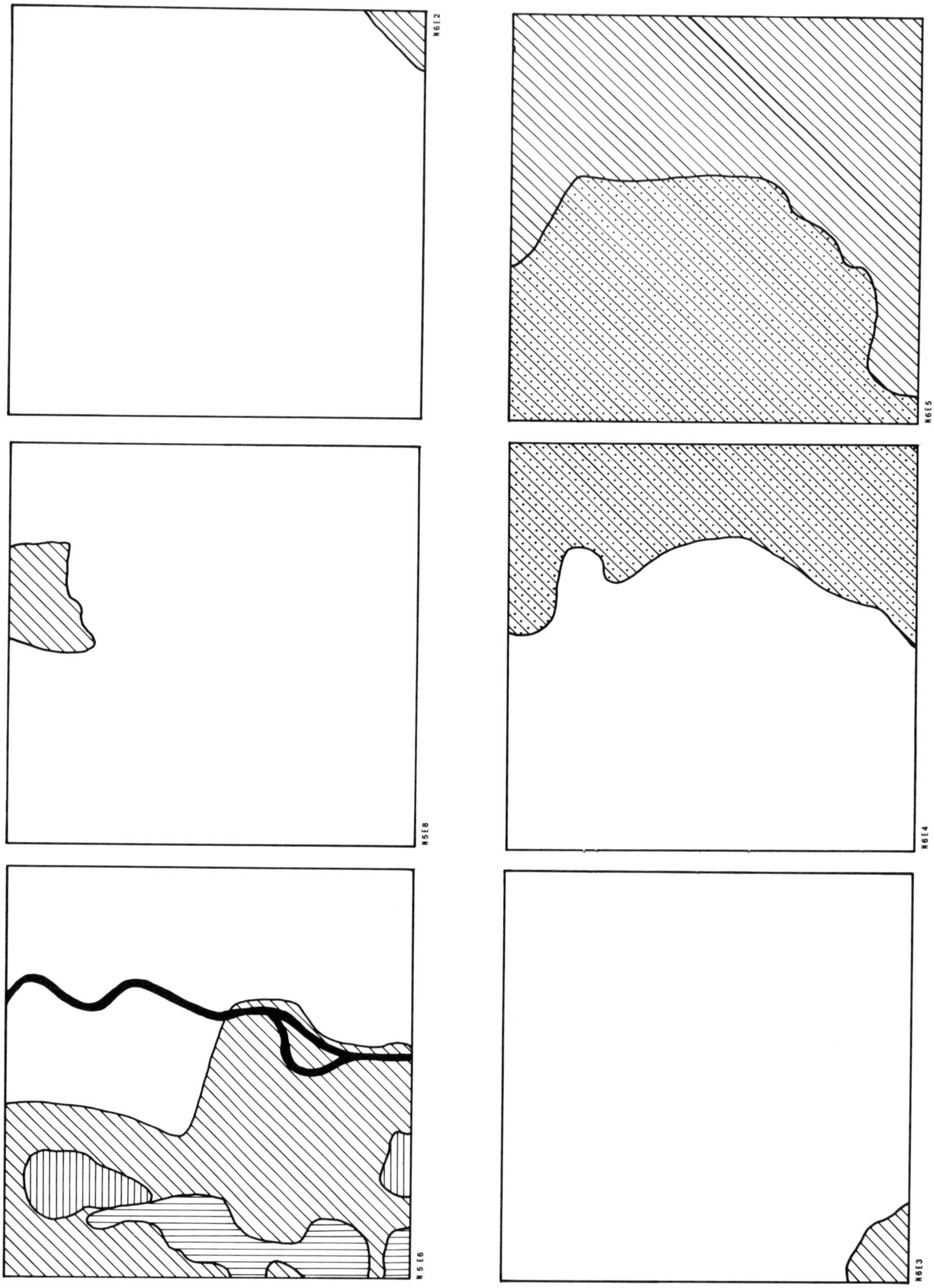
N6E2
N6E5
N5E8
N6E4
N5E6
N6E3

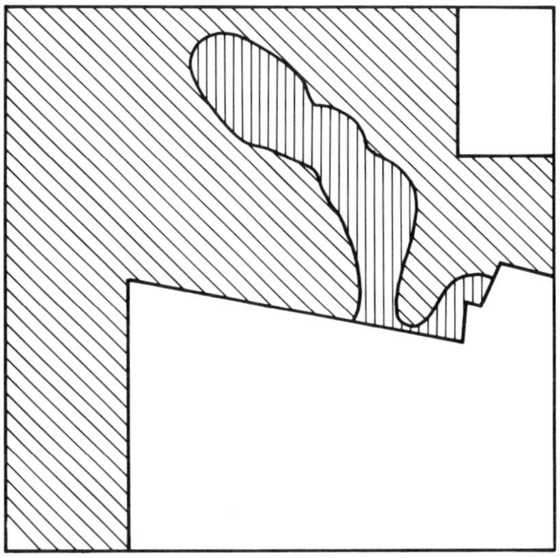

N6E8

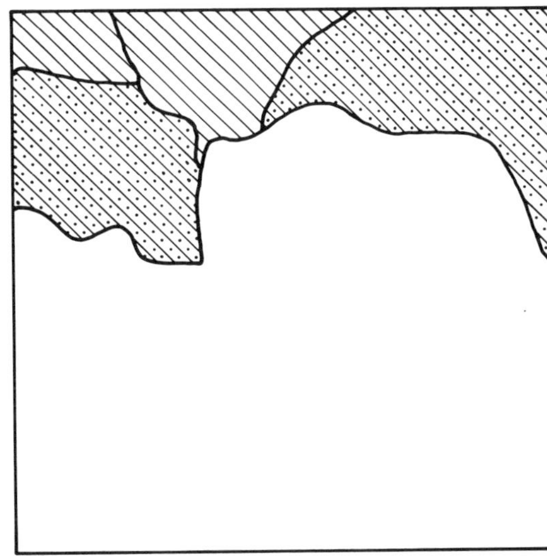

N7E4

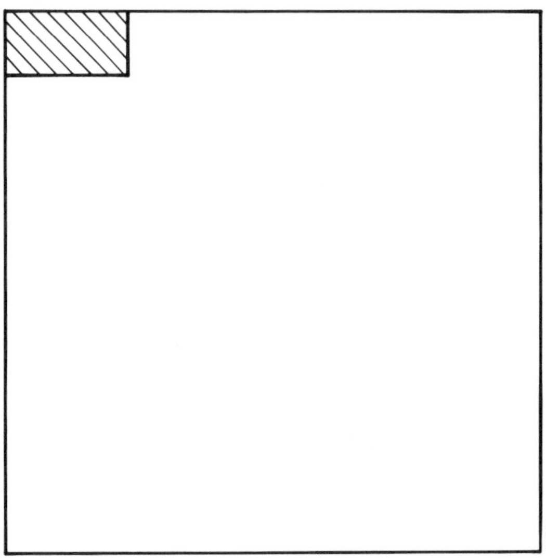

N6E7

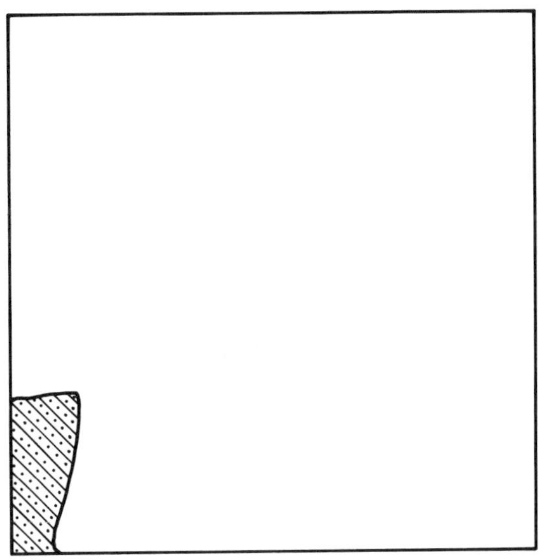

N6E10

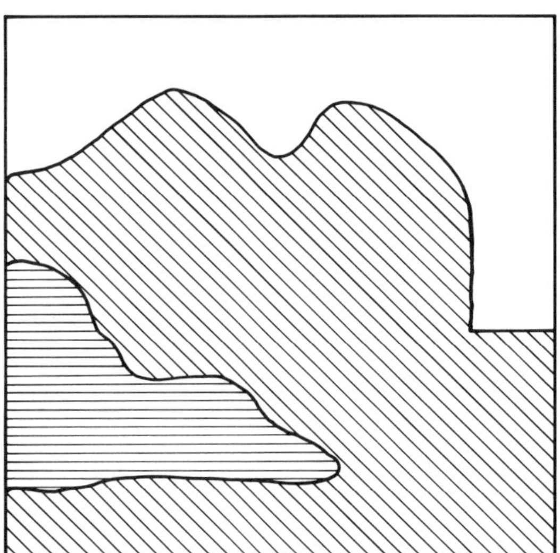

N6E6

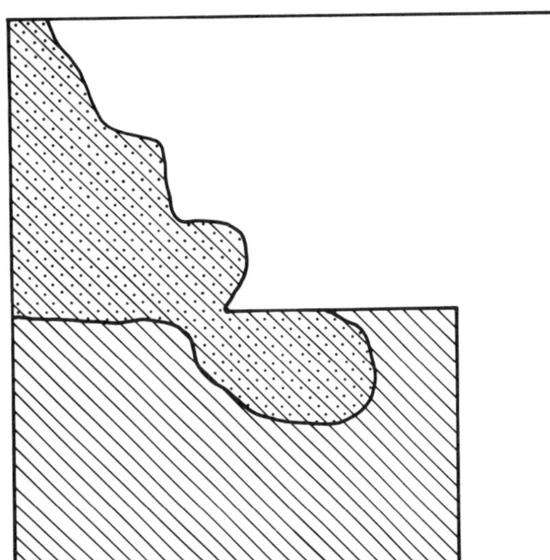

N6E9

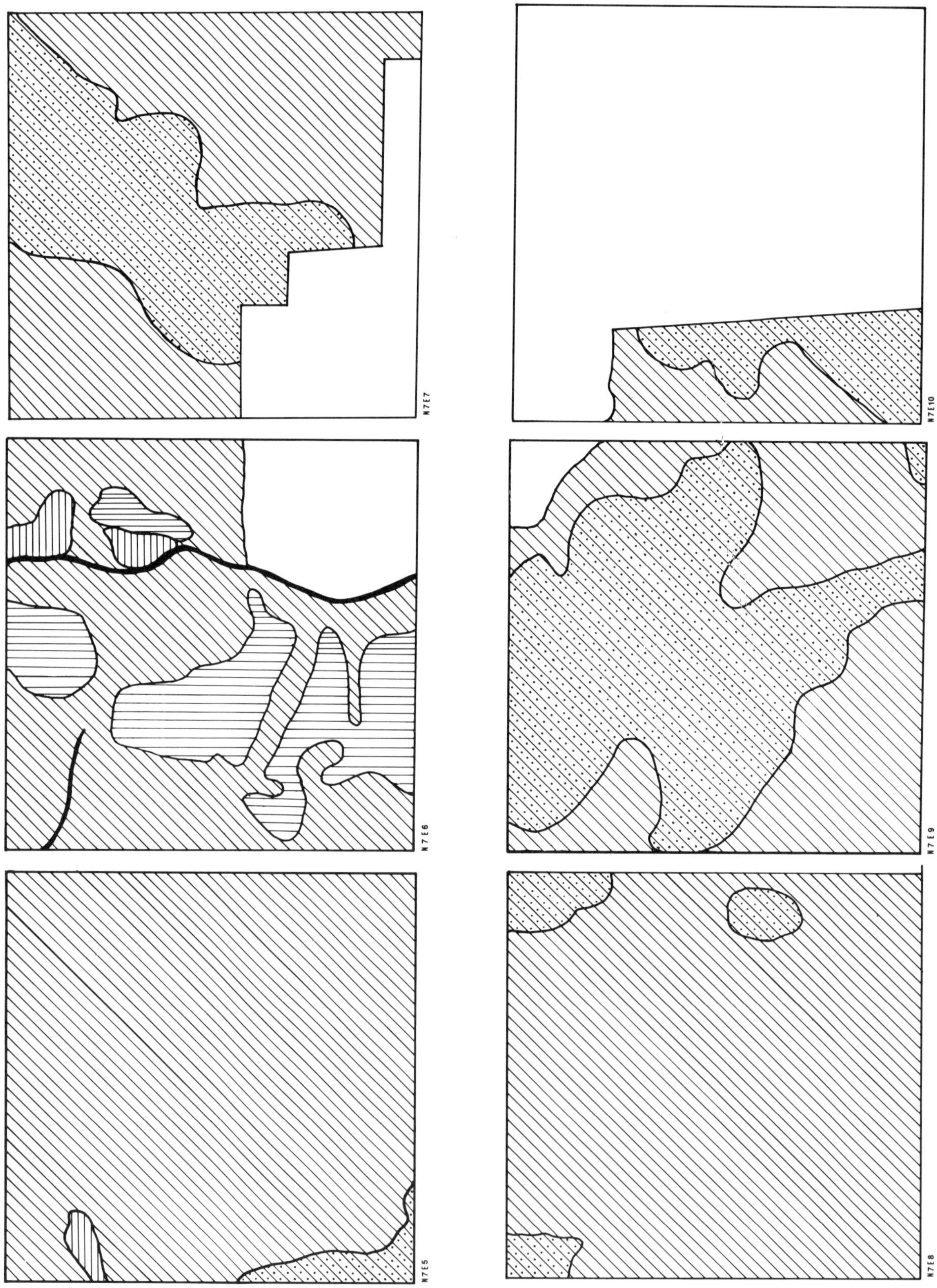
N7E7
N7E10
N7E6
N7E9
N7E5
N7E8

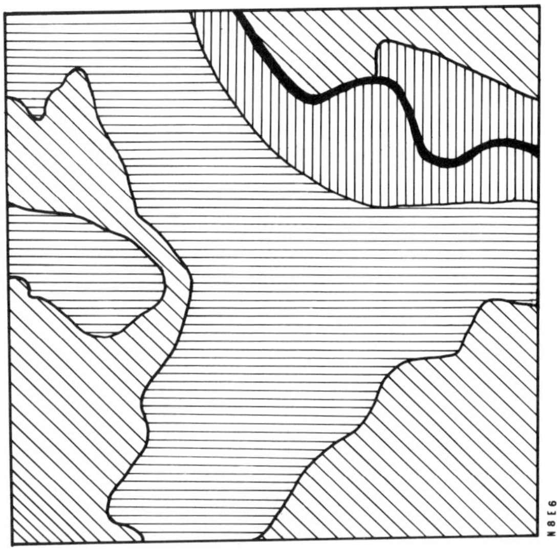
N8E6

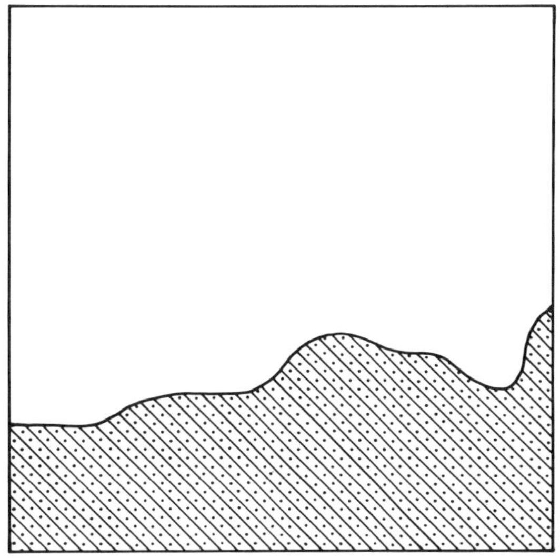
N8E9

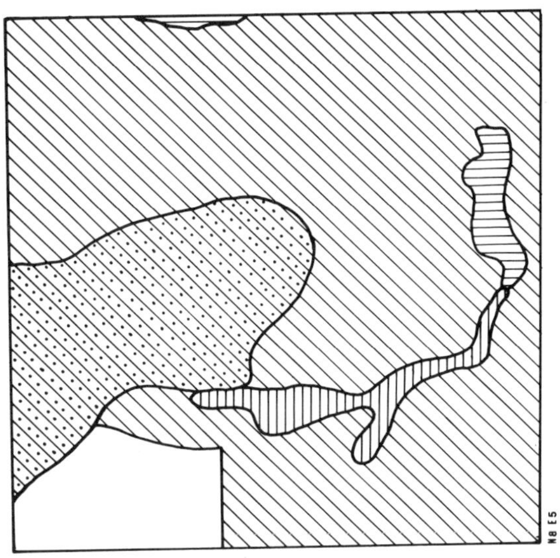
N8E5

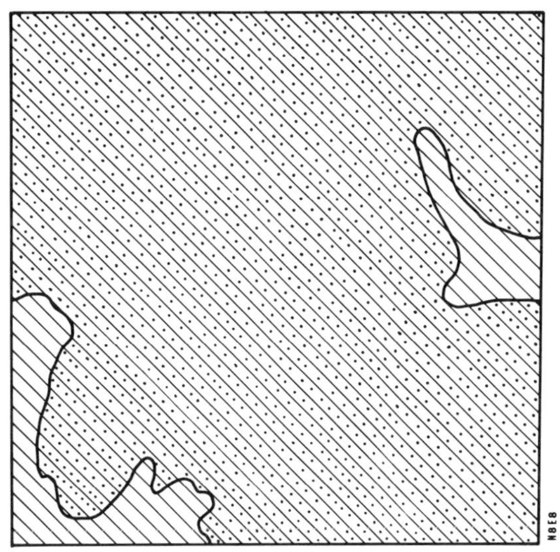
N8E8

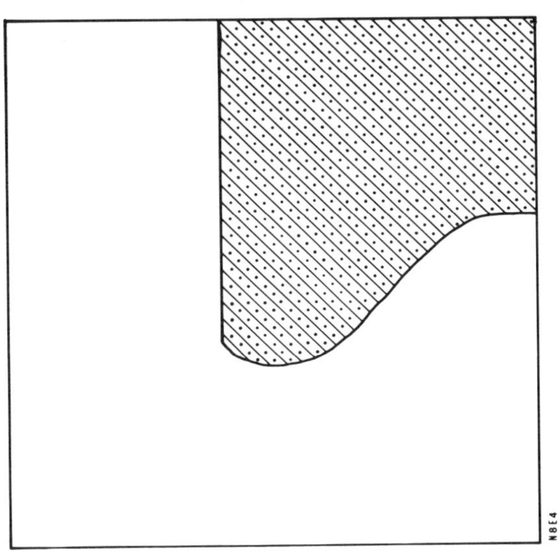
N8E4

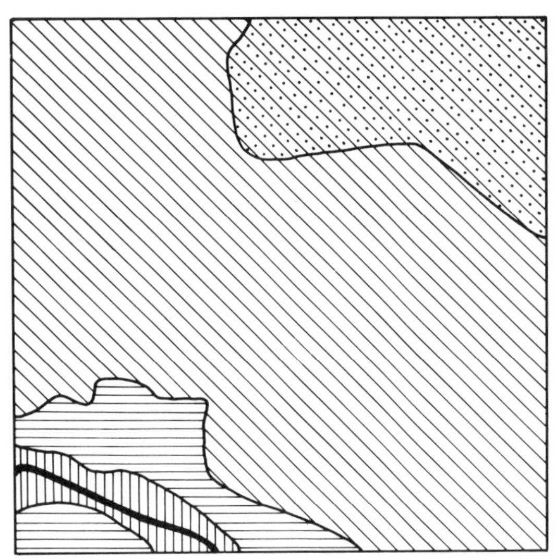
N8E7

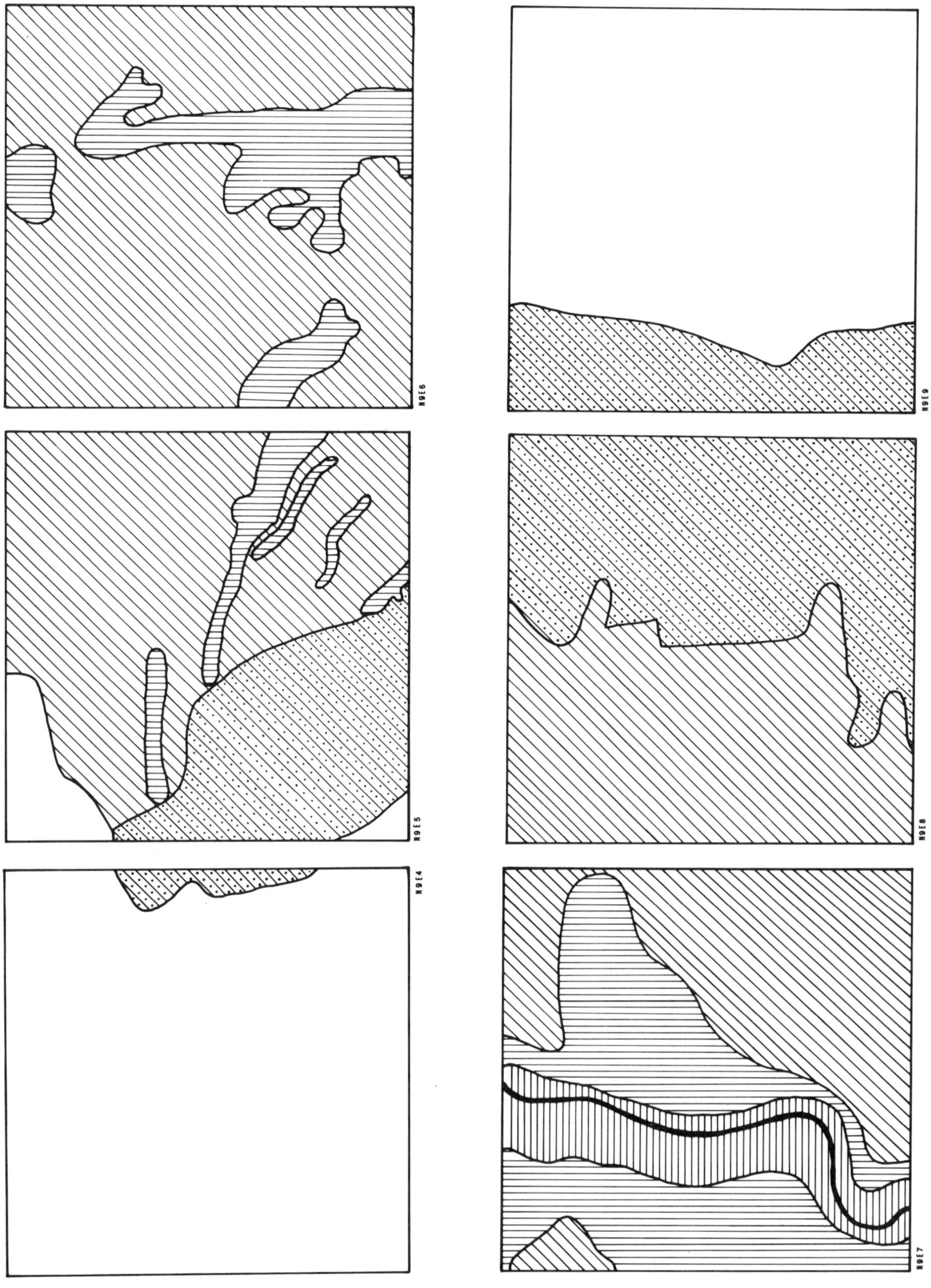
N9E6
N9E9
N9E5
N9E8
N9E4
N9E7

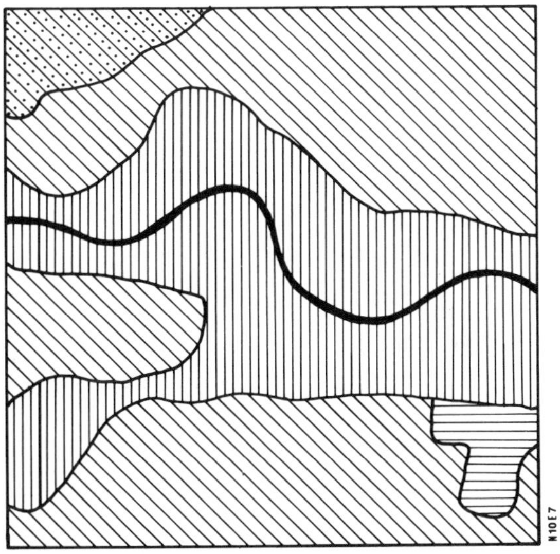
N10E7

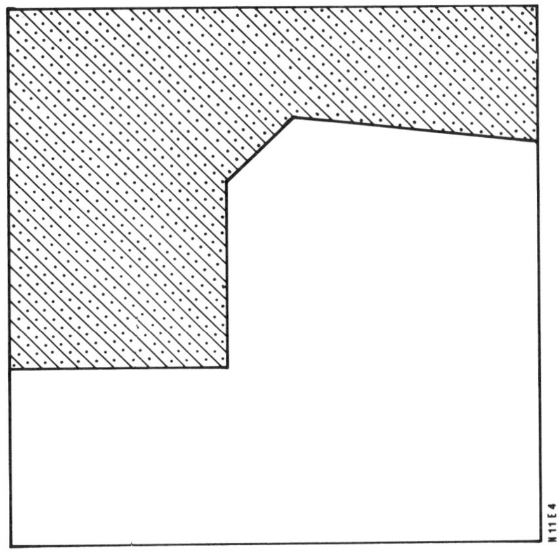
N11E4

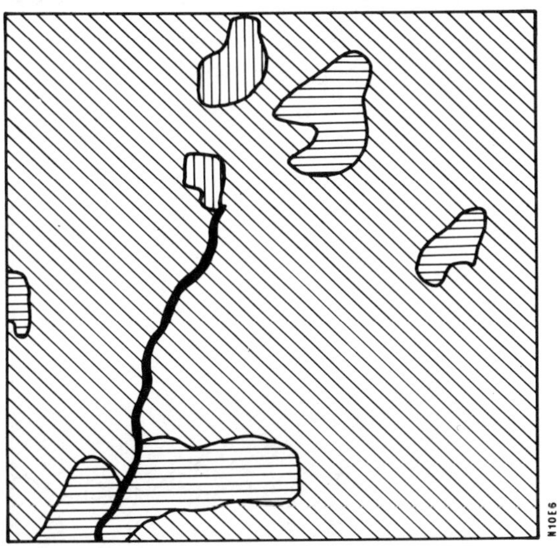
N10E6

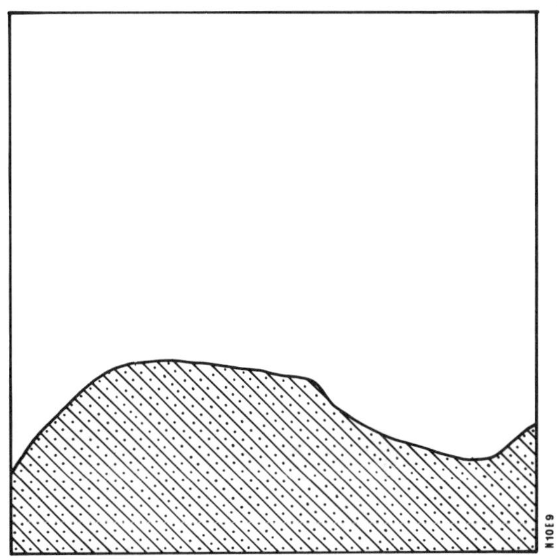
N10E9

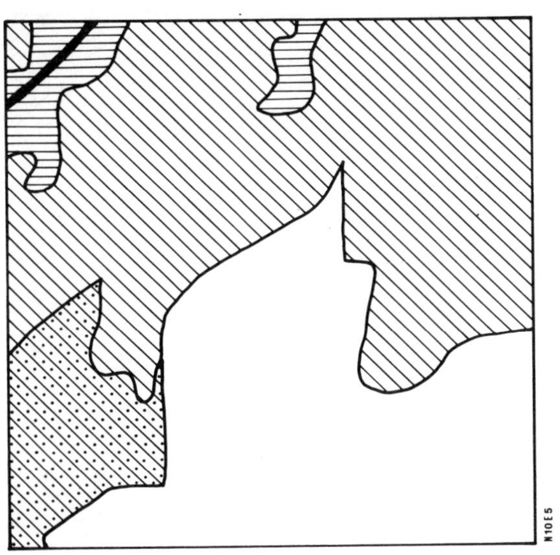
N10E5

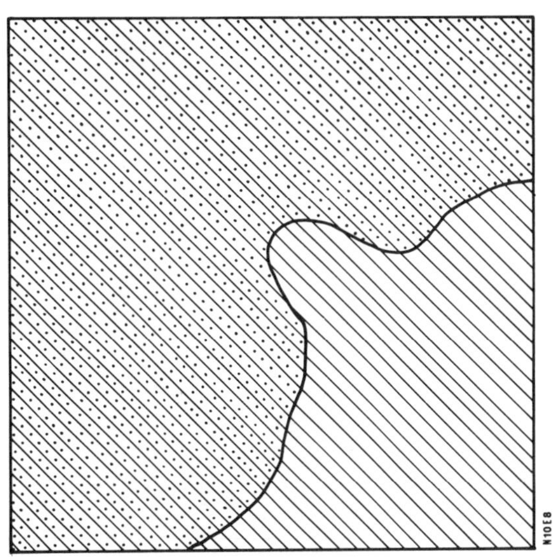
N10E8

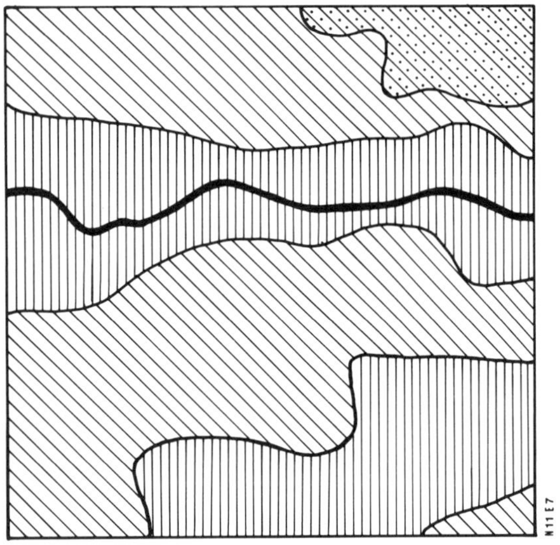
N11E7

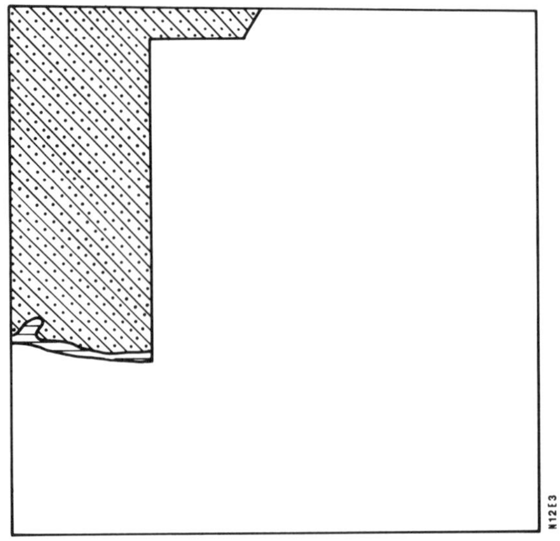
N12E3

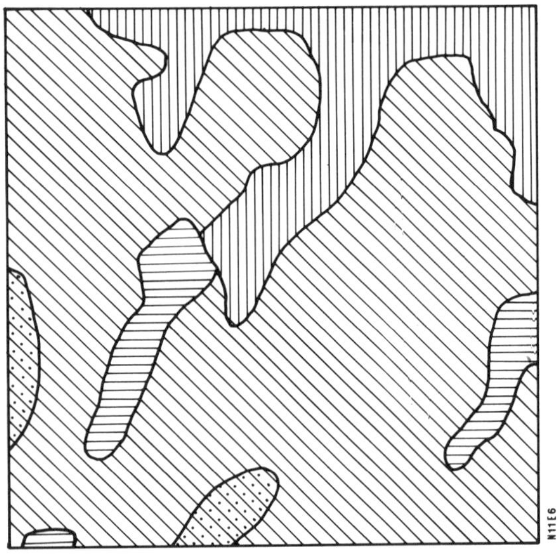
N11E6

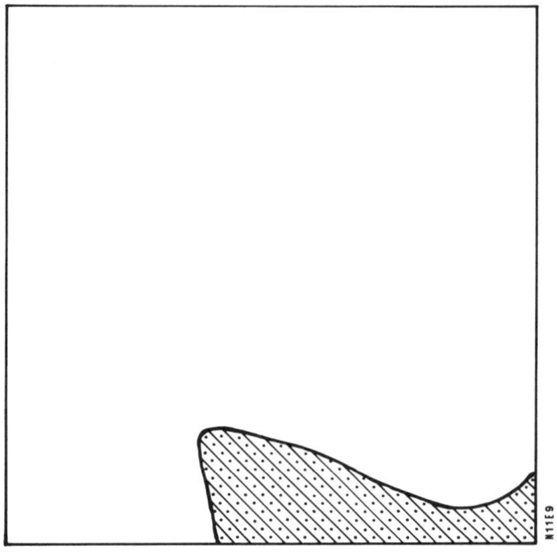
N11E9

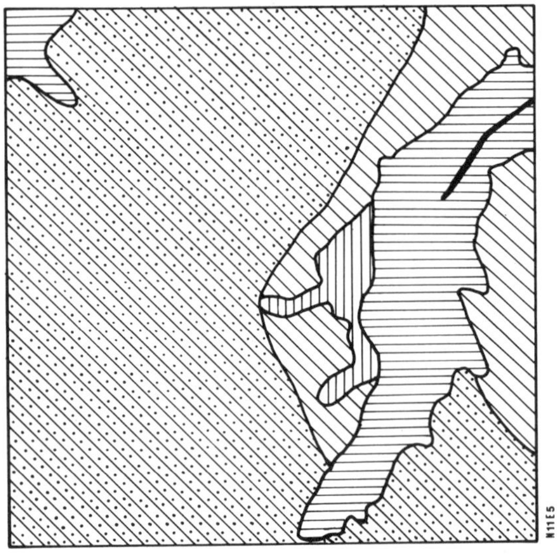
N11E5

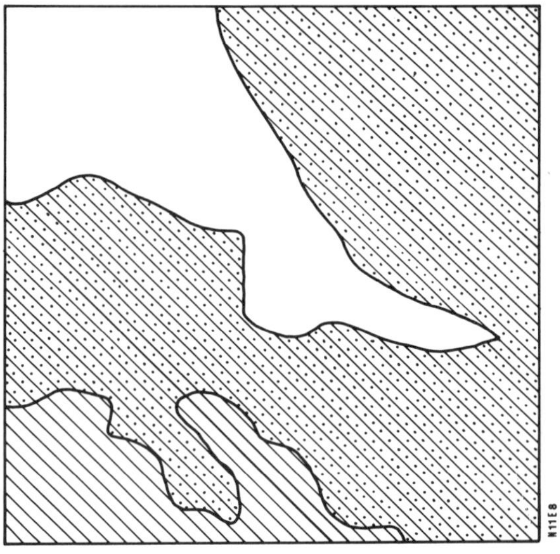
N11E8

N12E6

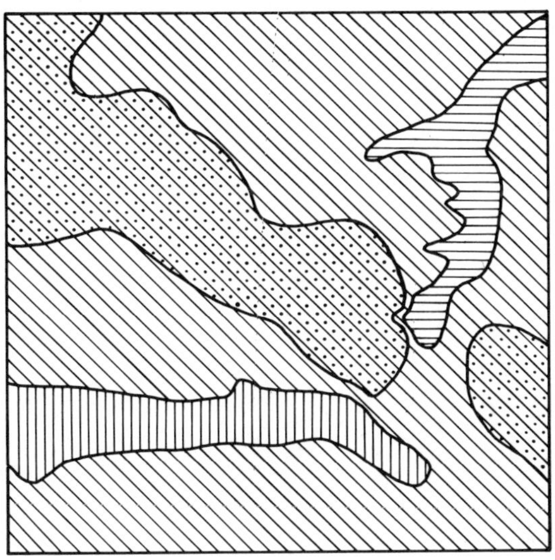

N12E5

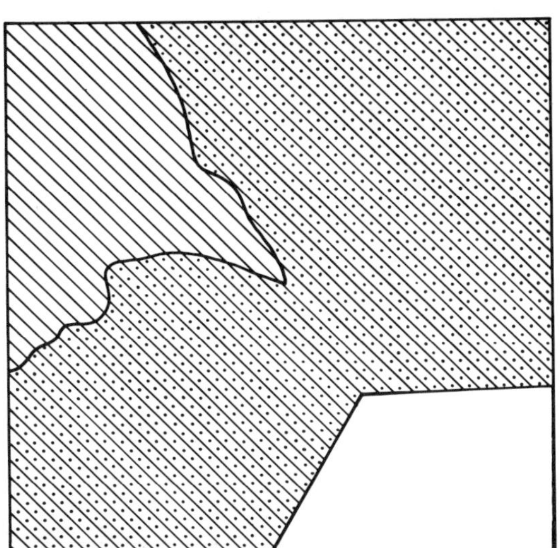

N12E4

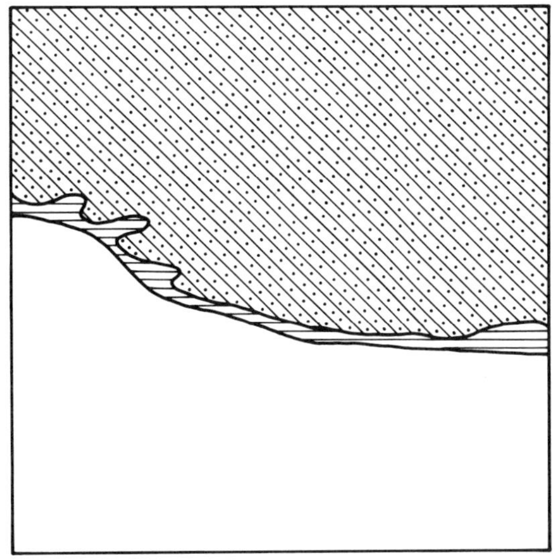

N13E3

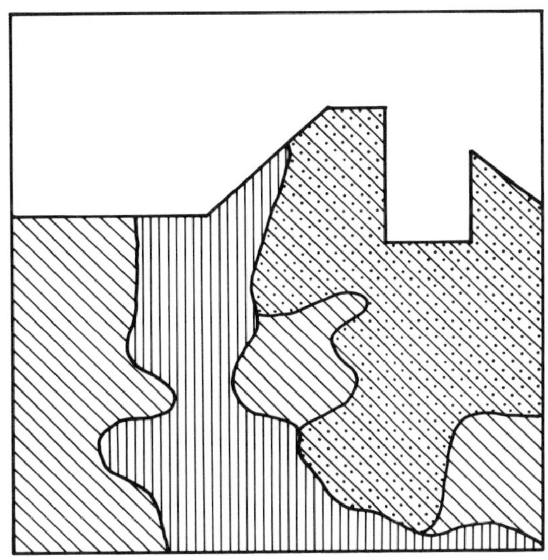

N12E8

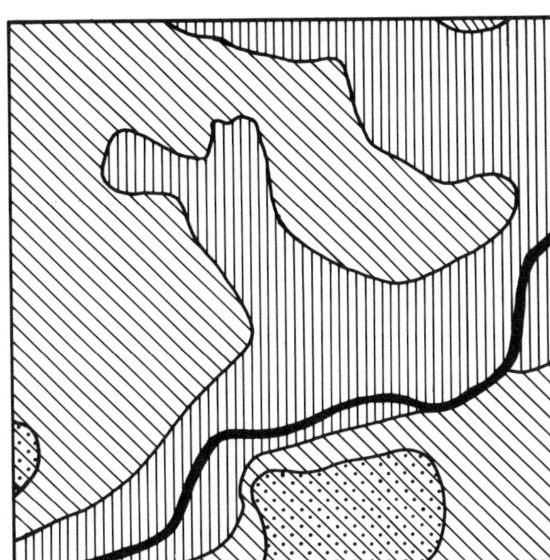

N12E7

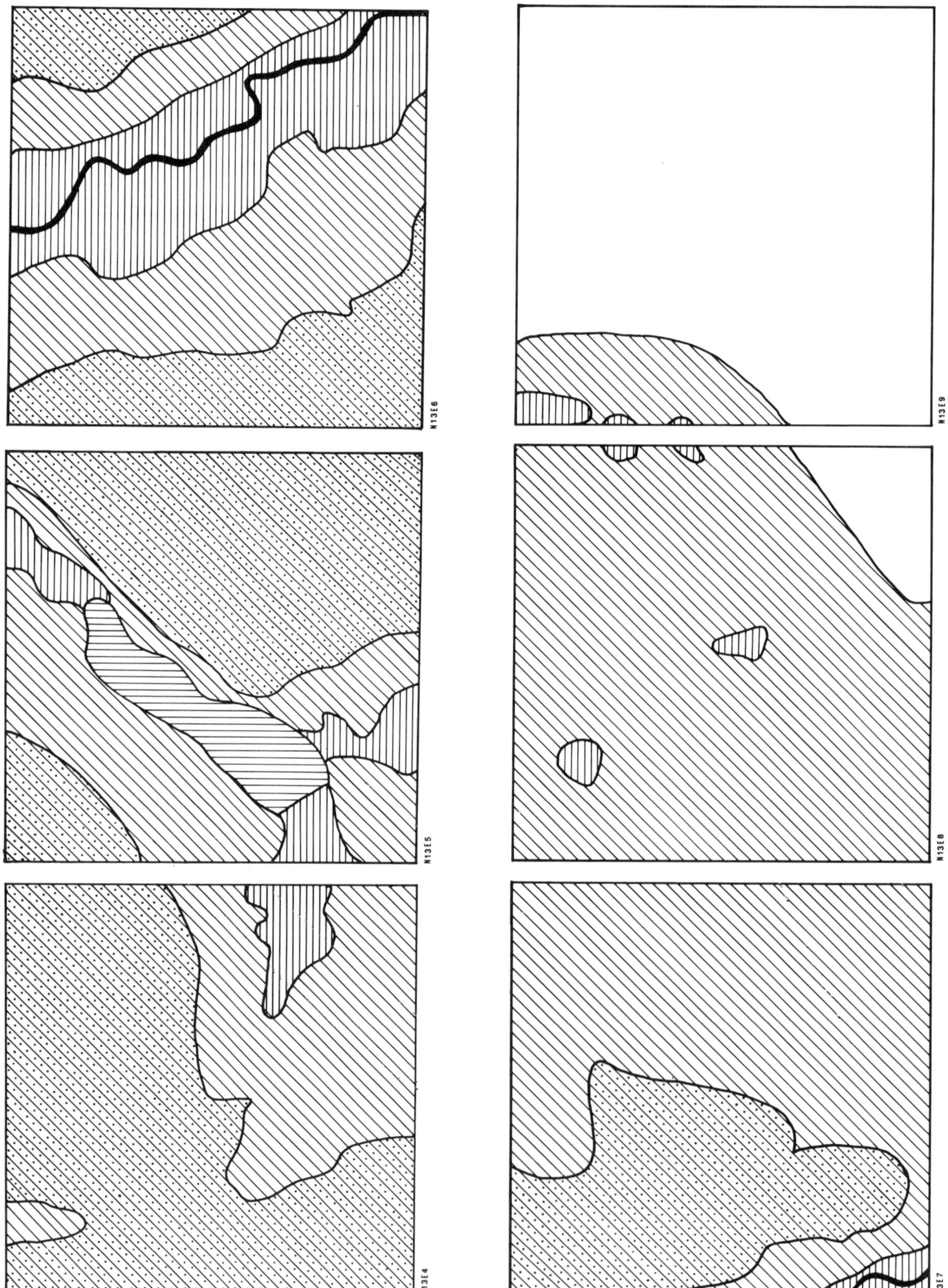
N13E6
N13E9
N13E5
N13E8
N13E4
N13E7

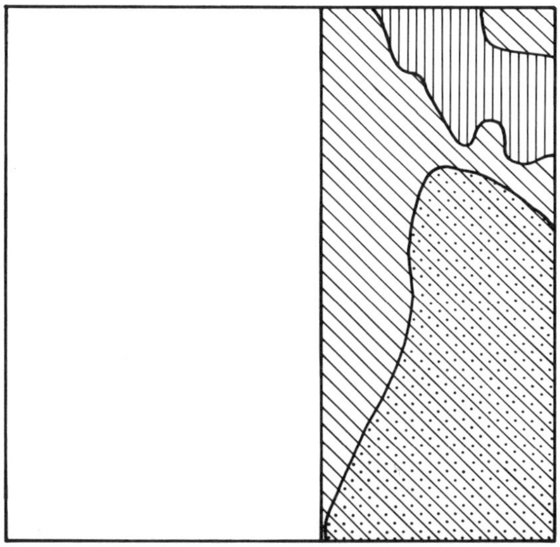

N14E5

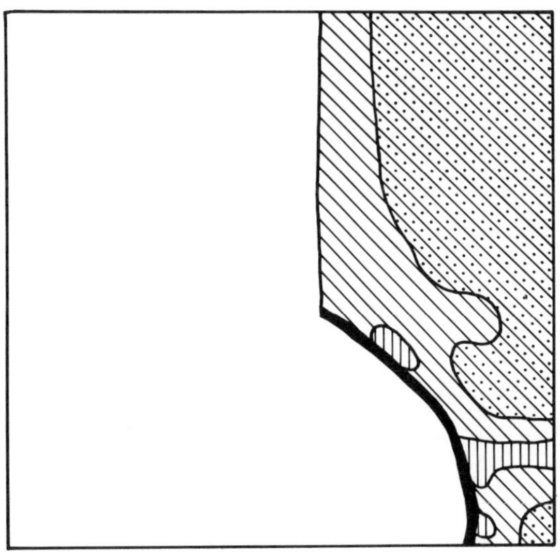

N14E4

N14E3

N14E8

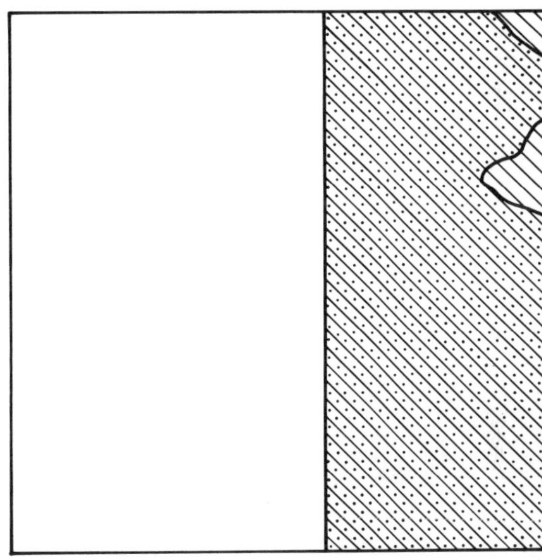

N14E7

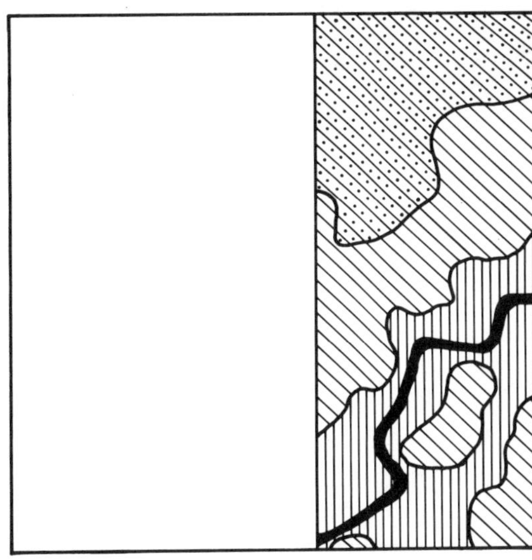

N14E6

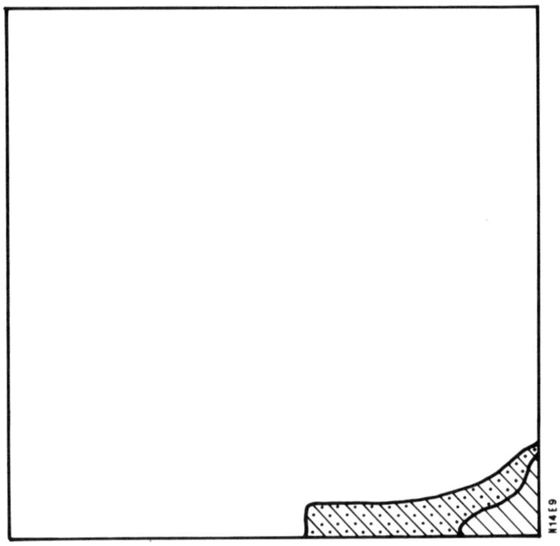
N14E9

Appendix IV

SITES THAT HAVE BEEN COMBINED

In Chapter 4 we described how some sites were combined for purposes of analysis, where we thought this would result in better approximations of actual sociological communities than does our site numbering system. The site numbering system can best be viewed as a means of collecting data in the field and then publishing it in coded form. The combined sites, we think, better represent entities that have meaning for analysis. This appendix includes sites we combined for that purpose, and the combined population estimates for each.

Sites that have been combined: Period Late I

Site Numbers	Population
0-6-1, 42-44, 46-49, 51, 52, 100-113, 115, 117, 118, 121, 153	17242
2-6-35, 36	141
2-6-87,90, 93	115
2-6-136-139	658
3-6-5, 8, 149	289
3-6-12-14	91
3-6-42,43	260
3-6-56, 57	51
3-6-68, 69	616
3-6-85, 86	879
3-6-107, 108, 122	137
3-6-109-114	138
3-6-129-131, 136	59

Sites that have been combined: Period II

Site Numbers	Population
0-7-1, 2-7-13	14492
2-7-15, 16	105
3-7-1-5, 7	423
3-7-9, 10	48
3-7-15-17	63
3-7-23, 24	132
3-7-29, 30, 37	83
3-7-32,33	40
3-7-41, 42	48
3-7-44-46	979
3-7-48, 49	115
3-7-54-56	29
3-7-69-71	29
3-7-77, 78, 84	161
3-7-79-82	87
3-7-85, 86	24
3-7-97-99	43

Sites That Have Been Combined: Period IIIa

Site Numbers	Population
3-8-2-6, 8	803
3-8-10-12	135
3-8-27-29	254
3-8-31-33	64
3-8-37-39, 283	1585
3-8-46, 48	211
3-8-57, 58	42
3-8-63, 64	81
3-8-67, 69-76	309
3-8-77-79	145
3-8-87, 89	286
3-8-114, 115	141
3-8-118-123	197
3-8-129-132	556
3-8-136, 150-152	12835
3-8-140-143	137
3-8-144, 153-164	296
3-8-167-170	83
3-8-177-179	3219
3-8-199, 200, 232	193
3-8-202-208	158
3-8-228-229	119
3-8-233-239, 241	1937
3-8-272-274	1320

Sites That Have Been Combined: Period IIIb

Site Numbers	Population
0-9-1, 2-9-120, 126, 128-131, 177-193, 198, 200, 202, 203, 206, 207, 209-212,214	24,189
2-9-1-3, 5-9, 69-89, 103, 104	1677
2-9-11-14	219
2-9-20, 25	385
2-9-29, 30	221
2-9-36-38, 44, 46, 47	525
2-9-50-61	1081
2-9-62, 136, 215	802
2-9-64, 65, 125	411
2-9-92-100	869
2-9-116-119	504
2-9-142, 156-158	257
3-9-8-18	839
3-9-21,22	53
3-9-25, 67	59
3-9-27-29	120
3-9-31, 37-42,71, 72	2135
3-9-47, 68	31
3-9-59, 60	35
3-9-62, 63	1215

Sites That Have Been Combined: Period IV

Site Numbers	Population
2-10-2-4	1929
2-10-11, 12, 16, 18	718
3-10-6-9	1121
3-10-10-13	43
3-10-28-30	95
3-10-34, 35	281
3-10-38-58, 60, 63, 64	16,117
3-10-67-72	1501
3-10-74, 75	25
3-10-83-91	4047

Sites That Have Been Combined: Period V

Site Numbers	Population
0-11-1, 2-11-126-132, 144-165, 247, 251-278, 281-283, 333, 34-47, 3-11-14-18, 21-38, 40-43, 46	13,573
2-11-1-13, 90-112, 120	1755
2-11-14-21, 142, 166-186, 188-195, 199-221, 223-227, 229-232	2506
2-11-23-25, 133	801
2-11-49-51	327
2-11-58-61, 63-69	775
2-11-71-75	1711
2-11-76-78, 323	199
2-11-81-85	329
2-11-88, 89, 124, 125	387
2-11-235-243	774
2-11-244-245	800
2-11-284-295	509
2-11-298-310, 315, 316	549
2-11-317-322, 332	506
3-11-1-5	97
3-11-48-50	51
3-11-51-54	119
3-11-56-59, 84-88, 117-132, 177	1968
3-11-64-69	172
3-11-94-96, 98	557
3-11-106, 111-113	97
3-11-107, 109, 153	81
3-11-115, 154-164, 514	585
3-11-133-136	65
3-11-144-145	63
3-11-146, 147	25
3-11-149-151	33
3-11-181-185	147
3-11-188-191	141
3-11-192, 209, 210	55
3-11-225, 226	183
3-11-228, 229	15
3-11-236-238	49
3-11-245, 259, 286, 288, 289, 292-296	6649
3-11-267, 268	78
3-11-270-272	76
3-11-276, 305-313, 317	486
3-11-281-283	99
3-11-324-332, 334	285
3-11-338, 339	95
3-11-341, 342, 344	47
3-11-347-348	30
3-11-356-359	793
3-11-368-369	55
3-11-378, 379	173
3-11-380, 523	199
3-11-382, 383	607
3-11-385, 414	851
3-11-387, 389	25
3-11-393-394, 399	23
3-11-395-398	30
3-11-404-407	100
3-11-408-410, 431, 432, 435	243
3-11-418, 419	25
3-11-426-428	30
3-11-433, 434	30
3-11-438, 439	115
3-11-442-444	39
3-11-447, 448	41
3-11-451-455, 458-462	1627
3-11-471, 473, 475-479	267
3-11-472, 474, 494-496	87
3-11-484, 485	55
3-11-501-503	40

Appendix V

SITE SURVEY FORM

VALLE GRAND SURVEY 1977

Site Number(s)____

Date________________Airphoto No.____________Recorder__________________

Topography

A. 1) Low Alluvium   2) High Alluvium

3) Piedmont   Low   Middle   Upper

4) Mountain

B. Slope   1) Flat   2) Shallow

3) Moderate   4) Steep

5) Hill or Ridgetop

Environment

A. Soils

1) Type(s)

2) Texture

3) Color

4) Degree of Erosion

5) Depth

B. Water

1) Distance to nearest source

2) Depth of water table

C. Vegetation (describe zone and species present)

Modern Use

A. Land utilization (mention crops)

B. Types of irrigation

C. Roads, Houses, etc.

D. Wells

(2) Site Number(s)____

Archaeological Remains

A.	Sherd Density	Trace	Very light
		Light	Moderate
		Heavy	
B.	Obsidian	Present	Absent
	1. Color		
	2. Density		
	3. Blades	Cores	Flakes
	Other (describe)		
C.	Ground Stone		
	Manos	Metates	Mortar
	Pestle	Celt	Other (describe)
D.	Chipped Stone other than Obsidian		
	Blades	Flakes	Cores
	Other (describe)		

E. Other
1. Adobes
2. Building stone
3. Plaster floors
4. Stone floors
5. Evidence for burning

F. Description of Structures (use back of sheet if necessary). Include base and top measurements, height, orientation, possible functions, access, and relations to other structures.

(3) Site Number(s)____

Archaeological Remains (cont.)

G. Terraces (use back of sheet if necessary). Number, dimensions, functions, access.

H. Other

1) Walls

2) Dams

3) Quarries

4) Workshop(s)

5) Other specialized activities

Collection Made Not Made

A. Description of Collection Area(s) (size[s], Location[s])

(4) Site Number(s)__________

B. Field Estimates of Periodization

	Trace	Present	Well Represented
Tierras Largas			
San José			
Guadalupe			
Rosario			
Early I			
Late I			
II			
IIIa			
IIIb-IV			
V			

Comments, ideas, relationships

Appendix VI

FIELD NUMBER DESIGNATIONS AND FIELD NUMBERS BY SITE

Beginning with the 1977 field season, we were asked by the Centro Regional in Oaxaca to list sites according to a site designation scheme they had developed. This scheme is described in Chapter 1 of this volume. This appendix lists the *Agencias* and *Municipio* abbreviations we used, then gives the field number using this system for all Valle Grande sites. Note that Zi and Zim both mean Zimatlán, and both Za and Zaa refer to Zaachila.

Field Number Designations

NAME	*AGENCIA*	*MUNICIPIO*
CE-AT-AT	ANIMAS TRUJANO	ANIMAS TRUJANO
CE-CUI-BG	BARRIO GRANDE	CUILAPAN
CE-CUI-CAR	CARRIZAL	CUILAPAN
CE-CUI-CUI	CUILAPAN	CUILAPAN
CE-CUI-RQ	RANCHO QUEMADO (BARRIO)	CUILAPAN
CE-CUI-SJ	SAN JOSE (BARRIO)	CUILAPAN
CE-CUI-SL	SAN LUCAS (BARRIO)	CUILAPAN
CE-SBC-RM	REYES MANTECON	S. BARTOLO COYOTEPEC
CE-SBC-SBC	SAN BARTOLO COYOTEPEC	S. BARTOLO COYOTEPEC
CE-SMC-SMC	SANTA MARIA COYOTEPEC	STA. MARIA COYOTEPEC
OC-OC-SJC	SAN JACINTO CHILATECA	OCOTLAN
OC-OC-TM	TEJAS DE MORELOS	OCOTLAN
OC-SA-SA	SAN ANTONINO	SAN ANTONINO
OC-SJC-SJC	SAN JUAN CHILATECA	S. JUAN CHILATECA
OC-SMT-SMT	SAN MARTIN TILCAJETE	SAN MARTIN TILCAJETE
OC-STJ-SDJ	SANTO DOMINGO JALIEZA	SANTO TOMAS JALIEZA
OC-STJ-SPG	SAN PEDRO GUEGOREXE	STO. TOMAS JALIEZA
OC-STJ-STJ	SANTO TOMAS JALIEZA	SANTO TOMAS JALIEZA

FIELD NUMBER DESIGNATIONS

NAME	*AGENCIA*	*MUNICIPIO*
ZA-SRJ-SRJ	SAN RAYMUNDO JALPAN	S. RAYMUNDO JALPAN
ZA-TRI-LAR	LA RAYA	TRINIDAD DE ZAACHILA
ZA-TRI-TRI	TRINIDAD DE ZAACHILA	TRINIDAD DE ZAACHILA
ZA-ZA-EZ	EMILIANO ZAPATA	ZAACHILA
ZA-ZA-ROA	ROALO	ZAACHILA (CORRECT: TRINIDAD DE ZAACHILA)
ZA-ZA-SMT	S. MIGUEL TLANICHICO	ZAACHILA (CORRECT: TRINIDAD DE ZAACHILA)
ZA-ZA-SPR	S. PEDRO LA REFORMA	ZAACHILA
ZA-ZA-TRI	TRINIDAD DE ZAACHILA	ZAACHILA (CORRECT: TRINIDAD DE ZAACHILA)
ZA-ZA-ZA	ZAACHILA	ZAACHILA
ZI-CIE-CIE	LA CIENAGA	LA CIENAGA
ZI-SAT-AB	AGUA BLANCA	STA. ANA TLAPACOYAN
ZI-SAT-ER	EL RINCON	STA. ANA TLAPACOYAN
ZI-SAT-SAT	SANTA ANA TLAPACOYAN	STA. ANA TLAPACOYAN
ZI-SBM-SBM	SAN BERNARDO MIXTEPEC	S. BERNARDO MIXTEPEC

ZI-SCM-EZ	EMILIANO ZAPATA	STA. CRUZ MIXTEPEC
ZI-SCM-SCM	SANTA CRUZ MIXTEPEC	STA. CRUZ MIXTEPEC
ZI-SCM-TR	TRAPICHE	STA. CRUZ MIXTEPEC
ZI-SCQ-LS	LA SOLEDAD	STA. CATARINA QUIANE (CORRECT: LA CIENEGA)
ZI-SCQ-SCQ	SANTA CATARINA QUIANE	STA. CATARINA QUIANE
ZI-SG-SG	SANTA GERTRUDIS	STA. GERTRUDIS
ZI-SG-SJ	SAN JOSE GUELATOVA	STA. GERTRUDIS
ZI-SG-PDP	PASO DE PIEDRAS	STA. GERTRUDIS
ZI-SIY-SIY	STA. INES YATZECHE	STA. INES YATZECHE
ZI-SMA-GUE	GUEGOVELA	STA. MARIA AYOQUEZCO
ZI-SMA-SMA	STA. MARIA AYOQUEZCO	STA. MARIA AYOQUEZCO
ZI-SMA-SJL	SAN JUAN LOGOLAVA	STA. MARIA AYOQUEZCO (CORRECT: EJUTLA DE CRESPO)
ZI-SPH-SPH	SAN PABLO HUIXTEPEC	SAN PABLO HUIXTEPEC
ZI-VDF-LB	LA BANDITA	VALDEFLORES
ZI-VDF-VDF	VALDEFLORES	VALDEFLORES
ZI-ZI-SN	SAN NICOLAS	ZIMATLAN
ZI-ZI-ZI	ZIMATLAN	ZIMATLAN

Field Numbers for Tierras Largas

SITE #	FIELD #
1	Zaa-Zaa-Ez-1
2	Ce-SBC-SBC-2
3	Ce-SBC-RM-3
4	Oc-SMT-SMT-12
5	Zi-SPH-SPH-6
6	Zim-SAT-SAT-2
7	Zaa-Zaa-2
8	Zim-SIY-SIY-1

Field Numbers for San José

SITE #	FIELD #
1	Zaa-Zaa-Ez-1
2	Ce-SBC-SBC-2
3	Ce-SBC-RM-3
4	OC-SMT-SMT-12
5	OC-SMT-SMT-4, 5
6	Zi-SPH-SPH-6
7	Zim-SAT-SAT-2
8	Zaa-Zaa-2
9	Zim-SIY-SIY-1

Field Numbers for Guadalupe

SITE #	FIELD #
1	Ce-Cui-RQ-10
2	Zaa-Zaa-Ez-1
3	Ce-SBC-SBC-2
4	CE-SBC-RM-3
5	OC-SMT-SMT-12
6	OC-SMT-SMT-4, 5
7	Zi-SPH-SPH-6
8	Zim-SAT-SAT-2
9	Zaa-Zaa-2

Field Numbers for Rosario

SITE #	FIELD #
1	Ce-Cui-SJ-5
2	Oc-SMT-SMT-11
3	CE-SBC-SBC-2
4	CE-SBC-SBC-9
5	CE-SBC-RM-26
6	OC-SMT-SMT-36
7	OC-SMT-SMT-12
8	Zim-Zim-Zim-1
9	Zim-Zim-Zim-5
10	Zim-Zim-SN-3
11	Zim-SIY-SIY-1
12	Zi-SPH-SPH-6
13	Zim-SG-SG-4
14	Oc-TM-TM-1, 2, 3
15	Zim-SAT-SAT-2
16	Zim-VDF-LB-1
17	Zi-SMA-GUE-3
18	Oc-SMT-SMT-11
19	Ce-SBC-RM-3
20	CE-SBC-SBC-9
21	Zaa-Zaa-2

Field Numbers for Early I

SITE #	FIELD #
1	Ce-Cui-SL-5; Ce-Cui-RQ-2
2	Ce-Cui-SL-5; Ce-Cui-RQ-2
3	Ce-Cui-SL-5; Ce-Cui-RQ-2
4	Ce-Cui-SL-3
5	Ce-Cui-SJ-5
6	Za-SRJ-SRJ-2
7	Xox-SJB-1
8	Xox-SJB-2
9	CE-AT-AT-1
10	CE-SMC-SMC-4, 5
11	CE-SMC-SMC-11

SITE #	FIELD #
12	CE-Cui-RQ-11
13	CE-Cui-RQ-13
14	Ce-SMC-SMC-19
15	Zaa-Zaa-Zaa-10
16	Zaa-Zaa-Zaa-12
17	Zaa-Zaa-Zaa-12
18	Zim-Cie-Cie-14
19	Ce-SBC-SBC-2
20	Cie-Cie-12
21	Ce-SBC-SBC-9
22	Zim-Cie-Cie-13
23	Zaa-Tri-Lar-5
24	Zaa-Roa-1
25	Ce-SBC-RM-3
26	Zim-Zim-Zim-5, 8
27	Zim-Zim-Zim-6
28	Oc-STJ-STJ-3
29	Zim-Zim-SN-1
30	Zim-Zim-SN-3
31	Zim-Zim-SN-4
32	Zim-SPH-SPH-5
33	Zim-SPH-SPH-19
34	Zim-SPH-SPH-10
35	Zim-SPH-SPH-9
36	Zim-SIY-SIY-1
37	Zi-SPH-SPH-6
38	Zi-SPH-SPH-6
39	Zim-SG-SG-4
40	Zim-SG-PDP-1
41	OC-TM-TM-1, 2, 3
42	Zim-SAT-SAT-4
43	Zim-SAT-SAT-2
44	Zim-VDF-LB-1
45	Zi-SMA-GUE-3
46	Zi-SAT-AB-44
47	Zim-SMA-SMA-39
48	Zi-SMA-SMA-36
49	Zi-SMA-SMA-35
50	Ce-Cui-RQ-13
51	Ce-SMC-SMC-19
52	Oc-SMT-SMT-11
53	Zi-SMA-SMA-35
54	Oc-SMT-SMT-11
55	Ce-SBC-RM-26
56	Zim-Cie-Cie-13
57	Ce-SBC-SBC-9
58	Zim-Zim-Zim-18
59	Zim-Cie-Cie-2
60	Oc-SMT-SMT-23
61	Oc-SMT-SMT-23
62	Zim-Zim-Zim-5
63	Zim-Zim-Zim-1
64	Zaa-Zaa-2
65	Zi-SAT-AB-2

Field Numbers for Late I

SITE #	FIELD #
1	Ce-Cui-Car-4
2	Ce-Cui-RQ-1
3	Ce-Cui-RQ-2; Ce-Cui-SL-5
4	Ce-Cui-RQ-2; Ce-Cui-SL-5
5	Ce-Cui-RQ-2; Ce-Cui-SL-5
6	Ce-Cui-SL-3
7	Ce-Cui-RQ-6
8	Ce-Cui-SJ-6
9	Ce-Cui-SL-2
10	Ce-Cui-SJ-2
11	Ce-Cui-SJ-1
12	Za-SRJ-1
13	Za-SRJ-SRJ-2
14	Za-SRJ-SRJ-2
15	Zim-SCM-SCM-12
16	Za-SRJ-SRJ-2
17	Za-SRJ-SRJ-2
18	Za-SRJ-SRJ-2
19	Za-SRJ-SRJ-2
20	Xox-SJB-1
21	Xox-SJB-2
22	CE-AT-AT-1
23	CE-SMC-SMC-5
24	CE-SMC-SMC-5
25	CE-SMC-SMC-4, 5
26	CE-SMC-SMC-8-10, 13-16, 23
27	CE-SMC-SMC-8-10, 13-16, 23
28	CE-SMC-SMC-8-10, 13-16, 23
29	CE-SMC-SMC-8-10, 13-16, 23
30	CE-SMC-SMC-11
31	Ce-Cui-RQ-15
32	Ce-Cui-RQ-14
33	Ce-Cui-RQ-13
34	Ce-SMC-SMC-6
35	Ce-SMC-SMC-19
36	Ce-SMC-SMC-19
37	Ce-SBC-SBC-7
38	Ce-SBC-SBC-7
39	Ce-SMC-SMC-25
40	Ce-SBC-SBC-15
41	Ce-SBC-SBC-16
42	Zaa-Zaa-Zaa-12
43	Zaa-Zaa-Zaa-12
44	Zaa-Zaa-Zaa-9
45	Zaa-Zaa-Zaa-8
46	Zaa-Zaa-Ez-1
47	Ce-SBC-SBC-2
48	Ce-SBC-SBC-9
49	Ce-SBC-SBC-27
50	Ce-SBC-SBC-24
51	Zim-Cie-Cie-13
52	Zaa-Roa-1
53	Zaa-Tri-2
54	Zaa-Tri-20
55	Ce-SBC-RM-5
56	Ce-SBC-RM-3
57	Ce-SBC-RM-3
58	Ce-SBC-RM-14
59	Ce-SBC-RM-12
60	Ce-SBC-RM-15
61	Ce-SBC-RM-15
62	Za-Za-Ez-32
63	Za-Za-Ez-20
64	Zim-Zim-Zim-20
65	Zim-Zim-Zim-19, 20
66	Zim-Cie-Cie-2
67	Zim-SCQ-LS-3
68	Zim-SCQ-LS-1
69	Zim-SCQ-LS-1
70	Zi-SCQ-LS-2
71	Ce-SBC-RM-16

Field Numbers for Late I (Con't)

SITE #	FIELD #
72	Oc-SMT-SMT-23
73	Oc-SMT-SMT-23
74	Oc-SMT-SMT-22
75	Oc-SMT-SMT-8
76	Oc-SMT-SMT-26
77	Zim-Zim-Zim-12, 14, 15
78	Zim-Zim-Zim-1
79	Zim-Zim-Zim-2
80	Zim-Zim-Zim-5
81	Zim-Zim-Zim-5
82	Zim-Zim-Zim-5, 8
83	Zim-Zim-Zim-6
84	Oc-SMT-SMT-10
85	Oc-SMT-SMT-11
86	Oc-SMT-SMT-11
87	Oc-SMT-SMT-33
88	Oc-STJ-STJ-2
89	Oc-SMT-SMT-34
90	Zim-Zim-SN-1
91	Zim-Zim-SN-3
92	Oc-STJ-STJ-1
93	Oc-STJ-STJ-1
94	Oc-STJ-STJ-1
95	Oc-STJ-STJ-8
96	Zim-SPH-SPH-15
97	Zim-Zim-SN-4
98	Zim-SPH-SPH-5
99	Zim-SPH-SPH-2
100	Zim-SIY-SIY-1
101	Zi-SAT-ER-9
102	Zi-SCM-SCM-5
103	Zi-SCM-SCM-3
104	Zim-VDF-VDF-5
105	Zim-VDF-VDF-7
106	Zim-VDF-VDF-10
107	Zim-SG-SG-2
108	Zim-SG-SG-3
109	Zi-SPH-SPH-6
110	Zi-SPH-SPH-6
111	Zi-SPH-SPH-6
112	Zi-SPH-SPH-6
113	Zi-SPH-SPH-6
114	Zi-SPH-SPH-6
115	Zim-SPH-SPH-8
116	Zim-SAT-ER-3
117	Zim-SAT-ER-7
118	Zim-SCM-TR-1
119	Zim-SCM-TR-3
120	Zim-SCM-TR-2
121	Zim-SCM-TR-10
122	Zim-SG-SG-4
123	Zim-SG-PDP-1
124	Oc-TM-TM-1, 2, 3
125	Oc-TM-TM-1, 2, 3
126	Oc-Oc-TM-2
127	Zim-SAT-SAT-1
128	Zim-SAT-SAT-14
129	Zim-SAT-SAT-16
130	Zim-SAT-SAT-2
131	Zim-SAT-SAT-15
132	Zim-VDF-LB-1
133	Zi-SMA-Gue-2
134	Zi-SMA-Gue-5
135	Zi-SAT-AB-42
136	Zim-SAT-SAT-2
137	Zi-SMA-SMA-8
138	Zi-SMA-SMA-20
139	Zi-SMA-SMA-11
140	Zi-SMA-SMA-21

Field Numbers for Late I (Con't)

SITE #	FIELD #
141	Zi-SMA-SMA-18
142	Zi-SMA-SMA-18
143	Zim-SMA-SMA-39
144	Zim-SMA-SMA-29
145	Zi-SMA-SMA-36
146	Zi-SMA-SMA-4
147	Zi-SMA-SMA-2
148	Zi-SMA-SMA-78
149	Ce-Cui-RQ-2; Ce-Cui-SL-5
150	CE-SMC-SMC-17
151	CE-Cui-RQ-11
152	Zaa-Zaa-2

Field Numbers for II

SITE #	FIELD #
1	Ce-Cui-RQ-2; Ce-Cui-SL-5
2	Ce-Cui-RQ-2; Ce-Cui-SL-5
3	Ce-Cui-RQ-2; Ce-Cui-SL-5
4	Ce-Cui-RQ-2; Ce-Cui-SL-5
5	Ce-Cui-RQ-2; Ce-Cui-SL-5
6	Ce-Cui-SL-3
7	Ce-Cui-SJ-6
8	Ce-Cui-SJ-1
9	Za-SRJ-SRJ-2
10	Za-SRJ-SRJ-2
11	Za-SRJ-3
12	Xox-SJB-2
13	Ce-AT-AT-2
14	Ce-Cui-RQ-12
15	Ce-Cui-RQ-13
16	Ce-Cui-RQ-13
17	Ce-Cui-RQ-13
18	Zaa-SPR-2
19	Ce-SMC-SMC-6
20	OC-STJ-STJ-8
21	Ce-SMC-SMC-19
22	Zaa-Zaa-Zaa-14
23	Zaa-Zaa-Zaa-12
24	Zaa-Zaa-Zaa-12
25	Zaa-Zaa-Zaa-9
26	Zaa-Zaa-Zaa-8
27	Ce-SBC-SBC-2
28	Ce-SBC-SBC-9
29	Zim-Cie-Cie-13
30	Zim-Cie-Cie-13
31	Za-Roa-1
32	Zaa-Tri-1
33	Zaa-Tri-2
34	Ce-SBC-RM-3
35	Zim-Zim-Zim-22
36	Zim-Cie-Cie-10
37	Zim-Cie-Cie-13
38	Zim-Zim-Zim-17
39	Zim-Zim-Zim-20
40	Zim-Cie-Cie-2
41	Zim-SCQ-LS-3
42	Zi-SCQ-LS-2
43	Ce-SBC-RM-20
44	Oc-SMT-SMT-23
45	Oc-SMT-SMT-21
46	Oc-SMT-SMT-46
47	Oc-SMT-SMT-18
48	Zim-Zim-Zim-12
49	Zim-Zim-Zim-13
50	Zim-Zim-Zim-7
51	Zim-Zim-Zim-1

Field Numbers for II (Con't)

SITE #	FIELD #
52	Zim-Zim-Zim-3,4
53	Zim-Zim-Zim-2
54	Zim-Zim-Zim-5
55	Zim-Zim-Zim-5
56	Zim-Zim-Zim-5
57	Zim-Zim-Zim-6
58	Oc-SMT-SMT-10
59	Zim-Zim-SN-1
60	Zim-Zim-SN-3
61	Oc-SMT-SMT-4,5
62	Oc-SMT-SMT-4,5
63	Oc-STJ-STJ-1
64	Oc-STJ-STJ-1
65	Oc-STJ-STJ-1
66	Oc-STJ-STJ-1
67	Zim-Zim-SN-4
68	Zim-SPH-SPH-5
69	Zim-SPH-SPH-2
70	Zim-SPH-SPH-2
71	Zim-SPH-SPH-2
72	Zim-SPH-SPH-1
73	Zim-SIY-SIY-1
74	Oc-SA-SA-1
75	Zim-SCM-SCM-21
76	Zi-SCM-SCM-5
77	Zim-SG-SG-2
78	Zim-SG-SG-3
79	Zi-SPH-SPH-6
80	Zi-SPH-SPH-6
81	Zi-SPH-SPH-6
82	Zi-SPH-SPH-6
83	Zim-SAT-AB-10
84	Zim-SG-SG-4
85	Zim-SG-PDP-1
86	Zim-SG-PDP-1
87	Oc-TM-TM-1,2,3
88	Zi-SAT-AB-4
89	Zi-SAT-AB-18
90	Zi-SAT-AB-12
91	Zi-SAT-AB-1
92	Zi-SAT-AB-20
93	Zim-SAT-SAT-2
94	Zim-VDF-VDF-1
95	Zim-VDF-LB-3
96	Zi-SMA-SMA-18
97	Zi-SMA-SMA-5
98	Zi-SMA-SMA-5
99	Zi-SMA-SMA-5
100	Zi-SMA-SMA-3
101	Zi-SMA-SMA-2
102	Zi-SMA-SMA-17
103	Zi-SMA-SMA-34
104	Zaa-Tri-20
105	Zim-SAT-ER-1
106	Zaa-Zaa-2

Field Numbers for IIIa

SITE #	FIELD#
1	Ce-Cui-RQ-1
2	Ce-Cui-RQ-2; Ce-Cui-SL-5
3	Ce-Cui-RQ-2; Ce-Cui-SL-5
4	Ce-Cui-RQ-2; Ce-Cui-SL-5
5	Ce-Cui-RQ-2; Ce-Cui-SL-5
6	Ce-Cui-RQ-3
7	Ce-Cui-SL-3

Field Numbers for IIIa (Con't)

SITE #	FIELD #	
8	Ce-Cui-SJ-5,6	
9	Ce-Cui-SJ-1	
10	Za-SRJ-1	
11	Za-SRJ-SRJ-2	
12	Za-SRJ-SRJ-2	
13	Za-SRJ-SRJ-3	
14	Xox-SJB-1	
15	Xox-SJB-2	
16	Xox-SJB3	
17	CE-AT-AT-4	
18	CE-SMC-SCM-5	
19	CE-SMC-SMC-4,5	
20	CE-SMC-SMC-5	
21	CE-SMC-SMC-5	
22	Ce-SBC-RM-18	
23	CE-SMC-SMC-8-10,13-16,23	
24	CE-SMC-SMC-8-10,13-16-23	
25	Ce-Cui-SL-9	
26	Ce-Cui-RQ-12	
27	Ce-Cui-RQ-9	
28	Ce-Cui-RQ-8	
29	Ce-Cui-RQ-8	
30	Ce-Cui-RQ-14	
31	Ce-Cui-RQ-13	
32	Ce-Cui-RQ-13	
33	Ce-Cui-RQ-13	
34	Zaa-Zaa-1	
35	Zaa-SPR-2	
36	Zaa-SPR-1	
37	Zaa-Zaa-2	
38	Zaa-Zaa-2	
39	Zaa-Zaa-2	
40	Ce-Xox-SJB-4	
41	Ce-SMC-SMC-6	
42	Ce-SBC-SBC-4	
43	Ce-SBC-SBC-5	
44	Ce-SBC-SBC-8	
45	Ce-SMC-SMC-19	
46	Ce-SMC-SMC-19	
47	Ce-SBC-SBC-14	Ce-SBC-SBC-6
48	Ce-SBC-SBC-13	
49	Ce-SBC-SBC-16	
50	Ce-SBC-SBC-19	
51	Zaa-Zaa-Zaa-14	
52	Zaa-Zaa-Zaa-9	
53	Zaa-Zaa-Zaa-8	
54	Zaa-Zaa-Ez-1	
55	Ce-SBC-SBC-2	
56	Ce-SBC-SBC-9	
57	Ce-SBC-SBC-9	
58	Zim-Cie-Cie-13	
59	Za-Tri-Lar-1	
60	Zim-Cie-Cie-3	
61	Zaa-Roa-1	
62	Zaa-Tri-1; Za-Tri-2	
63	Zaa-Tri-Tri-25	
64	Zaa-Tri-20	
65	Za-Ez-5	
66	Ce-SBC-RM-1	
67	Ce-SBC-RM-4	
68	Ce-SBC-RM-2,6	
69	Ce-SBC-RM-9	
70	Ce-SBC-RM-3	
71	Ce-SBC-RM-3	
72		
73	Ce-SBC-RM-14	
74	Ce-SBC-RM-10	
75	Ce-SBC-RM-12	
76	Ce-SBC-RM-13	

Field Numbers for IIIa (Con't)

SITE #	FIELD #
77	Ce-SBC-RM-15
78	Za-Za-Ez-32
79	Za-Za-Ez-31
80	Za-Za-Ez-20
81	Za-Za-Ez-23
82	Ce-SBC-SBC-12
83	Zim-Cie-Cie-17
84	Zim-Zim-Zim-21
85	Zim-Cie-Cie-10
86	Zim-Zim-Zim-20
87	Zim-Cie-Cie-4
88	Zim-Cie-Cie-6
89	Zim-Cie-Cie-2
90	Zim-Cie-Cie-1
91	Zi-Cie-Cie-5
92	Zim-SCQ-LS-1
93	Zi-SCQ-LS-5
94	Zi-SCQ-LS-2
95	Zi-SCQ-LS-4
96	Ce-SBC-RM-16
97	Ce-SBC-RM-21
98	Ce-SBC-RM-22
99	Ce-SBC-RM-23
100	Zi-SCQ-SCQ-24
101	Zi-SCQ-SCQ-23
102	Ce-SBC-RM-24
103	Oc-SMT-SMT-23
104	Oc-SMT-SMT-23
105	Oc-SMT-SMT-23
106	Oc-SMT-SMT-19
107	Oc-SMT-SMT-16
108	Oc-SMT-SMT-17
109	Oc-SMT-SMT-13
110	Oc-SMT-SMT-26
111	Oc-SMT-SMT-38
112	Oc-SMT-SMT-41
113	Oc-SMT-SMT-42
114	Zim-Zim-Zim-12
115	Zim-Zim-Zim-13
116	Zim-Zim-Zim-16
117	Zim-Zim-Zim-1
118	Zim-Zim-Zim-3
119	Zim-Zim-Zim-4
120	Zim-Zim-Zim-2
121	Zim-Zim-Zim-2
122	Zim-Zim-Zim-5
123	Zim-Zim-Zim-5,8
124	Zim-SCQ-SCQ-1
125	Zi-SCQ-SCQ-20
126	Oc-SMT-SMT-27
127	Oc-SMT-SMT-29
128	Oc-SMT-SMT-24
129	Oc-SMT-SMT-10
130	Oc-SMT-SMT-11
131	Oc-SMT-SMT-11
132	Oc-SMT-SMT-11
133	Oc-SMT-SMT-30
134	Oc-SMT-SMT-31
135	Oc-SMT-SMT-32
136	Oc-STJ-STJ-1
137	Oc-STJ-SPG-1
138	Oc-STJ-SPG-3
139	Zim-Zim-Zim-10
140	Zim-Zim-Zim-9
141	Zim-Zim-Zim-9
142	Zim-Zim-Zim-9
143	Zim-Zim-Zim-9
144	Zim-Zim-Zim-28
145	Zim-Zim-SN-1
146	Zim-Zim-SN-3
147	Oc-SMT-SMT-2
148	Oc-SMT-SMT-1
149	Oc-SMT-SMT-6
150	Oc-SMT-SMT-7
151	Oc-SMT-SMT-4,5
152	Oc-STJ-STJ-8
153	Zim-SPH-SPH-18
154	Zim-SPH-SPH-16
155	Zim-SPH-SPH-16
156	Zim-SPH-SPH-16
157	Zim-SPH-SPH-16
158	Zim-SPH-SPH-22
159	Zim-SPH-SPH-22
160	Zim-SPH-SPH-22
161	Zim-SPH-SPH-22
162	Zim-SPH-SPH-22
163	Zim-SPH-SPH-22
164	Zim-SPH-SPH-4
165	Zim-Zim-SN-4
166	Zim-SPH-SPH-5
167	Zim-SPH-SPH-2
168	Zim-SPH-SPH-2
169	Zim-SPH-SPH-2
170	Zim-SPH-SPH-2
171	Zim-SPH-SPH-1
172	Oc-Oc-SJC-2
173	OC-SJC-SJC-3
174	Zim-SPH-SPH-11
175	Zim-SIY-SIY-1
176	Oc-SA-SA-1
177	Zi-SBM-SBM-1
178	Zi-SBM-SBM-1
179	Zi-SBM-SBM-1; Zi-SBM-SCM-21,22
180	Zi-SCM-SCM-32
181	Zi-SCM-SCM-20
182	Zi-SCM-SCM-31
183	Zi-SCM-SCM-24
184	Zi-SCM-SCM-8
185	Zi-SCM-SCM-7
186	Zi-SCM-SCM-15
187	Zi-SCM-SCM-14
188	Zi-SCM-SCM-12
189	Zi-SCM-SCM-11
190	Zi-SAT-ER-9
191	Zi-SCM-SCM-4
192	Zi-SCM-TR-12
193	Zim-SCM-SCM-6
194	Zim-SCM-SCM-10
195	Zim-VDF-VDF-12
196	Zim-VDF-VDF-12
197	Zim-VDF-VDF-7
198	Zim-VDF-VDF-9
199	Zim-SG-SG-2
200	Zim-SG-SG-3
201	Zi-SG-SJ-1
202	Zi-SPH-SPH-6
203	Zi-SPH-SPH-6
204	Zi-SPH-SPH-6
205	Zi-SPH-SPH-6
206	Zi-SPH-SPH-6

Field Numbers for IIIa (Con't)

SITE #	FIELD #
207	Zi-SPH-SPH-6
208	Zi-SPH-SPH-6
209	Zim-SPH-SPH-8
210	Zim-SPH-SPH-7
211	Zim-SPH-SPH-12
212	Zim-SAT-AB-10
213	Zim-SAT-AB-10
214	Zim-SAT-ER-5
215	Zim-SAT-ER-1
216	Zim-SAT-ER-2
217	Zim-SAT-ER-3
218	Zim-SAT-ER-10
219	Zim-SAT-ER-6
220	Zim-SCM-TR-1
221	Zim-SCM-TR-5
222	Zim-SCM-TR-4
223	Zim-SCM-TR-3
224	Zim-SCM-TR-2
225	Zim-SCM-TR-8
226	Zim-SCM-TR-10
227	Zim-SCM-TR-10,16
228	Zim-VDF-VDF-3
229	Zim-VDF-VDF-3
230	Zim-VDF-VDF-1
231	Zim-SG-PDP-2
232	Zim-SG-SG-4
233	Zim-SG-PDP-1
234	Zim-SG-PDP-1
235	Oc-TM-TM-5
236	Oc-TM-TM-1,2,3
237	Oc-TM-TM-1,2,3
238	Zaa-Zaa-2; Oc-TM-TM-1,2,3
239	Oc-TM-TM-1,2,3
240	Zi-SG-SJ-2
241	Oc-Oc-TM-2
242	Zi-SAT-AB-30
243	Zi-SAT-AB-4
244	Zi-SAT-AB-17
245	Zi-SAT-AB-16
246	Zi-SAT-AB-1
247	Zi-SAT-AB-3
248	Zim-SAT-SAT-3
249	Zim-SAT-SAT-4
250	Zim-SAT-SAT-5
251	Zim-SAT-SAT-2
252	Zim-VDF-VDF-2
253	Zim-VDF-LB-2
254	Zim-SAT-SAT-9
255	Zim-SAT-SAT-10
256	Zim-VDF-LB-3
257	Zi-SMA-Gue-4
258	Zi-SMA-Gue-2
259	Zi-SAT-AB-34
260	Zi-SAT-AB-40
261	Zi-SAT-AB-41
262	Zi-SAT-AB-42
263	Zi-SAT-AB-44
264	Zi-SAT-AB-43
265	Zi-SMA-SMA-22
266	Zi-SMA-SMA-8
267	Zi-SMA-SMA-7
268	Zi-SMA-SMA-84
269	Zi-SMA-SMA-21
270	Zi-SMA-SMA-18
271	Zim-SMA-SJL-1

Field Number for IIIa (Con't)

SITE #	Field #
272	Zi-SMA-SMA-5
273	Zi-SMA-SMA-5
274	Zi-SMA-SMA-66
275	Zim-SMA-SMA-29
276	Zim-SMA-SMA-43
277	Zim-SMA-SMA-28
278	Zim-SMA-SMA-58
279	Zim-SMA-SMA-27
280	Zim-SMA-SMA-60
281	Zi-SMA-SMA-12
282	Zi-SMA-SMA-4,35
283	Zaa-Zaa-2
284	Zi-SMA-SMA-13
285	Zi-SMA-SMA-32
286	Zi-SMA-SMA-70
287	Zi-SMA-SMA-71
288	Zi-SMA-SMA-14
289	Zi-SMA-SMA-15
290	Zi-SMA-SMA-2
291	Zi-SMA-SMA-17
292	Zi-SMA-SMA-68
293	Zim-SMA-SMA-44
294	Zim-SMA-SMA-42
295	Zim-SMA-SMA-46
296	Zim-SMA-SMA-31
297	Zim-SMA-SMA-48
298	Zim-SMA-SMA-47
299	Zim-SMA-SMA-51,52
300	Zim-Cie-Cie-3
301	Zim-SMA-SMA-55
302	Zi-SMA-SMA-34
303	Zi-SMA-SMA-77
304	Zi-SMA-SMA-75
305	Zi-SMA-SMA-74
306	Zi-SMA-SMA-73
307	Zi-SMA-SMA-33
308	Zi-SMA-SMA-81
309	Zaa-Zaa-Zaa-12
310	Zi-SCQ-SCQ-22
311	Zim-Zim-Zim-6
312	Zi-SCQ-SCQ-20
313	Oc-SMT-SMT-10
314	Oc-Oc-TM-4
315	Oc-Oc-TM-4
316	Zim-SCM-TR-7
317	Zim-SCM-TR-13,14
318	Zim-SCM-TR-9
319	Zim-SMA-SMA-53

Field Numbers for IIIb

SITE #	FIELD #
1	Ce-Cui-Car-6
2	Ce-Cui-Car-2
3	Ce-Cui-Car-5
4	Ce-Cui-Car-4
5	Ce-Cui-Car-1
6	Ce-Cui-RQ-17
7	Ce-Cui-RQ-18
8	Ce-Cui-Cui-2
9	Ce-Cui-RQ-1
10	Ce-Cui-SL-5; Ce-Cui-RQ-2

Field Numbers for IIIb (con't)

SITE #	FIELD #
11	Ce-Cui-SL-5; Ce-Cui-RQ-2
12	Ce-Cui-SL-5; Ce-Cui-RQ-2
13	Ce-Cui-SL-5; Ce-Cui-RQ-2
14	Ce-Cui-SL-5; Ce-Cui-RQ-2
15	Ce-Cui-RQ-3
16	Ce-Cui-SL-6
17	Ce-Cui-SL-5
18	Ce-Cui-SJ-6
19	Ce-Cui-SJ-2
20	Ce-Cui-SJ-1
21	Za-SRJ-1
22	Za-SRJ-SRJ-2
23	Za-SRJ-2
24	Ce-SMC-SMC-3
25	CE-SMC-SMC-5
26	Ce-Cui-RQ-8
27	Ce-Cui-RQ-14
28	Ce-Cui-RQ-14
29	Ce-Cui-RQ-14
30	Ce-Cui-RQ-13
31	Zaa-Zaa-2
32	Ce-Xox-SJB-4
33	Ce-SBC-SBC-4
34	Ce-SBC-SBC-8
35	Ce-SMC-SMC-19
36	Zaa-Zaa-Zaa-9
37	Zaa-Zaa-Zaa-8
38	Zaa-Zaa-Zaa-22
39	Zaa-Zaa-Zaa-23
40	Zaa-Zaa-Zaa-24
41	Zaa-Zaa-Zaa-26
42	Zaa-Zaa-Zaa-27
43	Ce-SBC-SBC-24
44	Zaa-Zaa-SMT-2
45	Zaa-Zaa-SMT-2
46	Zaa-Zaa-SMT-2
47	Zaa-Roa-1; Za-Tri-2
48	Zaa-Tri-20
49	Ce-SBC-RM-1
50	Za-Za-Ez-35
51	Zim-Cie-Cie-2
52	Zim-Cie-Cie-1
53	CE-SMC-SMC-5
54	Zim-SCQ-SCQ-2
55	Zim-SCQ-SCQ-3
56	Zim-SPH-SPH-11
57	Zim-SG-SG-3
58	Zi-SG-SJ-1
59	Zi-SPH-SPH-6
60	Zi-SPH-SPH-6
61	Zim-SPH-SPH-8
62	OC-TM-TM-1,2,3
63	OC-TM-TM-1,2,3
64	Zi-SAT-AB-23
65	Zim-SAT-SAT-8
66	Zi-SMA-SMA-23
67	CE-AT-AT-2
68	Zaa-Tri-2
69	Zim-Zim-Zim-5
70	Zim-SAT-SAT-2
71	Zaa-Zaa-Zaa-7
72	Zaa-Zaa-Zaa-3
73	Zaa-Zaa-Zaa-4

Field Numbers for IV

SITE #	FIELD #
1	Ce-Cui-Car-6
2	Ce-Cui-RQ-2, Ce-Cui-SL-5
3	Ce-Cui-RQ-2, Ce-Cui-SL-5
4	Ce-Cui-RQ-2, Ce-Cui-SL-5
5	Ce-Cui-SL-2
6	Ce-AT-AT-3
7	CE-SMC-SMC-5
8	CE-SMC-SMC-5
9	CE-SMC-SMC-5
10	Ce-Cui-RQ-9
11	Ce-Cui-RQ-8
12	Ce-Cui-RQ-8
13	Ce-Cui-RQ-8
14	Ce-Cui-RQ-14
15	Ce-Cui-RQ-14
16	Ce-Cui-RQ-14
17	Ce-Cui-RQ-13
18	Ce-SMC-SMC-19
19	Ce-SMC-SMC-18
20	Zaa-Zaa-Zaa-8
24	Ce-SBC-SBC-1
25	Zaa-Zaa-SMT-2
26	Zaa-Zaa-SMT-2
27	Zaa-Zaa-SMT-2
28	Zaa-Tri-20
29	Zaa-Tri-20
30	Zaa-Tri-20
31	Za-Za-Ez-35
32	Za-Za-Ez-22
33	Oc-SMT-SMT-23
34	Oc-SMT-SMT-40
35	Oc-SMT-SMT-26
36	OC-SMT-SMT-25
37	Zim-Zim-Zim-3
38	Oc-STJ-SPG-2
39	Oc-STJ-SPG-4
40	Oc-STJ-SDJ-3
41	Oc-STJ-SPG-6
42	Oc-STJ-SPG-7
43	Oc-STJ-SPG-8
44	Oc-STJ-STJ-4,5
45	Oc-STJ-SDJ-12
46	Oc-STJ-SDJ-2; Oc-STJ-STJ-4,5
47	Oc-STJ-SDJ-16
48	Oc-STJ-SDJ-15
49	Oc-STJ-SDJ-14
50	Oc-STJ-SDJ-13
51	Oc-STJ-SDJ-17
52	Oc-STJ-SDJ-18
53	Oc-STJ-SDJ-10
54	Oc-STJ-SDJ-9
55	Oc-STJ-SDJ-8
56	Oc-STJ-SDJ-7
57	Oc-STJ-STJ-9
58	Oc-STJ-STJ-10
59	Oc-STJ-SDJ-4
60	Oc-STJ-SDJ-5
61	Oc-SJC-SJC-2
62	Zaa-Zaa-1
63	Oc-STJ-STJ-6
64	Oc-STJ-STJ-7
65	Zim-SPH-SPH-14
66	Zim-SPH-SPH-14
67	Zi-SBM-SBM-1

Field Numbers for IV (con't)

SITE #	FIELD #
68	Zi-SCM-SCM-21,22
69	Zi-SCM-SCM-21,22
70	Zim-SCM-SCM-21
71	Zim-SCM-SCM-21
72	Zim-SCM-SCM-30
73	Zi-SCM-SCM-4
74	Zi-SPH-SPH-6
75	Zi-SPH-SPH-6
76	Zim-SPH-SPH-12
77	Oc-TM-TM-1,2,3
78	Ce-SMC-SMC-21
79	Zim-SAT-SAT-8
80	Zi-SMA-SMA-25
81	Zi-SMA-SMA-26
82	Zi-SMA-SMA-21
83	Zi-SMA-SMA-5
84	Zi-SMA-SMA-41
85	Zi-SMA-SMA-5
86	Zi-SMA-SMA-65
87	Zi-SMA-SMA-64
88	Zi-SMA-SMA-63
89	Zi-SMA-SMA-62
90	Zi-SMA-SMA-61
91	Zi-SMA-SMA-66
92	Zim-SMA-SMA-30
93	Zim-SMA-SMA-40
94	Zim-SMA-SMA-31
95	Za-SRJ-SRJ-2
96	Zim-SAT-SAT-2

Field Numbers for V

SITE #	FIELD #
1	Ce-Cui-Car-9
2	Ce-Cui-Car-8
3	Ce-Cui-Car-7
4	Ce-Cui-Car-6
5	Ce-Cui-Car-2
6	Ce-Cui-Car-4
7	Ce-Cui-Car-3
8	Ce-Cui-RQ-17
9	Ce-Cui-RQ-19
10	Ce-Cui-RQ-16
11	Ce-Cui-RQ-21
12	Ce-Cui-RQ-22
13	Ce-Cui-RQ-20
14	Ce-Cui-Cui-4
15	Ce-Cui-Cui-3
16	Ce-Cui-Cui-1
17	Ce-Cui-Cui-2
18	Ce-Cui-RQ-1
19	Ce-Cui-SL-8
20	Ce-Cui-SL-7
21	Ce-Cui-RQ-2; Ce-Cui-SL-5
22	Ce-Cui-RQ-2; Ce-Cui-SL-5
23	Ce-Cui-RQ-2; Ce-Cui-SL-5
24	Ce-Cui-RQ-2; Ce-Cui-SL-5
25	Ce-Cui-RQ-2; Ce-Cui-SL-5
26	Ce-Cui-RQ-2; Ce-Cui-SL-5
27	Ce-Cui-RQ-3
28	Ce-Cui-RQ-3

Field Numbers for V (Con't)

SITE #	FIELD #
29	Ce-Cui-SL-5
30	Ce-Cui-SL-3
31	Ce-Cui-SL-4
32	Ce-Cui-RQ-4
33	Ce-Cui-RQ-6
34	Ce-Cui-BG-1
35	Ce-Cui-SJ-6
36	Ce-Cui-SJ-5
37	Ce-Cui-SJ-7
38	Ce-Cui-SL-1
39	Ce-Cui-SL-2
40	Ce-Cui-SJ-3
41	Ce-Cui-SJ-2
42	Ce-Cui-SJ-4
43	Ce-Cui-SJ-1
44	Za-SRJ-SRJ-2
45	Ce-Cui-RQ-13
46	Za-SRJ-3
47	Ce-AT-AT-4
48	Ce-AT-AT-2
49	Ce-AT-AT-2
50	Ce-AT-AT-2
51	CE-SMC-SMC-5
52	CE-SMC-SMC-5
53	CE-SMC-SMC-5
54	CE-SMC-SMC-5
55	CE-SMC-SMC-1
56	CE-SMC-SMC-8-10, 13-16, 23
57	CE-SMC-SMC-8-10, 13-16, 23
58	CE-SMC-SMC-6,7,14,17,19
59	CE-SMC-SMC-8-10,,0, 13-16, 23
60	Ce-Cui-RQ-12
61	Ce-Cui-RQ-12
62	Ce-Cui-RQ-12
63	Ce-Cui-RQ-11
64	Ce-Cui-RQ-9
65	Ce-Cui-RQ-9
66	Ce-Cui-RQ-8
67	Ce-Cui-RQ-8
68	Ce-Cui-RQ-8
69	Ce-Cui-RQ-8
70	Ce-Cui-RQ-15
71	Ce-Cui-RQ-15
72	Ce-Cui-RQ-14
73	Ce-Cui-RQ-14
74	Za-Za-2
75	Zaa-SRJ-SRJ-4
76	Zaa-Zaa-2
77	Zaa-Zaa-2
78	Zaa-Zaa-2
79	Ce-Xox-SJB-4
80	Ce-SMC-SMC-7
81	Ce-SBC-SBC-3
82	Ce-SBC-SBC-4
83	Ce-SBC-SBC-8
84	Ce-SMC-SMC-24
85	Ce-SBC-SBC-13
86	Ce-SBC-SBC-20
87	Ce-SBC-SBC-18
88	Ce3asbc-SBC-17
89	Zaa-Zaa-Zaa-14, 18
90	Zaa-Zaa-Zaa-19
91	Zaa-Zaa-Zaa-20
92	Zaa-Zaa-Zaa-21

Field Numbers for V (Con't)

SITE #	FIELD #
93	Zaa-Zaa-Zaa-11
94	Zaa-Zaa-Zaa-16
95	Zaa-Zaa-Zaa-17
96	Zaa-Zaa-Zaa-12
97	Zaa-Zaa-Zaa-15
98	Zaa-Zaa-SMT-1
99	Zaa-Zaa-Zaa-9
100	Zaa-Zaa-Zaa-9
101	Zaa-Zaa-Zaa-8
102	Zaa-Zaa-Zaa-7
103	Zaa-Zaa-Zaa-23
104	Zaa-Zaa-Zaa-6
105	Zaa-Zaa-Zaa-5
106	Zaa-Zaa-Ez-2
107	Zaa-Zaa-Ez-1
108	Zaa-Zaa-Ez-8
109	Zaa-Zaa-Ez-4
110	Ce-SBC-SBC-1
111	Ce-SBC-SBC-2
112	Ce-SBC-SBC-2
113	Ce-SBC-SBC-2
114	Ce-SBC-SBC-34
115	Za-Ez-7
116	Ce-SBC-SBC-33
117	Ce-SBC-SBC-23
118	Ce-SBC-SBC-9
119	Ce-SBC-SBC-9
120	Ce-SBC-SBC-9
121	Ce-SBC-SBC-9
122	Ce-SBC-SBC-22
123	Ce-SBC-SBC-25
124	Ce-SBC-SBC-26
125	Ce-SBC-SBC-24
126	Ce-SBC-SBC-32
127	Ce-SBC-SBC-10
128	Ce-SBC-SBC-28
129	Ce-SBC-SBC-29
130	Ce-SBC-SBC-11
131	Ce-SBC-SBC-30
132	Ce-SBC-SBC-31
133	Zaa-Tri-Lar-6
134	Zaa-Tri-Lar-6
135	Zaa-Tri-Lar-6
136	Zaa-Tri-Lar-6
137	Zaa-Zaa-Roa-2
138	Zaa-Zaa-Roa-2
139	Zaa-Zaa-Roa-3
140	Zaa-Zaa-Roa-4
141	Zim-Cie-Cie-3
142	Zaa-Tri-1; Za-Tri-2
143	Zaa-Tri-20
144	Zaa-Tri-20
145	Zaa-Tri-20
146	Zaa-Tri-20
147	Zaa-Tri-20
148	Zaa-Tri-21
149	Zaa-Tri-23
150	Zaa-Tri-22
151	Zaa-Tri-24
152	Zaa-Ez-6
153	Zaa-Ez-5
154	Ce-SBC-RM-1
155	Ce-SBC-RM-6
156	Ce-SBC-RM-4
157	Ce-SBC-RM-2, 6
158	Ce-SBC-RM-9
159	Ce-SBC-RM-3
160	Ce-SBC-RM-10
161	Ce-SBC-RM-11
162	Ce-SBC-RM-12
163	Ce-SBC-RM-13
164	Ce-SBC-RM-15
165	Ce-SBC-RM-28
166	Ce-SBC-RM-29
167	Za-Za-Ez-24
168	Za-Za-Ez-29
169	Za-Za-Ez-32
170	Za-Za-Ez-33
171	Za-Za-Ez-34
172	Za-Za-Ez-30
173	Za-Za-Ez-21
174	Za-Za-Ez-28
175	Za-Za-Ez-27
176	Za-Za-Ez-25
177	Za-Za-Ez-26
178	Zim-Zim-Zim-24
179	Zim-Zim-Zim-23
180	Zim-Cie-Cie-16
181	Zim-Zim-Zim-18
182	Zim-Zim-Zim-21
183	Zim-Cie-Cie-14
184	Zim-Cie-Cie-10
185	Zim-Cie-Cie-12
186	Zim-Zim-Zim-35
187	Zim-Zim-Zim-35
188	Zim-Zim-Zim-20
189	Zim-Zim-Zim-20
190	Zim-Zim-Zim-20
191	Zi-Cie-Cie-11
192	Oc-SMT-SMT-23
193	Zi-Cie-Cie-19
194	Zi-Cie-Cie-20
195	Zi-Cie-Cie-21
196	Zi-Cie-Cie-8
197	Zi-Cie-Cie-9
198	Zi-Cie-Cie-9
199	Zi-Cie-Cie-7
200	Zi-Cie-Cie-2
201	Zi-Cie-Cie-1
202	Zim-SCQ-LS-1
203	Zim-SCQ-LS-1
204	Zim-SCQ-LS-2
205	Ce-SBC-RM-17
206	Ce-SBC-RM-19
207	Ce-SBC-RM-25
208	OC-SMT-SMT-23
209	OC-SMT-SMT-23
210	OC-SMT-SMT-23
211	OC-SMT-SMT-9
212	OC-SMT-SMT-20
213	OC-SMT-SMT-19
214	OC-SMT-SMT-17
215	OC-SMT-SMT-15
216	OC-SMT-SMT-14
217	OC-SMT-SMT-39
218	OC-SMT-SMT-26
219	OC-SMT-SMT-26
220	OC-SMT-SMT-41
221	OC-SMT-SMT-42
222	Zim-Zim-Zim-11

Field Numbers for V (Con't)

SITE #	FIELD #
223	Zim-Zim-Zim-11
224	Zim-Zim-Zim-33
225	Zim-Zim-Zim-12
226	Zim-Zim-Zim-13
227	Zim-Zim-Zim-34
228	Zim-Zim-Zim-7
229	Zim-Zim-Zim-25
230	Zim-Zim-Zim-26
231	Zim-Zim-Zim-1
232	Zim-Zim-Zim-3,4
233	Zim-Zim-Zim-2
234	Zim-Zim-Zim-5
235	Zim-Zim-Zim-5
236	Zim-Zim-Zim-6
237	Zim-Zim-Zim-6
238	Zim-Zim-Zim-6
239	Zi-SCQ-SCQ-20
240	OC-SMT-SMT-27
241	Zim-SCQ-SCQ-21
242	OC-SMT-SMT-28
243	OC-SMT-SMT-24
244	OC-SMT-SMT-10
245	OC-STJ-STJ-8
246	Zim-Zim-SN-4
247	Oc-SMT-SMT-31
248	Oc-SMT-SMT-32
249	Oc-STJ-STJ-3
250	Oc-STJ-STJ-2
251	Oc-STJ-STJ-1
252	Oc-STJ-STJ-1
253	Oc-STJ-STJ-1
254	Oc-STJ-SPG-10
255	Oc-STJ-SPG-9
256	Oc-STJ-SPG-5
257	Oc-STJ-SPG-8
258	Oc-STJ-SPG-8
259	Oc-STJ-STJ-4,5
260	Oc-STJ-SDJ-2
261	Oc-STJ-SDJ-2
262	Oc-STJ-SDJ-2
263	Oc-STJ-SDJ-17
264	Oc-STJ-SDJ-11
265	Oc-STJ-SDJ-9
266	Oc-STJ-SDJ-8
267	Zim-Zim-Zim-10
268	Zim-Zim-Zim-10
269	Zim-Zim-Zim-32
270	Zim-Zim-Zim-9
271	Zim-Zim-Zim-9
272	Zim-Zim-Zim-9
273	Zim-Zim-Zim-31
274	Zim-Zim-Zim-27
275	Zim-Zim-Zim-30
276	Zim-Zim-Zim-29
277	Zim-Zim-SN-1
278	Oc-SMT-SMT-2
279	Oc-SMT-SMT-1
280	Oc-SMT-SMT-3
281	Oc-SMT-SMT-4,5
282	Oc-SMT-SMT-4,5
283	Oc-SMT-SMT-4,5
284	Oc-SMT-SMT-4,5
285	Oc-Oc-SJC-1
286	Oc-STJ-STJ-1
287	Oc-STJ-STJ-1

Field Numbers for V (Con't)

SITE #	FIELD #
288	Oc-STJ-STJ-1
289	Oc-STJ-STJ-1
290	Oc-STJ-STJ-1
291	Oc-STJ-STJ-8
292	Oc-STJ-STJ-8
293	Oc-STJ-STJ-2,4; Oc-STJ-SDJ-1,2
294	Oc-STJ-STJ-2,4; Oc-STJ-SDJ-1,2
295	Oc-STJ-STJ-2,4; Oc-STJ-SDJ-1,2
296	Oc-STJ-STJ-2,4; Oc-STJ-SDJ-1,2
297	Oc-STJ-STJ-2,4; Oc-STJ-SDJ-1,2
298	Oc-STJ-STJ-2,4; Oc-STJ-SDJ-1,2
299	Oc-STJ-STJ-2,4; Oc-STJ-SDJ-1,2
300	Zim-SAT-SAT-7
301	Oc-STJ-STJ-2,4; Oc-STJ-SDJ-1,2
302	Oc-STJ-STJ-2,4; Oc-STJ-SDJ-1,2
303	Oc-STJ-STJ-2,4; Oc-STJ-SDJ-1,2
304	OC-STJ-SDJ-6
305	Zim-SPH-SPH-16
306	Zim-SPH-SPH-16
307	Zim-SPH-SPH-16
308	Zim-SPH-SPH-16
309	Zim-SPH-SPH-16
310	Zim-SPH-SPH-16
311	Zim-SPH-SPH-22
312	Zim-SPH-SPH-22
313	Zim-SPH-SPH-4,22
314	Zim-SAT-SAT-6
315	Zim-SPH-SPH-17
316	Zim-SPH-SPH-21
317	Zim-Zim-SN-2
318	Zim-SPH-SPH-3
319	Zim-SPH-SPH-5
320	Zim-SPH-SPH-14
321	Zim-SPH-SPH-20
322	Zim-SPH-SPH-11
323	Oc-SA-SA-2
324	SCM-21,22
325	SCM-21,22
326	SCM-21,22
327	SCM-21,22
328	SCM-21,22
329	SCM-21,22
330	SCM-21,22
331	Zim-SCM-SCM-21
332	Zim-SCM-SCM-21
333	Zim-SCM-TR-1
334	Zim-SCM-SCM-30
335	Zim-SCM-SCM-21
336	Zi-SCM-SCM-17
337	Zi-SCM-SCM-23
338	Zi-SCM-SCM-8
339	Zi-SCM-SCM-7
340	Zi-SCM-SCM-16
341	Zi-SCM-SCM-15
342	Zi-SCM-SCM-15
343	Zi-SCM-SCM-31
344	Zi-SCM-SCM-19
345	Zi-SCM-SCM-18
346	Zi-SCM-SCM-13
347	Zi-SCM-SCM-14
348	Zi-SCM-SCM-14
349	Zi-SCM-SCM-12
350	Zi-SCM-SCM-11
351	Zi-SAT-ER-9
352	Zi-SCM-SCM-4

Field Numbers for V (Con't)

SITE #	FIELD #
353	Zi-SCM-SCM-5
354	Zi-SCM-SCM-1
355	Zi-SCM-TR-12
356	Zim-SCM-SCM-6
357	Zim-SCM-SCM-6
358	Zim-SCM-SCM-6; Zim-VDF-VDF-5
359	Zim-SCM-SCM-10
360	Zim-VDF-VDF-11
361	Zim-VDF-VDF-11
362	Zim-VDF-VDF-11
363	Zim-VDF-VDF-12
364	Zim-VDF-VDF-6
365	Zim-VDF-VDF-6
366	Zim-VDF-VDF-7
367	Zim-VDF-VDF-13
368	Zim-VDF-VDF-8
369	Zim-VDF-VDF-10
370	Zim-SG-SG-2
371	Zi-SPH-SPH-6
372	Zim-SPH-SPH-8
373	Zim-SAT-AB-10
374	Zim-SAT-ER-1
375	Zim-SAT-ER-4
376	Zim-SCM-TR-6
377	Zim-SCM-TR-1
378	Zim-SCM-TR-2
379	Zim-SCM-TR-2
380	Zim-SCM-TR-8,16
381	Zim-VDF-VDF-4
382	Zim-VDF-VDF-3
383	Zim-VDF-VDF-3
384	Zim-SCM-Ez-2
385	Zim-SCM-Ez-1
386	Zim-SG-SG-4
387	Zi-SAT-AB-26
388	Ce-SMC-SMC-22
389	Zi-SAT-AB-25
390	Zi-SAT-AB-8
391	Zi-SAT-AB-24,30
392	Zi-SAT-AB-31
393	Zi-SAT-AB-28
394	Zi-SAT-AB-29
395	Zi-SAT-AB-5
396	Zi-SAT-AB-6
397	Zi-SAT-AB-7
398	Zi-SAT-AB-27
399	Zi-SAT-AB-22
400	Zi-SAT-AB-47
401	Zi-SAT-AB-46
402	Zi-SAT-AB-22
403	Zi-SAT-AB-21
404	Zi-SAT-AB-19
405	Zi-SAT-AB-18
406	Zi-SAT-AB-15,16
407	Zi-SAT-AB-2,13,14
408	Zi-SAT-AB-12
409	Zi-SAT-AB-1
410	Zi-SAT-AB-3
411	Zim-SAT-SAT-1
412	Zim-SAT-SAT-6
413	Zim-SAT-SAT-21
414	Zim-VDF-VDF-2
415	Zim-SAT-SAT-7
416	Zim-SAT-SAT-7
417	Zim-SAT-SAT-4

Field Numbers for V (Con't)

SITE #	FIELD #
418	Zim-SAT-SAT-2
419	Zim-SAT-SAT-2
420	Zim-SAT-SAT-20
421	Zim-SAT-SAT-19
422	Zi-SMA-Gue-6
423	Zi-SMA-Gue-1
424	Zi-SAT-AB-33
425	Zi-SAT-AB-34
426	Zi-SAT-AB-38
427	Zi-SAT-AB-39
428	Zi-SAT-AB-45
429	Zi-SAT-AB-35
430	Zi-SAT-AB-32
431	Zi-SAT-AB-41
432	Zi-SAT-AB-42
433	Zi-SAT-AB-36
434	Zi-SAT-AB-37
435	Zi-SAT-AB-43
436	Zim-SAT-SAT-13
437	Zim-SAT-SAT-12
438	Zim-SAT-SAT-11
439	Zim-SAT-SAT-11
440	Zim-SAT-SAT-8
441	Zi-SMA-SMA-8
442	Zi-SMA-SMA-19
443	Zi-SMA-SMA-20
444	Zi-SMA-SMA-9
445	Zi-SMA-SMA-10
446	Zi-SMA-SMA-24
447	Zi-SMA-SMA-21
448	Zi-SMA-SMA-18
449	Zim-SMA-SMA-67
450	Zim-SMA-SMA-39
451	Zi-SMA-SMA-5,41
452	Zi-SMA-SMA-5
453	Zi-SMA-SMA-5
454	Zi-SMA-SMA-5
455	Zi-SMA-SMA-5
456	Zi-SMA-SMA-5
458	Zi-SMA-SMA-5
459	Zi-SMA-SMA-5
460	Zi-SMA-SMA-65
461	Zi-SMA-SMA-64
462	Zi-SMA-SMA-63
463	Zi-SMA-SMA-61
464	Zi-SMA-SMA-38
465	Zi-SMA-SMA-38
466	Zi-SMA-SMA-38
467	Zim-SMA-SMA-82
468	Zim-SMA-SMA-82
469	Zim-SMA-SMA-82
470	Zim-SMA-SMA-82
471	Zim-SMA-SMA-30
472	Zim-SMA-SMA-56
473	Zim-SMA-SMA-29
474	Zim-SMA-SMA-43
475	Zim-SMA-SMA-57
476	Zim-SMA-SMA-28
477	Zim-SMA-SMA-58
478	Zim-SMA-SMA-27
479	Zim-SMA-SMA-59
480	Zim-SMA-SMA-40
481	Zim-SMA-SMA-85
482	Zi-SMA-SMA-1
483	Zi-SMA-SMA-12

SITE #	FIELD #
484	Zi-SMA-SMA-4
485	Zi-SMA-SMA-35
486	Zi-SMA-SMA-35
487	Zi-SMA-SMA-72
488	Zi-SMA-SMA-13
489	Zi-SMA-SMA-32
490	Zi-SMA-SMA-71
491	Zi-SMA-SMA-16
492	Zi-SMA-SMA-17
493	Zi-SMA-SMA-69
494	Zim-SMA-SMA-44
495	Zim-SMA-SMA-42
496	Zim-SMA-SMA-45
497	Zim-SMA-SMA-46
498	Zim-SMA-SMA-31
499	Zim-SMA-SMA-49
500	Zim-SMA-SMA-47
501	Zim-SMA-SMA-50
502	Zim-SMA-SMA-51
503	Zim-SMA-SMA-52
504	Zi-SMA-SMA-78
505	Zi-SMA-SMA-79
506	Zi-SMA-SMA-34
507	Zi-SMA-SMA-77
508	Zi-SMA-SMA-80
509	Zi-SMA-SMA-76
510	Zi-SMA-SMA-37
511	Zi-SMA-SMA-75
512	Zi-SMA-SMA-74
513	Zi-SMA-SMA-73

SITE #	FIELD #
514	Ce-SBC-RM-3
515	Za-Za-Ez-3
516	SCQ-SCQ-22
517	Zi-SMA-SMA-5
518	Zim-SMA-SMA-53
519	Zim-SMA-SMA-54
520	Zim-SCM-TR-7
521	SAT-ER-8
522	Zim-SAT-AB-9
523	Zim-SCM-TR-13,14
524	Zim-SCM-SCM-9
526	Ce-Cui-RQ-8
527	Oc-STJ-STJ-2,4; Oc-STJ-SDJ-1,2
528	Zaa-Zaa-2
529	Zim-Cie-Cie-2

Field Numbers for Undated Sites

SITE #	FIELD #
1	Ce-SMC-SMC-20
2	Zaa-Zaa-Zaa-13
3	Zim-SG-SG-1
4	Zim-SAT-SAT-17
5	Zim-SAT-SAT-18
6	Zim-SAT-SAT-6
7	Zim-SMA-SMA-83
8	Zaa-Zaa-Zaa-10

Appendix VII

CERAMIC DESCRIPTIONS

Appendix II of the Monte Albán volume (Kowalewski, Spencer, and Redmond 1978) contains an explanation of our ceramic category numbering system, definitions of the descriptive terms used, and descriptions of most of the ceramic categories we use in the chronological placement of sites. What follows here includes: 1) descriptions of those pre-Monte Albán Early I categories we encountered during the valley survey and utilized in the dating of sites; 2) descriptions of a few categories dating to Early I or later that were not found on Monte Albán; and 3) some minor changes in the descriptions of a few of the Monte Albán categories, based on the experience we gained in the valley survey. Most of the latter changes involve a collapsing of some of the Early I *gris* incised categories into fewer categories. This was necessary because we found so few of these sherds in the valley survey, and often when we could collect them they were badly eroded or consisted of fragments so small we could not definitely fit them into the rather elaborate typological scheme we had developed for use with the Monte Albán collections.

In writing our descriptions of the pre-Monte Albán Early I categories, we depended largely on an unpublished first draft of "Early and Middle Formative Ceramics of the Valley of Oaxaca" (Flannery and Marcus, eds., in prep.). The basic source of information for the pottery of the Monte Albán sequence is Caso, Bernal, and Acosta (1967) (abbreviated as CBA below); in the following pages, figure and page references refer to that volume unless otherwise indicated.

CATEGORY: 0423
CBA DESIGNATION: See Fig. 387
PERIODIZATION: V
PASTE: *Gris Cremosa* or Sandy Cream
VESSEL FORM:
General Shape Mode: Jar
Specific Shape Mode: Common features are short, out-curved rims and incipient annular bases
SURFACE TREATMENT:
Interior: Variable
Exterior: Light raking (identical to 2221)

CATEGORY: 0424
PERIODIZATION: V
PASTE: *Gris Cremosa* or Sandy Cream
VESSEL FORM:
General Shape Mode: Bowl
Specific Shape Mode: Hemispherical, convex-walled bowls See G3M bowl description
SURFACE TREATMENT:
Interior: Burnished
Exterior: Burnished

CATEGORY: 0600
ALT. DESIGNATION: Tierras Largas Burnished Plain
PERIODIZATION: Tierras Largas phase
VESSEL FORM:
General Shape Mode: Bowl
Specific Shape Mode: Hemispherical bowls with plain or slightly incurved rims, thin walls
SURFACE TREATMENT: Streaky burnished
DECORATION: Some have punctations on the rim.

CATEGORY: 0601
ALT. DESIGNATION: Tierras Largas Burnished Plain
PERIODIZATION: Tierras Largas phase
VESSEL FORM:
General Shape Mode: Jar
Specific Shape Mode: Elongated jars with tall outcurving necks. Thin walls
SURFACE TREATMENT: Streaky burnished on exterior. Interiors are either pocked, smoothed or wiped

CATEGORY: 0602
ALT. DESIGNATION: Clementina Red-on-buff
PERIODIZATION: Tierras Largas phase
VESSEL FORM:
General Shape Mode: Bowl
Specific Shape Mode: Hemispherical bowls with flattened rims
SURFACE TREATMENT: Well burnished
DECORATION: Painting: Red (usually specular) paint applied either to the rim band alone in geometric designs or over the entire vessel
ADDITIONAL COMMENT: Relatively fine tempering

CATEGORY: 0603
ALTERNATIVE DESIGNATION: Avelina Red-on-buff
PERIODIZATION: Tierras Largas phase
VESSEL FORM:
General Shape Mode: Bowl
Specific Shape Mode: Hemispherical bowls with rounded bases
SURFACE TREATMENT: Burnished
DECORATION: Painting; red paint
ADDITIONAL COMMENTS: Usually fired at a low temperature and appears coarse

CATEGORY: 0604
ALTERNATIVE DESIGNATION: Avelina Red-on-buff
PERIODIZATION: Tierras Largas phase
VESSEL FORM:
General Shape Mode: Jar
Specific Shape Mode: Jars with outcurved necks.
SURFACE TREATMENT: Burnished
DECORATION: Painting; red painted
ADDITIONAL COMMENTS: Usually fired at a low temperature and appears coarse

CATEGORY: 0605
ALTERNATIVE DESIGNATION: Matadamas Orange
PERIODIZATION: Tierras Largas phase
VESSEL FORM:
General Shape Mode: Bowl
Specific Shape Mode: Hemispherical bowls with flattened bases
SURFACE TREATMENT: Burnished
DECORATION: Slipped surface: Orange on surface similar to Tierras Largas Burnished Plain

CATEGORY: 0606
ALTERNATIVE DESIGNATION: Matadamas Orange
PERIODIZATION: Tierras Largas phase
VESSEL FORM:
General Shape Mode: Jar
Specific Shape Mode: Elongated jars with high outcurved necks
SURFACE TREATMENT: Burnished
DECORATION: Slipped surface: Orange slip on surface similar to Tierras Largas Burnished Plain

CATEGORY: 0607
ALTERNATIVE DESIGNATION: Matadamas Orange
PERIODIZATION: Tierras Largas phase
VESSEL FORM:
General Shape Mode: Jar
Specific Shape Mode: Tecomate
SURFACE TREATMENT: Zoned dentate stamping on burnished surface
DECORATION: Slipped surface: Orange slip on surface similar to Tierras Largas Burnished Plain

CATEGORY: 0608
ALTERNATIVE DESIGNATION: Matadamas Red
PERIODIZATION: Tierras Largas phase
VESSEL FORM:
General Shape Mode: Bowl
Specific Shape Mode: Hemispherical bowls with flattened bases
SURFACE TREATMENT: Burnished
DECORATION: Slipped surface: Red slip on surface similar to Tierras Largas Burnished Plain

CATEGORY: 0609
ALTERNATIVE DESIGNATION: Matadamas Red
PERIODIZATION: Tierras Largas phase
VESSEL FORM:
General Shape Mode: Jar
Specific Shape Mode: Elongated jars with high outcurved necks
SURFACE TREATMENT: Burnished
DECORATION: Slipped surface: Red slip on surface similar to Tierras Largas Burnished Plain

CATEGORY: 0610
PERIODIZATION: II
VESSEL FORM:
General Shape Mode: Bowl
Specific Shape Mode: Various thin bowls though *not* cylindrical with hollow feet
SURFACE TREATMENT: Interior and exterior always treated. Usually burnished although occasionally surfaces are wiped or scraped. Slipping occurs on some vessels.
DECORATION: Plastic decoration may or may not be present.
ADDITIONAL COMMENTS: This category is for thin, Fine Paste, Period II Bowls that do not fit into already defined categories.

CATEGORY: 1108
CBA DESIGNATION: G3M. Form is similar to Fig. 384a.
PERIODIZATION: V
PASTE: *Gris*
VESSEL FORM:
General Shape Mode: Bowl
Specific Shape Mode: Cylindrical
SURFACE TREATMENT: Interior and exterior burnished.

CATEGORY: 1109
CBA DESIGNATION: G3M. See jar descriptions.
PERIODIZATION: V
PASTE: *Gris*
VESSEL FORM:
General Shape Mode: Jar
Specific Shape Mode: Unknown (Miscellaneous body sherds)
SURFACE TREATMENT:
Interior: Plain or wiped
Exterior: Burnished

CATEGORY: 1120
ADDITIONAL PERIODIZATION: IIIa

CATEGORY: 1137
ADDITIONAL PERIODIZATION: IIIa, IV

CATEGORY: 1138
ADDITIONAL PERIODIZATION: Rare in IIIa and IV

CATEGORY: 1274
ADDITIONAL PERIODIZATION: IV

CATEGORY: 1310
ADDITIONAL COMMENTS: In some cases it appears that the flaw would not have been serious enough to prevent normal use of vessel.

CATEGORY: 1400
CBA DESIGNATION: G3M (Page 451, Fig. 381)
PERIODIZATION: V
PASTE: *Gris*
VESSEL FORM:
General Shape Mode: Bowl

Specific Shape Mode: Thin hemispherical or outleaned wall bowl with slightly flared rim
SURFACE TREATMENT: Interior and exterior burnished

CATEGORY: 1500
ALTERNATIVE DESIGNATION: Delfina Fine Gray
PERIODIZATION: San José phase
VESSEL FORM:
General Shape Mode: Bowl
Specific Shape Mode: Cylindrical
SURFACE TREATMENT: Excised; often with Olmec style motifs
ADDITIONAL COMMENTS: Very hard, fine ware with metallic sheen

CATEGORY: 1501
ALTERNATIVE DESIGNATION: Socorro Fine Gray
PERIODIZATION: Guadalupe and Rosario phases; gradually evolves into G3 type of Monte Albán I
VESSEL FORM:
General Shape Mode: Bowls
Specific Shape Mode: Outleaned wall bowls
SURFACE TREATMENT: Streaky burnishings; usually plain

CATEGORY: 1502
ALTERNATIVE DESIGNATION: Socorro Fine Gray
PERIODIZATION: Guadalupe phase
VESSEL FORM:
General Shape Mode: Jar
Specific Shape Mode: Olla; some with wide mouths
SURFACE TREATMENT: Streaky burnished often with incising on either interior or exterior

CATEGORY: 1503
ALTERNATIVE DESIGNATION: Socorro Fine Gray
PERIODIZATION: Rosario phase (Elaborate versions of the line break motif can appear in Monte Albán Ia in *Gris* ware)
VESSEL FORM:
General Shape Mode: Bowl
Specific Shape Mode: Outleaned wall bowls.
SURFACE TREATMENT: Streaky burnished with incising on the interior rim or upper surface of everted and outcurving rims. Incised motifs include the pennant motif, the crescent motif, the line break motif and incised wavy lines (Drennan 1976:40, 56-58).

CATEGORY: 1507
CBA DESIGNATION: None
PERIODIZATION: II-IIIa
PASTE: *Gris*
VESSEL FORM:
General Shape Mode: Bowl
Specific Shape Mode: Various
SURFACE TREATMENT: Cream or brown slip on at least one surface of vessel

CATEGORY: 1508
PERIODIZATION: III-IV
PASTE: *Gris*
VESSEL FORM:
General Shape Mode: Jar
Specific Shape Mode: Large thick storage vessel. Shapes are various.
SURFACE TREATMENT: Exterior streaky burnished, scraped or wiped and interior rough

CATEGORY: 1509. Like 1333 and 1334 in being notched, but these are not everted.
CBA DESIGNATION: G-15, G-17 (pp. 25, 32, 35)
PERIODIZATION: I
PASTE: *Gris*
VESSEL FORM:
General Shape Mode: Bowl
Specific Shape Mode: Flaring or outcurving rims with notches
SURFACE TREATMENT:
Interior: Burnished
Exterior: Smoothed and/or burnished
DECORATION: Plastic Decoration: Fine or wide-line incising occasionally

CATEGORY: 1510 (Replaces 1331, 1336, 1340)
CBA DESIGNATION: G-15, G-17 (pp. 32, 35, Fig. 12, rows 1 and 2 and row 3, 2nd and 3rd from left)
PERIODIZATION: Late I
PASTE: *Gris*
VESSEL FORM:
General Shape Mode: Bowl
Specific Shape Mode: Rims everted or flaring
SURFACE TREATMENT:
Interior: Burnished
Exterior: Burnished or smoothed
DECORATION: Wide line incising

CATEGORY: 1511 (Replaces 1367, 1368, 1369)
CBA DESIGNATION: G-15, G-16 (pp. 26, 32; e.g., Fig. 10, 2nd row, 2nd from left)
PERIODIZATION: Ia mostly
PASTE: *Gris*
VESSEL FORM:
General Shape Mode: Jar
Specific Shape Mode: Tecomates or with straight or curved-back neck. (Most examples are body sherds.)
SURFACE TREATMENT:
Interior: Wiped or plain. Burnished around rim
Exterior: Burnished
DECORATION: Plastic Decoration: Various fine-line incising on exterior, occasionally with wide-line incising. Rarely red paint is rubbed into the incised areas.

CATEGORY: 1512
CBA DESIGNATION: G-15, G-16 (pp. 26, 32)
PERIODIZATION: Probably Ia
PASTE: *Gris*
VESSEL FORM:
General Shape Mode: Jar
Specific Shape Mode: Strap handles
SURFACE TREATMENT:
Exterior: Burnished
DECORATION: Fine-line incising is present.

CATEGORY: 1513 (combines M.A. 1335, 1346, 1347)
CBA DESIGNATION: G-15 (pp. 26, 32, Fig. 9, 4th row, 2nd from left)
PERIODIZATION: Ia
PASTE: *Gris*
VESSEL FORM:
General Shape Mode: Bowl
Specific Shape Mode: "Pinched In" rims
SURFACE TREATMENT:
Interior: Burnished
Exterior: Usually burnished
DECORATION: Plastic Decoration: Normally has fine-line incising on interior and/or exterior walls.

CATEGORY: 1514. (Combines M.A. 1336 and 1337)
CBA DESIGNATION: G-15 (pp. 26, 32; Fig. 8, 1st and 4th from left)
PERIODIZATION: I
PASTE: *Gris*
VESSEL FORM:
General Shape Mode: Bowl
Specific Shape Mode: Narrow everted rims
SURFACE TREATMENT:
Interior: Burnished
Exterior: Burnished or smoothed
DECORATION: Fine or wide-line incising on rim top and/or below rim interior

CATEGORY: 1515 (Replaced 1333, 1334, 1340)
CBA DESIGNATION: G-16 (pp. 32, Fig. 10, bottom row, 2nd from left)
PERIODIZATION: Ia possibly lasting into Late I.
PASTE: *Gris*
VESSEL FORM:
General Shape Mode: Bowl
Specific Shape Mode: Everted rims.
SURFACE TREATMENT:
Interior: Burnished
Exterior: Smoothed or burnished
DECORATION: Plastic Decoration: Plain or with fine-line incising. Some rims are notched; some are scalloped; some are thumb-impressed.

CATEGORY: 1516
CBA DESIGNATION: Probably G-15 or G-16 (pp. 26, 32)
PERIODIZATION: Ia
PASTE: *Gris*
VESSEL FORM:
General Shape Mode: Bowl
Specific Shape Mode: Outleaned wall, direct rims
SURFACE TREATMENT:
Interior: Burnished
Exterior: Usually burnished
DECORATION: Plastic Decoration: Fine-line incising in various simple designs below the rim interior

CATEGORY: 1517 (Replaces 1362, 1365)
CBA DESIGNATION: G-15 (Fig. 8; 2nd from left)
PERIODIZATION: Ia
PASTE: *Gris*
VESSEL FORM:
General Shape Mode: Bowl
Specific Shape Mode: Outcurving, rounded flaring, or slightly everted rims
SURFACE TREATMENT:
Interior: Burnished
Exterior: Usually burnished
DECORATION: Fine-line incising, simple patterns usually not bordered by parallel lines. Includes parallel lines and wavy lines

CATEGORY: 1518 (Combines 1339, 1342, 1344, 1357, 1363, 1364)
CBA DESIGNATION: G-15, G-16 (pp. 26, 32.; e.g. Fig. 10, 3rd row, first from left)
PERIODIZATION: Ia
PASTE: *Gris*
VESSEL FORM:
General Shape Mode: Bowl, plate
Specific Shape Mode: Outleaned wall, flaring, outleaned or everted rims
SURFACE TREATMENT:
Interior: Burnished
Exterior: Burnished or smoothed
DECORATION: Plastic Decoration: Fine and wide line incising, often in cross-hatching, diagonal lines, opposed lines or wavy lines bordered by wide or fine line borders

CATEGORY: 1519 (Replaces 1353, 1354, 1355, 1356, 1361)
CBA DESIGNATION G-12, G-15 (pp. 25, 26, 32; e.g. Fig. 8, 5th row, 3rd from left)
PERIODIZATION: I
PASTE: *Gris*
VESSEL FORM:
General Shape Mode: Bowl
Specific Shape Mode: Outleaned, direct, or flaring rim
SURFACE TREATMENT:
Interior: Burnished
Exterior: Burnished, smoothed, scraped, or wiped
DECORATION: Plastic Decoration: 2-3 parallel lines below the rim on the interior wall (rarely also on the exterior); additional fine or wide line incised designs between the lines or above the lines.

CATEGORY: 2083
ADDITIONAL PERIODIZATION: IV

CATEGORY: 2086
ADDITIONAL PERIODIZATION: IIIa

CATEGORY: 2220
PERIODIZATION: V
PASTE: *Café, Gris*
VESSEL FORM:
General Shape Mode: Handle
Specific Shape Mode: Narrow, hollow tube (*Sahumador*), nearly solid, with only a small-diameter hole running the length of the shaft

CATEGORY: 2221
CBA DESIGNATION: K-2, (pp. 50; Fig. 26; pp. 457; Fig. 387)
PERIODIZATION: V
PASTE: *Café*
VESSEL FORM:
General Shape Mode: Jar

Specific Shape Mode: Thin to medium thick globular ollas, with outcurved rims
SURFACE TREATMENT:
Interior: Variable
Exterior: Wiped or scraped
DECORATION: Plastic Decoration: Roughly scraped or incised while wet, resulting in shallow incisions or raking, usually closely spaced

CATEGORY: 2222
CBA DESIGNATION: None
PERIODIZATION: V
PASTE: *Café*. Contains moderate to heavy amount of mica particles ranging in size from small specks to large flakes. Finished vessel has distinct sparkling or glittering appearance. Some examples appear to have more mica than clay.
VESSEL FORM:
General Shape Mode: Jar
Specific Shape Mode: Olla
SURFACE TREATMENT:
Interior: Variable
Exterior: Wiped or scraped
DECORATION: Plastic Decoration: May be roughly scraped while wet. Treatment is identical to 2221.

CATEGORY: 2223
CBA DESIGNATION: None
PERIODIZATION: V
PASTE: Fine *Café*
VESSEL FORM:
General Shape Mode: Bowl
Specific Shape Mode: Thin hemispherical bowls
SURFACE TREATMENT: Interior and exterior burnished
DECORATION: Painting: Horizontal graphite stripes, usually on the interior
Plastic Decoration: One example had an incised design on the bowl exterior.

CATEGORY: 2224
CBA DESIGNATION: KlM, Kl0M, K19 (Table XVIII [pp. 449]; pp. 451; Fig. 380 [pp. 454])
PERIODIZATION: V
PASTE: *Café*
VESSEL FORM:
General Shape Mode: Bowl
Specific Shape Mode: Thin hemispherical or outleaned wall
SURFACE TREATMENT:
Interior: Smoothed or burnished or wiped
Exterior: Smoothed or burnished

CATEGORY: 2500
ALTERNATIVE DESIGNATION: Atoyac Yellow-white
PERIODIZATION: San José phase, Guadalupe phase; rare in Rosario
VESSEL FORM:
General Shape Mode: Bowl
Specific Shape Mode: Outleaned bowls with flat base
SURFACE TREATMENT: None
DECORATION: Slipped Surface: Yellow-white slip on exterior surface

CATEGORY: 2501
ALTERNATIVE DESIGNATION: Atoyac Yellow-white
PERIODIZATION: San José, Guadalupe; rare in Rosario
VESSEL FORM:
General Shape Mode: Bowl
Specific Shape Mode: Outleaned wall bowls with flat base
SURFACE TREATMENT: Incising, often with double-line break or excising, often raspada design
DECORATION: Slipped Surface: Yellow-white slip on exterior surface.

CATEGORY: 2502
ALTERNATIVE DESIGNATION: Atoyac Yellow-white
PERIODIZATION: San José, Guadalupe
VESSEL FORM:
General Shape Mode: Bowl
Specific Shape Mode: Bolstered rim bowls
DECORATION: Slipped Surface: Yellow-white slip on surface

CATEGORY: 2503
ALTERNATIVE DESIGNATION: Atoyac Yellow-white
PERIODIZATION: San José, Guadalupe; rare in Rosario
VESSEL FORM:
General Shape Mode: Bowl
Specific Shape Mode: Cylindrical
DECORATION: Slipped Surface: Yellow-white slip on exterior surface

CATEGORY: 2504
ALTERNATIVE DESIGNATION: Atoyac Yellow-white
PERIODIZATION: San José, Guadalupe phases
VESSEL FORM:
General Shape Mode: Jar
Specific Shape Mode: Vertical necked jar
DECORATION: Yellow-white slip on surface

CATEGORY: 2505
ALTERNATIVE DESIGNATION: Atoyac Yellow-white
PERIODIZATION: San José, Guadalupe
VESSEL FORM:
General Shape Mode: Jar
Specific Shape Mode: Tecomate
DECORATION: Slipped Surface: Yellow-white slip

CATEGORY: 2506
ALTERNATIVE DESIGNATION: Fidencio Coarse
PERIODIZATION: San José, Guadalupe, Rosario phases
VESSEL FORM:
General Shape Mode: Bowl
Specific Shape Mode: Outleaned wall bowls
SURFACE TREATMENT: Scraped or smoothed
DECORATION: Painting: Sloppily applied; dull red wash is diagnostic.

CATEGORY: 2507
ALTERNATIVE DESIGNATION: Fidencio Coarse
PERIODIZATION: San José, Guadalupe, Rosario phases
VESSEL FORM:
General Shape Mode: Bowl
Specific Shape Mode: Hemispherical
SURFACE TREATMENT: Scraped or smoothed
DECORATION: Painting: Sloppily applied dull red wash.

CATEGORY: 2508
ALTERNATIVE DESIGNATION: Fidencio Coarse
PERIODIZATION: San José, Guadalupe, Rosario phases
VESSEL FORM:
General Shape Mode: Jar
Specific Shape Mode: Ollas with outleaning rims
SURFACE TREATMENT: Plastic decorations including rosettes, herringbone incised, incised dashes, oblong punctations, cross-hatching and punctations in semi-circles mainly in Guadalupe
DECORATION: Painting: A carelessly applied dull red wash.

CATEGORY: 2509
ALTERNATIVE DESIGNATION: Fidencio Coarse
PERIODIZATION: San José, Guadalupe, Rosario phases
VESSEL FORM:
General Shape Mode: Jar
Specific Shape Mode: Tecomate
SURFACE TREATMENT: Scraped or smoothed
DECORATION: Painting: Carelessly applied dull red wash

CATEGORY: 2510
ALTERNATIVE DESIGNATION: Lupita Heavy Plain
PERIODIZATION: San José, Guadalupe, Rosario phases
VESSEL FORM:
General Shape Mode: Bowl
Specific Shape Mode: Outleaned wall bowl rims
SURFACE TREATMENT: Surface smoothed never burnished
ADDITIONAL COMMENT: No slip or wash applied.

CATEGORY: 2511
ALTERNATIVE DESIGNATION: Lupita Heavy Plain
PERIODIZATION: San José, Guadalupe, Rosario phases
VESSEL FORM:
General Shape Mode: Bowl
Specific Shape Mode: Hemispherical bowls
SURFACE TREATMENT: Smoothed, never burnished
ADDITIONAL COMMENT: No slip or wash applied.

CATEGORY: 2512
ALTERNATIVE DESIGNATION: Leandro Gray
PERIODIZATION: San José phase (occasionally occurs in Guadalupe phase)
VESSEL FORM:
General Shape Mode: Bowl
Specific Shape Mode: Outleaned wall bowls
SURFACE TREATMENT: Well burnished; often incised or excised
ADDITIONAL COMMENT: Softer than Socorro Fine Gray wares because they are fired at a lower temperature and have a different clay body.

CATEGORY: 2513
ALTERNATIVE DESIGNATION: Leandro Gray
PERIODIZATION: San José phase (Slight occurrence in Guadalupe phase)
VESSEL FORM:
General Shape Mode: Jar
Specific Shape Mode: Tecomate
SURFACE TREATMENT: Well burnished
ADDITIONAL COMMENT: Softer than Socorro Fine Gray wares due to firing at lower temperatures and use of different clay body.

CATEGORY: 2514
ALTERNATIVE DESIGNATION: Leandro Gray
PERIODIZATION: San José phase (occasionally occurs in Guadalupe phase.)
VESSEL FORM:
General Shape Mode: Jar
Specific Shape Mode: Ollas
SURFACE TREATMENT: Well burnished
ADDITIONAL COMMENT: Softer than Socorro Fine Gray wares since firing occurs at lower temperatures and a different clay body is used.

CATEGORY: 2515
ALTERNATIVE DESIGNATION: Leandro Gray
PERIODIZATION: San José phase (occasionally occurs in Guadalupe phase)
VESSEL FORM:
General Shape Mode: Bowl
Specific Shape Mode: Cylindrical
SURFACE TREATMENT: Well burnished
ADDITIONAL COMMENT: Softer than Socorro Fine Gray wares due to firing which occurs at lower temperatures and use of different clay body.

CATEGORY: 2516
ALTERNATIVE DESIGNATION: San José Black-and-white
PERIODIZATION: San José phase
VESSEL FORM:
General Shape Mode: Bowl
Specific Shape Mode: Outleaned wall bowls with flat bases, bolstered rim bowls, cylindrical bowls.
SURFACE TREATMENT: Differential firing; white with black rim or black with white rim. Some have Olmec style decoration, and some are excised or incised.
DECORATION: Slipped Surface: Differentially fired yellow-white slip

CATEGORY: 2517
ALTERNATIVE DESIGNATION: San José Black-and-white
PERIODIZATION: San José phase
VESSEL FORM:
General Shape Mode: Jar
Specific Shape Modes: 1) Tecomate
2) Vertical necked jars
SURFACE TREATMENT: Differential firing: Olmec style decoration
DECORATION: Slipped Surface: Differentially fired yellow-white slip

CATEGORY: 2518
ALTERNATIVE DESIGNATION: San José Red-on-white
PERIODIZATION: San José phase
VESSEL FORM:
General Shape Mode: Bowl

Specific Shape Mode: Often with bolstered rim
SURFACE TREATMENT: Often well burnished
DECORATION: Slipped Surface: Red hematite slip over yellow-white slip

CATEGORY: 2519
ALTERNATIVE DESIGNATION: San José Red-on-white
PERIODIZATION: San José phase
VESSEL FORM:
General Shape Mode: Jar
Specific Shape Mode: 1) Tecomate
2) Vertical necked jar
SURFACE TREATMENT: Often well burnished, sometimes with zoned rocker stamping
DECORATION: Slipped Surface: Red hematite slip over yellow-white slip

CATEGORY: 2520
ALTERNATIVE DESIGNATION: Guadalupe Burnished Brown
PERIODIZATION: Guadalupe, Rosario phases
VESSEL FORM:
General Shape Mode: Bowl
Specific Shape Mode: Outleaned wall bowls
SURFACE TREATMENT: Streaky burnished
DECORATION: Usually plain

CATEGORY: 2521
ALTERNATIVE DESIGNATION: Socorro Fine Gray
PERIODIZATION: Rosario phase
VESSEL FORM:
General Shape Mode: Bowl
Specific Shape Mode: Hemispherical, incurved, and composite silhouette bowls
SURFACE TREATMENT: Streaky burnished
DECORATION: Usually plain, appears gray
ADDITIONAL COMMENT: Bowl shapes other than outleaning wall and fluted bowls are rare in Guadalupe phase (Drennan 1976:65).

CATEGORY: 3035
ADDITIONAL PERIODIZATION: IIIa

CATEGORY: 5425
ALTERNATIVE DESIGNATION: Huitzo Polished Cream (Paddock 1966:208)
PERIODIZATION: V
PASTE: *Gris Cremosa* or Sandy Cream
VESSEL FORM:
General Shape Mode: Bowl
Specific Shape Mode: Thin hemispherical or outleaned wall bowls
SURFACE TREATMENT:
Interior: Burnished
Exterior: Burnished
DECORATION: Red paint, frequently in stripes

Appendix VIII

NUMBER OF CERAMIC TYPES PER SITE, BY ADMINISTRATIVE RANK

Early I

SITE	# OF TYPES	RANK
2-33	21	2
36	9	2
64	11	2
52,54	15	2
2-9	4	3
21,57	10	3
25	17	3
30	16	3
35	5	3
37,38	8	3
43	11	3
59	14	3
2-2	7	Non-Admin.
3	7	< 100
4	7	"
5	1	"
6	1	"
7	3	"
8	1	"
9	5	"
10	3	"
11	1	"
12	3	"
13	1	"
14	12	"
16	3	"

SITE	# OF TYPES	RANK
17	3	Non-Admin.
18	9	< 100
19	3	"
21	3	"
22	5	"
23	3	"
24	1	"
27	4	"
28	7	"
29	1	"
30	13	"
34	8	"
35	1	"
36	3	"
37	1	"
2-1	9	Non-Admin.
15	15	> 100
3-1	8	Non-Admin.
3	15	< 100
4	11	"
5	3	"
6	5	"
7	6	"
8	14	"
11	1	"
12	9	"

SITE	# OF TYPES	RANK
13	13	Non-Admin.
14	3	< 100
15	4	"
19	8	"
24	1	"
26,62	8	"
28	9	"
29	4	"
31	6	"
32	6	"
33	1	"
34	3	"
39	8	"
40	9	"
41	8	"
44	7	"
45	2	"
46	2	"
47	6	"
48	5	"
49	4	"
50	14	"
53	1	"
61,60	6	"
63	6	"
65	1	"

Early I

SITE	# OF TYPES	RANK
3-16,17	10	Non-Admin. > 100
27	8	"
56,58	9	"

Late I

SITE	# OF TYPES	RANK
3-85,86	12	2
2-136-139	22	3
3-5,8,149	43	3
100	15	3
152	26	3
2-8	14	4
42,43	19	4
51	22	4
90	13	4
142	2	4
3-13,14	20	4
48	18	4
52	22	4
73	14	4
91	23	4
107,8	28	4
109-114	22	4
2-128	14	5
152	3	5
3-22	2	5
33	32	5
34	10	5
47	26	5
53	11	5
56,57	20	5
66	12	5

SITE	# OF TYPES	RANK
3-70	8	5
87,90,93	7	5
97	13	5
98	11	5
104	12	5
105	7	5
119	9	5
130	16	5
147	11	5
2-13	12	Non-Admin. > 100
14	10	"
34	9	"
35,36	1	"
53	18	"
65	9	"
67	16	"
101	4	"
109	10	"
146	4	"
3-64	4	"
83	15	"
2-7	2	Non-Admin. < 100
12	2	"
17	1	"
19	2	"

SITE	# OF TYPES	RANK
2-20	3	Non-Admin. < 100
23	4	"
26	3	"
28	1	"
30	1	"
32	2	"
37	1	"
39	1	"
40	7	"
42	2	"
45	2	"
49	8	"
52	6	"
54	5	"
55	3	"
64	4	"
66	1	"
68	1	"
69	1	"
71	3	"
75	1	"
76	1	"
77	2	"
79	6	"
80	4	"

Late I (continued)

SITE	# OF TYPES	RANK
2-81	5	Non-Admin. < 100
85	3	"
86	3	"
91	1	"
95	5	"
98	5	"
100	9	"
112	2	"
113	1	"
122	9	"
144	2	"
145	1	"
147	2	"
3-3	7	"
6	12	"
7	3	"
9	4	"
10	4	"
11	1	"
12	4	"
19	13	"
20	10	"
22	8	"
24	6	"
26	1	"
30	1	"

SITE	# OF TYPES	RANK
35	8	Non-Admin. < 100
44	7	"
46	11	"
54	5	"
65	10	"
76	5	"
77	7	"
78	11	"
79	19	"
80	11	"
81	10	"
88	8	"
92	14	"
99	10	"
101	8	"
102	9	"
103	7	"
106	7	"
115	7	"
116	2	"
118	6	"
120	5	"
121	6	"
123	16	"
124	1	"
125	14	"

SITE	# OF TYPES	RANK
132	12	Non-Admin. < 100
133	1	"
135	6	"
139	2	"
141	5	"
143	10	"
145	6	"
151	7	"

Period II

SITE	# OF TYPES	RANK
VG-1-57	39	2
44-46	15	2
73	11	2
106	18	2
9,10	14	3
26	12	3
27	19	3
28	17	3
31	24	3
51	11	3
59	11	3
60	21	3
77,78,84	25	3
79-82	20	3
95	10	3
C-15,16	10	4
15-17	32	4
19	9	4
21	8	4
23,24	20	4
29,30,37	22	4
32,33	7	4
34	8	4
40	11	4
67	10	4
68	7	4

SITE	# OF TYPES	RANK
69-71	10	4
93	9	4
101	9	4
39	6	Non-Admin. > 100
48,49	10	"
C-1	12	Non-Admin. < 100
C-2	4	"
C-4	4	"
C-6	6	"
C-7	7	"
C-8	2	"
C-9	4	"
C-10	5	"
C-11	4	"
C-12	7	"
C-17	8	"
C-18	3	"
C-19	7	"
C-20	4	"
C-21	4	"
C-22	4	"
C-23	4	"
6	10	"
8	2	"
11	6	"

SITE	# OF TYPES	RANK
12	19	Non-Admin. < 100
13	5	"
14	10	"
18	4	"
20	3	"
22	3	"
25	5	"
35	3	"
36	10	"
38	13	"
43	7	"
50	11	"
52	7	"
53	22	"
54-56	25	"
57	6	"
58	6	"
62	0	"
63	5	"
65	14	"
66	2	"
74	6	"
75	2	"
76	9	"
83	2	"
85,86	19	"

Period II (continued)

SITE	# OF TYPES	RANK
87	14	Non-Admin. < 100
91	6	"
94	8	"
97-99	14	"
100	3	"
103	4	"
104	4	"
105	4	"

IIIA

SITE	# OF TYPES	RANK
VG-136,150-152	25	2
C-17	13	3
VG-2-6,8	28	3
37-39, 283	18	3
65	18	3
175	9	3
233-39, 241	20	3
10,11,12	16	4
27-29	18	4
40	6	4
56	19	4
62	18	4
67,69-76	16	4
87,89	18	4
90	10	4
118-123	27	4
129-132	12	4
177-179	17	4
199-200, 232	21	4
202-209	21	4
251	12	4
272-274	14	4
C-16	12	5
18	6	5

SITE	# OF TYPES	RANK
C-23	10	5
29	5	5
VG-30	6	5
31-33	20	5
35	2	5
36	4	5
41	8	5
46,48	6	5
54	10	5
55	8	5
57,58	12	5
63,64	13	5
66	5	5
117	9	5
144,153-164	4	5
145	14	5
165	14	5
166	9	5
167-170	16	5
188	2	5
190	7	5
197	9	5
201	9	5
211	8	5
220	16	5
222	2	5

SITE	# OF TYPES	RANK
VG-223	6	5
228-229	2	5
250	9	5
256	9	5
285	4	5
290	7	5
309	11	5
13	9	Non-Admin. > 100
59	20	"
114,115	14	"
282	4	"
C-1	7	Non-Admin. < 100
2	2	"
3	7	"
4	4	"
5	4	"
6	4	"
7	5	"
8	1	"
9	4	"
10	8	"
19	11	"
28	3	"
30	4	"
31	2	"

IIIA (continued)

SITE	# OF TYPES	RANK
C-32	3	Non-Admin. < 100
33	6	"
34	5	"
35	2	"
36	3	"
VG-9	3	"
14	7	"
15	14	"
17	4	"
21	3	"
24	2	"
25	4	"
26	7	"
34	4	"
42	3	"
52	3	"
53	5	"
68	1	"
84	5	"
86	5	"
104	7	"
105	5	"
110	7	"
116	6	"
125	5	"
139	4	"

SITE	# OF TYPES	RANK
VG-146	7	Non-Admin. < 100
147	5	"
148	2	"
173	3	"
174	3	"
176	6	"
182	6	"
184	7	"
185	0	"
187	3	"
189	1	"
191	2	"
192	4	"
193	4	"
194	3	"
212	2	"
213	4	"
215	2	"
224	5	"
226	8	"
227	2	"
230	6	"
246	7	"
247	3	"
252	4	"
254	2	"

SITE	# OF TYPES	RANK
VG-255	3	Non-Admin. < 100
258	4	"
262	4	"
263	3	"
267	2	"
296	4	"
302	5	"
307	4	"
311	10	"
316	3	"
317	1	"
318	1	"

IIIB

SITE	# OF TYPES	RANK
C-63	7	2
VG-31,37-42,71,72	10	2
C-1,5-9,69-89	8	3
VG-8-18	13	3
26	16	3
62-63	5	3
21-22	7	4
27-29	8	4
32	7	4
51	7	4
52	6	4
C-29-30	0	5
32	6	5
39	8	5
92,100	1	5
114	2	5
VG-25,67	3	5
47,68	7	5
48	8	5
49	4	5
57	7	5
59-60	7	5
61	7	5
65	3	5
70	3	5

SITE	# OF TYPES	RANK
C-16	0	Non-Admin. > 100
20,25	9	"
36-38,44,46,47	5	"
50-61	5	"
62,136,215	2	"
64,65,125	4	"
66	3	"
116-119	0	"
127	8	"
141	3	"
142-156,158	5	"
VG-20	5	"
C-17	5	Non-Admin. < 100
18	2	"
22	3	"
115	1	"
138	1	"
144	5	"
151	1	"
152	4	"
153	3	"
155	6	"
168	1	"
201	3	"

SITE	# OF TYPES	RANK
C-204	3	Non-Admin. < 100
205	1	"
208	3	"
213	1	"
VG-19	2	"
23	5	"
30	2	"
33	3	"
36	3	"
56	3	"
58	6	"
69	9	"

IV

SITE	# OF TYPES	RANK
3-38-58,60,63,64	18	1
Zaachila	7	2
3-83-91	14	2
2-2-4	8	3
3-6-9	9	3
67-72	10	3
2-5	3	4
3-33	5	4
94	3	4
2-11,12,16,18	3	5
3-5	4	5
10-13	11	5
16	8	5
20	3	5
28-30	10	5
74-75	7	5
76	7	5
79	3	5
93	2	5
95	5	5
2-1	4	Non-Admin. < 100
10	5	"
17	1	"
19	3	"

SITE	# OF TYPES	RANK
3-2	5	Non-Admin. < 100
36	4	"
37	6	"
62	3	"
66	3	"
73	1	"
92	3	"
96	5	"

V

SITE	# OF TYPES	RANK
Cuiban	19	1
C-14	9	2
VG-245	15	2
56	11	3
192	2	3
326	10	3
451	11	3
C-81	3	4
235	5	4
317	3	4
VG-297	3	5
498	1	5
358	11	5
C-1	11	Non-Admin. > 100
23	10	"
27	7	"
34	19	"
49	12	"
58	9	"
71	11	"
76	1	"
88	2	"
244	10	"
249	4	"
280	6	"
284	8	"

SITE	# OF TYPES	RANK
298	9	Non-Admin. > 100
G-94-96,98	4	"
VG-51	3	"
64	14	"
89	3	"
115	10	"
181	8	"
188	9	"
225	13	"
276	10	"
378	5	"
380	9	"
382	6	"
385	10	"
404	4	"
408	9	"
471	6	"
C-28	1	Non-Admin. < 100
30	6	"
32	3	"
54	4	"
62	6	"
87	3	"
121	1	"
134	4	"

SITE	# OF TYPES	RANK
139	3	Non-Admin. < 100
141	3	"
234	4	"
246	1	"
279	2	"
314	1	"
324	4	"
325	2	"
326	1	"
328	3	"
330	4	"
331	2	"
334	1	"
VG-39	1	"
44	9	"
45	8	"
47	1	"
48	4	"
60	5	"
63	2	"
72	2	"
82	4	"
93	5	"
99	2	"
102	3	"
104	5	"

V (continued)

SITE	# OF TYPES	RANK
VG-105	7	Non-Admin. < 100
106	6	"
107	6	"
142	5	"
143	0	"
144	9	"
146	3	"
148	4	"
152	5	"
200	10	"
201	5	"
204	6	"
219	1	"
228	5	"
231	2	"
232	9	"
233	11	"
235	10	"
236	7	"
239	7	"
241	0	"
246	6	"
249	3	"
250	3	"
267	5	"
277	5	"

SITE	# OF TYPES	RANK
VG-278	1	Non-Admin. < 100
279	5	
280	4	"
281	7	"
285	2	"
287	2	"
298	4	"
299	1	"
319	3	"
320	3	"
322	2	"
333	7	"
338	7	"
341	7	"
343	3	"
345	5	"
347	7	"
349	2	"
350	6	"
351	6	"
352	4	"
353	7	"
355	5	"
368	3	"
370	1	"
371	3	"

SITE	# OF TYPES	RANK
372	0	Non-Admin. < 100
373	1	"
374	2	"
375	1	"
381	3	"
386	4	"
418	1	"
423	3	"
440	3	"
447	3	"
465	4	"
480	4	"
489	1	"
510	5	"
520	5	"
521	6	"
527	4	"
528	9	"

Appendix IX

CERAMIC PRODUCTION SITES

by Gary Feinman

In the Valley of Oaxaca, evidence of ceramic production has been found at occupations dating to each of the seven Monte Albán phases. These loci of ceramic production were identified according to a two-step procedure. An initial identification was made based upon the field observations of our survey crews. When kiln wasters were recorded in the field notes as present at a given site, that occupation was described as a locus of production. Sites were also identified as ceramic production places when a road or barranca cut revealed evidence either of ceramic firing or of kiln. Sites initially identified as loci of ceramic production based on such field observations were coded accordingly (Appendix 1).

ic production was made after the coding of the 1055 ceramic collections from the valley survey (the data can be found in Feinman 1980). Using these data, it became possible to check the tentative field identifications of production sites with information on ceramic distributions. Densities and raw counts of certain types and wares were examined at four levels: the collection, the site and the 2 kilometer subsquare and the 4 kilometer grid square. It was expected that a site which produced pottery during a given period would have relatively high counts and densities (number of sherds of given type per collected area) of those types that field indications suggested were being made locally. For example, a site which field observations suggested was a locus for the production of Period I red painted *crema* ware would be expected to have relatively large quantities of the types made in that ware in its collection. In addition, spatial analyses of utilitarian artifact distributions (Hodder 1974; Hodder and Orton 1976; Johnson 1973, 1977:481-87; Rands 1967) have suggested that settlements located close to production sites should have higher quantities of the locally produced artifacts than should similar settlements located farther away. This expectation is supported by several descriptions of contemporary utilitarian ceramic production and distribution (Hendry 1957; Shepard 1977; Stolmaker 1976: 197-98). Consequently, I also expected that the 4 kilometer grid square in which a ceramic production site was located would contain larger quantities of locally produced ceramics than would most other grid squares within the survey area.

The second phase of the ceramic workshop identification then considered the seven following variables:

1) Presence of kiln wasters or clay concretions (Bordaz 1964:24, 75, 117). Kiln wasters were defined as sherds which had bubbles or cracks of the kind that most probably resulted from firing a vessel that was not totally dry. Some of the sherds that were defined as wasters could still have been part of vessels that were used as containers. Clay concretions were defined as the bricks or modeled lumps of fired clay which have often been associated with ceramic firing (i.e., Bordaz 1964:117).

2) Evidence of kilns or ceramic firing.

3) The presence of burnishing tools or other artifacts possibly used in ceramic manufacture.

4) The relative abundance of particular types and/or wares in specific collections.

5) The relative abundance of particular types and/or wares at specific sites.

6) The relative abundance of particular types and/or wares within 2 by 2 kilometer subsquares. The subsquare density of a given type for a particular phase was calculated by dividing the total number of that type within the collections dated to a particular phase in a specific subsquare by the total collected area of those same collections.

7) The relative abundance of particular types and/or wares within specific 4 kilometer grid squares. The grid square density of a given type for a particular phase was calculated by dividing the total number of that type within the collections dated to a particular phase in a specific grid square by the total collected area of those same collections. These densities were calculated in sherds per hectare.

In almost all cases, sites were not identified as ceramic producing sites unless at least two of these variables indicated that ceramic manufacture occurred there. The only exceptions were a few sites where the amount, density, and formal variability of a particular ware were so unusually high (compared to other contemporaneous occupations) that production of that ware was indicated. This latter interpretation was based upon contemporary studies of ceramic production in Oaxaca which indicated that the presence and use of the widest assortment of forms made of a given ware tended to occur near the site producing that ware (Hendry 1957:179, 236-39; Shanson, n.d.:11; Shepard 1977:18).

In general, analysis of ceramic distributional information supported the designation of loci of ceramic production based upon field evaluations. Most of the sites that were coded as locations of production initially were identified as ceramic production sites in this second stage of analysis. For the most part, it was multicomponent sites that were coded initially as loci of production and then were not identified as ceramic manufacturing sites after supplemental analysis. The periodization of the ceramic production at these multicomponent occupations was somewhat unclear in the field and so the location often was coded positively for all occupational periods. Ceramic distributional analysis enabled more accurate periodization of ceramic production at these sites and consequently, some components were deleted as production sites. The other discrepancies were created in cases where a site initially was coded as a ceramic production location because a single kiln waster was found. If no corroborative evidence was found, the site was removed from the ceramic production list. This was done because some of the collected kiln wasters, though flawed, possibly may have been part of functional vessels (Hendry 1957:120). These vessels therefore may have been distributed for use to the site where they were found rather than made and discarded there. Prior to listing the sites where the presence of ceramic production was observed it must be stated that we do not believe that we have found all the locations where ceramic production occurred within the survey area. We do believe, however, that for each phase we have a large enough sample of the major ceramic production sites to observe meaningful patterning in their size and location through time. Furthermore, we suggest that variability in the mean size and the location of the identified ceramic production sites when interpreted in conjunction with other data, will enable us to make certain tentative statements regarding changes in the strategies of ceramic production in the Oaxaca Valley over time.

In this appendix, I will list and describe the settlements that appear to be sites of ceramic production for each of the seven chronological phases between Early I and V. The specific collection area, within which evidence of ceramic manufacturing was noted, also will be listed in the description of each locus of production. Listing these collection numbers will enable the reader to determine the grid square that contains evidence of ceramic manufacture for each phase. The first four digits of each collection number refer to the grid square within which the collection was made. The other three numbers refer to the collection itself, as coded in Feinman (1980). After ceramic production sites are listed for each phase, a few additional remarks will be offered concerning ceramic production during that phase.

CERAMIC PRODUCTION SITES: MONTE ALBAN EARLY I

2-5-3: This site within the Central Valley Survey Area has been described by Kowalewski (1976:45-46). It sits just west of a source of fine textured clay used by the contemporary potters of Atzompa. The surface densities of Early I ceramics were described as light and one kiln waster was recorded in collection 1405404 at this site. The densities of almost all Period I *crema* types, within grid square 1405, were high compared to the other grid squares within the survey area and this suggests that ceramic production occurred locally. The number of both unpainted *crema* bowls (6) and non-diagnostic *crema* sherds (20) in collection area 1405404 were relatively high and it appears that this settlement may have been a *crema* ware ceramic production site in Early I.

2-5-14: This site also was previously described by Kowalewski (1976:56) who reported moderate to heavy densities (Parsons 1971:22-23) of surface ceramics over a 0.8 hectare area of the occupation. The dense surface concentration of pottery at this site could not be attributed to any specific erosional, agricultural, or habitational factors and so it was suggested that these unusual densities were related to prehispanic ceramic production. The nearly exclusive presence of a single ware (Period I *cremas*) in these surface concentrations also suggested that the densities were related to pottery production. A dense concentration of relatively homogeneous ceramic debris was found during the excavation of a known locus of ceramic production in the Netherlands (van der Leeuw 1976:115). The relationship between heavy surface densities of ceramics of a single ware and ceramic production was also noted by our survey crews who walked through the modern pottery producing town of San Bartolo Coyotepec in the Valley of Oaxaca. The accumulation of debris from black pottery production in the fields and in the barrancas within this village far surpassed the surface concentrations of modern pottery that were observed at any other location within the Valle Grande Survey Area.

In addition, 2-5-14 is located in grid square 1404 where the densities of most of the Period I crema ceramic types in the Early I collections were relatively high in relation to the rest of the survey area. It is also interesting to note that although *crema* pottery was plentiful and found in many formal varieties here, Early I *gris* pottery was almost absent.

2-5-33: Light-moderate surface densities of Early I ceramic types were observed over a portion of this occupation located within the Central Valley Survey Area (Kowalewski 1976:73–76). One probable kiln waster, an outleaned wall, flaring rim, Period I *gris* bowl was in a collection (1107410) from this site. In addition, unlike most collections from Early I occupations within the survey area, *gris* pottery seems to be predominant in collections from 2-5-33. The collected total of Early I incised *gris* bowls (Caso, Bernal, and Acosta 1967:32-35) from grid square 1107 was more than twice the collected total of these types from any other grid square (excluding those containing Monte Albán). Consequently, it seems very likely that these *gris* types were made in this grid unit. The unusual surface densities and the kiln waster found here suggest that this site was the locus of manufacture.

3-5-26, 62: The densities of unpainted Early I *café* pottery types found in the collections from the grid squares surrounding the contemporary town of Zimatlán (0805, 0806, 0705, 0706, 0606) were, for the most part, higher than the densities of those types from any other portion of the Central or Valle Grande Survey Areas. Consequently, it seems likely that some of this utilitarian ware was made in the general area. The presence of two unpainted *café* kiln wasters in collection 0706310 suggested that some of that ware was made at this site between Early I and II. Unfortunately, more refined dating of ceramic production at this site was not possible, and so this location was identified as a production location for all three phases.

3-5-27: The predominance of Period I *café* pottery types over other Period I types on the surface of this site suggested that unpainted Period I *café* ceramics were produced in this area. The relatively high densities of Early I unpainted *café* types in the collections from grid squares 0805, 0806, 0705, 0706, 0606 as compared to the densities of the same types in the central part of the valley also suggested that those types were produced around modern Zimatlán. The presence of two kiln wasters, both Period I plain *café* bowls, in collection 0706202 suggested that at least some of that production occurred at this occupation during either Early I or Late I.

3-5-45: The presence of a fired lump of clay along with the large amount of non-diagnostic *café* pottery (44 sherds) collected at this site suggested that it was a ceramic workshop in Rosario and/or Early I. This was suggested by the fairly high density of one *café* bowl type (T2079) in the collection from this site. The density of red painted *café* pottery (K-3) was higher in the grid square (0304) containing this site than in any other grid unit within the valley not including either Monte Albán or grid square 0606 (where one red painted *café* sherd was collected in the lone Early I collection made). Unfortunately, no red painted *café* pottery was picked up at 3-5-45.

Monte Albán Early I: Additional Comments

The site designated ET-SLC-SLC 5 in the field and located within the Etla Arm near the modern town of San Lorenzo Cacaotepec was an additional location where Early I ceramics were produced. The site lies several hundred meters from a modern riverbed source of clay. The density of surface pottery in two areas of the site was light-moderate. Most of the surface pottery was Period I *crema* ware. Clay concretions were observed scattered in collection area 1405303, the area where surface pottery was the most dense. These concretions, which were shaped like rounded clay bricks, were made in *crema* paste with diorite temper. Almost all Period I *crema* ware types were present in relatively high frequencies both at this site and within grid square 1405. In addition, at ET-SLC-SLC 5 the perid I *crema* types were far more abundant than were the Period I *gris* or *café* types.

3-5-3 was coded as a ceramic production site (Appendix I, Part II). A road cut into the site revealed evidence of two kilns. Each was more than a meter in diameter and at least two meters deep. The soil around these tubular features was baked bright red. No kiln wasters were found but Richard Blanton (personal communication) observed that ceramics were especially abundant near the kilns. It was noted that *crema* pottery was especially dense in the immediate vicinity of the kilns. A collection was made near the features. Since Early I through II pottery was found in this collection (1006101) the site was identified and coded as a workshop for each of the three phases. Upon further analysis, however, most of the collected *cremas* were found to date to Monte Albán II and so the periodization of the ceramic production at the occupation was re-evaluated to only include that latest epoch.

An analysis of the densities by grid unit of the various Early I types suggested that *café* pottery was also made at some location(s) within the Etla Arm during Early I. Densities of several of the *café* types were relatively high in the northern part of Etla area. The near absence of Early I *café* types in the intervening central part of the valley make it rather unlikely that the *café* pottery collected in Etla was produced at and distributed from the Valle Grande *café* pottery manufacturing sites. Unfortunately, no specific loci of Early I *café* pottery production, within the Etla Arm, have been found yet.

CERAMIC PRODUCTION SITES: MONTE ALBAN LATE I

2-6-136-139: This occupation was considered an Early I ceramic production loci (2-5-33). Once again, the *gris* pottery, dating to Late I, substantially outnumbered the other Late I types in the collections from this occupation. Seventy Type 1207's (Caso, Bernal, and Acosta 1967:25-27; Kowalewski, Spencer, and Redmond 1978:179) alone were collected at the site as compared to a total of only 11 Late I *cremas*. Since the kiln waster in collection 1107410 cannot be dated more finely than to Period I and since it was found in a collection which contains both Early I and Late I, it must be considered as possible evidence for Late I ceramic production. The relative abundance of certain Late I *gris* types in grid square 1007 also suggests that ceramic production continued at this location in Late I.

3-6-33: This occupation was apparently a loci of *café* utilitarian ware production in Late I and/or II. A kiln waster (a *café* ware *olla*) was found in area 0906102. More raked *café ollas* (T2009) were collected in area 0906104 than in any other Late I collection. In addition, considering only those collections dated to Late I, raked *ollas* were found in greater density in grid square 0906 than in any other grid square within the survey area.

3-6-51: There is considerable evidence that Late I *gris* paste combed bottomed bowls (Caso, Bernal, and Acosta 1967:26, 28; Kowalewski, Spencer, and Redmond 1978:181) were made at this site. Eighteen sherds of this type (T1297) were collected in area 0805101. This represents seven more examples of T1297's than were picked up in any other survey collection. In addition, 19 more T1297's were collected in the other collections made at this site. One of the combed-bottomed bowls collected in area 0805101 was a vessel that apparently was combed too deeply during production. An incision went through the bowl bottom causing the pot to break. It should be noted that more T1207's (Kowalewski, Spencer, and Redmond 1978:179) were picked up in collection area 0805101 than were found in any other valley survey collection.

3-6-80: This occupation was considered to be an area of plain *café* ceramic production in Early I (3-5-26). Two plain *café* kiln wasters were found in collection 0706310, and these sherds represented evidence of ceramic production. Unfortunately, this production could not be dated more finely than sometime from Early I to II. Consequently the occupation was considered a production site in all three phases. Additional evidence for *café* pottery production at this location was derived from the distributional data on certain *café olla* types within Late I collections. More plain *café ollas* with thin straight necks (T2013B) were collected in the Late I collections within grid square 0706 than within the Late I collections from any other grid square. In addition, the 47 plain *café ollas* with curved-back necks (T2013A) that were found within 0706 were the second largest amount of this type that were found in any grid square within the valley survey area.

3-6-83: The relatively high densities of unpainted Late I *café* vessels (T2013A, T2079) in certain grid squares (0805, 0806, 0705, 0706, 0605, and 0606) as compared to the densities of these types in other parts of the survey region, suggested that plain *café* pottery was made near Zimatlán in Late I. The presence of the two Period I plain *café* bowl wasters in the collection from the southern portion of 3-6-83 suggested that some of that manufacturing may have occurred at this site.

Monte Albán Late I: Additional Comments

Production of *crema* utility wares probably continued at ET-SLC-SLC 5 into Late I. Many of the ceramic types densely concentrated on the surface of the site and relatively abundant in the collections made at the site were known to have been used in Late I as well as Early I. In addition, the collection area at the site (1405303), in which the surface concentrations of *crema* ceramics were extremely dense and where several clay concretions were noted, included a G-12 (T1207) (Caso, Bernal, and Acosta 1967:25-26) which suggested that the occupation of this loci of production continued into Late I. Finally, the densities of many ceramic types (T0016, T0018, T0057, T0121, T0376, T0384, T0385, T0389, T0390, T0391, T0398) in collections dated to Late I were greater in grid unit 1405 than in any other grid square within the valley survey area and this also suggested that production occurred within this area. Since ET-SLC-SLC 5 was the only occupation in grid square 1405 at which there is some indication of ceramic manufacturing, it seems likely that Late I *crema* production occurred here.

Three suspected Period Late I ceramic production sites (3-6-5, 8, 149, 3-6-24, 3-6-118) were no longer considered to be loci of ceramic manufacturing after more careful analysis.

3-6-5, 8, 149: This site was coded initially as a ceramic production site; however, it is no longer believed to have been a Late I locus of production. A road cut into collection area 1006101 revealed evidence of several kilns. It was noted that *crema* ware ceramics were especially dense in the immediate vicinity of the kilns. Since pottery from phases Early I through II was present in this collection, the site was coded initially as a ceramic manufacturing site for each of these three phases. Upon further analysis, it was found that most of these *cremas* present dated to Period II. Consequently, the periodization of ceramic production at this location was re-evaluated to include only that latest phase.

3-6-24: One *gris* kiln waster was noted in this collection, which included a few ceramic types that date to Late I. Consequently the occupation was coded as a possible Late I ceramic production site. No corroborating evidence for Late I ceramic production at the site was found, however, and, in fact, the collection containing the waster (1007203) had hardly any Late I *gris* types. It seems more likely that the *gris* waster pertains to Monte Albán IIIb.

3-6-118: A *gris* kiln waster was found at this occupation in collection area 0403207, which was dated to several phases including Late I. The surface ceramic density at the site was for the most part sparse and an analysis of the distributional data on *gris* ceramic types did not provide any corroborating evidence of ceramic production for any occupation.

CERAMIC PRODUCTION SITES: MONTE ALBAN II

3-7-1-5, 7: The surface concentrations of ceramics were relatively dense over much of this site, which may have been a locus of ceramic production between phases II and IV. Two distinct collection areas were judged to be production locations in Monte Albán II. The collection from area 1005218 contained a single kiln waster made of *gris* alluvial clay. The collection also contained 48 non-diagnostic *gris* sherds. In addition, the collections from 3-7-1-5, 7 contained more examples of one Monte Albán II *gris* paste type (T1419-white rimmed black ware) than did any other site in the valley excluding Monte Albán.

Several kilns or areas of ceramic firing were observed in a road cut at this site. These features were each more than a meter in diameter and more than two meters deep. The areas surrounding these features were baked to a bright red color. A collection area (1006101) was positioned adjacent to the kilns in an area where *crema* pottery was abundant. The *cremas* from this collection area for the most part were dated to Monte Albán II and this suggested that II *crema* production occurred here as well.

3-7-15, 16: The presence of a *café* kiln waster in collection area 0906102 at this occupation suggested ceramic production. This was supported by the presence of eight *café* raked *ollas* with curved-back necks (T2013A) within this same collection. In addition, 46 T2013A *café ollas* (Kowalewski, Spencer, and Redmond 1978:188) were collected in grid square 0906 and this was the largest number of this type that was collected in II collections from any grid square within the survey area excluding Monte Albán. The 39 T2009's and the 18 T2013C's that were collected in grid square 0906 also represented the largest number of these types that were collected in II collections from any grid square, again excluding Monte Albán.

3-7-29, 30, 37: This occupation was a location of Late I *gris* production (3-6-51). One collection (0805101) made at this site also contained the second largest quantity of Period II type 1194 gray bowls in any collection other than those made at Monte Albán. This same collection also contained more Type 1207's than did any other II collection again excluding Monte Albán. Consequently, it is suggested that some II *gris* pottery was made at this site. This suggestion is supported by the fact that in contrast to the abundance of II *gris* types here, relatively few II *café* or *crema* sherds were collected here.

3-7-31: The relative abundance of the usually rare red painted *amarillo* pottery (T3408) on the surface of this site was noted by the survey crews. Twenty-five A-9 sherds (Caso, Bernal, and Acosta 1967:70) were picked up at this site in collection area 0806101 and this was more than twice the number of A-9's recorded in any other collection area. Six additional A-9's were collected in other parts of this site. As expected, the density of T3408's in grid square 0806 was one of the highest in the valley. Another category (T3066) of *amarillo* bowls (T3066) also was relatively abundant in the II collections from grid square 0806. Consequently, it seems likely that some II *amarillo* pottery was produced at this site.

3-7-55, 56: This occupation was identified as an area of plain *café* ceramic production in both Early I (3-5-26) and Late I (3-6-80). Two plain *café* kiln wasters were found in collection 0706310 and these sherds represent evidence of ceramic production. Unfortunately this production could not be dated more securely than to sometime between Early I and II and the occupation was judged to be a production site in all three phases. The relatively high densities of several *café* ware types (T2009, T2013B, T2414) in the collections dated to II within grid square 0706 also suggested that *café* ceramic production may have continued at this site during II.

Monte Albán II: Additional Comments

Some *cremas* were probably made during Period II in the Etla Arm of the valley. Some of this production of *crema* pottery may have occurred at ET-SLC-SLC 5 where Period I *cremas* were made. But, Period II production at ET-SLC-SLC 5 seems unlikely, given that most of the *crema* types diagnostic to II alone were not abundant in the collections from this site. Identification of specific II *crema* production sites awaits additional research in this arm of the valley. The wide variety of the highly decorated *crema* ware vessels and their rather distinctive spatial distributions within the survey area, however, does suggest that these types were produced at several distinct locations. Although a specific production location cannot yet be identified, it seems likely that II *amarillo* pottery was also made in Etla Arm. The *amarillo* sherds collected in Etla had a different paste color than did the *amarillo* pottery collected in the Valle Grande. Most of the Etla *amarillos* were beige (7.5 YR 7/4) while those in the Valle Grande had a more pinkish paste color (5 YR 7/6). Both *amarillo* varieties were found in the Monte Albán collections.

CERAMIC PRODUCTION SITES: MONTE ALBAN IIIa

2-8-23: At this site, the collection area 1107405 contained both a kiln waster and a bowl with an oddly formed rim that apparently was caused by a production error (Stephen Kowalewski: field notes). The kiln waster was an outleaned wall G-23 bowl (T1264), which indicated that ceramic manufacture probably occurred at this site during the Early Classic period. Some of the ceramics produced at this site may have been made in *amarillo* since the sherd with the oddly shaped rim was of that paste. In addition, more carved *amarillo* bowls (T3410) were collected at this site than at any other valley site except for Monte Albán. Bevelled rim bowls (T1268) were also relatively abundant in the collections from this site and more generally within the IIIa collections from grid unit 1107. The 24 non-diagnostic *gris* sherds found in collection area 1107405 also indicated that *gris* pottery was being produced in a wide variety of forms at this site. Based on comparisons with contemporary pottery making in modern Oaxaca, this also suggested that *gris* pottery may have been made here (Hendry 1957:236-239; Shanson, MS:11).

3-8-2-6: The surface concentrations of ceramics were relatively dense over much of this site, which may have been a locus of ceramic manufacture between II and IV. Collection 1005208 contained a single *gris* waster, which based upon the dating of the diagnostic pottery in the collection, may have been made either in II or IIIa. Further indication of *gris* production at this loci was suggested by the 48 non-diagnostic gray wares which were picked up in 1005218. Large quantities of non-diagnostic gray wares also were recorded in several other collections, dated to IIIa and made at this site. Several *gris* ceramic types (T1126, T1265, T1268) were also found in relatively high densities within IIIa collections in grid square 1005, also suggesting local ceramic production.

3-8-31, 32, 33: *Café* kiln wasters were found in both collections 0906205 and 0906102 at this site. The latter was a single component IIIa collection while the former was dated to several phases, including IIIa. This suggested that ceramic manufacturing may have occurred here during the Early Classic period. Eight *café* raked *ollas* (T2009) were noted in collection 0906102 while four more were found in 0906205. In addition, more (40) of these raked *ollas* were found in the IIIa collections from grid unit 0906 than from any other grid square, excluding Monte Albán. Another *café olla* type (T2013A) was also found to be relatively abundant in the IIIa collections from this site. Fifteen examples of this type were picked up in the Structure 2 collection (0906105) and this was the largest quantity of this type found in any IIIa collection other than those made at Monte Albán.

3-8-41: This occupation sits very close to the riverbed where alluvial clays could have been collected. Eight thick fired lumps of unfinished alluvial clay were picked up in the collection from this site (1007401). Five of these lumps were completely oxidized while the other three were gray. If the collections made at three of the valley's large Early Classic centers (3-8-136, 150, 152: 3-8-175 and 3-8-233-239, 241) are not included, the collection from this small occupation included the second largest number of outleaned wall, exteriorally carved *gris* bowls (T1264) picked up in any survey collection. The relative abundance of this decorated Early Classic type (T1264) at this small site suggested that outleaned wall G-23's were produced here.

3-8-63, 64: A lump of fired gray alluvial clay and one IIIa kiln waster were recovered in collection 0906302 at this occupation. In addition, each of the three IIIa collections from this site also contained at least twelve pieces of non-diagnostic *gris* pottery. Twenty-seven pieces of non-diagnostic *gris* pottery, much of it probably Classic period in date, were collected in collection area 0906393 alone. When this formal diversity in *gris* pottery is considered in conjunction with the fired lump and the waster, it was concluded that *gris* ceramics were produced here.

3-8-65: *Gris* kiln wasters were found in three different collections at this large Early Classic period site (0806201, 0806202, 0806216). Since two of the collections were single component (IIIa), it seems very likely that *gris* ceramics were produced here in the Early Classic period. The waster in 0906216 was a conical *cajete* (T1126); since 41 G-35 bowls (T1126) were collected in 0906216, it seems likely that these omnipresent bowls were one of the types manufactured here. The production of G-35 bowls (T1126) at this site during the Early Classic also is suggested by the presence of more T1126's in the IIIa collections from grid square 0806 than in the IIIa collections from any other grid square, excluding Monte Albán and Jalieza.

3-8-136, 150-152 (Jalieza): It seems apparent that ceramic manufacture was undertaken at this large center during the Early Classic period. Kiln wasters made out of alluvial gray clay were found in two single component IIIa collections at this site (0708405 and 0708422). Several types of Early Classic *gris* pottery were also very well represented in the collections from here. More outleaned-wall carved gray bowls (T1264) were collected at Jalieza than at any other site in the valley with the exception of Monte Albán. A clay mold, shaped like an ear of corn, also was found here and it probably was used in the manufacture of ceramic urns (Caso and Bernal 1952).

3-8-201: Some *gris* ceramic production may have occurred at this site during the Early Classic. Three kiln wasters were found in collection area 0505401. These dated to both IIIa and IIIb. Consequently, this occupation was considered to be a locus of ceramic production in both the Early and Late Classic periods. Although the densities of IIIa *gris* types in the collections from grid square 0505 were not particularly significant, the densities of several types within the two IIIa collections in sub-square 05054 were quite high. For example, the density of *gris* bowls with solid supports (T1274) within the Early Classic collections in sub-square 05054 was 11.19 per hectare, which was higher than the density of that type within any grid square except for grid unit 0502 and those grid squares containing Monte Albán. Non-diagnostic Classic period *gris* pottery and *gris* conical *cajetes* (T1126) were also relatively abundant in both the collection from this occupation (0505401) and the other collections dated to the Early Classic period within this subsquare.

3-8-177-179: It seems quite likely that ceramic production was undertaken at this large Early Classic ridgetop center. *Gris* kiln wasters were found in three separate collections from this site (0502202, 0502205, 0503101). The density of *gris* conical *cajetes* (T1126) within IIIa collections was higher in grid square 0502 than in any other grid unit other than 1705 and Monte Albán. The T1126's were also found in comparatively high density within grid square 0503. The densities of plain *gris* jars (T1120) within IIIa collections in grid squares 0502 and 0504 were also both relatively high as were the densities of *gris* bowls with both hollow (T1264) and solid supports (T1274).

Monte Albán IIIa: Additional Comments

A *gris* kiln waster was found at 3-8-220 in collection 0403207 which was dated to several periods including IIIa. The surface ceramic density throughout the site was sparse. An analysis of the distribution of *gris* ceramic types also did not show any significant evidence of ceramic production for this phase. This site consequently was not identified as a locus of ceramic manufacture.

CERAMIC PRODUCTION SITES: MONTE ALBAN IIIb

2-9-20, 25: This site lies only 250 meters southeast of a clay source for the contemporary potters of Atzompa. The surface ceramic density at the site varied from light through moderate with the heaviest densities noted at the center of the occupation (Kowalewski 1976:318). An abundance of *gris* and *gris cremosa* pottery at the site was noted and these wares were found in an unusual variety of forms (Kowalewski 1976:318). A hollow *sahumador* handle that may have been a kiln waster and a mold fragment for Classic period funerary urns were found in collection 1405316. A *gris* kiln waster also was found in collection area 1405308 at this occupation. The densities of *gris* types within the IIIb collections in grid square 1405 were not particularly high, although the actual count of conical *cajetes* (T1126) within these IIIb collections was fifth largest for any grid square within the survey area.

Monte Albán: Site Subdivision 11 (Atzompa): This subdivision of Monte Albán has a long occupational history, but most of its component terraces were only occupied in IIIb at the time when Monte Albán reached its greatest extent (Blanton 1978:88). Although Blanton (1978:91) noted that a relatively large number of kiln wasters were found within subdivision 11, he argued against the hypothesis that ceramic production was an important activity at prehispanic Atzompa. However, Blanton made his argument before he had the opportunity to compare the collections from Monte Albán with the collections from a large number of other valley sites. Based on these intra-valley comparisons one must suggest that at least during the Late Classic period the production of ceramics was an important activity within site subdivision 11. On the terraces at Atzompa, many of which were occupied only during the Late Classic period, 34 kiln wasters were found. In contrast, only 63 kiln wasters were noted in all of the collections made at valley occupations other than Monte Albán. Additional information collected during the Monte Albán survey also suggested that Atzompa may have been an important locus of *gris* production during the Late Classic period. Various ground stone tools, chipped stone tools, shell objects and Classic period *café* ware ceramic types (T2086, T2418) were not unusually abundant in site subdivision 11 (Blanton 1978:78-88). Yet several Classic period *gris* pottery types (T1125, T1137) as well as *gris* ceramic funerary urns were found in greater densities upon the collected terraces within site subdivision 11 than in the collected terraces in any other Monte Albán subdivision (Blanton 1978:80, 90; Kuttruff 1978:402). In addition, two of the six polishing or burnishing stones identified in the surface collections from Monte Albán were found on Atzompa terraces (Blanton 1978:95).

3-9-8-18: The surface concentrations of ceramics were relatively dense over much of this site, a possible locus of ceramic production between phases II and IV. At this site, two multicomponent collections (1005202, 1005294) that included IIIb components, contained single *gris* kiln wasters. The wasters could not be dated to any one epoch, and so the possibility that they were Late Classic in date had to be considered. The density of bevelled rim *gris* bowls (T1268) in period IIIb collections within grid square 1005 was one of the highest within the survey area, and this suggests that at least some Late Classic *gris* pottery was made locally.

3-9-25, 67: A *gris* kiln waster probably dating to the Classic period was found in collection area 1007203 at this site. Another collection area 1008301, also at this occupation, contained unusually high densities of several of the most common Late Classic *gris* types (T1120, T1126). Consequently, it seemed likely that some *gris* pottery was made here during the Late Classic period.

3-9-58: Three *gris* pottery kiln wasters and 17 non-diagnostic *gris* sherds were noted within collection area 0505401 at this site. The settlement was occupied in both IIIa and IIIb. Ceramic production may have taken place during both phases (see 3-8-201). The densities of several *gris* ceramic categories (T1140, T1274, T1263) were relatively high within IIIb collections within grid unit 0505 and this tentatively supported the suggestion that ceramic production occurred here during the Late Classic period.

3-9-69: A Classic period *gris* kiln waster was found in collection area 0706305 at this occupation. In addition, several Classic Period *gris* types (T1120, T1126, T1140, T1263, T1274) were collected in high densities from collection area 0706305, which is the sole IIIb collection within grid square 0706. Consequently, it is suggested that some ceramic production occurred here during the Late Classic period.

Monte Albán IIIb: Additional Comments

Although it is clear that a small percentage of the pottery used in the Valley of Oaxaca during the Late Classic period was made in *café* ware (i.e., T2083, T2086, T2418), no specific IIIb *café* pottery production site can yet be identified. Analysis of the ceramic collections from Monte Albán revealed that the dominant Late Classic *comal* type, in 10 of the 15 site subdivisions that were clustered in the southern and central portions of the site, was made in *café* ware (T2418) (Blanton 1978:88). Only seven of the *comals* (T2418) were found in IIIb collections from the rest of the valley, but all of these seven examples were collected at sites within 10 kilometers of Monte Albán. The second relatively common Late Classic *café* type, a conical *cajete* (T2086), apparently had a somewhat broader distribution. Yet, 91 out of the 113 examples of this type found in IIIb collections came from either Monte Albán or from sites within 10 kilometers of Monte Albán. The largest percentage of both of these types (T2418, T2086) found outside Monte Albán were collected in grid square 1006. Consequently, I would argue that at least some of the Late Classic *café* pottery was made either at Monte Albán and/or at some location within grid square 1006 (3-9-26?). A more specific identification awaits additional research.

Excavations near Terrace 634 (site subdivision 10) (Blanton 1978:88; Winter and Payne 1976) have provided some additional evidence for ceramic manufacturing at Monte Albán. Two small features were discovered and interpreted to have been ceramic kilns (Winter and Payne 1976). The kilns were dated to Monte Albán IIIb-IV.

The paste of most of the *gris* pottery collected at the site of Rancho Tejas (3-8-233-239, 241; 3-9-62, 63) was somewhat distinct from the *gris* pottery collected in other parts of the valley. A large amount of the gris pottery from the Tejas site had a greenish-gray color which was different from the ordinary *gris* pottery found at other sites within the Valley of Oaxaca. Based on this observation, it seems quite likely that some *gris* ceramic production occurred at or near Rancho Tejas during both the Early and Late Classic periods. The specific location, however, remains unknown.

Similarly, it seems likely that some Classic period *gris* pottery also was manufactured at a location(s) in the northern half of the Etla Arm of the valley. Classic period *gris* pottery collected in the Etla Arm, south of the modern town of Etla, was tempered with diorite and was very similar to the *gris* pottery found at the Classic period occupation of Atzompa. The altered diorite temper in this Classic period pottery from Atzompa was probably obtained from a mine just northwest of the modern village of Santa María Atzompa (Shepard 1967:477-78, 1977). Given the similarity in form and temper between the Atzompa pottery and the pottery from the southern half of the Etla Arm, one might postulate, subject to further investigation, that the pottery collected in the southern half of the Etla Arm was produced largely at Atzompa. Most of the Classic *gris* pottery collected in the northern half of the Etla Arm, however, though formally similar to the pottery from Atzompa, was sand rather than diorite tempered. Consequently one might suggest that at least one unidentified location produced sand-tempered *gris* pottery, in the northern half of the Etla Arm during the Classic period.

CERAMIC PRODUCTION SITES: MONTE ALBAN IV

2-10-2, 4: This site at the western edge of the Tlacolula Arm of the valley has been described as having surface densities of pottery that range from sparse to heavy (Kowalewski 1976:489). One *gris* waster was recovered in collection area 1208302 which is a single component IV collection. In addition, the density of *gris* bevelled rim bowls (T1268) was relatively high within the IV collections in grid square 1208.

3-10-2: Surface concentrations of ceramics were relatively dense over much of this site. One multicomponent collection (1005202) that included a IV component contained a single *gris* waster which may have dated to the Early Postclassic. Additionally, the densities of most *gris* types (T1120, T1126, T1268, T1277) that were found in the IV collections within grid square 1005, were quite high relative to the rest of the surveyed area. This suggested that production may have occurred in this area.

3-10-67-72: One undiagnostic *gris* kiln waster was found in a collection area 0502205 at this large hilltop settlement dated to both IIIa and IV. The possibility that this waster dated to IV cannot be dismissed. In addition, one *gris* type (T1274) was found at a higher density within IV collections in 0502 than in any other grid square within the valley excluding Monte Albán. Consequently, although the evidence is not overwhelming, phase IV *gris* production may have occurred at this site.

Monte Albán IV: Additional Comments

The IV occupation, 3-10-6-9, was coded initially as a ceramic production site. Upon further analysis, this identification could not be substantiated. No kiln wasters were found in the collections from the site and the densities of IV types were not unusually high in the two grid squares (1007 and 1008) which contain this site. The site collections also do not contain unusually large quantities of IV ceramic types.

Lambityeco, a large site in the Tlacolula Arm of the valley, apparently had a large Early Postclassic period occupation (Monte Albán IV). Clay beds exist in a low-lying area only several hundred meters from mounded architectural construction at the site. This clay deposit was apparently mined in the past (Paddock, Mogor, and Lind 1968; Payne 1970). In addition, Payne (1970) was able to very accurately duplicate the prehispanic IV ceramics from Lambityeco using clay mined from these deposits. Therefore, it is easy to understand why several scholars have concluded already that this site was a principal locus of IV ceramic manufacturing (Paddock, Mogor, and Lind 1968; Payne 1970; Swasey 1973).

Although four *café* ware ceramic types (T2014, T2083, T2086, T2418) have been dated to IV, we have not yet located a ceramic production site for *café* pottery in IV. One *café* bowl type (T2086) was found in relatively equal quantities within several grid squares that are rather widely dispersed. This suggested that some *café* pottery may have been produced at several different IV settlements within the valley.

Although we did not find any kiln wasters within the IV collections at 3-10-38 (Jalieza), it is quite possible that IV pottery was produced at or near this site. The pottery in the IV collections from this site was somewhat distinctive from the pottery in IV collections found in other parts of the valley. A fairly large amount of the IV pottery from 3-10-38 was made of alluvial clay and was tan or light gray-brown. Thus, it was quite distinct from the usual *grises* that were found in most IV survey collections.

CERAMIC PRODUCTION SITES: MONTE ALBAN V

3-11-57-59, 84-88, 117-132, 177: This V settlement includes two areas that seem to have been loci of *gris* ceramic production. Collection area 1008203 (3-11-57) contained two V *gris* wasters.

Three additional V kiln wasters were found in collection area 0908401 (3-11-130). One of these latter wasters was a composite silhouette bowl (T1105). Another waster was a hollow support (T1102) while the third was a G3M bowl (Caso, Bernal, and Acosta 1967:447-57) of indeterminate form. Collection area 0908401 also contained 12 composite silhouette bowls (T1105) and 17 hemispherical G3M bowls with incurved rims (T1104). Another collection at this site, 0908201, included 24 examples of Type 1104, which was one of the largest quantities of this type that was found in a single collection area.

3-11-64-69: Collection area 1006302 at this occupation included two V *gris* wasters. One of these wasters was described as being so misshapen that it could not have been used as a container. The collection area also included 11 pieces of polychrome (T5007) pottery which was the second largest quantity of polychrome ware found in any collection excluding the Monte Albán collections. Since the paste of most of the polychrome pottery picked up during Valley of Oaxaca survey was similar to the paste of local V *grises* (Caso, Bernal, and Acosta 1967:465), it was hypothesized that at least some of the polychrome pottery found in Oaxaca was locally produced. This notion was supported tentatively by the analysis of a single Mixteca-Puebla style polychrome sherd through neutron activation (Abascal, Harbottle, and Sayre 1974:93). This analysis showed that the clay used in the manufacturing of the polychrome sherd did not differ markedly in its trace element composition from the clay used in the manufacturing of Oaxacan style vessels found at sites within the valley (see also Bernal 1965). It was also postulated that at least some of the Oaxacan polychromes were made in one of three adjacent grid squares (1105, 1106, 1006) in which large quantities of polychrome pottery were found. Based upon the quantity of T5007's recovered in collection area 1006302, it was very tentatively suggested that some of the locally-produced polychrome was made at this occupation. Curiously, the distribution of polychrome pottery in the Oaxaca Valley was quite similar to the distribution of the V *gris* pottery. The largest concentrations of both were found at the valley's center. This similarity in polychrome and *gris* distributions, when considered along with the similarity in their paste compositions, supports the contention that both the V *grises* and polychromes could have been produced at the same locations within the valley. Of course, it is important also to note that some of the polychrome pottery collected during excavations at Monte Albán were found to have fine *café* paste (Caso, Bernal, and Acosta 1967:465-75). Polychromes made in this paste very possibly could have been produced outside the valley.

3-11-104: This small site was only 200 meters from the Río Atoyac where alluvial clay is available. The surface of the site was covered almost exclusively with V gray wares. Thirty hemispherical G3M's with incurved rims (T1104) were collected at the site while very few other types were found in the collection (0907302). Several kiln wasters were noted at the site by the survey crew that mapped the occupation and one *gris* waster was included within the collection.

3-11-105: This site was very similar to 3-11-104, another V settlement within the same subsquare (09073). This occupation lies just off the Atoyac where alluvial clay is available. Four kiln wasters of V *gris* hemispherical bowls were gathered in collection 0907301. Thirty-six hemispherical G3M bowls (T1104) were collected in 0907301, and this represented the largest quantity of this type in any collection excluding those made at Monte Albán. As with 3-11-104, very few ceramic categories other than hemispherical G3M's were observed on the site surface or included in the collection from this occupation. In addition, two thick, broken, semi-circular *gris* objects, plate-like in form, were found at this site. These objects were "warped" so that they could not have laid flat upon a horizontal surface. Interestingly, these objects closely resemble the concave molds or *moldes* which are used in present-day ceramic production at San Bartolo Coyotepec within the Valley of Oaxaca (Foster 1955:5-6; Shepard 1977; van de Velde and van de Velde 1939). The modern Coyotepec potters use these saucer-shaped *moldes* in forming canteens and jars, and this production technique may have been important prehistorically as well (Foster 1955).

3-11-115, 154-165, 514: The collection area (0907304) at this settlement in which evidence of V gris ceramic production was recorded was in the same subsquare as 3-11-104 and 3-11-105. This collection contained three kiln wasters as well as a lump of gray clay that was 9 x 9 x 5 centimeters and fired on only one side. This site also lies only several hundred meters from the Atoyac and a source of alluvial clay. As with 3-11-104 and 3-11-105, the collection that contained the kiln wasters was composed almost exclusively of *gris* hemispherical G3M bowls (T1104).

3-11-152: This occupation is also quite similar to 3-11-104 and 3-11-105 which are located within the same subsquare. The collection (0907303) from this site contained two *gris* wasters, one of which was a poorly fired body sherd with a rounded edge. This latter sherd may have been used in ceramic production (Bordaz 1964:105). This collection also contained a flat *gris* block of indeterminate use. As with the other pottery production sites in this subsquare, both the ground surface of the site and the collection made at the site contained almost exclusively V *gris* pottery.

3-11-245, 259, 286, 288, 289, 291, 296: Two collection areas at this occupation contained direct evidence of V *gris* ceramic production. Collection area 0709310 contained one *gris* kiln waster. A second ceramic collection, 0709319, also included a V gray ware waster. In addition, this second collection contained two poorly fired composite silhouette bowls (T1105). Large quantities of hemispherical G3M bowls (T1104) were collected in several collections made at the site. In fact, the total number of these bowls within the V collections in grid square 0709 was the largest amount of these bowls found within any grid unit excluding Monte Albán. The density of these hemispherical bowls (T1104) in the V collections within grid square 0709 was also relatively high in relation to the other grid squares within the Central and Valle Grande Survey Areas.

Monte Albán V: Additional Comments

The presence of a kiln waster was noted in the field notes made at 3-11-377. The site consequently was initially coded as a V ceramic production locus. This waster, however, was apparently Classic period in date, and the collection area in which it was found contained no V pottery. The site therefore was deleted from the list of V ceramic production sites.

All of the ceramic production sites that were identified for Monte Albán V were loci of *gris* ceramic manufacturing. This includes the evidence for *gris olla* manufacturing in the Late Postclassic from a dry cave near Mitla (Christopher Moser: personal communication). No loci of either *café* or sandy-cream ware production were found. Yet, it is suggested that the Late Postclassic sandy-cream (T4023, T4024, T5425) and *café* (T2221, T2222, T2223, G2224) vessels also probably were manufactured locally within the Valley of Oaxaca.

All of these V sandy-cream and *café* types were far more abundant in the valley survey collections than were the known exotic types. Aztec fine orange pottery (T5000), for example, did not appear in one of the surface collections that was made outside the limits of Monte Albán, and at Monte Albán only 13 examples of this ware were recovered. In comparison, 106 examples of Huitzo Red-on-Cream (T5425) and 63 examples of Graphite-on-Orange (T2223) were found in the V collections without even considering those from the Monte Albán collections. The sandy-cream (T0423) and the *café* (T2221, T2222) utility jar categories were even more abundant than were the two painted V types (T5425, T2223). In fact, in certain sections of the valley, the V sandy-cream and *café* ware utility jar types were significantly more numerous than were the *gris* jar (T1109). In our collections from the southern half of the Valle Grande Survey Area, and especially within grid squares 0503, 0504, and 0404, the *café* jars significantly outnumber the *gris* jars. In the survey collections from within the grid squares just west of Monte Albán (i.e.,

1303, 1304, 1203, 1204), the number of sandy-cream utility jars was much greater than the number of *gris* jars. Since these *café* and sandy-cream ware utility jars were the most numerous V jar types in certain parts of the valley, it seems likely that at least in these parts of the valley, these jars would have been an integral part of each household's ceramic assemblage. If this proposition is accepted, it would seem rather unlikely that these types would have been made outside the valley. The transportation of utilitarian pottery over the mountains into the valley, without mechanized transportation, would have been an extremely costly proposition. Also, what we do know about ceramic production within the Valley of Oaxaca suggests that during every phase between the Tierras Largas and the present, the utilitarian pottery was made locally. There is no obvious reason why this should not have been the case during the Late Postclassic as well. In fact, historical information that we do have about the Postclassic period suggests that relatively little pottery was exchanged over long distances (Bordaz 1964: 271-78).

The two V *café* bowl types (T2223, T2224) were distributed throughout the valley in a pattern which closely matched the distribution of V raked *café ollas* (T2221). All three of these *café* types were found to be most numerous in grid square 0503 and to be comparatively abundant in grid unit 0504 as well. If it is accepted that the raked *ollas* were made locally, it would seem likely that these two other *café* types would also have been manufactured within the valley. Although a specific location of production for these three types is unknown, one possible site is 3-11-356-359. The largest quantity (12) of raked *café ollas* (T2221) found in any one collection area came from 0504307 at this site. Two collection areas here (0504301 and 0504307) also contained five *café* V bowls (T2224), the largest quantity of this vessel type found in any single collection. Finally, with the exception of Monte Albán the greatest quantity (12 examples) of Graphite-on-Orange ware collected at any one site came from 3-11-356-359.

The mica *café ollas* (T2222) which were most numerous in grid square 0404 may have been made at 3-11-380,523. More than 25% of the total quantity of this type from survey collections, was collected at this site. Furthermore, the mica used as a tempering material in the production of this type would have been readily available from outcrops not too far from this settlement.

The distribution of the sandy-cream ware bowls (T0424) closely resembles that of the sandy-cream ware *ollas* (T0423). Both of these types were found to be abundant within adjacent grid units (1303, 1304, 1203, 1204). The sandy-cream ware *ollas* were the overwhelmingly predominant V jar type within these four grid units. If one accepts that the sandy-cream *ollas* were made locally, it would seem likely, given the similarity in distributions, that the sandy-cream bowls also were made within the valley. The specific location of sandy-cream plain ware production is unknown. The largest quantities of both of these types were found in the collections from 2-11-1-13, 90-112, 120, yet Kowalewski (personal communication) found no other basis on which to suggest ceramic production at this occupation within the Central Valley Survey Area.

The distribution of Huitzo Red-on-Cream (T5425) in our collections was similar to that of the plain sandy-cream ware *ollas* (T0423), in that they both occur most frequently in the areas immediately west and north of Monte Albán. Yet Huitzo Red-on-Cream was distributed somewhat more evenly than the plain sandy-cream ware types within the grid squares on the northern third of the valley. The highest density of this type, within our V collections, was found in grid square 1303, which also contained the highest densities of the two sandy-cream utility types. But the largest quantity of Huitzo Red-on-Cream bowls was found within grid square 1505 and only one example of sandy-cream utility ware was collected within that grid unit. Consequently, it remains unclear where the Huitzo Red-on-Creams were made. Although rather similar to the Yanhuitlán Red-on-Creams that Spores (1972:30-33) found in the Nochixtlán Valley, I would suggest that most of our examples of Huitzo Red-on-Cream were made locally within the northern third of the Valley of Oaxaca. The relative abundance of Huitzo Red-on-Cream in our collections and the stylistic differences between the Yanhuitlán and Huitzo Red-on-Creams suggest that the Oaxacan Red-on-Cream was not made in the Mixteca Alta.

Appendix X

SUMMARY OF TERRACED SITES

JALIEZA (3-IIIA-136, 3-IV-46, and 3-V-259 unless otherwise indicated)

TERRACE	SITE GRID SQUARE	LENGTH	WIDTH	PERIODIZATION	COMMENTS
1	1-3	10	5	IV	
2	1-3	10	4	IV	
3	1-3	10	7	IV	
4	1-3	9	8	IV	
5	1-3	10	10	IV	
6	1-3	14	10	IV	
7	1-3	13	6	IV	
8	1-3	9	9	IV	
9	1-3	18	8	IV	
10	1-3	10	10	IV	
11	1-3	15	6	IV	
12	1-3	10	7	IV	
13	1-3	14	13	IV	
14	1-3	19	5	IV	
15	1-3	18	7	IV	
16	1-3	12	4	IV	
17	1-3	10	4	IV	
18	1-3	12	8	IV	
19	1-3	13	7	IV	
20	1-3	11	6	IV	
21	1-3	23	5	IV	
22	1-3	10	6	IV	
23	1-3	16	14	IV	
24	1-3	14	7	IV	
25	1-3	16	10	IV	
26	1-3	20	5	IV	
27	1-3	13	5	IV	
28	1-3	9	3	IV	
29	1-3	13	5	IV	
30	1-3	12	7	IV	
31	1-3	10	4	IV	
32	1-3	8	8	IV	
33	1-3	11	5	IV	
34	1-3	10	5	IV	
35	1-3	8	3	IV	
36	1-3	9	5	IV	
37	1-3	7	3	IV	
38	1-3	18	4	IV	
39	1-3	7	7	IV	
40	1-3	24	5	IV	
41	1-3	13	10	IV	
42	1-3	7	3	IV	
43	1-3	11	5	IV	
44	1-3	8	4	IV	
45	1-3	17	5	IV	
46	1-3	20	7	IV	
47	1-3	12	7	IV	
48	1-3	6	3	IV	
49	1-3	22	7	IV	
50	1-3	17	5	IV	
51	1-3	8	3	IV	
52	1-3	19	4	IV	
53	1-3	14	10	IV	
54	1-3	9	8	IV	
55	1-3	15	5	IV	
56	1-3	9	3	IV	
57	1-3	10	9	IV	
58	1-3	11	6	IV	
59	1-3	7	3	IV	
60	1-3	10	9	IV	
61	1-3	11	3	IV	
62	1-3	7	5	IV	
63	1-3	10	7	IV	
64	1-3	12	6	IV	
65	1-3	11	6	IV	
66	1-3	14	13	IV	
67	1-3	17	5	IV	
68	1-3	10	10	IV, V	3-V-527, one green obsidian blade
69	1-3	32	6	IV	
70	1-3	16	4	IV	
71	1-3	22	4	IV	
72	1-3	14	6	IV	
73	1-3	12	7	IV	
74	1-3	11	7	IV	
75	1-3	10	5	IV	
76	1-3	21	10	IV	
77	1-3	9	5	IV	
78	1-3	9	3	IV	
79	1-3	9	7	IV	
80	1-3	13	7	IV	

JALIEZA (3-IIIA-136, 3-IV-46, and 3-V-259 unless otherwise indicated)

TERRACE	SITE GRID SQUARE	LENGTH	WIDTH	PERIODIZATION	COMMENTS
81	1-3	12	4	IV	
82	1-4	21	6	IV	
83	1-4	35	6	IV	
84	1-4	14	7	IV	
85	1-4	7	4	IV	
86	1-4	9	4	IV	
87	1-4	21	7	IV	
88	1-4	11	5	IV	
89	1-4	15	5	IV	
90	1-4	13	7	IV	
91	1-4	11	6	IV	
92	1-4	14	3	IV	
93	1-4	12	5	IV	
94	1-4	11	5	IV	
95	1-4	21	6	IV	
96	1-4	12	5	IV	
97	1-4	13	8	IV	
98	1-4	9	7	IV	
99	1-4	15	5	IV	
100	1-4	11	4	IV	
101	1-4	13	6	IV	
102	1-4	14	6	IV	
103	1-4	9	3	IV	
104	1-4	14	7	IV	
105	1-4	21	5	IV	
106	1-4	13	6	IV	One grey obsidian blade
107	1-4	8	7	IV	
108	1-4	9	3	IV	
109	1-4	11	7	IV	
110	1-4	14	9	IV	
111	1-4	9	5	IV	
112	1-4	20	4	IV	
113	1-4	11	5	IV	
114	1-4	10	5	IV	
115	1-4	17	4	IV	
116	1-4	10	7	IV	
117	1-4	8	4	IV	
118	1-4	9	9	IV	
119	1-4	14	6	IV	
120	1-4	14	7	IV	
121	1-4	22	4	IV	
122	1-4	12	5	IV	
123	1-4	7	3	IV	
124	1-4	13	5	IV	
125	1-4	14	13	IV	
126	1-4	7	6	IV	
127	1-4	7	7	IV	
128	1-4	10	7	IV	
129	1-4	12	6	IV	
130	1-4	14	6	IV	
131	1-4	11	4	IV	
132	1-4	8	6	IV	
133	1-4	11	7	IV	
134	1-4	21	6	IV	
135	1-4	8	7	IV	
136	1-4	14	7	IV	
137	1-4	17	7	IV	
138	1-4	14	10	IV	
139	1-4	18	11	IV	
140	1-4	10	7	IV	
141	1-4	14	8	IV	
142	1-4	15	11	IV	
143	1-4	18	5	IV	
144	1-4	8	4	IV	
145	1-4	14	7	IV	
146	1-4	5	4	IV	
147	1-4	8	7	IV	
148	1-4	7	7	IV	
149	1-4	7	6	IV	
150	1-4	25	11	IV	Two houses.
151	1-4	25	20	IV	Three houses.
152	1-4	53	35	IV	Four houses.
153	1-4	11	4	IV	
154	1-4	12	7	IV	
155	1-4	18	4	IV	
156	1-4	23	23	IV	One hammerstone.
157	1-4	25	8	IV	
158	1-4	13	4	IV	
159	1-4	13	4	IV	
160	1-4	12	4	IV	

JALIEZA (3-IIIA-136, 3-IV-46, and 3-V-259 unless otherwise indicated)

TERRACE	SITE GRID SQUARE	LENGTH	WIDTH	PERIODIZATION	COMMENTS
161	1-4	11	9	IV	
162	1-4	9	4	IV	"One hammerstone."
163	1-4	11	4	IV	
164	1-4	14	5	IV	
165	1-4	18	8	IV	
166	1-4	9	5	IV	
167	1-4	10	6	IV	
168	1-4	16	3	IV	
169	1-4	20	3	IV	
170	1-4	7	3	IV	
171	1-4	25	6	IV	
172	1-4	19	8	IV	
173	1-4	17	4	IV	
174	1-4	8	3	IV	
175	1-4	14	6	IV	
176	1-4	14	6	IV	
177	1-4	9	4	IV	
178	1-4	30	5	IV	
179	1-4	25	11	IV	
180	1-4	9	6	IV	Two manos.
181	1-4	10	7	IV	
182	1-4	21	13	IV	
183	1-4	21	5	IV	
184	1-4	43	11	IV	Four houses.
185	1-4	10	5	IV	
186	1-4	13	4	IV	
187	1-4	35	5	IV	
188	1-4	21	7	IV	
189	1-4	20	5	IV	
190	1-4	24	6	IV	
191	1-4	13	3	IV	
192	1-4	35	12	IV	
193	1-4	42	12	IV	
194	1-4	40	10	IV	
195	1-4	30	14	IV	
196	1-4	11	7	IV	
197	1-4	14	8	IV	
198	1-4	9	6	IV	
199	1-4	14	4	IV	
200	1-4	27	10	IV	
201	1-4	9	5	IV	
202	1-4	20	3	IV	
203	1-4	14	7	IV	
204	1-4	11	11	IV	
205	1-4	18	7	IV	
206	1-4	18	8	IV	
207	1-4	14	6	IV	
208	1-4	45	18	IV	Two houses.
209	1-4	30	10	IV	
210	1-4	10	4	IV	
211	1-4	20	14	IV	
212	1-4	15	8	IV	
213	1-4	90	10	IV	
214	1-4	14	5	IV	
215	1-4	22	14	IV	
216	1-4	12	11	IV	
217	1-4	10	7	IV	
218	1-4	28	7	IV	
219	1-4	14	5	IV	
220	1-4	13	6	IV	
221	1-4	10	7	IV	
222	1-4	9	4	IV	
223	1-4	7	4	IV	
224	1-4	10	5	IV	
225	1-4	8	4	IV	
226	1-4	7	5	IV	
227	1-4	14	4	IV	
228	1-4	17	4	IV	
229	1-4	35	4	IV	
230	1-4	9	6	IV	
231	1-4	12	8	IV	
232	1-4	17	7	IV	
233	1-4	11	5	IV	
234	1-4	15	7	IV	
235	1-4	7	6	IV	
236	1-4	7	7	IV	
237	1-4	7	6	IV	
238	1-4	15	6	IV	
239	1-4	14	5	IV	
240	1-4	8	4	IV	

JALIEZA (3-IIIA-136, 3-IV-46, and 3-V-259 unless otherwise indicated)

TERRACE	SITE GRID SQUARE	LENGTH	WIDTH	PERIODIZATION	COMMENTS
241	1-4	14	5	IV	
242	1-4	12	7	IV	
243	1-4	11	7	IV	
244	1-4	8	5	IV	
245	1-4	14	5	IV	
246	1-4	8	7	IV	
247	1-4	15	6	IV	
248	1-4	70	16	IV	Two houses.
249	1-4	126	14	IV	
250	1-4	124	17	IV	
251	1-4	30	7	IV	
252	1-4	18	3	IV	
253	1-4	20	8	IV	
254	1-4	23	18	IV	
255	1-4	21	9	IV	
256	1-4	12	9	IV	
257	1-4	28	28	IV	
258	1-4	28	7	IV	
259	1-4	31	5	IV	Very high ceramic density, two houses, two grey obsidian blades
260	1-4	14	6	IV	
261	1-4	20	12	IV	
262	1-4	7	3	IV	
263	1-4	14	5	IV	
264	1-4	19	7	IV	
265	1-4	20	4	IV	
266	1-4	9	3	IV	
267	1-4	22	12	IV	
268	1-4	16	12	IV	
269	1-4	15	3	IV	
270	1-4	10	9	IV	
271	1-4	15	14	IV	
272	1-4	25	10	IV	
273	1-4	12	5	IV	
274	1-4	10	4	IV	
275	1-4	20	12	IV	
276	1-4	15	7	IV	
277	1-4	13	7	IV	
278	1-4	18	14	IV	
279	1-4	11	7	IV	
280	1-4	14	8	IV	
281	1-4	14	8	IV	
282	1-4	20	9	IV	
283	1-4	15	6	IV	
284	1-4	22	12	IV	
285	1-4	10	8	IV	
286	1-4	10	7	IV	
287	1-4	11	4	IV	
288	1-4	21	5	IV	
289	1-4	14	10	IV	
290	1-4	25	9	IV	
291	1-4	21	14	IV	
292	1-4	21	15	IV	
293	1-4	14	11	IV	
294	1-4	42	22	IV	"One mano."
295	1-4	38	14	IV	
296	1-4	28	14	IV	
297	1-4	17	10	IV	
298	1-4	14	4	IV	
299	1-4	14	7	IV	
300	1-4	14	7	IV	
301	1-4	29	28	IV	
302	1-4	30	19	IV	
303	1-4	28	11	IV	
304	1-4	23	14	IV	
305	1-4	22	6	IV	
306	1-4	30	7	IV	Two houses
307	1-4	49	14	IV, V	Three houses, 3-V-298
308	1-4	13	5	IV	
309	1-4	18	3	IV	
310	1-4	34	27	IV	
311	1-4	45	22	IV, V	One piece polychrome, two houses, 3-V-298
312	1-4	90	22	IV	Four houses.
313	1-4	15	15	IV	
314	1-4	20	16	IV	
315	1-4	28	28	IV	

JALIEZA (3-IIIA-136, 3-IV-46, and 3-V-259 unless otherwise indicated)

TERRACE	SITE GRID SQUARE	LENGTH	WIDTH	PERIODIZATION	COMMENTS
316	1-4	105	18	IV	
317	1-4	35	28	IV	
318	1-4	28	11	IV	
319	1-4	14	7	IV	
320	1-4	12	8	IV	
321	1-4	35	23	IV	Two houses.
322	1-4	12	10	IV	
323	1-4	21	10	IV	
324	1-4	63	12	IV	Two manos.
325	1-4	14	10	IV	
326	1-4	14	10	IV	
327	1-4	28	6	IV	
328	1-4	100	62	IV	One metate, ten houses, one mano.
329	1-4	21	14	IV	Two houses.
330	1-4	16	4	IV	
331	1-4	50	6	IV	One grey obsidian blade
332	1-4	22	12	IV	
333	1-4	30	4	IV	
334	1-4	24	6	IV	
335	1-4	23	16	IV	
336	1-4	20	7	IV	
337	1-4	18	14	IV	
338	1-4	22	12	IV	One black obsidian blade, two houses.
339	1-4	12	5	IV	
340	1-4	40	5	IV	
341	1-4	40	10	IV	
342	1-4	16	3	IV	
343	1-4	40	7	IV	
344	1-4	12	3	IV	
345	1-4	64	40	IV	One grey obsidian blade.
346	1-4	20	14	IV	
347	1-4	22	10	IV	
348	1-4	30	4	IV	
349	1-4	10	10	IV	
350	1-4	12	5	IV	
351	2-4	14	12	IV	
352	2-4	24	10	IV	Two houses.
353	2-4	48	24	IV	
354	2-4	20	12	IV	
355	2-4	16	10	IV	
356	2-4	40	6	IV	
357	2-4	10	8	IV	
358	2-4	20	5	IV	
359	2-4	24	8	IV	
360	2-4	30	14	IV	
361	2-4	15	12	IV	One green obsidian blade.
362	2-4	20	5	IV	
363	2-4	20	12	IV	One A-7.
364	2-4	72	4	IV	One chert blade, three cores.
365	1-4	10	4	IV	
366	1-4	14	12	IV	
367	1-4	12	7	IV	
368	1-4	32	10	IV	One piece of black obsidian.
369	1-4	26	7	IV	
370	2-4	24	13	IV	
371	2-4	9	3	IV	
372	2-4	17	3	IV	
373	2-4	19	5	IV	
374	2-4	49	5	IV	One green obsidian blade.
375	1-4	13	4	IV	One metate.
376	2-4	8	8	IV	One chert core.
377	1-4	9	6	IV	
378	1-4	42	8	IV	
379	1-4	23	4	IV	
380	1-4	9	5	IV	One hammerstone.
381	1-4	48	34	IV	
382	1-4	26	10	IV	
383	1-4	32	26	IV	
384	1-4	46	16	IV	
385	1-4	20	17	IV	
386	1-4	28	12	IV	
387	1-4	32	20	IV	

JALIEZA (3-IIIA-136, 3-IV-46, and 3-V-259 unless otherwise indicated)

TERRACE	SITE GRID SQUARE	LENGTH	WIDTH	PERIODIZATION	COMMENTS
388	1-4	14	14	IV	
389	1-4	18	13	IV	
390	1-4	18	12	IV	
391	1-4	42	14	IV	
392	1-4	28	6	IV	
393	1-4	24	6	IV	
394	1-4	13	10	IV	
395	2-4	14	8	IV	
396	2-4	60	15	IV	
397	2-4	18	10	IV	
398	2-4	13	5	IV	
399	2-4	12	9	IV	
400	2-4	15	4	IV	
401	2-4	21	10	IV	
402	2-4	67	7	IV	
403	2-4	7	3	IV	
404	2-4	28	18	IV	Plaster floor.
405	2-4	48	47	IV	
406	2-4	46	18	IV	
407	2-4	22	3	IV	
408	2-4	15	3	IV	
409	2-4	20	4	IV	
410	2-4	20	14	IV	
411	2-4	16	6	IV	Plaster floor.
412	2-4	40	20	IV	
413	2-4	16	12	IV	
414	2-4	24	3	IV	
415	2-4	25	8	IV	
416	2-4	20	8	IV	
417	2-4	28	15	IV	
418	2-4	8	6	IV	
419	2-4	26	4	IV	
420	2-4	6	3	IV	
421	2-4	20	8	IV	
422	2-4	13	6	IV	
423	2-4	14	5	IV	
424	2-4	5	2	IV	
425	2-4	12	4	IV	
426	2-4	9	3	IV	
427	2-4	15	6	IV	
428	2-4	35	18	IV, V	3-V-297
429	2-4	32	27	IV	Three houses, interior courtyard house.
430	2-4	12	12	IV	
431	2-4	18	4	IV	
432	2-4	26	8	IV	
433	2-4	10	3	IV	
434	2-4	14	5	IV	
435	2-4	8	2	IV	
436	2-4	15	5	IV	
437	2-4	13	5	IV	
438	2-4	13	5	IV, V	3-V-297
439	2-4	12	5	IV	
440	2-4	11	4	IV	
441	2-4	13	4	IV	
442	2-4	8	3	IV	
443	2-4	10	7	IV	
444	2-4	11	3	IV	One A-7.
445	2-4	18	14	IV	
446	2-4	8	5	IV	
447	2-4	10	7	IV	
448	2-4	18	4	IV	
449	2-4	14	9	IV	
450	2-4	11	7	IV	
451	2-4	10	8	IV	
452	2-4	10	8	IV	
453	2-4	50	25	IV	
454	2-4	18	2	IV	
455	2-4	28	16	IV	
456	2-4	23	14	IV	
457	2-4	60	10	IV	
458	2-4	10	8	IV	
459	2-4	20	16	IV	
460	2-4	16	11	IV	
461	2-4	18	10	IV	
462	2-4	32	3	IV	
463	2-4	12	12	IV	One grey obsidian blade.
464	2-4	12	6	IV	One metate.

JALIEZA (3-IIIA-136, 3-IV-46, and 3-V-259 unless otherwise indicated)

TERRACE	SITE GRID SQUARE	LENGTH	WIDTH	PERIODIZATION	COMMENTS
465	2-4	24	20	IV	
466	2-4	18	6	IV	
467	2-4	8	6	IV	
468	2-4	7	3	IV	
469	2-4	14	3	IV	
470	2-4	16	3	IV	One striated grey obsidian blade.
471	2-4	25	12	IV	
472	2-4	18	14	IV	
473	2-4	32	14	IV	
474	2-4	20	6	IV	
475	2-4	8	7	IV	
476	2-4	8	3	IV	
477	2-4	12	12	IV	
478	2-4	13	10	IV	
479	2-4	46	9	IV	
480	2-4	25	10	IV	
481	2-4	20	14	IV	
482	2-4	20	16	IV	
483	2-4	24	10	IV	
484	2-4	10	8	IV	
485	2-4	18	5	IV	
486	2-4	85	10	IV	
487	2-4	20	8	IV	
488	2-4	15	12	IV	
489	2-4	20	3	IV	
490	2-4	18	10	IV	One metate.
491	2-4	24	8	IV	
492	2-4	36	7	IV	
493	2-4	20	10	IV	
494	2-4	14	4	IV	
495	2-4	115	15	IV	
496	2-4	18	4	IV	
497	2-4	10	8	IV	
498	2-4	35	10	IV	
499	2-4	56	20	IV	Sixteen by ten meter sherd concentration just north of the terrace.
500	2-4	25	6	IV	
501	2-4	14	3	IV	
502	2-4	15	6	IV	
503	2-4	22	5	IV	
504	2-4	7	6	IV	
505	2-4	14	6	IV	
506	2-4	12	9	IV	
507	2-4	20	4	IV	
508	2-4	20	4	IV	
509	2-4	18	7	IV	
510	2-4	26	8	IV	One mano.
511	2-4	26	12	IV	
512	2-4	10	8	IV	
513	2-4	13	3	IV	
514	2-4	28	7	IV	
515	2-4	24	9	IV	
516	2-4	14	6	IV	
517	2-4	7	6	IV	
518	2-4	22	5	IV	One grey obsidian blade.
519	2-4	20	6	IV	
520	2-4	10	8	IV	One A-7.
521	2-4	30	3	IV	
522	2-4	15	5	IV	
523	2-4	18	7	IV	
524	2-4	21	3	IV	
525	2-4	16	11	IV	
526	2-4	26	10	IV	
527	2-4	28	8	IV	
528	2-4	30	10	IV	
529	2-4	8	8	IV	
530	2-4	8	6	IV	
531	2-4	8	6	IV	
532	2-4	11	10	IV	
533	2-4	14	6	IV	
534	2-4	8	7	IV	
535	2-4	22	6	IV	
536	2-4	32	14	IV	
537	2-4	49	7	IV	
538	2-4	12	10	IV	
539	2-4	12	10	IV	

JALIEZA (3-IIIA-136, 3-IV-46, and 3-V-259 unless otherwise indicated)

TERRACE	SITE GRID SQUARE	LENGTH	WIDTH	PERIODIZATION	COMMENTS
540	2-4	16	8	IV	
541	2-4	28	4	IV	
542	2-4	52	10	IV	
543	2-4	20	10	IV	
544	2-4	16	6	IV	
545	2-4	21	9	IV	
546	2-4	19	5	IV	
547	2-4	28	10	IV	
548	2-4	22	8	IV	
549	2-4	16	10	IV	
550	2-4	24	16	IV	One metate.
551	2-4	26	16	IV	
552	2-4	19	14	IV	
553	2-4	10	6	IV	
554	2-4	28	24	IV	
555	2-4	14	6	IV	
556	2-4	24	16	IV	Plaster floor. One metate.
557	2-4	20	16	IV	Plaster floor, one metate, one A-7.
558	2-4	12	3	IV	
559	2-4	14	3	IV	
560	2-4	24	10	IV	
561	2-4	26	20	IV	
562	2-4	63	12	IV	Plaster floor.
563	2-4	12	7	IV	
564	2-4	45	40	IV	
565	2-4	45	25	IV	
566	2-4	12	12	IV	One grey obsidian blade.
567	2-4	20	6	IV	
568	2-4	10	6	IV	
569	2-4	20	16	IV	
570	2-4	42	5	IV	
571	2-4	14	6	IV	
572	2-4	10	4	IV	
573	2-4	4	4	IV	
574	2-4	14	5	IV	
575	2-4	16	6	IV	
576	2-4	10	6	IV	
577	2-4	53	10	IV	
578	2-4	11	10	IV	
579	2-4	6	5	IV	
580	2-4	35	10	IV	
581	2-4	27	5	IV	
582	2-4	11	3	IV	
583	2-4	10	3	IV	
584	2-4	9	5	IV	
585	2-4	19	3	IV	
586	2-4	21	5	IV	
587	2-4	16	5	IV	
588	2-4	7	4	IV	
589	2-4	16	3	IV	
590	2-4	12	5	IV	
591	2-4	37	5	IV	
592	2-4	36	10	IV	
593	2-4	20	14	IV	
594	2-4	14	6	IV	
595	2-4	13	3	IV	
596	2-4	53	8	IV	
597	2-4	55	16	IV	
598	2-4	32	18	IV	
599	2-4	4	4	IV	
600	2-4	22	10	IV	
601	2-4	28	26	IV	One metate.
602	2-4	27	6	IV	
603	2-4	15	14	IV	
604	2-4	36	10	IV	
605	2-4	45	34	IV	
606	2-4	40	4	IV	
607	2-4	18	6	IV	
608	2-4	10	6	IV	
609	2-4	14	8	IV	
610	2-4	36	12	IV	
611	2-3	10	10	IV	
612	2-4	20	16	IV	Plaster floor.
613	2-3	14	10	IV	One stone molcajete.
614	2-3	42	8	IV	
615	2-3	30	14	IV	
616	2-3	26	18	IV	

JALIEZA (3-IIIA-136, 3-IV-46, and 3-V-259 unless otherwise indicated)

TERRACE	SITE GRID SQUARE	LENGTH	WIDTH	PERIODIZATION	COMMENTS
617	2-3	11	10	IV, V	
618	2-3	11	10	IV, V	
619	2-3	20	4	IV, V	
620	2-3	14	6	IV, V	
621	2-3	12	10	IV, V	
622	2-3	30	10	IV	
623	2-3	6	5	IV	
624	2-3	10	6	IV	
625	2-3	8	6	IV	
626	2-3	16	7	IV	
627	2-3	10	6	IV	
628	2-3	11	7	IV	
629	2-3	20	4	IV	
630	2-3	20	16	IV, V	
631	2-3	15	8	IV, V	
632	2-3	36	10	IV, V	
633	2-3	22	4	IV, V	
634	2-3	12	8	IV, V	
635	2-3	11	6	IV, V	
636	2-3	20	14	IV, V	
637	2-3	20	7	IV, V	
638	2-3	14	11	IV, V	
639	2-3	12	7	IV, V	
640	2-3	45	20	IV, V	
641	2-3	12	12	IV, V	
642	2-3	32	16	IV, V	
643	2-3	16	14	IV, V	
644	2-3	10	8	IV, V	
645	2-3	26	8	IV, V	
646	2-3	14	12	IV, V	
647	2-3	34	12	IV, V	One mano.
648	2-3	17	10	IV, V	
649	2-3	18	17	IV, V	
650	2-3	16	8	IV, V	
651	2-3	14	14	IV, V	
652	2-3	16	16	IV, V	
653	2-3	11	7	IV	
654	2-3	22	10	IV	
655	2-3	12	9	IV	
656	2-3	20	2	IV	

TERRACE	SITE GRID SQUARE	LENGTH	WIDTH	PERIODIZATION	COMMENTS
657	2-3	12	11	IV, V	3-V-245
658	2-3	14	13	IV, V	3-V-245
659	2-3	24	12	IV	One metate
660	2-3	14	12	IV	
661	2-3	10	5	IV, V	3-V-245
662	2-3	13	4	IV	
663	2-4	9	7	IV	
664	2-3	13	4	IV	
665	2-3	14	4	IV	
666	2-4	23	5	IV	
667	2-4	10	3	IV	
668	2-4	22	14	IV	
669	2-4	10	6	IV	
670	2-4	45	3	IV	
671	2-4	9	3	IV	
672	2-4	8	5	IV	
673	2-4	12	8	IV	
674	2-4	18	8	IV	
675	2-4	28	20	IV	
676	2-4	10	3	IV	
677	2-4	26	8	IV	
678	2-4	17	3	IV	
679	2-4	17	7	IV	
680	2-4	13	3	IV	
681	2-4	22	13	IV	
682	2-4	22	4	IV	
683	2-4	5	3	IV	
684	2-4	10	4	IV	
685	2-4	14	11	IV	
686	2-4	40	8	IV	
687	2-4	12	6	IV	
688	2-4	12	6	IV	
689	2-4	16	10	IV	
690	2-4	18	6	IV	
691	2-4	18	3	IV	
692	2-4	16	7	IV	
693	2-4	18	12	IV	
694	2-4	70	10	IV	
695	2-4	16	7	IV	
696	2-4	36	4	IV	

JALIEZA (3-IIIA-136, 3-IV-46, and 3-V-259 unless otherwise indicated)

TERRACE	SITE GRID SQUARE	LENGTH	WIDTH	PERIODIZATION	COMMENTS
697	2-4	33	25	IV, V	3-V-297
698	2-4	12	4	IV	
699	2-4	18	3	IV	
700	2-4	85	10	IV, V	3-V-297
701	2-4	16	7	IV	
702	2-4	18	6	IV	
703	1-4	40	4	IV	
704	2-4	13	6	IV	
705	2-4	14	6	IV	
706	2-4	35	15	IV	
707	2-4	13	12	IV	
708	2-4	10	4	IV	
709	2-4	10	8	IV	
710	2-4	10	6	IV	
711	2-4	31	8	IV	
712	2-4	13	8	IV	
713	2-4	14	8	IV	
714	2-4	16	6	IV	
715	2-4	22	14	IV	
716	2-4	16	7	IV	
717	2-4	16	4	IV	Two grey obsidian blades.
718	2-4	7	6	IV	
719	2-4	17	6	IV	
720	2-4	23	6	IV	
721	2-4	12	5	IV	
722	2-4	10	8	IV	
723	2-4	13	12	IV	
724	2-4	6	6	IV	
725	2-4	13	8	IV	
726	2-4	93	20	IV	Two houses.
727	2-4	35	16	IV	
728	2-4	20	7	IV	
729	2-4	8	3	IV	
730	2-4	30	16	IV	
731	2-4	11	3	IV	
732	2-4	15	8	IV	
733	2-4	40	10	IV	
734	2-4	14	7	IV	Two black obsidian blades.

TERRACE	SITE GRID SQUARE	LENGTH	WIDTH	PERIODIZATION	COMMENTS
735	2-4	16	7	IV	Two grey obsidian blades.
736	2-4	8	4	IV	
737	2-4	14	4	IV	
738	2-4	12	8	IV	One grey obsidian blade.
739	2-4	10	4	IV	
740	2-4	42	14	IV	
741	2-4	52	20	IV	
742	2-4	17	10	IV	One black obsidian blade.
743	2-3	48	16	IV	Two houses.
744	2-4	8	7	IV	
745	2-4	5	4	IV	
746	2-4	23	10	IV	One black obsidian flake.
747	2-4	13	8	IV	One mano.
748	2-4	12	8	IV	
749	2-4	12	7	IV	
750	2-4	12	8	IV	
751	2-4	14	13	IV	
752	2-4	22	15	IV	
753	2-4	20	8	IV	
754	2-4	24	12	IV	
755	2-4	14	9	IV	
756	2-4	14	6	IV	
757	2-4	16	9	IV	
758	2-4	43	10	IV	
759	2-4	30	8	IV	
760	2-4	25	6	IV	
761	2-4	12	8	IV	
762	2-4	13	3	IV	
763	2-4	25	9	IV	
764	2-4	14	10	IV	
765	2-4	14	4	IV	
766	2-4	6	3	IV	
767	2-4	12	5	IV	
768	2-4	34	6	IV	
769	2-4	9	6	IV	
770	2-4	14	12	IV	

JALIEZA (3-IIIA-136, 3-IV-46, and 3-V-259 unless otherwise indicated)

TERRACE	SITE GRID SQUARE	LENGTH	WIDTH	PERIODIZATION	COMMENTS
771	2-4	25	8	IV	
772	2-4	12	8	IV	
773	2-4	36	18	IV	
774	2-4	12	10	IV	One mano.
775	2-4	9	4	IV	
776	2-4	22	14	IV	
777	2-4	40	12	IV	
778	2-4	12	3	IV	
779	2-4	24	8	IV	
780	2-4	6	5	IV	
781	2-4	15	5	IV	
782	2-4	18	5	IV	
783	2-4	6	2	IV	
784	2-4	12	10	IV	
785	2-4	14	2	IV	
786	2-4	20	7	IV	
787	1-4	24	8	IV	
788	1-4	18	4	IV	
789	1-4	31	3	IV	
790	1-4	13	5	IV	One corn cob urn.
791	1-4	13	4	IV	
792	1-4	11	8	IV	
793	104	60	5	IV	Three houses.
794	1-4	26	3	IV	Two houses.
795	1-4	8	6	IV	
796	1-4	10	4	IV	
797	1-4	8	2	IV	
798	1-4	23	7	IV	
799	1-4	24	3	IV	
800	1-4	6	2	IV	
801	1-4	14	3	IV	
802	1-4	8	4	IV	
803	1-4	14	3	IV	
804	1-4	26	3	IV	
805	1-4	32	8	IV	
806	1-4	12	10	IV	
807	1-4	8	6	IV	
808	1-4	40	3	IV	
809	1-4	14	4	IV	
810	1-4	14	4	IV	
811	1-4	9	3	IV	
812	1-3	34	26	IV	
813	1-3	22	11	IV	
814	1-3	13	10	IV	One green obsidian flake.
815	1-3	22	4	IV	
816	1-3	10	6	IV	
817	1-3	24	14	IV	
818	1-3	20	6	IV	
819	1-3	34	5	IV	
820	1-3	18	5	IV	
821	1-3	24	10	IV	
822	1-3	11	7	IV	
823	1-3	12	5	IV	
824	1-3	30	8	IV	
825	1-3	50	10	IV	
826	1-3	26	8	IV	
827	1-3	28	6	IV	
828	1-3	26	9	IV	
829	1-3	4	2	IV	
830	1-3	20	10	IV	
831	1-3	16	8	IV	
832	1-3	15	10	IV	
833	1-3	15	6	IV	
834	1-3	40	15	IV	
835	1-3	30	15	IV, V	Plaster floor. 3-V-294
836	1-3	20	15	IV	One green obsidian blade.
837	1-3	56	4	IV	
838	1-3	60	7	IV	
839	1-3	16	8	IV	One green obsidian blade.
840	1-3	28	10	IV	
841	1-3	25	5	IV	
842	1-3	58	5	IV	
843	1-3	15	6	IV	
844	1-3	12	4	IV	
845	1-3	10	10	IV	One green obsidian blade.

JALIEZA (3-IIIA-136, 3-IV-46, and 3-V-259 unless otherwise indicated)

TERRACE	SITE GRID SQUARE	LENGTH	WIDTH	PERIODIZATION	COMMENTS
846	1-3	12	6	IV	
847	1-3	20	5	IV	
848	1-3	20	6	IV	
849	1-3	16	3	IV	
850	1-3	14	8	IV	
851	1-3	6	4	IV	
852	1-3	54	2	IV	
853	1-3	10	3	IV	
854	1-3	20	6	IV	
855	1-3	23	3	IV	
856	1-3	18	6	IV	
857	1-3	14	10	IV	
858	1-3	9	6	IV	
859	1-3	8	3	IV	
860	1-3	11	7	IV	
861	1-3	9	4	IV	
862	1-3	14	4	IV	
863	1-3	22	3	IV	
864	1-3	23	8	IV	
865	1-3	22	6	IV	
866	1-3	21	6	IV	
867	1-3	25	9	IV	
868	2-3	18	10	IV	
869	2-3	20	7	IV	
870	2-3	16	6	IV	
871	2-3	20	6	IV	
872	2-3	13	8	IV	
873	2-3	27	3	IV	
874	2-3	10	7	IV	
875	2-3	14	6	IV	
876	2-3	38	6	IV	One grey obsidian blade.
877	2-3	14	6	IV	
878	2-3	21	5	IV	
879	2-4	44	9	IV	One hammerstone.
880	2-3	25	18	IV	One metate.
881	2-3	20	12	IV	
882	2-3	10	8	IV	
883	2-3	24	20	IV	
884	2-3	8	7	IV	
885	2-3	10	10	IV	
886	2-3	15	14	IV	
887	2-3	41	6	IV	
888	2-3	24	6	IV	
889	2-3	14	6	IV	
890	2-3	8	5	IV	
891	2-3	14	8	IV	
892	2-3	10	10	IV	
893	2-3	16	12	IV	
894	2-3	16	6	IV	
895	2-3	26	8	IV	
896	2-3	10	10	IV	
897	2-3	40	12	IV	
898	2-3	10	8	IV	
899	2-3	12	4	IV	
900	2-3	14	10	IV	Several grey obsidian blades.
901	2-3	7	5	IV	
902	2-3	14	4	IV	
903	2-3	18	8	IV	
904	2-3	10	6	IV	
905	2-3	10	4	IV	
906	2-3	45	10	IV	
907	2-3	18	12	IV	
908	2-3	14	10	IV	One metate.
909	2-3	20	14	IV	
910	2-3	16	6	IV	
911	2-3	13	7	IV	
912	2-3	14	8	IV	
913	2-3	22	10	IV	
914	2-3	25	7	IV	
915	2-3	12	10	IV	
916	2-3	14	7	IV	
917	2-3	14	12	IV	
918	2-3	12	6	IV	
919	2-3	7	6	IV	
920	2-3	8	6	IV	
921	2-3	20	9	IV	
922	2-3	9	4	IV	
923	2-3	25	5	IV	

JALIEZA (3-IIIA-136, 3-IV-46, and 3-V-259 unless otherwise indicated)

TERRACE	SITE GRID SQUARE	LENGTH	WIDTH	PERIODIZATION	COMMENTS
924	2-3	13	5	IV	
925	2-3	27	7	IV	
926	2-3	10	8	IV	
927	2-3	9	3	IV	
928	2-3	5	5	IV	
929	2-3	10	6	IV	
930	2-3	26	10	IV	
931	2-3	20	4	IV	
932	2-3	30	7	IV	
933	2-3	12	7	IV	
934	2-3	9	3	IV	
935	2-3	22	4	IV	
936	2-3	14	10	IV	
937	2-3	30	8	IV	
938	2-3	25	14	IV	
939	2-3	24	12	IV	
940	2-3	8	6	IV	
941	2-3	31	12	IV	
942	2-3	24	18	IV, V	
943	2-3	17	13	IV, V	
944	2-3	16	15	IV, V	
945	2-3	8	8	IV, V	
946	2-3	10	4	IV, V	
947	2-3	13	8	IV, V	
948	2-3	12	8	IV, V	
949	2-3	28	20	IV, V	
950	2-3	17	12	IV, V	
951	2-3	6	3	IV, V	
952	2-3	30	14	IV, V	
953	2-3	18	8	IV, V	
954	2-3	20	10	IV, V	
955	2-3	44	12	IV, V	
956	2-3	20	12	IV, V	
957	2-3	24	5	IV, V	
958	2-3	20	12	IV, V	
959	2-3	24	13	IV, V	
960	2-3	13	8	IV, V	
961	2-3	10	8	IV, V	
962	2-3	8	3	IV, V	
963	2-3	20	8	IV, V	
964	2-3	12	4	IV, V	
965	2-3	16	6	IV, V	
966	2-3	6	4	IV, V	
967	2-3	22	6	IV, V	
968	2-3	30	10	IV	
969	2-3	9	4	IV, V	
970	2-3	18	10	IV, V	
971	2-3	6	6	IV, V	
972	2-3	8	6	IV	
973	2-3	12	7	IV	
974	2-3	22	8	IV, V	
975	2-3	18	12	IV	
976	2-3	8	4	IV	
977	2-3	10	5	IV, V	
978	2-3	11	5	IV	
979	2-3	26	6	IV	
980	2-3	12	8	IV	
981	2-3	18	10	IV, V	
982	1-3	16	12	IV	
983	2-3	17	8	IV	
984	2-3	24	4	IV	
985	2-3	14	6	IV, V	
986	2-3	14	7	IV, V	One metate.
987	2-3	28	10	IV, V	
988	2-3	30	10	IV, V	
989	2-3	14	6	IV, V	
990	2-3	70	14	IV, V	
991	1-3	16	6	IV	
992	1-3	10	6	IV	
993	2-3	28	12	IV, V	
994	2-3	11	10	IV	
995	2-3	18	10	IV, V	
996	2-3	40	11	IV, V	One grey obsidian flake.
997	2-3	42	16	IV, V	
998	2-3	24	9	IV, V	
999	2-3	11	10	IV	
1000	2-3	28	12	IV, V	
1001	1-3	20	16	IV, V	
1002	1-3	52	20	IV, V	
1003	1-3	33	18	IV, V	Four green obsidian blades. Several A-7's.

JALIEZA (3-IIIA-136, 3-IV-46, and 3-V-259 unless otherwise indicated)

TERRACE	SITE GRID SQUARE	LENGTH	WIDTH	PERIODIZATION	COMMENTS
1004	1-3	22	12	IV, V	
1005	1-3	14	10	IV, V	
1006	1-3	12	11	IV, V	
1007	1-3	10	5	IV, V	
1008	1-3	80	32	IV, V	
1009	1-4	10	6	IV	
1010	2-3	10	6	IV	
1011	2-3	16	8	IV	
1012	2-3	17	5	IV, V	
1013	2-3	14	6	V	
1014	2-3	10	3	V	
1015	2-3	5	3	V	
1016	2-3	7	4	V	
1017	2-3	7	5	V	
1018	2-3	7	4	V	
1019	2-3	7	4	V	
1020	2-3	19	5	V	
1021	2-3	12	5	V	
1022	2-3	7	3	V	
1023	2-3	15	8	V	
1024	2-3	15	7	V	
1025	2-3	12	5	V	
1026	2-3	8	4	V	
1027	2-3	10	8	V	
1028	2-3	12	5	V	
1029	2-3	13	7	V	
1030	2-3	10	5	V	
1031	2-3	7	3	V	
1032	2-3	14	3	V	
1033	2-3	22	4	V	
1034	2-3	16	3	V	
1035	2-3	16	3	V	
1036	2-3	15	5	V	
1037	2-3	108	14	V	
1038	2-3	10	4	V	
1039	2-3	32	11	V	
1040	2-3	16	13	IV, V	
1041	2-3	13	12	V	
1042	2-3	16	8	V	
1043	2-3	19	8	V	
1044	2-3	13	11	IV, V	
1045	2-3	6	5	V	
1046	2-3	14	7	V	
1047	2-3	14	9	IV, V	
1048	2-3	36	15	IV, V	
1049	2-3	7	7	IV, V	
1050	1-3	10	10	IV, V	One chert blade.
1051	1-3	10	7	IV, V	
1052	1-3	19	7	IV, V	
1053	1-3	18	12	IV, V	
1054	1-3	12	4	IV, V	Three green obsidian blades.
1055	1-3	42	12	IV, V	
1056	1-3	6	5	IV, V	
1057	1-3	16	16	IV, V	
1058	1-3	20	18	IV, V	
1059	1-3	21	10	IV, V	
1060	1-3	14	5	IV, V	
1061	1-3	24	20	IV, V	
1062	1-3	14	9	IV, V	
1063	1-3	8	8	IV, V	
1064	1-3	18	9	IV, V	
1065	1-3	14	10	IV, V	
1066	1-3	38	4	IV, V	
1067	1-3	40	10	IV, V	
1068	1-3	27	4	IV, V	
1069	1-3	8	5	IV, V	
1070	1-3	46	6	IV, V	
1071	2-3	16	6	IV, V	
1072	2-3	30	3	IV, V	
1073	2-3	40	16	IV, V	
1074	2-3	27	20	IV, V	
1075	2-3	27	14	IV, V	
1076	1-3	10	4	IV, V	
1077	1-3	25	15	IV, V	
1078	1-3	31	15	IV, V	
1079	1-3	14	11	IV, V	
1080	1-3	40	15	IV, V	
1081	1-3	30	3	IV, V	
1082	1-3	16	4	IV, V	
1083	1-3	16	12	IV, V	

JALIEZA (3-IIIA-136, 3-IV-46, and 3-V-259 unless otherwise indicated)

TERRACE	SITE GRID SQUARE	LENGTH	WIDTH	PERIODIZATION	COMMENTS
1084	1-3	12	9	IV, V	
1085	1-3	20	10	IV, V	
1086	2-3	18	12	IV, V	
1087	2-3	21	10	IV, V	
1088	2-3	17	13	IV, V	
1089	2-3	8	7	IV, V	
1090	2-3	19	9	IV, V	
1091	2-3	22	5	IV	
1092	2-3	23	6	IV	
1093	2-3	19	19	IV	
1094	2-3	15	12	IV, V	
1095	2-3	48	7	IV, V	
1096	2-3	30	10	IV, V	
1097	2-3	24	20	IV, V	
1098	2-3	19	11	IV, V	
1099	2-3	16	13	IV, V	
1100	2-3	21	9	IV, V	
1101	2-3	15	6	IV, V	
1102	2-3	25	8	IV, V	
1103	1-3	36	15	IV, V	
1104	1-3	17	7	IV, V	
1105	2-3	19	18	IV, V	
1106	2-3	27	16	IV, V	
1107	1-3	17	16	IIIA, V	
1108	1-3	12	12	IIIA, V	
1109	2-3	54	23	IV, V	
1110	2-3	8	8	IV, V	
1111	2-3	13	7	IV, V	
1112	2-3	29	10	IV, V	
1113	2-3	21	15	IV, V	
1114	2-3	37	18	IV, V	
1115	2-3	40	3	IV, V	
1116	2-3	22	16	IV, V	One striated grey
1117	2-3	41	13	IV, V	obsidian flake.
1118	2-3	18	12	IV, V	
1119	2-3	12	4	IV, V	
1120	2-3	17	3	V	
1121	2-3	22	9	IV, V	One metate.
1122	2-3	12	11	V	
1123	2-3	17	3	V	

TERRACE	SITE GRID SQUARE	LENGTH	WIDTH	PERIODIZATION	COMMENTS
1124	2-3	44	31	V	
1125	2-3	26	14	IV, V	
1126	2-3	17	11	IV, V	
1127	2-3	13	12	IV, V	
1128	2-3	11	7	V	
1129	2-3	13	11	V	
1130	2-3	14	8	V	
1131	2-3	15	8	V	
1132	2-3	25	10	V	
1133	2-3	21	6	V	
1134	2-3	18	8	V	
1135	2-3	20	12	V	
1136	2-3	30	14	V	
1137	2-3	4	2	V	
1138	2-3	15	3	V	
1139	2-3	8	7	V	
1140	2-3	19	3	V	
1141	2-3	13	7	V	
1142	2-3	8	8	V	
1143	2-3	14	8	V	
1144	2-3	14	5	V	
1145	2-3	25	8	V	
1146	2-3	20	6	V	
1147	2-3	10	4	V	
1148	2-3	10	4	V	
1149	2-3	22	7	V	
1150	2-3	17	3	V	
1151	2-3	20	7	V	
1152	2-3	16	7	V	
1153	2-3	14	8	V	
1154	2-3	15	4	V	
1155	2-3	21	7	V	
1156	2-3	8	4	V	
1157	2-3	20	7	V	
1158	2-3	14	12	V	
1159	2-3	7	6	V	
1160	2-3	15	8	V	
1161	2-3	17	9	V	
1162	2-3	9	7	V	
1163	2-3	9	5	V	

JALIEZA (3-IIIA-136, 3-IV-46, and 3-V-259 unless otherwise indicated)

TERRACE	SITE GRID SQUARE	LENGTH	WIDTH	PERIODIZATION	COMMENTS
1164	2-3	17	5	V	
1165	2-3	11	7	V	
1166	2-3	9	7	V	
1167	2-3	8	6	V	
1168	2-3	14	4	V	
1169	2-3	15	12	V	
1170	2-3	10	3	V	
1171	2-3	14	6	IIIA, V	
1172	2-3	28	9	IIIA, V	
1173	2-3	12	3	V	
1174	2-3	10	3	V	
1175	2-3	22	10	V	
1176	2-3	42	9	IIIA, V	
1177	2-3	20	5	V	
1178	2-3	7	7	V	
1179	2-3	29	6	V	
1180	2-3	13	4	V	
1181	2-3	12	7	V	
1182	2-3	18	6	V	
1183	2-3	7	3	V	
1184	2-3	20	3	V	
1185	2-3	12	3	V	
1186	2-3	15	3	V	
1187	2-3	20	5	V	
1188	2-3	36	9	V	Two houses.
1189	2-3	8	6	V	
1190	2-3	20	10	V	
1191	2-3	7	3	V	
1192	2-3	8	3	V	
1193	2-3	9	5	V	
1194	2-3	20	10	IIIA, V	
1195	2-3	13	6	V	
1196	2-3	16	7	V	
1197	2-3	17	3	V	
1198	2-3	9	5	IIIA, V	
1199	2-3	13	11	V	
1200	2-3	18	12	V	
1201	2-3	10	9	IIIA, V	
1202	2-3	13	5	V	
1203	2-3	10	9	IIIA, V	

TERRACE	SITE GRID SQUARE	LENGTH	WIDTH	PERIODIZATION	COMMENTS
1204	2-3	14	7	IIIA, V	
1205	2-3	16	9	IIIA, V	
1206	2-3	14	12	IIIA, V	
1207	2-3	7	4	IIIA, V	
1208	2-3	12	6	IIIA, V	
1209	2-3	8	7	IIIA, V	
1210	2-3	12	12	IIIA, V	
1211	2-3	9	8	IIIA, V	
1212	2-3	7	7	IIIA, V	
1213	2-3	8	8	IIIA, V	
1214	2-3	18	6	IIIA, V	
1215	2-3	27	7	IIIA, V	
1216	2-3	18	6	IIIA, V	
1217	2-3	20	6	IIIA, V	
1218	2-3	10	7	IIIA, V	
1219	2-3	26	7	IIIA, V	
1220	1-3	32	26	IIIA, V	Two grey obsidian blades.
1221	2-3	20	7	IIIA, V	
1222	2-3	12	11	IIIA, V	
1223	2-3	10	9	IIIA, V	
1224	2-3	30	18	IIIA, V	
1225	2-3	26	18	IIIA, V	One green obsidian blade.
1226	2-3	21	11	IIIA, V	
1227	2-3	21	10	IIIA, V	
1228	1-3	14	10	IIIA, V	
1229	2-3	27	10	IIIA, V	
1230	2-3	17	8	IIIA, V	
1231	2-3	16	8	IIIA, V	
1232	2-3	10	7	IIIA, V	
1233	2-3	7	5	IIIA, V	
1234	2-3	12	10	IIIA, V	
1235	2-3	44	18	IIIA, V	
1236	2-3	19	10	IIIA, V	
1237	2-3	12	7	IIIA, V	
1238	2-3	18	10	IIIA, V	
1239	2-3	18	18	IIIA, V	
1240	2-3	15	10	IIIA, V	
1241	2-3	8	8	IIIA, V	

JALIEZA (3-IIIA-136, 3-IV-46, and 3-V-259 unless otherwise indicated)

TERRACE	SITE GRID SQUARE	LENGTH	WIDTH	PERIODIZATION	COMMENTS
1242	2-3	28	11	IIIA, V	One mano.
1243	2-3	12	7	IIIA, V	
1244	2-3	18	3	V	
1245	2-3	13	4	V	
1246	2-3	22	13	IIIA, V	
1247	2-3	24	9	IIIA, V	
1248	2-3	20	7	V	
1249	2-3	19	6	V	
1250	2-3	9	5	V	
1251	2-3	90	7	V	
1252	2-3	19	5	V	
1253	2-3	21	5	V	
1254	2-3	12	4	V	
1255	2-3	24	4	IIIA, V	
1256	2-3	12	6	IIIA, V	
1257	2-3	10	3	IIIA, V	One G-23.
1258	2-3	25	10	V	
1259	2-3	18	4	IIIA, V	
1260	2-3	6	5	V	
1261	2-3	21	5	V	
1262	2-3	21	3	V	
1263	2-3	27	9	V	
1264	2-3	14	3	V	
1265	2-3	17	4	V	
1266	2-3	14	4	V	
1267	2-3	12	3	V	
1268	2-3	22	8	V	
1269	2-3	8	3	V	
1270	2-3	8	3	V	
1271	2-3	18	6	V	
1272	2-3	12	4	V	
1273	2-3	18	6	V	
1274	2-3	15	3	V	
1275	2-3	18	8	V	
1276	2-3	10	4	V	
1277	2-3	56	10	IIIA, V	
1278	2-3	22	3	V	
1279	2-3	17	8	V	
1280	2-3	11	4	V	
1281	2-3	24	4	V	

TERRACE	SITE GRID SQUARE	LENGTH	WIDTH	PERIODIZATION	COMMENTS
1282	2-3	11	3	V	
1283	2-3	19	6	V	
1284	2-3	24	5	V	
1285	2-3	14	11	V	
1286	2-3	21	11	V	
1287	2-3	17	8	V	
1288	2-3	12	9	V	
1289	2-3	14	5	V	
1290	2-3	36	16	V	
1291	2-3	24	16	IIIA, V	One quartzite
1292	2-3	12	8	IIIA, V	flake.
1293	2-3	18	17	IIIA, V	
1294	2-3	25	19	IIIA, V	Plaster floor.
1295	2-3	29	15	IIIA, V	One mano.
1296	2-3	10	10	IIIA, V	
1297	2-3	30	16	IIIA, V	
1298	2-3	26	23	IIIA, V	
1299	2-3	40	20	IIIA, V	One unworked flint
1300	2-3	15	9	IIIA, V	chunk.
1301	2-3	24	9	IIIA, V	
1302	2-3	20	7	IIIA, V	One kiln waster, one flint chunk.
1303	2-3	34	8	IIIA, V	
1304	2-3	28	6	IIIA, V	
1305	2-2	16	12	IIIA, V	
1306	2-2	32	25	IIIA, V	
1307	2-2	65	63	IIIA, V	
1308	2-2	29	22	IIIA, V	One mano.
1309	2-2	21	10	IIIA, V	
1310	2-2	12	12	IIIA, V	
1311	2-2	20	12	IIIA, V	
1312	2-2	38	14	IIIA, V	
1313	2-2	14	9	IIIA, V	
1314	2-2	30	28	IIIA, V	
1315	2-2	35	20	IIIA, V	
1316	2-2	20	15	IIIA, V	
1317	2-2	26	14	IIIA, V	Two houses.
1318	2-2	23	12	IIIA, V	
1319	1-2	35	18	IIIA, V	
1320	1-2	23	18	IIIA, V	

JALIEZA (3-IIIA-136, 3-IV-46, and 3-V-259 unless otherwise indicated)

TERRACE	SITE GRID SQUARE	LENGTH	WIDTH	PERIODIZATION	COMMENTS
1321	1-2	15	13	IIIA, V	One mano, one G-23.
1322	1-2	65	16	IIIA, V	One green obsidian blade.
1323	1-2	13	8	IIIA	
1324	2-2	16	11	IIIA, V	
1325	2-2	22	9	IIIA, V	
1326	2-2	24	19	IIIA, V	
1327	2-2	31	18	IIIA, V	
1328	2-2	16	10	IIIA, V	
1329	2-2	28	13	IIIA, V	
1330	2-3	15	11	IIIA, V	
1331	2-2	15	9	V	
1332	2-2	20	13	V	
1333	2-2	17	15	V	
1334	2-2	25	8	V	
1335	2-2	15	7	V	
1336	2-2	21	14	V	
1337	2-2	15	11	V	
1338	2-2	9	8	V	
1339	2-2	11	8	V	
1340	2-2	35	10	V	
1341	2-2	26	4	V	
1342	2-2	13	7	V	
1343	2-2	25	3	V	
1344	2-2	17	3	V	
1345	2-3	8	3	V	
1346	2-3	7	3	V	
1347	2-3	8	3	V	
1348	2-3	6	3	V	
1349	2-3	22	7	IIIA, V	
1350	2-3	15	5	V	
1351	2-3	22	7	V	
1352	2-3	10	3	V	
1353	2-3	7	3	V	
1354	2-3	15	7	V	
1355	2-3	7	3	IIIA, V	
1356	2-3	9	3	V	
1357	2-3	40	6	V	One metate, three houses.

TERRACE	SITE GRID SQUARE	LENGTH	WIDTH	PERIODIZATION	COMMENTS
1358	2-3	18	3	V	
1359	2-3	14	3	V	
1360	2-3	27	3	V	
1361	2-3	25	5	V	
1362	2-3	14	7	V	
1363	2-3	11	7	V	
1364	2-3	11	3	V	
1365	2-3	21	5	V	
1366	2-3	40	7	V	
1367	2-3	7	3	V	
1368	2-3	14	7	V	
1369	2-3	12	8	V	
1370	2-3	13	3	V	
1371	2-3	15	5	V	
1372	2-3	28	6	V	
1373	2-3	7	6	V	
1374	2-3	17	3	V	
1375	2-3	7	6	V	
1376	2-3	12	8	V	
1377	2-3	14	5	V	One mano.
1378	2-2	14	6	V	
1379	2-2	40	3	V	
1380	2-2	10	4	V	One metate.
1381	2-3	14	4	V	
1382	2-3	27	4	V	
1383	2-2	10	3	V	
1384	2-3	32	14	V	
1385	2-2	19	9	V	
1386	2-2	14	5	V	
1387	2-2	12	3	V	
1388	2-2	12	3	V	
1389	2-2	24	10	V	
1390	2-2	8	4	V	
1391	2-2	9	3	V	
1392	2-2	19	6	V	
1393	2-2	20	8	V	
1394	2-2	11	9	V	
1395	2-2	8	7	V	
1396	2-2	21	4	V	
1397	2-2	32	7	V	

JALIEZA (3-IIIA-136, 3-IV-46, and 3-V-259 unless otherwise indicated)

TERRACE	SITE GRID SQUARE	LENGTH	WIDTH	PERIODIZATION	COMMENTS
1398	2-2	21	8	V	
1399	2-2	16	3	V	One mano.
1400	2-2	70	17	IIIA, V	Three houses.
1401	2-2	47	14	IIIA, V	
1402	2-2	24	9	IIIA, V	
1403	2-2	34	22	IIIA, V	
1404	2-2	15	15	IIIA, V	
1405	2-2	14	9	IIIA, V	
1406	2-2	14	10	IIIA, V	
1407	2-2	9	3	IIIA, V	
1408	2-2	16	5	IIIA, V	
1409	2-2	12	4	IIIA, V	
1410	2-2	14	11	IIIA, V	
1411	2-2	12	11	IIIA, V	
1412	2-2	20	15	IIIA, V	
1413	2-2	20	5	IIIA, V	
1414	2-2	10	6	IIIA, V	
1415	2-2	13	11	IIIA, V	
1416	2-2	17	2	IIIA, V	
1417	2-2	10	3	IIIA, V	
1418	2-2	12	5	IIIA, V	
1419	2-2	13	5	IIIA, V	
1420	2-2	20	3	IIIA, V	
1421	2-2	11	5	IIIA, V	
1422	2-2	14	10	IIIA, V	
1423	2-2	15	7	IIIA, V	
1424	2-2	13	4	IIIA, V	
1425	2-2	20	7	IIIA, V	
1426	2-2	9	7	IIIA, V	
1427	2-2	25	5	V	
1428	2-2	21	12	V	
1429	2-2	25	10	V	
1430	2-2	25	12	V	
1431	2-2	26	10	V	
1432	2-2	12	8	V	
1433	2-2	24	21	IIIA, V	Possibly functioned as a road.
1434	2-2	16	14	V	
1435	2-2	10	9	IIIA, V	
1436	2-2	38	24	IIIA, V	
1437	2-2	7	7	IIIA, V	
1438	2-2	12	9	IIIA, V	
1439	2-2	30	4	IIIA, V	
1440	2-2	15	3	IIIA, V	
1441	2-2	18	8	IIIA, V	
1442	2-2	23	14	IIIA, V	
1443	2-2	18	8	IIIA, V	
1444	2-2	30	12	IIIA, V	
1445	2-2	30	15	IIIA, V	
1446	2-2	38	8	IIIA, V	
1447	2-2	38	12	IIIA, V	
1448	2-2	17	10	IIIA, V	
1449	2-2	87	18	IIIA, V	Three houses.
1450	2-2	82	45	IIIA, V	Five houses.
1451	2-2	23	16	IIIA, V	
1452	2-2	22	12	IIIA, V	
1453	2-2	29	24	IIIA, V	Two houses.
1454	2-2	30	25	IIIA, V	
1455	2-2	80	75	IIIA, V	Five houses.
1456	2-2	35	25	IIIA, V	
1457	2-2	37	18	IIIA, V	
1458	2-2	25	12	V	
1459	2-2	25	18	V	
1460	2-2	30	10	V	
1461	2-2	18	8	V	
1462	2-2	20	18	V	
1463	2-2	23	10	V	
1464	2-2	13	11	V	
1465	2-2	28	13	V	
1466	2-2	40	5	V	
1467	2-2	17	5	V	
1468	2-2	13	9	V	
1469	2-2	75	12	V	
1470	2-2	38	22	V	
1471	2-2	25	15	V	
1472	2-2	8	2	V	
1473	2-2	24	10	V	One hammerstone.
1474	2-2	6	3	V	
1475	2-2	12	8	V	
1476	2-2	16	5	V	

JALIEZA (3-IIIA-136, 3-IV-46, and 3-V-259 unless otherwise indicated)

TERRACE	SITE GRID SQUARE	LENGTH	WIDTH	PERIODIZATION	COMMENTS
1477	2-2	8	3	V	
1478	2-2	39	8	V	
1479	2-2	20	19	V	One mano.
1480	2-2	17	8	V	
1481	2-2	13	8	V	
1482	2-2	16	14	IIIA, V	One celt, one mano.
1483	2-2	26	20	IIIA	
1484	2-2	31	12	IIIA	
1485	2-2	42	22	IIIA, V	
1486	2-2	20	20	IIIA, V	
1487	2-2	28	24	IIIA, V	
1488	2-2	40	12	IIIA, V	Two houses.
1489	2-2	23	21	IIIA, V	
1490	2-2	90	19	IIIA, V	
1491	2-2	38	20	IIIA, V	
1492	2-2	33	19	IIIA, V	
1493	2-2	43	26	IIIA	
1494	2-2	25	15	IIIA	
1495	2-2	34	22	IIIA	
1496	2-2	20	20	IIIA	
1497	2-2	24	9	IIIA	One grey chert blade.
1498	2-2	38	10	IIIA	Two houses.
1499	2-2	34	32	IIIA, V	
1500	2-2	28	10	IIIA, V	
1501	2-2	36	17	IIIA, V	
1502	2-2	42	10	IIIA, V	
1503	2-2	42	40	IIIA	
1504	2-2	22	17	IIIA, V	Several G-23's.
1505	2-2	21	20	IIIA, V	
1506	2-2	21	12	IIIA	
1507	2-2	24	21	IIIA	
1508	2-2	19	19	IIIA	One G-23.
1509	2-2	16	10	IIIA	
1510	2-2	25	21	IIIA, V	
1511	2-2	50	18	IIIA, V	One G-23.
1512	2-2	34	15	IIIA, V	Two houses.
1513	2-2	36	24	IIIA	
1514	2-2	27	11	IIIA	
1515	2-2	26	19	IIIA	
1516	2-2	32	6	IIIA	
1517	2-2	11	11	IIIA	
1518	2-2	18	17	IIIA	
1519	2-2	15	10	IIIA	
1520	2-2	40	4	IIIA	
1521	2-2	16	5	IIIA	
1522	2-2	7	3	IIIA	
1523	2-2	18	5	IIIA	
1524	2-2	4	2	IIIA	
1525	2-2	3	2	IIIA	
1526	2-2	35	11	IIIA	
1527	2-2	10	3	IIIA	
1528	2-2	32	5	IIIA	Two houses.
1529	2-2	26	6	IIIA	Two houses.
1530	2-2	58	25	IIIA	Two houses
1531	2-2	37	10	IIIA	
1532	2-2	75	30	IIIA	
1533	2-2	26	5	IIIA	
1534	2-2	24	9	IIIA	
1535	2-2	35	5	IIIA	Four houses.
1536	2-2	32	24	IIIA, V	Three houses.
1537	2-2	28	20	IIIA	
1538	2-2	18	6	IIIA	One hammerstone.
1539	2-2	12	9	IIIA	
1540	2-2	23	18	IIIA, V	
1541	2-2	28	16	IIIA	
1542	2-2	22	8	IIIA	
1543	2-2	24	4	IIIA	
1544	2-2	10	9	IIIA	
1545	2-2	48	18	IIIA	One G-23.
1546	2-2	22	9	IIIA	
1547	2-2	78	35	IIIA	Three houses.
1548	2-2	60	42	IIIA	
1549	2-2	50	21	IIIA	Several G-23's.
1550	2-2	11	10	IIIA	One G-23.
1551	2-2	12	10	IIIA	One G-23.
1552	2-2	85	57	IIIA	
1553	2-2	210	80	IIIA, V	3-V-286.
1554	2-2	65	15	IIIA, V	3-V-286.
1555	2-2	65	30	IIIA	Two houses
1556	2-2	35	20	IIIA	

JALIEZA (3-IIIA-136, 3-IV-46, and 3-V-259 unless otherwise indicated)

TERRACE	SITE GRID SQUARE	LENGTH	WIDTH	PERIODIZATION	COMMENTS
1557	2-2	32	27	IIIA	
1558	2-2	28	28	IIIA	
1559	2-2	38	35	IIIA	
1560	2-2	36	15	IIIA	
1561	2-2	45	17	IIIA	Two houses, many G-23's.
1562	2-2	17	6	IIIA	
1563	2-2	18	9	IIIA	
1564	2-2	23	21	IIIA	
1565	2-2	12	6	IIIA	
1566	2-2	18	8	IIIA	
1567	2-2	36	21	IIIA	
1568	2-2	18	18	IIIA	
1569	2-2	20	12	IIIA	
1570	2-2	50	20	IIIA	
1571	1-2	38	18	IIIA	
1572	1-2	68	18	IIIA	
1573	1-2	60	20	IIIA	
1574	2-2	28	19	IIIA	
1575	2-2	25	23	IIIA	
1576	2-2	44	29	IIIA	
1577	2-2	40	17	IIIA	
1578	2-2	65	8	IIIA	
1579	2-2	68	25	IIIA	
1580	2-2	32	12	IIIA	
1581	2-2	29	11	IIIA	
1582	2-2	37	12	IIIA	
1583	2-2	35	12	IIIA	
1584	2-2	22	20	IIIA	
1585	2-2	30	13	IIIA	
1586	2-2	30	22	IIIA	
1587	2-2	55	35	IIIA	
1588	2-2	25	10	IIIA	
1589	2-2	24	5	IIIA	
1590	2-2	27	25	IIIA	
1591	2-2	26	7	IIIA	
1592	2-2	40	9	IIIA	
1593	2-2	35	5	IIIA	
1594	2-2	30	17	IIIA	
1595	2-2	91	18	IIIA	
1596	2-2	68	17	IIIA	
1597	2-2	20	17	IIIA	
1598	2-2	38	10	IIIA	
1599	2-2	60	20	IIIA	Two houses.
1600	2-2	50	21	IIIA	
1601	2-2	35	6	IIIA	
1602	2-2	71	14	IIIA	
1603	2-2	17	13	IIIA	
1604	2-2	12	10	IIIA	
1605	2-2	25	12	IIIA	
1606	2-2	52	21	IIIA	Several G-23's.
1607	1-2	62	40	IIIA	
1608	1-2	35	25	IIIA	
1609	1-2	19	18	IIIA	
1610	1-2	37	15	IIIA	One G-23.
1611	1-2	33	20	IIIA	
1612	1-2	81	56	IIIA	
1613	1-2	30	5	IIIA	
1614	1-2	38	26	IIIA	Several G-23's.
1615	1-2	31	26	IIIA	
1616	2-2	25	11	IIIA	Several G-23's.
1617	2-2	26	21	IIIA	
1618	2-2	18	15	IIIA	
1619	2-2	28	14	IIIA	Several G-23's.
1620	2-2	20	16	IIIA	Several G-23's.
1621	2-2	30	27	IIIA	Several G-23's.
1622	2-2	38	12	IIIA	
1623	2-2	24	10	IIIA	
1624	2-2	50	15	IIIA	
1625	2-2	20	8	IIIA	
1626	2-2	26	25	IIIA	
1627	2-2	35	25	IIIA	
1628	2-2	38	18	IIIA	
1629	2-2	55	43	IIIA	Two houses.
1630	2-2	40	24	IIIA	Moderate concentration of sherds--10 meters in diameter.
1631	2-2	32	25	IIIA	
1632	2-2	45	38	IIIA	
1633	2-1	52	26	IIIA	
1634	2-2	25	25	IIIA	
1635	2-2	38	17	IIIA	
1636	2-2	20	13	IIIA	

JALIEZA (3-IIIA-136, 3-IV-46, and 3-V-259 unless otherwise indicated)

TERRACE	SITE GRID SQUARE	LENGTH	WIDTH	PERIODIZATION	COMMENTS
1637	2-2	28	16	IIIA	
1638	2-2	26	20	IIIA	
1639	2-2	75	32	IIIA	
1640	2-2	48	16	IIIA	
1641	2-2	44	9	IIIA	
1642	2-2	50	15	IIIA	
1643	2-2	48	15	IIIA	
1644	2-2	38	7	IIIA	
1645	2-2	45	8	IIIA	
1646	2-1	160	42	IIIA	Five houses.
1647	2-2	95	8	IIIA	
1648	2-2	75	18	IIIA	
1649	2-2	70	25	IIIA	One striated grey obsidian blade.
1650	2-2	41	30	IIIA	Two houses.
1651	2-2	55	6	IIIA	
1652	2-2	85	52	IIIA	Two houses
1653	2-2	65	30	IIIA	
1654	2-2	20	15	IIIA	
1655	2-2	26	12	IIIA	
1656	2-2	15	8	IIIA	One G-23.
1657	2-1	35	15	IIIA	
1658	2-2	18	12	IIIA	
1659	2-2	12	4	IIIA	
1660	2-2	17	12	IIIA	
1661	2-2	10	5	IIIA	
1662	2-2	24	18	IIIA	
1663	2-2	64	5	IIIA	
1664	2-2	30	11	IIIA	
1665	2-2	23	20	IIIA	
1666	2-2	70	18	IIIA	
1667	2-2	28	16	IIIA	
1668	2-2	45	16	IIIA	
1669	2-2	28	25	IIIA	
1670	2-2	14	6	IIIA	
1671	2-2	12	5	IIIA	
1672	2-2	25	12	IIIA	
1673	2-2	25	18	IIIA	
1674	2-2	25	12	IIIA, V	3-V-287
1675	2-2	5	3	IIIA	
1676	2-2	65	31	IIIA, V	3-V-287
1677	2-2	20	8	IIIA	
1678	2-2	44	12	IIIA	
1679	2-2	9	6	IIIA	
1680	2-2	17	17	IIIA	
1681	2-2	12	10	IIIA	
1682	2-2	15	6	IIIA	
1683	2-3	18	10	IV, V	
1684	2-3	8	8	IV, V	
1685	2-3	20	4	IV, V	
1686	2-3	12	10	IV, V	
1687	2-3	22	14	IV, V	
1688	2-3	34	12	IV, V	
1689	2-3	20	8	IV, V	
1690	2-3	14	8	IV, V	
1691	2-3	11	7	IV, V	
1692	2-3	33	14	IV, V	
1693	2-3	9	7	IV, V	
1694	2-3	17	10	IV, V	
1695	2-3	11	6	IV, V	
1696	2-3	9	5	IV, V	
1697	2-3	15	14	IV, V	
1698	2-3	20	10	IV, V	
1699	2-3	18	14	IV, V	
1700	2-3	7	4	IV, V	Several pieces of adobe.
1701	2-3	33	22	IV, V	
1702	2-3	22	16	IV, V	One metate.
1703	2-3	16	12	IV, V	
1704	2-3	16	5	IV, V	
1705	2-3	14	9	IV, V	
1706	2-3	37	13	IV, V	
1707	2-3	41	7	IV, V	
1708	2-3	22	13	IV, V	
1709	2-3	50	15	IV, V	
1710	2-3	11	10	IV, V	
1711	2-3	11	7	IV, V	
1712	2-3	21	9	IV, V	
1713	2-3	10	5	IV, V	
1714	2-3	61	43	IV, V	
1715	2-3	31	12	IV, V	

JALIEZA (3-IIIA-136, 3-IV-46, and 3-V-259 unless otherwise indicated)

TERRACE	SITE GRID SQUARE	LENGTH	WIDTH	PERIODIZATION	COMMENTS
1716	2-3	28	13	IV, V	
1717	2-3	19	7	V	
1718	2-3	41	5	IV, V	
1719	2-3	36	35	IV, V	
1720	2-3	30	16	IV, V	
1721	2-3	16	9	IV, V	
1722	2-3	23	16	IV, V	
1723	2-3	13	7	V	Possibly functioned to regulate traffic flow.
1724	2-3	19	17	IV, V	
1725	2-3	11	4	V	
1726	2-3	12	9	V	
1727	2-3	28	14	V	
1728	2-3	23	7	V	
1729	2-3	28	11	V	
1730	2-3	8	8	V	
1731	2-3	22	7	V	
1732	2-3	57	8	V	One mano, one metate.
1733	2-3	25	13	V	
1734	2-3	15	12	V	
1735	2-3	12	12	V	One metate.
1736	2-3	15	11	V	
1737	2-3	21	7	V	
1738	2-3	21	7	V	
1739	2-3	24	8	V	
1740	2-3	23	19	V	Structure, 11 x 4 meters.
1741	2-3	19	11	V	
1742	2-3	13	8	V	
1743	2-2	15	12	V	
1744	2-2	19	19	V	
1745	2-2	22	12	V	
1746	2-2	20	9	V	
1747	2-2	33	17	V	
1748	2-2	15	14	V	Stone floor.
1749	2-2	11	10	V	Stone floor.
1750	2-2	10	4	V	
1751	2-2	10	10	V	
1752	2-2	36	11	V	One black obsidian blade.

TERRACE	SITE GRID SQUARE	LENGTH	WIDTH	PERIODIZATION	COMMENTS
1753	2-2	15	9	V	
1754	2-2	37	15	V	
1755	2-2	15	10	V	
1756	2-2	26	6	V	
1757	2-2	12	11	V	
1758	2-2	26	14	V	
1759	2-2	22	12	V	
1760	2-2	21	17	V	
1761	2-2	15	11	V	
1762	2-2	28	9	V	
1763	2-2	17	6	V	
1764	2-2	28	19	V	
1765	2-2	40	17	V	
1766	2-2	25	12	V	
1767	2-2	20	12	V	One metate.
1768	2-2	18	17	V	
1769	2-2	15	12	V	
1770	2-2	16	15	V	
1771	2-2	18	16	V	
1772	2-2	17	7	IIIA	
1773	2-2	17	6	IIIA	
1774	2-2	11	6	IIIA	Not residential.
1775	2-2	24	8	IIIA	
1776	2-2	20	9	IIIA	
1777	2-2	14	9	IIIA	
1778	2-2	23	3	IIIA	
1779	2-2	5	2	IIIA	
1780	2-2	13	5	IIIA	
1781	2-2	14	3	IIIA	
1782	2-2	10	6	IIIA	
1783	2-2	7	2	IIIA	
1784	2-2	16	6	IIIA	
1785	2-2	22	5	IIIA	
1786	2-2	23	10	IIIA	One G-23.
1787	2-2	17	5	IIIA	
1788	2-2	17	3	IIIA	
1789	2-2	15	8	IIIA	
1790	2-2	18	3	IIIA	
1791	2-2	17	3	IIIA	
1792	2-2	23	4	IIIA	

JALIEZA (3-IIIA-136, 3-IV-46, and 3-V-259 unless otherwise indicated)

TERRACE	SITE GRID SQUARE	LENGTH	WIDTH	PERIODIZATION	COMMENTS
1793	2-2	18	7	IIIA	
1794	2-2	30	6	IIIA	
1795	2-2	22	3	IIIA	
1796	2-2	9	5	IIIA	
1797	2-2	13	3	IIIA	One mano, one metate
1798	2-2	9	3	IIIA	
1799	2-2	19	8	IIIA	
1800	2-2	21	3	IIIA	
1801	2-2	35	4	IIIA	
1802	2-2	35	16	IIIA	
1803	2-2	10	2	IIIA	
1804	2-2	8	3	IIIA	
1805	2-2	17	5	IIIA	
1806	2-2	25	11	IIIA	
1807	2-2	8	3	IIIA	
1808	2-2	15	4	IIIA	
1809	2-2	20	11	IIIA	
1810	2-2	25	3	IIIA	
1811	2-2	18	7	IIIA	
1812	2-2	28	16	IIIA	
1813	2-2	30	11	IIIA	
1814	2-2	33	14	IIIA	
1815	2-2	64	7	IIIA	Two houses.
1816	2-2	15	3	IIIA	One chisel.
1817	2-2	26	9	IIIA	One G-23.
1818	2-2	25	6	IIIA	
1819	2-2	25	12	IIIA, V	3-V-252, lots of chert flakes and cores.
1820	2-2	30	5	IIIA	One G-23.
1821	2-2	18	9	IIIA	One G-23.
1822	2-2	10	4	IIIA	
1823	2-2	22	8	IIIA	
1824	2-2	13	2	IIIA	
1825	2-2	20	2	IIIA	
1826	2-2	25	2	IIIA	
1827	2-2	22	8	IIIA	
1828	2-2	12	5	IIIA	
1829	2-2	19	12	IIIA	
1830	2-2	36	12	IIIA	
1831	2-2	14	13	IIIA	

TERRACE	SITE GRID SQUARE	LENGTH	WIDTH	PERIODIZATION	COMMENTS
1832	2-2	12	11	IIIA	
1833	2-2	25	23	IIIA	
1834	2-2	13	5	IIIA	One G-23.
1835	2-2	5	3	IIIA	One G-23.
1836	2-2	12	7	IIIA	One G-23.
1837	2-2	12	12	IIIA	
1838	2-2	34	19	IIIA	One grey obsidian blade.
1839	2-2	16	10	IIIA	
1840	2-2	12	9	IIIA	
1841	2-2	26	21	IIIA	
1842	2-2	14	14	IIIA	
1843	2-2	15	9	IIIA	One G-23.
1844	2-2	11	5	IIIA	
1845	2-2	23	11	IIIA	One G-23.
1846	2-2	14	6	IIIA	
1847	2-2	32	7	IIIA	Two G-23's.
1848	2-2	13	8	IIIA	
1849	2-2	13	3	IIIA	Functionally related to T. 1848.
1850	2-2	23	12	IIIA	
1851	2-2	21	10	IIIA	Two G-23's.
1852	2-2	17	5	IIIA	
1853	2-2	17	10	IIIA	
1854	2-2	16	7	IIIA	
1855	2-2	17	4	IIIA	
1856	2-2	12	5	IIIA	Four G-23's.
1857	2-2	17	14	IIIA	Two G-23's.
1858	2-2	12	4	IIIA	One projectile point.
1859	2-2	12	7	IIIA	
1860	2-2	22	4	IIIA	
1861	2-2	27	5	IIIA	
1862	2-2	28	5	IIIA	
1863	2-2	23	4	IIIA	
1864	2-2	24	14	IIIA	
1865	2-2	22	7	IIIA	
1866	2-2	10	5	IIIA	
1867	2-2	16	3	IIIA	
1868	2-2	20	8	IIIA	One G-23.

JALIEZA (3-IIIA-136, 3-IV-46, and 3-V-259 unless otherwise indicated)

TERRACE	SITE GRID SQUARE	LENGTH	WIDTH	PERIODIZATION	COMMENTS
1869	2-2	17	9	IIIA	
1870	2-2	9	5	IIIA	
1871	2-2	8	2	IIIA	
1872	2-2	7	4	IIIA	
1873	2-2	16	3	IIIA	One G-23.
1874	2-2	13	8	IIIA	Two G-23's.
1875	2-2	7	2	IIIA	
1876	2-2	11	3	IIIA	
1877	2-2	15	5	IIIA	
1878	2-2	24	3	IIIA	
1879	2-2	15	3	IIIA	One G-23.
1880	2-2	15	3	IIIA	
1881	2-2	19	3	IIIA	
1882	2-2	6	2	IIIA	
1883	2-1	15	6	IIIA	
1884	2-1	9	5	IIIA	One G-23.
1885	2-2	21	6	IIIA	
1886	2-1	36	5	IIIA	
1887	2-1	34	8	IIIA	Three G-23's.
1888	2-1	14	4	IIIA	
1889	2-1	31	5	IIIA	
1890	2-2	16	10	IIIA	One G-23, one mano.
1891	2-2	15	3	IIIA	One G-23.
1892	2-2	10	3	IIIA	
1893	2-1	10	3	IIIA	
1894	2-1	9	3	IIIA	
1895	2-1	25	6	IIIA	
1896	2-1	23	3	IIIA	One jasper biface.
1897	2-1	28	3	IIIA	
1898	2-1	23	3	IIIA	
1899	2-1	36	3	IIIA	
1900	2-1	9	3	IIIA	Chert, quartz flakes.
1901	2-2	10	4	IIIA	One G-23.
1902	2-2	13	9	IIIA	One G-23.
1903	2-2	9	3	IIIA	
1904	2-2	18	8	IIIA	One metate.
1905	2-2	17	3	IIIA	
1906	2-2	28	2	IIIA	
1907	2-2	18	3	IIIA	
1908	2-2	29	8	IIIA	One metate, one projectile point.
1909	2-2	25	7	IIIA	
1910	2-2	9	2	IIIA	
1911	2-2	9	3	IIIA	
1912	2-2	32	6	IIIA	
1913	2-2	30	7	IIIA	
1914	2-2	27	11	IIIA	
1915	2-1	18	4	IIIA	
1916	2-1	22	7	IIIA	
1917	2-1	37	6	IIIA	
1918	2-1	6	6	IIIA	
1919	2-1	17	10	IIIA	
1920	2-1	20	4	IIIA	
1921	2-1	10	3	IIIA	
1922	2-1	25	7	IIIA	
1923	2-1	46	16	IIIA, V	3-V-253, two houses.
1924	2-1	36	13	IIIA, V	3-V-253.
1925	2-1	44	3	IIIA	
1926	2-1	22	3	IIIA	
1927	2-1	16	3	IIIA	
1928	2-1	11	3	IIIA	
1929	2-1	9	5	IIIA	
1930	2-2	18	2	IIIA	
1931	2-2	60	4	IIIA	Three houses.
1932	2-2	28	3	IIIA	
1933	2-2	6	3	IIIA	
1934	2-2	10	3	IIIA	
1935	2-2	10	5	IIIA	
1936	2-2	7	3	IIIA	
1937	2-2	10	5	IIIA	
1938	2-2	23	3	IIIA	
1939	2-2	15	3	IIIA	
1940	2-2	45	4	IIIA	
1941	2-2	8	3	IIIA	
1942	1-2	38	30	IIIA	
1943	1-2	56	52	IIIA	One G-23.
1944	1-2	65	56	IIIA	
1945	1-1	42	37	IIIA	
1946	1-1	51	9	IIIA	
1947	1-1	76	29	IIIA	

JALIEZA (3-IIIA-136, 3-IV-46, and 3-V-259 unless otherwise indicated)

TERRACE	SITE GRID SQUARE	LENGTH	WIDTH	PERIODIZATION	COMMENTS
1948	1-1	32	24	IIIA	
1949	1-1	75	26	IIIA	
1950	1-1	26	25	IIIA	
1951	1-1	106	51	IIIA	Two houses.
1952	1-1	18	10	IIIA	
1953	1-1	59	18	IIIA	
1954	1-1	54	8	IIIA	
1955	2-1	75	68	IIIA	Several G-23's, two houses.
1956	2-1	51	20	IIIA	
1957	2-1	50	42	IIIA	
1958	2-1	12	9	IIIA	
1959	2-1	35	19	IIIA	
1960	2-1	37	18	IIIA	
1961	2-1	75	9	IIIA	
1962	2-1	23	20	IIIA	
1963	2-1	37	35	IIIA	
1964	2-1	20	5	IIIA	
1965	2-1	15	13	IIIA	
1966	2-1	19	7	IIIA	
1967	2-1	10	9	IIIA	
1968	2-1	28	21	IIIA	
1969	2-1	31	18	IIIA	Two G-23's.
1970	2-1	19	10	IIIA	
1971	2-1	24	20	IIIA	
1972	2-1	15	10	IIIA	
1973	2-1	12	10	IIIA	One chert scraper.
1974	2-1	22	9	IIIA	
1975	2-1	16	14	IIIA	
1976	2-1	131	23	IIIA	
1977	2-1	66	10	IIIA	
1978	2-1	210	110	IIIA	
1979	2-1	78	68	IIIA	
1980	2-1	33	25	IIIA	
1981	2-1	20	11	IIIA	
1982	2-1	110	45	IIIA	
1983	2-1	48	15	IIIA	
1984	2-1	40	10	IIIA	
1985	2-1	130	25	IIIA	
1986	2-1	53	30	IIIA	
1987	2-1	54	8	IIIA	
1988	2-1	60	11	IIIA	
1989	2-1	20	10	IIIA	
1990	2-1	32	14	IIIA	
1991	2-1	32	16	IIIA	
1992	2-1	26	9	IIIA	
1993	2-1	31	10	IIIA	
1994	2-1	28	16	IIIA	
1995	2-1	43	9	IIIA	
1996	2-1	32	16	IIIA	
1997	2-1	46	21	IIIA	
1998	2-1	67	15	IIIA	
1999	2-1	55	20	IIIA	
2000	2-1	16	16	IIIA	
2001	2-1	25	13	IIIA	
2002	2-1	113	35	IIIA	
2003	2-1	35	14	IIIA	
2004	2-1	315	35	IIIA	
2005	2-1	270	45	IIIA	
2006	2-1	15	7	IIIA	
2007	2-1	34	24	IIIA	
2008	2-1	60	16	IIIA, V	3-V-282
2009	2-1	38	20	IIIA	
2010	2-1	50	24	IIIA	
2011	2-1	52	20	IIIA	
2012	2-1	32	25	IIIA	
2013	2-1	42	40	IIIA, V	3-V-282
2014	2-1	35	30	IIIA	
2015	2-1	150	35	IIIA, V	3-V-282
2016	2-1	40	38	IIIA	
2017	2-1	75	45	IIIA, V	3-V-282
2018	2-1	30	18	IIIA	
2019	2-1	30	25	IIIA	
2020	2-1	40	27	IIIA	
2021	2-1	12	4	IIIA	
2022	2-1	32	6	IIIA, V	3-V-282
2023	2-1	20	10	IIIA	
2024	2-1	18	12	IIIA	
2025	2-1	120	20	IIIA	
2026	2-1	25	17	IIIA	

JALIEZA (3-IIIA-136, 3-IV-46, and 3-V-259 unless otherwise indicated)

TERRACE	SITE GRID SQUARE	LENGTH	WIDTH	PERIODIZATION	COMMENTS
2027	2-1	125	25	IIIA, V	3-V-282
2028	2-1	26	10	IIIA	
2029	2-1	31	9	IIIA	
2030	2-1	25	18	II, IIIA	3-II-61, one G-23, one mano.
2031	2-1	40	25	IIIA	
2032	2-1	37	26	IIIA	
2033	2-1	32	15	IIIA	
2034	2-1	32	12	IIIA	
2035	2-1	12	10	IIIA	
2036	2-1	15	3	IIIA	
2037	2-1	13	6	IIIA	
2038	2-1	25	20	IIIA	Several G-23's.
2039	2-1	25	5	IIIA	
2040	2-1	18	16	IIIA	Worked sherd discs, one G-23.
2041	2-1	39	27	IIIA, V	3-V-283, one G-23. one metate, three houses.
2042	2-1	30	15	IIIA	Several G-23's.
2043	2-1	50	15	IIIA	Several G-23's.
2044	2-1	25	25	IIIA, V	One G-23, 3-V-283.
2045	2-1	39	3	IIIA	
2046	2-1	38	13	IIIA	
2047	2-1	18	10	IIIA, V	3-V-283
2048	2-1	29	20	IIIA	One G-23. lots of chert debitage, two houses.
2049	2-1	32	18	IIIA	
2050	2-1	30	17	IIIA	One G-23.
2051	2-1	20	12	IIIA	One ground stone fragment.
2052	2-1	19	17	IIIA	One worked sherd disc.
2053	2-1	100	7	IIIA	Two houses, one G-23.
2054	2-1	87	75	IIIA	
2055	2-1	80	19	IIIA	Several G-23's.
2056	2-1	210	150	IIIA	
2057	2-1	140	100	IIIA	
2058	2-1	145	40	IIIA	
2059	2-1	13	9	IIIA	
2060	2-1	115	55	IIIA, V	One G-23, 3-V-282.
2061	2-1	38	12	IIIA, V	One G-23, 3-V-282.
2062	2-1	81	76	IIIA	
2063	2-1	81	25	IIIA	
2064	2-1	43	19	IIIA	
2065	2-1	57	26	IIIA	One metate, lots of chert and flint.
2066	2-1	32	11	IIIA	
2067	2-1	31	15	IIIA	One metate.
2068	2-1	23	9	IIIA	
2069	2-1	30	11	IIIA	
2070	2-1	40	18	IIIA	Several G-23's.
2071	2-1	34	9	IIIA	
2072	2-1	20	11	IIIA	
2073	2-1	50	36	IIIA	Several G-23's, lots of chert and flint.
2074	2-1	40	27	IIIA	Several G-23's.
2075	2-1	22	12	IIIA	
2076	2-1	16	6	IIIA	
2077	2-1	42	15	IIIA	
2078	2-1	25	7	IIIA	
2079	2-1	33	6	IIIA	One G-23, two houses.
2080	2-1	24	5	IIIA	
2081	2-1	20	8	IIIA	
2082	2-1	22	13	IIIA	
2083	2-1	22	12	IIIA	
2084	2-1	18	12	IIIA	
2085	2-1	14	10	IIIA	
2086	2-1	26	21	IIIA	Several G-23's.
2087	2-1	22	22	IIIA	
2088	2-1	51	34	IIIA	Several G-23's.
2089	2-1	25	11	IIIA	
2090	2-1	35	10	IIIA	Several G-23's.
2091	2-1	25	19	IIIA	Several G-23's.
2092	2-1	35	13	IIIA	
2093	2-1	22	15	IIIA	
2094	2-1	41	16	IIIA	

JALIEZA (3-IIIA-136, 3-IV-46, and 3-V-259 unless otherwise indicated)

TERRACE	SITE GRID SQUARE	LENGTH	WIDTH	PERIODIZATION	COMMENTS
2095	2-1	17	12	IIIA	
2096	2-1	32	12	IIIA	One flake tool.
2097	2-1	27	13	IIIA	
2098	2-1	21	7	IIIA	Two houses.
2099	2-1	15	11	IIIA	
2100	2-1	56	41	IIIA	One mano.
2101	2-1	35	20	IIIA	
2102	2-1	10	8	IIIA	
2103	2-1	20	17	IIIA	
2104	2-1	12	10	IIIA	Several G-23's.
2105	2-1	19	10	IIIA	
2106	2-1	10	10	IIIA	
2107	2-1	35	15	IIIA	Three G-23's.
2108	2-1	10	7	IIIA	
2109	2-4	18	6	IV	
2110	1-4	17	8	IV	
2111	1-4	17	11	IV	
2112	1-3	13	5	IV	
2113	1-3	19	10	IV	
2114	1-3	11	6	IV	
2115	2-4	16	10	IV	
2116	2-4	14	6	IV	
2117	1-3	26	16	IV	
2118	2-4	18	8	IV	
2119	1-4	8	2	IV	
2120	2-2	18	3	IIIA, V	
2121	2-3	24	6	V	One metate.
2122	1-3	24	8	IV	
2123	1-2	30	14	IIIA	
2124	2-2	30	26	IIIA	
2125	2-1	31	9	IIIA, V	3-V-253, one piece
2126					of polychrome.
2126	2-1	44	25	IIIA	One metate, one mano, three houses.
2127	2-3	14	10	IV	
2128	2-4	31	15	IV	
2129	2-4	13	10	IV	
2130	2-4	27	4	IV	
2131	2-4	9	7	IV	
2132	2-4	12	7	IV	
2133	2-4	17	10	IV	
2134	2-3	10	7	IV	
2135	2-3	13	6	IV	
2136	2-3	17	7	IV	
2137	2-4	10	8	IV	One grey obsidian blade, one mano, burnt soil.
2138	2-3	14	7	V	
2139	2-3	20	9	IIIA, V	
2140	1-3	10	5	IV, V	
2141	2-3	18	11	IV	
2142	2-2	22	5	IIIA	
2143	2-2	33	3	IIIA	
2144	2-3	10	7	IV	
2145	1-4	26	19	IV	
2146	2-4	14	5	IV	
2147	1-1	72	35	IIIA	One G-23.
2148	1-2	59	37	IIIA	One G-23.
2149	1-1	37	17	IIIA	

STA. CRUZ MIXTEPEC (Under periodization, all IIIa terraces belong to 3-IIIA-179, unless otherwise noted, and all IV terraces belong to 3-IV-68, unless otherwise noted.)

TERRACE	LENGTH	WIDTH	PERIODIZATION	COMMENTS
1	10	7	IIIA, IV	
2	12	11	IIIA, IV	
3	8	7	IIIA, IV	
4	8	5	IIIA, IV	
5	10	5	IIIA, IV	
6	8	6	IIIA, IV	
7	8	5	IIIA, IV	
8	8	5	IIIA, IV	
9	10	5	IIIA, IV	
10	10	4	IIIA, IV	
11	7	3	IIIA, IV	
12	9	7	IIIA, IV	
13	14	8	IIIA, IV	
14	23	12	IIIA, IV	
15	12	11	IIIA, IV	
16	12	8	IIIA, IV	
17	12	10	IIIA, IV	
18	12	12	IIIA, IV	
19	10	8	IIIA, IV	
20	20	14	IIIA, IV	
21	20	11	IIIA, IV	
22	12	11	IIIA, IV	
23	14	11	IIIA, IV	
24	14	14	IIIA, IV	
25	9	8	IIIA, IV	
26	23	20	IIIA, IV	
27	27	18	IIIA, IV	One tomb.
28	21	19	IIIA, IV	
29	18	13	IIIA, IV	
30	22	13	IIIA, IV	
31	12	4	IIIA, IV	
32	15	15	IIIA, IV, V	3-V-324
33	45	21	IIIA, IV, V	Two houses, 3-V-324 one chert projectile point, chert working area?
34	8	5	IIIA	
35	8	4	IIIA	
36	10	5	IIIA	
37	7	4	IIIA	
38	7	5	IIIA	
39	12	6	IIIA	
40	12	5	IIIA	
41	10	3	IIIA	
42	12	6	IIIA	
43	12	6	IIIA	3-IIIA-178
44	24	12	IIIA	3-IIIA-178
45	20	6	IIIA	3-IIIA-178
46	10	8	IIIA	3-IIIA-178
47	30	10	IIIA	3-IIIA-178
48	50	20	IIIA	3-IIIA-178
49	30	12	IIIA	3-IIIA-178
50	15	9	IIIA	3-IIIA-178
51	16	16	IIIA	Three houses. 3-IIIA-178
52	12	10	IIIA	3-IIIA-178
53	18	12	IIIA	3-IIIA-178
54	15	6	IIIA	3-IIIA-178
55	13	7	IIIA	One metate, 3-IIIA-178
56	16	13	IIIA	3-IIIA-178
57	12	8	IIIA	3-IIIA-178
58	14	8	IIIA	3-IIIA-178
59	12	12	IIIA	3-IIIA-178
60	70	30	IIIA	3-IIIA-177
61	10	10	IIIA	3-IIIA-177
62	15	10	IIIA	3-IIIA-177
63	12	3	IIIA	3-IIIA-177
64	20	15	IIIA	3-IIIA-177
65	50	40	IIIA	Three houses.
66	12	12	IIIA	
67	14	10	IIIA	
68	15	10	IIIA	
69	10	10	IIIA	
70	12	6	IIIA	
71	12	10	IIIA	
72	17	14	IIIA	
73	12	12	IIIA	
74	11	5	IIIA	

STA. CRUZ MIXTEPEC

TERRACE	LENGTH	WIDTH	PERIODIZATION	COMMENTS
75	40	4	IIIA, IV	One grey obsidian blade. 3-IV-67
76	15	3	IIIA	
77	16	8	IIIA	
78	10	5	IIIA	
79	26	12	IIIA, IV	One A-7. 3-IV-67
80	14	11	IIIA	
81	10	7	IIIA	
82	20	3	IIIA	
83	15	10	IIIA	
84	10	8	IIIA	
85	9	6	IIIA	
86	30	13	IIIA	
87	22	17	IIIA	
88	22	12	IIIA	
89	10	3	IIIA	
90	16	6	IIIA	
91	9	2	IIIA	
92	10	6	IIIA	
93	10	6	IIIA	
94	18	16	IIIA	
95	15	7	IIIA	
96	28	17	IIIA	
97	13	7	IIIA	
98	32	10	IIIA	One house, 6x6 meters
99	16	10	IIIA	One house, 10x5 meters
100	10	6	IIIA	
101	6	3	IIIA	
102	18	10	IIIA	
103	10	6	IIIA	
104	10	7	IIIA	
105	20	9	IIIA	One house, 4x2m
106	23	10	IIIA	
107	23	23	IIIA	One house, 5 meters long
108	18	4	IIIA	
109	17	7	IIIA	
110	15	5	IIIA	
111	15	10	IIIA	
112	10	10	IIIA	
113	18	6	IIIA, V	3-V-327
114	27	2	IIIA	
115	9	4	IIIA	
116	5	3	IIIA	
117	10	4	IIIA	
118	16	10	IIIA	
119	15	9	IIIA	
120	15	13	IIIA	
121	16	5	IIIA	
122	17	12	IIIA	
123	10	5	IIIA	
124	10	6	IIIA	Structure, 1.0x3.5 meters
125	25	9	IIIA	
126	28	12	IIIA	
127	14	9	IIIA,V	3-V-328
128	13	10	IIIA,V	3-V-328
129	27	10	IIIA,V	3-V-328
130	12	9	IIIA,V	3-V-329
131	22	6	IIIA,V	3-V-329
132	32	6	IIIA	
133	13	8	IIIA	
134	17	10	IIIA,V	3-V-329
135	20	9	IIIA,V	3-V-329
136	35	9	IIIA,V	3-V-329
137	36	8	IIIA,V	3-V-329
138	10	8	IIIA,IV	
139	12	12	IIIA,IV	
140	23	18	IIIA,IV	
141	16	12	IIIA,IV	
142	26	15	IIIA,IV,V	Two houses. 3-V-324
143	15	15	IIIA,IV	
144	16	6	IIIA	3-IIIA-178
145	10	4	IIIA,IV	3-IV-69
146	14	2	IIIA,IV	3-IV-69
147	15	5	IIIA	3-IIIA-178
148	9	8	IIIA,IV	3-IV-69
149	46	15	IIIA,V	3-V-329
150	23	5	IIIA,V	3-V-329
151	17	16	IIIA,IV,V	3-V-324
152	12	7	IIIA,IV	

STA. CRUZ MIXTEPEC

TERRACE	LENGTH	WIDTH	PERIODIZATION	COMMENTS
153	11	3	IIIA,IV,V	3-V-324
154	30	5	IIIA,IV	Five grey obsidian flakes.
155	14	3	IIIA,IV	
156	25	10	IIIA,IV	
157	25	6	IIIA,IV	
158	15	5	IIIA,IV	
159	30	8	IIIA,IV	
160	41	10	IIIA,IV	
161	30	8	IIIA,IV	
162	25	5	IIIA,IV	
163	32	7	IIIA,IV	
164	22	6	IIIA,IV	
165	25	4	IIIA,IV	
166	22	4	IIIA,IV	
167	22	12	IIIA,IV	
168	18	8	IIIA,IV	
169	26	6	IIIA,IV	
170	33	8	IIIA,IV	
171	31	3	IIIA,IV	
172	40	4	IIIA,IV	
173	25	7	IIIA,IV	
174	10	5	IIIA,IV	
175	21	3	IIIA,IV	
176	13	5	IIIA,IV,V	3-V-325
177	18	4	IIIA,IV,V	3-V-325
178	19	4	IIIA,IV,V	3-V-325
179	39	14	IIIA,IV,V	3-V-325
180	53	13	IIIA,IV	
181	27	5	IIIA,IV	
182	13	4	IIIA,IV	
183	22	3	IIIA,IV	
184	25	4	IIIA,IV	
185	4	1	IIIA,IV	
186	14	5	IIIA,IV	One mano.
187	13	5	IIIA,IV	
188	19	5	IIIA,IV	
189	15	5	IIIA,IV	
190	21	4	IIIA,IV	
191	12	3	IIIA,IV	
192	10	4	IIIA	
193	25	15	IIIA	
194	18	12	IIIA	
195	15	6	IIIA	
196	15	12	IIIA	
197	15	4	IIIA	
198	10	6	IIIA	
199	25	11	IIIA	
200	10	3	IIIA	
201	28	15	IIIA	
202	40	5	IIIA,IV	
203	17	16	IIIA,IV	
204	16	11	IIIA,IV	One house, 6x2 meters, 0.25 meters high.
205	51	19	IIIA,IV	
206	22	21	IIIA,IV	
207	25	7	IIIA,IV	
208	15	4	IIIA,IV	
209	16	6	IIIA,IV	
210	22	17	IIIA	
211	11	5	IIIA	
212	15	4	IIIA	
213	46	9	IIIA	
214	8	7	IIIA	
215	10	4	IIIA	
216	27	9	IIIA	
217	11	9	IIIA	
218	10	5	IIIA	
219	21	13	IIIA	
220	16	15	IIIA	
221	17	5	IIIA	
222	15	9	IIIA	
223	23	12	IIIA	
224	15	9	IIIA	
225	16	11	IIIA	
226	20	3	IIIA	
227	17	7	IIIA	
228	15	7	IIIA	

STA. CRUZ MIXTEPEC

TERRACE	SITE GRID SQUARE	LENGTH	WIDTH	PERIODIZATION	COMMENTS
229		11	8	IIIA	
230		34	7	IIIA	
231		10	9	IIIA	
232		16	11	IIIA	
233		35	14	IIIA,V	Five grey obsidian blades. One mano. One quartz flake. 3-V-326
234		34	11	IIIA	One large metate.
235		12	5	IIIA	
236		16	4	IIIA	
237		17	9	IIIA	
238		17	6	IIIA	
239		25	3	IIIA	
240		14	10	IIIA,V	3-V-326
241		19	5	IIIA	One large metate.
242		15	5	IIIA	
243		12	6	IIIA	
244		9	8	IIIA	
245		9	7	IIIA	
246		19	16	IIIA,V	3-V-326
247		9	2	IIIA,V	3-V-326
248		27	9	IIIA	
249		122	5	IIIA	One quartz core.
250		23	4	IIIA	
251		34	12	IIIA	One utilized quartz flake. Flint flakes.
252		18	5	IIIA,V	3-V-326
253		15	5	IIIA	
254		13	3	IIIA	
255		9	4	IIIA	
256		9	4	IIIA	
257		38	10	IIIA,V	One grey obsidian blade. 3-V-325
258		8	3	IIIA	
259		11	5	IIIA	
260		20	16	IIIA	
261		21	5	IIIA	One urn. One house, 10 x 5 meters.
262		21	4	IIIA	
263		29	8	IIIA	One mano.
264		10	3	IIIA	
265		16	8	IIIA	
266		17	3	IIIA	
267		50	8	IIIA	One grey obsidian blade.
268		20	5	IIIA	
269		31	18	IIIA,IV	One grey obsidian blade. 3-IV-70
270		10	7	IIIA	
271		15	6	IIIA	
272		10	6	IIIA	
273		16	5	IIIA	
274		17	7	IIIA	
275		25	17	IIIA,IV	3-IV-70
276		13	4	IIIA	
277		15	6	IIIA	
278		18	18	IIIA	
279		21	21	IIIA,V	3-V-331
280		11	5	IIIA,V	3-V-331
281		21	5	IIIA	One urn.
282		31	8	IIIA	
283		6	4	IIIA	
284		6	4	IIIA	
285		13	6	IIIA	
286		8	4	IIIA	
287		20	5	IIIA	
288		18	6	IIIA,V	3-V-331
289		12	9	IIIA,V	3-V-331
290		7	4	IIIA	
291		12	6	IIIA	
292		30	10	IIIA	
293		43	20	IIIA	
294		28	17	IIIA	One tomb.

STA. CRUZ MIXTEPEC

TERRACE	LENGTH	WIDTH	PERIODIZATION	COMMENTS
295	39	25	IIIA	Two houses.
296	13	7	IIIA	
297	27	3	IIIA	
298	12	5	IIIA	
299	8	6	IIIA	
300	15	6	IIIA	
301	25	8	IIIA	
302	12	6	IIIA	
303	13	4	IIIA	
304	15	8	IIIA	
305	18	4	IIIA	
306	12	5	IIIA	
307	18	9	IIIA	
308	17	8	IIIA	
309	11	3	IIIA	One grey obsidian blade.
310				
310	30	6	IIIA	Two houses.
311	44	20	IIIA	
312	30	9	IIIA,IV	One utilized chert flake. 3-IV-71
313	47	11	IIIA,IV, V	One grey obsidian blade. 3-IV-71, 3-V-332
314	20	6	IIIA	
315	24	4	IIIA	Plaster floor.
316	11	9	IIIA,IV, V	3-IV-71, 3-V-332 One urn. One sherd disc.
.				
317	18	10	IIIA,IV, V	3-IV-71, 3-V-332 One grey obsidian blade. One urn.
318	23	14	IIIA,IV, V	3-IV-71, 3-V-332 One grey obsidian blade.
319	23	12	IIIA,IV, V	3-IV-71, 3-V-332
320	20	12	IIIA,IV, V	3-IV-71, 3-V-332
321	16	9	IIIA,IV	3-IV-71
322	25	9	IIIA,IV	3-IV-71
323	50	9	II,IIIA,IV, V	3-II-75,3-IV-71, 3-V-332
324	20	8	II,IIIA,IV, V	3-II-75,3-IV-71, 3-V-332, One perforated pottery disc.
325	20	8	II,IIIA,IV, V	3-II-75,3-IV-71, 3-V-332
326	10	5	II,IIIA,IV, V	3-II-75,3-IV-71, 3-V-332
327	20	6	IIIA,IV	3-IV-71
328	16	3	IIIA,IV	3-IV-71
329	13	6	IIIA,IV	3-IV-71
330	13	3	IIIA,IV	3-IV-71
331	16	3	IIIA,IV	3-IV-71
332	17	3	IIIA,IV,V	3-IV-71,3-V-332
333	14	5	IIIA,IV	3-IV-71,3-V-332
334	17	3	IIIA,IV,V	3-IV-71
335	17	3	IIIA,IV	3-IV-71
336	14	8	IIIA	
337	10	3	IIIA,IV,V	3-IV-71,3-V-332
338	13	3	IIIA,IV	3-IV-71
339	23	7	IIIA,IV	One chert flake scraper. 3-IV-71
340	12	3	IIIA,IV	3-IV-71
341	18	7	IIIA,IV	3-IV-71
342	18	4	IIIA,IV	Two grey obsidian blades. 3-IV-71
343	6	3	IIIA	
344	15	8	IIIA,IV	
345	14	12	IIIA,IV	
346	25	6	IIIA,IV,V	3-IV-69,3-V-329
347	13	5	IIIA,IV,V	3-IV-69,3-V-329
348	15	10	IIIA,IV,V	3-IV-69,3-V-329
349	25	8	IIIA,IV,V	3-IV-69,3-V-329
350	30	8	IIIA,IV,V	3-IV-69,3-V-329

STA. CRUZ MIXTEPEC

TERRACE	LENGTH	WIDTH	PERIODIZATION	COMMENTS
351	29	6	IIIA,IV,V	3-IV-69, 3-V-329
352	15	14	IIIA,IV	3-IV-69
353	16	15	IIIA,IV	3-IV-69
354	9	3	IIIA,IV	3-IV-69
355	15	8	IIIA,IV	3-IV-69
356	16	4	IIIA,IV	2-IV-69
357	28	10	IIIA,IV	3-IV-69
358	62	15	IIIA,IV	3-IV-69
359	10	9	IIIA,IV	3-IV-69
360	12	4	IIIA,IV	3-IV-69
361	40	10	IIIA,IV	3-IV-69
362	5	4	IIIA,IV	3-IV-69
363	18	4	IIIA,IV	3-IV-69
364	60	19	IIIA,IV	3-IV-69
365	60	4	IIIA,IV,V	Quartz cores and flakes. 3-IV-69 3-V-330
366	36	4	IIIA,IV,V	3-IV-69,3-V-330
367	22	17	IIIA,IV,V	Quartz flakes. 3-IV-69,3-V-330
368	12	11	IIIA,IV,V	Quartz flakes,two quartz cores, utilized quartz scraper -workshop? Flint flakes. Jasper flake 3-IV-69, 3-V-330
369	27	4	IIIA,IV,V	3-IV-69,3-V-330
370	22	5	IIIA,IV,V	3-IV-69,3-V-330
371	6	5	IIIA,IV	Quartz chunks.3-IV-69
372	62	6	IIIA,IV,V	3-IV-69,3-V-330
373	25	18	IIIA,IV,V	Two utilized grey obsidian blades. 3-V-330 Quartz flakes and chunks. 3-IV-69
374	100	7	IIIA,IV	Lots of quartz. 3-IV-69
375	25	3	IIIA,IV	Quartz flakes and chunks. 3-IV-69
376	50	25	IIIA,IV	3-IV-69
377	17	5	IIIA,IV	3-IV-69
378	24	15	IIIA,IV	3-IV-69
379	34	5	IIIA,IV	3-IV-69
380	47	4	IIIA,IV	3-IV-69
381	12	11	IIIA,IV	3-IV-69
382	12	8	IIIA,IV	3-IV-69
383	32	23	IIIA,IV	3-IV-69
384	12	4	IIIA,IV	3-IV-69
385	12	4	IIIA,IV	3-IV-69
386	20	6	IIIA,IV	3-IV-69
387	15	6	IIIA,IV	3-IV-69
388	15	2	IIIA,IV	Quartz chunks. 3-IV-69
389	12	2	IIIA,IV	Quartz. 3-IV-69
390	12	3	IIIA,IV,V	Quartz flakes. 3-IV-69,3-V-330

EL CHOCO (All terraces assigned to period V are part of 3-11-451, except for some whose site numbers appear in the "comments" column.)

TERRACE	LENGTH	WIDTH	PERIODIZATION	COMMENTS
1	8	3	IV	
2	6	3	IV	
3	10	3	IV	
4	15	6	IV	
5	12	3	IV	
6	18	8	IV	
7	20	10	IV	
8	11	6	IV	
9	9	5	IV	
10	28	7	IV	
11	50	4	IV	
12	18	5	IV	
13	45	5	IV	
14	20	8	IV	
15	25	4	IV	
16	17	10	IV	
17	16	5	IV	
18	61	48	IV,V	Plaza.
19	16	5	IV,V	
20	20	7	IV	
21	24	8	IV,V	
22	27	12	IV	
23	21	5	IV	
24	11	3	IV	
25	30	6	IV,V	
26	40	8	IV,V	
27	32	10	IV	
28	18	16	IV,V	
29	50	5	IV,V	
30	31	28	IV	
31	24	16	IV,V	
32	17	9	IV	
33	11	9	IV	
34	33	18	IV,V	
35	25	8	IV	
36	78	18	IIIA,IV,V	
37	43	20	IV	
38	13	13	IV,V	
39	14	9	IV	
40	16	10	IV	
41	18	9	IV	
42	18	15	IV	
43	20	5	IV,V	
44	25	4	IV,V	
45	9	8	V	
46	18	12	IV,V	
47	16	11	IV,V	
48	71	25	IV	One green obsidian blade.
49	29	9	IV	
50	36	9	IV	
51	24	8	IV,V	
52	42	13	IV	
53	15	8	IV	
54	36	18	IV	
55	36	5	IV	
56	18	6	IV,V	V-458
57	24	8	IV	
58	16	8	IV	
59	80	6	IV	
60	20	16	IV	
61	22	13	IV	
62	19	6	IV	
63	16	8	IV	
64	8	6	IV	
65	24	13	IV	
66	30	9	IV	
67	21	7	IV	
68	85	10	IV	
69	18	7	IV	
70	11	2	IV	
71	12	5	IV	
72	20	9	IV	
73	11	6	IV	
74	3	3	IV	
75	16	8	IV	

EL CHOCO (All terraces assigned to period V are part of 3-11-451, except for some whose site numbers appear in the "comments" column.)

TERRACE	LENGTH	WIDTH	PERIODIZATION	COMMENTS
76	15	10	IV	
77	34	7	IV,V	V-458
78	20	6	IV	
79	31	16	IV	
80	25	9	IV	
81	40	10	IV	
82	10	4	IV	
83	18	9	IV	
84	25	13	IV,V	V-458
85	20	7	IV	
86	19	8	IV,V	
87	30	9	IV	
88	22	7	IV,V	
89	14	8	IV,V	
90	31	5	IV,V	
91	20	9	IV,V	
92	20	12	IV,V	
93	80	16	IV,V	
94	24	8	IV,V	
95	12	5	IV,V	
96	26	16	IV,V	
97	28	8	II,IIIA,V	One chert core. One worked sherd.
98	30	12	IV	
99	12	8	IV,V	
100	14	12	IV,V	
101	23	9	IV,V	
102	12	12	IV,V	
103	32	10	IV	
104	65	27	IV	
105	25	16	IV	
106	24	5	IV	
107	25	7	IV,V	
108	13	10	V	
109	62	20	IV	
110	30	8	IV,V	
111	26	8	IV,V	
112	32	11	IV,V	
113	12	8	V	
114	60	12	IV,V	
115	44	8	IV,V	
116	26	4	V	
117	25	5	V	
118	14	4	IV,V	
119	16	8	IV,V	
120	27	7	IV,V	
121	10	6	IV,V	
122	21	7	IV,V	
123	15	10	IV,V	
124	32	11	IV	
125	30	7	IV	
126	26	8	IV	
127	10	5	IV	
128	10	5	IV,V	
129	16	8	IV	
130	25	6	IV,V	
131	18	7	IV,V	
132	23	5	IV	
133	20	8	IV	
134	19	10	IV	
135	40	17	IV,V	
136	18	8	IV	
137	18	6	IV,V	
138	40	11	IV	
139	24	20	IV,V	
140	14	8	IV,V	
141	10	3	IV,V	
142	22	10	IV,V	
143	15	12	IV	
144	13	6	IV	
145	32	20	IV,V	
146	40	12	IV,V	
147	48	10	V	
148	35	11	IV,V	
149	30	4	IV,V	
150	25	15	IV,V	

EL CHOCO (All terraces assigned to period V are part of 3-11-451, except for some whose site numbers appear in the "comments" column.)

TERRACE	LENGTH	WIDTH	PERIODIZATION	COMMENTS
151	20	4	IV,V	
152	13	5	IV,V	
153	30	10	IV,V	
154	17	6	IV,V	
155	23	14	IV,V	
156	12	8	IV	
157	10	6	IV	
158	15	8	IV	One striated grey obsidian blade.
159	17	9	IV	
160	12	8	IV	
161	34	28	IV,V	
162	26	13	IV	
163	12	5	IV	
164	50	7	IV,V	V-452
165	17	10	IV,V	V-452
166	15	7	IV,V	V-452
167	38	5	IV	
168	14	5	IV	
169	16	14	IV	
170	25	12	IV	
171	63	7	IV,V	V-452
172	30	10	IV,V	V-452
173	25	10	IV	
174	14	10	IV	
175	12	10	IV	
176	17	8	IV	
177	12	10	IV,V	V-452
178	16	10	IV,V	V-452
179	20	15	IV,V	V-452
180	37	14	IV	
181	25	25	IV	
182	12	7	IV	
183	60	11	IV	
184	28	20	IV	
185	42	14	IV,V	V-454
186	18	14	IV	
187	27	5	IV	
188	12	7	IV	
189	18	11	IV	
190	17	5	IV	
191	21	16	IV	
192	18	10	IV	
193	35	21	IV	
194	13	11	IV	
195	16	6	IV	
196	17	8	IV	
197	50	8	IV	
198	72	12	IV	
199	88	6	IV	
200	24	9	IV	
201	45	16	IV,V	V-455
202	15	10	IV	
203	12	12	IV	
204	28	26	IV	
205	36	10	IV	One grey obsidian blade.
206	14	14	IV	
207	34	11	IV	
208	30	12	IV	
209	50	7	IV	
210	25	10	IV	
211	20	6	IV	
212	20	8	IV	
213	32	8	IV	
214	12	9	IV	One grey obsidian blade
215	15	5	IV	
216	22	9	IV	
217	16	7	IV	
218	16	17	IV	
219	12	11	IV	
220	21	7	IV	
221	10	6	IV	
222	17	6	IV	
223	12	8	IV	One mano.
224	33	6	IV	

EL CHOCO (All terraces assigned to period V are part of 3-11-451, except for some whose site numbers appear in the "comments" column.)

TERRACE	LENGTH	WIDTH	PERIODIZATION	COMMENTS
225	25	6	IV	
226	12	5	IV	
227	25	10	IV	
228	7	6	IV	
229	23	6	IV	
230	15	9	IV	
231	28	14	IV	
232	16	6	IV	
233	22	5	IV	
234	16	8	IV	
235	32	10	IV	
236	25	8	IV	
237	22	10	IV	One triangular chert point.
238	30	10	IV	
239	48	13	IV	
240	11	4	IV	
241	34	10	IV	
242	10	6	IV	
243	50	6	IV	
244	30	13	IV	
245	7	5	IV	
246	20	6	IV	
247	10	8	IV	
248	14	4	IV	
249	25	6	IV,V	
250	9	9	IV	
251	13	7	IV	
252	9	4	IV	
253	7	3	IV	
254	12	8	IV	
255	9	6	IV,V	V-453
256	9	8	IV	
257	12	6	IV	
258	11	8	IV	
259	27	12	IV	
260	21	7	IV	
261	19	11	IV	
262	18	5	IV	One worked sherd.
263	12	5	IV	
264	16	4	IV	
265	9	6	IV	
266	9	9	IV	
267	25	9	IV	
268	28	13	IV	
269	11	5	IV	
270	32	24	IV	Two houses.
271	12	12	IV	
272	25	7	IV	
273	16	13	IV	
274	18	5	IV,V	
275	15	5	IV	
276	12	5	IIIA,IV	
277	12	10	IIIA,IV	One G-23. One grey obsidian blade.
278	38	10	IIIA,IV,V	
279	11	7	IIIA,IV,V	
280	13	6	IIIA,IV	
281	28	12	IV,V	
282	18	8	IIIA,IV	
283	15	8	IIIA,IV	
284	13	7	IV	One chert core.
285	12	8	IIIA,IV	
286	18	6	IV	
287	23	6	IV	
288	87	5	IV	One chert core.
289	9	5	IV	
290	23	5	IIIA,IV	
291	45	6	IIIA,IV,V	
292	44	5	IV	One chert core.
293	17	5	IV	
294	62	7	IV,V	
295	28	5	IIIA,IV	
296	45	4	IIIA,IV	Two white chert flakes.
297	45	5	IIIA,IV	
298	31	6	IV	

EL CHOCO (All terraces assigned to period V are part of 3-11-451, except for some whose site numbers appear in the "comments" column.)

TERRACE	LENGTH	WIDTH	PERIODIZATION	COMMENTS
299	9	6	IV,V	
300	11	7	IV	One chert core.
301	10	3	IV	
302	13	5	IV	One chert flake.
303	14	4	IV	
304	10	5	IV	
305	23	9	IV	One chert core.
306	14	5	IV	
307	10	4	IIIA,IV,V	
308	16	4	IIIA,IV	
309	26	7	IIIA,IV,V	
310	17	7	IIIA,IV	
311	35	5	IIIA,IV,V	
312	36	7	IIIA,IV,V	
313	70	10	IIIA,IV,V	
314	30	6	IIIA,IV,V	
315	8	6	IIIA,IV	
316	18	11	IIIA,IV	One chert core.
317	32	9	IIIA,IV,V	
318	21	4	IIIA,IV,V	
319	13	5	IIIA,IV	
320	25	5	IIIA,IV,V	
321	7	5	IIIA,IV	
322	12	8	IIIA,IV,V	
323	10	5	IIIA,IV,V	
324	18	6	IIIA,IV,V	
325	25	6	IIIA,IV	
326	25	6	IIIA,IV	
327	20	6	IIIA,IV	
328	10	10	IIIA,IV,V	
329	60	10	IIIA,IV	
330	10	6	IIIA,IV	
331	20	7	IIIA,IV	
332	22	10	IIIA,IV	
333	30	7	IIIA,IV,V	
334	10	8	IIIA,IV	
335	25	12	IIIA,IV,V	
336	20	12	IIIA,IV,V	
337	24	7	IIIA,IV	
338	10	6	IIIA,IV	
339	40	8	IIIA,IV	
340	10	10	IIIA,IV	
341	12	12	IIIA,IV	
342	25	12	IIIA,IV	
343	30	10	IIIA,IV,V	
344	25	15	IIIA,IV,V	
345	16	8	IIIA,IV,V	
346	22	8	IIIA,IV,V	
347	30	11	IIIA,IV	One mano.
348	38	12	IIIA,IV	
349	15	8	IIIA,IV	
350	20	20	IIIA,IV	
351	15	10	IIIA,IV	
352	10	10	IIIA	
353	23	3	IIIA,IV	
354	8	3	IIIA,IV	
355	6	3	IIIA,IV	
356	13	3	IIIA	
357	38	5	IIIA	
358	24	5	IIIA	One mano.
359	15	3	IIIA	One G-23.
360	30	12	IIIA	
361	38	11	IIIA	
362	34	11	IIIA	
363	26	9	IIIA	
364	23	9	IIIA,V	
365	34	6	IIIA	
366	40	8	IIIA	
367	45	4	IIIA	
368	32	4	IIIA,V	
369	18	6	IIIA	
370	32	7	IIIA,V	
371	48	8	II,IIIA,V	Two G-23's.
372	52	10	II,IIIA,V	
373	25	10	IIIA,V	One green obsidian blade.
374	10	6	IIIA,V	
375	30	10	IIIA,V	One grey obsidian blade.

EL CHOCO (All terraces assigned to period V are part of 3-11-451, except for some whose site numbers appear in the "comments" column.)

TERRACE	LENGTH	WIDTH	PERIODIZATION	COMMENTS
376	40	7	IIIA,V	
377	17	9	II,IIIA	One chert core.
378	35	7	II,IIIA	Two G-23's.
379	25	10	II,IIIA	
380	15	8	IIIA,V	
381	20	10	II,IIIA	One mano.
382	7	6	IV	
383	18	5	IIIA,V	
384	25	7	IIIA	
385	18	18	IIIA,V	
386	25	6	IIIA	
387	13	7	IIIA,V	
388	14	4	II,IIIA	
389	36	5	IIIA,V	
390	24	7	II,IIIA,IV	One G-21 base.
391	12	6	IIIA	
392	30	10	II,IIIA,V	
393	20	7	IIIA	
394	18	8	IIIA	One mano.
395	10	10	IIIA	
396	20	5	IIIA,V	
397	72	5	II,IIIA	One chert core.
398	22	6	IIIA	
399	12	11	II,IIIA	
400	26	20	II,IIIA, IV,V	Two grey obsidian flakes.
401	22	10	IIIA	One G-23.
402	15	5	IIIA	
403	18	3	IIIA	One grey obsidian flake.
404	13	5	IIIA	
405	18	7	IIIA	
406	16	5	IIIA	
407	14	3	IIIA	
408	14	3	IIIA	
409	28	6	IIIA	
410	22	3	IIIA	
411	21	5	IIIA	
412	22	6	IIIA,V	
413	22	7	IIIA,V	
414	15	10	IIIA,V	
415	25	10	IIIA,V	
416	26	5	IIIA,V	
417	10	10	IIIA	
418	13	12	IIIA,V	
419	24	5	IIIA	
420	35	13	IIIA	
421	17	10	IIIA	
422	26	6	IIIA	
423	12	12	IIIA	
424	30	7	IIIA	
425	15	7	IIIA,V	
426	16	3	IIIA	
427	13	4	IIIA	
428	10	10	IIIA	
429	25	5	IIIA	
430	60	10	IIIA,V	
431	24	7	IIIA	
432	16	5	IIIA,V	
433	27	8	IIIA	
434	16	12	IIIA,V	
435	60	30	IIIA,IV,V	Three houses. V-459
436	34	20	IIIA,IV,V	V-459
437	18	12	IIIA,IV,V	V-459
438	18	8	IIIA,IV,V	V-459
439	15	8	IIIA,IV,V	V-459
440	22	7	IIIA,IV,V	One mano. V-459
441	75	14	IIIA,IV,V	V-459
442	26	10	IIIA,IV,V	V-459
443	16	3	IIIA	
444	67	8	IIIA,IV,V	V-459
445	12	3	IIIA,IV,V	V-459
446	20	17	IIIA,IV	
447	10	7	IIIA,IV,V	V-459
448	9	6	IIIA,IV,V	V-459
449	28	8	IIIA,IV,V	V-459

EL CHOCO (All terraces assigned to period V are part of 3-11-451, except for some whose site numbers appear in the "comments" column.)

TERRACE	LENGTH	WIDTH	PERIODIZATION	COMMENTS
450	8	3	IIIA,IV,V	V-459
451	30	13	IV	One mano.
452	90	7	IV	One chert piece.
453	26	13	IV	
454	23	9	IV	
455	30	10	IV,V	
456	22	11	IV,V	
457	17	9	IV	
458	32	11	IV	One mano.
459	33	12	IV,V	
460	30	11	IV	
461	60	11	IV,V	
462	21	10	IV	
463	18	8	IV	
464	20	13	IV,V	
465	27	21	IV,V	
466	18	12	IV,V	
467	27	16	IV,V	
468	30	15	IV,V	
469	29	7	IV,V	
470	21	7	IV	
471	15	5	IV	
472	19	10	IV	
473	15	5	IV	
474	31	4	IV	
475	10	6	IV	
476	9	4	IV	
477	17	8	IV	
478	13	12	IV	
479	10	5	IV	
480	17	6	II,IV,V	
481	25	12	IV	
482	32	7	IV	
483	19	12	IV	
484	16	5	IV	
485	24	12	IV	
486	30	9	IV,V	
487	45	15	IV	
488	12	5	IV	
489	10	8	IV	
490	19	13	IV,V	
491	29	10	IV	
492	21	8	IV	
493	22	10	IV	
494	15	8	IV	
495	15	7	IV	
496	12	9	IV	
497	13	5	IV	
498	20	7	IV	
499	10	5	IV	
500	20	9	IV,V	
501	15	5	IV,V	
502	25	9	V	
503	22	11	V	
504	42	8	V	
505	47	9	V	
506	60	8	IV	
507	22	12	IV	
508	32	15	V	
509	21	9	IV	
510	18	12	IV	
511	27	9	IV	
512	30	8	IV,V	
513	28	12	V	
514	15	9	IV,V	
515	23	12	IV,V	
516	18	12	IV,V	
517	20	7	IV	
518	12	5	IV	
519	15	12	IV,V	
520	20	11	IV,V	
521	10	7	IV	
522	9	9	IV	
523	10	4	IV	
524	10	7	IIIA,IV,V	V-459

2-IIIB-1

TERRACE	LENGTH	WIDTH	PERIODIZATION	COMMENTS
1	78	36	IIIB	Several manos. Plaster floor.
2	41	32	IIIB	
5	23	14	IIIB	
6	19	15	IIIB	Plaza.
7	22	9		
8	31	27	IIIB	Elaborate residence.
9	12	10	IIIB	
10	13	5	IIIB	
11	27	15	IIIB	One polishing stone.
12	52	8	IIIB	
13	20	17	IIIB	Plaza.
14	32	6	IIIB	One polishing stone.
15	14	6	IIIB	
16	11	8	IIIB	One chert flake.
17	12	7	IIIB	
18	20	17	IIIB	
19	32	9	IIIB	
20	46	19	IIIB	One projectile point.
21	27	12	IIIB	
22	22	10	IIIB	One metate.
23	24	21	IIIB	One mano. Plaza.
24	37	30	IIIB	
25	21	12	IIIB	One metate. Two manos.
26	25	3	IIIB	
27	65	10	IIIB	One chert core.
28	28	18	IIIB	One mano. One polishing stone.
29	82	10	IIIB	Two manos.
30	11	7	IIIB	
31	21	12	IIIB	One mano. One grey obsidian blade.
32	27	9	IIIB	One mano.
33	30	14	IIIB	
34	40	17	IIIB	
35	56	35	IIIB	Two manos.
36	22	12	IIIB	One mano.
37	70	20	IIIB	

2-IV-2

TERRACE	LENGTH	WIDTH	PERIODIZATION	COMMENTS
1	21	13	IV	
2	20	11	IV	
3	42	15	IV	
4	12	5	IV	
5	16	10	IV	
6	50	10	IV	
7	27	14	IV	
8	60	11	IV	Two houses.
9	52	10	IV,V	
10	70	10	IV	Three houses.
11	21	10	IV	
12	36	7	IV	One mano.
13	34	7	IV	One grey obsidian blade.
14	16	11	IV,V	
15	24	9	IV,V	
16	12	9	IV,V	
17	16	10	IV,V	
18	19	10	IV	
19	11	6	IV	
20	18	8	IV,V	
21	31	20	IV,V	
22	27	7	IV,V	
23	45	17	LI,IV,V	
24	30	10	IV,V	
25	17	10	IV	
26	15	9	IV,V	One mano.
27	25	10	IV	One celt.
28	19	10	IIIA,IV,V	
29	13	8	IV,V	
30	13	10	IV	
31	30	19	IV,V	
32	30	14	IV	
33	44	16	IV	Two houses.
34	20	12	IV	
35	9	8	IV	
36	18	12	IV	
37	27	14	LI,IV,V	
38	21	8	LI,IV,V	
39	21	11	IV,V	One metate.
40	100	20	IV,V	
41	20	14	IV,V	
42	20	9	IV,V	
43	15	9	IV	
44	13	9	IV	
45	13	3	IV	
46	17	10	IV,V	
47	53	5	IV,V	
48	47	10	IV	
49	24	5	IV	
50	45	10	IV,V	
51	34	9	IV	
52	42	20	IV,V	
53	18	12	IV,V	
54	22	10	IV,V	One metate.
55	36	9	IV,V	
56	19	16	IV	
57	23	15	IV	
58	127	14	IV,V	
59	20	18	IV,V	One green obsidian blade.
60	18	9	IV,V	
61	11	8	IV	
62	12	9	IV	
63	23	11	IV	
64	18	7	IV	
65	20	9	IV,V	
66	17	8	IV	
67	42	17	IV,V	
68	23	10	IV,V	
69	26	9	IV,V	
70	16	11	IV,V	
71	15	8	IV	
72	33	12	IV	One mano.
73	15	12	IV	
74	15	8	IV	

2-IV-2

TERRACE	LENGTH	WIDTH	PERIODIZATION	COMMENTS
75	9	4	IV,V	
76	85	15	IV,V	
77	18	7	IV	One metate.
78	26	12	IV,V	
79	8	5	IV	
80	17	6	IV	
81	20	8	IV,V	
82	9	4	IV,V	One metate.
83	12	3	IV,V	
84	21	8	IV	One metate.
85	15	12	IV	
86	38	36	IV	Elite residence.
87	29	14	IV	
88	18	15	IV	
89	35	21	IV,V	
90	33	15	IV	Two manos.
91	105	26	IV,V	
92	55	9	IV,v	
93	40	11	IV	
94	30	9	IV	
95	33	11	IV	
96	21	11	IV	
97	15	8	IV,V	
98	42	8	IV,V	
99	13	9	IV,V	
100	11	7	IV,V	
101	38	15	IV,V	
102	19	15	IV	
103	33	20	IV	
104	9	8	IV	
105	12	9	IV,V	
106	16	13	IV,V	
107	23	6	IV	
108	13	5	IV	
109	13	4	IV	
110	26	20	IV	
111	57	20	IV	
112	22	22	IV	
113	26	26	IV	
114	27	20	IV	
115	26	22	IV	
116	26	19	IV	
117	40	17	IV	
118	26	20	IV	
119	20	14	IV	
120	21	15	IV	
121	20	15	IV,V	
122	15	15	IV	
123	30	12	IIIA,IV	
124	18	9	IV	
125	15	12	IV	
126	12	11	IV	
127	17	9	IV	
128	15	8	IV	
129	15	6	IV	
130	21	9	IV	
131	14	13	IV	
132	17	10	IV	One mortar. Structure, 4x8 meters.
133	46	8	IV	

3-IIIA-220 (All on this sheet are periodization IIIA.)

TERRACE	LENGTH	WIDTH	PERIODIZATION	COMMENTS
1	37	32	IIIA	Plaza.
2	23	8	IIIA	
3	19	15	IIIA	Plaster floor. A lot of flaked quartz.
4	32	11	IIIA	One house, 13x5 m. Quartz flakes.
5	18	8	IIIA	
6	20	19	IIIA	
7	11	5	IIIA	
8	26	13	IIIA	One metate. Plaster floor. Quartz flakes.
9	14	3	IIIA	
10	17	4	IIIA	
11	8	5	IIIA	
12	9	6	IIIA	
13	10	6	IIIA	
14	11	5	IIIA	
15	13	5	IIIA	
16	17	8	IIIA	
17	25	6	IIIA	
18	17	6	IIIA	
19	18	5	IIIA	
20	16	7	IIIA	Two houses.
21	14	7	IIIA	
22	10	6	IIIA	
23	9	3	IIIA	
24	10	3	IIIA	
25	25	6	IIIA	
26	22	4	IIIA	
27	23	7	IIIA	
28	20	5	IIIA	
29	20	10	IIIA	
30	19	4	IIIA	
31	30	7	IIIA	
32	11	11	IIIA	
33	20	5	IIIA	
34	35	6	IIIA	
35	22	5	IIIA	
36	18	7	IIIA	
37	37	8	IIIA	
38	23	6	IIIA	
39	23	7	IIIA	
40	59	8	IIIA	One house, 8x8 m.
41	70	9	IIIA	Three houses.
42	24	3	IIIA	
43	9	3	IIIA	
44	11	5	IIIA	
45	7	6	IIIA	
46	23	8	IIIA	Two houses.
47	16	2	IIIA	
48	17	9	IIIA	Two houses.
49	10	3	IIIA	
50	14	6	IIIA	
51	24	7	IIIA	
52	7	6	IIIA	Quartz flakes.
53	11	6	IIIA	
54	14	6	IIIA	
55	14	3	IIIA	
56	9	4	IIIA	
57	20	5	IIIA	
58	15	4	IIIA	
59	14	4	IIIA	
60	8	3	IIIA	
61	14	4	IIIA	
62	12	3	IIIA	
63	23	5	IIIA	Quartz flakes.
64	16	4	IIIA	Quartz flakes.
65	15	5	IIIA	
66	7	3	IIIA	
67	7	2	IIIA	
68	11	6	IIIA	
69	8	3	IIIA	
70	13	3	IIIA	
71	20	5	IIIA	
72	7	3	IIIA	

3-IIIA-220 (All on this sheet are periodization IIIA; exceptions are noted in "comments" column.)

TERRACE	LENGTH	WIDTH	PERIODIZATION	COMMENTS
73	12	3	IIIA	Two houses. Quartz flakes.
74	10	2	IIIA	Quartz flakes.
75	11	4	IIIA	Quartz flakes.
76	15	6	IIIA	
77	14	5	IIIA	Quartz flakes.
78	7	4	IIIA	
79	16	11	IIIA	
80	18	10	IIIA	One house, 8x7 m.
81	10	5	IIIA	
82	15	9	IIIA	
83	37	14	IIIA	Two houses.
84	15	6	IIIA	
85	21	7	IIIA	
86	16	9	IIIA	
87	12	3	IIIA	
88	10	3	IIIA	
89	25	12	IIIA	Two houses.
90	10	6	IIIA	
91	13	9	IIIA	
92	21	8	IIIA	
93	26	5	IIIA	
94	28	9	IIIA	
95	15	8	IIIA	
96	47	10	IIIA	
97	14	6	IIIA	
98	24	9	IIIA	
99	15	4	IIIA	
100	25	6	IIIA	Two houses.
101	23	6	IIIA	
102	10	3	IIIA	
103	26	5	IIIA	Two houses.
104	14	4	IIIA	Two houses.
105	15	4	IIIA	Quartz flakes.
106	10	4	IIIA	
107	11	7	IIIA	
108	5	5	IIIA	
109	18	4	IIIA	
110	9	3	IIIA	
111	12	5	IIIA	
112	8	5	IIIA	
113	12	5	IIIA	
114	6	5	IIIA	
115	17	7	IIIA	
116	18	4	IIIA	
117	31	7	IIIA	
118	14	5	IIIA	
119	15	6	IIIA	
120	26	5	IIIA	
121	20	6	IIIA	Mica mine.
122	15	9	IIIA	
123	22	3	IIIA	
124	23	6	IIIA	
125	18	7	IIIA	
126	18	6	IIIA	
127	18	7	IIIA	
128	15	3	IIIA	
129	25	3	IIIA	
130	24	5	IIIA	
131	12	6	IIIA	
132	26	10	LI,IIIA,V	
133	32	13	LI,IIIA,V	
134	26	25	LI,IIIA,V	Kiln waster.
135	19	11	LI,IIIA,V	One mano.
136	26	9	LI,IIIA,V	
137	15	13	LI,IIIA	
138	31	16	LI,IIIA,V	
139	50	13	LI,IIIA	
140	34	26	LI,IIIA,V	
141	59	13	IIIA,V	Two houses, Abundant mica.

3-IIIA-222

TERRACE	LENGTH	WIDTH	PERIODIZATION	COMMENTS
1	48	32	IIIA	Plaza.
2	32	20	IIIA	
3	40	30	IIIA	Two houses.
4	7	3	IIIA	
5	30	24	IIIA	Two houses.
6	38	36	IIIA	Two houses, one mano.
7	42	8	IIIA	
8	43	7	IIIA	Two grey obsidian blades, quartz flakes.
9	50	12	IIIA	
10	25	7	IIIA	
11	56	8	IIIA	
12	13	3	IIIA	
13	6	3	IIIA	One mano.

3-IIIA-250

TERRACE	LENGTH	WIDTH	PERIODIZATION	COMMENTS
1	33	12	IIIA	
2	15	12	IIIA	
3	21	14	IIIA	
4	27	10	IIIA	
5	20	15	IIIA	
6	14	13	IIIA	
7	11	10	IIIA	
8	21	13	IIIA	
9	40	7	IIIA	
10	26	15	IIIA	
11	15	11	IIIA	
12	25	13	IIIA	
13	50	7	IIIA	
14	30	7	IIIA	
15	55	6	IIIA	
16	20	20	IIIA	
17	10	3	IIIA	
18	27	3	IIIA	Three houses.
19	40	5	IIIA	Two houses.
20	17	6	IIIA	
21	23	8	IIIA	
22	11	3	IIIA	
23	38	17	IIIA	
24	20	15	IIIA	
25	20	12	IIIA	
26	22	4	IIIA	
27	42	4	IIIA	Two houses.
28	37	10	IIIA	
29	13	6	IIIA	
30	47	3	IIIA	Two houses.
31	12	6	IIIA	
32	15	6	IIIA	
33	37	3	IIIA	
34	23	15	IIIA	
35	25	6	IIIA	
36	52	6	IIIA	Two houses.
37	45	5	IIIA	
38	17	14	IIIA	
39	11	5	IIIA	
40	15	9	IIIA	
41	23	16	IIIA	
42	13	12	IIIA	
43	20	10	IIIA	
44	12	10	IIIA	
45	15	10	IIIA	
46	14	13	IIIA	
47	17	6	IIIA	
48	34	14	IIIA	
49	34	15	IIIA	
50	84	10	IIIA	
51	14	12	IIIA	
52	11	7	IIIA	
53	29	3	IIIA	
54	45	7	IIIA	
55	55	5	IIIA	Two houses.
56	31	15	IIIA	
57	52	4	IIIA	
58	25	15	IIIA	
59	16	4	IIIA	
60	19	12	IIIA	
61	90	3	IIIA	Two houses.
62	25	12	IIIA	
63	38	18	IIIA	
64	20	8	IIIA	
65	62	3	IIIA	Two houses.
66	18	9	IIIA	
67	14	6	IIIA	
68	14	10	IIIA	
69	25	12	IIIA	
70	12	5	IIIA	
71	30	5	IIIA	Two houses.
72	16	5	IIIA	
73	17	7	IIIA	
74	13	9	IIIA	
75	25	8	IIIA	
76	60	3	IIIA	Two houses.

3-IIIA-250

TERRACE	LENGTH	WIDTH	PERIODIZATION	COMMENTS
77	38	4	IIIA	
78	14	8	IIIA	
79	21	7	IIIA	
80	11	10	IIIA	
81	8	6	IIIA	
82	9	5	IIIA	
83	22	7	IIIA	
84	8	4	IIIA	
85	14	7	IIIA	
86	14	6	IIIA	
87	20	10	IIIA	
88	20	12	IIIA	
89	36	15	IIIA	
90	20	6	IIIA	
91	45	15	IIIA	
92	20	17	IIIA	

3-IIIA-271

TERRACE	LENGTH	WIDTH	PERIODIZATION	COMMENTS
1	10	8	IIIA	
2	17	12	IIIA	
3	8	5	IIIA	
4	10	6	IIIA	
5	24	8	IIIA	Two houses.
6	12	6	IIIA	
7	16	4	IIIA	
8	17	4	IIIA	
9	6	5	IIIA	
10	4	3	IIIA	
11	12	6	IIIA	
12	24	7	IIIA	
13	18	14	IIIA	
14	9	7	IIIA	
15	8	6	IIIA	
16	20	5	IIIA	
17	22	4	IIIA	
18	8	6	IIIA	
19	18	6	IIIA	
20	12	5	IIIA	
21	8	4	IIIA	
22	10	6	IIIA	
23	8	5	IIIA	
24	9	6	IIIA	
25	10	8	IIIA	
26	10	6	IIIA	
27	8	4	IIIA	
28	21	5	IIIA	
29	24	8	IIIA	One house, 3x2.2 m.

3-IIIA-285

TERRACE	LENGTH	WIDTH	PERIODIZATION	COMMENTS
1	36	6	IIIA	
2	26	7	IIIA	
3	25	6	IIIA	
4	35	9	IIIA	
5	40	4	IIIA	
6	13	7	IIIA	
7	21	7	IIIA	One celt.
8	12	7	IIIA	
9	130	7	IIIA,V	One mano.
10	80	4	IIIA	
11	28	15	IIIA	
12	26	3	IIIA	
13	42	10	IIIA	
14	208	10	IIIA	One mano.
15	25	6	IIIA	Two chert cores.
16	23	6	IIIA	
17	18	7	IIIA	
18	8	4	IIIA	
19	17	12	IIIA	
20	7	5	IIIA	
21	8	8	IIIA	
22	11	8	IIIA	
23	85	2	IIIA	
24	35	15	IIIA	
25	24	9	IIIA	
26	25	13	IIIA	
27	39	37	IIIA	Three houses.
28	42	7	IIIA	
29	46	5	IIIA	
30	10	3	IIIA	
31	30	9	IIIA	
32	33	7	IIIA	One mano.
33	32	3	IIIA	
34	14	3	IIIA	
35	28	5	IIIA	
36	31	7	IIIA	One G-23.
37	58	6	IIIA	
38	12	7	IIIA	
39	23	8	IIIA	
40	24	5	IIIA	One large chert scraper.
41	15	6	IIIA	
42	11	3	IIIA	
43	5	5	IIIA	
44	37	10	IIIA	Three houses.
45	22	5	IIIA	
46	18	5	IIIA	
47	16	6	IIIA	
48	45	4	IIIA	
49	35	5	IIIA	
50	37	12	IIIA	
51	37	16	IIIA	
52	13	6	IIIA	
53	14	6	IIIA	
54	25	18	IIIA	

3-IV-7

TERRACE	LENGTH	WIDTH	PERIODIZATION	COMMENTS
1	28	11	IV	
2	14	7	IV	
3	26	6	IV	
4	24	5	IV	
5	17	6	IV	
6	22	8	IV	
7	27	5	IV	
8	10	5	IV	
9	10	4	IV	
10	12	3	IV	
11	13	11	IV	
12	15	12	IV	
13	13	12	IV	
14	28	12	IV	
15	13	8	IV	
16	13	4	IV	
17	12	9	IV	
18	12	12	IV	
19	21	14	IV	
20	28	18	IV	
21	24	9	IV	
22	25	6	IV	
23	12	4	IV	
24	34	21	IV	
25	18	10	IV	
26	13	11	IV	
27	13	13	IV	
28	60	20	IV	

Appendix XI

STRUCTURE SUMMARY AND STRUCTURE DRAWINGS

The first part of this appendix is a summary of base and top dimensions, and elevations, for mounded structures in the central places of the Valle Grande (for information on structures in the Central Survey Area, see Kowalewski, 1976). The second part of this appendix contains structure drawings of the major Central area sites, and most of the Valle Grande sites with mounded construction. These drawings allow the reader to see the orientation of the mounds, and their disposition with respect to other structures. A few of the Valle Grande sites, where only a few low mounds were present, are not included in the structure drawings. In these cases, to obtain information on orientation, note that the first value given in the structure summary is the north-south dimension.

As we mentioned in our section on methods in Chapter 1, data on structures were collected by pacing the base and top dimensions, and by using an eye level for mound height. Obviously, therefore, the measurements and drawings presented here should be considered as rough approximations. All contour lines are impressionistic, and cannot be used for measurement. Plane-table maps would of course be preferable but were outside the limits of our resources, given that over 500 mounded structures were located and mapped in the Valle Grande area alone.

An additional problem is that many of the mounds are so severely damaged by erosion or recent construction, or are so choked with vegetation, that any attempt to reconstruct what the buildings looked like (as we do in the structure drawings) faces numerous problems. In some cases, making a measurement in the field is difficult or impossible due to these same problems, which is why some dimensions are missing for some of the structures in the structure summary. In these cases, we used the following rules for estimating missing dimensions: 1) if a structure is less than 3 meters high, then the top area is calculated as 60% of the base area; 2) if a structure is 3 to 6 meters high, then the top area is 50% of the base area; and 3) if the structure is higher than 6 meters, the top area is 40% of the base area.

In the final drawings of the very large sites, the scales which we were forced to use made it difficult to draw structures accurately to scale. However, the structure summaries can be used to obtain accurate measurements.

STRUCTURE SUMMARY (1)

Field Number(s) or Site Name		St.#	Base(m)	Top(m)	Height(m)	Period-ization
CE-AT-AT-1 (Fig. A. XI-1)	EI-9	1	24 x 24	10 x 6	3.0	EI, LI
	LI-22	2	33 x 30	6 x 4.5	5.2	EI, LI
		3	43 x 30	15 x 6	8.5	EI, LI
		4	32 x 32	6 x 5	3.6	EI, LI
		5	21 x 17	19 x 5	3.0	EI, LI
		PLATFORM	20 x 27	21 x 6	1.5	EI, LI
		6 St.	10 x 15	2 x 5	1.5	LI
		PLATFORM	25 x 40	15 x 20	2.0	EI, LI
CE-AT-AT-2 (Fig. A. XI-2)	II-13 LI-23	1	50 x 22	29 x 10	4	II, IV
	IV-7	2	24 x 50	9 x 38	3.3	II, IV
	V-48, 49, 50					
		PLATFORM (under St. 1, 2, and 3)	50 x 77	30 x 50	8	II, IV
		3	19 x 23	4 x 14	1.7	II, IV
		4	11 x 3	?	1	IV
		5	50 x 45	12 x 10	4	IV, V
		6	20 x 34	3 x 12	3.6	II, IV
		7	44 x 26	35 x 18	1.75	II, IV
CE-AT-AT-3	IV-6	1	28 x 26	?	.25	IV
CUILAPAN (CE-CUI-RQ-2) (Figs. A. XI-3-7)		1	34 x 24	20 x 16	2	II, IIIA
		2	58 x 68	12 x 18	2.1	LI, II, IIIA
		3	75 x 62	18 x 12	3	II, IIIA, IIIB
		4	25 x 25	14 x 14	7.5	II, IIIA
		(4 platform)	56 x 50	close to same	1.5	" "
		5	30 x 56	13 x 10	1	II, IIIA
		6	37 x 38	7 x 7	8	LI, II, IIIA
		(6 platform)	41 x 43	40 x 42	1	" "

STRUCTURE SUMMARY (2)

Field Number(s) or Site Name		St.#	Base(m)	Top(m)	Height(m)	Period-ization
CUILAPAN (CE-CUI-RQ-2) (cont.)		7	30 x 34	22 x 25	1	II, IIIA
		8	38 x 38	20 x 25	7.5	II, IIIA, IV
		(8 platform)	50 x 40	almost same	3	" "
		9	40 x 12	12 x 15	6	LI, II, IIIA
		10	63 x 30	24 x 1	2.8	" "
		11	50 x 53	15 x 6	9	" "
		13	18 x 25	10 x 10	2	" "
		14	25 x 40	3 x 10	2	LI, II, IIIA
		15	30 x 25	1 x 1	5	" "
		16	26 x 26	8 x 8	3.5	IIIA, V
		18	42 x 44	6 x 6	7.5	LI, II, IIIA
		XX	40 x 30	10 x 10	8	" "
CE-CUI-RQ-8 (Fig. A. XI-8)	IIIA-29	1	38 x 31	8 x 8	3	IIIA
	IIIB-26	2	50 x 62	17 x 15	2	IIIB, V
	IV-13, 12, 11	3	38 x 50	16 x 20	2	IIIA, IIIB
	V-69, 68, 67, 66	4	29 x 45	6 x 10	5	IIIA, IIIB IV, V
		5	(49 x 53) (55 x 19) (23 x 17)	(6 x 14) (31 x 9) (9 x 7)	(18) (3) (1.5)	(IIIA, IIIB) (" ") (" ")
		6	45 x 50	11 x 18	10	IIIA
		7	35 x 40	13 x 6	2	IIIA
		8	18 x 20	7 x 10	2	IIIA, IIIB
		9	26 x 28	9 x 12	0.5	IIIA, IIIB
		10	56 x 20	3 x 3	?	IIIA, IIIB, IV, V
		11	50 x 45	8 x 8	0.75	IIIA, IIIB, IV, V
		12	35 x 37	6 x 6	1.5	IIIA, IIIB

STRUCTURE SUMMARY (3)

Field Number(s) or Site Name		St.#	Base(m)	Top(m)	Height(m)	Period-ization
CE-CUI-SJ-5 (east end of Cuilapan)		1	60 x 125	12 x 25	8	IIIA
(Fig. A. XI-3-7)		Platform under st. 1	135 x 135	close to same	1	"
		2	38 x 38	14 x 11	4.5	"
		3	90 x 125	50 x 55	1.8	"
CE-CUI-SJ-6 (part of Cuilapan) (Fig. A. XI-3-7)	LI-8	1	25 x 32	6 x 10	8	LI, II, IIIA, IIIB
	II-7	(1 platform)	45 x 68	?	2	LI, II, IIIA, IIIB
	IIIA-8	2	20 x 18	?	1	LI, II, IIIA, IIIB, V
	IIIB-18					
		3	30 x 36	10 x 15	7.5	LI, II, IIIA
	V-35					
		4	10 x 22	10 x 22	1.5	LI, II, IIIA
CE-CUI-SL-2	LI-9	1	37 x 60	roughly 3/4 the base	1.25	LI, IIIB, IV, V
	IV-5					
	V-39					
CE-SBC-RM-3 (Fig. A. XI-9)	TL-3	1	37.5 x 40	10 x 5	1.65	IIIA, IIIB
	SJ-3	2	37.5 x 40	5 x 10	3	IIIA, IIIB, V
	G-4	3	28 x 28	8 x 8	5.5	II, IIIA
	Ros-19					
	EI-25	4	40 x 44	11 x 23	4	II, IIIA, IIIB
	LI-56, 57	5	37.5 x 33	10 x 6	1	II, IIIA
	II-34	6	25 x 50	5 x 20	4.5	EI, LI, II, IIIA
	IIIA-71, 72					
		7	30 x 37.5	12 x 12	6	EI, LI, II, IIIA
	IIIB-49					
	V-159, 514	8	25 x 20	18 x 10	1	EI, LI, II, IIIA
		9	25 x 20	18 x 7	3	EI, LI, II, IIIA
		10	15 x 25	5 x 12	3	EI, LI, IIIA

STRUCTURE SUMMARY (4)

Field Number(s) or Site Name		St.#	Base (m)	Top(m)	Height(m)	Period-ization
CE-SBC-RM-3 (cont.)		11	35 x 45	6 x 12	1.25	TL, SJ, G, R, EI, LI, IIIA
		12	35 x 30	15 x 10	4.5	TL, EI, LI
		13	30 x 25	13 x 18	1.15	LI, IIIA, V
CE-SBC-SBC-2 (Fig. A. XI-10)	TL-2, SJ-2, G-3, Ros-3	1	35 x 58	12 x 13	7	TL, SJ, G, EI, LI, IIIA
	EI-19, LI-47	2	31 x 38	7 x 10	3.5	LI, II
	II-27, IIIA-56	3	32 x 22	4 x 2	3	EI, LI
	V-111, 112, 113	4	64 x 43	16 x 16	4.5	EI, LI IIIA
		5	45 x 55	25 x 30	2.25	II, IIIA, V
		6	25 x 42	19 x 33	1	LI, II, IIIA
		7	28 x 34	13 x 12	2.3	LI, II, IIIA
		8	56 x 30	20 x 10	1.5	LI, II, IIIA, V
		9	18 x 15	3 x 5.5	4.25	R, EI, LI
CE-SBC-SBC-9 (Fig. A. XI-11)	Ros-4, 20	1	30 x 21	11 x 9	4.4	LI, II, IIIA, V
	EI-21, 57	2	10 x 15	?	1.7	LI, II, IIIA
	LI-48	3	?	?	.5	LI, II
	II-28	4	23 x 23	7 x 6	4.75	R, EI, LI, II
	IIIA-57, 58	5	29 x 20	5 x 4	4.5	R, EI, LI, II
	V-118, 119, 120, 121	6	25 x 14	8 x 3	2.9	R, EI, LI, II
		7	15 x 27	3 x 14	1.5	R, EI, LI, II
		8	18 x 25	3 x 13	1.3	R, EI, LI, II

STRUCTURE SUMMARY (5)

Field Number(s) or Site Name		St.#	Base(m)	Top(m)	Height(m)	Period-ization
CE-SBC-SBC-9 (cont.)		9	28 x 22	10 x 6	1.3	LI, II
		10	19 x 22	12 x 14	1.5	R, EI, LI, II
		11	45 x 30	40 x 26.5	.5	V
		12				
		N St	26 x 9.5	11 x 4	1.0	V
		S St	26 x 9.5	11 x 4	1.0	V
		E St	27 x 15	15 x 4	1.1	V
		13	32 x 7	16 x 2	0.9	R, EI, LI, II
CE-SBC-SBC-10	V-127	1	26 x 26	?	1.75	V
		Platform (under st.)	55 x 90	?	2.0	V
CE-SMC-SMC-5	LI-24, 23 IIIA-18 IV-7 V-51, 52, 53	1	12 x 18	12 x 7	1.6	IIIB, IV, V
		2	18 x 18	10 x 13	2	IIIA
CE-SMC-SMC-6	LI-34 II-19 IIIA-41	1	43 x 34	14 x 5	10	LI, II, IIIA
		Platform (under st.)	90 x 100	?	1.7	LI, II, IIIA
CE-SMC-SMC-19	EI-14, 51 LI-35, 36 II-21 IIIA-45, 46 IIIB-35 IV-18	1	25 x 24	5 x 5	2	II, IIIA, V
		2	24 x 22	8 x 8	3	II, IIIA, V
CE-XOX-SJB-4	IIIA-40 IIIB-32 V-79	1	36 x 36	?	2.0	IIIA, IIIB
		2	32 x 32	?	1.0	IIIA, IIIB
		3	53 x 60	?	?	IIIA, IIIB
		4	45 x 34	?	1.5	IIIA, IIIB

STRUCTURE SUMMARY (6)

Field Number(s) or Site Name		St.#	Base(m)	Top(m)	Height(m)	Period-ization
OC-OC-TM-1, 2, 3 (Fig. A. XI-12)	Ros-14 EI-41 LI-125, 124 II-87 IIIA-236, 237, 238, 239 IIIB-62, 63 IV-77	1A	48 x 50	?	1	R-IIIB
		1	32 x 38	?	2	IIIA, IIIB
		2	43.5 x 54	5 x 10	12	IIIA
		3	31 x 25	3 x 8	3.9	IIIA
		4	41 x 37	7 x 3	2.2	IIIA
		5	23 x 28	5 x 9	1.0	IIIA
		6	33 x 53	9 x 9	3.25	IIIA
		7	31 x 45	17 x 18	5	IIIA, IIIB
		8	37 x 29	14 x 20	1.5	IIIA, IIIB
		9	36 x 15	6 x 6	3.1	IIIA, IIIB
		10	31 x 20	8 x 10	2	IIIA
		11	27 x 18	8 x 7	2.5	IIIA
		12	32 x 32	10 x 8	2.25	IIIA
		13	26 x 22	7 x 5	3	IIIA
		14	55 x 28	6 x 6	1.5	IIIA
		15	22 x 25	4 x 10	1	IIIA
		16	35 x 35	?	3.5	IIIA
		17	29 x 18	15 x 12	3.1	IIIA
		18	34 x 21	18 x 14	1	IIIA
		19	44 x 40	10 x 10	3.5	IIIA
		20	27 x 25	?	1.5	IIIA
		22	21 x 14	5.5 x 3.5	1.6	IIIA
		23	34 x 32	6 x 10	2.5	IIIA
		24	30 x 30	6 x 6	1	IIIA
		25	6 x 6	?	0.25	IIIA
		26	36 x 30	8 x 6	3.5	IIIA
		27	20 x 20	14 x 14	1	IIIA
		28	20 x 20	8 x 12	1	IIIA
		29	24 x 20	11 x 10	1	IIIA

STRUCTURE SUMMARY (7)

Field Number(s) or Site Name	St.#	Base(m)	Top(m)	Height(m)	Period-ization
OC-OC-TM-1, 2, 3 (cont.)	30	17 x 24	?	2	IIIA
	31	23 x 30	?	1.5	IIIA
	32	32 x 30	18 x 18	3	IIIA
	33	32 x 22	?	1.5	IIIA
	34	30 x 24	15 x 15	1	IIIA
	35	17 x 20	?	1	IIIA, IIIB
	36	29 x 21	8 x 11	2	IIIA
	Platform	21 x 50	10 x 11	1.9	IIIA
	40	24 x 24	16 x 12	1	IIIA
	41	19 x 19	4 x 4	0.25	IIIA
	42	9 x 9	8 x 8	0.25	IIIA
	43	27 x 20	10 x 4	0.75	IIIA
	44	18 x 16	10 x 9	0.5	IIIA
OC-SMT-SMT-11 (Fig A. XI-13) Ros-2, 18; EI-52, 54; LI-85, 86; IIIA-130, 131, 132	1	50 x 40	13 x 9	6	R, EI, LI
	2	30 x 60	?	2	EI, LI
	3	28 x 35	8 x 18	1.75	EI, LI
	4	26 x 38	6 x 9	4.25	EI, LI
	5	30 x 22	?	1	R, EI, LI, IIIA
	6	46 x 70	36 x 6	1.5	R, EI, LI, IIIA
	7	48 x 40	15 x 18	3	R, EI, LI, IIIA
	8	38 x 20	14 x 6	2.1	EI, LI
	9	20 x 15	?	0.6	EI, LI
	10	35 x 35	30 x 21	1	R, EI, LI
	11	28 x 35	7 x 10	6	EI, LI, IIIA
	12	39 x 6	35 x 3	2	EI, LI, IIIA
	13	17.5 x 11	11 x 7	1.7	EI, LI, IIIA

STRUCTURE SUMMARY (8)

Field Number(s) or Site Name	St.#	Base(m)	Top(m)	Height(m)	Period-ization
OC-SMT-SMT-11 (cont.)	14	30 x 14	22 x 7	2	EI, LI, IIIA
	15	70 x 12	almost same	2	EI, LI, IIIA
	16	30 x 40	20 x 22	8	EI, LI, IIIA
	17	28 x 11	6 x 22	2	EI, LI, IIIA
OC-SMT-SMT-23 (Fig. A. XI-14) EI-60, 61; LI-72, 73; II-44; IIIA-103, 104, 105; IV-33; V-192, 208, 209, 210	1	20 x 20	8 x 7	4	EI, LI, IIIA, V
	2	20 x 20	8 x 11	3	EI, LI, II, IV, V
	3	19 x 18	4 x 4	3	EI, LI, II, IV, V
	4	22 x 48	9 x 19	10	EI, LI, II, IV, V
	5	16 x 9	6 x 3	5	EI, LI, II, IV, V
	6	25 x 35	9 x 22	3.7	EI, LI, II, IV, V
	7	18 x 7	16 x 5	5	EI, LI, II, IV, V
	8	27 x 20	6 x 4	4	EI, LI, II, IV, V
	9	38 x 10	24 x 10	3	EI, LI, II, IV, V
	10	12 x 18	8 x 12	2	EI, LI, II, IV, V
	11	19 x 6	10 x 2	1	EI, LI, II, IV, V
	12	19 x 10	?	0.5	EI, LI, II, IV, V
	13	28 x 26	12 x 12	1	LI, II
	14	18 x 18	4 x 5	4	II
	15	16 x 21	11 x 11	2.5	II
	16	8 x 14	3 x 7	1	II

STRUCTURE SUMMARY (9)

Field Number(s) or Site Name		St.#	Base(m)	Top(m)	Height(m)	Period-ization
Jalieza (OC-STJ-STJ-1)	(1-4)	1	21 x 26	6 x 21	4.5	IV
(numbers in parentheses	"	2	25 x 18	16 x 8	2	"
are the Jalieza grid	"	3	40 x 14	7 x 6	3	"
square numbers)	"	4	8 x 9	2 x 2	1.75	"
(Figs. A. XI-15-24)	"	5	10 x 17	5 x 13	1	"
	"	6	21 x 25	7 x 10	6.75	"
	"	7	49 x 40	40 x 3	6	"
	"	8	25 x 18	16 x 8	12	"
	"	9	34 x 16	20 x 2.5	1	"
	"	10	40 x ?	30 x 2	4	"
	"	11	30 x 6	18 x 2	2.5	"
	"	12	12 x 36	2 x 34	2.5	"
	"	13	38 x 24	11 x 4.5	2.6	"
	"	14	14 x 14	3 x 5	4	"
	"	15	19 x 12	6 x 4	4	"
	"	16	12 x 6	3 x 1	2.5	"
	"	17	12 x 14	3 x 4	4.75	"
	(2-4)	18	12 x 14	7 x 7	1.5	"
	"	19	20 x 12	6 x 5	2.5	"
	"	20	12 x 8	6 x 3	1	"
	"	21	9 x 4	5 x 4	1	"
	"	22	N 25 x 30 E 53 x ? S ? x 35 W 30 x ?	15 x 25 28 x 6 3 x 25 25 x 3	2.4 4 2 1.5	IV, V
	"	23	12 x 15	8 x 5	3	IV
	"	24	14 x 9	8 x 14	2.5	"
	"	25	10 x 8	8 x 6	.5	"
	"	26	32 x 10	7 x 4	.5	"

STRUCTURE SUMMARY (10)

Field Number(s) or Site Name		St.#	Base(m)	Top(m)	Height(m)	Period-ization
Jalieza (cont.)	(2-4)	27	32 x 32	14 x 12	1.5	IV
	"	28	10 x 7	5 x 5	1	"
	"	29	10 x 12	4 x 4	1.25	"
	"	30	23 x 21	5 x 3	2.5	"
	"	31	8 x 12.5	6.5 x 6.5	1.75	"
	"	32	24 x 22	4.5 x 4.5	4.8	"
	"	33	15 x 15	4 x 5	1.5	"
	"	34	22 x 28	4 x 6	5	"
	"	35	34 x 20	12 x 2	1.5	"
	"	36	20 x 11	16 x 10	1.5	"
	"	37	18 x 6	12 x 1.5	1	"
	(1-3)	38	21 x 20	8 x 8	2	"
	"	39	22 x 30	10 x 12	3.75	"
	"	40	22 x 20	10 x 10	1.5	"
	"	41	10 x 13	8 x 9	.5	"
	(2-2)	42	26 x 30	10 x 10	2	IIIA
	"	43	18 x 18	3.5 x 5	1.5	"
	"	44	30 x 32	10 x 10	2.5	"
	"	45	6 x 10	3 x 5	1.2	"
	"	46	30 x 30	17 x 11	1	"
	"	47	8 x 15	33 x 52	3	"
	"	48	36 x 48	14 x 21	1.5	"
	"	49	50 x 30	30 x 18	3.25	IIIA, V
	"	50	38 x 34	8 x 5	3.75	" "
	"	51	38 x 28	18 x 10	2	II, IIIA
	"	52	50 x 50	5 x 5	4.5	IIIA
	(1-2)	53	34 x 34	12 x 12	1.75	IIIA
	(2-2)	54	?	15 x 18	2.5	IIIA, V?

STRUCTURE SUMMARY (11)

Field Number(s) or Site Name		St.#	Base(m)	Top(m)	Height(m)	Periodization
Jalieza (cont.)	(2-2)	55	18 x 26	11 x 12	.25	IIIA
	(1-2)	56	25 x 25	6 x 7	.5	"
	"	57	28 x 36	12 x 13	1	"
	(2-2)	58	10 x 16	8 x 10	1.6	"
	(1-2)	59	80 x 75	54 x 50	1	LI, II, IIIA, V
	(2-2)	60	27 x 23	10 x 8	4.25	IIIA
	"	61	21 x 16	8 x 5	2.3	"
	"	62	17 x 22	7 x 12	2.5	"
	"	63	19 x 10	10 x 9	4.5	"
	"	64	19 x 10	10 x 9	4	"
	"	65	14 x 17	3 x 14	3	"
	"	66	10 x 20	6 x 15	4	"
	(1-3)	67	8 x 18	3 x 14	1	IV
	"	68	14 x 16	6 x 8	2	IV
	(2-2)	69	16 x 10	8 x 5	2.5	IIIA
	"	70	21 x 10	12 x 4	1.5	"
	"	71	17 x 10	4 x 4	5	"
	"	72	10 x 12	4.5 x 4.5	.7	"
	"	73	18 x 12	9 x 7	1	"
	(2-1)	74	3 x 1.5	3 x 1.5	.5	"
	"	75	25 x 25	40 x 40	3	"
	"	76	32 x 30	24 x 24	2	"
	"	77	50 x 16	22 x 22	3	IIIA, V
	"	78	36 x 28	25 x 25	1	" "
	"	79	28 x 14	15 x 15	1	IIIA
	"	80	?	?	?	"
	"	81	28 x 21	10 x 5	.75	"
	"	82	28 x 35	20 x 29	.5	"

STRUCTURE SUMMARY (12)

Field Number(s) or Site Name		St.#	Base(m)	Top(m)	Height(m)	Periodization
Jalieza (cont.)	(2-1)	83	34 x 24	24 x 24	1	IIIA, V
	"	84	24 x 5	16 x 3	4	IIIA
	"	85	37 x 39	10 x 10	3	"
	"	86	36 x 30	25 x 25	1	"
	"	87	24 x 25	19 x 19	1	"
	(2-3)	88	12 x 15	2.5 x 3.5	3	IV
	"	89	21 x 17.5	7 x 7	1	IV
	(2-4)	90	21 x 40	7 x 12	1	IV
	(1-4)	91	21 x 26	5 x 5	2.25	IV

STRUCTURE SUMMARY (13)

Field Number(s) or Site Name		St.#	Base(m)	Top(m)	Height(m)	Period-ization
ZA-SRJ-SRJ-1 (Fig. A. XI-25)	LI-12, IIIA-10, IIIB-21	1	95 x 62	27 x 8	8	LI, IIIA, IIIB
ZA-SRJ-SRJ-2 (Fig. A. XI-25)	EI-6, LI-13, 14, II-9, 10, IIIA-11, 12, IIIB-22, IV-95, V-44	1	60 x 48	7 x 12	2.75	LI, IIIA, IIIB
		2	56 x 75	?	2.5	LI, IIIA, IIIB, V
		3	30 x 50	?	1.2	LI, IIIA, V
		4	30 x 35	?	1.0	IIIA
		5	54 x 54	6 x 14	19	EI, LI, II, IIIA
		6	48 x 38	5 x 8	2.75	EI, LI, II, IIIA
		7	35 x 82	?	1.25	EI, LI, II, IIIA
		8	22 x 38	?	1.25	EI, LI, II, IIIA
		9	67 x 43	24 x 25	9.5	IIIA
		10	30 x 32	8 x 8	2.25	IIIA
		11	26 x 26	10 x 10	2.5	II, IIIA, IV
		11 Platform	100 x 100	?	1.5	II, IIIA, IV
		12	50 x 50	20 x 25	2.5	LI, II, IIIA, V
ZA-TRI-LAR-2	LI-53, II-33	1B	21 x 20	8 x 7	3.0	LI, II
		2B	13 x 15	8 x 9	1.0	LI, II
ZA-TRI-TRI-20 (Fig. A. XI-26)	LI-54, II-104, IIIA-65, IIIB-48, IV-28, 29, 30, V-143, 144, 145, 146, 147	1	88 x 54	32 x 18	2.75	IIIA
		2	64 x 63	20 x 20	2.0	IIIA, IV, V
		3	86 x 80	28 x 24	2.0	IIIA
		4	94 x 65	?	1.75	IIIA
		5	30 x 72	60 x 17	.5	IIIA
		6	72 x 53	?	1.75	IIIA

STRUCTURE SUMMARY (14)

Field Number(s) or Site Name		St.#	Base(m)	Top(m)	Height(m)	Period-ization
ZA-TRI-TRI-20 (cont.)		7	87 x 66	25 x 25	2.0	IIIA, V
		8	50 x 54	33 x 26	1.8	II, IIIA, V
		9	66 x 75	18 x 26	2.25	IIIA, V
		10	120 x 100	40 x 25	3.0	IIIA
		11	75 x 70	45 x 35	1.8	LI, IIIA, V
		12	80 x 55	?	1.75	IIIA
		13	?	?	2.0	IIIA
		14	80 x 80	32 x 32	1.5	IIIA
		15	60 x 48	?	1.5	IIIA
		16	?	?	1.5	IIIA, IV
		17	63 x 50	10 x 13	3.25	IIIA, IV
		18	47 x 43	13 x 12	2.0	IIIA
		19	38 x 36	15 x 13	1.4	IIIA
		20	43 x 50	15 x 15	1.5	IIIA
		21	63 x 87	40 x 48	1.5	IIIA
		22	140 x 54	45 x 20	2.0	IIIA
		23	?	?	1.75	IIIA, V
		24	90 x 130	47 x 47	2.5	IIIA, IIIB
		25	?	?	1.75	IIIA
		26	95 x 80	55 x 32	1.8	IIIA, IV, V
ZA-ZA-EZ-1 (Fig. A. XI-27)	TL-1, SJ-1, G-2, LI-46, IIIA-55, V-107	1	74 x 50	42 x 30	1.5	TL, SJ, G, LI, IIIA
		2	40 x 60	?	1	TL, SJ, G, IIIA, V
		3	26 x 44	10 x 6	2.5	TL, SJ, G, IIIA, V
		4	37 x 37	20 x 20	1.5	LI, IIIA, V

STRUCTURE SUMMARY (15)

Field Number(s) or Site Name		St.#	Base(m)	Top(m)	Height(m)	Period-ization
ZA-ZA-ROA-1 (Fig. A. XI-28)	EI-24, LI-52, II-31, IIIA-62	1(st.)	28 x 34	10 x 8	4.5	LI, II, IIIA
		Bottom Platform 1	78 x 85	62 x 78	1.5	LI, II, IIIA
		Top Platform 1	46 x 76	28 x 66	3.0	LI, II, IIIA
		1 SW	60 x 60	25 x 10	3.0	LI, II
		2	65 x 60	20 x 20	1.35	II, IIIA
		3	42 x 40	15 x 6	8.5	EI, LI, II, IIIA
		4	44 x 30	5 x 4	9	LI, II,
		5	61 x 47	25 x 5	1.25	LI, II, IIIA
		6	96 x 44	64 x 20	1.6	LI, II, IIIA
ZA-ZA-TR-1	II-32, IIIA-63, IIIB-47, V-142	1	Roughly 50m in diameter		1.5	IIIA, IIIB, V
		2	60 x 37.5	7 x 14	1.5	IIIA, IIIB, V
ZA-ZA-TR-2	LI-53, II-33, IIIA-63, IIIB-47, 68, V-142	1	70 x 75	25 x 40	1.75	LI, II, V, IIIA, IIIB
		2	60 x 100	50 x 25	1	" "
ZA-ZA-ZA-2 (Zaachila) (Fig. A. XI-29)	TL-7, SJ-8, G-9, Ros-21, EI-64, LI-152, II-106, IIIA-37, 38, 39, 283, IIIB-31, V-76, 77, 78, 528	A	25 x 25	12 x 15	5	
		B north	35 x 22	20 x 12	2	
		B south	48 x 37	34 x 14	2	
		C	36 x 22	8 x 4	7	
		D	?	?	-	
		E	48 x 48	15 x 23	8	
		F	48 x 35	26 x 18	4	

STRUCTURE SUMMARY (16)

Field Number(s) or Site Name		St.#	Base(m)	Top(m)	Height(m)	Period-ization
ZA-ZA-ZA-2 (cont.) (Zaachila)		G	20 x 21	12 x 13	1	
		H	190 x 44	?	4	
		I	33 x 32	22 x 22	2	
		J	43 x 38	23 x 14	3	
		K	36 x 58	28 x 50	3.5	
		X	15 x ?	?	5	
ZA-ZA-ZA-3	IIIB-72	1	42 x 38	4 x 4	6.75	IIIB
		2	56 x 45	?	1.75	IIIB
ZA-ZA-ZA-7	IIIB-71, V-102	1	58 x 65	?	1.0	IIIB, V
ZAA-ZAA-ZA-8	LI-45, II-26, IIIA-54, IIIB-37, IV-20, V-101	1	31 x 29	11 x 6	4	II, IIIB, IV
		2	58 x 20	?	1.5	II, IIIA, IIIB
		3	75 x 50	10 x 10	0.5	II, IIIA
		4	50 x 30	5 x 5	0.5	II, IIIA
ZAA-ZAA-ZAA-12	EI-16, 17, LI-42, 43, II-23, 24, IIIA-309, V-96	1	24 x 22	10 x 8	3.5	EI, LI, II, IIIA
		2	20 x 21	12 x 15	1.35	EI, LI
		3	20 x 17	7 x 8	2.0	LI, II
		4	30 x 32	8 x 9	4	LI, II, IIIA, V
ZI-CIE-CIE-1	IIIA-90, IIIB-52, V-201	1	65 x 65	25 x 25	4.5	IIIA, IIIB, V
		2	50 x 52.5	20 x 5	14	IIIA, IIIB
ZI-CIE-CIE-2 (Fig. A. XI-30)	EI-59, LI-66, II-40, IIIA-89, IIIB-51, V-200, 529	1	25 x 25	6 x 5	5	EI, LI, IIIA, V
		2	101 x 82.5	7 x 7	4	EI, II, IIIA, IIIB
		3	?	?	1.6	IIIA, IIIB, V

STRUCTURE SUMMARY (17)

Field Number(s) or Site Name		St.#	Base(m)	Top(m)	Height(m)	Period-ization
ZI-CIE-CIE-2 (cont.)		4	75 x 75	50 x 50	.5	EI, IIIA, IIIB, V
		5	77.5 x 70	12 x 10	1.75	EI, II, IIIA, V
ZI-CIE-CIE-13 (Fig. A. XI-31)	EI-56, LI-51 II-37	1	20 x 28	6 x 5	6	EI, LI, II
		2	12 x 12	10 x 5	.65	EI, LI, II
		3	5 x 16	5 x 13	.5	EI, LI, II
		4	23 x 8	19 x 6	1.5	EI, LI, II
ZI-CIE-CIE-15 (Fig. A. XI-31)	LI-51	1A	48 x 32	10 x 14	4.6	LI
		2A	31 x 11	21 x 4	2.0	LI } possible ball court
		3A	31 x 11	21 x 4	2.0	LI }
ZI-SAT-SAT-2 (Fig. A. XI-32)	TL-6 SJ-7 G-8 Ros-15 EI-43 LI-130, 131, 136 II-93	1	38 x 54	7 x 3.5	10	ROS, EI, LI, II, IIIA, IIIB
		2	34 x 16	12 x 6	5	TL, SJ, G, ROS, EI, LI, II, IIIA
	IIIA-251 IV-96 V-418, 419	3	34 x 16	10 x 8	3	TL, SJ, G, ROS, EI, LI, II, IIIA
	IIIB-70	4	27 x 26	10 x 18	4	TL, SJ, G, ROS, EI, LI, II, IIIA
		5	59 x 25	17 x 8	2.65	" "
		6	42 x 40	10 x 13	3.0	" "
		7	30 x 20	10 x 10	.75	IIIA
ZI-SAT-SAT-5 (Fig. A. XI-33)	IIIA-250	1	22 x 16	11 x 3.5	2.25	IIIA
		2	30 x 16	7 x 7	2.0	"
		3	12 x 10	2.5 x 2.5	2.0	"
		4	12 x 12	4 x 7	2.5	"

STRUCTURE SUMMARY (18)

Field Number(s) or Site Name		St.#	Base(m)	Top(m)	Height(m)	Period-ization
ZI-SCM-SCM-22, SBM-2 SBM-1 SCM-21 (Santa Cruz Mixtepec)	II-75 IIIA-177, 178, 179	1	11 x 16	6 x 2	2.25	IIIA, IV
		2	18 x 18	10 x 10	3.0	IIIA, IV, V
		3	10 x 18	5 x 9	4.0	IIIA, IV
	IV-67, 68, 69, 70, 71	4	13 x 10	4 x 5	1.5	IIIA
	V-324, 325, 326, 327, 328, 329, 330, 331, 332, 335	5	10 x 20	10 x 12	1.5	IIIA
		6	9 x 12	4 x 4	1.0	IIIA
		7	16 x 9	8 x ?	8.0	IIIA, IV, V
		8	12 x 8	9 x 7	1.0	IIIA
		9	6 x 6	?	?	IIIA
		10	18 x 9	12 x 2	?	IIIA
		11	20 x 24	9 x 12	5.8	IIIA, IV
		12	23 x 18	15 x 7	4.25	IIIA, IV
		13	13 x 10	?	0.5	V
		14	35 x 15	?	3.5	IIIA, IV
		15	13 x 15	8 x 11	1.5	IIIA, IV, V
		16	13 x 13	13 x 13	0.25	IIIA, IV, V
		17	4 x 2	?	0.5	IIIA, IV, V
		18	11 x 11	11 x 11	0.2	IIIA, IV
		19	16 x 10	8 x 3.5	2.0	IIIA, IV
ZI-SCM-TR-1 (Fig. A. XI-35)	IIIA-220	1	20 x 14	10 x 5	3.5	IIIA
		2	22 x 12	11 x 6	3	"
ZI-SCM-TR-4 (Fig. A. XI-36)	IIIA-222	1	11 x 17	5 x 10	2.25	IIIA
		2	9 x 9	6 x 5	.5	IIIA
		(platform)	6 x 5	5 x 5	.5	IIIA

STRUCTURE SUMMARY (19)

Field Number(s) or Site Name		St.#	Base(m)	Top(m)	Height(m)	Period-ization
ZI-SCQ-LS-1 (Fig. A. XI-37)	LI-68, 69 IIIA-92	1	21 x 26	3.5 x 10	6	LI, IIIA
	V-202, 203	2	25 x 12	22 x 2.5	2	LI, IIIA
		3	12 x 22	7.5 x 20	3	LI, IIIA
		4	22 x 30	12 x 6.5	3	LI, IIIA
		5	4 x 20	2 x 12	1.5	LI, IIIA
		6	22 x 22	7 x 8	6	IIIA
		7	12 x 17.5	7 x 7	1.6	IIIA
		8	5 x 24	4 x 24	0.25	IIIA
ZI-SCQ-LS-2						
(Fig. A. XI-38)	LI-70 II-42	1	21 x 17	7 x 4	2	LI, II, V
	IIIA-94 V-204	2	31 x 26	2.5 x 7	1.75	LI, II, V
		3	25 x 22	7 x 3.5	3.6	LI, II, V
		4	10 x 12	4 x 6	?	LI, II, V
		5	40 x 50	?	1	LI, II, V
ZI-SG-PDP-1	EI-40 LI-123 II-85, 86	1	100 x 90	36 x 18	1.25	EI, LI, II, IIIA
	IIIA-233,234	2A	55 x 70	25 x 25	1.75	IIIA
		2B	55 x 25	14 x 18	0.5	IIIA
		3	50 x 60	8 x 8	1.5	II, IIIA
		4	29 x 31	8 x 6	2.75	IIIB, IV
ZI-SG-SG-2	LI-107 II-77	1	50 x 45	18 x 12	1.75	LI, IIIA
	IIIA-199 V-370	2	58 x 102	25 x 61	2.5	LI, II, IIIA
		3	25 x 35	10 x 20	0.25	LI, II, IIIA
		4	44 x 50	21 x 24	0.5	LI, II, IIIA
		5	25 x 25	12 x 12	.25	LI, II, IIIA, V

STRUCTURE SUMMARY (20)

Field Number(s) or Site Name		St.#	Base(m)	Top(m)	Height(m)	Period-ization
ZI-SG-SG-3	LI-108 II-78 IIIA-200	1	8 x 11	?	2.2	LI, II, IIIA
	IIIB-57	platform	26 x 67	?	1.5	" "
		2	71 x 68	23 x 22	1.5	LI, II, IIIA
		3	55 x 50	18 x 20	2.5	LI, II, IIIA, IIIB
ZI-SG-SG-4 (Fig. A. XI-39)	ROS-13 EI-39	1	50 x 59	21 x 22	1.0	II, IIIA
	LI-122 II-84 IIIA-232	2	52 x 45	9 x 9	2.5	ROS, EI, LI, II, IIIA, V
	V-386	3	35 x 40	25 x 19	0.5	IIIA

STRUCTURE SUMMARY (21)

Field Number(s) or Site Name		St.#	Base(m)	Top(m)	Height(m)	Period-ization
ZI-SMA-SJL-1 (Fig. A. XI-40)	IIIA-271	1	12 x 10	6 x 4	2	IIIA
		2	10 x 6	6 x 2	1	IIIA
ZI-SMA-SMA-2 (Fig. A. XI-41)	LI-147 II-101 IIIA-290	1	19 x 16	12 x 7	2	LI, II, IIIA
		2	27 x 14	14 x 13	1.5	LI, II, IIIA
		3	14 x 23	6.5 x 9	2	LI, II, IIIA
		4	11 x 11	4 x 5	1	LI, II, IIIA
ZI-SMA-SMA-5 (Figs. A. XI-42, 43)	II-97, 99 IIIA-272, 273 IV-83-85 V-451-455, 517	1	17 x 9	?	1.0	IIIA, IV
		2	19 x 21	7 x 7	3.3	IIIA, IV, V
		3	13 x 10	3.5 x 7	1.0	IIIA, IV, V
		4	22 x 22	6 x 11	3.0	IIIA, IV V
		5	25 x 25	10 x 12	6.75	IIIA, V
		6	17 x 15	8 x 6	3.25	IIIA, V
		7	24 x ?	10 x 12	8.25	IIIA, V
		ballcourt 8	overall 31 x 36.5		3.3	IIIA, V
		9	8 x 16	6 x 14	1.0	II, IIIA, IV, V
		10	10 x 13	6 x 10	1.0	II, IIIA, IV, V
		11	16 x 32	8 x 13	1.8	II, IIIA, IV, V
		12	20 x 12	12 x 2.5	5.0	II, IIIA, IV, V
		13	11 x 30	8 x 26	1.5	IV, V

STRUCTURE SUMMARY (22)

Field Number(s) or Site Name		St.#	Base(m)	Top(m)	Height(m)	Period-ization
ZI-SMA-SMA-5 (cont.)		14	19 x 19	8 x 6	4.25	IV, V
		15	4 x 10	2 x 4	1.25	IV, V
		16	11 x 9	6 x 3	1.0	IV, V
		17	?	12 x 6	0.5	IV
		18	?	15 x 2.5	0.5	IV
		19	?	3 x 15	0.5	IV
		20	?	7 x 3	2.5	IIIA, IV, V
		21	21 x 12	7 x 3.5	?	IV
		22	18 x 6	8 x 2	1.5	II, IV, V
		23	14 x 10	3 x 4	3.7	II, IV, V
		24	10 x 16	4 x 8	?	IV
		25	32 x 30	17 x 10	3.0	IV, V
		26	14 x 16	4 x 6	1.6	IV
		27	14 x 21	5 x 7	2.6	IV
		28	10 x 18	7 x 18	1.5	IV
		29	10 x 10	8 x 4	1.	IV
ZI-SMA-SMA-32 (Fig. A. XI-44)	IIIA-285 V-489	1	18 x 18	10 x 10	3	IIIA, V
		2	14 x 13.5	?	1.75	IIIA
ZI-SMA-SMA-40	IV-93 V-480	1	5 x 12	3 x 10	.5	IV, V
		2	5 x 12	5 x 12	0.25	IV, V
		3	15 x 5	13 x 3	0.5	IV, V
		4	5 x 5	5 x 5	0.25	IV, V
ZI-SPH-SPH-1	II-72 IIIA-171	1	65 x 40	?	1.50	II, IIIA
ZI-SPH-SPH-2	LI-99	1	71 x 56	32 x 24	0.75	LI, II, IIIA
	II-69, 70, 71	2	40 x 55	24 x 33	1.5	II, IIIA
	IIIA-167, 168, 169, 170	3	12 x 20	10 x 12	0.5	IIIA

STRUCTURE SUMMARY (23)

Field Number(s) or Site Name		St.#	Base(m)	Top(m)	Height(m)	Period-ization
ZI-SPH-SPH-2 (cont.)		4	40 x 35	8 x 9	3.8	II, IIIA
		5	35 x 35	?	1.0	II, IIIA
		6	55 x 65	?	1.0	IIIA
		7	69 x 55	35 x 20	1.5	LI, IIIA
		8	60 x 59	40 x 40	1.5	IIIA
		9	35 x 35	35 x 35	1.0	II, IIIA
ZI-SPH-SPH-5	EI-32 LI-98 II-68 IIIA-166 V-319	1	100 x 100	30 x 30	1.75	EI, LI, II, IIIA
ZI-SPH-SPH-6 (Fig. A. XI-45)	TL-5 SJ-6	1	25 x 25	4 x 4	1.5	II
	G-7 ROS-12 EI-37, 38 LI-109, 110, 111, 112, 113, 114	2	50 x 50	12 x 10	1.5	TL/SJ, G/R, EI, LI, IIIA, IV
		3	18 x 25	6 x 10	5.0	LI, IIIA, IIIB, IV
	II-79, 80, 81, 82	Platform	78 x 45	75 x 45	0.5	LI, IIIA, IIIB, IV
	IIIA-202, 203, 204, 205, 206, 207, 208 IIIB-58, 59, 60	4	80 x 75	25 x 20	1.25	LI, II, IIIA, V
		5	75 x 60	35 x 30	0.8	LI, II, IIIA
	IV-74, 75 V-371	6	60 x 42	25 x 25	0.5	EI, LI, II, IIIA
		7	85 x 35	?	2.0	LI, II, IIIA, V
		8	70 x 60	25 x 15	1.0	IIIA, IIIB
		9	75 x 67	40 x 40	1.0	IIIA, IIIB
		10	80 x 54	32 x 30	1.0	II, IIIA
		11	95 x 80	30 x 30	1.6	IIIA

STRUCTURE SUMMARY (24)

Field Number(s) or Site Name		St.#	Base(m)	Top(m)	Height(m)	Period-ization
ZI-SPH-SPH-9 (Fig. A. XI-46)	EI-35	1	41 x 40	14 x 23	2.5	EI
		2	37 x 62	15 x 30	1.5	EI
		3	80 x 37	25 x 31	1.25	EI
		4	58 x 85	18 x 50	2.75	EI
		5A	20 x 64	58 x 10	2.5	EI
		5B	26 x 20	16 x 10	2.0	EI
ZI-SPH-SPH-12	IIIA-211 IIIB-61 IV-76	1	46 x 20	20 x 10	2	IIIA, IIIB, IV
ZI-VDF-LB-3 (Fig. A. XI-47)	II-95 IIIA-256	1	15 x 15	10 x 9	?	II, IIIA
		2	20 x 18	9 x 10	?	" "
		3	18 x 9	12 x 3	?	" "
		4	25 x 18	12 x 13	5.25	" "
		5	18 x 18	8 x 6	3	" "
		6	20 x 20	4 x 5	1.5	" "
		7	19 x 15	8 x 5	2.5	" "
		8	15 x 10	6 x 6	2.5	" "
		9	20 x 20	?	1	" "
		10	21 x 10	13 x 11	2.25	" "
ZI-ZI-SN-1 (Fig. A. XI-48)	EI-29 LI-90 II-59 IIIA-145 V-277	1	75 x 60	45 x 40	1.5	LI, II, IIIA
		2	40 x 55	36 x 50	1.5	EI, LI, II, IIIA, V
		3	55 x 40	20 x 20	3.5	LI, II, IIIA
		4	60 x 60	?	0.8	LI, II, IIIA, V
ZI-ZI-SN-3 (Fig. A. XI-49)	ROS-10 EI-30 LI-91 II-60 IIIA-146	1	35 x 37.5	12 x 18	2.5	EI, LI, II
		2	60 x 32	21 x 30	2	ROS, EI, LI, II, IIIA
		3A	40 x 41	17 x 23	1.5	EI, LI, II

STRUCTURE SUMMARY (25)

Field Number(s) or Site Name		St.#	Base(m)	Top(m)	Height(m)	Period-ization
ZI-ZI-SN-3 (cont.)		3B	27 x 25	13 x 9	1.0	EI, LI, II
		4	22 x 18	12 x 8	2	EI, LI, II
		5	17 x 23	9 x 6	1.4	EI, LI, II
		6	60 x 45	35 x 30	.5	EI, LI, II
		7	17 x 13	15 x 13	.5	LI, II
ZI-ZI-SN-4 (Fig. A. XI-50)	EI-31, LI-97	1	40 x 42	11 x 20	3.0	II, IIIA
	II-67, IIIA-165	2	60 x 71	20 x 78	1.8	EI, LI, IIIA
	V-246	3	55 x 55	?	2.0	IIIA, V
		4	32 x 31	12 x 12	0.75	EI, LI, II, IIIA
ZI-ZI-ZI-1	ROS-8, EI-63, LI-78, II-51, IIIA-51, V-231	1	50 x 50	23 x 22	1.3	ROS, EI, LI, IIIA, V
ZI-ZI-ZI-2	LI-79, II-53	1	64 x 65	25 x 25	1.0	LI, II, IIIA
	IIIA-120, 121	2	37.5 x 37.5	12 x 12	?	LI, II, IIIA, V
	V-233	3	38 x 30	20 x 16	0.75	II, IIIA, V
		4	26 x 59	8 x 16	0.75	II, IIIA, V
		5	115 x 50	41.5 x 30	2.0	IIIA, V
		6	90 x 65	32 x 17	0.75	IIIA, V
		7	65 x 85	?	1.5	V
		8	20 x 20	?	0.25	IIIA
ZI-ZI-ZI-3	II-52, IIIA-118, IV-37, V-232	1	52 x 52	20 x 30	12	IIIA, IV, V

STRUCTURE SUMMARY (26)

Field Number(s) or Site Name		St.#	Base(m)	Top(m)	Height(m)	Period-ization
ZI-ZI-ZI-5 (Fig. A. XI-51)	EI-26, 62, LI-80, 81, 82	1	34 x 15	25 x 10	1.5	EI, II, IIIA
	II-54, 55, 56, IIIA-122, 123	2	28 x 22	12 x 8	1.6	II
	IIIB-69, V-234, 235	3	29 x 30	17 x 15	1.0	LI, V
		4	42 x 27	14 x 8	.75	II, IIIA
		5	30 x 30	?	.5	IIIA, V
		6	75 x 50	25 x 10	1.5	LI, IIIA
		7	50 x 26	?	1.5	IIIA, IIIB, V
		8	60 x 40	27 x 21	1.0	EI, LI, IIIA, V
ZI-ZI-ZI-8 (Fig. A. XI-51)	ROS-9, EI-26, LI-82	1N	20 x 30	15 x 10	1.0	ROS, EI, LI II, IIIA
	II-56, IIIA-123	1S	30 x 30	15 x 15	1.75	ROS, EI, LI II, IIIA

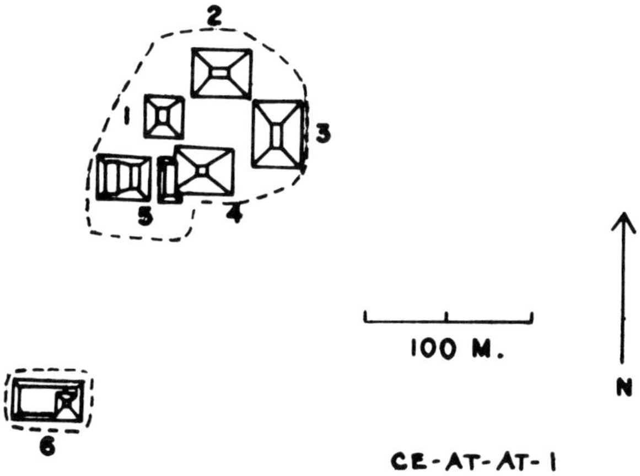

Figure A.XI-1. CE-AT-AT-1. 3-5-9, 3-6-22.

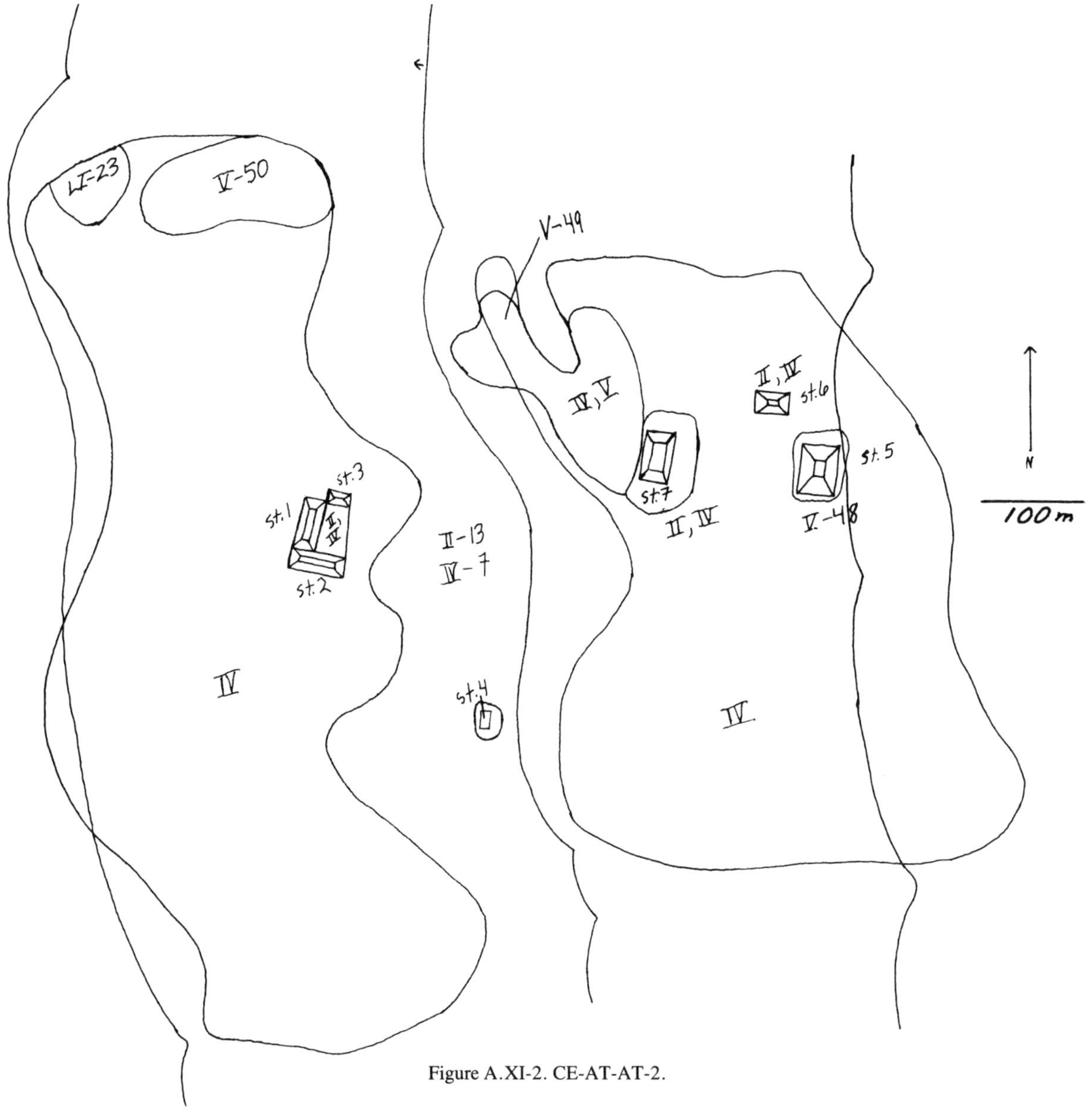

Figure A.XI-2. CE-AT-AT-2.

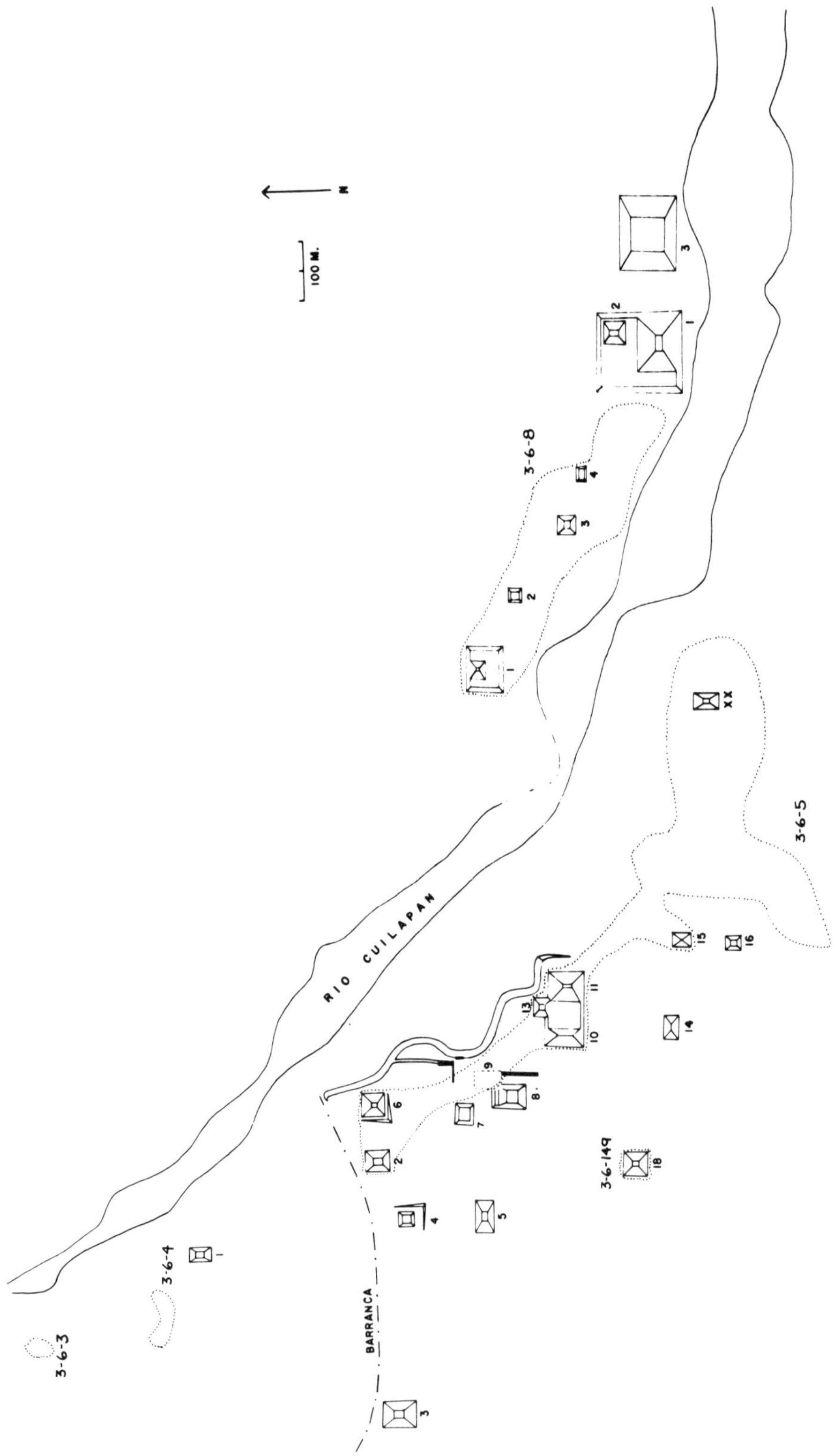

Figure A.XI-3. Cuilapan in Late I.

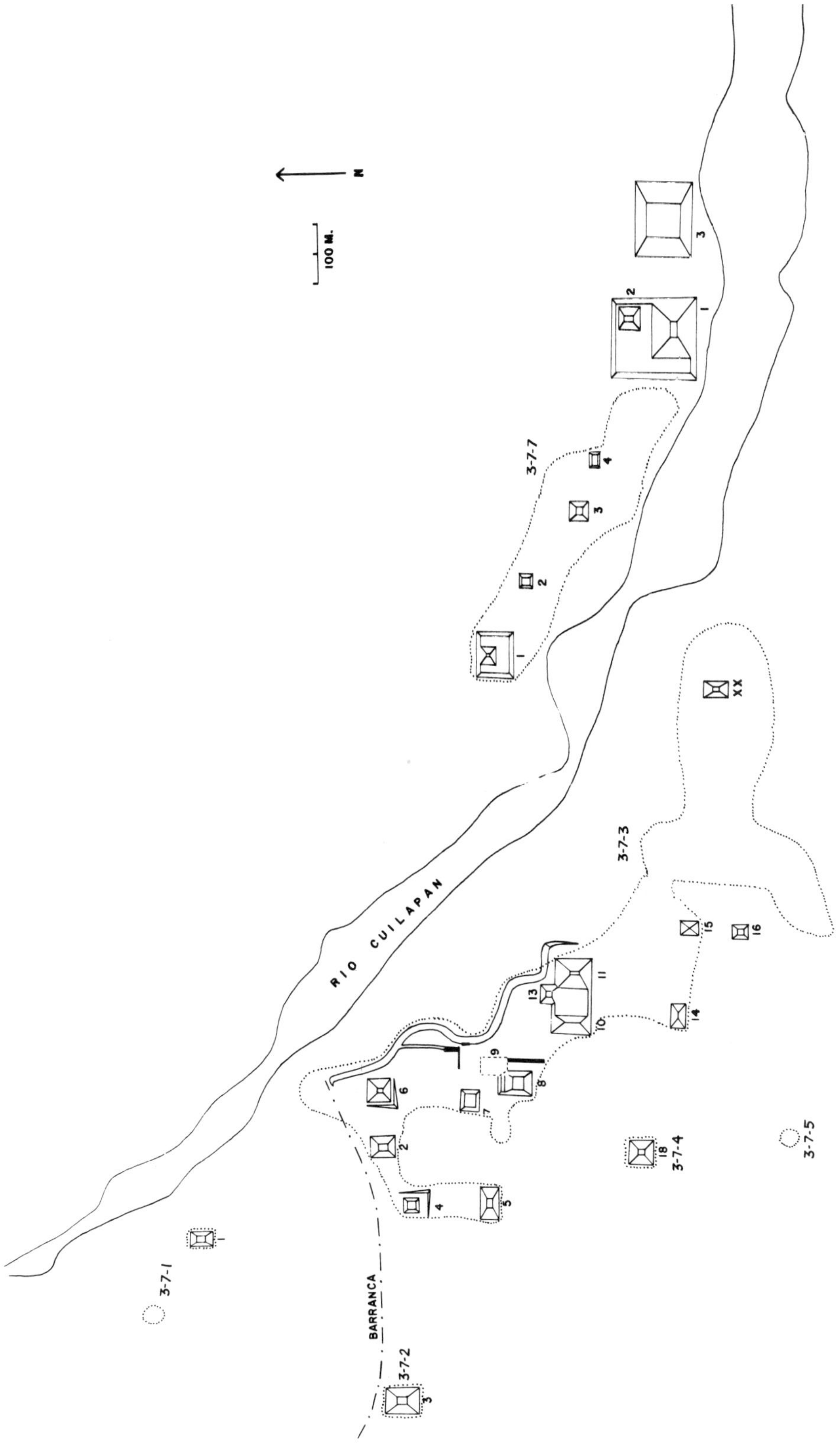

Figure A.XI-4. Cuilapan in Period II.

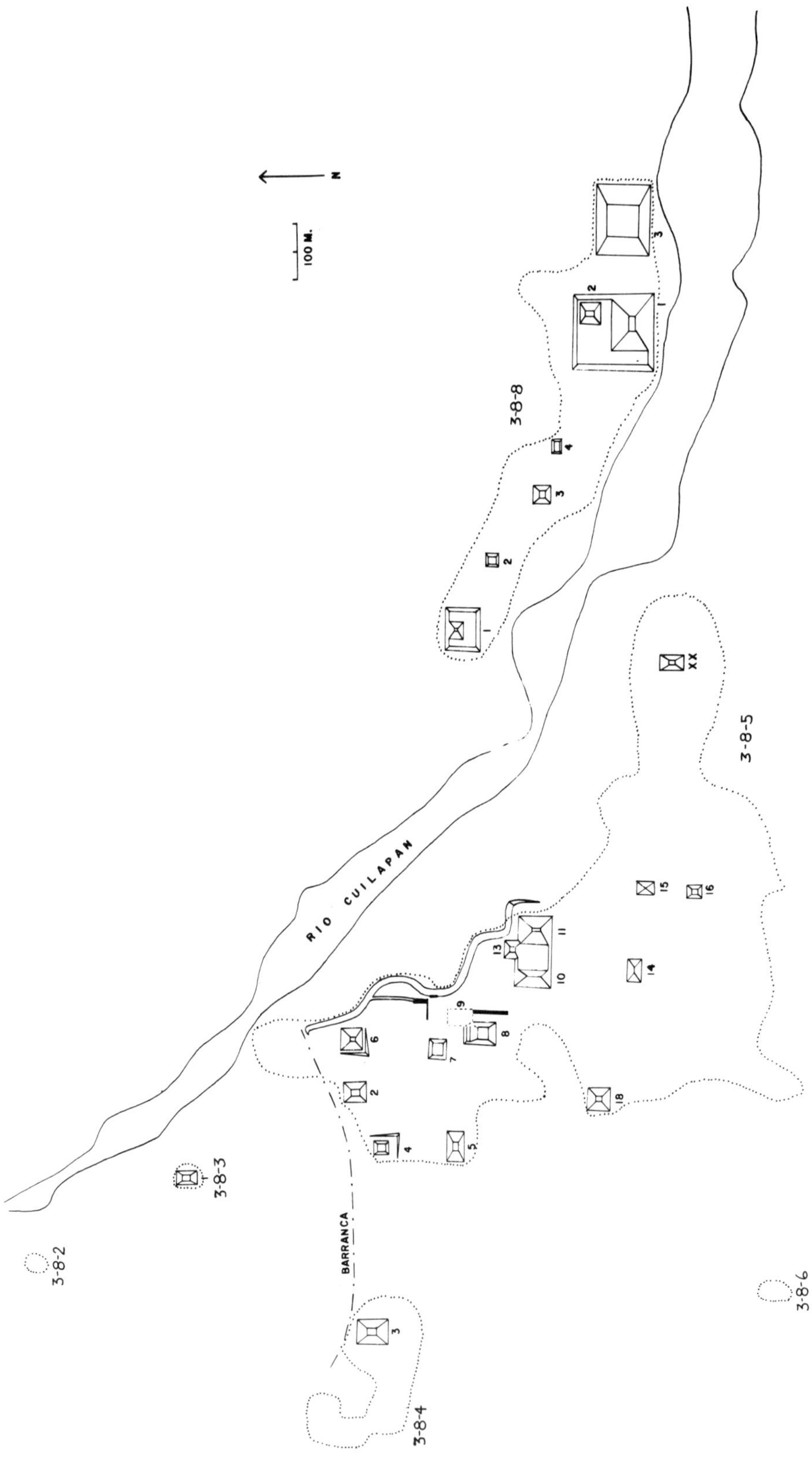

Figure A.XI-5. Cuilapan in Period IIIa.

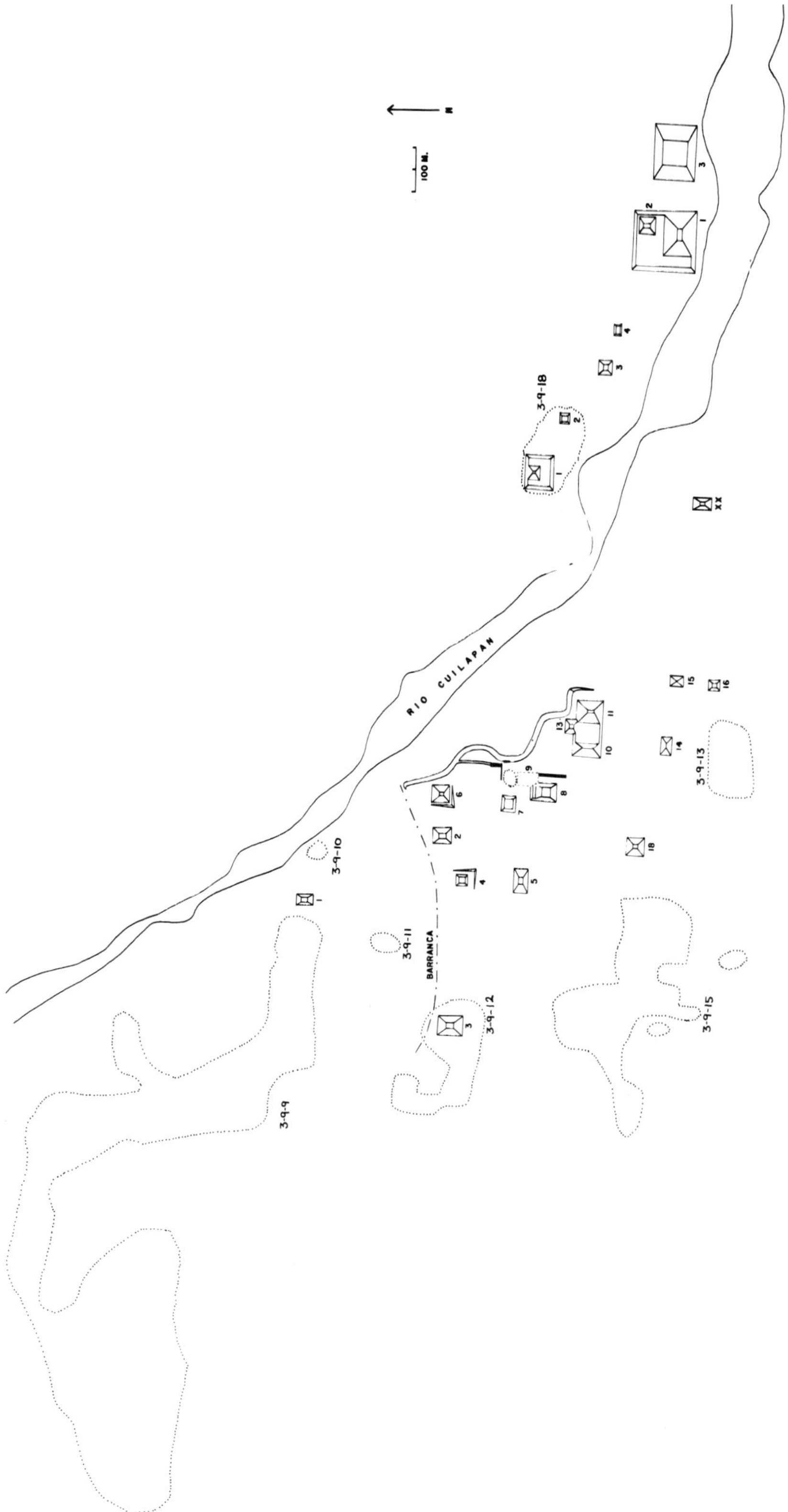

Figure A.XI-6. Cuilapan in Period IIIb.

Figure A.XI-7. Cuilapan in Period V.

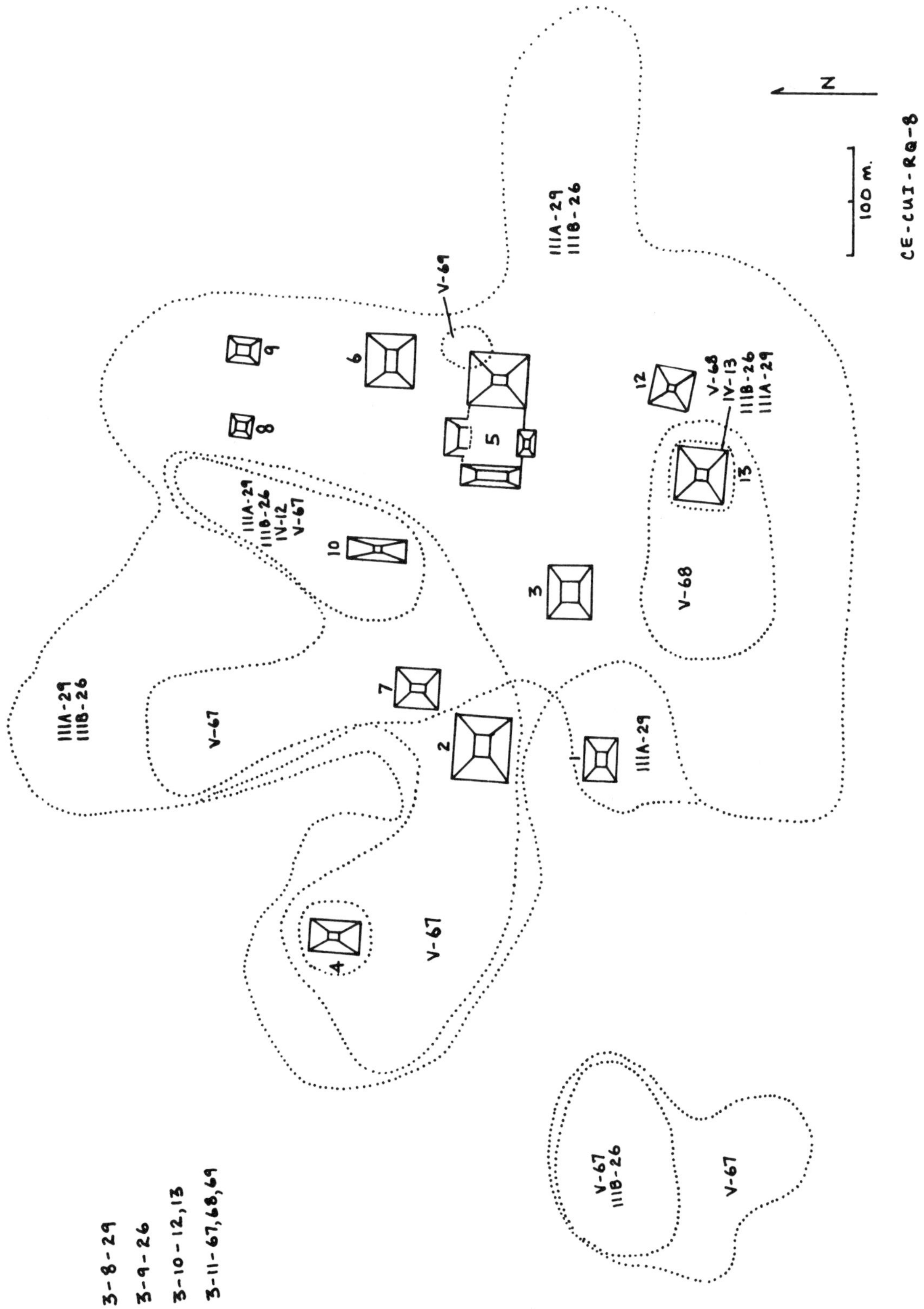

Figure A.XI-8. CE-CUI-RQ-8. Noriega.

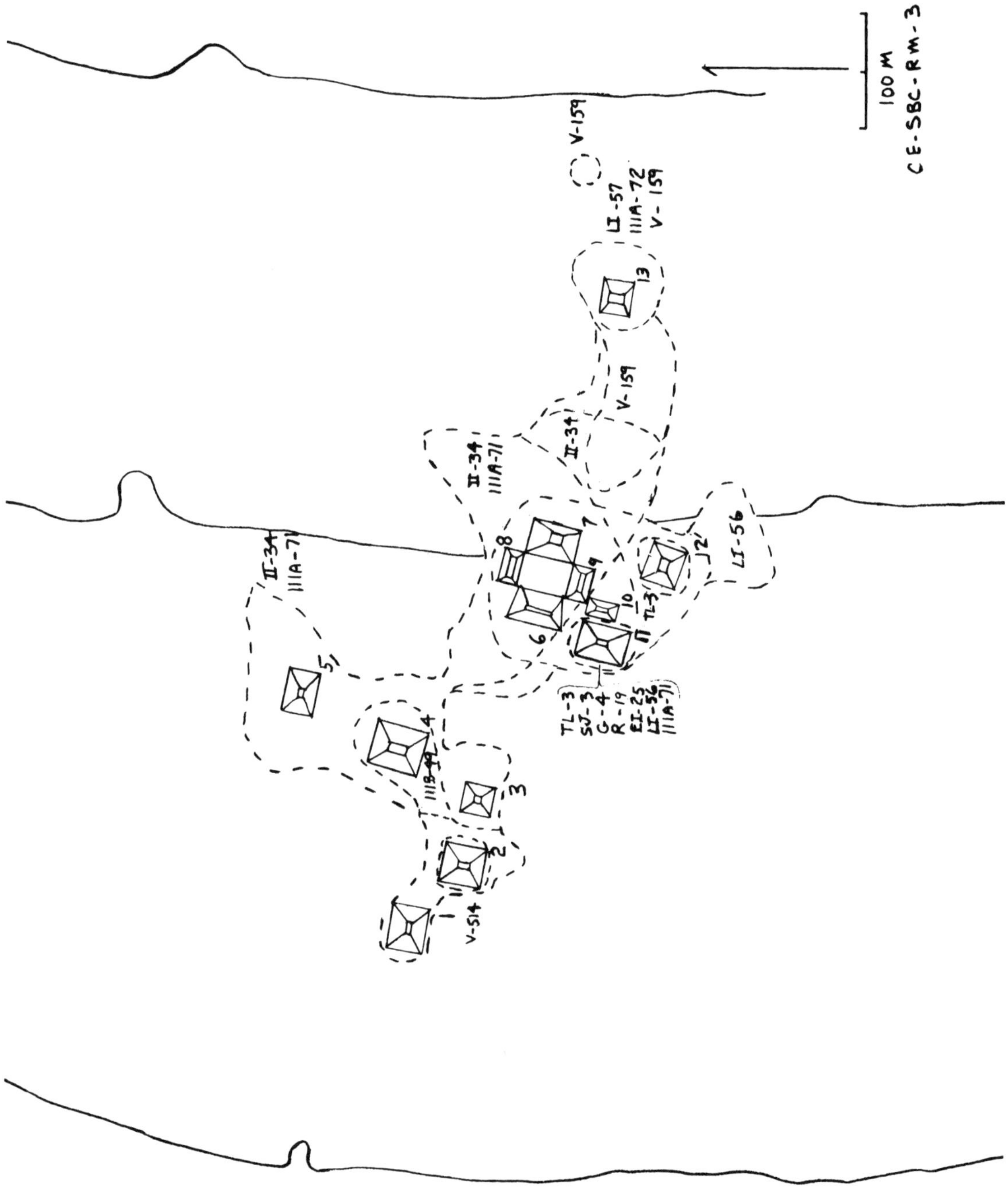

Figure A.XI-9. CE-SBC-RM-3.

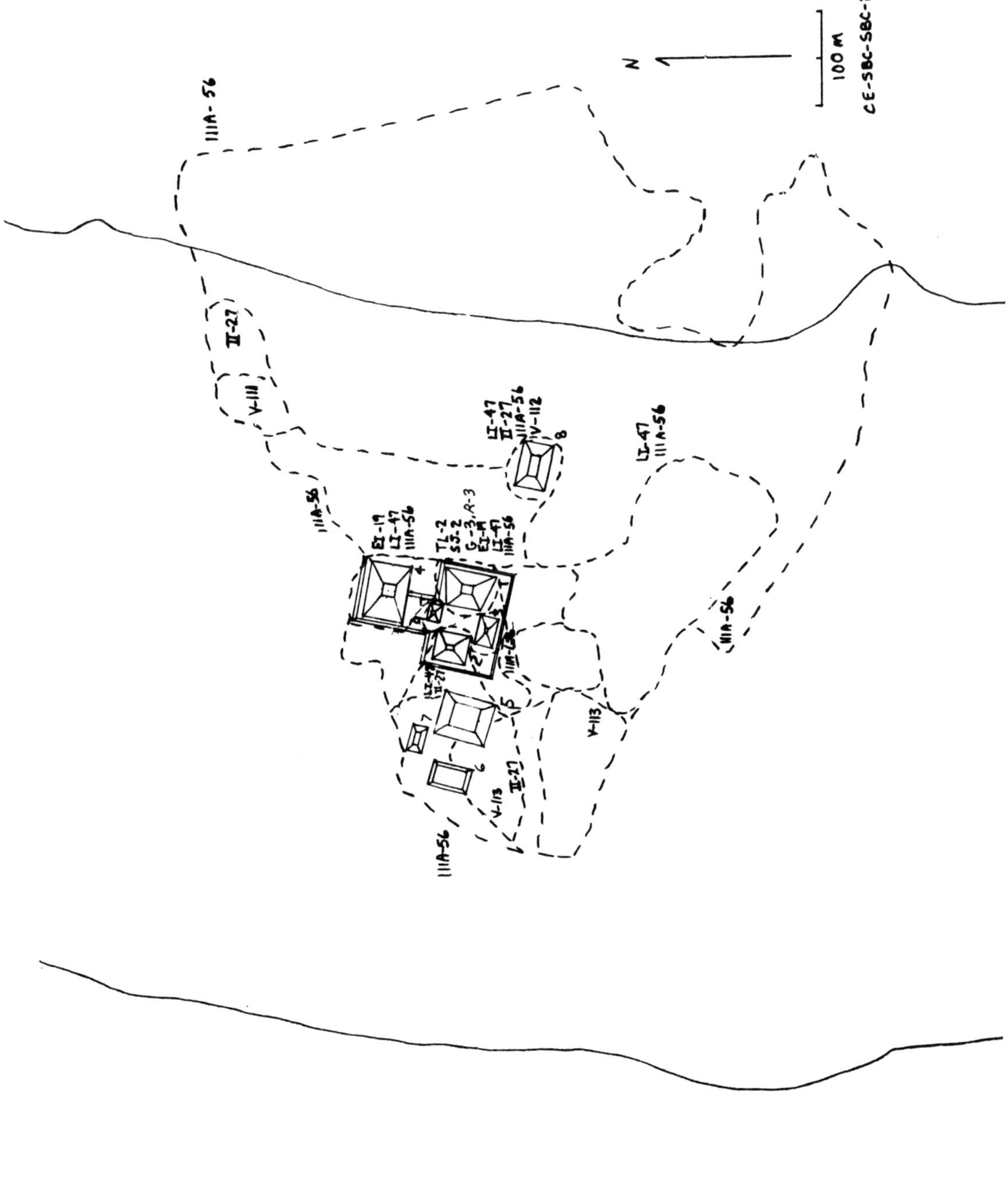

Figure A.XI-10. CE-SBC-SBC-2.

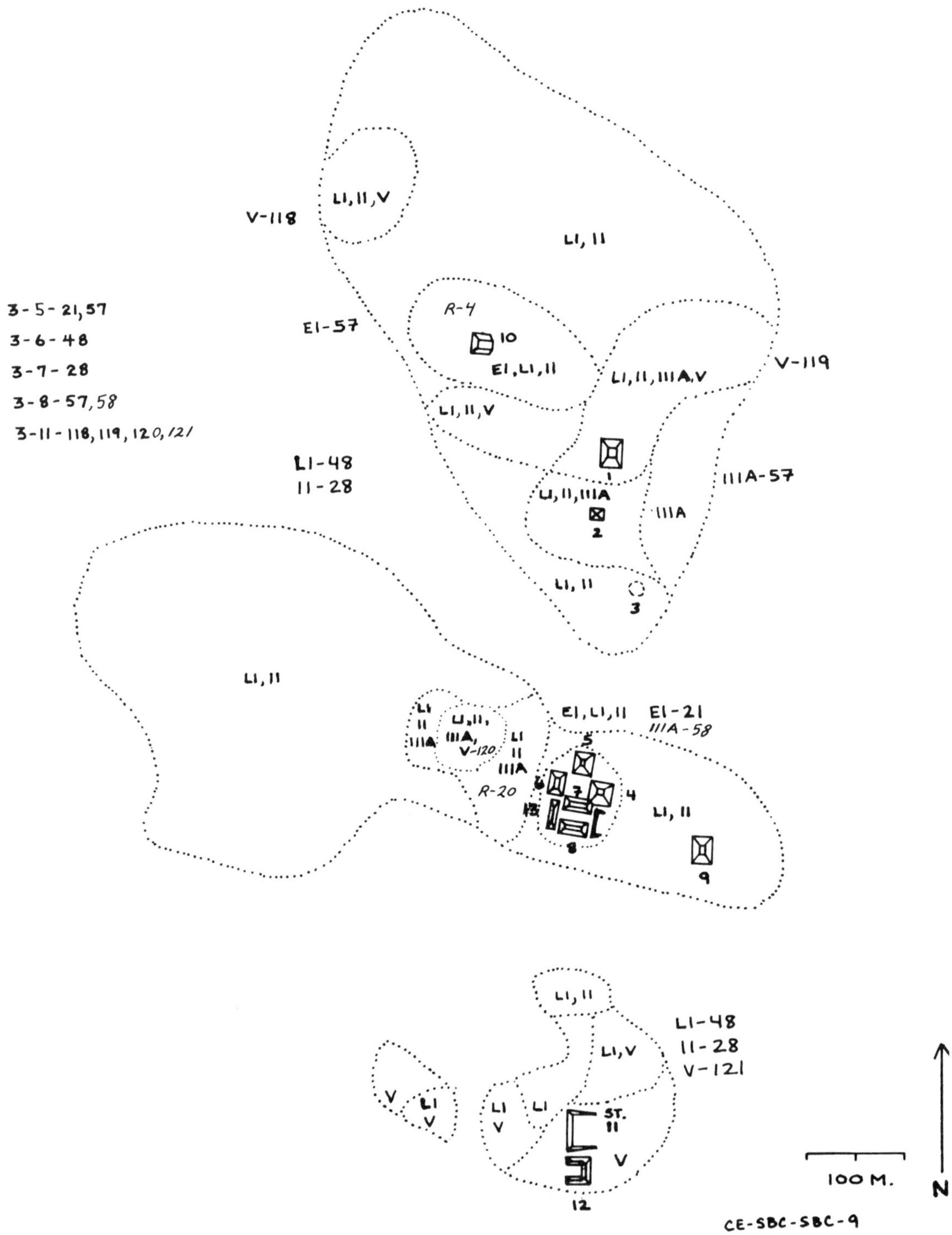

Figure A.XI-11. CE-SBC-SBC-9.

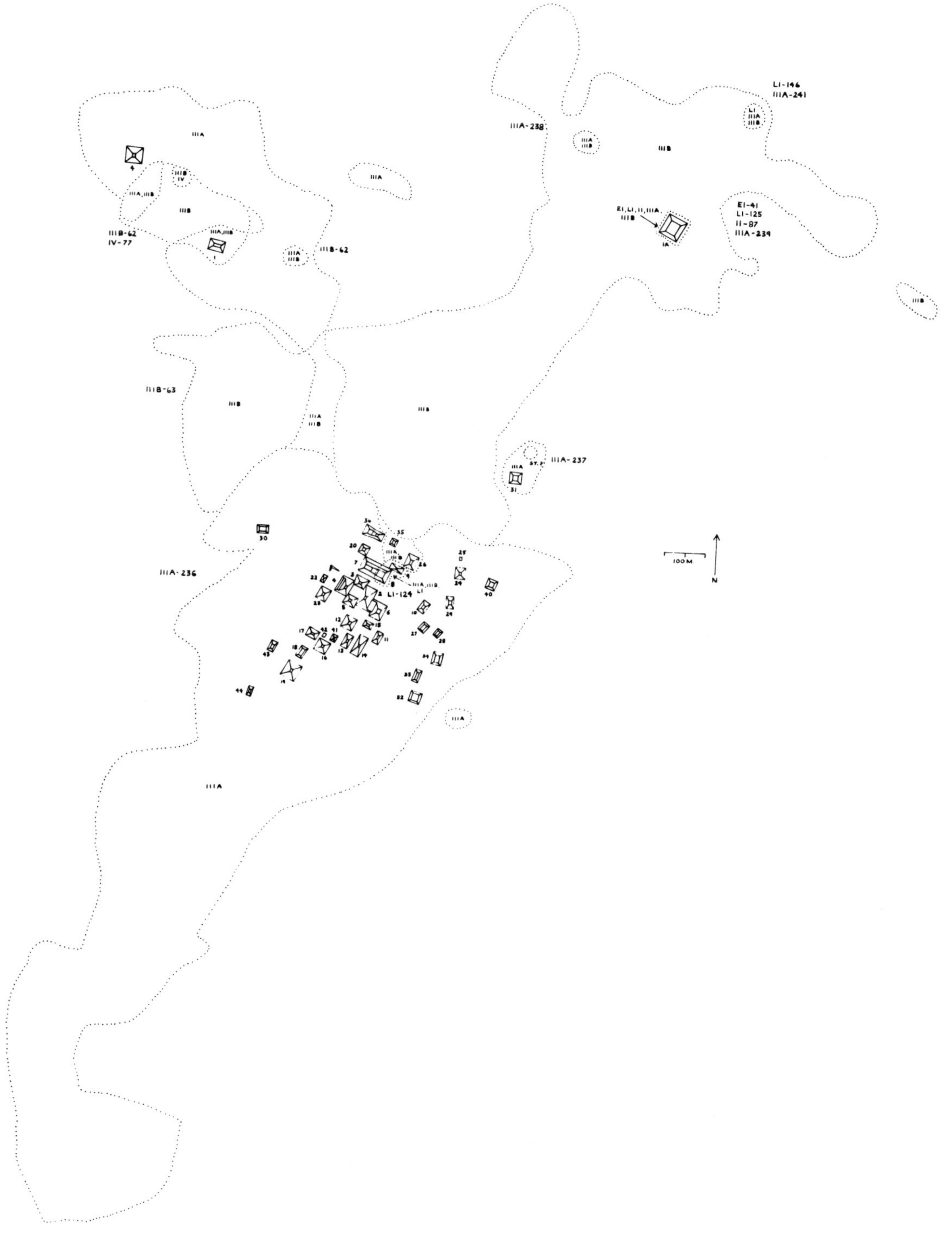

Figure A.XI-12. OC-OC-TM-1,2,3. Tejas de Morelos.

Figure A.XI-13. OC-SMT-SMT-11.

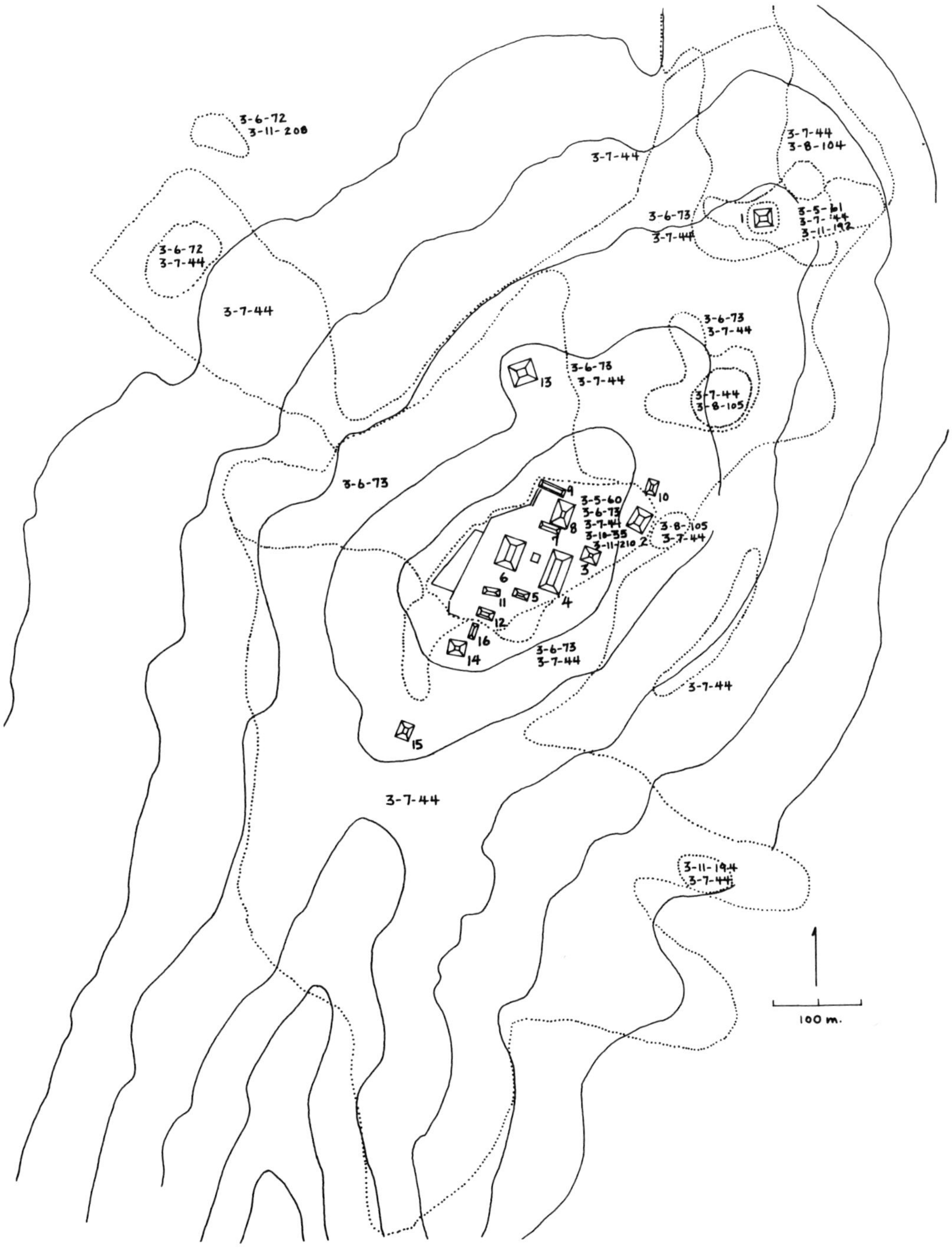

Figure A.XI-14. OC-SMT-SMT-23.

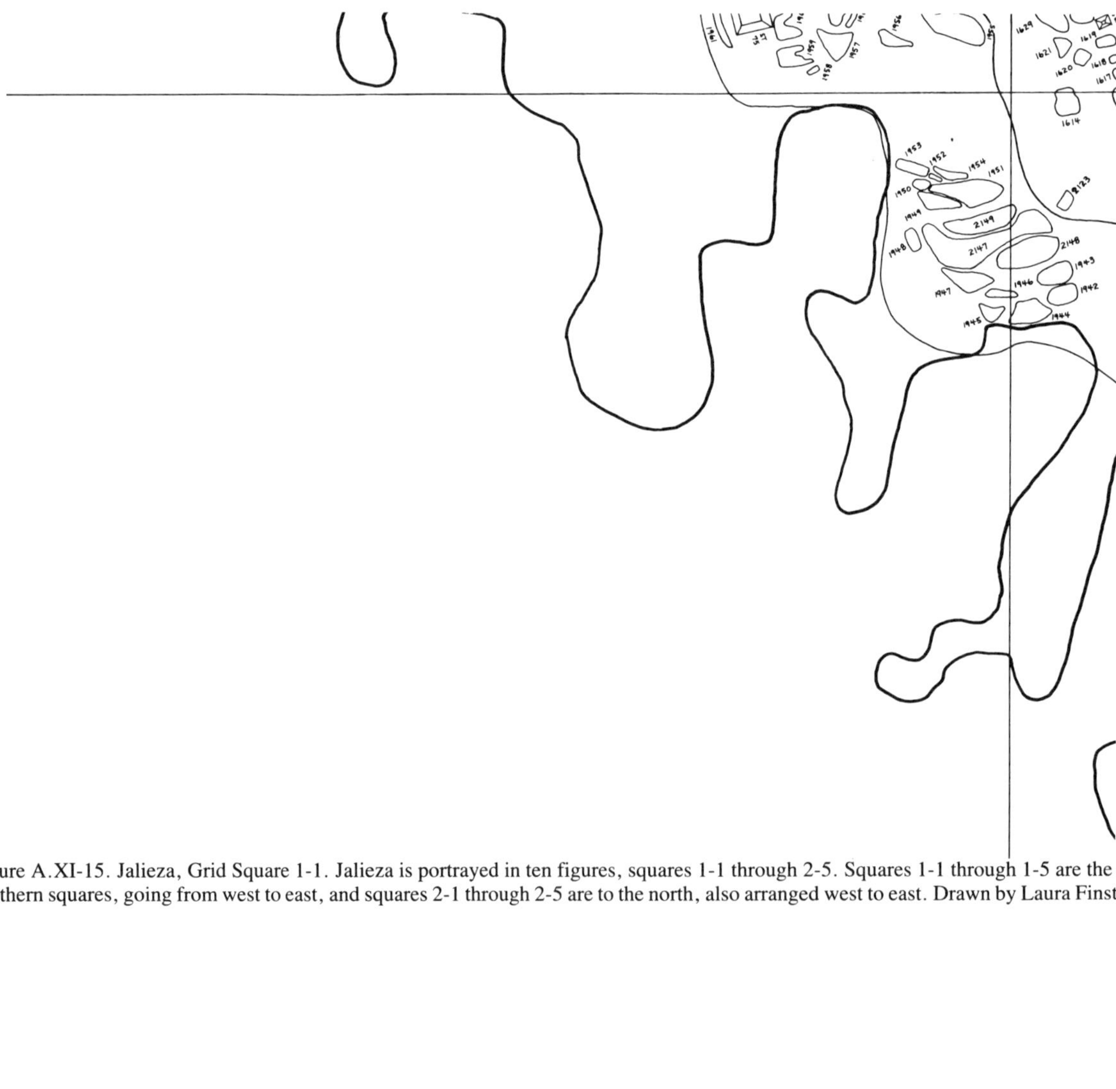

Figure A.XI-15. Jalieza, Grid Square 1-1. Jalieza is portrayed in ten figures, squares 1-1 through 2-5. Squares 1-1 through 1-5 are the five southern squares, going from west to east, and squares 2-1 through 2-5 are to the north, also arranged west to east. Drawn by Laura Finsten.

Figure A.XI-16. Jalieza, Grid Square 1-2. Drawn by Laura Finsten.

Figure A.XI-17. Jalieza, Grid Square 1-3. Drawn by Laura Finsten.

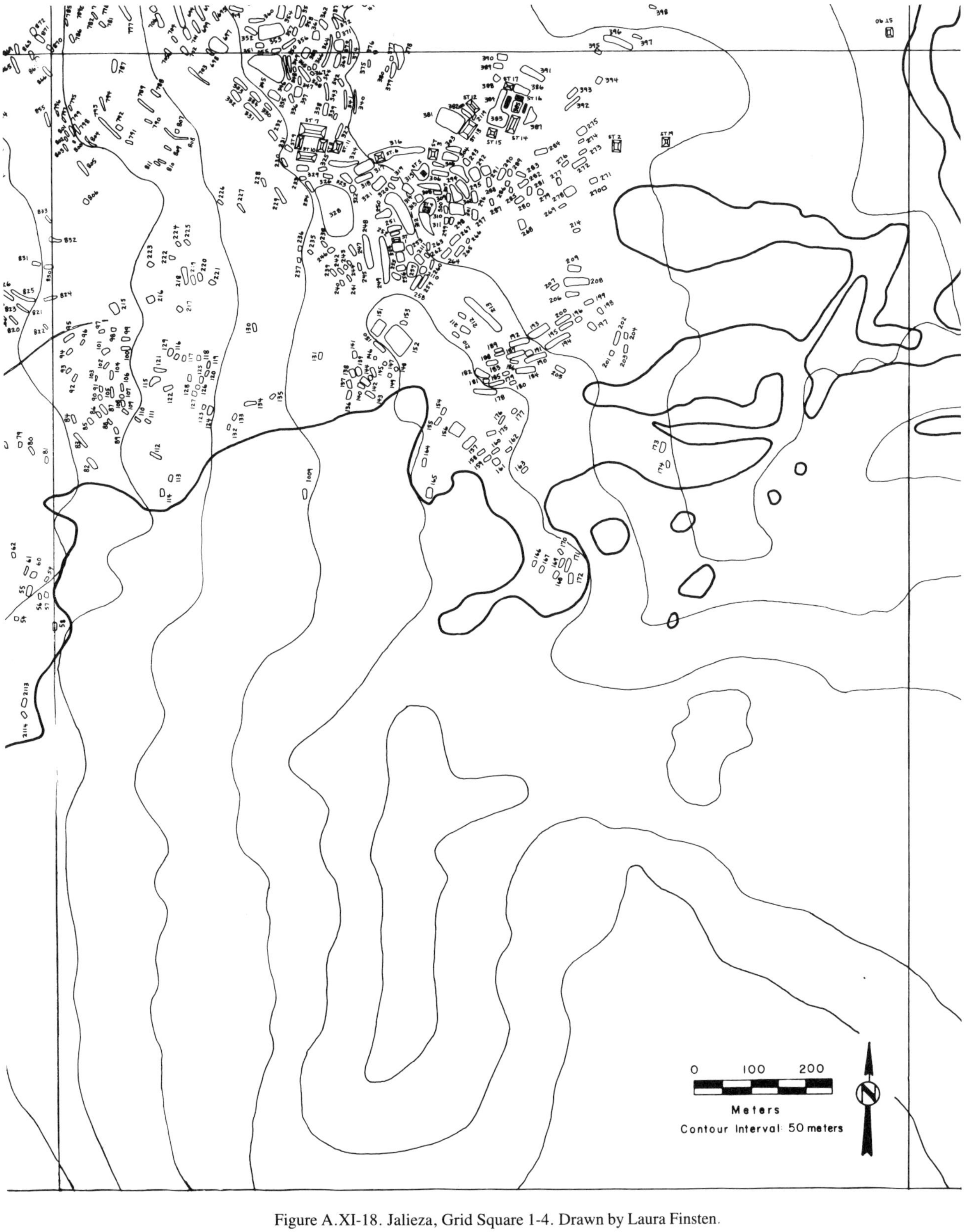

Figure A.XI-18. Jalieza, Grid Square 1-4. Drawn by Laura Finsten.

Figure A.XI-19. Jalieza, Grid Square 1-5. Drawn by Laura Finsten.

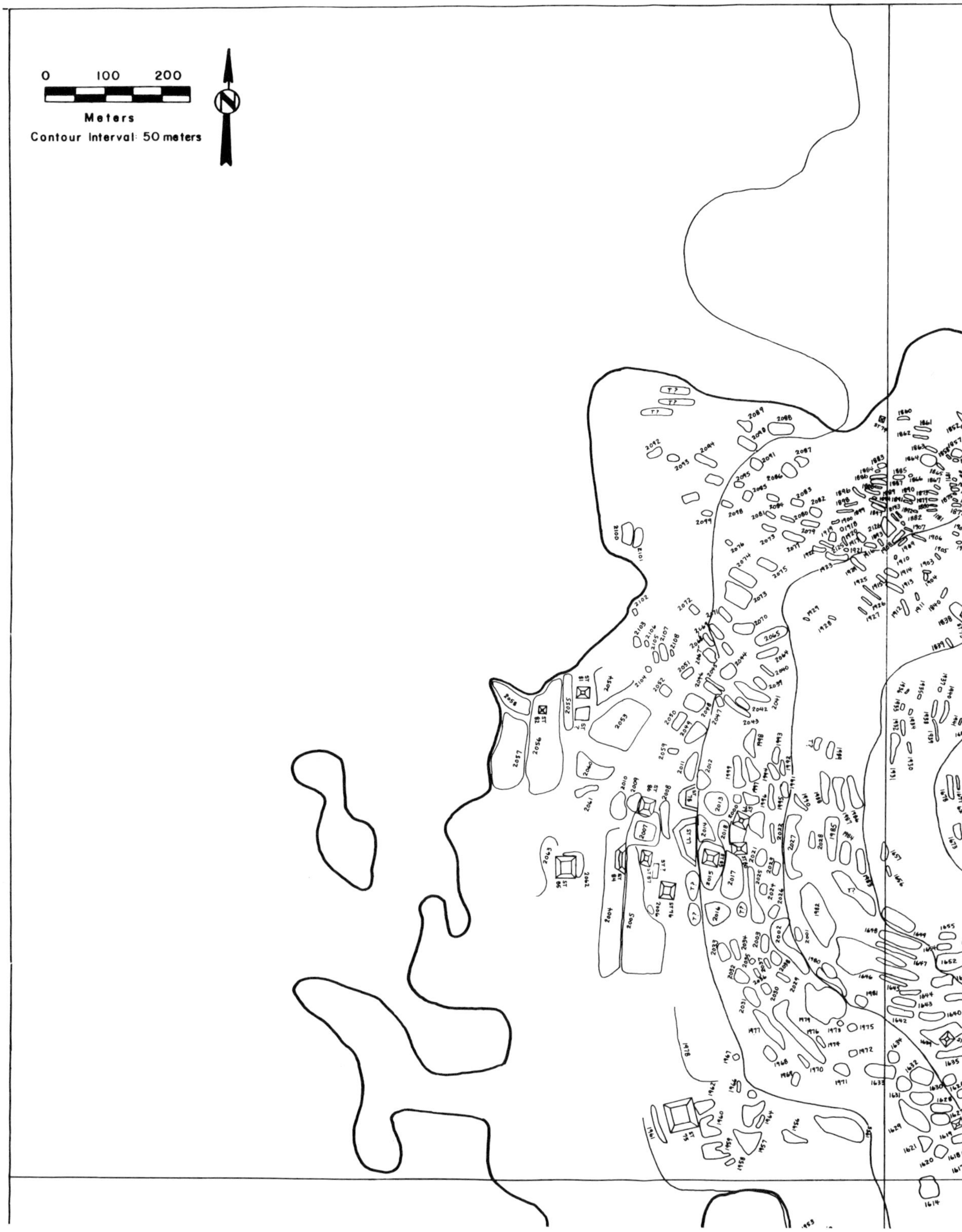

Figure A.XI-20. Jalieza, Grid Square 2-1. Drawn by Laura Finsten.

Figure A.XI-21. Jalieza, Grid Square 2-2. Drawn by Laura Finsten.

Figure A.XI-22. Jalieza, Grid Square 2-3. Drawn by Laura Finsten.

Figure A.XI-23. Jalieza, Grid Square 2-4. Drawn by Laura Finsten.

Figure A.XI-24. Jalieza, Grid Square 2-5. Drawn by Laura Finsten.

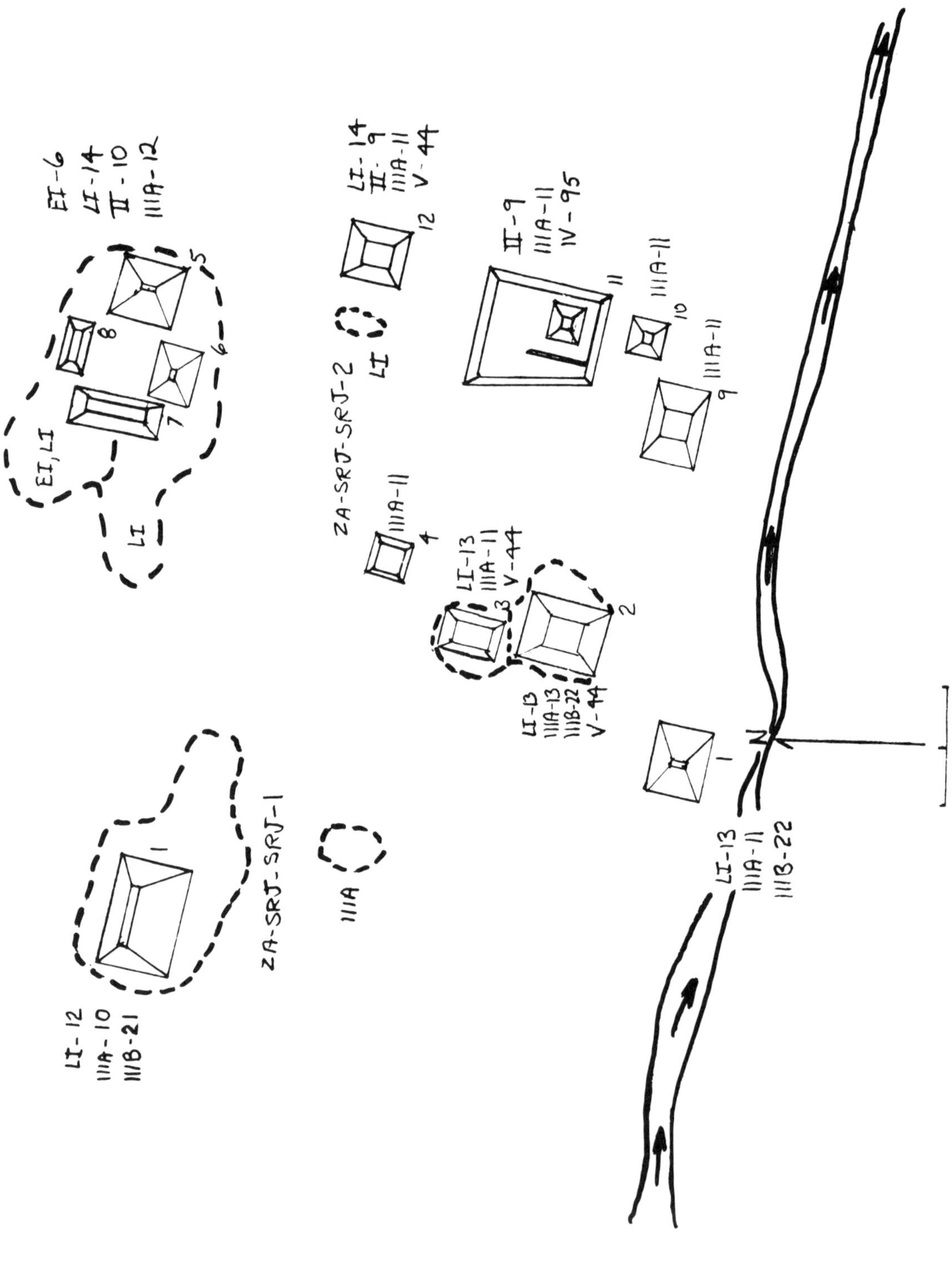

Figure A.XI-25. ZA-SRJ-SRJ-1 and 2.

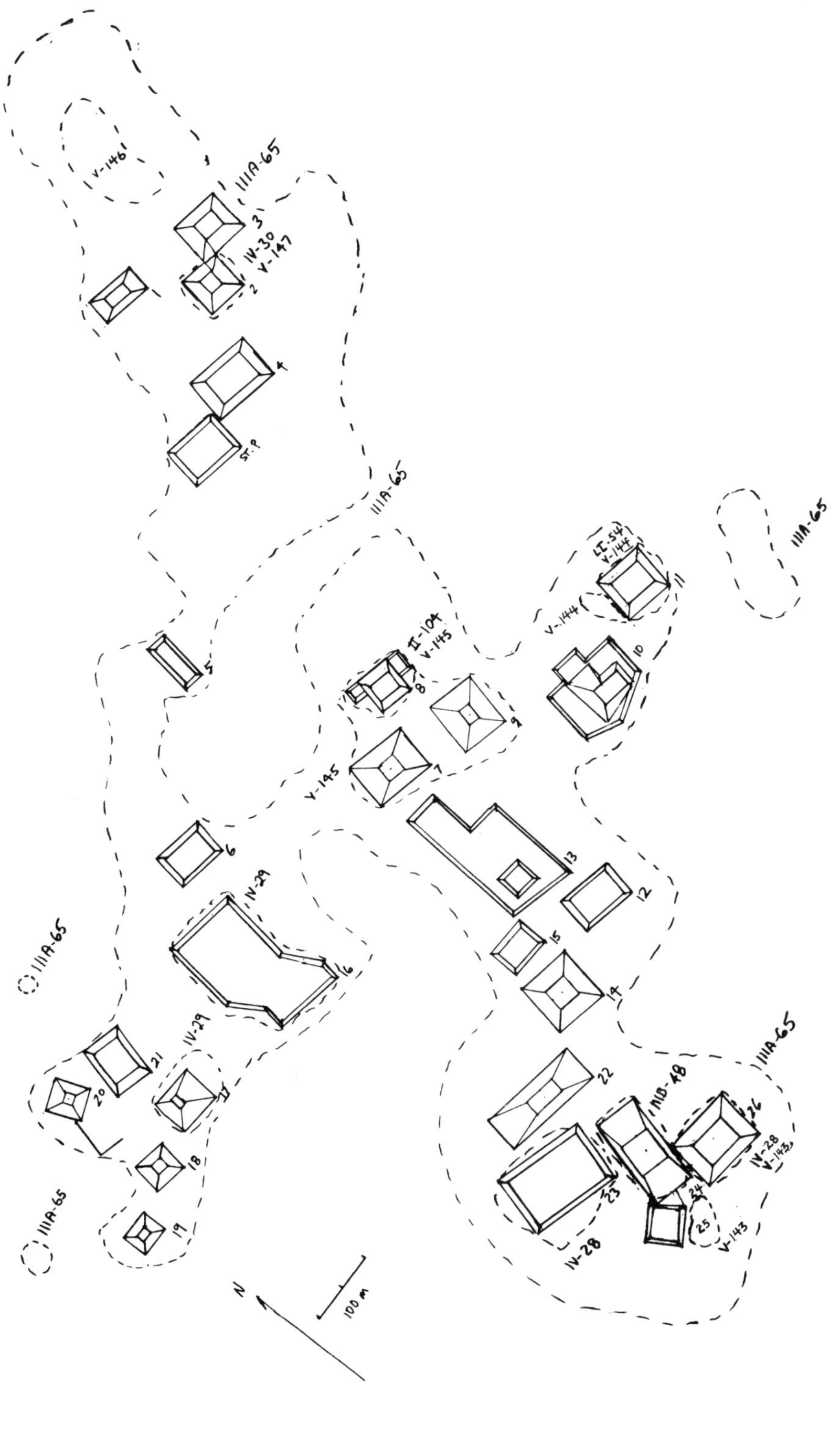

Figure A.XI-26. ZA-TRI-TRI-20.

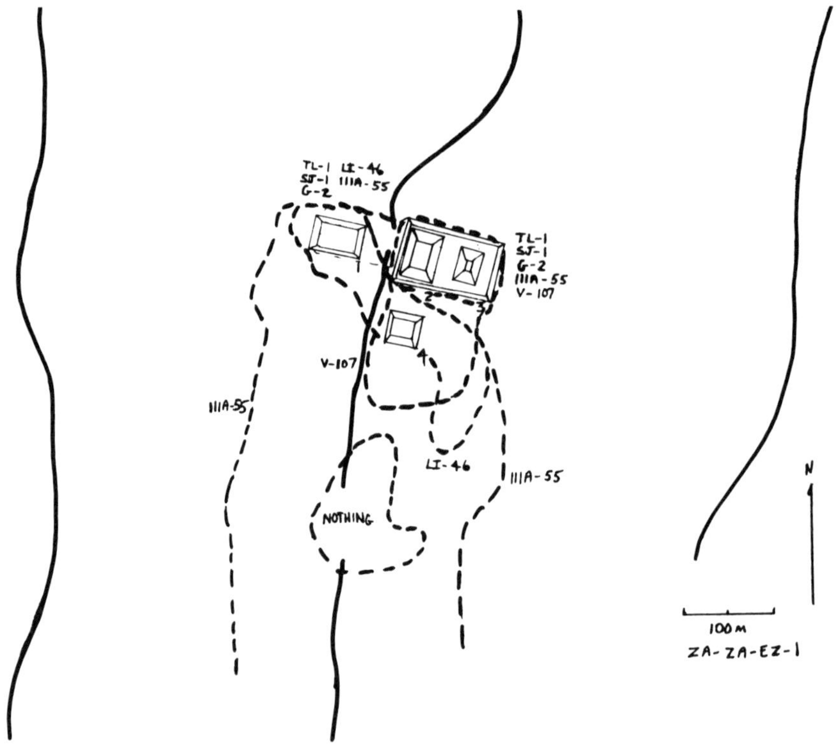

Figure A.XI-27. ZA-ZA-EZ-1.

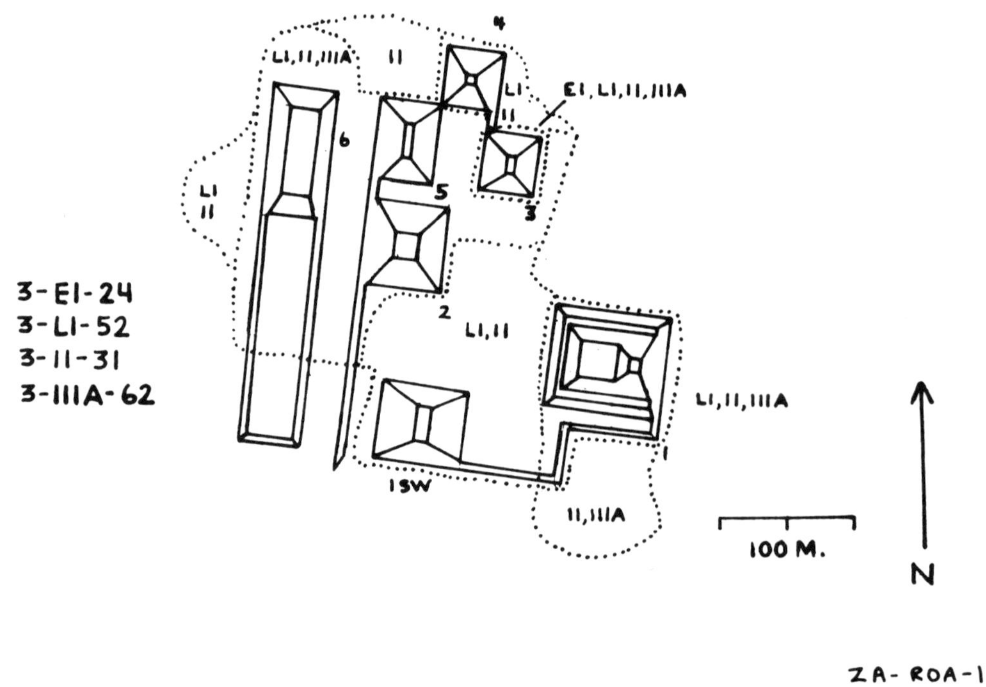

Figure A.XI-28. ZA-ZA-ROA-1. Roaló.

Figure A.XI-29. ZA-ZA-ZA-2. Zaachila (from Gallegos 1962, 1963). Numbers are contour intervals in meters. Structure A is the excavated Period V palace.

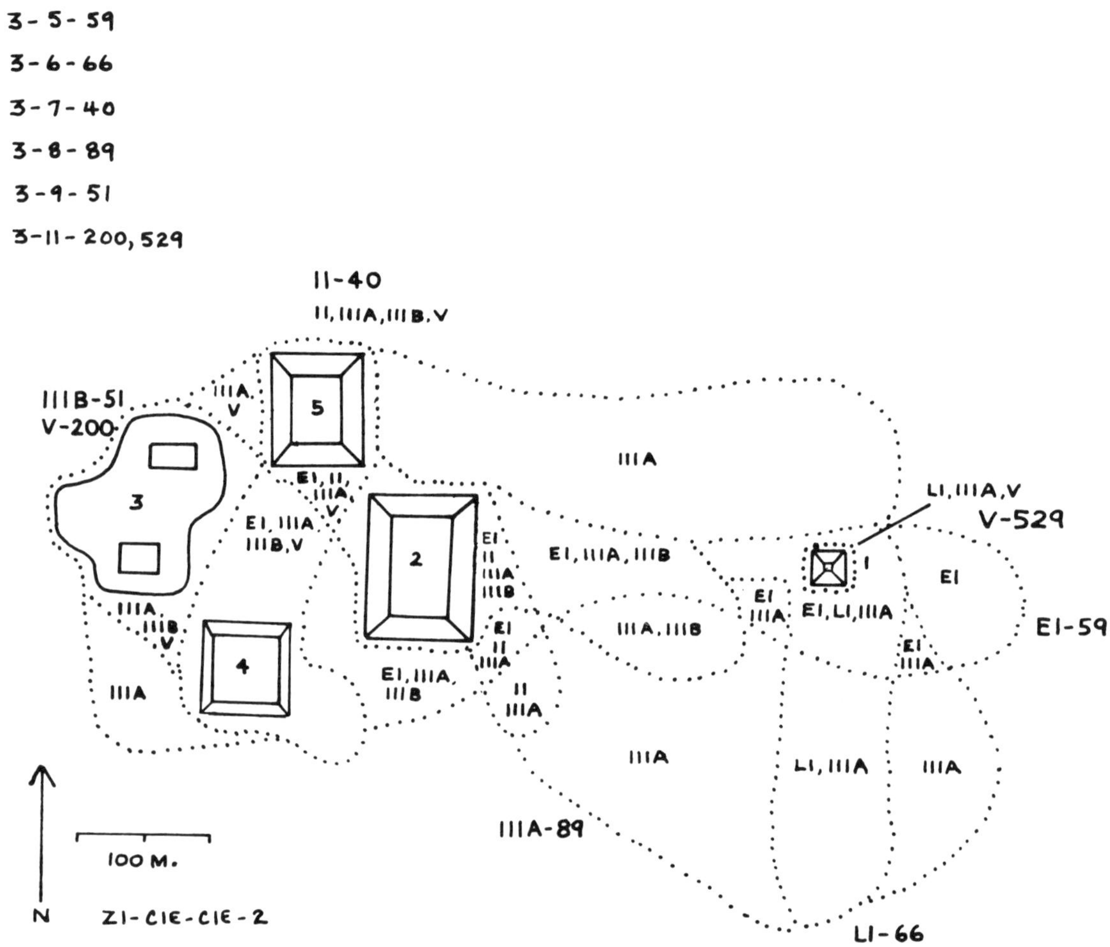

Figure A.XI-30. ZI-CIE-CIE-2.

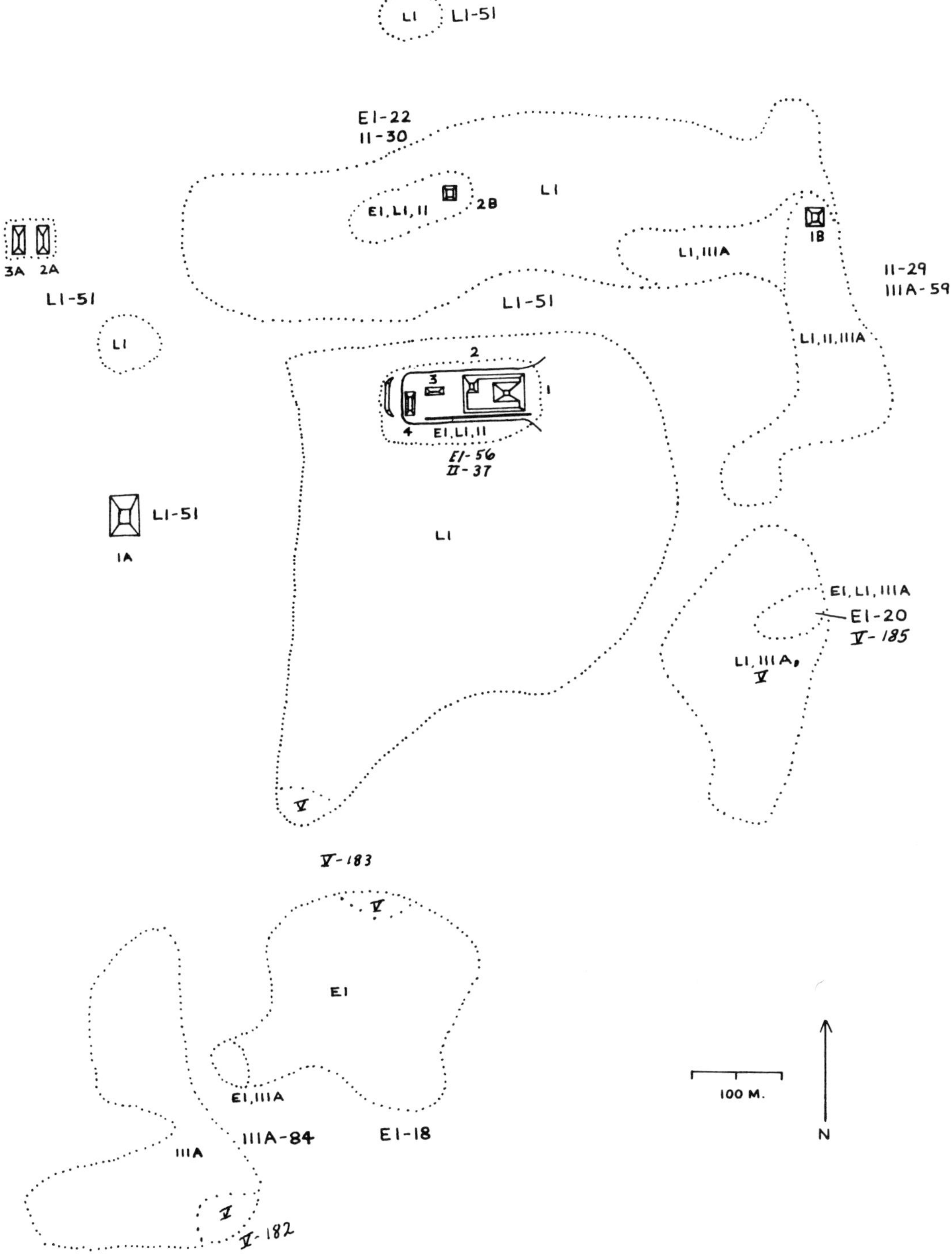

Figure A.XI-31. ZI-CIE-CIE-13,15.

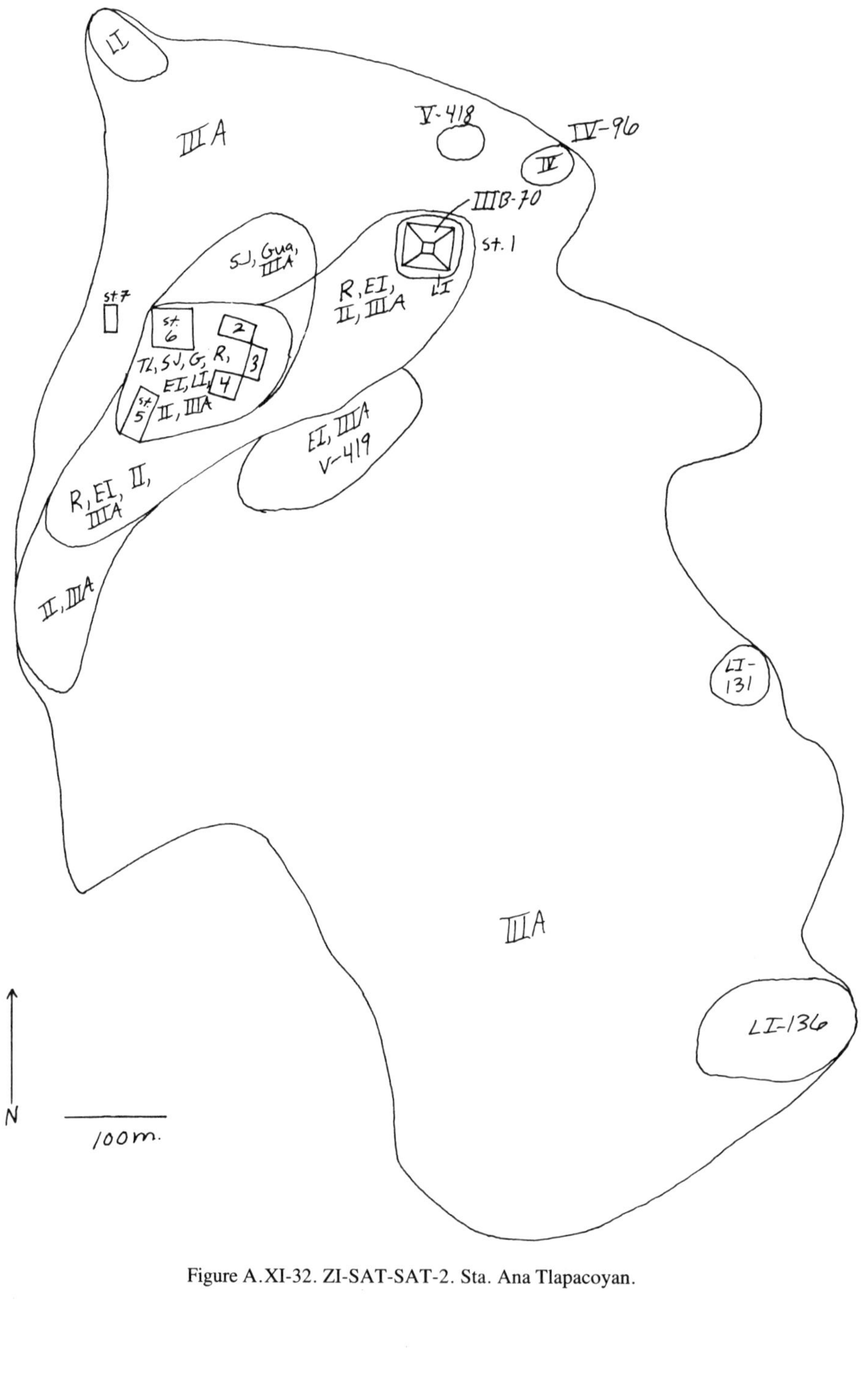

Figure A.XI-32. ZI-SAT-SAT-2. Sta. Ana Tlapacoyan.

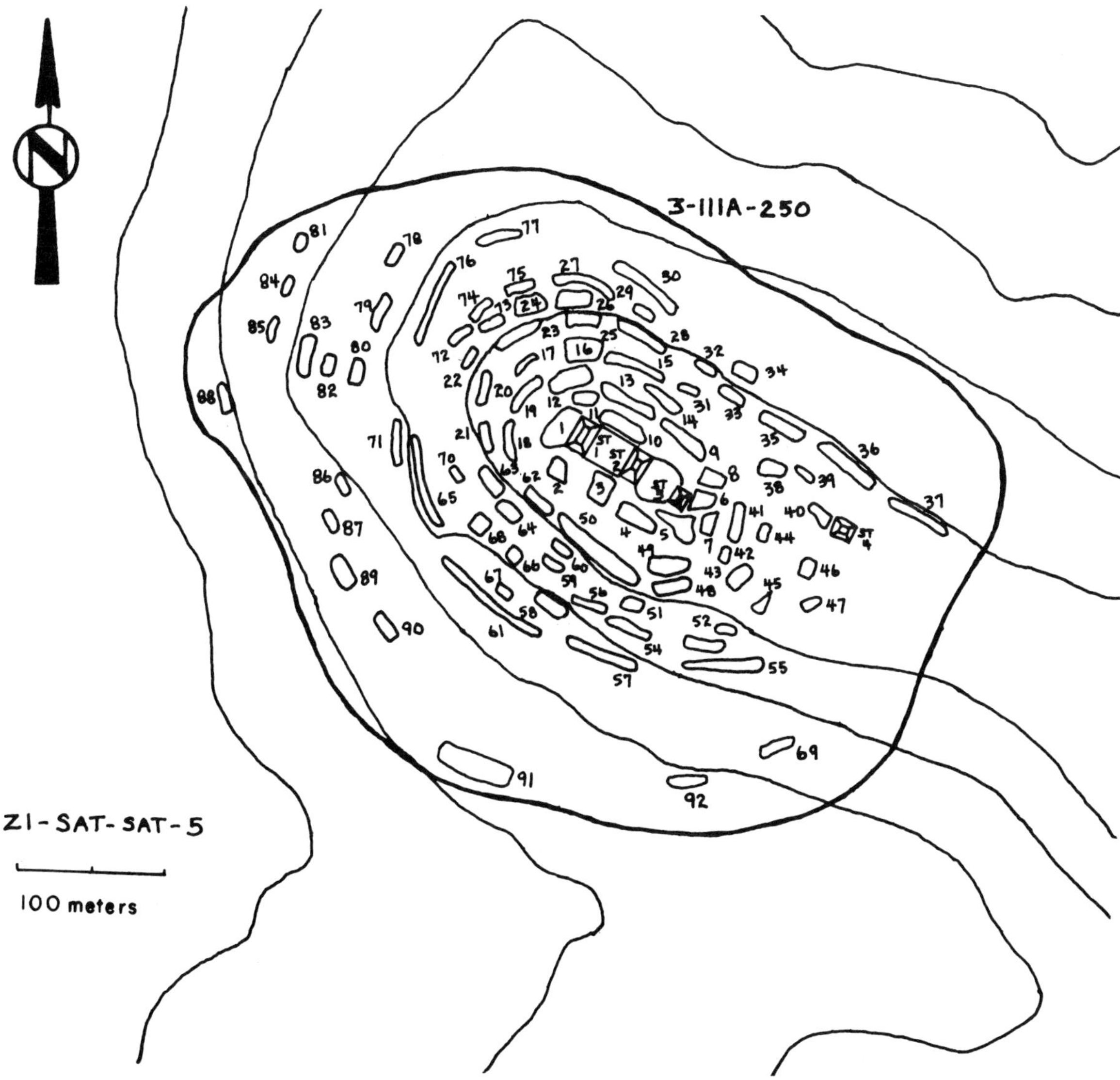

Figure A.XI-33. ZI-SAT-SAT-5.

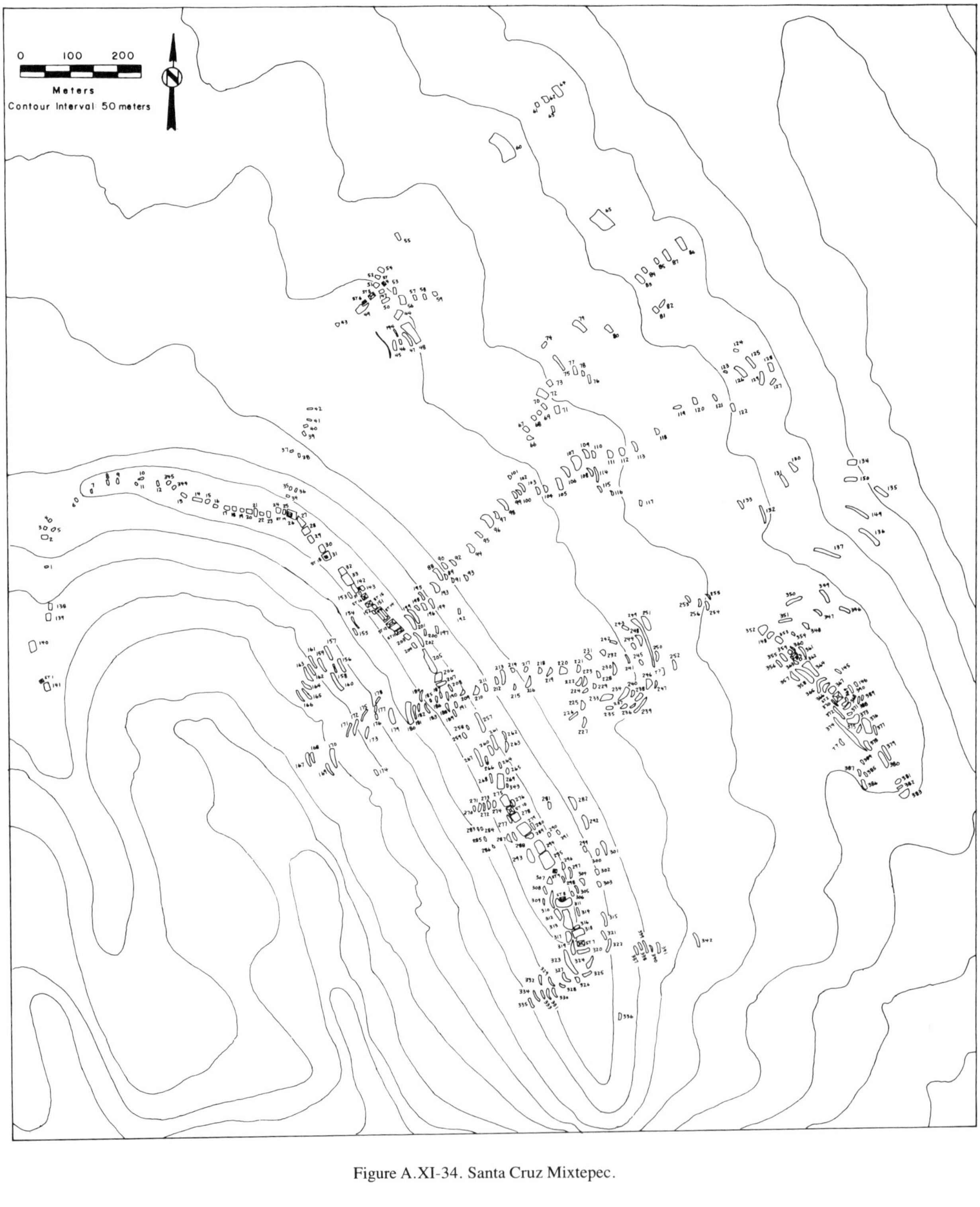

Figure A.XI-34. Santa Cruz Mixtepec.

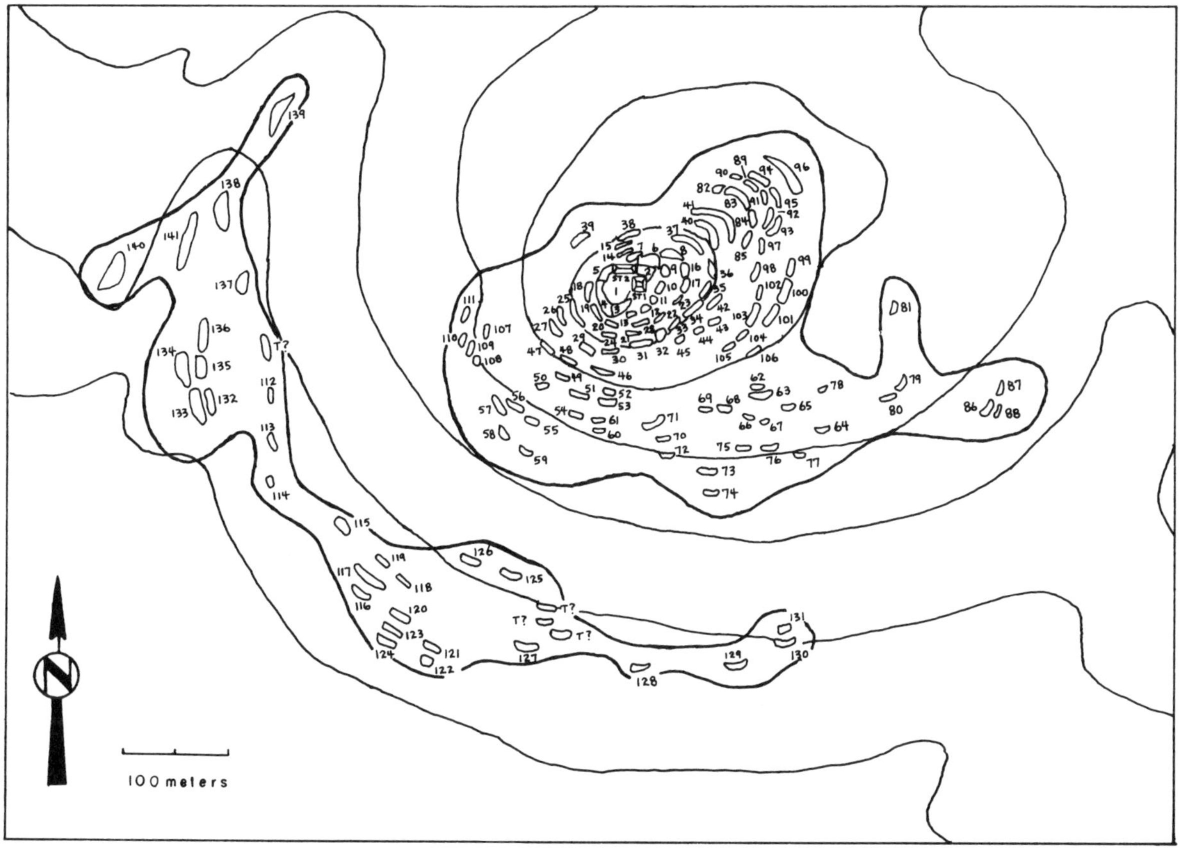

Figure A.XI-35. ZI-SCM-TR-1. El Trapiche.

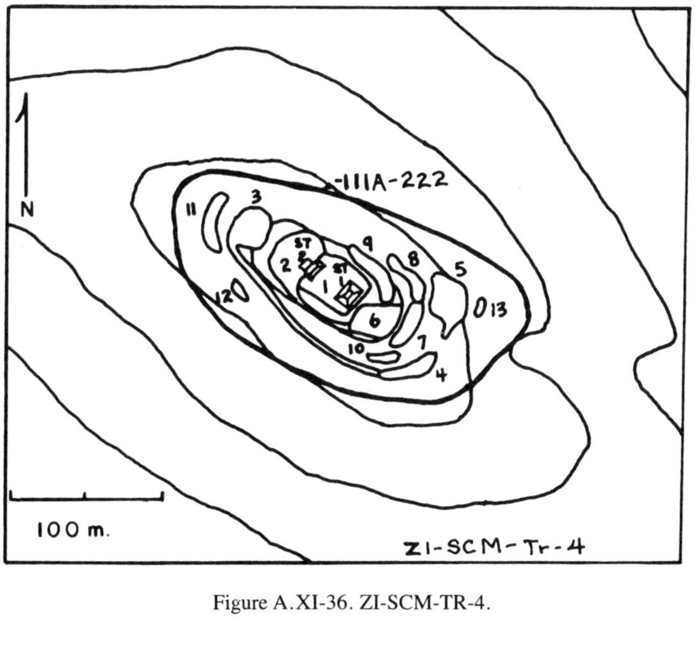

Figure A.XI-36. ZI-SCM-TR-4.

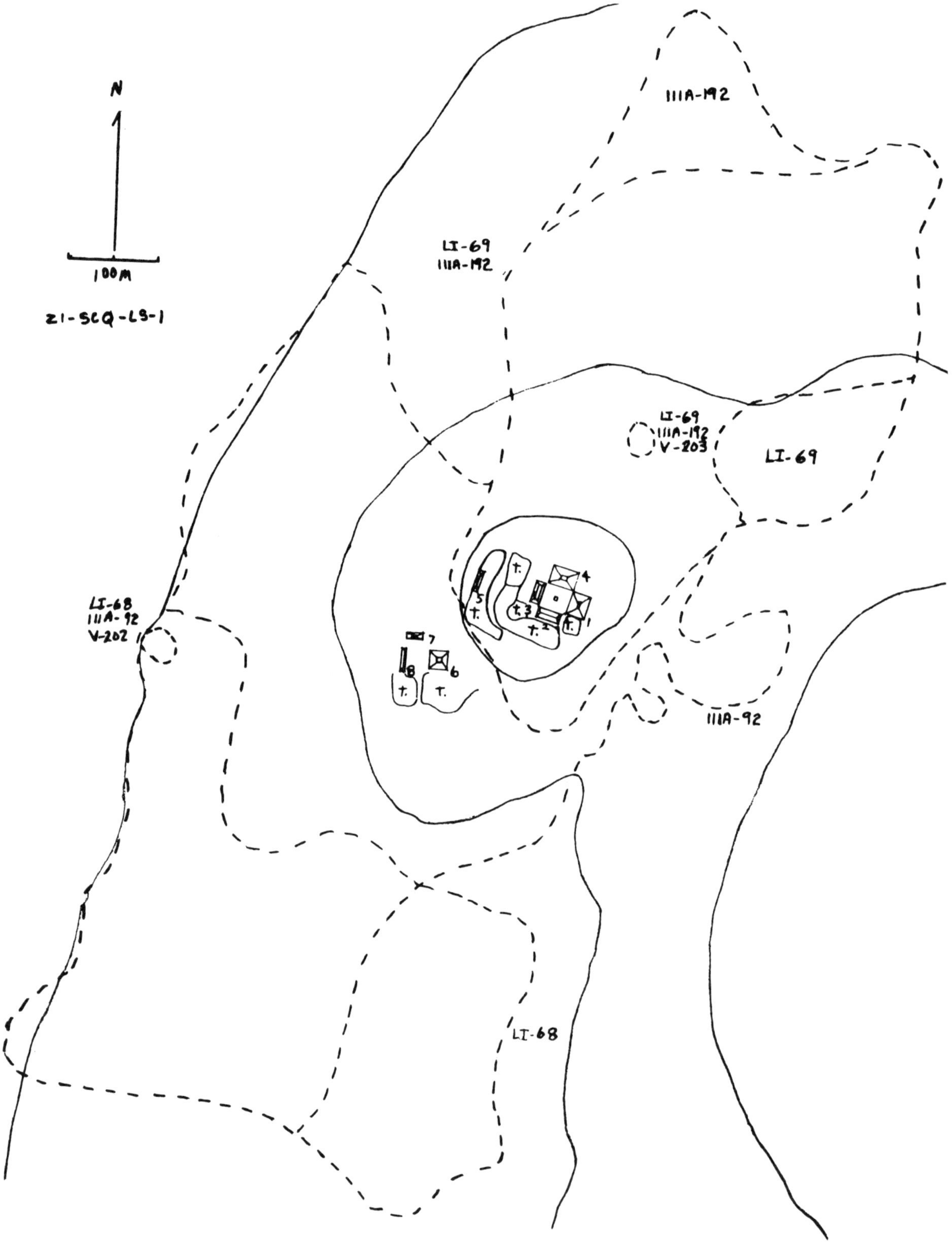

Figure A.XI-37. ZI-SCQ-LS-1.

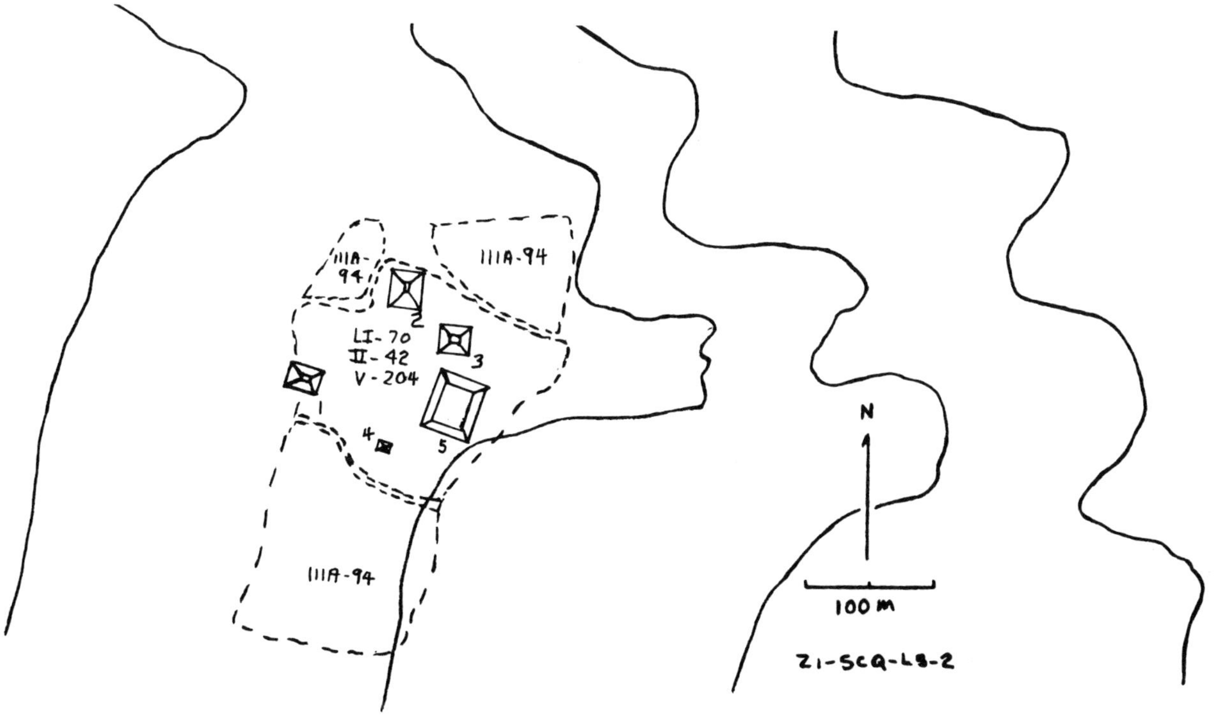

Figure A.XI-38. ZI-SCQ-LS-2.

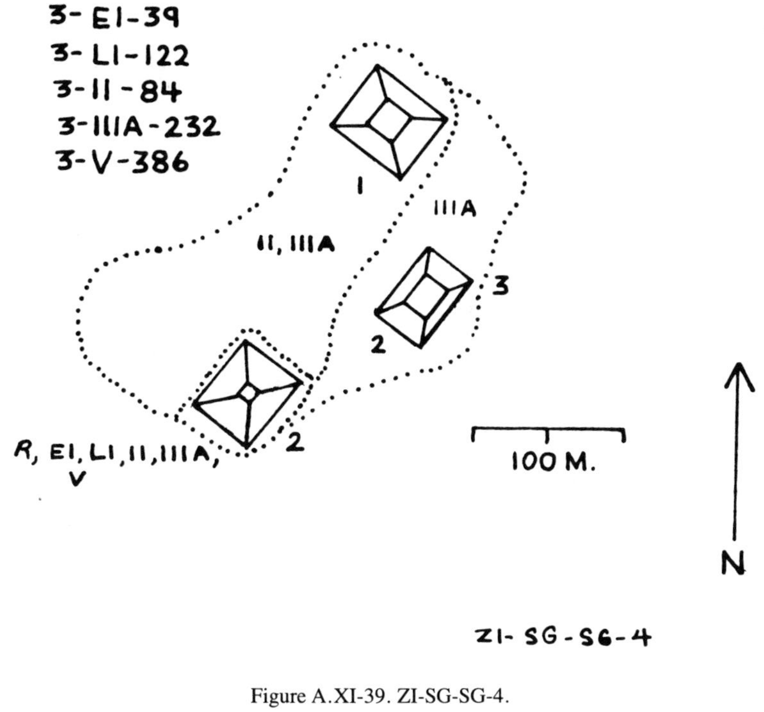

Figure A.XI-39. ZI-SG-SG-4.

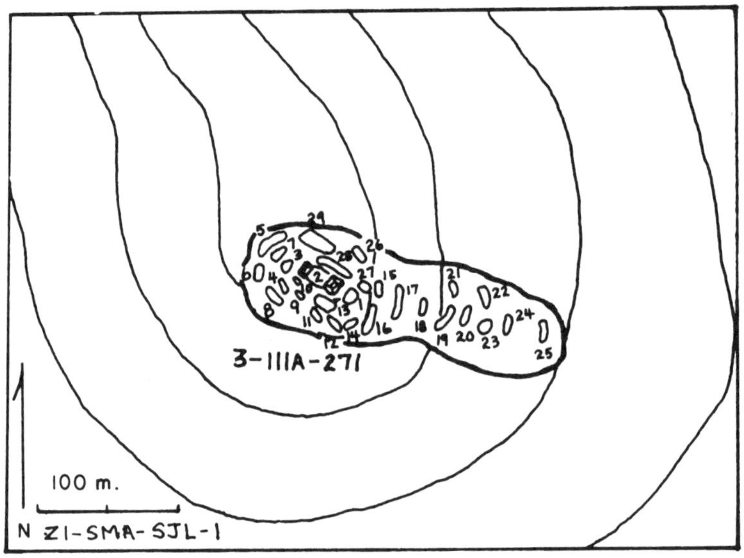

Figure A.XI-40. ZI-SMA-SJL-1.

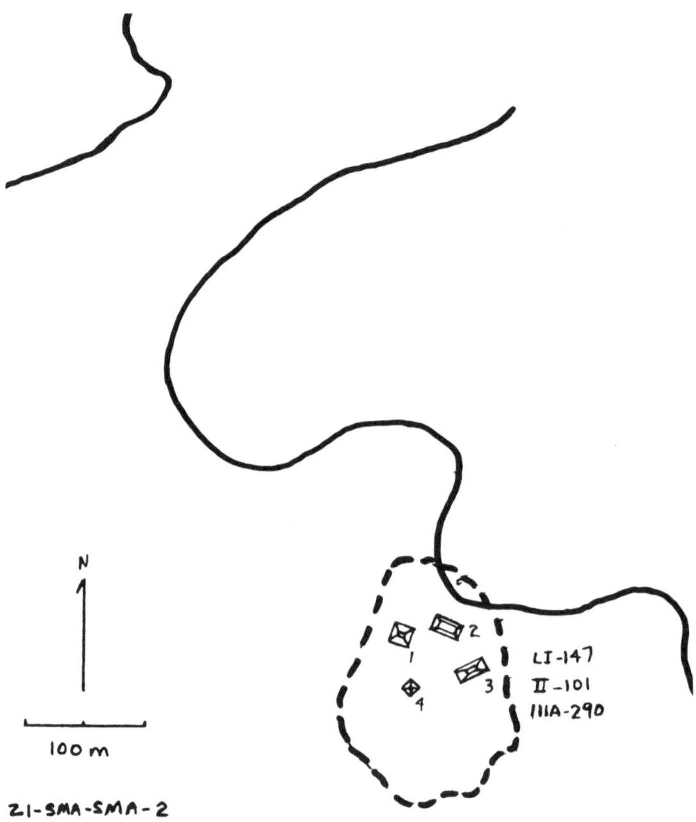

Figure A.XI-41. ZI-SMA-SMA-2.

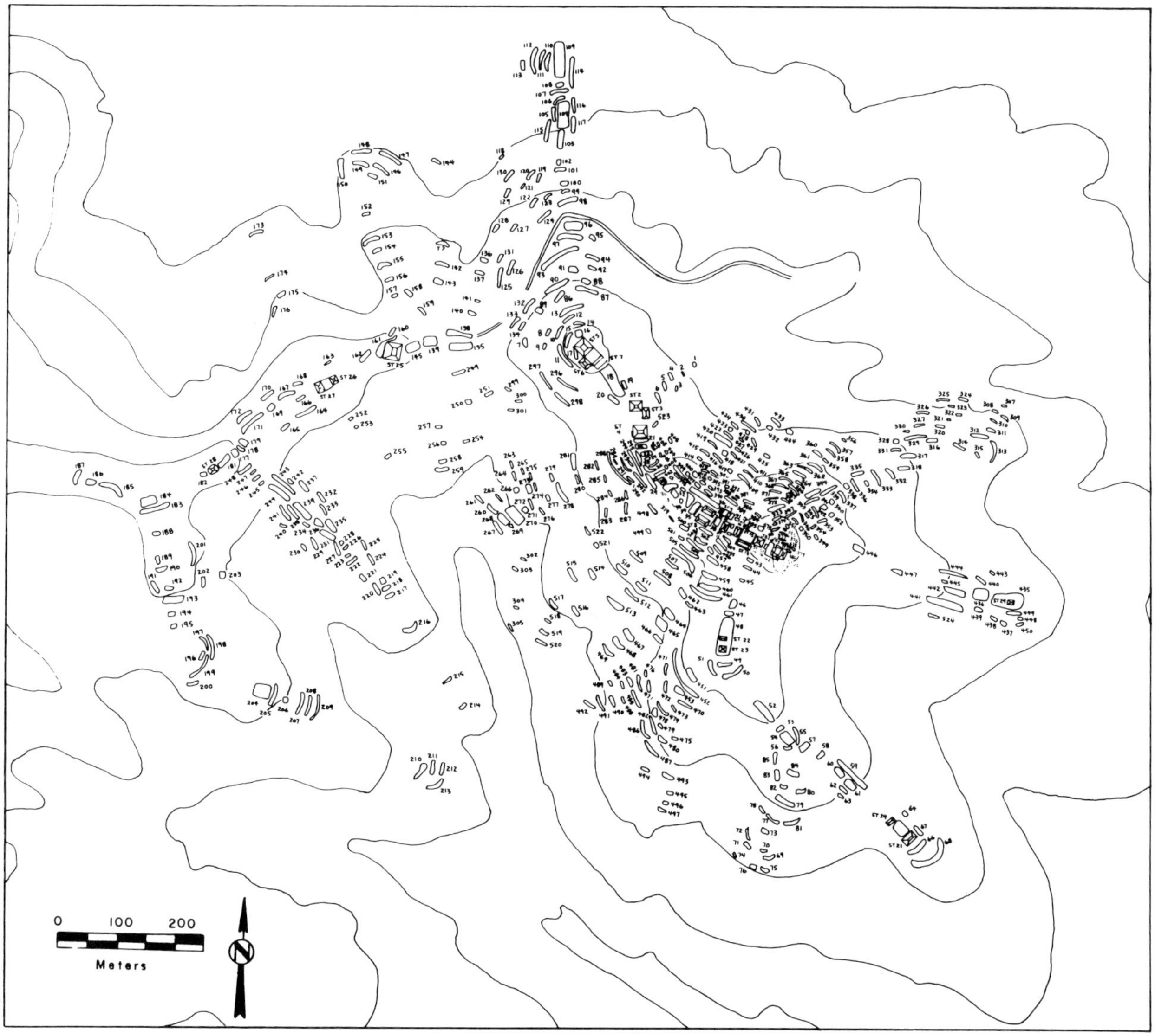

Figure A.XI-42. ZI-SMA-SMA-5. El Choco. The following figure is a detail of the congested civic-ceremonial core of the site.

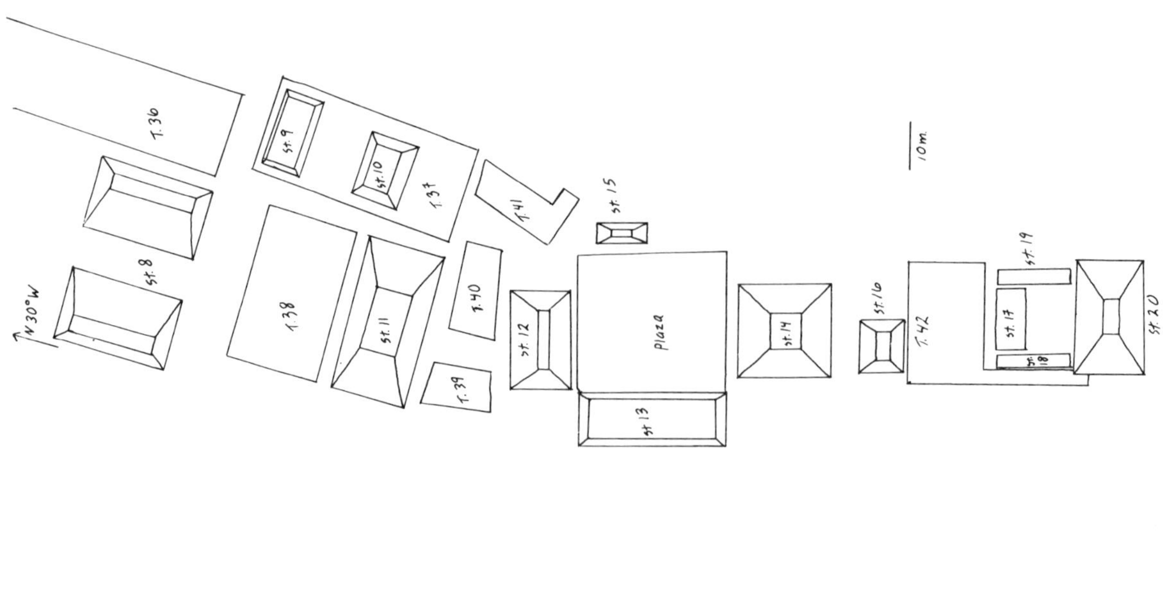

Figure A.XI-43. Detail of the civic-ceremonial core of El Choco, ZI-SMA-SMA-5.

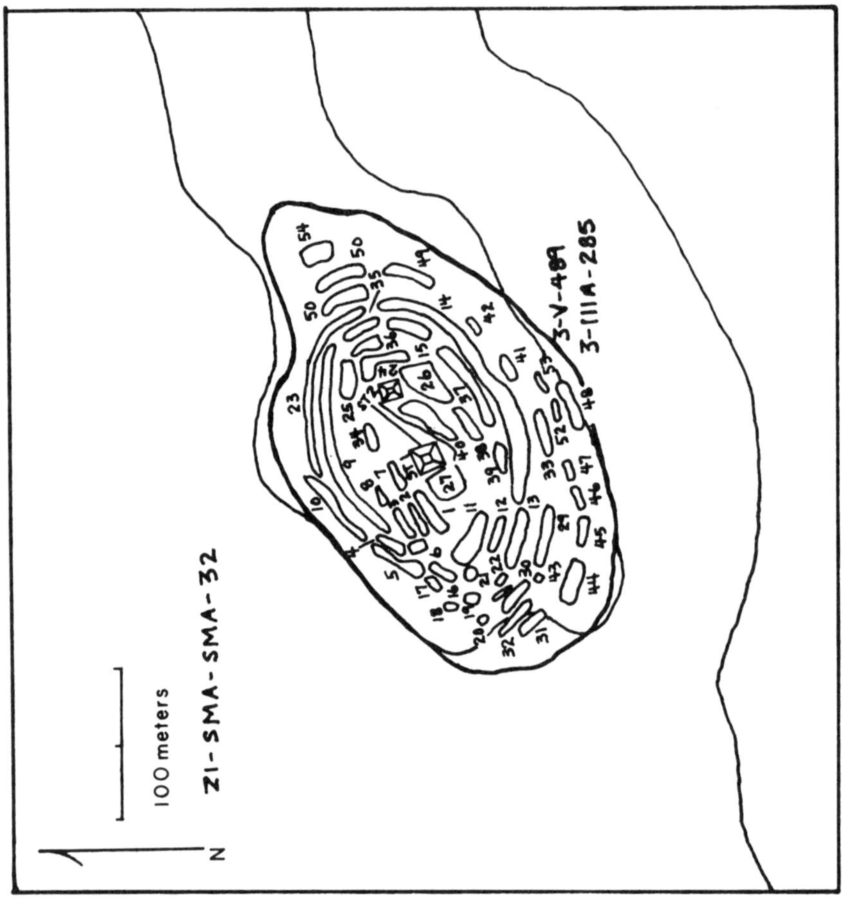

Figure A.XI-44. ZI-SMA-SMA-32.

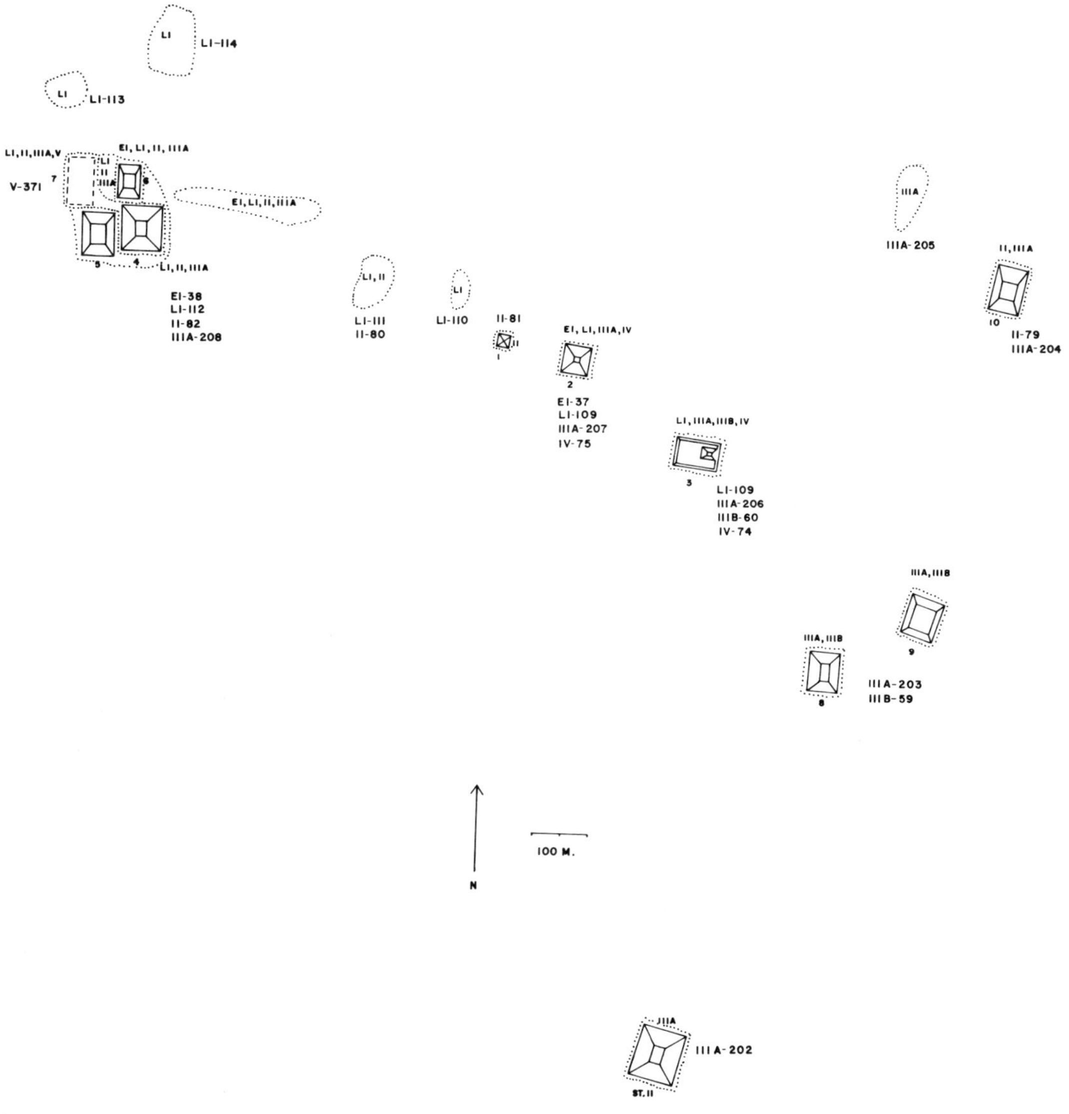

Figure A.XI-45. ZI-SPH-SPH-6. Shows probable dates of construction and use of mounds. For locations of the earlier periods on the site, see Grid Square 0506.

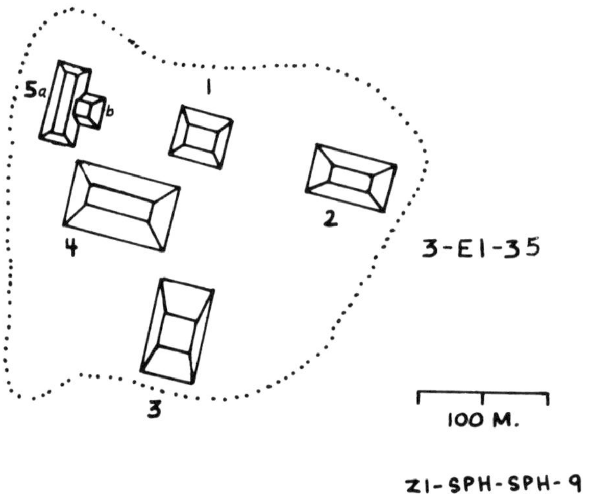

Figure A.XI-46. ZI-SPH-SPH-9.

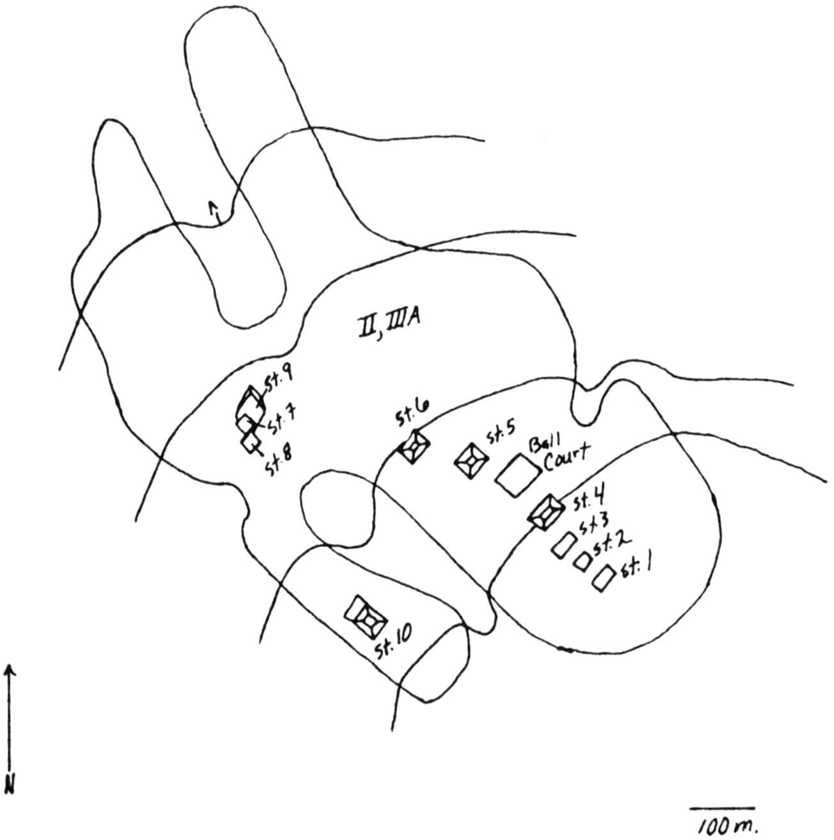

Figure A.XI-47. ZI-VDF-LB-3.

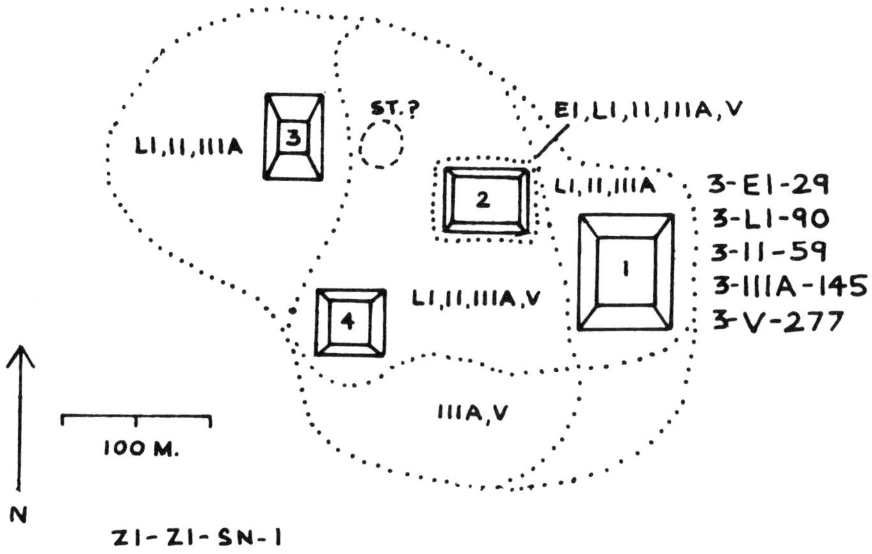

Figure A.XI-48. ZI-ZI-SN-1.

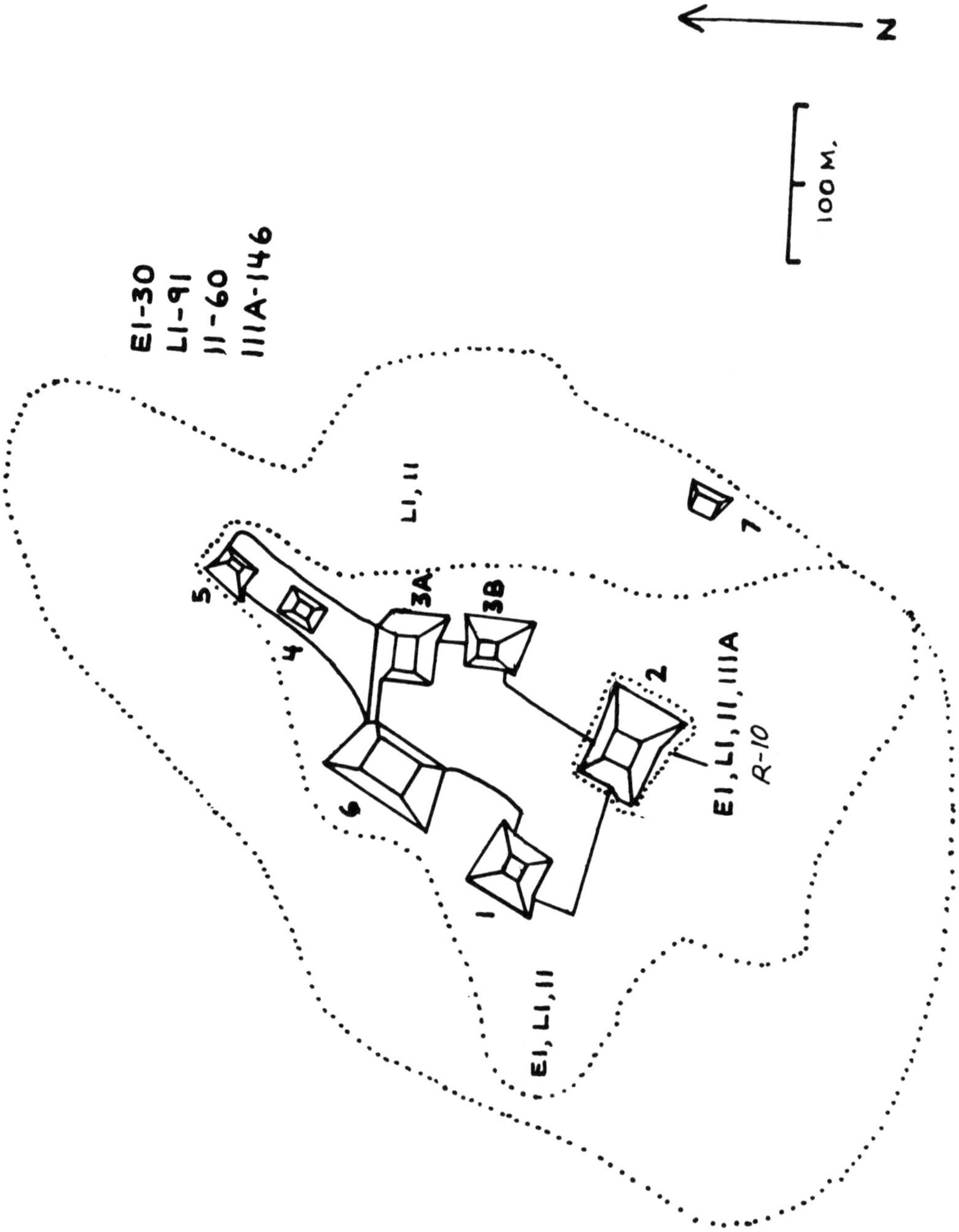

Figure A.XI-49. ZI-ZI-SN-3.

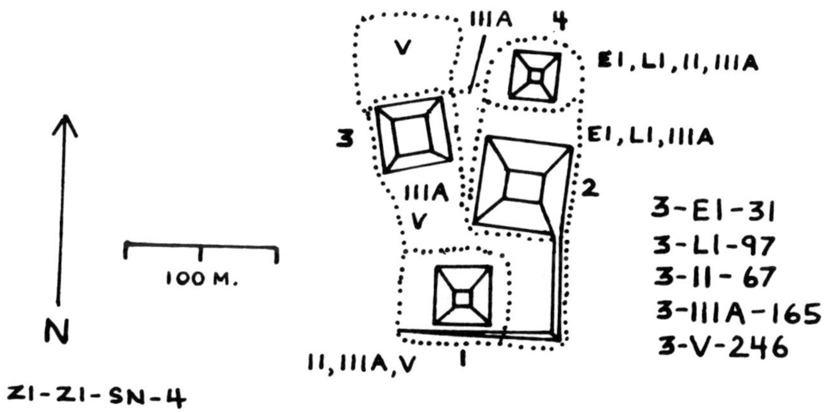

Figure A.XI-50. ZI-ZI-SN-4.

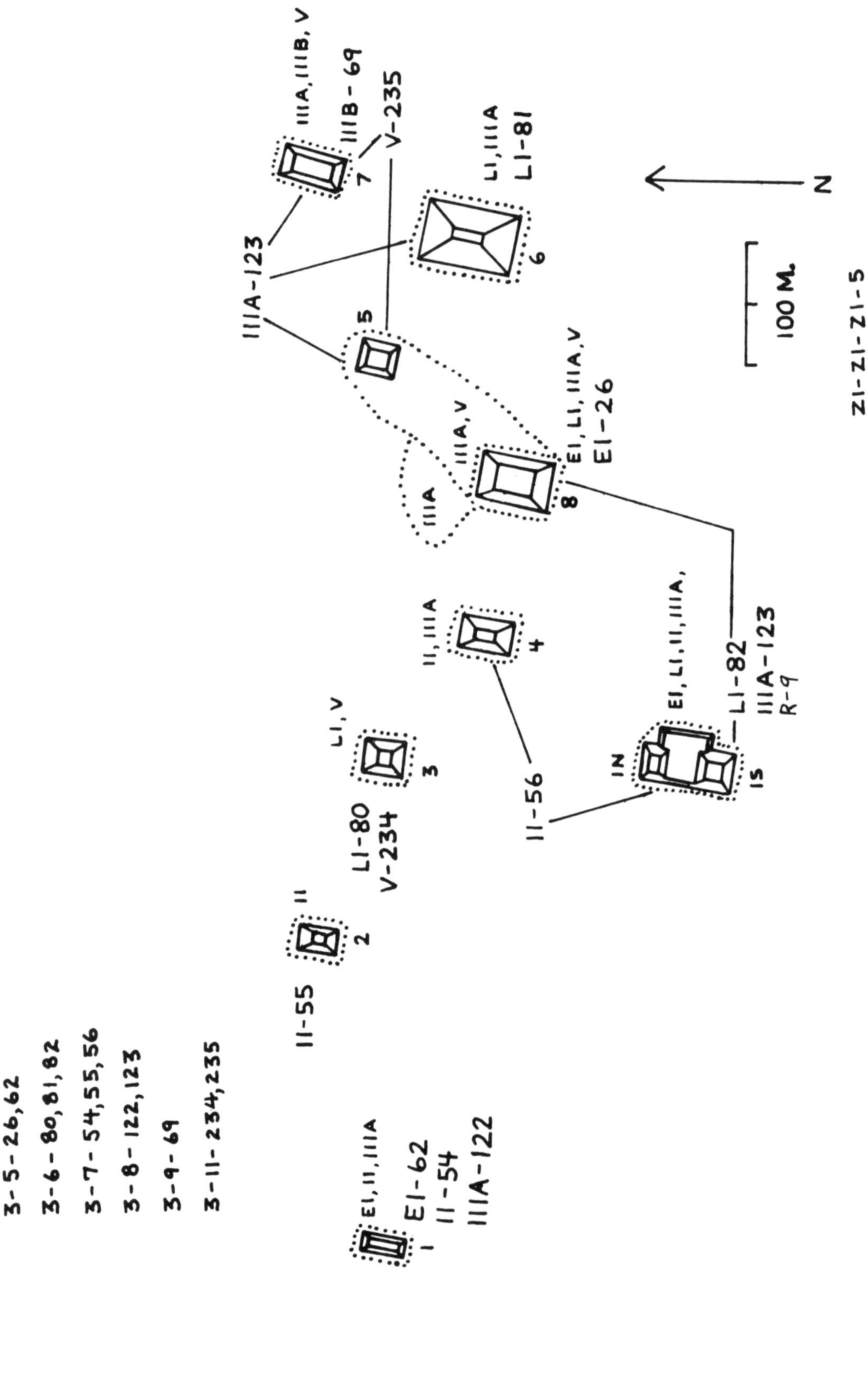

Figure A.XI-51. ZI-ZI-ZI-5, ZI-ZI-ZI-8.

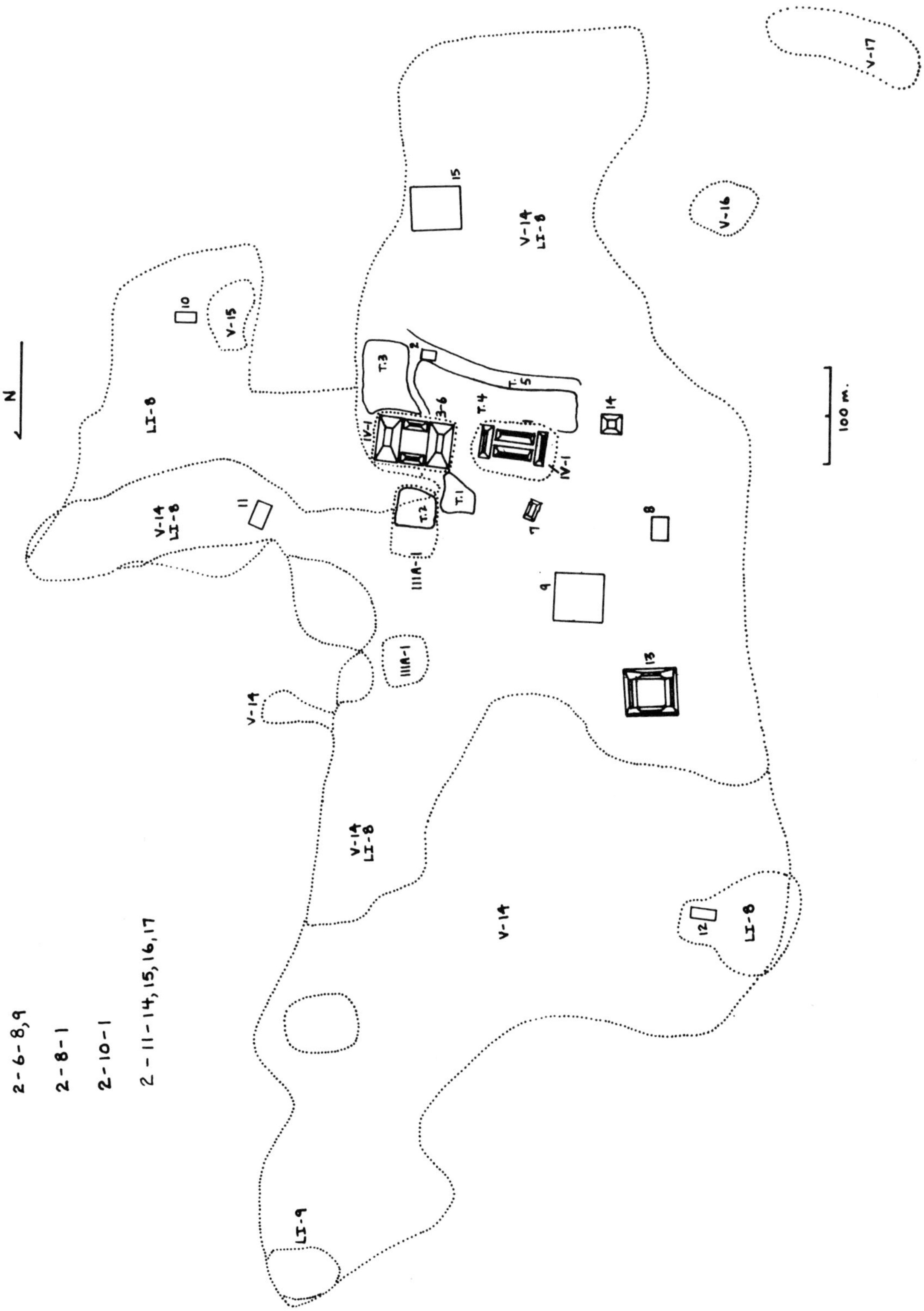

Figure A.XI-52. San Luís Beltrán.

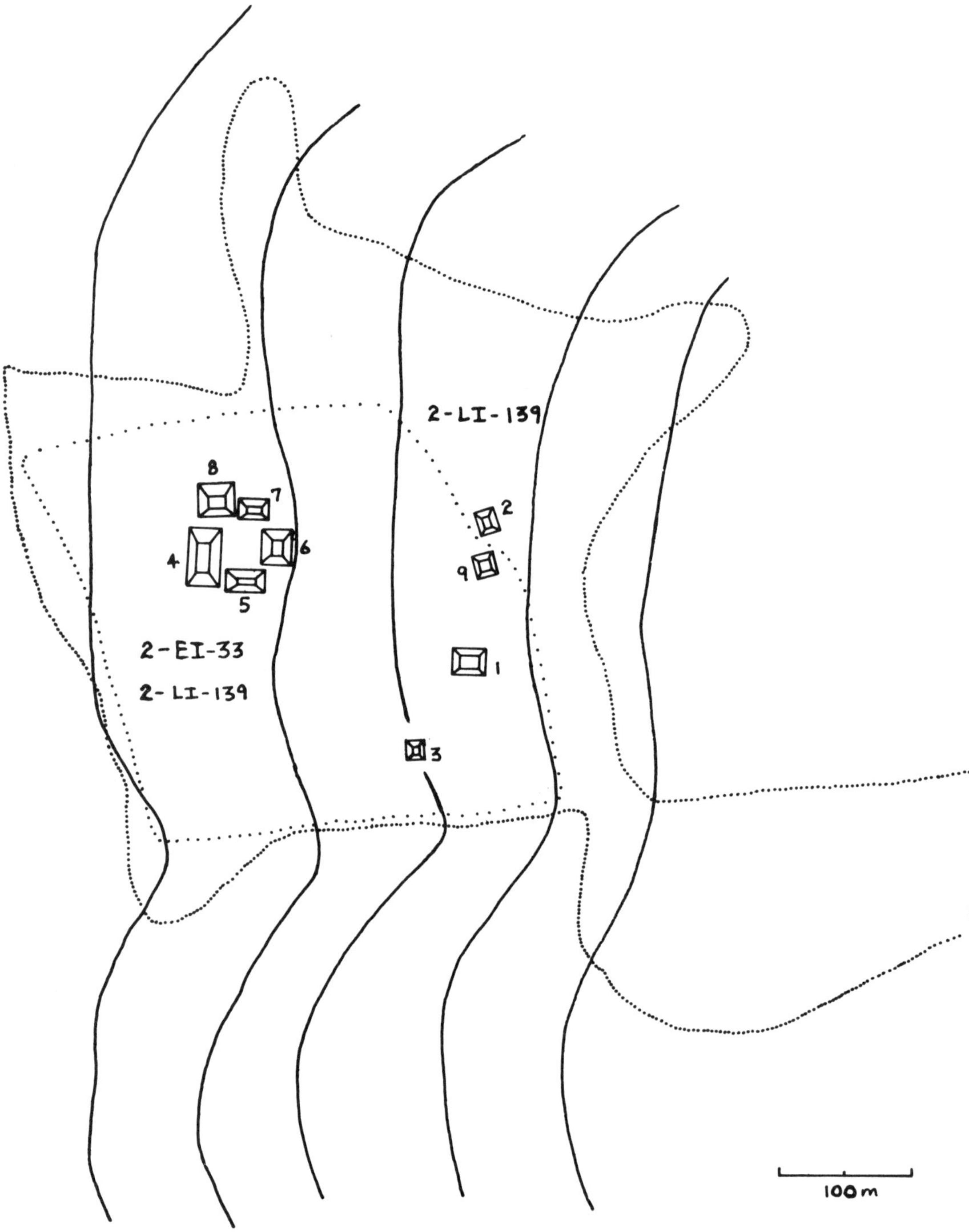

Figure A.XI-53. 2-5-33, 2-6-139.

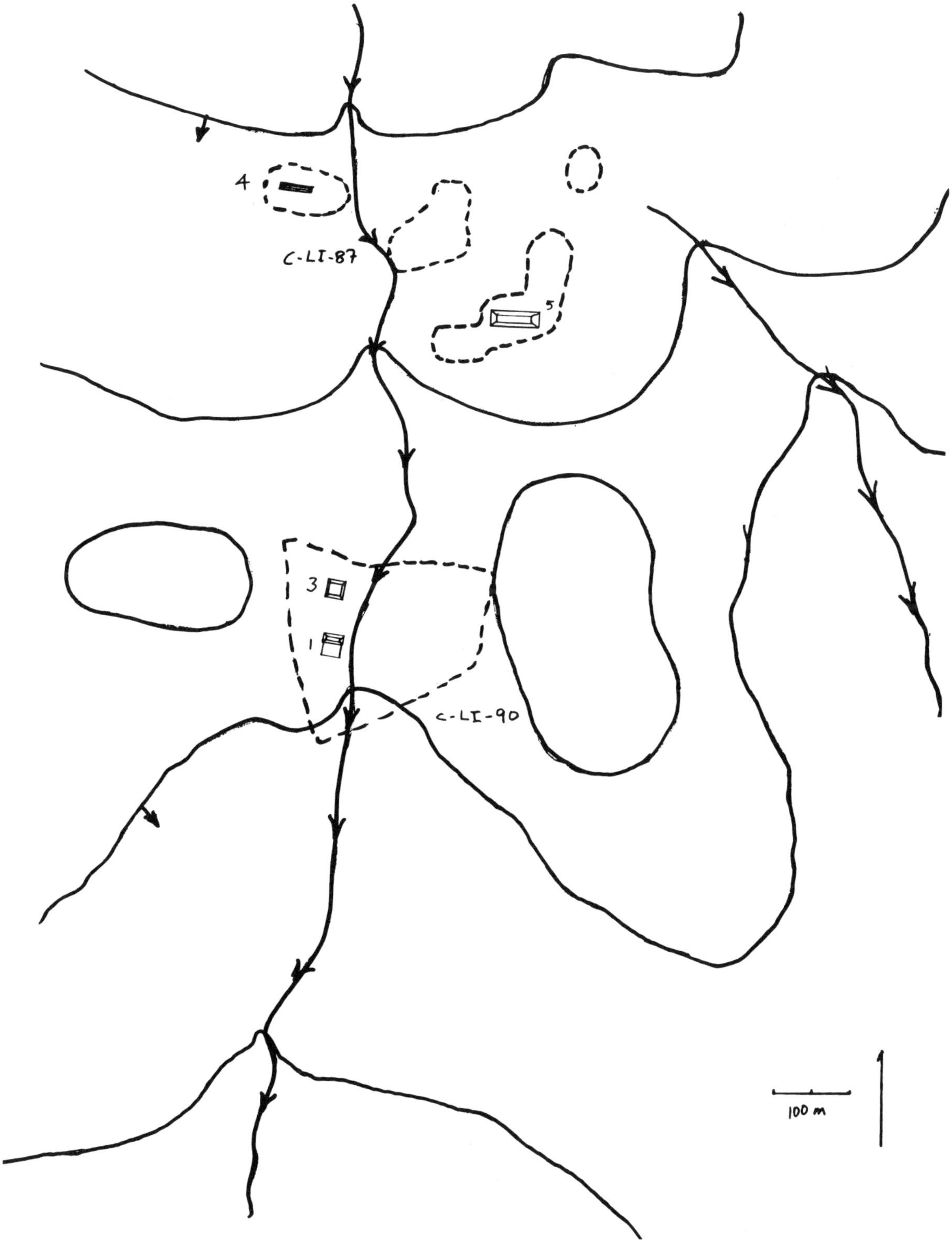

Figure A.XI-54. 2-6-87, 90.

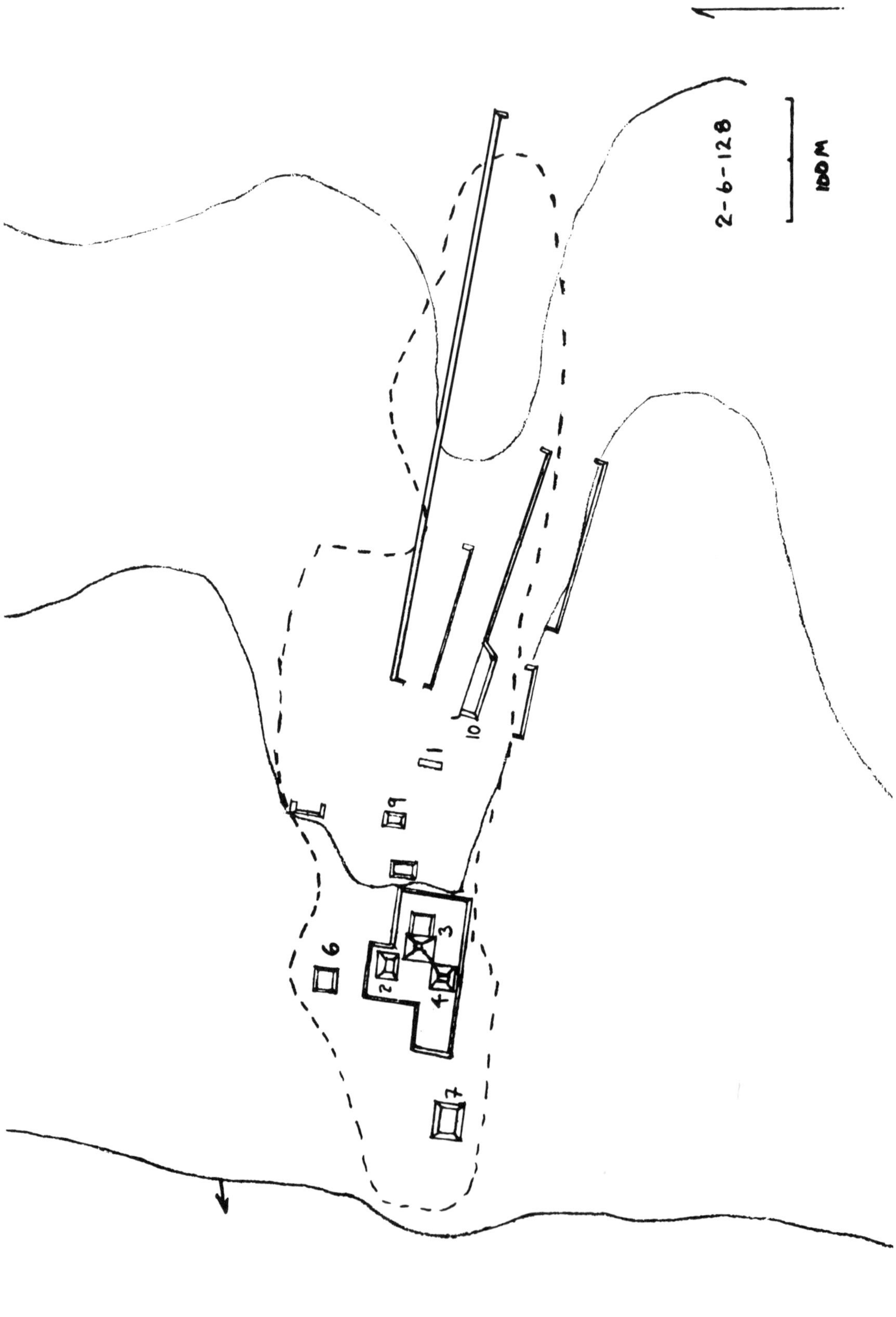

Figure A.XI-55. The Late I (2-6-128) mounds at Hacienda Experimental.

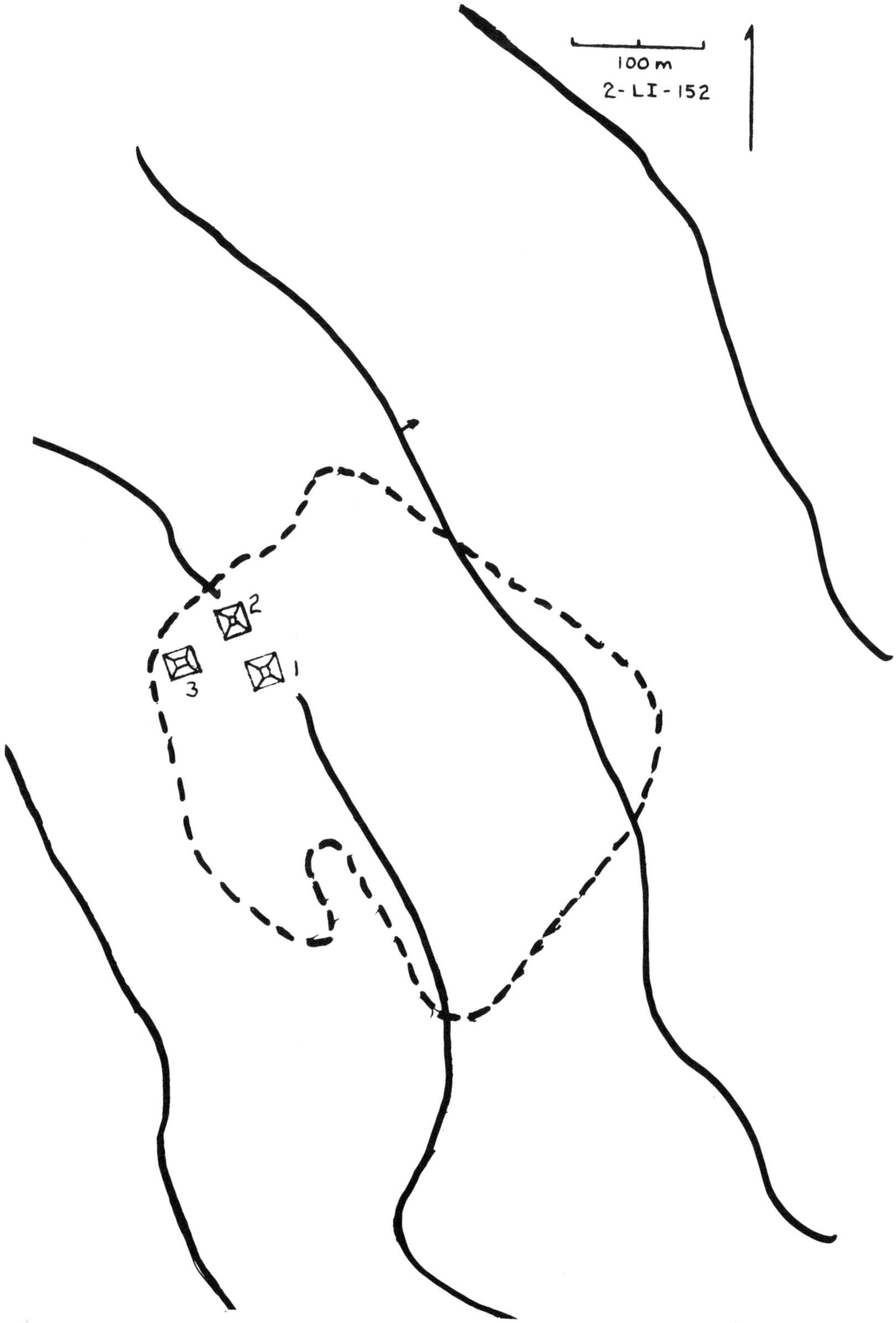

Figure A.XI-56. 2-6-152.

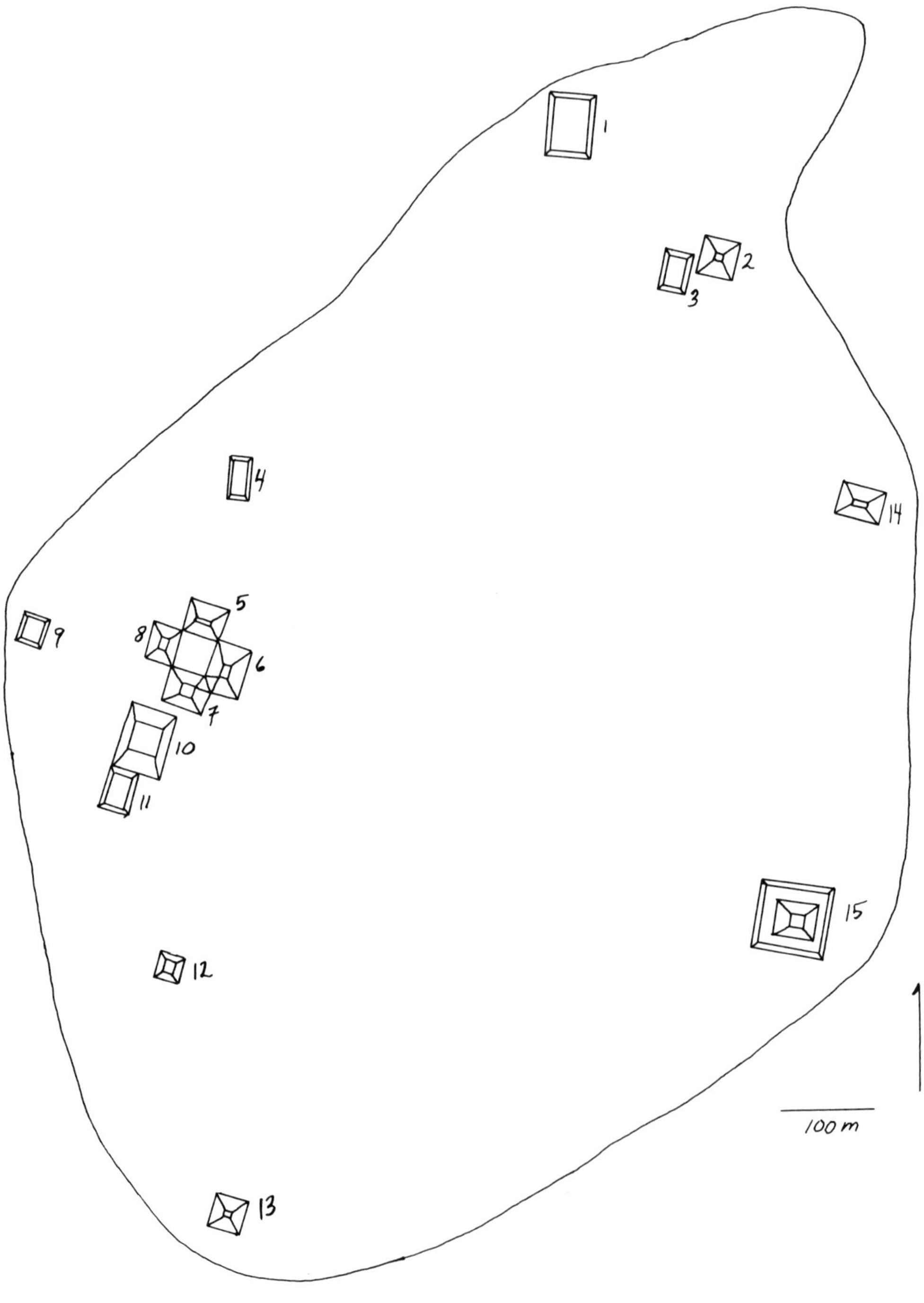

Figure A.XI-57. Xoxocotlán (2-8-17).

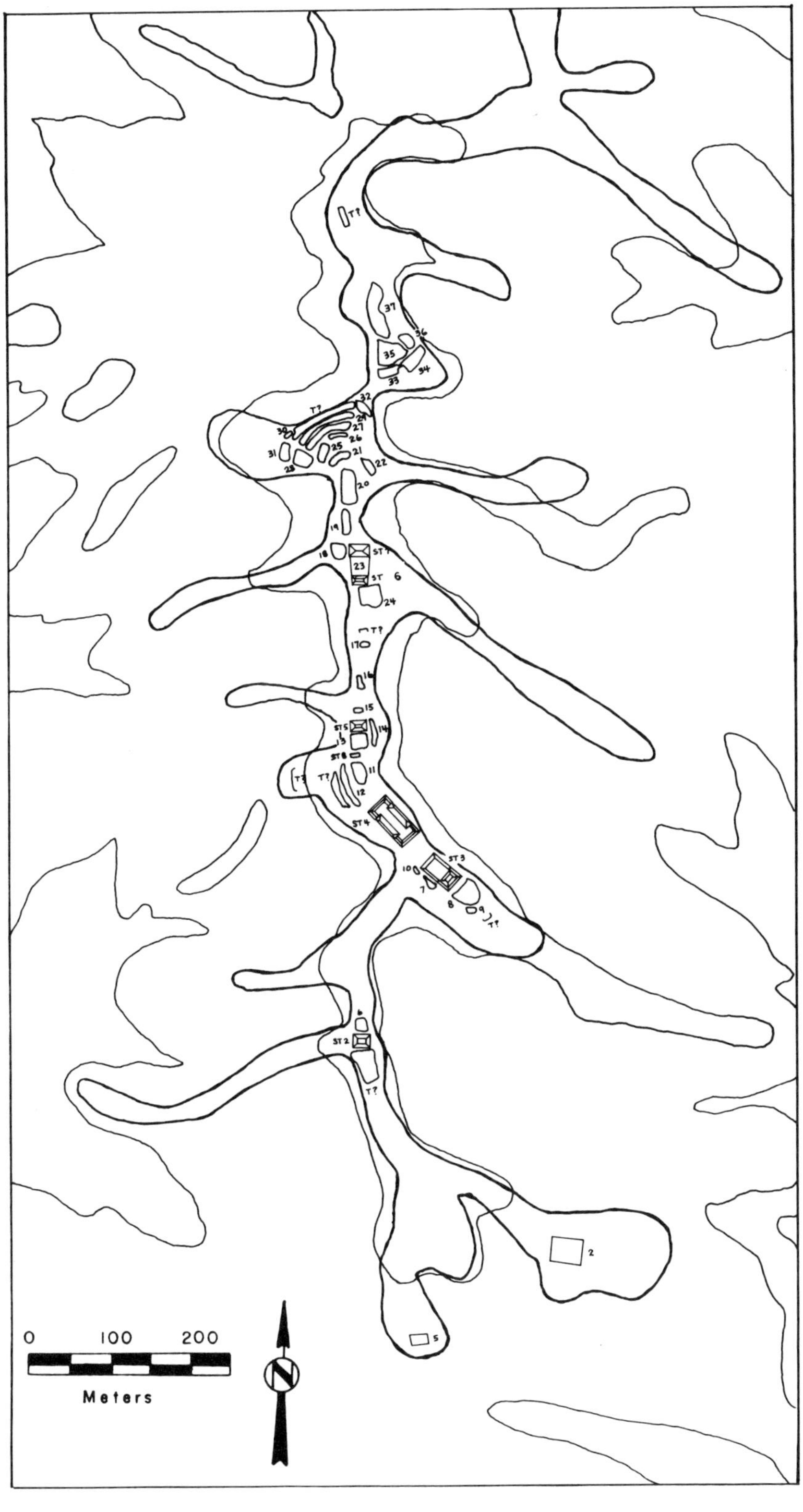

Figure A.XI-58. El Mirador (2-9-1).

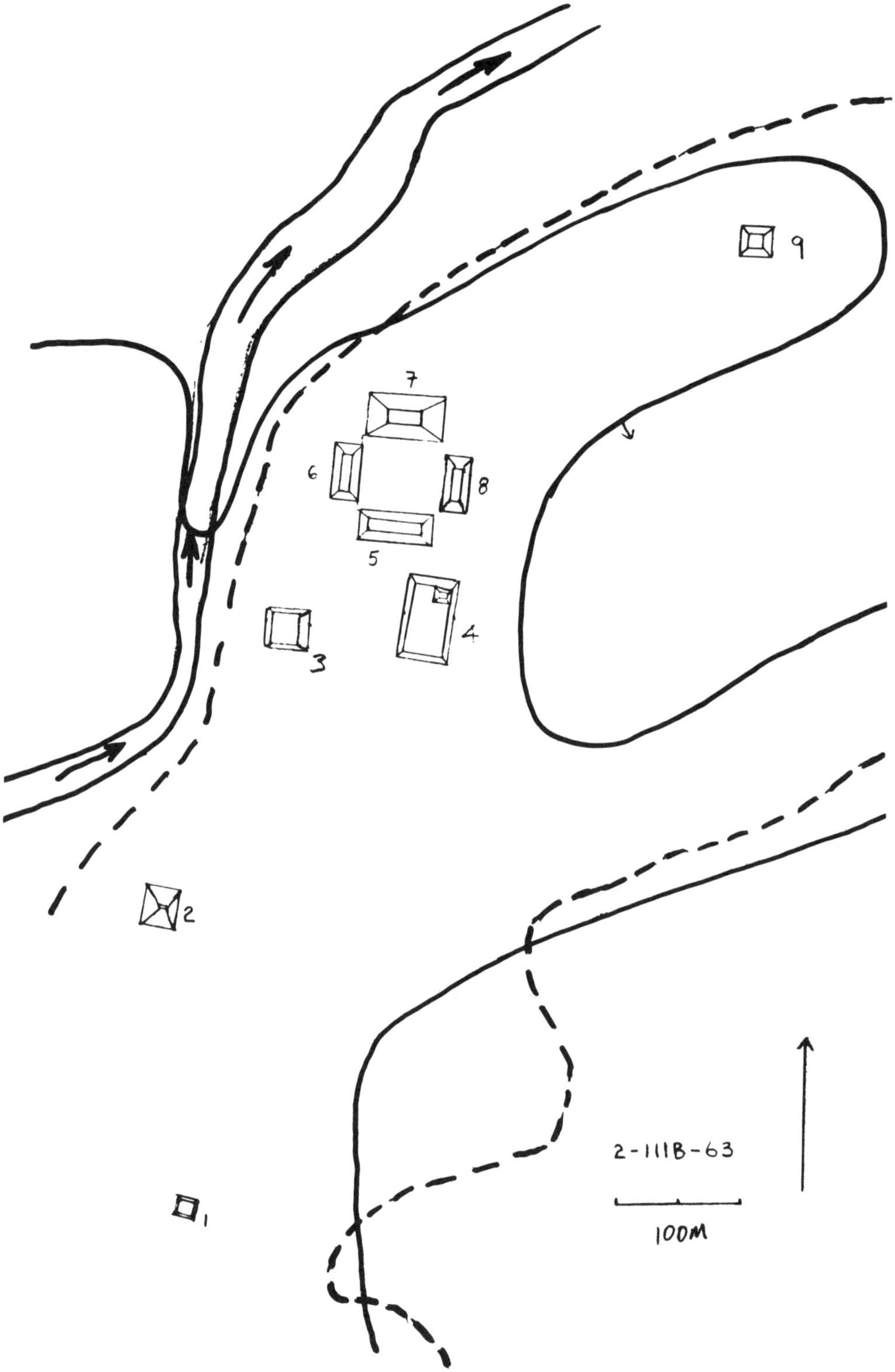

Figure A.XI-59. San Pedro Ixtlahuaca (2-9-63).

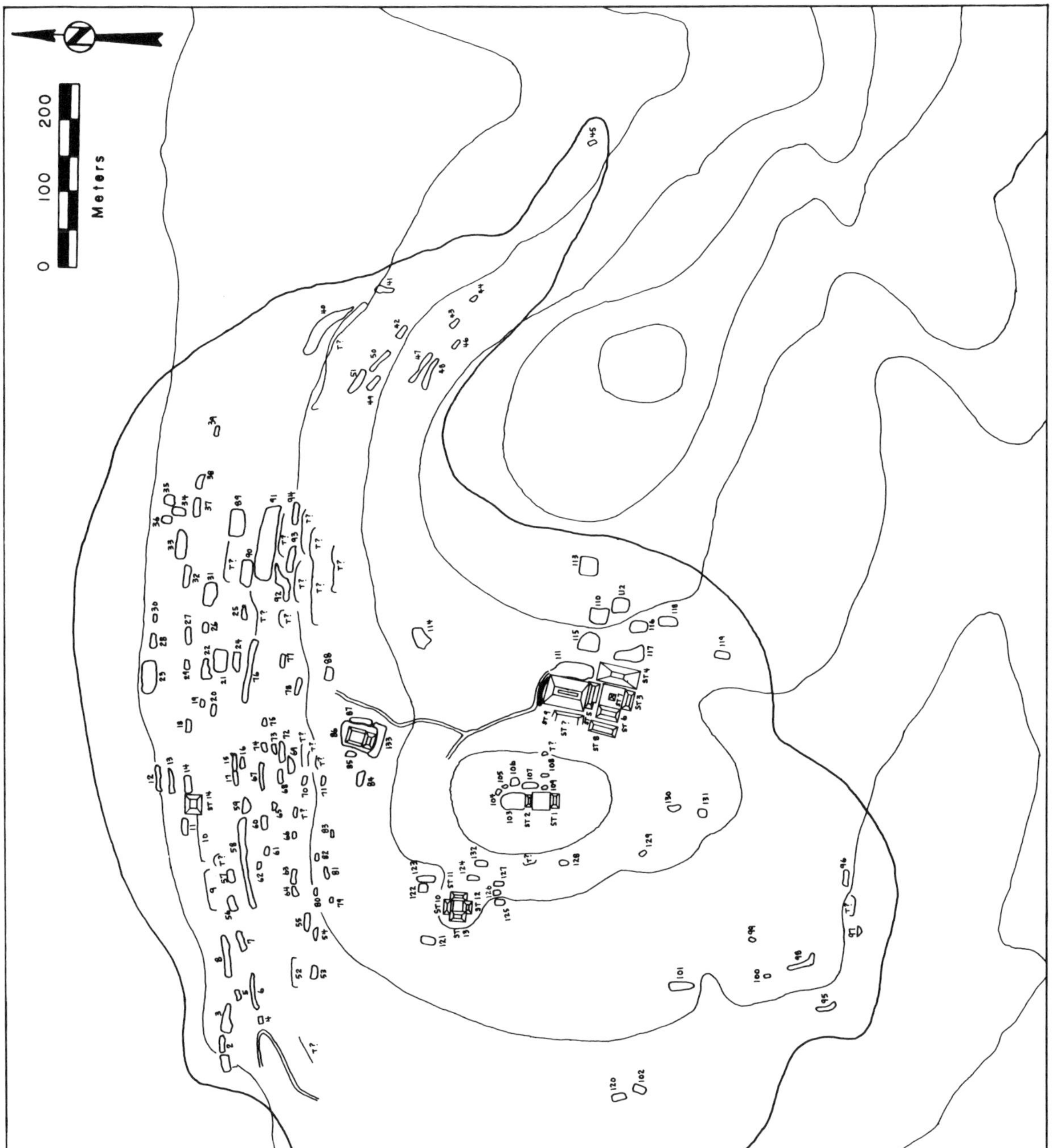

Figure A.XI-60. Loma de la Montura (2-10-2).

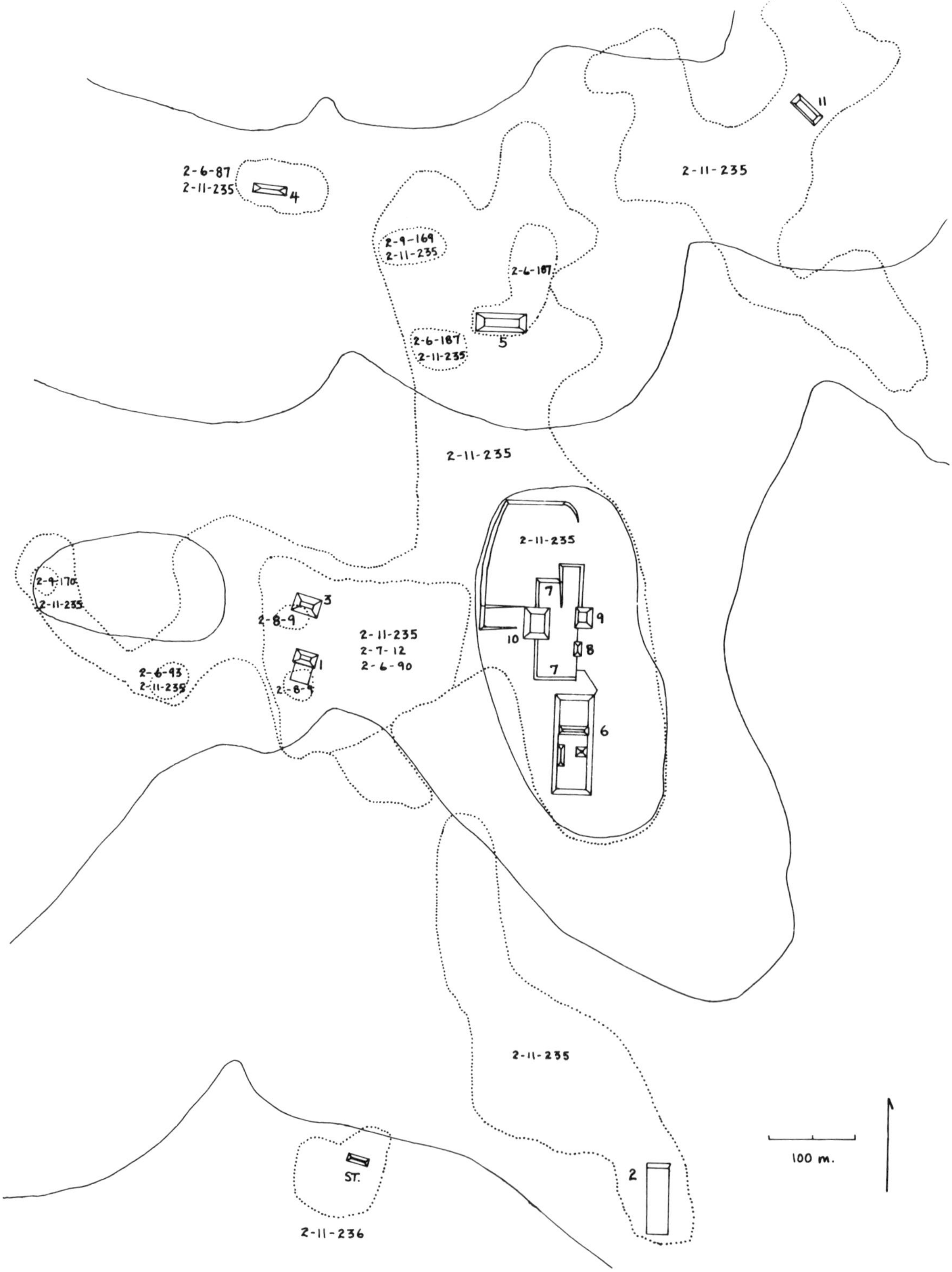

Figure A.XI-61. 2-11-235, etc.

REFERENCES

Abascal, Rafael M., Gordon Harbottle, and E.V. Sayre

1974 Correlation between Terra Cotta Figurines and Pottery from the Valley of Mexico and Source Clays by Activation Analysis. In *Archaeological Chemistry*, edited by Curt W. Beck, pp. 81-99, American Chemical Society, Washington.

Aceves de La Mora, J.L.

1976 *Climatología del Estado de Oaxaca*. Oaxaca, Indeco.

Acosta, Jorge R.

1965 Preclassic and Classic Architecture of Oaxaca. In *Handbook of Middle American Indians*, Vol. 3, edited by Robert Wauchope and Gordon R. Willey, pp. 814-36. University of Texas Press, Austin.

1972 Nuevas Descubrimientos en Zaachila: 1971. *Boletín del Instituto Nacional de Antropología e Historia*, Epoca 2 (3):27–34.

Adams, Robert McC.

1965 *Land Behind Baghdad*. University of Chicago Press, Chicago.

1966 *The Evolution of Urban Society*. Aldine-Atherton, Chicago.

Adams, Robert McC., and Hans Nissen

1972 *The Uruk Countryside*. University of Chicago Press, Chicago.

Ammerman, Albert J.

1975 Late Pleistocene Population Dynamics: An Alternative View. *Human Ecology* 3 (4):219-34.

Allan, Jim

1978 Fishing for Wallabies: Trade as a Mechanism for Social Interaction, Integration and Elaboration on the Central Papuan Coast. In *The Evolution of Social Systems*, edited by Jonathan Friedman and M.J. Rowlands, pp. 419-56. University of Pittsburgh Press, Pittsburgh.

Allan, William

1965 *The African Husbandman*. Oliver and Boyd, Edinburgh.

Andrews, E. Wyllys, IV

1965 Archaeology and Prehistory in the Northern Maya Lowlands: An Introduction. In *Handbook of Middle American Indians*, Vol. 2, edited by Robert Wauchope and Gordon R. Willey, pp. 288-330. University of Texas Press, Austin.

1968 Dzibilchaltún: A Northern Maya Metropolis. *Archaeology* 21:36-47.

Appel, Jill

1982 *Political and Economic Organization in the Valley of Oaxaca Late Postclassic: An Evolutionary Perspective*. Ph.D. dissertation, Department of Sociology and Anthropology, Purdue University.

Appleby, Gordon

1976 The Role of Urban Food Needs in Regional Development, Puno, Peru. In *Regional Analysis, Volume I: Economic Systems*, edited by Carol Smith, pp. 147-77. Academic Press, New York.

Armillas, Pedro

1971 Gardens on Swamps. *Science* 174:653-61.

Athens, J. Stephen

1978 Theory Building and the Study of Evolutionary Process in Complex Societies. In *For Theory Building in Archaeology*, Lewis Binford, editor, pp. 353-84. Academic Press, New York.

Baker, Hugh D.R.

1977 Extended Kinship in the Traditional City. In *The City in Late Imperial China*, edited by G. William Skinner, pp. 499-520. Stanford University Press, Stanford.

Balfet, Hélène

1965 Ethnographic Observations in North Africa and Archaeological Interpretation: The Pottery of the Maghreb. In *Ceramics and Man*, edited by Fred R. Matson, pp. 161-77. Aldine, Chicago.

Barlow, Robert H.

1945 Dos Relaciones Antiguas del Pueblo de Cuilapa, Estado de Oaxaca. *Tlalocan* 2:18-28.

1949 The Extent of the Empire of the Culhua Mexica. *Ibero-Americana, No*. 28. University of California Press, Berkeley.

Benet, Francisco

1957 Explosive Markets: The Berber Highlands. In *Trade and Market in the Early Empires*, edited by Karl Polanyi, Conrad Arensberg, and Harry Pearson, pp. 188-217. The Free Press, New York.

Bernal, Ignacio

1949 Exploraciones en Coixtlahuaca. *Revista Mexicana de Estudios Antropológicos* 10:5-76.

1965 Archaeological Synthesis of Oaxaca. In *Handbook of Middle American Indians*, Vol. 3, edited by Robert Wauchope and Gordon R. Willey, pp. 788-813. University of Texas Press, Austin.

Bernal, Ignacio, and Lorenzo Gamio

1974 *Yagul: El Palacio de los Seis Patios*. Universidad Nacional Autónoma de México, México.

Berry, Brian J.L.

1961 City Size Distribution and Economic Development. *Economic Development and Culture Change* 9:573-88.

1967 *Geography of Market Centers and Retail Distribution*. Prentice-Hall, Englewood Cliffs.

Birmingham, Judy

1975 Traditional Potters of the Kathmandu Valley: An Ethnoarchaeological Study. *Man* 10:370-86.

Blanton, Richard E.
1972 Prehispanic Settlement Patterns of the Ixtapalapa Peninsula Region, Mexico. *Occasional Papers in Anthropology, No.* 6. Pennsylvania State University, University Park.
1975 The Cybernetic Analysis of Human Population Growth. In: Population Studies in Archaeology and Biological Anthropology: A Symposium. *Memoirs of the Society for American Archaeology* 30:116-26.
1976a The Origins of Monte Albán. In *Cultural Change and Continuity*, edited by Charles Cleland, pp. 223-31. Academic Press, New York.
1976b Anthropological Studies of Cities. *Annual Review of Anthropology* 5:249-64.
1976c The Role of Symbiosis in Adaptation and Sociocultural Change in the Valley of Mexico. In *The Valley of Mexico*, edited by Eric R. Wolf, pp. 181-202. University of New Mexico Press, Albuquerque.
1978 *Monte Albán: Settlement Patterns at the Ancient Zapotec Capital*. Academic Press, New York.
1980 Cultural Ecology Reconsidered. *American Antiquity* 45:145-50.

Blanton, Richard E., Jill Appel, Laura Finsten, Steve Kowalewski, Gary Feinman, and Eva Fisch
1979 Regional Evolution in the Valley of Oaxaca, Mexico. *Journal of Field Archaeology* 6:369-90.

Blanton, Richard E., and Stephen Kowalewski
1981 Monte Albán and After in the Valley of Oaxaca. In *Supplement to the Handbook of Middle American Indian*, Vol. 1, edited by Jeremy A. Sabloff, pp. 94-116. University of Texas Press, Austin.

Blanton, Richard E.
in press Sections in *The Cloud People: Divergent Evolution of the Zapotec and Mixtec Civilizations*., edited by Kent V. Flannery and Joyce Marcus. New York: Academic Press.

Blau, Peter M.
1968 The Hierarchy of Authority in Organizations. *The American Journal of Sociology* 73:453-67.
1970 A Formal Theory of Differentiation in Organizations. *American Sociological Review* 35(2):201-18.

Bloch, Marc
1961 *Feudal Society, Volume II*. Routledge and Kegan Paul, London.

Borah, Woodrow, and Sherburne F. Cook
1963 The Aboriginal Population of Central Mexico on the Eve of the Spanish Conquest. *Ibero-Americana*, No. 45. University of California Press, Berkeley.

Bordaz, Jacques
1964 *Pre-Columbian Ceramic Kilns at Peñitas, a Post-Classic Site in Coastal Nayarit*. Ph.D. dissertation, Department of Anthropology, Columbia University.

Boulding, Kenneth
1956 Toward a General Theory of Growth. *General Systems* 1:66-75.

Bray, Warwick
1978 Civilising the Aztecs. In *The Evolution of Social Systems*, edited by Jonathan Friedman and M.J. Rowlands, pp. 373-400. University of Pittsburgh Press, Pittsburgh.

Brockington, Donald
1973 Archaeological Investigations at Miahuatlán, Oaxaca. *Vanderbilt University Publications in Anthropology*, 7, Nashville.

Brumfiel, Elizabeth
1976 *Specialization and Exchange at the Late Postclassic (Aztec) Community of Huexotla, Mexico*. Ph.D. dissertation, Department of Anthropology, The University of Michigan.
1982 An Ethnohistorical Synthesis of the Chaleo-Xochimilco Region. In: Prehispanic Settlement Patterns in the Southern Valley of Mexico: The Chalco-Xochimilco Region, by Jeffrey R. Parsons, Elizabeth Brumfiel, Mary H. Parsons, and David J. Wilson. *Memoirs of the Museum of Anthropology, University of Michigan,* No. 14. Ann Arbor.

Burgoa, Fray Francisco de
1934 *Geográfica Descripción*. 2 Vol. Archivo General de la Nación, México.

Byers, Douglas S.
1967 Climate and Hydrology. In *The Prehistory of the Tehuacán Valley, Volume I: Environment and Subsistence*, edited by Douglas S. Byers, pp. 48-65. University of Texas Press, Austin.

Caldwell, Joseph, and Robert Hall (eds.)
1964 Hopewellian Studies. *Illinois State Museum Scientific Papers, Vol. 12*. Springfield.

Calnek, Edward
1978 The Internal Structure of Cities in America: Pre-Columbian Cities; The Case of Tenochtitlán. In *Urbanization in the Americas from its Beginnings to the Present,* edited by Richard P. Schaedel, Jorge E. Hardoy, and Nora Scott Kinzer, pp. 315-26. Mouton, The Hague.

Carneiro, Robert
1970 A Theory of the Origin of the State. *Science* 169:733-38.

Carrasco, Pedro
1964 Family Structure of Sixteenth-Century Tepoztlan. In *Process and Pattern in Culture,* edited by Robert Manners, pp. 185-210. Aldine, Chicago.

Carrothers, George A.P.
1956 An Historical Review of the Gravity and Potential Concepts of Human Interaction. *Journal of the American Institute of Planning* 22:94-102.

Carta de Climas
1970 San Pedro Pochutla 14P-(II) Oaxaca 14Q-VIII. Dirección de Planeación, Comisión de Estudios de Territorio Nacional y Universidad Nacional Autónoma de México, Instituto de Geografía.

Caso, Alfonso

1928 *Las Estelas Zapotecas*. Monografías del Museo Nacional de Arqueología, Historia y Etnografía, No. 3. México.

1928a Relación de la Vicaria y Partido de Sta. Cruz Que en Mexicano Se Dice Iztepec y en Zapoteco Quialoo. *Revista Mexicana de Estudios Históricos* 2, Suplemento:180–84.

1928b Descripción de Tehuantepec. *Revista Mexicana de Estudios Históricos 2,* Suplemento:164-75.

1947 Calendario y Escritura de las Antiguas Culturas de Monte Albán. In *Obras Completas de Miguel Othón de Mendizábal* 1:115-43.

1965 Zapotec Writing and Calendar. In *Handbook of Middle American Indians*, Vol. 3, edited by Robert Wauchope and Gordon R. Willey, pp. 931-47. University of Texas Press, Austin.

1969 El Tesoro de Monte Albán. *Memorias del Instituto Nacional de Antropología e Historia 3*, México.

Caso, Alfonso, and Daniel F. Rubín de la Borbolla

1936 Exploraciones en Mitla, 1934-1935. *Instituto Panamericano de Geografía e Historia*, Pub. 21. México.

Caso, Alfonso, and Ignacio Bernal

1952 Urnas de Oaxaca. *Memorias del Instituto Nacional de Antropología e Historia 2*, México.

1965 Ceramics of Oaxaca. In *Handbook of Middle American Indians*, Vol. 3, edited by Robert Wauchope and Gordon R. Willey, pp. 871-95. University of Texas Press, Austin.

Caso, Alfonso, Ignacio Bernal, and Jorge R. Acosta

1967 La Cerámica de Monte Albán. *Memorias del Instituto Nacional de Antropología e Historia 13*. México.

Castetter, Edward F., and William H. Bell

1942 Pima and Papago Indian Agriculture. *Inter-American Studies*, 1:1-245. University of New Mexico Press, Albuquerque.

Chadwick, Robert

1971 Postclassic Pottery of the Central Valleys. In *Handbook of Middle American Indians*, Vol. 10, edited by Gordon Ekholm and Ignacio Bernal, pp. 228-57. The University of Texas Press, Austin.

Chagnon, Napoleon

1968 *Yanomamö, the Fierce People*. Holt, Rinehart, and Winston, New York.

Chapman, Kenneth

1970 *The Pottery of San Ildefonso Pueblo*. University of New Mexico Press, Albuquerque.

Charlton, Thomas

1976 Modern ceramics in the Teotihuacan Valley. In *Ethnic and Tourist Arts: Cultural Expressions from the Fourth World*, edited by Nelson H. Graburn, pp. 137-48. University of California Press, Berkeley.

1978 Teotihuacan, Tepeapulco, and Obsidian Exploitation. *Science* 200:1227-36.

Chisholm, Michael

1968 *Rural Settlement and Land Use*. 2nd ed. Hutchinson, London.

Christaller, Walter

1933 *Die Zentralen Orte in Süddeutschland*. Translated by C.W. Baskin (1966), *Central Places in Southern Germany*. Prentice Hall, Englewood Cliffs.

Cieza de León, Pedro de

1945 *La Crónica del Perú*. Colección Austral, Buenos Aires.

Claessen, Henri J.M., and Peter Skalník (eds.)

1978 *The Early State*. Mouton, The Hague.

Coe, Michael D.

1969 Photogrammetry and the Ecology of the Olmec Civilization. Paper read at a working conference on aerial photography and anthropology, Cambridge, Mass.

Coe, William R.

1967 *Tikal: A Handbook of Ancient Maya Ruins*. University Museum, University of Pennsylvania, Philadelphia.

Colección . . .

1864-1884 *Colección de Documentos Inéditos, Relativos al Descubrimiento, Conquista, y Organización de las Antiguas Posesiones Españolas de América y del Ultramar, Sacados de los Archivos de Indias*. 42 vols. Madrid.

Collier, George A.

1975 *Fields of the Tzotzil: The Ecological Bases of Tradition in Highland Chiapas*. University of Texas Press, Austin.

Cook, Scott, and Martin Diskin

1976 The Peasant Market Economy of the Valley of Oaxaca in Analysis and History. In *Markets in Oaxaca*, edited by Scott Cook and Martin Diskin, pp. 5-26. University of Texas Press, Austin.

Coontz, Sidney

1968 *Population Theories and the Economic Interpretation*. Routledge and Kegan Paul, London.

Cortés, Hernán

1971 *Letters from Mexico*. Translated and edited by A.R. Pagden. Orion Press, New York.

Cowgill, George

1975 On Causes and Consequences of Ancient and Modern Population Changes. *American Anthropologist* 77:505-25.

Crissman, Lawrence

1976 Specific Central-Place Models for an Evolving System of Market Towns on the Changhua Plain, Taiwan. In *Regional Analysis, Vol. I, Economic Systems*, edited by Carol Smith, pp. 183-218. Academic Press, New York.

Cruz, Wilfrido

1946 *Oaxaca Recóndita: Razas, Idiomas, Costumbres, Leyendas, y Tradiciones del Estado de Oaxaca, México*. México.

Culbert, T. Patrick

1974 *The Lost Civilization: The Story of the Classic Maya*. Harper and Row, New York.

Curran, Margaret
1978 An Examination of the Relationships between Population Density and Agricultural Productivity in the Prehispanic Valley of Oaxaca, Mexico. Paper presented to the 43rd annual meeting of the Society for American Archaeology.

David, Nicholas, and Hilke Hennig
1972 The Ethnography of Pottery: A Fulani Case Seen in Archaeological Perspective. *McCaleb Module in Anthropology*, 21.

Davies, Nigel
1973 *The Aztecs: A History*. MacMillan, London.

DeGlopper, Donald R.
1977 Social Structure in a Nineteenth-Century Taiwanese Port City. In *The City in Late Imperial China*, edited by G. William Skinner, pp. 633-50. Stanford University Press, Stanford.

Diakanov, Igor
1969 The Rise of the Despotic State in Ancient Mesopotamia. In *Ancient Mesopotamia, Socio-Economic History*, edited by Igor Diakanov, pp. 173-203. Nauka, Moscow.

Díaz del Castillo, Bernal
1956 *The Discovery and Conquest of Mexico*, translated by A.P. Maudslay, Farrar, Straus, and Giroux, New York.

Downing, Theodore
1974 Irrigation and Moisture Sensitive Periods: A Zapotec Case. In Irrigation's Impact on Society, edited by Theodore Downing and McGuire Gibson, pp. 113-22. *Anthropological Papers of the University of Arizona*, 25. Tucson.

Drennan, Robert
1976 Fábrica San José and Middle Formative Society in the Valley of Oaxaca. *Prehistory and Human Ecology of the Valley of Oaxaca*, Vol. 4, edited by Kent V. Flannery. *Memoirs of the Museum of Anthropology, University of Michigan*, No. 8. Ann Arbor.
in press Oaxaca Radiocarbon Dates Associated with Ceramic Phases, In *The Cloud People: Divergent Evolution of the Zapotec and Mixtec Civilizations,* edited by Kent V. Flannery and Joyce Marcus. New York: Academic Press. Albuquerque.

Drennan, Robert, and Judith Nowack
1977 El Posible Papel de Teotihuacan en el Desarrollo Clásico de Tehuacán. Paper presented at Mesa Redonda, Guanajuato, Mexico.

Dunn, Mary
1975 Ceramic Evidence for the Prehistoric Distribution of Maize in Mexico. *American Antiquity* 40:305-14.

Durán, Fray Diego
1951 *Historia de las Indias de Nueva España*. Editorial Nacional, México.

Earle, Timothy
1977 A Reappraisal of Redistribution: Complex Hawaiian Chiefdoms. In *Exchange Systems in Prehistory*, edited by Timothy Earle and Jonathon Ericson, pp. 213-29. Academic Press, New York.
1978 Economic and Social Organization of Complex Chiefdoms: the Halelea District, Kauai, Hawaii. *Anthropological Papers, Museum of Anthropology, University of Michigan*, No. 63. Ann Arbor.

Eisenstadt, Shmuel Noah
1963 *The Political Systems of Empires*. Free Press, New York.

Elvin, Mark
1977 Market Towns and Waterways: The County of Shang-hai from 1480 to 1910. In *The City in Late Imperial China*, edited by G. William Skinner, pp. 441-74. Stanford University Press, Stanford.

Farvar, M. Taghi, and John P. Milton (eds.)
1972 *The Careless Technology*. Natural History Press, Garden City, New York.

Feinman, Gary
1977 An Evaluation of Settlement Pattern Research Completed Within the State of Oaxaca. Paper presented at the Congreso de Evaluación de la Antropología en Oaxaca, Museo Regional de Oaxaca.
1980 *The Relationship Between Administrative Organization and Ceramic Production in the Valley of Oaxaca, Mexico*. Ph.D. dissertation, The City University of New York Graduate Center, Department of Anthropology.

Fesler, James
1968 Centralization and Decentralization. *International Encyclopedia of the Social Sciences* 2:370-79.

Finsten, Laura
1978 The Classic-Postclassic Transition in the Valley of Oaxaca: Evidence from Sto. Tomás Jalieza. Paper presented at the 43rd annual meeting of the Society for American Archaeology.
1982 *The Classic-Postclassic Transition in the Valley of Oaxaca, Mexico: A Regional Analysis of the Process of Political Decentralization in a Prehistoric Complex Society*. Ph.D. dissertation, Purdue University, Department of Sociology and Anthropology.

Firth, Raymond
1936 *We the Tikopia*. Allen and Unwin, London.
1939 *Primitive Polynesian Economy*. Routledge, London.
1959 *Social Change in Tikopia*. Allen and Unwin, London.
1961 *History and Traditions of Tikopia*. Polynesian Society, London.

Flannery, Kent V.
1968a The Olmec and the Valley of Oaxaca: A Model for Interregional Interaction in Formative Times. In *Dumbarton Oaks Conference on the Olmec*, edited by Elizabeth P. Benson, pp. 79-110. Dumbarton Oaks, Washington.
1968b Archaeological Systems Theory and Early Mesoamerica. In *Anthropological Archaeology in the Americas*, edited by Betty J. Meggers, pp. 67-87. Anthropological Society of Washington, Washington, D.C.

1972a The Cultural Evolution of Civilizations. *Annual Review of Ecology and Systematics* 3:399-426.

1972b Summary Comments: Evolutionary Trends in Social Exchange and Interaction. In Social Exchange and Interaction, edited by Edwin Wilmsen, pp. 129-36. *Anthropological Papers, Museum of Anthropology, University of Michigan*, No. 46. Ann Arbor.

1976a Sampling on the Regional Level. In *The Early Mesoamerican Village*, edited by Kent Flannery, pp. 131-36. Academic Press, New York.

1976b Empirical Determination of Site Catchments in Oaxaca and Tehuacán. In *The Early Mesoamerican Village*, edited by Kent Flannery, pp. 103-17. Academic Press, New York.

Flannery, Kent V. (ed.)
1976 *The Early Mesoamerican Village*. Academic Press, New York.

Flannery, Kent V., Anne V.T. Kirkby, Michael J. Kirkby, and Aubrey W. Williams, Jr.
1967 Farming Systems and Political Growth in Ancient Oaxaca. *Science* 158:445-54.

Flannery, Kent V., and James Schoenwetter
1970 Climate and Man in Formative Oaxaca. *Archaeology* 23:144-52.

Flannery, Kent V., Marcus C. Winter, Susan F. Lees, James A. Neely, James Schoenwetter, Suzanne Kitchen, and Jane C. Wheeler
1970 *Preliminary Archaeological Investigations in the Valley of Oaxaca, Mexico*. A report to the National Science Foundation and the Instituto Nacional de Antropología e Historia.

Flannery, Kent V., and Joyce Marcus
1976 Evolution of the Public Building in Formative Oaxaca. In *Cultural Change and Continuity*, edited by C. Cleland, pp. 205-22. Academic Press, New York.

Flannery, Kent V., and Marcus C. Winter
1976 Analyzing Household Activities. In *The Early Mesoamerican Village*, edited by Kent V. Flannery, pp. 34-47. Academic Press, New York.

Flannery, Kent V., Joyce Marcus, and Stephen Kowalewski
1981 The Preceramic and Formative of the Valley of Oaxaca. In *Supplement to the Handbook of Middle American Indians*, Vol. 1: Archaeology, edited by Jeremy Sabloff, pp. 48-93. University of Texas Press, Austin.

Flannery, Kent V., and Joyce Marcus (eds.)
in press *The Cloud People: Divergent Evolution of the Zapotec and Mixtec Civilizations*. New York: Academic Press.
in prep. Early and Middle Formative Ceramics of the Valley of Oaxaca. *Prehistory and Human Ecology of the Valley of Oaxaca, Memoirs of the Museum of Anthropology, University of Michigan* (future volume).

Fontana, Bernard, William Robinson, Charles Cormack, and Ernest Leavitt
1962 *Papago Indian Pottery* . University of Washington Press, Seattle.

Ford, Richard I.
1972 Barter, Gift, or Violence: An Analysis of Tewa Intertribal Exchange. In Social Exchange and Interaction, edited by Edwin Wilmsen, pp. 21-46. *Anthropological Papers, Museum of Anthropology, University of Michigan*, No. 46. Ann Arbor.

Foster, George M.
1955 *Contemporary Pottery Techniques in Southern and Central Mexico*. Middle American Research Institute, Tulane University, Publication 22.
1965 The Sociology of Pottery: Questions, Hypotheses, Arising from Contemporary Mexican Work. In *Ceramics and Man*, edited by F.R. Matson, pp. 43-61. Aldine, Chicago.

Fried, Morton
1965 *The Evolution of Political Society*. Random House, New York.

Friedman, Jonathan and M.J. Rowlands
1978 Notes Toward an Epigenetic Model of the Evolution of 'Civilization'. In *The Evolution of Social Systems*, edited by Jonathan Friedman and M.J. Rowlands, pp. 201-78. University of Pittsburgh Press, Pittsburgh.

Gall, Patricia, and Arthur Saxe
1977 The Ecological Evolution of Culture: The State as Predator in Succession Theory. In *Exchange Systems in Prehistory*, edited by Timothy Earle and Jonathon Ericson, pp. 255-68. Academic Press, New York.

Gallegos, Roberto
1962 Exploraciones en Zaachila, Oaxaca. *Boletín del Instituto Nacional de Antropología e Historia* 8:6-8.
1963 Zaachila: The First Season's Work, translated by Dudley Easby, Jr. *Archaeology* 16:226-33.

García Pimentel, Luis (ed.)
1904 *Relación de los Obispados de Tlaxcala, Michoacan, Oaxaca, y Otros Lugares en el Siglo XVI*. México.

Gerhard, Peter
1972 *A Guide to the Historical Geography of New Spain*. Cambridge University Press, Cambridge.

Golas, Peter J.
1977 Early Ch'ing Guilds. In *The City in Late Imperial China*, edited by G. William Skinner, pp. 555-80. Stanford University Press, Stanford.

Granskog, Jane
1974 *Agricultural Efficiency in a Zapotec Indian Village*. Ph.D. dissertation, The University of Texas, Department of Anthropology, Austin.

Haggett, Peter
1966 *Locational Analysis in Human Geography*. St. Martin's Press, New York.

Hall, Peter (ed.)
1966 *Von Thunen's Isolated State*, translated by C.M. Wartenberg. Pergamon Press, Oxford.

Hammond, Norman
1972 Locational Models and the Site of Lubaantún: A Classic Maya Centre. In *Models in Archaeology*, edited by David Clarke, pp. 757-800. Methuen, London.

Harding, Thomas G.
1967 *Voyagers of the Vitiaz Strait*. University of Washington Press, Seattle.
Harner, Michael
1970 Population Pressure and the Social Evolution of Agriculturalists. *Southwestern Journal of Anthropology* 26: 67-68.
Helms, Mary
1979 *Ancient Panama*. University of Texas Press, Austin.
Hendry, Jean
1957 *Atzompa: A Pottery Producing Village of Southern Mexico*. Ph.D. dissertation, Department of Anthropology. Cornell University.
Herrera y Tordesillas, Antonio de
1947 *Historia General de los Hechos de los Castellanos en las Islas de Tierrafirme del Mar Océano*. 15 Vols. México.
Hodder, Ian
1974 Some Marketing Models for Romano-British Coarse Pottery. *Britannia* 5:340-59.
Hodder, Ian R., and U.I. Ukwu
1969 *Markets in West Africa*. Ibadan University Press, Ibadan.
Hodder, Ian R., and M. Hassall
1971 The Non-Random Spacing of Romano-British Walled Towns. *Man* 6:391-407.
Hodder, Ian R., and Clive Orton
1976 *Spatial Analysis in Archaeology*. Cambridge University Press, Cambridge.
Holland, John
1975 *Adaptation in Natural And Artificial Systems*. University of Michigan Press, Ann Arbor.
Holling, C.S., and M. Goldberg
1971 Ecology and Planning. *Journal of the American Institute of Planners* 37:221-30.
Holmes, William H.
1897 *Archaeological Studies among the Ancient Cities of Mexico, Part II, Monuments of Chiapas, Oaxaca, and the Valley of Mexico*. Field Columbian Museum, Anthropological Series Vol. 1, No. 1. Pub. 16. Chicago.
Hunt Eva, and Robert Hunt
1974 Irrigation, Conflict, and Politics: A Mexican Case. In Irrigation's Impact on Society, edited by Theodore Downing and McGuire Gibson, pp. 129-57. *Anthropological Papers of the University of Arizona*, 25.
Irwin, Geoffrey
1978 Pots and Entrêpots: A Study of Settlement, Trade, and the Development of Economic Specialization in Papuan Prehistory. *World Archaeology* 9:299-319.
Isbell, William
1978 Environmental Perturbations and the Origin of the Andean State. In *Social Archaeology*, edited by Charles Redman et al., pp. 303-13. Academic Press, New York.

Johnson, E.A.J.
1970 *The Organization of Space in Developing Countries*. Harvard University Press, Cambridge, Mass.
Johnson, Gregory
1973 Local Exchange and Early State Development in Southwestern Iran. *Anthropological Papers, Museum of Anthropology, University of Michigan*, No. 51. Ann Arbor.
1977 Aspects of Regional Analysis in Archaeology. *Annual Review of Anthropology* 6:429-508.
in press The Changing Organization of Uruk Administration on the Susiana Plain. In *Archaeological Perspectives on Iran: From Prehistory to the Islamic Conquest*, edited by Frank Hole. University of New Mexico Press, Albuquerque.
Jones, E.L., and S.J. Woolf
1969 The Historic Role of Agrarian Change in Economic Development. In *Agrarian Change and Economic Development*, edited by E.L. Jones and S.J. Woolf, pp. 1-21. Methuen, London.
Jorde, L. B.
1978 Precipitation Cycles and Cultural Buffering in the Prehistoric Southwest. In *For Theory Building in Archaeology*, edited by Lewis Binford, pp. 385-95. Academic Press, New York.
Kappel, Wayne
1977 Alternative Adaptive Strategies in Three Mexican Towns. Ph.D. dissertation, The University of Arizona, Department of Anthropology.
Kasarda, J.D.
1974 The Structural Implications of Social Systems Size: A Three-Level Analysis. *American Sociological Review* 39 (1):19-28.
Katz, Friedrich
1978 A Comparison of Some Aspects of the Evolution of Cuzco and Tenochtitlán. In *Urbanization in the Americas from Its Beginnings to the Present*, edited by Richard P. Schaedel, Jorge E. Hardoy, and Nora Scott Kinzer, pp. 203-14. Mouton, The Hague.
Kelley, Klara
1976 Dendritic Central-Place Systems and the Organization of Navajo Trading Posts. In *Regional Analysis, Volume I, Economic Systems*, edited by Carol Smith, pp. 219-54. Academic Press, New York.
Kirkby, Anne V.T.
1973 The Use of Land and Water Resources in the Past and Present Valley of Oaxaca, Mexico. *Prehistory and Human Ecology of the Valley of Oaxaca*, Vol. 1, edited by Kent V. Flannery. *Memoirs of the Museum of Anthropology, University of Michigan*, No. 5. Ann Arbor.
Kowalewski, Stephen A.
1976 *Prehispanic Settlement Patterns of the Central Part of the Valley of Oaxaca, Mexico*. Ph.D. dissertation, The University

of Arizona, Department of Anthropology.
1980 Population Resource Balances in Period I of Oaxaca, Mexico. *American Antiquity* 45:151-64.

Kowalewski, Stephen A., Charles Spencer, and Elsa Redmond
1978 Description of Ceramic Categories. Appendix II in *Monte Albán: Settlement Patterns at the Ancient Zapotec Capital*, by Richard E. Blanton. Academic Press, New York.

Kurtz, Donald
1974 Peripheral and Transitional Markets: The Aztec Case. *American Ethnologist* 1:685-705.

Kuttruff, Carl
1978 Figurines and Urn Fragments from the Monte Albán Survey. Appendix VIII in *Monte Albán: Settlement Patterns at the Ancient Zapotec Capital*, by Richard E. Blanton. Academic Press, New York.

Lane, Frederic
1966 Economic Consequences of Organized Violence. In *Venice and History,* pp. 412–28. John Hopkins Press, Baltimore.

Lee, Richard
1968 What Hunters Do for a Living, or, How to Make Out on Scarce Resources. In *Man the Hunter*, edited by Richard Lee and Irven DeVore, pp. 30-48. Aldine, Chicago.

Lees, Susan
1973 Sociopolitical Aspects of Canal Irrigation in the Valley of Oaxaca. *Prehistory and Human Ecology of the Valley of Oaxaca*, Vol. 2, edited by Kent V. Flannery. *Memoirs of the Museum of Anthropology, The University of Michigan*, No. 6. Ann Arbor.
1974 Hydraulic Development as a Process of Response. *Human Ecology* 2:159-75.

Lightfoot, Kent
n.d. Multi-Site Communities in the Prehistoric Southwest: An Example from Pinedale, Arizona. Manuscript on file, Department of Anthropology, Arizona State University, Tempe.

Lind, Michael
1967 *Mixtec Polychrome Pottery: A Comparison of the Late Preconquest Polychrome Pottery from Cholula, Oaxaca, and the Chinantla*. M.A. thesis, The University of the Americas, Mexico.

Lopez, Robert
1976 *The Commercial Revolution of the Middle Ages, 950-1350*. Cambridge University Press, Cambridge.

Lorenzo, José Luis
1960 Aspectos Físicos del Valle de Oaxaca. *Revista Mexicana de Estudios Antropológicos* 16:49-65.

Lowe, Gareth W., and J. Alden Mason
1965 Archaeological Survey of the Chiapas Coast, Highlands, and Upper Grijalva Basin. In *Handbook of Middle American Indians*, Vol. 2, edited by Robert Wauchope and Gordon R. Willey, pp. 195-236. University of Texas Press, Austin.

MacCluer, Jean W., James V. Neel, and Napoleon A. Chagnon
1971 Demographic Structure of a Primitive Population: A Simulation. *American Journal of Physical Anthropology* 35:193-207.

MacNeish, Richard S., Frederick A. Peterson, and Kent V. Flannery
1970 *The Prehistory of the Tehuacan Valley, Volume 3: Ceramics*. University of Texas Press, Austin.

Malinowski, Bronislaw
1922 *Argonauts of the Western Pacific*. Dutton, New York.

Marcus, Joyce
1976a The Iconography of Militarism at Monte Albán and Neighboring Sites in the Valley of Oaxaca. In *Origins of Religious Art and Iconography in Preclassic Mesoamerica*, edited by H.B. Nicholson, pp. 123-39. Latin American Center, University of California, Los Angeles.
1976b The Origins of Mesoamerican Writing. *Annual Review of Anthropology* 5:35–67.
1976c The Size of the Early Mesoamerican Village. In *The Early Mesoamerican Village*, edited by Kent V. Flannery, pp. 79-90. Academic Press, New York.
1980 Zapotec Writing. *Scientific American* 242:50-64.

Mason, Roger, Dennis Lewarch, Michael O'Brien, and James Neely
1977 An Archaeological Survey on the Xoxocotlán Piedmont, Oaxaca, Mexico. *American Antiquity* 42:567-74.

Meggitt, Mervyn J.
1971 The Pattern of Leadership among the Mae-Enga of New Guinea. In *Politics in New Guinea*, edited by Ronald Berndt and Peter Lawrence, pp. 191-206. University of Western Australia Press.
1972 System and Subsystem: The Te Exchange Cycle among the Mae Enga. *Human Ecology* 1:111-23.

Messer, Ellen
1978 Zapotec Plant Knowledge: Classification, Uses, and Communication about Plants in Mitla, Oaxaca, Mexico. *Prehistory and Human Ecology of the Valley of Oaxaca*, Vol. 5, edited by Kent V. Flannery and Richard E. Blanton. *Memoirs of the Museum of Anthropology, University of Michigan*, No. 10, Part 2. Ann Arbor.

Millon, René
1973 *Urbanization at Teotihuacan, Mexico, Volume 1, The Teotihuacan Map, Part 1: Text*. University of Texas Press, Austin.
1976 Social Relations in Ancient Teotihuacan. In *The Valley of Mexico*, edited by Eric R. Wolf, pp. 205-48. University of New Mexico Press, Albuquerque.

Millon, René, Clara Hall, and May Díaz
1962 Conflict in the Modern Teotihuacan Irrigation System. *Comparative Studies in Society and History* 4:494-521.

Molíns Fábrega, N.
1956 *El Códice Mendocino y la Economía de Tenochtitlan*. Ediciones Libro-Mex, México.

Moseley, Michael, and Carol J. Mackey
1974 *Twenty-four Architectural Plans of Chan-Chan, Peru*. Peabody Museum Press, Cambridge, Massachusetts.

Motolinía, Toribio de Benavente
1950 *History of the Indians of New Spain*. Translated and edited by Elizabeth Foster. The Cortés Society, Documents and Narratives Concerning the Discovery and Conquest of Latin America, 4. Berkeley.

Murra, John
1956 *The Economic Organization of the Inca State*. Ph.D. dissertation, The University of Chicago, Department of Anthropology.

Nash, Manning
1958 Machine Age Maya: The Industrialization of a Guatemalan Community. *American Anthropological Association, Memoir* 87.

Nef, John U.
1977 An Early Energy Crisis and Its Consequences. *Scientific American* 237 (5):140-51.

Odum, Eugene
1969 The Strategy of Ecosystem Development. *Science* 164:262-70.

Olmstead, Albert T.
1923 *History of Assyria*. Charles Scribner's Sons, New York.

Olsson, Gunnar
1965 *Distance and Human Interaction*. The Regional Science Research Institute, Bibliography Series 2. Philadelphia.

Oppenheim, A. Leo
1964 *Ancient Mesopotamia*. The University of Chicago Press, Chicago.

Orlandini, Richard
1967 A Formative Well from the Valley of Oaxaca. Paper presented to the 32nd annual meeting of the Society for American Archaeology.

Oviedo y Valdés, Gonzalo Fernández de
1851-1855 *Historia General y Natural de las Indias, Islas, y Tierra-Firme del Mar Océano*. 4 vol. Seville.

Paddock, John
1966 Oaxaca in Ancient Mesoamerica. In *Ancient Oaxaca*, edited by John Paddock, pp. 83-242. Stanford University Press, Stanford.
in press Sections in *The Cloud People: Evolution of the Zapotec and Mixtec Civilizations of Oaxaca, Mexico*, edited by Kent V. Flannery and Joyce Marcus. University of New Mexico Press, Albuquerque.

Paddock, John (ed.)
1966 *Ancient Oaxaca*. Stanford University Press, Stanford.

Paddock, John, Joseph Mogor, and Michael Lind
1968 Lambityeco Tomb 2: A Preliminary Report. *Boletín de Estudios Oaxaqueños* 25:1-24.

Parsons, Jeffrey
1971 Prehistoric Settlement Patterns of the Texcoco Region, Mexico. *Memoirs of the Museum of Anthropology, University of Michigan*, No. 3. Ann Arbor.
1976 The Role of Chinampa Agriculture in the Food Supply of Aztec Tenochtitlan. In *Cultural Change and Continuity*, edited by C. Cleland, pp. 233-62. Academic Press, New York.

Paso y Troncoso, Francisco del (ed.)
1905-1908 *Papeles de Nueva España*. Segunda Serie, Volumes I and IV. Sucesores de Rivadeneyra, Madrid.
1940 *Epistolario de Nueva España*. 16 Vols. Biblioteca Histórica Méxicana de Obras Inéditas, Serie 2, México.

Payne, William O.
1970 A Potter's Analysis of the Pottery from Lambityeco, Tomb 2. *Boletín de Estudios Oaxaqueños* 29:1-8.

Peebles, Christopher, and Susan Kus
1977 Some Archaeological Correlates of Ranked Societies. *American Antiquity* 42:421-48.

Peterson, David
1976 *Ancient Commerce*. Ph.D. dissertation, State University of New York at Binghamton, Department of Anthropology.

Pirenne, Henri
1936 *Economic and Social History of Medieval Europe*. Routledge and Kegan Paul, London.
1957 *Mohammed and Charlemagne*. World Publishing Co., Cleveland and New York.

Pires-Ferreira, Jane W.
1975 Formative Exchange Networks with Special Reference to the Valley of Oaxaca. *Prehistory and Human Ecology of the Valley of Oaxaca*, Vol. 3, edited by Kent V. Flannery. *Memoirs of the Museum of Anthropology, University of Michigan*, No. 7. Ann Arbor.

Plog, Fred
1979 Alternative Models of Prehistoric Change. In *Transformations: Mathematical Approaches to Culture Change*, edited by Colin Renfrew and Kenneth L. Cooke, pp. 221-36. Academic Press, New York.

Plog, Stephen
1976 Measurement of Prehistoric Interaction between Communities. In *The Early Mesoamerican Village*, edited by Kent V. Flannery, pp. 255-72. Academic Press, New York.

Polanyi, Karl
1944 *The Great Transformation*. Holt, Rinehart, and Winston, New York.

Polanyi, Karl, Conrad W. Arensberg, and Harry W. Pearson (eds.)
1957 *Trade and Market in the Early Empires*. The Free Press, New York.

Prigogine, Ilya
1976 Order through Fluctuation: Self-organization and Social System. In *Evolution and Consciousness*, edited by E. Jantsch and C. Waddington, pp. 93-133. Addison-Wesley, New York.

Pyne, Nanette
1976 The Fire-serpent and Were-jaguar in Formative Oaxaca: A Contingency Table Analysis. In *The Early Mesoamerican Village*, edited by Kent V. Flannery, pp. 272-80. Academic Press, New York.

Rabin, Emily
1970 The Lambityeco Friezes: Notes on Their Content, with an Appendix on C^{14} Dates. *Boletín de Estudios Oaxaqueños* 33.

Rands, Robert
1967 Ceramic Technology and Trade in the Palenque Region, Mexico. In *American Historical Archaeology*, edited by C. Riley and W. Taylor, pp. 137-51. Southern Illinois University Press, Carbondale.

Rappaport, Roy A.
1969 Sanctity and Adaptation. Paper presented for Wenner-Gren Symposium 44, The Moral and Aesthetic Structure of Human Adaptation.
1978 Maladaptation in Social Systems. In *The Evolution of Social Systems*, edited by Jonathan Friedman and M.J. Rowlands, pp. 49-72. University of Pittsburgh Press, Pittsburgh.

Rathje, William
1971 The Origin and Development of Lowland Classic Maya Civilization. *American Antiquity* 36:275-85.
1975 Last Tango in Mayapan: A Tentative Trajectory of Production-distribution Systems. In *Ancient Civilization and Trade*, edited by Jeremy A. Sabloff and C.C. Lamberg-Karlovsky, pp. 409-48. University of New Mexico Press, Albuquerque.

Redfield, Robert, and Alfonso Villa Rojas
1962 *Chan Kom: A Maya Village*. Abridged Ed. The University of Chicago Press. Chicago.

Renfrew, Colin
1972 *The Emergence of Civilization*. Methuen, London.
1979 Transformations. In *Transformations: Mathematical Approaches to Culture Change*, edited by Colin Renfrew and Kenneth L. Cooke, pp. 3-44. Academic Press, New York.

Rowe, John
1967 What Kind of Settlement was Inca Cuzco? *Ñawpa Pacha* 5:59-76.

Sahagún, Fray Bernardino de
1952 *General History of the Things of New Spain (Florentine Codex)*. Book 4, translated and edited by Arthur J. O. Anderson and Charles E. Dibble. University of Utah Press.

Sahlins, Marshall D.
1972 *Stone Age Economics*. Aldine-Atherton, Chicago.

Saindon, Jacqueline
1977 *Cotton Production and Exchange in Mexico, 1427-1580*. M.A. thesis, Hunter College, City University of New York.

Sanders, William T.
1956 The Central Mexican Symbiotic Region. In *Prehistoric Settlement Patterns in the New World*, edited by Gordon R. Willey, pp. 115-27. Viking Fund Publications in Anthropology 23. Wenner-Gren Foundation, New York.
1965 *The Cultural Ecology of the Teotihuacan Valley*. Ms. on file, the Department of Anthropology, The Pennsylvania State University.
1970 The Population of the Teotihuacan Valley, The Basin of Mexico and the Central Mexican Symbiotic Region in the 16th century. In *Occasional Papers in Anthropology*, Pennsylvania State University, 3:385-457.
1972 Population, Agricultural History, and Societal Evolution in Mesoamerica. In *Population Growth: Anthropological Implications*, edited by Brian Spooner, pp. 101-53. Massachusetts Institute of Technology Press, Cambridge.

Sanders, William T., Jeffrey Parsons, and Michael Logan
1976 Summary and Conclusions. In *The Valley of Mexico*, edited by Eric R. Wolf, pp. 161-78. University of New Mexico Press, Albuquerque.

Sanders, William T., and Robert Santley
1978 Review of *Monte Albán* by Richard E. Blanton. *Science* 202:303-04.

Sanders, William T., Jeffrey Parsons, and Robert Santley
1979 *The Basin of Mexico*. Academic Press, New York.

Santley, Robert
1980 Disembedded Capitals Reconsidered. *American Antiquity* 45:132-45.

Saville, Marshall
1899a Exploration of Zapotecan Tombs in Southern Mexico. *American Anthropologist* 1:350-62.
1899b Field notes filed in the American Museum of Natural History, New York.

Schalk, Randall
1978 The Structure of an Anadromous Fish Resource. In *For Theory Building in Archaeology*, edited by Lewis Binford, pp. 207-44. Academic Press, New York.

Schipper, Kristofer M.
1977 Neighborhood Cult Associations in Traditional Tainan. In *The City in Late Imperial China*, edited by G. William Skinner, pp. 651-78. Stanford University Press, Stanford.

Schmieder, Oscar
1930 *The Settlements of the Tzapotec and Mije Indians, State of Oaxaca, Mexico*. University of California Press, Berkeley.

Schoenwetter, James
1974 Pollen Records of Guilá Naquitz Cave. *American Antiquity* 39:292-303.

Schwimmer, Brian
1976 Periodic Markets and Urban Development in Southern Ghana. In *Regional Analysis, Volume I, Economic Systems*, edited by Carol Smith, pp. 123-46. Academic Press, New York.

Service, Elman
1955 Indian-European Relations in Colonial Latin America. *American Anthropologist* 57:411-25.
1975 *The Origins of the State and Civilization: The Process of Cultural Evolution*. Norton, New York.
1978 Classical and Modern Theories of the Origin of Government. In: *Origins of the State: The Anthropology of Political Evolution,* edited by Ronald Cohen and Elman Service, pp. 21–34. ISHI, Philadelphia.

Shanson, Linda
MS Upgrading Proposal. University College, London University.

Shepard, Anna O.
1967 Preliminary Notes on the Paste Compositions of the Monte Albán Pottery. In *La Cerámica de Monte Albán*, by Alfonso Caso, Ignacio Bernal, and Jorge R. Acosta, *Memorias del Instituto Nacional de Antropología e Historia*, 13. México.
1977 Beginnings of Ceramic Industrialization: An Example from the Oaxaca Valley. In *Notes from a Ceramic Laboratory*, Carnegie Institution of Washington, Washington, D.C. (originally published in 1963).

Simon, Herbert
1944 Decision-Making and Administrative Organization. *Public Administration Review* 4: 16-30.
1955 On a Class of Skew Distribution Functions. *Biometrica* 42:425-40.
1969 The Architecture of Complexity. In *The Sciences of the Artificial*, by Herbert Simon, pp. 85-118. Massachusetts Institute of Technology Press, (originally published in the *Proceedings of the American Philosophical Society* 106:467-82, 1962).
1976 *Administrative Behavior*, 3rd ed. The Free Press, New York.

Skinner, G. William
1964 Marketing and Social Structure in Rural China, Part I. *Journal of Asian Studies* 24:195-228.
1965 Marketing and Social Structure in Rural China, Part II. *Journal of Asian Studies* 24:3-43.
1976 Mobility strategies in Late Imperial China: A Regional Systems Analysis. In *Regional Analysis, Volume I, Economic Systems*, edited by Carol Smith, pp. 327-64. Academic Press, New York.
1977a Introduction: Urban Development in Imperial China. In *The City in Late Imperial China*, edited by G. William Skinner, pp. 3-31. Stanford University Press, Stanford.
1977b Cities and the Hierarchy of Local Systems. In *The City in Late Imperial China*, edited by G. William Skinner, pp. 275-351. Stanford University Press, Stanford.

Skinner, G. William (ed.)
1977 *The City in Late Imperial China*. Stanford University Press, Stanford.

Skolnick, M.H., and C. Cannings
1972 Natural Regulation of Numbers in Primitive Human Populations. *Nature* 239(No. 5370):287-88.

Slobodkin, Lawrence B.
1968 Toward a Predictive Theory of Evolution. In *Population, Biology, and Evolution*, edited by Richard O. Lewontin, Syracuse University Press, Syracuse.

Smith, A. Ledyard
1950 *Uaxactún, Guatemala: Excavations of 1931-1937*. Carnegie Institution of Washington, Publication 588.

Smith, C. Earle, Jr.
1978 The vegetational history of the Oaxaca Valley. *Prehistory and Human Ecology of the Valley of Oaxaca*, Vol. 5, edited by Kent V. Flannery and Richard E. Blanton. *Memoirs of the Museum of Anthropology, University of Michigan*, No. 10, Part 1. Ann Arbor.

Smith, Carol
1974 Economics of Marketing Systems: Models from Economic Geography. *Annual Review of Anthropology* 3:167-201.
1976 Regional Economic Systems: Linking Geographical Models and Socioeconomic Problems. In *Regional Analysis, Volume I, Economic Systems*, edited by Carol Smith, pp. 3-67. Academic Press, New York.

Smith, Carol (ed.)
1976 *Regional Analysis, 2 Vols*. Academic Press, New York.

Smith, Michael
1979 The Aztec Marketing System and Settlement Pattern in the Valley of Mexico: A Central Place Analysis. *American Antiquity* 44:110-24.

Smith, Philip, and T.C. Young, Jr.
1972 The Evolution of Early Agriculture and Culture in Greater Mesopotamia: A Trial Model. In *Population Growth: Anthropological Implications*, edited by Brian Spooner, pp. 1-59. Massachusetts Institute of Technology Press, Cambridge.

Soustelle, Jacques
1961 *Daily Life of the Aztecs on the Eve of the Spanish Conquest*. Stanford University Press, Stanford.

Spence, Michael
1967 The Obsidian Industry of Teotihuacan. *American Antiquity* 32:507-14.
1974 The Development of the Teotihuacan Production System. Manuscript.
1978 The Archaeological Objectives of Obsidian Characterization Studies in Mesoamerica. Paper presented at the symposium titled Obsidian Characterization and Exchange Systems in Prehistory, sponsored by the National Bureau of Standards and the U.S. Department of Commerce, Washington, D.C.
1979 Obsidian Production and the State in Teotihuacan, Mexico. Paper presented at the symposium and workshop, Preshistoric Craft Production, The Department of Anthropology, Arizona State University.

Spencer, Charles, and Elsa Redmond
1979 Formative and Classic Developments in the Cuicatlán Cañada, Oaxaca: A Preliminary Report. Ms.

Spooner, Brian (ed.)
1972 *Population Growth: Anthropological Implications*. Massachusetts Institute of Technology Press, Cambridge.

Spores, Ronald
1965 The Zapotecs and Mixtecs at Spanish Conquest. In *Handbook of Middle American Indians, Vol. 3*, edited by Robert Wauchope and Gordon R. Willey, pp. 962-87. University of Texas Press, Austin.
1967 *Mixtec Kings and Their People*. University of Oklahoma Press, Norman.
1972 An Archaeological Settlement Survey of the Nochixtlan Valley, Oaxaca. *Vanderbilt University Publications in Anthropology*, 1. Nashville.
1974 Marital Alliances in the Political Integration of Mixtec Kingdoms. *American Anthropologist* 76:297-311.

Steponaitis, Vincas
1978 Location Theory and Complex Chiefdoms: A Mississippian Example. In *Mississippian Settlement Patterns*, edited by Bruce Smith, pp. 417-53. Academic Press, New York.

Stolmaker, Charlotte
1976 Examples of Stability and Change from Sta. María Atzompa. In *Markets in Oaxaca*, edited by Scott Cook and Martin Diskin, pp. 189-207. University of Texas Press, Austin.

Stross, Fred, Thomas Hester, Robert Heizer, and Robert Jack
1976 Chemical and Archaeological Studies of Mesoamerican Obsidians. In *Advances in Obsidian Glass Studies: Archaeological and Geochemical Perspectives*, edited by R.E. Taylor, pp. 240-58. Noyes Press, Park Ridge.

Swasey, William
1973 Mound 91, Lambityeco, a Description of an Ancient Kiln. *Mesa Redonda de Antropología XIII*. Sociedad Mexicana de Antropología, México.

Tambiah, S.J.
1976 *World Conqueror and World Renouncer*. Cambridge University Press, Cambridge and New York.

Taylor, William
1971 The Colonial Background to Peasant Economy in the Valley of Oaxaca. Paper presented at the joint annual meetings of the Southwestern Anthropological Association and the American Ethnological Society, Tucson.
1972 *Landlord and Peasant in Colonial Oaxaca*. Stanford University Press, Stanford.

Thomas, David
1976 *Figuring Anthropology: First Principles of Probability and Statistics*. Holt, Rinehart, and Winston, New York.

Tilly, Charles
1975 Food Supply and Public Order in Modern Europe. In *The Formation of Nation States in Western Europe*, edited by Charles Tilly, pp. 380-455. Princeton University Press, Princeton.

Torquemada, Fray Juan de
1944 *Los Veinte y un Libros Rituales y Monarchía Indiana*. 3 Vol. Chávez Hayhoe. México.
1969 *Monarquía Indiana*. Vol. 2. Editorial Porrúa, México.

Twitchett, Denis
1966 The T'ang Market System. *Asia Minor* 12:202-48.

Udy, Stanley Jr.
1959 *Organization of Work: A Comparative Analysis of Production among Nonindustrial Peoples*. HRAF Press, New Haven.

Uzoiqwe, G.N.
1972 Precolonial Markets in Bunyaro-Kitara. *Comparative Studies in Society and History* 14:422-55.

Vance, James
1970 *The Merchant's World*. Prentice-Hall, Englewood Cliffs.

van der Leeuw, Sander (ed.)
1976 *Studies in the Technology of Ancient Pottery*. Organization for the Advancement of Pure Research, Amsterdam, Netherlands.

van der Leeuw, Sander, and J. Schimmer
1976 The Archaeological Situation. In *Studies in the Technology of Ancient Pottery,* edited by Sander van der Leeuw. Organization for the Advancement of Pure Research, Amsterdam, Netherlands.

van der Sprenkel, Sybille
1977 Urban Social Control. In *The City in Late Imperial China*, edited by G. William Skinner, pp. 609-32. Stanford University Press, Stanford.

van de Velde, Paul, and Henriette Romieke van de Velde
1939 The Black Pottery of Coyotepec, Mexico. *Southwest Museum Papers*, 13. Highland Park, Los Angeles.

van Zantwijk, Rudolf A.M.
1973 Politics and Ethnicity in a Prehispanic Mexican State between the 13th and 15th Centuries. *Plural Societies* 4:23-52.

Varner, Dudley
1974 *Prehispanic Settlement Patterns in the Valley of Oaxaca, Mexico: The Etla Arm*. Ph.D. dissertation, The University of Arizona, Department of Anthropology.

Vita-Finzi, Claudio, and E.S. Higgs
1970 Prehistoric Economy in the Mount Carmel Area of Palestine: Site Catchment Analysis. *Proceedings of the Prehistoric Society* 36:1-37

Waddell, Eric
1972 *The Mound Builders*. University of Washington Press, Seattle.

Wallerstein, Immanuel
1974 *The Modern World-system*. Academic Press, New York.

Wasserstrom, Robert
1977 Land and Labor in Central Chiapas: A Regional Analysis. *Development and Change* 8:441-63.

Webber, Michael J.
1972 *Impact of Uncertainty on Location*. Massachusetts Institute of Technology Press, Cambridge.
Welte, Cecil
1975 *Ready Reference Release Number 3*. Oficina de Estudios de la Humanidad del Valle de Oaxaca. Mimeo.
Whalen, Michael
1974 Community Development and Integration during the Formative Period in the Valley of Oaxaca, Mexico. Paper presented at the 73rd annual meeting of the American Anthropological Association.
1981 Excavations at Santo Domingo Tomaltepec: Evolution of a Formative Community in the Valley of Oaxaca. *Prehistory and Human Ecology of the Valley of Oaxaca*, Vol. 6, edited by Kent V. Flannery and Richard E. Blanton. *Memoirs of the Museum of Anthropology, University of Michigan*, No. 12. Ann Arbor.
Wheatley, Paul
1971 *The Pivot of the Four Quarters*. Aldine, Chicago.
Wheeler, Sir Mortimer
1968 *The Indus Civilization*. 3rd ed. Cambridge University Press, Cambridge.
White, Benjamin
1973 Demand for Labor and Population Growth in Colonial Java. *Human Ecology* 1:217-36.
White, Leslie
1959 *The Evolution of Culture*. McGraw-Hill, New York.
Whitecotton, Joseph
1977 *The Zapotecs: Princes, Priests, and Peasants*. University of Oklahoma Press, Norman.
Whittlesey, Stephanie M.
1974 Identification of Imported Ceramics through Functional Analysis of Attributes. *The Kiva* 40:1-2.
Willey, Gordon
1962 The Early Great Styles and the Rise of Precolumbian Civilizations. *American Anthropologist* 64:1-14.
Winter, Marcus
1972 *Tierras Largas: A Formative Community in the Valley of Oaxaca, Mexico*. Ph.D. dissertation, The University of Arizona, Department of Anthropology.
1974 Late Formative Society in the Valley of Oaxaca and the Mixteca Alta, Mexico. Paper presented at the 41st International Congress of Americanists.
1976 Cerámica de la Fase Rosario Encontrada en Dos Pozos Tronco-Cónicos en el Sitio de Tierras Largas, Valle de Oaxaca, México. Centro Regional de Oaxaca, Instituto Nacional de Antropología e Historia, México. Mimeo.
Winter, Marcus, and Willim O. Payne
1976 Hornos para Cerámica Hallados en Monte Albán. *Boletín del Instituto Nacional de Antropología e Historia* 16:37-40.
Wittfogel, Karl
1957 *Oriental Despotism*. Yale University Press, New Haven.
Wobst, Martin
1974 Boundary Conditions for Paleolithic Social Systems: A Simulation Approach. *American Antiquity* 39:147-78.
Wolf, Eric (ed.)
1976 *The Valley of Mexico*. University of New Mexico Press, Albuquerque.
Wright, Henry T.
1969 The Administration of Rural Production in an Early Mesopotamian Town. *Anthropological Papers, Museum of Anthropology, University of Michigan*, No. 38. Ann Arbor.
1977 Recent Research on the Origin of the State. *Annual Review of Anthropology* 6:379-97.
Wright, Henry T., and Gregory Johnson
1975 Population, Exchange, and Early State Formation in Southwestern Iran. *American Anthropologist* 77:267-89.
Zipf, George K.
1949 *Human Behavior and the Principle of Least Effort*. Harvard University Press, Cambridge.

RESUMEN EN ESPAÑOL

por Richard E. Blanton y Stephen Kowalewski

En 1977 se completó la segunda etapa de un programa de reconocimientos superficiales en el Valle de Oaxaca. La primera etapa fué el reconocimiento superficial de Monte Albán (Blanton 1978). La tercera etapa va a incluir el reconocimiento de las regiones Tlacolula y Etla. En la segunda etapa del programa, varios equipos de arqueólogos entrenados en la secuencia arqueológica de Oaxaca examinaron toda la superficie actual de la parte central y sur (Valle Grande) del valle, una área de unos 800 kilómetros cuadrados. Se registraron sistemáticamente observaciones sobre la localización y extensión de cada sitio antiguo en cada fase de la secuencia cerámica, incluyendo información sobre ambiente, recursos, y restos arqueológicos así como artefactos y arquitectura.

En estas zonas se conocen más de 2000 sitios arqueológicos. Con estos datos podemos contribuir a dar solución a ciertos problemas de la prehistoria cultural del Valle de Oaxaca. Entre ellos tenemos tales como la ocupación pre-Monte Albán y él de la fundación de este gran centro urbano. En los tiempos siguientes, ¿Qué efecto tuvo la ciudad de Monte Albán en la ocupación y uso de la región circundante y al sur de ésta? ¿Qué pasó con la población rural cuando Monte Albán fué abandonado?, ¿Se pueden relacionar los pueblos mencionados en las fuentes etnohistóricas con específicos sitios arqueológicos? En el nivel teórico estas investigaciones contribuirán a mejorar el entendimiento de los factores y procesos que influyeron el desarrollo del ecosistema humano del Valle de Oaxaca. Es decir, la reconstrucción de los factores más importantes desde el punto de vista de la evolución de la cultura de las etapas anteriores, especialmente en el campo de la economía, política, y la relación de las poblaciones con su medio ambiente. Nuestros principales descubrimientos son los siguientes:

1400-500 a.C.: En Oaxaca las etapas formativa temprana y media se dividen en las fases Tierras Largas, San José, Guadalupe, y Rosario. Lo que se sabe de la sociedad antigua durante estas fases está basado principalmente en las investigaciones hechas por Kent Flannery y otros miembros de su proyecto. Hemos encontrado algunos sitios nuevos, pero los de mayor importancia están situados en la zona de Etla, no en las zonas central o Valle Grande. La población total de estas zonas no fué muy numerosa. El número de sitios por fase es: Tierras Largas (10), San José (13), Guadalupe (15), Rosario (26).

Monte Albán I Temprano (500-300 a.C.), Tardío (300-100 a.C.): El Valle de Oaxaca aparece más poblado durante la fase Monte Albán I (Temprano, 103 sitios; Tardío, 307 sitios) en las zonas central y Valle Grande, aunque el crecimiento es desigual, éste se concentra en la zona central y en el nuevo centro urbano: Monte Albán. El análisis indica otros aspectos en la evolución de la cultura en estas fases: 1) cambio en la organización de producción y distribución de la cerámica, que indica más producción por especialistas y quizás un sistema de mercados; 2) el establecimiento de un sistema más complejo de administración regional; y 3) un sistema agrícola más intensivo que antes, con mucho más uso de las lomas de la zona central.

Monte Albán II (100 a.C.-200 d.C.): Durante los tres o cuatro siglos de Monte Albán II la organización regional parece ser menos centralizada que en la época anterior. Solamente unos 14,000 vivían en Monte Albán comparado con 17,000 durante Período I Tardío. El área central, alrededor de Monte Albán, casi estuvo abandonada. Los centros administrativos locales continuan desde el período anterior con pocos cambios.

Monte Albán IIIa (200-400 d.C.): El período IIIa es la fase prehispánica más desarrollada en el Valle Grande. Esta región experimenta un gran incremento demográfico de 20,000 en Monte Albán II a más que 40,000 en IIIa. Jalieza, en el cuadro N7E8 representa el extremo de esta tendencia. Crece de casi nada en Monte Albán II a 12,800 habitantes en IIIa, segundo después de Monte Albán. Creemos que IIIa es el período mas centralizado de todas las fases prehispánicas y también es la fase más poblada de todas, con unos 60,000 habitantes.

Monte Albán IIIb (400-700 d.C.): La población total de la región (central y Valle Grande) decrece en este período a un poco más que 40,000, pero crece la población de Monte Albán a 24,000, el número más grande en la historia de este centro urbano. Muchos de los sitios ocupados en IIIa fueron abandonados en IIIb. Sin embargo, hubieron sitios grandes en este período cercanos a Monte Albán.

Monte Albán IV (700-1000 d.C.): En esta fase se quiebra la autoridad de Monte Albán. Disminuye más la población total de la región (a un poco más que 30,000). Grandes comunidades se establecen en el sur (por ejemplo, otra vez, en Jalieza, con 16,000 habitantes), separados por corredores no habitados. Los datos sugieren un mundo fragmentado, sin la integración que hemos visto en fases anteriores.

Monte Albán V (1000-1520 d.C.): Creemos que esta fase no tuvo integración política centralizada, pero con más integración de tipo económico. Hay mas población, más sitios, más obsidiana, mejor calidad en la cerámica, indicios de actividades comerciales más que nunca, pero casi nada de construcción de pirámides y otros edificios monumentales. Pensamos en que este período es muy interesante desde el punto de vista de la evolución de un sistema de mercados.

Tenemos nuestras conclusiones más globales adentro de capítulos 8, suplemento (sobre cosas etnohistóricas, por Jill Appel), 9 (población y recursos agrícolas, por Stephen Kowalewski), 10 (sobre la producción y distribución de la cerámica, por Gary Feinman), y 11 (síntesis). Los datos se presentan en una serie de once apéndices.